The Writer's Presence
A Pool of Readings

The Writer's Presence

A Pool of Readings
Fourth Edition

EDITED BY

Donald McQuade
University of California, Berkeley

Robert Atwan
Series Editor, The Best American Essays

Director, The Blue Hills Writing Institute at Curry College

Bedford / St. Martin's   Boston   ◆   New York

For Bedford/St. Martin's

Developmental Editor: Ellen Thibault
Assistant Editor, Publishing Services: Maria Teresa Burwell
Senior Production Supervisor: Joe Ford
Marketing Manager: Brian Wheel
Project Management: Books By Design, Inc.
Cover Design: Hannus Design Associates
Cover Art: F. Scott Hess, *Ms. Jacqueline Vincent-Millais, "Writing Table Suite 6A, 9/22, 10:01 pm"*
Composition: Pine Tree Composition, Inc.
Printing and Binding: Haddon Craftsmen, an R.R. Donnelley & Sons Company

President: Joan E. Feinberg
Editorial Director: Denise B. Wydra
Editor in Chief: Karen S. Henry
Director of Marketing: Karen R. Melton
Director of Editing, Design, and Production: Marcia Cohen
Manager, Publishing Services: Emily Berleth

Library of Congress Control Number: 2002110817

For information, write: Bedford/St. Martin's, 75 Arlington Street, Boston, MA 02116   (617-399-4000)

ISBN: 0–312–40027–6

Acknowledgments

Sherman Alexie, "The Joy of Reading and Writing: Superman and Me" from *The Most Wonderful Books,* edited by Michael Dorris and Emilie Buchwald. Copyright © 1997 by Milkweed Editions. Reprinted by permission of the author. "The Toughest Indian in the World" from *The Toughest Indian in the World* by Sherman Alexie. Copyright © 1999 by Sherman Alexie. Used by permission of Grove/Atlantic, Inc.
Dorothy Allison, "This Is Our World" from *DoubleTake* 13, Summer 1998. Copyright © 1998 by Dorothy Allison. Reprinted by permission of The Frances Goldin Agency, Inc.

Preface
for Instructors _____

This new edition of *The Writer's Presence* is designed to achieve three fundamental objectives: to allow writing instructors maximum flexibility in assigning reading materials and writing models; to introduce students to a wide range of prose genres emphasizing a strong authorial presence and voice; and to support composition teachers and students as effectively as possible with helpful, though unobtrusive, editorial and pedagogical features. We are confident that the reading material we have selected, the ways we have chosen to arrange that material, and the instructional resources we have provided both within the book and in the comprehensive instructor's manual will make this a uniquely useful collection that will satisfy the requirements of most first year writing programs.

Following is a description of the established features of *The Writer's Presence*. For information on what's new to this edition see page viii.

FLEXIBLE ORGANIZATION

The organization of *The Writer's Presence* displays a broad range of private, personal, expository, argumentative, and creative writing without imposing an order or specifying an instructional context in which to work with individual selections. In that sense, the contents of *The Writer's Presence* can truly be called "A Pool of Readings." The nonfiction selections that constitute the first four parts are roughly divided into the four most commonly taught types of nonfiction—informal writing, personal essays, exposition, and argumentation. That is the extent of the book's overarching structure. Within each part, we present the writers in alphabetical order and number the selections consecutively. This loose arrangement frees the instructor from an overly engineered text that locks its readers into a particular compositional pedagogy. The selections are easy to retrieve, assign, and interpret, regardless of instructional emphasis. To make it even easier to explore different approaches, *The Writer's Presence* includes several alternate tables of contents in the front and back of the book. Embedded within the collection is a variety of organizational options: *The Writer's Presence* was carefully designed to be used as a thematic reader, a rhetorical reader, a contemporary argument reader, and a research/interdisciplinary reader. Each selection was scrupulously chosen to play multiple roles.

DIVERSE SELECTIONS WITH A STRONG WRITER'S PRESENCE

Each of the selections in *The Writer's Presence* displays the distinctive signature that characterizes memorable prose: the presence of a lively individual imagination attempting to explore the self, shape information into meaning, or contend with issues through discussion and debate. Ranging widely across subjects, methods of development, and stylistic patterns, the selections illustrate the expectations as well as the uncertainties that surface when a writer attempts to create a memorable presence in prose. We have built the book — like previous editions — around first-rate teaching material, much of it proven to work in the writing classroom. We continue to feature a large number of authors whose works instructors have repeatedly enjoyed teaching over the years. These classroom favorites include essays and other nonfiction selections from such respected writers as Maya Angelou, James Baldwin, Joan Didion, Annie Dillard, Loren Eiseley, Edward Hoagland, Langston Hughes, Zora Neale Hurston, Jamaica Kincaid, N. Scott Momaday, George Orwell, Adrienne Rich, Scott Russell Sanders, Jonathan Swift, Mark Twain, Virginia Woolf, Alice Walker, and E. B. White. In fact, as this list of writers clearly indicates, *The Writer's Presence* could be used as an introduction to the essay or to literary nonfiction in general. For instructors with even more literary ambitions, we have included paired selections so that certain writers can be shown working in two different genres. These writers are Virginia Woolf, Raymond Carver, Jamaica Kincaid, Alice Walker, Stephen King, John Edgar Wideman, Sherman Alexie, and Amy Tan.

HELPFUL AND UNOBTRUSIVE APPARATUS

As in previous editions, we continue to keep instructional apparatus to a minimum, striving for a middle ground between too much and too little. In our opinion, student readers profit from brief headnotes that provide useful and accessible information about a particular writer's background, relevant publications, and compositional practices and goals. Many selections provide interesting stories in themselves, and readers understandably want to know when a piece was written and how and where it originally appeared. Our headnotes are as attentive as possible to a selection's original source. We don't want readers to infer mistakenly that an excerpt is actually an essay. This distorts one's approach to the selection and may be unfair to the author. For example, we want readers to know at the outset that Maya Angelou's well-known selection, "What's Your Name, Girl?" is taken from her award-winning autobiography, *I Know Why the Caged Bird Sings,* and was never intended to be an essay in itself. The selection requires a certain amount of preliminary context (and a few notes) to clarify the dramatic situation she so vividly describes.

It is our experience, too, that many students can be guided in their assessment or rereading of a selection by carefully constructed follow-up questions. In this edition we have retained "The Reader's Presence," the small collection of questions after every numbered selection. These questions can be used privately by student readers and writers to enhance their understanding of the selection, or in the classroom to stimulate group discussion and evaluation. We have designed the questions to cover some of the dominant features of the selection and refer to matters of content, style, and structure. As their title indicates, the questions will often draw attention to the specific ways in which readers are present in a piece of writing — either as an implied reader (the reader imagined by the writer) or as an actual reader (oneself). The concept of presence — both the writer's and the reader's — is discussed more fully in the "Introduction for Students."

RESOURCES FOR TEACHING *THE WRITER'S PRESENCE*

Carefully managing the amount of instructional apparatus in *The Writer's Presence* does not weaken our commitment to provide you with a wealth of specific instructional activities. In 320 spiral-bound pages, *Resources for Teaching* THE WRITER'S PRESENCE is the most extensive instructor's manual available for any composition reader.

This resource-full guide to *The Writer's Presence* includes the following four parts in each entry:

- "Approaching the Essay" provides a thorough overview of the pedagogical prospects of working with the essay in the classroom.
- "Additional Activities" offers imaginative classroom activities, including writing-before reading exercises, connections to other essays in the book, and collaborative projects.

- "Generating Writing" includes a range of writing exercises — from suggestions for informal writing to essay assignments and ideas for research papers.

- "The Reader's Presence" addresses the questions that follow each selection in the text, pointing to illuminating passages in the selection and anticipating possible responses from students.

NEW TO THIS EDITION

For the fourth edition of *The Writer's Presence,* while we have retained the book's key features (its flexible format and its emphasis on authorial presence and cultural diversity), we have also made a number of changes that we believe will enhance the book's appeal and utility. We have:

- **Added fifty-two new selections, bringing the total number of readings to 153.** These compelling essays include works by such well-known contemporaries as Julia Alvarez, Don DeLillo, bell hooks, and John Updike, and fresh selections from such classic writers as Sylvia Plath and James Baldwin. **New fiction selections** include stories by Sherman Alexie and John Edgar Wideman.

- **Included an essay by Richard Wright that has never before been published.** We are honored to be the first to print "I Choose Exile," an essay that Richard Wright submitted to *Ebony* magazine in 1951, but that was rejected by the publisher. In this work Wright explains his reasons for leaving America to live as an expatriate in Paris: "My decision is predicated upon this simple fact. I *need* freedom."

- **Included two new research-based essays,** Malcolm Gladwell on the phenomena of "tipping points" and Veronica Boix-Mansilla and Howard Gardner on how we understand history and literature. These selections — which include footnotes and bibliographies — add to the book's examples of writing that requires outside sources.

- **Introduced a number of emerging authors who are relatively new to anthologies.** In addition to many established and frequently anthologized authors, this edition features the work of many writers who are now finding their way into major collections: Eric Liu, Andrew Sullivan, Jane Eaton Hamilton, David Sedaris, Martha Nussbaum, and Eric Schlosser, to name a few. We have also included two relatively unknown writers, Adam Mayblum and Tim Townsend, whose essays reflect their personal responses to the events of September 11, 2001. We hope that readers will be as delighted as we are with the selections from these outstanding authors. Further, we've made an effort to include authors who, though more established, are not often included in composition readers; in this edition, we are pleased to introduce essays by such well-known writers as the cultural and literary critic Harold Bloom, the poet June Jordan, the dramatist and fiction writer, Wole Soyinka, and the novelists Salman Rushdie and Stephen King.

- **Placed a greater emphasis on issues.** The fourth edition offers more readings that represent a range of topics, including race, class, sexuality, privacy, and the media, and that provide students with models for expository and argumentative essays. These engaging new selections include Stanley Fish on affirmative action, Jane Eaton Hamilton on gay marriage, and Wendy Kaminer on sex, gender, and language.

- **Added more "Writer at Work" selections.** These twenty-three readings, eleven of which are new, include excerpts from interviews and essays in which authors discuss their writing process and their identities as writers; we chose each to show students that good writing is thoughtful work done by real people. This popular feature — introduced in the third edition — now includes such new selections as Julia Alvarez on writing in English and John Edgar Wideman on the value of storytelling.

- **Provided new questions probing connections between essays.** At the request of instructors, we have added after each selection a new type of question aimed at helping students see the many links between and among the selections.

- **Revised a new *Writer's Presence* Web site** (bedfordstmartins.com /writerspresence). The companion site for the fourth edition offers biographies and research links for every author in the book and online resources for the major topics represented, providing students with starting points for their research.

ACKNOWLEDGMENTS

Revisions of *The Writer's Presence* have grown out of correspondence and conversations — on the phone, in person, in letters, and on the Internet — with the many teachers and an appreciable number of students who have worked with *The Writer's Presence* in their writing classes. We continue to learn a great deal from these discussions, and we are grateful to the colleagues and friends who graciously have allowed us into their already crowded lives to seek advice and encouragement. Since its inception, *The Writer's Presence* has been and continues to be a truly collaborative enterprise.

In the same way we originally developed *The Writer's Presence,* revisions have emerged from spirited discussions with instructors who prefer to pick and choose—at their own discretion and with their own instructional purposes—from among a wide range of eminently readable and teachable essays. We are grateful to these colleagues across the country who took the time to tell us about what did—and did not—work well when they used the third edition: James Adams, Boston College; Susan J. Allspaw, Boston College; Bette Bauer, College of Saint Mary; Ann Lightcap Bruno, Boston College; Ruth Elizabeth Burks, Tufts University; Susan M. Cannata, University of North Carolina—Pembroke; Rosanne Colosi, Boston College; Ellen Davis, Boston University; Emily Dial-Driver, Rogers State University; Trevor Dodge, Boise State University; Jamye Doerfler, Virginia Commonwealth University; Lori Harrison-Kahan, Boston College; Benjamin Hoffman, Boston College; Elizabeth Klem, Atlantic Cape Community College; Donna Levy, University of Richmond and J. Sargeant Reynolds Community College; Anthony W. Lilly II, Tufts University; Robert Rogan, University of North Carolina—Wilmington; Larry Severeid, College of Eastern Utah; Nancy Sorenson, California State University; Kathleen G. White, Bellevue Community College; Mary Robin Whitney, John Jay College of Criminal Justice, City University of New York.

We would also like to acknowledge those instructors who gave us feedback about the second edition: Linda Baker, Portland Community College; Jennifer Buckley, John Carroll University; Eileen Donovan-Kranz, Boston College; Susan M. Eisenthal, University of Massachusetts—Boston; Jack Jacobs, Auburn University; Michael M. Walker, Palomar College; Genoveva Llosa, Boston College; Lolly Ockerstrom, Virginia Commonwealth University; Jean Pace, Emerson College; Jan Zlotnick Schmidt, State University of New York, New Paltz; Joanne Sibicky, Virginia Commonwealth University; Robert Singleton, State University of New York, New Paltz; Robert L. Stapleton, Long Beach City College; and Chad R. Stockton, Emerson College.

We would like to thank those who commented on the first edition: Lisa Altomari, Vermont Technical College; Maurice H. Barr, Spokane Community College; Todd W. Bersley, California State University—Northridge; Gerri Black, Stockton State College; Scott Brookman, Virginia Commonwealth University; Larry Brunt, Highline Community College; Irene Burgess, SUC Cortland; Dolores M. Burton, Boston University; Diane Challis, Virginia Commonwealth University; Jimmy Cheshire, Wright State University; Chet Childress, Virginia Commonwealth University; Alice Cleveland, College of Mareu; Michel S. Connell, University of Iowa; Chase Crossingham, University of South Carolina; Ruth Y. Davidson, Pennsylvania State University—Schuylkill Campus; Michael G. Davros, University of Illinois at Chicago; Peggy C. de Broux, Peninsula College; Jessica Deforest, Michigan State University; Mary Devaney, Rutgers University—Newark Campus; Debra DiPiazza, Bernard M. Baruch College, City University of New York; Maria Rowena P. Dolorico, Bristol Community College; Alex Fagan, Virginia Commonwealth University;

Grace Farrell, Butler University; Joan Gabriele, University of Colorado; Christie Anderson Garcia, Spokane Falls Community College; Jane Gatewood, Mary Washington College; Rae Greiner, Radford University; Brian Hale, University of South Carolina; Sarah Hanselman, Tufts University; Dave Hendrickson, Virginia Commonwealth University; Curtis W. Herr, Kutztown University; Goldie Johnson, Winona State University; Nancy B. Johnson, Pace University; Ronald L. King, Virginia Commonwealth University; Harriet Malinowitz, Hunter College, City University of New York; Barbara Mallonee, Loyola College; Denice Martone, New York University; Ilene Miele, Moorpark College; Andrew Mossin, Temple University; Cathryn A. Myers, Virginia Commonwealth University; Cheryl Pallant, Virginia Commonwealth University; Marty Patton, University of Missouri—Columbia; Gary D. Pratt, Brandeis University; Catherine S. Quick, University of Missouri—Columbia; Larry Rodgers, Kansas State University; Colleen Richmond, George Fox College; Lissa Schneider, University of Miami; Marilyn S. Scott, California State University—Hayward; Constance Fletcher Smith, Mary Washington College; Roger Sorkin, University of Massachusetts—Dartmouth; J. F. Stenerson, Pace University; Steven Strang, Massachusetts Institute of Technology; Pamela Topping, Long Island University—Southampton Campus; Mary Turnbull, University of Puget Sound; Donna M. Turner, University of North Dakota; Sandra Urban, Loyola University of Chicago; Jennifer Lynne Von Ammon, Florida State University; and Ed Wiltse, Tufts University.

We would especially like to acknowledge our colleagues in the Expository Writing Program at New York University—Alfred Guy, Lisa Altomari, Karen Boiko, Darlene Forrest, Mary Helen Kolisnyk, Jim Marcall, Denice Martone, and Will McCormack—for taking the time to talk with us and for sharing their ideas during the planning stages of the first edition of this book.

We also extend our thanks to all the people at Bedford/St. Martin's for their innumerable contributions to this revision. We deeply appreciate the continuous support and intelligent suggestions we received from our editor, Ellen Thibault. She made this a better book in every conceivable way. We are also grateful to Christine Turnier-Vallecillo, who helped bring together all the inevitable loose ends as we neared the publication date. Many thanks, too, to Herb Nolan for deftly moving an enormous and complex manuscript through production and to Emily Berleth for managing the entire process with great attentiveness.

As ever, Chuck Christensen, the recently retired president of Bedford/St. Martin's, and his successor, Joan Feinberg, offered us spirited encouragement, first-rate and rigorous advice, as well as numerous suggestions for improving the project. They never hesitated to urge us to explore an idea or an instructional feature of the book if it might make our purposes clearer and more useful to teachers and students. And when our conversations veered occasionally toward uncertainty, we relied on their steady editorial presence to help us convert pedagogical principle into sound instructional practice.

The comprehensive instructor's guide that accompanies this collection, *Resources for Teaching THE WRITER'S PRESENCE,* was prepared this year by Cassandra Cleghorn of Williams College. Cassandra also supplied many of "The Reader's Presence" questions and has linked these closely to the entries in the manual. We appreciate her intelligent contributions and her remarkable ability to assess the classroom potential of such a wide variety of texts. We continue to be grateful to Shelley Salamensky of Williams College, Alfred Guy of New York University, Jon Roberts of St. Thomas Aquinas College, and Alix Schwartz of University of California, Berkeley for their work in previous editions; their very helpful suggestions are still amply evident in the instructor's manual. We also continue to appreciate the help received from Greg Mullins, who provided a considerable amount of the biographical and compositional information contained in the headnotes to selections carried over from previous editions. The new headnote research and writing for this edition was handled by Andrew Wilson; we are enormously grateful to him for all of his efforts. We extend our thanks, too, to Elisabeth Gehrlein, who adroitly managed the challenging process of securing reprint permissions.

Finally, we hope that Hélène, Gregory, and Emily Atwan, along with Susanne, Christine, and Marc McQuade, will once again share our satisfaction in seeing this project in print and our pleasure in continuing our productive collaboration.

Donald McQuade
Robert Atwan

Contents _____

I. THE INFORMAL VOICE: Diaries, Journals, Notebooks, Testimony   11

"I let the tension stay in my body. I go home and sit with myself for an hour, trying to grasp the feeling — the odor of self-hatred, the biting stench of shame."

"My first notebook was a Big Five tablet, given to me by my mother with the sensible suggestion that I stop whining and learn to amuse myself by writing down my thoughts."

"Oh, so many things bubble up inside me as I lie in bed, having to put up with people I'm fed up with, who always misinterpret my intentions. That's why in the end I always come back to my diary."

"We stood in the street, uncertain and afraid, until a house across from us began to sway and then with a rending motion fell almost at our feet. Our own house began to sway, and in a minute it, too, collapsed in a cloud of dust."

"On the forty-fourth floor my phone rang again. It was my parents. They were hysterical. I said relax, I'm fine. My father said get out, there is a third plane coming. I still did not understand."

"I was very conscious of his nearness. His blue eyes were startlingly close, looking at me boldly, with flecks of laughter in them.
'I really have to go. They will be waiting. The picture was lovely.'
Smiling, he was between me and the door. A motion. His hand closed around my arm."

"In the seconds, minutes, and hours following the World Trade Center attacks, hundreds—maybe thousands—of ordinary people would find their best selves and become heroes. And then there were the rest of us, running hard, wanting only to live and to talk to someone we loved, even if it meant leaving an old guy lying in the street, glasses gone, a cloud of death and destruction creeping up on him."

"Future years will never know the seething hell and the black infernal background of countless minor scenes and interiors . . . of the Secession war; and it is best they should not—the real war will never get in the books."

"What sort of diary should I like mine to be? Something loose knit and yet not slovenly, so elastic that it will embrace anything, solemn, slight or beautiful that comes into my mind. I should like it to resemble some deep old desk, or capacious hold-all, in which one flings a mass of odds and ends without looking them through."

"A smart Indian is a dangerous person, widely feared and ridiculed by Indians and non-Indians alike. I fought with my classmates on a daily basis. They wanted me to stay quiet when the non-Indian teacher asked for answers, for volunteers, for help. We were Indian children who were expected to be stupid."

"I would bow my head, humiliated by the smiles and snickers of the American children around me. I grew insecure about Spanish. My native tongue was not quite as good as English, as if words like *columpio* were illegal immigrants trying to cross a border into another language. But Teacher's discerning grammar-and-vocabulary-patrol ears could tell and send them back."

THE WRITER AT WORK:

"I am not a Dominican writer. I have no business writing in a language that I can speak but have not studied deeply enough to craft. I can't ride its wild horses. . . . I know the tender mouth of English, just how to work the reins."

"Every person I knew had a hellish horror of being 'called out of his name.' It was a dangerous practice to call a Negro anything that could be loosely construed as insulting because of the centuries of their having been called niggers, jigs, dinges, blackbirds, crows, boots, and spooks."

"I had never met a writer, had shown no previous urge to write, and hadn't a notion how to become a writer, but I loved stories and thought that making up stories must surely be almost as much fun as reading them."

"My Dad walked, hitched rides, and rode in empty boxcars when he went from Arkansas to Washington State in 1934, looking for work. I don't know whether he was pursuing a dream when he went out to Washington. I doubt it. I don't think he dreamed much."

"My father's Navy check provided us with financial security and a standard of life that the factory workers envied. The only thing his money could not buy us was a place to live away from the barrio — his greatest wish, Mother's greatest fear."

THE WRITER AT WORK:

"Much of my writing begins as a meditation on past events. But memory for me is the 'jumping off' point; I am not, in my poetry and my fiction writing, a slave to memory."

"My longing was wrong in the eyes of my mother, whose hazel eyes were

the eyes of the world, and if that longing continued unchecked, the unwieldy
shape of my fate would be cast, and I'd be subjected to a lifetime of scorn."

"The more I read, the more I was led to abhor and detest my enslavers. I
could regard them in no other light than a band of successful robbers, who
had left their homes, and gone to Africa, and stolen us from our homes,
and in a strange land reduced us to slavery. I loathed them as being the
meanest as well as the most wicked of men."

"And I knew that no one would ever want to marry me. I had no breasts. I
would never have breasts."

"The 'kitchen' I'm speaking of now is the very kinky bit of hair at the back
of the head, where the neck meets the shirt collar. If there ever was one
part of our African past that resisted assimilation, it was the kitchen. No
matter how hot the iron, no matter how powerful the chemical, no matter
how stringent the mashed-potatoes-and-lye formula of a man's 'process,'
neither God nor woman nor Sammy Davis, Jr., could straighten the
kitchen."

"I've always had two conflicting voices within me, one that wants to be
outrageous and on the edge, always breaking new ground, and another
that wants to be loved by the community for that outrageousness."

"I've stuttered for more than 60 years, and the mysteries of the encumbrance
still catch me up: being reminded every morning that it's engrained in my
fiber, although I had forgotten in my dreams. Life can become a matter of
measuring the importance of anything you have to say."

"Essays are how we speak to one another in print – caroming thoughts not
merely in order to convey a certain packet of information, but with a
special edge or bounce of personal character in a kind of public letter."

"Slowly I began to understand fully that there was no place in academe for
folks from working-class backgrounds who did not wish to leave the past
behind. That was the price of the ticket."

"Suddenly the whole room broke into a sea of shouting, as they saw me rise. Waves of rejoicing swept the place. Women leaped in the air. My aunt threw her arms around me. The minister took me by the hand and led me to the platform."

"Have nothing to say, but use a great many words, particularly high-sounding words, to say it."

"Among the thousand white persons, I am a dark rock surged upon, and overswept, but through it all, I remain myself. When covered by the waters, I am; and the ebb but reveals me again."

"The dress I am wearing in this black-and-white photograph, taken when I was two years old, was a yellow dress made of cotton poplin (a fabric with a slightly unsmooth texture first manufactured in the French town of Avignon and brought to England by the Huguenots, but I could not have known that at the time), and it was made for me by my mother."

"We are inventors, all. We assemble ourselves from fragments of story. Every identity is a social construction, a drawing of arbitrary lines. But are all identities *equally* arbitrary—and equally necessary?"

"First, the matter of semantics. I am a cripple. I choose this word to name me. I choose from among several possibilities, the most common of which are 'handicapped' and 'disabled.' I made the choice a number of years ago, without thinking, unaware of my motives for doing so."

"The question I am most often asked when I speak to students and others interested in writing is, How did you find your voice?"

"I spent my first month in town with my mouth hanging open. The sharp-dressed young 'cats' who hung on the corners and in the poolrooms, bars and restaurants, and who obviously didn't work anywhere, completely entranced me. I couldn't get over marveling at how their hair was straight and shiny like white men's hair; Ella told me this was called a 'conk.'"

fellow students and I engaged in the sort of conversation commonly
overheard in refugee camps.
'Sometimes me cry alone at night.'
'That be common for I, also, but be more strong, you. Much work and
someday you talk pretty. People start love you soon. Maybe tomorrow,
okay.'"

"She cast back a worried glance. To her, the youngish black man—a
broad six feet two inches with a beard and billowing hair, both hands
shoved into the pockets of a bulky military jacket—seemed menacingly
close. After a few more quick glimpses, she picked up her pace and was
soon running in earnest."

THE WRITER AT WORK:
Another Version of "Just Walk on By"   258

"She looked back at me once, then again, and picked up her pace. She
looked back again and started to run. I stopped where I was and looked
up at the surrounding windows. What did this look like to people peeking
out through their blinds?"

"Lately, I've been giving more thought to the kind of English my mother
speaks. Like others, I have described it to people as 'broken' or 'fractured'
English. But I wince when I say that. It has always bothered me that I can
think of no way to describe it other than 'broken,' as if it were damaged
and needed to be fixed, as if it lacked a certain wholeness and
soundness."

"I passed all the other courses that I took at my University, but I could
never pass botany. This was because all botany students had to spend
several hours a week in a laboratory looking through a microscope at
plant cells, and I could never see through a microscope. I never once saw a
cell through a microscope."

"For the rest of my days, I shall be a recovering short person. Even from
my lofty perch of something over six feet (as if I don't know within a
micron), I have the soul of a shrimp."

"Where the BB pellet struck there is a glob of whitish scar tissue, a hideous
cataract, on my eye. Now when I stare at people—a favorite pastime, up
to now—they will stare back. Not at the 'cute' little girl, but at her scar."

"One of my favorite passages, really, in theology, is Emily Dickinson saying, 'I believe and disbelieve one hundred times in an hour which keeps believing nimble.' That contending with doubt and ambivalence is one of the things that evidently kept her faith alive."

"Psychologists identify ten as roughly the age at which many boys experience the gender-linked normative developmental trauma that leaves them, as adult men, at risk for specific psychological sequelae often manifest as deficits in the arenas of intimacy, empathy, and struggles with commitment in relationships. In other words, this is around the age when guys get screwed up about girls."

"Political language — and with variations this is true of all political parties, from Conservatives to Anarchists — is designed to make lies sound truthful and murder respectable, and to give an appearance of solidity to pure wind."

"Putting aside the need to earn a living, I think there are four great motives for writing, at any rate for writing prose."

"Instead of looking at kids to 'prove' that differences in behavior by sex are innate, we can look at the ways we raise kids as an index to how unfinished the feminist revolution really is, and how tentatively it is embraced even by adults who fully expect their daughters to enter previously male-dominated professions and their sons to change diapers."

"It's no secret that television has *become* the public sphere for Americans, the one central source of information and public debate on matters of national import."

"Bono called me. 'I've written this melody for your words, and I think it might be one of the best things I've done.' I was astonished."

"Secrets purvey affordable glamour, suggest danger without presenting an actual threat. . . . Secrets hold out the promise, false but necessary, that death will be deferred until their unveiling."

"Wonderful smells drifted through the hallways, men and women in neat white lab coats cheerfully went about their work, and hundreds of little glass bottles sat on laboratory tables and shelves. . . . The long chemical names on the little white labels were as mystifying to me as medieval Latin. These odd-sounding things would be mixed and poured and turned into new substances, like magic potions."

"When we let people grow up feeling that cruelty is all right provided they know it is make-believe, or provided they sufficiently disapprove of certain individuals or groups, or provided the cruelty is in the service of their country (whether the country is right or wrong), we make it easier for them to go berserk when the provocation comes."

"Whoever he is, it's likely he first saw the city from the air, looked out and saw the Twin Towers mirroring each other's dizzying rise. Maybe he stood at the window of some safe house in Queens or Jersey and looked at them. Thrusting so immodestly more than a thousand feet in the air, they mocked his passionate intensity, he no doubt thought."

"My skin sticks a little to the syringe as I pull it out, and then an odd mix of oil and blackish blood usually trickles down my hip. . . . The chemical I am putting into myself is synthetic testosterone. . . . Twenty years ago, as it surged through my pubescent body, it deepened my voice, grew hair on my face and chest, strengthened my limbs, made me a man. So what, I wonder, is it doing to me now?"

"For many women, as for girls, talk is the glue of close relationships; your best friend is the one you tell your secrets to, the one you discuss your troubles with. For many men, as for boys, activities are central; your best friend is the one you do everything with (and the one who will stick up for you if there is a fight)."

"Dieting is hatred — of self and others. Women, fat and thin both, hate fat women. We hate one another, say cruel things to and about one another, judge, cut apart. We sympathize with one another, but the battle is about survival."

"The brutal truth is that the bulk of white people in America never had any interest in educating black people, except as this could serve white purposes. It is not the black child's language that is in question, it is not his language that is despised: It is his experience."

"Imaginative literature is otherness, and as such alleviates loneliness. We read not only because we cannot know enough people, but because friendship is so vulnerable, so likely to diminish or disappear, overcome by space, time, imperfect sympathies, and all the sorrows of familial and passional life."

"Watching the news reports, it is often hard to tell whether there are real living and breathing women in conflict-stricken places like Haiti. The evening news broadcasts only allow us a brief glimpse of presidential coups, rejected boat people, and sabotaged elections. The women's stories never manage to make the front page. However they do exist."

"Writing was a dangerous activity. Perhaps it was that danger that attracted me, the feeling of doing a high-wire act between stretching the limits of silence and telling the whole truth."

"We can live any way we want. People take vows of poverty, chastity, and obedience—even of silence—by choice. The thing is to stalk your calling in a certain skilled and supple way, to locate the most tender and live spot and plug into that pulse. This is yielding, not fighting."

"Don't use any extra words. A sentence is a machine; it has a job to do. An extra word in a sentence is like a sock in a machine."

"In the fairly near future, a standard item in the trunks of American police cruisers—perhaps even on each officer's belt—may be a DNA analyzer. As a suspect is arrested, police will quickly swipe the inside of his cheek with a cotton swab and pop the results into the scanner."

THE WRITER AT WORK:

"I believe that a writer does have to think about the responsibilities. . . .
But I don't think that writers should censor themselves and I don't think
that readers should censor writers."

"'Sammy, you don't want to do this to your Mom and Dad,' he tells me.
It's true, I don't. But it seems to me that once you begin a gesture it's fatal
not to go through with it."

"In real life I am a large, big-boned woman with rough, man-working
hands. In the winter I wear flannel nightgowns to bed and overalls during
the day. I can kill and clean a hog as mercilessly as a man. My fat keeps
me hot in zero weather."

"My mother is a weightlifter. You know what I mean. She understands
that the best laid plans, the sweetest beginnings have a way of turning to
shit. Bad enough when life fattens you up just so it can turn around and
gobble you down."

THE WRITER AT WORK:

"Stories that do mount a challenge to our everyday conventions and
assumptions stir my blood. Not only because they are exciting formally
and philosophically, but because they retain for fiction its special
subversive, radically democratic role."

Selections Arranged by Theme ———

CHILDHOOD AND FAMILY

A SENSE OF PLACE

PSYCHOLOGY AND HUMAN BEHAVIOR

ETHICS AND MORALITY

PHILOSOPHY, SPIRITUALITY, AND RELIGION

THE NATURAL ENVIRONMENT

HISTORY AND BIOGRAPHY

EDUCATION

POPULAR CULTURE AND MASS MEDIA

LANGUAGE AND LITERATURE

SCIENCES AND TECHNOLOGY

LAW, POLITICS, AND SOCIETY

The Writer's Presence
A Pool of Readings

Introduction for Students:
The Writer's Presence

Presence is a word—like *charisma*—that we reserve for people who create powerful and memorable impressions. Many public figures and political leaders are said to "have presence" (John F. Kennedy and Martin Luther King Jr. were two superb examples) as well as many athletes, dancers, and musicians. In fact, the quality of presence is found abundantly in the performing arts; think of Michael Jackson or Madonna, two entertainers who have self-consciously fashioned—through style, costume, and gesture—an instantly recognizable public presence. Clearly, people with presence are able to command our attention. How do they do it?

Presence is far easier to identify than it is to define. We recognize it when we see it, but how do we capture it in words? Virtually everyone would agree, for example, that when Michael Jordan steps onto a basketball court, he displays an exceptional degree of presence; we acknowledge this whether or not we are basketball fans. But what is it about such individuals that commands our attention? How can we begin to understand this elusive characteristic known as presence?

On one level, *presence* simply means "being present." But the word is more complex than that; it suggests much more than the mere fact of being physically present. Most dictionaries define *presence* as an ability to project a sense of self-assurance, poise, ease, or dignity. We thus speak of someone's "stage presence" or "presence of mind." But the word is also used today to suggest an impressive personality, an individual who can make his or her presence felt. As every college student knows, to be present in a classroom is not the same thing as *having a presence* there. We may be present in body, but not in spirit. In that sense, presence is also a matter of individual energy and exertion, of putting something of ourselves into whatever it is we do.

Presence is especially important in writing, which is what this book is about. Just as we notice individual presence in sports, or music, or conversation, so too we discover it in good writing. If what we read seems dreary, dull, or dead, it's usually because the writer forgot to include an

1

important ingredient: *personal presence.* That doesn't mean that your essays should be written *in* the first-person singular (this book contains many exceptional essays that aren't), but that your essays should be written *by* the first-person singular—by *you.* Interesting essays are produced by a real and distinct person, not an automaton following a set of mechanical rules and abstract principles.

PRESENCE IN WRITING

How can someone be present in writing? How can you project yourself into an essay so that it seems that you're personally there, even though all your reader sees are words on a piece of paper?

The Writer's Presence shows you how this is done. It shows how a wide variety of talented writers establish a distinct presence in many different kinds of writing and for many different purposes and audiences. Though the book offers numerous examples of how presence is compositionally established, there are several methods that nearly all experienced writers observe and that are worth pointing out at the start. Let's examine four of the chief ways a writer can be present in an essay.

1. Personal Experience. One of the most straightforward ways of making your presence felt in an essay is to include appropriate personal experiences. Of course, many assignments may call for a personal essay, and in those cases you will naturally be putting episodes from your own life at the center of your writing. But writers also find ways to build their personal experiences into essays that are basically informative or argumentative, essays on topics other than the self. They do this to show their close connection with a subject, to offer testimony, or to establish their personal authority on a subject. Many of the essays in this collection offer clear illustrations of how writers incorporate personal experience into an essay on a specific topic or issue.

Look, for example, at the essay by Amy Cunningham, "Why Women Smile" (page 335). This essay is primarily an explanation of a cultural phenomenon—the way women are socially conditioned to maintain a smiling attitude. But note that Cunningham begins the essay not with a general observation but with a personal anecdote: "After smiling brilliantly for nearly four decades, I now find myself trying to quit." Though her essay is not "personal," her opening sentence, besides establishing her own connection with the topic, provides readers with a personal motive for her writing.

One of the first places to look for the writer's presence is in the motive, the purpose, for putting pen to paper. Virginia Woolf calls this a "fierce attachment to an idea." The extent of our success in making clear our motive for writing will largely depend on our interest both in our subject as well as in our idea about the subject. It will prove extremely difficult for any writer to establish a presence when he or she is either bored with—or simply uninterested in—the subject at hand. Investing in a clearly articulated purpose will yield an attractive return in reader attention.

2. *Voice.* Another way a writer makes his or her presence felt is through creating a distinctive and identifiable *voice.* All words are composed of sounds, and language itself is something nearly all of us originally learned through *hearing.* Any piece of writing can be read aloud, though many readers have developed such ingrained habits of silent reading that they no longer *hear* the writing. Good writers, however, want their words to be heard. They want their sentences to have rhythm, cadence, and balance. Experienced authors revise a great deal of their writing just to make sure the sentences *sound* right. They're writing for the reader's ear as well as the reader's mind.

In many respects, voice is the writer's "signature," what finally distinguishes the work of one writer from another. Consider how quickly we recognize voice. We only *hear* the opening lines of a humorous sketch on television, yet we instantly recognize the comedian. So, too, whenever we read a piece of writing, we ought to think of it as an experience similar to listening to someone speak aloud. Doing so adds drama to writing and reading. Here is what the poet Robert Frost has to say on the subject:

> Everything written is as good as it is dramatic. . . . A dramatic necessity goes deep into the nature of the sentence. Sentences are not different enough to hold the attention unless they are dramatic. No ingenuity of varying structure will do. All that can save them is the speaking tone of voice somehow entangled in the words and fastened to the page for the ear of the imagination. That is all that can save poetry from singing, all that can save prose from itself. (Preface to *A Way Out,* in *Selected Prose of Robert Frost,* 1)

Frost spent a good portion of his celebrated public life encouraging people to cultivate what he called "the hearing imagination."

A writer's voice is usually fairly consistent from essay to essay and can be detected quickly by an experienced reader who pays attention to "the hearing imagination." To be distinctive and effective, a writer's voice need not be strange, artificial, or self-consciously literary. Many essayists develop a casual, familiar, flexible tone of voice that allows them to range easily from the intimate to the intellectual. Sentence rhythm and word choice play a large part in determining a writer's tone of voice. Observe how Raymond Carver begins an essay about his father (page 86):

> My dad's name was Clevie Raymond Carver. His family called him Raymond and friends called him C.R. I was named Raymond Clevie Carver, Jr. I hated the "Junior" part. When I was little my dad called me Frog, which was okay. . . .

Carver's voice here is casual and almost childlike, a quality he is striving for in an essay intended to be candid, intimate, and low-key.

Throughout the essay, for example, he rarely uses the word *father* but always the more colloquial *dad*. If you read this passage aloud, you will get the feeling that someone is speaking directly to you.

A more specific dimension of voice is *tone*, which refers not only to the implied social relationship of the writer to the reader, but also to the manner the writer adopts in addressing the reader. When considering tone as a feature of the writer's presence, it is useful to remember that tone addresses the ways in which writers convey attitudes. In this respect, tone does not speak to the attitudes themselves but to the manner in which those attitudes are revealed. In either projecting or analyzing the writer's tone, writers and readers ought to consider its intensity, the force with which the writer's attitudes are expressed. The strength of the writer's tone depends on such factors as the seriousness of the situation, the nature and extent of the writer's involvement in the situation, and the control the writer exercises over expression. In practical terms, tone is usually a matter of diction and individual word choice.

3. Point of View. Another sure way to establish presence is in the point of view we adopt toward a subject. In this sense, point of view comprises the "whereness" of the writer's presence. Sometimes a point of view can be a literal reality, an actual place or situation in which we physically locate ourselves as writers. This occurs most frequently in autobiographical essays in which the writer is present both as the narrator and as a character. For example, in "A Clack of Tiny Sparks: Remembrances of a Gay Boyhood" (page 104), Bernard Cooper is always meticulous about telling us his actual location at any given moment in his writing. The essay begins: "Theresa Sanchez sat behind me in ninth-grade algebra."

Note, too, how extremely important point of view is to another essayist in the volume, Brent Staples, in "Just Walk on By: A Black Man Ponders His Power to Alter Public Space" (page 254). Here is how Staples opens his essay:

> My first victim was a woman—white, well dressed, probably in her early twenties. I came upon her late one evening on a deserted street in Hyde Park, a relatively affluent neighborhood in an otherwise mean, impoverished section of Chicago. As I swung onto the avenue behind her, there seemed to be a discreet, uninflammatory distance between us. Not so. She cast back a worried glance. To her, the youngish black man—a broad six feet two inches with a beard and billowing hair, both hands shoved into the pockets of a bulky military jacket—seemed menacingly close. After a few more quick glimpses, she picked up her pace and was soon running in earnest. Within seconds she disappeared into a cross street.

Point of view in this essay is crucial to Staples, since, in order to see why he frightens people, he needs to see himself in the stereotypical ways that others see him. Thus, by the middle of this opening paragraph (in the sentence beginning "To her"), he literally switches the point of view from his own perspective to that of the young and terrified white woman, describing his appearance as she would perceive it.

Point of view is not always a matter of a specific location or position. Writers are not always present in their essays as dramatic characters. In many reflective, informative, or argumentative essays, the point of view is determined more by a writer's intellectual attitude or opinions—an angle of vision—than by a precise physical perspective. As an example of how a writer establishes a personal perspective without introducing a first-person narrator or a characterized self, note the following passage from Wole Soyinka's "Every Dictator's Nightmare." The author prefaces his essay in support of universal human rights with a clear position against authoritarianism and fanaticism, praising Martin Luther's famous theses against religious absolutism. He goes on to argue that religion and Western philosophy have functioned to exclude some populations from basic rights:

> Polarizations within various micro-worlds—us versus the inferior them—have long been armed with industrious rationalizations. Christian and Islamic theologians throughout history have quarried their scriptures for passages that stress the incontestable primacy of an unseen and unknowable Supreme Deity who has conferred authority on them. And to what end? Largely to divide the world into us and the rest. The great philosophical minds of Europe, like Hume, Hegel, and Kant, bent their prodigious talents to separating the species into those with rights and those with none, founded on the convenient theory that some people were human and others less so (page 767).

With the exception of the first paragraph of the essay, there is no first person singular here, nor a dramatically rendered self. Yet this passage conveys a very distinct point of view.

4 *Patterns* A writer can also be present in an essay as a *writer*—that is, a person consciously crafting and shaping his or her work. This artistic presence is not always obvious. Yet when we begin to detect in our reading certain kinds of repeated elements—a metaphor or an image, a twist on an earlier episode, a conclusion that echoes the opening—we become aware that someone is deliberately shaping experience or ideas in a special manner. We often find this type of presence in imaginative literature—especially in novels and poems—as well as in essays that possess a distinct literary flavor.

As an example of creating a presence through patterns, look at the opening paragraph of E. B. White's now-classic essay, "Once More to the Lake" (page 281).

> One summer, along about 1904, my father rented a camp on a lake in Maine and took us all there for the month of August. We all got ringworm from some kittens and had to rub Pond's Extract on our arms and legs night and morning, and my father rolled over in a canoe with all his clothes on; but outside of that the vacation was a success and from then

on none of us ever thought there was any place in the world like that lake in Maine. We returned summer after summer—always on August 1st for one month. I have since become a salt-water man, but sometimes in summer there are days when the restlessness of the tides and the fearful cold of the sea water and the incessant wind that blows across the afternoon and into the evening make me wish for the placidity of a lake in the woods. A few weeks ago this feeling got so strong I bought myself a couple of bass hooks and a spinner and returned to the lake where we used to go, for a week's fishing and to revisit old haunts.

If in rereading this opening, you circle every use of the word *and*, you will clearly see a pattern of repetition. *And,* of course, is a very unobtrusive word, and you may not notice right off how White keeps it present throughout the passage. This repetition alone may strike you at first as of no special importance, but as you read through the essay and see how much of White's central theme depends on the idea of return and repetition, you will get a better sense of why the little word *and*—a word that subtly reinforces the idea of repetition itself—is so significant.

E. B. White is present in his essay in more obvious ways—he is both telling us the story and he appears in it as a character. But he is also present to us as a writer, someone consciously shaping the language and form of his essay. We are dealing here with three levels of presence (which might also be described as three levels of "I"). If this sounds confusing, just think of a movie in which a single person directs the film, writes the script, and plays a leading role. It's not that uncommon. If you watch the 1987 film *Hannah and Her Sisters,* for example, you can observe the three presences of Woody Allen. Allen is not only visibly present in the film as one of the chief characters, but we also can detect his creative and shaping presence as the author of the screenplay (for which he won an Oscar) and as the director. The audience can directly see him on the screen as an actor; but the audience can also infer his presence as a scriptwriter and especially as a director—presences that, though less directly observable, are still original and powerful.

THE SELECTIONS IN THIS BOOK

Many of the selections in this book feature the first-person point of view directly. These selections appear mostly in the first two parts, "The Informal Voice: Diaries, Journals, Notebooks, Testimony" and "Personal Writing: Exploring Our Own Lives." In most of these journal entries and essays, the writer will appear as both narrator and main character, and the writer's presence will be quite observable.

But private and personal writing provide only a fraction of the different types of nonfiction that appear regularly in books, newspapers, and magazines. Many essays are written on specific topics and deal with specific issues. Most of the essays appearing in America's dominant periodicals, for example, are intended to be either informative or persuasive; the author wants to convey information about a particular subject (a Civil War battle) or wants to express an opinion about a particular issue (how to deal with the homeless). The book's third and fourth parts, "Expository Writing: Shaping Information" and "Argumentative Writing: Contending with Issues," contain a large number of selections that illustrate writing intended to inform, argue, and persuade.

You'll notice, however, a strong writer's presence in many of the informative and persuasive essays. This is deliberate. To write informatively or persuasively about subjects other than yourself doesn't mean that you have to disappear as a writer. Sometimes you will want to insert your own experiences and testimony into an argumentative essay; at other times you will want to assume a distinct viewpoint concerning a piece of information; and at still other times—though you may not introduce the first-person singular—you will make your presence strongly felt in your tone of voice or simply in the way you arrange your facts and juxtapose details. At the heart of the word *information* is *form*. Writers don't passively receive facts and information in a totally finished format; they need to shape their information, to give it form. This shaping or patterning is something the writer *contributes*. A large part of the instructional purpose of this collection is to encourage you to pay more attention to the different ways writers are present in their work.

An individual writer's presence and voice are perhaps more easily discerned in nonfiction than in fiction. The reason for this is that a novelist or short story writer invents and gives voices to numerous characters who should not be confused with the author. Sometimes, a story is told by an invented character who also should not be closely identified with his or her author. A good example of this technique can be found in John Updike's "A & P" (see page 888), in which a story is narrated in the distinctive voice of its main character, Sammy, a teenager who is working at a small suburban supermarket. Although the story is written in the first-person singular—exactly like most personal essays—the character and voice are fictional and do not correspond to any real person. Sammy is not John Updike nor does he necessarily speak like John Updike would if we met him.

To further complicate matters, this biographical gap between narrator and author remains even when a story that is told in the third person appears to be written in the voice of the author. The third-person narrator is also invented and the narrative voice and presence may have little to do with the life of the author who created it. So in what ways can the writer's presence be observed in a story if we cannot attach to its teller any biographical connection with its author? In fiction, we often find a writer's presence in a distinctive style of writing, in certain repeated patterns, in the dynamics of structure and plot, and of course in the ethical, spiritual, or intellectual values a story may be intended to illustrate. In certain stories, to be sure, a particular character may clearly represent the author's own values, and in those cases we might argue that the writer becomes "present" in that character. As can be seen in Part V, "The Voices of Fiction: Ten Modern Short Stories," an author may refuse to locate his or her moral and psychological values within a particular character but will expect instead that the reader will derive these values from the overall perspective of the story itself. Unlike essayists, short story writers rarely state their ethical or aesthetic values directly and explicitly. As the novelist D. H. Lawrence aptly put it, in fiction we must trust the tale and not the teller. We have included in *The Writer's Presence* several examples of fiction and nonfiction by the same author (e.g., Raymond Carver, Jamaica Kincaid, Amy Tan, and Alice Walker) so that readers can explore the different ways a writer's values are conveyed in different genres.

THE READER'S PRESENCE

Because almost all writing (and *all* published writing) is intended to be read, we can't dismiss the importance of the reader. Just as we find different levels of a writer's presence in a given piece of writing, so too can we detect different ways in which a reader can be present.

An author writes a short essay offering an opinion about gun control. The author herself has been the victim of a shooting, and her piece, though it includes her personal experiences, is largely made up of a concrete plan to eliminate all guns—even hunting rifles—from American life. She would like lawmakers to adopt her plan. Yet, in writing her essay, she imagines a great deal of resistance to her argument. In other words, she imagines a reader who will most likely disagree with her and who needs to be won over. Let's imagine she gets her essay published in *Newsweek*.

Now imagine three people in a dentist's office who within the same afternoon pick up this issue of *Newsweek* and read the essay. One of them has also been victimized by guns (her son was accidentally wounded by a hunter), and she reads the essay with great sympathy and conviction. She understands perfectly what this woman has gone through and believes in her plan completely. The next reader, a man who has never once in his life committed a crime and has no tolerance for criminals, is outraged by the essay. He was practically brought up in the woods and loves to hunt. He could never adopt a gun control plan that would in effect criminalize hunting. He's ready to fire off a letter attacking this woman's plan. The third reader also enjoys hunting and has always felt that hunting rifles should be exempt from any government regulation of firearms. But he finds the woman's plan convincing and feasible. He spends the rest of the day trying to think of counterarguments.

Obviously, these are only three of many possibilities. But you should be able to see from this example the differences between the reader imagined by the writer and some actual readers. The one person who completely agreed with the writer was not the kind of reader the author had originally imagined or was trying to persuade; she was already persuaded. And though the other two readers were part of her intended audience, one of them could never be persuaded to her point of view, whereas the other one might.

The differences briefly outlined here are distinctions between what can be called implied readers and actual readers. The implied reader is the reader imagined by the writer for a particular piece of writing. In constructing arguments, for example, it is usually effective to imagine readers we are *trying* to win over to our views. Otherwise, we are simply asking people who already agree with us to agree with us—what's commonly known as "preaching to the converted."

In informative or critical essays, a writer also needs to be careful about the implied reader. For example, it's always important to ask how much your intended audience may already know about your subject. Here's a practical illustration. If you were asked to write a review of a recent film for your college newspaper, you would assume your readers had not yet seen it (or else you might annoy them by giving away some surprises). On the other hand, if you were asked to write a critical essay about the same movie for a film course, you could assume your readers had seen it. It's the same movie, and you have the same opinions about it, but your two essays had two different purposes, and in the process of writing them you imagined readers with two different levels of knowledge about the film.

Actual readers, of course, differ from implied readers in that they are real people who read the writing—not readers intended or imagined by the writer. As you read the essays in this collection, you should be aware of at least two readers—(1) the reader you think the writer imagines for the essay, and (2) the reader you are in actuality. Sometimes you will seem very close to the kind of reader the writer is imagining. In those cases, you might say that you "identify" with a particular writer, essay, or point of view. At other times, however, you will notice a great deal of distance between the reader the author imagines and you as an actual reader. For example, you may feel excluded by the author on the basis of race, gender, class, or expected knowledge and educational level. Or you may feel you know more than the author does about a particular topic.

To help you get accustomed to your role as a reader, each selection in the book is followed by a set of questions, "The Reader's Presence." These questions are designed to orient you to the various levels of reading suggested by the selection. Some of the questions will ask you to identify the kind of reader you think the author imagines; other questions will prompt you to think about specific ways you may differ from the author's intended reader; others will help you to make connections between and among the selections and authors. In general, the questions are intended to make you more deeply aware of your *presence* as a reader.

In this brief introduction, we covered only two levels of readers (imagined and actual), but some literary essays demand more complex consideration. Whenever we think more than these two types of readers need to be identified in an essay, we will introduce this information in the questions.

We hope you will find *The Writer's Presence* a stimulating book to read and think about. To make our presence felt as writers is as much a matter of self-empowerment as it is of faith. It requires the confidence that we can affect others, or determine a course of action, or even surprise ourselves by new ideas or by acquiring new powers of articulation. Part of the enduring pleasure of writing is precisely that element of surprise, of originality—that lifelong pleasure of discovering new resources of language, finding new means of knowing ourselves, and inventing new ways to be present in the world.

Part I

The Informal Voice: Diaries, Journals, Notebooks, Testimony

1

Toi Derricotte

From *The Black Notebooks*

In the 1970s Toi Derricotte, a well-known and award-winning African American poet, moved with her husband and young son to an upscale, all-white New Jersey suburb. She soon began keeping a sketchy yet intimate journal of her experiences with friends, neighbors, and family as complex and unpleasant tensions developed. As she wrote, she realized that her disclosures were bringing her face to face with her own shame, her own "internalized racism." She worked at the notebooks for twenty-five years, slowly revising them until they captured "the language of self-hate, the pain of re-emerging thought and buried memory and consciousness." The Black Notebooks: An Interior Journey, *from which the following selections were extracted, was published in 1997. It won a number of important awards and was a* New York Times *Notable Book of the Year. "October" recounts an episode that took place while Derricotte and her husband were house-hunting in New Jersey; the incident in "July" occurred after they had moved to the all-white community.*

Born in Detroit, Michigan, in 1941, Derricotte is also the author of four collections of poetry: Natural Birth, The Empress of the Death House, Captivity, *and* Tender. *She currently teaches at the University of Pittsburgh.*

OCTOBER

It's the overriding reality I must get through. Each time I drive down the streets and see only whites, each time I notice no blacks in the local supermarket or walking on the streets, I think, *I'm not supposed to be here.* When I go into real estate agents' offices, I put on a mask. At first they hope you are in for a quick sell. They show you houses they want to get rid of. But if you stick around, and if you are the "right kind," they show you ones just newly listed, and sometimes not even on the market. There are neighborhoods that even most white people are not supposed to be in.

I make myself likable, optimistic. I am married, a woman who belongs to a man. Sometimes I reveal I am Catholic, if it might add a feeling of connection. It is not entirely that I am acting. I am myself but slightly strained, like you might strain slightly in order to hear something whispered.

Yesterday an agent took me into the most lily-white neighborhood imaginable, took me right into the spotless kitchen, the dishwasher rumbling, full of the children's dishes. I opened the closets as if I were a thief, as if I were filthying them, as if I believe about myself what they believe: that I'm "passing," that my silence is a crime.

The first woman I knew about who "passed" was the bronze-haired daughter of insurance money, one of the wealthiest black families in the United States. I remember my mother telling me stories of her white roadster, how she wrote plays and opened a theater. She had directed several of the plays in which my mother and father had acted. She went to New York to "make it" and was published in the *New York Times*. I was seven when my father went down to meet the midnight train that brought her home: people said she had confessed to her rich fiancé that she was black and he had jilted her. They dressed her in a long bronze dress, a darkened tone of her long auburn hair. She looked like Sleeping Beauty in a casket made especially for her with a glass top.

My mother told me how, when she was young, her mother used to   5
get great pleasure when she would seat her daughter in the white part of the train and then depart, as if she were her servant. She said her mother would stand alongside the train and wave good-bye with a smile on her face, like a kid who has gotten away with the cookies. And my father told how, during the Detroit riots of 1943, when black men were being pulled off the buses and beaten to death, he used to walk down East Grand Boulevard as a dare.

Of course, we are never caught; it is absolutely inconceivable that we could go unrecognized, that we are that much like them. In fact, we are the same.

When Bruce and I first got married, I had been looking for an apartment for months. Finally, I found a building in a nice neighborhood with a playground nearby, and a school that was integrated. I rang the bell and was relieved when the supervisor who came to the door was black. I loved the apartment. Then I became terrified. Should I tell *him* we're black? Would that make my chances of getting the apartment greater? I wondered if he would be glad to have another black family in the building, or if maybe his job was dependent on his keeping us out. I decided to be silent, to take the chance that he liked me.

When I left, sailing over the George Washington Bridge, I had my first panic attack. I thought I might drive my car right over the edge. I felt so high up there, so disconnected, so completely at my own mercy. Some part of me doesn't give a fuck about boundaries — in fact, sees the boundaries and is determined to dance over them no matter what the consequences are. I am so precarious, strung out between two precipices, that even when I get to the other side, I am still not down, still not so low I can't harm myself.

I could hardly control my car, my heart pounding, my hands sweaty on the wheel. I had to pull off the West Side Highway as soon as I could, and I went into the first place I could find, a meat-packing house. The kind white man let me use the phone to call Bruce before he took me in a big meat truck to the nearest hospital. The doctor said it was anxiety, and I should just go home and rest. For days I was afraid to come out of my house, and even now, though I push myself to do it, every time I go over a high place, or am in a strange territory, I fear I will lose control, that something horrible and destructive will come out of me.

Each night Bruce and I don't talk about it, as if there were no cost to   10
what I'm doing, or as if whatever the cost is I've got to pay.

JULY

This morning I put my car in the shop. The neighborhood shop. When I went to pick it up I had a conversation with the man who had worked on it. I told him I had been afraid to leave the car there at night with the keys in it. "Don't worry," he said. "You don't have to worry about stealing as long as the niggers don't move in." I couldn't believe it. I hoped I had heard him wrong. "What did you say?" I asked. He repeated the same thing without hesitation.

In the past, my anger would have swelled quickly. I would have blurted out something, hotly demanded he take my car down off the rack immediately, though he had not finished working on it, and taken off in a blaze. I love that reaction. The only feeling of power one can possibly have in a situation in which there is such a sudden feeling of powerlessness is to "do" something, handle the situation. When you "do" something, everything is clear. But this is the only repair shop in the city. Might I have to come back here someday in an emergency?

Blowing off steam is supposed to make you feel better. But in this situation it *doesn't!* After responding in anger, I often feel sad, guilty, frightened, and confused. Perhaps my anger isn't just about race. Perhaps it's like those rapid-fire responses to Bruce—a way of dulling the edge of feelings that lie even deeper.

I let the tension stay in my body. I go home and sit with myself for an hour, trying to grasp the feeling—the odor of self-hatred, the biting stench of shame.

The Reader's Presence

1. In what ways does Derricotte try to fit into a white community? What features of an all-white community does she appear to find desirable? What features worry her? What does she mean by "passing"? How does she feel about the act of "passing"?

2. Why doesn't Derricotte express her anger to the auto mechanic? What explanations does she offer? What feelings does her silence lead to?

3. Compare Derricotte's growing awareness of "the odor of self-hatred, the biting stench of shame" to Malcolm X's insights at the end of "Homeboy." How do the tones of the two pieces compare? What does this comparison tell you about the differences between a journal entry and an essay?

2

Joan Didion

On Keeping a Notebook

The author of novels, short stories, screenplays, and essays, Joan Didion (b. 1934) began her career in 1956 as a staff writer at Vogue *magazine in New York. In 1963 she published her first novel,* Run River, *and the following year returned to her native California. Didion's essays have appeared in periodicals ranging from* Mademoiselle *to the* National Review. *Her essay "On Keeping a Notebook" can be found in her collection of essays,* Slouching Towards Bethlehem *(1968). Didion's other nonfiction publications include* The White Album *(1979),* Salvador *(1983),* Miami *(1987),* After Henry *(1992), and* Political Fictions *(2001).*

Didion has defined a writer as "a person whose most absorbed and passionate hours are spent arranging words on pieces of paper. I write entirely to find out what's on my mind, what I'm thinking, what I'm looking at, what I'm seeing and what it means, what I want and what I'm afraid of." She has also said that "all writing is an attempt to find out what matters, to find the pattern in disorder, to find the grammar in the shimmer. Actually I don't know whether you find the grammar in the shimmer or you impose a grammar on the shimmer, but I am quite specific about the grammar—I mean it literally. The scene that you see in your mind finds its own structure; the structure dictates the arrangement of the words. . . . All the writer has to do really is to find the words." However, she warns, "You have to be alone to do this."

"'That woman Estelle,'" the note reads, "'is partly the reason why George Sharp and I are separated today.' *Dirty crepe-de-Chine wrapper, hotel bar, Wilmington RR, 9:45 a.m. August Monday morning.*"

Since the note is in my notebook, it presumably has some meaning to me. I study it for a long while. At first I have only the most general notion of what I was doing on an August Monday morning in the bar of the hotel across from the Pennsylvania Railroad station in Wilmington, Delaware (waiting for a train? missing one? 1960? 1961? why Wilmington?), but I do remember being there. The woman in the dirty crepe-de-Chine wrapper had come down from her room for a beer, and the bartender had heard before the reason why George Sharp and she were separated today. "Sure," he said, and went on mopping the floor. "You told me." At the other end of the bar is a girl. She is talking, pointedly, not to the man beside her but to a cat lying in the triangle of sunlight cast through the open door. She is wearing a plaid silk dress from Peck & Peck, and the hem is coming down.

Here is what it is: The girl has been on the Eastern Shore, and now she is going back to the city, leaving the man beside her, and all she can see ahead are the viscous summer sidewalks and the 3 A.M. long-distance calls that will make her lie awake and then sleep drugged through all the steaming mornings left in August (1960? 1961?). Because she must go directly from the train to lunch in New York, she wishes that she had a safety pin for the hem of the plaid silk dress, and she also wishes that she could forget about the hem and the lunch and stay in the cool bar that smells of disinfectant and malt and make friends with the woman in the crepe-de-Chine wrapper. She is afflicted by a little self-pity, and she wants to compare Estelles. That is what that was all about.

Why did I write it down? In order to remember, of course, but exactly what was it I wanted to remember? How much of it actually happened? Did any of it? Why do I keep a notebook at all? It is easy to deceive oneself on all those scores. The impulse to write things down is a peculiarly compulsive one, inexplicable to those who do not share it, useful only accidentally, only secondarily, in the way that any compulsion tries to justify itself. I suppose that it begins or does not begin in the cradle. Although I have felt compelled to write things down since I was five years old, I doubt that my daughter ever will, for she is a singularly blessed and accepting child, delighted with life exactly as life presents itself to her, unafraid to go to sleep and unafraid to wake up. Keepers of private notebooks are a different breed altogether, lonely and resistant rearrangers of things, anxious malcontents, children afflicted apparently at birth with some presentiment of loss.

My first notebook was a Big Five tablet, given to me by my mother   5
with the sensible suggestion that I stop whining and learn to amuse myself by writing down my thoughts. She returned the tablet to me a few years ago; the first entry is an account of a woman who believed herself to be freezing to death in the Arctic night, only to find, when day broke, that she had stumbled onto the Sahara Desert, where she would die of the heat before lunch. I have no idea what turn of a five-year-old's mind could have prompted so insistently "ironic" and exotic a story, but it does reveal a certain predilection for the extreme which has dogged me

into adult life; perhaps if I were analytically inclined I would find it a truer story than any I might have told about Donald Johnson's birthday party or the day my cousin Brenda put Kitty Litter in the aquarium.

So the point of my keeping a notebook has never been, nor is it now, to have an accurate factual record of what I have been doing or thinking. That would be a different impulse entirely, an instinct for reality which I sometimes envy but do not possess. At no point have I ever been able successfully to keep a diary; my approach to daily life ranges from the grossly negligent to the merely absent, and on those few occasions when I have tried dutifully to record a day's events, boredom has so overcome me that the results are mysterious at best. What is this business about "shopping, typing piece, dinner with E, depressed"? Shopping for what? Typing what piece? Who is E? Was this "E" depressed, or was I depressed? Who cares?

In fact I have abandoned altogether that kind of pointless entry; instead I tell what some would call lies. "That's simply not true," the members of my family frequently tell me when they come up against my memory of a shared event. "The party was *not* for you, the spider was *not* a black widow, *it wasn't that way at all.*" Very likely they are right, for not only have I always had trouble distinguishing between what happened and what merely might have happened, but I remain unconvinced that the distinction, for my purposes, matters. The cracked crab that I recall having for lunch the day my father came home from Detroit in 1945 must certainly be embroidery, worked into the day's pattern to lend verisimilitude; I was ten years old and would not now remember the cracked crab. The day's events did not turn on cracked crab. And yet it is precisely that fictitious crab that makes me see the afternoon all over again, a home movie run all too often, the father bearing gifts, the child weeping, an exercise in family love and guilt. Or that is what it was to me. Similarly, perhaps it never did snow that August in Vermont; perhaps there never were flurries in the night wind, and maybe no one else felt the ground hardening and summer already dead even as we pretended to bask in it, but that was how it felt to me, and it might as well have snowed, could have snowed, did snow.

How it felt to me: that is getting closer to the truth about a notebook. I sometimes delude myself about why I keep a notebook, imagine that some thrifty virtue derives from preserving everything observed. See enough and write it down, I tell myself, and then some morning when the world seems drained of wonder, some day when I am only going through the motions of doing what I am supposed to do, which is write — on that bankrupt morning I will simply open my notebook and there it will all be, a forgotten account with accumulated interest, paid passage back to the world out there: dialogue overheard in hotels and elevators and at the hatcheck counter in Pavillon (one middle-aged man shows his hat check to another and says, "That's my old football number"); impressions of

Bettina Aptheker and Benjamin Sonnenberg and Teddy ("Mr. Acapulco") Stauffer; careful *aperçus*[1] about tennis bums and failed fashion models and Greek shipping heiresses, one of whom taught me a significant lesson (a lesson I could have learned from F. Scott Fitzgerald, but perhaps we all must meet the very rich for ourselves) by asking, when I arrived to interview her in her orchid-filled sitting room on the second day of a paralyzing New York blizzard, whether it was snowing outside.

I imagine, in other words, that the notebook is about other people. But of course it is not. I have no real business with what one stranger said to another at the hatcheck counter in Pavillon; in fact I suspect that the line "That's my old football number" touched not my own imagination at all, but merely some memory of something once read, probably "The Eighty-Yard Run."[2] Nor is my concern with a woman in a dirty crepe-de-Chine wrapper in a Wilmington bar. My stake is always, of course, in the unmentioned girl in the plaid silk dress. *Remember what it was to be me:* that is always the point.

It is a difficult point to admit. We are brought up in the ethic that others, any others, all others, are by definition more interesting than ourselves; taught to be diffident, just this side of self-effacing. ("You're the least important person in the room and don't forget it," Jessica Mitford's[3] governess would hiss in her ear on the advent of any social occasion; I copied that into my notebook because it is only recently that I have been able to enter a room without hearing some such phrase in my inner ear.) Only the very young and the very old may recount their dreams at breakfast, dwell upon self, interrupt with memories of beach picnics and favorite Liberty lawn dresses and the rainbow trout in a creek near Colorado Springs. The rest of us are expected, rightly, to affect absorption in other people's favorite dresses, other people's trout.

And so we do. But our notebooks give us away, for however dutifully we record what we see around us, the common denominator of all we see is always, transparently, shamelessly, the implacable "I." We are not talking here about the kind of notebook that is patently for public consumption, a structural conceit for binding together a series of graceful *pensées;*[4] we are talking about something private, about bits of the mind's string too short to use, an indiscriminate and erratic assemblage with meaning only for its maker.

And sometimes even the maker has difficulty with the meaning. There does not seem to be, for example, any point in my knowing for the rest of my life that, during 1964, 720 tons of soot fell on every square mile of New York City, yet there it is in my notebook, labeled "FACT."

10

---

[1]*aperçus:* Summarizing glimpse or insight (French). —EDS.
[2]*"The Eighty-Yard Run":* Popular short story by Irwin Shaw. —EDS.
[3]*Jessica Mitford* (b. 1917): British satirical writer. —EDS.
[4]*pensées:* Thoughts or reflections (French). —EDS.

Nor do I really need to remember that Ambrose Bierce liked to spell Leland Stanford's[5] name "£eland $tanford" or that "smart women almost always wear black in Cuba," a fashion hint without much potential for practical application. And does not the relevance of these notes seem marginal at best?:

> In the basement museum of the Inyo County Courthouse in Independence, California, sign pinned to a mandarin coat: "This MANDARIN COAT was often worn by Mrs. Minnie S. Brooks when giving lectures on her TEAPOT COLLECTION."

> Redhead getting out of car in front of Beverly Wilshire Hotel, chinchilla stole, Vuitton bags with tags reading:

> > MRS. LOU FOX
> > HOTEL SAHARA
> > VEGAS

Well, perhaps not entirely marginal. As a matter of fact, Mrs. Minnie S. Brooks and her MANDARIN COAT pull me back into my own childhood, for although I never knew Mrs. Brooks and did not visit Inyo County until I was thirty, I grew up in just such a world, in houses cluttered with Indian relics and bits of gold ore and ambergris and the souvenirs my Aunt Mercy Farnsworth brought back from the Orient. It is a long way from that world to Mrs. Lou Fox's world, where we all live now, and is it not just as well to remember that? Might not Mrs. Minnie S. Brooks help me to remember what I am? Might not Mrs. Lou Fox help me to remember what I am not?

But sometimes the point is harder to discern. What exactly did I have in mind when I noted down that it cost the father of someone I know $650 a month to light the place on the Hudson in which he lived before the Crash? What use was I planning to make of this line by Jimmy Hoffa:[6] "I may have my faults, but being wrong ain't one of them"? And although I think interesting to know where the girls who travel with the Syndicate have their hair done when they find themselves on the West Coast, will I ever make suitable use of it? Might I not be better off just passing it on to John O'Hara?[7] What is a recipe for sauerkraut doing in my notebook? What kind of magpie keeps this notebook? "*He was born the night the* Titanic *went down.*" That seems a nice enough line, and I even recall who said it, but is it not really a better line in life than it could ever be in fiction?

---

[5]*Bierce . . . Stanford's:* Ambrose Bierce (1842–1914?), American journalist and short story writer known for his savage wit; Leland Stanford (1824–1893), wealthy railroad builder who was a governor of California and the founder of Stanford University. —EDS.

[6]*Jimmy Hoffa* (1913–1975?): Controversial leader of the Teamsters Union who disappeared in the mid-seventies. —EDS.

[7]*John O'Hara* (1905–1970): American novelist who wrote several books about gangsters. —EDS.

But of course that is exactly it: not that I should ever use the line, but   15
that I should remember the woman who said it and the afternoon I heard
it. We were on her terrace by the sea, and we were finishing the wine left
from lunch, trying to get what sun there was, a California winter sun.
The woman whose husband was born the night the *Titanic* went down
wanted to rent her house, wanted to go back to her children in Paris. I remember wishing that I could afford the house, which cost $1,000 a
month. "Someday you will," she said lazily. "Someday it all comes."
There in the sun on her terrace it seemed easy to believe in someday, but
later I had a low-grade afternoon hangover and ran over a black snake on
the way to the supermarket and was flooded with inexplicable fear when
I heard the checkout clerk explaining to the man ahead of me why she
was finally divorcing her husband. "He left me no choice," she said over
and over as she punched the register. "He has a little seven-month-old
baby by her, he left me no choice." I would like to believe that my dread
then was for the human condition, but of course it was for me, because I
wanted a baby and did not then have one and because I wanted to own
the house that cost $1,000 a month to rent and because I had a hangover.

It all comes back. Perhaps it is difficult to see the value in having
one's self back in that kind of mood, but I do see it; I think we are well
advised to keep on nodding terms with the people we used to be whether
we find them attractive company or not. Otherwise they turn up unan-
nounced and surprise us, come hammering on the mind's door at 4 A.M.
of a bad night and demand to know who deserted them, who betrayed
them, who is going to make amends. We forget all too soon the things we
thought we could never forget. We forget the loves and the betrayals
alike, forget what we whispered and what we screamed, forget who we
were. I have already lost touch with a couple of people I used to be; one
of them, a seventeen-year-old, presents little threat, although it would be
of some interest to me to know again what it feels like to sit on a river
levee drinking vodka-and-orange-juice and listening to Les Paul and
Mary Ford[8] and their echoes sing "How High the Moon" on the car
radio. (You see I still have the scenes, but I no longer perceive myself
among those present, no longer could even improvise the dialogue.) The
other one, a twenty-three-year-old, bothers me more. She was always a
good deal of trouble, and I suspect she will reappear when I least want to
see her, skirts too long, shy to the point of aggravation, always the injured party, full of recriminations and little hurts and stories I do not
want to hear again, at once saddening me and angering me with her vulnerability and ignorance, an apparition all the more insistent for being so
long banished.

It is a good idea, then, to keep in touch, and I suppose that keeping in
touch is what notebooks are all about. And we are all on our own when it

[8]*Les Paul and Mary Ford:* Husband-and-wife musical team of the forties and fifties
who had many hit records. —EDS.

comes to keeping those lines open to ourselves: your notebook will never help me, nor mine you. "*So what's new in the whiskey business?*" What could that possibly mean to you? To me it means a blonde in a Pucci bathing suit sitting with a couple of fat men by the pool at the Beverly Hills Hotel. Another man approaches, and they all regard one another in silence for a while. "So what's new in the whiskey business?" one of the fat men finally says by way of welcome, and the blonde stands up, arches one foot and dips it in the pool, looking all the while at the cabaña where Baby Pignatari is talking on the telephone. That is all there is to that, except that several years later I saw the blonde coming out of Saks Fifth Avenue in New York with her California complexion and a voluminous mink coat. In the harsh wind that day she looked old and irrevocably tired to me, and even the skins in the mink coat were not worked the way they were doing them that year, not the way she would have wanted them done, and there is the point of the story. For a while after that I did not like to look in the mirror, and my eyes would skim the newspapers and pick out only the deaths, the cancer victims, the premature coronaries, the suicides, and I stopped riding the Lexington Avenue IRT because I noticed for the first time that all the strangers I had seen for years—the man with the seeing-eye dog, the spinster who read the classified pages every day, the fat girl who always got off with me at Grand Central—looked older than they once had.

It all comes back. Even that recipe for sauerkraut: even that brings it back. I was on Fire Island when I first made that sauerkraut, and it was raining, and we drank a lot of bourbon and ate the sauerkraut and went to bed at ten, and I listened to the rain and the Atlantic and felt safe. I made the sauerkraut again last night and it did not make me feel any safer, but that is, as they say, another story.

The Reader's Presence

1. Notice that Didion begins her essay not with a general comment about notebooks but with an actual notebook entry. What does the entry sound like at first? What effect do you think Didion wants it to have on you as a reader?

2. Consider the comparison Didion makes in paragraph 6 between a notebook and a diary. How do they differ? Why is she fond of one and not the other? How does her example of a diary entry support her distinction?

3. Didion's notebook entries were never intended to have an audience. How is that apparent from the entries themselves? Compare Didion's ideas about keeping a notebook to Virginia Woolf's diary entries on the writing process. Focus especially on the first paragraph, in which Woolf discusses the advantages of a form of

writing that is for "[her] own eye only." Where do you fit in as a reader of Didion's work? of Woolf's work? Do you think the two writers would agree about the uses of private diaries?

3

Anne Frank
From *The Diary of a Young Girl*

On her thirteenth birthday (June 12, 1942), and as WW II raged on, Anne Frank began a diary that she called "Kitty." Less than a month later, she and her family went into hiding in a cramped attic in Amsterdam, Holland, in hopes of escaping the Nazis. She continued to keep her diary, addressing it in the form of letters that candidly and freely expressed her most personal thoughts and feelings. Living in conditions that allowed for little privacy, she cherished the secrecy her diary provided: "Who besides me will ever read these letters?" she writes, never dreaming that after her death her intimate diary would be found, published, and read by millions throughout the world.

In August 1944 the Frank family's hiding place was discovered by the Nazis and in March 1945, three months before her sixteenth birthday, Anne died in the concentration camp at Bergen-Belsen. As they searched the attic for valuables and important documents, the Nazis left behind on the floor an insignificant-looking little red-checkered cloth book. Anne Frank: The Diary of a Young Girl *was first published in 1952.*

THINGS THAT LIE BURIED DEEP IN MY HEART

Saturday, June 20, 1942

I haven't written for a few days, because I wanted first of all to think about my diary. It's an odd idea for someone like me to keep a diary; not only because I have never done so before, but because it seems to me that neither I—nor for that matter anyone else—will be interested in the unbosomings of a thirteen-year-old schoolgirl. Still, what does that matter? I want to write, but more than that, I want to bring out all kinds of things that lie buried deep in my heart.

There is a saying that "paper is more patient than man"; it came back to me on one of my slightly melancholy days, while I sat chin in hand, feeling too bored and limp even to make up my mind whether to go out or stay at home. Yes, there is no doubt that paper is patient and as I don't intend to show this cardboard-covered notebook, bearing the proud name of "diary," to anyone, unless I find a real friend, boy or girl, probably nobody cares. And now I come to the root of the matter, the reason for my starting a diary: it is that I have no such real friend.

Let me put it more clearly, since no one will believe that a girl of thirteen feels herself quite alone in the world, nor is it so. I have darling parents and a sister of sixteen. I know about thirty people whom one might call friends—I have strings of boy friends, anxious to catch a glimpse of me and who, failing that, peep at me through mirrors in class. I have relations, aunts and uncles, who are darlings too, a good home, no—I don't seem to lack anything. But it's the same with all my friends, just fun and joking, nothing more. I can never bring myself to talk of anything outside the common round. We don't seem to be able to get any closer, that is the root of the trouble. Perhaps I lack confidence, but anyway, there it is, a stubborn fact and I don't seem to be able to do anything about it.

Hence, this diary. In order to enhance in my mind's eye the picture of the friend for whom I have waited so long, I don't want to set down a series of bald facts in a diary like most people do, but I want this diary itself to be my friend, and I shall call my friend Kitty. No one will grasp what I'm talking about if I begin my letters to Kitty just out of the blue, so albeit unwillingly, I will start by sketching in brief the story of my life.

My father was thirty-six when he married my mother, who was then   5
twenty-five. My sister Margot was born in 1926 in Frankfort-on-Main, I followed on June 12, 1929, and, as we are Jewish, we emigrated to Holland in 1933, where my father was appointed Managing Director of Travies N.V. This firm is in close relationship with the firm of Kolen & Co. in the same building, of which my father is a partner.

The rest of our family, however, felt the full impact of Hitler's anti-Jewish laws, so life was filled with anxiety. In 1938 after the pogroms, my two uncles (my mother's brothers) escaped to the U.S.A. My old grandmother came to us, she was then seventy-three. After May 1940 good times rapidly fled: first the war, then the capitulation, followed by the arrival of the Germans, which is when the sufferings of us Jews really began. Anti-Jewish decrees followed each other in quick succession. Jews must wear a yellow star,[1] Jews must hand in their bicycles, Jews are banned from trains and are forbidden to drive. Jews are only allowed to do their shopping between three and five o'clock and then only in shops which bear the placard "Jewish shop." Jews must be indoors by eight o'clock and cannot even sit in their own gardens after that hour. Jews are forbidden to visit theaters, cinemas, and other places of entertainment. Jews may not take part in public sports. Swimming baths, tennis courts, hockey fields, and other sports grounds are all prohibited to them. Jews may not visit Christians. Jews must go to Jewish schools, and many more restrictions of a similar kind.

---

[1]All Jews were ordered to wear a yellow six-pointed star.—EDS.

So we could not do this and were forbidden to do that. But life went on in spite of it all. Jopie[2] used to say to me, "You're scared to do anything, because it may be forbidden." Our freedom was strictly limited. Yet things were still bearable.

Granny died in January 1942; no one will ever know how much she is present in my thoughts and how much I love her still.

In 1934 I went to school at the Montessori Kindergarten and continued there. It was at the end of the school year, I was in form 6B, when I had to say good-by to Mrs. K. We both wept, it was very sad. In 1941 I went, with my sister Margot, to the Jewish Secondary School, she into the fourth form and I into the first.

So far everything is all right with the four of us and here I come to the present day.   10

I ALWAYS COME BACK TO MY DIARY

Saturday, November 7, 1942

Dear Kitty,

Mummy is frightfully irritable and that always seems to herald unpleasantness for me. Is it just chance that Daddy and Mummy never rebuke Margot and that they always drop on me for everything? Yesterday evening, for instance: Margot was reading a book with lovely drawings in it; she got up and went upstairs, put the book down ready to go on with it later. I wasn't doing anything, so picked up the book and started looking at the pictures. Margot came back, saw "her" book in my hands, wrinkled her forehead and asked for the book back. Just because I wanted to look a little further on, Margot got more and more angry. Then Mummy joined in: "Give the book to Margot; she was reading it," she said. Daddy came into the room. He didn't even know what it was all about, but saw the injured look on Margot's face and promptly dropped on me: "I'd like to see what you'd say if Margot ever started looking at one of your books!" I gave way at once, laid the book down, and left the room — offended, as they thought. It so happened I was neither offended nor cross, just miserable. It wasn't right of Daddy to judge without knowing what the squabble was about. I would have given Margot the book myself, and much more quickly, if Mummy and Daddy hadn't interfered. They took Margot's part at once, as though she were the victim of some great injustice.

It's obvious that Mummy would stick up for Margot; she and Margot always do back each other up. I'm so used to that that I'm utterly indifferent to both Mummy's jawing and Margot's moods.

I love them; but only because they are Mummy and Margot. With Daddy it's different. If he holds Margot up as an example, approves of

---

[2]*Jopie:* A girlfriend. — EDS.

what she does, praises and caresses her, then something gnaws at me inside, because I adore Daddy. He is the one I look up to. I don't love anyone in the world but him. He doesn't notice that he treats Margot
differently from me. Now Margot is just the prettiest, sweetest, most
beautiful girl in the world. But all the same I feel I have some right to be
taken seriously too. I have always been the dunce, the ne'er-do-well of the
family, I've always had to pay double for my deeds, first with the scolding
and then again because of the way my feelings are hurt. Now I'm not satisfied with this apparent favoritism any more. I want something from
Daddy that he is not able to give me.

I'm not jealous of Margot, never have been. I don't envy her good
looks or her beauty. It is only that I long for Daddy's real love: not only
as his child, but for me—Anne, myself.

I cling to Daddy because it is only through him that I am able to re-   15
tain the remnant of family feeling. Daddy doesn't understand that I need
to give vent to my feelings over Mummy sometimes. He doesn't want to
talk about it; he simply avoids anything which might lead to remarks
about Mummy's failings. Just the same, Mummy and her failings are
something I find harder to bear than anything else. I don't know how to
keep it all to myself. I can't always be drawing attention to her untidiness,
her sarcasm, and her lack of sweetness, neither can I believe that I'm always in the wrong.

We are exact opposites in everything; so naturally we are bound to
run up against each other. I don't pronounce judgment on Mummy's
character, for that is something I can't judge. I only look at her as a
mother, and she just doesn't succeed in being that to me; I have to be my
own mother. I've drawn myself apart from them all; I am my own skipper
and later on I shall see where I come to land. All this comes about particularly because I have in my mind's eye an image of what a perfect mother
and wife should be; and in her whom I must call "Mother" I find no trace
of that image.

I am always making resolutions not to notice Mummy's bad example. I want to see only the good side of her and to seek in myself what
I cannot find in her. But it doesn't work; and the worst of it is that neither
Daddy nor Mummy understands this gap in my life, and I blame them for
it. I wonder if anyone can ever succeed in making their children absolutely content.

Sometimes I believe that God wants to try me, both now and later on;
I must become good through my own efforts, without examples and without good advice. Then later on I shall be all the stronger. Who besides me
will ever read these letters? From whom but myself shall I get comfort?
As I need comforting often, I frequently feel weak, and dissatisfied with
myself; my shortcomings are too great. I know this, and every day I try to
improve myself, again and again.

My treatment varies so much. One day Anne is so sensible and is allowed to know everything; and the next day I hear that Anne is just a silly
little goat who doesn't know anything at all and imagines that she's

learned a wonderful lot from books. I'm not a baby or a spoiled darling any more, to be laughed at, whatever she does. I have my own views, plans, and ideas, though I can't put them into words yet. Oh, so many things bubble up inside me as I lie in bed, having to put up with people I'm fed up with, who always misinterpret my intentions. That's why in the end I always come back to my diary. That is where I start and finish, because Kitty is always patient. I'll promise her that I shall persevere, in spite of everything, and find my own way through it all, and swallow my tears. I only wish I could see the results already or occasionally receive encouragement from someone who loves me.

Don't condemn me; remember rather that sometimes I too can reach   20
the bursting point.

Yours, Anne

A SWEET SECRET

Wednesday, January 5, 1944

Dear Kitty,

I have two things to confess to you today, which will take a long time. But I must tell someone and you are the best one to tell, as I know that, come what may, you always keep a secret.

The first is about Mummy. You know that I've grumbled a lot about Mummy, yet still tried to be nice to her again. Now it is suddenly clear to me what she lacks. Mummy herself has told us that she looked upon us more as her friends than her daughters. Now that is all very fine, but still, a friend can't take a mother's place. I need my mother as an example which I can follow, I want to be able to respect her. I have the feeling that Margot thinks differently about these things and would never be able to understand what I've just told you. And Daddy avoids all arguments about Mummy.

I imagine a mother as a woman who, in the first place, shows great tact, especially towards her children when they reach our age, and who does not laugh at me if I cry about something—not pain, but other things—like "Mums" does.

One thing, which perhaps may seem rather fatuous, I have never forgiven her. It was on a day that I had to go to the dentist. Mummy and Margot were going to come with me, and agreed that I should take my bicycle. When we had finished at the dentist, and were outside again, Margot and Mummy told me that they were going into the town to look at something or buy something—I don't remember exactly what. I wanted to go, too, but was not allowed to, as I had my bicycle with me. Tears of rage sprang into my eyes, and Mummy and Margot began laughing at me. Then I became so furious that I stuck my tongue out at them in the street just as an old woman happened to pass by, who looked very shocked! I rode home on my bicycle, and I know I cried for a long time.

It is queer that the wound that Mummy made then still burns, when I   25
think of how angry I was that afternoon.

The second is something that is very difficult to tell you, because it is
about myself.

Yesterday I read an article about blushing by Sis Heyster. This article
might have been addressed to me personally. Although I don't blush very
easily, the other things in it certainly all fit me. She writes roughly something like this—that a girl in the years of puberty becomes quiet within
and begins to think about the wonders that are happening to her body.

I experience that, too, and that is why I get the feeling lately of being
embarrassed about Margot, Mummy, and Daddy. Funnily enough, Margot, who is much more shy than I am, isn't at all embarrassed.

I think what is happening to me is so wonderful, and not only what
can be seen on my body, but all that is taking place inside. I never discuss
myself or any of these things with anybody; that is why I have to talk to
myself about them.

Each time I have a period—and that has only been three times—I   30
have the feeling that in spite of all the pain, unpleasantness, and nastiness,
I have a sweet secret, and that is why, although it is nothing but a nuisance to me in a way, I always long for the time that I shall feel that secret
within me again.

Sis Heyster also writes that girls of this age don't feel quite certain of
themselves, and discover that they themselves are individuals with ideas,
thoughts, and habits. After I came here, when I was just fourteen, I began
to think about myself sooner than most girls, and to know that I am a
"person." Sometimes, when I lie in bed at night, I have a terrible desire to
feel my breasts and to listen to the quiet rhythmic beat of my heart.

I already had these kinds of feelings subconsciously before I came
here, because I remember that once when I slept with a girl friend I had a
strong desire to kiss her, and that I did do so. I could not help being terribly inquisitive over her body, for she had always kept it hidden from me.
I asked her whether, as proof of our friendship, we should feel one another's breasts, but she refused. I go into ecstasies every time I see the
naked figure of a woman, such as Venus, for example. It strikes me as so
wonderful and exquisite that I have difficulty in stopping the tears rolling
down my cheeks.

If only I had a girl friend!

Yours, Anne

The Reader's Presence

1. Why do you think the thirteen-year-old Frank feels compelled to
   write? Does she have a purpose for keeping a diary?

2. Speculate why her diary is addressed to "Kitty." What is the effect
   of personalizing her diary in this way? What does that personalization allow her to do as a person and as a writer?

3. Anne Frank wrote during wartime, but the bulk of her diary is devoted to her relationships with family and friends, and to her experiences as a teenager whose mind and body are changing. Walt Whitman, Virginia Woolf, and Michihiko Hachiya also kept journals during war. How do these writers deal with what is going on around them? How do they deal with their feelings? How do their ways of expressing context and feelings compare to Anne Frank's?

4

Michihiko Hachiya

From *Hiroshima Diary*

On August 6, 1945, the United States dropped an atomic bomb on the Japanese city of Hiroshima and introduced a new, devastating weapon into modern war. Two days later, the military dropped another bomb on Nagasaki, forcing the Japanese government into an unconditional surrender. For years, the Japanese survivors of the blasts suffered from unhealing burns, radiation poisoning, cancers, and a score of other illnesses. At first, the Japanese had no idea what had hit them, though rumors of a new secret weapon circulated rapidly. Most Americans today know of the bombing mainly through repeated images of the mushroom cloud itself; rarely do they see photographs or footage of the destruction and casualties. One of the most vivid accounts of the bombing and its immediate aftermath can be found in a diary kept by a Hiroshima physician, Michihiko Hachiya, who, though severely injured himself, miraculously found the time to record both his professional observations of a medical nightmare and his human impressions of an utterly destroyed community. Published on the tenth anniversary of the bombing of Hiroshima, Hiroshima Diary (1955) gained widespread attention. The diary runs only for some two months, from the moment of the blast on the sunny morning of August 6 to the end of September, when the American occupation was well under way.

WHAT HAD HAPPENED?
August 6, 1945

Badly injured from the blast, Dr. Hachiya managed to make his way to the hospital where he served as director and which, fortunately, was quite near his house. He spent several days in bed and did not begin writing his diary until August 8. As we can see from the following passage, however, the events were still fresh in his mind.

The hour was early; the morning still, warm, and beautiful. Shimmering leaves, reflecting sunlight from a cloudless sky, made a pleasant contrast with shadows in my garden as I gazed absently through wide-flung doors opening to the south.

Clad in drawers and undershirt, I was sprawled on the living room floor exhausted because I had just spent a sleepless night on duty as an air warden in my hospital.

Suddenly, a strong flash of light startled me — and then another. So well does one recall little things that I remember vividly how a stone lantern in the garden became brilliantly lit and I debated whether this light was caused by a magnesium flare or sparks from a passing trolley.

Garden shadows disappeared. The view where a moment before all had been so bright and sunny was now dark and hazy. Through swirling dust I could barely discern a wooden column that had supported one corner of my house. It was leaning crazily and the roof sagged dangerously.

Moving instinctively, I tried to escape, but rubble and fallen timbers   5
barred the way. By picking my way cautiously I managed to reach the *rōka*[1] and stepped down into my garden. A profound weakness overcame me, so I stopped to regain my strength. To my surprise I discovered that I was completely naked. How odd! Where were my drawers and undershirt?

What had happened?

All over the right side of my body I was cut and bleeding. A large splinter was protruding from a mangled wound in my thigh, and something warm trickled into my mouth. My cheek was torn, I discovered as I felt it gingerly, with the lower lip laid wide open. Embedded in my neck was a sizable fragment of glass which I matter-of-factly dislodged, and with the detachment of one stunned and shocked I studied it and my blood-stained hand.

Where was my wife?

Suddenly thoroughly alarmed, I began to yell for her: "Yaeko-san! Yaeko-san! Where are you?"

Blood began to spurt. Had my carotid artery been cut? Would I bleed   10
to death? Frightened and irrational, I called out again: "It's a five-hundred-ton bomb! Yaeko-san, where are you? A five-hundred-ton bomb has fallen!"

Yaeko-san, pale and frightened, her clothes torn and blood-stained, emerged from the ruins of our house holding her elbow. Seeing her, I was reassured. My own panic assuaged, I tried to reassure her.

"We'll be all right," I exclaimed. "Only let's get out of here as fast as we can."

She nodded, and I motioned for her to follow me.

The shortest path to the street lay through the house next door so through the house we went — running, stumbling, falling, and then

[1]*rōka:* A narrow outside hall. — EDS.

running again until in headlong flight we tripped over something and fell sprawling into the street. Getting to my feet, I discovered that I had tripped over a man's head.

"Excuse me! Excuse me, please!" I cried hysterically.   15

There was no answer. The man was dead. The head had belonged to a young officer whose body was crushed beneath a massive gate.

We stood in the street, uncertain and afraid, until a house across from us began to sway and then with a rending motion fell almost at our feet. Our own house began to sway, and in a minute it, too, collapsed in a cloud of dust. Other buildings caved in or toppled. Fires sprang up and whipped by a vicious wind began to spread.

It finally dawned on us that we could not stay there in the street, so we turned our steps towards the hospital. Our home was gone; we were wounded and needed treatment; and after all, it was my duty to be with my staff. This latter was an irrational thought—what good could I be to anyone, hurt as I was.

We started out, but after twenty or thirty steps I had to stop. My breath became short, my heart pounded, and my legs gave way under me. An overpowering thirst seized me and I begged Yaeko-san to find me some water. But there was no water to be found. After a little my strength somewhat returned and we were able to go on.

I was still naked, and although I did not feel the least bit of shame, I   20
was disturbed to realize that modesty had deserted me. On rounding a corner we came upon a soldier standing idly in the street. He had a towel draped across his shoulder, and I asked if he would give it to me to cover my nakedness. The soldier surrendered the towel quite willingly but said not a word. A little later I lost the towel, and Yaeko-san took off her apron and tied it around my loins.

Our progress towards the hospital was interminably slow, until finally, my legs, stiff from drying blood, refused to carry me farther. The strength, even the will, to go on deserted me, so I told my wife, who was almost as badly hurt as I, to go on alone. This she objected to, but there was no choice. She had to go ahead and try to find someone to come back for me.

Yaeko-san looked into my face for a moment, and then, without saying a word, turned away and began running towards the hospital. Once, she looked back and waved and in a moment she was swallowed up in the gloom. It was quite dark now, and with my wife gone, a feeling of dreadful loneliness overcame me.

I must have gone out of my head lying there in the road because the next thing I recall was discovering that the clot on my thigh had been dislodged and blood was again spurting from the wound. I pressed my hand to the bleeding area and after a while the bleeding stopped and I felt better.

Could I go on?

I tried. It was all a nightmare—my wounds, the darkness, the road   25 ahead. My movements were ever so slow; only my mind was running at top speed.

In time I came to an open space where the houses had been removed to make a fire lane. Through the dim light I could make out ahead of me the hazy outlines of the Communications Bureau's big concrete building, and beyond it the hospital. My spirits rose because I knew that now someone would find me; and if I should die, at least my body would be found.

I paused to rest. Gradually things around me came into focus. There were the shadowy forms of people, some of whom looked like walking ghosts. Others moved as though in pain, like scarecrows, their arms held out from their bodies with forearms and hands dangling. These people puzzled me until I suddenly realized that they had been burned and were holding their arms out to prevent the painful friction of raw surfaces rubbing together. A naked woman carrying a naked baby came into view. I averted my gaze. Perhaps they had been in the bath. But then I saw a naked man, and it occurred to me that, like myself, some strange thing had deprived them of their clothes. An old woman lay near me with an expression of suffering on her face; but she made no sound. Indeed, one thing was common to everyone I saw—complete silence. . . .

PIKADON
August 9, 1945

As the wounded poured into Dr. Hachiya's hospital, the physicians tried to make sense of the symptoms and injuries, which did not resemble those of ordinary bombings. Because many of the patients with horrible symptoms showed no obvious signs of injuries, Dr. Hachiya could only speculate about what might have occurred. He had no idea as yet what type of weapon had been used against them.

Today, Dr. Hanaoka's[2] report on the patients was more detailed. One observation particularly impressed me. Regardless of the type of injury, nearly everybody had the same symptoms. All had a poor appetite, the majority had nausea and gaseous indigestion, and over half had vomiting.

Not a few had shown improvement since yesterday. Diarrhea, though, continued to be a problem and actually appeared to be increasing. Distinctly alarming was the appearance of blood in the stools of patients who earlier had only diarrhea. The isolation of these people was becoming increasingly difficult.

One seriously ill man complained of a sore mouth yesterday, and today, numerous small hemorrhages began to appear in his mouth and

30

---

[2]*Dr. Hanaoka:* Head of Internal Medicine. —EDS.

under his skin. His case was the more puzzling because he came to the hospital complaining of weakness and nausea and did not appear to have been injured at all.

This morning, other patients were beginning to show small subcutaneous hemorrhages, and not a few were coughing and vomiting blood in addition to passing it in their stools. One poor woman was bleeding from her privates. Among these patients there was not one with symptoms typical of anything we knew, unless you could excuse those who developed signs of severe brain disease before they died.

Dr. Hanaoka believed the patients could be divided into three groups:

1. Those with nausea, vomiting, and diarrhea who were improving.
2. Those with nausea, vomiting, and diarrhea who were remaining stationary.
3. Those with nausea, vomiting, and diarrhea who were developing hemorrhage under the skin or elsewhere.

Had these patients been burned or otherwise injured, we might have tried to stretch the logic of cause and effect and assume that their bizarre symptoms were related to injury, but so many patients appeared to have received no injury whatsoever that we were obliged to postulate an insult heretofore unknown.

The only other possible cause for the weird symptoms observed was a sudden change in atmospheric pressure. I had read somewhere about bleeding that follows ascent to high altitudes and about bleeding in deep sea divers who ascend too rapidly from the depths. Having never seen such injury I could not give much credence to my thoughts.

Still, it was impossible to dismiss the thought that atmospheric pressure had had something to do with the symptoms of our patients. During my student days at Okayama University, I had seen experiments conducted in a pressure chamber. Sudden, temporary deafness was one symptom everyone complained of if pressure in the chamber was abruptly altered.

Now, I could state positively that I heard nothing like an explosion when we were bombed the other morning, nor did I remember any sound during my walk to the hospital as houses collapsed around me. It was as though I walked through a gloomy, silent motion picture. Others whom I questioned had had the same experience.

Those who experienced the bombing from the outskirts of the city characterized it by the word: *pikadon*.[3]

How then could one account for my failure and the failure of others to hear an explosion except on the premise that a sudden change in at-

[3]***Pika*** means a glitter, sparkle, or bright flash of light, like a flash of lightning. ***Don*** means a boom! or loud sound. Together, the words came to mean to the people of Hiroshima an explosion characterized by a flash and a boom. Hence: "flash-boom!" Those who remember the flash only speak of the *"pika"*; those who were far enough from the hypocenter to experience both speak of the *"pikadon."*

mospheric pressure had rendered those nearby temporarily deaf: Could the bleeding we were beginning to observe be explained on the same basis?

Since all books and journals had been destroyed, there was no way to corroborate my theories except by further appeal to the patients. To that end Dr. Katsube[4] was asked to discover what else he could when he made ward rounds.

It was pleasing to note my scientific curiosity was reviving, and I lost no opportunity to question everyone who visited me about the bombing of Hiroshima. Their answers were vague and ambiguous, and on one point only were they in agreement: a new weapon had been used. *What* the new weapon was became a burning question. Not only had our books been destroyed, but our newspapers, telephones, and radios as well. . . .

The Reader's Presence

1. In many ways it is fortunate that one of the diaries kept immediately after the atomic blast was written by a medical doctor. Why? How does it contribute to the diary's historical value? Could this be a disadvantage? Would you have preferred to read a patient's diary instead? If so, why?

2. Dr. Hachiya's first entry on August 6 was written a few days after the events it depicts. What indications do you receive from the writing that the entry was predated? Can you detect any differences from the second entry (August 9), which was apparently composed on the stated day?

3. Hachiya's confusion reveals itself in his writing in many ways: short paragraphs, multiple questions, and unconfirmed guesses. Throughout, his matter-of-fact language belies his panic. How does Hachiya's characterization of the bombing of Hiroshima compare with Don DeLillo's account of the attack on the World Trade Center (page 341)? Is a survivor's account necessarily more vivid than that of a firsthand witness?

[4]*Dr. Katsube:* Chief of Surgery. — EDS.

5

Adam Mayblum

The Price We Pay

Adam Mayblum, the 36-year-old managing director of the May Davis Group private investment firm, was in his office on the eighty-seventh floor of the North Tower of the World Trade Center when one of the hijacked planes struck on September 11, 2001. He escaped just before the tower's collapse. The following day, at his home in New Rochelle, New York, Mayblum composed a terse, harrowing e-mail describing his experience and sent the 2,100-word piece out to friends and family. This e-mail quickly circulated throughout the world, bringing Mayblum over 1,000 responses from strangers offering thanks, sympathy, and prayers. One woman wrote, "The fact that you survived . . . helped to lift the terrible weight from my heart." Mayblum, who disclaims the label of "hero" by pointing out that firefighters and police officers were the ones who rushed in to save lives, attributes the enormous outpouring of support to the fact that his e-mail "helped a lot of people understand what was going on inside the building at the same time they had seen what was going on outside."

My name is Adam Mayblum. I am alive today. I am committing this to "paper" so I never forget. SO WE NEVER FORGET. I am sure that this is one of thousands of stories that will emerge over the next several days and weeks.

I arrived as usual a little before 8 A.M. My office was on the eighty-seventh floor of 1 World Trade Center, aka: Tower 1, aka: the North Tower. Most of my associates were in by 8:30 A.M. We were standing around, joking around, eating breakfast, checking e-mails, and getting set for the day when the first plane hit just a few stories above us. I must stress that we did not know that it was a plane. The building lurched violently and shook as if it were an earthquake. People screamed. I watched out my window as the building seemed to move ten to twenty feet in each direction. It rumbled and shook long enough for me to get my wits about myself and grab a coworker and seek shelter under a doorway. Light fixtures and parts of the ceiling collapsed. The kitchen was destroyed. We were certain that it was a bomb. We looked out the windows. Reams of paper were flying everywhere, like a ticker tape parade. I looked down at the street. I could see people in Battery Park City looking up. Smoke started billowing in through the holes in the ceiling. I believe that there were thirteen of us.

We did not panic. I can only assume that we thought that the worst was over. The building was standing and we were shaken but alive. We checked the halls. The smoke was thick and white and did not smell like I imagined smoke should smell. Not like your BBQ or your fireplace or even a bonfire. The phones were working. My wife had taken our nine-month-old for his checkup. I called my nanny at home and told her to page my wife, tell her that a bomb went off, I was O.K., and on my way out, I grabbed my laptop. Took off my T-shirt and ripped it into three pieces. Soaked it in water. Gave two pieces to my friends. Tied my piece around my face to act as an air filter. And we all started moving to the staircase. One of my dearest friends said that he was staying until the police or firemen came to get him. In the halls there were tiny fires and sparks. The ceiling had collapsed in the men's bathroom. It was gone along with anyone who may have been in there. We did not go in to look. We missed the staircase on the first run and had to double back. Once in the staircase we picked up fire extinguishers just in case. On the eighty-fifth floor a brave associate of mine and I headed back up to our office to drag out my partner who stayed behind. There was no air, just white smoke. We made the rounds through the office calling his name. No response. He must have succumbed to the smoke. We left defeated in our efforts and made our way back to the stairwell. We proceeded to the seventy-eighth floor where we had to change over to a different stairwell. Seventy-eight is the main junction to switch to the upper floors. I expected to see more people. There were some fifty to sixty more. Not enough. Wires and fires all over the place. Smoke too. A brave man was fighting a fire with the emergency hose. I stopped with friends to make sure that everyone from our office was accounted for. We ushered them and confused people into the stairwell. In retrospect, I recall seeing Harry, my head trader, doing the same several yards behind me. I am only thirty-five. I have known him for over fourteen years. I headed into the stairwell with two friends.

We were moving down very orderly in Stairwell A. Very slowly. No panic. At least not overt panic. My legs could not stop shaking. My heart was pounding. Some nervous jokes and laughter. I made a crack about ruining a brand new pair of Merrells. Even still, they were right, my feet felt great. We all laughed. We checked our cell phones. Surprisingly, there was a very good signal, but the Sprint network was jammed. I heard that the BlackBerry two-way e-mail devices worked perfectly. On the phones, one out of twenty dial attempts got through. I knew I could not reach my wife so I called my parents. I told them what happened and that we were all O.K. and on the way down. Soon, my sister-in-law reached me. I told her we were fine and moving down. I believe that was about the sixty-fifth floor. We were bored and nervous. I called my friend Angel in San Francisco. I knew he would be watching. He was amazed I was on the phone. He told me to get out, that there was another plane on its way. I did not know what he was talking about. By now the second plane had struck Tower 2. We were so deep into the middle of our building that we did not hear or feel anything. We had no idea what was really going on. We kept making way for wounded to go down ahead of us. Not many of them, just a few. No one seemed seriously wounded. Just some cuts and scrapes. Everyone cooperated. Everyone was a hero yesterday. No questions asked. I had coworkers in another office on the seventy-seventh floor. I tried dozens of times to get them on their cell phones or office lines. It was futile. Later I found that they were alive. One of the many miracles on a day of tragedy.

On the fifty-third floor we came across a very heavyset man sitting on the stairs. I asked if he needed help or was he just resting. He needed help. I knew I would have trouble carrying him because I have a very bad back. But my friend and I offered anyway. We told him he could lean on us. He hesitated, I don't know why. I said do you want to come or do you want us to send help for you. He chose for help. I told him he was on the fifty-third floor in Stairwell A and that's what I would tell the rescue workers. He said O.K. and we left.

On the forty-fourth floor my phone rang again. It was my parents. They were hysterical. I said relax, I'm fine. My father said get out, there is a third plane coming. I still did not understand. I was kind of angry. What did my parents think? Like I needed some other reason to get going? I couldn't move the thousand people in front of me any faster. I know they love me, but no one inside understood what the situation really was. My parents did. Starting around this floor the firemen, policemen, WTC K-9 units without the dogs, anyone with a badge, started coming up as we were heading down. I stopped a lot of them and told them about the man on Fifty-three and my friend on Eighty-seven. I later felt terrible about this. They headed up to find those people and met death instead.

On the thirty-third floor I spoke with a man who somehow knew most of the details. He said two small planes hit the building. Now we all started talking about which terrorist group it was. Was it an internal organization or an external one? The overwhelming but uninformed opinion was Islamic fanatics. Regardless, we now knew that it was not a bomb and there were potentially more planes coming. We understood.

On the third floor the lights went out and we heard and felt this rumbling coming towards us from above. I thought the staircase was collapsing upon itself. It was 10 a.m. now and that was Tower 2 collapsing next door. We did not know that. Someone had a flashlight. We passed it forward and left the stairwell and headed down a dark and cramped corridor to an exit. We could not see at all. I recommended that everyone place a hand on the shoulder of the person in front of them and call out if they hit an obstacle so others would know to avoid it. They did. It worked perfectly. We reached another stairwell and saw a female officer emerge soaking wet and covered in soot. She said we could not go that way, it was blocked. Go up to Four and use the other exit. Just as we started up she said it was O.K. to go down instead. There was water everywhere. I called out for hands on shoulders again and she said that was a great idea. She stayed behind instructing people to do that. I do not know what happened to her.

We emerged into an enormous room. It was light but filled with smoke. I commented to a friend that it must be under construction. Then we realized where we were. It was the second floor. The one that overlooks the lobby. We were ushered out into the courtyard, the one where the fountain used to be. My first thought was of a TV movie I saw once about nuclear winter and fallout. I could not understand where all of the debris came from. There was at least five inches of this gray pasty dusty drywall soot on the ground as well as a thickness of it in the air. Twisted steel and wires. I heard there were bodies and body parts as well, but I did not look. It was bad enough. We hid under the remaining overhangs and moved out to the street. We were told to keep walking towards Houston Street. The odd thing is that there were very few rescue workers around. Less than five. They all must have been trapped under the debris when Tower 2 fell. We did not know that and could not understand where all of that debris came from. It was just my friend Kern and I now. We were hugging but sad. We felt certain that most of our friends ahead of us died and we knew no one behind us.

We came upon a post office several blocks away. We stopped and looked up. Our building, exactly where our office is (was), was engulfed in flame and smoke. A postal worker said that Tower 2 had fallen down. I looked again and sure enough it was gone. My heart was racing. We kept trying to call our families. I could not get in touch with my wife. Finally I got through to my parents. Relieved is not the word to explain their feelings. They got through to my wife, thank G–d, and let her know I was alive. We sat down. A girl on a bike offered us some water. Just as she took the cap off her bottle we heard a rumble. We looked up and our building, Tower 1, collapsed. I did not note the time but I am told it was 10:30 A.M. We had been out less than fifteen minutes. 10

We were mourning our lost friends, particularly the one who stayed in the office, as we were now sure that he had perished. We started walking towards Union Square. I was going to Beth Israel Medical Center to be looked at. We stopped to hear the president speaking on the radio. My phone rang. It was my wife. I think I fell to my knees crying when I heard her voice. Then she told me the most incredible thing. My partner who had stayed behind called her. He was alive and well. I guess we just lost him in the commotion. We started jumping and hugging and shouting. I told my wife that my brother had arranged for a hotel in midtown. He can be very resourceful in that way. I told her I would call her from there.

My brother and I managed to get a gypsy cab to take us home to West-chester instead. I cried on my son and held my wife until I fell asleep. As it turns out, my partner, the one who I thought had stayed behind, was behind us with Harry Ramos, our head trader. This is now secondhand information. They came upon Victor, the heavyset man on the fifty-third floor. They helped him. He could barely move. My partner bravely/stupidly tested the elevator on the fifty-second floor. He rode it down to the sky lobby on Forty-four. The doors opened, it was fine. He rode it back up and got Harry and Victor. I don't yet know if anyone else joined them. Once on Forty-four they made their way back into the stairwell. Someplace around the thirty-ninth to thirty-sixth floors they felt the same rumble I felt on the third floor. It was 10 A.M. and Tower 2 was coming down. They had about thirty minutes to get out. Victor said he could no longer move. They offered to have him lean on them. He said he couldn't do it. My partner hollered at him to sit on his butt and scooch down the steps. He said he was not capable of doing it. Harry told my partner to go ahead of them. Harry once had a heart attack and was worried about this man's heart. It was his nature to be this way. He was/is one of the kindest people I know. He would not leave a man behind. My partner went ahead and made it out. He said he was out maybe ten minutes before the building came down. This means that Harry had maybe twenty-five minutes to move Victor thirty-six floors. I guess they moved one floor every 1.5 minutes. Just a guess. This means Harry was around the twentieth floor when the building collapsed. As of now twelve of thirteen people are accounted for. As of 6 P.M. yesterday his wife had not heard from him. I fear that Harry is lost. However, a short while ago I heard that he may be alive. Apparently there is a Web site with survivor names on it and his appears there. Unfortunately, Ramos is not an uncommon name in New York. Pray for him and all those like him.

With regards to the firemen heading upstairs, I realize that they were going up anyway. But it hurts to know that I may have made them move quicker to find my friend. Rationally, I know this is not true and that I am not the responsible one. The responsible ones are in hiding somewhere on this planet and damn them for making me feel like this. But they should know that they failed in terrorizing us. We were calm. Those men and women that went up were heroes in the face of it all. They must have known what was going on and they did their jobs. Ordinary people were heroes, too. Today the images that people around the world equate with power and democracy are gone, but "America" is not an image, it is a concept. That concept is only strengthened by our pulling together as a team. If you want to kill us, leave us alone because we will try to do it by ourselves. If you want to make us stronger, attack and we unite. This is the ultimate failure of terrorism against the United States and the ultimate price we pay to be free, to decide where we want to work, what we want to eat, and when and where we want to go on vacation. The very moment the first plane was hijacked, democracy won.

The Reader's Presence

1. Whom does Mayblum talk to as he moves down the stairs? What subject(s) do they discuss? Whom did you talk to following the attacks on the World Trade Center? To what extent do these conversations confirm Mayblum's claim that "If you want to make us stronger, attack and we unite" (paragraph 12).

2. As Mayblum mentions the floors he passes in his descent, how does the countdown affect his overall story? Point to specific parts of his story that are more hurried than other parts. What about the moments in which he pauses? How do these moments affect your reading?

3. Compare Mayblum's account with Tim Townsend's in "The First Hours" (see page 44). How does each person think of his actions after the disaster? Which account do you find more moving? Why?

6

Sylvia Plath

From Her *Journals* and "Bitter Strawberries"

One of the twentieth century's most gifted poets, Sylvia Plath (1932–1963) was born in Massachusetts to a financially strapped but educated family. Plath, an outstanding student who won a scholarship to Smith College, suffered from severe depression and was hospitalized after attempting suicide during her junior year. Upon graduating summa cum laude *in 1955, Plath went on to Cambridge University where she met and married the English poet Ted Hughes. In 1962, after learning of her husband's infidelity, she took her own life. Her finest poetry was published in three posthumous volumes,* Ariel *(1966),* Crossing the Water *(1971), and* Winter Trees *(1972).*

An extraordinary child and talented young writer, Plath began keeping a journal from age 11, a practice that she would continue throughout her life. The journal entry and poem reprinted here are from The Unabridged Journals of Sylvia Plath *(2000), edited by Karen V. Kukil, a volume that covers 1950 through 1962.*

In the summer of 1950, just before she entered Smith College, Plath worked as a field hand on a farm near her home in Wellesley. In the following entry, she describes an encounter with an Estonian refugee, Ilo, an artistic young man who

*also worked on the farm and whom she occasionally dated. She would repeatedly
deal with the encounter in stories and poems.*

*Plath also wrote the poem "Bitter Strawberries" that summer, describing her
experiences on the farm where she met refugees from countries invaded by the Soviet Union—and who presumably expressed the anti-Russian feelings that we
hear in the poem. Plath was troubled by the outbreak of the Korean War (in late
June), the new military draft, and the threat of nuclear war. Not many seventeen-
year-old poets would have worked these concerns into a poem ostensibly based
on a summer job picking strawberries.*

Some things are hard to write about. After something happens to
you, you go to write it down, and either you over dramatize it or under-
play it, exaggerate the wrong parts or ignore the important ones. At any
rate, you never write it quite the way you want to. I've just got to put
down what happened to me this afternoon. I can't tell mother, not yet,
anyway. She was in my room when I came home, fussing with clothes,
and she didn't even sense that something had happened. She just kept
scolding and chattering on and on. So I couldn't stop her and tell her. No
matter how it comes out, I have to write it.

It rained all afternoon at the farm, and I was cold and wet, my hair
under a silk print kerchief, my red ski jacket over my sweatshirt. I had
worked hard on beans all afternoon and picked over three bushels. Since
it was five o'clock, people were leaving, and I was waiting beside the cars
for my ride home. Kathy had just come up, and as she got on her bike she
called, "Here comes Ilo."

I looked, and sure enough, there he was, coming up the road in his
old khaki shirt with his familiar white handkerchief tied around his head.
I was on conversational terms with him since that day we worked together in the strawberry field. He had given me a pen and ink sketch of
the farm, drawn with detail and assurance. Now he was working on a
sketch of one of the boys.

So I called, "Have you finished John's picture?"

"Oh, ya, ya," he smiled. "Come and see. Your last chance." He had   5
promised to show it to me when he was done, so I ran out and got in step
with him on his way to the barn. That's where he lives.

On the way, we passed Mary Coffee. I felt her looking at me rather
strangely. Somehow I couldn't meet her eyes.

"Hullo, Mary," Ilo said.

"Hello, Ilo," Mary said in an oddly colorless voice.

We walked by Ginny, Sally, and a crowd of kids keeping dry in the
tractor shed. A roar went up as we passed. A singsong, "Oh Sylvia." My
cheeks burned.

"Why do they have to tease me?" I asked. Ilo just laughed. He was   10
walking very fast.

"We're going home in a little while," Milton yelled from the washroom. I nodded and kept walking, looking at the ground. Then we were

at the barn, a huge place, a giant high ceilinged room smelling of horses and damp hay. It was dim inside; I thought I saw the figure of a person on the other side of the stalls, but I couldn't be sure. Without saying a word, Ilo had begun to mount a narrow flight of wooden stairs.

"You live up there? All these stairs?"

He kept walking up, so I followed him, hesitating at the top.

"Come in, come in," he said, opening a door. The picture was there, in his room. I walked over the threshold. It was a narrow place with two windows, a table full of drawing things, and a cot, covered with a dark blanket. Oranges and milk were set out on a table with a radio.

"Here," he held out the picture. It was a fine pencil sketch of John's head.   15

"Why, how do you do it? With the side of the pencil?"

It seemed of no significance then, but now I remember how Ilo had shut the door, had turned on the radio so that music came out.

He talked very fast, showing me a pencil. "See, here the lead comes out, any size." I was very conscious of his nearness. His blue eyes were startlingly close, looking at me boldly, with flecks of laughter in them.

"I really have to go. They will be waiting. The picture was lovely."

Smiling, he was between me and the door. A motion. His hand closed   20
around my arm. And suddenly his mouth was on mine, hard, vehement, his tongue darting between my lips, his arms like iron around me.

"Ilo, Ilo!" I don't know whether I screamed or whispered, struggling to break free, my hands striking wildly, futilely against his great strength. At last he let me go, and stood back. I held my hand against my mouth, warm and bruised from his kiss. He looked at me quizzically, with something like surprised amusement as he saw that I was crying, frightened. No one ever kissed me that way before, and I stood there, flooded with longing, electric, shivering.

"Why, why," he made sympathetic, depreciating little noises. "I get you some water."

He poured me out a glass, and I drank it. He opened the door, and I stumbled blindly downstairs, past Maybelle and Robert, the little colored children, who called my name in the corrupted way kids have of pronouncing things. Past Mary Lou, their mother, who stood there, a silent, dark presence.

And I was outdoors. A truck was going by. Coming from behind the barn. In it was Bernie — the horrible, short, muscular boy from the washroom. His eyes glittered with malicious delight, and he drove fast, so I could not catch up with him. Had he been in the barn? Had he seen Ilo shut the door, seen me come out? I think he must have.

I walked up past the washroom to the cars. Bernie yelled out, "Why   25
are you crying?" I wasn't crying. Kenny and Freddy came by on the tractor. A group of boys, going home, looked at me with a light flickering somewhere in their eyes. "Did he kiss you?" one asked, with a knowing smile.

I felt sick. I couldn't have spoken if someone had talked to me. My voice was stuck in my throat, thick and furry.

Mr. Tompkins came up to the pump to watch Kenny and Freddy run the old stock car. They were nice, but they knew. They all must know.

"There's cutie pie," Kenny said.

"Cutie pie and angel face," Freddy said.

So I stood there, arms folded, staring at the whirring engine, smiling   30
as if I was all right, as if nothing had happened.

Milton sat in the rumble seat with me going home. David drove, and Andy was in front. They all looked at me with that dancing light in their eyes. David said in a stiff, strained voice, "Everybody in the washroom was watching you go into the barn and making wisecracks."

Milton asked about the picture. We talked a little about art and drawing. They were all so nice. I think they may have been relieved at my narrow escape; they may have expected me to cry. They knew, though, they knew.

So, I'm home. And tomorrow I have to face the whole damn farm. Good Lord, it might have happened in a dream. Now I can almost believe it did. But tomorrow my name will be on the tip of every tongue. I wish I could be smart, or flip, but I'm too scared. If only he hadn't kissed me. I'll have to lie and say he didn't. But they know. They all know. And what am I against so many. . . ?

BITTER STRAWBERRIES

All morning in the strawberry field
They talked about the Russians.
Squatted down between the rows
We listened.
We heard the head woman say,   5
"Bomb them off the map."

Horseflies buzzed, paused and stung.
And the taste of strawberries
Turned thick and sour.

Mary said slowly, "I've got a fella   10
Old enough to go.
If anything should happen . . ."

The sky was high and blue.
Two children laughed at tag
In the tall grass,   15
Leaping awkward and long-legged
Across the rutted road.
The fields were full of bronzed young men
Hoeing lettuce, weeding celery.

"The draft is passed," the woman said.   20
"We ought to have bombed them long ago."
"Don't," pleaded the little girl
With blond braids.

Her blue eyes swam with vague terror.
She added pettishly, "I can't see why   25
You're always talking this way . . ."
"Oh, stop worrying, Nelda,"
Snapped the woman sharply.
She stood up, a thin commanding figure
In faded dungarees.   30
Businesslike she asked us, "How many quarts?"
She recorded the total in her notebook,
And we all turned back to picking.

Kneeling over the rows,
We reached among the leaves   35
With quick practiced hands,
Cupping the berry protectively before
Snapping off the stem
Between thumb and forefinger.

The Reader's Presence

1. At the same time that she kept her journals, Plath was also writing
   and publishing poems and short stories. Can you see any connections between her journal writing and her literary endeavors?
   What storytelling or fictional techniques appear in the journal entries? What poetic elements do you find in her prose?

2. What links can you find between the poem "Bitter Strawberries"
   and the journal entries reprinted here? What experiences appear
   to be contained in both the journal and the poem?

7 _____

Tim Townsend

The First Hours

*Tim Townsend is a 32-year-old financial reporter. He was only a few blocks
away from his office at the World Financial Center when the first hijacked plane
crashed into the World Trade Center tower on September 11, 2001. The follow-*

ing selection, which appeared in Rolling Stone *(October 25, 2001), is based on notes he wrote immediately following the attack.*

The first thing I saw in the parking lot across Liberty Street from the South Tower was luggage. Burned luggage. A couple of cars were on fire. Half a block east, a man who'd been working out in a South Tower fitness club was walking barefoot over shards of glass, wearing only a white towel around his waist; he still had shaving cream on the left side of his face. Bits of glass were falling to the ground like hail. I ventured a block south, away from the towers, and that's when I started seeing body parts. At first, just scattered lumps of mangled flesh dotting the road and the sidewalks, then a leg near the gutter. Someone mentioned a severed head over by a fire hydrant. Hunks of metal—some silver and the size of a fist, others green and as big as toasters—were strewn for blocks south of the building. Shoes were everywhere.

"Oh, Jesus," I heard someone say. "They're jumping." Every few moments a body would fall from the North Tower, from about ninety floors up. The jumpers all seemed to come from the floors that were engulfed in flames. Sometimes they jumped in pairs—one just after the other. They were up so high, it took ten to twelve seconds for each of them to hit the ground. I counted.

What must have been going through their minds, to choose certain death? Was it a decision between one death and another? Or maybe it wasn't a decision at all, their bodies involuntarily recoiling from the heat, the way you pull your hand off a hot stove.

Moments later, a low metallic whine, quickly followed by a high-pitched whoosh, came out of the south. I looked up to see the white belly of an airplane much closer than it should have been. The South Tower of the Trade Center seemed to suck the plane into itself. For an instant it looked like there would be no trauma to the building—it was as if the plane just slipped through a mail slot in the side of the tower, or simply vanished. But then a fireball ballooned out of the top of the building just five blocks from where we stood.

People were running south down West Street toward Battery Park— the southern tip, the end, of Manhattan—and west toward the Hudson River. I ran with the crowd that veered toward the river, looking back over my shoulder at the new gash in the Trade Center. Once relatively safe among the tree-lined avenues of Battery Park City, people hugged each other and some cried.

After about ten minutes, a wave of calm returned to the streets. Police were trying to get the thousands of people south of the World Trade Center off the West Street, east to the FDR Drive, over the Brooklyn Bridge. And still people were throwing themselves out of the North Tower: You could see suit jackets fluttering in the wind and women's dresses billowing like failed parachutes.

But about five minutes later, a sharp cracking sound momentarily replaced the shrill squeal of sirens, and the top half of the South Tower imploded, bringing the entire thing down. It was the most frightened I've ever been. Screaming and sprinting south toward Battery Park, we all flew from the dark cloud that was slowly funneling toward us. At that moment I believed two things about this cloud. One, that it was made not just of ash and soot, but of metal, glass and concrete; and two, that soon this shrapnel would be whizzing by — and perhaps through — my head. A woman next to me turned to run. Her black bag came off her shoulder and a CD holder went flying, sending bright silver discs clattering across the ground. An older man to my right tripped and took a face-first dive across the pavement, glasses flying off his face.

In the seconds, minutes, and hours following the World Trade Center attacks, hundreds — maybe thousands — of ordinary people would find their best selves and become heroes. And then there were the rest of us, running hard, wanting only to live and to talk to someone we loved, even if it meant leaving an old guy lying in the street, glasses gone, a cloud of death and destruction creeping up on him.

I'd always wondered what I'd do in a life-or-death situation. Until that moment, I'd believed I'd do the right thing, would always help the helpless, most likely without regard for my own well-being. All across lower Manhattan at that moment, people were making similar decisions, so many of them so much more critical than mine. September 11th, 2001, at 9:45 A.M. was not my finest moment. As I turned back to help, I saw two younger guys scoop the fallen man up, and we all continued running south.

After about three blocks, I hid for a moment behind a large Dumpster   10
on the west side of the street. But when I looked back toward the towers, I could see that my Dumpster was no match for the cloud, and I took off again. I ran the last few blocks into Battery Park, where the cloud finally did catch up with the thousands of us fleeing it. I could see only a few feet in front of me, and so I followed the silhouettes I could make out. Because Battery Park is the tip of the island, it wasn't much of a surprise that the crowd would wind up dead-ending at the water. When it happened, the people in the front panicked. So they turned around, screamed and ran back toward us in a stampede. We had nowhere to go — there were thousands of people behind us and hundreds coming back the other way.

As the crowd doubled back on itself, I jumped over a wrought-iron fence and landed in a flower bed. I stayed down for a second, thinking I'd wait out the panic low to the ground. But then I felt other people jumping the fence and landing near me. Thinking I was about to be trampled, I got up and ran behind a nearby tree. In a minute or two the panic subdued, and I hopped back over the fence and onto a park path. But now the air was heavier with debris and there was no clear path out of the park. I took off my tie with wrapped it around my face. People were coughing and stumbling. Some were crying, others screaming. It was difficult to breathe or even keep my eyes open.

Soon, there was another wave of calm and quiet, and the ash that fell from the sky and settled on the grass and trees gave the park the peaceful feel of a light evening snowfall. Eventually, I found a path that led me out to the east side of the Battery area, and I followed a crowd to the FDR. Thousands participated in the exodus up the highway and into Brooklyn. It was now just past ten, and we looked like refugees. In a way, we were. My tie wasn't doing much good against the ash, so I took off my shirt and tied it around my head. We walked in the falling gray dust for fifteen minutes, still hacking, and rubbing our eyes. Then the cloud broke, and, covered in soot, we were in the sunlight again. There wasn't a lot of talking. Some walked in groups, desperately trying to stay together. Others walked alone, crying out the names of friends, co-workers, or loved ones from whom they'd been separated.

At 10:25, as I was getting ready to cross the bridge, another cracking sound came out of the west. We looked behind us and to the left to see the remaining tower collapse. Soon, that ash reached the Manhattan foot of the Brooklyn Bridge, and the bridge was closed. Three hours later, I was finally back in my apartment in Brooklyn. It was nearly one o'clock. There was a thin layer of ash all over my kitchen from the blast. I made my phone calls and cried with my fiancée. Then I called some friends who'd left messages, checking on me. I called my friend Sully in Boston, and we went through the list of names of our friends who worked in the financial district. I was one of the last to be accounted for. When we'd gotten through most of the names—Sims, Kane, T-Bone, Molloy—Sully said, "It's not all good news. Beezo called his wife from high up in the second building to say he was OK, but she hasn't heard from him since it fell." Beezo—Tom Brennan to those he didn't go to high school or college with—still hasn't been heard from.

As it turns out, when I was watching that tower fall, I was watching my friend die. His wife was at home, in their brand-new house in Westchester County, amid their still boxed-up life. She'd already turned off the TV when Beezo's building collapsed. Their seventeen-month-old daughter is too young to have seen the images of her father's death, but someday— maybe on a distant anniversary of September 11th when each network commemorates the tragedy—I'm sure she'll be able to see it, along with her little brother or sister who is due in two months.

I hung up with Sully and turned on the television to see what I had 15
seen. Places where I once ate lunch or shopped for a sweater or bought stamps were now buried under piles of concrete and metal, as were thousands of people—some of whom I probably rode the subway with every day. One of whom was my friend.

Since then, I've been freakishly fine, given what I'd seen. Maybe it's because I realize how lucky I was—my experience was like Christmas morning compared to what other people went through. Maybe it's because I lack the imagination, or the will, to realize the scope of what I'd seen. But sadness works in bizarre ways. The second night after the attack, I sat in front of the news, alone with my eighth or ninth beer, and I listened to a report about NFL officials considering a postponement of the second week of games. I thought about what a nice gesture that would be, and I cried and cried.

The Reader's Presence

1. How would you characterize Townsend's actions after the World Trade Center disaster? To what extent do you agree with his assessment that he didn't find his best self or act heroically like so many others? What did he do, or not do, that showed him at less than his best? What made him seem less than a hero? Townsend describes his movements and thoughts step by step — what would you have done differently? What would you have thought differently?

2. Examine the structure of the first paragraph carefully. What significance can you find in the order in which Townsend presents details? Or in how he describes relatively mundane sights ("[b]urned luggage") compared to how he describes gruesome sights ("mangled flesh")? Does he seem more affected by some things than others? Or does each thing he encounters seem to affect him similarly? What indicates his level of emotion or detachment throughout the essay? Townsend reports twice during the narrative that he cried: the first time, when he talked to his fiancée, he "cried" (paragraph 13); the second time, when he heard that the NFL was considering canceling games, he "cried and cried" (paragraph 16). What effect(s) does he produce by repeating "cried" in the second instance? What was it about the more trivial instance that makes him emphasize how much he cried?

3. Compare Townsend's account with Adam Mayblum's in "The Price We Pay" (page 35). What kinds of writing strategies do these writers adopt to mark the passing of time? What are the similarities and differences in how they interact with other people trying to escape? How does each person think of his actions after the disaster? Which account do you find more moving? Why?

8

Walt Whitman

From *Specimen Days: Civil War Diary*

If the United States can be said to have a national poet, it would be Walt Whitman. No other American poet has represented the national experience more fully and has had a deeper influence on the shape of our literature. His major work, Leaves of Grass, *is almost universally considered a world masterpiece, though when it first appeared in 1855, it was loudly condemned as incoherent and obscene. Born into a working-class family near Huntington, Long Island, in 1819, Whitman grew up in Brooklyn, New York, where he attended public schools until he dropped out at the age of eleven to start work as an office boy and later as a printer's apprentice. Whitman enjoyed a successful career in newspaper journalism but by the late 1840s decided to concentrate on more literary endeavors, while supporting himself with various jobs and freelance writing. In 1862, as the Civil War intensified, Whitman visited the front in Virginia, where his brother had been wounded. Feeling great sympathy for the average soldier, he settled in Washington, D.C., to perform volunteer work nursing the wounded in military hospitals. He kept notes of this experience and years later included them (with some slight revision) in a volume of reminiscence,* Specimen Days *(1882), from which the following few passages have been taken. Whitman died in Camden, New Jersey, in 1892.*

DOWN AT THE FRONT
Falmouth, Va., opposite Fredericksburgh, December 21, 1862

Whitman kept a diary of his Civil War experiences among the sick and wounded. It now represents one of our literature's most moving on-the-spot accounts of the war's human devastation. Whitman, however, did not intend to be composing a literary work when he recorded his entries, which were often written in a hurry and during a pause from emergency duties. When he returned to this diary years later, he sometimes added information in parentheses (his titles, too, are later additions), as you will note in the following passages, but he never allowed himself to edit out the immediacy of his observations and feelings of the moment.

Begin my visits among the camp hospitals in the army of the Potomac. Spend a good part of the day in a large brick mansion on the banks of the Rappahannock, used as a hospital since the battle — seems to have receiv'd only the worst cases. Out doors, at the foot of a tree, within ten yards of the front of the house, I notice a heap of amputated feet, legs, arms, hands, &c., a full load for a one-horse cart. Several dead bodies lie near, each cover'd with its brown woolen blanket. In the dooryard, towards the river, are fresh graves, mostly of officers, their names on pieces of barrel-staves or broken boards, stuck in the dirt. (Most of these bodies were subsequently taken up and transported north to their friends.) The large mansion is quite crowded upstairs and down, everything impromptu, no system, all bad enough, but I have no doubt the best that can be done; all the wounds pretty bad, some frightful, the men in their old clothes, unclean and bloody. Some of the wounded are rebel soldiers and officers, prisoners. One, a Mississippian, a captain, hit badly in leg, I talk'd with some time; he ask'd me for papers, which I gave him. (I saw him three months afterward in Washington, with his leg amputated, doing well.) I went through the rooms, downstairs and up. Some of the men were dying. I had nothing to give at that visit, but wrote a few letters to folks home, mothers, &c. Also talk'd to three or four, who seem'd most susceptible to it, and needing it.

FIFTY HOURS LEFT WOUNDED ON THE FIELD
[undated; most likely late January 1863]

One of the horrors of the war that especially disturbed Whitman was the army's inability to rescue wounded soldiers quickly. Many died unnecessarily in the field on both sides because of inadequate first aid. Whitman noted the following example shortly after he went to the front. Though Whitman was fiercely committed to the Union cause, the entry shows his unwillingness to demonize the Confederate soldier, whom he frequently refers to in his diary as a "secesh" (secessionist).

Here is a case of a soldier I found among the crowded cots in the Patent-office. He likes to have some one to talk to, and we will listen to him. He got badly hit in his leg and side at Fredericksburgh that eventful Saturday, 13th of December. He lay the succeeding two days and nights helpless on the field, between the city and those grim terraces of batteries; his company and regiment had been compell'd to leave him to his fate. To make matters worse, it happen'd he lay with his head slightly down hill, and could not help himself. At the end of some fifty hours he was brought off, with other wounded, under a flag of truce. I ask him how the rebels treated him as he lay during those two days and nights within reach of them — whether they came to him — whether they abused him? He answers that several of the rebels, soldiers and others, came to him at one time and another. A couple of them, who were together, spoke roughly and sarcastically, but nothing worse. One middle-aged man, however, who seem'd to be moving around the field, among the dead and wounded, for benevolent purposes, came to him in a way he will never forget; treated our soldier kindly, bound up his wounds, cheer'd him, gave him a couple of biscuits and a drink of whiskey and water; asked him if he could eat some beef. This good secesh, however, did not change our soldier's position, for it might have caused the blood to burst from the wounds, clotted and stagnated. Our soldier is from Pennsylvania; has had a pretty severe time; the wounds proved to be bad ones. But he retains a good heart, and is at present on the gain. (It is not uncommon for the men to remain on the field this way, one, two, or even four or five days.)

ABRAHAM LINCOLN
August 12, 1863

Whitman was a fervent supporter and great admirer of Lincoln, and throughout his later years often lectured on the assassinated president. His poem on the assassination, "When Lilacs Last in the Dooryard Bloom'd" remains one of America's finest elegies. While in Washington, Whitman saw Lincoln on numerous occasions, though the two never met. In this entry, Whitman obtains a close glimpse of a somber leader.

I see the President almost every day, as I happen to live where he passes to or from his lodgings out of town. He never sleeps at the White House during the hot season, but has quarters at a healthy location some three miles north of the city, the Soldiers' home, a United States military establishment. I saw him this morning about 8½ coming in to business, riding on Vermont avenue, near L street. He always has a company of twenty-five or thirty cavalry, with sabres drawn and held upright over their shoulders. They say this guard was against his personal wish, but he let his counselors have their way. The party makes no great show in uniform or horses. Mr. Lincoln on the saddle generally rides a good-sized, easy-going gray horse, is dress'd in plain black, somewhat rusty and dusty, wears a black stiff hat, and looks about as ordinary in attire, &c., as the commonest man. A lieutenant, with yellow straps, rides at his left, and following behind, two by two, come the cavalry men, in their yellow-striped jackets. They are generally going at a slow trot, as that is the pace set them by the one they wait upon. The sabres and accoutrements clank, and the entirely unornamental *cortège* as it trots towards Lafayette square arouses no sensation, only some curious stranger stops and gazes. I see very plainly Abraham Lincoln's dark brown face, with the deep-cut lines, the eyes, always to me with a deep latent sadness in the expression. We have got so that we exchange bows, and very cordial ones. Sometimes the President goes and comes in an open barouche. The cavalry always accompany him, with drawn sabres. Often I notice as he goes out evenings—and sometimes in the morning, when he returns early—he turns off and halts at the large and handsome residence of the Secretary of War, on K street, and holds conference there. If in his barouche, I can see from my window he does not alight, but sits in his vehicle, and Mr. Stanton comes out to attend him. Sometimes one of his sons, a boy of ten or twelve, accompanies him, riding at his right on a pony. Earlier in the summer I occasionally saw the President and his wife, toward the latter part of the afternoon, out in a barouche, on a pleasure ride through the city. Mrs. Lincoln was dress'd in complete black, with a long crape veil. The equipage is of the plainest kind, only two horses, and they nothing extra. They pass'd me once very close, and I saw the President in the face fully, as they were moving slowly, and his look, though abstracted, happen'd to be directed steadily in my eye. He bow'd and smiled, but far beneath his smile I noticed well the expression I have alluded to. None of the artists or pictures has caught the deep, though subtle and indirect expression of this man's face. There is something else there. One of the great portrait painters of two or three centuries ago is needed.

TWO BROTHERS, ONE SOUTH, ONE NORTH
May 28–29, 1865

Whitman stayed on to help with the wounded after the South surrendered. In the following entry he personally experiences one of the war's distressing incidents—the way it sometimes resulted in brother battling brother.

I staid to-night a long time by the bedside of a new patient, a young Baltimorean, aged about 19 years, W. S. P., (2d Maryland, southern,) very feeble, right leg amputated, can't sleep hardly at all—has taken a great deal of morphine, which, as usual, is costing more than it comes to. Evidently very intelligent and well bred—very affectionate—held on to my hand, and put it by his face, not willing to let me leave. As I was lingering, soothing him in his pain, he says to me suddenly, "I hardly think you know who I am—I don't wish to impose upon you—I am a rebel soldier." I said I did not know that, but it made no difference. Visiting him daily for about two weeks after that, while he lived, (death had mark'd him, and he was quite alone,) I loved him much, always kiss'd him, and he did me. In an adjoining ward I found his brother, an officer of rank, a Union soldier, a brave and religious man, (Col. Clifton K. Prentiss, sixth Maryland infantry, Sixth corps, wounded in one of the engagements at Petersburgh, April 2—linger'd, suffer'd much, died in Brooklyn, Aug. 20, '65.) It was in the same battle both were hit. One was a strong Unionist, the other Secesh; both fought on their respective sides, both badly wounded, and both brought together here after a separation of four years. Each died for his cause.

THE REAL WAR WILL NEVER GET IN THE BOOKS
[undated]

As he reviewed the page proofs of Specimen Days, *Whitman worried that his "diary would prove, at best, but a batch of convulsively written reminiscences." Yet he decided to leave it that way, for the notes "are but parts of the actual distraction, heat, smoke, and excitement of those times." The war itself, he realized, could only be described by the word* convulsiveness. *In other words, the real war—as he suggests in this famous passage from* Specimen Days *—will never properly be seen by writers or historians in retrospect. It can perhaps best be conveyed by the spontaneous and fragmentary jottings of a diary.*

And so good-bye to the war. I know not how it may have been, or   5
may be, to others—to me the main interest I found, (and still, on recollection, find,) in the rank and file of the armies, both sides, and in those specimens amid the hospitals, and even the dead on the field. To me the points illustrating the latent personal character and eligibilities of these States, in the two or three millions of American young and middle-aged men, North and South, embodied in those armies—and especially the one-third or one-fourth of their number, stricken by wounds or disease at some time in the course of the contest—were of more significance even than the political interests involved. (As so much of a race depends on how it faces death, and how it stands personal anguish and sickness. As, in the glints of emotions under emergencies, and the indirect traits and asides in Plutarch, we get far profounder clues to the antique world than all its more formal history.)

Future years will never know the seething hell and the black infernal background of countless minor scenes and interiors, (not the official surface-courteousness of the Generals, not the few great battles) of the Secession war; and it is best they should not—the real war will never get in the books. In the mushy influences of current times, too, the fervid atmosphere and typical events of those years are in danger of being totally forgotten. I have at night watch'd by the side of a sick man in the hospital, one who could not live many hours. I have seen his eyes flash and burn as he raised himself and recurr'd to the cruelties of his surrender'd brother, and mutilations of the corpse afterward. . . .

Such was the war. It was not a quadrille in a ball-room. Its interior history will not only never be written—its practicality, minutiæ of deeds and passions, will never be even suggested. The actual soldier of 1862–'65, North and South, with all his ways, his incredible dauntlessness, habits, practices, tastes, language, his fierce friendship, his appetite, rankness, his superb strength and animality, lawless gait, and a hundred unnamed lights and shades of camp, I say, will never be written—perhaps must not and should not be.

The preceding notes may furnish a few stray glimpses into that life, and into those lurid interiors, never to be fully convey'd to the future. The hospital part of the drama from '61 to '65, deserves indeed to be recorded. Of that many-threaded drama, with its sudden and strange surprises, its confounding of prophecies, its moments of despair, the dread of foreign interference, the interminable campaigns, the bloody battles, the mighty and cumbrous and green armies, the drafts and bounties—the immense money expenditure, like a heavy-pouring constant rain—with, over the whole land, the last three years of the struggle, an unending, universal mourning-wail of women, parents, orphans—the marrow of the tragedy concentrated in those Army Hospitals—(it seem'd sometimes as if the whole interest of the land, North and South, was one vast central hospital, and all the rest of the affair but flanges)—those forming the untold and unwritten history of the war—infinitely greater (like life's) than the few scraps and distortions that are ever told or written. Think how much, and of importance, will be—how much, civic and military, has already been—buried in the grave, in eternal darkness.

The Reader's Presence

1. In your opinion, what aspects of Whitman's Civil War diary help make the experience of the war vivid and realistic? How are these aspects captured in Whitman's writing?

2. Formulate in your own words what Whitman means by his expression "the real war will never get in the books." What sort of book is he thinking about? Do you think he means that it could never be conveyed in language at all?

3. Whitman's poetry is characterized by long lines in which he incorporates the speech of real Americans, or what he called "the blab of the pave." Do you see these stylistic features in his prose? Compare Whitman's long last sentence (paragraph 8) to one of Jamaica Kincaid's long sentences. Does the stylistic similarity produce similar effects? If not, why not? How do the two writers work pauses into their prose?

9

Virginia Woolf
From *A Writer's Diary*

At the time of her death, Virginia Woolf (1882–1941), one of modern litera-ture's outstanding creative voices, left twenty-six volumes of a handwritten diary that she had started in 1915. Her diary records her daily activities, social life, reading, and, most importantly, her thoughts about the writing process. In 1953, her husband, Leonard Woolf, extracted her remarks about writing and published them in a separate volume called A Writer's Diary. *The following diary entries are taken from this edition. They show Virginia Woolf struggling with creative doubts and aesthetic demands, as well as with social obligations, depression, and, with the onset of World War II, the Nazi bombing of England. For more infor-mation on Virginia Woolf, see page 583.*

THIS LOOSE, DRIFTING MATERIAL OF LIFE
Easter Sunday, April 20, 1919

One of the pleasures of keeping a diary is rereading what we've writ-ten. Here, just having completed a newspaper article on the novelist Daniel Defoe, Virginia Woolf decides to take a break and think about the different ways she composes when she writes in her diary as opposed to when she writes more formally for publication.

In the idleness which succeeds any long article, and Defoe is the sec-ond leader this month, I got out this diary and read, as one always does read one's own writing, with a kind of guilty intensity. I confess that the rough and random style of it, often so ungrammatical, and crying for a word altered, afflicted me somewhat. I am trying to tell whichever self it is that reads this hereafter that I can write very much better; and take no time over this; and forbid her to let the eye of man behold it. And now I may add my little compliment to the effect that it has a slapdash and vigour and sometimes hits an unexpected bull's eye. But what is more to the point is my belief that the habit of writing thus for my own eye only is good practice. It loosens the ligaments. Never mind the misses and the stumbles. Going at such a pace as I do I must make the most direct and instant shots at my object, and thus have to lay hands on words, choose them and shoot them with no more pause than is needed to put my pen in the ink. I believe that during the past year I can trace some increase of ease in my professional writing which I attribute to my casual half hours after tea. Moreover there looms ahead of me the shadow of some kind of form which a diary might attain to. I might in the course of time learn what it is that one can make of this loose, drifting material of life; finding another use for it than the use I put it to, so much more consciously and scrupulously, in fiction. What sort of diary should I like mine to be? Something loose knit and yet not slovenly, so elastic that it will embrace anything, solemn, slight, or beautiful that comes into my mind. I should like it to resemble some deep old desk, or capacious hold-all, in which one flings a mass of odds and ends without looking them through. I should like to come back, after a year or two, and find that the collection had sorted itself and refined itself and coalesced, as such deposits so mysteriously do, into a mould, transparent enough to reflect the light of our life, and yet steady, tranquil compounds with the aloofness of a work of art. The main requisite, I think on re-reading my old volumes, is not to play the part of censor, but to write as the mood comes or of anything whatever; since I was curious to find how I went for things put in haphazard, and found the significance to lie where I never saw it at the time. But looseness quickly becomes slovenly. A little effort is needed to face a character or an incident which needs to be recorded. . . .

CHAINED TO MY ROCK
Thursday, August 18, 1921

In 1919, Virginia and Leonard (referred to throughout the diaries as L.) purchased a small country house in Sussex. For many years, they divided their time between there and London. In 1921, Virginia Woolf suffered a bout of nervous depression and was advised by a local doctor (who, she wrote, thought of her as a "chronic invalid") to rest and do nothing for a while. In an irritable state of mind, the day after the doctor's visit, she wrote the following entry in which she compares herself to Prometheus, the Greek mythic hero who was chained to a rock by Zeus as punishment for stealing fire from the gods and giving it to human beings.

Nothing to record; only an intolerable fit of the fidgets to write away. Here I am chained to my rock; forced to do nothing; doomed to let every worry, spite, irritation, and obsession scratch and claw and come again. This is a day that I may not walk and must not work. Whatever book I read bubbles up in my mind as part of an article I want to write. No one in the whole of Sussex is so miserable as I am; or so conscious of an infinite capacity of enjoyment hoarded in me, could I use it. The sun streams (no, never streams; floods rather) down upon all the yellow fields and the long low barns; and what wouldn't I give to be coming through Firle woods, dirty and hot, with my nose turned home, every muscle tired and the brain laid up in sweet lavender, so sane and cool, and ripe for the morrow's task. How I should notice everything—the phrase for it coming the moment after and fitting like a glove; and then on the dusty road, as I ground my pedals, so my story would begin telling itself; and then the sun would be down; and home, and some bout of poetry after dinner, half read, half lived, as if the flesh were dissolved and through it the flowers burst red and white. There! I've written out half my irritation. I hear poor L. driving the lawn mower up and down, for a wife like I am should have a latch to her cage. She bites! And he spent all yesterday running round London for me. Still if one is Prometheus, if the rock is hard and the gadflies pungent, gratitude, affection, none of the nobler feelings have sway. And so this August is wasted.

Only the thought of people suffering more than I do at all consoles; and that is an aberration of egotism, I suppose. I will now make out a time table if I can to get through these odious days. . . .

THEY GET CLOSER EVERY TIME
Wednesday, October 2, 1940

The Woolfs lost their London house during the Nazi bombing raids in 1940. But even in their Sussex house they experienced the incessant raids. They often witnessed air battles above their home. On one occasion, having watched an enemy plane being shot down, Woolf wrote that it "would have been a peaceful matter of fact death to be popped off on the terrace . . . this very fine cool sunny August evening." The thought of death returned during another bombing raid in October. Six months later, on March 28, 1941, she took her own life.

Ought I not to look at the sunset rather than write this? A flush of red in the blue; the haystack on the marsh catches the glow; behind me, the apples are red in the trees. L. is gathering them. Now a plume of smoke goes from the train under Caburn. And all the air a solemn stillness holds. Till 8:30 when the cadaverous twanging in the sky begins; the planes going to London. Well it's an hour still to that. Cows feeding. The elm tree sprinkling its little leaves against the sky. Our pear tree swagged with pears; and the weathercock above the triangular church tower above it. Why try again to make the familiar catalogue, from which something escapes. Should I think of death? Last night a great heavy plunge of bomb under the window. So near we both started. A plane had passed dropping this fruit. We went on to the terrace. Trinkets of stars sprinkled and glittering. All quiet. The bombs dropped on Itford Hill. There are two by the river, marked with white wooden crosses, still unburst. I said to L.: I don't want to die yet. The chances are against it. But they're aiming at the railway and the power works. They get closer every time. Caburn was crowned with what looked like a settled moth, wings extended—a Messerschmitt it was, shot down on Sunday. . . . Oh I try to imagine how one's killed by a bomb. I've got it fairly vivid—the sensation: but can't see anything but suffocating nonentity following after. I shall think—oh I wanted another 10 years—not this—and shan't, for once, be able to describe it. It—I mean death; no, the scrunching and scrambling, the crushing of my bone shade in on my very active eye and brain: the process of putting out the light—painful? Yes. Terrifying. I suppose so. Then a swoon; a drain; two or three gulps attempting consciousness—and then dot dot dot.

The Reader's Presence

1. In the first entry from Woolf's diaries, what positive qualities does she discover about her diary as she rereads it? Does she note any negative tendencies? In what ways does her diary offer her a means of self-discovery?

2. Woolf observed that one of the problems with diaries is that we usually turn to them only in certain moods (for example, loneliness, depression) and that therefore they provide only a limited view of someone's personality. Do you think, from the three excerpts reprinted here, that this observation would pertain to her own diaries? Can you apply her observation to some of the other diary entries in this chapter?

3. In the Writer at Work selection on page 137, Edward Hoagland characterizes the essay as "serendipitous or domestic satire or testimony, tongue-in-cheek or wail of grief." What do Woolf's criteria for diaries share with Hoagland's criteria for essays? What are the possible relationships between the "raw material" of an event recorded in a diary, and an account of that same event offered in an essay?

Part II

Personal Writing: Exploring Our Own Lives

10

Sherman Alexie

The Joy of Reading and Writing: Superman and Me

Sherman Alexie (b. 1966) is a Spokane/Coeur d'Arelene Indian who grew up on the Spokane Indian Reservation in Wellpinit, Washington. He was born hydrocephalic and underwent a brain operation at the age of six months, which he was not expected to survive. As a youth, Alexie left the reservation for a public high school where he excelled in academics and became a star player on the basketball team. He attended Gonzaga University in Spokane on a scholarship, then transferred to Washington State University, where his experience in a poetry workshop encouraged him to become a writer. Soon after graduation he received the Washington State Arts Commission Poetry Fellowship and a National Endowment for the Arts Poetry Fellowship. His first collection of short stories, The Lone Ranger and Tonto Fistfight in Heaven, *received both a PEN/Hemingway Award for Best First Book of Fiction and a Lila Wallace–Reader's Digest Writer's Award. He was subsequently named one of Granta's Best Young American Novelists, and published a novel titled* Reservation Blues *(1995), followed the next year by* Indian Killer *(1996). Since 1997 Alexie has written for the screen; his screenplay for a movie based on his own short story, "Smoke Signals," received the Christopher Award in 1999. Including poetry, he has now published fourteen books, including his most recent collection of short stories,* The Toughest Indian in the World *(2000), the title story of which appears on page 827.*

Sherman Alexie has commented on his own work, "I'm a good writer who may be a great writer one day. I'm harder on myself than anybody."

I learned to read with a Superman comic book. Simple enough, I suppose. I cannot recall which particular Superman comic book I read, nor can I remember which villain he fought in that issue. I cannot remember the plot, nor the means by which I obtained the comic book. What I can remember is this: I was 3 years old, a Spokane Indian boy living with his family on the Spokane Indian Reservation in eastern Washington state. We were poor by most standards, but one of my parents usually managed to find some minimum-wage job or another, which made us middle-class by reservation standards. I had a brother and three sisters. We lived on a combination of irregular paychecks, hope, fear, and government surplus food.

My father, who is one of the few Indians who went to Catholic school on purpose, was an avid reader of westerns, spy thrillers, murder mysteries, gangster epics, basketball player biographies, and anything else he could find. He bought his books by the pound at Dutch's Pawn Shop, Goodwill, Salvation Army, and Value Village. When he had extra money, he bought new novels at supermarkets, convenience stores, and hospital gift shops. Our house was filled with books. They were stacked in crazy piles in the bathroom, bedrooms, and living room. In a fit of unemployment-inspired creative energy, my father built a set of bookshelves and soon filled them with a random assortment of books about the Kennedy assassination, Watergate, the Vietnam War, and the entire 23-book series of the Apache westerns. My father loved books, and since I loved my father with an aching devotion, I decided to love books as well.

I can remember picking up my father's books before I could read. The words themselves were mostly foreign, but I still remember the exact moment when I first understood, with a sudden clarity, the purpose of a paragraph. I didn't have the vocabulary to say "paragraph," but I realized that a paragraph was a fence that held words. The words inside a paragraph worked together for a common purpose. They had some specific reason for being inside the same fence. This knowledge delighted me. I began to think of everything in terms of paragraphs. Our reservation was a small paragraph within the United States. My family's house was a paragraph, distinct from the other paragraphs of the LeBrets to the north, the Fords to our South, and the Tribal School to the west. Inside our house, each family member existed as a separate paragraph but still had genetics and common experiences to link us. Now, using this logic, I can see my changed family as an essay of seven paragraphs: mother, father, older brother, the deceased sister, my younger twin sisters, and our adopted little brother.

At the same time I was seeing the world in paragraphs, I also picked up that Superman comic book. Each panel, complete with picture, dialogue, and narrative was a three-dimensional paragraph. In one panel, Superman breaks through a door. His suit is red, blue, and yellow. The brown door shatters into many pieces. I look at the narrative above the picture. I cannot read the words, but I assume it tells me that "Superman is breaking down the door." Aloud, I pretend to read the words and say, "Superman is breaking down the door." Words, dialogue, also float out of Superman's mouth. Because he is breaking down the door, I assume he says, "I am breaking down the door." Once again, I pretend to read the words and say aloud, "I am breaking down the door." In this way, I learned to read.

This might be an interesting story all by itself. A little Indian boy   5
teaches himself to read at an early age and advances quickly. He reads "Grapes of Wrath" in kindergarten when other children are struggling

through "Dick and Jane." If he'd been anything but an Indian boy living on the reservation, he might have been called a prodigy. But he is an Indian boy living on the reservation and is simply an oddity. He grows into a man who often speaks of his childhood in the third person, as if it will somehow dull the pain and make him sound more modest about his talents.

A smart Indian is a dangerous person, widely feared and ridiculed by Indians and non-Indians alike. I fought with my classmates on a daily basis. They wanted me to stay quiet when the non-Indian teacher asked for answers, for volunteers, for help. We were Indian children who were expected to be stupid. Most lived up to those expectations inside the classroom but subverted them on the outside. They struggled with basic reading in school but could remember how to sing a few dozen powwow songs. They were monosyllabic in front of their non-Indian teachers but could tell complicated stories and jokes at the dinner table. They submissively ducked their heads when confronted by a non-Indian adult but would slug it out with the Indian bully who was 10 years older. As Indian children, we were expected to fail in the non-Indian world. Those who failed were ceremonially accepted by other Indians and appropriately pitied by non-Indians.

I refused to fail. I was smart. I was arrogant. I was lucky. I read books late into the night, until I could barely keep my eyes open. I read books at recess, then during lunch, and in the few minutes left after I had finished my classroom assignments. I read books in the car when my family traveled to powwows or basketball games. In shopping malls, I ran to the bookstores and read bits and pieces of as many books as I could. I read the books my father brought home from the pawnshops and secondhand. I read the books I borrowed from the library. I read the backs of cereal boxes. I read the newspaper. I read the bulletins posted on the walls of the school, the clinic, the tribal offices, the post office. I read junk mail. I read auto-repair manuals. I read magazines. I read anything that had words and paragraphs. I read with equal parts joy and desperation. I loved those books, but I also knew that love had only one purpose. I was trying to save my life.

Despite all the books I read, I am still surprised I became a writer. I was going to be a pediatrician. These days, I write novels, short stories, and poems. I visit schools and teach creative writing to Indian kids. In all my years in the reservation school system, I was never taught how to write poetry, short stories, or novels. I was certainly never taught that Indians wrote poetry, short stories, and novels. Writing was something beyond Indians. I cannot recall a single time that a guest teacher visited the reservation. There must have been visiting teachers. Who were they? Where are they now? Do they exist? I visit the schools as often as possible. The Indian kids crowd the classroom. Many are writing their own poems, short stories, and novels. They have read my books. They have read many other books. They look at me with bright eyes and arrogant wonder. They are trying to save their lives. Then there are the sullen and already defeated Indian kids who sit in the back rows and ignore me with theatrical precision.

The pages of their notebooks are empty. They carry neither pencil nor pen. They stare out the window. They refuse and resist. "Books," I say to them. "Books," I say. I throw my weight against their locked doors. The door holds. I am smart. I am arrogant. I am lucky. I am trying to save our lives.

The Reader's Presence

1. What does literacy mean to Alexie? What are his associations with reading? with writing? How does he use his reading and his writing to establish his ties to the community? What aspects of his identity are bound up with reading and writing?

2. How did the young Alexie use popular culture to educate himself? What did comic books teach him? How does Alexie use the figure of Superman, and aspects of action-hero stories more generally, to give structure and coherence to his essay?

3. Alexie uses the metaphor of "breaking down the door" to describe the act of learning to read. What are the connotations of this metaphor? How does it compare with Frederick Douglass's account of his acquisition of literacy in "Learning to Read and Write" (see page 112) in which he says that he sometimes felt as though "learning to read had been a curse rather than a blessing"? As he encountered arguments for and against slavery in the books he read, Douglass felt that reading deepened his already vivid experience of slavery: "It had given me a view of my wretched condition, without the remedy" (paragraph 6). Is literacy a means to freedom for Alexie as it was, ultimately, for Douglass? If so, freedom from what and/or freedom to do what?

11

Julia Alvarez

My English

Julia Alvarez was born in New York City in 1950 but raised in the Dominican Republic. Because her father, a medical doctor, was active in the underground movement against dictator General Rafael Trujilo, her family was forced to flee the Dominican Republic when she was ten years old, and resettled permanently in New York. She attended Connecticut College, Middlebury College, and Syracuse University. Besides creative writing, she has had a long-standing involvement with education: Alvarez has taught in Kentucky, Delaware, North Carolina, Massachusetts, and Vermont. She is best known for her novels: How the Garcia Girls Lost Their Accents *(1991),* In the Time of Butterflies *(1994), which was an American Library Association Notable Book and a finalist for the National Book Critics Circle Award,* ¡Yo! *(1997), and* In the Name of Salome *(2000). She has also written many novels for children and adolescents. She is now a tenured professor at Middlebury College in Vermont.*

Alvarez comments, "I came late to the [English] language but I came early into the writing profession. In high school, I fell in love with how words can make you feel complete in a way that I hadn't felt complete since leaving the island. Early on, I fell in love with books, which I didn't have at all growing up."

Mami and Papi used to speak it when they had a secret they wanted to keep from us children. We lived then in the Dominican Republic, and the family as a whole spoke only Spanish at home, until my sisters and I started attending the Carol Morgan School, and we became a bilingual family. Spanish had its many tongues as well. There was the castellano of Padre Joaquín from Spain, whose lisp we all loved to imitate. Then the educated español my parents' families spoke, aunts and uncles who were always correcting us children, for we spent most of the day with the maids and so had picked up their "bad Spanish." Campesinas, they spoke a lilting, animated campuno, ss swallowed, endings chopped off, funny turns of phrases. This campuno was my true mother tongue, not the Spanish of Calderón de la Barca or Cervantes or even Neruda, but of Chucha and Iluminada and Gladys and Ursulina from Juncalito and Licey and Boca de Yuma and San

Juan de la Maguana. Those women yakked as they cooked, they storytold, they gossiped, they sang—boleros, merengues, canciones, salves. Theirs were the voices that belonged to the rain and the wind and the teeny, teeny stars even a small child could blot out with her thumb.

Besides all these versions of Spanish, every once in a while another strange tongue emerged from my papi's mouth or my mami's lips. What I first recognized was not a language, but a tone of voice, serious, urgent, something important and top secret being said, some uncle in trouble, someone divorcing, someone dead. *Say it in English so the children won't understand.* I would listen, straining to understand, thinking that this was not a different language but just another and harder version of Spanish. *Say it in English so the children won't understand.* From the beginning, English was the sound of worry and secrets, the sound of being left out.

I could make no sense of this "harder Spanish," and so I tried by other means to find out what was going on. I knew my mother's face by heart. When the little lines on the corners of her eyes crinkled, she was amused. When her nostrils flared and she bit her lips, she was trying hard not to laugh. She held her head down, eyes glancing up, when she thought I was lying. Whenever she spoke that gibberish English, I translated the general content by watching the Spanish expressions on her face.

Soon, I began to learn more English, at the Carol Morgan School. That is, when I had stopped gawking. The teacher and some of the American children had the strangest coloration: light hair, light eyes, light skin, as if Ursulina had soaked them in bleach too long, to' deteñío. I did have some blond cousins, but they had deeply tanned skin, and as they grew older, their hair darkened, so their earlier paleness seemed a phase of their acquiring normal color. Just as strange was the little girl in my reader who had a *cat* and a *dog,* that looked just like un gatito y un perrito. Her mami was *Mother* and her papi *Father.* Why have a whole new language for school and for books with a teacher who could speak it teaching you double the amount of words you really needed?

Butter, butter, butter, butter. All day, one English word that had par-   5
ticularly struck me would go round and round in my mouth and weave through all the Spanish in my head until by the end of the day, the word did sound like just another Spanish word. And so I would say, "Mami, please pass la mantequilla." She would scowl and say in English, "I'm sorry, I don't understand. But would you be needing some butter on your bread?"

Why my parents didn't first educate us in our native language by en-rolling us in a Dominican school, I don't know. Part of it was that Mami's family had a tradition of sending the boys to the States to boarding school and college, and she had been one of the first girls to be allowed to join her brothers. At Abbot Academy, whose school song was our lullaby as babies ("Although Columbus and Cabot never heard of Abbot, it's quite the place for you and me"), she had become quite Americanized. It was very impor-tant, she kept saying, that we learn our English. She always used the possessive pronoun: *your* English, an inheritance we had come into and must wisely use. Unfortunately, my English became all mixed up with our Spanish.

Mix-up, or what's now called Spanglish, was the language we spoke for several years. There wasn't a sentence that wasn't colonized by an English word. At school, a Spanish word would suddenly slide into my English like someone butting into line. Teacher, whose face I was learning to read as minutely as my mother's, would scowl but no smile played on her lips. Her pale skin made her strange countenance hard to read, so that I often misjudged how much I could get away with. Whenever I made a mistake, Teacher would shake her head slowly, "In English, YU-LEE-AH, there's no such word as *columpio*. Do you mean a *swing?*"

I would bow my head, humiliated by the smiles and snickers of the American children around me. I grew insecure about Spanish. My native tongue was not quite as good as English, as if words like *columpio* were illegal immigrants trying to cross a border into another language. But Teacher's discerning grammar-and-vocabulary-patrol ears could tell and send them back.

Soon, I was talking up an English storm. "Did you eat English parrot?" my grandfather asked one Sunday. I had just enlisted yet one more patient servant to listen to my rendition of "Peter Piper picked a peck of pickled peppers" at breakneck pace. "Huh?" I asked impolitely in English, putting him in his place. *Cat got your tongue? No big deal! So there! Take that! Holy Toledo!* (Our teacher's favorite "curse word.") *Go jump in the lake! Really dumb. Golly. Gosh.* Slang, clichés, sayings, hotshot language that our teacher called, ponderously, idiomatic expressions. Riddles, jokes, puns, conundrums. *What is yellow and goes click-click? Why did the chicken cross the road? See you later, alligator.* How wonderful to call someone an alligator and not be scolded for being disrespectful. In fact, they were supposed to say back, *In a while, crocodile.*

There was also a neat little trick I wanted to try on an English-speaking 10 adult at home. I had learned it from Elizabeth, my smart-alecky friend in fourth grade, whom I alternately worshiped and resented. I'd ask her a question that required an explanation, and she'd answer, "Because . . ." "Elizabeth, how come you didn't go to Isabel's birthday party?" "Because . . ." "Why didn't you put your name in your reader?" "Because . . ." I thought that such a cool way to get around having to come up with answers. So, I practiced saying it under my breath, planning for the day I could use it on an unsuspecting English-speaking adult.

One Sunday at our extended family dinner, my grandfather sat down at the children's table to chat with us. He was famous, in fact, for the way he could carry on adult conversations with his grandchildren. He often spoke to us in English so that we could practice speaking it outside the classroom. He was a Cornell man, a United Nations representative from our country. He gave speeches in English. Perfect English, my mother's phrase. That Sunday, he asked me a question. I can't even remember what it was because I wasn't really listening but lying in wait for my chance. "Because . . . ," I answered him. Papito waited a second for the rest of my sentence and then gave me a thumbnail grammar lesson, "*Because* has to be followed by a clause."

"Why's that?" I asked, nonplussed.

"Because," he winked, "Just because."

A beginning wordsmith, I had so much left to learn; sometimes it was disheartening. Once Tío Gus, the family intellectual, put a speck of salt on my grandparents' big dining table during Sunday dinner. He said, "Imagine this whole table is the human brain. Then this teensy grain is all we ever use of our intelligence!" He enumerated geniuses who had perhaps used two grains, maybe three: Einstein, Michelangelo, da Vinci, Beethoven. We children believed him. It was the kind of impossible fact we thrived on, proving as it did that the world out there was not drastically different from the one we were making up in our heads.

Later, at home, Mami said that you had to take what her younger   15
brother said "with a grain of salt." I thought she was still referring to Tío Gus's demonstration, and I tried to puzzle out what she was saying. Finally, I asked what she meant. "Taking what someone says with a grain of salt is an idiomatic expression in English," she explained. It was pure voodoo is what it was — what later I learned poetry could also do: a grain of salt could symbolize both the human brain and a condiment for human nonsense. And it could be itself, too: a grain of salt to flavor a bland plate of American food.

When we arrived in New York, I was shocked. A country where everyone spoke English! These people must be smarter, I thought. Maids, waiters, taxi drivers, doormen, bums on the street, all spoke this difficult language. It took some time before I understood that Americans were not necessarily a smarter, superior race. It was as natural for them to learn their mother tongue as it was for a little Dominican baby to learn Spanish. It came with "mother's milk," my mother explained, and for a while I thought a mother tongue was a mother tongue because you got it from your mother's breast, along with proteins and vitamins.

Soon it wasn't so strange that everyone was speaking in English instead of Spanish. I learned not to hear it as English, but as sense. I no longer strained to understand, I understood. I relaxed in this second language. Only when someone with a heavy southern or British accent spoke in a movie, or at church when the priest droned his sermon — only then did I experience that little catch of anxiety. I worried that I would not be able to understand, that I wouldn't be able to "keep up" with the voice speaking in this acquired language. I would be like those people from the Bible we had studied in religion class, whom I imagined standing at the foot of an enormous tower that looked just like the skyscrapers around me. They had been punished for their pride by being made to speak different languages so that they didn't understand what anyone was saying.

But at the foot of those towering New York skyscrapers, I began to understand more and more — not less and less — English. In sixth grade, I had one of the first in a lucky line of great English teachers who began to nurture in me a love of language, a love that had been there since my childhood of listening closely to words. Sister Marie Generosa did not make our class interminably diagram sentences from a workbook or learn a catechism of grammar rules. Instead, she asked us to write little stories imagining we were snowflakes, birds, pianos, a stone in the pavement, a star in the sky. What would it feel like to be a flower with roots in the ground? If the clouds could talk, what would they say? She had an expressive, dreamy look that was accentuated by the wimple that framed her face.

Supposing, just supposing . . . My mind would take off, soaring into possibilities, a flower with roots, a star in the sky, a cloud full of sad, sad tears, a piano crying out each time its back was tapped, music only to our ears.

Sister Maria stood at the chalkboard. Her chalk was always snapping   20
in two because she wrote with such energy, her whole habit shaking with the swing of her arm, her hand tap-tap-tapping on the board. "Here's a simple sentence: 'The snow fell.' " Sister pointed with her chalk, her eyebrows lifted, her wimple poked up. Sometimes I could see wisps of gray hair that strayed from under her headdress. "But watch what happens if we put an adverb at the beginning and a prepositional phrase at the end: 'Gently, the snow fell on the bare hills.' "

I thought about the snow. I saw how it might fall on the hills, tapping lightly on the bare branches of trees. Softly, it would fall on the cold, bare fields. On toys children had left out in the yard, and on cars and on little birds and on people out late walking on the streets. Sister Marie filled the chalkboard with snowy print, on and on, handling and shaping and moving the language, scribbling all over the board until English, those verbal gadgets, those tricks and turns of phrases, those little fixed units and counters, became a charged, fluid mass that carried me in its great fluent waves, rolling and moving onward, to deposit me on the shores of my new homeland. I was no longer a foreigner with no ground to stand on. I had landed in the English language.

The Reader's Presence

1. At the beginning of the essay, Alvarez identifies English as "the sound of being left out" (paragraph 2). What is the sound of being left out? Think about conversations in which you have deliberately been left out. How did they sound? Compare your experience of the sound with Alvarez's. As the story goes on, Alvarez becomes fluent enough in English to leave other people out. What strategies does she use to exclude others? In a similar vein, consider the instances when you have purposely left someone else out of a conversation (parents, friends, teachers, etc.). Did you use similar strategies or different ones? Which did you find most effective? Why?

2. This story is partly about becoming more competent in English. Review carefully — and then compare — the first and last paragraphs. What written signs of development can you find? Would you argue in support of — or against — the assertion that the final paragraph is written in better English than the first? What specifically do you look at to judge the two paragraphs? Foreign words? Sentence structure? Punctuation? Something else? Please explain.

3. Alvarez talks about words in her native language as "illegal immigrants" (paragraph 8) that have to be erased from her speech before she knows she has "landed in the English language" (paragraph 19). Read carefully Eric Liu's essay, "Creating an Asian American Identity" (see page 162), or others in this collection that focus on the process of becoming an American. What do other authors think becoming an American involves? Are these beliefs and customs they must leave behind because they are not American? What are the authors' attitudes toward foods, accents, and culture? To what extent do the authors argue that being American involves maintaining one's ethnic heritage?

THE WRITER AT WORK

Julia Alvarez on Her Identity as a Writer

Even before her family fled to the United States from the Dominican Republic in 1960 when she was ten years old, Julia Alvarez had to come to terms with her American-ness. In the Dominican Republic, Alvarez had what she calls "an American childhood," in which American food, American goods, and American cars were part of everyday life; she and her sisters attended an American school. "At night," Alvarez wrote in an essay in American Scholar, *"my prayers were full of blond hair and blue eyes and snow." And yet her actual arrival on American soil marked the beginning of a difficult period of adjustment for Alvarez. "In New York City, I was suddenly thrown back on myself," she wrote, and that self was deeply homesick for the Island. As for many writers, her feeling of isolation and alienation led Alvarez to reading, and sensitive teachers pushed her toward writing for which she had obvious gifts. In reading and writing Alvarez found a place to belong. Alvarez likes to quote Czeslow Milosz, the exiled Polish poet: "Language is the only homeland." Alvarez adds, "And that was where I landed when we left the Dominican Republic, not in the United States but in the English language." In the following piece, originally titled "Doña Aida, with Your Permission," Alvarez defends her "homeland" of English in the place of her birth, and expresses the power of the "synthesizing consciousness" that has made her one of America's most vivid writers.*

A few years ago the Caribbean Studies Association had its annual meeting in Santo Domingo, and they asked me if I would be its keynote speaker as a Dominican American writer along with Aída Cartagena Portalatín, the grand woman of letters in the Dominican Republic. She read in Spanish, and then I read in English, and then—as a kind of crowning moment—we were both brought together on stage to meet each other in front of everyone.

Doña Aída embraced me, but then in front of the mikes, she reamed me out. "Eso parece mentira que una dominicana se ponga a escribir en inglés. Vuelve a tu país, vuelve a tu idioma. Tú eres dominicana." ("It doesn't seem possible that a Dominican should write in English. Come back to your country, to your language. You are a Dominican.") Since she was grand and old—and I was raised to have respeto for the old people—but also because she was arguing in Spanish—and I can usually only win my fights in English—I kept my mouth shut. What is it that I would have said?

This is what this short essay is about.

Doña Aída, con su permiso. Doña Aída, with your permission.

I am *not* a Dominican writer. I have no business writing in a language   5
that I can speak but have not studied deeply enough to craft. I can't ride its
wild horses. Just the subjunctive would throw me off. I know the tender
mouth of English, just how to work the reins. I've taken lessons from Emily
Dickinson and Walt Whitman and Toni Morrison and William Carlos
Williams, whose Mami was Puerto Rican. And though I have read Pablo
Neruda and César Vallejo and Julia de Burgos and Ana Lydia Vega and
Aída Cartagena Portalatín, I can only admire what they do in Spanish. I
cannot emulate their wonderful mastery of that language.

No, I am not a Dominican writer or really a Dominican in the traditional sense. I don't live on the Island, breathing its daily smells, enduring its particular burdens, speaking its special dominicano. In fact, I would tell a different story and write poems with a different rhythm if I lived and worked there, ate there, made love there, voted there, dried my tears there, laughed my laughter there. If daily what I heard was *Ay* instead of *Oh*, if instead of that limited palette of colors in Vermont, gray softening into green, what I saw were colors so bright I'd have to look twice at things to believe that they were real.

But, you're right, Doña Aída, I'm also not una norteamericana. I am not a mainstream American writer with my roots in a small town in Illinois or Kentucky or even Nuevo México. I don't hear the same rhythms in English as a native speaker of English. Sometimes I hear Spanish in English (and, of course, vice versa). That's why I describe myself as a Dominican American writer. That's not just a term. I'm mapping a country that's not on the map, and that's why I'm trying to put it down on paper.

It's a world formed of contradictions, clashes, cominglings—the gringa and the Dominican, and it is precisely that tension and richness that interests me. Being in and out of both worlds, looking at one side from the other side—thus the title of one of my books of poems, *The Other Side/El Otro Lado*. These unusual perspectives are often what I write about. A duality that I hope in the writing transcends itself and becomes a new consciousness, a new place on the map, a synthesizing way of looking at the world.

And I would propose that this multicultural perspective—and forgive me that word because it has become such a catchphrase, a lap for every baby—this multicultural perspective is the perspective of some of the most interesting writers of this late twentieth century: Salman Rushdie in London, Michael Ondaatje in Toronto, Maxine Hong Kingston in San Francisco, Seamus Heaney in Boston, Bharati Mukherjee in Berkeley, Marjorie Agosin in Wellesley, Edwidge Danticat in Brooklyn. We're a mobile world; borders are melting; nationalities are on the move, often for devastating reasons. A multicultural perspective is more and more the way to understand the world.

So Doña Aída, I'm a mixed breed, as are many of us U.S.A. Latino/a   10
writers. With our finger-snapping, gum-chewing English, sometimes slipping in una palabrita o frase español. With our roots reaching down deep to the Latin American continent and the Caribbean where our parents or abuelitos or we ourselves came from. With our asabaches and SAT scores; our fast-paced, watch-checking rhythms combining with the slower eternal wavings of the palm trees.

And though I complain sometimes about the confusion resulting from being of neither world, and about the marginalizations created on both sides—the Americans considering me a writer of ethnic interest, a Latina writer (meaning a writer for Latinos and of sociological interest to mainstream Americans), or the Dominicans reaming me out, saying she's not one of us, she's not Dominican enough—though I complain about the confusion and rootlessness of being this mixed breed, I also think it's what confirmed me as a writer, particularly because I am a woman.

This is probably true for many of us Caribbean women writers. Our emigrations from our native countries and families helped us to achieve an important separation from a world in which it might not have been as easy for us to strike out on our own, to escape the confining definitions of our traditional gender roles. We also, many of us, achieved a measure of economic security, jobs in universities, say, that released us from the control of our papis and brothers and husbands and a patriarchal system that doesn't even pretend to be something else. For me, anyhow, as a writer, I had to free myself from certain restrictions—physical and mental—of being a Dominican female before I could rediscover and embrace the Latina in my writing.

"So what are you doing here in Santo Domingo?" you ask me, Doña Aída.

To know who I am, I have to know where I come from. So I keep coming back to the Island. And for fuerza, I go back to this thought: it really is in my Caribbean roots, in my island genes to be a pan-American, a gringa-dominicana, a synthesizing consciousness.

Think of it, the Caribbean . . . a string of islands, a sieve of the conti-   15
nents, north and south, a sponge, as most islands are, absorbing those who come and go, whether indios in canoes from the Amazon, or conquistadors from Spain, or African princes brought in chains in the holds of ships to be slaves, or refugees from China or central Europe or other islands. We are not a big continental chunk, a forbidding expanse that takes forever to pen-

etrate, which keeps groups solidly intact, for a while anyhow. Our beaches welcome the stranger with their carpets of white sand. In an hour you reach the interior; in another hour you arrive at the other coast. We are islands, permeable countries. It's in our genes to be a world made of many worlds. ¿No es así?

Ay, Doña Aída, you who carry our mixtures in the color of your skin, who also left the island as an exile many times and so understand what it is to be at home nowhere and everywhere, I know I don't really have to ask your pardon or permission. Beneath our individual circumstances and choices, we have fought many of the same struggles and have ended up in the same place, on paper.

12

Maya Angelou

"What's Your Name, Girl?"

Maya Angelou (b. 1928) grew up in St. Louis, Missouri, and in Stamps, Arkansas, a victim of poverty, discrimination, and abuse. Angelou confronts the pain and injustice of her childhood in I Know Why the Caged Bird Sings *(1969), from which the selection "What's Your Name, Girl?" is taken. James Baldwin, who suggested she write about her childhood, praised this book as the mark of the "beginning of a new era in the minds and hearts of all black men and women." Angelou, who has received over a hundred honorary degrees, is currently Reynolds Professor of American Studies at Wake Forest University. In addition to the several volumes of her autobiography, she is the author of articles, short stories, and poetry. Her most recent publications are a collection of essays,* Even the Stars Look Lonesome *(1997), and a children's book,* Kofi and His Magic *(1996). She has also directed her first feature-length film,* Down in the Delta, *released in 1998.*

Angelou describes a typical day in her life as a writer in this way: "When I'm writing, everything shuts down. I get up about five. . . . I get in my car and drive off to a hotel room: I can't write in my house, I take a hotel room and ask them to take everything off the walls so there's me, the Bible, Roget's Thesaurus, and some good, dry sherry and I'm at work by 6:30. I write on the bed lying down— one elbow is darker than the other, really black from leaning on it—and I write in longhand on yellow pads. Once into it, all disbelief is suspended, it's beautiful. I hate to go, but I've set for myself 12:30 as the time to leave, because after that it's an indulgence, it becomes stuff I am going to edit out anyway. . . . After dinner I re-read what I have written . . . if April is the cruellest month, then 8:00 at night is the cruellest hour because that's when I start to edit and all that pretty stuff I've written gets axed out. So if I've written ten or twelve pages in six hours, it'll end up as three or four if I'm lucky."

Recently a white woman from Texas, who would quickly describe herself as a liberal, asked me about my hometown. When I told her that in Stamps[1] my grandmother had owned the only Negro general merchandise store since the turn of the century, she exclaimed, "Why, you were a debutante." Ridiculous and even ludicrous. But Negro girls in small Southern towns, whether poverty-stricken or just munching along on a few of life's necessities, were given as extensive and irrelevant preparations for adulthood as rich white girls shown in magazines. Admittedly the training was not the same. While white girls learned to waltz and sit gracefully with a teacup balanced on their knees, we were lagging behind, learning the mid-Victorian values with very little money to indulge them. (Come and see Edna Lomax spending the money she made picking cotton on five balls of ecru tatting thread. Her fingers are bound to snag the work and she'll have to repeat the stitches time and time again. But she knows that when she buys the thread.)

We were required to embroider and I had trunkfuls of colorful dishtowels, pillowcases, runners, and handkerchiefs to my credit. I mastered the art of crocheting and tatting, and there was a lifetime's supply of dainty doilies that would never be used in sacheted dresser drawers. It went without saying that all girls could iron and wash, but the finer touches around the home, like setting a table with real silver, baking roasts, and cooking vegetables without meat, had to be learned elsewhere. Usually at the source of those habits. During my tenth year, a white woman's kitchen became my finishing school.

Mrs. Viola Cullinan was a plump woman who lived in a three-bedroom house somewhere behind the post office. She was singularly unattractive until she smiled, and then the lines around her eyes and mouth which made her look perpetually dirty disappeared, and her face looked like the mask of an impish elf. She usually rested her smile until late afternoon when her women friends dropped in and Miss Glory, the cook, served them cold drinks on the closed-in porch.

The exactness of her house was inhuman. This glass went here and only here. That cup had its place and it was an act of impudent rebellion to place it anywhere else. At twelve o'clock the table was set. At 12:15 Mrs. Cullinan sat down to dinner (whether her husband had arrived or not). At 12:16 Miss Glory brought out the food.

It took me a week to learn the difference between a salad plate, a bread plate, and a dessert plate.   5

Mrs. Cullinan kept up the tradition of her wealthy parents. She was from Virginia. Miss Glory, who was a descendant of slaves that had

---

[1]*Stamps:* A town in southwestern Arkansas. — EDS.

worked for the Cullinans, told me her history. She had married beneath her (according to Miss Glory). Her husband's family hadn't had their money very long and what they had "didn't 'mount to much."

As ugly as she was, I thought privately, she was lucky to get a husband above or beneath her station. But Miss Glory wouldn't let me say a thing against her mistress. She was very patient with me, however, over the housework. She explained the dishware, silverware, and servants' bells.

The large round bowl in which soup was served wasn't a soup bowl, it was a tureen. There were goblets, sherbet glasses, ice-cream glasses, wine glasses, green glass coffee cups with matching saucers, and water glasses. I had a glass to drink from, and it sat with Miss Glory's on a separate shelf from the others. Soup spoons, gravy boat, butter knives, salad forks, and carving platter were additions to my vocabulary and in fact almost represented a new language. I was fascinated with the novelty, with the fluttering Mrs. Cullinan and her Alice-in-Wonderland house.

Her husband remains, in my memory, undefined. I lumped him with all the other white men that I had ever seen and tried not to see.

On our way home one evening, Miss Glory told me that Mrs. Cullinan   10
couldn't have children. She said that she was too delicate-boned. It was hard to imagine bones at all under those layers of fat. Miss Glory went on to say that the doctor had taken out all her lady organs. I reasoned that a pig's organs included the lungs, heart, and liver, so if Mrs. Cullinan was walking around without these essentials, it explained why she drank alcohol out of unmarked bottles. She was keeping herself embalmed.

When I spoke to Bailey[2] about it, he agreed that I was right, but he also informed me that Mr. Cullinan had two daughters by a colored lady and that I knew them very well. He added that the girls were the spitting image of their father. I was unable to remember what he looked like, although I had just left him a few hours before, but I thought of the Coleman girls. They were very light-skinned and certainly didn't look very much like their mother (no one ever mentioned Mr. Coleman).

My pity for Mrs. Cullinan preceded me the next morning like the Cheshire cat's smile. Those girls, who could have been her daughters, were beautiful. They didn't have to straighten their hair. Even when they were caught in the rain, their braids still hung down straight like tamed snakes. Their mouths were pouty little cupid's bows. Mrs. Cullinan didn't know what she missed. Or maybe she did. Poor Mrs. Cullinan.

For weeks after, I arrived early, left late, and tried very hard to make up for her barrenness. If she had had her own children, she wouldn't have had to ask me to run a thousand errands from her back door to the back door of her friends. Poor old Mrs. Cullinan.

Then one evening Miss Glory told me to serve the ladies on the porch. After I set the tray down and turned toward the kitchen, one of the

[2]*Bailey:* Her brother. — EDS.

women asked, "What's your name, girl?" It was the speckled-face one.
Mrs. Cullinan said, "She doesn't talk much. Her name's Margaret."

"Is she dumb?"   15

"No. As I understand it, she can talk when she wants to but she's
usually quiet as a little mouse. Aren't you, Margaret?"

I smiled at her. Poor thing. No organs and couldn't even pronounce
my name correctly.[3]

"She's a sweet little thing, though."

"Well, that may be, but the name's too long. I'd never bother myself.
I'd call her Mary if I was you."

I fumed into the kitchen. That horrible woman would never have the   20
chance to call me Mary because if I was starving I'd never work for her. I
decided I wouldn't pee on her if her heart was on fire. Giggles drifted in
off the porch and into Miss Glory's pots. I wondered what they could be
laughing about.

Whitefolks were so strange. Could they be talking about me? Everybody knew that they stuck together better than the Negroes did. It was
possible that Mrs. Cullinan had friends in St. Louis who heard about a
girl from Stamps being in court and wrote to tell her. Maybe she knew
about Mr. Freeman.[4]

My lunch was in my mouth a second time and I went outside and relieved myself on the bed of four-o'clocks. Miss Glory thought I might be
coming down with something and told me to go on home, that Momma
would give me some herb tea, and she'd explain to her mistress.

I realized how foolish I was being before I reached the pond. Of
course Mrs. Cullinan didn't know. Otherwise she wouldn't have given me
the two nice dresses that Momma cut down, and she certainly wouldn't
have called me a "sweet little thing." My stomach felt fine, and I didn't
mention anything to Momma.

That evening I decided to write a poem on being white, fat, old, and
without children. It was going to be a tragic ballad. I would have to
watch her carefully to capture the essence of her loneliness and pain.

The very next day, she called me by the wrong name. Miss Glory and   25
I were washing up the lunch dishes when Mrs. Cullinan came to the doorway. "Mary?"

Miss Glory asked, "Who?"

Mrs. Cullinan, sagging a little, knew and I knew. "I want Mary to go
down to Mrs. Randall's and take her some soup. She's not been feeling
well for a few days."

Miss Glory's face was a wonder to see. "You mean Margaret,
ma'am. Her name's Margaret."

"That's too long. She's Mary from now on. Heat that soup from last

---

[3]Angelou's first name is actually Marguerite. — EDS.
[4]**Mr. Freeman:** A friend of Angelou's mother; he was convicted of raping Angelou
when she was a child. — EDS.

night and put it in the china tureen and, Mary, I want you to carry it carefully."

Every person I knew had a hellish horror of being "called out of his   30
name." It was a dangerous practice to call a Negro anything that could be loosely construed as insulting because of the centuries of their having been called niggers, jigs, dinges, blackbirds, crows, boots, and spooks.

Miss Glory had a fleeting second of feeling sorry for me. Then as she handed me the hot tureen she said, "Don't mind, don't pay that no mind. Sticks and stones may break your bones, but words . . . You know, I been working for her for twenty years."

She held the back door open for me. "Twenty years; I wasn't much older than you. My name used to be Hallelujah. That's what Ma named me, but my mistress give me 'Glory,' and it stuck. I likes it better too."

I was in the little path that ran behind the houses when Miss Glory shouted. "It's shorter too."

For a few seconds it was a tossup over whether I would laugh (imagine being named Hallelujah) or cry (imagine letting some white woman rename you for her convenience). My anger saved me from either outburst. I had to quit the job, but the problem was going to be how to do it. Momma wouldn't allow me to quit for just any reason.

"She's a peach. That woman is a real peach." Mrs. Randall's maid   35
was talking as she took the soup from me, and I wondered what her name used to be and what she answered to now.

For a week I looked into Mrs. Cullinan's face as she called me Mary. She ignored my coming late and leaving early. Miss Glory was a little annoyed because I had begun to leave egg yolk on the dishes and wasn't putting much heart in polishing the silver. I hoped that she would complain to our boss, but she didn't.

Then Bailey solved my dilemma. He had me describe the contents of the cupboard and the particular plates she liked best. Her favorite piece was a casserole shaped like a fish and the green glass coffee cups. I kept his instructions in mind, so on the next day when Miss Glory was hanging out clothes and I had again been told to serve the old biddies on the porch, I dropped the empty serving tray. When I heard Mrs. Cullinan scream, "Mary!" I picked up the casserole and two of the green glass cups in readiness. As she rounded the kitchen door I let them fall on the tiled floor.

I could never absolutely describe to Bailey what happened next, because each time I got to the part where she fell on the floor and screwed up her ugly face to cry, we burst out laughing. She actually wobbled around on the floor and picked up shards of the cups and cried, "Oh, Momma. Oh, dear Gawd. It's Momma's china from Virginia. Oh, Momma, I sorry."

Miss Glory came running in from the yard and the women from the porch crowded around. Miss Glory was almost as broken up as her mistress. "You mean to say she broke our Virginia dishes? What we gone do?"

Mrs. Cullinan cried louder. "That clumsy nigger. Clumsy little black   40
nigger."

Old speckled-face leaned down and asked, "Who did it, Viola? Was it Mary? Who did it?"

Everything was happening so fast I can't remember whether her action preceded her words, but I know that Mrs. Cullinan said, "Her name's Margaret, goddamn it, her name's Margaret!" And she threw a wedge of the broken plate at me. It could have been the hysteria which put her aim off, but the flying crockery caught Miss Glory right over her ear and she started screaming.

I left the front door wide open so all the neighbors could hear.

Mrs. Cullinan was right about one thing. My name wasn't Mary.

The Reader's Presence

1. At the center of this autobiographical episode is the importance of people's names in African American culture. Where does Angelou make this point clear? If she hadn't explained the problem of names directly, how might your interpretation of the episode be different? To what extent do the names of things also play an important role in the essay? What does it mean to be "called out of [one's] name" (paragraph 30)?

2. Consider Margaret's final act carefully. What turns her sympathetic feelings for Mrs. Cullinan to anger? Why does she respond by deliberately destroying Mrs. Cullinan's china? What else could she have done? Why was that act especially appropriate? What does the china represent? How does Angelou establish our sympathy, or lack thereof, for Margaret in the final paragraphs?

3. Many coming-of-age stories involve an account of the child's acquisition of language, but also, and perhaps more importantly, of the importance of social context to communication. Miss Glory's training of Marguerite as a maid involves "additions to [her] vocabulary and in fact almost represented a new language" (paragraph 8). How does Margaret's education compare to that of Malcolm X in "Homeboy" (see page 178) when he arrives in the Roxbury ghetto (paragraph 15 and following). What is the relation between language and power in each essay?

13

Russell Baker

Gumption

From 1962 to 1998, Russell Baker (b. 1925) wrote the "Observer" column in the New York Times, *a column that is syndicated to over four hundred and fifty newspapers across the nation. Baker's articles on contemporary American politics, culture, and language are consistently funny and often sharply satiric. Collections of his articles have been published in several volumes, including* So This Is Depravity (1980) *and* There's a Country in My Cellar (1990). *He is also the author of fiction and children's literature. Baker hosted* Masterpiece Theater *on public television until his retirement in 1998.*

Among other professional honors, he has twice been awarded the Pulitzer Prize, in 1979 for commentary and in 1983 for his autobiography, Growing Up (1982), *from which the selection "Gumption" is taken, and was awarded the George Polk Career Award in 1998. Baker's second volume of memoirs,* The Good Times, *was published in 1989. Baker engaged in extensive research efforts in preparation for writing these memoirs. After all, he explains, "I was writing about a world that seemed to exist 200 years ago. I had one foot back there in this primitive country life where the women did the laundry running their knuckles on scrub boards and heated irons on coal stoves."*

I began working in journalism when I was eight years old. It was my mother's idea. She wanted me to "make something" of myself and, after a levelheaded appraisal of my strengths, decided I had better start young if I was to have any chance of keeping up with the competition.

The flaw in my character which she had already spotted was the lack of "gumption." My idea of a perfect afternoon was lying in front of the radio rereading my favorite Big Little Book, *Dick Tracy Meets Stooge Viller.* My mother despised inactivity. Seeing me having a good time in repose, she was powerless to hide her disgust. "You've got no more gumption than a bump on a log," she said. "Get out in the kitchen and help Doris do those dirty dishes."

My sister Doris, though two years younger than I, had enough gumption for a dozen people. She positively enjoyed washing dishes, making beds, and cleaning the house. When she was only seven she could carry a piece of short-weighted cheese back to the A&P, threaten the manager with legal action, and come back triumphantly with the full quarter-pound we'd paid for and a few extra ounces thrown in for forgiveness. Doris could have made something of herself if she hadn't been a girl. Because of this defect, however, the best she could hope for was a career as a nurse or schoolteacher, the only work that capable females were considered up to in those days.

This must have saddened my mother, this twist of fate that had allocated all the gumption to the daughter and left her with a son who was content with Dick Tracy and Stooge Viller. If disappointed, though, she wasted no energy on self-pity. She would make me make something of myself whether I wanted to or not. "The Lord helps those who help themselves," she said. That was the way her mind worked.

She was realistic about the difficulty. Having sized up the material the   5
Lord had given her to mold, she didn't overestimate what she could do with it. She didn't insist that I grow up to be president of the United States.

Fifty years ago parents still asked boys if they wanted to grow up to be president, and asked it not jokingly but seriously. Many parents who were hardly more than paupers still believed their sons could do it. Abraham Lincoln had done it. We were only sixty-five years from Lincoln. Many a grandfather who walked among us could remember Lincoln's time. Men of grandfatherly age were the worst for asking if you wanted to grow up to be president. A surprising number of little boys said yes and meant it.

I was asked many times myself. No, I would say, I didn't want to grow up to be president. My mother was present during one of these interrogations. An elderly uncle, having posed the usual question and exposed my lack of interest in the presidency, asked, "Well, what *do* you want to be when you grow up?"

I loved to pick through trash piles and collect empty bottles, tin cans with pretty labels, and discarded magazines. The most desirable job on earth sprang instantly to mind. "I want to be a garbage man," I said.

My uncle smiled, but my mother had seen the first distressing evidence of a bump budding on a log. "Have a little gumption, Russell," she said. Her calling me Russell was a signal of unhappiness. When she approved of me I was always "Buddy."

When I turned eight years old she decided that the job of starting me   10
on the road toward making something of myself could no longer be safely delayed. "Buddy," she said one day, "I want you to come home right after school this afternoon. Somebody's coming and I want you to meet him."

When I burst in that afternoon she was in conference in the parlor with an executive of the Curtis Publishing Company. She introduced me. He bent low from the waist and shook my hand. Was it true as my mother had told him, he asked, that I longed for the opportunity to conquer the world of business?

My mother replied that I was blessed with a rare determination to make something of myself.

"That's right," I whispered.

"But have you got the grit, the character, the never-say-quit spirit it takes to succeed in business?"

My mother said I certainly did.   15

"That's right," I said.

He eyed me silently for a long pause, as though weighing whether I could be trusted to keep his confidence, then spoke man-to-man. Before taking a crucial step, he said, he wanted to advise me that working for the Curtis Publishing Company placed enormous responsibility on a young man. It was one of the great companies of America. Perhaps the greatest publishing house in the world. I had heard, no doubt, of the *Saturday Evening Post*?

Heard of it? My mother said that everyone in our house had heard of the *Saturday Post* and that I, in fact, read it with religious devotion.

Then doubtless, he said, we were also familiar with those two monthly pillars of the magazine world, the *Ladies Home Journal* and the *Country Gentleman*.

Indeed we were familiar with them, said my mother.   20

Representing the *Saturday Evening Post* was one of the weightiest honors that could be bestowed in the world of business, he said. He was personally proud of being a part of that great corporation.

My mother said he had every right to be.

Again he studied me as though debating whether I was worthy of a knighthood. Finally: "Are you trustworthy?"

My mother said I was the soul of honesty.

"That's right," I said.   25

The caller smiled for the first time. He told me I was a lucky young man. He admired my spunk. Too many young men thought life was all play. Those young men would not go far in this world. Only a young man willing to work and save and keep his face washed and his hair neatly combed could hope to come out on top in a world such as ours. Did I truly and sincerely believe that I was such a young man?

"He certainly does," said my mother.

"That's right," I said.

He said he had been so impressed by what he had seen of me that he was going to make me a representative of the Curtis Publishing Company. On the following Tuesday, he said, thirty freshly printed copies of the *Saturday Evening Post* would be delivered at our door. I would place these magazines, still damp with the ink of the presses, in a handsome canvas bag, sling it over my shoulder, and set forth through the streets to bring the best in journalism, fiction, and cartoons to the American public.

He had brought the canvas bag with him. He presented it with a reverence fit for a chasuble. He showed me how to drape the sling over my   30 left shoulder and across the chest so that the pouch lay easily accessible to my right hand, allowing the best in journalism, fiction, and cartoons to be swiftly extracted and sold to a citizenry whose happiness and security depended upon us soldiers of the free press.

The following Tuesday I raced home from school, put the canvas bag over my shoulder, dumped the magazines in, and, tilting to the left to balance their weight on my right hip, embarked on the highway of journalism.

We lived in Belleville, New Jersey, a commuter town at the northern fringe of Newark. It was 1932, the bleakest year of the Depression. My father had died two years before, leaving us with a few pieces of Sears, Roebuck furniture and not much else, and my mother had taken Doris and me to live with one of her younger brothers. This was my Uncle Allen. Uncle Allen had made something of himself by 1932. As salesman for a soft-drink bottler in Newark, he had an income of $30 a week; wore pearl-gray spats, detachable collars, and a three-piece suit; was happily married; and took in threadbare relatives.

With my load of magazines I headed toward Belleville Avenue. That's where the people were. There were two filling stations at the intersection with Union Avenue, as well as an A&P, a fruit stand, a bakery, a barbershop, Zuccarelli's drugstore, and a diner shaped like a railroad car. For several hours I made myself highly visible, shifting position now and then from corner to corner, from shop window to shop window, to make sure everyone could see the heavy black lettering on the canvas bag that said THE SATURDAY EVENING POST. When the angle of the light indicated that it was suppertime, I walked back to the house.

"How many did you sell, Buddy?" my mother asked.

"None."   35

"Where did you go?"

"The corner of Belleville and Union Avenues."

"What did you do?"

"Stood on the corner waiting for somebody to buy a *Saturday Evening Post.*"

"You just stood there?"   40

"Didn't sell a single one."

"For God's sake, Russell!"

Uncle Allen intervened. "I've been thinking about it for some time," he said, "and I've about decided to take the *Post* regularly. Put me down as a regular customer." And I handed him a magazine and he paid me a nickel. It was the first nickel I earned.

Afterwards my mother instructed me in salesmanship. I would have to ring doorbells, address adults with charming self-confidence, and break down resistance with a sales talk pointing out that no one, no matter how poor, could afford to be without the *Saturday Evening Post* in the home.

I told my mother I'd changed my mind about wanting to succeed in   45
the magazine business.

"If you think I'm going to raise a good-for-nothing," she replied, "you've got another thing coming." She told me to hit the streets with the canvas bag and start ringing doorbells the instant school was out the next day. When I objected that I didn't feel any aptitude for salesmanship, she asked how I'd like to lend her my leather belt so she could whack some sense into me. I bowed to superior will and entered journalism with a heavy heart.

My mother and I had fought this battle almost as long as I could remember. It probably started even before memory began, when I was a country child in northern Virginia and my mother, dissatisfied with my father's plain workman's life, determined that I would not grow up like him and his people, with calluses on their hands, overalls on their backs, and fourth-grade educations in their heads. She had fancier ideas of life's possibilities. Introducing me to the *Saturday Evening Post,* she was trying to wean me as early as possible from my father's world where men left with their lunch pails at sunup, worked with their hands until the grime ate into the pores, and died with a few sticks of mail-order furniture as their legacy. In my mother's vision of the better life there were desks and white collars, well-pressed suits, evenings of reading and lively talk, and perhaps—if a man were very, very lucky and hit the jackpot, really made something important of himself—perhaps there might be a fantastic salary of $5,000 a year to support a big house and a Buick with a rumble seat and a vacation in Atlantic City.

And so I set forth with my sack of magazines. I was afraid of the dogs that snarled behind the doors of potential buyers. I was timid about ringing the doorbells of strangers, relieved when no one came to the door, and scared when someone did. Despite my mother's instructions, I could not deliver an engaging sales pitch. When a door opened I simply asked, "Want to buy a *Saturday Evening Post?*" In Belleville few persons did. It was a town of thirty thousand people, and most weeks I rang a fair majority of its doorbells. But I rarely sold my thirty copies. Some weeks I canvassed the entire town for six days and still had four or five unsold magazines on Monday evening; then I dreaded the coming of Tuesday morning, when a batch of thirty fresh *Saturday Evening Posts* was due at the front door.

"Better get out there and sell the rest of those magazines tonight," my mother would say.

I usually posted myself then at a busy intersection where a traffic   50
light controlled commuter flow from Newark. When the light turned red I stood on the curb and shouted my sales pitch at the motorists.

"Want to buy a *Saturday Evening Post?*"

One rainy night when car windows were sealed against me I came back soaked and with not a single sale to report. My mother beckoned to Doris.

"Go back down there with Buddy and show him how to sell these magazines," she said.

Brimming with zest, Doris, who was then seven years old, returned with me to the corner. She took a magazine from the bag, and when the light turned red she strode to the nearest car and banged her small fist against the closed window. The driver, probably startled at what he took to be a midget assaulting his car, lowered the window to stare, and Doris thrust a *Saturday Evening Post* at him.

"You need this magazine," she piped, "and it only costs a nickel."   55

Her salesmanship was irresistible. Before the light changed half a dozen times she disposed of the entire batch. I didn't feel humiliated. To the contrary. I was so happy I decided to give her a treat. Leading her to the vegetable store on Belleville Avenue, I bought three apples, which cost a nickel, and gave her one.

"You shouldn't waste your money," she said.

"Eat your apple." I bit into mine.

"You shouldn't eat before supper," she said. "It'll spoil your appetite."

Back at the house that evening, she dutifully reported me for wasting   60 a nickel. Instead of a scolding, I was rewarded with a pat on the back for having the good sense to buy fruit instead of candy. My mother reached into her bottomless supply of maxims and told Doris, "An apple a day keeps the doctor away."

By the time I was ten I had learned all my mother's maxims by heart. Asking to stay up past normal bedtime, I knew the refusal would be explained with, "Early to bed and early to rise, makes a man healthy, wealthy, and wise." If I whimpered about having to get up early in the morning, I could depend on her to say, "The early bird gets the worm."

The one I most despised was, "If at first you don't succeed, try, try again." This was the battle cry with which she constantly sent me back into the hopeless struggle whenever I moaned that I had rung every doorbell in town and knew there wasn't a single potential buyer left in Belleville that week. After listening to my explanation, she handed me the canvas bag and said, "If at first you don't succeed . . ."

Three years in that job, which I would gladly have quit after the first day except for her insistence, produced at least one valuable result. My mother finally concluded that I would never make something of myself by pursuing a life in business and started considering careers that demanded less competitive zeal.

One evening when I was eleven I brought home a short "composition" on my summer vacation which the teacher had graded with an A. Reading it with her own schoolteacher's eye, my mother agreed that it was top-drawer seventh grade prose and complimented me. Nothing more was said about it immediately, but a new idea had taken life in her mind. Halfway through supper she suddenly interrupted the conversation.

"Buddy," she said, "maybe you could be a writer."   65

I clasped the idea to my heart. I had never met a writer, had shown no previous urge to write, and hadn't a notion how to become a writer, but I loved stories and thought that making up stories must surely be almost as much fun as reading them. Best of all, though, and what really gladdened my heart, was the ease of a writer's life. Writers did not have to trudge through the town peddling from canvas bags, defending themselves against angry dogs, being rejected by surly strangers. Writers did not have to ring doorbells. So far as I could make out, what writers did couldn't even be classified as work.

I was enchanted. Writers didn't have to have any gumption at all. I did not dare tell anybody for fear of being laughed at in the schoolyard, but secretly I decided that what I'd like to be when I grew up was a writer.

The Reader's Presence

1. Baker writes that his sister "could have made something of herself if she hadn't been a girl. Because of this defect, however, the best she could hope for was a career as a nurse or schoolteacher, the only work that capable females were considered up to in those days" (paragraph 3). How would you describe Baker's tone in this passage? Do you think he really believes his sister's gender is a "defect"?

2. Baker's autobiographical essay is sprinkled with maxims and clichés (for example, "an apple a day," "bump on a log"). Such language is usually considered a flaw in writing; how can you tell that Baker is using these phrases intentionally? What effect on the reader do you think they are intended to have?

3. What sort of word is *gumption*? What synonyms can you think of for the term? How does Baker convey what his mother meant by the word without resorting to definitions? Do you believe Baker when he says in the final paragraph that writers don't need any gumption at all?

4. In paragraphs 11 through 28 Baker describes a conversation between his mother and the salesman for the magazine company. Although Baker is present, his mother speaks for him; Baker simply affirms her claims about him, saying "That's right" repeatedly. Compare this humorous scene to Jamaica Kincaid's description of the moment she is photographed (paragraph 7) in "Biography of a Dress" (see page 160). What are Baker and Kincaid saying about the dreams these two mothers have for their children?

14

Raymond Carver

My Father's Life

Son of a laborer and a homemaker in Clatskanie, Oregon, Raymond Carver (1938–1988) resembled the characters in the short stories for which he is widely acclaimed. Once a manual laborer, a gas station attendant, and a janitor himself, Carver acquired his vision of the working class and the desperate lives of ordinary folk through direct experience. The Pacific Northwest of Carver's writing is peopled with types such as "the waitress, the bus driver, the mechanic, the hotel keeper"—people Carver feels are "good people." First published in Esquire *in 1984, "My Father's Life," Carver's account of his father's hardships during the Great Depression, puts a biographical spin on these "good people." Carver's short story collections,* Will You Please Be Quiet, Please? *(1976),* Cathedral *(1984), and* Where I'm Calling From *(1988), were all nominated for the National Book Critics Circle Award. The latter two collections were also nominated for the Pulitzer Prize for fiction in 1985 and 1989, respectively. Carver's poetry is collected in* Where Water Comes Together with Other Water *(1985), recipient of the 1986 Los Angeles Times Book Prize;* Ultramarine *(1986); and* A New Path to the Waterfall *(1989).*

In his essay "On Writing," Carver states, "Writers don't need tricks or gimmicks or even necessarily to be the smartest fellows on the block. At the risk of appearing foolish, a writer sometimes needs to be able to just stand and gape at this or that thing—a sunset or an old shoe—in absolute and simple amazement."

My dad's name was Clevie Raymond Carver. His family called him Raymond and friends called him C. R. I was named Raymond Clevie Carver, Jr. I hated the "Junior" part. When I was little my dad called me Frog, which was okay. But later, like everybody else in the family, he began calling me Junior. He went on calling me this until I was thirteen or fourteen and announced that I wouldn't answer to that name any longer. So he began calling me Doc. From then until his death, on June 17, 1967, he called me Doc, or else Son.

When he died, my mother telephoned my wife with the news. I was away from my family at the time, between lives, trying to enroll in the School of Library Science at the University of Iowa. When my wife answered the phone, my mother blurted out, "Raymond's dead!" For a moment, my wife thought my mother was telling her that I was dead. Then my mother made it clear *which* Raymond she was talking about and my wife said, "Thank God. I thought you meant *my* Raymond."

My dad walked, hitched rides, and rode in empty boxcars when he went from Arkansas to Washington State in 1934, looking for work. I don't know whether he was pursuing a dream when he went out to Washington. I doubt it. I don't think he dreamed much. I believe he was simply looking for steady work at decent pay. Steady work was meaningful work. He picked apples for a time and then landed a construction laborer's job on the Grand Coulee Dam. After he'd put aside a little money, he bought a car and drove back to Arkansas to help his folks, my grandparents, pack up for the move west. He said later that they were about to starve down there, and this wasn't meant as a figure of speech. It was during that short while in Arkansas, in a town called Leola, that my mother met my dad on the sidewalk as he came out of a tavern.

"He was drunk," she said. "I don't know why I let him talk to me. His eyes were glittery. I wish I'd had a crystal ball." They'd met once, a year or so before, at a dance. He'd had girlfriends before her, my mother told me. "Your dad always had a girlfriend, even after we married. He was my first and last. I never had another man. But I didn't miss anything."

They were married by a justice of the peace on the day they left for Washington, this big, tall country girl and a farmhand-turned-construction worker. My mother spent her wedding night with my dad and his folks, all of them camped beside the road in Arkansas.

In Omak, Washington, my dad and mother lived in a little place not much bigger than a cabin. My grandparents lived next door. My dad was still working on the dam, and later, with the huge turbines producing electricity and the water backed up for a hundred miles into Canada, he stood in the crowd and heard Franklin D. Roosevelt when he spoke at the construction site. "He never mentioned those guys who died building that dam," my dad said. Some of his friends had died there, men from Arkansas, Oklahoma, and Missouri.

He then took a job in a sawmill in Clatskanie, Oregon, a little town alongside the Columbia River. I was born there, and my mother has a picture of my dad standing in front of the gate to the mill, proudly holding me up to face the camera. My bonnet is on crooked and about to come untied. His hat is pushed back on his forehead, and he's wearing a big grin. Was he going in to work or just finishing his shift? It doesn't matter. In either case, he had a job and a family. These were his salad days.

In 1941 we moved to Yakima, Washington, where my dad went to work as a saw filer, a skilled trade he'd learned in Clatskanie. When war broke out, he was given a deferment because his work was considered necessary to the war effort. Finished lumber was in demand by the armed services, and he kept his saws so sharp they could shave the hair off your arm.

After my dad had moved us to Yakima, he moved his folks into the same neighborhood. By the mid-1940s the rest of my dad's family—his brother, his sister, and her husband, as well as uncles, cousins, nephews, and most of their extended family and friends—had come out from Arkansas. All because my dad came out first. The men went to work at Boise Cascade, where my dad worked, and the women packed apples in the canneries. And in just a little while, it seemed—according to my mother—everybody was better off than my dad. "Your dad couldn't keep money," my mother said. "Money burned a hole in his pocket. He was always doing for others."

The first house I clearly remember living in, at 1515 South Fifteenth Street, in Yakima, had an outdoor toilet. On Halloween night, or just any night, for the hell of it, neighbor kids, kids in their early teens, would carry our toilet away and leave it next to the road. My dad would have to get somebody to help him bring it home. Or these kids would take the toilet and stand it in somebody else's backyard. Once they actually set it on fire. But ours wasn't the only house that had an outdoor toilet. When I was old enough to know what I was doing, I threw rocks at the other toilets when I'd see someone go inside. This was called bombing the toilets. After a while, though, everyone went to indoor plumbing until, suddenly, our toilet was the last outdoor one in the neighborhood. I remember the shame I felt when my third-grade teacher, Mr. Wise, drove me home from school one day. I asked him to stop at the house just before ours, claiming I lived there.

I can recall what happened one night when my dad came home late to find that my mother had locked all the doors on him from the inside. He was drunk, and we could feel the house shudder as he rattled the door. When he'd managed to force open a window, she hit him between the eyes with a colander and knocked him out. We could see him down there on the grass. For years afterward, I used to pick up this colander—it was as heavy as a rolling pin—and imagine what it would feel like to be hit in the head with something like that.

It was during this period that I remember my dad taking me into the bedroom, sitting me down on the bed, and telling me that I might have to go live with my Aunt LaVon for a while. I couldn't understand what I'd done that meant I'd have to go away from home to live. But this, too—whatever prompted it—must have blown over, more or less, anyway, because we stayed together, and I didn't have to go live with her or anyone else.

I remember my mother pouring his whiskey down the sink. Sometimes she'd pour it all out and sometimes, if she was afraid of getting caught, she'd only pour half of it out and then add water to the rest. I tasted some of his whiskey once myself. It was terrible stuff, and I don't see how anybody could drink it.

After a long time without one, we finally got a car, in 1949 or 1950, a 1938 Ford. But it threw a rod the first week we had it, and my dad had to have the motor rebuilt.

"We drove the oldest car in town," my mother said. "We could have   15
had a Cadillac for all he spent on car repairs." One time she found someone else's tube of lipstick on the floorboard, along with a lacy handkerchief. "See this?" she said to me. "Some floozy left this in the car."

Once I saw her take a pan of warm water into the bedroom where
my dad was sleeping. She took his hand from under the covers and held it
in the water. I stood in the doorway and watched. I wanted to know
what was going on. This would make him talk in his sleep, she told me.
There were things she needed to know, things she was sure he was keeping from her.

Every year or so, when I was little, we would take the North Coast
Limited across the Cascade Range from Yakima to Seattle and stay in the
Vance Hotel and eat, I remember, at a place called the Dinner Bell Cafe.
Once we went to Ivar's Acres of Clams and drank glasses of warm clam
broth.

In 1956, the year I was to graduate from high school, my dad quit his
job at the mill in Yakima and took a job in Chester, a little sawmill town
in northern California. The reasons given at the time for his taking the
job had to do with a higher hourly wage and the vague promise that he
might, in a few years' time, succeed to the job of head filer in this new
mill. But I think, in the main, that my dad had grown restless and simply
wanted to try his luck elsewhere. Things had gotten a little too predictable for him in Yakima. Also, the year before, there had been the
deaths, within six months of each other, of both his parents.

But just a few days after graduation, when my mother and I were
packed to move to Chester, my dad penciled a letter to say he'd been sick
for a while. He didn't want us to worry, he said, but he'd cut himself on a
saw. Maybe he'd got a tiny sliver of steel in his blood. Anyway, something had happened and he'd had to miss work, he said. In the same mail
was an unsigned postcard from somebody down there telling my mother
that my dad was about to die and that he was drinking "raw whiskey."

When we arrived in Chester, my dad was living in a trailer that be-   20
longed to the company. I didn't recognize him immediately. I guess for a
moment I didn't want to recognize him. He was skinny and pale and
looked bewildered. His pants wouldn't stay up. He didn't look like my
dad. My mother began to cry. My dad put his arm around her and patted
her shoulder vaguely, like he didn't know what this was all about, either.
The three of us took up life together in the trailer, and we looked after
him as best we could. But my dad was sick, and he couldn't get any better. I worked with him in the mill that summer and part of the fall. We'd
get up in the mornings and eat eggs and toast while we listened to the
radio, and then go out the door with our lunch pails. We'd pass through
the gate together at eight in the morning, and I wouldn't see him again
until quitting time. In November I went back to Yakima to be closer to
my girlfriend, the girl I'd made up my mind I was going to marry.

He worked at the mill in Chester until the following February, when he collapsed on the job and was taken to the hospital. My mother asked if I would come down there and help. I caught a bus from Yakima to Chester, intending to drive them back to Yakima. But now, in addition to being physically sick, my dad was in the midst of a nervous breakdown, though none of us knew to call it that at the time. During the entire trip back to Yakima, he didn't speak, not even when asked a direct question. ("How do you feel, Raymond?" "You okay, Dad?") He'd communicate, if he communicated at all, by moving his head or by turning his palms up as if to say he didn't know or care. The only time he said anything on the trip, and for nearly a month afterward, was when I was speeding down a gravel road in Oregon and the car muffler came loose. "You were going too fast," he said.

Back in Yakima a doctor saw to it that my dad went to a psychiatrist. My mother and dad had to go on relief, as it was called, and the county paid for the psychiatrist. The psychiatrist asked my dad, "Who is the President?" He'd had a question put to him that he could answer. "Ike," my dad said. Nevertheless, they put him on the fifth floor of Valley Memorial Hospital and began giving him electroshock treatment. I was married by then and about to start my own family. My dad was still locked up when my wife went into this same hospital, just one floor down, to have our first baby. After she had delivered, I went upstairs to give my dad the news. They let me in through a steel door and showed me where I could find him. He was sitting on a couch with a blanket over his lap. *Hey,* I thought. *What in hell is happening to my dad?* I sat down next to him and told him he was a grandfather. He waited a minute and then he said, "I feel like a grandfather." That's all he said. He didn't smile or move. He was in a big room with a lot of other people. Then I hugged him, and he began to cry.

Somehow he got out of there. But now came the years when he couldn't work and just sat around the house trying to figure what next and what he'd done wrong in his life that he'd wound up like this. My mother went from job to crummy job. Much later she referred to that time he was in the hospital, and those years just afterward, as "when Raymond was sick." The word *sick* was never the same for me again.

In 1964, through the help of a friend, he was lucky enough to be hired on at a mill in Klamath, California. He moved down there by himself to see if he could hack it. He lived not far from the mill, in a one-room cabin not much different from the place he and my mother had started out living in when they went west. He scrawled letters to my mother, and if I called she'd read them aloud to me over the phone. In the letters, he said it was touch and go. Every day that he went to work, he felt like it was the most important day of his life. But every day, he told her, made the next day that much easier. He said for her to tell me he said hello. If he couldn't sleep at night, he said, he thought about me and the good times we used to have. Finally, after a couple of months, he regained some of his confidence. He could do the work and didn't think he had to worry that he'd let anybody down ever again. When he was sure, he sent for my mother.

He'd been off from work for six years and had lost everything in that 25 time—home, car, furniture, and appliances, including the big freezer that had been my mother's pride and joy. He'd lost his good name too—Raymond Carver was someone who couldn't pay his bills—and his self-respect was gone. He'd even lost his virility. My mother told my wife, "All during that time Raymond was sick we slept together in the same bed, but we didn't have relations. He wanted to a few times, but nothing happened. I didn't miss it, but I think he wanted to, you know."

During those years I was trying to raise my own family and earn a living. But, one thing and another, we found ourselves having to move a lot. I couldn't keep track of what was going down in my dad's life. But I did have a chance one Christmas to tell him I wanted to be a writer. I might as well have told him I wanted to become a plastic surgeon. "What are you going to write about?" he wanted to know. Then, as if to help me out, he said, "Write about stuff you know about. Write about some of those fishing trips we took." I said I would, but I knew I wouldn't. "Send me what you write," he said. I said I'd do that, but then I didn't. I wasn't writing anything about fishing, and I didn't think he'd particularly care about, or even necessarily understand, what I was writing in those days. Besides, he wasn't a reader. Not the sort, anyway, I imagined I was writing for.

Then he died. I was a long way off, in Iowa City, with things still to say to him. I didn't have the chance to tell him goodbye, or that I thought he was doing great at his new job. That I was proud of him for making a comeback.

My mother said he came in from work that night and ate a big supper. Then he sat at the table by himself and finished what was left of a bottle of whiskey, a bottle she found hidden in the bottom of the garbage under some coffee grounds a day or so later. Then he got up and went to bed, where my mother joined him a little later. But in the night she had to get up and make a bed for herself on the couch. "He was snoring so loud I couldn't sleep," she said. The next morning when she looked in on him, he was on his back with his mouth open, his cheeks caved in. *Graylooking*, she said. She knew he was dead—she didn't need a doctor to tell her that. But she called one anyway, and then she called my wife.

Among the pictures my mother kept of my dad and herself during those early days in Washington was a photograph of him standing in front of a car, holding a beer and a stringer of fish. In the photograph he is wearing his hat back on his forehead and has this awkward grin on his face. I asked her for it and she gave it to me, along with some others. I put it up on my wall, and each time we moved, I took the picture along and put it up on another wall. I looked at it carefully from time to time, trying to figure out some things about my dad, and maybe myself in the process. But I couldn't. My dad just kept moving further and further away from me and back into time. Finally, in the course of another move, I lost the photograph. It was then that I tried to recall it, and at the same time make an attempt to say something about my dad, and how I thought that in some important ways we might be alike. I wrote the poem when I was living in an apartment house in an urban area south of San Francisco, at a time when I found myself, like my dad, having trouble with alcohol. The poem was a way of trying to connect up with him.

PHOTOGRAPH OF MY FATHER IN HIS TWENTY-SECOND YEAR

October. Here in this dank, unfamiliar kitchen
I study my father's embarrassed young man's face.
Sheepish grin, he holds in one hand a string
of spiny yellow perch, in the other
a bottle of Carlsberg beer.

In jeans and flannel shirt, he leans
against the front fender of a 1934 Ford.
He would like to pose brave and hearty for his posterity,
wear his old hat cocked over his ear.
All his life my father wanted to be bold.

But the eyes give him away, and the hands
that limply offer the string of dead perch
and the bottle of beer. Father, I love you,
yet how can I say thank you, I who can't hold my liquor either
and don't even know the places to fish.

The poem is true in its particulars, except that my dad died in June   30
and not October, as the first word of the poem says. I wanted a word
with more than one syllable to it to make it linger a little. But more than
that, I wanted a month appropriate to what I felt at the time I wrote the
poem—a month of short days and failing light, smoke in the air, things
perishing. June was summer nights and days, graduations, my wedding
anniversary, the birthday of one of my children. June wasn't a month
your father died in.

After the service at the funeral home, after we had moved outside,
a woman I didn't know came over to me and said, "He's happier
where he is now." I stared at this woman until she moved away. I still remember the little knob of a hat she was wearing. Then one of my dad's
cousins—I didn't know the man's name—reached out and took my
hand. "We all miss him," he said, and I knew he wasn't saying it just to
be polite.

I began to weep for the first time since receiving the news. I hadn't
been able to before. I hadn't had the time, for one thing. Now, suddenly,
I couldn't stop. I held my wife and wept while she said and did what she
could do to comfort me there in the middle of that summer afternoon.

I listened to people say consoling things to my mother, and I was glad
that my dad's family had turned up, had come to where he was. I thought
I'd remember everything that was said and done that day and maybe find
a way to tell it sometime. But I didn't. I forgot it all, or nearly. What I do
remember is that I heard our name used a lot that afternoon, my dad's

name and mine. But I knew they were talking about my dad. *Raymond,* these people kept saying in their beautiful voices out of my childhood. *Raymond.*

The Reader's Presence

1. You may have noticed that Carver begins and ends his essay with a reference to his and his father's name. Of what importance is this information at the opening? What do we learn about his relationship with his father through their names? How do names matter in the final paragraph?

2. Try rereading the essay with particular attention to the conversations between father and son. How many reported conversations can you find? What do the conversations sound like? Can you find any pattern to them? To what extent do these conversations help you understand Carver's relationship with his father?

3. Carver includes one of his own poems in his essay, as do Alice Walker in "Beauty: When the Other Dancer Is the Self" (page 274) and Gloria Anzaldua in "How to Tame a Wild Tongue" (page 299). Alberto Ríos ("Green Cards," page 217) is a poet whose essay contains very lyrical passages. How do these writers explore the margins between poetry and prose? What do you think a poem communicates that a passage of prose may not?

15

Judith Ortiz Cofer

Silent Dancing

Born in Puerto Rico in 1952, Judith Ortiz Cofer moved to the United States in 1960. Her poetry has appeared in numerous literary magazines, and several collections of her poems have been published. Her first novel, The Line of the Sun *(1989), was nominated for the Pulitzer Prize. "Silent Dancing" is from Cofer's 1990 essay collection,* Silent Dancing: A Partial Remembrance of a Puerto Rican Childhood, *which won a PEN/Martha Albrand special citation for nonfiction. Her most recent books are* The Latin Deli: Prose and Poetry *(1993), An Island Like You: Stories of the Barrio (1995),* The Year of Our Revolution *(1998), and* Woman in Front of the Sun *(2000).*

Reflecting on her life as a writer, Cofer has said, "The 'infinite variety' and power of language interest me. I never cease to experiment with it. As a native Puerto Rican, my first language was Spanish. It was a challenge, not only to learn English, but to master it enough to teach it and—the ultimate goal—to write poetry in it." Cofer is professor of English and creative writing at the University of Georgia.

We have a home movie of this party. Several times my mother and I have watched it together, and I have asked questions about the silent revelers coming in and out of focus. It is grainy and of short duration, but it's a great visual aid to my memory of life at that time. And it is in color—the only complete scene in color I can recall from those years.

We lived in Puerto Rico until my brother was born in 1954. Soon after, because of economic pressures on our growing family, my father joined the United States Navy. He was assigned to duty on a ship in Brooklyn Yard—a place of cement and steel that was to be his home base in the States until his retirement more than twenty years later. He left the Island first, alone, going to New York City and tracking down his uncle who lived with his family across the Hudson River in Paterson, New Jersey. There my father found a tiny apartment in a huge tenement that had once housed Jewish families but was just being taken over and transformed by Puerto Ricans, overflowing from New York City. In 1955 he sent for us. My mother was only twenty years old, I was not quite three, and my brother was a toddler when we arrived at *El Building,* as the place had been christened by its newest residents.

My memories of life in Paterson during those first few years are all in shades of gray. Maybe I was too young to absorb vivid colors and details, or to discriminate between the slate blue of the winter sky and the darker hues of the snow-bearing clouds, but that single color washes over the whole period. The building we lived in was gray, as were the streets, filled with slush the first few months of my life there. The coat my father had bought for me was similar in color and too big; it sat heavily on my thin frame.

I do remember the way the heater pipes banged and rattled, startling all of us out of sleep until we got so used to the sound that we automatically shut it out or raised our voices above the racket. The hiss from the valve punctuated my sleep (which has always been fitful) like a nonhuman presence in the room—a dragon sleeping at the entrance of my childhood. But the pipes were also a connection to all the other lives being lived around us. Having come from a house designed for a single family back in Puerto Rico—my mother's extended-family home—it was curious to know that strangers lived under our floor and above our heads, and that the heater pipe went through everyone's apartments. (My first spanking in Paterson came as a result of playing tunes on the pipes in my room to see if there would be an answer.) My mother was as new to this concept of beehive life as I was, but she had been given strict orders by my father to keep the doors locked, the noise down, ourselves to ourselves.

It seems that Father had learned some painful lessons about prejudice 5
while searching for an apartment in Paterson. Not until years later did I
hear how much resistance he had encountered with landlords who were
panicking at the influx of Latinos into a neighborhood that had been Jewish for a couple of generations. It made no difference that it was the
American phenomenon of ethnic turnover which was changing the urban
core of Paterson, and that the human flood could not be held back with
an accusing finger.

"You Cuban?" one man had asked my father, pointing at his name
tag on the Navy uniform—even though my father had the fair skin and
light-brown hair of his northern Spanish background, and the name Ortiz
is as common in Puerto Rico as Johnson is in the United States.

"No," my father had answered, looking past the finger into his ad-
versary's angry eyes. "I'm Puerto Rican."

"Same shit." And the door closed.

My father could have passed as European, but we couldn't. My
brother and I both have our mother's black hair and olive skin, and so we
lived in El Building and visited our great-uncle and his fair children on the
next block. It was their private joke that they were the German branch of
the family. Not many years later that area too would be mainly Puerto
Rican. It was as if the heart of the city map were being gradually colored
brown—*café con leche*[1] brown. Our color.

The movie opens with a sweep of the living room. It is "typical" im- 10
migrant Puerto Rican decor for the time: The sofa and chairs are square
and hard looking, upholstered in bright colors (blue and yellow in this in-
stance), and covered with the transparent plastic that furniture salesmen
then were so adept at convincing women to buy. The linoleum on the
floor is light blue; if it had been subjected to spike heels (as it was in most
places), there were dime-sized indentations all over it that cannot be seen
in this movie. The room is full of people dressed up: dark suits for the
men, red dresses for the women. When I have asked my mother why most
of the women are in red that night, she has shrugged, "I don't remember.
Just a coincidence." She doesn't have my obsession for assigning symbol-
ism to everything.

The three women in red sitting on the couch are my mother, my
eighteen-year-old cousin, and her brother's girlfriend. The novia *is just up*
from the Island, which is apparent in her body language. She sits up for-
mally, her dress pulled over her knees. She is a pretty girl, but her posture
makes her look insecure, lost in her full-skirted dress, which she has care-
fully tucked around her to make room for my gorgeous cousin, her future
sister-in-law. My cousin has grown up in Paterson and is in her last year
of high school. She doesn't have a trace of what Puerto Ricans call la

[1]*café con leche:* Coffee with cream. In Puerto Rico it is sometimes prepared with
boiled milk.

mancha *(literally, the stain: the mark of the new immigrant — something about the posture, the voice, or the humble demeanor that makes it obvious to everyone the person has just arrived on the mainland). My cousin is wearing a tight, sequined, cocktail dress. Her brown hair has been lightened with peroxide around the bangs, and she is holding a cigarette expertly between her fingers, bringing it up to her mouth in a sensuous arc of her arm as she talks animatedly. My mother, who has come up to sit between the two women, both only a few years younger than herself, is somewhere between the poles they represent in our culture.*

It became my father's obsession to get out of the barrio, and thus we were never permitted to form bonds with the place or with the people who lived there. Yet El Building was a comfort to my mother, who never got over yearning for *la isla.* She felt surrounded by her language: The walls were thin, and voices speaking and arguing in Spanish could be heard all day. *Salsas* blasted out of radios, turned on early in the morning and left on for company. Women seemed to cook rice and beans perpetually — the strong aroma of boiling red kidney beans permeated the hallways.

Though Father preferred that we do our grocery shopping at the supermarket when he came home on weekend leaves, my mother insisted that she could cook only with products whose labels she could read. Consequently, during the week I accompanied her and my little brother to *La Bodega* — a hole-in-the-wall grocery store across the street from El Building. There we squeezed down three narrow aisles jammed with various products. Goya's and Libby's — those were the trademarks that were trusted by *her mamá,* so my mother bought many cans of Goya beans, soups, and condiments, as well as little cans of Libby's fruit juices for us. And she also bought Colgate toothpaste and Palmolive soap. (The final *e* is pronounced in both these products in Spanish, so for many years I believed that they were manufactured on the Island. I remember my surprise at first hearing a commercial on television in which Colgate rhymed with "ate.") We always lingered at La Bodega, for it was there that Mother breathed best, taking in the familiar aromas of the foods she knew from Mamá's kitchen. It was also there that she got to speak to the other women of El Building without violating outright Father's dictates against fraternizing with our neighbors.

Yet Father did his best to make our "assimilation" painless. I can still see him carrying a real Christmas tree up several flights of stairs to our apartment, leaving a trail of aromatic pine. He carried it formally, as if it were a flag in a parade. We were the only ones in El Building that I knew of who got presents on both Christmas day AND *dia de Reyes,* the day when the Three Kings brought gifts to Christ and to Hispanic children.

Our supreme luxury in El Building was having our own television set.   15
It must have been a result of Father's guilt feelings over the isolation he had imposed on us, but we were among the first in the barrio to have one.

My brother quickly became an avid watcher of Captain Kangaroo and Jungle Jim, while I loved all the series showing families. By the time I started first grade, I could have drawn a map of Middle America as exemplified by the lives of characters in "Father Knows Best," "The Donna Reed Show," "Leave It to Beaver," "My Three Sons," and (my favorite) "Bachelor Father," where John Forsythe treated his adopted teenage daughter like a princess because he was rich and had a Chinese houseboy to do everything for him. In truth, compared to our neighbors in El Building, *we* were rich. My father's Navy check provided us with financial security and a standard of life that the factory workers envied. The only thing his money could not buy us was a place to live away from the barrio—his greatest wish, Mother's greatest fear.

In the home movie the men are shown next, sitting around a card table set up in one corner of the living room, playing dominoes. The clack of the ivory pieces was a familiar sound. I heard it in many houses on the Island and in many apartments in Paterson. In "Leave It to Beaver," the Cleavers played bridge in every other episode; in my childhood, the men started every social occasion with a hotly debated round of dominoes. The women would sit around and watch, but they never participated in the games.

Here and there you can see a small child. Children were always brought to parties and, whenever they got sleepy, were put to bed in the host's bedroom. Babysitting was a concept unrecognized by the Puerto Rican women I knew: A responsible mother did not leave her children with any stranger. And in a culture where children are not considered intrusive, there was no need to leave the children at home. We went where our mother went.

Of my preschool years I have only impressions: the sharp bite of the wind in December as we walked with our parents toward the brightly lit stores downtown; how I felt like a stuffed doll in my heavy coat, boots, and mittens; how good it was to walk into the five-and-dime and sit at the counter drinking hot chocolate. On Saturdays our whole family would walk downtown to shop at the big department stores on Broadway. Mother bought all our clothes at Penney's and Sears, and she liked to buy her dresses at the women's specialty shops like Lerner's and Diana's. At some point we'd go into Woolworth's and sit at the soda fountain to eat.

We never ran into other Latinos at these stores or when eating out, and it became clear to me only years later that the women from El Building shopped mainly in other places—stores owned by other Puerto Ricans or by Jewish merchants who had philosophically accepted our presence in the city and decided to make us their good customers, if not real neighbors and friends. These establishments were located not downtown but in the blocks around our street, and they were referred to generically as *La Tienda, El Bazar, La Bodega, La Botánica.* Everyone knew what was meant. These were the stores where your face did not turn a clerk to stone, where your money was as green as anyone else's.

One New Year's Eve we were dressed up like child models in the   20
Sears catalogue: my brother in a miniature man's suit and bow tie, and I
in black patent-leather shoes and a frilly dress with several layers of
crinoline underneath. My mother wore a bright red dress that night, I remember, and spike heels; her long black hair hung to her waist. Father,
who usually wore his Navy uniform during his short visits home, had put
on a dark civilian suit for the occasion: We had been invited to his
uncle's house for a big celebration. Everyone was excited because my
mother's brother Hernan—a bachelor who could indulge himself with
luxuries—had bought a home movie camera, which he would be trying
out that night.

Even the home movie cannot fill in the sensory details such a gathering left imprinted in a child's brain. The thick sweetness of women's perfumes mixing with the ever-present smells of food cooking in the kitchen:
meat and plantain *pasteles,* as well as the ubiquitous rice dish made special with pigeon peas—*gandules*—and seasoned with precious *sofrito*[2]
sent up from the Island by somebody's mother or smuggled in by a recent
traveler. *Sofrito* was one of the items that women hoarded, since it was
hardly ever in stock at La Bodega. It was the flavor of Puerto Rico.

The men drank Palo Viejo rum, and some of the younger ones got
weepy. The first time I saw a grown man cry was at a New Year's Eve
party: He had been reminded of his mother by the smells in the kitchen.
But what I remember most were the boiled *pasteles*—plantain or yucca
rectangles stuffed with corned beef or other meats, olives, and many other
savory ingredients, all wrapped in banana leaves. Everybody had to fish
one out with a fork. There was always a "trick" pastel—one without
stuffing—and whoever got that one was the "New Year's Fool."

There was also the music. Long-playing albums were treated like precious china in these homes. Mexican recordings were popular, but the
songs that brought tears to my mother's eyes were sung by the melancholy
Daniel Santos, whose life as a drug addict was the stuff of legend. Felipe
Rodríguez was a particular favorite of couples, since he sang about faithless
women and brokenhearted men. There is a snatch of one lyric that has
stuck in my mind like a needle on a worn groove: *De piedra ha de ser mi
cama, de piedra la cabezera . . . la mujer que a mi me quiera . . . ha de
quererme de veras. Ay, Ay, Ay, corazón, porque no amas.*[3] . . . I must have
heard it a thousand times since the idea of a bed made of stone, and its connection to love, first troubled me with its disturbing images.

---

[2]*sofrito:* A cooked condiment. A sauce composed of a mixture of fatback, ham, tomatoes, and many island spices and herbs. It is added to many typical Puerto Rican dishes for a
distinctive flavor.

[3]*De piedra ha de ser . . . amas:* Lyrics from a popular romantic ballad (called a *bolero*
in Puerto Rico). Freely translated: "My bed will be made of stone, of stone also my headrest
(or pillow), the woman who (dares to) loves me, will have to love me for real. Ay, Ay, Ay,
my heart, why can't you (let me) love. . . ."

The five-minute home movie ends with people dancing in a circle—the creative filmmaker must have set it up, so that all of them could file past him. It is both comical and sad to watch silent dancing. Since there is no justification for the absurd movements that music provides for some of us, people appear frantic, their faces embarrassingly intense. It's as if you were watching sex. Yet for years I've had dreams in the form of this home movie. In a recurring scene, familiar faces push themselves forward into my mind's eyes, plastering their features into distorted close-ups. And I'm asking them: "Who is *she*? Who is the old woman I don't recognize? Is she an aunt? Somebody's wife? Tell me who she is."

"See the beauty mark on her cheek as big as a hill on the lunar landscape of her face—well, that runs in the family. The women on your father's side of the family wrinkle early; it's the price they pay for that fair skin. The young girl with the green stain on her wedding dress is *La Novia*—just up from the Island. See, she lowers her eyes when she approaches the camera, as she's supposed to. Decent girls never look at you directly in the face. *Humilde*, humble, a girl should express humility in all her actions. She will make a good wife for your cousin. He should consider himself lucky to have met her only weeks after she arrived here. If he marries her quickly, she will make him a good Puerto Rican–style wife; but if he waits too long, she will be corrupted by the city—just like your cousin there."

"She means me. I do what I want. This is not some primitive island I live on. Do they expect me to wear a black mantilla on my head and go to mass every day? Not me. I'm an American woman, and I will do as I please. I can type faster than anyone in my senior class at Central High, and I'm going to be a secretary to a lawyer when I graduate. I can pass for an American girl anywhere—I've tried it. At least for Italian, anyway—I never speak Spanish in public. I hate these parties, but I wanted the dress. I look better than any of these *humildes* here. My life is going to be different. I have an American boyfriend. He is older and has a car. My parents don't know it, but I sneak out of the house late at night sometimes to be with him. If I marry him, even my name will be American. I hate rice and beans—that's what makes these women fat."

"Your *prima*[4] is pregnant by that man she's been sneaking around with. Would I lie to you? I'm your *Tía Política*,[5] your great-uncle's common-law wife—the one he abandoned on the Island to go marry your cousin's mother. *I* was not invited to this party, of course, but I came anyway. I came to tell you that story about your cousin that you've always wanted to hear. Do you remember the comment your mother made to a neighbor that has always haunted you? The only thing you heard was your cousin's name, and then you saw your mother pick up your doll from the couch and say: 'It was as big as this doll when

[4]*prima:* Female cousin.
[5]*Tía Política:* Aunt by marriage.

they flushed it down the toilet.' This image has bothered you for years, hasn't it? You had nightmares about babies being flushed down the toilet, and you wondered why anyone would do such a horrible thing. You didn't dare ask your mother about it. She would only tell you that you had not heard her right, and yell at you for listening to adult conversations. But later, when you were old enough to know about abortions, you suspected.

"I am here to tell you that you were right. Your cousin was growing an *Americanito* in her belly when this movie was made. Soon after she put something long and pointy into her pretty self, thinking maybe she could get rid of the problem before breakfast and still make it to her first class at the high school. Well, *Niña*,[6] her screams could be heard downtown. Your aunt, her mamá, who had been a midwife on the Island, managed to pull the little thing out. Yes, they probably flushed it down the toilet. What else could they do with it—give it a Christian burial in a little white casket with blue bows and ribbons? Nobody wanted that baby—least of all the father, a teacher at her school with a house in West Paterson that he was filling with real children, and a wife who was a natural blonde.

"Girl, the scandal sent your uncle back to the bottle. And guess where your cousin ended up? Irony of ironies. She was sent to a village in Puerto Rico to live with a relative on her mother's side: a place so far away from civilization that you have to ride a mule to reach it. A real change in scenery. She found a man there—women like that cannot live without male company—but believe me, the men in Puerto Rico know how to put a saddle on a woman like her. *La Gringa*,[7] they call her. Ha, ha, ha. *La Gringa* is what she always wanted to be. . . ."

The old woman's mouth becomes a cavernous black hole I fall into. And as I fall, I can feel the reverberations of her laughter. I hear the echoes of her last mocking words: *La Gringa, La Gringa!* And the conga line keeps moving silently past me. There is no music in my dream for the dancers.

When Odysseus visits Hades to see the spirit of his mother, he makes   25 an offering of sacrificial blood, but since all the souls crave an audience with the living, he has to listen to many of them before he can ask questions. I, too, have to hear the dead and the forgotten speak in my dream. Those who are still part of my life remain silent, going around and around in their dance. The others keep pressing their faces forward to say things about the past.

My father's uncle is last in line. He is dying of alcoholism, shrunken and shriveled like a monkey, his face a mass of wrinkles and broken arteries. As he comes closer I realize that in his features I can see my whole family. If you were to stretch that rubbery flesh, you could find my father's face, and deep within *that* face—my own. I don't want to look into those eyes ringed in purple. In a few years he will retreat into silence, and

[6]*Niña:* Girl.
[7]*La Gringa:* Derogatory epithet used here to ridicule a Puerto Rican girl who wants to look like a blonde North American.

take a long, long time to die. *Move back, Tio,* I tell him. *I don't want to hear what you have to say. Give the dancers room to move. Soon it will be midnight. Who is the New Year's Fool this time?*

The Reader's Presence

1. "Silent Dancing" explores the personal, familial, and communal transformations that resulted from moving in the 1950s to Paterson, New Jersey—to "a huge tenement that had once housed Jewish families," and to a new community that emerged from the sprawling barrio that Puerto Ricans "overflowing from New York City" called home. Reread the essay carefully, and summarize the transformations that occurred in the life of the narrator, her family, and their larger Puerto Rican community.

2. Cofer uses an account of a home movie to create a structure for her essay. What are the specific advantages and disadvantages of this strategy? How, for example, does the home movie serve as "a great visual aid" to recounting life in the barrio of Paterson, New Jersey? What effect does the fact that the home movie is in color have on what she notices? on how she writes?

3. Because Cofer's essay is built around the occasion of watching a home movie, the narrator assumes the position of an observer of the scenes and people she describes. What specific strategies as a writer does Cofer use to establish a presence for herself in this narrative and descriptive account of growing up?

4. In his attempt to aid the family's "assimilation" into American culture, Cofer's father forbids his relatives from making friends in "El Building." Cofer and her mother were expected "to keep the doors locked, the noise down, ourselves to ourselves" (paragraph 4). How do the father's strategies and goals compare with those of Adrienne Rich's father in "Split at the Root: An Essay on Jewish Identity" (see page 205)? How do the two essays become part of the writers' responses to their fathers? Cofer at times feels alienated from her own relatives. How does her situation compare to that of the narrator of Maxine Hong Kingston's "No Name Woman" (see page 434)?

THE WRITER AT WORK

Judith Ortiz Cofer on Memory and Personal Essays

In setting out to write essays recounting her family history, Judith Ortiz Cofer found in Virginia Woolf a brilliant mentor and guide who taught her how to release the creative power of memory. In the following preface to Silent

Dancing: A Partial Remembrance of a Puerto Rican Childhood, *she pays tribute
to Woolf, who "understood that the very act of reclaiming her memories could
provide a writer with confidence in the power of art to discover meaning and
truth in ordinary events." How do Cofer's remarks in the preface (which she
called "Journey to a Summer's Afternoon") along with Woolf's "The Death of
the Moth" (see page 583) help illuminate the artistry of Cofer's own essay,
"Silent Dancing"?*

As one gets older, childhood years are often conveniently consoli-
dated into one perfect summer's afternoon. The events can be projected
on a light blue screen; the hurtful parts can be edited out, and the moments of joy brought in sharp focus to the foreground. It is our show. But
with all that on the cutting room floor, what remains to tell?

Virginia Woolf, whose vision guided my efforts as I tried to recall the
faces and words of the people who are a part of my "summer's afternoon," wrote of the problem of writing truth from memory. In "A Sketch
of the Past" she says, "But if I turn to my mother, how difficult it is to
single her out as she really was; to imagine what she was thinking, to put
a single sentence into her mouth." She accepts the fact that in writing
about one's life, one often has to rely on that combination of memory,
imagination, and strong emotion that may result in "poetic truth." In
preparing to write her memoirs Woolf said, "I dream, I make up pictures
of a summer's afternoon."

In one of her essays from her memoir *Moments of Being,* Woolf recalls the figure of her beautiful and beloved mother who died while the
author was still a child, leaving her a few precious "moments of being"
from which the mature woman must piece together a childhood. And she
does so not to showcase her life, extraordinary as it was, but rather out of
a need most of us feel at some point to study ourselves and our lives in
retrospect; to understand what people and events formed us (and, yes,
what and who hurt us, too).

From "A Sketch of the Past": "Many bright colors; many distinct
sounds; some human beings, caricatures; several violent moments of
being, always including a circle of the scene they cut out: and all surrounded by a vast space—that is a rough visual description of childhood.
This is how I shape it; and how I see myself as a child . . ."

This passage illustrates the approach that I was seeking in writing   5
about my family. I wanted the essays to be, not just family history, but
also creative explorations of known territory. I wanted to trace back
through scenes based on my "moments of being" the origins of my creative imagination. As a writer, I am, like most artists, interested in the
genesis of ideas: How does a poem begin? Can the process be triggered at
will? What compels some of us to examine and re-examine our lives in
poems, stories, novels, memoirs?

Much of my writing begins as a meditation on past events. But memory for me is the "jumping off" point; I am not, in my poetry and my fiction writing, a slave to memory. I like to believe that the poem or story

contains the "truth" of art rather than the factual, historical truth that the journalist, sociologist, scientist — most of the rest of the world — must adhere to. Art gives me that freedom. But in writing these "essays" (the Spanish word for essay, *ensayo*, suits my meaning here better — it can mean "a rehearsal," an exercise or practice), I faced the possibility that the past is mainly a creation of the imagination also, although there are facts one can research and confirm. The biographer's time-honored task can be employed on one's own life too. There are birth, marriage, and death certificates on file, there are letters and family photographs in someone's desk or attic; and there are the relatives who have assigned themselves the role of genealogist or family bard, recounting at the least instigation the entire history of your clan. One can go to these sources and come up with a *Life* in several volumes that will make your mother proud and give you the satisfaction of having "preserved" something. I am not interested in merely "canning" memories, however, and Woolf gave me the focus that I needed to justify this work. Its intention is not to chronicle my life — which in my case is still very much "in-progress," nor are there any extraordinary accomplishments to showcase; neither is it meant to be a record of public events and personal histories (in fact, since most of the characters in these essays are based on actual, living persons and real places, whenever I felt that it was necessary to protect their identities, I changed names, locations, etc.). Then, what is the purpose of calling this collection non-fiction or a memoir? Why not just call it fiction? Once again I must turn to my literary mentor for this project, Virginia Woolf, for an answer: like her, I wanted to try to connect myself to the threads of lives that have touched mine and at some point converged into the tapestry that is my memory of childhood. Virginia Woolf understood that the very act of reclaiming her memories could provide a writer with confidence in the power of art to discover meaning and truth in ordinary events. She was a time-traveler who saw the past as a real place one could return to by following the tracks left by strong emotions: "I feel that strong emotion must leave its trace; and it is only a question of discovering how we can get ourselves attached to it, so that we shall be able to live our lives through from the start."[1]

It was this winding path of memory, marked by strong emotions that I followed in my *ensayos* of a life.

---

[1] All quotes by Virginia Woolf are from *Moments of Being* (Harcourt Brace Jovanovich, Inc.). — COFER'S NOTE.

16

Bernard Cooper

A Clack of Tiny Sparks:
Remembrances of a Gay Boyhood

Born (1951), raised, and still residing in Los Angeles, Bernard Cooper received his B.F.A. and M.F.A. from the California Institute of the Arts. He has taught at the Otis/Parsons Institute of Art and Design and Southern California Institute of Architecture, Los Angeles, at the UCLA writing program, and he is now an art critic for Los Angeles Magazine. *His collection of essays,* Maps to Anywhere *(1990), covers a wide range of topics as varying as the aging of his father, the extinction of the dinosaur, and the future of American life and culture. Cooper contributes to various periodicals such as* Harper's, *where "A Clack of Tiny Sparks: Remembrances of a Gay Boyhood" first appeared in January 1991. His most recent collection of short stories is* Guess Again *(2000).*

Commenting on his 1993 novel, A Year of Rhymes, *Cooper notes, "One of the reasons why there is so much detail in my work is that I'm a person that essentially shies away from abstractions, from Large Issues and Big Ideas. The world only seems real and vivid and meaningful to me in the smaller details, what's heard and felt and smelled and tasted."*

Theresa Sanchez sat behind me in ninth-grade algebra. When Mr. Hubbley faced the blackboard, I'd turn around to see what she was reading; each week a new book was wedged inside her copy of *Today's Equations*. The deception worked; from Mr. Hubbley's point of view, Theresa was engrossed in the value of X, but I knew otherwise. One week she perused *The Wisdom of the Orient*, and I could tell from Theresa's contemplative expression that the book contained exotic thoughts, guidelines handed down from high. Another week it was a paperback novel whose title, *Let Me Live My Life*, appeared in bold print atop every page, and whose cover, a gauzy photograph of a woman biting a strand of pearls, head thrown back in an attitude of ecstasy, confirmed my suspicion that Theresa Sanchez was mature beyond her years. She was the tallest girl in school. Her bouffant hairdo, streaked with blond, was higher than the flaccid bouffants of other girls. Her smooth skin, plucked eyebrows, and painted fingernails suggested hours of pampering, a worldly and sensual vanity that placed her within the domain of adults. Smiling dimly, steeped in daydreams, Theresa moved through the crowded halls with a languid, self-satisfied indifference to those around her. "You are merely children," her posture seemed to say. "I can't be bothered." The week Theresa hid *101 Ways to Cook Hamburger* behind her algebra book, I could stand it no longer and, after the bell rang, ventured a question.

"Because I'm having a dinner party," said Theresa. "Just a couple of intimate friends."

No fourteen-year-old I knew had ever given a dinner party, let alone used the word "intimate" in conversation. "Don't you have a mother?" I asked.

Theresa sighed a weary sigh, suffered my strange inquiry. "Don't be so naive," she said. "Everyone has a mother." She waved her hand to indicate the brick school buildings outside the window. "A higher education should have taught you that." Theresa draped an angora sweater over her shoulders, scooped her books from the graffiti-covered desk, and just as she was about to walk away, she turned and asked me, "Are you a fag?"

There wasn't the slightest hint of rancor or condescension in her voice. The tone was direct, casual. Still I was stunned, giving a sidelong glance to make sure no one had heard. "No," I said. Blurted really, with too much defensiveness, too much transparent fear in my response. Octaves lower than usual, I tried a "Why?"   5

Theresa shrugged. "Oh, I don't know. I have lots of friends who are fags. You remind me of them." Seeing me bristle, Theresa added, "It was just a guess." I watched her erect, angora back as she sauntered out the classroom door.

She had made an incisive and timely guess. Only days before, I'd invited Grady Rogers to my house after school to go swimming. The instant Grady shot from the pool, shaking water from his orange hair, freckled shoulders shining, my attraction to members of my own sex became a matter I could no longer suppress or rationalize. Sturdy and boisterous and gap-toothed, Grady was an inveterate backslapper, a formidable arm wrestler, a wizard at basketball. Grady was a boy at home in his body.

My body was a marvel I hadn't gotten used to; my arms and legs would sometimes act of their own accord, knocking over a glass at dinner or flinching at an oncoming pitch. I was never singled out as a sissy, but I could have been just as easily as Bobby Keagan, a gentle, intelligent, and introverted boy reviled by my classmates. And although I had always been aware of a tacit rapport with Bobby, a suspicion that I might find with him a rich friendship, I stayed away. Instead, I emulated Grady in the belief that being seen with him, being like him, would somehow vanquish my self-doubt, would make me normal by association.

Apart from his athletic prowess, Grady had been gifted with all the trappings of what I imagined to be a charmed life: a fastidious, aproned mother who radiated calm, maternal concern; a ruddy, stoic father with a knack for home repairs. Even the Rogerses' small suburban house in Hollywood, with its spindly Colonial furniture and chintz curtains, was a testament to normalcy.

Grady and his family bore little resemblance to my clan of Eastern   10
European Jews, a dark and vociferous people who ate with abandon—
matzo and halvah and gefilte fish; foods the goyim couldn't pronounce—
who cajoled one another during endless games of canasta, making the
simplest remark about the weather into a lengthy philosophical discourse
on the sun and the seasons and the passage of time. My mother was a
chain-smoker, a dervish in a frowsy housedress. She showed her love in
the most peculiar and obsessive ways, like spending hours extracting
every seed from a watermelon before she served it in perfectly bite-sized,
geometric pieces. Preoccupied and perpetually frantic, my mother succumbed to bouts of absentmindedness so profound she'd forget what she
was saying midsentence, smile and blush and walk away. A divorce attorney, my father wore roomy, iridescent suits, and the intricacies, the de-
ceits inherent in his profession, had the effect of making him forever tense
and vigilant. He was "all wound up," as my mother put it. But when he
relaxed, his laughter was explosive, his disposition prankish: "Walk this
way," a waitress would say, leading us to our table, and my father would
mimic the way she walked, arms akimbo, hips liquid, while my mother
and I were wracked with laughter. Buoyant or brooding, my parents'
moods were unpredictable, and in a household fraught with extravagant
emotion it was odd and awful to keep my longing secret.

One day I made the mistake of asking my mother what a "fag" was. I
knew exactly what Theresa had meant but hoped against hope it was not
what I thought; maybe "fag" was some French word, a harmless term
like "naive." My mother turned from the stove, flew at me, and grabbed
me by the shoulders. "Did someone call you that?" she cried.

"Not me," I said. "Bobby Keagan."

"Oh," she said, loosening her grip. She was visibly relieved. And
didn't answer. The answer was unthinkable.

For weeks after, I shook with the reverberations from that afternoon
in the kitchen with my mother, pained by the memory of her shocked expression and, most of all, her silence. My longing was wrong in the eyes
of my mother, whose hazel eyes were the eyes of the world, and if that
longing continued unchecked, the unwieldy shape of my fate would be
cast, and I'd be subjected to a lifetime of scorn.

During the remainder of the semester, I became the scientist of my   15
own desire, plotting ways to change my yearning for boys into a yearning
for girls. I had enough evidence to believe that any habit, regardless of
how compulsive, how deeply ingrained, could be broken once and for all:
The plastic cigarette my mother purchased at the Thrifty pharmacy—one
end was red to approximate an ember, the other tan like a filtered tip—
was designed to wean her from the real thing. To change a behavior re-

quired self-analysis, cold resolve, and the substitution of one thing for another: plastic, say, for tobacco. Could I also find a substitute for Grady? What I needed to do, I figured, was kiss a girl and learn to like it.

This conclusion was affirmed one Sunday morning when my father, seeing me wrinkle my nose at the pink slabs of lox he layered on a bagel, tried to convince me of its salty appeal. "You should try some," he said. "You don't know what you're missing."

"It's loaded with protein," added my mother, slapping a platter of sliced onions onto the dinette table. She hovered above us, cinching her housedress, eyes wet from onion fumes, the mock cigarette dangling from her lips.

My father sat there chomping with gusto, emitting a couple of hearty grunts to dramatize his satisfaction. And still I was not convinced. After a loud and labored swallow, he told me I may not be fond of lox today, but sooner or later I'd learn to like it. One's tastes, he assured me, are destined to change.

"Live," shouted my mother over the rumble of the Mixmaster. "Expand your horizons. Try new things." And the room grew fragrant with the batter of a spice cake.

The opportunity to put their advice into practice, and try out my plan   20
to adapt to girls, came the following week when Debbie Coburn, a member of Mr. Hubbley's algebra class, invited me to a party. She cornered me in the hall, furtive as a spy, telling me her parents would be gone for the evening and slipping into my palm a wrinkled sheet of notebook paper. On it were her address and telephone number, the lavender ink in a tidy cursive. "Wear cologne," she advised, wary eyes darting back and forth. "It's a make-out party. Anything can happen."

The Santa Ana wind blew relentlessly the night of Debbie's party, careening down the slopes of the Hollywood hills, shaking the road signs and stoplights in its path. As I walked down Beachwood Avenue, trees thrashed, surrendered their leaves, and carob pods bombarded the pavement. The sky was a deep but luminous blue, the air hot, abrasive, electric. I had to squint in order to check the number of the Coburns' apartment, a three-story building with glitter embedded in its stucco walls. Above the honeycombed balconies was a sign that read BEACH-WOOD TERRACE in lavender script resembling Debbie's.

From down the hall, I could hear the plaintive strains of Little Anthony's "I Think I'm Going Out of My Head." Debbie answered the door bedecked in an Empire dress, the bodice blue and orange polka dots, the rest a sheath of black and white stripes. "Op art," proclaimed Debbie. She turned in a circle, then proudly announced that she'd rolled her hair in orange juice cans. She patted the huge unmoving curls and dragged me inside. Reflections from the swimming pool in the courtyard, its surface ruffled by wind, shuddered over the ceiling and walls. A dozen of my classmates were seated on the sofa or huddled together in corners, their whispers full of excited imminence, their bodies barely discernible in the dim light. Drapes flanking the sliding glass doors bowed out with every gust of wind, and it seemed that the room might lurch from its foundations and sail with its cargo of silhouettes into the hot October night.

Grady was the last to arrive. He tossed a six-pack of beer into Debbie's arms, barreled toward me, and slapped my back. His hair was slicked back with Vitalis, lacquered furrows left by the comb. The wind hadn't shifted a single hair. "Ya ready?" he asked, flashing the gap between his front teeth and leering into the darkened room. "You bet," I lied.

Once the beers had been passed around, Debbie provoked everyone's attention by flicking on the overhead light. "Okay," she called. "Find a partner." This was the blunt command of a hostess determined to have her guests aroused in an orderly fashion. Everyone blinked, shuffled about, and grabbed a member of the opposite sex. Sheila Garabedian landed beside me — entirely at random, though I wanted to believe she was driven by passion — her timid smile giving way to plain fear as the light went out. Nothing for a moment but the heave of the wind and the distant banter of dogs. I caught a whiff of Sheila's perfume, tangy and sweet as Hawaiian Punch. I probed her face with my own, grazing the small scallop of an ear, a velvety temple, and though Sheila's trembling made me want to stop, I persisted with my mission until I found her lips, tightly sealed as a private letter. I held my mouth over hers and gathered her shoulders closer, resigned to the possibility that, no matter how long we stood there, Sheila would be too scared to kiss me back. Still, she exhaled through her nose, and I listened to the squeak of every breath as though it were a sigh of inordinate pleasure. Diving within myself, I monitored my heartbeat and respiration, trying to will stimulation into being, and all the while an image intruded, an image of Grady erupting from our pool, rivulets of water sliding down his chest. "Change," shouted Debbie, switching on the light. Sheila thanked me, pulled away, and continued her routine of gracious terror with every boy throughout the evening. It didn't matter whom I held — Margaret Sims, Betty Vernon, Elizabeth Lee — my experiment was a failure; I continued to picture Grady's wet chest, and Debbie would bellow "change" with such fervor, it could have been my own voice, my own incessant reprimand.

Our hostess commandeered the light switch for nearly half an hour.   25
Whenever the light came on, I watched Grady pivot his head toward the newest prospect, his eyebrows arched in expectation, his neck blooming with hickeys, his hair, at last, in disarray. All that shuffling across the carpet charged everyone's arms and lips with static, and eventually, between low moans and soft osculations, I could hear the clack of tiny sparks and see them flare here and there in the dark like meager, short-lived stars.

I saw Theresa, sultry and aloof as ever, read three more books — *North American Reptiles, Bonjour Tristesse,* and *MGM: A Pictorial History* — before she vanished early in December. Rumors of her fate abounded. Debbie Coburn swore that Theresa had been "knocked up" by an older man, a traffic cop, she thought, or a grocer. Nearly quivering with relish, Debbie told me and Grady about the home for unwed mothers in the San Fernando Valley, a compound teeming with pregnant girls who had nothing to do but touch their stomachs and contemplate their mistake. Even Bobby Keagan, who took Theresa's place behind me in algebra, had a theory regarding her disappearance colored by his own wish for escape; he imagined that Theresa, disillusioned with society, booked passage to a tropical island, there to live out the rest of her days without restrictions or ridicule. "No wonder she flunked out of school," I overheard Mr. Hubbley tell a fellow teacher one afternoon. "Her head was always in a book."

Along with Theresa went my secret, or at least the dread that she might divulge it, and I felt, for a while, exempt from suspicion. I was, however, to run across Theresa one last time. It happened during a period of torrential rain that, according to reports on the six o'clock news, washed houses from the hillsides and flooded the downtown streets. The halls of Joseph Le Conte Junior High were festooned with Christmas decorations: crepe-paper garlands, wreaths studded with plastic berries, and one requisite Star of David twirling above the attendance desk. In Arts and Crafts, our teacher, Gerald (he was the only teacher who allowed us —*required* us—to call him by his first name), handed out blocks of balsa wood and instructed us to carve them into bugs. We would paint eyes and antennae with tempera and hang them on a Christmas tree he'd made the previous night. "Voilà," he crooned, unveiling his creation from a burlap sack. Before us sat a tortured scrub, a wardrobe-worth of wire hangers that were bent like branches and soldered together. Gerald credited his inspiration to a Charles Addams cartoon he's seen in which Morticia, grimly preparing for the holidays, hangs vampire bats on a withered pine. "All that red and green," said Gerald. "So predictable. So *boring*."

As I chiseled a beetle and listened to rain pummel the earth, Gerald handed me an envelope and asked me to take it to Mr. Kendrick, the drama teacher. I would have thought nothing of his request if I hadn't seen Theresa on my way down the hall. She was cleaning out her locker, blithely dropping the sum of its contents—pens and textbooks and mimeographs—into a trash can. "Have a nice life," she sang as I passed. I mustered the courage to ask her what had happened. We stood alone in the silent hall, the reflections of wreaths and garlands submerged in brown linoleum.

"I transferred to another school. They don't have grades or bells, and you get to study whatever you want." Theresa was quick to sense my incredulity. "Honest," she said. "The school is progressive." She gazed into a glass cabinet that held the trophies of track meets and intramural spelling bees. "God," she sighed, "this place is so . . . barbaric." I was still trying to decide whether or not to believe her story when she asked me where I was headed. "Dear," she said, her exclamation pooling in the silence, "that's no ordinary note, if you catch my drift." The envelope was blank and white; I looked up at Theresa, baffled. "Don't be so naive," she muttered, tossing an empty bottle of nail polish into the trash can. It struck bottom with a resolute thud. "Well," she said, closing her locker and breathing deeply, "bon voyage." Theresa swept through the double doors and in seconds her figure was obscured by rain.

As I walked toward Mr. Kendrick's room, I could feel Theresa's in-   30
sinuation burrow in. I stood for a moment and watched Mr. Kendrick through the pane in the door. He paced intently in front of the class, handsome in his shirt and tie, reading from a thick book. Chalked on the blackboard behind him was THE ODYSSEY BY HOMER. I have no recollection of how Mr. Kendrick reacted to the note, whether he accepted it with pleasure or embarrassment, slipped it into his desk drawer or the pocket of his shirt. I have scavenged that day in retrospect, trying to see Mr. Kendrick's expression, wondering if he acknowledged me in any way as his liaison. All I recall is the sight of his mime through a pane of glass, a lone man mouthing an epic, his gestures ardent in empty air.

Had I delivered a declaration of love? I was haunted by the need to know. In fantasy, a kettle shot steam, the glue released its grip, and I read the letter with impunity. But how would such a letter begin? Did the common endearments apply? This was a message between two men, a message for which I had no precedent, and when I tried to envision the contents, apart from a hasty, impassioned scrawl, my imagination faltered.

Once or twice I witnessed Gerald and Mr. Kendrick walk together into the faculty lounge or say hello at the water fountain, but there was nothing especially clandestine or flirtatious in their manner. Besides, no matter how acute my scrutiny, I wasn't sure, short of a kiss, exactly what to look for—what semaphore of gesture, what encoded word. I suspected there were signs, covert signs that would give them away, just as I'd unwittingly given myself away to Theresa.

In the school library, a *Webster's* unabridged dictionary lay on a wooden podium, and I padded toward it with apprehension; along with clues to the bond between my teachers, I risked discovering information that might incriminate me as well. I had decided to consult the dictionary during lunch period, when most of the students would be on the playground. I clutched my notebook, moving in such a way as to appear both studious and nonchalant, actually believing that, unless I took precautions, someone would see me and guess what I was up to. The closer I came to the podium, the more obvious, I thought, was my endeavor; I felt like the model of The Visible Man in our science class, my heart's undulations, my overwrought nerves legible through transparent skin. A couple of kids riffled through the card catalogue. The librarian, a skinny woman whose perpetual whisper and rubber-soled shoes caused her to drift through the room like a phantom, didn't seem to register my presence. Though I'd looked up dozens of words before, the pages felt strange beneath my fingers. *Homer* was the first word I saw. *Hominid. Homogenize.* I feigned interest and skirted other words before I found the word I was after. Under the heading

HO•MO•SEX•U•AL was the terse definition: *adj. Pertaining to, characteristic of, or exhibiting homosexuality.—n. A homosexual person.* I read the definition again and again, hoping the words would yield more than they could. I shut the dictionary, swallowed hard, and, none the wiser, hurried away.

As for Gerald and Mr. Kendrick, I never discovered evidence to prove or dispute Theresa's claim. By the following summer, however, I had overheard from my peers a confounding amount about homosexuals: They wore green on Thursday, couldn't whistle, hypnotized boys with a piercing glance. To this lore, Grady added a surefire test to ferret them out.

"A test?" I said.   35

"You ask a guy to look at his fingernails, and if he looks at them like this" — Grady closed his fingers into a fist and examined his nails with manly detachment — "then he's okay. But if he does this" — he held out his hands at arm's length, splayed his fingers, and coyly cocked his head — "you'd better watch out." Once he'd completed his demonstration, Grady peeled off his shirt and plunged into our pool. I dove in after. It was early June, the sky immense, glassy, placid. My father was cooking spareribs on the barbecue, an artist with a basting brush. His apron bore the caricature of a frazzled French chef. Mother curled on a chaise lounge, plumes of smoke wafting from her nostrils. In a stupor of contentment she took another drag, closed her eyes, and arched her face toward the sun.

Grady dog-paddled through the deep end, spouting a fountain of chlorinated water. Despite shame and confusion, my longing for him hadn't diminished; it continued to thrive without air and light, like a luminous fish in the dregs of the sea. In the name of play, I swam up behind him, encircled his shoulders, astonished by his taut flesh. The two of us flailed, pretended to drown. Beneath the heavy press of water, Grady's orange hair wavered, a flame that couldn't be doused.

I've lived with a man for seven years. Some nights, when I'm half-asleep and the room is suffused with blue light, I reach out to touch the expanse of his back, and it seems as if my fingers sink into his skin, and I feel the pleasure a diver feels the instant he enters a body of water.

I have few regrets. But one is that I hadn't said to Theresa, "Of course I'm a fag." Maybe I'd have met her friends. Or become friends with her. Imagine the meals we might have concocted: hamburger Stroganoff, Swedish meatballs in a sweet translucent sauce, steaming slabs of Salisbury steak.

The Reader's Presence

1. Cooper's first stirrings of attraction for his friend Grady occur in a swimming pool. What importance does swimming play in Cooper's essay? How does it provide him with a cluster of images for sexual experience?

2. Why does Cooper attend the "make-out party"? What does he hope will happen? Why do you think he ends his description of the party with the observation of the "clack of tiny sparks"? Why do you think he used that image for his title?

3. In paragraph 15, Cooper writes that he became "the scientist of [his] own desire," as he tried to understand—and to resist—his "yearning for boys." Adrienne Rich determines as a young woman to understand her parents' seeming denial of her Jewish heritage: "I have to face the sources and the flickering presence of my own ambivalence as a Jew" (paragraph 3, "Split at the Root: An Essay on Jewish Identity," page 205). Both writers feel shame and a sense of betrayal in the writing of their essays. What more do you find in common between the two? What are key differences between them? Children often turn to dictionaries to solve mysteries they are too shy to ask people about. How does Cooper's discovery of the definition of "homosexual" compare to Frederick Douglass's attempt to discover the meaning of "abolition" in "Learning to Read and Write" (see the following selection)?

17

Frederick Douglass

Learning to Read and Write

Born into slavery, Frederick Douglass (1817?–1895) was taken from his mother as an infant and denied any knowledge of his father's identity. He escaped to the north at the age of twenty-one and created a new identity for himself as a free man. He educated himself and went on to become one of the most eloquent orators and persuasive writers of the nineteenth century. He was a national leader in the abolition movement and, among other activities, founded and edited the North Star *and* Douglass' Monthly. *His public service included appointments as United States marshal and consul general to the Republic of Haiti. His most lasting literary accomplishment was his memoirs, which he revised several times before they were published as the* Life and Times of Frederick Douglass *(1881 and 1892). "Learning to Read and Write" is taken from these memoirs.*

Douglass overcame his initial reluctance to write his memoirs because, as he put it, "not only is slavery on trial, but unfortunately, the enslaved people are also on trial. It is alleged that they are, naturally, inferior; that they are so low in the scale of humanity, and so utterly stupid, that they are unconscious of their wrongs, and do not apprehend their rights." Therefore, wishing to put his talents to work "to the benefit of my afflicted people," Douglass agreed to write the story of his life.

I lived in Master Hugh's family about seven years. During this time, I succeeded in learning to read and write. In accomplishing this, I was compelled to resort to various stratagems. I had no regular teacher. My mistress, who had kindly commenced to instruct me, had, in compliance with the advice and direction of her husband, not only ceased to instruct, but had set her face against my being instructed by anyone else. It is due, however, to my mistress to say of her, that she did not adopt this course of treatment immediately. She at first lacked the depravity indispensable to shutting me up in mental darkness. It was at least necessary for her to have some training in the exercise of irresponsible power, to make her equal to the task of treating me as though I were a brute.

My mistress was, as I have said, a kind and tender-hearted woman; and in the simplicity of her soul she commenced, when I first went to live with her, to treat me as she supposed one human being ought to treat another. In entering upon the duties of a slaveholder, she did not seem to perceive that I sustained to her the relation of a mere chattel, and that for her to treat me as a human being was not only wrong, but dangerously so. Slavery proved as injurious to her as it did to me. When I went there, she was a pious, warm, and tender-hearted woman. There was no sorrow or suffering for which she had not a tear. She had bread for the hungry, clothes for the naked, and comfort for every mourner that came within her reach. Slavery soon proved its ability to divest her of these heavenly qualities. Under its influence, the tender heart became stone, and the lamb-like disposition gave way to one of tiger like fierceness. The first step in her downward course was in her ceasing to instruct me. She now commenced to practice her husband's precepts. She finally became even more violent in her opposition than her husband himself. She was not satisfied with simply doing as well as he had commanded; she seemed anxious to do better. Nothing seemed to make her more angry than to see me with a newspaper. She seemed to think that here lay the danger. I have had her rush at me with a face made all up of fury, and snatch from me a newspaper, in a manner that fully revealed her apprehension. She was an apt woman; and a little experience soon demonstrated, to her satisfaction, that education and slavery were incompatible with each other.

From this time I was most narrowly watched. If I was in a separate room any considerable length of time, I was sure to be suspected of having a book, and was at once called to give an account of myself. All this, however, was too late. The first step had been taken. Mistress, in teaching me the alphabet, had given me the *inch,* and no precaution could prevent me from taking the *ell.*

The plan which I adopted, and the one by which I was most success-ful, was that of making friends of all the little white boys whom I met in the street. As many of these as I could, I converted into teachers. With their kindly aid, obtained at different times and in different places, I fi-nally succeeded in learning to read. When I was sent to errands, I always took my book with me, and by doing one part of my errand quickly, I found time to get a lesson before my return. I used also to carry bread with me, enough of which was always in the house, and to which I was always welcome; for I was much better off in this regard than many of the poor white children in our neighborhood. This bread I used to bestow upon the hungry little urchins, who, in return, would give me that more valuable bread of knowledge. I am strongly tempted to give the names of two or three of those little boys, as a testimonial of the gratitude and af-fection I bear them; but prudence forbids—not that it would injure me, but it might embarrass them; for it is almost an unpardonable offense to teach slaves to read in this Christian country. It is enough to say of the dear little fellows, that they lived on Philpot Street, very near Durgin and Bailey's ship-yard. I used to talk this matter of slavery over with them. I would sometimes say to them, I wished I could be as free as they would be when they got to be men. "You will be free as soon as you are twenty-one, *but I am a slave for life!* Have not I as good a right to be free as you have?" These words used to trouble them; they would express for me the liveliest sympathy, and console me with the hope that something would occur by which I might be free.

I was now about twelve years old, and the thought of being *a slave*   5 *for life* began to bear heavily upon my heart. Just about this time, I got hold of a book entitled "The Columbian Orator." Every opportunity I got, I used to read this book. Among much of other interesting matter, I found in it a dialogue between a master and his slave. The slave was rep-resented as having run away from his master three times. The dialogue represented the conversation which took place between them, when the slave was retaken the third time. In this dialogue, the whole argument in behalf of slavery was brought forward by the master, all of which was disposed of by the slave. The slave was made to say some very smart as well as impressive things in reply to his master—things which had the de-sired though unexpected effect; for the conversation resulted in the volun-tary emancipation of the slave on the part of the master.

In the same book, I met with one of Sheridan's[1] mighty speeches on and in behalf of Catholic emancipation. These were choice documents to me. I read them over and over again with unabated interest. They gave tongue to interesting thoughts of my own soul, which had frequently flashed through my mind, and died away for want of utterance. The

---

[1]*Sheridan's:* Richard Brinsley Butler Sheridan (1751–1816), Irish dramatist and ora-tor. — EDS.

moral which I gained from the dialogue was the power of truth over the conscience of even a slaveholder. What I got from Sheridan was a bold denunciation of slavery, and a powerful vindication of human rights. The reading of these documents enabled me to utter my thoughts, and to meet the arguments brought forward to sustain slavery; but while they relieved me of one difficulty, they brought on another even more painful than the one of which I was relieved. The more I read, the more I was led to abhor and detest my enslavers. I could regard them in no other light than a band of successful robbers, who had left their homes, and gone to Africa, and stolen us from our homes, and in a strange land reduced us to slavery. I loathed them as being the meanest as well as the most wicked of men. As I read and contemplated the subject, behold! that very discontentment which Master Hugh had predicted would follow my learning to read had already come, to torment and sting my soul to unutterable anguish. As I writhed under it, I would at times feel that learning to read had been a curse rather than a blessing. It had given me a view of my wretched condition, without the remedy. It opened my eyes to the horrible pit, but to no ladder upon which to get out. In moments of agony, I envied my fellow-slaves for their stupidity. I have often wished myself a beast. I preferred the condition of the meanest reptile to my own. Anything, no matter what, to get rid of thinking! It was this everlasting thinking of my condition that tormented me. There was no getting rid of it. It was pressed upon me by every object within sight or hearing, animate or inanimate. The silver trump of freedom had roused my soul to eternal wakefulness. Freedom now appeared, to disappear no more forever. It was heard in every sound, and seen in every thing. It was ever present to torment me with a sense of my wretched condition. I saw nothing without seeing it, I heard nothing without hearing it, and felt nothing without feeling it. It looked from every star, it smiled in every calm, breathed in every wind, and moved in every storm.

I often found myself regretting my own existence, and wishing myself dead; and but for the hope of being free, I have no doubt but that I should have killed myself, or done something for which I should have been killed. While in this state of mind, I was eager to hear anyone speak of slavery. I was a ready listener. Every little while, I could hear something about the abolitionists. It was some time before I found what the word meant. It was always used in such connections as to make it an interesting word to me. If a slave ran away and succeeded in getting clear, or if a slave killed his master, set fire to a barn, or did anything very wrong in the mind of a slaveholder, it was spoken of as the fruit of *abolition*. Hearing the word in this connection very often, I set about learning what it meant. The dictionary afforded me little or no help. I found it was "the act of abolishing"; but then I did not know what was to be abolished. Here I was perplexed. I did not dare to ask anyone about its meaning, for I was satisfied that it was something they wanted me to know very little about. After a patient waiting, I got one of our city papers, containing an account of the number of

petitions from the North, praying for the abolition of slavery in the District
of Columbia, and of the slave trade between the States. From this time I understood the words *abolition* and *abolitionist,* and always drew near when
that word was spoken, expecting to hear something of importance to myself and fellow-slaves. The light broke in upon me by degrees. I went one
day down on the wharf of Mr. Waters; and seeing two Irishmen unloading
a scow of stone, I went, unasked, and helped them. When we had finished,
one of them came to me and asked me if I were a slave. I told him I was. He
asked, "Are ye a slave for life?" I told him that I was. The good Irishman
seemed to be deeply affected by the statement. He said to the other that it
was a pity so fine a little fellow as myself should be a slave for life. He said
it was a shame to hold me. They both advised me to run away to the
North; that I should find friends there, and that I should be free. I pretended not to be interested in what they said, and treated them as if I did
not understand them; for I feared they might be treacherous. White men
have been known to encourage slaves to escape, and then, to get the reward, catch them and return them to their masters. I was afraid that these
seemingly good men might use me so; but I nevertheless remembered their
advice, and from that time I resolved to run away. I looked forward to a
time at which it would be safe for me to escape. I was too young to think of
doing so immediately; besides, I wished to learn how to write, as I might
have occasion to write my own pass. I consoled myself with the hope that I
should one day find a good chance. Meanwhile, I would learn to write.

The idea as to how I might learn to write was suggested to me by
being in Durgin and Bailey's ship-yard, and frequently seeing the ship carpenters, after hewing, and getting a piece of timber ready for use, write on
the timber the name of that part of the ship for which it was intended.
When a piece of timber was intended for the larboard side, it would be
marked thus—"L." When a piece was for the starboard side, it would
be marked thus—"S." A piece for the larboard side forward, would be
marked thus—"L.F." When a piece was for starboard side forward, it
would be marked thus—"S.F." For larboard aft, it would be marked thus
—"L.A." For starboard aft, it would be marked thus—"S.A." I soon
learned the names of these letters, and for what they were intended when
placed upon a piece of timber in the shipyard. I immediately commenced
copying them, and in a short time was able to make the four letters
named. After that, when I met with any boy who I knew could write, I
would tell him I could write as well as he. The next word would be, "I
don't believe you. Let me see you try it." I would then make the letters
which I had been so fortunate as to learn, and ask him to beat that. In this
way I got a good many lessons in writing, which it is quite possible I
should never have gotten in any other way. During this time, my copy-
book was the board fence, brick wall, and pavement; my pen and ink was
a lump of chalk. With these, I learned mainly how to write. I then commenced and continued copying the Italics in *Webster's Spelling Book,* until
I could make them all without looking in the book. By this time, my little

Master Thomas had gone to school, and learned how to write, and had written over a number of copy-books. These had been brought home, and shown to some of our near neighbors, and then laid aside. My mistress used to go to class meeting at the Wilk Street meeting-house every Monday afternoon, and leave me to take care of the house. When left thus, I used to spend the time in writing in the spaces left in master Thomas's copy-book, copying what he had written. I continued to do this until I could write a hand very similar to that of Master Thomas. Thus, after a long, tedious effort for years, I finally succeeded in learning how to write.

The Reader's Presence

1. What sort of audience does Douglass anticipate for his reminiscence? How much does he assume his readers know about the conditions of slavery?

2. What books seem to matter to Douglass most? Why? What are his motives for wanting to read and write? What is the relation to Douglass between literacy and freedom? How does he move from curiosity to anguish to "eternal wakefulness" in paragraph 6? What is the relation between learning to read and learning to write?

3. How does Douglass's education compare to that of Helen Keller in "Living Words" (see page 424)? How do their accounts differ in detail, in style, and in tone?

18

Nora Ephron

A Few Words about Breasts

Nora Ephron (b. 1941) started her writing career as a reporter for the New York Post, *and since then has written for numerous magazines, including* New York, McCall's, *and* Cosmopolitan. *Ephron has published four collections of essays on popular culture, including* Crazy Salad *(1975), from which the essay "A Few Words about Breasts" is taken. She also wrote the screenplays for* Silkwood *(with Alice Arlen),* When Harry Met Sally, *and* Sleepless in Seattle. *In 1992 she directed her first movie,* This Is My Life, *written with her sister Delia Ephron; since then she has directed the films* Michael *(1996),* You've Got Mail *(1998),* and Lucky Numbers *(2000). Her most recent books are* Heartburn *(1983), and* Nora Ephron Collected *(1991).*

Ephron relies heavily on events from her own life to inspire her writing. She told an interviewer, "I've always written about my life. That's how I grew up. 'Take notes. Everything is copy.' All that stuff my mother said to us." As you read the essay that follows, notice the way that Ephron draws on her personal experience.

I have to begin with a few words about androgyny. In grammar school, in the fifth and sixth grades, we were all tyrannized by a rigid set of rules that supposedly determined whether we were boys or girls. The episode in *Huckleberry Finn* where Huck is disguised as a girl and gives himself away by the way he threads a needle and catches a ball—that kind of thing. We learned that the way you sat, crossed your legs, held a cigarette, and looked at your nails—the way you did these things instinctively was absolute proof of your sex. Now obviously most children did not take this literally, but I did. I thought that just one slip, just one incorrect cross of my legs or flick of an imaginary cigarette ash would turn me from whatever I was into the other thing; that would be all it took, really. Even though I was outwardly a girl and had many of the trappings generally associated with girldom—a girl's name, for example, and dresses, my own telephone, an autograph book—I spent the early years of my adolescence absolutely certain that I might at any point gum it up. I did not feel at all like a girl. I was boyish. I was athletic, ambitious, outspoken, competitive, noisy, rambunctious. I had scabs on my knees and my socks slid into my loafers and I could throw a football. I wanted desperately not to be that way, not to be a mixture of both things, but instead just one, a girl, a definite indisputable girl. As soft and as pink as a nursery. And nothing would do that for me, I felt, but breasts.

I was about six months younger than everyone else in my class, and so for about six months after it began, for six months after my friends had begun to develop (that was the word we used, develop), I was not particularly worried. I would sit in the bathtub and look down at my breasts and know that any day now, any second now, they would start growing like everyone else's. They didn't. "I want to buy a bra," I said to my mother one night. "What for?" she said. My mother was really hateful about bras, and by the time my third sister had gotten to the point where she was ready to want one, my mother had worked the whole business into a comedy routine. "Why not use a Band-Aid instead?" she would say. It was a source of great pride to my mother that she had never even had to wear a brassiere until she had her fourth child, and then only because her gynecologist made her. It was incomprehensible to me that anyone could ever be proud of something like that. It was the 1950s, for God's sake. Jane Russell. Cashmere sweaters. Couldn't my mother see that? *"I am too old to wear an undershirt."* Screaming. Weeping. Shouting. "Then don't wear an undershirt," said my mother. "But I want to buy a bra." "What for?"

I suppose that for most girls, breasts, brassieres, that entire thing, has more trauma, more to do with the coming of adolescence, with becoming a woman, than anything else. Certainly more than getting your period, although that, too, was traumatic, symbolic. But you could see breasts; they were there; they were visible. Whereas a girl could claim to have her period for months before she actually got it and nobody would ever know the difference. Which is exactly what I did. All you had to do was make a great fuss over having enough nickels for the Kotex machine and walk around clutching your stomach and moaning for three to five days a month about The Curse and you could convince anybody. There is a school of thought somewhere in the women's lib/women's mag/gynecology establishment that claims that menstrual cramps are purely psychological, and I lean toward it. Not that I didn't have them finally. Agonizing cramps, heating-pad cramps, go-down-to-the-school-nurse-and-lie-on-the-cot cramps. But unlike any pain I had ever suffered, I adored the pain of cramps, welcomed it, wallowed in it, bragged about it. "I can't go. I have cramps." "I can't do that. I have cramps." And most of all, gigglingly, blushingly: "I can't swim. I have cramps." Nobody ever used the hard-core word. Menstruation. God, what an awful word. Never that. "I have cramps."

The morning I first got my period, I went into my mother's bedroom to tell her. And my mother, my utterly-hateful-about-bras mother, burst into tears. It was really a lovely moment, and I remember it so clearly not just because it was one of the two times I ever saw my mother cry on my account (the other was when I was caught being a six-year-old kleptomaniac), but also because the incident did not mean to me what it meant to her. Her little girl, her firstborn, had finally become a woman. That was what she was crying about. My reaction to the event, however, was that I might well be a woman in some scientific, textbook sense (and could at least stop faking every month and stop wasting all those nickels). But in another sense—in a visible sense—I was as androgynous and as liable to tip over into boyhood as ever.

I started with a 28 AA bra. I don't think they made them any smaller in those days, although I gather that now you can buy bras for five-year-olds that don't have any cups whatsoever in them; trainer bras they are called. My first brassiere came from Robinson's Department Store in Beverly Hills. I went there alone, shaking, positive they would look me over and smile and tell me to come back next year. An actual fitter took me into the dressing room and stood over me while I took off my blouse and tried the first one on. The little puffs stood out on my chest. "Lean over," said the fitter. (To this day, I am not sure what fitters in bra departments do except to tell you to lean over.) I leaned over, with the fleeting hope that my breasts would miraculously fall out of my body and into the puffs. Nothing.

"Don't worry about it," said my friend Libby some months later, when things had not improved. "You'll get them after you're married."

"What are you talking about?" I said.

"When you get married," Libby explained, "your husband will touch your breasts and rub them and kiss them and they'll grow."

That was the killer. Necking I could deal with. Intercourse I could deal with. But it had never crossed by mind that a man was going to touch my breasts, that breasts had something to do with all that, petting, my God, they never mentioned petting in my little sex manual about the fertilization of the ovum. I became dizzy. For I knew instantly—as naïve as I had been only a moment before—that only part of what she was saying was true: the touching, rubbing, kissing part, not the growing part. And I knew that no one would ever want to marry me. I had no breasts. I would never have breasts.

My best friend in school was Diana Raskob. She lived a block from   10
me in a house full of wonders. English muffins, for instance. The Raskobs were the first people in Beverly Hills to have English muffins for breakfast. They also had an apricot tree in the back, and a badminton court, and a subscription to *Seventeen* magazine, and hundreds of games, like Sorry and Parcheesi and Treasure Hunt and Anagrams. Diana and I spent three or four afternoons a week in their den reading and playing and eating. Diana's mother's kitchen was full of the most colossal assortment of junk food I have ever been exposed to. My house was full of apples and peaches and milk and homemade chocolate-chip cookies—which were nice, and good for you, but-not-right-before-dinner-or-you'll-spoil-your-appetite. Diana's house had nothing in it that was good for you, and what's more, you could stuff it in right up until dinner and nobody cared. Bar-B-Q potato chips (they were the first in them, too), giant bottles of ginger ale, fresh popcorn with melted butter, hot fudge sauce on Baskin-Robbins jamoca ice cream, powdered-sugar doughnuts from Van de Kamp's. Diana and I had been best friends since we were seven; we were about equally popular in school (which is to say, not particularly), we had about the same success with boys (extremely intermittent), and we looked much the same. Dark. Tall. Gangly.

It is September, just before school begins. I am eleven years old, about to enter the seventh grade, and Diana and I have not seen each other all summer. I have been to camp and she has been somewhere like Banff with her parents. We are meeting, as we often do, on the street midway between our two houses, and we will walk back to Diana's and eat junk and talk about what has happened to each of us that summer. I am walking down Walden Drive in my jeans and my father's shirt hanging out and my old red loafers with the socks falling into them and coming toward me is . . . I take a deep breath . . . a young woman. Diana. Her hair is curled and she has a waist and hips and a bust and she is wearing a straight skirt, an article of clothing I have been repeatedly told I will be unable to wear until I have the hips to hold it up. My jaw drops, and suddenly I am crying, crying hysterically, can't catch my breath sobbing. My best friend has betrayed me. She has gone ahead without me and done it. She has shaped up.

Here are some things I did to help:
Bought a Mark Eden Bust Developer.
Slept on my back for four years.
Splashed cold water on them every night because some French ac-   15
tress said in *Life* magazine that that was what *she* did for her perfect bustline.

Ultimately, I resigned myself to a bad toss and began to wear padded bras. I think about them now, think about all those years in high school that I went around in them, my three padded bras, every single one of them with different-sized breasts. Each time I changed bras I changed sizes: one week nice perky but not too obtrusive breasts, the next medium-sized slightly pointy ones, the next week knockers, true knockers; all the time, whatever size I was, carrying around this rubberized appendage on my chest that occasionally crashed into a wall and was poked inward and had to be poked outward—I think about all that and wonder how anyone kept a straight face through it. My parents, who normally had no restraints about needling me—why did they say nothing as they watched my chest go up and down? My friends, who would periodically inspect my breasts for signs of growth and reassure me—why didn't they at least counsel consistency?

And the bathing suits. I die when I think about the bathing suits. That was the era when you could lay an uninhabited bathing suit on the beach and someone would make a pass at it. I would put one on, an absurd swimsuit with its enormous bust built into it, the bones from the suit stabbing me in the rib cage and leaving little red welts on my body, and there I would be, my chest plunging straight downward absolutely vertically from my collarbone to the top of my suit and then suddenly, wham, out came all that padding and material and wiring absolutely horizontally.

Buster Klepper was the first boy who ever touched them. He was my boyfriend my senior year of high school. There is a picture of him in my high-school yearbook that makes him look quite attractive in a Jewish, horn-rimmed-glasses sort of way, but the picture does not show the pimples, which were air-brushed out, or the dumbness. Well, that isn't really fair. He wasn't dumb. He just wasn't terribly bright. His mother refused to accept it, refused to accept the relentlessly average report cards, refused to deal with her son's inevitable destiny in some junior college or other. "He was tested," she would say to me, apropos of nothing, "and it came out a hundred and forty-five. That's near-genius." Had the word "underachiever" been coined, she probably would have lobbed that one at me, too. Anyway, Buster was really very sweet—which is, I know, damning with faint praise, but there it is. I was the editor of the front page of the high-school newspaper and he was editor of the back page;

we had to work together, side by side, in the print shop, and that was how it started. On our first date, we went to see *April Love,* starring Pat Boone. Then we started going together. Buster had a green coupe, a 1950 Ford with an engine he had hand-chromed until it shone, dazzled, reflected the image of anyone who looked into it, anyone usually being Buster polishing it or the gas-station attendants he constantly asked to check the oil in order for them to be overwhelmed by the sparkle on the valves. The car also had a boot stretched over the back seat for reasons I never understood; hanging from the rearview mirror, as was the custom, was a pair of angora dice. A previous girlfriend named Solange, who was famous throughout Beverly Hills High School for having no pigment in her right eyebrow, had knitted them for him. Buster and I would ride around town, the two of us seated to the left of the steering wheel. I would shift gears. It was nice.

There was necking. Terrific necking. First in the car, overlooking Los Angeles from what is now the Trousdale Estates. Then on the bed of his parents' cabana at Ocean House. Incredibly wonderful, frustrating necking, I loved it, really, but no further than necking, please don't, please, because there I was absolutely terrified of the general implications of going-a-step-further with a near-dummy and also terrified of his finding out there was next to nothing there (which he knew, of course; he wasn't that dumb).

I broke up with him at one point. I think we were apart for about   20 two weeks. At the end of that time, I drove down to see a friend at a boarding school in Palos Verdes Estates and a disc jockey played "April Love" on the radio four times during the trip. I took it as a sign. I drove straight back to Griffith Park to a golf tournament Buster was playing in (he was the sixth-seeded teenage golf player in southern California) and presented myself back to him on the green of the eighteenth hole. It was all very dramatic. That night we went to a drive-in and I let him get his hand under my protuberances and onto my breasts. He really didn't seem to mind at all.

> "Do you want to marry my son?" the woman asked me.
>
> "Yes," I said.
>
> I was nineteen years old, a virgin, going with this woman's son, this big strange woman who was married to a Lutheran minister in New Hampshire and pretended she was gentile and had this son, by her first husband, this total fool of a son who ran the hero-sandwich concession at Harvard Business School and whom for one moment one December in New Hampshire I said—as much out of politeness as anything else—that I wanted to marry.
>
> "Fine," she said. "Now, here's what you do. Always make sure you're on top of him so you won't seem so small. My bust is very large, you see, so I always lie on my back to make it look smaller, but you'll have to be on top most of the time."
>
> I nodded. "Thank you," I said.

"I have a book for you to read," she went on. "Take it with you when you leave. Keep it." She went to the bookshelf, found it, and gave it to me. It was a book on frigidity.

"Thank you," I said.

That is a true story. Everything in this article is a true story, but I feel I have to point out that that story in particular is true. It happened on December 30, 1960. I think about it often. When it first happened, I naturally assumed that the woman's son, my boyfriend, was responsible. I invented a scenario where he had had a little heart-to-heart with his mother and had confessed that his only objection to me was that my breasts were small; his mother then took it upon herself to help out. Now I think I was wrong about the incident. The mother was acting on her own, I think: That was her way of being cruel and competitive under the guise of being helpful and maternal. You have small breasts, she was saying; therefore you will never make him as happy as I have. Or you have small breasts; therefore you will doubtless have sexual problems. Or you have small breasts; therefore you are less woman than I am. She was, as it happens, only the first of what seems to me to be a never-ending string of women who have made competitive remarks to me about breast size. "I would love to wear a dress like that," my friend Emily says to me, "but my bust is too big." Like that. Why do women say these things to me? Do I attract these remarks the way other women attract married men or alcoholics or homosexuals? This summer, for example. I am at a party in East Hampton and I am introduced to a woman from Washington. She is a minor celebrity, very pretty and Southern and blond and outspoken, and I am flattered because she has read something I have written. We are talking animatedly, we have been talking no more than five minutes, when a man comes up to join us. "Look at the two of us," the woman says to the man, indicating me and her. "The two of us together couldn't fill an A cup." Why does she say that? It isn't even true, dammit, so why? Is she even more addled than I am on this subject? Does she honestly believe there is something wrong with her size breasts, which, it seems to me, now that I look hard at them, are just right? Do I unconsciously bring out competitiveness in women? In that form? What did I do to deserve it?

As for men.

There were men who minded and let me know that they minded. There were men who did not mind. In any case, *I* always minded.

And even now, now that I have been countlessly reassured that my figure is a good one, now that I am grown-up enough to understand that most of my feelings have very little to do with the reality of my shape, I am nonetheless obsessed by breasts. I cannot help it. I grew up in the terrible fifties—with rigid stereotypical sex roles, the insistence that men be men and dress like men and women be women and dress like women, the intolerance of androgyny—and I cannot shake it, cannot shake my feelings of inadequacy. Well, that time is gone, right? All those exaggerated examples of breast worship are gone, right? Those women were freaks, right? I know all that. And yet here I am, stuck with the psychological remains of it all, stuck with my own peculiar version of breast worship. You probably think I am crazy to go on like this: Here I have set out to write a confession that is meant to hit you with the shock of recognition, and instead you are sitting there thinking I am thoroughly warped. Well, what can I tell you? If I had had them, I would have been a completely different person. I honestly believe that.

After I went into therapy, a process that made it possible for me to tell   25
total strangers at cocktail parties that breasts were the hang-up of my life, I was often told that I was insane to have been bothered by my condition. I was also frequently told, by close friends, that I was extremely boring on the subject. And my girlfriends, the ones with nice big breasts, would go on endlessly about how their lives had been far more miserable than mine. Their bra straps were snapped in class. They couldn't sleep on their stomachs. They were stared at whenever the word "mountain" cropped up in geography. And *Evangeline,* good God what they went through every time someone had to stand up and recite the Prologue to Longfellow's *Evangeline:* "...stand like druids of eld.../ With beards that rest on their bosoms." It was much worse for them, they tell me. They had a terrible time of it, they assure me. I don't know how lucky I was, they say.

I have thought about their remarks, tried to put myself in their place, considered their point of view. I think they are full of shit.

The Reader's Presence

1. "That is a true story. Everything in this article is a true story ..." Ephron maintains in paragraph 21. Why does she feel she must say this? What attitude does she anticipate in her reader? Why might she think her readers would doubt her story? Do you?

2. In paragraph 24, Ephron addresses her readers directly: "You probably think I am crazy to go on like this: Here I have set out to write a confession that is meant to hit you with the shock of recognition, and instead you are sitting there thinking I am thoroughly warped." What are her assumptions about her readers at this point? What does she seem worried about? What is your response as a reader? How closely do you fit into the role she is assigning for her readers?

3. How does Ephron make small breasts a matter of identity as well as appearance? Do you agree with her? Do you think her reasons for this are well founded? How does her sense of her body compare with that of Nancy Mairs in "On Being a Cripple" (see page 166)? Mairs writes: "Physical imperfection, even freed of moral disapprobation, still defies and violates the ideal, especially for

women, whose confinement in their bodies as objects of desire is far from over" (paragraph 20). Despite such acute and often painful self-examination, both writers use humor; how do their uses of it compare?

19

Henry Louis Gates Jr.

In the Kitchen

The critic, educator, writer, and activist Henry Louis Gates Jr. (b. 1950) is perhaps the most recent in a long line of African American intellectuals who are also public figures. In 1979 he became the first African American to earn a Ph.D. from Cambridge University in its eight-hundred year history. He has been the recipient of countless honors, including a Carnegie Foundation Fellowship, a Mellon Fellowship, a MacArthur "genius" grant for his work in literary theory, and the 1998 National Medal for the Humanities. Gates is currently the W. E. B. Du Bois Professor of the Humanities at Harvard University, where he also chairs the department of Afro-American Studies. He has been at the forefront of the movement to expand the literary canon that is studied in American schools to include the works of non-European authors. He is also known for his work as a "literary archaeologist," uncovering literally thousands of previously unknown stories, poems, and reviews written by African American authors between 1829 and 1940, and making those texts available to modern readers. Much of his writing, in particular for publications such as the New York Times, Newsweek, *and* Sports Illustrated, *is accessible to general audiences. His testimony on behalf of the rap group 2 Live Crew helped earn them an acquittal in their trial for obscenity, because he was able to bring his understanding of the history of black culture—specifically the language game known as "signifying"—to bear on their contemporary lyrics.*

Gates's publications include Figures in Black: Words, Signs, and the "Racial" Self *(1987),* The Signifying Monkey: A Theory of African-American Literary Criticism *(1988),* Loose Canons: Notes on the Culture Wars *(1992), and* Colored People: A Memoir *(1994), from which "In the Kitchen" is taken. About this book, Gates says, "I'm trying to recollect a lost era, what I can call a sepia time, a whole world that simply no longer exists." His most recent book is* Wonders of the African World *(1999).*

We always had a gas stove in the kitchen, though electric cooking became fashionable in Piedmont, like using Crest toothpaste rather than Colgate, or watching Huntley and Brinkley rather than Walter Cronkite.

But for us it was gas, Colgate, and good ole Walter Cronkite, come what may. We used gas partly out of loyalty to Big Mom, Mama's mama, because she was mostly blind and still loved to cook, and she could feel her way better with gas than with electric.

But the most important thing about our gas-equipped kitchen was that Mama used to do hair there. She had a "hot comb"—a fine-tooth iron instrument with a long wooden handle—and a pair of iron curlers that opened and closed like scissors: Mama would put them into the gas fire until they glowed. You could smell those prongs heating up.

I liked what that smell meant for the shape of my day. There was an intimate warmth in the women's tones as they talked with my mama while she did their hair. I knew what the women had been through to get their hair ready to be "done," because I would watch Mama do it herself. How that scorched kink could be transformed through grease and fire into a magnificent head of wavy hair was a miracle to me. Still is.

Mama would wash her hair over the sink, a towel wrapped round her shoulders, wearing just her half-slip and her white bra. (We had no shower until we moved down Rat Tail Road into Doc Wolverton's house, in 1954.) After she had dried it, she would grease her scalp thoroughly with blue Bergamot hair grease, which came in a short, fat jar with a picture of a beautiful colored lady on it. It's important to grease your scalp real good, my mama would explain, to keep from burning yourself.

Of course, her hair would return to its natural kink almost as soon as   5 the hot water and shampoo hit it. To me, it was another miracle how hair so "straight" would so quickly become kinky again once it even approached some water.

My mama had only a "few" clients whose heads she "did"—and did, I think, because she enjoyed it, rather than for the few dollars it brought in. They would sit on one of our red plastic kitchen chairs, the kind with the shiny metal legs, and brace themselves for the process. Mama would stroke that red-hot iron, which by this time had been in the gas fire for a half hour or more, slowly but firmly through their hair, from scalp to strand's end. It made a scorching, crinkly sound, the hot iron did, as it burned its way through the damp kink, leaving in its wake the straightest of hair strands, each of them standing up long and tall but drooping at the end, like the top of a heavy willow tree. Slowly, steadily, with deftness and grace, Mama's hands would transform a round mound of Odetta kink[1] into a darkened swamp of everglades. The Bergamot made the hair shiny; the heat of the hot iron gave it a brownish-red cast. Once all the hair was as straight as God allows kink to get, Mama would take the well-heated curling iron and twirl the straightened strands into

[1] *Odetta kink:* A reference to Odetta Holmes Felious Gorden, a popular African American folk singer of the 1960s who helped popularize the hairstyle known as the "afro." —EDS.

more or less loosely wrapped curls. She claimed that she owed her strength and skill as a hairdresser to her wrists, and her little finger would poke out the way it did when she sipped tea. Mama was a southpaw, who wrote upside down and backwards to produce the cleanest, roundest letters you've ever seen.

The "kitchen" she would all but remove from sight with a pair of shears bought for this purpose. Now, the *kitchen* was the room in which we were sitting, the room where Mama did hair and washed clothes, and where each of us bathed in a galvanized tub. But the word has another meaning, and the "kitchen" I'm speaking of now is the very kinky bit of hair at the back of the head, where our neck meets the shirt collar. If there ever was one part of our African past that resisted assimilation, it was the kitchen. No matter how hot the iron, no matter how powerful the chemical, no matter how stringent the mashed-potatoes-and-lye formula of a man's "process," neither God nor woman nor Sammy Davis, Jr., could straighten the kitchen. The kitchen was permanent, irredeemable, invincible kink. Unassimilably African. No matter what you did, no matter how hard you tried, nothing could dekink a person's kitchen. So you trimmed it off as best you could.

When hair had begun to "turn," as they'd say, or return to its natural kinky glory, it was the kitchen that turned first. When the kitchen started creeping up the back of the neck, it was time to get your hair done again. The kitchen around the back, and nappy edges at the temples.

Sometimes, after dark, Mr. Charlie Carroll would come to have his hair done. Mr. Charlie Carroll was very light-complected and had a ruddy nose, the kind of nose that made me think of Edmund Gwenn playing Kris Kringle in *Miracle on 34th Street*. At the beginning, they did it after Rocky and I had gone to sleep. It was only later that we found out he had come to our house so Mama could iron his hair — not with a comb and curling iron but with our very own Proctor-Silex steam iron. For some reason, Mr. Charlie would conceal his Frederick Douglass mane[2] under a big white Stetson hat, which I never saw him take off. Except when he came to our house, late at night, to have his hair pressed.

(Later, Daddy would tell us about Mr. Charlie's most prized piece of   10
knowledge, which the man would confide only after his hair had been pressed, as a token of intimacy. "Not many people know this," he'd say in a tone of circumspection, "but George Washington was Abraham Lincoln's daddy." Nodding solemnly, he'd add the clincher: "A white man told me." Though he was in dead earnest, this became a humorous refrain around the house — "a white man told me" — used to punctuate especially preposterous assertions.)

---

[2]*Frederick Douglass mane:* Frederick Douglass (1817?–1895), an escaped slave who became a prominent African American writer, abolitionist, and orator (see page 112). His photographs reveal an impressive head of hair. — EDS.

My mother furtively examined my daughters' kitchens whenever we went home for a visit in the early eighties. It became a game between us. I had told her not to do it, because I didn't like the politics it suggested of "good" and "bad" hair. "Good" hair was straight. "Bad" hair was kinky. Even in the late sixties, at the height of Black Power, most people could not bring themselves to say "bad" for "good" and "good" for "bad." They still said that hair like white hair was "good," even if they encapsulated it in a disclaimer like "what we used to call 'good.'"

Maggie would be seated in her high chair, throwing food this way and that, and Mama would be cooing about how cute it all was, remembering how I used to do the same thing, and wondering whether Maggie's flinging her food with her left hand meant that she was going to be a southpaw too. When my daughter was just about covered with Franco-American SpaghettiOs, Mama would seize the opportunity and wipe her clean, dipping her head, tilted to one side, down under the back of Maggie's neck. Sometimes, if she could get away with it, she'd even rub a curl between her fingers, just to make sure that her bifocals had not deceived her. Then she'd sigh with satisfaction and relief, thankful that her prayers had been answered. No kink . . . yet. "Mama!" I'd shout, pretending to be angry. (Every once in a while, if no one was looking, I'd peek too.)

I say "yet" because most black babies are born with soft, silken hair. Then, sooner or later, it begins to "turn," as inevitably as do the seasons or the leaves turn on a tree. And if it's meant to turn, it *turns,* no matter how hard you try to stop it. People once thought baby oil would stop it. They were wrong.

Everybody I knew as a child wanted to have good hair. You could be as ugly as homemade sin dipped in misery and still be thought attractive if you had good hair. Jesus Moss was what the girls at Camp Lee, Virginia, had called Daddy's hair during World War II. I know he played that thick head of hair for all it was worth, too. Still would, if he could.

My own hair was "not a bad grade," as barbers would tell me when they cut my head for the first time. It's like a doctor reporting the overall results of the first full physical that he had given you. "You're in good shape" or "Blood pressure's kind of high; better cut down on salt."

I spent much of my childhood and adolescence messing with my hair. I definitely wanted straight hair. Like Pop's.

When I was about three, I tried to stick a wad of Bazooka bubble gum to that straight hair of his. I suppose what fixed that memory for me is the spanking I got for doing so: he turned me upside down, holding me by the feet, the better to paddle my behind. Little *nigger,* he shouted, walloping away. I started to laugh about it two days later, when my behind stopped hurting.

When black people say "straight," of course, they don't usually mean "straight" literally, like, say, the hair of Peggy Lipton (the white girl on *The Mod Squad*) or Mary of Peter, Paul and Mary fame; black people call that "stringy" hair. No, "straight" just means not kinky, no matter what contours the curl might take. Because Daddy had straight hair, I would have done *anything* to have straight hair — and I used to try everything to make it straight, short of getting a process, which only riffraff were dumb enough to do.

Of the wide variety of techniques and methods I came to master in the great and challenging follicle prestidigitation, almost all had two things in common: a heavy, oil-based grease and evenly applied pressure. It's no accident that many of the biggest black companies in the fifties and sixties made hair products. Indeed, we do have a vast array of hair grease. And I have tried it all, in search of that certain silky touch, one that leaves neither the hand nor the pillow sullied by grease.

I always wondered what Frederick Douglass put on *his* hair, or Phillis Wheatley.[3] Or why Wheatley has that rag on her head in the little engraving in the frontispiece of her book. One thing is for sure: you can bet that when Wheatley went to England to see the Countess of Huntington, she did not stop by the Queen's Coiffeur on the way. So many black people still get their hair straightened that it's a wonder we don't have a national holiday for Madame C. J. Walker, who invented the process for straightening kinky hair, rather than for Dr. King. Jheri-curled or "relaxed" — it's still fried hair.

I used all the greases, from sea-blue Bergamot, to creamy vanilla Duke (in its orange-and-white jar), to the godfather of grease, the formidable Murray's. Now, Murray's was some *serious* grease. Whereas Bergamot was like oily Jell-O and Duke was viscous and sickly sweet, Murray's was light brown and *hard*. Hard as lard and twice as greasy, Daddy used to say whenever the subject of Murray's came up. Murray's came in an orange can with a screw-on top. It was so hard that some people would put a match to the can, just to soften it and make it more manageable. In the late sixties, when Afros came into style, I'd use Afro-Sheen. From Murray's to Duke to Afro-Sheen: that was my progression in black consciousness.

We started putting hot towels or washrags over our greased-down Murray's-coated heads, in order to melt the wax into the scalp and follicles. Unfortunately, the wax had a curious habit of running down your neck, ears, and forehead. Not to mention your pillowcase.

Another problem was that if you put two palmfuls of Murray's on your head, your hair turned white. Duke did the same thing. It was a challenge: if you got rid of the white stuff, you had a magnificent head of wavy hair. Murray's turned kink into waves. Lots of waves. Frozen waves. A hurricane couldn't have blown those waves around.

That was the beauty of it. Murray's was so hard that it froze your hair into the wavy style you brushed it into. It looked really good if you wore a part. A lot of guys had parts *cut* into their hair by a barber, with clippers or

---

[3]*Phillis Wheatley* (1753?–1784): An African-born slave who became America's first major black poet. — EDS.

20

a straight-edge razor. Especially if you had kinky hair—in which case you'd generally wear a short razor cut, or what we called a Quo Vadis.

Being obsessed with our hair, we tried to be as innovative as possible. Everyone knew about using a stocking cap, because your father or your uncle or the older guys wore them whenever something really big was about to happen, secular or sacred, a funeral or a dance, a wedding or a trip in which you confronted official white people, or when you were trying to look really sharp. When it was time to be clean, you wore a stocking cap. If the event was really a big one, you made a new cap for the occasion.

A stocking cap was made by asking your mother for one of her hose, cutting it with a pair of scissors about six inches or so from the open end, where the elastic goes to the top of the thigh. Then you'd knot the cut end, and behold—a conical-shaped hat or cap, with an elastic band that you pulled down low on your forehead and down around your neck in the back. A good stocking cap, to work well, had to fit tight and snug, like a press. And it had to fit that tightly because it *was* a press: it pressed your hair with the force of the hose's elastic. If you greased your hair down real good and left the stocking cap on long enough—*voilà:* you got a head of pressed-against-the-scalp waves. If you used Murray's, and if you wore a stocking cap to sleep, you got a *whole lot* of waves. (You also got a ring around your forehead when you woke up, but eventually that disappeared.)

And then you could enjoy your concrete 'do. Swore we were bad, too, with all that grease and those flat heads. My brother and I would brush it out a bit in the morning so it would look—ahem—"natural."

Grown men still wear stocking caps, especially older men, who generally keep their caps in their top drawer, along with their cuff links and their see-through silk socks, their Maverick tie, their silk handkerchief, and whatever else they prize most.

A Murrayed-down stocking cap was the respectable version of the process, which, by contrast, was most definitely not a cool thing to have, at least if you weren't an entertainer by trade.

Zeke and Keith and Poochie and a few other stars of the basketball team all used to get a process once or twice a year. It was expensive, and to get one you had to go to Pittsburgh or D.C. or Uniontown, someplace where there were enough colored people to support a business. They'd disappear, then reappear a day or two later, strutting like peacocks, their hair burned slightly red from the chemical lye base. They'd also wear "rags" or cloths or handkerchiefs around it when they slept or played basketball. Do-rags, they were called. But the result was *straight* hair with a hint of wave. No curl. Do-it-yourselfers took their chances at home with a concoction of mashed potatoes and lye.

The most famous process, outside of what Malcolm X describes in his *Autobiography* and maybe that of Sammy Davis, Jr., was Nat King Cole's. Nat King Cole had patent-leather hair.

"That man's got the finest process money can buy." That's what Daddy said the night Cole's TV show aired on NBC, November 5, 1956.

I remember the date because everyone came to our house to watch it and to celebrate one of Daddy's buddies' birthdays. Yeah, Uncle Joe chimed in, they can do shit to his hair that the average Negro can't even *think* about—secret shit.

Nat King Cole was *clean*. I've had an ongoing argument with a Nigerian friend about Nat King Cole for twenty years now. Not whether or not he could sing; any fool knows that he could sing. But whether or not he was a handkerchief-head for wearing that patent-leather process.

Sammy Davis's process I detested. It didn't look good on him. Worse still, he liked to have a fried strand dangling down the middle of his forehead, shaking it out from the crown when he sang. But Nat King Cole's hair was a thing unto itself, a beautifully sculpted work of art that he and he alone should have had the right to wear.

The only difference between a process and a stocking cap, really, was taste; yet Nat King Cole—unlike, say, Michael Jackson—looked *good* in his process. His head looked like Rudolph Valentino's in the twenties, and some say it was Valentino that the process imitated. But Nat King Cole wore a process because it suited his face, his demeanor, his name, his style. He was as clean as he wanted to be.

I had forgotten all about Nat King Cole and that patent-leather look until the day in 1971 when I was sitting in an Arab restaurant on the island of Zanzibar, surrounded by men in fezzes and white caftans, trying to learn how to eat curried goat and rice with the fingers of my right hand, feeling two million miles from home, when all of a sudden the old transistor radio sitting on top of a china cupboard stopped blaring out its Swahili music to play "Fly Me to the Moon" by Nat King Cole. The restaurant's din was not affected at all, not even by half a decibel. But in my mind's eye, I saw it: the King's sleek black magnificent tiara. I managed, barely, to blink back the tears.

The Reader's Presence

1. At what point in the essay do you, as a reader, begin to become aware of the social or political significance of the hair-straightening process? At what point in his own development does Gates begin to ascribe a political significance to hair? How would you describe his attitude toward the "kitchen"? toward the "process"? toward the prominent black Americans whom he names in the essay?

2. How would you characterize the author's voice in this essay? Which words and phrases hark back to the language of his home and family? How does Gates integrate these words and phrases into the text? What difference, if any, does it make to you as a reader when he puts certain words, such as *kitchen* or *good*, in quotation marks, as opposed to the passages in which phrases

(such as "ugly as homemade sin dipped in misery" [paragraph 14]) are not set off in the text in this way?

3. Gates makes explicit reference to Malcolm X's description of his own first home hair-straightening process (paragraph 31). Reread that description in "Homeboy" (page 189, paragraph 69 to end). How do the two descriptions compare in terms of detail and tone? Are both essays staging an argument? If so, what are their main assertions, and what do they use as evidence? Might Gates's essay be read as a response to Malcolm X's admission of shame? If so, what sort of response is it?

THE WRITER AT WORK

Henry Louis Gates Jr. on the Writer's Voice

Skilled at critical and academic writing, the Harvard English professor Henry Louis Gates Jr. hoped to find ways to tell stories about his growing up in a small West Virginia community. In writing his memoir, Colored People, *from which "In the Kitchen" is taken, Gates found the voice he wanted. The following comments appeared in a collection,* Swing Low: Black Men Writing, *edited by Rebecca Carroll in 1995.*

My father told stories all the time when I was growing up. My mother used to call them "lies." I didn't know that "lies" was the name for stories in the black vernacular, I just thought it was her own word that she had made up. I was inspired by those "lies," though, and knew that I wanted to tell some too one day.

When I was ten or twelve, I had a baseball column in the local newspaper. I was the scorekeeper for the minor-league games in my town—I would compile all of the facts, and then the editor and I would put together a narrative. I did that every week during the summer. The best part was seeing my name in print. After that, I was hooked—hooked to seeing my name in black and white on paper.

At fourteen or fifteen, I read James Baldwin's work and became fascinated with the idea of writing. When I started reading about black people through the writings of black people, suddenly I was seized by the desire to write. I was in awe of how writers were able to take words and create an illusion of the world that people could step into—a world where people opened doors and shut doors, fell in love and out of love, where people lived and died. I wanted to be able to create those worlds too. I knew I had a voice even before I knew what a "writer's voice" meant. I didn't know what it was, but I could hear it, and I knew when my rhythm was on—it was almost as if I could hear myself write. I thought I had a unique take on the world and trusted my sensibility. It struck me that perhaps it would be a good thing to share it with other people. . . .

I don't think that the prime reason for writing is to save the world, or to save black people. I do it because it makes me feel good. I want to record my vision and to entertain people. When I was writing reviews, although it was an intriguing way to discuss literature, I would have a lot of black people say to me, "I'm having a hard time understanding you, brother." I've always had two conflicting voices within me, one that wants to be outrageous and on the edge, always breaking new ground, and another that wants to be loved by the community for that outrageousness. It is very difficult to expect that people will let you have it both ways like that. Those who really care about a community are the ones who push the boundaries and create new definitions, but generally they get killed for doing that, which is what I mean when I refer to myself as a griot in the black community — the one who makes the wake-up call, who loves his people enough to truly examine the status quo.

The wonderful thing about *Colored People* is that everybody gets it and can appreciate it because it is a universal story. It is my segue from nonfiction to fiction. I wrote it to preserve a world that has passed away, and to reveal some secrets — not for the shock value, but because I want to re-create a voice that black people use when there are no white people around. Oftentimes in black literature, black authors get all lockjawed in their writing because they are doing it for a white audience, and not for themselves. You don't hear the voice of black people when it's just us in the kitchen, talking out the door and down the road, and that is the voice that I am trying to capture in *Colored People*. Integration may have cost us that voice. We cannot take it for granted and must preserve it whenever possible. I don't know what kind of positive language and linguistic rituals are being passed down in the fragmented, dispossessed black underclass. I think it's very different from when and where I was raised, when there was a stronger sense of community, and that language was everywhere I turned.

20

Edward Hoagland

On Stuttering

Edward Hoagland (b. 1932) is an essayist, nature writer, and novelist. Before his graduation from Harvard University, his first novel, Cat Man (1956), was accepted for publication and won the Houghton-Mifflin Literary Fellowship Award. He has received several other honors, including a Guggenheim Fellowship, an

O. Henry Award, an award from the American Academy of Arts and Letters, and
a Lannan Foundation Award, and has taught for over fifteen years at Bennington
College in Vermont. Hoagland's essays cover a wide range of topics, such as per-
sonal experiences, wild animals, travels to other countries, and ecological crisis.
Among his many highly regarded books are Walking the Dead Diamond River
(1973), African Calliope: A Journey to the Sudan *(1979),* Balancing Acts *(1992),*
and Tigers and Ice: Essays on Life and Nature *(1999). Hoagland also served as*
guest editor for Best American Essays: 1999. *In his memoir,* Compass Points
(2001), Hoagland writes: "Most of us live like stand-up comedians on a vaude-
ville stage—the way an essayist does—by our humble wits, messing up, swallow-
ing an aspirin, knowing Hollywood won't call, thinking no one we love will die
today, just another day of sunshine and rain."

Stuttering is like trying to run with loops of rope around your feet.
And yet you feel that you do want to run because you may get more
words out that way before you trip: an impulse you resist so other people
won't tell you to "calm down" and "relax." Because they themselves may
stammer a little bit when jittery or embarrassed, it's hard for a real stutterer like me to convince a new acquaintance that we aren't perpetually in
such a nervous state and that it's quite normal for us to be at the mercy of
strangers. Strangers are usually civilized, once the rough and sometimes
inadvertently hurtful process of recognizing what is wrong with us is over
(that we're not laughing, hiccuping, coughing, or whatever) and in a way
we plumb them for traces of schadenfreude. A stutterer knows who the
good guys are in any crowded room, as well as the location of each
mocking gleam, and even the St. Francis type, who will wait until he
thinks nobody is looking to wipe a fleck of spittle off his face.

I've stuttered for more than 60 years, and the mysteries of the encumbrance still catch me up: being reminded every morning that it's engrained in my fiber, although I had forgotten in my dreams. Life can
become a matter of measuring the importance of anything you have to
say. Is it better to remain a pleasant cipher who ventures nothing in particular but chuckles immoderately at everyone else's conversation, or instead to subject your several companions to the ordeal of watching you
struggle to expel opinions that are either blurred and vitiated, or made to
sound too emphatic, by all the huffing and puffing, the facial contortions,
tongue biting, blushing, and suffering? "Write it down," people often
said to me in school; indeed I sold my first novel before I left college.

Self-confidence can reduce a stutter's dimensions (in that sense you do
"outgrow" it), as will affection (received or felt), anger, sexual arousal,
and various other hormonal or pheromonal states you may dip into in the
shorter term. Yet it still lurks underfoot, like a trapdoor. I was determined
not to be impeded and managed to serve a regular stint in the Army by
telling the draft-board psychiatrist that I wanted to and was only stammering from "nervousness" with him. Later I also contrived to become a
college professor, thanks to the patience of my early students. Nevertheless, through childhood and adolescence, when I was almost mute in pub-

lic, I could talk without much difficulty to one or two close friends, and then to the particular girl I was necking with. In that case, an overlapping trust was then the lubricant, but if it began to evaporate as our hopes for permanence didn't pan out, I'd start regretfully, apologetically but willy-nilly, to stutter with her again. Adrenaline, when I got mad, operated in a similar fashion, though only momentarily. That is, if somebody made fun of me or treated me cavalierly and a certain threshold was crossed, a spurt of chemistry would suddenly free my mouth and—like Popeye grabbing a can of spinach—I could answer him. Poor Billy Budd didn't learn this technique (and his example frightened me because of its larger implications). Yet many stutterers develop a snappish temperament, and from not just sheer frustration but the fact that being more than ready to "lose one's temper" (as Billy wasn't) actually helps. As in jujitsu, you can trap an opponent by employing his strength and cruelty against him; and bad guys aren't generally smart enough to know that if they wait me out, I'll bog down helplessly all over again.

Overall, however, stuttering is not so predictable. Whether rested or exhausted, fibbing or speaking the Simon-pure truth, and when in the company of chums or people whom I don't respect, I can be fluent or tied in knots. I learned young to be an attentive listener, both because my empathy for others' worries was honed by my handicap and because it was in my best interest that they talk a lot. And yet a core in you will hemorrhage if you become a mere assenter. How many opinions can you keep to yourself before you choke on them (and turn into a stick of furniture for everybody else)? So, instead, you measure what's worth specifying. If you agree with two-thirds of what's being suggested, is it worth the labor of breathlessly elaborating upon the one-third where you differ? There were plenty of times when a subject might come up that I knew more about than the rest of the group, and it used to gall me if I had held my peace till maybe closeted afterward with a close friend. A stymieing bashfulness can also slide a stutterer into slack language because accurate words are so much harder to say than bland ones. You're tempted to be content with an approximation of what you mean in order to escape the scourge of being exact. A sort of football game is going on in your head—the tacklers live there too—and the very effort of pausing to figure out the right way to describe something will alert them to how to pull you down. Being glib and sloppy generates less blockage.

A tuning fork. But it's important not to err in the opposite direction, on the side of tendentiousness, and insist on equal time only because you are a pain in the neck with a problem. You can stutter till your tongue bleeds and your chest is sore from heaving, but so what, if you haven't anything to say that's worth the humiliation? Better to function as a kind of tuning fork, vibrating to other people's anguish or apprehensiveness, as well as your own. A handicap can be cleansing. My scariest moments as a stutterer have been (1) when my daughter was learning to talk and briefly got the impression that she was supposed to do the same; (2) once

5

when I was in the woods and a man shot in my direction and I had to make myself heard loud and fast; and (3) when anticipating weddings where I would need either to propose a toast or say "I do." Otherwise my impediment ceased to be a serious blight about the time I lost my virginity: just a sort of cleft to step around—a squint and gasp of hesitation that indicated to people I might want to be friends with or interview that I wasn't perfect either and perhaps they could trust me.

At worst, during my teens, when I was stuttering on vowels as well as consonants and spitting a few words out could seem interminable, I tried some therapies. But "Slow Speech" was as slow as the trouble itself; and repeatedly writing the first letter of the word that I was stuttering on with my finger in my pocket looked peculiar enough to attract almost as much attention. It did gradually lighten with my maturity and fatherhood, professional recognition, and the other milestones that traditionally help. Nothing "slew" it, though, until at nearly 60 I went semiblind for a couple of years, and this emergency eclipsed—completely trumped—the lesser difficulty. I felt I simply had to talk or die, and so I talked. Couldn't do it gratuitously or lots, but I talked enough to survive. The stutter somehow didn't hold water and ebbed away, until surgery restored my vision and then it returned, like other normalcies.

Such variations can make a stutter seem like a sort of ancillary eccentricity, or a personal Godzilla. But the ball carrier in your head is going to have his good days too—when he can swivel past the tacklers, improvising a broken-field dash so that they are out of position—or even capture their attention with an idea so intriguing that they stop and listen. Not for long, however: The message underlying a stutter is rather like mortality, after all. Real reprieves and fluency are not for you and me. We blunder along, stammering—then not so much—through minor scrapes and scares, but not unscathed. We're not Demosthenes, of course. And poor Demosthenes, if you look him up, ended about as sadly as Billy Budd. People tend to.

The Reader's Presence

1. Why does Hoagland compare his stutter to a football game (paragraph 4)? Explore the metaphor fully. For example, what position does Hoagland play? Who are the tacklers who are trying to pull him down? How many touchdowns does he score in his life, according to his essay? What strategies does he develop to avoid anticipated blockers? Would you say he's winning or losing? Why?

2. In what specific ways do Hoagland's sentences and paragraphs begin and end as you might have anticipated? Can you detect written signs of his stutter? What kinds of verbal hesitations and restatements happen when someone stutters? Where—and with what effects—are there similar hesitations and restatements in

Hoagland's essay? Imagine Hoagland speaking this essay. At which points do you think that he would hesitate? Rewrite a paragraph to include the imagined stuttering and compare it to the original paragraph. What changes in meaning occur in the rewritten version?

3. Read David Sedaris's "Me Talk Pretty One Day" (page 249) and compare the two authors' approaches to handling difficulties with speech. What strategies do they use to deal with being less than fluent? To what extent do their limitations affect their feelings about themselves? about the world around them? Who deals more effectively with not being able to communicate fluently? Why?

THE WRITER AT WORK

Edward Hoagland on What an Essay Is

Known as one of America's finest essayists, Edward Hoagland began his career writing fiction. In this passage from his Introduction to The Best American Essays 1999, *Hoagland describes how he thinks essays work and the idiosyncratic ways essayists—like himself—approach the act of writing them. Essays, he reminds us, are different from articles and documents: They don't necessarily offer objective information and they don't require their writers to be authorities about anything other than their own experiences. All good essays, he suggests, encapsulate their writer's presence. In these literary beliefs he is a direct descendent of Montaigne (1533–1592), whom many consider the inventor of the modern essay. Montaigne, too, was skeptical of authority and wrote essays that appear to follow the drifts of an interior dialogue carried on with himself. After reading Hoagland's brief but thoughtful passage, consider how it comments on his essay on stuttering.*

Essays are how we speak to one another in print—caroming thoughts not merely in order to convey a certain packet of information, but with a special edge or bounce of personal character in a kind of public letter. You multiply yourself as a writer, gaining height as though jumping on a trampoline, if you can catch the gist of what other people have also been feeling and clarify it for them. Classic essay subjects, like the flux of friendship, "On Greed," "On Religion," "On Vanity," or solitude, lying, self-sacrifice, can be major-league yet not require Bertrand Russell to handle them. A layman who has diligently looked into something, walking in the mosses of regret after the death of a parent, for instance, may acquire an intangible authority, even without being memorably angry or funny or possessing a beguiling equanimity. *He* cares; therefore, if he has tinkered enough with his words, we do too.

An essay is not a scientific document. It can be serendipitous or domestic, satire or testimony, tongue-in-cheek or a wail of grief. Mulched perhaps in its own contradictions, it promises no sure objectivity, just the condiment of opinion on a base of observation, and sometimes such leaps of illogic or superlogic that they may work a bit like magic realism in a novel: namely, to simulate the mind's own processes in a murky and incongruous world. More than being instructive, as a magazine article is, an essay has a slant, a seasoned personality behind it that ought to weather well. Even if we think the author is telling us the earth is flat, we might want to listen to him elaborate upon the fringes of his premise because the bristle of his narrative and what he's seen intrigues us. He has a cutting edge, yet balance too. A given body of information is going to be eclipsed, but what lives in art is spirit, not factuality, and we respond to Montaigne's human touch despite four centuries of technological and social change.

21

bell hooks

Learning in the Shadow of Race and Class

Born Gloria Watkins in Hopkinsville, Kentucky, in 1952, bell hooks (a pen name taken to honor both her grandmother and her mother) is a widely known writer, feminist thinker, and critic of media representations. The Atlantic Monthly *has celebrated hooks as one of the nation's leading public intellectuals. She is the author of over seventeen books, including* Ain't I a Woman: Black Women and Feminism *(1981),* Feminist Theory: From Margin to Center *(1984),* Breaking Bread, All about Love *(2000), and* A Woman's Mourning Song *(2001). Her most recent book is a children's story,* Bee Boy Buzz *(2001). She lives in New York City.*

In a recent interview, hooks said, "I started out writing plays and poetry, but then felt I'd received this 'message from the spirits': that I really needed to do feminist work which would challenge the universalized category of 'Woman.' I remember people being enraged because the book challenged the whole construction of white woman as victim, or white woman as the symbol of the most oppressed. Because I was saying, 'Wait a minute. What about class differences between women? What about racial differences that in fact make some women more powerful than others?' So that's how I started out. I continued to do my plays and my poetry, but my feminist theory and writings became better known."

As a child, I often wanted things money could buy that my parents could not afford and would not get. Rather than tell us we did not get some material thing because money was lacking, mama would frequently manipulate us in an effort to make the desire go away. Sometimes she would belittle and shame us about the object of our desire. That's what I remember most. That lovely yellow dress I wanted would become in her storytelling mouth a really ugly mammy-made thing that no girl who cared about her looks would desire. My desires were often made to seem worthless and stupid. I learned to mistrust and silence them. I learned that the more clearly I named my desires, the more unlikely those desires would ever be fulfilled.

I learned that my inner life was more peaceful if I did not think about money, or allow myself to indulge in any fantasy of desire. I learned the art of sublimation and repression. I learned it was better to make do with acceptable material desires than to articulate the unacceptable. Before I knew money mattered, I had often chosen objects to desire that were costly, things a girl of my class would not ordinarily desire. But then I was still a girl who was *unaware of class,* who did not think my desires were stupid and wrong. And when I found they were, I let them go. I concentrated on *survival,* on making do.

When I was choosing a college to attend, the issue of money surfaced and had to be talked about. While I would seek loans and scholarships, even if everything related to school was paid for, there would still be transportation to pay for, books, and a host of other hidden costs. Letting me know that there was no extra money to be had, mama urged me to attend any college nearby that would offer financial aid. My first year of college, I went to a school close to home. A plain-looking white woman recruiter had sat in our living room and explained to my parents that everything would be taken care of, that I would be awarded a full academic scholarship, that they would have to pay nothing. They knew better. Still they found this school acceptable.

After my parents dropped me at the predominately white women's college, I saw the terror in my roommate's face that she was going to be housed with someone black, and I requested a change. She had no doubt also voiced her concern. I was given a tiny single room by the stairs—a room usually denied a first-year student—but I was a first-year black student, a scholarship girl who could never in a million years have afforded to pay her way or absorb the cost of a single room. My fellow students kept their distance from me. I ate in the cafeteria and did not have to worry about who would pay for pizza and drinks in the world outside. I kept my desires to myself, my lacks, and my loneliness; I made do.

I rarely shopped. Boxes came from home, with brand-new clothes   5
mama had purchased. Even though it was never spoken, she did not want me to feel ashamed among privileged white girls. I was the only black girl in my dorm. There was no room in me for shame. I felt contempt and disinterest. With their giggles and their obsession to marry, the white girls at the women's college were aliens. We did not reside on the same planet. I lived in the world of books. The one white woman who became my close friend found me there reading. I was hiding under the shadows of a tree

with huge branches, the kinds of trees that just seemed to grow effort-lessly on well-to-do college campuses. I sat on the "perfect" grass reading poetry, wondering how the grass around me could be so lovely, and yet, when daddy had tried to grow grass in the front yard of Mr. Porter's house, it always turned yellow or brown and then died. Endlessly, the yard defeated him, until finally he gave up. The outside of the house looked good, but the yard always hinted at the possibility of endless ne-glect. The yard looked poor.

Foliage and trees on the college grounds flourished. Greens were lush and deep. From my place in the shadows, I saw a fellow student sitting alone weeping. Her sadness had to do with all the trivia that haunted our day's classwork, the fear of not being smart enough, of losing financial aid (like me she had loans and scholarships, though her family paid some), and boys. Coming from an Illinois family of Czechoslovakian im-migrants, she understood class.

When she talked about the other girls who flaunted their wealth and family background, there was a hard edge of contempt, anger, and envy in her voice. Envy was always something I pushed away from my psyche. Kept too close for comfort, envy could lead to infatuation and on to de-sire. I desired nothing that they had. She desired everything, speaking her desires openly, without shame. Growing up in the kind of community where there was constant competition to see who could buy the bigger better whatever, in a world of organized labor, of unions and strikes, she understood a world of bosses and workers, of haves and have-nots.

White friends I had known in high school wore their class privilege modestly. Raised, like myself, in church traditions that taught us to iden-tify only with the poor, we knew that there was evil in excess. We knew rich people were rarely allowed into heaven. God had given them a par-adise of bounty on earth, and they had not shared. The rare ones, the rich people who shared, were the only ones able to meet the divine in par-adise, and even then it was harder for them to find their way. According to the high-school friends we knew, flaunting wealth was frowned upon in our world, frowned upon by God and community.

The few women I befriended my first year in college were not wealthy. They were the ones who shared with me stories of the other girls flaunting the fact that they could buy anything expensive—clothes, food, vacations. There were not many of us from working-class backgrounds; we knew who we were. Most girls from poor backgrounds tried to blend in, or fought back by triumphing over wealth with beauty or style or some combination of the above. Being black made me an automatic out-sider. Holding their world in contempt pushed me further to the edge. One of the fun things the "in" girls did was choose someone and trash their room. Like so much else deemed cute by insiders, I dreaded the thought of strangers entering my space and going through my things. Being outside the in crowd made me an unlikely target. Being contemptu-ous made me first on the list. I did not understand. And when my room was trashed, it unleashed my rage and deep grief over not being able to protect my space from violation and invasion. I hated the girls who had so much, took so much for granted, never considered that those of us who did not have mad money would not be able to replace broken things, perfume poured out, or talcum powder spread everywhere—that we did not know everything could be taken care of at the dry cleaner's, because we never took our clothes there. My rage fueled by contempt was deep, strong, and long lasting. Daily it stood as a challenge to their fun, to their habits of being.

Nothing they did to win me over worked. It came as a great surprise.   10
They had always believed black girls wanted to be white girls, wanted to possess their world. My stony gaze, silence, and absolute refusal to cross the threshold of their world was total mystery; it was for them a violation they needed to avenge. After trashing my room, they tried to win me over with apologies and urges to talk and understand. There was nothing about me I wanted them to understand. Everything about their world was overexposed, on the surface.

One of my English professors had attended Stanford University. She felt that was the place for me to go—a place where intellect was valued over foolish fun and games and dress up, and finding a husband did not overshadow academic work. I had never thought about the state of California. Getting my parents to agree to my leaving Kentucky to attend a college in a nearby state had been hard enough. They had accepted a college they could reach by car, but a college thousands of miles away was beyond their imagination. Even I had difficulty grasping going that far away from home. The lure for me was the promise of journeying and arriving at a destination where I would be accepted and understood.

All the barely articulated understandings of class privilege that I had learned my first year of college had not hipped me to the reality of class shame. It still had not dawned on me that my parents, especially mama, resolutely refused to acknowledge any difficulties with money because her sense of shame around class was deep and intense. And when this shame was coupled with her need to feel that she had risen above the low-class backwoods culture of her family, it was impossible for her to talk in a straightforward manner about the strains it would put on the family for me to attend Stanford.

All I knew then was that, as with all my desires, I was told that this desire was impossible to fulfill. At first, it was not talked about in relation to money, it was talked about in relation to sin. California was an evil place, a modern-day Babylon where souls were easily seduced away from the path of righteousness. It was not a place for an innocent young girl to go on her own. Mama brought the message back that my father had absolutely refused to give permission.

I expressed my disappointment through ongoing unrelenting grief. I explained to mama that other parents wanted their children to go to good schools. It still had not dawned on me that my parents knew nothing about "good" schools. Even though I knew mama had not graduated from high school, I still held her in awe.

When my parents refused to permit me to attend Stanford, I accepted   15
the verdict for awhile. Overwhelmed by grief, I could barely speak for weeks. Mama intervened and tried to change my father's mind, as folks she respected in the outside world told her what a privilege it was for me to have this opportunity, that Stanford University was a good school for a smart girl. Without their permission, I decided I would go. And even though she did not give her approval, mama was willing to help.

My decision made conversations about money necessary. Mama explained that California was too far away, that it would always "cost" to get there, that if something went wrong, they would not be able to come and rescue me, that I would not be able to come home for holidays. I heard all this, but its meaning did not sink in. I was just relieved I would not be returning to the women's college, to the place where I had truly been an outsider.

There were other black students at Stanford. There was even a dormitory where many black students lived. I did not know I could choose to live there. I went where I was assigned. Going to Stanford was the first time I flew somewhere. Only mama stood and waved farewell as I left to take the bus to the airport. I left with a heavy heart, feeling both excitement and dread. I knew nothing about the world I was journeying to. Not knowing made me afraid, but my fear of staying in place was greater.

I had no idea what was ahead of me. In small ways, I was ignorant. I had never been on an escalator, a city bus, an airplane, or a subway. I arrived in San Francisco with no understanding that Palo Alto was a long drive away—that it would take money to find transportation there. I decided to take the city bus. With all my cheap overpacked bags, I must have seemed like just another innocent immigrant when I struggled to board the bus.

This was a city bus with no racks for luggage. It was filled with immigrants. English was not spoken. I felt lost and afraid. Without words the strangers surrounding me understood the universal language of need and distress. They reached for my bags, holding and helping. In return, I told them my story—that I had left my village in the South to come to Stanford University and that, like them, my family were workers.

On arriving, I called home. Before I could speak, I began to weep   20
as I heard the faraway sound of mama's voice. I tried to find the words, to slow down, to tell her how it felt to be a stranger, to speak my uncertainty and longing. She told me this is the lot I had chosen. I must live with it. After her words, there was only silence. She had hung up on me—let me go into this world where I am a stranger still.

Stanford University was a place where one could learn about class from the ground up. Built by a man who believed in hard work, it was to have been a place where students of all classes would come, women and men, to work together and learn. It was to be a place of equality and communalism. His vision was seen by many as almost communist. The fact that he was rich made it all less threatening. Perhaps no one really believed the vision could be realized. The university was named after his son, who had died young, a son who had carried his name but who had no future money could buy. No amount of money can keep death away. But it could keep memory alive.

Everything in the landscape of my new world fascinated me, the plants brought from a rich man's travels all over the world back to this place of water and clay. At Stanford University, adobe buildings blend with Japanese plum trees and leaves of kumquat. On my way to study medieval literature, I ate my first kumquat. Surrounded by flowering cactus and a South American shrub bougainvillea of such trailing beauty it took my breath away, I was in a landscape of dreams, full of hope and possibility. If nothing else would hold me, I would not remain a stranger to the earth. The ground I stood on would know me.

Class was talked about behind the scenes. The sons and daughters from rich, famous, or notorious families were identified. The grown-ups in charge of us were always looking out for a family who might give their millions to the college. At Stanford, my classmates wanted to know me, thought it hip, cute, and downright exciting to have a black friend. They invited me on the expensive vacations and ski trips I could not afford. They offered to pay. I never went. Along with other students who were not from privileged families, I searched for places to go during the holiday times when the dormitory was closed. We got together and talked about the assumption that everyone had money to travel and would necessarily be leaving. The staff would be on holiday as well, so all students had to leave. Now and then the staff did not leave, and we were allowed to stick around. Once, I went home with one of the women who cleaned for the college.

Now and then, when she wanted to make extra money, mama would work as a maid. Her decision to work outside the home was seen as an act of treason by our father. At Stanford, I was stunned to find that there were maids who came by regularly to vacuum and tidy our rooms. No one had ever cleaned up behind me, and I did not want them to. At first I roomed with another girl from a working-class background—a beautiful white girl from Orange County who looked like pictures I had seen on the cover of *Seventeen* magazine. Her mother had died of cancer during her high-school years, and she had since been raised by her father. She had been asked by the college officials if she would find it problematic to have a black roommate. A scholarship student like myself, she knew her preferences did not matter and, as she kept telling me, she did not really care.

Like my friend during freshman year, she shared the understanding of   25
what it was like to be a have-not in a world of haves. But unlike me, she was determined to become one of them. If it meant she had to steal nice

clothes to look the same as they did, she had no problem taking these risks. If it meant having a privileged boyfriend who left bruises on her body now and then, it was worth the risk. Cheating was worth it. She believed the world the privileged had created was all unfair—all one big cheat; to get ahead, one had to play the game. To her, I was truly an innocent, a lamb being led to the slaughter. It did not surprise her one bit when I began to crack under the pressure of contradictory values and longings.

Like all students who did not have seniority, I had to see the school psychiatrists to be given permission to live off campus. Unaccustomed to being around strangers, especially strangers who did not share or understand my values, I found the experience of living in the dorms difficult. Indeed, almost everyone around me believed working-class folks had no values. At the university where the founder, Leland Stanford, had imagined different classes meeting on common ground, I learned how deeply individuals with class privilege feared and hated the working classes. Hearing classmates express contempt and hatred toward people who did not come from the right backgrounds shocked me.

To survive in this new world of divided classes, this world where I was also encountering for the first time a black bourgeois elite that was as contemptuous of working people as their white counterparts were, I had to take a stand, to get clear my own class affiliations. This was the most difficult truth to face. Having been taught all my life to believe that black people were inextricably bound in solidarity by our struggles to end racism, I did not know how to respond to elitist black people who were full of contempt for anyone who did not share their class, their way of life.

At Stanford, I encountered for the first time a black diaspora. Of the few black professors present, the vast majority were from African or Caribbean backgrounds. Elites themselves, they were only interested in teaching other elites. Poor folks like myself, with no background to speak of, were invisible. We were not seen by them or anyone else. Initially, I went to all meetings welcoming black students, but when I found no one to connect with, I retreated. In the shadows, I had time and books to teach me about the nature of class—about the ways black people were divided from themselves.

Despite this rude awakening, my disappointment at finding myself estranged from the group of students I thought would understand, I still looked for connections. I met an older black male graduate student who also came from a working-class background. Even though he had gone to the right high school, a California school for gifted students, and then to Princeton as an undergraduate, he understood intimately the intersections of race and class. Good in sports and in the classroom, he had been slotted early on to go far, to go where other black males had not gone. He understood the system. Academically, he fit. Had he wanted to, he could have been among the elite, but he chose to be on the margins, to hang with an intellectual artistic avant-garde. He wanted to live in a world of the mind where there was no race or class. He wanted to worship at the throne of art and knowledge. He became my mentor, comrade, and companion.

Slowly, I began to understand fully that there was no place in aca-   30
deme for folks from working-class backgrounds who did not wish to
leave the past behind. That was the price of the ticket. Poor students
would be welcome at the best institutions of higher learning only if they
were willing to surrender memory, to forget the past and claim the assimilated present as the only worthwhile and meaningful reality.

Students from nonprivileged backgrounds who did not want to forget
often had nervous breakdowns. They could not bear the weight of all the
contradictions they had to confront. They were crushed. More often than
not, they dropped out with no trace of their inner anguish recorded, no
institutional record of the myriad ways their take on the world was assaulted by an elite vision of class and privilege. The records merely indicated that, even after receiving financial aid and other support, these
students simply could not make it, simply were not good enough.

At no time in my years as a student did I march in a graduation ceremony. I was not proud to hold degrees from institutions where I had been
constantly scorned and shamed. I wanted to forget these experiences, to
erase them from my consciousness. Like a prisoner set free, I did not want
to remember my years on the inside. When I finished my doctorate, I felt
too much uncertainty about who I had become. Uncertain about whether
I had managed to make it through without giving up the best of myself,
the best of the values I had been raised to believe in—hard work, honesty,
and respect for everyone no matter their class—I finished my education
with my allegiance to the working class intact. Even so, I had planted my
feet on the path leading in the direction of class privilege. There would always be contradictions to face. There would always be confrontations
around the issue of class. I would always have to reexamine where I stand.

The Reader's Presence

1. Hooks writes that she "began to crack under the pressure of contradictory values and longings" (paragraph 25). How would you
   define these opposing pressures? In what way are they central to the
   essay? Does she resolve these contradictions by the end of the essay?

2. According to hooks, why is it difficult to succeed in academia and at
   the same time retain one's allegiance to a working-class background? Why do you think she believes it is valuable to do so?
   What values does she find inherent in the working class that other
   classes apparently lack?

3. How do hooks's attitudes about class compare with those of two
   other African American writers whose essays appear in this part
   of the book, Maya Angelou (see page 73) and Jamaica Kincaid
   (see page 154)? In what ways do these three writers view race and
   class as separate modes of identity?

22

Langston Hughes

Salvation

One of the leading figures of the Harlem Renaissance, Langston Hughes (1902–1967) was a prolific writer. He started his career as a poet, but he also wrote fiction, autobiography, biography, history, and plays, and he worked at various times as a journalist. One of his most famous poems, "The Negro Speaks of Rivers," was written while he was a high school student. Although Langston Hughes traveled widely, most of his writings are concerned with the lives of urban working-class African Americans.

Hughes used the rhythms of blues and jazz to bring to his writing a distinctive expression of black culture and experience. His work continues to be popular today, especially collections of short stories such as The Ways of White Folks (1934), volumes of poetry such as Montage of a Dream Deferred (1951), and his series of vignettes on the character Jesse B. Simple, collected and published from 1950 to 1965. Hughes published two volumes of autobiography; "Salvation" is taken from the first of these, The Big Sea (1940).

Throughout his work, Hughes refused to idealize his subject. "Certainly," he said, "I personally knew very few people anywhere who were wholly beautiful and wholly good. Besides I felt that the masses of our people had as much in their lives to put into books as did those more fortunate ones who had been born with some means and the ability to work up to a master's degree at a Northern college." Expressing the writer's truism about writing about what one knows best, he continued, "Anyway, I didn't know the upper-class Negroes well enough to write much about them. I only knew the people I had grown up with, and they weren't the people whose shoes were always shined, who had been to Harvard, or who had heard of Bach. But they seemed to me good people too."

I was saved from sin when I was going on thirteen. But not really saved. It happened like this. There was a big revival at my Auntie Reed's church. Every night for weeks there had been much preaching, singing, praying, and shouting, and some very hardened sinners had been brought to Christ, and the membership of the church had grown by leaps and bounds. Then just before the revival ended, they held a special meeting for children, "to bring the young lambs to the fold." My aunt spoke of it for days ahead. That night I was escorted to the front row and placed on the mourners' bench with all the other young sinners, who had not yet been brought to Jesus.

My aunt told me that when you were saved you saw a light, and something happened to you inside! And Jesus came into your life! And God was with you from then on! She said you could see and hear and feel Jesus in your soul. I believed her. I had heard a great many old people say the same thing and it seemed to me they ought to know. So I sat there calmly in the hot, crowded church, waiting for Jesus to come to me.

The preacher preached a wonderful rhythmical sermon, all moans and shouts and lonely cries and dire pictures of hell, and then he sang a song about the ninety and nine safe in the fold, but one little lamb was left out in the cold. Then he said: "Won't you come? Won't you come to Jesus? Young lambs, won't you come?" And he held out his arms to all us young sinners there on the mourners' bench. And the little girls cried. And some of them jumped up and went to Jesus right away. But most of us just sat there.

A great many old people came and knelt around us and prayed, old women with jet-black faces and braided hair, old men with work-gnarled hands. And the church sang a song about the lower lights are burning, some poor sinners to be saved. And the whole building rocked with prayer and song.

Still I kept waiting to *see* Jesus.   5

Finally all the young people had gone to the altar and were saved, but one boy and me. He was a rounder's son named Westley. Westley and I were surrounded by sisters and deacons praying. It was very hot in the church, and getting late now. Finally Westley said to me in a whisper: "God damn! I'm tired o' sitting here. Let's get up and be saved." So he got up and was saved.

Then I was left all alone on the mourners' bench. My aunt came and knelt at my knees and cried, while prayers and song swirled all around me in the little church. The whole congregation prayed for me alone, in a mighty wail of moans and voices. And I kept waiting serenely for Jesus, waiting, waiting—but he didn't come. I wanted to see him, but nothing happened to me. Nothing! I wanted something to happen to me, but nothing happened.

I heard the songs and the minister saying: "Why don't you come? My dear child, why don't you come to Jesus? Jesus is waiting for you. He wants you. Why don't you come? Sister Reed, what is this child's name?"

"Langston," my aunt sobbed.

"Langston, why don't you come? Why don't you come and be saved?   10 Oh, Lamb of God! Why don't you come?"

Now it was really getting late. I began to be ashamed of myself, holding everything up so long. I began to wonder what God thought about Westley, who certainly hadn't seen Jesus either, but who was now sitting proudly on the platform, swinging his knickerbockered legs and grinning down at me, surrounded by deacons and old women on their knees praying. God had not struck Westley dead for taking his name in vain or for lying in the temple. So I decided that maybe to save further trouble, I'd better lie, too, and say that Jesus had come, and get up and be saved.

So I got up.

Suddenly the whole room broke into a sea of shouting, as they saw me rise. Waves of rejoicing swept the place. Women leaped in the air. My aunt threw her arms around me. The minister took me by the hand and led me to the platform.

When things quieted down, in a hushed silence, punctuated by a few ecstatic "Amens," all the new young lambs were blessed in the name of God. Then joyous singing filled the room.

That night, for the first time in my life but one — for I was a big boy   15
twelve years old — I cried. I cried, in bed alone, and couldn't stop. I buried my head under the quilts, but my aunt heard me. She woke up and told my uncle I was crying because the Holy Ghost had come into my life, and because I had seen Jesus. But I was really crying because I couldn't bear to tell her that I had lied, that I had deceived everybody in the church, that I hadn't seen Jesus, and that now I didn't believe there was a Jesus anymore, since he didn't come to help me.

The Reader's Presence

1. Pay close attention to Hughes's two opening sentences. How would you describe their tone? How do they suggest the underlying pattern of the essay? How do they introduce the idea of deception right from the start? Who is being deceived in the essay? Is it the congregation? God? Hughes's aunt? the reader?

2. Hughes's essay is full of hyperbole, much of it expressing the heightened emotion of religious conversion. What is the purpose of the exclamation points Hughes uses in paragraph 2? Who is speaking these sentences? Where are other examples of overstatement? How does Hughes incorporate lyrics from songs into his prose (see especially paragraph 3. Why not simply quote from the songs directly? How do these stylistic decisions affect your sense of the scene? Do you feel aligned with Hughes? Why or why not?

3. How does Hughes use the character of Westley? Is he essential to the narrative? If so, why? How does his role compare to secondary characters in other essays; for example, Theresa in Bernard Cooper's "A Clack of Tiny Sparks" (page 104) or Shorty in Malcolm X's "Homeboy" (page 178)?

THE WRITER AT WORK

Langston Hughes on "How to Be a Bad Writer (in Ten Easy Lessons)"

Established authors are frequently asked for tips on writing. Here Langston Hughes reverses the practice and offers young writers some memorable advice on how to write poorly. "How to Be a Bad Writer" first appeared in The Harlem Quarterly *(Spring 1950). Some of his suggestions no longer seem applicable today, thanks in part to his own literary efforts. But which lessons do you think are still worth paying attention to?*

1. Use all the clichés possible, such as "He had a gleam in his eye," or "Her teeth were white as pearls."

2. If you are a Negro, try very hard to write with an eye dead on the white market—use modern stereotypes of older stereotypes—big burly Negroes, criminals, low-lifers, and prostitutes.

3. Put in a lot of profanity and as many pages as possible of near-pornography and you will be so modern you pre-date Pompei in your lonely crusade toward the best seller lists. By all means be misunderstood, unappreciated, and ahead of your time in print and out, then you can be felt-sorry-for by your own self, if not the public.

4. Never characterize characters. Just name them and then let them go for themselves. Let all of them talk the same way. If the reader hasn't imagination enough to make something out of cardboard cut-outs, shame on him!

5. Write about China, Greece, Tibet, or the Argentine pampas—anyplace you've never seen and know nothing about. Never write about anything you know, your home town, or your home folks, or yourself.

6. Have nothing to say, but use a great many words, particularly high-sounding words, to say it.

7. If a playwright, put into your script a lot of hand-waving and spirituals, preferably the ones everybody has heard a thousand times from Marion Anderson to the Golden Gates.

8. If a poet, rhyme June with moon as often and in as many ways as possible. Also use *thee*'s and *thou*'s and *'tis* and *o'er,* and invert your sentences all the time. Never say, "The sun rose, bright and shining." But, rather, "Bright and shining rose the sun."

9. Pay no attention to spelling or grammar or the neatness of the manuscript. And in writing letters, never sign your name so anyone can read it. A rapid scrawl will better indicate how important and how busy you are.

10. Drink as much liquor as possible and always write under the influence of alcohol. When you can't afford alcohol yourself, or even if you can, drink on your friends, fans, and the general public.

If you are white, there are many more things I can advise in order to be a bad writer, but since this piece is for colored writers, there are some things I know a Negro just will not do, not even for writing's sake, so there is no use mentioning them.

23

Zora Neale Hurston
How It Feels to Be Colored Me

Born in Eatonville, Florida, in a year that she never remembered the same way twice, Zora Neale Hurston (1901?–1960) entered Howard University in 1923. In 1926 she won a scholarship to Barnard College, where she was the first black woman to be admitted. There Hurston developed an interest in anthropology, which was cultivated by Columbia University's distinguished anthropologist, Frank Boas. From 1928 to 1931 she collected voodoo folklore in the South and published her findings in Mules and Men *(1935). Two successive Guggenheim Fellowships allowed her to do field work in the Caribbean, resulting in another anthropological study,* Tell My Horse *(1938). She also collected folklore about Florida for the Work Projects Administration and published the two novels for which she is justly famous,* Jonah's Gourd Vine *(1934), and* Their Eyes Were Watching God *(1937).*

Langston Hughes said that "she was always getting scholarships and things from wealthy white people." But when the economy collapsed and brought the famous Harlem Renaissance down with it, Hurston's patrons all but disappeared. She managed to publish two more books, Moses, Man of the Mountain *(1939) and* Seraph on the Suwanee *(1948), and her autobiography,* Dust Tracks on a Road *(1942), before her reputation suffered a serious decline during the 1950s. After working as a librarian, part-time teacher, and maid near the end of her life, Hurston died in a county welfare home in Florida in virtual obscurity. The rediscovery of her work is largely attributed to Alice Walker, who edited a collection of Hurston's writings,* I Love Myself When I'm Laughing *(1975). "How It Feels to Be Colored Me" originally appeared in* The World Tomorrow *in 1928.*

Hurston said, "I regret all my books. It is one of the tragedies of life that one cannot have all the wisdom one is ever to possess in the beginning. Perhaps, it is just as well to be rash and foolish for a while. If writers were too wise, perhaps no books would be written at all. It might be better to ask yourself 'Why?' afterwards than before. Anyway, the force from somewhere in Space which commands you to write in the first place, gives you no choice. You take up the pen when you are told, and write what is commanded. There is no agony like bearing an untold story inside you."

I am colored but I offer nothing in the way of extenuating circumstances except the fact that I am the only Negro in the United States whose grandfather on the mother's side was *not* an Indian chief.

I remember the very day that I became colored. Up to my thirteenth year I lived in the little Negro town of Eatonville, Florida. It is exclusively a colored town. The only white people I knew passed through the town going to or coming from Orlando. The native whites rode dusty horses, the Northern tourists chugged down the sandy village road in automobiles. The town knew the Southerners and never stopped cane chewing[1] when they passed. But the Northerners were something else again. They were peered at cautiously from behind curtains by the timid. The more venturesome would come out on the porch to watch them go past and got just as much pleasure out of the tourists as the tourists got out of the village.

The front porch might seem a daring place for the rest of the town, but it was a gallery seat for me. My favorite place was atop the gate-post. Proscenium box for a born first-nighter. Not only did I enjoy the show, but I didn't mind the actors knowing that I liked it. I usually spoke to them in passing. I'd wave at them and when they returned my salute, I would say something like this: "Howdy-do-well-I-thank-you-where-you-goin'?" Usually automobile or the horse paused at this, and after a queer exchange of compliments, I would probably "go a piece of the way" with them, as we say in farthest Florida. If one of my family happened to come to the front in time to see me, of course negotiations would be rudely broken off. But even so, it is clear that I was the first "welcome-to-our-state" Floridian, and I hope the Miami Chamber of Commerce will please take notice.

During this period, white people differed from colored to me only in that they rode through town and never lived there. They liked to hear me "speak pieces" and sing and wanted to see me dance the parse-me-la,[2] and gave me generously of their small silver for doing these things, which seemed strange to me for I wanted to do them so much that I needed bribing to stop. Only they didn't know it. The colored people gave no dimes. They deplored any joyful tendencies in me, but I was their Zora nevertheless. I belonged to them, to the nearby hotels, to the county—everybody's Zora.

But changes came in the family when I was thirteen, and I was sent to school in Jacksonville. I left Eatonville, the town of the oleanders, as Zora. When I disembarked from the river-boat at Jacksonville, she was no more. It seemed that I had suffered a sea change. I was not Zora of Orange County any more, I was now a little colored girl. I found it out in certain ways. In my heart as well as in the mirror, I became a fast brown—warranted not to rub nor run.

But I am not tragically colored. There is no great sorrow dammed up in my soul, nor lurking behind my eyes. I do not mind at all. I do not belong to the sobbing school of Negrohood who hold that nature somehow

5

---

[1] *cane chewing:* Chewing on sugar cane. — EDS.
[2] *parse-me-la:* Probably an old dance song. — EDS.

has given them a lowdown dirty deal and whose feelings are all hurt about it. Even in the helter-skelter skirmish that is my life, I have seen that the world is to the strong regardless of a little pigmentation more or less. No, I do not weep at the world—I am too busy sharpening my oyster knife.

Someone is always at my elbow reminding me that I am the grand-daughter of slaves. It fails to register depression with me. Slavery is sixty years in the past. The operation was successful and the patient is doing well, thank you. The terrible struggle that made me an American out of a potential slave said "On the line!" The Reconstruction[3] said "Get set!"; and the generation before said "Go!" I am off to a flying start and I must not halt in the stretch to look behind and weep. Slavery is the price I paid for civilization, and the choice was not with me. It is a bully adventure and worth all that I have paid through my ancestors for it. No one on earth ever had a greater chance for glory. The world to be won and noth-ing to be lost. It is thrilling to think—to know that for any act of mine, I shall get twice as much praise or twice as much blame. It is quite exciting to hold the center of the national stage, with the spectators not knowing whether to laugh or to weep.

The position of my white neighbor is much more difficult. No brown specter pulls up a chair beside me when I sit down to eat. No dark ghost thrusts its leg against mine in bed. The game of keeping what one has is never so exciting as the game of getting.

I do not always feel colored. Even now I often achieve the uncon-scious Zora of Eatonville before the Hegira.[4] I feel most colored when I am thrown against a sharp white background.

For instance at Barnard. "Beside the waters of the Hudson" I feel my race. Among the thousand white persons, I am a dark rock surged upon, and overswept, but through it all, I remain myself. When covered by the waters, I am; and the ebb but reveals me again.   10

Sometimes it is the other way around. A white person is set down in our midst, but the contrast is just as sharp for me. For instance, when I sit in the drafty basement that is The New World Cabaret with a white per-son, my color comes. We enter chatting about any little nothing that we have in common and are seated by the jazz waiters. In the abrupt way that jazz orchestras have, this one plunges into a number. It loses no time in circumlocutions, but gets right down to business. It constricts the tho-rax and splits the heart with its tempo and narcotic harmonies. This or-chestra grows rambunctious, rears on its hind legs and attacks the tonal veil with primitive fury, rending it, clawing it until it breaks through to

---

[3]***Reconstruction:*** The period of rebuilding and reorganizing immediately following the Civil War. — EDS.

[4]***Hegira:*** A journey to safety. Historically it refers to Mohammed's flight from Mecca in A.D. 622. — EDS.

the jungle beyond. I follow those heathen—follow them exultingly. I dance wildly inside myself; I yell within, I whoop; I shake my assegai[5] above my head, I hurl it true to the mark *yeeeeooww!* I am in the jungle and living in the jungle way. My face is painted red and yellow and my body is painted blue. My pulse is throbbing like a war drum. I want to slaughter something—give pain, give death to what, I do not know. But the piece ends. The men of the orchestra wipe their lips and rest their fingers. I creep back slowly to the veneer we call civilization with the last tone and find the white friend sitting motionless in his seat, smoking calmly.

"Good music they have here," he remarks, drumming the table with his fingertips.

Music. The great blobs of purple and red emotion have not touched him. He has only heard what I felt. He is far away and I see him but dimly across the ocean and the continent that have fallen between us. He is so pale with his whiteness then and I am *so* colored.

At certain times I have no race, I am *me.* When I set my hat at a certain angle and saunter down Seventh Avenue, Harlem City, feeling as snooty as the lions in front of the Forty-Second Street Library, for instance. So far as my feelings are concerned, Peggy Hopkins Joyce[6] on the Boule Mich[7] with her gorgeous raiment, stately carriage, knees knocking together in a most aristocratic manner, has nothing on me. The cosmic Zora emerges. I belong to no race nor time. I am the eternal feminine with its string of beads.

I have no separate feeling about being an American citizen and colored. I am merely a fragment of the Great Soul that surges within the boundaries. My country, right or wrong.   15

Sometimes, I feel discriminated against, but it does not make me angry. It merely astonishes me. How *can* any deny themselves the pleasure of my company? It's beyond me.

But in the main, I feel like a brown bag of miscellany propped against a wall. Against a wall in company with other bags, white, red, and yellow. Pour out the contents, and there is discovered a jumble of small things priceless and worthless. A first-water diamond, an empty spool, bits of broken glass, lengths of string, a key to a door long since crumbled away, a rusty knife-blade, old shoes saved for a road that never was and never will be, a nail bent under the weight of things too heavy for any nail, a dried flower or two still a little fragrant. In your hand is the brown bag. On the ground before you is the jumble it held—so much like the jumble in the bags, could they be emptied, that all might be dumped in a single heap and

---

[5]*assegai:* A hunting spear.—EDS.

[6]*Peggy Hopkins Joyce:* A fashionable American who was a celebrity in the 1920s.—EDS.

[7]*Boule Mich:* The Boulevard Saint-Michel in Paris.—EDS.

the bags refilled without altering the content of any greatly. A bit of colored glass more or less would not matter. Perhaps that is how the Great Stuffer of Bags filled them in the first place—who knows?

The Reader's Presence

1. How much does being "colored" inform Hurston's identity? Does it seem to matter throughout the essay? At what points does color seem deeply important to Hurston? When does it seem less important? What do you think the reasons are for these differences?

2. Consider Hurston's startling image in the final paragraph: "But in the main, I feel like a brown bag of miscellany propped against a wall." Try rereading the essay with this image in mind. In what ways does it help you understand Hurston's sense of personal identity? In what ways can it be said to describe the form and style of the essay itself?

3. Hurston uses an extended description of jazz at The New World Cabaret to illustrate the claim: "I feel most colored when I am thrown against a sharp white background" (paragraph 9). Does Malcolm X's experience at the Roseland State Ballroom in Boston teach him the same lesson in "Homeboy" (see page 178)? How might Malcolm X respond to Hurston's claim that at times she has "no race" (paragraph 14)? What might he say to her statement, "I do not belong to the sobbing school of Negrohood" (paragraph 6)? What are Hurston's and Malcolm X's definitions of "race"? How do these definitions compare to that of Richard Rodriguez, who says that he has been "liberated . . . from the black-and-white checkerboard" (see page 240)?

24

Jamaica Kincaid
Biography of a Dress

Jamaica Kincaid was born in Antigua in 1949 and came to the United States at the age of seventeen to work for a New York family as an au pair. Her novel Lucy *(1990) is an imaginative account of her experience of coming into adult-*

hood in a foreign country and continues the narrative of her personal history begun in the novel Annie John *(1985). She has also published a collection of short stories,* At the Bottom of the River *(1983), a collection of essays,* A Small Place *(1988), and a third novel,* The Autobiography of My Mother *(1995). Her most recent publications include* My Brother *(1997), which was a National Book Award Finalist for Nonfiction,* My Favorite Plant: Writers and Gardeners on the Plants They Love *(1998),* My Garden *(2001), and* Mr. Potter *(2002). Her writing also appears in national magazines, especially the* New Yorker, *where she worked as a staff writer until 1995.*

"I'm someone who writes to save her life," Kincaid says, "I mean, I can't imagine what I would do if I didn't write. I would be dead or I would be in jail because—what else could I do? I can't really do anything but write. All the things that were available to someone in my position involved being a subject person. And I'm very bad at being a subject person."

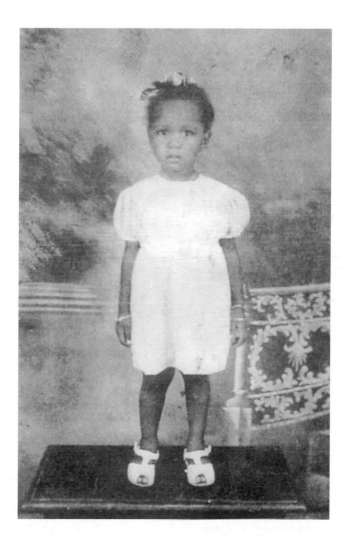

The dress I am wearing in this black-and-white photograph, taken when I was two years old, was a yellow dress made of cotton poplin (a fabric with a slightly unsmooth texture first manufactured in the French town of Avignon and brought to England by the Huguenots, but I could not have known that at the time), and it was made for me by my mother. This shade of yellow, the color of my dress that I am wearing when I was two years old, was the same shade of yellow as boiled cornmeal, a food that my mother was always eager for me to eat in one form (as a porridge) or another (as fongie, the starchy part of my midday meal) because it was cheap and therefore easily available (but I did not know that at the time), and because she thought that foods bearing the colors yellow, green or orange were particularly rich in vitamins and so boiled cornmeal would be particularly good for me. But I was then (not so now) extremely particular about what I would eat, not knowing then (but I do now) of shortages and abundance, having no consciousness of the idea of rich and poor (but I know now that we were poor then), and would eat only boiled beef (which I required my mother to chew for me first and, after she had made it soft, remove it from her mouth and place it in mine), certain kinds of boiled fish (doctor or angel), hard-boiled eggs (from hens, not ducks), poached calf's liver and the milk from cows, and so would not even look at the boiled cornmeal (porridge or fongie). There was not one single thing that I could isolate and say I did not like about the boiled cornmeal (porridge or fongie) because I could not isolate parts of things then (though I can and do now), but whenever I saw this bowl of trembling yellow substance before me I would grow still and silent, I did not cry, that did not make me cry. My mother told me this then (she does not tell me this now, she does not remember this now, she does not remember telling me this now): she knew of a man who had eaten boiled cornmeal at least once a day from the time he was my age then, two years old, and he lived for a very long time, finally dying when he was almost one hundred years old, and when he died he had looked rosy and new, with the springy wrinkles of the newborn, not the slack pleats of skin of the aged; as he lay dead his stomach was cut open, and all his insides were a beautiful shade of yellow, the same shade of yellow as boiled cornmeal. I was powerless then (though not so now) to like or dislike this story; it was beyond me then (though not so now) to understand the span of my lifetime then, two years old, and it was beyond me then (though not so now), the span of time called almost one hundred years old; I did not know then (though I do now) that there was such a thing as an inside to anybody, and that this inside would have a color, and that if the insides were the same shade of yellow as the yellow of boiled cornmeal my mother would want me to know about it.

On a day when it was not raining (that would have been unusual, that would have been out of the ordinary, ruining the fixed form of the day), my mother walked to one of the Harneys stores (there were many Harneys who owned stores, and they sold the same things, but I did not know then and I do not know now if they were all of the same people) and bought one-and-a-half yards of this yellow cotton poplin to make a dress for me, a dress I would wear to have my picture taken on the day I turned two years old. Inside, the store was cool and dark, and this was a good thing because outside was hot and overly bright. Someone named Harney did not wait on my mother, but someone named Miss Verna did and she was very nice still, so nice that she tickled my cheek as she spoke to my mother, and I reached forward as if to kiss her, but when her cheek met my lips I opened my mouth and bit her hard with my small child's teeth. Her cry of surprise did not pierce the air, but she looked at me hard, as if she knew me very, very well; and later, much later, when I was about twelve years old or so and she was always in and out of the crazy house, I would pass her on the street and throw stones at her, and she would turn and look at me hard, but she did not know who I was, she did not know who anyone was at all, not at all. Miss Verna showed my mother five flat thick bolts of cloth, white, blue (sea), blue (sky), yellow and pink, and my mother chose the yellow after holding it up against the rich copper color that my hair was then (it is not so now); she paid for it with a one-pound note that had an engraving of the king George Fifth on it (an ugly man with a cruel, sharp, bony nose, not the kind, soft, fleshy noses I was then used to), and she received change that included crowns, shillings, florins, and farthings.

My mother, carrying me and the just-bought piece of yellow poplin wrapped in coarse brown paper in her arms, walked out of Mr. Harney's store, up the street a few doors away, and into a store called Murdoch's (because the family who owned it were the Murdochs), and there my mother bought two skeins of yellow thread, the kind used for embroidering and a shade of yellow almost identical to the yellow poplin. My mother not only took me with her everywhere she went, she carried me, sometimes in her arms, sometimes on her back; for this errand she carried me in her arms; she did not complain, she never complained (but later she refused to do it anymore and never gave an explanation, at least not one that I can remember now); as usual, she spoke to me and sang to me in French patois (but I did not understand French patois then and I do not now and so I can never know what exactly she said to me then). She walked back to our house on Dickenson Bay Street, stopping often to hold conversations with people (men and women) she knew, speaking to them sometimes in English, sometimes in French; and if after they said how beautiful I was (for people would often say that about me then but they do not say that about me now), she would laugh and say that I did not like to be kissed (and I don't know if that was really true then but it is not so now). And that night after we had eaten our supper (boiled fish in a butter-and-lemon-juice sauce) and her husband (who was not my father but I did not know that at the time, I know that now) had gone for a walk (to the jetty), she removed her yellow poplin from its brown wrapper and folded and made creases in it and with scissors made holes (for the arms and neck) and slashes (for an opening in the back and the shoulders); she then placed it along with some ordinary thread (yellow), the thread for embroidering, the scissors and a needle in a basket that she had brought with her from her home in Dominica when she first left it at sixteen years of age.

For days afterward, my mother, after she had finished her usual chores (clothes washing, dish washing, floor scrubbing, bathing me, her only child, feeding me a teaspoon of cod-liver-oil), sat on the sill of the doorway, half in the sun, half out of the sun, and sewed together the various parts that would make up altogether my dress of yellow poplin; she gathered and hemmed and made tucks; she was just in the early stages of teaching herself how to make smocking and so was confined to making straight stitches (up-cable, down-cable, outline, stem, chain); the bodice of the dress appeared simple, plain, and the detail and pattern can only be seen close up and in real life, not from far away and not in a photograph; and much later, when she grew in confidence with this craft, the bodice of my dresses became overburdened with the stitches, chevron, trellis, diamonds, Vandyke, and species of birds she had never seen (swan) and species of flowers she had never seen (tulip) and species of animals she had never seen (bear) in real life, only in a picture in a book.

My skin was not the color of cream in the process of spoiling, my   5
hair was not the texture of silk and the color of flax, my eyes did not gleam like blue jewels in a crown, the afternoons in which I sat watching my mother make me this dress were not cool, and verdant lawns and pastures and hills and dales did not stretch out before me; but it was the picture of such a girl at two years old—a girl whose skin was the color of cream in the process of spoiling, whose hair was the texture of silk and the color of flax, a girl whose eyes gleamed like blue jewels in a crown, a girl whose afternoons (and mornings and nights) were cool, and before whom stretched verdant lawns and pastures and hills and dales—that my mother saw, a picture on an almanac advertising a particularly fine and scented soap (a soap she could not afford to buy then but I can now), and this picture of this girl wearing a yellow dress with smocking on the front bodice perhaps created in my mother the desire to have a daughter who looked like that or perhaps created the desire in my mother to try and make the daughter she already had look like that. I do not know now and I did not know then. And who was that girl really? (I did not ask then because I could not ask then but I ask now.) And who made her dress? And this girl would have had a mother; did the mother then have some friends, other women, did they sit together under a tree (or sit somewhere else) and compare strengths of potions used to throw away a child, or weigh the satisfactions to be had from the chaos of revenge or the smooth order of forgiveness; and this girl with skin of cream on its way to spoiling and hair the color of flax, what did her insides look like, what did she eat? (I did not ask then because I could not ask then and I ask now but no one can answer me, really answer me.)

My second birthday was not a major event in anyone's life, certainly not my own (it was not my first and it was not my last, I am now forty-three years old), but my mother, perhaps because of circumstances (I would not have known then and to know now is not a help), perhaps only because of an established custom (but only in her family, other people didn't do this), to mark the occasion of my turning two years old had my ears pierced. One day, at dusk (I would not have called it that then), I was taken to someone's house (a woman from Dominica, a woman who was as dark as my mother was fair, and yet they were so similar that I am sure now as I was then that they shared the same tongue), and two thorns that had been heated in a fire were pierced through my earlobes. I do not now know (and could not have known then) if the pain I experienced resembled in any way the pain my mother experienced while giving birth to me or even if my mother, in having my ears bored in that way, at that time, meant to express hostility or aggression toward me (but without meaning to and without knowing that it was possible to mean to). For days afterward my earlobes were swollen and covered with a golden crust (which might have glistened in the harsh sunlight, but I can only imagine that now), and the pain of my earlobes must have filled up all that made up my entire being then and the pain of my earlobes must have been unbearable, because it was then that was the first time that I separated myself from myself, and I became two people (two small children then, I was two years old), one having the experience, the other observing the one having the experience. And the observer, perhaps because it was an act of my own will (strong then, but stronger now), my first and only real act of self-invention, is the one of the two I most rely on, the one of the two whose voice I believe to be the true voice; and of course it is the observer who cannot be relied on as the final truth to be believed, for the observer has woven between myself and the person who is having an experience a protective membrane, which allows me to see but only feel as much as I can handle at any given moment. And so . . .

. . . On the day I turned two years old, the twenty-fifth of May 1951, a pair of earrings, small hoops made of gold from British Guiana (it was called that then, it is not called that now), were placed in the bored holes in my earlobes (which by then had healed); a pair of bracelets made of silver from someplace other than British Guiana (and that place too was called one thing then, something else now) was placed one on each wrist; a pair of new shoes bought from Bata's was placed on my feet. That afternoon, I was bathed and powdered, and the dress of yellow poplin, completed, its seams all stitched together with a certainty found only in the natural world (I now realize), was placed over my head, and it is quite possible that this entire act had about it the feeling of being draped in a shroud. My mother, carrying me in her arms (as usual), took me to the studio of a photographer, a man named Mr. Walker, to have my picture taken. As she walked along with me in her arms (not complaining), with the heat of the sun still so overwhelming that it, not gravity, seemed to be the force that kept us pinned to the earth's surface, I placed my lips against one side of her head (the temple) and could feel the rhythm of the blood pulsing through her body; I placed my lips against her throat and could hear her swallow saliva that had collected in her mouth; I placed my face against her neck and inhaled deeply a scent that I could not identify then (how could I, there was nothing to compare it to) and cannot now, because it is not of animal or place or thing, it was (and is) a scent unique to her, and it left a mark of such depth that it eventually became a part of my other senses, and even now (yes, now) that scent is also taste, touch, sight, and sound.

And Mr. Walker lived on Church Street in a house that was mysterious to me (then, not now) because it had a veranda (unlike my own house) and it had many rooms (unlike my own house, but really Mr. Walker's house had only four rooms, my own house had one) and the windows were closed (the windows in my house were always open). He spoke to my mother, I did not understand what they said, they did not share the same tongue. I knew Mr. Walker was a man, but how I knew that I cannot say (now, then, sometime to come). It is possible that because he touched his hair often, smoothing down, caressing, the forcibly straightened strands, and because he admired and said that he admired my dress of yellow poplin with its simple smocking (giving to me a false air of delicacy), and because he admired and said that he admired the plaid taffeta ribbon in my hair, I thought that he perhaps wasn't a man at all, I had never seen a man do or say any of those things, I had then only seen a woman do or say those things. He (Mr. Walker) stood next to a black box which had a curtain at its back (this was his camera but I did not know that at the time, I only know it now) and he asked my mother to stand me on a table, a small table, a table that made me taller, because the scene in the background, against which I was to be photographed, was so vast, it overwhelmed my two-year-old frame, making me seem a mere figurine, not a child at all; and when my mother picked me up, holding me by the armpits with her hands, her thumb accidentally (it could have been deliberate, how could someone who loved me inflict so much pain just in passing?) pressed deeply into my shoulder, and I cried out and then (and still now) looked up at her face and couldn't find any reason in it, and could find no malice in it, only that her eyes were full of something, a feeling that I thought then (and am convinced now) had nothing to do with me; and of course it is possible that just at that moment she had realized that she was exhausted, not physically, but just exhausted by this whole process, celebrating my second birthday, commemorating an event, my birth, that she may not have wished to occur in the first place and may have tried repeatedly to prevent, and then, finally, in trying to find some beauty in it, ended up with a yard and a half of yellow poplin being shaped into a dress, teaching herself smocking and purchasing gold hoops from places whose names never remained the same and silver bracelets from places whose names never remained the same. And Mr.

Walker, who was not at all interested in my mother's ups and downs and would never have dreamed of taking in the haphazard mess of her life (but there was nothing so unusual about that, every life, I now know, is a haphazard mess), looked on for a moment as my mother, belying the look in her eyes, said kind and loving words to me in a kind and loving voice, and he then walked over to a looking glass that hung on a wall and squeezed with two of his fingers a lump the size of a pinch of sand that was on his cheek; the lump had a shiny white surface and it broke, emitting a tiny plap sound, and from it came a long ribbon of thick, yellow pus that curled on Mr. Walker's cheek imitating, almost, the decoration on the birthday cake that awaited me at home, and my birthday cake was decorated with a series of species of flora and fauna my mother had never seen (and still has not seen to this day, she is seventy-three years old).

After that day I never again wore my yellow poplin dress with the smocking my mother had just taught herself to make. It was carefully put aside, saved for me to wear to another special occasion; but by the time another special occasion came (I could say quite clearly then what the special occasion was and can say quite clearly now what the special occasion was but I do not want to), the dress could no longer fit me, I had grown too big for it.

The Reader's Presence

1. Kincaid's prose style is unusual. Read the first few sentences of the essay aloud. How does Kincaid use repetition? What is the relation of the parenthetical phrases to the main sentences? Are Kincaid's sentences "run-on" sentences? What is the effect of their length and sweep? Summarize the essay's "plot." What details beyond simple actions matter to Kincaid? Compare Kincaid's style in this essay to her style in the short story "Girl" (page 840).

2. The writer's early surroundings are evoked through objects and sensations; she never identifies the locale nor explicitly describes it. The reader is forced to absorb potentially unfamiliar background material in the course of following the plot. How might this experience parallel that of the young Kincaid, navigating a world full of alien images? How might Kincaid's stylistic approach serve to challenge traditional colonial hierarchies?

3. Kincaid interrupts her primary story, set in the past, with parenthetical references to the present. How does the writer's adult perspective enhance or detract from the story of childhood? What does Kincaid think of her younger self? Do the interjections interpret the earlier story, or simply add another layer of narrative? Can you infer how memory works for Kincaid? How does Kincaid's essay compare to E. B. White's meditation upon memory in "Once More to the Lake" (see page 281)?

25

Eric Liu

Creating an Asian American Identity

Eric Liu was born in 1968 in Poughkeepsie, New York, and attended Yale University, graduating in 1990. In the year of his Yale graduation, Liu founded The Next Progressive, *a quarterly journal of Democratic party politics and culture. In 1993 he joined the speech-writing staff of President Clinton as its youngest and only Asian American member. Liu currently attends Harvard Law School. He has contributed many articles and essays to magazines, including the* Washington Post *and* USA Weekend, *and edited an influential anthology titled* Next: Young American Writers on the New Generation *(1994). The Accidental Asian: Notes of a Native Speaker (1998) is a collection of related essays on the personal and sociological implications of being Asian American. Liu treats the subject of racial identity with marked ambivalence, at one point describing himself as "someone who has stumbled onto a sense of race; who wonders now what to do with it." The following essay is excerpted from* The Accidental Asian.

The Asian American identity was born, as I was, roughly thirty years ago. In those three decades it has struggled to find relevance and a coherent voice. As I have. It has tried to adapt itself to the prevailing attitudes about race—namely, that one matters in this society, if one is colored, mainly to the extent that one claims a race for oneself. I, too, have tried to accommodate these forces. The Asian American identity, like me, renounces whiteness. It draws strength from the possibility of transcending the fear and blindness of the past. So do I. It is the so very American product of a rejection of history's limitations, rooted in little more than its own creation a generation ago. As I am.

What I am saying is that I can identify with the Asian American identity. I understand why it does what it does. It is as if this identity and I were twin siblings, separated at birth but endowed with uncanny foreknowledge of each other's motives. The problem is, I disagree with it often. I become frustrated by it, even disappointed. The feeling is mutual, I suspect. We react to the same world in very different ways.

And yes, I do think of this identity as something that reacts, something almost alive, in the way that a shadow, or a mirror image — or a conscience — is almost alive. It has, if not a will of its own, then at least a highly developed habit of asserting its existence. It is like a storm, a beautiful, swirling weather pattern that moves back and forth across my mind. It draws me in, it repulses me. I am ever aware of its presence. There is always part of me that believes I will find deliverance if I merge with this identity. Yet still I hold it at a remove. For I fear that in the middle of this swirl, this great human churn, lies emptiness. . . .

Thirty-some years ago, there were no "Asian Americans." Not a single one. There were Japanese Americans, Chinese Americans, Filipino Americans, and so on: a disparate lot who shared only yellow-to-brown skin tones and the experience of bigotry that their pigmentation provoked. Though known to their countrymen, collectively, as "Orientals," and assumed to share common traits and cultures, they didn't think of themselves at all as a collective. It really wasn't until the upheavals of the late 1960s that some of them began to.

Stirred by the precedent of Black Power, a cadre of Asian student activists, mostly in California, performed an act of conceptual jujitsu: they would create a positive identity out of the unhappy fact that whites tend to lump all Asians together. Their first move was to throw off the "Oriental" label, which, to their thinking, was the cliché-ridden product of a colonial European gaze. They replaced it with "Yellow," and after protests from their darker-hued constituents, they replaced "Yellow" with "Asian American." In their campaign for semantic legitimacy, the ex-Orientals got an unlikely assist from bean counting federal bureaucrats. Looking to make affirmative action programs easier to document, the Office of Management and Budget in 1973 christened the term *Asian and Pacific Islander* for use in government forms. In the eyes of the feds, all Asians now looked alike. But this was a *good* thing.

The greatest problem for "Asian America," at least initially, was that this place existed mostly in the arid realm of census figures. It was a statistical category more than a social reality. In the last few decades, though, Asian American activists, intellectuals, artists, and students have worked, with increasing success, to transform their label into a lifestyle and to create, by every means available, a truly pan-ethnic identity for their ten million members. They have begun to build a nation.

The scholar Benedict Anderson has aptly defined the nation as an "imagined community," a grouping that relies for cohesion on an intangible, exclusive sense of connection among its far-flung members. Sometimes a nation has a state to enforce its will, sometimes it does not. But it must *always* have a mythology, a quasi-official culture that is communicated to all who belong, wherever they may be.

The Asian American narrative is rooted deeply in threat. That is one of the main things polyglot Americans of Asian descent have had in common: the fear of being discriminated against simply on account of being, metaphorically if not genetically, Chinamen. It is no accident that an early defining skirmish for Asian American activists was the push for Asian American Studies programs at San Francisco State and Berkeley in 1968. For what these programs did, in part, was to record and transmit the history of mistreatment that so many immigrants from Asia had endured over the centuries. Today, in the same vein, one of the most powerful allegories in Asian American lore is the tale of Vincent Chin, a Chinese American beaten to death in 1982 by two laid-off white auto workers who took him to be Japanese. The Chin story tells of a lingering strain of vicious, indiscriminate racism that can erupt without warning.

Yet no race can live on threat alone. To sustain a racial identity, there must be more than other people's racism, more than a negation. There must also be an affirmative sensibility, an aesthetic that emerges through the fusing of arts and letters with politics. Benedict Anderson again, in *Imagined Communities,* points to vernacular "print-capitalism" — books, newspapers, pamphlets — as the driving force of an incipient national consciousness. On the contemporary scene, perhaps no periodical better epitomizes the emerging aesthetic than the New York-based bimonthly *A. Magazine: Inside Asian America.*

Founded eight years ago by a Harvard graduate and entrepreneurial dynamo named Jeff Yang, *A. Magazine* covers fashion, politics, film, books, and trends in a style one might call Multiculti Chic. To flip through the glossy pages of this publication is to be swept into a cosmopolitan, cutting-edge world where Asians *matter.* It is to enter a realm populated by Asian and Asian American luminaries: actors like Jackie Chan and Margaret Cho, athletes like Michael Chang and Kristi Yamaguchi. It is to see everyday spaces and objects — sporting events, television shows, workplaces, bookstores, boutiques — through the eyes of a well-educated, socially conscious, politically aware, media-savvy, left-of-center, twenty-to-thirty-something, second-generation Asian American. It is to create, and be created by, an Ideal Asian.

There is something fantastic about all this, and I mean that in every way. That the children of Chinese and Japanese immigrants, or Korean and Japanese, or Indian and Pakistani, should so heedlessly disregard the animosities of their ancestors; that they should prove it possible to reinvent themselves as one community; that they should catalog their collective contributions to society so very sincerely: what can you say, really, but "Only in America?" There is an impressive, defiant ambition at work here: an assertion of ownership, a demand for respect. But there is also, on occasion, an under-oxygenated air of fantasy, a shimmering mirage of whitelessness and Asian self-sufficiency. A *dream.*

The dream of a nation-race called Asian America makes the most sense if you believe that the long-discredited "melting pot" was basically

10

replaced by a "quintuple melting pot." This is the multicultural method at its core: liquefy the differences *within* racial groups, solidify those *among* them. It is a method that many self-proclaimed Asian Americans, with the most meliorative of intentions, have applied to their own lives. They have thrown the *chink* and the *jap* and the *gook* and the *flip* into the same great bubbling cauldron. Now they await the emergence of a new and superior being, the *Asian American.* They wish him into existence. And what's troubling about this, frankly, is precisely what's inspiring: that it is possible.

The invention of a race testifies not only to the power of the human imagination but also to its limits. There is something awesome about the coalescence of a sprawling conglomerate identity. There is something frustrating as well, the sense that all this creativity and energy could have been harnessed to a greater end. For the challenge today is not only to announce the arrival of color. It is also to form combinations that lie beyond color. The creators of Asian America suggest that racial nationalism is the most meaningful way of claiming American life. I worry that it defers the greater task of confronting American life.

The Reader's Presence

1. At various points in his essay, Liu accepts and rejects the idea of an Asian American identity. What reasons does he give for accepting himself as an Asian American? What reasons does he give for not identifying himself as Asian American? If you were to attempt to change his mind about either viewpoint, what counterarguments would you make?

2. Go through each sentence in Liu's essay, changing the word *Asian* in the phrase *Asian American* to *African,* or *Latino,* or *Italian.* To what extent do Liu's claims still hold true? Which explanations of these various American identities continue to be applicable? Explain why. Which explanations no longer work? Why?

26

Nancy Mairs

On Being a Cripple

Nancy Mairs (b. 1943) has contributed poetry, short stories, articles, and essays to numerous journals. "On Being a Cripple" comes from, Plaintext, *which was published in 1986. More recent publications include* Remembering the Bone House: An Erotics of Time and Space *(1989),* Carnal Acts: Essays *(1990),* Ordinary Time: Cycles in Marriage, Faith, and Renewal *(1993), and* Waist High in the World: A Life Among the Nondisabled *(1996). Her current project is titled* Life's Worth: Rethinking How We Live and Die. *From 1983 to 1985 she served as assistant director of the Southwest Institute for Research on Women, and has also taught at the University of Arizona and at UCLA.*

In Voice Lessons: On Becoming a (Woman) Writer *(1994), she writes, "I want a prose that is allusive and translucent, that eases you into me and embraces you, not one that baffles you or bounces you around so that you can't even tell where I am. And so I have chosen to work, very, very carefully, with the language we share, faults and all, choosing each word for its capacity, its ambiguity, the space it provides for me to live my life within it, relating rather than opposing each word to the next, each sentence to the next, 'starting on all sides at once . . . twenty times, thirty times, over': the stuttering adventure of the essay."*

> To escape is nothing. Not to escape is nothing.
>
> —Louise Bogan

The other day I was thinking of writing an essay on being a cripple. I was thinking hard in one of the stalls of the women's room in my office building, as I was shoving my shirt into my jeans and tugging up my zipper. Preoccupied, I flushed, picked up my book bag, took my cane down from the hook, and unlatched the door. So many movements unbalanced me, and as I pulled the door open I fell over backward, landing fully clothed on the toilet seat with my legs splayed in front of me: the old beetle-on-its-back routine. Saturday afternoon, the building deserted, I was free to laugh aloud as I wriggled back to my feet, my voice bouncing off the yellowish tiles from all directions. Had anyone been there with me, I'd have been still and faint and hot with chagrin. I decided that it was high time to write the essay.

First, the matter of semantics. I am a cripple. I choose this word to name me. I choose from among several possibilities, the most common of which are "handicapped" and "disabled." I made the choice a number of years ago, without thinking, unaware of my motives for doing so. Even now, I'm not sure what those motives are, but I recognize that they are complex and not entirely flattering. People—crippled or not—wince at the word "cripple," as they do not at "handicapped" or "disabled." Perhaps I want them to wince. I want them to see me as a tough customer, one to whom the fates/gods/viruses have not been kind, but who can face the brutal truth of her existence squarely. As a cripple, I swagger.

But, to be fair to myself, a certain amount of honesty underlies my choice. "Cripple" seems to me a clean word, straightforward and precise. It has an honorable history, having made its first appearance in the Lindisfarne Gospel in the tenth century. As a lover of words, I like the accuracy with which it describes my condition: I have lost the full use of my limbs. "Disabled," by contrast, suggests any incapacity, physical or mental. And I certainly don't like "handicapped," which implies that I have deliberately been put at a disadvantage, by whom I can't imagine (my God is not a Handicapper General), in order to equalize chances in the great race of life. These words seem to me to be moving away from my condition, to be widening the gap between word and reality. Most remote is the recently coined euphemism "differently abled," which partakes of the same semantic hopefulness that transformed countries from "undeveloped" to "underdeveloped," then to "less developed," and finally to "developing" nations. People have continued to starve in those countries during the shift. Some realities do not obey the dictates of language.

Mine is one of them. Whatever you call me, I remain crippled. But I don't care what you call me, so long as it isn't "differently abled," which strikes me as pure verbal garbage designed, by its ability to describe anyone, to describe no one. I subscribe to George Orwell's thesis that "the slovenliness of our language makes it easier for us to have foolish thoughts."[1] And I refuse to participate in the degeneration of the language to the extent that I deny that I have lost anything in the course of this calamitous disease; I refuse to pretend that the only differences between you and me are the various ordinary ones that distinguish any one person from another. But call me "disabled" or "handicapped" if you like. I have long since grown accustomed to them; and if they are vague, at least they hint at the truth. Moreover, I use them myself. Society is no readier to accept crippledness than to accept death, war, sex, sweat, or wrinkles. I would never refer to another person as a cripple. It is the word I use to name only myself.

---

[1] *Orwell:* From his essay "Politics and The English Language" (see page 481). —EDS.

I haven't always been crippled, a fact for which I am soundly grateful.   5
To be whole of limb is, I know from experience, infinitely more pleasant
and useful than to be crippled: and if that knowledge leaves me open to
bitterness at my loss, the physical soundness I once enjoyed (though I did
not enjoy it half enough) is well worth the occasional stab of regret.
Though never any good at sports, I was a normally active child and young
adult. I climbed trees, played hopscotch, jumped rope, skated, swam, rode
my bicycle, sailed. I despised team sports, spending some of the
wretchedest afternoons of my life, sweaty and humiliated, behind a field-
hockey stick and under a basketball hoop. I tramped alone for miles along
the bridle paths that webbed the woods behind the house I grew up in. I
swayed through countless dim hours in the arms of one man or another
under the scattered shot of light from mirrored balls, and gyrated through
countless more as Tab Hunter and Johnny Mathis gave way to the Rolling
Stones, Creedance Clearwater Revival, Cream. I walked down the aisle. I
pushed baby carriages, changed tires in the rain, marched for peace.

When I was twenty-eight I started to trip and drop things. What at
first seemed my natural clumsiness soon became too pronounced to shrug
off. I consulted a neurologist, who told me that I had a brain tumor. A
battery of tests, increasingly disagreeable, revealed no tumor. About a
year and a half later I developed a blurred spot in one eye. I had, at last,
the episodes "disseminated in space and time" requisite for a diagnosis:
multiple sclerosis. I have never been sorry for the doctor's initial misdiag-
nosis, however. For almost a week, until the negative results of the tests
were in, I thought that I was going to die right away. Every day for the
past nearly ten years, then, has been a kind of gift. I accept all gifts.

Multiple sclerosis is a chronic degenerative disease of the central nervous system, in which the myelin that sheathes the nerves is somehow
eaten away and scar tissue forms in its place, interrupting the nerves' signals. During its course, which is unpredictable and uncontrollable, one
may lose vision, hearing, speech, the ability to walk, control of bladder
and/or bowels, strength in any or all extremities, sensitivity to touch, vibration, and/or pain, potency, coordination of movements—the list of
possibilities is lengthy and, yes, horrifying. One may also lose one's sense
of humor. That's the easiest to lose and the hardest to survive without.

In the past ten years, I have sustained some of these losses. Characteristic of MS are sudden attacks, called exacerbations, followed by
remissions, and these I have not had. Instead, my disease has been slowly
progressive. My left leg is now so weak that I walk with the aid of a brace
and a cane; and for distances I use an Amigo, a variation on the electric
wheelchair that looks rather like an electrified kiddie car. I no longer have
much use of my left hand. Now my right side is weakening as well. I still
have the blurred spot in my right eye. Overall, though, I've been lucky so
far. My world has, of necessity, been circumscribed by my losses, but the
terrain left me has been ample enough for me to continue many of the activities that absorb me: writing, teaching, raising children and cats and
plants and snakes, reading, speaking publicly about MS and depression,

even playing bridge with people patient and honorable enough to let me scatter cards every which way without sneaking a peek.

Lest I begin to sound like Pollyanna, however, let me say that I don't like having MS. I hate it. My life holds realities—harsh ones, some of them—that no right-minded human being ought to accept without grumbling. One of them is fatigue. I know of no one with MS who does not complain of bone-weariness; in a disease that presents an astonishing variety of symptoms, fatigue seems to be a common factor. I wake up in the morning feeling the way most people do at the end of a bad day, and I take it from there. As a result, I spend a lot of time *in extremis* and, impatient with limitation, I tend to ignore my fatigue until my body breaks down in some way and forces rest. Then I miss picnics, dinner parties, poetry readings, the brief visits of old friends from out of town. The offspring of a puritanical tradition of exceptional venerability, I cannot view these lapses without shame. My life often seems a series of small failures to do as I ought.

I lead, on the whole, an ordinary life, probably rather like the one I would have led had I not had MS. I am lucky that my predilections were already solitary, sedentary, and bookish—unlike the world-famous French cellist I have read about, or the young woman I talked with one long afternoon who wanted only to be a jockey. I had just begun graduate school when I found out something was wrong with me, and I have remained, interminably, a graduate student. Perhaps I would not have if I'd thought I had the stamina to return to a full-time job as a technical editor; but I've enjoyed my studies.   10

In addition to studying, I teach writing courses. I also teach medical students how to give neurological examinations. I pick up freelance editing jobs here and there. I have raised a foster son and sent him into the world, where he has made me two grandbabies, and I am still escorting my daughter and son through adolescence. I go to Mass every Saturday. I am a superb, if messy, cook. I am also an enthusiastic laundress, capable of sorting a hamper full of clothes into five subtly differentiated piles, but a terrible housekeeper. I can do italic writing and, in an emergency, bathe an oil-soaked cat. I play a fiendish game of Scrabble. When I have the time and the money, I'd like to sit on my front steps with my husband, drinking Amaretto and smoking a cigar, as we imagine our counterparts in Leningrad and make sure that the sun gets down once more behind the sharp childish scrawl of the Tucson Mountains.

This lively plenty has its bleak complement, of course, in all the things I can no longer do. I will never run again, except in dreams, and one day I may have to write that I will never walk again. I like to go camping, but I can't follow George and the children along the trails that wander out of a campsite through the desert or into the mountains. In fact, even on the level I've learned never to check the weather or try to hold a coherent conversation: I need all my attention for my wayward feet. Of late, I have begun to catch myself wondering how people can propel themselves without canes. With only one usable hand, I have to select my clothing with care not so much for style as for ease of ingress and egress, and even so, dressing can be laborious. I can no longer do fine stitchery, pick up babies, play the piano, braid my hair. I am immobilized by acute attacks of depression, which may or may not be physiologically related to MS but are certainly its logical concomitant.

These two elements, the plenty and the privation, are never pure, nor are the delight and wretchedness that accompany them. Almost every pickle that I get into as a result of my weakness and clumsiness—and I get into plenty—is funny as well as maddening and sometimes painful. I recall one May afternoon when a friend and I were going out for a drink after finishing up at school. As we were climbing into opposite sides of my car, chatting, I tripped and fell, flat and hard, onto the asphalt parking lot, my abrupt departure interrupting him in mid-sentence. "Where'd you go?" he called as he came around the back of the car to find me hauling myself up by the door frame. "Are you all right?" Yes, I told him, I was fine, just a bit rattly, and we drove off to find a shady patio and some beer. When I got home an hour or so later, my daughter greeted me with "What have you done to yourself?" I looked down. One elbow of my white turtleneck with the green froggies, one knee of my white trousers, one white kneesock were blood-soaked. We peeled off the clothes and inspected the damage, which was nasty enough but not alarming. That part wasn't funny: The abrasions took a long time to heal, and one got a little infected. Even so, when I think of my friend talking earnestly, suddenly, to the hot thin air while I dropped from his view as though through a trap door, I find the image as silly as something from a Marx Brothers movie.

I may find it easier than other cripples to amuse myself because I live propped by the acceptance and the assistance and, sometimes, the amusement of those around me. Grocery clerks tear my checks out of my checkbook for me, and sales clerks find chairs to put into dressing rooms when I want to try on clothes. The people I work with make sure I teach at times when I am least likely to be fatigued, in places I can get to, with the materials I need. My students, with one anonymous exception (in an end-of-the-semester evaluation), have been unperturbed by my disability. Some even like it. One was immensely cheered by the information that I paint my own fingernails; she decided, she told me, that if I could go to such trouble over fine details, she could keep on writing essays. I suppose I became some sort of bright-fingered muse. She wrote good essays, too.

The most important struts in the framework of my existence, of course, are my husband and children. Dismayingly few marriages survive the MS test, and why should they? Most twenty-two- and nineteen-year-olds, like George and me, can vow in clear conscience, after a childhood of chicken pox and summer colds, to keep one another in sickness and in health so long as they both shall live. Not many are equipped for catastrophe: the dismay, the depression, the extra work, the boredom that a degenerative disease can insinuate into a relationship. And our society, with its emphasis on fun and its association of fun with physical performance, offers little encouragement for a whole spouse to stay with a crippled partner. Children experience similar stresses when faced with a crippled parent, and they are more helpless, since parents and children can't usually get divorced. They hate, of course, to be different from their peers, and the child whose mother is tacking down the aisle of a school auditorium packed with proud parents like a Cape Cod dinghy in a stiff breeze jolly well stands out in a crowd. Deprived of legal divorce, the child can at least deny the mother's disability, even her existence, forgetting to tell her about recitals and PTA meetings, refusing to accompany her to stores or church or the movies, never inviting friends to the house. Many do.

But I've been limping along for ten years now, and so far George and the children are still at my left elbow, holding tight. Anne and Matthew vacuum floors and dust furniture and haul trash and rake up dog droppings and button my cuffs and bake lasagna and Toll House cookies with just enough grumbling so I know that they don't have brain fever. And far from hiding me, they're forever dragging me by racks of fancy clothes or through teeming school corridors, or welcoming gaggles of friends while I'm wandering through the house in Anne's filmy pink babydoll pajamas. George generally calls before he brings someone home, but he does just as many dumb thankless chores as the children. And they all yell at me, laugh at some of my jokes, write me funny letters when we're apart—in short, treat me as an ordinary human being for whom they have some use. I think they like me. Unless they're faking. . . .

Faking. There's the rub. Tugging at the fringes of my consciousness always is the terror that people are kind to me only because I'm a cripple. My mother almost shattered me once, with that instinct mothers have—blind, I think, in this case, but unerring nonetheless—for striking blows along the fault lines of their children's hearts, by telling me, in an attack on my selfishness, "We all have to make allowances for you, of course, because of the way you are." From the distance of a couple of years, I have to admit that I haven't any idea just what she meant, and I'm not sure that she knew either. She was awfully angry. But at the time, as the words thudded home, I felt my worst fear, suddenly realized. I could bear being called selfish: I am. But I couldn't bear the corroboration that those around me were doing in fact what I'd always suspected them of doing, professing fondness while silently putting up with me because of the way I am. A cripple. I've been a little cracked ever since.

Along with this fear that people are secretly accepting shoddy goods comes a relentless pressure to please—to prove myself worth the burdens I impose, I guess, or to build a substantial account of good will against which I may write drafts in times of need. Part of the pressure arises from social expectations. In our society, anyone who deviates from the norm had better find some way to compensate. Like fat people, who are expected to be jolly, cripples must bear their lot meekly and cheerfully. A grumpy cripple isn't playing by the rules. And much of the pressure is self-generated. Early on I vowed that, if I had to have MS, by God I was going to do it well. This is a class act, ladies and gentlemen. No tears, no recriminations, no faint-heartedness.

One way and another, then, I wind up feeling like Tiny Tim,[2] peering over the edge of the table at the Christmas goose, waving my crutch, piping down God's blessing on us all. Only sometimes I don't want to play Tiny Tim, I'd rather be Caliban,[3] a most scurvy monster. Fortunately, at home no one much cares whether I'm a good cripple or a bad cripple as long as I make vichyssoise with fair regularity. One evening several years ago, Anne was reading at the dining-room table while I cooked dinner. As I opened a can of tomatoes, the can slipped in my left hand and juice spattered me and the counter with bloody spots. Fatigued and infuriated, I bellowed, "I'm so sick of being crippled!" Anne glanced at me over the top of her book. "There now," she said, "do you feel better?" "Yes," I said, "yes, I do." She went back to her reading. I felt better. That's about all the attention my scurviness ever gets.

Because I hate being crippled, I sometimes hate myself for being a crip-   20
ple. Over the years I have come to expect—even accept—attacks of violent self-loathing. Luckily, in general our society no longer connects deformity and disease directly with evil (though a charismatic once told me that I have MS because a devil is in me) and so I'm allowed to move largely at will, even among small children. But I'm not sure that this revision of attitude has been particularly helpful. Physical imperfection, even freed of moral disapprobation, still defies and violates the ideal, especially for women, whose confinement in their bodies as objects of desire is far from over. Each age, of course, has its ideal, and I doubt that ours is any better or worse than any other. Today's ideal woman, who lives on the glossy pages of dozens of magazines, seems to be between the ages of eighteen and twenty-five; her hair has body, her teeth flash white, her breath smells minty, her underarms are dry; she has a career but is still a fabulous cook, especially of meals that take less than twenty minutes to prepare; she does not ordinarily appear to have a husband or children; she is trim and deeply tanned; she jogs, swims, plays tennis, rides a bicycle, sails, but does not bowl; she travels widely, even to out-of-the-way places like Finland and Samoa, always in the company of the ideal man, who possesses a nearly identical set of characteristics. There are a few exceptions. Though usually white and often blonde, she may be black, Hispanic, Asian, or Native American, so long as she is unusually sleek. She may be old, provided she is selling a laxative or is Lauren Bacall. If she is selling a detergent, she may be married and have a flock of strikingly messy children. But she is never a cripple.

Like many women I know, I have always had an uneasy relationship with my body. I was not a popular child, largely, I think now, because I was peculiar: intelligent, intense, moody, shy, given to unexpected actions and inexplicable notions and emotions. But as I entered adolescence, I believed

[2]***Tiny Tim:*** Crippled boy in Charles Dickens's *A Christmas Carol.*—EDS.
[3]***Caliban:*** A character in Shakespeare's play, *The Tempest.*—EDS.

myself unpopular because I was homely; my breasts too flat, my mouth too wide, my hips too narrow, my clothing never quite right in fit or style. I was not, in fact, particularly ugly, old photographs inform me, though I was well off the ideal; but I carried this sense of self-alienation with me into adulthood, where it regenerated in response to the depredations of MS. Even with my brace I walk with a limp so pronounced that, seeing myself on the videotape of a television program on the disabled, I couldn't believe that anything but an inchworm could make progress humping along like that. My shoulders droop and my pelvis thrusts forward as I try to balance myself upright, throwing my frame into a bony S. As a result of contractures, one shoulder is higher than the other and I carry one arm bent in front of me, the fingers curled into a claw. My left arm and leg have wasted into pipe-stems, and I try always to keep them covered. When I think about how my body must look to others, especially to men, to whom I have been trained to display myself, I feel ludicrous, even loathsome.

At my age, however, I don't spend much time thinking about my appearance. The burning egocentricity of adolescence, which assures one that all the world is looking all the time, has passed, thank God, and I'm generally too caught up in what I'm doing to step back, as I used to, and watch myself as though upon a stage. I'm also too old to believe in the accuracy of self-image. I know that I'm not a hideous crone, that in fact, when I'm rested, well dressed, and well made up, I look fine. The self-loathing I feel is neither physically nor intellectually substantial. What I hate is not me but a disease.

I am not a disease.

And a disease is not—at least not singlehandedly—going to determine who I am, though at first it seemed to be going to. Adjusting to a chronic incurable illness, I have moved through a process similar to that outlined by Elizabeth Kübler-Ross in *On Death and Dying*. The major difference—and it is far more significant than most people recognize—is that I can't be sure of the outcome, as the terminally ill cancer patient can. Research studies indicate that, with proper medical care, I may achieve a "normal" life span. And in our society, with its vision of death as the ultimate evil, worse even than decrepitude, the response to such news is, "Oh well, at least you're not going to *die*." Are there worse things than dying? I think that there may be.

I think of two women I know, both with MS, both enough older than   25
I to have served me as models. One took to her bed several years ago and has been there ever since. Although she can sit in a high-backed wheelchair, because she is incontinent she refuses to go out at all, even though incontinence pants, which are readily available at any pharmacy, could protect her from embarrassment. Instead, she stays at home and insists that her husband, a small quiet man, a retired civil servant, stay there with her except for a quick weekly foray to the supermarket. The other woman, whose illness was diagnosed when she was eighteen, a nursing student engaged to a young doctor, finished her training, married her

doctor, accompanied him to Germany when he was in the service, bore three sons and a daughter, now grown and gone. When she can, she travels with her husband; she plays bridge, embroiders, swims regularly; she works, like me, as a symptomatic-patient instructor of medical students in neurology. Guess which woman I hope to be.

At the beginning, I thought about having MS almost incessantly. And because of the unpredictable course of the disease, my thoughts were always terrified. Each night I'd get into bed wondering whether I'd get out again the next morning, whether I'd be able to see, to speak, to hold a pen between my fingers. Knowing that the day might come when I'd be physically incapable of killing myself, I thought perhaps I ought to do so right away, while I still had the strength. Gradually I came to understand that the Nancy who might one day lie inert under a bedsheet, arms and legs paralyzed, unable to feed or bathe herself, unable to reach out for a gun, a bottle of pills, was not the Nancy I was at present, and that I could not presume to make decisions for that future Nancy, who might well not want in the least to die. Now the only provision I've made for the future Nancy is that when the time comes—and it is likely to come in the form of pneumonia, friend to the weak and the old—I am not to be treated with machines and medications. If she is unable to communicate by then, I hope she will be satisfied with these terms.

Thinking all the time about having MS grew tiresome and intrusive, especially in the large and tragic mode in which I was accustomed to considering my plight. Months and even years went by without catastrophe (at least without one related to MS), and really I was awfully busy, what with George and children and snakes and students and poems, and I hadn't the time, let alone the inclination, to devote myself to being a disease. Too, the richer my life became, the funnier it seemed, as though there were some connection between largesse and laughter, and so my tragic stance began to waver until, even with the aid of a brace and a cane, I couldn't hold it for very long at a time.

After several years I was satisfied with my adjustment. I had suffered my grief and fury and terror, I thought, but now I was at ease with my lot. Then one summer day I set out with George and the children across the desert for a vacation in California. Part way to Yuma I became aware that my right leg felt funny. "I think I've had an exacerbation," I told George. "What shall we do?" he asked. "I think we'd better get the hell to California," I said, "because I don't know whether I'll ever make it again." So we went on to San Diego and then to Orange, up the Pacific Coast Highway to Santa Cruz, across to Yosemite, down to Sequoia and Joshua Tree, and so back over the desert to home. It was a fine two-week trip, filled with friends and fair weather, and I wouldn't have missed it for the world, though I did in fact make it back to California two years later. Nor would there have been any point in missing it, since in MS, once the symptoms have appeared, the neurological damage has been done, and there's no way to predict or prevent that damage.

The incident spoiled my self-satisfaction, however. It renewed my grief and fury and terror, and I learned that one never finishes adjusting to MS. I don't know now why I thought one would. One does not, after all, finish adjusting to life, and MS is simply a fact of my life—not my favorite fact, of course—but as ordinary as my nose and my tropical fish and my yellow Mazda station wagon. It may at any time get worse, but no amount of worry or anticipation can prepare me for a new loss. My life is a lesson in losses. I learn one at a time.

And I had best be patient in the learning, since I'll have to do it like it or not. As any rock fan knows, you can't always get what you want. Particularly when you have MS. You can't, for example, get cured. In recent years researchers and the organizations that fund research have started to pay MS some attention even though it isn't fatal; perhaps they have begun to see that life is something other than a quantitative phenomenon, that one may be very much alive for a very long time in a life that isn't worth living. The researchers have made some progress toward understanding the mechanism of the disease: It may well be an autoimmune reaction triggered by a slow-acting virus. But they are nowhere near its prevention, control, or cure. And most of us want to be cured. Some, unable to accept incurability, grasp at one treatment after another, no matter how bizarre: megavitamin therapy, gluten-free diet, injections of cobra venom, hypothermal suits, lymphocytopharesis, hyperbaric chambers. Many treatments are probably harmless enough, but none are curative.

The absence of a cure often makes MS patients bitter toward their doctors. Doctors are, after all, the priests of modern society, the new shamans, whose business is to heal, and many an MS patient roves from one to another, searching for the "good" doctor who will make him well. Doctors too think of themselves as healers, and for this reason many have trouble dealing with MS patients, whose disease in its intransigence defeats their aims and mocks their skills. Too few doctors, it is true, treat their patients as whole human beings, but the reverse is also true. I have always tried to be gentle with my doctors, who often have more at stake in terms of ego than I do. I may be frustrated, maddened, depressed by the incurability of my disease, but I am not diminished by it, and they are. When I push myself up from my seat in the waiting room and stumble toward them, I incarnate the limitation of their powers. The least I can do is refuse to press on their tenderest spots.

This gentleness is part of the reason that I'm not sorry to be a cripple. I didn't have it before. Perhaps I'd have developed it anyway—how could I know such a thing?—and I wish I had more of it, but I'm glad of what I have. It has opened and enriched my life enormously, this sense that my frailty and need must be mirrored in others, that in searching for and shaping a stable core in a life wrenched by change and loss, change and loss, I must recognize the same process, under individual conditions, in the lives around me. I do not deprecate such knowledge, however I've come by it.

All the same, if a cure were found, would I take it? In a minute. I may be a cripple, but I'm only occasionally a loony and never a saint. Anyway, in my brand of theology God doesn't give bonus points for a limp. I'd take a cure; I just don't need one. A friend who also has MS startled me once by asking, "Do you ever say to yourself, 'Why me, Lord?'" "No, Michael, I don't," I told him, "because whenever I try, the only response I can think of is 'Why not?'" If I could make a cosmic deal, who would I put in my place? What in my life would I give up in exchange for sound limbs and a thrilling rush of energy? No one. Nothing. I might as well do the job myself. Now that I'm getting the hang of it.

The Reader's Presence

1. Mairs's approach to her multiple sclerosis may come across as ironic, jaunty, or tough. Near the beginning of the essay she assumes that her reader is fundamentally alienated from her: "I refuse to pretend that the only differences between you and me are the various ordinary ones that distinguish any one person from another" (paragraph 4). What are those differences? How does the essay attempt to move the reader away from awkwardness or suspicion or hostility? Does it succeed?

2. What does the epigraph from Louise Bogan mean to you? What might it signify in relation to Mairs's essay? What is "escape," in Mairs's context? What meanings might the word *nothing* have?

3. "Lest I begin to sound like Polyanna, however, let me say that I don't like having MS. I hate it" (paragraph 9). Discuss Mairs's admission of hatred for the disease—and for herself (paragraph 20)—in relation to Alice Walker's "abuse" of her injured eye (paragraph 30) in "Beauty: When the Other Dancer Is the Self (see page 274)." What is the role of self-loathing in personal growth?

THE WRITER AT WORK

Nancy Mairs on Finding a Voice

In writing workshops and lectures, the essayist Nancy Mairs is often asked what appears to be a simple question: How did you find your voice as a writer? Yet is the question truly an easy one? In the following passage from her book "on becoming a (woman) writer," Voice Lessons, Mairs closely examines the question and suggests a way it might be answered. You might want to compare her concern about finding a voice to that of Henry Louis Gates Jr. on page 132.

The question I am most often asked when I speak to students and others interested in writing is, How did you find your voice? I have some trouble with this locution because "find" always suggests to me the discovery, generally fortuitous, of some lack or loss. I have found an occasional four-leaf clover. I have found a mate. I have, more than once, found my way home. But is a voice susceptible of the same sort of revelation or retrieval? Hasn't mine simply always been there, from my earliest lallation to the "I love you" I called after my husband on his way to school several hours ago?

But of course, I remind myself, the question doesn't concern *my* voice at all but the voice of another woman (also named Nancy Mairs, confusingly enough) whose "utterances" are, except for the occasional public reading, literally inaudible: not, strictly speaking, a voice at all, but a fabrication, a device. And when I look again at the dictionary, I see that "find" can indeed also mean "devise." The voice in question, like the woman called into being to explain its existence, is an invention.

But of whom? For simplicity's sake, we assume that the voice in a work is that of the writer (in the case of nonfiction) or one invented by her (in the case of fiction). This assumption describes the relationship between writer (the woman in front of a luminous screen) and persona (whoever you hear speaking to you right now) adequately for most readers. And maybe for most writers, too. Until that earnest student in the second row waves a gnawed pencil over her head and asks, timidly as a rule because hers is the first question, "How did you find your voice?"

As though "you" were a coherent entity already existing at some original point, who had only to open her mouth and agitate her vocal chords—or, to be precise, pick up her fingers and diddle the keys—to call the world she had in mind into being. Not just a writer, an Author. But I've examined this process over and over in myself, and the direction of this authorial plot simply doesn't ring true. In the beginning, remember, was the *Word*. Not me. And the question, properly phrased, should probably be asked of my voice: How did you find (devise, invent, contrive) your Nancy?

27

Malcolm X

Homeboy

Malcolm X (1925–1965) is regarded as one of the most influential figures in the struggle for racial equality. Born Malcolm Little in Omaha, Nebraska, his family was frequently the target of racist violence: white supremacists burned their home, and his father, a Baptist minister, was horribly murdered. After his father's death, his mother was hospitalized for mental illness, and he and his seven brothers and sisters were placed in foster homes. Although a gifted student, Malcolm was discouraged by a racist teacher and quit high school. He later moved to Boston, where he engaged in various illegal activities, became addicted to narcotics, and was imprisoned for robbery. While in jail Malcolm made extensive use of the prison library and studied philosophy, politics, and the teachings of the Black Muslims' Nation of Islam. After his release from prison, Malcolm worked with Elijah Muhammad, founder and leader of the Nation of Islam, and changed his name to Malcolm X. He became known as an outspoken and articulate minister, championing racial separatism, faith in Allah, and rejection of white society, and quickly rose to a position of prominence within the organization. While on a pilgrimage to Mecca in 1964, Malcolm X became an orthodox Muslim, adopted the name El-Hajj Malik El-Shabazz, and formed his own religious organization. Hostilities grew between his followers and the Black Muslims, and in 1965 Malcolm X was assassinated in a Harlem ballroom. The Autobiography of Malcolm X (1965), from which "Homeboy" is taken, was written with Alex Haley and was published posthumously.

I looked like Li'l Abner. Mason, Michigan, was written all over me. My kinky, reddish hair was cut hick style, and I didn't even use grease in it. My green suit's coat sleeves stopped above my wrists, the pants legs showed three inches of socks. Just a shade lighter green than the suit was my narrow-collared, three-quarter length Lansing department store topcoat. My appearance was too much for even Ella.[1] But she told me later

---

[1]*Ella:* Malcolm's older sister. He left Lansing, Michigan, and moved to her house in the Roxbury section of Boston in 1948. — EDS.

she had seen countrified members of the Little family come up from Georgia in even worse shape than I was.

Ella had fixed up a nice little upstairs room for me. And she was truly a Georgia Negro woman when she got into the kitchen with her pots and pans. She was the kind of cook who would heap up your plate with such as ham hock, greens, black-eyed peas, fried fish, cabbage, sweet potatoes, grits and gravy, and cornbread. And the more you put away, the better she felt. I worked out at Ella's kitchen table like there was no tomorrow.

Ella still seemed to be as big, black, outspoken, and impressive a woman as she had been in Mason and Lansing. Only about two weeks before I arrived, she had split up with her second husband—the soldier, Frank, whom I had met there the previous summer; but she was taking it right in stride. I could see, though I didn't say, how any average man would find it almost impossible to live for very long with a woman whose every instinct was to run everything and everybody she had anything to do with—including me. About my second day there in Roxbury, Ella told me that she didn't want me to start hunting for a job right away, like most newcomer Negroes did. She said that she had told all those she'd brought North to take their time, to walk around, to travel the buses and the subway, and get the feel of Boston, before they tied themselves down working somewhere, because they would never again have the time to really see and get to know anything about the city they were living in. Ella said she'd help me find a job when it was time for me to go to work.

So I went gawking around the neighborhood—the Waumbeck and Humboldt Avenue Hill section of Roxbury, which is something like Harlem's Sugar Hill, where I'd later live. I saw those Roxbury Negroes acting and living differently from any black people I'd ever dreamed of in my life. This was the snooty-black neighborhood; they called themselves the "Four Hundred," and looked down their noses at the Negroes of the black ghetto, or so-called "town" section where Mary, my other half-sister, lived.

What I thought I was seeing there in Roxbury were high-class, edu-   5
cated, important Negroes, living well, working in big jobs and positions. Their quiet homes sat back in their mowed yards. These Negroes walked along the sidewalks looking haughty and dignified, on their way to work, to shop, to visit, to church. I know now, of course, that what I was really seeing was only a big-city version of those "successful" Negro bootblacks and janitors back in Lansing. The only difference was that the ones in Boston had been brainwashed even more thoroughly. They prided themselves on being incomparably more "cultured," "cultivated," "dignified," and better off than their black brethren down in the ghetto, which was no further away than you could throw a rock. Under the pitiful misapprehension that it would make them "better," these Hill Negroes were breaking their backs trying to imitate white people.

Any black family that had been around Boston long enough to own the home they lived in was considered among the Hill elite. It didn't make any difference that they had to rent out rooms to make ends meet. Then the native-born New Englanders among them looked down upon recently migrated Southern home-owners who lived next door, like Ella. And a big percentage of the Hill dwellers were in Ella's category — Southern strivers and scramblers, and West Indian Negroes, whom both the New Englanders and the Southerners called "Black Jews." Usually it was the Southerners and the West Indians who not only managed to own the places where they lived, but also at least one other house which they rented as income property. The snooty New Englanders usually owned less than they.

In those days on the Hill, any who could claim "professional" status — teachers, preachers, practical nurses — also considered themselves superior. Foreign diplomats could have modeled their conduct on the way the Negro postmen, Pullman porters, and dining car waiters of Roxbury acted, striding around as if they were wearing top hats and cutaways.

I'd guess that eight out of ten of the Hill Negroes of Roxbury, despite the impressive-sounding job titles they affected, actually worked as menials and servants. "He's in banking," or "He's in securities." It sounded as though they were discussing a Rockefeller or a Mellon — and not some grayheaded, dignity-posturing bank janitor, or bond-house messenger. "I'm with an old family" was the euphemism used to dignify the professions of white folks' cooks and maids who talked so affectedly among their own kind in Roxbury that you couldn't even understand them. I don't know how many forty- and fifty-year-old errand boys went down the Hill dressed like ambassadors in black suits and white collars, to downtown jobs "in government," "in finance," or "in law." It has never ceased to amaze me how so many Negroes, then and now, could stand the indignity of that kind of self-delusion.

Soon I ranged out of Roxbury and began to explore Boston proper. Historic buildings everywhere I turned, and plaques and markers and statues for famous events and men. One statue in the Boston Commons astonished me: a Negro named Crispus Attucks, who had been the first man to fall in the Boston Massacre. I had never known anything like that.

I roamed everywhere. In one direction, I walked as far as Boston University. Another day, I took my first subway ride. When most of the people got off, I followed. It was Cambridge, and I circled all around in the Harvard University campus. Somewhere, I had already heard of Harvard — though I didn't know much more about it. Nobody that day could have told me I would give an address before the Harvard Law School Forum some twenty years later.

I also did a lot of exploring downtown. Why a city would have *two* big railroad stations — North Station and South Station — I couldn't understand. At both of the stations, I stood around and watched people arrive and leave. And I did the same thing at the bus station where Ella had met me. My wanderings even led me down along the piers and docks

10

where I read plaques telling about the old sailing ships that used to put into port there.

In a letter to Wilfred, Hilda, Philbert, and Reginald back in Lansing, I told them about all this, and about the winding, narrow, cobblestoned streets, and the houses that jammed up against each other. Downtown Boston, I wrote them, had the biggest stores I'd ever seen, and white people's restaurants and hotels. I made up my mind that I was going to see every movie that came to the fine, air-conditioned theaters.

On Massachusetts Avenue, next door to one of them, the Loew's State Theater, was the huge, exciting Roseland State Ballroom. Big posters out in front advertised the nationally famous bands, white and Negro, that had played there. "COMING NEXT WEEK," when I went by that first time, was Glenn Miller.[2] I remember thinking how nearly the whole evening's music at Mason High School dances had been Glenn Miller's records. What wouldn't that crowd have given, I wondered, to be standing where Glenn Miller's band was actually going to play? I didn't know how familiar with Roseland I was going to become.

Ella began to grow concerned, because even when I had finally had enough sight-seeing, I didn't stick around very much on the Hill. She kept dropping hints that I ought to mingle with the "nice young people my age" who were to be seen in the Townsend Drugstore two blocks from her house, and a couple of other places. But even before I came to Boston, I had always felt and acted toward anyone my age as if they were in the "kid" class, like my younger brother Reginald. They had always looked up to me as if I were considerably older. On weekends back in Lansing where I'd go to get away from the white people in Mason, I'd hung around in the Negro part of town with Wilfred's and Philbert's set. Though all of them were several years older than me, I was bigger, and I actually looked older than most of them.

I didn't want to disappoint or upset Ella, but despite her advice, I   15
began going down into the town ghetto section. That world of grocery stores, walk-up flats, cheap restaurants, poolrooms, bars, storefront churches, and pawnshops seemed to hold a natural lure for me.

Not only was this part of Roxbury much more exciting, but I felt more relaxed among Negroes who were being their natural selves and not putting on airs. Even though I did live on the Hill, my instincts were never—and still aren't—to feel myself any better than any other Negro.

I spent my first month in town with my mouth hanging open. The sharp-dressed young "cats" who hung on the corners and in the pool-rooms, bars and restaurants, and who obviously didn't work anywhere, completely entranced me. I couldn't get over marveling at how their hair was straight and shiny like white men's hair; Ella told me this was called a "conk." I had never tasted a sip of liquor, never even smoked a ciga-

[2]*Miller:* One of America's most popular band leaders of the 1940s.—EDS.

rette, and here I saw little black children, ten and twelve years old, shooting craps, playing cards, fighting, getting grown-ups to put a penny or a
nickel on their number for them, things like that. And these children
threw around swear words I'd never heard before, even, and slang expressions that were just as new to me, such as "stud" and "cat" and "chick"
and "cool" and "hip." Every night as I lay in bed I turned these new
words over in my mind. It was shocking to me that in town, especially
after dark, you'd occasionally see a white girl and a Negro man strolling
arm in arm along the sidewalk, and mixed couples drinking in the neon-
lighted bars—not slipping off to some dark corner, as in Lansing. I wrote
Wilfred and Philbert about that, too.

I wanted to find a job myself, to surprise Ella. One afternoon, something told me to go inside a poolroom whose window I was looking
through. I had looked through that window many times. I wasn't yearning
to play pool; in fact, I had never held a cue stick. But I was drawn by the
sight of the cool-looking "cats" standing around inside, bending over
the big, green, felt-topped tables, making bets and shooting the bright-
colored balls into the holes. As I stared through the window this particular afternoon, something made me decide to venture inside and talk to a
dark, stubby, conk-headed fellow who racked up balls for the pool-players,
whom I'd heard called "Shorty." One day he had come outside and
seen me standing there and said "Hi, Red," so that made me figure he was
friendly.

As inconspicuously as I could, I slipped inside the door and around
the side of the poolroom, avoiding people, and on to the back, where
Shorty was filling an aluminum can with the powder that pool players
dust on their hands. He looked up at me. Later on, Shorty would enjoy
teasing me about how with that first glance he knew my whole story.
"Man, that cat still *smelled* country!" he'd say, laughing. "Cat's legs was
so long and his pants so short his knees showed—an' his head looked
like a briar patch!"

But that afternoon Shorty didn't let it show in his face how "country" I appeared when I told him I'd appreciate it if he'd tell me how could
somebody go about getting a job like his.

"If you mean racking up balls," said Shorty, "I don't know of no
pool joints around here needing anybody. You mean you just want any
slave you can find?" A "slave" meant work, a job.

He asked what kind of work I had done. I told him that I'd washed
restaurant dishes in Mason, Michigan. He nearly dropped the powder
can. "My homeboy! Man, gimme some skin! I'm from Lansing!"

I never told Shorty—and he never suspected—that he was about ten
years older than I. He took us to be about the same age. At first I would
have been embarrassed to tell him, later I just never bothered. Shorty had
dropped out of first-year high school in Lansing, lived a while with an
uncle and aunt in Detroit, and had spent the last six years living with his

cousin in Roxbury. But when I mentioned the names of Lansing people and places, he remembered many, and pretty soon we sounded as if we had been raised in the same block. I could sense Shorty's genuine gladness, and I don't have to say how lucky I felt to find a friend as hip as he obviously was.

"Man, this is a swinging town if you dig it," Shorty said. "You're my homeboy—I'm going to school you to the happenings." I stood there and grinned like a fool. "You got to go anywhere now? Well, stick around until I get off."

One thing I liked immediately about Shorty was his frankness. When I told him where I lived, he said what I already knew—that nobody in town could stand the Hill Negroes. But he thought a sister who gave me a "pad," not charging me rent, not even running me out to find "some slave," couldn't be all bad. Shorty's slave in the poolroom, he said, was just to keep ends together while he learned his horn. A couple of years before, he'd hit the numbers and bought a saxophone. "Got it right in there in the closet now, for my lesson tonight." Shorty was taking lessons "with some other studs," and he intended one day to organize his own small band. "There's a lot of bread to be made gigging right around here in Roxbury," Shorty explained to me. "I don't dig joining some big band, one-nighting all over just to say I played with Count or Duke or somebody." I thought that was smart. I wished I had studied a horn; but I never had been exposed to one.

All afternoon, between trips up front to rack balls, Shorty talked to me out of the corner of his mouth: which hustlers—standing around, or playing at this or that table—sold "reefers," or had just come out of prison, or were "second-story men." Shorty told me that he played at least a dollar a day on the numbers. He said as soon as he hit a number, he would use the winnings to organize his band.

I was ashamed to have to admit that I had never played the numbers. "Well, you ain't never had nothing to play with," he said, excusing me, "but you start when you get a slave, and if you hit, you got a stake for something."

He pointed out some gamblers and some pimps. Some of them had white whores, he whispered. "I ain't going to lie—I dig them two-dollar white chicks," Shorty said. "There's a lot of that action around here, nights: you'll see it." I said I already had seen some. "You ever had one?" he asked.

My embarrassment at my inexperience showed. "Hell, man," he said, "don't be ashamed. I had a few before I left Lansing—them Polack chicks that used to come over the bridge. Here, they're mostly Italians and Irish. But it don't matter what kind, they're something else! Ain't no different nowhere—there's nothing they love better than a black stud."

Through the afternoon, Shorty introduced me to players and

25

30

loungers. "My homeboy," he'd say, "he's looking for a slave if you hear anything." They all said they'd look out.

At seven o'clock, when the night ball-racker came on, Shorty told me he had to hurry to his saxophone lesson. But before he left, he held out to me the six or seven dollars he had collected that day in nickel and dime tips. "You got enough bread, homeboy?"

I was okay, I told him—I had two dollars. But Shorty made me take three more. "Little fattening for your pocket," he said. Before we went out, he opened his saxophone case and showed me the horn. It was gleaming brass against the green velvet, an alto sax. He said, "Keep cool, homeboy, and come back tomorrow. Some of the cats will turn you up a slave."

When I got home, Ella said there had been a telephone call from somebody named Shorty. He had left a message that over at the Roseland State Ballroom, the shoeshine boy was quitting that night, and Shorty had told him to hold the job for me.

"Malcolm, you haven't had any experience shining shoes," Ella said. Her expression and tone of voice told me she wasn't happy about my taking that job. I didn't particularly care, because I was already speechless thinking about being somewhere close to the greatest bands in the world. I didn't even wait to eat any dinner.

The ballroom was all lighted when I got there. A man at the front   35
door was letting in members of Benny Goodman's band. I told him I wanted to see the shoeshine boy, Freddie.

"You're going to be the new one?" he asked. I said I thought I was, and he laughed, "Well, maybe you'll hit the numbers and get a Cadillac, too." He told me that I'd find Freddie upstairs in the men's room on the second floor.

But downstairs before I went up, I stepped over and snatched a glimpse inside the ballroom. I just couldn't believe the size of that waxed floor! At the far end, under the soft, rose-colored lights, was the bandstand with the Benny Goodman musicians moving around, laughing and talking, arranging their horns and stands.

A wiry, brown-skinned, conked fellow upstairs in the men's room greeted me. "You Shorty's homeboy?" I said I was, and he said he was Freddie. "Good old boy," he said. "He called me, he just heard I hit the big number, and he figured right I'd be quitting." I told Freddie what the man at the front door had said about a Cadillac. He laughed and said, "Burns them white cats up when you get yourself something. Yeah, I told them I was going to get me one—just to bug them."

Freddie then said for me to pay close attention, that he was going to be busy and for me to watch but not get in the way, and he'd try to get me ready to take over at the next dance, a couple of nights later.

As Freddie busied himself setting up the shoeshine stand, he told me,   40
"Get here early . . . your shoeshine rags and brushes by this footstand . . . your polish bottles, paste wax, suede brushes over here . . . everything in place, you get rushed, you never need to waste motion. . . ."

While you shined shoes, I learned, you also kept watch on customers inside, leaving the urinals. You darted over and offered a small white hand towel. "A lot of cats who ain't planning to wash their hands, sometimes you can run up with a towel and shame them. Your towels are really your best hustle in here. Cost you a penny apiece to launder—you always get at least a nickel tip."

The shoeshine customers, and any from the inside rest room who took a towel, you whiskbroomed a couple of licks. "A nickel or a dime tip, just give 'em that," Freddie said. "But for two bits, Uncle Tom a little—white cats especially like that. I've had them to come back two, three times a dance."

From down below, the sound of the music had begun floating up. I guess I stood transfixed. "You never seen a big dance?" asked Freddie. "Run on awhile, and watch."

There were a few couples already dancing under the rose-colored lights. But even more exciting to me was the crowd thronging in. The most glamorous-looking white women I'd ever seen—young ones, old ones, white cats buying tickets at the window, sticking big wads of green bills back into their pockets, checking the women's coats, and taking their arms and squiring them inside.

Freddie had some early customers when I got back upstairs. Between the shoeshine stand and thrusting towels to me just as they approached the wash basin, Freddie seemed to be doing four things at once. "Here, you can take over the whiskbroom," he said, "just two or three licks—but let 'em feel it."

When things slowed a little, he said, "You ain't seen nothing tonight. You wait until you see a spooks' dance! Man, our own people carry *on!*" Whenever he had a moment, he kept schooling me. "Shoelaces, this drawer here. You just starting out, I'm going to make these to you as a present. Buy them for a nickel a pair, tell cats they need laces if they do, and charge two bits."

Every Benny Goodman record I'd ever heard in my life, it seemed, was filtering faintly into where we were. During another customer lull, Freddie let me slip back outside again to listen. Peggy Lee was at the mike singing. Beautiful! She had just joined the band and she was from North Dakota and had been singing with a group in Chicago when Mrs. Benny Goodman discovered her, we had heard some customers say. She finished the song and the crowd burst into applause. She was a big hit.

"It knocked me out, too, when I first broke in here," Freddie said, grinning, when I went back in there. "But, look, you ever shined any shoes?" He laughed when I said I hadn't excepting my own. "Well, let's go to work. I never had neither." Freddie got on the stand and went to work on his own shoes. Brush, liquid polish, brush, paste wax, shine rag, lacquer sole dressing . . . step by step, Freddie showed me what to do.

"But you got to get a whole lot faster. You can't waste time!" Freddie showed me how fast on my own shoes. Then, because business was tapering off, he had time to give me a demonstration of how to make the shine rag pop like a firecracker. "Dig the action?" he asked. He did it in slow motion. I got down and tried it on his shoes. I had the principle of it. "Just got to do it faster," Freddie said. "It's a jive noise, that's all. Cats tip better, they figure you're knocking yourself out!"

By the end of the dance, Freddie had let me shine the shoes of three   50
or four stray drunks he talked into having shines, and I had practiced picking up my speed on Freddie's shoes until they looked like mirrors. After we had helped the janitors to clean up the ballroom after the dance, throwing out all the paper and cigarette butts and empty liquor bottles, Freddie was nice enough to drive me all the way home to Ella's on the Hill in the second-hand maroon Buick he said he was going to trade in on his Cadillac. He talked to me all the way. "I guess it's all right if I tell you, pick up a couple of dozen packs of rubbers, two-bits apiece. You notice some of those cats that came up to me around the end of the dance? Well, when some have new chicks going right, they'll come asking you for rubbers. Charge a dollar, generally you'll get an extra tip."

He looked across at me. "Some hustles you're too new for. Cats will ask you for liquor, some will want reefers. But you don't need to have nothing except rubbers—until you can dig who's a cop.

"You can make ten, twelve dollars a dance for yourself if you work everything right," Freddie said, before I got out of the car in front of Ella's. "The main thing you got to remember is that everything in the world is a hustle. So long, Red."

The next time I ran into Freddie I was downtown one night a few weeks later. He was parked in his pearl gray Cadillac, sharp as a tack, "cooling it."

"Man, you sure schooled me!" I said, and he laughed; he knew what I meant. It hadn't taken me long on the job to find out that Freddie had done less shoeshining and towel-hustling than selling liquor and reefers, and putting white "Johns" in touch with Negro whores. I also learned that white girls always flocked to the Negro dances—some of them whores whose pimps brought them to mix business and pleasure, others who came with their black boy friends, and some who came in alone, for a little freelance lusting among a plentiful availability of enthusiastic Negro men.

At the white dances, of course, nothing black was allowed, and that's   55
where the black whores' pimps soon showed a new shoeshine boy what he could pick up on the side by slipping a phone number or address to the white Johns who came around the end of the dance looking for "black chicks."

Most of Roseland's dances were for whites only, and they had white bands only. But the only white band ever to play there at a Negro dance

to my recollection, was Charlie Barnet's. The fact is that very few white
bands could have satisfied the Negro dancers. But I know that Charlie
Barnet's "Cherokee" and his "Redskin Rhumba" drove those Negroes
wild. They'd jampack that ballroom, the black girls in way-out silk and
satin dresses and shoes, their hair done in all kinds of styles, the men
sharp in their zoot suits and crazy conks, and everybody grinning and
greased and gassed.

Some of the bandsmen would come up to the men's room at about
eight o'clock and get shoeshines before they went to work. Duke Elling-
ton, Count Basie, Lionel Hampton, Cootie Williams, Jimmie Lunceford
were just a few of those who sat in my chair. I would really make my
shine rag sound like someone had set off Chinese firecrackers. Duke's
great alto saxman, Johnny Hodges—he was Shorty's idol—still owes me
for a shoeshine I gave him. He was in the chair one night, having a
friendly argument with the drummer, Sonny Greer, who was standing
there, when I tapped the bottom of his shoes to signal that I was finished.
Hodges stepped down, reaching his hand in his pocket to pay me, but
then snatched his hand out to gesture, and just forgot me, and walked
away. I wouldn't have dared to bother the man who could do what he
did with "Daydream" by asking him for fifteen cents.

I remember that I struck up a little shoeshine-stand conversation with
Count Basie's great blues singer, Jimmie Rushing. (He's the one famous
for "Sent For You Yesterday, Here You Come Today" and things like
that.) Rushing's feet, I remember, were big and funny-shaped—not long
like most big feet, but they were round and roly-poly like Rushing. Anyhow, he even introduced me to some of the other Basie cats, like Lester
Young, Harry Edison, Buddy Tate, Don Byas, Dickie Wells, and Buck
Clayton. They'd walk in the rest room later, by themselves. "Hi, Red."
They'd be up there in my chair, and my shine rag was popping to the beat
of all of their records, spinning in my head. Musicians never have had,
anywhere, a greater shoeshine-boy fan than I was. I would write to
Wilfred and Hilda and Philbert and Reginald back in Lansing, trying to
describe it.

I never got any decent tips until the middle of the Negro dances,
which is when the dancers started feeling good and getting generous.
After the white dances, when I helped to clean out the ballroom,
we would throw out perhaps a dozen empty liquor bottles. But after
the Negro dances, we would have to throw out cartons full of empty
fifth bottles—not rotgut, either, but the best brands, and especially
Scotch.

During lulls up there in the men's room, sometimes I'd get in five   60
minutes of watching the dancing. The white people danced as though
somebody had trained them—left, one, two; right, three, four—the same
steps and patterns over and over, as though somebody had wound them
up. But those Negroes—nobody in the world could have choreographed

the way they did whatever they felt—just grabbing partners, even the white chicks who came to the Negro dances. And my black brethren today may hate me for saying it, but a lot of black girls nearly got run over by some of those Negro males scrambling to get at those white women; you would have thought God had lowered some of his angels. Times have sure changed; if it happened today, those same black girls would go after those Negro men—and the white women, too.

Anyway, some couples were so abandoned—flinging high and wide, improvising steps and movements—that you couldn't believe it. I could feel the beat in my bones, even though I had never danced.

"*Showtime!*" people would start hollering about the last hour of the dance. Then a couple of dozen really wild couples would stay on the floor, the girls changing to low white sneakers. The band now would really be blasting, and all the other dancers would form a clapping, shouting circle to watch that wild competition as it began, covering only a quarter or so of the ballroom floor. The band, the spectators and the dancers, would be making the Roseland Ballroom feel like a big rocking ship. The spotlight would be turning, pink, yellow, green, and blue, picking up the couples lindy-hopping as if they had gone mad. "*Wail, man, wail!*" people would be shouting at the band; and it *would* be wailing, until first one and then another couple just ran out of strength and stumbled off toward the crowd, exhausted and soaked with sweat. Sometimes I would be down there standing inside the door jumping up and down in my gray jacket with the whiskbroom in the pocket, and the manager would have to come and shout at me that I had customers upstairs.

The first liquor I drank, my first cigarettes, even my first reefers, I can't specifically remember. But I know they were all mixed together with my first shooting craps, playing cards, and betting my dollar a day on the num- bers, as I started hanging out at night with Shorty and his friends. Shorty's jokes about how country I had been made us all laugh. I still was country, I know now, but it all felt so great because I was accepted. All of us would be in somebody's place, usually one of the girls', and we'd be turning on, the reefers making everybody's head light, or the whiskey aglow in our middles. Everybody understood that my head had to stay kinky a while longer, to grow long enough for Shorty to conk it for me. One of these nights, I remarked that I had saved about half enough to get a zoot.

"*Save?*" Shorty couldn't believe it. "Homeboy, you never heard of credit?" He told me he'd call a neighborhood clothing store the first thing in the morning, and that I should be there early.

A salesman, a young Jew, met me when I came in. "You're Shorty's   65
friend?" I said I was; it amazed me—all of Shorty's contacts. The sales- man wrote my name on a form, and the Roseland as where I worked, and Ella's address as where I lived. Shorty's name was put down as re- commending me. The salesman said, "Shorty's one of our best customers."

I was measured, and the young salesman picked off a rack a zoot suit that was just wild: sky-blue pants thirty inches in the knee and angle-narrowed down to twelve inches at the bottom, and a long coat that pinched my waist and flared out below my knees.

As a gift, the salesman said, the store would give me a narrow leather belt with my initial "L" on it. Then he said I ought to also buy a hat, and I did—blue, with a feather in the four-inch brim. Then the store gave me another present: a long, thick-lined, gold-plated chain that swung down lower than my coat hem. I was sold forever on credit.

When I modeled the zoot for Ella, she took a long look and said, "Well, I guess it had to happen." I took three of those twenty-five-cent sepia-toned, while-you-wait pictures of myself, posed the way "hipsters" wearing their zoots would "cool it"—hat dangled, knees drawn close together, feet wide apart, both index fingers jabbed toward the floor. The long coat and swinging chain and the Punjab pants were much more dramatic if you stood that way. One picture, I autographed and airmailed to my brothers and sisters in Lansing, to let them see how well I was doing. I gave another one to Ella, and the third to Shorty, who was really moved: I could tell by the way he said, "Thanks, homeboy." It was part of our "hip" code not to show that kind of affection.

Shorty soon decided that my hair was finally long enough to be conked. He had promised to school me in how to beat the barbershops' three- and four-dollar price by making up congolene, and then conking ourselves.

I took the little list of ingredients he had printed out for me, and went to a grocery store, where I got a can of Red Devil lye, two eggs, and two medium-sized white potatoes. Then at a drugstore near the poolroom, I asked for a large jar of vaseline, a large bar of soap, a large-toothed comb and a fine-toothed comb, one of those rubber hoses with a metal spray-head, a rubber apron, and a pair of gloves.

"Going to lay on that first conk?" the drugstore man asked me. I proudly told him, grinning, "Right!"

Shorty paid six dollars a week for a room in his cousin's shabby apartment. His cousin wasn't at home. "It's like the pad's mine, he spends so much time with his woman," Shorty said. "Now, you watch me—"

He peeled the potatoes and thin-sliced them into a quart-sized Mason fruit jar, then started stirring them with a wooden spoon as he gradually poured in a little over half the can of lye. "Never use a metal spoon; the lye will turn it black," he told me.

A jelly-like, starchy-looking glop resulted from the lye and potatoes, and Shorty broke in the two eggs, stirring real fast—his own conk and dark face bent down close. The congolene turned pale-yellowish. "Feel the jar," Shorty said. I cupped my hand against the outside, and snatched it away. "Damn right, it's hot, that's the lye," he said. "So you know it's going to burn when I comb it in—it burns *bad*. But the longer you can stand it, the straighter the hair."

He made me sit down, and he tied the string of a new rubber apron   75
tightly around my neck, and combed up my bush of hair. Then, from the big vaseline jar, he took a handful and massaged it hard all through my hair and into the scalp. He also thickly vaselined my neck, ears and forehead. "When I get to washing out your head, be sure to tell me anywhere you feel any little stinging," Shorty warned me, washing his hands, then pulling on the rubber gloves, and tying on his own rubber apron. "You always got to remember that any congolene left in burns a sore into your head."

The congolene just felt warm when Shorty started combing it in. But then my head caught fire.

I gritted my teeth and tried to pull the sides of the kitchen table together. The comb felt as if it was raking my skin off.

My eyes watered, my nose was running. I couldn't stand it any longer; I bolted to the washbasin. I was cursing Shorty with every name I could think of when he got the spray going and started soap-lathering my head.

He lathered and spray-rinsed, lathered and spray-rinsed, maybe ten or twelve times, each time gradually closing the hot-water faucet, until the rinse was cold, and that helped some.

"You feel any stinging spots?"   80

"No," I managed to say. My knees were trembling.

"Sit back down, then. I think we got it all out okay."

The flame came back as Shorty, with a thick towel, started drying my head, rubbing hard. *"Easy, man, easy!"* I kept shouting.

"The first time's always worst. You get used to it better before long. You took it real good, homeboy. You got a good conk."

When Shorty let me stand up and see in the mirror, my hair hung   85
down in limp, damp strings. My scalp still flamed, but not as badly; I could bear it. He draped the towel around my shoulders, over my rubber apron, and began again vaselining my hair.

I could feel him combing, straight back, first the big comb, then the fine-tooth one.

Then, he was using a razor, very delicately, on the back of my neck. Then, finally, shaping the sideburns.

My first view in the mirror blotted out the hurting. I'd seen some pretty conks, but when it's the first time, on your *own* head, the transformation, after the lifetime of kinks, is staggering.

The mirror reflected Shorty behind me. We both were grinning and sweating. And on top of my head was this thick, smooth sheen of shining red hair—real red—as straight as any white man's.

How ridiculous I was! Stupid enough to stand there simply lost in ad-   90 miration of my hair now looking "white," reflected in the mirror in Shorty's room. I vowed that I'd never again be without a conk, and I never was for many years.

This was my first really big step toward self-degradation: when I endured all of that pain, literally burning my flesh to have it look like a white man's hair. I had joined that multitude of Negro men and women in America who are brainwashed into believing that the black people are "inferior" —and white people "superior"—that they will even violate and mutilate their God-created bodies to try to look "pretty" by white standards.

Look around today, in every small town and big city, from two-bit catfish and soda-pop joints into the "integrated" lobby of the Waldorf-Astoria, and you'll see conks on black men. And you'll see black women wearing these green and pink and purple and red and platinum-blond wigs. They're all more ridiculous than a slapstick comedy. It makes you wonder if the Negro has completely lost his sense of identity, lost touch with himself.

You'll see the conk worn by many, many so-called "upper class" Negroes, and, as much as I hate to say it about them, on all too many Negro entertainers. One of the reasons that I've especially admired some of them, like Lionel Hampton and Sidney Poitier, among others, is that they have kept their natural hair and fought to the top. I admire any Negro man who has never had himself conked, or who has had the sense to get rid of it—as I finally did.

I don't know which kind of self-defacing conk is the greater shame— the one you'll see on the heads of the black so-called "middle class" and "upper class," who ought to know better, or the one you'll see on the heads of the poorest, most downtrodden, ignorant black men. I mean the legal-minimum-wage ghetto-dwelling kind of Negro, as I was when I got my first one. It's generally among these poor fools that you'll see a black kerchief over the man's head, like Aunt Jemima; he's trying to make his conk last longer, between trips to the barbershop. Only for special occasions is this kerchief-protected conk exposed—to show off how "sharp" and "hip" its owner is. The ironic thing is that I have never heard any woman, white or black, express any admiration for a conk. Of course, any white woman with a black man isn't thinking about his hair. But I don't see how on earth a black woman with any race pride could walk down the street with any black man wearing a conk—the emblem of his shame that he is black.

To my own shame, when I say all of this I'm talking first of all about myself—because you can't show me any Negro who ever conked more faithfully than I did. I'm speaking from personal experience when I say of any black man who conks today, or any white-wigged black woman, that if they gave the brains in their heads just half as much attention as they do their hair, they would be a thousand times better off.

95

The Reader's Presence

1. The young Malcolm resists Ella's pressure to imitate white lifestyles in order to get ahead. Instead, he seeks the company of his "brethren" in the black ghetto (paragraph 15) from whom he learns that "everything in the world is a hustle" (paragraph 52). What might this resistance signify politically? What relation might it bear to his later name changes, from Malcolm Little to Malcolm X and, finally, to El-Hajj Malik El-Shabazz (see introduction)? What elements of African American identity appeal to the young Malcolm X?

2. The writer, of course, was a courageous African American leader who was assassinated in 1965, when he was only forty years old. How does this knowledge affect your reading of this account of his early years? How does Malcolm himself indicate the difference in time between the events he is relating and the time at which he is writing?

3. Despite his awareness of the horrors of racism, Malcolm X describes some of the events of his politically naïve youth with gentleness, humor, and a degree of nostalgia. He is willing to poke fun at himself, as in his portrait of himself in his first zoot suit (paragraph 68). Compare Malcolm X's essay to "In the Kitchen" by Henry Louis Gates Jr. How do the essays compare in substance and in tone?

28

David Mamet

The Rake: A Few Scenes from My Childhood

David Mamet (b. 1947) is a playwright, screenwriter, and director whose work is appreciated for the attention he pays to language as it is spoken by ordinary people in the contemporary world. His Pulitzer Prize–winning play, Glengarry Glen Ross, *explores the psychology of ambition, competition, failure, and despair among a group of Chicago real estate agents who are driven to sell worthless property to unsuspecting customers. He has written and directed several films, including* State and Main *(2000); and* The Heist *(2001).*

Mamet has said that "playwriting is simply showing how words influence actions and vice versa. All my plays attempt to bring out the poetry in the plain, everyday language people use. That's the only way to put art back in the theater." Mamet's sensitivity to working-class language and experience is due in part to his own work experience in factories, at a real estate agency, and as a window washer, office cleaner, and taxi driver. More recently, he has taught theater at several leading universities and has published two collections of essays. His most recent publications include a play, The Old Neighborhood (1997), *a collection of essays,* Jafsie and John Henry (1999), *and two nonfiction books,* True and False: Heresy and Common Sense for the Actor (1997) *and* Three Uses of the Knife (1998). *"The Rake: A Few Scenes from My Childhood" appeared in* Harper's *in 1992.*

There was the incident of the rake and there was the incident of the school play, and it seems to me that they both took place at the round kitchen table.

The table was not in the kitchen proper but in an area called "the nook," which held its claim to that small measure of charm by dint of a waist-high wall separating it from an adjacent area known as the living room.

All family meals were eaten in the nook. There was a dining room to the right, but, as in most rooms of that name at the time and in those surroundings, it was never used.

The round table was of wrought iron and topped with glass; it was noteworthy for that glass, for it was more than once and rather more than several times, I am inclined to think, that my stepfather would grow so angry as to bring some object down on the glass top, shattering it, thus giving us to know how we had forced him out of control.

And it seems that most times when he would shatter the table, as   5 often as that might have been, he would cut some portion of himself on the glass, or that he or his wife, our mother, would cut their hands on picking up the glass afterward, and that we children were to understand, and did understand, that these wounds were our fault.

So the table was associated in our minds with the notion of blood.

The house was in a brand-new housing development in the southern suburbs. The new community was built upon, and now bordered, the remains of what had once been a cornfield. When our new family moved in, there were but a few homes in the development completed, and a few more under construction. Most streets were mud, and boasted a house here or there, and many empty lots marked out by white stakes.

The house we lived in was the development's Model Home. The first time we had seen it, it had signs plastered on the front and throughout the interior telling of the various conveniences it contained. And it had a lawn, and was one of the only homes in the new community that did.

My stepfather was fond of the lawn, and he detailed me and my sister to care for it, and one fall afternoon we found ourselves assigned to rake the leaves.

Why this chore should have been so hated I cannot say, except that we children, and I especially, felt ourselves less than full members of this new, cobbled-together family, and disliked being assigned to the beautification of a home that we found unbeautiful in all respects, and for which we had neither natural affection nor a sense of proprietary interest.

We went to the new high school. We walked the mile down the open two-lane road on one side of which was the just-begun suburban community and on the other side of which was the cornfield.

The school was as new as the community, and still under construction for the first three years of its occupancy. One of its innovations was the notion that honesty would be engendered by the absence of security, and so the lockers were designed and built both without locks and without the possibility of attaching locks. And there was the corresponding rash of thievery and many lectures about the same from the school administration, but it was difficult to point with pride to any scholastic or community tradition supporting the suggestion that we, the students, pull together in this new, utopian way. We were, in school, in an uncompleted building in the midst of a mud field in the midst of a cornfield. Our various sports teams were called The Spartans; and I played on those teams, which were of a wretchedness consistent with their novelty.

Meanwhile my sister interested herself in the drama society. The year after I had left the school she obtained the lead in the school play. It called for acting and singing, both of which she had talent for, and it looked to be a signal triumph for her in her otherwise unremarkable and unenjoyed school career.

On the night of the play's opening, she sat down to dinner with our mother and our stepfather. It may be that they ate a trifle early to allow her to get to the school to enjoy the excitement of opening night. But however it was, my sister had no appetite, and she nibbled a bit at her food, and then she got up from the table to carry her plate back to scrape it in the sink, when my mother suggested that she sit down, as she had not finished her food. My sister said she really had no appetite, but my mother insisted that, as the meal had been prepared, it would be good form to sit and eat it.

My sister sat down with the plate and pecked at her food and she tried to eat a bit, and told my mother that, no, really, she possessed no appetite whatever, and that was due, no doubt, not to the food, but to her nervousness and excitement at the prospect of opening night.

My mother, again, said that, as the food had been cooked, it had to be eaten, and my sister tried and said that she could not; at which my mother nodded. She then got up from the table and went to the telephone and looked the number up and called the school and got the drama teacher and identified herself and told him that her daughter wouldn't be coming to school that night, that, no, she was not ill, but that she would not be coming in. Yes, yes, she said, she knew her daughter had the lead in the play, and, yes, she was aware that many children and teachers had worked hard for it, et cetera, and so my sister did not play the lead in her school play. But I was long gone, out of the house by that time, and well out of it. I heard that story, and others like, at the distance of twenty-five years.

In the model house our rooms were separated from their room, the master bedroom, by a bathroom and a study. On some weekends I would go alone to visit my father in the city and my sister would stay and sometimes grow frightened or lonely in her part of the house. And once, in the period when my grandfather, then in his sixties, was living with us, she became alarmed at a noise she had heard in the night; or perhaps she just became lonely, and she went out of her room and down the hall, calling for my mother, or my stepfather, or my grandfather, but the house was dark, and no one answered.

And, as she went farther down the hall, toward the living room, she heard voices, and she turned the corner, and saw a light coming from under the closed door in the master bedroom, and heard my stepfather crying, and the sound of my mother weeping. So my sister went up to the door, and she heard my stepfather talking to my grandfather and saying, "Jack. Say the words. Just say the words . . ." And my grandfather in his Eastern European accent, saying with obvious pain and difficulty, "No. No. I can't. Why are you making me do this? Why?" And the sound of my mother crying convulsively.

My sister opened the door, and she saw my grandfather sitting on the bed, and my stepfather standing by the closet and gesturing. On the floor of the closet she saw my mother, curled in a fetal position, moaning and crying and hugging herself. My stepfather was saying, "Say the words. Just say the words." And my grandfather was breathing fast and repeating, "I can't. She knows how I feel about her. I can't." And my stepfather said, "Say the words, Jack. Please. Just say you love her." At which my mother would moan louder. And my grandfather said, "I can't."

My sister pushed the door open farther and said—I don't know what she said, but she asked, I'm sure, for some reassurance, or some explanation, and my stepfather turned around and saw her and picked up a hairbrush from a dresser that he passed as he walked toward her, and he hit her in the face and slammed the door on her. And she continued to hear "Jack, say the words."

She told me that on weekends when I was gone my stepfather ended every Sunday evening by hitting or beating her for some reason or other. He would come home from depositing his own kids back at their mother's house after their weekend visitation, and would settle down tired and angry, and, as a regular matter on those evenings, would find out some intolerable behavior on my sister's part and slap or hit or beat her.

Years later, at my mother's funeral, my sister spoke to our aunt, my mother's sister, who gave a footnote to this behavior. She said when they were young, my mother and my aunt, they and their parents lived in a small flat on the West Side. My grandfather was a salesman on the road from dawn on Monday until Friday night. Their family had a fiction, and that fiction, that article of faith, was that my mother was a naughty child. And each Friday, when he came home, his first question as he climbed the stairs was, "What has she done this week . . . ?" At which my grandmother would tell him the terrible things that my mother had done, after which she, my mother, was beaten.

This was general knowledge in my family. The footnote concerned my grandfather's behavior later in the night. My aunt had a room of her own, and it adjoined her parents' room. And she related that each Friday, when the house had gone to bed, she, through the thin wall, heard my grandfather pleading for sex. "Cookie, please." And my grandmother responding, "No, Jack." "Cookie, please." "No, Jack." "Cookie, please."

And once, my grandfather came home and asked, "What has she done this week?" and I do not know, but I imagine that the response was not completed, and perhaps hardly begun; in any case, he reached and grabbed my mother by the back of the neck and hurled her down the stairs.

And once, in our house in the suburbs there had been an outburst   25
by my stepfather directed at my sister. And she had, somehow, prevailed. It was, I think, that he had the facts of the case wrong, and had accused her of the commission of something for which she had demonstrably had no opportunity, and she pointed this out to him with what I can imagine, given the circumstances, was an understandable, and, given my prejudice, a commendable degree of freedom. Thinking the incident closed she went back to her room to study, and, a few moments later, saw him throw open her door, bat the book out of her hands, and pick her up and throw her against the far wall, where she struck the back of her neck on the shelf.

She was told, the next morning, that her pain, real or pretended, held no weight, and that she would have to go to school. She protested that she could not walk, or, if at all, only with the greatest of difficulty and in great pain; but she was dressed and did walk to school, where she fainted, and was brought home. For years she suffered various headaches; an X ray taken twenty years later for an unrelated problem revealed that when he threw her against the shelf he had cracked her vertebrae.

When we left the house we left in good spirits. When we went out to dinner, it was an adventure, which was strange to me, looking back, because many of these dinners ended with my sister or myself being banished, sullen or in tears, from the restaurant, and told to wait in the car, as we were in disgrace.

These were the excursions that had ended, due to her or my intolerable arrogance, as it was explained to us.

The happy trips were celebrated and capped with a joke. Here is the joke: My stepfather, my mother, my sister, and I would exit the restaurant, my stepfather and mother would walk to the car, telling us that they would pick us up. We children would stand by the restaurant entrance. They would drive up in the car, open the passenger door, and wait until my sister and I had started to get in. They would then drive away.

They would drive ten or fifteen feet, and open the door again, and we   30
would walk up again, and they would drive away again. They sometimes would drive around the block. But they would always come back, and by that time the four of us would be laughing in camaraderie and appreciation of what, I believe, was our only family joke.

We were raking the lawn, my sister and I. I was raking, and she was stuffing the leaves into a bag. I loathed the job, and my muscles and my mind rebelled, and I was viciously angry, and my sister said something, and I turned and threw the rake at her and hit her in the face.

The rake was split bamboo and metal, and a piece of metal caught her lip and cut her badly.

We were both terrified, and I was sick with guilt, and we ran into the house, my sister holding her hand to her mouth, and her mouth and her hand and the front of her dress covered in blood.

We ran into the kitchen where my mother was cooking dinner, and my mother asked what happened.

Neither of us, myself out of guilt, of course, and my sister out of a de-   35
sire to avert the terrible punishment she knew I would receive, neither of us would say what occurred.

My mother pressed us, and neither of us would answer. She said that until one or the other answered, we would not go to the hospital; and so the family sat down to dinner where my sister clutched a napkin to her face and the blood soaked the napkin and ran down onto her food, which she had to eat; and I also ate my food and we cleared the table and went to the hospital.

I remember the walks home from school in the frigid winter, along the cornfield that was, for all its proximity to the city, part of the prairie. The winters were viciously cold. From the remove of years, I can see how the area might and may have been beautiful. One could have walked in the stubble of the cornfields, or hunted birds, or enjoyed any of a number of pleasures naturally occurring.

The Reader's Presence

1. Interwoven through Mamet's essay are descriptions of suburban developments and model homes; he even uses the word "utopian" (paragraph 12). What is Mamet's attitude toward these ideals? What is his tone in discussing them? Mamet says that he and his sister hate doing chores, in part because they "had neither natural

affection nor a sense of proprietary interest" (paragraph 10) toward their house. What does this mean?

2. Near the end of the essay, Mamet recalls a "joke" that his family
   shared. How does he present the joke to the reader? Do you think
   Mamet wants the reader to think the joke is funny? Would the joke
   seem different if Mamet had told it at the beginning of the essay?
   How does he connect this joke back to the story about the rake?

3. Mamet says that "the table was associated in our minds with the
   notion of blood" (paragraph 6). Do you think the rake also has
   symbolic value? If so, what does it represent? How does Mamet's
   use of symbolic objects compare to George Orwell's treatment of
   the gun and the elephant in "Shooting an Elephant" (see the following selection)? How does Mamet's account of his relationship
   with his sister compare to Alice Walker's account of her brothers'
   role in the "accident" in which she lost one of her eyes in "Beauty:
   When the Other Dancer Is the Self (see page 274)?

29

George Orwell

Shooting an Elephant

*George Orwell (1903–1950) was born Eric Arthur Blair in Bengal, India, the
son of a colonial administrator. He was sent to England for his education and attended Eton on a scholarship, but rather than go on to university in 1922 he returned to the East and served with the Indian Imperial Police in Burma. Orwell
hated his work and the colonial system; published posthumously, the essay
"Shooting an Elephant" was based on his experience in Burma and is found in*
Shooting an Elephant and Other Essays *(1950). In 1927 Orwell returned to England and began a career as a professional writer. He served briefly in the Spanish
Civil War until he was wounded and then settled in Hertfordshire. Best remembered for his novels* Animal Farm *(1945) and* Nineteen Eighty-Four *(1949), Orwell also wrote articles, essays, and reviews, usually with a political point in
mind. In 1969 Irving Howe honored Orwell as "the best English essayist since
Hazlitt, perhaps since Dr. Johnson. He was the greatest moral force in English letters during the last several decades: craggy, fiercely polemical, sometimes mistaken, but an utterly free man."*

*In his 1946 essay "Why I Write," Orwell said that from a very early age "I
knew that when I grew up I should be a writer." At first he saw writing as a remedy for loneliness, but as he grew up his reasons for writing expanded: "Looking*

back through my work, I see it is invariably when I lacked a political purpose that I wrote lifeless books." In his mature work, he relied on simple, clear prose to express his political and social convictions: "Good prose," he once wrote, "is like a windowpane."

In Moulmein, in Lower Burma, I was hated by large numbers of people—the only time in my life that I have been important enough for this to happen to me. I was subdivisional police officer of the town, and in an aimless, petty kind of way anti-European feeling was very bitter. No one had the guts to raise a riot, but if a European woman went through the bazaars alone somebody would probably spit betel juice over her dress. As a police officer I was an obvious target and was baited whenever it seemed safe to do so. When a nimble Burman tripped me up on the football field and the referee (another Burman) looked the other way, the crowd yelled with hideous laughter. This happened more than once. In the end the sneering yellow faces of young men that met me everywhere, the insults hooted after me when I was at a safe distance, got badly on my nerves. The young Buddhist priests were the worst of all. There were several thousands of them in the town and none of them seemed to have anything to do except stand on street corners and jeer at Europeans.

All this was perplexing and upsetting. For at that time I had already made up my mind that imperialism was an evil thing and the sooner I chucked up my job and got out of it the better. Theoretically—and secretly, of course—I was all for the Burmese and all against the oppressors, the British. As for the job I was doing, I hated it more bitterly than I can perhaps make clear. In a job like that you see the dirty work of Empire at close quarters. The wretched prisoners huddling in the stinking cages of the lockups, the grey, cowed faces of the long-term convicts, the scarred buttocks of the men who had been flogged with bamboos—all these oppressed me with an intolerable sense of guilt. But I could get nothing into perspective. I was young and ill-educated and I had had to think out my problems in the utter silence that is imposed on every Englishman in the East. I did not even know that the British Empire is dying, still less did I know that it is a great deal better than the younger empires that are going to supplant it. All I knew was that I was stuck between my hatred of the empire I served and my rage against the evil-spirited little beasts who tried to make my job impossible. With one part of my mind I thought of the British Raj[1] as an unbreakable tyranny, as something clamped down, in *saecula saeculorum*,[2] upon the will of prostrate peoples; with another part I thought that the greatest joy in the world would be to drive a bayonet into a Buddhist priest's guts. Feelings like these are the normal by-products of imperialism; ask any Anglo-Indian official, if you can catch him off duty.

[1]*Raj:* The British administration. — EDS.
[2]*saecula saeculorum:* Forever and ever (Latin). — EDS.

One day something happened which in a roundabout way was enlightening. It was a tiny incident in itself, but it gave me a better glimpse than I
had had before of the real nature of imperialism—the real motives for
which despotic governments act. Early one morning the subinspector at a
police station the other end of town rang me up on the phone and said that
an elephant was ravaging the bazaar. Would I please come and do something about it? I did not know what I could do, but I wanted to see what
was happening and I got on to a pony and started out. I took my rifle, an
old .44 Winchester and much too small to kill an elephant, but I thought
the noise might be useful *in terrorem*.[3] Various Burmans stopped me on
the way and told me about the elephant's doings. It was not, of course, a
wild elephant, but a tame one which had gone "must."[4] It had been
chained up, as tame elephants always are when their attack of "must" is
due, but on the previous night it had broken its chain and escaped. Its mahout,[5] the only person who could manage it when it was in that state, had
set out in pursuit, but had taken the wrong direction and was now twelve
hours' journey away, and in the morning the elephant had suddenly reappeared in the town. The Burmese population had no weapons and were
quite helpless against it. It had already destroyed somebody's bamboo hut,
killed a cow, and raided some fruit stalls and devoured the stock; also it
had met the municipal rubbish van and, when the driver jumped out and
took to his heels, had turned the van over and inflicted violences upon it.

The Burmese subinspector and some Indian constables were waiting
for me in the quarter where the elephant had been seen. It was a very
poor quarter, a labyrinth of squalid bamboo huts, thatched with palm-
leaf, winding all over a steep hillside. I remember that it was a cloudy,
stuffy morning at the beginning of the rains. We began questioning the
people as to where the elephant had gone and, as usual, failed to get any
definite information. That is invariably the case in the East; a story always sounds clear enough at a distance, but the nearer you get to the
scene of events the vaguer it becomes. Some of the people said that the
elephant had gone in one direction, some said that he had gone in another, some professed not even to have heard of any elephant. I had almost made up my mind that the whole story was a pack of lies, when we
heard yells a little distance away. There was a loud, scandalized cry of
"Go away, child! Go away this instant!" and an old woman with a
switch in her hand came round the corner of a hut, violently shooing
away a crowd of naked children. Some more women followed, clicking
their tongues and exclaiming; evidently there was something that the children ought not to have seen. I rounded the hut and saw a man's dead
body sprawling in the mud. He was an Indian, a black Dravidian[6] coolie,

---

[3]*in terrorem:* As a warning (Latin). — EDS.
[4]*"must":* Sexual arousal. — EDS.
[5]*mahout:* Keeper (Hindi). — EDS.
[6]*Dravidian:* A populous Indian group. — EDS.

almost naked, and he could not have been dead many minutes. The people said that the elephant had come suddenly upon him round the corner of the hut, caught him with its trunk, put its foot on his back, and ground him into the earth. This was the rainy season and the ground was soft, and his face had scored a trench a foot deep and a couple of yards long. He was lying on his belly with arms crucified and head sharply twisted to one side. His face was coated with mud, the eyes wide open, the teeth bared and grinning with an expression of unendurable agony. (Never tell me, by the way, that the dead look peaceful. Most of the corpses I have seen looked devilish.) The friction of the great beast's foot had stripped the skin from his back as neatly as one skins a rabbit. As soon as I saw the dead man I sent an orderly to a friend's house nearby to borrow an elephant rifle. I had already sent back the pony, not wanting it to go mad with fright and throw me if it smelled the elephant.

The orderly came back in a few minutes with a rifle and five cartridges, and meanwhile some Burmans had arrived and told us that the elephant was in the paddy fields below, only a few hundred yards away. As I started forward practically the whole population of the quarter flocked out of the houses and followed me. They had seen the rifle and were all shouting excitedly that I was going to shoot the elephant. They had not shown much interest in the elephant when he was merely ravaging their homes, but it was different now that he was going to be shot. It was a bit of fun to them, as it would be to an English crowd; besides they wanted the meat. It made me vaguely uneasy. I had no intention of shooting the elephant—I had merely sent for the rifle to defend myself if necessary—and it is always unnerving to have a crowd following you. I marched down the hill, looking and feeling a fool, with the rifle over my shoulder and an ever-growing army of people jostling at my heels. At the bottom, when you got away from the huts, there was a metalled road and beyond that a miry waste of paddy fields a thousand yards across, not yet ploughed but soggy from the first rains and dotted with coarse grass. The elephant was standing eight yards from the road, his left side towards us. He took not the slightest notice of the crowd's approach. He was tearing up bunches of grass, beating them against his knees to clean them and stuffing them into his mouth.

I had halted on the road. As soon as I saw the elephant I knew with perfect certainty that I ought not to shoot him. It is a serious matter to shoot a working elephant—it is comparable to destroying a huge and costly piece of machinery—and obviously one ought not to do it if it can possibly be avoided. And at that distance, peacefully eating, the elephant looked no more dangerous than a cow. I thought then and I think now that his attack of "must" was already passing off; in which case he would merely wander harmlessly about until the mahout came back and caught him. Moreover, I did not in the least want to shoot him. I decided that I would watch him for a little while to make sure that he did not turn savage again, and then go home.

5

But at that moment, I glanced round at the crowd that had followed me. It was an immense crowd, two thousand at the least and growing every minute. It blocked the road for a long distance on either side. I looked at the sea of yellow faces above the garish clothes—faces all happy and excited over this bit of fun, all certain that the elephant was going to be shot. They were watching me as they would watch a conjuror about to perform a trick. They did not like me, but with the magical rifle in my hands I was momentarily worth watching. And suddenly I realized that I should have to shoot the elephant after all: The people expected it of me and I had got to do it; I could feel their two thousand wills pressing me forward, irresistibly. And it was at this moment, as I stood there with the rifle in my hands, that I first grasped the hollowness, the futility of the white man's dominion in the East. Here was I, the white man with his gun, standing in front of the unarmed native crowd—seemingly the leading actor of the piece; but in reality I was only an absurd puppet pushed to and fro by the will of those yellow faces behind. I perceived in this moment that when the white man turns tyrant it is his own freedom that he destroys. He becomes a sort of hollow, posing dummy, the conventionalized figure of a sahib. For it is the condition of his rule that he shall spend his life in trying to impress the "natives," and so in every crisis he has got to do what the "natives" expect of him. He wears a mask, and his face grows to fit it. I had got to shoot the elephant. I had committed myself to doing it when I sent for the rifle. A sahib has got to act like a sahib; he has got to appear resolute, to know his own mind and do definite things. To come all that way, rifle in hand, with two thousand people marching at my heels, and then to trail feebly away, having done nothing—no, that was impossible. The crowd would laugh at me. And my whole life, every white man's life in the East, was one long struggle not to be laughed at.

But I did not want to shoot the elephant. I watched him beating his bunch of grass against his knees, with that preoccupied grandmotherly air that elephants have. It seemed to me that it would be murder to shoot him. At that age I was not squeamish about killing animals, but I had never shot an elephant and never wanted to. (Somehow it always seems worse to kill a *large* animal.) Besides, there was the beast's owner to be considered. Alive, the elephant was worth at least a hundred pounds; dead, he would only be worth the value of his tusks, five pounds, possibly. But I had got to act quickly. I turned to some experienced-looking Burmans who had been there when we arrived, and asked them how the elephant had been behaving. They all said the same thing: He took no notice of you if you left him alone, but he might charge if you went too close to him.

It was perfectly clear to me what I ought to do. I ought to walk up to within, say, twenty-five yards of the elephant and test his behavior. If he charged, I could shoot; if he took no notice of me, it would be safe to leave him until the mahout came back. But also I knew that I was going to do no such thing. I was a poor shot with a rifle and the ground was soft mud into which one would sink at every step. If the elephant charged and I missed him, I should have about as much chance as a toad under a steamroller. But even then I was not thinking particularly of my own skin, only of the watchful yellow faces behind. For at that moment, with the crowd watching me, I was not afraid in the ordinary sense, as I would have been if I had been alone. A white man mustn't be frightened in front of "natives"; and so, in general, he isn't frightened. The sole thought in my mind was that if anything went wrong those two thousand Burmans would see me pursued, caught, trampled on, and reduced to a grinning corpse like that Indian up the hill. And if that happened it was quite probable that some of them would laugh. That would never do. There was only one alternative. I shoved the cartridges into the magazine and lay down on the road to get a better aim.

The crowd grew very still, and a deep, low, happy sigh, as of people   10
who see the theatre curtain go up at last, breathed from innumerable throats. They were going to have their bit of fun after all. The rifle was a beautiful German thing with cross-hair sights. I did not then know that in shooting an elephant one would shoot to cut an imaginary bar running from ear-hole to ear-hole. I ought, therefore, as the elephant was side-ways on, to have aimed straight at his ear-hole; actually I aimed several inches in front of this, thinking the brain would be further forward.

When I pulled the trigger I did not hear the bang or feel the kick — one never does when a shot goes home — but I heard the devilish roar of glee that went up from the crowd. In that instant, in too short a time, one would have thought, even for the bullet to get there, a mysterious, terrible change had come over the elephant. He neither stirred nor fell, but every line of his body had altered. He looked suddenly stricken, shrunken, immensely old, as though the frightful impact of the bullet had para-lyzed him without knocking him down. At last, after what seemed a long time — it might have been five seconds, I dare say — he sagged flabbily to his knees. His mouth slobbered. An enormous senility seemed to have settled upon him. One could have imagined him thousands of years old. I fired again into the same spot. At the second shot he did not collapse but climbed with desperate slowness to his feet and stood weakly upright, with legs sagging and head drooping. I fired a third time. That was the shot that did for him. You could see the agony of it jolt his whole body and knock the last remnant of strength from his legs. But in falling he seemed for a moment to rise, for as his hind legs collapsed beneath him he seemed to tower upward like a huge rock toppling, his trunk reaching skywards like a tree. He trumpeted, for the first and only time. And then down he came, his belly towards me, with a crash that seemed to shake the ground even where I lay.

I got up. The Burmans were already racing past me across the mud. It was obvious that the elephant would never rise again, but he was not dead. He was breathing very rhythmically with long rattling gasps, his great mound of a side painfully rising and falling. His mouth was wide open. I could see far down into caverns of pale pink throat. I waited a long time for him to die, but his breathing did not weaken. Finally, I fired my two remaining shots into the spot where I thought his heart must be. The thick blood welled out of him like red velvet, but still he did not die. His body did not even jerk when the shots hit him, the tortured breathing continued without a pause. He was dying, very slowly and in great agony, but in some world remote from me where not even a bullet could damage him further. I felt I had got to put an end to that dreadful noise. It seemed dreadful to see the great beast lying there, powerless to move and yet powerless to die, and not even to be able to finish him. I sent back for my small rifle and poured shot after shot into his heart, and down his throat. They seemed to make no impression. The tortured gasps continued as steadily as the ticking of a clock.

In the end I could not stand it any longer and went away. I heard later that it took him half an hour to die. Burmans were bringing dahs[7] and baskets even before I left, and I was told they had stripped his body almost to the bones by the afternoon.

Afterwards, of course, there were endless discussions about the shooting of the elephant. The owner was furious, but he was only an Indian and could do nothing. Besides, legally I had done the right thing, for a mad elephant has to be killed, like a mad dog, if its owner fails to control it. Among the Europeans opinion was divided. The older men said I was right, the younger men said it was a damn shame to shoot an elephant for killing a coolie, because the elephant was worth more than any damn Coringhee coolie. And afterwards I was very glad that the coolie had been killed; it put me legally in the right and it gave me sufficient pretext for shooting the elephant. I often wondered whether any of the others grasped that I had done it solely to avoid looking a fool.

The Reader's Presence

1. At the end of paragraph 2, Orwell gives the perfect expression of ambivalence, the simultaneous holding of two opposed feelings or opinions: "With one part of my mind . . . with another part . . ." How would you describe Orwell's dilemma? How would you react in such a situation? Is Orwell recommending that readers see his behavior as a model of what to do in such a conflict? To what extent is Orwell responsible for the situation in which he finds himself? What does he mean when he says that his conflicted feelings "are the normal by-products of imperialism"?

[7]*dahs:* Large knives. — EDS.

2. Some literary critics doubt that Orwell really did shoot an elephant in Burma. No external historical documentation has ever been found to corroborate Orwell's account. Yet what *internal* elements in the essay—what details or features—help persuade you that the episode is fact and not fiction? In other words, what makes you think that you are reading an essay and not a short story?

3. Orwell's essay describes a state of extreme personal self-consciousness, even vigilance, in a situation in which one's behavior feels somehow "scripted" by society. Orwell writes, "in reality I was only an absurd puppet pushed to and fro by the will of those yellow faces behind" (paragraph 7). How does Orwell's essay compare with Brent Staples's essay "Just Walk on By" (see page 254)? Compare especially Orwell's use of the word *fool* in his last paragraph and Staples's use of the same word in the second paragraph of the alternate version of his essay. Do you believe both authors?

30

Adrienne Rich

Split at the Root: An Essay on Jewish Identity

Adrienne Rich (b. 1929) has published numerous volumes of poetry and her work has appeared in many anthologies. She received her first award for poetry, a Yale Series of Younger Poets Award, while a student at Radcliffe College in 1951. Since then Rich has received many other professional honors, including a National Institute of Art and Letters Award (1961), a National Book Award (1974), a Fund for Human Dignity Award from the National Gay Task Force (1981), and the Lenore Marshall Nation Poetry Prize for her 1991 book, An Atlas of the Difficult World. *Her most recent books of poems are* Midnight Salvage *(1999) and* Fox *(2001). Adrienne Rich's poetics are informed by her political work against the oppression of women and against homophobia.*

Besides poetry, Rich has published five prose collections, including Blood, Bread and Poetry: Selected Prose *(1986), from which "Split at the Root" is excerpted,* What Is Found There: Notebooks on Poetry and Politics *(1993), and* Arts of the Possible *(2001). She has taught at many colleges and universities, most recently as a professor of English and feminist studies at Stanford University, and as the Marjorie Kouler visiting fellow at the University of Chicago.*

Rich has written about a pivotal moment in her life as a writer: "To write directly and overtly as a woman, out of a woman's body and experience, to take women's existence seriously as theme and source for art, was something I had been hungering to do, needing to do, all my writing life. It placed me nakedly face to face with both terror and anger; it did indeed imply the breakdown of the world as I had always known it, the end of safety, to paraphrase Baldwin. . . . But it released tremendous energy in me, as in many other women, to have that way of writing affirmed and validated in a growing political community. I felt for the first time the closing of the gap between poet and woman."

For about fifteen minutes I have been sitting chin in hand in front of the typewriter, staring out at the snow. Trying to be honest with myself, trying to figure out why writing this seems to be so dangerous an act, filled with fear and shame, and why it seems so necessary. It comes to me that in order to write this I have to be willing to do two things: I have to claim my father, for I have my Jewishness from him and not from my gentile mother, and I have to break his silence, his taboos; in order to claim him I have in a sense to expose him.

And there is, of course, the third thing: I have to face the sources and the flickering presence of my own ambivalence as a Jew; the daily, mundane anti-Semitisms of my entire life.

These are stories I have never tried to tell before. Why now? Why, I asked myself sometime last year, does this question of Jewish identity float so impalpably, so ungraspably around me, a cloud I can't quite see the outlines of, which feels to me to be without definition?

And yet I've been on the track of this longer than I think.

In a long poem written in 1960, when I was thirty-one years old, I described myself as "Split at the root, neither Gentile nor Jew, / Yankee nor Rebel."[1] I was still trying to have it both ways: to be neither/nor, trying to live (with my Jewish husband and three children more Jewish in ancestry than I) in the predominantly gentile Yankee academic world of Cambridge, Massachusetts.

But this begins, for me, in Baltimore, where I was born in my father's workplace, a hospital in the black ghetto, whose lobby contained an immense white marble statue of Christ.

My father was then a young teacher and researcher in the department of pathology at the Johns Hopkins Medical School, one of the very few Jews to attend or teach at that institution. He was from Birmingham, Alabama; his father, Samuel, was Ashkenazic,[2] an immigrant from Austria-

---

[1]Adrienne Rich, "Readings of History," in *Snapshots of a Daughter-in-Law* (New York: W. W. Norton, 1967), pp. 36–40.

[2]*Ashkenazic:* Descendants of the Jews, generally Yiddish-speaking, who settled in middle and northern Europe. — EDS.

Hungary and his mother, Hattie Rice, a Sephardic[3] Jew from Vicksburg, Mississippi. My grandfather had had a shoe store in Birmingham, which did well enough to allow him to retire comfortably and to leave my grandmother income on his death. The only souvenirs of my grandfather, Samuel Rich, were his ivory flute, which lay on our living-room mantel and was not to be played with; his thin gold pocket watch, which my father wore; and his Hebrew prayer book, which I discovered among my father's books in the course of reading my way through his library. In this prayer book there was a newspaper clipping about my grandparents' wedding, which took place in a synagogue.

My father, Arnold, was sent in adolescence to a military school in the North Carolina mountains, a place for training white southern Christian gentlemen. I suspect that there were few, if any, other Jewish boys at Colonel Bingham's, or at "Mr. Jefferson's university" in Charlottesville, where he studied as an undergraduate. With whatever conscious forethought, Samuel and Hattie sent their son into the dominant southern WASP culture to become an "exception," to enter the professional class. Never, in describing these experiences, did he speak of having suffered — from loneliness, cultural alienation, or outsiderhood. Never did I hear him use the word *anti-Semitism.*

It was only in college, when I read a poem by Karl Shapiro beginning "To hate the Negro and avoid the Jew / is the curriculum," that it flashed on me that there was an untold side to my father's story of his student years. He looked recognizably Jewish, was short and slender in build with dark wiry hair and deep-set eyes, high forehead, and curved nose.

My mother is a gentile. In Jewish law I cannot count myself a Jew. If   10
it is true that "we think back through our mothers if we are women" (Virginia Woolf) — and I myself have affirmed this — then even according to lesbian theory, I cannot (or need not?) count myself a Jew.

The white southern Protestant woman, the gentile, has always been there for me to peel back into. That's a whole piece of history in itself, for my gentile grandmother and my mother were also frustrated artists and intellectuals, a lost writer and a lost composer between them. Readers and annotators of books, note takers, my mother a good pianist still, in her eighties. But there was also the obsession with ancestry, with "background," the southern talk of family, not as people you would necessarily know and depend on, but as heritage, the guarantee of "good breeding." There was the inveterate romantic heterosexual fantasy, the mother telling the daughter how to attract men (my mother often used the word "fascinate"); the assumption that relations between the sexes could only be romantic, that it was in the woman's interest to cultivate "mystery,"

---

[3]*Sephardic:* Descendants of the Jews who settled for the most part in Spain, Portugal, and northern Africa. — EDS.

conceal her actual feelings. Survival tactics of a kind, I think today, knowing what I know about the white woman's sexual role in the southern racist scenario. Heterosexuality as protection, but also drawing white women deeper into collusion with white men.

It would be easy to push away and deny the gentile in me — that white southern woman, that social christian. At different times in my life I have wanted to push away one or the other burden of inheritance, to say merely *I am a woman; I am a lesbian.* If I call myself a Jewish lesbian, do I thereby try to shed some of my southern gentile white woman's culpability? If I call myself only through my mother, is it because I pass more easily through a world where being a lesbian often seems like outsiderhood enough?

According to Nazi logic, my two Jewish grandparents would have made me a *Mischling, first-degree* — nonexempt from the Final Solution.[4]

The social world in which I grew up was christian virtually without needing to say so — christian imagery, music, language, symbols, assumptions everywhere. It was also a genteel, white, middle-class world in which "common" was a term of deep opprobrium. "Common" white people might speak of "niggers"; *we* were taught never to use that word — *we* said "Negroes" (even as we accepted segregation, the eating taboo, the assumption that black people were simply of a separate species). Our language was more polite, distinguishing us from the "rednecks" or the lynch-mob mentality. But so charged with negative meaning was even the word "Negro" that as children we were taught never to use it in front of black people. We were taught that any mention of skin color in the presence of colored people was treacherous, forbidden ground. In a parallel way, the word *Jew* was not used by polite gentiles. I sometimes heard my best friend's father, a Presbyterian minister, allude to "the Hebrew people" or "people of the Jewish faith." The world of acceptable folk was white, gentile (christian, really), and had "ideals" (which colored people, white "common" people, were not supposed to have). "Ideals" and "manners" included not hurting someone's feelings by calling her or him a Negro or a Jew — naming the hated identity. This is the mental framework of the 1930s and 1940s in which I was raised.

(Writing this, I feel dimly like the betrayer: of my father, who did not   15
speak the word; of my mother, who must have trained me in the messages; of my caste and class; of my whiteness itself.)

Two memories: I am in a play reading at school of *The Merchant of Venice.* Whatever Jewish law says, I am quite sure I was *seen* as Jewish (with a reassuringly gentile mother) in that double vision that bigotry al-

[4]*Final Solution:* The Nazi plan to exterminate the Jews. — EDS.

lows. I am the only Jewish girl in the class, and I am playing Portia. As always, I read my part aloud for my father the night before, and he tells me to convey, with my voice, more scorn and contempt with the word *Jew:* "Therefore, Jew . . ." I have to say the word out, and say it loudly. I was encouraged to pretend to be a non-Jewish child acting a non-Jewish character who has to speak the word *Jew* emphatically. Such a child would not have had trouble with the part. But *I* must have had trouble with the part, if only because the word itself was really taboo. I can see that there was a kind of terrible, bitter bravado about my father's way of handling this. And who would not dissociate from Shylock in order to identify with Portia? As a Jewish child who was also a female, I loved Portia—and, like every other Shakespearean heroine, she proved a treacherous role model.

A year or so later I am in another play, *The School for Scandal,* in which a notorious spendthrift is described as having "many excellent friends . . . among the Jews." In neither case was anything explained, either to me or to the class at large, about this scorn for Jews and the disgust surrounding Jews and money. Money, when Jews wanted it, had it, or lent it to others, seemed to take on a peculiar nastiness; Jews and money had some peculiar and unspeakable relation.

At the same school—in which we had Episcopalian hymns and prayers, and read aloud through the Bible morning after morning—I gained the impression that Jews were in the Bible and mentioned in English literature, that they had been persecuted centuries ago by the wicked Inquisition, but that they seemed not to exist in everyday life. These were the 1940s, and we were told a great deal about the Battle of Britain, the noble French Resistance fighters, the brave, starving Dutch—but I did not learn of the resistance of the Warsaw ghetto until I left home.

I was sent to the Episcopal church, baptized and confirmed, and attended it for about five years, though without belief. That religion seemed to have little to do with belief or commitment; it was liturgy that mattered, not spiritual passion. Neither of my parents ever entered that church, and my father would not enter *any* church for any reason—wedding or funeral. Nor did I enter a synagogue until I left Baltimore. When I came home from church, for a while, my father insisted on reading aloud to me from Thomas Paine's *The Age of Reason*—a diatribe against institutional religion. Thus, he explained, I would have a balanced view of these things, a choice. He—they—did not give me the choice to be a Jew. My mother explained to me when I was filling out forms for college that if any question was asked about "religion," I should put down "Episcopalian" rather than "none"—to seem to have no religion was, she implied, dangerous.

But it was white social christianity, rather than any particular christian sect, that the world was founded on. The very word *Christian* was used as a synonym for virtuous, just, peace-loving, generous, etc., 20 etc.[5] The norm was christian: "Religion: none" was indeed not acceptable. Anti-Semitism was so intrinsic as not to have a name. I don't recall exactly being taught that the Jews killed Jesus — "Christ killer" seems too strong a term for the bland Episcopal vocabulary — but certainly we got the impression that the Jews had been caught out in a terrible mistake, failing to recognize the true Messiah, and were thereby less advanced in moral and spiritual sensibility. The Jews had actually allowed *money-lenders in the Temple* (again, the unexplained obsession with Jews and money). They were of the past, archaic, primitive, as older (and darker) cultures are supposed to be primitive; christianity was lightness, fairness, peace on earth, and combined the feminine appeal of "The meek shall inherit the earth" with the masculine stride of "Onward, Christian Soldiers."

Sometime in 1946, while still in high school, I read in the newspaper that a theater in Baltimore was showing films of the Allied liberation of the Nazi concentration camps. Alone, I went downtown after school one afternoon and watched the stark, blurry, but unmistakable newsreels. When I try to go back and touch the pulse of that girl of sixteen, growing up in many ways so precocious and so ignorant, I am overwhelmed by a memory of despair, a sense of inevitability more enveloping than any I had ever known. Anne Frank's diary and many other personal narratives of the Holocaust were still unknown or unwritten. But it came to me that every one of those piles of corpses, mountains of shoes and clothing had contained, simply, individuals, who had believed, as I now believed of myself, that they were intended to live out a life of some kind of meaning, that the world possessed some kind of sense and order; yet *this* had happened to them. And I, who believed my life was intended to be so interesting and meaningful, was connected to those dead by something — not just mortality but a taboo name, a hated identity. Or was I — did I really have to be? Writing this now, I feel belated rage that I was so impoverished by the family and social worlds I lived in, that I had to try to figure out by myself what this did indeed mean for me. That I had never been taught about resistance, only about passing. That I had no language for anti-Semitism itself.

When I went home and told my parents where I had been, they were not pleased. I felt accused of being morbidly curious, not healthy, sniffing around death for the thrill of it. And since, at sixteen, I was often not sure of the sources of my feelings or of my motives for doing what I did, I probably accused myself as well. One thing was clear: There was nobody in my world with whom I could discuss those films. Probably at the same time, I was reading accounts of the camps in magazines and newspapers;

[5]In a similar way the phrase *That's white of you* implied that you were behaving with the superior decency and morality expected of white but not of black people.

what I remember were the films and having questions that I could not even phrase, such as *Are those men and women "them" or "us"?*

To be able to ask even the child's astonished question *Why do they hate us so?* means knowing how to say "we." The guilt of not knowing, the guilt of perhaps having betrayed my parents or even those victims, those survivors, through mere curiosity — these also froze in me for years the impulse to find out more about the Holocaust.

1947: I left Baltimore to go to college in Cambridge, Massachusetts, left (I thought) the backward, enervating South for the intellectual, vital North. New England also had for me some vibration of higher moral rectitude, of moral passion even, with its seventeenth-century Puritan self-scrutiny, its nineteenth-century literary "flowering," its abolitionist righteousness, Colonel Shaw and his black Civil War regiment depicted in granite on Boston Common. At the same time, I found myself, at Radcliffe, among Jewish women. I used to sit for hours over coffee with what I thought of as the "real" Jewish students, who told me about middle-class Jewish culture in America. I described my background — for the first time to strangers — and they took me on, some with amusement at my illiteracy, some arguing that I could never marry into a strict Jewish family, some convinced I didn't "look Jewish," others that I did. I learned the names of holidays and foods, which surnames are Jewish and which are "changed names"; about girls who had had their noses "fixed," their hair straightened. For these young Jewish women, students in the late 1940s, it was acceptable, perhaps even necessary, to strive to look as gentile as possible; but they stuck proudly to being Jewish, expected to marry a Jew, have children, keep the holidays, carry on the culture.

I felt I was testing a forbidden current, that there was danger in these 25
revelations. I bought a reproduction of a Chagall portrait of a rabbi in striped prayer shawl and hung it on the wall of my room. I was admittedly young and trying to educate myself, but I was also doing something that *is* dangerous: I was flirting with identity.

One day that year I was in a small shop where I had bought a dress with a too-long skirt. The shop employed a seamstress who did alterations, and she came in to pin up the skirt on me. I am sure that she was a recent immigrant, a survivor. I remember a short, dark woman wearing heavy glasses, with an accent so foreign I could not understand her words. Something about her presence was very powerful and disturbing to me. After marking and pinning up the skirt, she sat back on her knees, looked up at me, and asked in a hurried whisper: "You Jewish?" Eighteen years of training in assimilation sprang into the reflex by which I shook my head, rejecting her, and muttered, "No."

What was I actually saying "no" to? She was poor, older, struggling with a foreign tongue, anxious; she had escaped the death that had been intended for her, but I had no imagination of her possible courage and foresight, her resistance—I did not see in her a heroine who had perhaps saved many lives, including her own. I saw the frightened immigrant, the seamstress hemming the skirts of college girls, the wandering Jew. But I was an American college girl having her skirt hemmed. And I was frightened myself, I think, because she had recognized me ("It takes one to know one," my friend Edie at Radcliffe had said) even if I refused to recognize myself or her, even if her recognition was sharpened by loneliness or the need to feel safe with me.

But why should she have felt safe with me? I myself was living with a false sense of safety.

There are betrayals in my life that I have known at the very moment were betrayals: this was one of them. There are other betrayals committed so repeatedly, so mundanely, that they leave no memory trace behind, only a growing residue of misery, of dull, accreted self-hatred. Often these take the form not of words but of silence. Silence before the joke at which everyone is laughing: the anti-woman joke, the racist joke, the anti-Semitic joke. Silence and then amnesia. Blocking it out when the oppressor's language starts coming from the lips of one we admire, whose courage and eloquence have touched us: *She didn't really mean that; he didn't really say that.* But the accretions build up out of sight, like scale inside a kettle.

1948: I come home from my freshman year at college, flaming with   30
new insights, new information. I am the daughter who has gone out into the world, to the pinnacle of intellectual prestige, Harvard, fulfilling my father's hopes for me, but also exposed to dangerous influences. I have already been reproved for attending a rally for Henry Wallace[6] and the Progressive party. I challenge my father: "Why haven't you told me that I am Jewish? Why do you never talk about being a Jew?" He answers measuredly, "You know that I have never denied that I am a Jew. But it's not important to me. I am a scientist, a deist. I have no use for organized religion. I choose to live in a world of many kinds of people. There are Jews I admire and others whom I despise. I am a person, not simply a Jew." The words are as I remember them, not perhaps exactly as spoken. But that was the message. And it contained enough truth—as all denial drugs itself on partial truth—so that it remained for the time being unanswerable, leaving me high and dry, split at the root, gasping for clarity, for air.

At that time Arnold Rich was living in suspension, waiting to be appointed to the professorship of pathology at Johns Hopkins. The appointment was delayed for years, no Jew ever having held a professional chair in that medical school. And he wanted it badly. It must have been a very

---

[6]*Henry Wallace* (1888–1965): American journalist, agriculturist, and politician, as well as the 1948 Progressive party's candidate for the presidency. — EDS.

bitter time for him, since he had believed so greatly in the redeeming power of excellence, of being the most brilliant, inspired man for the job. With enough excellence, you could presumably make it stop mattering that you were Jewish; you could become the *only* Jew in the gentile world, a Jew so "civilized," so far from "common," so attractively combining southern gentility with European cultural values that no one would ever confuse you with the raw, "pushy" Jews of New York, the "loud, hysterical" refugees from eastern Europe, the "overdressed" Jews of the urban South.

We—my sister, mother, and I—were constantly urged to speak quietly in public, to dress without ostentation, to repress all vividness or spontaneity, to assimilate with a world which might see us as too flamboyant. I suppose that my mother, pure gentile though she was, could be seen as acting "common" or "Jewish" if she laughed too loudly or spoke aggressively. My father's mother, who lived with us half the year, was a model of circumspect behavior, dressed in dark blue or lavender, retiring in company, ladylike to an extreme, wearing no jewelry except a good gold chain, a narrow brooch, or a string of pearls. A few times, within the family, I saw her anger flare, felt the passion she was repressing. But when Arnold took us out to a restaurant or on a trip, the Rich women were always tuned down to some WASP level my father believed, surely, would protect us all—maybe also make us unrecognizable to the "real Jews" who wanted to seize us, drag us back to the *shtetl,* the ghetto, in its many manifestations.

For, yes, that *was* a message—that some Jews would be after you, once they "knew," to rejoin them, to re-enter a world that was messy, noisy, unpredictable, maybe poor—"even though," as my mother once wrote me, criticizing my largely Jewish choice of friends in college, "some of them will be the most brilliant, fascinating people you'll ever meet." I wonder if that isn't one message of assimilation—of America—that the unlucky or the unachieving want to pull you backward, that to identify with them is to court downward mobility, lose the precious chance of passing, of token existence. There was always within this sense of Jewish identity a strong class discrimination. Jews might be "fascinating" as individuals but came with huge unruly families who "poured chicken soup over everyone's head" (in the phrase of a white southern male poet). Anti-Semitism could thus be justified by the bad behavior of certain Jews; and if you did not effectively deny family and community, there would always be a remote cousin claiming kinship with you who was the "wrong kind" of Jew.

I have always believed his attitude toward other Jews depended on who they were. . . . It was my impression that Jews of this background looked down on Eastern European Jews, including Polish Jews and Russian Jews, who generally were not as well educated. This from a letter written to me recently by a gentile who had worked in my father's department, whom I had asked about anti-Semitism there and in particular regarding my father. This informant also wrote me that it was hard to perceive anti-Semitism in Baltimore because the racism made so much more intense an impression: *I would almost have to think that blacks went to a different heaven than the whites, because the bodies were kept in a separate morgue, and some white persons did not even want blood transfusions from black donors.* My father's mind was predictably racist and misogynist; yet as a medical student he noted in his journal that southern male chivalry stopped at the point of any white man in a streetcar giving his seat to an old, weary black woman standing in the aisle. Was this a Jewish insight—an outsider's insight, even though the outsider was striving to be on the inside?

Because what isn't named is often more permeating than what is, I   35
believe that my father's Jewishness profoundly shaped my own identity and our family existence. They were shaped both by external anti-Semitism and my father's self-hatred, and by his Jewish pride. What Arnold did, I think, was call his Jewish pride something else: achievement, aspiration, genius, idealism. Whatever was unacceptable got left back under the rubric of Jewishness or the "wrong kind" of Jews—uneducated, aggressive, loud. The message I got was that we were really superior: Nobody else's father had collected so many books, had traveled so far, knew so many languages. Baltimore was a musical city, but for the most part, in the families of my school friends, culture was for women. My father was an amateur musician, read poetry, adored encyclopedic knowledge. He prowled and pounced over my school papers, insisting I use "grown-up" sources; he criticized my poems for faulty technique and gave me books on rhyme and meter and form. His investment in my intellect and talent was egotistical, tyrannical, opinionated, and terribly wearing. He taught me, nevertheless, to believe in hard work, to mistrust easy inspiration, to write and rewrite; to feel that I *was* a person of the book, even though a woman; to take ideas seriously. He made me feel, at a very young age, the power of language and that I could share in it.

The Riches were proud, but we also had to be very careful. Our behavior had to be more impeccable than other people's. Strangers were not to be trusted, nor even friends; family issues must never go beyond the family; the world was full of potential slanderers, betrayers, *people who could not understand.* Even within the family, I realize that I never in my whole life knew what my father was really feeling. Yet he spoke—monologued—with driving intensity. You could grow up in such a house mesmerized by the local electricity, the crucial meanings assumed by the merest things. This used to seem to me a sign that we were all living on some high emotional plane. It was a difficult force field for a favored daughter to disengage from.

Easy to call that intensity Jewish; and I have no doubt that passion is one of the qualities required for survival over generations of persecution. But what happens when passion is rent from its original base, when the white gentile world is softly saying "Be more like us and you can be almost one of us"? What happens when survival seems to mean closing off one emotional artery after another? His forebears in Europe had been forbidden to travel or expelled from one country after another, had special taxes levied on them if they left the city walls, had been forced to wear special clothes and badges, restricted to the poorest neighborhoods. He had wanted to be a "free spirit," to travel widely, among "all kinds of people." Yet in his prime of life he lived in an increasingly withdrawn world, in his house up on a hill in a neighborhood where Jews were not supposed to be able to buy property, depending almost exclusively on interactions with his wife and daughters to provide emotional connectedness. In his home, he created a private defense system so elaborate that even as he was dying, my mother felt unable to talk freely with his colleagues or others who might have helped her. Of course, she acquiesced in this.

The loneliness of the "only," the token, often doesn't feel like loneliness but like a kind of dead echo chamber. Certain things that ought to don't resonate. Somewhere Beverly Smith writes of women of color "inspiring the behavior" in each other. When there's nobody to "inspire the behavior," act out of the culture, there is an atrophy, a dwindling, which is partly invisible. . . .

Sometimes I feel I have seen too long from too many disconnected angles: white, Jewish, anti-Semite, racist, anti-racist, once-married, lesbian, middle-class, feminist, exmatriate southerner, *split at the root*—that I will never bring them whole. I would have liked, in this essay, to bring together the meanings of anti-Semitism and racism as I have experienced them and as I believe they intersect in the world beyond my life. But I'm not able to do this yet. I feel the tension as I think, make notes: *If you really look at the one reality, the other will waver and disperse.* Trying in one week to read Angela Davis and Lucy Davidowicz,[7] trying to hold throughout to a feminist, a lesbian, perspective—what does this mean? Nothing has trained me for this. And sometimes I feel inadequate to make any statement as a Jew; I feel the history of denial within me like an injury, a scar. For assimilation has affected *my* perceptions; those early lapses in meaning, those blanks, are with me still. My ignorance can be dangerous to me and to others.

Yet we can't wait for the undamaged to make our connections for us;   40
we can't wait to speak until we are perfectly clear and righteous. There is no purity and, in our lifetimes, no end to this process.

This essay, then, has no conclusions: It is another beginning for me. Not just a way of saying, in 1982 Right Wing America, *I, too, will wear the yellow star.* It's a moving into accountability, enlarging the range of

---

[7]Angela Y. Davis, *Women, Race and Class* (New York: Random House, 1981); Lucy S. Davidowicz, *The War against the Jews 1933–1945* (New York: Bantam, 1979).

accountability. I know that in the rest of my life, the next half century or so, every aspect of my identity will have to be engaged. The middle-class white girl taught to trade obedience for privilege. The Jewish lesbian raised to be a heterosexual gentile. The woman who first heard oppression named and analyzed in the black Civil Rights struggle. The woman with three sons, the feminist who hates male violence. The woman limping with a cane, the woman who has stopped bleeding are also accountable. The poet who knows that beautiful language can lie, that the oppressor's language sometimes sounds beautiful. The woman trying, as part of her resistance, to clean up her act.

The Reader's Presence

1. Why does Rich feel she needs to "claim" her father in order to come to terms with her identity? What does she mean by "claim"? How do we make such claims? Why is her father so closely tied to her sense of identity?

2. In rereading Rich's essay, pay close attention to her use of time. Try to construct a chronology for the essay. How does she organize that chronology in the essay itself? Can you think of some explanations for why Rich does not proceed in an orderly and straightforward manner? Can you discover any patterns in the procedure she chose to follow?

3. In paragraph 30 Rich writes that "all denial drugs itself on partial truth." What is Rich saying about her father? about herself? She writes in the previous paragraph about the danger of silence in the face of bigotry: "Silence and then amnesia." Read Alberto Ríos's essay "Green Cards" (see page 217) in the context of these statements. How do they affect how you read Rich's strategies of self-protection?

31

Alberto Alvaro Ríos

Green Cards

Alberto Alvaro Ríos (b. 1952) is a first-generation American; his father was born in Mexico, and his mother in England. His writing reflects this double heritage and the experience of living in the borderlands between languages and cultures. Ríos was raised and educated in Arizona, where he now teaches in the English department at Arizona State University. He has received, among other honors, a fellowship from the National Endowment for the Arts. He has published several collections of poetry, including Whispering to Fool the Wind *(1982) and* The Warrington Poems *(1989), and fiction, including* The Iguana Killer: Twelve Stories of the Heart *(1984) and* Pig Cookies and Other Stories *(1995). His most recent collection of fiction is* The Curtain of Trees: Stories *(1999). Ríos has recently published* Caprirotada: A Nogales Memoir *(2002). "Green Cards" appeared in* Indiana Review *in 1995.*

Reflecting on his relationship to language, writing, and translation, Ríos talks "about the duality of language using the metaphor of binoculars, how by using two lenses one might see something better, closer, with more detail. The apparatus, the binoculars, are of course physically clumsy—as is the learning of two languages . . . but once put to the eyes a new world in that moment opens up to us. And it's not a new world at all—it's the same world, but simply better seen, and therefore better understood."

All colors exist to satisfy the longing for blue.

There's a folk saying in Spanish, *el que quiera azul que le cueste*. One must pay for what one wants; it's a variation of the older Spanish proverb, "Take what you want and pay for it, says God." But the phrase means, more literally, *he who wants blue, let it cost him.*

A green card is what you get if you are a citizen of another country but you find yourself in, or cross over to, the United States. The card is a first step toward applying for citizenship. My wife, who was born in Mexico, had one. My mother, who was born in England, had one. My father, who was born in Mexico, didn't have one. But that's another story, involving some curious papers and shady explanations. My mother-in-law, after more than forty years here, still has one. She's never been quite sure what to do next. But she's learned well that you don't raise your hand to ask the Immigration Service anything. They notice you then. Everybody knows that.

They notice you, and then they do something. And they're everywhere, maybe. So you don't speak loudly, you don't ask questions, you don't make trouble. Run away when you have to. Don't sign anything. Get a job only where everybody else is getting one, where it's safe.

There were all kinds of stories. The one my mother-in-law lived with the longest was how, her sister in Guaymas told her, they had heard that when you become a citizen of the United States, you have to spit on the flag of Mexico. And they would all shake their heads in a *no*.

My mother, when she became a citizen, recalls a curious moment.   5
After the ceremony, the high-school band came in to the courtroom and, because she was special—which is to say, in this border town with Mexico, she was not Mexican—they played the British national anthem. Someone thought it was a good idea. At that moment, though, she says she felt a little funny. She never forgot.

None of this is easy, and nobody knows what will happen when you come, and everybody is not treated the same. And things do happen. I think, finally, they were right.

Crossing over from Mexico, for example, was more than just being there and then being here. It was a change in how one walked, and a change in color. Over there, the ground moved one way, coiled and trailed and offered itself. Here was not there, and the coiling and trailing and offering were to the left and to the right, but never the same. To this, the legs and the body had to adjust. It was not the same ground.

And in Mexico, the color was green. Here, it is blue. And that Latin-American green is not the green of here, in the way that this blue is not the same blue in Mexico. The eyes, like the legs, have to learn over.

It is more than the music and the food and the clothing. It is the walk, and the color. And smell—not of food, but of things. And if one walked this other walk, and smells were new so the nose had to accommodate itself, one then began to look different. The body and the mirror made their changes.

I remember something from the middle of all this, from the middle of   10
color and the middle of the century. During the '50s, I remember driving through town and seeing pickup trucks full of men dressed in white. They were *braceros,* the workers imported specifically from Mexico for a brief time, sometimes only a day, just to work. After work, either at the end of the day or the end of the growing season, they had to go back to Mexico. What that meant was taking the pickup truck to the border and dropping them all off.

Arizona was the last state to hold out against minimum wage, championing the *laissez-faire* system of government oversight: in this case, let the growers pay what the workers will accept and don't get in the way.

And these workers worked for almost nothing. It seemed, for a while, like a good idea to the growers and to the government, whose program this was.

As a kid, I remember only all these men dressed in white. It was a color that meant they didn't belong anywhere.

Crossing over from Mexico to the United States is not a small thing, but not large either. This is an incorrect vocabulary. To cross over was big, but that part was easy. The big is like that. It was the small that was difficult.

To cross the border was made up of these smaller things, then. It was lived as these more difficult-to-explain changes in color, more like that, more something of the body than one might suspect. It was the different way of walking because the ground was new, in all things. A different way of walking or a different way of hiding. More surprise, or more dullness, dullness or quiet. Something.

It is a movement from green, but who would know it? How to explain it? This is what I've heard all my life. It is a movement like the planet's, a movement that is there absolute, but who can feel it? A movement from green, from green to what is next. 15

For my family, crossing over was crossing over from green, not from Mexico. Green from before, but sorted out, from all the moments of green in a life, sorted and lifted out and then assembled together, into a big green, into green only. Fresh from the inhuman jungles of Chiapas and farther still, somewhere middle on the Western-hemisphere map, into the green day, into the green night, into the in-between—the light and the dark greens, the green that is brown and the green that is white—but green, and inside green, green incarnate, from the back and from the front, from the shoulders and the feet, green from yesterday and green from before yesterday, all of it ocean-like, all of it water, all of it moving as claws and tendrils and tongues, as eyes, as webs, and as base and rough flight, so that to navigate upon it one needed to ride above it to move through it, and even then to be careful and to look around. One needed to paddle and to chart, the paddle as a half-weapon and a half-tool, remembering never to dangle foolishly—for the one moment green takes—an arm into it.

From green utterly and in whispers, green eyes and green tongue, green taste and green sound; green from tea, but then from coffee; from bitter, but then from sweet; green from garden, and a little then from bean and root and tuber, but then from sky and from air, and from light.

But at light, and in dream, sound and strong, four-square and, yet, in that moment of pellucid strength, in that moment also inexplicably tinged with rue, there it is that green wavers and is for a moment inconstant, is for a moment green that is hollowed, or absent; is, for a moment, blue. There is the pivotal point, the narrows in this repeating hourglass of colors, in this life. There for a second, but there absolutely: green shifts to blue, and it is done.

It is Blue. Only and just blue. It is the log sawed and in its moment of breaking. It is the yawn pushed fully and then fully engaged. It is a blue. Blue and not green. Only blue. Only blue and the memory of green. Not a desire yet—green is too close—but a memory.

So much was the green.   20

On the far other side of green was a yellow, somewhere out there, somewhere only in imagination perhaps, yellow and red and some other colors on the other side of memory. Yellow, then the green, but now blue. It was the end at last, or the beginning. It was not the middle. But it was the discovery of the middle.

In this way, the green stayed, the way the Virgin Mary was painted, and in the shades of the hillside houses. It stayed in the Chinese teas, in the *yerba buena*,[1] how that green was a cure for things, and in the afternoons, in talk. Green stayed, and had a place in my family, but always as a memory. It stayed as a sadness for something.

It stayed as what used to be.

The Reader's Presence

1. Ríos begins his essay with a Spanish phrase that he translates in several different ways. How does this opening amplify the essay's central themes? What difference would it make if Ríos were to give the phrase only in its English version?

2. How does Ríos use color as a metaphor in this essay? In what ways does he suggest that the border between Mexico and the United States is like the border between blue and green? What do you think Ríos is saying in general about boundaries and divisions?

3. How does Ríos's account of the immigrant experience compare to the images we often see of immigrants in the media? Do you think he is pro- or anti-immigration? Do you think that Ríos's use of literary and poetic language diminishes the political elements of the essay, or enhances them?

4. Paragraph 17 is closer to poetry than to prose. Consider Ríos's highly metaphorical meditation. His essay ends with an allusion to a distant place in the imagination, *from* which one is safe but *for* which one may still long. How would you describe Ríos's relation to his American-ness?

---

[1] *yerba buena:* A mint tea. — EDS.

32

Richard Rodriguez

Aria: A Memoir of a Bilingual Childhood

> *Richard Rodriguez (b. 1944) has contributed articles to many magazines and newspapers, including* Harper's, American Scholar, *the* Los Angeles Times, *and the* New York Times. *He is an editor at Pacific News Service, and a contributing editor for* Harper's, U.S. News & World Report, *and the* Los Angeles Times. *He is also a regular essayist for the* News Hour with Jim Lehrer, *for which he received the 1997 George Foster Peabody Award. His most sensational literary accomplishment, however, is his autobiography,* Hunger of Memory: The Education of Richard Rodriguez *(1982). In it, Rodriguez outlines his positions on issues such as bilingualism, affirmative action, and assimilation, and concludes that current policies in these areas are misguided and only serve to reinforce current social inequalities. Other books include* Days of Obligation: An Argument with My Mexican Father *(1992), and* Brown: The Last Discovery of America *(2002).*
>
> *About the experience of writing his autobiography, Rodriguez comments, "By finding public words to describe one's feelings, one can describe oneself to oneself.... I have come to think of myself as engaged in writing graffiti."*
>
> *The following essay originally appeared in* The American Scholar *(winter 1980/81) and later served as the opening chapter in his intellectual autobiography* Hunger of Memory *(1982).*

I remember, to start with, that day in Sacramento, in a California now nearly thirty years past, when I first entered a classroom—able to understand about fifty stray English words. The third of four children, I had been preceded by my older brother and sister to a neighborhood Roman Catholic school. But neither of them had revealed very much about their classroom experiences. They left each morning and returned each afternoon, always together, speaking Spanish as they climbed the five steps to the porch. And their mysterious books, wrapped in brown shopping-bag paper, remained on the table next to the door, closed firmly behind them.

An accident of geography sent me to a school where all my classmates were white and many were the children of doctors and lawyers and business executives. On that first day of school, my classmates must certainly have been uneasy to find themselves apart from their families, in the first institution of their lives. But I was astonished. I was fated to be the "problem student" in class.

The nun said, in a friendly but oddly impersonal voice: "Boys and girls, this is Richard Rodriguez." (I heard her sound it out: *Rich-heard Road-ree-guess.*) It was the first time I had heard anyone say my name in English. "Richard," the nun repeated more slowly, writing my name down in her book. Quickly I turned to see my mother's face dissolve in a watery blur behind the pebbled-glass door.

Now, many years later, I hear of something called "bilingual education" — a scheme proposed in the late 1960s by Hispanic-American social activists, later endorsed by a congressional vote. It is a program that seeks to permit non-English-speaking children (many from lower class homes) to use their "family language" as the language of school. Such, at least, is the aim its supporters announce. I hear them, and am forced to say no: It is not possible for a child, any child, ever to use his family's language in school. Not to understand this is to misunderstand the public uses of schooling and to trivialize the nature of intimate life.

Memory teaches me what I know of these matters. The boy reminds the adult. I was a bilingual child, but of a certain kind: "socially disadvantaged," the son of working-class parents, both Mexican immigrants.   5

In the early years of my boyhood, my parents coped very well in America. My father had steady work. My mother managed at home. They were nobody's victims. When we moved to a house many blocks from the Mexican-American section of town, they were not intimidated by those two or three neighbors who initially tried to make us unwelcome. ("Keep your brats away from my sidewalk!") But despite all they achieved, or perhaps because they had so much to achieve, they lacked any deep feeling of ease, of belonging in public. They regarded the people at work or in crowds as being very distant from us. Those were the others, *los gringos*. That term was interchangeable in their speech with another, even more telling: *los americanos*.

I grew up in a house where the only regular guests were my relations. On a certain day, enormous families of relatives would visit us, and there would be so many people that the noise and the bodies would spill out to the backyard and onto the front porch. Then for weeks no one would come. (If the doorbell rang, it was usually a salesman.) Our house stood apart — gaudy yellow in a row of white bungalows. We were the people with the noisy dog, the people who raised chickens. We were the foreigners on the block. A few neighbors would smile and wave at us. We waved back. But until I was seven years old, I did not know the name of the old couple living next door or the names of the kids living across the street.

In public, my father and mother spoke a hesitant, accented, and not always grammatical English. And then they would have to strain, their bodies tense, to catch the sense of what was rapidly said by *los gringos*. At home, they returned to Spanish. The language of their Mexican past sounded in counterpoint to the English spoken in public. The words would come quickly, with ease. Conveyed through those sounds was the pleasing, soothing, consoling reminder that one was at home.

During those years when I was first learning to speak, my mother and father addressed me only in Spanish; in Spanish I learned to reply. By contrast, English (*inglés*) was the language I came to associate with gringos, rarely heard in the house. I learned my first words of English overhearing my parents speaking to strangers. At six years of age, I knew just enough words for my mother to trust me on errands to stores one block away — but no more.

I was then a listening child, careful to hear the very different sounds of   10 Spanish and English. Wide-eyed with hearing, I'd listen to sounds more than to words. First, there were English (gringo) sounds. So many words still were unknown to me that when the butcher or the lady at the drugstore said something, exotic polysyllabic sounds would bloom in the midst of their sentences. Often the speech of people in public seemed to me very loud, booming with confidence. The man behind the counter would literally ask, "What can I do for you?" But by being so firm and clear, the sound of his voice said that he was a gringo; he belonged in public society. There were also the high, nasal notes of middle-class American speech — which I rarely am conscious of hearing today because I hear them so often, but could not stop hearing when I was a boy. Crowds at Safeway or at bus stops were noisy with the birdlike sounds of *los gringos*. I'd move away from them all — all the chirping chatter above me.

My own sounds I was unable to hear, but I knew that I spoke English poorly. My words could not extend to form complete thoughts. And the words I did speak I didn't know well enough to make distinct sounds. (Listeners would usually lower their heads to hear better what I was trying to say.) But it was one thing for *me* to speak English with difficulty; it was more troubling to hear my parents speaking in public: their high-whining vowels and guttural consonants; their sentences that got stuck with "eh" and "ah" sounds; the confused syntax; the hesitant rhythm of sounds so different from the way gringos spoke. I'd notice, moreover, that my parents' voices were softer than those of gringos we would meet.

I am tempted to say now that none of this mattered. (In adulthood I am embarrassed by childhood fears.) And, in a way, it didn't matter very much that my parents could not speak English with ease. Their linguistic difficulties had no serious consequences. My mother and father made themselves understood at the county hospital clinic and at government offices. And yet, in another way, it mattered very much. It was unsettling to hear my parents struggle with English. Hearing them, I'd grow nervous, and my clutching trust in their protection and power would be weakened.

There were many times like the night at a brightly lit gasoline station (a blaring white memory) when I stood uneasily hearing my father talk to a teenage attendant. I do not recall what they were saying, but I cannot forget the sounds my father made as he spoke. At one point his words slid together to form one long word—sounds as confused as the threads of blue and green oil in the puddle next to my shoes. His voice rushed through what he had left to say. Toward the end, he reached falsetto notes, appealing to his listener's understanding. I looked away at the lights of passing automobiles. I tried not to hear any more. But I heard only too well the attendant's reply, his calm, easy tones. Shortly afterward, headed for home, I shivered when my father put his hand on my shoulder. The very first chance that I got, I evaded his grasp and ran on ahead into the dark, skipping with feigned boyish exuberance.

But then there was Spanish: *español,* the language rarely heard away from the house; *español,* the language which seemed to me therefore a private language, my family's language. To hear its sounds was to feel myself specially recognized as one of the family, apart from *los otros.* A simple remark, an inconsequential comment could convey that assurance. My parents would say something to me and I would feel embraced by the sounds of their words. Those sounds said: *I am speaking with ease in Spanish. I am addressing you in words I never use with* los gringos. *I recognize you as someone special, close, like no one outside. You belong with us. In the family. Ricardo.*

At the age of six, well past the time when most middle-class children   15 no longer notice the difference between sounds uttered at home and words spoken in public, I had a different experience. I lived in a world compounded of sounds. I was a child longer than most. I lived in a magical world, surrounded by sounds both pleasing and fearful. I shared with my family a language enchantingly private—different from that used in the city around us.

Just opening or closing the screen door behind me was an important experience. I'd rarely leave home all alone or without feeling reluctance. Walking down the sidewalk, under the canopy of tall trees, I'd warily notice the (suddenly) silent neighborhood kids who stood warily watching me. Nervously, I'd arrive at the grocery store to hear there the sounds of the gringo, reminding me that in this so-big world I was a foreigner. But if leaving home was never routine, neither was coming back. Walking toward our house, climbing the steps from the sidewalk, in summer when the front door was open, I'd hear voices beyond the screen door talking in Spanish. For a second or two I'd stay, linger there listening. Smiling, I'd hear my mother call out, saying in Spanish, "Is that you, Richard?" Those were her words, but all the while her sounds would assure me: *You are home now. Come closer inside. With us.* "Sí," I'd reply.

Once more inside the house, I would resume my place in the family. The sounds would grow harder to hear. Once more at home, I would grow less conscious of them. It required, however, no more than the blurt of the doorbell to alert me all over again to listen to sounds. The house would turn instantly quiet while my mother went to the door. I'd hear her hard English sounds. I'd wait to hear her voice turn to soft-sounding Spanish, which assured me, as surely as did the clicking tongue of the lock on the door, that the stranger was gone.

Plainly it is not healthy to hear such sounds so often. It is not healthy to distinguish public from private sounds so easily. I remained cloistered by sounds, timid and shy in public, too dependent on the voices at home. And yet I was a very happy child when I was at home. I remember many nights when my father would come back from work, and I'd hear him call out to my mother in Spanish, sounding relieved. In Spanish, his voice would sound the light and free notes that he never could manage in English. Some nights I'd jump up just hearing his voice. My brother and I would come running into the room where he was with our mother. Our laughing (so deep was the pleasure!) became screaming. Like others who feel the pain of public alienation, we transformed the knowledge of our public separateness into a consoling reminder of our intimacy. Excited, our voices joined in a celebration of sounds. *We are speaking now the way we never speak out in public—we are together,* the sounds told me. Some nights no one seemed willing to loosen the hold that sounds had on us. At dinner we invented new words that sounded Spanish, but made sense only to us. We pieced together new words by taking, say, an English verb and giving it Spanish endings. My mother's instructions at bedtime would be lacquered with mock-urgent tones. Or a word like *sí,* sounded in several notes, would convey added measures of feeling. Tongues lingered around the edges of words, especially fat vowels. And we happily sounded that military drum roll, the twirling roar of the Spanish *r.* Family language, my family's sounds: the voices of my parents and sisters and brother. Their voices insisting: *You belong here. We are family members. Related. Special to one another. Listen!* Voices singing and sighing, rising and straining, then surging, teeming with pleasure which burst syllables into fragments of laughter. At times it seemed there was steady quiet only when, from another room, the rustling whispers of my parents faded and I edged closer to sleep.

Supporters of bilingual education imply today that students like me miss a great deal by not being taught in their family's language. What they seem not to recognize is that, as a socially disadvantaged child, I regarded Spanish as a private language. It was a ghetto language that deepened and strengthened my feeling of public separateness. What I needed to learn in school was that I had the right, and the obligation, to speak the public language. The odd truth is that my first-grade classmates could have become bilingual, in the conventional sense of the word, more easily than I. Had they been taught early (as upper middle-class children often are taught) a "second language" like Spanish or French, they could have regarded it simply as another public language. In my case, such bilingualism could not have been so quickly achieved. What I did not believe was that I could speak a single public language.

Without question, it would have pleased me to have heard my teach-   20
ers address me in Spanish when I entered the classroom. I would have felt
much less afraid. I would have imagined that my instructors were somehow "related" to me; I would indeed have heard their Spanish as my family's language. I would have trusted them and responded with ease. But I
would have delayed—postponed for how long?—having to learn the
language of public society. I would have evaded—and for how long?—
learning the great lesson of school: that I had a public identity.

Fortunately, my teachers were unsentimental about their responsibility. What they understood was that I needed to speak public English. So
their voices would search me out, asking me questions. Each time I heard
them I'd look up in surprise to see a nun's face frowning at me. I'd
mumble, not really meaning to answer. The nun would persist. "Richard,
stand up. Don't look at the floor. Speak up. Speak to the entire class, not
just to me!" But I couldn't believe English could be my language to use.
(In part, I did not want to believe it.) I continued to mumble. I resisted the
teacher's demands. (Did I somehow suspect that once I learned this public
language my family life would be changed?) Silent, waiting for the bell to
sound, I remained dazed, diffident, afraid.

Because I wrongly imagined that English was intrinsically a public language and Spanish was intrinsically private, I easily noted the difference between classroom language and the language of home. At school, words
were directed to a general audience of listeners. ("Boys and girls . . .")
Words were meaningfully ordered. And the point was not self-expression
alone, but to make oneself understood by many others. The teacher
quizzed: "Boys and girls, why do we use that word in this sentence? Could
we think of a better word to use there? Would the sentence change its
meaning if the words were differently arranged? Isn't there a better way of
saying much the same thing?" (I couldn't say. I wouldn't try to say.)

Three months passed. Five. A half year. Unsmiling, ever watchful, my
teachers noted my silence. They began to connect my behavior with the
slow progress my brother and sisters were making. Until, one Saturday
morning, three nuns arrived at the house to talk to our parents. Stiffly
they sat on the blue living-room sofa. From the doorway of another
room, spying on the visitors, I noted the incongruity, the clash of two
worlds, the faces and voices of school intruding upon the familiar setting
of home. I overheard one voice gently wondering, "Do your children
speak only Spanish at home, Mrs. Rodriguez?" While another voice
added, "That Richard especially seems so timid and shy."

That Rich-heard!

With great tact, the visitors continued, "Is it possible for you and   25
your husband to encourage your children to practice their English when
they are home?" Of course my parents complied. What would they not
do for their children's well-being? And how could they question the
Church's authority which those women represented? In an instant they
agreed to give up the language (the sounds) which had revealed and ac-

centuated our family's closeness. The moment after the visitors left, the change was observed. *"Ahora,* speak to us only *en inglés,"* my father and mother told us.

At first, it seemed a kind of game. After dinner each night, the family gathered together to practice "our" English. It was still then *inglés,* a language foreign to us, so we felt drawn to it as strangers. Laughing, we would try to define words we could not pronounce. We played with strange English sounds, often over-anglicizing our pronunciations. And we filled the smiling gaps of our sentences with familiar Spanish sounds. But that was cheating, somebody shouted, and everyone laughed.

In school, meanwhile, like my brother and sisters, I was required to attend a daily tutoring session. I needed a full year of this special work. I also needed my teachers to keep my attention from straying in class by calling out, *"Rich-heard!"*—their English voices slowly loosening the ties to my other name, with its three notes, *Ri-car-do.* Most of all, I needed to hear my mother and father speak to me in a moment of seriousness in "broken"—suddenly heartbreaking—English. This scene was inevitable. One Saturday morning I entered the kitchen where my parents were talking, but I did not realize that they were talking in Spanish until, the moment they saw me, their voices changed and they began speaking English. The gringo sounds they uttered startled me. Pushed me away. In that moment of trivial misunderstanding and profound insight, I felt my throat twisted by unsounded grief. I simply turned and left the room. But I had no place to escape to where I could grieve in Spanish. My brother and sisters were speaking English in another part of the house.

Again and again in the days following, as I grew increasingly angry, I was obliged to hear my mother and father encouraging me: "Speak to us *en inglés.*" Only then did I determine to learn classroom English. Thus, sometime afterward it happened: one day in school, I raised my hand to volunteer an answer to a question. I spoke out in a loud voice and I did not think it remarkable when the entire class understood. That day I moved very far from being the disadvantaged child I had been only days earlier. Taken hold at last was the belief, the calming assurance, that I *belonged* in public.

Shortly after, I stopped hearing the high, troubling sounds of *los gringos.* A more and more confident speaker of English, I didn't listen to how strangers sounded when they talked to me. With so many English-speaking people around me, I no longer heard American accents. Conversations quickened. Listening to persons whose voices sounded eccentrically pitched, I might note their sounds for a few seconds, but then I'd concentrate on what they were saying. Now when I heard someone's tone of voice—angry or questioning or sarcastic or happy or sad—I didn't distinguish it from the words it expressed. Sound and word were thus tightly wedded. At the end of each day I was often bemused, and always relieved, to realize how "soundless," though crowded with words, my day in public had been. An eight-year-old boy, I finally came to accept what had been technically true since my birth: I was an American citizen.

But diminished by then was the special feeling of closeness at home.   30
Gone was the desperate, urgent, intense feeling of being at home among
those with whom I felt intimate. Our family remained a loving family, but
one greatly changed. We were no longer so close, no longer bound tightly
together by the knowledge of our separateness from *los gringos*. Neither
my older brother nor my sisters rushed home after school any more. Nor
did I. When I arrived home, often there would be neighborhood kids in
the house. Or the house would be empty of sounds.

Following the dramatic Americanization of their children, even my
parents grew more publicly confident—especially my mother. First she
learned the names of all the people on the block. Then she decided we
needed to have a telephone in our house. My father, for his part, continued to use the word gringo, but it was no longer charged with bitterness
or distrust. Stripped of any emotional content, the word simply became a
name for those Americans not of Hispanic descent. Hearing him, sometimes, I wasn't sure if he was pronouncing the Spanish word *gringo,* or
saying gringo in English.

There was a new silence at home. As we children learned more and
more English, we shared fewer and fewer words with our parents. Sentences needed to be spoken slowly when one of us addressed our mother
or father. Often the parent wouldn't understand. The child would need to
repeat himself. Still the parent misunderstood. The young voice, frustrated, would end up saying, "Never mind"—the subject was closed.
Dinners would be noisy with the clinking of knives and forks against
dishes. My mother would smile softly between her remarks; my father, at
the other end of the table, would chew and chew his food while he stared
over the heads of his children.

My mother! My father! After English became my primary language, I
no longer knew what words to use in addressing my parents. The old
Spanish words (those tender accents of sound) I had earlier used—*mamá*
and *papá*—I couldn't use any more. They would have been all-too-
painful reminders of how much had changed in my life. On the other
hand, the words I heard neighborhood kids call their parents seemed
equally unsatisfactory. "Mother" and "father," "ma," "papa," "pa,"
"dad," "pop" (how I hated the all-American sound of that last word)—
all these I felt were unsuitable terms of address for *my* parents. As a result, I never used them at home. Whenever I'd speak to my parents, I
would try to get their attention by looking at them. In public conversations, I'd refer to them as my "parents" or my "mother" and "father."

My mother and father, for their part, responded differently, as their
children spoke to them less. My mother grew restless, seemed troubled
and anxious at the scarceness of words exchanged in the house. She
would question me about my day when I came home from school. She
smiled at my small talk. She pried at the edges of my sentences to get me
to say something more. ("What . . . ?") She'd join conversations she overheard, but her intrusions often stopped her children's talking. By con-

trast, my father seemed to grow reconciled to the new quiet. Though his English somewhat improved, he tended more and more to retire into silence. At dinner he spoke very little. One night his children and even his wife helplessly giggled at his garbled English pronunciation of the Catholic "Grace Before Meals." Thereafter he made his wife recite the prayer at the start of each meal, even on formal occasions when there were guests in the house.

Hers became the public voice of the family. On official business it   35 was she, not my father, who would usually talk to strangers on the phone or in stores. We children grew so accustomed to his silence that years later we would routinely refer to his "shyness." (My mother often tried to explain: Both of his parents died when he was eight. He was raised by an uncle who treated him as little more than a menial servant. He was never encouraged to speak. He grew up alone—a man of few words.) But I realized my father was not shy whenever I'd watch him speaking Spanish with relatives. Using Spanish, he was quickly effusive. Especially when talking with other men, his voice would spark, flicker, flare alive with varied sounds. In Spanish he expressed ideas and feelings he rarely revealed when speaking English. With firm Spanish sounds he conveyed a confidence and authority that English would never allow him.

The silence at home, however, was not simply the result of fewer words passing between parents and children. More profound for me was the silence created by my inattention to sounds. At about the time I no longer bothered to listen with care to the sounds of English in public, I grew careless about listening to the sounds made by the family when they spoke. Most of the time I would hear someone speaking at home and didn't distinguish his sounds from the words people uttered in public. I didn't even pay much attention to my parents' accented and ungrammatical speech—at least not at home. Only when I was with them in public would I become alert to their accents. But even then their sounds caused me less and less concern. For I was growing increasingly confident of my own public identity.

I would have been happier about my public success had I not recalled, sometimes, what it had been like earlier, when my family conveyed its intimacy through a set of conveniently private sounds. Sometimes in public, hearing a stranger, I'd hark back to my lost past. A Mexican farm worker approached me one day downtown. He wanted directions to some place. "*Hijito*, . . ." he said. And his voice stirred old longings. Another time I was standing beside my mother in the visiting room of a Carmelite convent, before the dense screen which rendered the nuns shadowy figures. I heard several of them speaking Spanish in their busy, singsong, overlapping voices, assuring my mother that, yes, yes, we were remembered, all our family was remembered, in their prayers. Those voices echoed faraway family sounds. Another day a dark-faced old woman touched my shoulder lightly to steady herself as she boarded a bus. She murmured something to me I couldn't quite comprehend. Her

Spanish voice came near, like the face of a never-before-seen relative in the instant before I was kissed. That voice, like so many of the Spanish voices I'd hear in public, recalled the golden age of my childhood.

Bilingual educators say today that children lose a degree of "individuality" by becoming assimilated into public society. (Bilingual schooling is a program popularized in the seventies, that decade when middle-class "ethnics" began to resist the process of assimilation—the "American melting pot.") But the bilingualists oversimplify when they scorn the value and necessity of assimilation. They do not seem to realize that a person is individualized in two ways. So they do not realize that, while one suffers a diminished sense of *private* individuality by being assimilated into public society, such assimilation makes possible the achievement of *public* individuality.

Simplistically again, the bilingualists insist that a student should be reminded of his difference from others in mass society, of his "heritage." But they equate mere separateness with individuality. The fact is that only in private—with intimates—is separateness from the crowd a prerequisite for individuality; an intimate "tells" me that I am unique, unlike all others, apart from the crowd. In public, by contrast, full individuality is achieved, paradoxically, by those who are able to consider themselves members of the crowd. Thus it happened for me. Only when I was able to think of myself as an American, no longer an alien in gringo society, could I seek the rights and opportunities necessary for full public individuality. The social and political advantages I enjoy as a man began on the day I came to believe that my name is indeed *Rich-heard Road-ree-guess*. It is true that my public society today is often impersonal; in fact, my public society is usually mass society. But despite the anonymity of the crowd, and despite the fact that the individuality I achieve in public is often tenuous—because it depends on my being one in a crowd—I celebrate the day I acquired my new name. Those middle-class ethnics who scorn assimilation seem to me filled with decadent self-pity, obsessed by the burden of public life. Dangerously, they romanticize public separateness and trivialize the dilemma of those who are truly socially disadvantaged.

If I rehearse here the changes in my private life after my Americanization, it is finally to emphasize a public gain. The loss implies the gain. The house I returned to each afternoon was quiet. Intimate sounds no longer greeted me at the door. Inside there were other noises. The telephone rang. Neighborhood kids ran past the door of the bedroom where I was reading my schoolbooks—covered with brown shopping-bag paper. Once I learned the public language, it would never again be easy for me to hear intimate family voices. More and more of my day was spent hearing words, not sounds. But that may only be a way of saying that on the day I raised my hand in class and spoke loudly to an entire roomful of faces, my childhood started to end.

40

I grew up the victim of a disconcerting confusion. As I became fluent in English, I could no longer speak Spanish with confidence. I continued to understand spoken Spanish, and in high school I learned how to read and write Spanish. But for many years I could not pronounce it. A powerful guilt blocked my spoken words; an essential glue was missing whenever I would try to connect words to form sentences. I would be unable to break a barrier of sound, to speak freely. I would speak, or try to speak, Spanish, and I would manage to utter halting, hiccuping sounds which betrayed my unease. (Even today I speak Spanish very slowly, at best.)

When relatives and Spanish-speaking friends of my parents came to the house, my brother and sisters would usually manage to say a few words before being excused. I never managed so gracefully. Each time I'd hear myself addressed in Spanish, I couldn't respond with any success. I'd know the words I wanted to say, but I couldn't say them. I would try to speak, but everything I said seemed to me horribly anglicized. My mouth wouldn't form the sounds right. My jaw would tremble. After a phrase or two, I'd stutter, cough up a warm, silvery sound, and stop.

My listeners were surprised to hear me. They'd lower their heads to grasp better what I was trying to say. They would repeat their questions in gentle, affectionate voices. But then I would answer in English. No, no, they would say, we want you to speak to us in Spanish ("*en español*"). But I couldn't do it. Then they would call me *Pocho*. Sometimes playfully, teasing, using the tender diminutive—*mi pochito*. Sometimes not so playfully but mockingly, *pocho*. (A Spanish dictionary defines that word as an adjective meaning "colorless" or "bland." But I heard it as a noun, naming the Mexican-American who, in becoming an American, forgets his native society.) "*¡Pocho!*" my mother's best friend muttered, shaking her head. And my mother laughed, somewhere behind me. She said that her children didn't want to practice "our Spanish" after they started going to school. My mother's smiling voice made me suspect that the lady who faced me was not really angry at me. But searching her face, I couldn't find the hint of a smile.

Embarrassed, my parents would often need to explain their children's inability to speak fluent Spanish during those years. My mother encountered the wrath of her brother, her only brother, when he came up from Mexico one summer with his family and saw his nieces and nephews for the very first time. After listening to me, he looked away and said what a disgrace it was that my siblings and I couldn't speak Spanish, "*su propria idioma.*" He made that remark to my mother, but I noticed that he stared at my father.

One other visitor from those years I clearly remember: a long-time   45
friend of my father from San Francisco who came to stay with us for several days in late August. He took great interest in me after he realized that I couldn't answer his questions in Spanish. He would grab me, as I started to leave the kitchen. He would ask me something. Usually he wouldn't bother to wait for my mumbled response. Knowingly, he'd murmur, "*¿Ay*

pocho, pocho, donde vas?" And he would press his thumbs into the upper part of my arms, making me squirm with pain. Dumbly I'd stand there, waiting for his wife to notice us and call him off with a benign smile. I'd giggle, hoping to deflate the tension between us, pretending that I hadn't seen the glittering scorn in his glance.

I recount such incidents only because they suggest the fierce power that Spanish had over many people I met at home, how strongly Spanish was associated with closeness. Most of those people who called me a *pocho* could have spoken English to me, but many wouldn't. They seemed to think that Spanish was the only language we could use among ourselves, that Spanish alone permitted our association. (Such persons are always vulnerable to the ghetto merchant and the politician who have learned the value of speaking their clients' "family language" so as to gain immediate trust.) For my part, I felt that by learning English I had somehow committed a sin of betrayal. But betrayal against whom? Not exactly against the visitors to the house. Rather, I felt I had betrayed my immediate family. I knew that my parents had encouraged me to learn English. I knew that I had turned to English with angry reluctance. But once I spoke English with ease, I came to feel guilty. I sensed that I had broken the spell of intimacy which had once held the family so close together. It was this original sin against my family that I recalled whenever anyone addressed me in Spanish and I responded, confounded.

Yet even during those years of guilt, I was coming to grasp certain consoling truths about language and intimacy — truths that I learned gradually. Once, I remember playing with a friend in the backyard when my grandmother appeared at the window. Her face was stern with suspicion when she saw the boy (the *gringo* boy) I was with. She called out to me in Spanish, sounding the whistle of her ancient breath. My companion looked up and watched her intently as she lowered the window and moved (still visible) behind the light curtain, watching us both. He wanted to know what she had said. I started to tell him, to translate her Spanish words into English. The problem was, however, that though I knew how to translate exactly what she had told me, I realized that any translation would distort the deepest meaning of her message: it had been directed only to me. This message of intimacy could never be translated because it did not lie in the actual words she had used but passed through them. So any translation would have seemed wrong; the words would have been stripped of an essential meaning. Finally I decided not to tell my friend anything — just that I didn't hear all she had said.

This insight was unfolded in time. As I made more and more friends outside my house, I began to recognize intimate messages spoken in English in a close friend's confidential tone or secretive whisper. Even more remarkable were those instances when, apparently for no special reason, I'd become conscious of the fact that my companion was speaking *only to me*. I'd marvel then, just hearing his voice. It was a stunning event to be able to break through the barrier of public silence, to be able to hear the voice of the other, to realize that it was directed just to me. After such moments of intimacy outside the house, I began to trust what I heard intimately conveyed through my family's English. Voices at home at last punctured sad confusion. I'd hear myself addressed as an intimate — in English. Such moments were never as raucous with sound as in past times, when we had used our "private" Spanish. (Our English-sounding house was never to be as noisy as our Spanish-sounding house had been.) Intimate moments were usually moments of soft sound. My mother would be ironing in the dining room while I did my homework nearby. She would look over at me, smile, and her voice sounded to tell me that I was her son. *Richard.*

Intimacy thus continued at home; intimacy was not stilled by English. Though there were fewer occasions for it — a change in my life that I would never forget — there were also times when I sensed the deep truth about language and intimacy: *Intimacy is not created by a particular language; it is created by intimates.* Thus the great change in my life was not linguistic but social. If, after becoming a successful student, I no longer heard intimate voices as often as I had earlier, it was not because I spoke English instead of Spanish. It was because I spoke public language for most of my day. I moved easily at last, a citizen in a crowded city of words.

As a man I spend most of my day in public, in a world largely devoid   50
of speech sounds. So I am quickly attracted by the glamorous quality of certain alien voices. I still am gripped with excitement when someone passes me on the street, speaking in Spanish. I have not moved beyond the range of the nostalgic pull of those sounds. And there is something very compelling about the sounds of lower-class blacks. Of all the accented versions of English that I hear in public, I hear theirs most intently. The Japanese tourist stops me downtown to ask me a question and I inch my way past his accent to concentrate on what he is saying. The eastern European immigrant in the neighborhood delicatessen speaks to me and, again, I do not pay much attention to his sounds, nor to the Texas accent of one of my neighbors or the Chicago accent of the woman who lives in the apartment below me. But when the ghetto black teenagers get on the city bus, I hear them. Their sounds in my society are the sounds of the outsider. Their voices annoy me for being so loud — so self-sufficient and unconcerned by my presence, but for the same reason they are glamorous: a romantic gesture against public acceptance. And as I listen to their shouted laughter, I realize my own quietness. I feel envious of them — envious of their brazen intimacy.

I warn myself away from such envy, however. Overhearing those teenagers, I think of the black political activists who lately have argued in favor of using black English in public schools — an argument that varies only slightly from that of foreign-language bilingualists. I have heard "radical" linguists make the point that black English is a complex and intricate version of English. And I do not doubt it. But neither do I think that black English should be a language of public instruction. What makes it inappropriate in classrooms is not something in the language itself but, rather, what lower-class speakers make of it. Just as Spanish would have been a dangerous language for me to have used at the start of my education, so black English would be a dangerous language to use in the schooling of teenagers for whom it reinforces feelings of public separateness.

This seems to me an obvious point to make, and yet it must be said. In recent years there have been many attempts to make the language of the alien a public language. "Bilingual education, two ways to understand . . ." television and radio commercials glibly announce. Proponents of bilingual education are careful to say that above all they want every student to acquire a good education. Their argument goes something like this: Children permitted to use their family language will not be so alienated and will be better able to match the progress of English-speaking students in the crucial first months of schooling. Increasingly confident of their ability, such children will be more inclined to apply themselves to their studies in the future. But then the bilingualists also claim another very different goal. They say that children who use their family language in school will retain a sense of their ethnic heritage and their family ties. Thus the supporters of bilingual education want it both ways. They propose bilingual schooling as a way of helping students acquire the classroom skills crucial for public success. But they likewise insist that bilingual instruction will give students a sense of their identity apart from the English-speaking public.

Behind this scheme gleams a bright promise for the alien child: One can become a public person while still remaining a private person. Who would not want to believe such an appealing idea? Who can be surprised that the scheme has the support of so many middle-class ethnic Americans? If the barrio or ghetto child can retain his separateness even while being publicly educated, then it is almost possible to believe that no private cost need be paid for public success. This is the consolation offered by any of the number of current bilingual programs. Consider, for example, the bilingual voter's ballot. In some American cities one can cast a ballot printed in several languages. Such a document implies that it is possible for one to exercise that most public of rights—the right to vote—while still keeping oneself apart, unassimilated in public life.

It is not enough to say that such schemes are foolish and certainly doomed. Middle-class supporters of public bilingualism toy with the confusion of those Americans who cannot speak standard English as well as they do. Moreover, bilingual enthusiasts sin against intimacy. A Hispanic-American tells me, "I will never give up my family language," and he clutches a group of words as though they were the source of his family ties. He credits to language what he should credit to family members. This is a convenient mistake, for as long as he holds on to certain familiar words, he can ignore how much else has actually changed in his life.

It has happened before. In earlier decades, persons ambitious for social mobility, and newly successful, similarly seized upon certain "family
words." Workingmen attempting to gain political power, for example,
took to calling one another "brother." The word as they used it, however, could never resemble the word (the sound) "brother" exchanged by
two people in intimate greeting. The context of its public delivery made it
at best a metaphor; with repetition it was only a vague echo of the intimate sound. Context forced the change. Context could not be overruled.
Context will always protect the realm of the intimate from public misuse.
Today middle-class white Americans continue to prove the importance of
context as they try to ignore it. They seize upon idioms of the black
ghetto, but their attempt to appropriate such expressions invariably
changes the meaning. As it becomes a public expression, the ghetto idiom
loses its sound, its message of public separateness and strident intimacy.
With public repetition it becomes a series of words, increasingly lifeless.

The mystery of intimate utterance remains. The communication of intimacy passes through the word and enlivens its sound, but it cannot be
held by the word. It cannot be retained or ever quoted because it is too
fluid. It depends not on words but on persons.

My grandmother! She stood among my other relations mocking me
when I no longer spoke Spanish. *Pocho,* she said. But then it made no difference. She'd laugh, and our relationship continued because language
was never its source. She was a woman in her eighties during the first
decade of my life—a mysterious woman to me, my only living grandparent, a woman of Mexico in a long black dress that reached down to her
shoes. She was the one relative of mine who spoke no word of English.
She had no interest in gringo society and remained completely aloof from
the public. She was protected by her daughters, protected even by me
when we went to Safeway together and I needed to act as her translator.
An eccentric woman. Hard. Soft.

When my family visited my aunt's house in San Francisco, my grandmother would search for me among my many cousins. When she found
me, she'd chase them away. Pinching her granddaughters, she would
warn them away from me. Then she'd take me to her room, where she had
prepared for my coming. There would be a chair next to the bed, a dusty
jellied candy nearby, and a copy of *Life en Español* for me to examine.
"There," she'd say. And I'd sit content, a boy of eight. *Pocho,* her
favorite. I'd sift through the pictures of earthquake-destroyed Latin-
American cities and blonde-wigged Mexican movie stars. And all the
while I'd listen to the sound of my grandmother's voice. She'd pace
around the room, telling me stories of her life. Her past. They were stories so familiar that I couldn't remember when I'd heard them for the first
time. I'd look up sometimes to listen. Other times she'd look over at me,
but she never expected a response. Sometimes I'd smile or nod. (I understood exactly what she was saying.) But it never seemed to matter to her
one way or the other. It was enough that I was there. The words she

spoke were almost irrelevant to that fact. We were content. And the great mystery remained: intimate utterance.

I learn nothing about language and intimacy listening to those social activists who propose using one's family language in public life. I learn much more simply by listening to songs on a radio, or hearing a great voice at the opera, or overhearing the woman downstairs at an open window singing to herself. Singers celebrate the human voice. Their lyrics are words, but, animated by voice, those words are subsumed into sounds. (This suggests a central truth about language: All words are capable of becoming sounds as we fill them with the "music" of our life.) With excitement I hear the words yielding their enormous power to sound, even though their meaning is never totally obliterated. In most songs, the drama or tension results from the way that the singer moves between words (sense) and notes (song). At one moment the song simply "says" something; at another moment the voice stretches out the words and moves to the realm of pure sound. Most songs are about love: lost love, celebrations of loving, pleas. By simply being occasions when sounds soar through words, however, songs put me in mind of the most intimate moments of life.

Finally, among all types of music, I find songs created by lyric poets 60
most compelling. On no other public occasion is sound so important for me. Written poems on a page seem at first glance a mere collection of words. And yet, without musical accompaniment, the poet leads me to hear the sounds of the words that I read. As song, a poem moves between the levels of sound and sense, never limited to one realm or the other. As a public artifact, the poem can never offer truly intimate sound, but it helps me to recall the intimate times of my life. As I read in my room, I grow deeply conscious of being alone, sounding my voice in search of another. The poem serves, then, as a memory device; it forces remembrance. And it refreshes; it reminds me of the possibility of escaping public words, the possibility that awaits me in intimate meetings.

The child reminds the adult: To seek intimate sounds is to seek the company of intimates. I do not expect to hear those sounds in public. I would dishonor those I have loved, and those I love now, to claim anything else. I would dishonor our intimacy by holding on to a particular language and calling it my family language. Intimacy cannot be trapped within words; it passes through words. It passes. Intimates leave the room. Doors close. Faces move away from the window. Time passes, and voices recede into the dark. Death finally quiets the voice. There is no way to deny it, no way to stand in the crowd claiming to utter one's family language.

The last time I saw my grandmother I was nine years old. I can tell you some of the things she said to me as I stood by her bed, but I cannot quote the message of intimacy she conveyed with her voice. She laughed, holding my hand. Her voice illumined disjointed memories as it passed them again. She remembered her husband—his green eyes, his magic name of Narcissio, his early death. She remembered the farm in Mexico, the eucalyptus trees nearby (their scent, she remembered, like incense). She remembered the family cow, the bell around its neck heard miles away. A dog. She remembered working as a seamstress, how she'd leave her daughters and son for long hours to go into Guadalajara to work. And how my mother would come running toward her in the sun—in her bright yellow dress—on her return. "MMMAAAAMMMMÁÁÁÁÁ," the old lady mimicked her daughter (my mother) to her daughter's son. She laughed. There was the snap of a cough. An aunt came into the room and told me it was time I should leave. "You can see her tomorrow," she promised. So I kissed my grandmother's cracked face. And the last thing I saw was her thin, oddly youthful thigh, as my aunt rearranged the sheet on the bed.

At the funeral parlor a few days after, I remember kneeling with my relatives during the rosary. Among their voices I traced, then lost, the sounds of individual aunts in the surge of the common prayer. And I heard at that moment what since I have heard very often—the sound the women in my family make when they are praying in sadness. When I went up to look at my grandmother, I saw her through the haze of a veil draped over the open lid of the casket. Her face looked calm—but distant and unyielding to love. It was not the face I remembered seeing most often. It was the face she made in public when the clerk at Safeway asked her some question and I would need to respond. It was her public face that the mortician had designed with his dubious art.

The Reader's Presence

1. The writer blames the intrusion of English into his family's private language, Spanish, for a breakdown of communication, and even of caring. How does the Spanish language appear in the essay? What associations does it have for the author? Why does Rodriguez end the essay with the scene of his dying grandmother followed by a glimpse of her corpse?

2. Rodriguez's rhetorical style alternates between persuasive argument and personal drama. Find examples of each. Do these divergent tactics undercut or reinforce each other? Why? What is the purpose of the exclamation points at the beginning of paragraph 33?

3. Rodriguez opposes proposals to teach bilingual children in their native languages, wishing to keep native language "private" and fearing it will further contribute to the marginalization of minorities. In contrast, Gloria Anzaldúa, in "How to Tame a Wild Tongue" (see page 299), considers Spanish one of America's native languages and wishes to see it publicly accepted and promoted. Whose argument do you find more persuasive, and why?

THE WRITER AT WORK

Richard Rodriguez on a Writer's Identity

How important is cultural or ethnic identity to a writer? Some writers clearly draw creative strength from their allegiances and affiliations, whereas others prefer to remain independent of groups, even those they are undeniably part of. In the following passage from a recent interview published in Sun Magazine, *Scott London asks Richard Rodriguez some tough questions about his various "identities." Could you have anticipated his responses based on his essay, "Aria: A Memoir of a Bilingual Childhood"?*

London: Many people feel that the call for diversity and multiculturalism is one reason the American educational system is collapsing.

Rodriguez: It's no surprise that at the same time that American universities have engaged in a serious commitment to diversity, they have been thought-prisons. We are not talking about diversity in any real way. We are talking about brown, black, and white versions of the same political ideology. It is very curious that the United States and Canada both assume that diversity means only race and ethnicity. They never assume it might mean more Nazis, or more Southern Baptists. That's diversity, too, you know.

London: What do *you* mean by diversity?

Rodriguez: For me, diversity is not a value. Diversity is what you find in Northern Ireland. Diversity is Beirut. Diversity is brother killing brother. Where diversity is *shared*—where I share with you my difference—that can be valuable. But the simple fact that we are unlike each other is a terrifying notion. I have often found myself in foreign settings where I became suddenly aware that I was not like the people around me. That, to me, is not a pleasant discovery.

London: You've said that it's tough in America to lead an intellectual life outside the universities. Yet you made a very conscious decision to leave academia.   5

Rodriguez: My decision was sparked by affirmative action. There was a point in my life when affirmative action would have meant something to me—when my family was working-class, and we were struggling. But very early in life I became part of the majority culture and now don't think of myself as a minority. Yet the university said I was one. Anybody who has met a real minority—in the economic sense, not the numerical sense—would understand how ridiculous it is to describe a young man who is already at the university, already well into his studies in Italian and English Renaissance literature, as a minority. Affirmative action ignores our society's real minorities—members of the disadvantaged classes, no matter what their race. We have this ludicrous, bureaucratic sense that certain racial groups, regardless of class, are minorities. So what happens is those "minorities" at the very top of the ladder get chosen for everything.

London: Is that what happened to you?

Rodriguez: Well, when it came time for me to look for jobs, the jobs came looking for me. I had teaching offers from the best universities in the country. I was about to accept one from Yale when the whole thing collapsed on me.

London: What do you mean?

Rodriguez: I had all this anxiety about what it meant to be a minor- 10 ity. My professors—these same men who taught me the intricacies of language—just shied away from the issue. They didn't want to talk about it, other than to suggest I could be a "role model" to other Hispanics— when I went back to my barrio, I suppose. I came from a white, middle-class neighborhood. Was I expected to go back there and teach the woman next door about Renaissance sonnets? The embarrassing truth of the matter was that I was being chosen because Yale University had some peculiar idea about what my skin color or ethnicity signified. Who knows what Yale thought it was getting when it hired Richard Rodriguez? The people who offered me the job thought there was nothing wrong with that. I thought there was something very wrong. I still do. I think race-based affirmative action is crude and absolutely mistaken.

London: I noticed that some university students put up a poster outside the lecture hall where you spoke the other night. It said, "Richard Rodriguez is a disgrace to the Chicano community."

Rodriguez: I sort of like that. I don't think writers should be convenient examples. I don't think we should make people feel settled. I don't try to be a gadfly, but I do think that real ideas are troublesome. There should be something about my work that leaves the reader unsettled. I intend that. The notion of the writer as a kind of sociological sample of a community is ludicrous. Even worse is the notion that writers should provide an example of how to live. Virginia Woolf ended her life by putting a rock in her sweater one day and walking into a lake. She is not a model for how I want to live my life. On the other hand, the bravery of her syntax, of her sentences, written during her deepest depression, is a kind of example for me. But I do not want to become Virginia Woolf. That is not why I read her.

London: What's wrong with being a role model?

Rodriguez: The popular idea of a role model implies that an adult's influence on a child is primarily occupational, that all a black child needs is to see a black doctor, and then this child will think, "Oh, I can become a doctor, too." I have a good black friend who is a doctor, but he didn't become a doctor because he saw other black men who were doctors. He became a doctor because his mother cleaned office buildings at night, and because she loved her children. She grew bowlegged from cleaning office buildings at night, and in the process she taught him something about courage and bravery and dedication to others. I became a writer not because my father was one—my father made false teeth for a living. I became a writer because the Irish nuns who educated me taught me something about bravery with their willingness to give so much to me.

London: There used to be a category for writers and thinkers and in-   15
tellectuals — "the intelligentsia." But not anymore.

Rodriguez: No, I think the universities have co-opted the intellectual,
by and large. But there is an emerging intellectual set coming out of
Washington think tanks now. There are people who are leaving the universities and working for the government or in think tanks, simply looking for freedom. The university has become so stultified since the sixties.
There is so much you can't do at the university. You can't say this, you
can't do that, you can't think this, and so forth. In many ways, I'm free to
range as widely as I do intellectually precisely because I'm not at a university. The tiresome Chicanos would be after me all the time. You know:
"We saw your piece yesterday, and we didn't like what you said," or,
"You didn't sound happy enough," or, "You didn't sound proud
enough."

London: You've drawn similar responses from the gay community, I
understand.

Rodriguez: Yes, I've recently gotten in trouble with certain gay activists because I'm not gay enough! I am a morose homosexual. I'm
melancholy. *Gay* is the last adjective I would use to describe myself. The
idea of being gay, like a little sparkler, never occurs to me. So if you ask
me if I'm gay, I say no.

After the second chapter of *Days of Obligation,* which is about the
death of a friend of mine from AIDS, was published in *Harper's,* I got this
rather angry letter from a gay-and-lesbian group that was organizing a
protest against the magazine. It was the same old problem: political
groups have almost no sense of irony. For them, language has to say exactly what it means. "Why aren't you proud of being gay?" they wanted
to know. "Why are you so dark? Why are you so morbid? Why are you
so sad? Don't you realize, we're all OK? Let's celebrate that fact." But
that is not what writers do. We don't celebrate being "OK." If you want
to be OK, take an aspirin.

London: Do you consider yourself more Mexican, or more American?   20

Rodriguez: In some ways I consider myself more Chinese, because I
live in San Francisco, which is becoming a predominantly Asian city. I
avoid falling into the black-and-white dialectic in which most of America
still seems trapped. I have always recognized that, as an American, I am
in relationships with other parts of the world; that I have to measure myself against the Pacific, against Asia. Having to think of myself in relationship to that horizon has liberated me from the black-and-white
checkerboard.

33

Judy Ruiz

Oranges and Sweet Sister Boy

Judy Ruiz (b. 1944) earned an M.F.A. in poetry from the University of Arkansas in 1988, has taught writing at Southwest Missouri State University in Springfield, Missouri, and won an Arkansas Arts Fellowship in 1991. Her poems have been widely published in various literary journals and have been collected in her book, Talking Razzmatazz *(1991). "Oranges and Sweet Sister Boy," which originally appeared in* Iowa Woman *in 1988, was selected for* The Best American Essays 1989. *Her nonfiction writing has most recently been included in the anthologies* Surviving Crisis *(1997) and* Connecting *(1998).*

When asked by an interviewer about her writing process, Ruiz replied: "Part of writing for me is that what happens, always, is what I don't expect. I may get a sentence in my head that is a beginning. I go from there. Sometimes I think I may be some sort of savant because I pretty much doot-de-doot around, writing on scraps of paper and in various journals and on napkins, etc.; then, when it comes time, I start gathering what I've written."

I am sleeping, hard, when the telephone rings. It's my brother, and he's calling to say that he is now my sister. I feel something fry a little, deep behind my eyes. Knowing how sometimes dreams get mixed up with not-dreams, I decide to do a reality test at once. "Let me get a cigarette," I say, knowing that if I reach for a Marlboro and it turns into a trombone or a snake or anything else on the way to my lips that I'm still out in the large world of dreams.

The cigarette stays a cigarette. I light it. I ask my brother to run that stuff by me again.

It is the Texas Zephyr[1] at midnight—the woman in a white suit, the man in a blue uniform; she carries flowers—I know they are flowers. The petals spill and spill into the aisle, and a child goes past this couple who have just come from their own wedding—goes past them and past them, going always to the toilet but really just going past them;

[1]*Texas Zephyr:* A passenger train.—EDS.

and the child could be a horse or she could be the police and they'd not notice her any more than they do, which is not at all—the man's hands high up on the woman's legs, her skirt up, her stockings and garters, the petals and finally all the flowers spilling out into the aisle and his mouth open on her. My mother. My father. I am conceived near Dallas in the dark while a child passes, a young girl who knows and doesn't know, who witnesses, in glimpses, the creation of the universe, who feels an odd hurt as her own mother, fat and empty, snores with her mouth open, her false teeth slipping down, snores and snores just two seats behind the Creators.

News can make a person stupid. It can make you think you can do something. So I ask The Blade question, thinking that if he hasn't had the operation yet that I can fly to him, rent a cabin out on Puget Sound. That we can talk. That I can get him to touch base with reality.

"Begin with an orange," I would tell him. "Because oranges are mildly intrusive by nature, put the orange somewhere so that it will not bother you—in the cupboard, in a drawer, even a pocket or a handbag will do. The orange, being a patient fruit, will wait for you much longer than say a banana or a peach."

I would hold an orange out to him. I would say, "This is the one that will save your life." And I would tell him about the woman I saw in a bus station who bit right into her orange like it was an apple. She was wild looking, as if she'd been outside for too long in a wind that blew the same way all the time. One of the dregs of humanity, our mother would have called her, the same mother who never brought fruit into the house except in cans. My children used to ask me to "start" their oranges for them. That meant to make a hole in the orange so they could peel the rind away, and their small hands weren't equipped with fingernails that were long enough or strong enough to do the job. Sometimes they would suck the juice out of the hole my thumbnail had made, leaving the orange flat and sad.

5

The earrings are as big as dessert plates, filigree gold-plated with thin dangles hanging down that touch her bare shoulders. She stands in front of the Alamo while a bald man takes her picture. The sun is absorbed by the earrings so quickly that by the time she feels the heat, it is too late. The hanging dangles make small blisters on her shoulders, as if a centipede had traveled there. She takes the famous river walk in spiked heels, rides in a boat, eats some Italian noodles, returns to the motel room, soaks her feet, and applies small band-aids to her toes. She is briefly concerned about the gun on the nightstand. The toilet flushes. She pretends to be sleeping. The gun is just large and heavy. A .45? A .357 magnum? She's never been good with names. She hopes he doesn't try to. Or that if he does, that it's not loaded. But he'll say it's loaded just for fun. Or he'll pull the trigger and the bullet will lodge in her medulla oblongata, ripping through her womb first, taking everything else vital on the way.

In the magazine articles, you don't see this: "Well, yes. The testicles have to come out. And yes. The penis is cut off." What you get is tonsils. So-and-so has had a "sex change" operation. A sex change operation. How precious. How benign. Doctor, just what do you people do with those penises?

News can make a person a little crazy also. News like, "We regret to inform you that you have failed your sanity hearing."

The bracelet on my wrist bears the necessary information about me, but there is one small error. The receptionist typing the information asked me my religious preference. I said, "None." She typed, "Neon."

Pearl doesn't have any teeth and her tongue looks weird. She says "Pumpkin pie." That's all she says. Sometimes she runs her hands over my bed sheets and says pumpkin pie. Sometimes I am under the sheets. Marsha got stabbed in the chest, but she tells everyone she fell on a knife. Elizabeth—she's the one who thinks her shoe is a baby—hit me in the back with a tray right after one of the cooks gave me extra toast. There's a note on the bulletin board about a class for the nurses: "How Putting A Towel On Someone's Face Makes Them Stop Banging Their Spoon/OR Reduction of Disruptive Mealtime Behavior By Facial Screening—7 P.M.—Conference Room." Another note announces the topic for remotivation class: "COWS." All the paranoid schizophrenics will be there.

Here, in the place for the permanently bewildered, I fit right in. Not because I stood at the window that first night and listened to the trains. Not because I imagined those trains were bracelets, the jewelry of earth. Not even because I imagined that one of those bracelets was on my own arm and was the Texas Zephyr where a young couple made love and conceived me. I am eighteen and beautiful and committed to the state hospital by a district court judge for a period of one day to life. Because I am a paranoid schizophrenic.

I will learn about cows.

So I'm being very quiet in the back of the classroom, and I'm peeling an orange. It's the smell that makes the others begin to turn around, that mildly intrusive nature. The course is called "Women and Modern Literature," and the diaries of Virginia Woolf are up for discussion except nobody has anything to say. I, of course, am making a mess with the orange; and I'm wanting to say that my brother is now my sister.

Later, with my hands still orangey, I wander in to leave something on   10
a desk in a professor's office, and he's reading so I'm being very quiet, and then he says, sort of out of nowhere, "Emily Dickinson up there in her room making poems while her brother was making love to her best friend right downstairs on the dining room table. A regular thing. Think of it. And Walt Whitman out sniffing around the boys. Our two great American poets." And I want to grab this professor's arm and say, "Listen. My brother called me and now he's my sister, and I'm having trouble making sense out of my life right now, so would you mind not

telling me any more stuff about sex." And I want my knuckles to turn white while the pressure of my fingers leaves imprints right through his jacket, little indentations he can interpret as urgent. But I don't say anything. And I don't grab his arm. I go read a magazine. I find this:

> "I've never found an explanation for why the human race has so many languages. When the brain became a language brain, it obviously needed to develop an intense degree of plasticity. Such plasticity allows languages to be logical, coherent systems and yet be extremely variable. The same brain that thinks in words and symbols is also a brain that has to be freed up with regard to sexual turn-on and partnering. God knows why sex attitudes have not been subject to the corresponding degrees of modification and variety as language. I suspect there's a close parallel between the two. The brain doesn't seem incredibly efficient with regard to sex."

John Money said that. The same John Money who, with surgeon Howard W. Jones, performed the first sex change operation in the United States in 1965 at Johns Hopkins University and Hospital in Baltimore.

Money also tells about the *hijra* of India who disgrace their families because they are too effeminate: "The ultimate stage of the *hijra* is to get up the courage to go through the amputation of penis and testicles. They had no anesthetic." Money also answers anyone who might think that "heartless members of the medical profession are forcing these poor darlings to go and get themselves cut up and mutilated," or who think the medical profession should leave them alone. "You'd have lots of patients willing to get a gun and blow off their own genitals if you don't do it. I've had several who got knives and cut themselves trying to get rid of their sex organs. That's their obsession!"

Perhaps better than all else, I understand obsession. It is of the mind. And it is language-bound. Sex is of the body. It has no words. I am stunned to learn that someone with an obsession of the mind can have parts of the body surgically removed. This is my brother I speak of. This is not some lunatic named Carl who becomes Carlene. This is my brother.

So while we're out in that cabin on Puget Sound, I'll tell him about LuAnn. She is the sort of woman who orders the in-season fruit and a little cottage cheese. I am the sort of woman who orders a double cheeseburger and fries. LuAnn and I are sitting in her car. She has a huge orange, and she peels it so the peel falls off in one neat strip. I have a sack of oranges, the small ones. The peel of my orange comes off in hunks about the size of a baby's nail. "Oh, you bought the *juice* oranges," LuAnn says to me. Her emphasis on the word "juice" makes me want to die or something. I lack the courage to admit my ignorance, so I smile and breathe "yes," as if I know some secret, when I'm wanting to scream at her about how my mother didn't teach me about fruit and my own blood pounds in my head wanting out, out.

There is a pattern to this thought as there is a pattern for a jump-suit. Sew the sleeve to the leg, sew the leg to the collar. Put the garment on. Sew the mouth shut. This is how I tell about being quiet because I am bad, and because I cannot stand it when he beats me or my brother.

"The first time I got caught in your clothes was when I was four years old and you were over at Sarah what's-her-name's babysitting. Dad beat me so hard I thought I was going to die. I really thought I was going to die. That was the day I made up my mind I would *never* get caught again. And I never got caught again." My brother goes on to say he continued to go through my things until I was hospitalized. A mystery is solved.

He wore my clothes. He played in my makeup. I kept saying, back   15
then, that someone was going through my stuff. I kept saying it and saying it. I told the counselor at school. "Someone goes in my room when I'm not there, and I *know* it—goes in there and wears my clothes and goes through my stuff." I was assured by the counselor that this was not so. I was assured by my mother that this was not so. I thought my mother was doing it, snooping around for clues like mothers do. It made me a little crazy, so I started deliberately leaving things in a certain order so that I would be able to prove to myself that someone, indeed, was going through my belongings. No one, not one person, ever believed that my room was being ransacked; I was accused of just making it up. A paranoid fixation.

And all the time it was old Goldilocks.

So I tell my brother to promise me he'll see someone who counsels adult children from dysfunctional families. I tell him he needs to deal with the fact that he was physically abused on a daily basis. He tells me he doesn't remember being beaten except on three occasions. He wants me to get into a support group for families of people who are having a sex change. Support groups are people who are in the same boat. Except no one has any oars in the water.

I tell him I know how it feels to think you are in the wrong body. I tell him how I wanted my boyfriend to put a gun up inside me and blow the woman out, how I thought wearing spiked heels and low-cut dresses would somehow help my crisis, that putting on an ultrafeminine outside would mask the maleness I felt needed hiding. I tell him it's the rule, rather than the exception, that people from families like ours have very spooky sexual identity problems. He tells me that his sexuality is a birth defect. I recognize the lingo. It's support-group-for-transsexuals lingo. He tells me he sits down to pee. He told his therapist that he used to wet all over the floor. His therapist said, "You can't aim the bullets if you don't touch the gun." Lingo. My brother is hell-bent for castration, the castration that started before he had language: the castration of abuse. He will simply finish what was set in motion long ago.

I will tell my brother about the time I took ten sacks of oranges into a school so that I could teach metaphor. The school was for special students—those who were socially or intellectually impaired. I had planned to have them peel the oranges as I spoke about how much the world is like the orange. I handed out the oranges. The students refused to peel them, not because they wanted to make life difficult for me—they were enchanted with the gift. One child asked if he could have an orange to take home to his little brother. Another said he would bring me ten dollars the next day if I would give him a sack of oranges. And I knew I was at home, that these children and I shared something that *makes* the leap of mind the metaphor attempts. And something in me healed.

A neighbor of mine takes pantyhose and cuts them up and sews them   20 up after stuffing them. Then she puts these things into Mason jars and sells them, you know, to put out on the mantel for conversation. They are little penises and little scrotums, complete with hair. She calls them "Pickled Peters."

A friend of mine had a sister who had a sex change operation. This young woman had her breasts removed and ran around the house with no shirt on before the stitches were taken out. She answered the door one evening. A young man had come to call on my friend. The sex-changed sister invited him in and offered him some black bean soup as if she were perfectly normal with her red surgical wounds and her black stitches. The young man left and never went back. A couple years later, my friend's sister/brother died when s/he ran a car into a concrete bridge railing. I hope for a happier ending. For my brother, for myself, for all of us.

My brother calls. He's done his toenails: Shimmering Cinnamon. And he's left his wife and children and purchased some nightgowns at a yard sale. His hair is getting longer. He wears a special bra. Most of the people he works with know about the changes in his life. His voice is not the same voice I've heard for years; he sounds happy.

My brother calls. He's always envied me, my woman's body. The same body I live in and have cursed for its softness. He asks me how I feel about myself. He says, "You know, you are really our father's first-born son." He tells me he used to want to be me because I was the only person our father almost loved.

The drama of life. After I saw that woman in the bus station eat an orange as if it were an apple, I went out into the street and smoked a joint with some guy I'd met on the bus. Then I hailed a cab and went to a tattoo parlor. The tattoo artist tried to talk me into getting a nice bird or butterfly design; I had chosen a design on his wall that appealed to me— a symbol I didn't know the meaning of. It is the Yin-Yang, and it's tattooed above my right ankle bone. I supposed my drugged, crazed consciousness knew more than I knew: that yin combines with yang to produce all that comes to be. I am drawn to androgyny.

Of course there is the nagging possibility that my brother's dilemma is   25
genetic. Our father used to dress in drag on Halloween, and he made a beautiful woman. One year, the year my mother cut my brother's blond curls off,
my father taped those curls to his own head and tied a silk scarf over the
tape. Even his close friends didn't know it was him. And my youngest
daughter was a body builder for a while, her lean body as muscular as a
man's. And my sons are beautiful, not handsome: they look androgynous.

Then there's my grandson. I saw him when he was less than an hour
old. He was naked and had hiccups. I watched as he had his first bath,
and I heard him cry. He had not been named yet, but his little crib had a
blue card affixed to it with tape. And on the card were the words "Baby
Boy." There was no doubt in me that the words were true.

When my brother was born, my father was off flying jets in Korea. I
went to the hospital with my grandfather to get my mother and this new
brother. I remember how I wanted a sister, and I remember looking at
him as my mother held him in the front seat of the car. I was certain he
was a sister, certain that my mother was joking. She removed his diaper
to show me that he was a boy. I still didn't believe her. Considering what
has happened lately, I wonder if my child-skewed consciousness knew
more than the anatomical proof suggested.

I try to make peace with myself. I try to understand his decision to
alter himself. I try to think of him as her. I write his woman name, and I
feel like I'm betraying myself. I try to be open-minded, but something in
me shuts down. I think we humans are in big trouble, that many of us
don't really have a clue as to what acceptable human behavior is. Something in me says no to all this, that this surgery business is the ultimate
betrayal of the self. And yet, I want my brother to be happy.

It was in the city of San Antonio that my father had his surgery. I
rode the bus from Kansas to Texas, and arrived at the hospital two days
after the operation to find my father sitting in the solarium playing soli-
taire. He had a type of cancer that particularly thrived on testosterone.
And so he was castrated in order to ease his pain and to stop the growth
of tumors. He died six months later.

Back in the sleep of the large world of dreams, I have done surgeries   30
under water in which I float my father's testicles back into him, and he—
the brutal man he was—emerges from the pool a tan and smiling man,
parting the surface of the water with his perfect head. He loves all the
grief away.

I will tell my brother all I know of oranges, that if you squeeze the orange peel into a flame, small fires happen because of the volatile oil in the
peel. Also, if you squeeze the peel and it gets into your cat's eyes, the cat
will blink and blink. I will tell him there is no perfect rhyme for the word

"orange," and that if we can just make up a good word we can be immortal. We will become obsessed with finding the right word, and I will be joyous at our legitimate pursuit.

I have purchased a black camisole with lace to send to my new sister. And a card. On the outside of the card there's a drawing of a woman sitting by a pond and a zebra is off to the left. Inside are these words: "The past is ended. Be happy." And I have asked my companions to hold me and I have cried. My self is wet and small. But it is not dark. Sometimes, if no one touches me, I will die.

Sister, you are the best craziness of the family. Brother, love what you love.

The Reader's Presence

1. The essay opens with the author asleep. How do sleep and dreams figure throughout the essay? How might they help account for the odd jumps and connections that sometimes make the essay hard to follow?

2. Note the moments in the essay where Ruiz inserts paragraphs in smaller type. What are these moments? What have they to do with the main body of the essay? What do those moments have in common? How are you intended to read them? What would the essay be like without these paragraphs?

3. In rereading the essay, make a note of all references to the body. In what ways is the human body present? According to Ruiz, how does the body differ from the mind? (See paragraph 12.) What does she mean when she says, "I think we humans are in big trouble" (paragraph 28)? In "A Clack of Tiny Sparks," (page 104), Bernard Cooper describes his early attempts to redirect his sexual desire for boys to girls: "To change a behavior required self-analysis, cold resolve, and the substitution of one thing for another" (paragraph 15). How does Ruiz's brother's voice come through her essay? What is the relation between gender and sexuality? How do Ruiz and Cooper resolve or fail to resolve their problems by the conclusions of their essays?

34

David Sedaris

Me Talk Pretty One Day

David Sedaris was born in 1956 in Johnson City, New York, and raised in Raleigh, North Carolina. He is a dramatist whose plays, written in collaboration with his sister, Amy (one of which won an Obie Award), have been produced at La Mama and Lincoln Center. Sedaris launched his career as a wry, neurotically self-disparaging humorist on National Public Radio's Morning Edition, *when he read aloud from "The Santa Land Diaries," an autobiographical piece about working as a Christmas elf at Macy's. He has since published a number of best-selling collections, including* Barrel Fever (1994), Naked (1997), Holiday on Ice (1997), *and his latest book,* Me Talk Pretty One Day (2000). *His essays appear regularly in the* New Yorker *and* Esquire. *In 2001, Sedaris was named Humorist of the Year by* Time Magazine *and received the Thurber Prize for American Humor.* New York Magazine *had dubbed Sedaris "the most brilliantly witty New Yorker since Dorothy Parker." He currently resides in Paris, where he collected material for his latest book.*

Sedaris, who for two years taught writing at the Art Institute of Chicago, laments that the students in his writing classes "were ashamed of their middle-class background . . . they felt like unless they grew up in poverty, they had nothing to write about." Sedaris feels that "it doesn't really matter what your life was like, you can write about anything. It's just the writing of it that is the challenge."

At the age of forty-one, I am returning to school and have to think of myself as what my French textbook calls "a true debutant." After paying my tuition, I was issued a student ID, which allows me a discounted entry fee at movie theaters, puppet shows, and Festyland, a far-flung amusement park that advertises with billboards picturing a cartoon stegosaurus sitting in a canoe and eating what appears to be a ham sandwich.

I've moved to Paris with hopes of learning the language. My school is an easy ten-minute walk from my apartment, and on the first day of class I arrived early, watching as the returning students greeted one another in the school lobby. Vacations were recounted, and questions were raised concerning mutual friends with names like Kang and Vlatnya. Regardless of their nationalities, everyone spoke in what sounded to me like excellent French. Some accents were better than others, but the students exhibited an ease and confidence I found intimidating. As an added discomfort, they were all young, attractive, and well dressed, causing me to feel not unlike Pa Kettle trapped backstage after a fashion show.

The first day of class was nerve-racking because I knew I'd be expected to perform. That's the way they do it here — it's everybody into the language pool, sink or swim. The teacher marched in, deeply tanned from a recent vacation, and proceeded to rattle off a series of administrative announcements. I've spent quite a few summers in Normandy, and I took a monthlong French class before leaving New York. I'm not completely in the dark, yet I understood only half of what this woman was saying.

"If you have not *meimslsxp* or *lgpdmurct* by this time, then you should not be in this room. Has everyone *apzkiubjxow?* Everyone? Good, we shall begin." She spread out her lesson plan and sighed, saying, "All right, then, who knows the alphabet?"

It was startling because (a) I hadn't been asked that question in a   5
while and (b) I realized, while laughing, that I myself did *not* know the alphabet. They're the same letters, but in France they're pronounced differently. I know the shape of the alphabet but had no idea what it actually sounded like.

"Ahh." The teacher went to the board and sketched the letter *a.* "Do we have anyone in the room whose first name commences with an *ahh?*"

Two Polish Annas raised their hands, and the teacher instructed them to present themselves by stating their names, nationalities, occupations, and a brief list of things they liked and disliked in this world. The first Anna hailed from an industrial town outside of Warsaw and had front teeth the size of tombstones. She worked as a seamstress, enjoyed quiet times with friends, and hated the mosquito.

"Oh, really," the teacher said. "How very interesting. I thought that everyone loved the mosquito, but here, in front of all the world, you claim to detest him. How is it that we've been blessed with someone as unique and original as you? Tell us, please."

The seamstress did not understand what was being said but knew that this was an occasion for shame. Her rabbity mouth huffed for breath, and she stared down at her lap as though the appropriate comeback were stitched somewhere alongside the zipper of her slacks.

The second Anna learned from the first and claimed to love sunshine   10
and detest lies. It sounded like a translation of one of those Playmate of the Month data sheets, the answers always written in the same loopy handwriting: "Turn-ons: Mom's famous five-alarm chili! Turnoffs: insecurity and guys who come on too strong!!!!"

The two Polish Annas surely had clear notions of what they loved and hated, but like the rest of us, they were limited in terms of vocabulary, and this made them appear less than sophisticated. The teacher forged on, and we learned that Carlos, the Argentine bandonion player, loved wine, music, and, in his words, "making sex with the womens of the world." Next came a beautiful young Yugoslav who identified herself as an optimist, saying that she loved everything that life had to offer.

The teacher licked her lips, revealing a hint of the saucebox we would later come to know. She crouched low for her attack, placed her hands on the young woman's desk, and leaned close, saying, "Oh yeah? And do you love your little war?"

While the optimist struggled to defend herself, I scrambled to think of an answer to what had obviously become a trick question. How often is one asked what he loves in this world? More to the point, how often is one asked and then publicly ridiculed for his answer? I recalled my mother, flushed with wine, pounding the tabletop late one night, saying, "Love? I love a good steak cooked rare. I love my cat, and I love . . ." My sisters and I leaned forward, waiting to hear our names. "Tums," our mother said. "I love Tums."

The teacher killed some time accusing the Yugoslavian girl of masterminding a program of genocide, and I jotted frantic notes in the margins of my pad. While I can honestly say that I love leafing through medical textbooks devoted to severe dermatological conditions, the hobby is beyond the reach of my French vocabulary, and acting it out would only have invited controversy.

When called upon, I delivered an effortless list of things that I detest: 15
blood sausage, intestinal pâtés, brain pudding. I'd learned these words the hard way. Having given it some thought, I then declared my love for IBM typewriters, the French word for *bruise,* and my electric floor waxer. It was a short list, but still I managed to mispronounce *IBM* and assign the wrong gender to both the floor waxer and the typewriter. The teacher's reaction led me to believe that these mistakes were capital crimes in the country of France.

"Were you always this *palicmkrexis?"* she asked. "Even a *fiuscrzsa ticiwelmun* knows that a typewriter is feminine."

I absorbed as much of her abuse as I could understand, thinking— but not saying—that I find it ridiculous to assign a gender to an inanimate object incapable of disrobing and making an occasional fool of itself. Why refer to Lady Crack Pipe or Good Sir Dishrag when these things could never live up to all that their sex implied?

The teacher proceeded to belittle everyone from German Eva, who hated laziness, to Japanese Yukari, who loved paintbrushes and soap. Italian, Thai, Dutch, Korean, and Chinese—we all left class foolishly believing that the worst was over. She'd shaken us up a little, but surely that was just an act designed to weed out the deadweight. We didn't know it then, but the coming months would teach us what it was like to spend time in the presence of a wild animal, something completely unpredictable. Her temperament was not based on a series of good and bad days but, rather, good and bad moments. We soon learned to dodge chalk and protect our heads and stomachs whenever she approached us with a question. She hadn't yet punched anyone, but it seemed wise to protect ourselves against the inevitable.

Though we were forbidden to speak anything but French, the teacher would occasionally use us to practice any of her five fluent languages.

"I hate you," she said to me one afternoon. Her English was flawless. 20
"I really, really hate you." Call me sensitive, but I couldn't help but take
it personally.

After being singled out as a lazy *kfdtinvfm,* I took to spending four
hours a night on my homework, putting in even more time whenever we
were assigned an essay. I suppose I could have gotten by with less, but I
was determined to create some sort of identity for myself: David the hard
worker, David the cut-up. We'd have one of those "complete this sentence" exercises, and I'd fool with the thing for hours, invariably settling
on something like "A quick run around the lake? I'd love to! Just give me
a moment while I strap on my wooden leg." The teacher, through word
and action, conveyed the message that if this was my idea of an identity,
she wanted nothing to do with it.

My fear and discomfort crept beyond the borders of the classroom
and accompanied me out onto the wide boulevards. Stopping for a coffee,
asking directions, depositing money in my bank account: these things
were out of the question, as they involved having to speak. Before beginning school, there'd been no shutting me up, but now I was convinced
that everything I said was wrong. When the phone rang, I ignored it. If
someone asked me a question, I pretended to be deaf. I knew my fear was
getting the best of me when I started wondering why they don't sell cuts
of meat in vending machines.

My only comfort was the knowledge that I was not alone. Huddled
in the hallways and making the most of our pathetic French, my fellow
students and I engaged in the sort of conversation commonly overheard
in refugee camps.

"Sometime me cry alone at night."

"That be common for I, also, but be more strong, you. Much work 25
and someday you talk pretty. People start love you soon. Maybe tomorrow, okay."

Unlike the French class I had taken in New York, here there was no
sense of competition. When the teacher poked a shy Korean in the eyelid
with a freshly sharpened pencil, we took no comfort in the fact that, unlike Hyeyoon Cho, we all knew the irregular past tense of the verb *to defeat.* In all fairness, the teacher hadn't meant to stab the girl, but neither
did she spend much time apologizing, saying only, "Well, you should
have been *vkkdyo* more *kdeynfulh.*"

Over time it became impossible to believe that any of us would ever
improve. Fall arrived and it rained every day, meaning we would now be
scolded for the water dripping from our coats and umbrellas. It was mid-
October when the teacher singled me out, saying, "Every day spent with
you is like having a cesarean section." And it struck me that, for the first
time since arriving in France, I could understand every word that someone was saying.

Understanding doesn't mean that you can suddenly speak the language. Far from it. It's a small step, nothing more, yet its rewards are in-

toxicating and deceptive. The teacher continued her diatribe and I settled back, bathing in the subtle beauty of each new curse and insult.

"You exhaust me with your foolishness and reward my efforts with nothing but pain, do you understand me?"

The world opened up, and it was with great joy that I responded, "I know the thing that you speak exact now. Talk me more, you, plus, please, plus."   30

The Reader's Presence

1. How did Sedaris take a potentially boring experience—auditing a beginner's language class—and turn it into a humorous essay? What were the funniest parts of the essay? An interviewer wrote that Sedaris's signature is "deadpan" humor. What is deadpan humor? Identify—and characterize the effectiveness of—examples of it in "Me Talk Pretty One Day."

2. Which English words would you substitute for the nonsense words that represent Sedaris's difficulties understanding his teacher's French? Have a classmate tell you what he or she thinks such words as *meimslsxp* (paragraph 4) *palicmkrexis* (paragraph 16), or *kdeynfulh* (paragraph 26) might mean? Did he or she pick the same or similar words to the ones you picked? Point to the clues Sedaris includes in the essay to hint at what such words mean. How would you rewrite the passage with different clues to indicate a different possible meaning for the nonsense words?

3. How surprised were you by the last line in the essay? To what extent did you expect that Sedaris would speak fluently because he understood his teacher's French perfectly? Look at some other unexpected last lines that you've read in this collection. Choose two surprising last lines and identify how each author goes about setting up the surprise. When you look back, at what point in each essay should you have been expecting the unexpected? If there were clues beforehand, identify them. Or, did the last lines come out of nowhere?

35

Brent Staples

Just Walk on By: A Black Man Ponders His Power to Alter Public Space

As he describes in Parallel Time: Growing Up in Black and White *(1994), Brent Staples (b. 1951) escaped a childhood of urban poverty through success in school and his determination to be a writer. Although Staples earned a Ph.D. in psychology from the University of Chicago in 1982, his love of journalism led him to leave the field of psychology and start a career that has taken him to his current position on the editorial board of the* New York Times. *Staples contributes to several national magazines, including* Harper's, *the* New York Times Magazine, *and* Ms., *in which "Just Walk on By" appeared in 1986.*

In his autobiography, which won the Anisfield Wolff Book Award, previously won by such writers as James Baldwin, Ralph Ellison, and Zora Neale Hurston, Staples remembers how in Chicago he prepared for his writing career by keeping a journal. "I wrote on buses, on the Jackson Park el — though only at the stops to keep the writing legible. I traveled to distant neighborhoods, sat on their curbs, and sketched what I saw in words. Thursdays meant free admission at the Art Institute. All day I attributed motives to people in paintings, especially people in Rembrandts. At closing time I went to a nightclub in The Loop and spied on patrons, copied their conversations and speculated about their lives. The journal was more than 'a record of my inner transactions.' It was a collection of stolen souls from which I would one day construct a book."

My first victim was a woman — white, well dressed, probably in her early twenties. I came upon her late one evening on a deserted street in Hyde Park, a relatively affluent neighborhood in an otherwise mean, impoverished section of Chicago. As I swung onto the avenue behind her, there seemed to be a discreet, uninflammatory distance between us. Not so. She cast back a worried glance. To her, the youngish black man — a broad six feet two inches with a beard and billowing hair, both hands shoved into the pockets of a bulky military jacket — seemed menacingly close. After a few more quick glimpses, she picked up her pace and was soon running in earnest. Within seconds she disappeared into a cross street.

That was more than a decade ago. I was twenty-two years old, a graduate student newly arrived at the University of Chicago. It was in the echo of that terrified woman's footfalls that I first began to know the unwieldy inheritance I'd come into—the ability to alter public space in ugly ways. It was clear that she thought herself the quarry of a mugger, a rapist, or worse. Suffering a bout of insomnia, however, I was stalking sleep, not defenseless wayfarers. As a softy who is scarcely able to take a knife to a raw chicken—let alone hold it to a person's throat—I was surprised, embarrassed, and dismayed all at once. Her flight made me feel like an accomplice in tyranny. It also made it clear that I was indistinguishable from the muggers who occasionally seeped into the area from the surrounding ghetto. That first encounter, and those that followed, signified that a vast, unnerving gulf lay between nighttime pedestrians—particularly women—and me. And I soon gathered that being perceived as dangerous is a hazard in itself. I only needed to turn a corner into a dicey situation, or crowd some frightened, armed person in a foyer somewhere, or make an errant move after being pulled over by a policeman. Where fear and weapons meet—and they often do in urban America—there is always the possibility of death.

In that first year, my first away from my hometown, I was to become thoroughly familiar with the language of fear. At dark, shadowy intersections in Chicago, I could cross in front of a car stopped at a traffic light and elicit the *thunk, thunk, thunk, thunk* of the driver—black, white, male, or female—hammering down the door locks. On less traveled streets after dark, I grew accustomed to but never comfortable with people who crossed to the other side of the street rather than pass me. Then there were the standard unpleasantries with police, doormen, bouncers, cabdrivers, and others whose business is to screen out troublesome individuals *before* there is any nastiness.

I moved to New York nearly two years ago and I have remained an avid night walker. In central Manhattan, the near-constant crowd cover minimizes tense one-on-one street encounters. Elsewhere—visiting friends in SoHo,[1] where sidewalks are narrow and tightly spaced buildings shut out the sky—things can get very taut indeed.

Black men have a firm place in New York mugging literature. Norman Podhoretz[2] in his famed (or infamous) 1963 essay, "My Negro Problem—And Ours," recalls growing up in terror of black males; they "were tougher than we were, more ruthless," he writes—and as an adult on the Upper West Side of Manhattan, he continues, he cannot constrain his nervousness when he meets black men on certain streets. Similarly, a decade later, the essayist and novelist Edward Hoagland extols a New York where once "Negro bitterness bore down mainly on other Negroes." Where some see mere panhandlers, Hoagland sees "a mugger who is clearly screwing up his nerve to do more than

5

---

[1]*Soho:* A district of lower Manhattan known for its art galleries.—EDS.
[2]*Norman Podhoretz:* A well-known literary critic and editor of *Commentary* magazine.—Eds.

just *ask* for money." But Hoagland has "the New Yorker's quick-hunch posture for broken-field maneuvering," and the bad guy swerves away.

I often witness that "hunch posture," from women after dark on the warrenlike streets of Brooklyn where I live. They seem to set their faces on neutral and, with their purse straps strung across their chests bandolier style, they forge ahead as though bracing themselves against being tackled. I understand, of course, that the danger they perceive is not a hallucination. Women are particularly vulnerable to street violence, and young black males are drastically overrepresented among the perpetrators of that violence. Yet these truths are no solace against the kind of alienation that comes of being ever the suspect, against being set apart, a fearsome entity with whom pedestrians avoid making eye contact.

It is not altogether clear to me how I reached the ripe old age of twenty-two without being conscious of the lethality nighttime pedestrians attributed to me. Perhaps it was because in Chester, Pennsylvania, the small, angry industrial town where I came of age in the 1960s, I was scarcely noticeable against a backdrop of gang warfare, street knifings, and murders. I grew up one of the good boys, had perhaps a half-dozen fistfights. In retrospect, my shyness of combat has clear sources.

Many things go into the making of a young thug. One of those things is the consummation of the male romance with the power to intimidate. An infant discovers that random flailings send the baby bottle flying out of the crib and crashing to the floor. Delighted, the joyful babe repeats those motions again and again, seeking to duplicate the feat. Just so, I recall the points at which some of my boyhood friends were finally seduced by the perception of themselves as tough guys. When a mark cowered and surrendered his money without resistance, myth and reality merged — and paid off. It is, after all, only manly to embrace the power to frighten and intimidate. We, as men, are not supposed to give an inch of our lane on the highway; we are to seize the fighter's edge in work and in play and even in love; we are to be valiant in the face of hostile forces.

Unfortunately, poor and powerless young men seem to take all this nonsense literally. As a boy, I saw countless tough guys locked away; I have since buried several, too. They were babies, really — a teenage cousin, a brother of twenty-two, a childhood friend in his midtwenties — all gone down in episodes of bravado played out in the streets. I came to doubt the virtues of intimidation early on. I chose, perhaps even unconsciously, to remain a shadow — timid, but a survivor.

The fearsomeness mistakenly attributed to me in public places often has   10
a perilous flavor. The most frightening of these confusions occurred in the late 1970s and early 1980s when I worked as a journalist in Chicago. One day, rushing into the office of a magazine I was writing for with a deadline story in hand, I was mistaken for a burglar. The office manager called security and, with an ad hoc posse, pursued me through the labyrinthine halls, nearly to my editor's door. I had no way of proving who I was. I could only move briskly toward the company of someone who knew me.

Another time I was on assignment for a local paper and killing time before an interview. I entered a jewelry store on the city's affluent Near North Side. The proprietor excused herself and returned with an enormous red Doberman pinscher straining at the end of a leash. She stood, the dog extended toward me, silent to my questions, her eyes bulging nearly out of her head. I took a cursory look around, nodded, and bade her good night. Relatively speaking, however, I never fared as badly as another black male journalist. He went to nearby Waukegan, Illinois, a couple of summers ago to work on a story about a murderer who was born there. Mistaking the reporter for the killer, police hauled him from his car at gunpoint and but for his press credentials would probably have tried to book him. Such episodes are not uncommon. Black men trade tales like this all the time.

In "My Negro Problem—And Ours," Podhoretz writes that the hatred he feels for blacks makes itself known to him through a variety of avenues—one being his discomfort with that "special brand of paranoid touchiness" to which he says blacks are prone. No doubt he is speaking here of black men. In time, I learned to smother the rage I felt at so often being taken for a criminal. Not to do so would surely have led to madness—via that special "paranoid touchiness" that so annoyed Podhoretz at the time he wrote the essay.

I began to take precautions to make myself less threatening. I move about with care, particularly late in the evening. I give a wide berth to nervous people on subway platforms during the wee hours, particularly when I have exchanged business clothes for jeans. If I happen to be entering a building behind some people who appear skittish, I may walk by, letting them clear the lobby before I return, so as not to seem to be following them. I have been calm and extremely congenial on those rare occasions when I've been pulled over by the police.

And on late-evening constitutionals along streets less traveled by, I employ what has proved to be an excellent tension-reducing measure: I whistle melodies from Beethoven and Vivaldi and the more popular classical composers. Even steely New Yorkers hunching toward nighttime destinations seem to relax, and occasionally they even join in the tune. Virtually everybody seems to sense that a mugger wouldn't be warbling bright, sunny selections from Vivaldi's *Four Seasons*. It is my equivalent of the cowbell that hikers wear when they know they are in bear country.

The Reader's Presence

1. Why does Staples use the word *victim* in his opening sentence? In what sense is the white woman a "victim"? How is he using the term? As readers, how might we interpret the opening sentence upon first reading? How does the meaning of the term change in rereading?

2. In rereading the essay, pay close attention to the way Staples handles point of view. When does he shift viewpoints or perspectives? What is his purpose in doing so? What are some of the connections Staples makes in this essay between the point of view one chooses and one's identity?

3. How does Staples behave on the street? How does he deal with the woman's anxiety? How has he "altered" his own public behavior? In what ways is his behavior on the street similar to his "behavior" as a writer? Compare this version of the essay to the alternate version that follows. What are the changes and how do those changes influence the essay's effect on the reader? How do you compare Staples's strategies—in both versions—to those of Zora Neale Hurston in "How It Feels to Be Colored Me" (see page 150)?

THE WRITER AT WORK

Another Version of "Just Walk on By"

When he published his memoir, Parallel Time, *in 1994, Brent Staples decided to incorporate his earlier essay into the book. He also decided to revise it substantially. As you compare the two versions, note the passages Staples retained and those he chose not to carry forward into book form. Do you agree with his changes? Why in general do you think he made them? If you had been his book editor, what revision strategy would you have suggested?*

At night, I walked to the lakefront whenever the weather permitted. I was headed home from the lake when I took my first victim. It was late fall, and the wind was cutting. I was wearing my navy pea jacket, the collar turned up, my hands snug in the pockets. Dead leaves scuttled in shoals along the streets. I turned out of Blackstone Avenue and headed west on 57th Street, and there she was, a few yards ahead of me, dressed in business clothes and carrying a briefcase. She looked back at me once, then again, and picked up her pace. She looked back again and started to run. I stopped where I was and looked up at the surrounding windows. What did this look like to people peeking out through their blinds? I was out walking. But what if someone had thought they'd seen something they hadn't and called the police. I held back the urge to run. Instead, I walked south to The Midway, plunged into its darkness, and remained on The Midway until I reached the foot of my street.

I'd been a fool. I'd been walking the streets grinning good evening at people who were frightened to death of me. I did violence to them by just being. How had I missed this? I kept walking at night, but from then on I paid attention.

I became expert in the language of fear. Couples locked arms or reached for each other's hand when they saw me. Some crossed to the other side of the street. People who were carrying on conversations went mute and stared straight ahead, as though avoiding my eyes would save them. This reminded me of an old wives' tale: that rabid dogs didn't bite if you avoided their eyes. The determination to avoid my eyes made me invisible to classmates and professors whom I passed on the street.

It occurred to me for the first time that I was big. I was 6 feet 1 ½ inches tall, and my long hair made me look bigger. I weighed only 170 pounds. But the navy pea jacket that Brian had given me was broad at the shoulders, high at the collar, making me look bigger and more fearsome than I was.

I tried to be innocuous but didn't know how. The more I thought   5 about how I moved, the less my body belonged to me; I became a false character riding along inside it. I began to avoid people. I turned out of my way into side streets to spare them the sense that they were being stalked. I let them clear the lobbies of buildings before I entered, so they wouldn't feel trapped. Out of nervousness I began to whistle and discovered I was good at it. My whistle was pure and sweet—and also in tune. On the street at night I whistled popular tunes from the Beatles and Vivaldi's *Four Seasons*. The tension drained from people's bodies when they heard me. A few even smiled as they passed me in the dark.

Then I changed. I don't know why, but I remember when. I was walking west on 57th Street, after dark, coming home from the lake. The man and the woman walking toward me were laughing and talking but clammed up when they saw me. The man touched the woman's elbow, guiding her toward the curb. Normally I'd have given way and begun to whistle, but not this time. This time I veered toward them and aimed myself so that they'd have to part to avoid walking into me. The man stiffened, threw back his head and assumed the stare: eyes dead ahead, mouth open. His face took on a bluish hue under the sodium vapor streetlamps. I suppressed the urge to scream into his face. Instead I glided between them, my shoulder nearly brushing his. A few steps beyond them I stopped and howled with laughter. I called this game Scatter the Pigeons.

Fifty-seventh Street was too well lit for the game to be much fun; people didn't feel quite vulnerable enough. Along The Midway were heart-stopping strips of dark sidewalk, but these were so frightening that few people traveled them. The stretch of Blackstone between 57th and 55th provided better hunting. The block was long and lined with young trees that blocked out the streetlight and obscured the heads of people coming toward you.

One night I stooped beneath the branches and came up on the other side, just as a couple was stepping from their car into their town house. The woman pulled her purse close with one hand and reached for her husband with the other. The two of them stood frozen as I bore down on them. I felt a surge of power: these people were mine; I could do with them as I wished. If I'd been younger, with less to lose, I'd have robbed them, and it would have been easy. All I'd have to do was stand silently before them until they surrendered their money. I thundered, "Good evening!" into their bleached-out faces and cruised away laughing.

I held a special contempt for people who cowered in their cars as they waited for the light to change at 57th and Woodlawn. The intersection was always deserted at night, except for a car or two stuck at the red. *Thunk! Thunk! Thunk!* they hammered down the door locks when I came into view. Once I had hustled across the street, head down, trying to seem harmless. Now I turned brazenly into the headlights and laughed. Once across, I paced the sidewalk, glaring until the light changed. They'd made me terrifying. Now I'd show them how terrifying I could be.

36

Amy Tan

Mother Tongue

Amy Tan (b. 1952) was born in California shortly after her parents immigrated to the United States from China. She started writing as a child and won a writing contest at age eight. As an adult, Tan made her living as a free-lance business writer for many years, but started to write fiction in 1985. In 1987, Tan traveled to China for the first time, an experience that helped shape her consciousness of both her American and Chinese identities. In 1989 she published her best-selling first novel, The Joy Luck Club, *followed by* The Kitchen God's Wife *(1991), the children's books* The Moon Lady *(1992) and* The Chinese Siamese Cat *(1994),* The Hundred Secret Senses *(1995), and* The Bonesetter's Daughter *(2001). "Mother Tongue" originally appeared in the* Threepenny Review *in 1990.*

Commenting on the art of writing, Tan has said, "I had a very unliterary background, but I had a determination to write for myself." She believes that the goal of every serious writer of literature is "to try to find your voice and your art, because it comes from your own experiences, your own pain."

I am not a scholar of English or literature. I cannot give you much more than personal opinions on the English language and its variations in this country or others.

I am a writer. And by that definition, I am someone who has always loved language. I am fascinated by language in daily life. I spend a great deal of my time thinking about the power of language—the way it can evoke an emotion, a visual image, a complex idea, or a simple truth. Language is the tool of my trade. And I use them all—all the Englishes I grew up with.

Recently, I was made keenly aware of the different Englishes I do use.

I was giving a talk to a large group of people, the same talk I had already given to half a dozen other groups. The nature of the talk was about my writing, my life, and my book, *The Joy Luck Club*. The talk was going along well enough, until I remembered one major difference that made the whole talk sound wrong. My mother was in the room. And it was perhaps the first time she had heard me give a lengthy speech, using the kind of English I have never used with her. I was saying things like "The intersection of memory upon imagination" and "There is an aspect of my fiction that relates to thus-and-thus"—a speech filled with carefully wrought grammatical phrases, burdened, it suddenly seemed to me, with nominalized forms, past perfect tenses, conditional phrases, all the forms of standard English that I had learned in school and through books, the forms of English I did not use at home with my mother.

Just last week, I was walking down the street with my mother, and I again found myself conscious of the English I was using, the English I do use with her. We were talking about the price of new and used furniture and I heard myself saying this: "Not waste money that way." My husband was with us as well, and he didn't notice any switch in my English. And then I realized why. It's because over the twenty years we've been together I've often used that same kind of English with him, and sometimes he even uses it with me. It has become our language of intimacy, a different sort of English that relates to family talk, the language I grew up with.

So you'll have some idea of what this family talk I heard sounds like,   5 I'll quote what my mother said during a recent conversation which I videotaped and then transcribed. During this conversation, my mother was talking about a political gangster in Shanghai who had the same last name as her family's, Du, and how the gangster in his early years wanted to be adopted by her family, which was rich by comparison. Later, the gangster became more powerful, far richer than my mother's family, and one day showed up at my mother's wedding to pay his respects. Here's what she said in part:

"Du Yusong having business like fruit stand. Like off the street kind. He is Du like Du Zong—but not Tsung-ming Island people. The local people call putong, the river east side, he belong to that side local people. That man want to ask Du Zong father take him in like become own family. Du Zong father wasn't look down on him, but didn't take seriously, until that man big like become a mafia. Now important person, very hard to inviting him. Chinese way, came only to show respect, don't stay for dinner. Respect for making big celebration, he shows up. Mean gives lots of respect. Chinese custom. Chinese social life that way. If too important won't have to stay too long. He come to my wedding. I didn't see, I heard it. I gone to boy's side, they have YMCA dinner. Chinese age I was nineteen."

You should know that my mother's expressive command of English belies how much she actually understands. She reads the *Forbes* report, listens to *Wall Street Week*, converses daily with her stockbroker, reads all of Shirley MacLaine's books with ease—all kinds of things I can't begin to understand. Yet some of my friends tell me they understand 50 percent of what my mother says. Some say they understand 80 to 90 percent. Some say they understand none of it, as if she were speaking pure Chinese. But to me, my mother's English is perfectly clear, perfectly natural. It's my mother tongue. Her language, as I hear it, is vivid, direct, full of observation and imagery. That was the language that helped shape the way I saw things, expressed things, made sense of the world.

Lately, I've been giving more thought to the kind of English my mother speaks. Like others, I have described it to people as "broken" or "fractured" English. But I wince when I say that. It has always bothered me that I can think of no other way to describe it other than "broken," as if it were damaged and needed to be fixed, as if it lacked a certain wholeness and soundness. I've heard other terms used, "limited English," for example. But they seem just as bad, as if everything is limited, including people's perceptions of the limited English speaker.

I know this for a fact, because when I was growing up, my mother's "limited" English limited *my* perception of her. I was ashamed of her English. I believed that her English reflected the quality of what she had to say. That is, because she expressed them imperfectly her thoughts were imperfect. And I had plenty of empirical evidence to support me: the fact that people in department stores, at banks, and at restaurants did not take her seriously, did not give her good service, pretended not to understand her, or even acted as if they did not hear her.

My mother has long realized the limitations of her English as well.   10
When I was fifteen, she used to have me call people on the phone to pretend I was she. In this guise, I was forced to ask for information or even to complain and yell at people who had been rude to her. One time it was a call to her stockbroker in New York. She had cashed out her small portfolio and it just so happened we were going to go to New York the next week, our very first trip outside California. I had to get on the phone and say in an adolescent voice that was not very convincing, "This is Mrs. Tan."

And my mother was standing in the back whispering loudly, "Why he don't send me check, already two weeks late. So mad he lie to me, losing me money."

And then I said in perfect English, "Yes, I'm getting rather concerned. You had agreed to send the check two weeks ago, but it hasn't arrived."

Then she began to talk more loudly. "What he want, I come to New York tell him front of his boss, you cheating me?" And I was trying to calm her down, make her be quiet, while telling the stockbroker, "I can't tolerate any more excuses. If I don't receive the check immediately, I am going to have to speak to your manager when I'm in New York next week." And sure enough, the following week there we were in front of this astonished stockbroker, and I was sitting there red-faced and quiet, and my mother, the real Mrs. Tan, was shouting at his boss in her impeccable broken English.

We used a similar routine just five days ago, for a situation that was far less humorous. My mother had gone to the hospital for an appointment, to find out about a benign brain tumor a CAT scan had revealed a month ago. She said she had spoken very good English, her best English, no mistakes. Still, she said, the hospital did not apologize when they said they had lost the CAT scan and she had come for nothing. She said they did not seem to have any sympathy when she told them she was anxious to know the exact diagnosis, since her husband and son had both died of brain tumors. She said they would not give her any more information until the next time and she would have to make another appointment for that. So she said she would not leave until the doctor called her daughter. She wouldn't budge. And when the doctor finally called her daughter, me, who spoke in perfect English—lo and behold—we had assurances the CAT scan would be found, promises that a conference call on Monday would be held, and apologies for any suffering my mother had gone through for a most regrettable mistake.

I think my mother's English almost had an effect on limiting my possibilities in life as well. Sociologists and linguists probably will tell you that a person's developing language skills are more influenced by peers. But I do think that the language spoken in the family, especially in immigrant families which are more insular, plays a large role in shaping the language of the child. And I believe that it affected my results on achievement tests, IQ tests, and the SAT. While my English skills were never judged as poor, compared to math, English could not be considered my strong suit. In grade school I did moderately well, getting perhaps B's, sometimes B pluses, in English and scoring perhaps in the sixtieth or seventieth percentile on achievement tests. But those scores were not good enough to override the opinion that my true abilities lay in math and science, because in those areas I achieved A's and scored in the ninetieth percentile or higher. 15

This was understandable. Math is precise; there is only one correct answer. Whereas, for me at least, the answers on English tests were always a judgment call, a matter of opinion and personal experience. Those tests were constructed around items like fill-in-the-blank sentence completion, such as "Even though Tom was _____, Mary thought he was _____." And the correct answer always seemed to be the most bland combinations of thoughts, for example, "Even though Tom was shy, Mary thought he was charming," with the grammatical structure "even though" limiting the correct answer to some sort of semantic opposites, so you wouldn't get answers like, "Even though Tom was foolish, Mary thought he was ridiculous." Well, according to my mother, there were very few limitations as to what Tom could have been and what Mary might have thought of him. So I never did well on tests like that.

The same was true with word analogies, pairs of words in which you were supposed to find some sort of logical, semantic relationship—for example, "*Sunset* is to *nightfall* as _____ is to _____." And here you would be presented with a list of four possible pairs, one of which showed the same kind of relationship: *red* is to *stoplight, bus* is to *arrival, chills* is to *fever, yawn* is to *boring.* Well, I could never think that way. I knew what the tests were asking, but I could not block out of my mind the images already created by the first pair, *"sunset* is to *nightfall"*—and I would see a burst of colors against a darkening sky, the moon rising, the lowering of a curtain of stars. And all the other pairs of words—red, bus, stoplight, boring—just threw up a mass of confusing images, making it impossible for me to sort out something as logical as saying: "A sunset precedes nightfall" is the same as "a chill precedes a fever." The only way I would have gotten that answer right would have been to imagine an associative situation, for example, my being disobedient and staying out past sunset, catching a chill at night, which turns into feverish pneumonia as punishment, which indeed did happen to me.

I have been thinking about all this lately, about my mother's English, about achievement tests. Because lately I've been asked, as a writer, why there are not more Asian Americans represented in American literature. Why are there few Asian Americans enrolled in creative writing programs? Why do so many Chinese students go into engineering? Well, these are broad sociological questions I can't begin to answer. But I have noticed in surveys—in fact, just last week—that Asian students, as a whole, always do significantly better on math achievement tests than in English. And this makes me think that there are other Asian-American students whose English spoken in the home might also be described as "broken" or "limited." And perhaps they also have teachers who are steering them away from writing and into math and science, which is what happened to me.

Fortunately, I happen to be rebellious in nature and enjoy the challenge of disproving assumptions made about me. I became an English major my first year in college, after being enrolled as pre-med. I started writing nonfiction as a freelancer the week after I was told by my former boss that writing was my worst skill and I should hone my talents toward account management.

But it wasn't until 1985 that I finally began to write fiction. And at   20
first I wrote using what I thought to be wittily crafted sentences, sentences that would finally prove I had mastery over the English language. Here's an example from the first draft of a story that later made its way into *The Joy Luck Club,* but without this line: "That was my mental quandary in its nascent state." A terrible line, which I can barely pronounce.

Fortunately, for reasons I won't get into today, I later decided I should envision a reader for the stories I would write. And the reader I decided upon was my mother, because these were stories about mothers. So with this reader in mind—and in fact she did read my early drafts—I began to write stories using all the Englishes I grew up with: the English I spoke to my mother, which for lack of a better term might be described as "simple": the English she used with me, which for lack of a better term might be described as "broken"; my translation of her Chinese, which could certainly be described as "watered down"; and what I imagined to be her translation of her Chinese if she could speak in perfect English, her internal language, and for that I sought to preserve the essence, but neither an English nor a Chinese structure. I wanted to capture what language ability tests can never reveal: her intent, her passion, her imagery, the rhythms of her speech, and the nature of her thoughts.

Apart from what any critic had to say about my writing, I knew I had succeeded where it counted when my mother finished reading my book and gave me her verdict: "So easy to read."

The Reader's Presence

1. In her second paragraph, Tan mentions "all the Englishes" she grew up with. What were those "Englishes"? What is odd about the term? How does the oddity of the word reinforce the point of her essay?

2. In paragraph 20, Tan gives an example of a sentence that she once thought showed her "mastery" of English. What does she now find wrong with that sentence? What do you think of it? What would her mother have thought of it? What sort of reader does that sentence anticipate?

3. What exactly is Tan's "mother tongue"? What does the phrase usually mean? Would you call her mother's English "broken English"? What does that phrase imply? Why does Tan write with her mother in mind as her ideal reader? How does Tan's determination to keep her mother linked to her writing compare with Rodriguez's profound sense of having irrecoverably lost a connection with his parents in "Aria: A Memoir of a Bilingual Childhood" (see page 221)? Does Rodriguez's distinction between private and public languages hold for Tan?

37

James Thurber

University Days

A short story writer, essayist, author of children's books, and cartoonist, James Thurber (1894–1961), is known for his outlandish and humorous characterizations of both urban and domestic life. Thurber, proclaimed by Alistair Cooke as "one of the world's greatest humorists," worked for the New Yorker *for most of his career and helped establish its urbane tone. While at the* New Yorker, *Thurber worked with E. B. White (see page 281), and together they wrote* Is Sex Necessary? *(1929), a spoof of sex manuals. One of Thurber's most famous short stories, "The Secret Life of Walter Mitty," depicts a man whose heroic daydreams help him escape from a dull job and a domineering wife. His publications include a collection of pieces from the* New Yorker, The Owl in the Attic and Other Perplexities *(1931); a book of drawings,* The Seal in the Bedroom and Other Predicaments *(1931); short stories,* My World—and Welcome to It *(1942); and an account of his days at the* New Yorker, The Years with Ross *(1959). "University Days" appeared in* The Thurber Carnival *(1931).*

I passed all the other courses that I took at my University, but I could never pass botany. This was because all botany students had to spend several hours a week in a laboratory looking through a microscope at plant cells, and I could never see through a microscope. I never once saw a cell through a microscope. This used to enrage my instructor. He would wander around the laboratory pleased with the progress all the students were making in drawing the involved and, so I am told, interesting structure of flower cells, until he came to me. I would just be standing there. "I can't see anything," I would say. He would begin patiently enough, explaining how anybody can see through a microscope, but he would always end up in a fury, claiming that I could *too* see through a microscope but just pretended that I couldn't. "It takes away from the beauty of flowers anyway," I used to tell him. "We are not concerned with beauty in this course," he would say. "We are concerned solely with what I may call the *mechanics* of flars." "Well," I'd say, "I can't see anything." "Try it just once again," he'd say, and I would put my eye to the microscope and see nothing at all, except now and again a nebulous milky substance—a phenomenon of maladjustment. You were supposed to see a vivid, restless clockwork of sharply defined plant cells. "I see what looks like a lot of milk," I would tell him. This, he claimed, was the result of my not having adjusted the microscope properly, so he would readjust it for me, or rather, for himself. And I would look again and see milk.

I finally took a deferred pass, as they called it, and waited a year and tried again. (You had to pass one of the biological sciences or you couldn't graduate.) The professor had come back from vacation brown as a berry, bright-eyed, and eager to explain cell-structure again to his classes. "Well," he said to me, cheerily, when we met in the first laboratory hour of the semester, "we're going to see cells this time, aren't we?" "Yes, sir," I said. Students to right of me and to left of me and in front of me were seeing cells; what's more, they were quietly drawing pictures of them in their notebooks. Of course, I didn't see anything.

"We'll try it," the professor said to me, grimly, "with every adjustment of the microscope known to man. As God is my witness, I'll arrange this glass so that you see cells through it or I'll give up teaching. In twenty-two years of botany, I—" He cut off abruptly for he was beginning to quiver all over, like Lionel Barrymore, and he genuinely wished to hold onto his temper; his scenes with me had taken a great deal out of him.

So we tried it with every adjustment of the microscope known to man. With only one of them did I see anything but blackness or the familiar lacteal opacity, and that time I saw, to my pleasure and amazement, a variegated constellation of flecks, specks, and dots. These I hastily drew. The instructor, noting my activity, came back from an adjoining desk, a smile on his lips and his eyebrows high in hope. He looked at my cell drawing. "What's that?" he demanded, with a hint of a squeal in his voice. "That's what I saw," I said. "You didn't, you didn't, you *didn't!*" he screamed, losing control of his temper instantly, and he bent over and squinted into the microscope. His head snapped up. "That's your eye!" he shouted. "You've fixed the lens so that it reflects! You've drawn your eye!"

Another course that I didn't like, but somehow managed to pass, was   5
economics. I went to that class straight from the botany class, which didn't help me any in understanding either subject. I used to get them mixed up. But not as mixed up as another student in my economics class who came there direct from a physics laboratory. He was a tackle on the football team, named Bolenciecwcz. At that time Ohio State University had one of the best football teams in the country, and Bolenciecwcz was one of its outstanding stars. In order to be eligible to play it was necessary for him to keep up in his studies, a very difficult matter, for while he was not dumber than an ox he was not any smarter. Most of his professors were lenient and helped him along. None gave him more hints, in answering questions, or asked him simpler ones than the economics professor, a thin, timid man named Bassum. One day when we were on the subject of

transportation and distribution, it came Bolenciecwcz's turn to answer a question. "Name one means of transportation," the professor said to him. No light came into the big tackle's eyes. "Just any means of transportation," said the professor. Bolenciecwcz sat staring at him. "That is," pursued the professor, "any medium, agency, or method of going from one place to another." Bolenciecwcz had the look of a man who is being led into a trap. "You may choose among steam, horse-drawn, or electrically propelled vehicles," said the instructor. "I might suggest the one which we commonly take in making long journeys across land." There was a profound silence in which everybody stirred uneasily, including Bolenciecwcz and Mr. Bassum. Mr. Bassum abruptly broke this silence in an amazing manner. "Choo-choo-choo," he said, in a low voice, and turned instantly scarlet. He glanced appealingly around the room. All of us, of course, shared Mr. Bassum's desire that Bolenciecwcz should stay abreast of the class in economics, for the Illinois game, one of the hardest and most important of the season, was only a week off. "Toot, toot, too-tooooooot!" some student with a deep voice moaned, and we all looked encouragingly at Bolenciecwcz. Somebody else gave a fine imitation of a locomotive letting off steam. Mr. Bassum himself rounded off the little show. "Ding, dong, ding, dong," he said, hopefully. Bolenciecwcz was staring at the floor now, trying to think, his great brow furrowed, his huge hands rubbing together, his face red.

"How did you come to college this year, Mr. Bolenciecwcz?" asked the professor. "*Chuf*fa chuffa, *chuf*fa chuffa."

"M'father sent me," said the football player.

"What on?" asked Bassum.

"I git an 'lowance," said the tackle, in a low, husky voice, obviously embarrassed.

"No, no," said Bassum. "Name a means of transportation. What did   10
you *ride* here on?"

"Train," said Bolenciecwcz.

"Quite right," said the professor. "Now, Mr. Nugent, will you tell us——"

If I went through anguish in botany and economics—for different reasons—gymnasium work was even worse. I don't even like to think about it. They wouldn't let you play games or join in the exercises with your glasses on and I couldn't see with mine off. I bumped into professors, horizontal bars, agricultural students, and swinging iron rings. Not being able to see, I could take it but I couldn't dish it out. Also, in order to pass gymnasium (and you had to pass it to graduate) you had to learn to swim if you didn't know how. I didn't like the swimming pool, I didn't like swimming, and I didn't like the swimming instructor, and after all these years I still don't. I never swam but I passed my gym work anyway, by having another student give my gymnasium number (978) and swim across the pool in my place. He was a quiet, amiable blond youth, number 473, and he would have seen through a microscope for me if we could have got away with it, but we couldn't get away with it. Another thing I didn't like about gymnasium work was that they made you strip the day you registered. It is impossible for me to be happy when I am stripped and being asked a lot of questions. Still, I did better than a lanky agricultural student who was cross-examined just before I was. They asked each student what college he was in — that is, whether Arts, Engineering, Commerce, or Agriculture. "What college are you in?" the instructor snapped at the youth in front of me. "Ohio State University," he said promptly.

It wasn't that agricultural student but it was another a whole lot like him who decided to take up journalism, possibly on the ground that when farming went to hell he could fall back on newspaper work. He didn't realize, of course, that that would be very much like falling back full-length on a kit of carpenter's tools. Haskins didn't seem cut out for journalism, being too embarrassed to talk to anybody and unable to use a typewriter, but the editor of the college paper assigned him to the cow barns, the sheep house, the horse pavilion, and the animal husbandry department generally. This was a genuinely big "beat," for it took up five times as much ground and got ten times as great a legislative appropriation as the College of Liberal Arts. The agricultural student knew animals, but nevertheless his stories were dull and colorlessly written. He took all afternoon on each of them, on account of having to hunt for each letter on the typewriter. Once in a while he had to ask somebody to help him hunt. "C" and "L," in particular, were hard letters for him to find. His editor finally got pretty much annoyed at the farmer-journalist because his pieces were so uninteresting. "See here, Haskins," he snapped at him one day, "why is it we never have anything hot from you on the horse pavilion? Here we have two hundred head of horses on this campus — more than any other university in the Western Conference except Purdue — and yet you never get any real low down on them. Now shoot over to the horse barns and dig up something lively." Haskins shambled out and came back in about an hour; he said he had something. "Well, start it off snappily," said the editor. "Something people will read." Haskins set to work and in a couple of hours brought a sheet of typewritten paper to the desk; it was a two-hundred word story about some disease that had broken out among the horses. Its opening sentence was simple but arresting. It read: "Who has noticed the sores on the tops of the horses in the animal husbandry building?"

Ohio State was a land grant university and therefore two years of 15 military drill was compulsory. We drilled with old Springfield rifles and studied the tactics of the Civil War even though the World War was going on at the time. At 11 o'clock each morning thousands of freshmen and sophomores used to deploy over the campus, moodily creeping up on the old chemistry building. It was good training for the kind of warfare that was waged at Shiloh but it had no connection with what was going on in Europe. Some people used to think there was German money behind it, but they didn't dare say so or they would have been thrown in jail as German spies. It was a period of muddy thought and marked, I believe, the decline of higher education in the Middle West.

As a soldier I was never any good at all. Most of the cadets were glumly indifferent soldiers, but I was no good at all. Once General Littlefield, who was commandant of the cadet corps, popped up in front of me during regimental drill and snapped, "You are the main trouble with this university!" I think he meant that my type was the main trouble with the university but he may have meant me individually. I was mediocre at drill, certainly — that is, until my senior year. By that time I had drilled longer than anybody else in the Western Conference, having failed at military at the end of each preceding year so that I had to do it all over again. I was the only senior still in uniform. The uniform which, when new, had made me look like an interurban railway conductor, now that it had become faded and too tight made me look like Bert Williams in his bellboy act. This had a definitely bad effect on my morale. Even so, I had become by sheer practice little short of wonderful at squad maneuvers.

One day General Littlefield picked our company out of the whole regiment and tried to get it mixed up by putting it through one movement after another as fast as we could execute them: squads right, squads left, squads on right into line, squads right about, squads left front into line etc. In about three minutes one hundred and nine men were marching in one direction and I was marching away from them at an angle of forty degrees, all alone. "Company, halt!" shouted General Littlefield, "That man is the only man who has it right!" I was made a corporal for my achievement.

The next day General Littlefield summoned me to his office. He was swatting flies when I went in. I was silent and he was silent too, for a long time. I don't think he remembered me or why he had sent for me, but he didn't want to admit it. He swatted some more flies, keeping his eyes on them narrowly before he let go with the swatter. "Button up your coat!" he snapped. Looking back on it now I can see that he meant me although he was looking at a fly, but I just stood there. Another fly came to rest on a paper in front of the general and began rubbing its hind legs together. The General lifted the swatter cautiously. I moved restlessly and the fly flew away. "You startled him!" barked General Littlefield, looking at me severely. I said I was sorry. "That won't help the situation!" snapped the General, with cold military logic. I didn't see what I could do except offer to chase some more flies toward his desk, but I didn't say anything. He stared out the window at the faraway figures of co-eds crossing the campus toward the library. Finally, he told me I could go. So I went. He either didn't know which cadet I was or else he forgot what he wanted to see me about. It may have been that he wished to apologize for having called me the main trouble with the university; or maybe he had decided to compliment me on my brilliant drilling of the day before and then at the last minute decided not to. I don't know. I don't think about it much any more.

The Reader's Presence

1. How does Thurber's depiction of his college life contrast with common expectations of the educational experience? What does he seem to have learned?

2. Thurber is able to render fairly ordinary events in a highly comedic manner. List the events of his "choo-choo" story as simply as possible and then determine what sorts of verbal tools he uses to build and maintain humor in the scene. To what extent is humor determined by form alone?

3. Compare this piece with Russell Baker's "Gumption" (see page 79). What similarities in comic style do the pieces share? How do they differ? Do you think the younger Russell Baker learned any humorous techniques from the popular Thurber?

38

Garry Trudeau

My Inner Shrimp

Garry Trudeau (b. 1948), creator of the popular comic strip "Doonesbury," has also contributed articles to such publications as Harper's, Rolling Stone, *the* New Republic, *the* New Yorker, New York, *and the* Washington Post. *He received bachelor's and master's degrees from Yale University. Trudeau won a Pulitzer Prize in 1975 and in 1994 received the award for best comic strip from the National Cartoonists Society. For five years he was an occasional columnist for the* New York Times *opinion and editorial page. Currently, he is a contributing essayist for* Time *magazine. He lives in New York City with his wife, Jane Pauley, and their three children.*

For the rest of my days, I shall be a recovering short person. Even from my lofty perch of something over six feet (as if I don't know within a micron), I have the soul of a shrimp. I feel the pain of the diminutive, irrespective of whether they feel it themselves, because my visit to the planet of the teenage midgets was harrowing, humiliating, and extended. I even perceive my last-minute escape to have been flukish, somehow unearned—as if the Commissioner of Growth Spurts had been an old classmate of my father.

My most recent reminder of all this came the afternoon I went hunting for a new office. I had noticed a building under construction in my neighborhood—a brick warren of duplexes, with wide, westerly-facing windows, promising ideal light for a working studio. When I was ushered into the model unit, my pulse quickened: The soaring, twenty-two-foot living room walls were gloriously aglow with the remains of the day. I bonded immediately.

Almost as an afterthought, I ascended the staircase to inspect the loft, ducking as I entered the bedroom. To my great surprise, I stayed ducked: The room was a little more than six feet in height. While my head technically cleared the ceiling, the effect was excruciatingly oppressive. This certainly wasn't a space I wanted to spend any time in, much less take out a mortgage on.

Puzzled, I wandered down to the sales office and asked if there were any other units to look at. No, replied a resolutely unpleasant receptionist, it was the last one. Besides, they were all exactly alike.

"Are you aware of how low the bedroom ceilings are?" I asked.   5

She shot me an evil look. "Of course we are," she snapped. "There were some problems with the building codes. The architect knows all about the ceilings.

"He's not an idiot, you know," she added, perfectly anticipating my next question.

She abruptly turned away, but it was too late. She'd just confirmed that a major New York developer, working with a fully licensed architect, had knowingly created an entire twelve-story apartment building virtually uninhabitable by anyone of even average height. It was an exclusive highrise for shorties.

Once I knew that, of course, I couldn't stay away. For days thereafter, as I walked to work, some perverse, unreasoning force would draw me back to the building. But it wasn't just the absurdity, the stone silliness of its design that had me in its grip; it was something far more compelling. Like some haunted veteran come again to an ancient battlefield, I was revisiting my perilous past.

When I was fourteen, I was the third-smallest in a high school class of   10
one hundred boys, routinely mistaken for a sixth grader. My first week of school, I was drafted into a contingent of students ignominiously dubbed the "Midgets," so grouped by taller boys presumably so they could taunt us with more perfect efficiency. Inexplicably, some of my fellow Midgets refused to be diminished by the experience, but I retreated into self-pity. I sent away for a book on how to grow tall, and committed to memory its tips on overcoming one's genetic destiny—or at least making the most of a regrettable situation. The book cited historical figures who had gone the latter route—Alexander the Great, Caesar, Napoleon (the mind involuntarily added Hitler). Strategies for stretching the limbs were suggested—hanging from door frames, sleeping on your back, doing assorted floor exercises—all of which I incorporated into my daily routine (get up, brush teeth, hang from

door frame). I also learned the importance of meeting girls early in the day, when, the book assured me, my rested spine rendered me perceptibly taller.

For six years, my condition persisted; I grew, but at nowhere near the rate of my peers. I perceived other problems as ancillary, and loaded up the stature issue with freight shipped in daily from every corner of my life. Lack of athletic success, all absence of a social life, the inevitable run-ins with bullies—all could be attributed to the missing inches. The night I found myself sobbing in my father's arms was the low point; we both knew it was one problem he couldn't fix.

Of course what we couldn't have known was that he and my mother already had. They had given me a delayed developmental timetable. In my seventeenth year, I miraculously shot up six inches, just in time for graduation and a fresh start. I was, in the space of a few months, reborn—and I made the most of it. Which is to say that thereafter, all of life's disappointments, reversals, and calamities still arrived on schedule—but blissfully free of subtext.

Once you stop being the butt, of course, any problem recedes, if only to give way to a new one. And yet the impact of being literally looked down on, of being *made* to feel small, is forever. It teaches you how to stretch, how to survive the scorn of others for things that are beyond your control. Not growing forces you to grow up fast.

Sometimes I think I'd like to return to a high-school reunion to surprise my classmates. Not that they didn't know me when I finally started catching up. They did, but I doubt they'd remember. Adolescent hierarchies have a way of enduring; I'm sure I am still recalled as the Midget I myself have never really left behind.

Of course, if I'm going to show up, it'll have to be soon. I'm starting   15
to shrink.

The Reader's Presence

1. It is said that "beauty is in the eye of the beholder"; Trudeau's testimony challenges this old saw. Does Trudeau's piece convince you that one's imagined shortcomings are nearly as ruinous as those apparent to others? Why or why not?

2. Locate examples in the essay of exaggeration or hyperbole. Does this descriptive technique support or weaken Trudeau's case, and why? What phrase does Trudeau's title intentionally echo? Why?

3. "Not growing forces you to grow up fast" (paragraph 13), Trudeau writes near the end of the essay—a general truth that can apply to any reader, tall or short. Compare this essay to Nancy Mairs's "On Being a Cripple" (see page 166). Their respective subjects differ, of course, but both writers strive to make their essays speak to a wide audience. How do they do this?

39

Alice Walker

Beauty: When the Other Dancer Is the Self

Alice Walker (b. 1944) was awarded the Pulitzer Prize and the American Book Award for her second novel, The Color Purple *(1982), which was made into a popular film. This novel helped establish Walker's reputation as one of America's most important contemporary writers. In both her fiction and nonfiction, she shares her compassion for the black women of America whose lives have long been largely excluded from or distorted in literary representation. Walker is also the author of other novels, short stories, several volumes of poetry, a children's biography of Langston Hughes, essays, and criticism. Her most recent books are* The Same River Twice *(1996),* Anything We Love Can Be Saved: A Writer's Activism *(1997),* By the Light of My Father's Smile: A Novel *(1998), and* The Way Forward Is with a Broken Heart *(2000). "Beauty: When the Other Dancer Is the Self" comes from her 1983 collection,* In Search of Our Mothers' Gardens.*

When asked by an interviewer about her writing habits, Walker replied, "Generally speaking I work in the morning and then I garden—I do watering. Writing is just a part of my life. I don't like to emphasize it so much it becomes a distortion. I think it was Hemingway who said that each day that you write, you don't try to write to the absolute end of what you feel and think. You leave a little, you know, so that the next day you have something else to go on. And I would take it a little further—the thing is being able to create out of fullness, and that in order to create out of fullness, you have to let it well up. You cannot do what is done so much in this culture and the world. You know, the image of what has happened to the planet is of a man and mankind just grabbing the earth by the throat and shaking it and saying 'give, give, give,' and just squeezing it until the last drop of life leaves it. That, needless to say, is very uncreative. It can only lead to death. . . . In creation you must always leave something. You have to go to the bottom of the well with creativity. You have to give it everything you've got, but at the same time you have to leave that last drop for the creative spirit or for the earth itself."

It is a bright summer day in 1947. My father, a fat, funny man with beautiful eyes and a subversive wit, is trying to decide which of his eight children he will take with him to the county fair. My mother, of course, will not go. She is knocked out from getting most of us ready: I hold my neck stiff against the pressure of her knuckles as she hastily completes the braiding and the beribboning of my hair.

My father is the driver for the rich old white lady up the road. Her name is Miss Mey. She owns all the land for miles around, as well as the house in which we live. All I remember about her is that she once offered to pay my mother thirty-five cents for cleaning her house, raking up piles of her magnolia leaves, and washing her family's clothes, and that my mother — she of no money, eight children, and a chronic earache — refused it. But I do not think of this in 1947. I am two-and-a-half years old. I want to go everywhere my daddy goes. I am excited at the prospect of riding in a car. Someone has told me fairs are fun. That there is room in the car for only three of us doesn't faze me at all. Whirling happily in my starchy frock, showing off my biscuit-polished patent-leather shoes and lavender socks, tossing my head in a way that makes my ribbons bounce, I stand, hands on hips, before my father. "Take me, Daddy," I say with assurance; "I'm the prettiest!"

Later, it does not surprise me to find myself in Miss Mey's shiny black car, sharing the back seat with the other lucky ones. Does not surprise me that I thoroughly enjoy the fair. At home that night I tell the unlucky ones all I can remember about the merry-go-round, the man who eats live chickens, and the teddy bears, until they say: that's enough, baby Alice. Shut up now, and go to sleep.

It is Easter Sunday, 1950. I am dressed in a green, flocked, scalloped-hem dress (handmade by my adoring sister, Ruth) that has its own smooth satin petticoat and tiny hot-pink roses tucked into each scallop. My shoes, new T-strap patent leather, again highly biscuit-polished. I am six years old and have learned one of the longest Easter speeches to be heard that day, totally unlike the speech I said when I was two: "Easter lilies / pure and white / blossom in / the morning light." When I rise to give my speech I do so on a great wave of love and pride and expectation. People in the church stop rustling their new crinolines. They seem to hold their breath. I can tell they admire my dress, but it is my spirit, bordering on sassiness (womanishness), they secretly applaud.

"That girl's a little *mess*," they whisper to each other, pleased.   5

Naturally I say my speech without stammer or pause, unlike those who stutter, stammer, or, worst of all, forget. This is before the word "beautiful" exists in people's vocabulary, but "Oh, isn't she the *cutest* thing!" frequently floats my way. "And got so much sense!" they gratefully add . . . for which thoughtful addition I thank them to this day.

It was great fun being cute. But then, one day, it ended.

I am eight years old and a tomboy. I have a cowboy hat, cowboy boots, checkered shirt and pants, all red. My playmates are my brothers, two and four years older than I. Their colors are black and green, the only difference in the way we are dressed. On Saturday nights we all go to the picture show, even my mother; Westerns are her favorite kind of movie. Back home, "on the ranch," we pretend we are Tom Mix, Hopalong Cassidy, Lash LaRue (we've even named one of our dogs Lash LaRue); we chase each other for hours rustling cattle, being outlaws, delivering damsels from distress. Then my parents decide to buy my brothers guns. These are not "real" guns. They shoot BBs, copper pellets my brothers say will kill birds. Because I am a girl, I do not get a gun. Instantly I am relegated to the position of Indian. Now there appears a great distance between us. They shoot and shoot at everything with their new guns. I try to keep up with my bow and arrows.

One day while I am standing on top of our makeshift "garage" — pieces of tin nailed across some poles — holding my bow and arrow and looking out toward the fields, I feel an incredible blow in my right eye. I look down just in time to see my brother lower his gun.

Both brothers rush to my side. My eye stings, and I cover it with my   10
hand. "If you tell," they say, "we will get a whipping. You don't want that to happen, do you?" I do not. "Here is a piece of wire," says the older brother, picking it up from the roof; "say you stepped on one end of it and the other flew up and hit you." The pain is beginning to start. "Yes," I say. "Yes, I will say that is what happened." If I do not say this is what happened, I know my brothers will find ways to make me wish I had. But now I will say anything that gets me to my mother.

Confronted by our parents we stick to the lie agreed upon. They place me on a bench on the porch and I close my left eye while they examine the right. There is a tree growing from underneath the porch that climbs past the railing to the roof. It is the last thing my right eye sees. I watch as its trunk, its branches, and then its leaves are blotted out by the rising blood.

I am in shock. First there is intense fever, which my father tries to break using lily leaves bound around my head. Then there are chills: my mother tries to get me to eat soup. Eventually, I do not know how, my parents learn what has happened. A week after the "accident" they take me to see a doctor. "Why did you wait so long to come?" he asks, looking into my eye and shaking his head. "Eyes are sympathetic," he says. "If one is blind, the other will likely become blind too."

This comment of the doctor's terrifies me. But it is really how I look that bothers me most. Where the BB pellet struck there is a glob of whitish scar tissue, a hideous cataract, on my eye. Now when I stare at people — a favorite pastime, up to now — they will stare back. Not at the "cute" little girl, but at her scar. For six years I do not stare at anyone, because I do not raise my head.

Years later, in the throes of a mid-life crisis, I ask my mother and sister whether I changed after the "accident." "No," they say, puzzled. "What do you mean?"

What do I mean?   15

I am eight, and, for the first time, doing poorly in school, where I have been something of a whiz since I was four. We have just moved to the place where the "accident" occurred. We do not know any of the people around us because this is a different county. The only time I see the friends I knew is when we go back to our old church. The new school is the former state penitentiary. It is a large stone building, cold and drafty, crammed to over-flowing with boisterous, ill-disciplined children. On the third floor there is a huge circular imprint of some partition that has been torn out.

"What used to be here?" I ask a sullen girl next to me on our way past it to lunch.

"The electric chair," says she.

At night I have nightmares about the electric chair, and about all the people reputedly "fried" in it. I am afraid of the school, where all the students seem to be budding criminals.

"What's the matter with your eye?" they ask, critically.   20

When I don't answer (I cannot decide whether it was an "accident" or not), they shove me, insist on a fight.

My brother, the one who created the story about the wire, comes to my rescue. But then brags so much about "protecting" me, I become sick.

After months of torture at the school, my parents decide to send me back to our old community, to my old school. I live with my grandparents and the teacher they board. But there is no room for Phoebe, my cat. By the time my grandparents decide there *is* room, and I ask for my cat, she cannot be found. Miss Yarborough, the boarding teacher, takes me under her wing, and begins to teach me to play the piano. But soon she marries an African—a "prince," she says—and is whisked away to his continent.

At my old school there is at least one teacher who loves me. She is the teacher who "knew me before I was born" and bought my first baby clothes. It is she who makes life bearable. It is her presence that finally helps me turn on the one child at the school who continually calls me "one-eyed bitch." One day I simply grab him by his coat and beat him until I am satisfied. It is my teacher who tells me my mother is ill.

My mother is lying in bed in the middle of the day, something I have   25
never seen. She is in too much pain to speak. She has an abscess in her ear. I stand looking down on her, knowing that if she dies, I cannot live. She is being treated with warm oils and hot bricks held against her cheek. Finally a doctor comes. But I must go back to my grandparents' house. The weeks pass but I am hardly aware of it. All I know is that my mother might die, my father is not so jolly, my brothers still have their guns, and I am the one sent away from home.

"You did not change," they say.

Did I imagine the anguish of never looking up?

I am twelve. When relatives come to visit I hide in my room. My cousin Brenda, just my age, whose father works in the post office and whose mother is a nurse, comes to find me. "Hello," she says. And then she asks, looking at my recent school picture, which I did not want taken, and on which the "glob," as I think of it, is clearly visible, "You still can't see out of that eye?"

"No," I say, and flop back on the bed over my book.

That night, as I do almost every night, I abuse my eye. I rant and rave   30
at it, in front of the mirror. I plead with it to clear up before morning. I tell it I hate and despise it. I do not pray for sight. I pray for beauty.

"You did not change," they say.

I am fourteen and baby-sitting for my brother Bill, who lives in Boston. He is my favorite brother and there is a strong bond between us. Understanding my feelings of shame and ugliness he and his wife take me to a local hospital, where the "glob" is removed by a doctor named O. Henry. There is still a small bluish crater where the scar tissue was, but the ugly white stuff is gone. Almost immediately I become a different person from the girl who does not raise her head. Or so I think. Now that I've raised my head I win the boyfriend of my dreams. Now that I've raised my head I have plenty of friends. Now that I've raised my head classwork comes from my lips as faultlessly as Easter speeches did, and I leave high school as valedictorian, most popular student, and *queen*, hardly believing my luck. Ironically, the girl who was voted most beautiful in our class (and was) was later shot twice through the chest by a male companion, using a "real" gun, while she was pregnant. But that's another story in itself. Or is it?

"You did not change," they say.

It is now thirty years since the "accident." A beautiful journalist comes to visit and to interview me. She is going to write a cover story for her magazine that focuses on my latest book. "Decide how you want to look on the cover," she says. "Glamorous, or whatever."

Never mind "glamorous," it is the "whatever" that I hear. Suddenly   35
all I can think of is whether I will get enough sleep the night before the photography session: If I don't, my eye will be tired and wander, as blind eyes will.

At night in bed with my lover I think up reasons why I should not appear on the cover of a magazine. "My meanest critics will say I've sold out," I say. "My family will now realize I write scandalous books."

"But what's the real reason you don't want to do this?" he asks.

"Because in all probability," I say in a rush, "my eye won't be straight."

"It will be straight enough," he says. Then, "Besides, I thought you'd made your peace with that."

And I suddenly remember that I have.   40

I remember:

I am talking to my brother Jimmy, asking if he remembers anything unusual about the day I was shot. He does not know I consider that day the last time my father, with his sweet home remedy of cool lily leaves, chose me, and that I suffered and raged inside because of this. "Well," he says, "all I remember is standing by the side of the highway with Daddy, trying to flag down a car. A white man stopped, but when Daddy said he needed somebody to take his little girl to the doctor, he drove off."

I remember:

I am in the desert for the first time. I fall totally in love with it. I am so overwhelmed by its beauty, I confront for the first time, consciously, the meaning of the doctor's words years ago: "Eyes are sympathetic. If one is blind, the other will likely become blind too." I realize I have dashed about the world madly, looking at this, looking at that, storing up images against the fading of the light. *But I might have missed seeing the desert!* The shock of that possibility—and gratitude for over twenty-five years of sight—sends me literally to my knees. Poem after poem comes—which is perhaps how poets pray.

ON SIGHT

I am so thankful I have seen
The Desert
And the creatures in the desert
And the desert Itself.

The desert has its own moon
Which I have seen
With my own eye.
There is no flag on it.

Trees of the desert have arms
All of which are always up
That is because the moon is up
The sun is up
Also the sky
The Stars
Clouds
None with flags.

If there were flags, I doubt
the trees would point.
Would you?

But mostly, I remember this:　　　　　　　　　　　　　　　　　45

I am twenty-seven, and my baby daughter is almost three. Since her birth I have worried about her discovery that her mother's eyes are different from other people's. Will she be embarrassed? I think. What will she say? Every day she watches a television program called *Big Blue Marble*. It begins with a picture of the earth as it appears from the moon. It is bluish, a little battered-looking, but full of light, with whitish clouds swirling around it. Every time I see it I weep with love, as if it is a picture of Grandma's house. One day when I am putting Rebecca down for her nap, she suddenly focuses on my eye. Something inside me cringes, gets ready to try to protect myself. All children are cruel about physical differences, I know from experience, and that they don't always mean to be is another matter. I assume Rebecca will be the same.

But no-o-o-o. She studies my face intently as we stand, her inside and me outside her crib. She even holds my face maternally between her dimpled little hands. Then, looking every bit as serious and lawyerlike as her father, she says, as if it may just possibly have slipped my attention: "Mommy, there's a *world* in your eye." (As in, "Don't be alarmed, or do anything crazy.") And then, gently, but with great interest: "Mommy, where did you *get* that world in your eye?"

For the most part, the pain left then. (So what, if my brothers grew up to buy even more powerful pellet guns for their sons and to carry real guns themselves. So what, if a young "Morehouse[1] man" once nearly fell off the steps of Trevor Arnett Library because he thought my eyes were blue.) Crying and laughing I ran to the bathroom, while Rebecca mumbled and sang herself to sleep. Yes indeed, I realized, looking into the mirror. There *was* a world in my eye. And I saw that it was possible to love it: that in fact, for all it had taught me of shame and anger and inner vision, I *did* love it. Even to see it drifting out of orbit in boredom, or rolling up out of fatigue, not to mention floating back at attention in excitement (bearing witness, a friend has called it), deeply suitable to my personality, and even characteristic of me.

That night I dream I am dancing to Stevie Wonder's song "Always" (the name of the song is really "As," but I hear it as "Always"). As I dance, whirling and joyous, happier than I've ever been in my life, another bright-faced dancer joins me. We dance and kiss each other and hold each other through the night. The other dancer has obviously come through all right, as I have done. She is beautiful, whole, and free. And she is also me.

The Reader's Presence

1. In her opening paragraph, Walker refers to her father's "beautiful eyes." How does that phrase take on more significance in rereading? Can you find other words, phrases, or images that do the same? For example, why might Walker have mentioned the pain of having her hair combed?

2. Note that Walker uses the present tense throughout the essay. Why might this be unusual, given her subject? What effect does it have for both writer and reader? Try rewriting the opening paragraph in the past tense. What difference do you think it makes?

[1]*Morehouse:* Morehouse College, a black men's college in Atlanta, Georgia. — EDS.

3. What is the meaning of Walker's occasional italicized comments? What do they have in common? Whose comments are they? To whom do they seem addressed? What time frame do they seem to be in? What purpose do you think they serve? How do they compare to those of Judith Ortiz Cofer in "Silent Dancing"?

40

E. B. White

Once More to the Lake

Elwyn Brooks White (1899–1985) started contributing to the New Yorker *soon after the magazine began publication in 1925, and in the "Talk of the Town" and other columns helped establish the magazine's reputation for precise and brilliant prose. Collections of his contributions can be found in* Every Day Is Saturday *(1934),* Quo Vadimus? *(1939), and* The Wild Flag *(1946). He also wrote essays for* Harper's *on a regular basis; these essays include "Once More to the Lake" and are collected in* One Man's Meat *(1941). In his comments on this work, the critic Jonathan Yardley observed that White is "one of the few writers of this or any century who has succeeded in transforming the ephemera of journalism into something that demands to be called literature."*

Capable of brilliant satire, White could also be sad and serious, as in his compilation of forty years of writing, Essays *(1977). Among his numerous awards and honors, White received the American Academy of Arts and Letters Gold Medal (1960), a Presidential Medal of Freedom (1963), and a National Medal for Literature (1971). He made a lasting contribution to children's literature with* Stuart Little *(1945),* Charlotte's Web *(1952), and* The Trumpet of the Swan *(1970).*

White has written, "I have always felt that the first duty of a writer was to ascend—to make flights, carrying others along if he could manage it." According to White, the writer needs not only courage, but also hope and faith to accomplish this goal: "Writing itself is an act of faith, nothing else. And it must be the writer, above all others, who keeps it alive—choked with laughter, or with pain."

One summer, along about 1904, my father rented a camp on a lake in Maine and took us all there for the month of August. We all got ringworm from some kittens and had to rub Pond's Extract on our arms and legs night and morning, and my father rolled over in a canoe with all his clothes on; but outside of that the vacation was a success and from then on none of us ever thought there was any place in the world like that lake in Maine. We returned summer after summer—always on August 1st for one month. I have since become a salt-water man, but sometimes in summer there are days when the restlessness of the tides and the fearful cold of the sea water and the incessant wind that blows across the afternoon and into the evening make me wish for the placidity of a lake in the woods. A few weeks ago this feeling got so strong I bought myself a couple of bass hooks and a spinner and returned to the lake where we used to go, for a week's fishing and to revisit old haunts.

I took along my son, who had never had any fresh water up his nose and who had seen lily pads only from train windows. On the journey over to the lake I began to wonder what it would be like. I wondered how time would have marred this unique, this holy spot—the coves and streams, the hills that the sun set behind, the camps and the paths behind the camps. I was sure that the tarred road would have found it out and I wondered in what other ways it would be desolated. It is strange how much you can remember about places like that once you allow your mind to return into the grooves that lead back. You remember one thing, and that suddenly reminds you of another thing. I guess I remembered clearest of all the early mornings, when the lake was cool and motionless, remembered how the bedroom smelled of the lumber it was made of and the wet woods whose scent entered through the screen. The partitions in the camp were thin and did not extend clear to the top of the rooms, and as I was always the first up I would dress softly so as not to wake the others, and sneak out into the sweet outdoors and start out in the canoe, keeping close along the shore in the long shadows of the pines. I remembered being very careful never to rub my paddle against the gunwale for fear of disturbing the stillness of the cathedral.

The lake had never been what you would call a wild lake. There were cottages sprinkled about the shores, and it was in farming country although the shores of the lake were quite heavily wooded. Some of the cottages were owned by nearby farmers, and you would live at the shore and eat your meals at the farmhouse. That's what our family did. But although it wasn't wild, it was a fairly large and undisturbed lake and there were places in it which, to a child at least, seemed infinitely remote and primeval.

I was right about the tar: It led to within half a mile of the shore. But when I got back there, with my boy, and we settled into a camp near a farmhouse and into the kind of summertime I had known, I could tell that it was going to be pretty much the same as it had been before—I knew it, lying in bed the first morning, smelling the bedroom, and hearing the boy sneak quietly out and go off along the shore in a boat. I began to sustain the illusion that he was I, and therefore, by simple transposition, that I was my father. This sensation persisted, kept cropping up all the time we were there. It was not an entirely new feeling, but in this setting it grew much stronger. I seemed to be living a dual existence. I would be in the middle of some simple act, I would be picking up a bait box or laying down a table fork, or I would be saying something, and suddenly it would be not I but my father who was saying the words or making the gesture. It gave me a creepy sensation.

We went fishing the first morning. I felt the same damp moss cover-   5
ing the worms in the bait can, and saw the dragonfly alight on the tip of my rod as it hovered a few inches from the surface of the water. It was the arrival of this fly that convinced me beyond any doubt that everything was as it always had been, that the years were a mirage and there had been no years. The small waves were the same, chucking the rowboat under the chin as we fished at anchor, and the boat was the same boat, the same color green and the ribs broken in the same places, and under the floor-boards the same fresh-water leavings and debris — the dead hell-grammite, the wisps of moss, the rusty discarded fishhook, the dried blood from yesterday's catch. We stared silently at the tips of our rods, at the dragonflies that came and went. I lowered the tip of mine into the water, tentatively, pensively dislodging the fly, which darted two feet away, poised, darted two feet back, and came to rest again a little farther up the rod. There had been no years between the ducking of this dragon-fly and the other one — the one that was part of memory. I looked at the boy, who was silently watching his fly, and it was my hands that held his rod, my eyes watching. I felt dizzy and didn't know which rod I was at the end of.

We caught two bass, hauling them in briskly as though they were mackerel, pulling them over the side of the boat in a businesslike manner without any landing net, and stunning them with a blow on the back of the head. When we got back for a swim before lunch, the lake was ex-actly where we had left it, the same number of inches from the dock, and there was only the merest suggestion of a breeze. This seemed an utterly enchanted sea, this lake you could leave to its own devices for a few hours and come back to, and find that it had not stirred, this constant and trustworthy body of water. In the shallows, the dark, watersoaked sticks and twigs, smooth and old, were undulating in clusters on the bot-tom against the clean ribbed sand, and the track of the mussel was plain. A school of minnows swam by, each minnow with its small individual shadow, doubling the attendance, so clear and sharp in the sunlight. Some of the other campers were in swimming, along the shore, one of them with a cake of soap, and the water felt thin and clear and unsub-stantial. Over the years there had been this person with the cake of soap, this cultist, and here he was. There had been no years.

Up to the farmhouse to dinner through the teeming, dusty field, the road under our sneakers was only a two-track road. The middle track was missing, the one with the marks of the hooves and splotches of dried, flaky manure. There had always been three tracks to choose from in choosing which track to walk in; now the choice was narrowed down to two. For a moment I missed terribly the middle alternative. But the way led past the tennis court, and something about the way it lay there in the sun reassured me; the tape had loosened along the backline, the alleys were green with plantains and other weeds, and the net (installed in June and removed in September) sagged in the dry noon, and the whole place steamed with midday heat and hunger and emptiness. There was a choice of pie for dessert, and one was blueberry and one was apple, and the waitresses were the same country girls, there having been no passage of time, only the illusion of it as in a dropped curtain—the waitresses were still fifteen; their hair had been washed, that was the only difference—they had been to the movies and seen the pretty girls with the clean hair.

Summertime, oh summertime, pattern of life indelible, the fade-proof lake, the woods unshatterable, the pasture with the sweetfern and the juniper forever and ever, summer without end; this was the background, and the life along the shore was the design, the cottages with their innocent and tranquil design, their tiny docks with the flagpole and the American flag floating against the white clouds in the blue sky, the little paths over the roots of the trees leading from camp to camp and the paths leading back to the outhouses and the can of lime for sprinkling, and at the souvenir counters at the store the miniature birch-bark canoes and the post cards that showed things looking a little better than they looked. This was the American family at play, escaping the city heat, wondering whether the newcomers in the camp at the head of the cove were "common" or "nice," wondering whether it was true that the people who drove up for Sunday dinner at the farmhouse were turned away because there wasn't enough chicken.

It seemed to me, as I kept remembering all this, that those times and those summers had been infinitely precious and worth saving. There had been jollity and peace and goodness. The arriving (at the beginning of August) had been so big a business in itself, at the railway station the farm wagon drawn up, the first smell of the pine-laden air, the first glimpse of the smiling farmer, and the great importance of the trunks and your father's enormous authority in such matters, and the feel of the wagon under you for the long ten-mile haul, and at the top of the last long hill catching the first view of the lake after eleven months of not seeing this cherished body of water. The shouts and cries of the other campers when they saw you, and the trunks to be unpacked, to give up their rich burden. (Arriving was less exciting nowadays, when you sneaked up in your car and parked it under a tree near the camp and took out the bags and in five minutes it was all over, no fuss, no loud wonderful fuss about trunks).

Peace and goodness and jollity. The only thing that was wrong now, really, was the sound of the place, an unfamiliar nervous sound of the outboard motors. This was the note that jarred, the one thing that would sometimes break the illusion and set the years moving. In those other summertimes all motors were inboard; and when they were at a little distance, the noise they made was a sedative, an ingredient of summer sleep. They were one-cylinder and two-cylinder engines, and some were make-and-break and some were jump-spark, but they all made a sleepy sound across the lake. The one-lungers throbbed and fluttered, and the twin-cylinder

10

ones purred and purred, and that was a quiet sound too. But now the campers all had outboards. In the daytime, in the hot mornings, these motors made a petulant, irritable sound; at night, in the still evening when the afterglow lit the water, they whined about one's ears like mosquitoes. My boy loved our rented outboard, and his great desire was to achieve single-handed mastery over it, and authority, and he soon learned the trick of choking it a little (but not too much), and the adjustment of the needle valve. Watching him I would remember the things you could do with the old one-cylinder engines with the heavy flywheel, how you could have it eating out of your hand if you got really close to it spiritually. Motor boats in those days didn't have clutches, and you would make a landing by shutting off the motor at the proper time and coasting in with a dead rudder. But there was a way of reversing them, if you learned the trick, by cutting the switch and putting it on again exactly on the final dying revolution of the flywheel, so that it would kick back against compression and begin reversing. Approaching a dock in a strong following breeze, it was difficult to slow up sufficiently by the ordinary coasting method, and if a boy felt he had complete mastery over his motor, he was tempted to keep it running beyond its time and then reverse it a few feet from the dock. It took a cool nerve, because if you threw the switch a twentieth of a second too soon you could catch the flywheel when it still had speed enough to go up past center, and the boat would leap ahead, charging bull-fashion at the dock.

We had a good week at the camp. The bass were biting well and the sun shone endlessly, day after day. We would be tired at night and lie down in the accumulated heat of the little bedrooms after the long hot day and the breeze would stir almost imperceptibly outside and the smell of the swamp drift in through the rusty screens. Sleep would come easily and in the morning the red squirrel would be on the roof, tapping out his gay routine. I kept remembering everything, lying in bed in the mornings—the small steamboat that had a long rounded stern like the lip of a Ubangi, and how quietly she ran on the moonlight sails, when the older boys played their mandolins and the girls sang and we ate doughnuts dipped in sugar, and how sweet the music was on the water in the shining night, and what it had felt like to think about girls then. After breakfast we would go up to the store and the things were in the same place—the minnows in a bottle, the plugs and spinners disarranged and pawed over by the youngsters from the boys' camp, the Fig Newtons and the Beeman's gum. Outside, the road was tarred and cars stood in front of the store. Inside, all was just as it had always been, except there was more Coca-Cola and not so much Moxie and root beer and birch beer and sarsaparilla. We would walk out with a bottle of pop apiece and sometimes the pop would backfire up our noses and hurt. We explored the streams, quietly, where the turtles slid off the sunny logs and dug their way into the soft bottom; and we lay on the town wharf and fed worms to the tame bass. Everywhere we went I had trouble making out which was I, the one walking at my side, the one walking in my pants.

One afternoon while we were there at that lake a thunderstorm came up. It was like the revival of an old melodrama that I had seen long ago with childish awe. The second-act climax of the drama of the electrical disturbance over a lake in America had not changed in any important respect. This was the big scene, still the big scene. The whole thing was so familiar, the first feeling of oppression and heat and a general air around camp of not wanting to go very far away. In midafternoon (it was all the same) a curious darkening of the sky, and a lull in everything that had made life tick; and then the way the boats suddenly swung the other way at their moorings with the coming of a breeze out of the new quarter, and the premonitory rumble. Then the kettle drum, then the snare, then the bass drum and cymbals, then crackling light against the dark, and the gods grinning and licking their chops in the hills. Afterward the calm, the rain steadily rustling in the calm lake, the return of light and hope and spirits, and the campers running out in joy and relief to go swimming in the rain, their bright cries perpetuating the deathless joke about how they were getting simply drenched, and the children screaming with delight at the new sensation of bathing in the rain, and the joke about getting drenched linking the generations in a strong indestructible chain. And the comedian who waded in carrying an umbrella.

When the others went swimming my son said he was going in too. He pulled his dripping trunks from the line where they had hung all through the shower, and wrung them out. Languidly, and with no thought of going in, I watched him, his hard little body, skinny and bare, saw him wince slightly as he pulled up around his vitals the small, soggy, icy garment. As he buckled the swollen belt suddenly my groin felt the chill of death.

The Reader's Presence

1. In paragraph 2, White begins to reflect on the way his memory works. How does he follow the process of remembering throughout the essay? Are his memories of the lake safely stored in the past? If not, why not?

2. Go through the essay and identify words and images having to do with the sensory details of seeing, hearing, touching, and so on. How do these details contribute to the overall effect of the essay? How do they anticipate White's final paragraph?

3. In paragraph 4, White refers to a "creepy sensation." What is the basis of that sensation? Why is it "creepy"? What is the "dual existence" White feels he is living? How does the essay build the story of White's relationships with both his father and his son? Compare this account of intergenerational intimacy to Raymond Carver's essay "My Father's Life" (see page 86).

THE WRITER AT WORK

E. B. White on the Essayist

For several generations, E. B. White has remained America's best known essayist, his works widely available and widely anthologized. Yet in the foreword to his 1977 collected essays when he addresses the role of the essayist, he sounds wholly modest not only about his career but about his chosen genre: In the world of literature, he writes, the essayist is a "second-class citizen." Why do you think White thinks of himself that way, and how might that self-deprecation be reconciled with the claims of his final two paragraphs? Do you think White's description of himself as an essayist matches the actual essayist we encounter in "Once More to the Lake"? Also, do you think his persistent use of the male pronoun is merely for grammatical convenience (the essay was written in 1977) or reflects a gender bias on his part?

The essayist is a self-liberated man, sustained by the childish belief that everything he thinks about, everything that happens to him, is of general interest. He is a fellow who thoroughly enjoys his work, just as people who take bird walks enjoy theirs. Each new excursion of the essayist, each new "attempt," differs from the last and takes him into new country. This delights him. Only a person who is congenitally self-centered has the effrontery and the stamina to write essays.

There are as many kinds of essays as there are human attitudes or poses, as many essay flavors as there are Howard Johnson ice creams. The essayist arises in the morning and, if he has work to do, selects his garb from an unusually extensive wardrobe: he can pull on any sort of shirt, be any sort of person, according to his mood or his subject matter—philosopher, scold, jester, raconteur, confidant, pundit, devil's advocate, enthusiast. I like the essay, have always liked it, and even as a child was at work, attempting to inflict my young thoughts and experiences on others by putting them on paper. I early broke into a print in the pages of *St. Nicholas*. I tend still to fall back on the essay form (or lack of form) when an idea strikes me, but I am not fooled about the place of the essay in twentieth century American letters—it stands a short distance down the line. The essayist, unlike the novelist, the poet, and the playwright, must be content in his self-imposed role of second-class citizen. A writer who has his sights trained on the Nobel Prize or other earthly triumphs had best write a novel, a poem, or a play, and leave the essayist to ramble about, content with living a free life and enjoying the satisfactions of a somewhat undisciplined existence. (Dr. Johnson called the essay "an irregular, undigested piece"; this happy practitioner has no wish to quarrel with the good doctor's characterization.)

There is one thing the essayist cannot do, though—he cannot indulge himself in deceit or in concealment, for he will be found out in no time. Desmond MacCarthy, in his introductory remarks to the 1928 E. P. Dutton & Company edition of Montaigne, observes that Montaigne "had the gift of natural candour. . . ." It is the basic ingredient. And even the essayist's escape from discipline is only a partial escape: the essay, although a relaxed form, imposes its own disciplines, raises its own problems, and these disciplines and problems soon become apparent and (we all hope) act as a deterrent to anyone wielding a pen merely because he entertains random thoughts or is in a happy or wandering mood.

I think some people find the essay the last resort of the egoist, a much too self-conscious and self-serving form for their tastes; they feel that it is presumptuous of a writer to assume that his little excursions or his small observations will interest the reader. There is some justice in their complaint. I have always been aware that I am by nature self-absorbed and egoistical; to write of myself to the extent I have done indicates a too great attention to my own life, not enough to the lives of others. I have worn many shirts, and not all of them have been a good fit. But when I am discouraged or downcast I need only fling open the door of my closet, and there, hidden behind everything else, hangs the mantle of Michel de Montaigne, smelling slightly of camphor.

41

Richard Wright

I Choose Exile

Richard Wright (1908–1960) experienced the life of poor black sharecroppers in Mississippi as a child and the life of the urban poor in Chicago and New York as an adult. A novelist, short story writer, poet, and essayist, he spent his writing career coming to terms with poverty, violence, and racism. During the 1930s Wright wrote for communist newspapers and was active in the Communist party; he eventually became disillusioned with communism and severed his ties in 1944. In 1947 Wright moved to Paris and lived there until his death. Wright first gained critical acclaim with his depiction of the dehumanization of blacks in a racist society in his novel Native Son *(1940). His autobiography,* Black Boy, *was published in 1945 and became a national best-seller.*

In 1951 Wright submitted "I Choose Exile" to Ebony *magazine. The magazine, despite having commissioned the piece, ultimately rejected it. According to Ben Burns, an* Ebony *editor who wanted to publish Wright's essay, the publisher "refused to publish it because he felt it would offend advertisers." In a letter to Burns that accompanied the manuscript Wright wrote: "You asked me to write about my life in Paris; now, such a subject covers a wide field. . . . I tried to give a general idea of what life in Paris is like, but only in contrast to what Negro life in America is like."*

We are pleased to print this essay—which appears in its entirety for the first time—and thank the Richard Wright estate for the opportunity to do so.

I am a native born American Negro. The first 38 years of my life were spent exclusively on the soil of my native land. But, at the moment of this writing, I live in voluntary exile in France and I like it. There is nothing in the life of America that I miss or yearn for. Barring war or catastrophe, I intend to remain in exile. I shall, of course, keep my American citizenship, my American passport; but I prefer to live out my days among a civilized people.

Why have I decided to live beyond the shores of my native land? It is because I love freedom, and I tell you frankly that there is more freedom in one square block of Paris than there is in the entire United States of America! These words of mine are not designed to provoke dissatisfaction in other whites or Negroes with America; I am not trying to persuade other Negroes to live abroad. My decision is predicated upon this simple fact: I *need* freedom. Yes, some people need more freedom than others, and I am one of them. Unless I feel free to let my instincts range, free to come and go as I please, free to probe and examine my environment, I languish, I wither, I die. In short, freedom, to me, is equated to concrete reality, to life; it is not something abstract, something to be won or hoped for; it is life itself, each day, each hour, each moment. . . .

Most Frenchmen I've met feel as I do about this; they love their personal and civil freedom. Yet, I've heard but few Frenchmen speak of freedom during the five years I've lived in Paris. People are not prone to speak of that which they already have. It was only in America where so much freedom is lacking that one hears long and impassioned arguments about freedom . . . It is like listening to a starving man tell of his need for food.

So well do I know white and black Americans that I can almost predict their reactions to my attitude. There are those who will immediately say, "Oh, yes; he is a Negro and he feels better in France where there is no racial segregation." But I hasten to declare that any such interpretations of my motives are wrong and shallow. True, it was in part the desire to escape the racial pressure of the United States that decided me to flee my native land, but it was not racial reasons alone that decided me to remain. What was it then?

During the years of my life in America I felt that in time my country would settle down to humane living with a code of civilized values. But my sojourn in France made me realize that I had deceived myself. I know now that America has no such future, that it is inescapably different from Europe and that no conceivable stretch of historical time will make it like Europe. Indeed, time will only emphasize the differences between the two value systems which are moving in completely opposed directions. My temperament made me elect to choose the side containing the deepest ele-

5

ments of humanity—France and Europe. On the Continent the individual is placed at the top of a carefully graded scale of values, and most all decisions and actions are based upon those values which are taught rigidly in the schools, reflected in the church, and depicted in art and literature. In the United States, despite its idealistic origins, the desire for materialistic power dominates all. Utilitarian motives claim, to the exclusion of all else, the hearts and minds of its citizens.

My life in America had been spent in fighting for the rights of the Negro people and I knew that that fight was, morally and legally, a correct one; that it was supported by our democratic traditions and our Constitution. Yet, deep down, during all of those years, I felt that there was something organically wrong with a nation that could so cynically violate its own laws in meting out cruelties upon a helpless minority. America's barbaric treatment of the Negro is not one-half so bad or inhuman as the destructive war which she wages against the concept of the free person, against the Rights of Man, and against herself!

But enough of generalizations; let me glance back and describe the last personal event which resolved me to leave America.

In New York, in the winter of 1946, I was seized by a longing for the countryside, for rolling landscapes. I was, as they say, "fed up" with city living, though city living certainly offers the American Negro his best possible haven from race prejudice, casting him into a vast anonymity which drapes about him a somewhat negative cloak of protection. Now, when an American Negro starts yearning for a landscape, it wisely behooves him to be careful to choose the *right* one, for most American landscapes have been robbed, for him, of their beauty and innocence by the fact that almost every lynching in America has taken place in such a setting. To go South, then, was unthinkable. The West Coast had never appealed to me, being too fruity and nutty. New England! That was it! Had not the dauntless abolitionists risen in that transcendentalistic atmosphere? And had not Hawthorne, Emerson, and Thoreau sprung from that stubborn but free soil? I was decided.

I discussed this all-too-normal desire to buy a home in New England with two well-bred and cultured white friends of mine who lived in Hanover, New Hampshire. They urged me to stay in their home and use it as a base from which to scout for a piece of property. I was grateful for their hospitality and I accepted.

Wintry New Hampshire greeted me magnificently. A heavy, gleaming snow carpeted the plunging hills. The eye could see for miles through the sharp, pure, bracing air. A deep quiet hung in the tranquil valleys. Proud pines pointed skywards. Here was what I wanted.   10

Two days of searching brought me a "dream" house, located in Connecticut just across the New Hampshire state line. The house was empty, sturdy, wooden, roomy, and ready for occupancy, and was half a mile from the nearest neighbor. The mere look of that house, as the salesmen say, "sold" me. The price was six thousand dollars. I'd buy it, cash.

I looked up the real estate agent and found him to be a seemingly friendly man. I told him what I wanted. His eyes became shifty. He smiled and scratched his chin.

"All right," he said. "I'll communicate with the owner and let you know."

"Why is that necessary?" I asked, sensing an air of unquiet in him.

"Oh, it's simply routine," he assured me.   15

"When will you let me know?" I asked. I told myself that I must not leap to premature conclusions.

"In a couple of days," he said. "I'll 'phone you."

In the comfortable home of my host I sat for four days in front of a blazing log fire and waited to hear from the real estate agent. My frequent 'phone calls merely elicited a polite:

"I've no word yet, Mr. Wright."

Finally I became certain in my own mind as to what was happening.   20 The dreadful issue of "race" was hovering somewhere over those beautiful, snow-clad hills of New Hampshire. At last I asked my host to see the real estate agent and get the truth. He made an appointment with the agent and when he returned to the house I saw at once a hurt, stunned look in his brooding eyes. I knew the truth before he spoke. A curious, sensitive scene followed, a scene which has haunted American history for 300 years: A white man wrestling with his conscience because he has to tell a Negro something which he knows will cause him pain. My host was trying to spare my feelings and the agony in him made me try to spare his feelings! I tried to assure him that this was a "normal thing" in the life of an American Negro and that he should not be too upset about it. The "truth" turned out to be that the white owner did not want to sell his house to a Negro. . . .

I sat the next day in a New York bound train and felt rather than thought. What was there to think about? A feeling welled up in me, springing from the depths of my life. I'd had enough of this. To hell with it. I would get out of it. I'd go to France at once. I'd try living a spell away from this racial nightmare. I'd leave the land of my birth, my home, my friends, everything. I'd leave the culture that had shaped me. I'd try something different.

I arrived at my New York apartment and announced to my wife:

"This is the first of April. We are leaving America on the first of May. Take the child out of school. Put the furniture in storage. Buy tickets for Paris. We're through here."

She was stunned, but she agreed.

To leave America in 1946 was not easy. My application for a pass-   25 port was rejected by the Department of State on the grounds that the conditions in post-war Europe were so bad that the government feared that United States citizens would become stranded abroad. I assured the government that I had enough money to care for my needs, but the answer was still no. I was packed, ready to leave, but no passport was forthcoming. I discovered, in consulting lawyers, that, as an American citizen, I had no legal right to a passport, that a passport could be given or withheld at the discretion of the government, in this case the government was personified by a distant woman named Miss Shipley whom I'd never seen.

I was determined not to give up. I appealed for help to French friends of mine in New York and they in turn appealed to the French Government. From Paris Gertrude Stein, with whom I was in close contact, wrote that she would do her utmost. On the 15th of April, 1946, the French Government responded graciously, giving me an official invitation to visit France. I've done it, I said. I air-mailed the invitation to the Passport Division of the Department of State in Washington and waited for a reply. None came. I 'phoned them by long distance and was dismayed to learn that the invitation "had been lost."

I was angry. I appealed again to the French Government for a duplicate invitation! They sent it. Again I 'phoned Washington long distance and told them that I was flying down with another invitation and that I wanted my passport. A suave voice tried to dissuade me from coming to Washington, but I insisted that I'd be there in person.

I began to pull every political string in sight. Through the good offices of a famous American doctor I got a pipe-line into the set of Evalyn Walsh MacLean, a set which was rumored to be sympathetic to facism. I did not give a damn about their political sympathies; I wanted my passport and I was ready to accept help from the devil himself. I was told to see a "certain man" in Washington. I saw him and told him to "put in the fix." He did. I got my passport an hour later.

I was not sorry when my ship sailed past the Statue of Liberty!

Irony of ironies! When I descended from the boat-train in Paris in   30
May, 1946, not only was Gertrude Stein on hand to greet me, but the United States Embassy had sent its public relations man with two sleek cars to aid me. I found that abroad the United States Government finds it convenient to admit that even Negroes are Americans! (Read between the lines!)

A swarm of French newsmen crowded about me, asking a thousand questions about the American Negro. I answered their questions and answered them straight. As these men pumped me I became aware of the smooth flow of a ritual of politeness that imbued me with a sense of social confidence. I was already beginning to feel the mellow influence of a deeply humane culture.

My first week in Paris taught me that the fight I had made back home for Negro rights was right, but somehow futile. The deep contrast between French and American racial attitudes demonstrated that it was barbarousness that incited such militant racism in white Americans. In discussing this matter with André Gide, he told me:

"The more uncivilized a white man, the more he fears and hates all those people who differ from him. With us in France, the different, the variant is prized; our curiosity to know other people is the hallmark of our civilized state. In America it is precisely the variant, the different who is hounded down by mobs and killed. The American is a terribly socially insecure man who feels threatened by the mere existence of men different from himself."

I was eager to find out how did these Frenchmen "get that way." I soon realized that the impartiality with which Frenchmen viewed people with dark skins had nothing whatsoever to do with their love of these dark people themselves. It was the love and respect which Frenchmen held toward their own history, culture, and achievements that braced the French to a stance of fairness in racial matters. What restrained a French-man from humiliating a Negro was not sentimental idealism, but a deep reverence for French dignity and worth.

One of the most gifted and remarkable men I've met in Paris is Jean-Paul Sartre, playwright, novelist, and philosophical spokesman for atheis-tic existentialism. Sartre is a free man who feels it is his duty, and not on moral or metaphysical grounds, to take a stand against anti-Semitism, against racism, against imperialism. Sartre is not the member of any polit-ical party and it cannot be maintained that his motives are dictated by selfish interests. In talking with Sartre I was made to understand that a French writer considers it a vital part of his growth as an artist and a human being to shed infantile prejudices. Albert Camus, Jean Cocteau, Si-mone de Beauvoir, and a host of other French writers share the same pas-sion to defend the dignity of man.

During my years of activity in various writers' and artists' organiza-tions in the United States, I've had the honor to meet most of the so-called great white American writers of my time, and I do not know of a single white American writer who has felt the humane compulsion to make a public declaration against racism, against anti-Semitism and against im-perialism, and to weave such concepts into his work as a part of his artis-tic creed.

In due time I became tired of my cramped hotel room and decided to look for an apartment. Living space was as scarce in Paris as elsewhere. But, as an American Negro living in Paris, I had an advantage over Ne-groes living in the United States. There is no Black Belt in which a Negro must confine his domicile. Paris is racially a free city. I state here that as an American Negro I am a highly sensitized person in racial matters. Dur-ing a period of three months I crossed and recrossed Paris in my car, en-tering hundreds of French homes to ask about apartments. And not once during my goings and comings did I so much as observe the lift of an eye-lid at the color of my skin. There was no anger or surprise when a dark face stood framed in the doorway of a French home!

Luck was with me and finally I found the apartment of my choice. My prospective landlord, an aristocratic woman of some 80 years, invited me to tea. When tea was over, she gave me her answer. It was yes.

There is one anecdote that I can relate that will illustrate the basic at-titudes of the average Frenchman to racial issues more graphically than a

35

thousand pages of argument. One winter I was motoring from Zurich to Paris and just over the Swiss border I lost my way in a driving rain. I got out of my car and ran into a little country cafe and asked a young girl behind the counter the main road to Paris. The girl did not answer; she gaped at me in astonishment. I repeated my request for information about the highways, and then she gasped:

"Attendez!" (Wait.)   40

She ran out of the cafe through a back doorway. I was baffled, wondering if I had offended her in some way. But a moment later she returned with another girl, a year or two younger, seemingly her sister. This newcomer gaped at me too, as though I'd been a man from Mars. She whirled and started calling:

"Maman! Maman!"

In another minute a big fat mama, wiping her hands on a dish towel, appeared in the back doorway, smiling, measuring me from my head to my feet. Again I asked for the road to Paris, but no one answered. Then the mother yelled, turning back toward the doorway:

"Vite! Vite, mon garçon!" (Quick, quick, my boy.)

Another minute passed, and then I could hardly credit my eyes, for   45 there stood in the back doorway a tall brownskin Negro, wearing a stocking cap, sleepily rubbing his eyes. Meanwhile, the oldest girl ran to the Negro and put her arm fondly about his neck and beamed at me. The mother and the other daughter stared at me proudly.

"Regardez, monsieur," the fat French mother told me, pointing to the Negro.

"Hy, Daddy-O," the young Negro said, smiling.

"What in hell are you doing way out here?" I asked him.

"Me? Hell, I live here," he said, kissing the girl who held him.

"This is my wife," he explained. "Man, I checked outta that army   50 and settled down here to do some living. You see, I gotta garage next door. I own this cafe too. I work nights in the garage; that's how come I was sleeping when you came." He shook his head with indulgent sadness. "Shucks, these people is crazy, man. Every time they see a spook, they go wild and wake me up . . . They so proud to have a spook in the family, they just wanted to show me off to you."

"Well, that's better than what happens back home, isn't it?" I asked.

"You sure can say that again," he said, lighting a cigarette.

I left behind me in the rain a smiling French peasant family doting on their colored boy!

To live in Paris is to allow one's sensibilities to be nourished by physical beauty. To me the most startling things in Paris are its trees which are to be found, not just in rich, residential areas, but in all sections of the city. A Parisian would find it criminal to make a Park Avenue and leave, say, Spanish Harlem to rot in dirt and garbage. Shaped to human ends, Paris is not terrifyingly "big"; there is a monumental grandeur in the uniform heights of its buildings. Two-story houses do not stand next to sixteen-story apartment hotels, an arrangement which gives so ragged an appearance even to New York City.

I love my adopted city. Its sunsets, its teeming boulevards, its slow and humane tempo of life have entered deeply into my heart. Yet, make no mistake, there is grim reality here. There is the danger of war and the Parisians have no illusions about it. But they refuse to become hysterical. From somewhere out of their 2,000-year-old history, Frenchmen have found a way to take the grim along with the beautiful.

France is, above all, a land of refuge. Even when there is a shortage of food, Frenchmen will share their crusts of bread with strangers. Yet, nowhere do you see so much gaiety as in Paris, nowhere can you hear so much spirited talk. Each contemporary event is tasted, chewed, digested. There is no first-rate French novelist specializing in creating unreal, romantic historical novels! The present is to be understood and they find it exciting enough. "The problems of philosophy," says Jean-Paul Sartre, "are to be found in the streets."

I have encountered among the French no social snobbery. The more individualistic a man is, the more acceptable he is. The spirit of the mob, whether intellectual, racial, or moral, is the very opposite of the spirit of French life. SOIT RAISONNABLE, (be reasonable) is their motto.

The Reader's Presence

1. Why does Wright leave America? What incident causes him to make this decision? Why do you think this incident pushes him to make the decision? How does Wright justify his decision to his wife? What sense of his character do you get from this account?

2. How does the story about the family in the French countryside function in the essay? What is its relation to the Connecticut real estate story? Why does Wright use these anecdotes?

3. How does Wright's account of his expatriation to France compare with that of James Baldwin in "Equal in Paris"? What reasons do the two Black writers give for leaving? How might they respond to one another?

Part III

Expository Writing: Shaping Information

42

Gloria Anzaldúa

How to Tame a Wild Tongue

Gloria Anzaldúa, born in south Texas in 1942, is a poet, cultural theorist, essayist, and editor who uses her writings to explore issues such as racism, Chicano culture, lesbianism, and feminism. In addition to writing and editing, Anzaldúa has taught creative writing, literature, and feminist studies at San Francisco State University, Oakes College at the University of California in Santa Cruz, and Norwich University. She is coeditor of This Bridge Called My Back: Writings by Radical Women of Color *(1981), which received the Before Columbus Foundation American Book Award. She is also the editor of* Making Face, Making Soul/ Haciendo Caras: Creative and Critical Perspectives by Women of Color *(1990), and, most recently, coeditor of* Cassell's Encyclopedia of Queer Myth, Symbol, and Spirit: Gay, Lesbian, Bisexual, and Transgender Lore *(1997). She is the author of three bilingual children's books,* Prietita Tiene un Amigo/Prietita Has a Friend *(1991),* Friends from the Other Side/Amigos del Otro Lado *(1993) and Prietita and the Ghost Woman/Prietita y la Ilorona *(1995). Her more recent works are* La Prieta *(1997) and* Interviews/Entrevistas *(2000). Her first book,* Borderlands/La Frontera: The New Mestiza *(1987), from which "How to Tame a Wild Tongue" is taken, is a blend of poetry, memoir, and historical analysis. Anzaldúa lives in Santa Cruz, California, and frequently participates in panel discussions, teaches workshops, and gives lectures.*

"We're going to have to control your tongue," the dentist says, pulling out all the metal from my mouth. Silver bits plop and tinkle into the basin. My mouth is a motherlode.

The dentist is cleaning out my roots. I get a whiff of the stench when I gasp. "I can't cap that tooth yet, you're still draining," he says.

"We're going to have to do something about your tongue," I hear the anger rising in his voice. My tongue keeps pushing out the wads of cotton, pushing back the drills, the long thin needles. "I've never seen anything as strong or as stubborn," he says. And I think how do you tame a wild tongue, train it to be quiet, how do you bridle and saddle it? How do you make it lie down?

"Who is to say that robbing a people of its language is less violent than war?"

—Ray Gwyn Smith[1]

I remember being caught speaking Spanish at recess—that was good for three licks on the knuckles with a sharp ruler. I remember being sent to the corner of the classroom for "talking back" to the Anglo teacher when all I was trying to do was tell her how to pronounce my name. "If you want to be American, speak 'American.' If you don't like it, go back to Mexico where you belong."

"I want you to speak English. *Pa' hallar buen trabajo tienes que*   5 *saber hablar el inglés bien. Qué vale toda tu educación si todavía hablas inglés con un* 'accent,'" my mother would say, mortified that I spoke English like a Mexican. At Pan American University, I, and all Chicano students were required to take two speech classes. Their purpose: to get rid of our accents.

Attacks on one's form of expression with the intent to censor are a violation of the First Amendment. *El Anglo con cara de inocente nos arrancó la lengua.* Wild tongues can't be tamed, they can only be cut out.

OVERCOMING THE TRADITION OF SILENCE

> *Ahogadas, escupimos el oscuro.*
> *Peleando con nuestra propia sombra*
> *el silencio nos sepulta.*

En boca cerrada no entran moscas. "Flies don't enter a closed mouth" is a saying I kept hearing when I was a child. *Ser habladora* was to be a gossip and a liar, to talk too much. *Muchachitas bien criadas,* well-bred girls don't answer back. *Es una falta de respeto* to talk back to one's mother or father. I remember one of the sins I'd recite to the priest in the confession box the few times I went to confession: talking back to my mother, *hablar pa' 'tras, repelar. Hocicona, repelona, chismosa,* having a big mouth, questioning, carrying tales are all signs of being *mal criada.* In my culture they are all words that are derogatory if applied to women—I've never heard them applied to men.

The first time I heard two women, a Puerto Rican and a Cuban, say the word *"nosotras,"* I was shocked. I had not known the word existed. Chicanas use *nosotros* whether we're male or female. We are robbed of our female being by the masculine plural. Language is a male discourse.

> And our tongues have become
> dry   the wilderness has

---

[1]Ray Gwyn Smith, *Moorland Is Cold Country,* unpublished book.

dried out our tongues   and
we have forgotten speech.

—Irena Klepfisz[2]

Even our own people, other Spanish speakers *nos quieren poner candados en la boca.* They would hold us back with their bag of *reglas de academia.*

OYÉ COMO LADRA: EL LENGUAJE DE LA FRONTERA

Quien tiene boca se equivoca.

—Mexican saying

"*Pocho,* cultural traitor, you're speaking the oppressor's language by speaking English, you're ruining the Spanish language," I have been accused by various Latinos and Latinas. Chicano Spanish is considered by the purist and by most Latinos deficient, a mutilation of Spanish.

But Chicano Spanish is a border tongue which developed naturally. Change, *evolución, enriquecimiento de palabras nuevas por invención o adopción* have created variants of Chicano Spanish, *un nuevo lenguaje. Un lenguaje que corresponde a un modo de vivir.* Chicano Spanish is not incorrect, it is a living language.

For people who are neither Spanish nor live in a country in which Spanish is the first language; for a people who live in a country in which English is the reigning tongue but who are not Anglo; for a people who cannot entirely identify with either standard (formal, Castillian) Spanish nor standard English, what recourse is left to them but to create their own language? A language which they can connect their identity to, one capable of communicating the realities and values true to themselves—a language with terms that are neither *español ni inglés,* but both. We speak a patois, a forked tongue, a variation of two languages.

Chicano Spanish sprang out of the Chicanos' need to identify ourselves as a distinct people. We needed a language with which we could communicate with ourselves, a secret language. For some of us, language is a homeland closer than the Southwest—for many Chicanos today live in the Midwest and the East. And because we are a complex, heterogeneous people, we speak many languages. Some of the languages we speak are:

1. Standard English
2. Working class and slang English

---

[2]Irena Klepfisz, "*Di rayze aheym*/The Journey Home," in *The Tribe of Dina: A Jewish Women's Anthology,* Melanie Kaye/Kantrowitz and Irena Klepfisz, eds. (Montpelier, VT: Sinister Wisdom Books, 1986), 49.

3. Standard Spanish
4. Standard Mexican Spanish
5. North Mexican Spanish dialect
6. Chicano Spanish (Texas, New Mexico, Arizona and California have regional variations)
7. Tex-Mex
8. *Pachuco* (called *caló*)

My "home" tongues are the languages I speak with my sister and brothers, with my friends. They are the last five listed, with 6 and 7 being closest to my heart. From school, the media, and job situations, I've picked up standard and working class English. From Mamagrande Locha and from reading Spanish and Mexican literature, I've picked up Standard Spanish and Standard Mexican Spanish. From *los recién llegados,* Mexican immigrants, and *braceros,* I learned the North Mexican dialect. With Mexicans I'll try to speak either Standard Mexican Spanish or the North Mexican dialect. From my parents and Chicanos living in the Valley, I picked up Chicano Texas Spanish, and I speak it with my mom, younger brother (who married a Mexican and who rarely mixes Spanish with English), aunts and older relatives.

With Chicanas from *Nuevo México* or *Arizona* I will speak Chicano 15 Spanish a little, but often they don't understand what I'm saying. With most California Chicanas I speak entirely in English (unless I forget). When I first moved to San Francisco, I'd rattle off something in Spanish, unintentionally embarrassing them. Often it is only with another Chicana *tejana* that I can talk freely.

Words distorted by English are known as anglicisms or *pochismos.* The *pocho* is an anglicized Mexican or American of Mexican origin who speaks Spanish with an accent characteristic of North Americans and who distorts and reconstructs the language according to the influence of English.[3] Tex-Mex, or Spanglish, comes most naturally to me. I may switch back and forth from English to Spanish in the same sentence or in the same word. With my sister and my brother Nune and with Chicano *tejano* contemporaries I speak in Tex-Mex.

From kids and people my own age I picked up *Pachuco. Pachuco* (the language of the zoot suiters) is a language of rebellion, both against Standard Spanish and Standard English. It is a secret language. Adults of the culture and outsiders cannot understand it. It is made up of slang words from both English and Spanish. *Ruca* means girl or woman, *vato* means guy or dude, *chale* means no, *simón* means yes, *churro* is sure, talk is *periquiar, pigionear* means petting, *que gacho* means how nerdy, *ponte águila* means

---

[3]R. C. Ortega, *Dialectología Del Barrio,* trans. Hortencia S. Alwan (Los Angeles, CA: R. C. Ortega Publisher & Bookseller, 1977), 132.

watch out, death is called *la pelona*. Through lack of practice and not having others who can speak it, I've lost most of the *Pachuco* tongue.

CHICANO SPANISH

Chicanos, after 250 years of Spanish/Anglo colonization have developed significant differences in the Spanish we speak. We collapse two adjacent vowels into a single syllable and sometimes shift the stress in certain words such as *maíz/maiz, cohete/cuete*. We leave out certain consonants when they appear between vowels: *lado/lao, mojado/majao*. Chicanos from South Texas pronounce *f* as *j* as in *jue (fue)*. Chicanos use "archaisms," words that are no longer in the Spanish language, words that have been evolved out. We say *semos, truje, haiga, ansina,* and *naiden*. We retain the "archaic" *j,* as in *jalar,* that derives from an earlier *h,* (the French *halar* or the Germanic *halon* which was lost to standard Spanish in the 16th century), but which is still found in several regional dialects such as the one spoken in South Texas. (Due to geography, Chicanos from the Valley of South Texas were cut off linguistically from other Spanish speakers. We tend to use words that the Spaniards brought over from Medieval Spain. The majority of the Spanish colonizers in Mexico and the Southwest came from Extremadura—Hernán Cortés was one of them—and Andalucía. Andalucians pronounce *ll* like a *y,* and their *d*'s tend to be absorbed by adjacent vowels: *tirado* becomes *tirao*. They brought *el lenguaje popular, dialectos y regionalismos*.[4])

Chicanos and other Spanish speakers also shift *ll* to *y* and *z* to *s*.[5] We leave out initial syllables, saying *tar* for *estar, toy* for *estoy, hora* for *ahora* (*cubanos* and *puertorriqueños* also leave out initial letters of some words.) We also leave out the final syllable such as *pa* for *para*. The intervocalic *y,* the *ll* as in *tortilla, ella, botella,* gets replaced by *tortia* or *tortiya, ea, botea*. We add an additional syllable at the beginning of certain words: *atocar* for *tocar, agastar* for *gastar*. Sometimes we'll say *lavaste las vacijas,* other times *lavates* (substituting the *ates* verb endings for the *aste*).

We use anglicisms, words borrowed from English: *bola* from ball, *carpeta* from carpet, *máchina de lavar* (instead of *lavadora*) from washing machine. Tex-Mex argot, created by adding a Spanish sound at the beginning or end of an English word such as *cookiar* for cook, *watchar* for watch, *parkiar* for park, and *rapiar* for rape, is the result of the pressures on Spanish speakers to adapt to English. 20

We don't use the word *vosotros/as* or its accompanying verb form. We don't say *claro* (to mean yes), *imagínate,* or *me emociona,* unless we picked up Spanish from Latinas, out of a book, or in a classroom. Other

---

[4]Eduardo Hernández-Chávez, Andrew D. Cohen, and Anthony F. Beltramo, *El Lenguaje de los Chicanos: Regional and Social Characteristics of Language Used By Mexican Americans* (Arlington, VA: Center for Applied Linguistics, 1975), 39.

[5]Hernández-Chávez, xvii.

Spanish-speaking groups are going through the same, or similar, development in their Spanish.

LINGUISTIC TERRORISM

> *Deslenguadas. Somos los del español deficiente.* We are your linguistic nightmare, your linguistic aberration, your linguistic *mestisaje,* the subject of your *burla.* Because we speak with tongues of fire we are culturally crucified. Racially, culturally and linguistically *somos huérfanos*—we speak an orphan tongue.

Chicanas who grew up speaking Chicano Spanish have internalized the belief that we speak poor Spanish. It is illegitimate, a bastard language. And because we internalize how our language has been used against us by the dominant culture, we use our language differences against each other.

Chicana feminists often skirt around each other with suspicion and hesitation. For the longest time I couldn't figure it out. Then it dawned on me. To be close to another Chicana is like looking into the mirror. We are afraid of what we'll see there. *Pena.* Shame. Low estimation of self. In childhood we are told that our language is wrong. Repeated attacks on our native tongue diminish our sense of self. The attacks continue throughout our lives.

Chicanas feel uncomfortable talking in Spanish to Latinas, afraid of their censure. Their language was not outlawed in their countries. They had a whole lifetime of being immersed in their native tongue; generations, centuries in which Spanish was a first language, taught in school, heard on radio and TV, and read in the newspaper.

If a person, Chicana or Latina, has a low estimation of my native 25 tongue, she also has a low estimation of me. Often with *mexicanas y latinas* we'll speak English as a neutral language. Even among Chicanas we tend to speak English at parties or conferences. Yet, at the same time, we're afraid the others will think we're *agringadas* because we don't speak Chicano Spanish. We oppress each other trying to out-Chicano each other, vying to be the "real" Chicanas, to speak like Chicanos. There is no one Chicano language just as there is no one Chicano experience. A monolingual Chicana whose first language is English or Spanish is just as much a Chicana as one who speaks several variants of Spanish. A Chicana from Michigan or Chicago or Detroit is just as much a Chicana as one from the southwest. Chicano Spanish is as diverse linguistically as it is regionally.

By the end of this century, Spanish speakers will comprise the biggest minority group in the U.S., a country where students in high schools and colleges are encouraged to take French classes because French is considered more "cultured." But for a language to remain alive it must be used.[6]

---

[6]Irena Klepfisz, "Secular Jewish Identity: Yidishkayt in America," in *The Tribe of Dina,* Kaye/Kantrowitz and Klepfisz, eds., 43.

By the end of this century English, and not Spanish, will be the mother tongue of most Chicanos and Latinos.

So, if you want to really hurt me, talk badly about my language. Ethnic identity is twin skin to linguistic identity—I am my language. Until I can take pride in my language, I cannot take pride in myself. Until I can accept as legitimate Chicano Texas Spanish, Tex-Mex and all the other languages I speak, I cannot accept the legitimacy of myself. Until I am free to write bilingually and to switch codes without having always to translate, while I still have to speak English or Spanish when I would rather speak Spanglish, and as long as I have to accommodate the English speakers rather than having them accommodate me, my tongue will be illegitimate.

I will no longer be made to feel ashamed of existing. I will have my voice: Indian, Spanish, white. I will have my serpent's tongue—my woman's voice, my sexual voice, my poet's voice. I will overcome the tradition of silence.

> My fingers
> move sly against your palm
> Like women everywhere, we speak in code. . . .
>
> —Melanie Kaye/Kantrowitz[7]

"VISTAS," CORRIDOS, Y COMIDA: MY NATIVE TONGUE

In the 1960s, I read my first Chicano novel. It was *City of Night* by John Rechy, a gay Texan, son of a Scottish father and a Mexican mother. For days I walked around in stunned amazement that a Chicano could write and could get published. When I read *I Am Joaquín*[8] I was surprised to see a bilingual book by a Chicano in print. When I saw poetry written in Tex-Mex for the first time, a feeling of pure joy flashed through me. I felt like we really existed as a people. In 1971, when I started teaching High School English to Chicano students, I tried to supplement the required texts with works by Chicanos, only to be reprimanded and forbidden to do so by the principal. He claimed that I was supposed to teach "American" and English literature. At the risk of being fired, I swore my students to secrecy and slipped in Chicano short stories, poems, a play. In graduate school, while working toward a Ph.D., I had to "argue" with one advisor after the other, semester after semester, before I was allowed to make Chicano literature an area of focus.

---

[7]Melanie Kaye/Kantrowitz, "Sign," in *We Speak In Code: Poems and Other Writings* (Pittsburgh, PA: Motheroot Publications, Inc., 1980), 85.

[8] Rodolfo Gonzales, *I Am Joaquín/Yo Soy Joaquín* (New York, NY: Bantam Books, 1972). It was first published in 1967.

Even before I read books by Chicanos or Mexicans, it was the Mexican movies I saw at the drive-in—the Thursday night special of $1.00 a carload—that gave me a sense of belonging. "*Vámonos a las vistas,*" my mother would call out and we'd all—grandmother, brothers, sister and cousins—squeeze into the car. We'd wolf down cheese and bologna white bread sandwiches while watching Pedro Infante in melodramatic tear-jerkers like *Nosotros los pobres,* the first "real" Mexican movie (that was not an imitation of European movies). I remember seeing *Cuando los hijos se van* and surmising that all Mexican movies played up the love a mother has for her children and what ungrateful sons and daughters suffer when they are not devoted to their mothers. I remember the singing-type "westerns" of Jorge Negrete and Miquel Aceves Mejía. When watching Mexican movies, I felt a sense of homecoming as well as alienation. People who were to amount to something didn't go to Mexican movies, or *bailes* or tune their radios to *bolero, rancherita,* and *corrido* music.

The whole time I was growing up, there was *norteño* music sometimes called North Mexican border music, or Tex-Mex music, or Chicano music, or *cantina* (bar) music. I grew up listening to *conjuntos,* three- or four-piece bands made up of folk musicians playing guitar, *bajo sexto,* drums and button accordion, which Chicanos had borrowed from the German immigrants who had come to Central Texas and Mexico to farm and build breweries. In the Rio Grande Valley, Steve Jordan and Little Joe Hernández were popular, and Flaco Jiménez was the accordian king. The rhythms of Tex-Mex music are those of the polka, also adapted from the Germans, who in turn had borrowed the polka from the Czechs and Bohemians.

I remember the hot, sultry evenings when *corridos*—songs of love and death on the Texas-Mexican borderlands—reverberated out of cheap amplifiers from the local *cantinas* and wafted in through my bedroom window.

Corridos first became widely used along the South Texas/Mexican border during the early conflict between Chicanos and Anglos. The *corridos* are usually about Mexican heroes who do valiant deeds against the Anglo oppressors. Pancho Villa's song, "*La cucaracha,*" is the most famous one. *Corridos* of John F. Kennedy and his death are still very popular in the Valley. Older Chicanos remember Lydia Mendoza, one of the great border *corrido* singers who was called *la Gloria de Tejas.* Her "*El tango negro,*" sung during the Great Depression, made her a singer of the people. The ever-present *corridos* narrated one hundred years of border history, bringing news of events as well as entertaining. These folk musicians and folk songs are our chief cultural myth-makers, and they made our hard lives seem bearable.

I grew up feeling ambivalent about our music. Country-western and rock-and-roll had more status. In the 50s and 60s, for the slightly educated and *agringado* Chicanos, there existed a sense of shame at being caught listening to our music. Yet I couldn't stop my feet from thumping to the music, could not stop humming the words, nor hide from myself the exhilaration I felt when I heard it.

There are more subtle ways that we internalize identification, especially in the forms of images and emotions. For me food and certain smells are tied to my identity, to my homeland. Woodsmoke curling up to an immense blue sky; woodsmoke perfuming my grandmother's clothes, her skin. The stench of cow manure and the yellow patches on the ground; the crack of a .22 rifle and the reek of cordite. Homemade white cheese sizzling in a pan, melting inside a folded *tortilla*. My sister Hilda's hot, spicy *menudo, chile colorado* making it deep red, pieces of *panza* and hominy floating on top. My brother Carito barbequing *fajitas* in the backyard. Even now and 3,000 miles away, I can see my mother spicing the ground beef, pork and venison with *chile*. My mouth salivates at the thought of the hot steaming *tamales* I would be eating if I were home. 35

SI LE PREGUNTAS A MI MAMÁ, "¿QUÉ ERES?"

> "Identity is the essential core of who
> we are as individuals, the conscious
> experience of the self inside."
>
> —Kaufman[9]

Nosotros los Chicanos straddle the borderlands. On one side of us, we are constantly exposed to the Spanish of the Mexicans, on the other side we hear the Anglos' incessant clamoring so that we forget our language. Among ourselves we don't say *nosotros los americanos, o nosotros los españoles, o nosotros los hispanos.* We say *nosotros los mexicanos* (by *mexicanos* we do not mean citizens of Mexico; we do not mean a national identity, but a racial one). We distinguish between *mexicanos del otro lado* and *mexicanos de este lado.* Deep in our hearts we believe that being Mexican has nothing to do with which country one lives in. Being Mexican is a state of soul—not one of mind, not one of citizenship. Neither eagle nor serpent, but both. And like the ocean, neither animal respects borders.

> *Dime con quien andas y te diré quien eres.*
> (Tell me who your friends are and I'll tell you who you are.)
>
> —Mexican saying

Si le preguntas a mi mamá, "¿Qué eres?" te dirá, "Soy mexicana." My brothers and sister say the same. I sometimes will answer *"soy mexi-*

[9]Kaufman, 68.

cana" and at others will say *"soy Chicana" o "soy tejana."* But I identified as "Raza" before I ever identified as *"mexicana"* or "Chicana."

As a culture, we call ourselves Spanish when referring to ourselves as a linguistic group and when copping out. It is then that we forget our predominant Indian genes. We are 70–80% Indian.[10] We call ourselves Hispanic[11] or Spanish-American or Latin American or Latin when linking ourselves to other Spanish-speaking peoples of the Western hemisphere and when copping out. We call ourselves Mexican-American[12] to signify we are neither Mexican nor American, but more the noun "American" than the adjective "Mexican" (and when copping out).

Chicanos and other people of color suffer economically for not acculturating. This voluntary (yet forced) alienation makes for psychological conflict, a kind of dual identity—we don't identify with the Anglo-American cultural values and we don't totally identify with the Mexican cultural values. We are a synergy of two cultures with various degrees of Mexicanness or Angloness. I have so internalized the borderland conflict that sometimes I feel like one cancels out the other and we are zero, nothing, no one. *A veces no soy nada ni nadie. Pero hasta cuando no lo soy, lo soy.*

When not copping out, when we know we are more than nothing, we   40
call ourselves Mexican, referring to race and ancestry; *mestizo* when affirming both our Indian and Spanish (but we hardly ever own our Black ancestry); Chicano when referring to a politically aware people born and/or raised in the U.S.; *Raza* when referring to Chicanos; *tejanos* when we are Chicanos from Texas.

Chicanos did not know we were a people until 1965 when César Chávez and the farmworkers united and *I Am Joaquín* was published and *la Raza Unida* party was formed in Texas. With that recognition, we became a distinct people. Something momentous happened to the Chicano soul—we became aware of our reality and acquired a name and a language (Chicano Spanish) that reflected that reality. Now that we had a name, some of the fragmented pieces began to fall together—who we were, what we were, how we had evolved. We began to get glimpses of what we might eventually become.

Yet the struggle of identities continues, the struggle of borders is our reality still. One day the inner struggle will cease and a true integration take place. In the meantime, *tenémos que hacer la lucha. ¿Quién está protegiendo los ranchos de mi gente? ¿Quién está tratando de cerrar la fisura entre la india y el blanco en nuestra sangre? El Chicano, si, el Chicano que anda como un ladrón en su propia casa.*

---

[10]Chávez, 88–90.

[11]"Hispanic" is derived from *Hispanis (España,* a name given to the Iberian Peninsula in ancient times when it was a part of the Roman Empire) and is a term designated by the U.S. government to make it easier to handle us on paper.

[12]The Treaty of Guadalupe Hidalgo created the Mexican-American in 1848.

Los Chicanos, how patient we seem, how very patient. There is the quiet of the Indian about us.[13] We know how to survive. When other races have given up their tongue, we've kept ours. We know what it is to live under the hammer blow of the dominant *norteamericano* culture. But more than we count the blows, we count the days the weeks the years the centuries the eons until the white laws and commerce and customs will rot in the deserts they've created, lie bleached. *Humildes* yet proud, *quietos* yet wild, *nosotros los mexicanos-Chicanos* will walk by the crumbling ashes as we go about our business. Stubborn, persevering, impenetrable as stone, yet possessing a malleability that renders us unbreakable, we, the *mestizas* and *mestizos,* will remain.

The Reader's Presence

1. The writer links her dentist's literal use of the word *tongue* to a metaphorical meaning. What connotations do the two senses of the word share? How does the tongue-as-organ/tongue-as-language pun relate to the quotation from Ray Gwyn Smith and questions of cultural silencing?

2. Anzaldúa peppers her English prose with untranslated Spanish words and phrases. How does this formal innovation influence the reader's experience of the text? How does the reader's experience mirror Anzaldúa's own in English-speaking America? In what ways might this technique underline the writer's insistence on the importance of keeping different languages active and alive?

3. Anzaldúa champions Spanish as the language of Mexican Americans. Spanish, of course, was brought to native Mexicans by colonizing conquistadors. The writer also distinguishes numerous dialects of Spanish and "Spanglish" as tongues in their own right. Cultural identity, in Anzaldúa's formulation, seems at once a unified and divided entity. How does this condition compare to the one suggested by Richard Rodriguez's "Aria: A Memoir of a Bilingual Childhood" (see page 221)? or to that of Julia Alvarez in "Doña Aida, with Your Permission" (see page 70)? For all their differences of politics and style, are there ideas held in common by these three Spanish- and English-speaking Americans? Do you think each of these writers would agree with your assessment?

---

[13]Anglos, in order to alleviate their guilt for dispossessing the Chicano, stressed the Spanish part of us and perpetrated the myth of the Spanish Southwest. We have accepted the fiction that we are Hispanic, that is Spanish, in order to accommodate ourselves to the dominant culture and its abhorrence of Indians. Chávez, 88–91.

43

Veronica Boix-Mansilla and Howard Gardner

Cognition and Understanding

Veronica Boix-Mansilla was born in Argentina and received a doctorate in education from Harvard. She is now Principal Investigator at Harvard's Project Zero. Boix-Mansilla has published several articles in academic journals examining how students understand the concept of truth in history and science, and is now collaborating with Howard Gardner on a study of "model cases" of interdisciplinary work and education. As director of the Latitud initiative, she is also working to extend Project Zero's frameworks to meet the educational needs of people in developing countries.

Howard Gardner was born in Scranton, Pennsylvania in 1943, the son of refugees from Nazi Germany. He was educated at Harvard University, where he trained as a developmental psychologist and then as a neuropsychologist. His efforts to synthesize the two lines of work led him to develop and introduce his theory of "multiple intelligences" in Frames of Mind *(1983). His published works include numerous articles and academic papers, and titles such as* Multiple Intelligences *(1993),* The Disciplined Mind *(1999), and most recently,* Good Work: When Excellence and Ethics Meet *(2001). He received a MacArthur Prize Fellowship in 1981 and is currently the John H. and Elizabeth A. Hobbs Professor in Cognition and Education at the Harvard Graduate School of Education.*

Gardner has remarked, "In my own work, I'm a proponent of teaching for understanding, which means going deeply into topics so that students can really make use of knowledge in new situations. This is very, very different from most teaching, where people memorize material and can reproduce it on demand but can't make use of it in new situations. If you favor education for understanding the way I do, then MI [multiple intelligences] can be extremely helpful. Because when you are teaching a topic, you can approach the topic in many different ways, thereby activating different intelligences."

The Holocaust, the systematic mass murder of European Jewry by the Nazis, has transformed humanity's image of itself. It has engendered caution about prevailing nationalisms, about conceptions of race, and about the reaches of state power. Contemporary efforts to guard civil liberties and human rights around the world are rooted to a significant degree in this horrendous chapter of human history.

The Holocaust has also challenged students, scholars, and educators. Historians, novelists, poets, and artists have sought to make sense of this most ghastly episode of modern times.[1] Educators have tried to draw important lessons from this period as they develop history curricula. Teachers recognize the importance of examining the Holocaust with their students in the hope that they will come to understand it.[2] And yet, in all of our minds the question lingers: What does it *mean* to understand this episode in depth?

In the Holocaust and in our cultural responses to it, issues of identity, morality, political power, state and society, dehumanization, media, and art are intricately intertwined. A deep understanding may emerge only after one has approached this complex nexus of topics through multiple domains and symbol systems. Educators combine historical or political accounts with poetic, pictorial, or sculptural renderings of the experiences of the victims.

But to be effective, we believe, this multidisciplinary approach must not mix these domains and their symbol systems haphazardly; rather, it must honor the specific contributions of each domain to a fuller understanding of the experience.[3] What role does each of these artistic or disciplinary entry points play in understanding? How does creating a monument or writing a poem demonstrate our understanding of the Holocaust? What kinds of understanding can one draw from reading a historical account or a fictional story? And how do these forms of understanding relate to, and differ from, one another?

In this article we focus on history and literature—two domains that use language in different ways—to examine the specific kinds of understanding they elicit. We deliberately use two linguistic domains in order to underscore the importance of the ways symbols are used in each case. If differences in understanding emerge between the "neighboring" domains of history and literature, then we may assume that even greater distinctions exist between those disciplines that use more disparate sets of symbols.

We begin by portraying the multidimensional nature of disciplinary understanding as we have come to formulate it in our own research. We compare understanding in each domain, illustrating our analysis with an important piece of historical work and a highly acclaimed novel. In the end, we examine the educational implications of recognizing the specific qualities of disciplinary understanding in history and literature.

UNDERSTANDING:
A MULTIDIMENSIONAL TASK

Understanding refers to an individual's ability to use knowledge in novel situations — e.g., to solve problems, fashion products, or create stories — in ways akin to those modeled by knowledgeable practitioners in specific domains. Students demonstrate their understanding when they are able to go beyond accumulating information and engage in performances that are valued by the communities in which they live. For example, they demonstrate their understanding of the Holocaust when they can compare and contrast it with current policies of genocide in Bosnia, when they can empathize with particular aspects of the survivors' experiences, and when they can offer plausible explanations of why and how it happened. In this *performance-centered* view, understanding is not merely a representation of the world in our minds or a set of loosely organized actions. Rather, understanding is the ability to *think with* knowledge, according to the standards of good practice within a specific domain, such as math, history, ceramics, or dance.[4]

Understanding *within* a discipline, such as history or literature, is in itself a multidimensional enterprise. As such, it goes beyond the specific mastery of one or more symbol systems or the recall of a series of facts. To demonstrate understanding, students need to be able to use important concepts, findings, or theories. However, they also need to appreciate the carefully crafted methods and criteria that knowledgeable people have developed to build a comprehensive historical account or to write a compelling novel. They need to communicate according to the specific rules of their chosen genres of performance — oral presentation, written text, theater performance. And, at best, they need to appreciate the purposes that inspire the writing of a historical account or a fictional work, and they need to be able to use samples of such work to orient their own actions or perceptions of the world.[5]

Two dimensions of understanding underlie our description: 1) understanding of domain-specific *knowledge* and 2) understanding of the *disciplinary models of thinking* embodied in the methods by which knowledge is constructed, the forms in which knowledge is made public, and the purposes that drive inquiry in the domain. Our main thesis here is that history and literature represent distinct kinds of understanding that cannot be merged uncritically without the loss of important contributions.

ONE HOLOCAUST: TWO KEY TEXTS

To illustrate this point we examine Daniel Goldhagen's *Hitler's Willing Executioners* and William Styron's *Sophie's Choice*.[6] In his study of Nazi Germany during the Holocaust, Goldhagen posits the provocative thesis that the killers who participated in the Holocaust were not primarily mem-

10

bers of the SS or fervent supporters of the Nazi party, as most previous interpreters had proposed. Instead, Goldhagen argues that anti-Semitism was
deeply pervasive in German society even before Hitler rose to power. Ordinary Germans regarded Jews as a demonic people who had to be extermi-
nated. Germans were predisposed to an active and voluntary participation
in this process. Unlike other historians, Goldhagen does not attribute the
actions of the German people to Nazi coercion, or to brutal social pressure,
or to the anonymity afforded by a bureaucratic system.[7] Instead, he proposes that the common people willingly joined in the brutalization and murder of Jews. To bolster his dramatic and controversial thesis, Goldhagen
examines the murderers' world views and values, their institutional means
of killing—police battalions, "work camps," and death marches—and the
broader social contexts in which the participants in the mass murders lived.

Sophie's Choice examines the experience of a Polish Holocaust survivor through the lens of a young American writer from the South who is
determined to render her story. The novel foregrounds three characters:
Sophie; Stingo, the writer; and Nathan, Sophie's emotionally unstable
lover. Looming in the background is a character from the past based on
Rudolf Höss, commandant of Auschwitz. In the novel readers confront
the Holocaust as Sophie reveals, bit by bit, the pieces of her story. Toward the end, she bares her most painful secret: the anguish of having
been forced to send her daughter to her death in order to save her son.
Styron chooses Stingo, the writer, as the narrator whose consciousness
determines what and how much of Sophie's anguish—loss of her children, her friends, and her health—will be revealed at each moment in the
text. The Holocaust serves as a background against which readers interpret the characters' beliefs and conduct.

Needless to say, Goldhagen's and Styron's books share some features:
their use of linguistic symbol systems, their reference to historical facts,
and their intention to uncover "truth." However, under closer scrutiny,
these two pieces are seen as emerging from different disciplinary enterprises; their value in helping us understand the Holocaust depends more
on the ways in which they differ than on the ways in which they are similar. Language, facts, and aesthetics not only carry different weights but
also play dramatically different roles in each domain. Shorn of these disciplinary distinctions, students' understanding is likely to be reduced to
propaganda or stereotypical opinion. We illustrate this point by compar-
ing these two works through our principal dimensions of understanding.

UNDERSTANDING IN HISTORY
AND LITERATURE

Understanding knowledge. Understanding the Holocaust as a historical phenomenon entails integrating what we can determine about specific
events and the particular world views of people involved in them with

more general interpretations of events during the period. For example, Goldhagen examines the intricacies of life in the "work camps" and the process by which members of the police battalions were selected. He draws our attention to the superficiality of the ideological and military training that police battalion members received, in order to support his broader thesis—that the mass murder of Jews was driven by the already existing anti-Semitism of the German people. In his account, factual information alone would be devoid of historical significance if it were detached from the broader thesis he is putting forth. Conversely, his interpretations would become mere opinions if they were devoid of the facts that give them substance.[8]

In history, such expressions as "final solution," "police battalions," or "Nazi regime" correspond to a world that existed in Germany in the 1930s and 1940s. Although the past is only indirectly accessible to historians, and historical narratives are necessarily interpretations, historical accounts aim to mold our present interpretations to a past that we know existed. Historical narratives strive for comprehensiveness and clarity. They seek to describe and explain what happened and why, in a mode of discourse that is as accessible and unambiguous as possible. Given these features of knowledge in the domain, students demonstrate their understanding of the Holocaust when they are able to integrate findings about different agents, goals, contexts, and circumstances into one or more comprehensive and unambiguous interpretations or when they are able to test broad interpretations against the details and evidence that are relevant to those claims.

Unlike history, which aims at portraying what the world was like in the past, literature aims at expressing aspects of human experience. In *Sophie's Choice,* the past operates as a frame, not as Styron's object of study. The novel is about the experiences of guilt, silence, and survival. But it is also about the sensuality of youth and the discovery of writing. For poets and novelists, the Holocaust provides a diabolical stimulus for speculating about the experience of dehumanization or the motives of evil and for pushing fictional and poetic language to its expressive and evocative limits, surpassing the more strictly constrained descriptive language of history. Understanding the Holocaust through literature entails exploring the themes and experiences created by the writer and appreciating his or her sensitive use of language in portraying events that drive many observers to silence.

Understanding disciplinary modes of thinking. Unlike novelists, historians consider past events as central to their work. They aim to capture events in as fair a manner as possible. Goldhagen's convictions about the Holocaust emerged from careful interpretations of texts, documents, and eyewitness reports of the period, leavened by accounts or interpretations proposed by other historians in more recent times. For example, he examined materials amassed during the investigations of Nazi crimes. He used documentation compiled by the German justice system as well as records

15

of extensive interrogations of the perpetrators themselves, surviving victims, and bystanders. He treated these sources cautiously, recognizing such limitations as memory's natural deficiency and the perpetrators' desire to conceal information. Confronted with euphemistic sources that were often fragmentary, he sought to uncover people's actual intentions, world views, and contexts and test them against competing accounts of similar data.

Despite the power of the questions that historians bring to sources, the intricacies of the selection of documents, or the ideologies that inspire them, historians' recourse to original documents marks the dividing line between history and fiction. Unlike novelists (who may pilfer from or radically alter original source materials), historians aim at reconstructing the past. Through the critical examination of documents, historians' imaginations are subject to the limits of what once was.[9] In contrast to novelists' imaginations, historians' imaginations are rigorously constrained by the evidence they extract from available sources. Goldhagen's text of 622 pages dedicates 22 pages to a framing introduction and 225 pages to notes and references. In a novel, such appendages could only be seen as ironic.

How do novelists produce worthy pieces of literature? For novelists, past events constitute only an instrumental aspect of their work. Unlike historians, they are not concerned with issues of evidence. Instead, they engage in such procedures as portraying and developing fictional characters, producing the effects of verisimilitude, and developing texts that are enriched by ambiguity and invite multiple interpretations.

For example, prior to depicting Höss' tenure at Auschwitz, Styron examined Höss' autobiography, consulted a series of testimonies from the war-crime trials, and visited the site of the death camp. However, Styron feels no commitment to keep facts unmodified. For the sake of enhancing the dramatic power of his narrative, Styron imaginatively creates Commandant Höss' motives, dialogues, and gestures. Rather than portray him as a public figure, Styron emphasizes the private man, surrounded by his wife, children, and friends. He spices up his character with periodic attacks of migraine—a carefully crafted strategy to complete the picture of a privately human Höss. Novelists are primarily concerned with the internal *coherence* of their narratives, rather than with the *correspondence* between their accounts and the data of the past. To be sure, Styron's novel honors the stability of settings and characters throughout. It establishes a "sense of truth" by referring successively, though in nonrepetitive ways, to settings, images, and characters that were previously introduced to the reader. While the trustworthiness of historical narratives relies chiefly on the proficient use of primary sources, the believability of novels rests, in part, on this effect of déjà vu embedded in their structure.[10]

Like most novels, *Sophie's Choice* is polysemous: its symbols invite multiple interpretations. Unlike historical accounts, novels benefit from such allusiveness. For example, Sophie explains that she is slowly becom-

20

ing human again as she learns how to cry when she listens to music. She associates her humanity with a deep sense of guilt and a certain skepticism about the possibility of human redemption. In describing her feelings when listening to "The Redeemer," Sophie confesses, "I know that my body will be destroyed by worms and my eyes will never see God." Styron chooses language that mimics the Genesis story of Adam and Eve and the loss of paradise. Sophie's Holocaust is for Styron both the story of a fictional individual and an emblem of the human species.[11] Literary writing relies on its ability to play with ambiguity, to invite the reader to grasp multiple layers of meaning, uncover multiple themes, and allow his or her imagination to proceed along idiosyncratic paths. In contrast, the theses put forth in historical accounts seek to avoid ambiguity in order to convince readers of a given interpretation of the past.

In moving from the unprocessed historical record to chronicles and stories, scholars like Goldhagen organize events in time and into the components of a "spectacle" with a discernible beginning, middle, and end.[12] Historians' definitions of the periods they cover emerge from a dynamic interaction between milestone events in the past and the interpretive frameworks that historians bring to their study.

For example, Goldhagen portrays a process that he calls the evolution of a European Eliminationist Anti-Semitism mentality. He marks its beginning in the earliest days of Christianity and its end in the Second World War. On the one hand, the beginning and ending dates are determined by milestones in the past, such as Christianity's consolidation of its hold over the Roman Empire. On the other hand, they are defined by Goldhagen's framework, in which German anti-Semitic beliefs need to be explored beyond the particular circumstances of Nazi Germany. In *Sophie's Choice* Styron unfolds the story from Stingo's arrival in Brooklyn, New York, to his reflections after the deaths of Sophie and Nathan. Such a time frame is an expression of Styron's imaginative design. The survivors of the Holocaust continue to live with their experiences after Goldhagen has ended his account, and the events of the Nazi regime continue to reverberate in the present, but Stingo ceases to live after page 562.

Narratives are a natural way for historians to represent the unfolding of events over time.[13] But unlike novelists, historians see narrative only as a tool to enhance the quality of their reports, not as their primary focus. Historians have learned about the ways in which the stories they produce shape and are shaped by canonical narrative codes long studied by linguists and discourse analysts.[14] For historians, compelling narratives function to convey their reconstructions of the past. For novelists, compelling narratives are the end product and center of their endeavor. Unlike understanding a history text, understanding a novel is primarily a matter of appreciating the ways in which narratives themselves are crafted (e.g., the use of metaphors, the creation of a character, the continuity of a scene, and so on).

In sum, when students are challenged to grasp the *disciplinary modes of thinking* on which historical and literary accounts of the Holocaust are based, they engage in two very different enterprises. Sources, layers of meaning, narrative structures, correspondence with facts, and coherence not only have different relevance in each domain, but also have different functions.

Students demonstrate their understanding of the Holocaust as a his-   25
torical phenomenon when they are able to interpret historical claims critically—not as transparent manifestations of the past or idiosyncratic
inventions of a creative historian, but as the product of an intricate
process of inquiry and marshaling of evidence. They demonstrate their
understanding of history when they are able to write accounts that satisfy
the standards of evidence and the norms of reference and citation that are
institutionalized in historical writing.

In literature, students demonstrate their understanding of *Sophie's
Choice* when they critique or produce a piece of fiction—e.g., showing
how figurative language can convey dehumanization in evocative ways,
demonstrating the role of symbolism in conveying the maturation of the
protagonist, or illustrating how the structure of the work conveys important themes and contrasts. In this case, reporting the sources of evidence
or clarifying the main thesis of the work would diminish the qualities of
suggestiveness and speculation embedded in literary performances.

THE PAYOFF FOR EDUCATION

So far we have described what expert historians, writers, and critics
perceive to be the central features of their tasks. We have shown how, despite sharing a verbal symbol system, understanding in history and understanding in literature pose different challenges to the mind. But the
question remains: Why should this matter to educators?

Here it becomes relevant to consider the developing mind. By the
time students encounter a topic like the Holocaust, they have already developed a series of beliefs and theories about the past, about this particular episode, and about knowledge—all of which are likely to reflect the
"unschooled mind" at work.[15] For instance, students create imaginative
accounts of the past on the basis of only a few events they may have encountered in earlier grades, in the media, or in everyday life (e.g., Jews
lived in ghettos, or Germans hated Jews). Often students interpret historical sources literally and build stereotypical portraits of historical actors.[16]
In literature, students often expect a story to end on a happy note and
characters to be depicted as unambiguously good or evil. Transforming
these intuitive but inadequate beliefs requires careful instruction. Only in
this way can students progressively replace their sometimes too imaginative versions of the past with the evidence-based historical ones that are
held as trustworthy by their culture. And only in this way can students
grasp the hidden symbolism in literary texts, enjoy the process of sharp-

ening human experience through language, and appreciate the formal structures that shape powerful meanings.

Students also bring their unique combinations of intelligences to their encounter with a topic; they might favor musical, bodily, logical/mathematical, or linguistic modes of thinking.[17] In order to motivate them to pursue their studies, educators face the challenge of devising a variety of "entry points" that honor each student's idiosyncratic ways of representing the world. Some students might be inclined to draw a Jewish scene in the ghetto as it is portrayed in a particular source; others might prefer to write a poem from the point of view of one of the characters; still others might be inclined to use their bodies to mimic the physical and ideological postures of those in the scene.

Such entry points invite students to use symbol systems that they find   30
comfortable and familiar as they engage in complex tasks.[18] In doing so they open up the possibilities for deeper understanding. Their limitation lies in the fact that they only partially represent understanding in history or literature. For example, drawing or mimicking a scene requires that students go beyond the literal meaning of the text to grasp the situation depicted, to assess its plausibility, to interpret the point of view from which it is described. By using familiar symbol systems, such as drawing or body language, students may be encouraged to engage in these complex interpretive tasks. Visual representations or mimicking may "take us to the scene," but they tell us little about the broader historical interpretations in which these situations must be inscribed. The metaphoric language of poetry resonates with our personal experience, but it is still too ambiguous to meet the standards of historical description and explanation.

To demonstrate full-fledged *historical* understanding, students have to place the scene in a broader context and interpretive frame. Why did it happen? What did it mean to the people at the time? What would these people soon find out? Questions of this sort invite students to produce historical accounts that integrate facts and interpretations, accounts that are respectful of the characteristics of past times and are grounded in carefully marshaled evidence. To demonstrate full-fledged *literary* understanding, students have to grasp the essential aspects of human experience embodied in the scene and use figurative language to portray them in a novel, a short story, or a poem. What does this incident say about human experience? What does it symbolize? How can the story be told? Questions of this sort invite students to produce literary accounts that hold multiple layers of meaning and play with the expressive limits of language.

There is one vital reason for stressing the distinctions between these two modes of presentation. The recent success of docudramas, of historical fiction, and of various movies, such as *JFK* or *Nixon*, has had the effect of blurring the boundaries between what happened, what might have happened, and what has clearly been invented by a writer, director, or actor. Such blurred genres actually revel in collapsing history and literature, truth and fiction. Young students can only be confused by such a mixing of modes of knowing. Indeed, at their most extreme, these blur-rings encourage the creation of myths, including the frightening myth that "there was no Holocaust."

Ideally, after approaching the Holocaust through "entry points" that are tuned to their individual intellectual profiles, students will come to produce historical and literary accounts that are exemplary "exit points" of a course or a project. At best, these final performances or demonstrations of understanding will fully show students' mastery of knowledge and disciplinary modes of thinking in each domain.

What forms of representation should these performances take? As Elliot Eisner reminds us, different forms of representation allow us "to construct meanings that might otherwise elude us."[19] In searching for generative final performances for their students, teachers face an important challenge: the challenge of assessing different forms of representation for what students gain and what they lose in the process of building deeper understanding in distinct domains. By viewing understanding as both the ability to *use knowledge* and the ability to *engage in disciplinary modes of thinking*, we have sought to provide an initial framework that may facilitate such nuanced assessment.

NOTES

1. See Lawrence Langer, "Fictional Facts and Factual Fictions: History in Holocaust Literature," in Randolph L. Braham, ed., *Reflections of the Holocaust in Art and Literature* (New York: Columbia University Press, 1993).

2. See *Facing History and Ourselves: Holocaust and Human Behavior Resource Book* (Brookline, Mass.: Facing History and Ourselves National Foundation, 1994).

3. For a careful analysis of the challenges and possibilities of cross-disciplinary curricula, see College Board and the Getty Center for Education in the Arts, *Connections: The Arts and the Integration of High School Curriculum* (New York: College Board Publications, 1996).

4. David Perkins, "What Is Understanding?," in M. Stone Wiske, ed., *Teaching for Understanding: A Practical Framework* (San Francisco: Jossey-Bass, forthcoming).

5. For a detailed analysis of "dimensions of understanding," see Veronica Boix-Mansilla and Howard Gardner, "Assessing Qualities of Understanding," in Wiske, op. cit. See also Veronica Boix-Mansilla, "Bridging Meaning and Rigor in Teaching for Understanding," paper presented at ATLAS seminar, Cambridge, Mass., 1995.

6. Daniel Goldhagen, *Hitler's Willing Executioners: Ordinary Germans and the Holocaust* (New York: Knopf, 1996); and William Styron, *Sophie's Choice* (New York: Vintage Books, 1992).

7. See Michael Marrus, *The Holocaust in History* (Hanover, N.H.: University Press of New England, 1987). See also Charles Maier, *The Unmasterable Past: History, Holocaust, and German National Identity* (Cambridge: Mass.: Harvard University Press, 1988).

8. See Bernard Bailyn, *On the Teaching and Writing of History: Responses to a Series of Questions* (Hanover, N.H.: Dartmouth College, 1994). See also Neil R. Stout, *Getting the Most out of Your U.S. History Course* (Lexington, Mass.: D. C. Heath, 1994).

9. Paul Ricoeur, *Time and Narrative*, Vol. 2 (Chicago: University of Chicago Press, 1985), pp. 142–43.

10. See Michael Riffaterre, *Fictional Truth* (Baltimore: Johns Hopkins University Press, 1990).

11. Styron, pp. 93–94.

12. Hayden White, *Metahistory: The Historical Imagination in Nineteenth-Century Europe* (Baltimore: Johns Hopkins University Press, 1973).

13. Louis Mink, "Narrative Form as a Cognitive Instrument," in Eugene Golob, Brian Fray, and Richard Vannin, eds., *Historical Understanding* (Ithaca, N.Y.: Cornell University Press, 1987).

14. See William Cronon, "A Place for Stories: Nature, History, and Narrative," *Journal of American History*, March 1992, pp. 1347–76.

15. Howard Gardner, *The Unschooled Mind: How Children Think and How Schools Should Teach* (New York: Basic Books, 1991); and Howard Gardner and Veronica Boix-Mansilla, "Teaching for Understanding in the Disciplines and Beyond," *Teachers College Record*, Winter 1994, pp. 198–218.

16. See Peter Lee, Rosalyn Ashby, and Alaric Dickinson, "Children's Understanding of History," paper presented at the Second International Seminar on History Learning and Instruction, Las Navas, Spain, June 1994.

17. Howard Gardner, *Frames of Mind* (New York: Basic Books, 1983).

18. Howard Gardner, *Multiple Intelligences: A Theory in Practice* (New York: Basic Books, 1993).

19. Elliot W. Eisner, "Forms of Understanding and the Future of Educational Research," *Educational Researcher*, October 1993, p. 6.

The Reader's Presence

1. Boix-Mansilla and Gardner refer to the "multidisciplinary approach" required to arrive at a deep understanding of the Holocaust (paragraph 4). Understanding itself, as they define it, is a "multidimensional" process whereby one comes to "the ability to think with knowledge, according to the standards of good practice within a specific domain" (paragraph 7). What are the "disciplines" and "dimensions" to which these writers refer? Restate their definition of understanding in language that makes sense to you. What are "standards of good practice"? Give examples of how such standards might vary from context to context. In respect to the Holocaust, what might "understanding" mean to the families of survivors? What might the term mean to an author writing a novel based on accounts of Hitler's youth? How does this essay help you make these distinctions?

2. At the end of paragraph 20 the authors offer a clear distinction between the uses of ambiguity in "literary writing" and in "historical accounts." Review this distinction. Do you agree with their characterization of the disciplines? What are the advantages or disadvantages of ambiguity according to Boix-Mansilla and Gardner? Have you read novels that attempt to stave off uncertainty? Have you read historical accounts that bring out multiple, even contradictory, layers of evidence? What is the authors' main argument, and how does their assertion of the boundaries between disciplines support that argument?

3. Apply Boix-Mansilla's and Gardner's model of understanding to your reading of Don DeLillo's essay "In the Ruins of the Future" (page 341). Is DeLillo's essay a work of history or of imaginative writing? Do you read the different sections of his essay (each of

which is written in a different mode, aimed at expressing a different kind of awareness) in ways that correspond with Boix-Mansilla's and Gardner's models? What are your "entry points" into the event—both in the reading of DeLillo's essay, and in your reading or experience beyond the essay?

44

Stephen L. Carter
The Insufficiency of Honesty

Law professor and writer Stephen L. Carter (b. 1954) is an insightful and incisive critic of contemporary cultural politics. His first book, Reflections of an Affirmative Action Baby *(1992), criticizes affirmative action policies that reinforce racial stereotypes rather than break down structures of discrimination. Carter's critique emerges from his own experience as an African American student at Stanford University and at Yale University Law School. After graduating from Yale, he served as a law clerk for Supreme Court Justice Thurgood Marshall and eventually joined the faculty at Yale as professor of law, where he has served since 1991 as the William Cromwell Professor of Law. Carter has published widely on legal and social topics, including his books* The Culture of Disbelief: How American Law and Politics Trivialize Religious Devotion *(1993),* The Confirmation Mess: Cleaning Up the Federal Appointments Process *(1994),* Civility: Manners, Morals, and the Etiquette of Democracy *(1998),* The Dissent of the Governed: A Meditation on Law, Religion, and Loyalty *(1998), and* God's Name in Vain *(2000). "The Insufficiency of Honesty" appears in* Integrity *(1996). Carter's most recent work is the best-selling novel,* The Emperor of Ocean Park *(2002).*

A couple of years ago I began a university commencement address by telling the audience that I was going to talk about integrity. The crowd broke into applause. Applause! Just because they had heard the word "integrity": that's how starved for it they were. They had no idea how I was using the word, or what I was going to say about integrity, or, indeed, whether I was for it or against it. But they knew they liked the idea of talking about it.

Very well, let us consider this word "integrity." Integrity is like the weather: everybody talks about it but nobody knows what to do about it. Integrity is that stuff that we always want more of. Some say that we need to return to the good old days when we had a lot more of it. Others say that we as a nation have never really had enough of it. Hardly anybody stops to explain exactly what we mean by it, or how we know it is a good thing, or why everybody needs to have the same amount of it. Indeed, the only trouble with integrity is that everybody who uses the word seems to mean something slightly different.

For instance, when I refer to integrity, do I mean simply "honesty"? The answer is no; although honesty is a virtue of importance, it is a different virtue from integrity. Let us, for simplicity, think of honesty as not lying; and let us further accept Sissela Bok's definition of a lie: "any intentionally deceptive message which is *stated*." Plainly, one cannot have integrity without being honest (although, as we shall see, the matter gets complicated), but one can certainly be honest and yet have little integrity.

When I refer to integrity, I have something very specific in mind. Integrity, as I will use the term, requires three steps: discerning what is right and what is wrong; acting on what you have discerned, even at personal cost; and saying openly that you are acting on your understanding of right and wrong. The first criterion captures the idea that integrity requires a degree of moral reflectiveness. The second brings in the ideal of a person of integrity as steadfast, a quality that includes keeping one's commitments. The third reminds us that a person of integrity can be trusted.

The first point to understand about the difference between honesty   5
and integrity is that a person may be entirely honest without ever engaging in the hard work of discernment that integrity requires; she may tell us quite truthfully what she believes without ever taking the time to figure out whether what she believes is good and right and true. The problem may be as simple as someone's foolishly saying something that hurts a friend's feelings; a few moments of thought would have revealed the likelihood of the hurt and the lack of necessity for the comment. Or the problem may be more complex, as when a man who was raised from birth in a society that preaches racism states his belief in one race's inferiority as a fact, without ever really considering that perhaps this deeply held view is wrong. Certainly the racist is being honest--he is telling us what he actually thinks—but his honesty does not add up to integrity.

TELLING EVERYTHING YOU KNOW

A wonderful epigram sometimes attributed to the filmmaker Sam Goldwyn goes like this: "The most important thing in acting is honesty; once you learn to fake that, you're in." The point is that honesty can be something one *seems* to have. Without integrity, what passes for honesty often is nothing of the kind; it is fake honesty—or it is honest but irrelevant and perhaps even immoral.

Consider an example. A man who has been married for fifty years confesses to his wife on his deathbed that he was unfaithful thirty-five years earlier. The dishonesty was killing his spirit, he says. Now he has cleared his conscience and is able to die in peace.

The husband has been honest—sort of. He has certainly unburdened himself. And he has probably made his wife (soon to be his widow) quite miserable in the process, because even if she forgives him, she will not be able to remember him with quite the vivid image of love and loyalty that she had hoped for. Arranging his own emotional affairs to ease his transition to death, he has shifted to his wife the burden of confusion and pain, perhaps for the rest of her life. Moreover, he has attempted his honesty at the one time in his life when it carries no risk; acting in accordance with what you think is right and risking no loss in the process is a rather thin and unadmirable form of honesty.

Besides, even though the husband has been honest in a sense, he has now twice been unfaithful to his wife: once thirty-five years ago, when he had his affair, and again when, nearing death, he decided that his own peace of mind was more important than hers. In trying to be honest he has violated his marriage vow by acting toward his wife not with love but with naked and perhaps even cruel self-interest.

As my mother used to say, you don't have to tell people everything   10
you know. Lying and nondisclosure, as the law often recognizes, are not the same thing. Sometimes it is actually illegal to tell what you know, as, for example, in the disclosure of certain financial information by market insiders. Or it may be unethical, as when a lawyer reveals a confidence entrusted to her by a client. It may be simple bad manners, as in the case of a gratuitous comment to a colleague on his or her attire. And it may be subject to religious punishment, as when a Roman Catholic priest breaks the seal of the confessional—an offense that carries automatic excommunication.

In all the cases just mentioned, the problem with telling everything you know is that somebody else is harmed. Harm may not be the intention, but it is certainly the effect. Honesty is most laudable when we risk harm to ourselves; it becomes a good deal less so if we instead risk harm to others when there is no gain to anyone other than ourselves. Integrity may counsel keeping our secrets in order to spare the feelings of others. Sometimes, as in the example of the wayward husband, the reason we want to tell what we know is precisely to shift our pain onto somebody else—a course of action dictated less by integrity than by self-interest. Fortunately, integrity and self-interest often coincide, as when a politician of integrity is rewarded with our votes. But often they do not, and it is at those moments that our integrity is truly tested.

ERROR

Another reason that honesty alone is no substitute for integrity is that if forthrightness is not preceded by discernment, it may result in the expression of an incorrect moral judgment. In other words, I may be honest about what I believe, but if I have never tested my beliefs, I may be wrong. And here I mean "wrong" in a particular sense: the proposition in question is wrong if I would change my mind about it after hard moral reflection.

Consider this example. Having been taught all his life that women are not as smart as men, a manager gives the women on his staff less-challenging assignments than he gives the men. He does this, he believes, for their own benefit: he does not want them to fail, and he believes that they will if he gives them tougher assignments. Moreover, when one of the women on his staff does poor work, he does not berate her as harshly as he would a man, because he expects nothing more. And he claims to be acting with integrity because he is acting according to his own deepest beliefs.

The manager fails the most basic test of integrity. The question is not whether his actions are consistent with what he most deeply believes but whether he has done the hard work of discerning whether what he most deeply believes is right. The manager has not taken this harder step.

Moreover, even within the universe that the manager has constructed   15
for himself, he is not acting with integrity. Although he is obviously wrong to think that the women on his staff are not as good as the men, even were he right, that would not justify applying different standards to their work. By so doing he betrays both his obligation to the institution that employs him and his duty as a manager to evaluate his employees.

The problem that the manager faces is an enormous one in our practical politics, where having the dialogue that makes democracy work can seem impossible because of our tendency to cling to our views even when we have not examined them. As Jean Bethke Elshtain has said, borrowing from John Courtney Murray, our politics are so fractured and contentious that we often cannot reach *disagreement*. Our refusal to look closely at our own most cherished principles is surely a large part of the reason. Socrates thought the unexamined life not worth living. But the unhappy truth is that few of us actually have the time for constant reflection on our views—on public or private morality. Examine them we must, however, or we will never know whether we might be wrong.

None of this should be taken to mean that integrity as I have described it presupposes a single correct truth. If, for example, your integrity-guided search tells you that affirmative action is wrong, and my integrity-guided search tells me that affirmative action is right, we need not conclude that one of us lacks integrity. As it happens, I believe—both as a Christian and as a secular citizen who struggles toward moral understanding—that we *can* find true and sound answers to our moral questions. But I do not pretend to have found very many of them, nor is an exposition of them my purpose here.

It is the case not that there aren't any right answers but that, given human fallibility, we need to be careful in assuming that we have found them. However, today's political talk about how it is wrong for the government to impose one person's morality on somebody else is just mindless chatter. *Every* law imposes one person's morality on somebody else, because law has only two functions: to tell people to do what they would rather not or to forbid them to do what they would.

And if the surveys can be believed, there is far more moral agreement in America than we sometimes allow ourselves to think. One of the reasons that character education for young people makes so much sense to so many people is precisely that there seems to be a core set of moral understandings—we might call them the American Core—that most of us accept. Some of the virtues in this American Core are, one hopes, relatively noncontroversial. About 500 American communities have signed on to Michael Josephson's program to emphasize the "six pillars" of good character: trustworthiness, respect, responsibility, caring, fairness, and citizenship. These virtues might lead to a similarly noncontroversial set of political values: having an honest regard for ourselves and others, protecting freedom of thought and religious belief, and refusing to steal or murder.

HONESTY AND COMPETING RESPONSIBILITIES

A further problem with too great an exaltation of honesty is that it 20 may allow us to escape responsibilities that morality bids us bear. If honesty is substituted for integrity, one might think that if I say I am not planning to fulfill a duty, I need not fulfill it. But it would be a peculiar morality indeed that granted us the right to avoid our moral responsibilities simply by stating our intention to ignore them. Integrity does not permit such an easy escape.

Consider an example. Before engaging in sex with a woman, her lover tells her that if she gets pregnant, it is her problem, not his. She says that she understands. In due course she does wind up pregnant. If we believe, as I hope we do, that the man would ordinarily have a moral responsibility toward both the child he will have helped to bring into the world and the child's mother, then his honest statement of what he intends does not spare him that responsibility.

This vision of responsibility assumes that not all moral obligations stem from consent or from a stated intention. The linking of obligations to promises is a rather modern and perhaps uniquely Western way of looking at life, and perhaps a luxury that the well-to-do can afford. As Fred and Shulamit Korn (a philosopher and an anthropologist) have pointed out, "If one looks at ethnographic accounts of other societies, one finds that, while obligations everywhere play a crucial role in social life, promising is not preeminent among the sources of obligation and is not even mentioned by most anthropologists." The Korns have made a study of Tonga, where promises are virtually unknown but the social order is remarkably stable. If life without any promises seems extreme, we Americans sometimes go too far the other way, parsing not only our contracts but even our marriage vows in order to discover the absolute minimum obligation that we have to others as a result of our promises.

That some societies in the world have worked out evidently functional structures of obligation without the need for promise or consent does not tell us what *we* should do. But it serves as a reminder of the basic proposition that our existence in civil society creates a set of mutual responsibilities that philosophers used to capture in the fiction of the social contract. Nowadays, here in America, people seem to spend their time thinking of even cleverer ways to avoid their obligations, instead of doing what integrity commands and fulfilling them. And all too often honesty is their excuse.

The Reader's Presence

1. If Carter intends his essay to be a discussion of honesty, why does he begin with a consideration of the concept of integrity? How are the terms related? In what important ways are they different? What does integrity involve that honesty doesn't?

2. Notice that in this essay Carter never once offers a dictionary definition of the words *honesty* or *integrity*. Look up each term in a standard dictionary. As a reader, do you think such definitions would have made Carter's distinctions more clear? Why do you think he chose not to define the words according to their common dictionary meanings? How does he define them? How are his considerations of honesty and integrity related to his conclusion?

3. Compare Carter's discussion of honesty to Russell Baker's essay "Gumption" (page 79). How are the two qualities related? How does each writer incorporate his own experiences? How do they move between personal idiosyncracies and ideas they hold to be generally true? Are the essays similarly interested in persuading the reader?

45

K. C. Cole

Calculated Risks

K. C. Cole (b. 1946) is a highly regarded science writer for the Los Angeles Times. *Born in Detroit, Michigan, she received a B. A. from Columbia University and has taught at the University of California and the University of Wisconsin. She began writing about science while affiliated with the Exploratorium in San Francisco in the 1970s. Using vivid examples and a clear writing style, Cole makes science accessible to a broad audience and is a frequent contributor to periodicals such as* Smithsonian, Omni, *and* Discover. *She has published a number of books, including* Vision: In the Eye of the Beholder *(1978),* What Only a Mother Can Tell You about Having a Baby *(1980), and* Sympathetic Vibrations: Reflections on Physics as a Way of Life *(1985). Her most recent books are* First You Build a Cloud and Other Reflections on Physics as a Way of Life *(1999), and* The Hole in the Universe: How Scientists Peered Over the Edge of Emptiness and Found Everything *(2001). In* The Universe and the Teacup: The Mathematics of Truth and Beauty *(1998), in which "Calculated Risks" appears, Cole explains exponential growth, quantum theory, optics, astrophysics, and the influence of mathematics on everyday life.*

Newsweek magazine plunged American women into a state of near panic some years ago when it announced that the chance of a college-educated thirty-five-year-old woman finding a husband was less than her chance of being killed by a terrorist. Although Susan Faludi made mincemeat of this so-called statistic in her book *Backlash*, the notion that we can precisely quantify risk has a strong hold on the Western psyche. Scientists, statisticians, and policy makers attach numbers to the risk of getting breast cancer or AIDS, to flying and food additives, to getting hit by lightning or falling in the bathtub.

Yet despite (or perhaps because of) all the numbers floating around, most people are quite properly confused about risk. I know people who live happily on the San Andreas Fault and yet are afraid to ride the New York subways (and vice versa). I've known smokers who can't stand to be in the same room with a fatty steak, and women afraid of the side effects of birth control pills who have unprotected sex with strangers. Risk assessment is rarely based on purely rational considerations—even if people could agree on what those considerations were. We worry about negligible quantities of Alar in apples, yet shrug off the much higher probability of dying from smoking. We worry about flying, but not driving. We worry about getting brain cancer from cellular phones, although the link is quite tenuous. In fact, it's easy to make a statistical argument—albeit a fallacious one—that cellular phones prevent cancer, because the proportion of people with brain tumors is smaller among cell phone users than among the general population.[1]

Even simple pleasures such as eating and breathing have become suspect. Love has always been risky, and AIDS has made intimacy more perilous than ever. On the other hand, not having relationships may be riskier still. According to at least one study, the average male faces three times the threat of early death associated with not being married as he does from cancer.

Of course, risk isn't all bad. Without knowingly taking risks, no one would ever walk out the door, much less go to school, drive a car, have a baby, submit a proposal for a research grant, fall in love, or swim in the ocean. It's hard to have any fun, accomplish anything productive, or experience life without taking on risks—sometimes substantial ones. Life, after all, is a fatal disease, and the mortality rate for humans, at the end of the day, is 100 percent.

Yet, people are notoriously bad at risk assessment. I couldn't get over this feeling watching the aftermath of the crash of TWA Flight 800 and the horror it spread about flying, with the long lines at airports, the increased security measures, the stories about grieving families day after day in the newspaper, the ongoing attempt to figure out why and who and what could be done to prevent such a tragedy from happening again.

Meanwhile, tens of thousands of children die every day around the world from common causes such as malnutrition and disease. That's roughly the same as a hundred exploding jumbo jets full of children every single day. People who care more about the victims of Flight 800 aren't callous or ignorant. It's just the way our minds work. Certain kinds of tragedies make an impact; others don't. Our perceptual apparatus is geared toward threats that are exotic, personal, erratic, and dramatic. This doesn't mean we're ignorant; just human.

This skewed perception of risk has serious social consequences, however. We aim our resources at phantoms, while real hazards are ignored. Parents, for example, tend to rate drug abuse and abduction by strangers as the greatest threats to their children. Yet hundreds of times more children die each year from choking, burns, falls, drowning, and other accidents that public safety efforts generally ignore.

---

[1]John Allen Paulos was the first person I know of to make this calculation; it is probably related to the fact that people who use cellular phones are on average richer, and therefore healthier, than people who don't.

We spend millions to fight international terrorism and wear combat fatigues for a morning walk to protect against Lyme disease. At the same time, "we see several very major problems that have received relatively little attention," write Bernard Cohen and I-Sing Lee in *Health Physics*. The physicists suggest—not entirely tongue in cheek—that resources might be far more efficiently spent on programs such as government-organized computer dating services. "Favorable publicity on the advantages of marriage might be encouraged."

It's as if we incarcerated every petty criminal with zeal, while inviting mass murderers into our bedrooms. If we wanted to put the money on the real killers, we'd go after suicide, not asbestos.

Even in terms of simple dollars, our policies don't make any sense. It's   10
well known, for example, that prenatal care for pregnant women saves enormous amounts of money—in terms of care infants need in the first year of life—and costs a pittance. Yet millions of low-income women don't get it.

Numbers are clearly not enough to make sense of risk assessment. Context counts, too. Take cancer statistics. It's always frightening to hear that cancer is on the rise. However, at least one reason for the increase is simply that people are living longer—long enough to get the disease.

Certain conclusions we draw from statistics are downright silly. Physicist Hal Lewis writes in *Technological Risk* that per mile traveled a person is more likely to be killed by a car as a pedestrian than as a driver or passenger. Should we conclude that driving is safer than walking and therefore that all pedestrians should be forced into cars?

Charles Dickens made a point about the absurdity of misunderstanding numbers associated with risk by refusing to ride the train. One day late in December, the story goes, Dickens announced that he couldn't travel by train any more that year, "on the grounds that the average annual quota of railroad accidents in Britain had not been filled and therefore further disasters were obviously imminent."

Purely numerical comparisons also may be socially unacceptable. When the state of Oregon decided to rank its medical services according to benefit-cost ratios, some results had to be thrown out—despite their statistical validity. Treatment for thumb sucking, crooked teeth, and headaches, for example, came out on the priorities list ahead of therapy for cystic fibrosis and AIDS.

What you consider risky, after all, depends somewhat on the circum-   15
stances of your life and lifestyle. People who don't have enough to eat don't worry about apples contaminated with Alar. People who face daily violence at their front door don't worry about hijackings on flights to the Bahamas. Attitudes toward risk evolve in cultural contexts and are influenced by everything from psychology to ethics to beliefs about personal responsibility.

In addition to context, another factor needed to see through the maze of conflicting messages about risk is human psychology. For example, imminent risks strike much more fear in our hearts than distant ones; it's much harder to get a teenager than an older person to take long-term dangers like smoking seriously.

Smoking is also a habit people believe they can control, which makes the risk far more acceptable. (People seem to get more upset about the effects of passive smoking than smoking itself—at least in part because smokers get to choose, and breathers don't.)

As a general principle, people tend to grossly exaggerate the risk of any danger perceived to be beyond their control, while shrugging off risks they think they can manage. Thus, we go skiing and skydiving, but fear asbestos. We resent and fear the idea that anonymous chemical companies are putting additives into our food; yet the additives we load onto our own food—salt, sugar, butter—are millions of times more dangerous.

This is one reason that airline accidents seem so unacceptable—because strapped into our seats in the cabin, what happens is completely beyond our control. In a poll taken soon after the TWA Flight 800 crash, an overwhelming majority of people said they'd be willing to pay up to fifty dollars more for a round-trip ticket if it increased airline safety. Yet the same people resist moves to improve automobile safety, for example, especially if it costs money.

The idea that we can control what happens also influences who we   20
blame when things go wrong. Most people don't like to pay the costs for treating people injured by cigarettes or riding motorcycles because we think they brought these things on themselves. Some people also hold these attitudes toward victims of AIDS, or mental illness, because they think the illness results from lack of character or personal morals.

In another curious perceptual twist, risks associated with losing something and gaining something appear to be calculated in our minds according to quite different scales. In a now-classic series of studies, Stanford psychologist Amos Tversky and colleague Daniel Kahneman concluded that most people will bend over backward to avoid small risks, even if that means sacrificing great potential rewards. "The threat of a loss has a greater impact on a decision than the possibility of an equivalent gain," they concluded.

In one of their tests, Tversky and Kahneman asked physicians to choose between two strategies for combating a rare disease, expected to kill 600 people. Strategy A promised to save 200 people (the rest would die), while Strategy B offered a one-third probability that everyone would be saved, and a two-thirds probability that no one would be saved. Betting on a sure thing, the physicians choose A. But presented with the identical choice, stated differently, they choose B. The difference in language was simply this: Instead of stating that Strategy A would guarantee 200 out of 600 saved lives, it stated that Strategy A would mean 400 sure deaths.

People will risk a lot to prevent a loss, in other words, but risk very little for possible gain. Running into a burning house to save a pet or fighting back when a mugger asks for your wallet are both high-risk gambles that people take repeatedly in order to hang on to something they care about. The same people might not risk the hassle of, say, fastening a seat belt in a car even though the potential gain might be much higher.

The bird in the hand always seems more attractive than the two in the bush. Even if holding on to the one in your hand comes at a higher risk and the two in the bush are gold-plated.

The reverse situation comes into play when we judge risks of com-   25
mission versus risks of omission. A risk that you assume by actually doing something seems far more risky than a risk you take by not doing something, even though the risk of doing nothing may be greater.

Deaths from natural causes, like cancer, are more readily acceptable than deaths from accidents or murder. That's probably one reason it's so much easier to accept thousands of starving children than the death of one in a drive-by shooting. The former is an act of omission—a failure to step in and help, send food or medicine. The latter is the commission of a crime—somebody pulled the trigger.

In the same way, the Food and Drug Administration is far more likely to withhold a drug that might help a great number of people if it threatens to harm a few; better to hurt a lot of people by failing to do something than act with the deliberate knowledge that some people will be hurt. Or as the doctors' credo puts it: First do no harm.

For obvious reasons, dramatic or exotic risks seem far more dangerous than more familiar ones. Plane crashes and AIDS are risks associated with ambulances and flashing lights, sex and drugs. While red dye #2 strikes terror in our hearts, that great glob of butter melting into our baked potato is accepted as an old friend. "A woman drives down the street with her child romping around in the front seat," says John Allen Paulos. "Then they arrive at the shopping mall, and she grabs the child's hand so hard it hurts, because she's afraid he'll be kidnapped."

Children who are kidnapped are far more likely to be whisked away by relatives than strangers, just as most people are murdered by people they know.

Familiar risks creep up on us like age and are often difficult to see until   30
it's too late to take action. Mathematician Sam C. Saunders of Washington State University reminds us that a frog placed in hot water will struggle to escape, but the same frog placed in cool water that's slowly warmed up will sit peacefully until it's cooked. "One cannot anticipate what one does not perceive," he says, which is why gradual accumulations of risk due to lifestyle choices (like smoking or eating) are so often ignored. We're in hot water, but it's gotten hot so slowly that no one notices.

To bring home his point, Saunders asks us to imagine that cigarettes are not harmful—with the exception of an occasional one that has been packed with explosives instead of tobacco. These dynamite-stuffed cigarettes look just like normal ones. There's only one hidden away in every 18,250 packs—not a grave risk, you might say. The only catch is, if you smoke one of those explosive cigarettes, it might blow your head off.

The mathematician speculates, I think correctly, that given such a situation, cigarettes would surely be banned outright. After all, if 30 million packs of cigarettes are sold each day, an average of 1,600 people a day would die in gruesome explosions. Yet the number of deaths is the same to be expected from normal smoking. "The total expected loss of life or health to smokers using dynamite-loaded (but otherwise harmless) cigarettes over forty years would not be as great as with ordinary filtered cigarettes," says Saunders.

We can accept getting cooked like a frog, in other words, but not getting blown up like a firecracker.

It won't come as a great surprise to anyone that ego also plays a role in the way we assess risks. Psychological self-protection leads us to draw consistently wrong conclusions. In general, we overestimate the risks of bad things happening to others, while vastly underrating the possibility that they will happen to ourselves. Indeed, the lengths people go to minimize their own perceived risks can be downright "ingenious," according to Rutgers psychologist Neil Weinstein. For example, people asked about the risk of finding radon in their houses always rate their risk as "low" or "average," never "high." "If you ask them why," says Weinstein, "they take anything and twist it around in a way that reassures them. Some say their risk is low because the house is new; others, because the house is old. Some will say their risk is low because their house is at the top of a hill; others, because it's at the bottom of a hill."

Whatever the evidence to the contrary, we think: "It won't happen to me." Weinstein and others speculate that this has something to do with preservation of self-esteem. We don't like to see ourselves as vulnerable. We like to think we've got some magical edge over the others. Ego gets involved especially in cases where being vulnerable to risk implies personal failure—for example, the risk of depression, suicide, alcoholism, drug addiction. "If you admit you're at risk," says Weinstein, "you're admitting that you can't handle stress. You're not as strong as the next person."

Average people, studies have shown, believe that they will enjoy longer lives, healthier lives, and longer marriages than the "average" person. Despite the obvious fact that they themselves are, well, average people, too. According to a recent poll, 3 out of 4 baby boomers (those born between 1946 and 1964) think they look younger than their peers, and 4 out of 5 say they have fewer wrinkles than other people their age—a statistical impossibility.

Kahneman and Tversky studied this phenomenon as well and found that people think they'll beat the odds because they're special. This is no doubt a necessary psychological defense mechanism, or no one would

ever get married again without thinking seriously about the potential for
divorce. A clear view of personal vulnerability, however, could go a long
way toward preventing activities like drunken driving. But then again,
most people think they are better than average drivers—even when intoxicated.

We also seem to believe it won't happen to us if it hasn't happened
yet. That is, we extrapolate from the past to the future. "I've been taking
that highway at eighty miles per hour for ten years and I haven't crashed
yet," we tell ourselves. This is rather like reasoning that flipping a coin
ten times that comes up heads guarantees that heads will continue to
come up indefinitely.

Curiously, one advertising campaign against drunken driving that
was quite successful featured the faces of children killed by drunken drivers. These children looked real to us. We could identify with them. In
the same way as we could identify with the people on TWA Flight 800.
It's much easier to empathize with someone who has a name and a face
than a statistic.

That explains in part why we go to great expense to rescue children   40
who fall down mine shafts, but not children dying from preventable diseases. Economists call this the "rule of rescue." If you know that someone
is in danger and you know that you can help, you have a moral obligation to do so. If you don't know about it, however, you have no obligation. Columnist Roger Simon speculates that's one reason the National
Rifle Association lobbied successfully to eliminate the program at the
Centers for Disease Control that keeps track of gun deaths. If we don't have
to face what's happening, we won't feel obligated to do anything about it.

Even without the complication of all these psychological factors,
however, calculating risks can be tricky because not everything is known
about every situation. "We have to concede that a single neglected or unrecognized risk can invalidate all the reliability calculations, which are
based on known risk," writes Ivar Ekeland. There is always a risk, in
other words, that the risk assessment itself is wrong.

Genetic screening, like tests for HIV infection, has a certain probability of being wrong. If your results come back positive, how much should
you worry? If they come back negative, how safe should you feel?

The more factors involved, the more complicated the risk assessment
becomes. When you get to truly complex systems like nationwide telephone networks and power grids, worldwide computer networks and
hugely complex machines like space shuttles, the risk of disaster becomes
infinitely harder to pin down. No one knows when a minor glitch will set
off a chain reaction of events that will culminate in disaster. Potential
risks in complex systems, in other words, are subject to the same kinds of
exponential amplification discussed in the previous chapter.

Needless to say, the way a society assesses risk is very different from
the way an individual views the same choices. Whether or not you wish

to ride a motorcycle is your own business. Whether society pays the bills for the thousands of people maimed by cycle accidents, however, is everybody's business. Any one of us might view our own survival on a transatlantic flight as more important than the needs of the nation's children. Governments, one presumes, ought to have a somewhat different agenda.

But how far does society want to go in strictly numerical accounting?   45
It certainly hasn't helped much in the all-important issue of health care, where an ounce of prevention has been proven again and again to be worth many pounds of cures. Most experts agree that we should be spending much more money preventing common diseases and accidents, especially in children. But no one wants to take health dollars away from precarious newborns or the elderly — where most of it goes. These are decisions that ultimately will not be made by numbers alone. Calculating risk only helps us to see more clearly what exactly is going on.

According to anthropologist Melvin Konner, author of *Why the Reckless Survive,* our poor judgment about potential risks may well be the legacy of evolution. Early peoples lived at constant risk from predators, disease, accidents. They died young. And in evolutionary terms, "winning" means not longevity, but merely sticking around long enough to pass on your genes to the next generation. Taking risk was therefore a "winning" strategy, especially if it meant a chance to mate before dying. Besides, decisions had to be made quickly. If going for a meal of ripe berries meant risking an attack from a saber-toothed tiger, you dove for the berries. For a half-starved cave dweller, this was a relatively simple choice. Perhaps our brains are simply not wired, speculates Konner, for the careful calculations presented by the risks of modern life.

Indeed, some of our optimistic biases toward personal risk may still serve important psychological purposes. In times of stress and danger, they help us to put one foot in front of the other; they help us to get on with our lives, and out the door.

In the end, Konner, the cautious professor, ruminates somewhat wistfully about his risk-taking friends — who smoke, and ride motorcycles, and drive with their seat belts fastened behind them. Beside them, he feels "safe and virtuous," yet somehow uneasy. "I sometimes think," he muses, "that the more reckless among us may have something to teach the careful about the sort of immortality that comes from living fully every day."

The Reader's Presence

1. Cole posits the notion of risk as relative. For example, she argues that suicide takes more lives than asbestos poisoning and that people without food do not worry about contaminants. What

rhetorical techniques does Cole use to support her argument? Do you find them convincing? Why or why not?

2. What does Cole see as the difference between individual risks versus those taken by society as a whole? Which risks receive more attention and why?

3. In paragraph 33, Cole writes, "We can accept getting cooked like a frog, in other words, but not getting blown up like a firecracker." This is an example of the writer's technique of restating a common fact with a provocative, exaggerated analogy. Cole also makes frequent use of the first person plural pronoun, "we," to align herself with her (often foolish) readers. Find examples of these techniques. Do they work for you? What do you think Cole's intention is in using them? Compare Cole's use of "we" to that of Amy Cunningham in the following essay, "Why Women Smile." How is the reader's gender accounted for or discounted in both cases?

46

Amy Cunningham

Why Women Smile

Amy Cunningham (b. 1955) has been writing on psychological issues and modern life for magazines such as Redbook, Glamour, *and the* Washington Post Magazine *since she graduated from the University of Virginia in 1977 with a bachelor's degree in English. Cunningham says that the essay reprinted here grew out of her own experience as an "easy to get along with person" who was raised by Southerners in the suburbs of Chicago. She also recalls that when writing it, "I was unhappy with myself for taking too long, for not being efficient the way I thought a professional writer should be—but the work paid off and now I think it is one of the best essays I've written." "Why Women Smile" originally appeared in* Lear's *in 1993.*

Looking back on her writing career, Cunningham notes, "When I was younger I thought if you had talent you would make it as a writer. I'm surprised to realize now that good writing has less to do with talent and more to do with the discipline of staying seated in the chair, by yourself, in front of the computer and getting the work done."

After smiling brilliantly for nearly four decades, I now find myself trying to quit. Or, at the very least, seeking to lower the wattage a bit.

Not everyone I know is keen on this. My smile has gleamed like a cheap plastic night-light so long and so reliably that certain friends and relatives worry that my mood will darken the moment my smile dims. "Gee," one says, "I associate you with your smile. It's the essence of you. I should think you'd want to smile more!" But the people who love me best agree that my smile—which springs forth no matter where I am or how I feel—hasn't been serving me well. Said my husband recently, "Your smiling face and unthreatening demeanor make people like you in a fuzzy way, but that doesn't seem to be what you're after these days."

Smiles are not the small and innocuous things they appear to be: Too many of us smile in lieu of showing what's really on our minds. Indeed, the success of the women's movement might be measured by the sincerity—and lack of it—in our smiles. Despite all the work we American women have done to get and maintain full legal control of our bodies, not to mention our destinies, we still don't seem to be fully in charge of a couple of small muscle groups in our faces.

We smile so often and so promiscuously—when we're angry, when we're tense, when we're with children, when we're being photographed, when we're interviewing for a job, when we're meeting candidates to employ—that the Smiling Woman has become a peculiarly American archetype. This isn't entirely a bad thing, of course. A smile lightens the load, diffuses unpleasantness, redistributes nervous tension. Women doctors smile more than their male counterparts, studies show, and are better liked by their patients.

Oscar Wilde's old saw that "a woman's face is her work of fiction" is often quoted to remind us that what's on the surface may have little connection to what we're feeling. What is it in our culture that keeps our smiles on automatic pilot? The behavior seems to be an equal blend of nature and nurture. Research has demonstrated that since females often mature earlier than males and are less irritable, girls smile more than boys from the very beginning. But by adolescence, the differences in the smiling rates of boys and girls are so robust that it's clear the culture has done more than its share of the dirty work. Just think of the mothers who painstakingly embroidered the words ENTER SMILING on little samplers, and then hung their handiwork on doors by golden chains. Translation: "Your real emotions aren't welcome here."

Clearly, our instincts are another factor. Our smiles have their roots in the greetings of monkeys, who pull their lips up and back to show their fear of attack, as well as their reluctance to vie for a position of dominance. And like the opossum caught in the light by the clattering garbage cans, we, too, flash toothy grimaces when we make major mistakes. By declaring ourselves nonthreatening, our smiles provide an extremely versatile means of protection.

Our earliest baby smiles are involuntary reflexes having only the vaguest connection to contentment or comfort. In short, we're genetically

5

wired to pull on our parents' heartstrings. As Desmond Morris explains in *Babywatching*, this is our way of attaching ourselves to our caretakers, as truly as baby chimps clench their mothers' fur. Even as babies we're capable of projecting onto others (in this case, our parents) the feelings we know we need to get back in return.

Bona fide social smiles occur at two-and-a-half to three months of age, usually a few weeks after we first start gazing with intense interest into the faces of our parents. By the time we are six months old, we are smiling and laughing regularly in reaction to tickling, feedings, blown raspberries, hugs, and peekaboo games. Even babies who are born blind intuitively know how to react to pleasurable changes with a smile, though their first smiles start later than those of sighted children.

Psychologists and psychiatrists have noted that babies also smile and laugh with relief when they realize that something they thought might be dangerous is not dangerous after all. Kids begin to invite their parents to indulge them with "scary" approach-avoidance games; they love to be chased or tossed up into the air. (It's interesting to note that as adults, we go through the same gosh-that's-shocking-and-dangerous-but-it's-okay-to-laugh-and-smile cycles when we listen to raunchy stand-up comics.)

From the wilds of New Guinea to the sidewalks of New York, smiles   10
are associated with joy, relief, and amusement. But smiles are by no means limited to the expression of positive emotions: People of many different cultures smile when they are frightened, embarrassed, angry, or miserable. In Japan, for instance, a smile is often used to hide pain or sorrow.

Psychologist Paul Ekman, the head of the University of California's Human Interaction Lab in San Francisco, has identified 18 distinct types of smiles, including those that show misery, compliance, fear, and contempt. The smile of true merriment, which Dr. Ekman calls the Duchenne Smile, after the nineteenth-century French doctor who first studied it, is characterized by heightened circulation, a feeling of exhilaration, and the employment of two major facial muscles: the zygomaticus major of the lower face, and the orbicularis oculi, which crinkles the skin around the eyes. But since the average American woman's smile often has less to do with her actual state of happiness than it does with the social pressure to smile no matter what, her baseline social smile isn't apt to be a felt expression that engages the eyes like this. Ekman insists that if people learned to read smiles, they could see the sadness, misery, or pain lurking there, plain as day.

Evidently, a woman's happy, willing deference is something the world wants visibly demonstrated. Woe to the waitress, the personal assistant or receptionist, the flight attendant, or any other woman in the line of public service whose smile is not offered up to the boss or client as proof that there are no storm clouds—no kids to support, no sleep that's been missed—rolling into the sunny workplace landscape. Women are expected to smile no matter where they line up on the social, cultural, or economic ladder: College professors are criticized for not smiling, political spouses are pilloried for being too serious, and women's roles in films have historically been smiling ones. It's little wonder that men on the street still call out, "Hey, baby, smile! Life's not *that* bad, is it?" to women passing by, lost in thought.

A friend remembers being pulled aside by a teacher after class and asked, "What is wrong, dear? You sat there for the whole hour looking so sad!" "All I could figure," my friend says now, "is that I wasn't smiling. And the fact that *she* felt sorry for me for looking normal made me feel horrible."

Ironically, the social laws that govern our smiles have completely reversed themselves over the last two thousand years. Women weren't always expected to seem animated and responsive; in fact, immoderate laughter was once considered one of the more conspicuous vices a woman could have, and mirth was downright sinful. Women were kept apart, in some cultures even veiled, so that they couldn't perpetuate Eve's seductive, evil work. The only smile deemed appropriate on a privileged woman's face was the serene, inward smile of the Virgin Mary at Christ's birth, and even that expression was best directed exclusively at young children. Cackling laughter and wicked glee were the kinds of sounds heard only in hell.

What we know of women's facial expressions in other centuries   15 comes mostly from religious writings, codes of etiquette, and portrait paintings. In fifteenth century Italy, it was customary for artists to paint lovely, blank-faced women in profile. A viewer could stare endlessly at such a woman, but she could not gaze back. By the Renaissance, male artists were taking some pleasure in depicting women with a semblance of complexity, Leonardo da Vinci's Mona Lisa, with her veiled enigmatic smile, being the most famous example.

The Golden Age of the Dutch Republic marks a fascinating period for studying women's facial expressions. While we might expect the drunken young whores of Amsterdam to smile devilishly (unbridled sexuality and lasciviousness were *supposed* to addle the brain), it's the faces of the Dutch women from fine families that surprise us. Considered socially more free, these women demonstrate a fuller range of facial expressions than their European sisters. Frans Hals's 1622 portrait of Stephanus Geraerdt and Isabella Coymans, a married couple, is remarkable not just for the full, friendly smiles on each face, but for the frank and mutual pleasure the couple take in each other.

In the 1800s, sprightly, pretty women began appearing in advertisements for everything from beverages to those newfangled Kodak Land cameras. Women's faces were no longer impassive, and their willingness to bestow status, to offer, proffer, and yield, was most definitely promoted by their smiling images. The culture appeared to have turned the smile, originally a bond shared between intimates, into a socially required display that sold capitalist ideology as well as kitchen appliances. And female viewers soon began to emulate these highly idealized pictures. Many longed to be more like her, that perpetually smiling female. She seemed so beautiful. So content. So whole.

By the middle of the nineteenth century, the bulk of America's smile burden was falling primarily to women and African-American slaves, providing a very portable means of protection, a way of saying, "I'm harmless. I won't assert myself here." It reassured those in power to see signs of gratitude and contentment in the faces of subordinates. As long ago as 1963, adman David Ogilvy declared the image of a woman smiling approvingly at a product clichéd, but we've yet to get the message. Cheerful Americans still appear in ads today, smiling somewhat less disingenuously than they smiled during the middle of the century, but smiling broadly nonetheless.

Other countries have been somewhat reluctant to import our "Don't worry, be happy" American smiles. When McDonald's opened in Moscow not long ago and when EuroDisney debuted in France last year, the Americans involved in both business ventures complained that they couldn't get the natives they'd employed to smile worth a damn.

Europeans visiting the United States for the first time are often surprised at just how often Americans smile. But when you look at our history, the relentless good humor (or, at any rate, the pretense of it) falls into perspective. The American wilderness was developed on the assumption that this country had a shortage of people in relation to its possibilities. In countries with a more rigid class structure or caste system, fewer people are as captivated by the idea of quickly winning friends and influencing people. Here in the States, however, every stranger is a potential associate. Our smiles bring new people on board. The American smile is a democratic version of a curtsy or doffed hat, since, in this land of free equals, we're not especially formal about the ways we greet social superiors. 20

The civil rights movement never addressed the smile burden by name, but activists worked on their own to set new facial norms. African-American males stopped smiling on the streets in the 1960s, happily aware of the unsettling effect this action had on the white population. The image of the simpleminded, smiling, white-toothed black was rejected as blatantly racist, and it gradually retreated into the distance. However, like the women of Sparta and the wives of samurai, who were expected to look happy upon learning their sons or husbands had died in battle, contemporary American women have yet to unilaterally declare their faces their own property.

For instance, imagine a woman at a morning business meeting being asked if she could make a spontaneous and concise summation of a complicated project she's been struggling to get under control for months. She might draw the end of her mouth back and clench her teeth—Eek!—in a protective response, a polite, restrained expression of her surprise, not unlike the expression of a conscientious young schoolgirl being told to get out paper and pencil for a pop quiz. At the same time, the woman might be feeling resentful of the supervisor who sprang the request, but she fears taking that person on. So she holds back a comment. The whole performance resolves in a weird grin collapsing into a nervous smile that conveys discomfort and unpreparedness. A pointed remark by way of explanation or self-defense might've worked better for her—but her mouth was otherwise engaged.

We'd do well to realize just how much our smiles misrepresent us, and swear off for good the self-deprecating grins and ritual displays of deference. Real smiles have beneficial physiological effects, according to Paul Ekman. False ones do nothing for us at all.

"Smiles are as important as sound bites on television," insists producer and media coach Heidi Berenson, who has worked with many of Washington's most famous faces. "And women have always been better at understanding this than men. But the smile I'm talking about is not a cutesy smile. It's an authoritative smile. A genuine smile. Properly timed, it's tremendously powerful."

To limit a woman to one expression is like editing down an orchestra   25
to one instrument. And the search for more authentic means of expression isn't easy in a culture in which women are still expected to be magnanimous smilers, helpmates in crisis, and curators of everybody else's morale. But change is already floating in the high winds. We see a boon in assertive female comedians who are proving that women can *dish out* smiles, not just wear them. Actress Demi Moore has stated that she doesn't like to take smiling roles. Nike is running ads that show unsmiling women athletes sweating, reaching, pushing themselves. These women aren't overly concerned with issues of rapport; they're not being "nice" girls—they're working out.

If a woman's smile were truly her own, to be smiled or not, according to how the *woman* felt, rather than according to what someone else needed, she would smile more spontaneously, without ulterior, hidden motives. As Rainer Maria Rilke wrote in *The Journal of My Other Self*, "Her smile was not meant to be seen by anyone and served its whole purpose in being smiled."

That smile is my long-term aim. In the meantime, I hope to stabilize on the smile continuum somewhere between the eliciting grin of Farrah Fawcett and the haughty smirk of Jeane Kirkpatrick.

The Reader's Presence

1. Cunningham presents an informative précis of the causes and effects of smiling in Western culture. Consider the points of view from which she addresses this subject. Summarize and evaluate her treatment of smiling from a psychological, physiological, sociological, and historical point of view. Which do you find most

incisive? Why? What other points of view does she introduce into her discussion of smiling? What effects do they create? What does she identify as the benefits (and the disadvantages) of smiling?

2. At what point in this essay does Cunningham address the issue of gender? Characterize the language she uses to introduce this issue. She distinguishes between the different patterns—and the consequences—experienced by men and women who smile. Summarize these differences and assess the nature and the extent of the evidence she provides for each of her points. What more general distinctions does she make about various kinds of smiles? What are their different purposes and degrees of intensity? What information does she provide about smiling as an issue of nationality and race? What is the overall purpose of this essay? Where—and how—does Cunningham create and sustain a sense of her own presence in this essay? What does she set as her personal goal in relation to smiling?

3. Cunningham presents an explanation of the causes of an activity that few of her readers think of in either scientific or historical terms. Compare her use of science and history to that of Vicki Hearne in "What's Wrong with Animal Rights" (page 665) and to that of Stephen Jay Gould in "Sex, Drugs, Disasters, and the Extinction of Dinosaurs" (page 401). How does each writer establish her or his authority in these fields? What is each writer's argument? To what extent does each argument depend upon factual evidence?

47

Don DeLillo

In the Ruins of the Future: Reflections on Terror, Loss, and Time in the Shadow of September

Don DeLillo was born in the Bronx, New York, in 1936, the son of Italian immigrants, and grew up in an Italian-American neighborhood. He attended Cardinal Hayes High School and then majored in communication arts at Fordham University, graduating with a B.A. in 1958. During the 1960s, he worked as a copywriter for the renowned ad agency Ogilvy and Mather. He did not start writing his first novel, Americana, *until about 1967. But after it appeared in print in 1971, he continued to write prolifically, publishing five novels in only seven years:* End Zone *(1972),* Great Jones Street *(1973),* Ratner's Star *(1976),* Players *(1977), and* Running Dog *(1978). Although popular with reviewers and a small but fanatical readership, DeLillo had difficulty reaching a wide audience until the publication of* White Noise *(1985), which won the National Book Award, and* Mao II *(1991), which won the PEN/Faulkner Award. DeLillo's work surveys recent history and portrays American culture since the 1950s, dealing with such themes as paranoia, terrorist violence, and consumerism. His novels include* Libra *(1988),* Underworld *(1997), and most recently,* The Body Artist *(2001). "In the Ruins of the Future" first appeared in* Harper's Magazine *in December 2001.*

As DeLillo once commented, "Writing is a concentrated form of thinking. I don't know what I think about certain subjects, even today, until I sit down and try to write about them.

In a 1997 essay, "The Power of History," DeLillo characterizes the writer and identifies the importance of language: ". . . the writer will reconfigure things the way his own history demands. He has his themes and biases and limitations. He has the small crushed pearl of his anger. He has his teaching job, his middling reputation, and the one radical idea that he has been waiting for all his life. The other thing he has is a flat surface that he will decorate, fitfully, with words . . . Let language shape the world." Indeed DeLillo's work reflects a fascination with language — its power to free the writer and to shape narrative and history. "Language lives in everything it touches and can be an agent of redemption, the thing that delivers us, paradoxically, from history's flat, thin, tight, and relentless designs, its arrangement of stark pages, and that allows us to find an unconstraining otherness, a free veer from time and place and fate."

In the following essay, DeLillo reflects on the losses of September 11, 2001. Consider his commentary on writing, the role of the writer, and the power of language. Do these ideas surface in "In the Ruins of the Future"?

I

In the past decade the surge of capital markets has dominated discourse and shaped global consciousness. Multinational corporations have come to seem more vital and influential than governments. The dramatic climb of the Dow and the speed of the Internet summoned us all to live permanently in the future, in the utopian glow of cyber-capital, because there is no memory there and this is where markets are uncontrolled and investment potential has no limit.

All this changed on September 11. Today, again, the world narrative belongs to terrorists. But the primary target of the men who attacked the Pentagon and the World Trade Center was not the global economy. It is America that drew their fury. It is the high gloss of our modernity. It is the thrust of our technology. It is our perceived godlessness. It is the blunt force of our foreign policy. It is the power of American culture to penetrate every wall, home, life, and mind.

Terror's response is a narrative that has been developing over years, only now becoming inescapable. It is *our* lives and minds that are occupied now. This catastrophic event changes the way we think and act, moment to moment, week to week, for unknown weeks and months to come, and steely years. Our world, parts of our world, have crumbled into theirs, which means we are living in a place of danger and rage.

The protesters in Genoa, Prague, Seattle, and other cities want to decelerate the global momentum that seemed to be driving unmindfully toward a landscape of consumer-robots and social instability, with the chance of self-determination probably diminishing for most people in most countries. Whatever acts of violence marked the protests, most of the men and women involved tend to be a moderating influence, trying to slow things down, even things out, hold off the white-hot future.

The terrorists of September 11 want to bring back the past.

II

Our tradition of free expression and our justice system's provisions for the rights of the accused can only seem an offense to men bent on suicidal terror.

We are rich, privileged, and strong, but they are willing to die. This is the edge they have, the fire of aggrieved belief. We live in a wide world, routinely filled with exchange of every sort, an open circuit of work, talk, family, and expressible feeling. The terrorist, planted in a Florida town, pushing his supermarket cart, nodding to his neighbor, lives in a far narrower format. This is his edge, his strength. Plots reduce the world. He builds a plot around his anger and our indifference. He lives a certain kind of apartness, hard and tight. This is not the self-watcher, the soft white dangling boy who shoots someone to keep from disappearing into himself. The terrorist shares a secret and a self. At a certain point he and his brothers may begin to feel less motivated by politics and personal hatred than by brotherhood itself. They share the codes and protocols of their mission here and something deeper as well, a vision of judgment and devastation.

Does the sight of a woman pushing a stroller soften the man to her humanity and vulnerability, and her child's as well, and all the people he is here to kill?

This is his edge, that he does not see her. Years here, waiting, taking flying lessons, making the routine gestures of community and home, the credit card, the bank account, the post-office box. All tactical, linked, layered. He knows who we are and what we mean in the world—an idea, a righteous fever in the brain. But there is no defenseless human at the end of his gaze.

The sense of disarticulation we hear in the term "Us and Them" has never been so striking, at either end.

We can tell ourselves that whatever we've done to inspire bitterness, distrust, and rancor, it was not so damnable as to bring this day down on our heads. But there is no logic in apocalypse. They have gone beyond the bounds of passionate payback. This is heaven and hell, a sense of armed martyrdom as the surpassing drama of human experience.

He pledges his submission to God and meditates on the blood to come.

III

The Bush Administration was feeling a nostalgia for the Cold War. This is over now. Many things are over. The narrative ends in the rubble, and it is left to us to create the counter-narrative.

There are a hundred thousand stories crisscrossing New York, Washington, and the world. Where we were, whom we know, what we've seen or heard. There are the doctors' appointments that saved lives, the cell phones that were used to report the hijackings. Stories generating others and people running north out of the rumbling smoke and ash. Men running in suits and ties, women who'd lost their shoes, cops running from the skydive of all that towering steel.

People running for their lives are part of the story that is left to us.

There are stories of heroism and encounters with dread. There are   15
stories that carry around their edges the luminous ring of coincidence, fate, or premonition. They take us beyond the hard numbers of dead and missing and give us a glimpse of elevated being. For a hundred who are arbitrarily dead, we need to find one person saved by a flash of forewarning. There are configurations that chill and awe us both. Two women on two planes, best of friends, who die together and apart, Tower 1 and Tower 2. What desolate epic tragedy might bear the weight of such juxtaposition? But we can also ask what symmetry, bleak and touching both, takes one friend, spares the other's grief?

The brother of one of the women worked in one of the towers. He managed to escape.

In Union Square Park, about two miles north of the attack site, the improvised memorials are another part of our response. The flags, flower beds, and votive candles, the lamppost hung with paper airplanes, the passages from the Koran and the Bible, the letters and poems, the cardboard John Wayne, the children's drawings of the Twin Towers, the hand-painted signs for Free Hugs, Free Back Rubs, the graffiti of love and peace on the tall equestrian statue.

There are many photographs of missing persons, some accompanied by hopeful lists of identifying features. (Man with panther tattoo, upper right arm.) There is the saxophonist, playing softly. There is the sculptured flag of rippling copper and aluminum, six feet long, with two young people still attending to the finer details of the piece.

Then there are the visitors to the park. The artifacts on display represent the confluence of a number of cultural tides, patriotic and multidevotional and retro hippie. The visitors move quietly in the floating aromas of candlewax, roses, and bus fumes. There are many people this mild evening, and in their voices, manner, clothing, and in the color of their skin they recapitulate the mix we see in the photocopied faces of the lost.

For the next fifty years, people who were not in the area when the at-   20
tacks occurred will claim to have been there. In time, some of them will believe it. Others will claim to have lost friends or relatives, although they did not.

This is also the counter-narrative, a shadow history of false memories and imagined loss.

The Internet is a counter-narrative, shaped in part by rumor, fantasy, and mystical reverberation.

The cell phones, the lost shoes, the handkerchiefs mashed in the faces of running men and women. The box cutters and credit cards. The paper that came streaming out of the towers and drifted across the river to Brooklyn back yards: status reports, résumés, insurance forms. Sheets of paper driven into concrete, according to witnesses. Paper slicing into truck tires, fixed there.

These are among the small objects and more marginal stories in the sifted ruins of the day. We need them, even the common tools of the terrorists, to set against the massive spectacle that continues to seem unmanageable, too powerful a thing to set into our frame of practiced response.

IV

Ash was spattering the windows. Karen was half dressed, grabbing 25 the kids and trying to put on some clothes and talking with her husband and scooping things to take out to the corridor, and they looked at her, twin girls, as if she had fourteen heads.

They stayed in the corridor for a while, thinking there might be secondary explosions. They waited, and began to feel safer, and went back to the apartment.

At the next impact, Marc knew in the sheerest second before the shock wave broadsided their building that it was a second plane, impossible, striking the second tower. Their building was two blocks away, and he'd thought the first crash was an accident.

They went back to the hallway, where others began to gather, fifteen or twenty people.

Karen ran back for a cell phone, a cordless phone, a charger, water, sweaters, snacks for the kids, and then made a quick dash to the bedroom for her wedding ring.

From the window she saw people running in the street, others locked 30 shoulder to shoulder, immobilized, with debris coming down on them. People were trampled, struck by falling objects, and there was ash and paper everywhere, paper whipping through the air, no sign of light or sky.

Cell phones were down. They talked on the cordless, receiving information measured out in eyedrops. They were convinced that the situation outside was far more grave than it was here.

Smoke began to enter the corridor.

Then the first tower fell. She thought it was a bomb. When she talked to someone on the phone and found out what had happened, she felt a surreal relief. Bombs and missiles were not falling everywhere in the city. It was not all-out war, at least not yet.

Marc was in the apartment getting chairs for the older people, for the woman who'd had hip surgery. When he heard the first low drumming rumble, he stood in a strange dead calm and said, "Something is happening." It sounded exactly like what it was, a tall tower collapsing.

The windows were surfaced with ash now. Blacked out completely, 35 and he wondered what was out there. What remained to be seen and did he want to see it?

They all moved into the stairwell, behind a fire door, but smoke kept coming in. It was gritty ash, and they were eating it.

He ran back inside, grabbing towels off the racks and washcloths out of drawers and drenching them in the sink, and filling his bicycle water bottles, and grabbing the kids' underwear.

He thought the crush of buildings was the thing to fear most. This is what would kill them.

Karen was on the phone, talking to a friend in the district attorney's office, about half a mile to the north. She was pleading for help. She begged, pleaded, and hung up. For the next hour a detective kept calling with advice and encouragement.

Marc came back out to the corridor. I think we *might* die, he told 40 himself, hedging his sense of what would happen next.

The detective told Karen to stay where they were.

When the second tower fell, my heart fell with it. I called Marc, who is my nephew, on his cordless. I couldn't stop thinking of the size of the towers and the meager distance between those buildings and his. He answered, we talked. I have no memory of the conversation except for his final remark, slightly urgent, concerning someone on the other line, who might be sending help.

Smoke was seeping out of the elevator shaft now. Karen was saying goodbye to her father in Oregon. Not hello-goodbye. But goodbye-I-think-we-are-going-to-die. She thought smoke would be the thing that did it.

People sat on chairs along the walls. They chatted about practical matters. They sang songs with the kids. The kids in the group were cooperative because the adults were damn scared.

There was an improvised rescue in progress. Karen's friend and a col- 45 league made their way down from Centre Street, turning up with two policemen they'd enlisted en route. They had dust masks and a destination, and they searched every floor for others who might be stranded in the building.

They came out into a world of ash and near night. There was no one else to be seen now on the street. Gray ash covering the cars and pavement, ash falling in large flakes, paper still drifting down, discarded shoes, strollers, briefcases. The members of the group were masked and toweled, children in adults' arms, moving east and then north on Nassau Street, trying not to look around, only what's immediate, one step and then another, all closely focused, a pregnant woman, a newborn, a dog.

They were covered in ash when they reached shelter at Pace University, where there was food and water, and kind and able staff members, and a gas-leak scare, and more running people.

Workers began pouring water on the group. *Stay wet, stay wet.* This was the theme of the first half hour.

Later a line began to form along the food counter.

Someone said, "I don't want cheese on that."

Someone said, "I like it better not so cooked."

Not so incongruous really, just people alive and hungry, beginning to be themselves again.

V

Technology is our fate, our truth. It is what we mean when we call ourselves the only superpower on the planet. The materials and methods we devise make it possible for us to claim our future. We don't have to depend on God or the prophets or other astonishments. We are the astonishment. The miracle is what we ourselves produce, the systems and networks that change the way we live and think.

But whatever great skeins of technology lie ahead, ever more complex, connective, precise, micro-fractional, the future has yielded, for now, to medieval expedience, to the old slow furies of cutthroat religion.

Kill the enemy and pluck out his heart.

If others in less scientifically advanced cultures were able to share, wanted to share, some of the blessings of our technology, without a threat to their faith or traditions, would they need to rely on a God in whose name they kill the innocent? Would they need to invent a God who rewards violence against the innocent with a promise of "infinite paradise," in the words of a handwritten letter found in the luggage of one of the hijackers?

For all those who may want what we've got, there are all those who do not. These are the men who have fashioned a morality of destruction. They want what they used to have before the waves of Western influence. They surely see themselves as the elect of God whether or not they follow the central precepts of Islam. It is the presumptive right of those who choose violence and death to speak directly to God. They will kill and then die. Or they will die first, in the cockpit, in clean shoes, according to instructions in the letter.

Six days after the attacks, the territory below Canal Street is hedged with barricades. There are few civilians in the street. Police at some checkpoints, troops in camouflage gear at others, wearing gas masks, and a pair of state troopers in conversation, and ten burly men striding east in hard hats, work pants, and NYPD jackets. A shop owner tries to talk a cop into letting him enter his place of business. He is a small elderly man with a Jewish accent, but there is no relief today. Garbage bags are everywhere in high broad stacks. The area is bedraggled and third-worldish, with an air of permanent emergency, everything surfaced in ash.

It is possible to pass through some checkpoints, detour around others.

At Chambers Street I look south through the links of the National Rent-A-Fence barrier. There stands the smoky remnant of filigree that marks the last tall thing, the last sign in the mire of wreckage that there were towers here that dominated the skyline for over a quarter of a century.

Ten days later and a lot closer, I stand at another barrier with a group   60
of people, looking directly into the strands of openwork facade. It is almost too close. It is almost Roman, I-beams for stonework, but not nearly so salvageable. Many here describe the scene to others on cell phones.

"Oh my god I'm standing here," says the man next to me.

The World Trade towers were not only an emblem of advanced technology but a justification, in a sense, for technology's irresistible will to realize in solid form whatever becomes theoretically allowable. Once defined, every limit must be reached. The tactful sheathing of the towers was intended to reduce the direct threat of such straight-edge enormity, a giantism that eased over the years into something a little more familiar and comfortable, even dependable in a way.

Now a small group of men have literally altered our skyline. We have fallen back in time and space. It is their technology that marks our moments, the small lethal devices, the remote-control detonators they fashion out of radios, or the larger technology they borrow from us, passenger jets that become manned missiles.

Maybe this is a grim subtext of their enterprise. They see something innately destructive in the nature of technology. It brings death to their customs and beliefs. Use it as what it is, a thing that kills.

VI

Nearly eleven years ago, during the engagement in the Persian Gulf,   65
people had trouble separating the war from coverage of the war. After the first euphoric days, coverage became limited. The rush of watching all that eerie green night-vision footage, shot from fighter jets in combat, had been so intense that it became hard to honor the fact that the war was still going on, untelevised. A layer of consciousness had been stripped away. People shuffled around, muttering. They were lonely for their war.

The events of September 11 were covered unstintingly. There was no confusion of roles on TV. The raw event was one thing, the coverage another. The event dominated the medium. It was bright and totalizing, and some of us said it was unreal. When we say a thing is unreal, we mean it is too real, a phenomenon so unaccountable and yet so bound to the power of objective fact that we can't tilt it to the slant of our perceptions. First the planes struck the towers. After a time it became possible for us to absorb this, barely. But when the towers fell. When the rolling smoke began moving downward, floor to floor. This was so vast and terrible that it was outside imagining even as it happened. We could not catch up to it. But it was real, punishingly so, an expression of the physics of structural limits and a void in one's soul, and there was the huge antenna falling out of the sky, straight down, blunt end first, like an arrow moving backward in time.

The event itself has no purchase on the mercies of analogy or simile. We have to take the shock and horror as it is. But living language is not diminished. The writer wants to understand what this day has done to us. Is it too soon? We seem pressed for time, all of us. Time is scarcer now. There is a sense of compression, plans made hurriedly, time forced and distorted. But language is inseparable from the world that provokes it. The writer begins in the towers, trying to imagine the moment, desperately. Before politics, before history and religion, there is the primal terror. People falling from the towers hand in hand. This is part of the counter-narrative, hands and spirits joining, human beauty in the crush of meshed steel.

In its desertion of every basis for comparison, the event asserts its singularity. There is something empty in the sky. The writer tries to give memory, tenderness, and meaning to all that howling space.

VII

We like to think America invented the future. We are comfortable with the future, intimate with it. But there are disturbances now, in large and small ways, a chain of reconsiderations. Where we live, how we travel, what we think about when we look at our children. For many people, the event has changed the grain of the most routine moment.

We may find that the ruin of the towers is implicit in other things. 70
The new PalmPilot at fingertip's reach, the stretch limousine parked outside the hotel, the midtown skyscraper under construction, carrying the name of a major investment bank—all haunted in a way by what has happened, less assured in their authority, in the prerogatives they offer.

There is fear of other kinds of terrorism, the prospect that biological and chemical weapons will contaminate the air we breathe and the water we drink. There wasn't much concern about this after earlier terrorist acts. This time we are trying to name the future, not in our normally hopeful way but guided by dread.

What has already happened is sufficient to affect the air around us, psychologically. We are all breathing the fumes of lower Manhattan, where traces of the dead are everywhere, in the soft breeze off the river, on rooftops and windows, in our hair and on our clothes.

Think of a future in which the components of a microchip are the size of atoms. The devices that pace our lives will operate from the smart quantum spaces of pure information. Now think of people in countless thousands massing in anger and vowing revenge. Enlarged photos of martyrs and holy men dangle from balconies, and the largest images are those of a terrorist leader.

Two forces in the world, past and future. With the end of Communism, the ideas and principles of modern democracy were seen clearly to prevail, whatever the inequalities of the system itself. This is still the case. But now there is a global theocratic state, unboundaried and floating and so obsolete it must depend on suicidal fervor to gain its aims.

Ideas evolve and de-evolve, and history is turned on end.   75

VIII

On Friday of the first week a long series of vehicles moves slowly west on Canal Street. Dump trucks, flatbeds, sanitation sweepers. There are giant earthmovers making a tremendous revving sound. A scant number of pedestrians, some in dust masks, others just standing, watching, the indigenous people, clinging to walls and doorways, unaccustomed to traffic that doesn't bring buyers and sellers, goods and cash. The fire rescue car and state police cruiser, the staccato sirens of a line of police vans. Cops stand at the sawhorse barriers, trying to clear the way. Ambulances, cherry pickers, a fleet of Con Ed trucks, all this clamor moving south a few blocks ahead, into the cloud of sand and ash.

One month earlier I'd taken the same walk, early evening, among crowds of people, the panethnic swarm of shoppers, merchants, residents and passersby, with a few tourists as well, and the man at the curbstone doing acupoint massage, and the dreadlocked kid riding his bike on the sidewalk. This was the spirit of Canal Street, the old jostle and stir unchanged for many decades and bearing no sign of SoHo just above, with its restaurants and artists' lofts, or TriBeCa below, rich in architectural textures. Here were hardware bargains, car stereos, foam rubber and industrial plastics, the tattoo parlor and the pizza parlor.

Then I saw the woman on the prayer rug. I'd just turned the corner, heading south to meet some friends, and there she was, young and slender, in a silk headscarf. It was time for sunset prayer, and she was kneeling, upper body pitched toward the edge of the rug. She was partly concealed by a couple of vendors' carts, and no one seemed much to notice her. I think there was another woman seated on a folding chair near the curbstone. The figure on the rug faced east, which meant most immediately a storefront just a foot and a half from her tipped head but more distantly and pertinently toward Mecca, of course, the holiest city of Islam.

Some prayer rugs include a *mihrab* in their design, an arched element representing the prayer niche in a mosque that indicates the direction of Mecca. The only locational guide the young women needed was the Manhattan grid.

I looked at her in prayer and it was clearer to me than ever, the daily   80
sweeping taken-for-granted greatness of New York. The city will accommodate every language, ritual, belief, and opinion. In the rolls of the dead

of September 11, all these vital differences were surrendered to the impact and flash. The bodies themselves are missing in large numbers. For the survivors, more grief. But the dead are their own nation and race, one identity, young or old, devout or unbelieving—a union of souls. During the *hadj,* the annual pilgrimage to Mecca, the faithful must eliminate every sign of status, income, and nationality, the men wearing identical strips of seamless white cloth, the women with covered heads, all recalling in prayer their fellowship with the dead.

Allahu akbar. God is great.

The Reader's Presence

1. From the title's linking of the past and the future to statements such as "history is turned on end" (paragraph 74), DeLillo's essay is absorbed with time. Trace the way time is used in the piece. How does the writer make schematic use of past and future to evoke the warring forces of the world? How does he vary tenses and points of view to report the events of September 11 and their aftermath? Why is time central to DeLillo's understanding of these events?

2. For the most part, DeLillo's discussion of the terrorists themselves is unspecific with respect to nationality, religion, or political affiliation. He first mentions Islam several pages into the essay, in section 5. How does DeLillo build the reader's sense of "the enemy"? How is Islam woven through the essay? Why might DeLillo resist giving too narrow an articulation of "us" and "them"?

3. Compare DeLillo's account of the very recent past to Barbara Tuchman's history of the distant past in " 'This Is the End of the World': The Black Death" (page 564). Which sections of DeLillo's essay read like a historian's account and which read more like the primary accounts of the plague's disastrous effects? Compare section IV to Michihiko Hachiya's journal of the days immediately following the bombing of Hiroshima in "From *Hiroshima Diary*" (page 29). Why do you think DeLillo varies his style so dramatically from section to section? What are the advantages and disadvantages of writing about an event whose meaning is still being discovered?

48

Lars Eighner

On Dumpster Diving

Lars Eighner (b. 1948) was born in Texas and attended the University of Texas at Austin. An essayist and fiction writer, he contributes regularly to the Threepenny Review, Advocate Men, The Guide, *and* Inches. *He has published several collections of short stories, essays, and gay erotica. His most recent publications include a camp novel,* Pawn to Queen Four *(1995); a collection of essays,* Gay Cosmos *(1995); an erotic short story collection,* Whispered in the Dark *(1995); and* WANK: The Tapes *(1998).*

Eighner became homeless in 1988, after he lost his job as a mental-hospital attendant. "On Dumpster Diving" is Eighner's prize-winning essay based on this experience, later reprinted as part of his full-length book about homelessness, Travels with Lizbeth: Three Years on the Road and on the Streets *(1993). Eighner and Lizbeth, Eighner's dog, became homeless again in 1996. Friends organized a fund under the auspices of the* Texas Observer *and obtained an apartment for Eighner and Lizbeth in Austin. Lizbeth recently passed away.*

On what is required to find success as a writer, Eighner has said, "I was not making enough money to support myself as a housed person, but I was writing well before I became homeless. . . . A writer needs talent, luck, and persistence. You can make do with two out of three, and the more you have of one, the less you need of the others."

Long before I began Dumpster diving I was impressed with Dumpsters, enough so that I wrote the Merriam-Webster research service to discover what I could about the word "Dumpster." I learned from them that "Dumpster" is a proprietary word belonging to the Dempster Dumpster company.

Since then I have dutifully capitalized the word although it was lowercased in almost all of the citations Merriam-Webster photocopied for me. Dempster's word is too apt. I have never heard these things called anything but Dumpsters. I do not know anyone who knows the generic name for these objects. From time to time, however, I hear a wino or hobo give some corrupted credit to the original and call them Dipsy Dumpsters.

I began Dumpster diving about a year before I became homeless.

I prefer the term "scavenging" and use the word "scrounging" when I mean to be obscure. I have heard people, evidently meaning to be polite, using the word "foraging," but I prefer to reserve that word for gathering nuts and berries and such which I do also according to the season and the opportunity. "Dumpster diving" seems to me to be a little too cute and, in my case, inaccurate because I lack the athletic ability to lower myself into the Dumpsters as the true divers do, much to their increased profit.

I like the frankness of the word "scavenging," which I can hardly   5
think of without picturing a big black snail on an aquarium wall. I live from the refuse of others. I am a scavenger. I think it a sound and honorable niche, although if I could I would naturally prefer to live the comfortable consumer life, perhaps—and only perhaps—as a slightly less wasteful consumer owing to what I have learned as a scavenger.

While my dog Lizbeth and I were still living in the house on Avenue B in Austin, as my savings ran out, I put almost all my sporadic income into rent. The necessities of daily life I began to extract from Dumpsters. Yes, we ate from Dumpsters. Except for jeans, all my clothes came from Dumpsters. Boom boxes, candles, bedding, toilet paper, medicine, books, a typewriter, a virgin male love doll, change sometimes amounting to many dollars: I acquired many things from the Dumpsters.

I have learned much as a scavenger. I mean to put some of what I have learned down here, beginning with the practical art of Dumpster diving and proceeding to the abstract.

What is safe to eat?

After all, the finding of objects is becoming something of an urban art. Even respectable employed people will sometimes find something tempting sticking out of a Dumpster or standing beside one. Quite a number of people, not all of them of the bohemian type, are willing to brag that they found this or that piece in the trash. But eating from Dumpsters is the thing that separates the dilettanti from the professionals.

Eating safely from the Dumpsters involves three principles: using the   10
senses and common sense to evaluate the condition of the found materials, knowing the Dumpsters of a given area and checking them regularly, and seeking always to answer the question "Why was this discarded?"

Perhaps everyone who has a kitchen and a regular supply of groceries has, at one time or another, made a sandwich and eaten half of it before discovering mold on the bread or got a mouthful of milk before realizing the milk had turned. Nothing of the sort is likely to happen to a Dumpster diver because he is constantly reminded that most food is discarded for a reason. Yet a lot of perfectly good food can be found in Dumpsters.

Canned goods, for example, turn up fairly often in the Dumpsters I frequent. All except the most phobic people would be willing to eat from a can even if it came from a Dumpster. Canned goods are among the safest of foods to be found in Dumpsters, but are not utterly foolproof.

Although very rare with modern canning methods, botulism is a possibility. Most other forms of food poisoning seldom do lasting harm to a healthy person. But botulism is almost certainly fatal and often the first symptom is death. Except for carbonated beverages, all canned goods should contain a slight vacuum and suck air when first punctured. Bulging, rusty, dented cans and cans that spew when punctured should be avoided, especially when the contents are not very acidic or syrupy.

Heat can break down the botulin, but this requires much more cooking than most people do to canned goods. To the extent that botulism occurs at all, of course, it can occur in cans on pantry shelves as well as in cans from Dumpsters. Need I say that home-canned goods found in Dumpsters are simply too risky to be recommended.

From time to time one of my companions, aware of the source of my   15
provisions, will ask, "Do you think these crackers are really safe to eat?" For some reason it is most often the crackers they ask about.

This question always makes me angry. Of course I would not offer my companion anything I had doubts about. But more than that I wonder why he cannot evaluate the condition of the crackers for himself. I have no special knowledge and I have been wrong before. Since he knows where the food comes from, it seems to me he ought to assume some of the responsibility for deciding what he will put in his mouth.

For myself I have few qualms about dry foods such as crackers, cookies, cereal, chips, and pasta if they are free of visible contaminates and still dry and crisp. Most often such things are found in the original packaging, which is not so much a positive sign as it is the absence of a negative one.

Raw fruits and vegetables with intact skins seem perfectly safe to me, excluding of course the obviously rotten. Many are discarded for minor imperfections which can be pared away. Leafy vegetables, grapes, cauliflower, broccoli, and similar things may be contaminated by liquids and may be impractical to wash.

Candy, especially hard candy, is usually safe if it has not drawn ants. Chocolate is often discarded only because it has become discolored as the cocoa butter de-emulsified. Candying after all is one method of food preservation because pathogens do not like very sugary substances.

All of these foods might be found in any Dumpster and can be evalu-   20
ated with some confidence largely on the basis of appearance. Beyond these are foods which cannot be correctly evaluated without additional information.

I began scavenging by pulling pizzas out of the Dumpster behind a pizza delivery shop. In general prepared food requires caution, but in this case I knew when the shop closed and went to the Dumpster as soon as the last of the help left.

Such shops often get prank orders, called "bogus." Because help seldom stays long at these places pizzas are often made with the wrong topping, refused on delivery for being cold, or baked incorrectly. The products to be discarded are boxed up because inventory is kept by counting boxes: A boxed pizza can be written off; an unboxed pizza does not exist.

I never placed a bogus order to increase the supply of pizzas and I believe no one else was scavenging in this Dumpster. But the people in the shop became suspicious and began to retain their garbage in the shop overnight.

While it lasted I had a steady supply of fresh, sometimes warm pizza. Because I knew the Dumpster I knew the source of the pizza, and because I visited the Dumpster regularly I knew what was fresh and what was yesterday's.

The area I frequent is inhabited by many affluent college students. I   25
am not here by chance; the Dumpsters in this area are very rich. Students throw out many good things, including food. In particular they tend to throw everything out when they move at the end of a semester, before and after breaks, and around midterm when many of them despair of college. So I find it advantageous to keep an eye on the academic calendar.

The students throw food away around the breaks because they do not know whether it has spoiled or will spoil before they return. A typical discard is a half jar of peanut butter. In fact nonorganic peanut butter does not require refrigeration and is unlikely to spoil in any reasonable time. The student does not know that, and since it is Daddy's money, the student decides not to take a chance.

Opened containers require caution and some attention to the question "Why was this discarded?" But in the case of discards from student apartments, the answer may be that the item was discarded through carelessness, ignorance, or wastefulness. This can sometimes be deduced when the item is found with many others, including some that are obviously perfectly good.

Some students, and others, approach defrosting a freezer by chucking out the whole lot. Not only do the circumstances of such a find tell the story, but also the mass of frozen goods stays cold for a long time and items may be found still frozen or freshly thawed.

Yogurt, cheese, and sour cream are items that are often thrown out while they are still good. Occasionally I find a cheese with a spot of mold, which of course I just pare off, and because it is obvious why such a cheese was discarded, I treat it with less suspicion than an apparently perfect cheese found in similar circumstances. Yogurt is often discarded, still sealed, only because the expiration date on the carton had passed. This is one of my favorite finds because yogurt will keep for several days, even in warm weather.

Students throw out canned goods and staples at the end of semesters   30
and when they give up college at midterm. Drugs, pornography, spirits, and the like are often discarded when parents are expected—Dad's day, for example. And spirits also turn up after big party weekends, presumably discarded by the newly reformed. Wine and spirits, of course, keep perfectly well even once opened.

My test for carbonated soft drinks is whether they still fizz vigorously. Many juices or other beverages are too acid or too syrupy to cause much concern provided they are not visibly contaminated. Liquids, however, require some care.

One hot day I found a large jug of Pat O'Brien's Hurricane mix. The jug had been opened, but it was still ice cold. I drank three large glasses before it became apparent to me that someone had added the rum to the mix, and not a little rum. I never tasted the rum and by the time I began to feel the effects I had already ingested a very large quantity of the beverage. Some divers would have considered this a boon, but being suddenly and thoroughly intoxicated in a public place in the early afternoon is not my idea of a good time.

I have heard of people maliciously contaminating discarded food and even handouts, but mostly I have heard of this from people with vivid imaginations who have had no experience with the Dumpsters themselves. Just before the pizza shop stopped discarding its garbage at night, jalapeños began showing up on most of the discarded pizzas. If indeed this was meant to discourage me it was a wasted effort because I am native Texan.

For myself, I avoid game, poultry, pork, and egg-based foods whether I find them raw or cooked. I seldom have the means to cook what I find, but when I do I avail myself of plentiful supplies of beef which is often in very good condition. I suppose fish becomes disagreeable before it becomes dangerous. The dog is happy to have any such thing that is past its prime and, in fact, does not recognize fish as food until it is quite strong.

Home leftovers, as opposed to surpluses from restaurants, are very often bad. Evidently, especially among students, there is a common type of personality that carefully wraps up even the smallest leftover and shoves it into the back of the refrigerator for six months or so before discarding it. Characteristic of this type are the reused jars and margarine tubs which house the remains.   35

I avoid ethnic foods I am unfamiliar with. If I do not know what it is supposed to look like when it is good, I cannot be certain I will be able to tell if it is bad.

No matter how careful I am I still get dysentery at least once a month, oftener in warm weather. I do not want to paint too romantic a picture. Dumpster diving has serious drawbacks as a way of life.

I learned to scavenge gradually, on my own. Since then I have initiated several companions into the trade. I have learned that there is a predictable series of stages a person goes through in learning to scavenge.

At first the new scavenger is filled with disgust and self-loathing. He is ashamed of being seen and may lurk around, trying to duck behind things, or he may try to dive at night.

(In fact, most people instinctively look away from a scavenger. By   40
skulking around, the novice calls attention to himself and arouses suspicion. Diving at night is ineffective and needlessly messy.)

Every grain of rice seems to be a maggot. Everything seems to stink. He can wipe the egg yolk off the found can, but he cannot erase the stigma of eating garbage out of his mind.

That stage passes with experience. The scavenger finds a pair of running shoes that fit and look and smell brand new. He finds a pocket calculator in perfect working order. He finds pristine ice cream, still frozen, more than he can eat or keep. He begins to understand: People do throw away perfectly good stuff, a lot of perfectly good stuff.

At this stage, Dumpster shyness begins to dissipate. The diver, after all, has the last laugh. He is finding all manner of good things which are his for the taking. Those who disparage his profession are the fools, not he.

He may begin to hang onto some perfectly good things for which he has neither a use nor a market. Then he begins to take note of the things which are not perfectly good but are nearly so. He mates a Walkman with broken earphones and one that is missing a battery cover. He picks up things which he can repair.

At this stage he may become lost and never recover. Dumpsters are   45
full of things of some potential value to someone and also of things which never have much intrinsic value but are interesting. All the Dumpster divers I have known come to the point of trying to acquire everything they touch. Why not take it, they reason, since it is all free.

This is, of course, hopeless. Most divers come to realize that they must restrict themselves to items of relatively immediate utility. But in some cases the diver simply cannot control himself. I have met several of these pack-rat types. Their ideas of the values of various pieces of junk verge on the psychotic. Every bit of glass may be a diamond, they think, and all that glistens, gold.

I tend to gain weight when I am scavenging. Partly this is because I always find far more pizza and doughnuts than water-packed tuna, nonfat yogurt, and fresh vegetables. Also I have not developed much faith in the reliability of Dumpsters as a food source, although it has been proven to me many times. I tend to eat as if I have no idea where my next meal is coming from. But mostly I just hate to see food go to waste and so I eat much more than I should. Something like this drives the obsession to collect junk.

As for collecting objects, I usually restrict myself to collecting one kind of small object at a time, such as pocket calculators, sunglasses, or campaign buttons. To live on the street I must anticipate my needs to a certain extent: I must pick up and save warm bedding I find in August because it will not be found in Dumpsters in November. But even if I had a home with extensive storage space I could not save everything that might be valuable in some contingency.

I have proprietary feelings about my Dumpsters. As I have suggested, it is no accident that I scavenge from Dumpsters where good finds are common. But my limited experience with Dumpsters in other areas suggests to me that it is the population of competitors rather than the affluence of the dumpers that most affects the feasibility of survival by scavenging. The large number of competitors is what puts me off the idea of trying to scavenge in places like Los Angeles.

Curiously, I do not mind my direct competition, other scavengers, so much as I hate the can scroungers.   50

People scrounge cans because they have to have a little cash. I have tried scrounging cans with an able-bodied companion. Afoot a can scrounger simply cannot make more than a few dollars a day. One can extract the necessities of life from the Dumpsters directly with far less effort than would be required to accumulate the equivalent value in cans.

Can scroungers, then, are people who *must* have small amounts of cash. These are drug addicts and winos, mostly the latter because the amounts of cash are so small.

Spirits and drugs do, like all other commodities, turn up in Dumpsters and the scavenger will from time to time have a half bottle of a rather good wine with his dinner. But the wino cannot survive on these occasional finds; he must have his daily dose to stave off the DTs. All the cans he can carry will buy about three bottles of Wild Irish Rose.

I do not begrudge them the cans, but can scroungers tend to tear up the Dumpsters, mixing the contents and littering the area. They become so specialized that they can see only cans. They earn my contempt by passing up change, canned goods, and readily hockable items.

There are precious few courtesies among scavengers. But it is a common practice to set aside surplus items: pairs of shoes, clothing, canned goods, and such. A true scavenger hates to see good stuff go to waste and what he cannot use he leaves in good condition in plain sight.   55

Can scroungers lay waste to everything in their path and will stir one of a pair of good shoes to the bottom of a Dumpster, to be lost or ruined in the muck. Can scroungers will even go through individual garbage cans, something I have never seen a scavenger do.

Individual garbage cans are set out on the public easement only on garbage days. On other days going through them requires trespassing close to a dwelling. Going through individual garbage cans without scattering litter is almost impossible. Litter is likely to reduce the public's tolerance of scavenging. Individual garbage cans are simply not as productive as Dumpsters; people in houses and duplexes do not move as often and for some reason do not tend to discard as much useful material. Moreover, the time required to go through one garbage can that serves one household is not much less than the time required to go through a Dumpster that contains the refuse of twenty apartments.

But my strongest reservation about going through individual garbage cans is that this seems to me a very personal kind of invasion to which I would object if I were a householder. Although many things in Dumpsters are obviously meant never to come to light, a Dumpster is somehow less personal.

I avoid trying to draw conclusions about the people who dump in the Dumpsters I frequent. I think it would be unethical to do so, although I know many people will find the idea of scavenger ethics too funny for words.

Dumpsters contain bank statements, bills, correspondence, and other documents, just as anyone might expect. But there are also less obvious sources of information. Pill bottles, for example. The labels on pill bottles contain the name of the patient, the name of the doctor, and the name of the drug. AIDS drugs and antipsychotic medicines, to name but two groups, are specific and are seldom prescribed for any other disorders. The plastic compacts for birth control pills usually have complete label information. 60

Despite all of this sensitive information, I have had only one apartment resident object to my going through the Dumpster. In that case it turned out the resident was a university athlete who was taking bets and who was afraid I would turn up his wager slips.

Occasionally a find tells a story. I once found a small paper bag containing some unused condoms, several partial tubes of flavored sexual lubricant, a partially used compact of birth control pills, and the torn pieces of a picture of a young man. Clearly she was through with him and planning to give up sex altogether.

Dumpster things are often sad—abandoned teddy bears, shredded wedding books, despaired-of sales kits. I find many pets lying in state in Dumpsters. Although I hope to get off the streets so that Lizbeth can have a long and comfortable old age, I know this hope is not very realistic. So I suppose when her time comes she too will go into a Dumpster. I will have no better place for her. And after all, for most of her life her livelihood has come from the Dumpster. When she finds something I think is safe that has been spilled from the Dumpster I let her have it. She already knows the route around the best Dumpsters. I like to think that if she survives me she will have a chance of evading the dog catcher and of finding her sustenance on the route.

Silly vanities also come to rest in the Dumpsters. I am a rather accomplished needleworker. I get a lot of materials from the Dumpsters. Evidently sorority girls, hoping to impress someone, perhaps themselves, with their mastery of a womanly art, buy a lot of embroider-by-number kits, work a few stitches horribly, and eventually discard the whole mess. I pull out their stitches, turn the canvas over, and work an original design. Do not think I refrain from chuckling as I make original gifts from these kits.

I find diaries and journals. I have often thought of compiling a book of literary found objects. And perhaps I will one day. But what I find is hopelessly commonplace and bad without being, even unconsciously, camp. College students also discard their papers. I am horrified to discover the kind of paper which now merits an A in an undergraduate course. I am grateful, however, for the number of good books and magazines the students throw out. 65

In the area I know best I have never discovered vermin in the Dumpsters, but there are two kinds of kitty surprise. One is alley cats which I meet as they leap, claws first, out of Dumpsters. This is especially thrilling when I have Lizbeth in tow. The other kind of kitty surprise is a plastic garbage bag filled with some ponderous, amorphous mass. This always proves to be used cat litter.

City bees harvest doughnut glaze and this makes the Dumpster at the doughnut shop more interesting. My faith in the instinctive wisdom of animals is always shaken whenever I see Lizbeth attempt to catch a bee in her mouth, which she does whenever bees are present. Evidently some birds find Dumpsters profitable, for birdie surprise is almost as common as kitty surprise of the first kind. In hunting season all kinds of small game turn up in Dumpsters, some of it, sadly, not entirely dead. Curiously, summer and winter, maggots are uncommon.

The worst of the living and near-living hazards of the Dumpsters are the fire ants. The food that they claim is not much of a loss, but they are vicious and aggressive. It is very easy to brush against some surface of the Dumpster and pick up half a dozen or more fire ants, usually in some sensitive area such as the underarm. One advantage of bringing Lizbeth along as I make Dumpster rounds is that, for obvious reasons, she is very alert to ground-based fire ants. When Lizbeth recognizes the signs of fire ant infestation around our feet she does the Dance of the Zillion Fire Ants. I have learned not to ignore this warning from Lizbeth, whether I perceive the tiny ants or not, but to remove ourselves at Lizbeth's first pas de bourrée.[1] All the more so because the ants are the worst in the months I wear flip-flops, if I have them.

(Perhaps someone will misunderstand the above. Lizbeth does the Dance of the Zillion Fire Ants when she recognizes more fire ants than she cares to eat, not when she is being bitten. Since I have learned to react promptly, she does not get bitten at all. It is the isolated patrol of fire ants that falls in Lizbeth's range that deserves pity. Lizbeth finds them quite tasty.)

By far the best way to go through a Dumpster is to lower yourself   70
into it. Most of the good stuff tends to settle at the bottom because it is usually weightier than the rubbish. My more athletic companions have often demonstrated to me that they can extract much good material from a Dumpster I have already been over.

To those psychologically or physically unprepared to enter a Dumpster, I recommend a stout stick, preferably with some barb or hook at one end. The hook can be used to grab plastic garbage bags. When I find canned goods or other objects loose at the bottom of a Dumpster I usually can roll them into a small bag that I can then hoist up. Much Dump-

[1]*pas de bourrée:* A transitional ballet step. — EDS.

ster diving is a matter of experience for which nothing will do except practice.

Dumpster diving is outdoor work, often surprisingly pleasant. It is not entirely predictable; things of interest turn up every day and some days there are finds of great value. I am always very pleased when I can turn up exactly the thing I most wanted to find. Yet in spite of the element of change, scavenging more than most other pursuits tends to yield returns in some proportion to the effort and intelligence brought to bear. It is very sweet to turn up a few dollars in change from a Dumpster that has just been gone over by a wino.

The land is now covered with cities. The cities are full of Dumpsters. I think of scavenging as a modern form of self-reliance. In any event, after ten years of government service, where everything is geared to the lowest common denominator, I find work that rewards initiative and effort refreshing. Certainly I would be happy to have a sinecure again, but I am not heartbroken not to have one anymore.

I find from the experience of scavenging two rather deep lessons. The first is to take what I can use and let the rest go by. I have come to think that there is no value in the abstract. A thing I cannot use or make useful, perhaps by trading, has no value however fine or rare it may be. I mean useful in a broad sense—so, for example, some art I would think useful and valuable, but other art might be otherwise for me.

I was shocked to realize that some things are not worth acquiring, 75 but now I think it is so. Some material things are white elephants that eat up the possessor's substance.

The second lesson is of the transience of material being. This has not quite converted me to a dualist, but it has made some headway in that direction. I do not suppose that ideas are immortal, but certainly mental things are longer-lived than other material things.

Once I was the sort of person who invests material objects with sentimental value. Now I no longer have those things, but I have the sentiments yet.

Many times in my travels I have lost everything but the clothes I was wearing and Lizbeth. The things I find in Dumpsters, the love letters and ragdolls of so many lives, remind me of this lesson. Now I hardly pick up a thing without envisioning the time I will cast it away. This I think is a healthy state of mind. Almost everything I have now has already been cast out at least once, proving that what I own is valueless to someone.

Anyway, I find my desire to grab for the gaudy bauble has been largely sated. I think this is an attitude I share with the very wealthy—we both know there is plenty more where what we have came from. Between us are the rat-race millions who have confounded their selves with the objects they grasp and who nightly scavenge the cable channels looking for they know not what.

I am sorry for them. 80

The Reader's Presence

1. At the center of "On Dumpster Diving" is Lars Eighner's effort to bring out from the shadows of contemporary American life the lore and practices of scavenging, what he calls "a modern form of self-reliance." His essay also provides a compelling account of his self-education as he took to the streets for "the necessities of life." Outline the stages in this process, and summarize the ethical and moral issues and the questions of decorum that Eighner confronted along the way. Show how this process reflects the structure of his essay, "beginning with the practical art of Dumpster diving and proceeding to the abstract."

2. One of the most remarkable aspects of Eighner's essay is the tone (the attitude) he expresses toward his subject. Select a paragraph from Eighner's essay. Read it aloud. How would you characterize the sound of his voice? Does he sound, for example, tough-minded? polite? strident? experienced? cynical? something else? Consider, for example, paragraph 34, where he notes: "For myself, I avoid game, poultry, pork, and egg-based foods whether I find them raw or cooked." Where have you heard talk like this before? Do you notice any changes as the essay develops, or does Eighner maintain the same tone in discussing his subject? What responses does he elicit from his readers when he speaks of scavenging as a "profession" and a "trade"?

3. Consider Eighner's relationship with his readers. Does he consider himself fundamentally different from or similar to his audience? In what specific ways? Consider, for example, the nature of the information Eighner provides in the essay. Does he expect his readers to be familiar with the information? How does he characterize his own knowledgeability about this often-noticed but rarely discussed activity in urban America? Comment on his use of irony in presenting information about Dumpster diving and in anticipating his readers' responses to the circumstances within which he does the work of his trade.

4. Compare Eighner's description of trash to John Hollander's in his essay, "Mess" (page 419). How do both writers work from lists to build their essays?

49

Ralph Ellison

What America Would Be Like without Blacks

*Ralph Ellison (1914–1994), one of the most influential writers of the twenti-
eth century, wrote novels, short stories, essays, and social criticism. His novel
about a black man's struggle for identity,* Invisible Man *(1952), received the National Book Award and is considered to be a landmark of modern fiction. Ellison
was born in Oklahoma City and in his twenties moved to New York City, where
he met Langston Hughes (see page 146) and Richard Wright (see page 288). He
began writing his second novel in 1954, but a large portion of the manuscript was
destroyed in a fire in 1967. For the last forty years of his life, he rewrote hundreds
and hundreds of pages in an effort to complete this second novel. With the help of
editor John Callahan, this long-awaited book,* Juneteenth, *was finally published
in 1999. "What America Would Be Like without Blacks" first appeared in* Time
in 1970.

The fantasy of an America free of blacks is at least as old as the
dream of creating a truly democratic society. While we are aware that
there is something inescapably tragic about the cost of achieving our democratic ideals, we keep such tragic awareness segregated to the rear of
our minds. We allow it to come to the fore only during moments of great
national crisis.

On the other hand, there is something so embarrassingly absurd
about the notion of purging the nation of blacks that it seems hardly a
product of thought at all. It is more like a primitive reflex, a throwback to
the dim past of tribal experience, which we rationalize and try to make
respectable by dressing it up in the gaudy and highly questionable trappings of what we call the "concept of race." Yet, despite its absurdity, the
fantasy of a blackless America continues to turn up. It is a fantasy born
not merely of racism but of petulance, of exasperation, of moral fatigue.
It is like a boil bursting forth from impurities in the bloodstream of
democracy.

In its benign manifestations, it can be outrageously comic — as in the picaresque adventures of Percival Brownlee who appears in William Faulkner's story "The Bear." Exasperating to his white masters because his aspirations and talents are for preaching and conducting choirs rather than for farming, Brownlee is "freed" after much resistance and ends up as the prosperous proprietor of a New Orleans brothel. In Faulkner's hands, the uncomprehending drive of Brownlee's owners to "get shut" of him is comically instructive. Indeed, the story resonates certain abiding, tragic themes of American history with which it is interwoven, and which are causing great turbulence in the social atmosphere today. I refer to the exasperation and bemusement of the white American with the black, the black American's ceaseless (and swiftly accelerating) struggle to escape the misconceptions of whites, and the continual confusing of the black American's racial background with his individual culture. Most of all, I refer to the recurring fantasy of solving one basic problem of American democracy by "getting shut" of the blacks through various wishful schemes that would banish them from the nation's bloodstream, from its social structure, and from its conscience and historical consciousness.

This fantastic vision of a lily-white America appeared as early as 1713, with the suggestion of a white "native American," thought to be from New Jersey, that all the Negroes be given their freedom and returned to Africa. In 1777, Thomas Jefferson, while serving in the Virginia legislature, began drafting a plan for the gradual emancipation and exportation of the slaves. Nor were Negroes themselves immune to the fantasy. In 1815, Paul Cuffe, a wealthy merchant, shipbuilder, and landowner from the New Bedford area, shipped and settled at his own expense thirty-eight of his fellow Negroes in Africa. It was perhaps his example that led in the following year to the creation of the American Colonization Society, which was to establish in 1821 the colony of Liberia. Great amounts of cash and a perplexing mixture of motives went into the venture. The slave owners and many Border-state politicians wanted to use it as a scheme to rid the country not of slaves but of the militant free Negroes who were agitating against the "peculiar institution." The abolitionists, until they took a lead from free Negro leaders and began attacking the scheme, also participated as a means of righting a great historical injustice. Many blacks went along with it simply because they were sick of the black and white American mess and hoped to prosper in the quiet peace of the old ancestral home.

Such conflicting motives doomed the Colonization Society to failure,   5
but what amazes one even more than the notion that anyone could have believed in its success is the fact that it was attempted during a period when the blacks, slave and free, made up eighteen percent of the total population. When we consider how long blacks had been in the New World and had been transforming it and being Americanized by it, the scheme appears not only fantastic, but the product of a free-floating irrationality. Indeed, a national pathology.

Nevertheless, some of the noblest of Americans were bemused. Not only Jefferson but later Abraham Lincoln was to give the scheme credence. According to historian John Hope Franklin, Negro colonization seemed as important to Lincoln as emancipation. In 1862, Franklin notes, Lincoln called a group of prominent free Negroes to the White House and urged them to support colonization, telling them, "Your race suffers greatly, many of them by living among us, while ours suffers from your presence. If this is admitted, it affords a reason why we should be separated."

In spite of his unquestioned greatness, Abraham Lincoln was a man of his times and limited by some of the less worthy thinking of his times. This is demonstrated both by his reliance upon the concept of race in his analysis of the American dilemma and by his involvement in a plan of purging the nation of blacks as a means of healing the badly shattered ideals of democratic federalism. Although benign, his motive was no less a product of fantasy. It envisaged an attempt to relieve an inevitable suffering that marked the growing pains of the youthful body politic by an operation which would have amounted to the severing of a healthy and indispensable member.

Yet, like its twin, the illusion of secession, the fantasy of a benign amputation that would rid the country of black men to the benefit of a nation's health not only persists; today, in the form of neo-Garveyism, it fascinates black men no less than it once hypnotized whites. Both fantasies become operative whenever the nation grows weary of the struggle toward the ideal of American democratic equality. Both would use the black man as a scapegoat to achieve a national catharsis, and both would, by way of curing the patient, destroy him.

What is ultimately intriguing about the fantasy of "getting shut" of the Negro American is the fact that no one who entertains it seems ever to have considered what the nation would have become had Africans *not* been brought to the New World, and had their descendants not played such a complex and confounding role in the creation of American history and culture. Nor do they appear to have considered with any seriousness the effect upon the nation of having any of the schemes for exporting blacks succeed beyond settling some fifteen thousand or so in Liberia.

We are reminded that Daniel Patrick Moynihan,[1] who has recently aggravated our social confusion over the racial issue while allegedly attempting to clarify it, is co-author of a work which insists that the American melting pot didn't melt because our white ethnic groups have resisted all assimilative forces that appear to threaten their identities. The problem here is that few Americans know who and what they really are. That is why few of these groups—or at least few of the children of these groups—have been able to resist the movies, television, baseball, jazz, football, drum-majoretting, rock, comic strips, radio commercials, soap operas, book clubs, slang, or any of a thousand other expressions and carriers of our plu-   10

---

[1]*Moynihan:* Moynihan wrote extensively on issues of poverty and welfare; he retired as senator of New York in 2000.—EDS.

ralistic and easily available popular culture. And it is here precisely that ethnic resistance is least effective. On this level the melting pot did indeed melt, creating such deceptive metamorphoses and blending of identities, values, and life-styles that most American whites are culturally part Negro American without even realizing it.

If we can resist for a moment the temptation to view everything having to do with Negro Americans in terms of their racially imposed status, we become aware of the fact that for all the harsh reality of the social and economic injustices visited upon them, these injustices have failed to keep Negroes clear of the cultural mainstream; Negro Americans are in fact one of its major tributaries. If we can cease approaching American social reality in terms of such false concepts as white and nonwhite, black culture and white culture, and think of these apparently unthinkable matters in the realistic manner of Western pioneers confronting the unknown prairie, perhaps we can begin to imagine what the United States would have been, or not been, had there been no blacks to give it—if I may be so bold as to say—color.

For one thing, the American nation is in a sense the product of the American language, a colloquial speech that began emerging long before the British colonials and Africans were transformed into Americans. It is a language that evolved from the king's English but, basing itself upon the realities of the American land and colonial institutions—or lack of institutions, began quite early as a vernacular revolt against the signs, symbols, manners, and authority of the mother country. It is a language that began by merging the sounds of many tongues, brought together in the struggle of diverse regions. And whether it is admitted or not, much of the sound of that language is derived from the timbre of the African voice and the listening habits of the African ear. So there is a *de'z* and *do'z* of slave speech sounding beneath our most polished Harvard accents, and if there is such a thing as a Yale accent, there is a Negro wail in it— doubtlessly introduced there by Old Yalie John C. Calhoun, who probably got it from his mammy.

Whitman viewed the spoken idiom of Negro Americans as a source for a native grand opera. Its flexibility, its musicality, its rhythms, free-wheeling diction, and metaphors, as projected in Negro American folklore, were absorbed by the creators of our great nineteenth-century literature even when the majority of blacks were still enslaved. Mark Twain celebrated it in the prose of *Huckleberry Finn;* without the presence of blacks, the book could not have been written. No Huck and Jim, no American novel as we know it. For not only is the black man a co-creator of the language that Mark Twain raised to the level of literary eloquence, but Jim's condition as American and Huck's commitment to freedom are at the moral center of the novel.[2]

---

[2]Ellison's observations on *Huckleberry Finn* became the basis of much subsequent literary criticism.—EDS.

In other words, had there been no blacks, certain creative tensions arising from the cross-purposes of whites and blacks would also not have existed. Not only would there have been no Faulkner; there would have been no Stephen Crane, who found certain basic themes of his writing in the Civil War. Thus, also, there would have been no Hemingway, who took Crane as a source and guide. Without the presence of Negro American style, our jokes, our tall tales, even our sports would be lacking in the sudden turns, the shocks, the swift changes of pace (all jazz-shaped) that serve to remind us that the world is ever unexplored, and that while a complete mastery of life is mere illusion, the real secret of the game is to make life swing. It is its ability to articulate this tragic-comic attitude toward life that explains much of the mysterious power and attractiveness of that quality of Negro American style known as "soul." An expression of American diversity within unity, of blackness with whiteness, soul announces the presence of a creative struggle against the realities of existence.

Without the presence of blacks, our political history would have been 15 otherwise. No slave economy, no Civil War; no violent destruction of the Reconstruction; no K.K.K. and no Jim Crow system. And without the disenfranchisement of black Americans and the manipulation of racial fears and prejudices, the disproportionate impact of white Southern politicians upon our domestic and foreign policies would have been impossible. Indeed, it is almost impossible to conceive of what our political system would have become without the snarl of forces—cultural, racial, religious—that make our nation what it is today.

Absent, too, would be the need for that tragic knowledge which we try ceaselessly to evade: that the true subject of democracy is not simply material well-being but the extension of the democratic process in the direction of perfecting itself. And that the most obvious test and clue to that perfection is the inclusion—*not* assimilation—of the black man.

Since the beginning of the nation, white Americans have suffered from a deep inner uncertainty as to who they really are. One of the ways that has been used to simplify the answer has been to seize upon the presence of black Americans and use them as a marker, a symbol of limits, a metaphor for the "outsider." Many whites could look at the social position of blacks and feel that color formed an easy and reliable gauge for determining to what extent one was or was not American. Perhaps that is why one of the first epithets that many European immigrants learned when they got off the boat was the term "nigger"—it made them feel instantly American. But this is tricky magic. Despite his racial difference and social status, something indisputably American about Negroes not only raised doubts about the white man's value system but aroused the troubling suspicion that whatever else the true American is, he is also somehow black.

Materially, psychologically, and culturally, part of the nation's heritage is Negro American, and whatever it becomes will be shaped in part by the Negro's presence. Which is fortunate, for today it is the black American who puts pressure upon the nation to live up to its ideals. It is he who gives creative tension to our struggle for justice and for the elimination of those factors, social and psychological, which make for slums and shaky suburban communities. It is he who insists that we purify the American language by demanding that there be a closer correlation between the meaning of words and reality, between ideal and conduct, our assertions and our actions. Without the black American, something irrepressibly hopeful and creative would go out of the American spirit, and the nation might well succumb to the moral slobbism that has ever threatened its existence from within.

When we look objectively at how the dry bones of the nation were hung together, it seems obvious that some one of the many groups that compose the United States had to suffer the fate of being allowed no easy escape from experiencing the harsh realities of the human condition as they were to exist under even so fortunate a democracy as ours. It would seem that some one group had to be stripped of the possibility of escaping such tragic knowledge by taking sanctuary in moral equivocation, racial chauvinism, or the advantage of superior social status. There is no point in complaining over the past or apologizing for one's fate. But for blacks, there are no hiding places down here, not in suburbia or in penthouse, neither in country nor in city. They are an American people who are geared to what *is* and who yet are driven by a sense of what it is possible for human life to be in this society. The nation could not survive being deprived of their presence because, by the irony implicit in the dynamics of American democracy, they symbolize both its most stringent testing and the possibility of its greatest human freedom.

The Reader's Presence

1. Ellison recounts little known information about Abraham Lincoln. What might Ellison's purpose be in challenging the common view of history? How might he hope to influence the future by uncovering unsettling aspects of the past? He also argues that white people in America are culturally part black. Why might this notion have seemed radical at the time of this essay's writing?

2. What does Ellison mean by describing certain aspects of mainstream American culture as "jazz-shaped"? Where else does Ellison's writing venture from the literal to the figurative? Are Ellison's metaphors more or less effective than his straightforward statements in advancing his argument? Why? Where does Ellison write from a basis of cool reason, and where does emotion seem to arise? Which style of expression do you find more effective? Why?

3. What connections can you find in the essay between cultural difference and invisibility? By what means, according to Ellison, do African American lives and their contributions to mainstream culture become and remain hidden? Does Ellison represent America's notion of itself as a great "melting-pot"? Why or why not? Compare this essay to Mary Gordon's "The Ghosts of Ellis Island" (see page 397). How does Ellison's account of African Americans' place in American culture compare with that of Zora Neale Hurston in "How It Feels to Be Colored Me" (page 150)? Ellison makes a pun on the idea of "mainstream" America by saying that "Negro Americans are in fact one of its major tributaries" (paragraph 11). What is Hurston's central metaphor and how does it compare to Ellison's?

50

Kai Erikson

The Witches of Salem Village

Kai Erikson (b. 1931), son of renowned psychoanalyst Erik Erikson, has been a professor of sociology and American studies at Yale University since 1966. A noted scholar, Erikson has published several books and received numerous professional awards. His interests in communities and the effects of human disasters are reflected in Everything in Its Path: Destruction of Community in the Buffalo Creek Flood *(1976) and* A New Species of Trouble: Explorations in Disaster, Trauma, and Community *(1994). Most recently, Erikson edited* Sociological Vision *(1997), a collection of writings on social problems. "The Witches of Salem Village" is from his study of Puritan New England,* Wayward Puritans: A Study in the Sociology of Deviance *(1966).*

No one really knows how the witchcraft hysteria began, but it originated in the home of the Reverend Samuel Parris, minister of the local church. In early 1692, several girls from the neighborhood began to spend their afternoons in the Parris' kitchen with a slave named Tituba, and it was not long before a mysterious sorority of girls, aged between nine and twenty, became regular visitors to the parsonage. We can only speculate what was going on behind the kitchen door, but we know that Tituba had been brought to Massachusetts from Barbados and enjoyed a reputation in the neighborhood for her skills in the magic arts. As the girls grew closer together, a remarkable change seemed to come over them: perhaps it is not true, as someone later reported, that they went out into the forest to celebrate their own version of a black mass, but it is apparent that they began to live in a state of high tension and shared secrets with one another which were hardly becoming to quiet Puritan maidens.

Before the end of winter, the two youngest girls in the group succumbed to the shrill pitch of their amusements and began to exhibit a most unusual malady. They would scream unaccountably, fall into grotesque convulsions, and sometimes scamper along on their hands and knees making noises like the barking of a dog. No sooner had word gone around about this extraordinary affliction than it began to spread like a contagious disease. All over the community young girls were groveling on the ground in a panic of fear and excitement, and while some of the less credulous townspeople were tempted to reach for their belts in the hopes of strapping a little modesty into them, the rest could only stand by in helpless horror as the girls suffered their torments.

The town's one physician did what he could to stem the epidemic, but he soon exhausted his meagre store of remedies and was forced to conclude that the problem lay outside the province of medicine. The Devil had come to Salem Village, he announced; the girls were bewitched. At this disturbing news, ministers from many of the neighboring parishes came to consult with their colleague and offer what advice they might. Among the first to arrive was a thoughtful clergyman named Deodat Lawson, and he had been in town no more than a few hours when he happened upon a frightening exhibition of the devil's handiwork. "In the beginning of the evening," he later recounted of his first day in the village,

> I went to give Mr. Parris a visit. When I was there, his kinswoman, Abigail Williams, (about 12 years of age,) had a grievous fit; she was at first hurried with violence to and fro in the room, (though Mrs. Ingersoll endeavored to hold her,) sometimes making as if she would fly, stretching up her arms as high as she could, and crying "whish, whish, whish!" several times. . . . After that, she run to the fire, and began to throw fire brands about the house; and run against the back, as if she would run up the chimney, and, as they said, she had attempted to go into the fire in other fits.[1]

Faced by such clear-cut evidence, the ministers quickly agreed that Satan's new challenge would have to be met with vigorous action, and this meant that the afflicted girls would have to identify the witches who were harassing them.

It is hard to guess what the girls were experiencing during those early days of the commotion. They attracted attention everywhere they went and exercised a degree of power over the adult community which would have been exhilarating under the sanest of circumstances. But whatever else was

---

[1]Deodat Lawson, "A Brief and True Narrative of Witchcraft at Salem Village," 1692, in *Narratives of the Witchcraft Cases, 1648–1706*, edited by George Lincoln Burr (New York: Scribner's, 1914), p. 154.

going on in those young minds, the thought seems to have gradually occurred to the girls that they were indeed bewitched, and after they had
been coaxed over and over again to name their tormentors, they finally singled out three women in the village and accused them of witchcraft.

Three better candidates could not have been found if all the gossips in   5
New England had met to make the nominations. The first, understandably, was Tituba herself, a woman who had grown up among the rich colors and imaginative legends of Barbados and who was probably
acquainted with some form of voodoo. The second, Sarah Good, was a
proper hag of a witch if Salem Village had ever seen one. With a pipe
clenched in her leathery face she wandered around the countryside neglect-
ing her children and begging from others, and on more than one occasion
the old crone had been overheard muttering threats against her neighbors
when she was in an unusually sour humor. Sarah Osburne, the third suspect, had a higher social standing than either of her alleged accomplices,
but she had been involved in a local scandal a year or two earlier when a
man moved into her house some months before becoming her husband.

A preliminary hearing was set at once to decide whether the three accused women should be held for trial. The girls were ushered to the front
row of the meeting house, where they took full advantage of the space afforded them by rolling around in apparent agony whenever some personal fancy (or the invisible agents of the devil) provoked them to it. It
was a remarkable show. Strange creatures flew about the room pecking at
the girls or taunting them from the rafters, and it was immediately obvious to everyone that the women on trial were responsible for all the disorder and suffering. When Sarah Good and Sarah Osburne were called to
the stand and asked why they sent these spectres to torment the girls, they
were too appalled to say much in their defense. But when Tituba took the
stand she had a ready answer. A lifetime spent in bondage is poor training for standing up before a bench of magistrates, and anyway Tituba
was an excitable woman who had breathed the warmer winds of the
Caribbean and knew things about magic her crusty old judges would
never learn. Whatever the reason, Tituba gave her audience one of the
most exuberant confessions ever recorded in a New England courtroom.
She spoke of the creatures who inhabit the invisible world, the dark rituals which bind them together in the service of Satan; and before she had
ended her astonishing recital she had convinced everyone in Salem Village
that the problem was far worse than they had dared imagine. For Tituba
not only implicated Sarah Good and Sarah Osburne in her own confession but announced that many other people in the colony were engaged in
the devil's conspiracy against the Bay.

So the hearing that was supposed to bring a speedy end to the affair
only stirred up a hidden hornet's nest, and now the girls were urged to
identify other suspects and locate new sources of trouble. Already the
girls had become more than unfortunate victims: in the eyes of the community they were diviners, prophets, oracles, mediums, for only they

could see the terrible spectres swarming over the countryside and tell
what persons had sent them on their evil errands. As they became caught
up in the enthusiasm of their new work, then, the girls began to reach
into every corner of the community in a search for likely suspects. Martha
Corey was an upstanding woman in the village whose main mistake was
to snort incredulously at the girls' behavior. Dorcas Good, five years old,
was a daughter of the accused Sarah. Rebecca Nurse was a saintly old
woman who had been bedridden at the time of the earlier hearings. Mary
Esty and Sarah Cloyce were Rebecca's younger sisters, themselves accused when they rose in energetic defense of the older woman. And so it
went—John Proctor, Giles Corey, Abigail Hobbs, Bridgit Bishop, Sarah
Wild, Susanna Martin, Dorcas Hoar, the Reverend George Burroughs: as
winter turned into spring the list of suspects grew to enormous length and
the Salem jail was choked with people awaiting trial. We know nothing
about conditions of life in prison, but it is easy to imagine the tensions
which must have echoed within those grey walls. Some of the prisoners
had cried out against their relatives and friends in a desperate effort to divert attention from themselves, others were witless persons with scarcely
a clue as to what had happened to them, and a few (very few, as it turned
out) were accepting their lot with quiet dignity. If we imagine Sarah Good
sitting next to Rebecca Nurse and lighting her rancid pipe or Tituba sharing views on supernatural phenomena with the Reverend George Burroughs, we may have a rough picture of life in those crowded quarters.

By this time the hysteria had spread well beyond the confines of
Salem Village, and as it grew in scope so did the appetites of the young
girls. They now began to accuse persons they had never seen from places
they had never visited (in the course of which some absurd mistakes were
made),[2] yet their word was so little questioned that it was ordinarily war-
rant enough to put respected people in chains.

From as far away as Charlestown, Nathaniel Cary heard that his wife
had been accused of witchcraft and immediately traveled with her to
Salem "to see if the afflicted did know her." The two of them sat through
an entire day of hearings, after which Cary reported:

> I observed that the afflicted were two girls of about ten years old,
> and about two or three others, of about eighteen. . . . The prisoners were
> called in one by one, and as they came in were cried out of [at]. . . . The
> prisoner was placed about seven or eight feet from the Justices, and the
> accusers between the Justices and them; the prisoner was ordered to
> stand right before the Justices, with an officer appointed to hold each
> hand, lest they should therewith afflict them, and the prisoner's eyes
> must be constantly on the Justices; for if they looked on the afflicted,

---

[2]John Alden later reported in his account of the affair that the girls pointed their fingers at the wrong man when they first accused him of witchcraft and only realized their mistake when an obliging passer-by corrected them. See Robert Calef, "More Wonders of the
Invisible World," Boston, 1701, in Burr, *Narratives*, p. 353.

they would either fall into their fits, or cry out of being hurt by them. . . . Then the Justices said to the accusers, "which of you will go and touch the prisoner at the bar?" Then the most courageous would adventure, but before they had made three steps would ordinarily fall down as in a fit. The Justices ordered that they should be taken up and carried to the prisoner, that she might touch them; and as soon as they were touched by the accused, the Justices would say "they are well," before I could discern any alteration. . . . Thus far I was only as a spectator, my wife also was there part of the time, but no notice taken of her by the afflicted, except once or twice they came to her and asked her name.

After this sorry performance the Carys retired to the local inn for   10
dinner, but no sooner had they taken seats than a group of afflicted girls burst into the room and "began to tumble about like swine" at Mrs. Cary's feet, accusing her of being the cause of their miseries. Remarkably, the magistrates happened to be sitting in the adjoining room — "waiting for this," Cary later decided — and an impromptu hearing took place on the spot.

> Being brought before the Justices, her chief accusers were two girls. My wife declared to the Justices that she never had any knowledge of them before that day; she was forced to stand with her arms stretched out. I did request that I might hold one of her hands, but it was denied me; then she desired me to wipe the tears from her eyes, and the sweat from her face, which I did; then she desired she might lean herself on me, saying she should faint. Justice Hathorne replied, she had strength enough to torment those persons, and she should have strength enough to stand I speaking something against their cruel proceedings, they commanded me to be silent, or else I should be turned out of the room. An Indian . . . was also brought in to be one of her accusers; being come in, he now (when before the Justices) fell down and tumbled about like a hog, but said nothing. The Justices asked the girls, "who afflicted the Indian?", they answered "she" (meaning my wife). . . . The Justices ordered her to touch him, in order of his cure . . . but the Indian took hold of her in a barbarous manner; then his hand was taken off, and her hand put on his, and the cure was quickly wrought. . . . Then her mittimus was writ.[3]

For another example of how the hearings were going, we might listen for a moment to the examination of Mrs. John Proctor. This record was taken down by the Reverend Samuel Parris himself, and the notes in parentheses are his. Ann Putnam and Abigail Williams were two of the most energetic of the young accusers.

> Justice: Ann Putnam, doth this woman hurt you?
> Putnam: Yes, sir, a good many times. (Then the accused looked upon them and they fell into fits.)
> Justice: She does not bring the book to you, does she?[4]

[3]Reproduced in Calef, "More Wonders," in Burr, *Narratives*, pp. 350–352.
[4]The "book" refers to the Devil's registry. The girls were presumably being tormented because they refused to sign the book and ally themselves with Satan.

Putnam: Yes, sir, often, and saith she hath made her maid set her hand to it.

Justice: Abigail Williams, does this woman hurt you?

Williams: Yes, sir, often.

Justice: Does she bring the book to you?

Williams: Yes.

Justice: What would she have you do with it?

Williams: To write in it and I shall be well.

Putnam to Mrs. Proctor: Did you not tell me that your maid had written?

Mrs. Proctor: Dear child, it is not so. There is another judgment, dear child. (Then Abigail and Ann had fits. By and by they cried out, "look you, there is Goody Proctor upon the beam." By and by both of them cried out of Goodman Proctor himself, and said he was a wizard. Immediately, many, if not all of the bewitched, had grievous fits.)

Justice: Ann Putnam, who hurt you?

Putnam: Goodman Proctor and his wife too. (Some of the afflicted cried, "there is Proctor going to take up Mrs. Pope's feet" — and her feet were immediately taken up.)

Justice: What do you say Goodman Proctor to these things?

Proctor: I know not. I am innocent.

Williams: There is Goodman Proctor going to Mrs. Pope (and immediately said Pope fell into a fit).

Justice: You see, the Devil will deceive you. The children could see what you was going to do before the woman was hurt. I would advise you to repentance, for the devil is bringing you out.[5]

This was the kind of evidence the magistrates were collecting in readiness for the trials; and it was none too soon, for the prisons were crowded with suspects. In June the newly arrived Governor of the Bay, Sir William Phips, appointed a special court of Oyer and Terminer to hear the growing number of witchcraft cases pending, and the new bench went immediately to work. Before the month was over, six women had been hanged from the gallows in Salem. And still the accused poured in.

As the court settled down to business, however, a note of uncertainty began to flicker across the minds of several thoughtful persons in the colony. To begin with, the net of accusation was beginning to spread out in wider arcs, reaching not only across the surface of the country but up the social ladder as well, so that a number of influential people were now among those in the overflowing prisons. Nathaniel Cary was an important citizen of Charlestown, and other men of equal rank (including the almost legendary Captain John Alden) were being caught up in the widening circle of panic and fear. Slowly but surely, a faint glimmer of skepticism was introduced into the situation; and while it was not to assert a modifying influence on the behavior of the court for some time to come, this new voice had become a part of the turbulent New England climate of 1692.

[5]Hutchinson, *History*, II, pp. 27–28.

Meantime, the girls continued to exercise their extraordinary powers. Between sessions of the court, they were invited to visit the town of Andover and help the local inhabitants flush out whatever witches might still remain at large among them. Handicapped as they were by not knowing anyone in town, the girls nonetheless managed to identify more than fifty witches in the space of a few hours. Forty warrants were signed on the spot, and the arrest total only stopped at that number because the local Justice of the Peace simply laid down his pen and refused to go on with the frightening charade any longer — at which point, predictably, he became a suspect himself.

Yet the judges worked hard to keep pace with their young representatives in the field. In early August five persons went to the gallows in Salem. A month later fifteen more were tried and condemned, of which eight were hung promptly and the others spared because they were presumably ready to confess their sins and turn state's evidence. Nineteen people had been executed, seven more condemned, and one pressed to death under a pile of rocks for standing mute at his trial. At least two more persons had died in prison, bringing the number of deaths to twenty-two. And in all that time, not one suspect brought before the court had been acquitted.

At the end of this strenuous period of justice, the whole witchcraft mania began to fade. For one thing, the people of the Bay had been shocked into a mood of sober reflection by the deaths of so many persons. For another, the afflicted girls had obviously not learned very much from their experience in Andover and were beginning to display an ambition which far exceeded their credit. It was bad enough that they should accuse the likes of John Alden and Nathaniel Cary, but when they brought up the name of Samuel Willard, who doubled as pastor of Boston's First Church and President of Harvard College, the magistrates flatly told them they were mistaken. Not long afterwards, a brazen finger was pointed directly at the executive mansion in Boston, where Lady Phips awaited her husband's return from an expedition to Canada, and one tradition even has it that Cotton Mather's mother was eventually accused.[6]

This was enough to stretch even a Puritan's boundless credulity. One by one the leading men of the Bay began to reconsider the whole question and ask aloud whether the evidence accepted in witchcraft hearings was really suited to the emergency at hand. It was obvious that people were being condemned on the testimony of a few excited girls, and responsible minds in the community were troubled by the thought that the girls' excitement may have been poorly diagnosed in the first place. Suppose the girls were directly possessed by the devil and not touched by intermediate witches? Suppose they were simply out of their wits altogether? Suppose, in fact, they were lying? In any of these events the rules of evidence used in court would have to be reviewed — and quickly.

[6]Burr, *Narratives*, p. 377.

Deciding what kinds of evidence were admissible in witchcraft cases was a thorny business at best. When the court of Oyer and Terminer had first met, a few ground rules had been established to govern the unusual situation which did not entirely conform to ordinary Puritan standards of trial procedure. In the first place, the scriptural rule that two eye-witnesses were necessary for conviction in capital cases was modified to read that any two witnesses were sufficient even if they were testifying about different events—on the interesting ground that witchcraft was a "habitual" crime. That is, if one witness testified that he had seen Susanna Martin bewitch a horse in 1660 and another testified that she had broken uninvited into his dreams twenty years later, then both were witnesses to the same general offense. More important, however, the court accepted as an operating principle the old idea that Satan could not assume the shape of an innocent person, which meant in effect that any spectres floating into view which resembled one of the defendants must be acting under his direct instruction. If an afflicted young girl "saw" John Proctor's image crouched on the window sill with a wicked expression on his face, for example, there could be no question that Proctor himself had placed it there, for the devil could not borrow that disguise without the permission of its owner. During an early hearing, one of the defendants had been asked: "How comes your appearance to hurt these [girls]?" "How do I know," she had answered testily, "He that appeared in the shape of Samuel, a glorified saint, may appear in anyone's shape."[7] Now this was no idle retort, for every man who read his Bible knew that the Witch of Endor had once caused the image of Samuel to appear before Saul, and this scriptural evidence that the devil might indeed be able to impersonate an innocent person proved a difficult matter for the court to handle. Had the defendant been able to win her point, the whole machinery of the court might have fallen in pieces at the magistrates' feet; for if the dreadful spectres haunting the girls were no more than free-lance apparitions sent out by the devil, then the court would have no prosecution case at all.

All in all, five separate kinds of evidence had been admitted by the court during its first round of hearings. First were trials by test, of which repeating the Lord's Prayer, a feat presumed impossible for witches to perform, and curing fits by touch were the most often used. Second was the testimony of persons who attributed their own misfortunes to the sorcery of a neighbor on trial. Third were physical marks like warts, moles, scars, or any other imperfection through which the devil might have sucked his gruesome quota of blood. Fourth was spectral evidence, of the sort just noted; and fifth were the confessions of the accused themselves.

Now it was completely obvious to the men who began to review the court's proceedings that the first three types of evidence were quite inconclusive. After all, anyone might make a mistake reciting the Lord's Prayer, particularly if the floor was covered with screaming, convulsive girls, and it   20

---

[7]Cotton Mather, "Wonders of the Invisible World," in Drake, *The Witchcraft Delusion*, p. 176.

did not make much sense to execute a person because he had spiteful neighbors or a mark upon his body. By those standards, half the people in Massachusetts might qualify for the gallows. This left spectral evidence and confessions. As for the latter, the court could hardly maintain that any real attention had been given to that form of evidence, since none of the executed witches had confessed and none of the many confessors had been executed. Far from establishing guilt, a well-phrased and tearfully delivered confession was clearly the best guarantee against hanging. So the case lay with spectral evidence, and legal opinion in the Bay was slowly leaning toward the theory that this form of evidence, too, was worthless.

In October, Governor Phips took note of the growing doubts by dismissing the special court of Oyer and Terminer and releasing several suspects from prison. The tide had begun to turn, but still there were 150 persons in custody and some 200 others who had been accused.

In December, finally, Phips appointed a new session of the Superior Court of Judicature to try the remaining suspects, and this time the magistrates were agreed that spectral evidence would be admitted only in marginal cases. Fifty-two persons were brought to trial during the next month, and of these, forty-nine were immediately acquitted. Three others were condemned ("two of which," a contemporary observer noted, "were the most senseless and ignorant creatures that could be found"),[8] and in addition death warrants were signed for five persons who had been condemned earlier. Governor Phips responded to these carefully reasoned judgments by signing reprieves for all eight of the defendants anyway, and at this, the court began to empty the jails as fast as it could hear cases. Finally Phips ended the costly procedure by discharging every prisoner in the colony and issuing a general pardon to all persons still under suspicion.

The witchcraft hysteria had been completely checked within a year of the day it first appeared in Salem Village.

The Reader's Presence

1. This essay appears in a larger work on social deviance. What is social deviance, in Erikson's perspective? How has it been perceived and controlled? Why might Erikson view the long-past historical events of Salem as relevant to questions of deviance today?

2. Erikson retells a familiar American story in a deceptively straightforward manner. Does his tone endorse or undercut the surface meaning of his tale? What position toward the events does the essay appear to encourage in the reader? By what means?

[8]Calef, "More Wonders," in Burr, *Narratives*, p. 382.

3. Erikson's essay has a neat timeline: The essay begins at the beginning of the witchcraft hysteria in 1692, and ends at the end of that year by which point the "hysteria had been completely checked." Barbara Tuchman's historical account of the Black Death (page 564) covers a similarly brief period. Reread the essays together and note how each historian paces the telling of the historical narrative. When is primary evidence included? What comment does the writer offer, or withhold, and why? How is each essay's sense of momentum established? What makes you keep reading?

51

James Fallows

Throwing Like a Girl

James Fallows (b. 1949) is a defense reporter, economic theorist, and media critic. He attended Harvard University and received a diploma in economic development from Queen's College, Oxford. He has been editor of the Washington Monthly, Texas Monthly, *the* Atlantic Monthly, *and, most recently,* U.S. News and World Report. *In addition to* National Defense, *which won the National Book Award, he has written* Looking at the Sun *(1995),* Breaking the News: How the Media Undermines American Democracy *(1996), and* Free Fight *(2001). The following article first appeared in the* Atlantic Monthly *for August 1996.*

Most people remember the 1994 baseball season for the way it ended—with a strike rather than a World Series. I keep thinking about the way it began. On opening day, April 4, Bill Clinton went to Cleveland and, like many Presidents before him, threw out a ceremonial first pitch. That same day Hillary Rodham Clinton went to Chicago and, like no First Lady before her, also threw out a first ball, at a Cubs game in Wrigley Field.

The next day photos of the Clintons in action appeared in newspapers around the country. Many papers, including the *New York Times* and the *Washington Post,* chose the same two photos to run. The one of Bill Clinton showed him wearing an Indians cap and warm-up jacket. The President throwing lefty, had turned his shoulders sideways to the plate in preparation for delivery. He was bringing the ball forward from behind his head in a clean-looking throwing action as the photo was snapped. Hillary Clinton was pictured wearing a dark jacket, a scarf, and an oversized Cubs hat. In preparation for her throw she was standing directly facing the plate. A right-hander, she had the elbow of her throwing arm pointed out in front of her. Her forearm was tilted back, toward her shoulder. The ball rested on her upturned palm. As the picture was taken, she was in the middle of an action that can only be described as throwing like a girl.

The phrase "throwing like a girl" has become an embattled and offensive one. Feminists smart at its implication that to do something "like a girl" is to do it the wrong way. Recently, on the heels of the O. J. Simpson case, a book appeared in which the phrase was used to help explain why male athletes, especially football players, were involved in so many assaults against women. Having been trained (like most American boys) to dread the accusation of doing anything "like a girl," athletes were said to grow into the assumption that women were valueless, and natural prey.

I grant the justice of such complaints. I am attuned to the hurt caused by similar broad-brush stereotypes when they apply to groups I belong to—"dancing like a white man," for instance, or "speaking foreign languages like an American," or "thinking like a Washingtonian."

Still, whatever we want to call it, the difference between the two Clin- 5
tons in what they were doing that day is real, and it is instantly recognizable. And since seeing those photos I have been wondering, Why, exactly, do so many women throw "like a girl"? If the motion were easy to change, presumably a woman as motivated and self-possessed as Hillary Clinton would have changed it. (According to her press secretary, Lisa Caputo, Mrs. Clinton spent the weekend before opening day tossing a ball in the Rose Garden with her husband, for practice.) Presumably, too, the answer to the question cannot be anything quite as simple as, because they *are* girls.

A surprising number of people think that there is a structural difference between male and female arms or shoulders—in the famous "rotator cuff," perhaps—that dictates different throwing motions. "It's in the shoulder joint," a well-educated woman told me recently. "They're hinged differently." Someday researchers may find evidence to support a biological theory of throwing actions. For now, what you'll hear if you ask an orthopedist, an anatomist, or (especially) the coach of a women's softball team is that there is no structural reason why men and women should throw in different ways. This point will be obvious to any male who grew up around girls who liked to play baseball and became good at it. It should be obvious on a larger scale this summer, in broadcasts of the Olympic Games. This year, for the first time, women's fast-pitch softball teams will compete in the Olympics. Although the pitchers in these games will deliver the ball underhand, viewers will see female shortstops, center fielders, catchers, and so on pegging the ball to one another at speeds few male viewers could match.

Even women's tennis is a constant if indirect reminder that men's and women's shoulders are "hinged" the same way. The serving motion in tennis is like a throw—but more difficult, because it must be coordinated with the toss of the tennis ball. The men in professional tennis serve harder than the women, because they are bigger and stronger. But women pros serve harder than most male amateurs have ever done, and the service motion for good players is the same for men and women alike. There is no expectation in college or pro tennis that because of their anatomy female players must "serve like a girl." "I know many women who can throw a lot harder and better than the normal male," says Linda Wells, the coach of the highly successful women's softball team at Arizona State University. "It's not gender that makes the difference in how they throw."

So what is it, then? Since Hillary Clinton's ceremonial visit to Wrigley Field, I have asked men and women how they learned to throw, or didn't. Why did I care? My impetus was the knowledge that eventually my sons would be grown and gone. If my wife, in all other ways a talented athlete, could learn how to throw, I would still have someone to play catch with. My research left some women, including my wife, thinking that I am some kind of obsessed lout, but it has led me to the solution to the mystery. First let's be clear about what there is to be explained.

At a superficial level it's easy to tick off the traits of an awkward-looking throw. The fundamental mistake is the one Mrs. Clinton appeared to be making in the photo: trying to throw a ball with your body facing the target, rather than rotating your shoulders and hips ninety degrees away from the target and then swinging them around in order to accelerate the ball. A throw looks bad if your elbow is lower than your shoulder as your arm comes forward (unless you're throwing sidearm). A throw looks really bad if, as the ball leaves your hand, your wrist is "inside your elbow"—that is, your elbow joint is bent in such a way that your forearm angles back toward your body and your wrist is closer to your head than your elbow is. Slow-motion film of big-league pitchers shows that when they release the ball, the throwing arm is fully extended and straight from shoulder to wrist. The combination of these three elements—head-on stance, dropped elbow, and wrist inside the elbow—mechanically dictates a pushing rather than a hurling motion, creating the familiar pattern of "throwing like a girl."

It is surprisingly hard to find in the literature of baseball a deeper explanation of the mechanics of good and bad throws. Tom Seaver's pitching for the Mets and the White Sox got him into the Hall of Fame, but his book *The Art of Pitching* is full of bromides that hardly clarify the process of throwing, even if they might mean something to accomplished pitchers. His chapter "The Absolutes of Pitching Mechanics," for instance, lays out these four unhelpful principles: "Keep the Front Leg Flexible!" "Rub Up the Baseball." "Hide the Baseball!" "Get it Out, Get it Up!" (The fourth refers to the need to get the ball out of the glove and into the throwing hand in a quick motion.)

10

A variety of other instructional documents, from *Little League's Official How-to-Play Baseball Book* to *Softball for Girls & Women,* mainly reveal the difficulty of finding words to describe a simple motor activity that everyone can recognize. The challenge, I suppose, is like that of writing a manual on how to ride a bike, or how to kiss. Indeed, the most useful description I've found of the mechanics of throwing comes from a man whose specialty is another sport: Vic Braden made his name as a tennis coach, but he has attempted to analyze the physics of a wide variety of sports so that they all will be easier to teach.

Braden says that an effective throw involves connecting a series of links in a "kinetic chain." The kinetic chain, which is Braden's tool for analyzing most sporting activity, operates on a principle like that of crack-the-whip. Momentum builds up in one part of the body. When that part is suddenly stopped, as the end of the "whip" is stopped in crack-the-whip, the momentum is transferred to and concentrated in the next link in the chain. A good throw uses six links of chain, Braden says. The first two links involve the lower body, from feet to waist. The first motion of a throw (after the body has been rotated away from the target) is to rotate the legs and hips back in the direction of the throw, building up momentum as large muscles move body mass. Then those links stop—a pitcher stops turning his hips once they face the plate—and the momentum is transferred to the next link. This is the torso, from waist to shoulders, and since its mass is less than that of the legs, momentum makes it rotate faster than the hips and legs did. The torso stops when it is facing the plate, and the momentum is transferred to the next link—the upper arm. As the upper arm comes past the head, it stops moving forward, and the momentum goes into the final links—the forearm and wrist, which snap forward at tremendous speed.

This may sound arcane and jerkily mechanical, but it makes perfect sense when one sees Braden's slow-mo movies of pitchers in action. And it explains why people do, or don't, learn how to throw. The implication of Braden's analysis is that throwing is a perfectly natural action (millions and millions of people can do it) but not at all innate. A successful throw involves an intricate series of actions coordinated among muscle groups, as each link of the chain is timed to interact with the next. Like bike riding or skating, it can be learned by anyone—male or female. No one starts out knowing how to ride a bike or throw a ball. Everyone has to learn.

Readers who are happy with their throwing skills can prove this to themselves in about two seconds. If you are right-handed, pick up a ball with your left hand and throw it. Unless you are ambidextrous or have some other odd advantage, you will throw it "like a girl." The problem is not that your left shoulder is hinged strangely or that you don't know what a good throw looks like. It is that you have not spent time training your leg, hip, shoulder, and arm muscles on that side to work together as required for a throw. The actor John Goodman, who played football seriously and baseball casually when he was in high school, is right-handed. When cast in the 1992 movie *The Babe,* he had to learn to bat and throw left-handed, for realism in the role of Babe Ruth. For weeks before the filming began, he would arrive an hour early at the set of his TV show, *Roseanne,* so that he could practice throwing a tennis ball against a wall left-handed. "I made damn sure no one could see me," Goodman told me recently. "I'm hard enough on myself without the derisive laughter of my so-called friends." When *The Babe* was released, Goodman told a newspaper interviewer, "I'll never say something like 'He throws like a girl' again. It's not easy to learn how to throw."

What Goodman discovered is what most men have forgotten: that if   15 they know how to throw now, it is because they spent time learning at some point long ago. (Goodman says that he can remember learning to ride a bicycle but not learning to throw with his right hand.) This brings us back to the roots of the "throwing like a girl" phenomenon. The crucial factor is not that males and females are put together differently but that they typically spend their early years in different ways. Little boys often learn how to throw without noticing that they are learning. Little girls are more rarely in environments that encourage them to learn in the same way. A boy who wonders why a girl throws the way she does is like a Frenchman who wonders why so many Americans speak French "with an accent."

"For young boys it is culturally acceptable and politically correct to develop these skills," says Linda Wells, of the Arizona State softball team. "They are mentored and networked. Usually girls are not coached at all, or are coached by Mom—or if it's by Dad, he may not be much of an athlete. Girls are often stuck with the bottom of the male talent pool as examples. I would argue that rather than learning to 'throw like a girl,' they learn to throw like poor male athletes. I say that a bad throw is 'throwing like an old man.' This is not gender, its acculturation."

Almost any motor skill, from doing handstands to dribbling a basketball, is easier to learn if you start young, which is why John Goodman did not realize that learning to throw is difficult until he attempted it as an adult. Many girls reach adulthood having missed the chance to learn to throw when that would have been easiest to do. And as adults they have neither John Goodman's incentive to teach their muscles a new set of skills nor his confidence that the feat is possible. Five years ago, Joseph Russo, long a baseball coach at St. John's University, gave athletic-talent tests to actresses who were trying out for roles in *A League of Their Own,* a movie about women's baseball. Most of them were "well coordinated in general, like for dancing," he says. But those who had not happened to play baseball or softball when they were young had a problem: "It sounds silly to say it, but they kept throwing like girls." (The best ball-field talents, by the way, were Madonna, Demi Moore, and the rock singer Joan Jett, who according to Russo "can really hit it hard." Careful viewers of *A League of Their Own* will note that only in a fleeting instant in one scene is the star, Geena Davis, shown actually throwing a ball.)

I'm not sure that I buy Linda Wells' theory that most boys are "mentored" or "networked" into developing ball skills. Those who make the baseball team, maybe. But for a far larger number the decisive ingredient seems to be the hundreds of idle hours spent throwing balls, sticks, rocks, and so on in the playground or the back yard. Children on the playground, I think, demonstrate the moment when the kinetic chain begins to work. It is when a little boy tries to throw a rock farther than his friend can or to throw a stick over a telephone wire thirty feet up. A toddler's first, instinctive throw is a push from the shoulder, showing the essential traits of "throwing like a girl." But when a child is really trying to put some oomph into the throw, his natural instinct is to wind up his body and let fly with the links of the chain. Little girls who do the same thing—compete with each other in distance throwing—learn the same way, but whereas many boys do this, few girls do. Tammy Richards, a woman who was raised on a farm in central California, says that she learned to throw by trying to heave dried cow chips farther than her brother could. It may have helped that her father, Bob Richards, was a former Olympic competitor in the decathlon (and two-time Olympic champion in the pole vault) and that he taught all his sons and daughters to throw not only the ball but also the discus, the shotput, and the javelin.

Is there a way to make up for lost time if you failed to invest those long hours on the playground years ago? Of course. Adults may not be able to learn to speak unaccented French, but they can learn to ride a bike, or skate, or throw. All that is required for developing any of these motor skills is time for practice—and spending that time requires overcoming the sense of embarrassment and futility that adults often have when attempting something new. Here are two tips that may help.

One is a surprisingly valuable drill suggested by the Little League's 20 *How-to-Play* handbook. Play catch with a partner who is ten or fifteen feet away—but do so while squatting with the knee of your throwing side touching the ground. When you start out this low, you have to keep the throw high to get the ball to your partner without bouncing it. This encourages a throw with the elbow held well above the shoulder, where it belongs.

The other is to play catch with a person who can throw like an athlete but is using his or her off hand. The typical adult woman hates to play catch with the typical adult man. She is well aware that she's not looking graceful and reacts murderously to the condescending tone in his voice ("That's more like it, honey!"). Forcing a right-handed man to throw left-handed is the great equalizer. He suddenly concentrates his attention on what it takes to get hips, shoulder, and elbow working together. He is suddenly aware of the strength of character needed to ignore the snickers of onlookers while learning new motor skills. He can no longer be condescending. He may even be nervous, wondering what he'll do if his partner makes the breakthrough first and he's the one still throwing like a girl.

The Reader's Presence

1. Fallows acknowledges the objections of feminists to the phrase "throwing like a girl." What other activities are linked to one gender or the other? Which gender gathers more negative associations? Why might feminists challenge the phrase? In your opinion, does Fallows satisfactorily answer such objections?

2. As a reporter, Fallows has covered many serious issues. Where does his use of language indicate that this essay is a lighter piece? Where does Fallows use an exaggerated or self-mocking tone? How does his use of humor affect the reader's reception of his message?

3. Reread the essay, focusing your attention on Fallows's descriptions of physical movement, especially paragraphs 9 to 14. Is it possible to understand his idea of the "kinetic chain" just by reading a description of it or must the reader also enact it with her or his body? Compare Fallows's anatomically detailed account to George Orwell's description of the dying elephant in "Shooting an Elephant" (page 198). How does each writer integrate such "close focus" descriptions into his larger argument? Do these passages slow down the essays? If not, why not?

52 _____

Ian Frazier

Tracks

The journalist and essayist Ian Frazier (b. 1951) started his career on the staff of the New Yorker, *writing "Talk of the Town" pieces as well as signed essays. Many of these essays can be found in his first two books:* Dating Your Mom *(1986) and* Nobody Better, Better Than Nobody *(1987). In the mid-1980s Frazier left his job in New York and embarked on a journey across the North American prairies to Montana. The book that emerged after several years spent exploring this region,* Great Plains *(1989), was a huge success with both critics and readers. In* Family *(1994), Frazier turns to a subject closer to home and tells the story of twelve generations of his family. His most recent collection is of comic essays,* Coyote v. Acme *(1996); his latest book is* On the Rez *(2000). "Tracks" was orginally published in* Audubon *magazine in November–December 1996.*

In all of his writing Frazier pays close attention to detail and location. "If you know something about a place it can save your sanity," he says, and a writer can find that knowledge through observation. "With a lot of writing, what you see is the top, the pinnacle, and the rest is invisible — all of these observations are ways of keeping yourself from flying off into space."

When I lived in New York City, I liked to walk in the park right after a snowfall. For a few hours the new snow held tracks — of rats, pigeons, squirrels, dogs, and the sewing machine tracks of sparrows. Always, someone had been there already on cross-country skis. Within a day or so, other tracks, most of them human, would cover the parks so thoroughly that it seemed not a square foot remained untouched, while the snow took on the complicated texture of a sheet of metal struck by millions of blows. On sloppy days there I sometimes studied the floors of subway cars, their dingy linoleum a palimpsest of shoe tracks, of treads and lugs and zigzag patterns, of lightning streaks and logos and brand names. Many shoes print advertisements beneath them with every step. Not only are there a lot more of us on the planet than in former times, but nowadays we make different marks on it with our feet.

I look at what is under and around my feet more often than is common, probably because of all the time I spent as a boy searching for four-leaf clovers and arrowheads and rifle shells and golf balls. One summer evening back then, in suburban Ohio, I suggested to my brothers and sisters that we go look for arrowheads on a newly seeded lawn. They agreed, we strolled over, and within a few minutes my sister Suzan picked up a perfect arrowhead about two inches long. It was shaped like a poplar leaf, and its flint was a dark gray marked with flecks and swirls of white. I could hardly have been more excited if she had found a piece of spaceman's antenna made from an element unknown on earth. The numen of this piece of stone — I snatched it from her immediately — overwhelmed me. The shaft it had once been attached to, the unknowable circumstances that had deposited it there, the chipped fingernails of the hand that had made it, all swirled around me in a romantic infinitude of suggestion. It drove me nuts that she had spotted it and I hadn't. Maybe simply because of this, I have kept my eyes to the ground ever since. At the rate of about once a decade, I have found arrowheads, a hide scraper, and what may be a tool for arrow making. I've also found money, mushrooms, pencils, love notes. Mostly, though, what I find are tracks.

Arrowheads and tracks are similar, in a way. Both are relics; both imply motion and direction. Both are larger in what they conjure for the imagination than in their actual physical reality. The bear track still filling with water at a wet place on the trail hits the imagination, inflaming speculation; the sight of the bear herself around the next bend registers in the gut and nerve endings and adrenal glands — no speculation is involved. I have to say, most of the time I prefer to speculate. I watch the track filling with water, my mind veers to speculation, and I retreat to a more comfortable spot to pursue it.

Of the places where I've lived in Montana, the most remote was in a neighborhood among foothills of fir and lodgepole pine—prime mountain lion habitat. Not long after I'd moved there, the people across the way told me that they'd heard a mountain lion scream, and that something had clawed one of their goats. Hiking logging roads through the woods, I began to see mountain lion tracks; they're like dog or coyote tracks but rounder, more elegant and catlike. The animal always traveled alone, keeping to a single wheel rut, cruising along like a car in the express lane. Even when it cut its foot and marked the same red spot in the snow for miles, the pace of the tracks hardly varied.

I never saw the lion itself, and it assumed the predictable configuration   5
of spirit lion in my mind. Then, on a logging road not nearby, when my thoughts were on the river I was hoping to fish and whether or not the vehicle I was driving would make it there, suddenly broadside across the road in front of me was a mountain lion. I stopped, quietly opened the door, slid from the car. Still the lion watched, an expression of mild curiosity on its face. I took a step toward it. It turned and lopingly ran, gawky as a teenager. I had never seen a big cat run like that—unimpeded, without a wall or bars to stop it. It jumped the shoulder of the road and disappeared. The last I saw was the question mark of its tail moving along above the weeds. Somehow, the tail alone was more evocative of the lion than clear sight of the animal itself had been. On the hard gravel road, the lion's paws had left not a whisper of a track. I paced back and forth, longing for a replay button, telling myself over and over that I'd seen what I'd seen, flummoxed at how undocumented the experience had been. I wanted a receipt; I wanted a track.

Of course, if there had been tracks, I would have just stared at them and daydreamed until the experience began to resemble something I'd made up. Then maybe the real lion would have come back and leaped on me in irritation at my preferring the imaginary to the real. It's like the time I was tracking a deer on an icy path with an overlay of light snow; the tracks showed the deer putting down each foot carefully, skidding a bit now and then. At a sudden steep decline, I saw that its feet had gone completely out from under in a fall that had sent it sliding. I was imagining this wipeout, enjoying a chuckle, when my own feet slipped. I landed hard, skidded, and wound up at the bottom not far from the sitzmark of the deer.

Now I live in Montana in a small city—the richest place for tracks so far. It has the expected city-country wildlife, the usual encirclement of raccoon tracks around the garbage cans. Skunks enter houses through pet doors; a friend came into her kitchen early one morning and found a skunk eating from her cat's bowl. Skunk tracks—the hind feet with elongated digits, like simian hands—cross the snow in our front yard. Coyotes

yip and howl from the bare hillsides east of town, so I assume the ubiquitous dog tracks I see are not all made by dogs. I haven't seen mountain lion
tracks, although a few years ago the local paper ran a photo of a mountain
lion curled up in a window well in town. That deer browse along the back
alley from compost pile to compost pile does not surprise me, nor that
their tracks continue along the chainlink fence by the elementary school.
As human enterprise takes up more and more of the landscape, animals
will certainly remain in it, at large if not exactly wild. Probably developers
will one day build them semiofficial housing of their own.

As in New York, most of the tracks here are human. But here the
numbers are fewer, and individuality doesn't get trampled out. I know of
course the tracks of my own family—the thin, wavy lines of tread on my
wife's rain boots, the flat sole and heel of her cowboy boots, my daughter's ice skate cross-hatching in the backyard, the thick zigzag tread of
what my three-year-old son calls his "big-heavy boots." Because my profession is solitary and I work at home, I live for the mail. I quickly learned
to identify the track of the mailman. The soles of our mailman's shoes
have regularly spaced short spikes in the shape of hemispheres, which
leave crisp concave holes like holes in a tea biscuit. No one else around
here wears such a shoe. His neat tracks proceeding door-to-door up our
street in new snow depict the hopefulness and civic rectitude I have always associated with the mail. One day I happened to meet him on the
front stoop, and I asked about his shoes. He told me that they were his
special winter shoes, that no others were as good on snow and ice, that
after he started wearing them he hadn't fallen once, that he recommended
them highly. He told me where I could buy a pair and how much they
cost. As far as relating goes, we far outdid the usual between mailman
and addressee.

I regret that birds don't leave tracks in the air. The fact that only
man-made things—fireworks and tracer bullets and jet planes—leave
any sign of their airborne passage seems somehow wrong. It would be
cool if peregrine falcons, say, left streaks in the sky as they came down on
their prey. The sky above certain parts of rivers would be hung with the
feathery hover marks of kingfishers. You wouldn't want too many, like
graffiti scratched in the windows of subway cars; but a few would be
nice. Because of the medium, they would quickly fade.

Once after a snowstorm had piled new powder everywhere, a squirrel   10
jumped onto a telephone wire behind our house. As he bounded along the
wire, his feet knocked snow loose each time they came down. Against the
bright blue sky the snow he dislodged fell in vertical white lines, a blue-
and-white bar code indicating *squirrel;* nothing else would have set the
snow falling in that particular way. The lines were most distinct a step or
two behind him. Farther behind they merged into a glittering curtain, and
farther still they had already vanished in the sky.

Some tracks are gone like that, in an instant. But a track is a mark,
and like all marks it can exist independent of time. Geographic circum-

stances can preserve a track for a minute or a week or unknown millions of years. Among my favorites are some dinosaur tracks 200 million years old. Two dinosaurs made them—one a large, plant-eating dinosaur, and the other a smaller, meat-eating dinosaur that came after it across a patch of calcareous mud, possibly in pursuit. Mud hardened, geology ensued, and eventually the tracks wound up in the dinosaur wing of the American Museum of Natural History in New York City. Whenever I get a chance, I revisit them there. No other tracks provoke me to fantasize the way these do. To begin with, they're sort of messy, with ragged edges and muddy flourishes: I imagine the squish of the big feet going in, the suck of them coming out. The dinosaurs that made these tracks were as real as the dented taxicab that brought me. Trying to summon them, I imagine that through some time-travel miracle I actually come upon the dinosaurs in a muddy place 50 yards or so up ahead; and I imagine that when I do, I am disappointed. I'm always disappointed when I see what made the tracks I'm fantasizing about. These two wouldn't be Dinosaur; they would just be a couple of individual dinosaurs—muddy-footed, maybe with nicks in their hide and missing teeth—mortal beings lit by the same ordinary sunlight as I am. Picturing them as slightly disappointing, almost boring, somehow brings them closer. Tracks let you do that, let you approach the fantastic by way of the mundane. A track is a place where the fantastic and the mundane coincide.

The Reader's Presence

1. Why are tracks important to Frazier? Does he use them the way a hunter or tracker would? What happens when he discovers them? How are they related to his imagination? to speculation?

2. Note that Frazier refers to big cities, small cities, the suburbs, prehistoric forests, and remote rural areas. How do these places get woven into the essay? How does each display different sorts of tracks? Watch Frazier's descriptions closely: How does he occasionally merge these different places into a single description of a track? Why do you think he does this?

3. Compare Frazier's essay with Mary Gordon's "The Ghosts of Ellis Island" (see page 397). Although their topics are very different, what do both essays have in common? How do both writers project their presence into the different environments they are studying?

53

Malcolm Gladwell

The Tipping Point

Malcolm Gladwell was born in 1963 in England, and grew up in Canada. He graduated with a degree in history from the University of Toronto in 1984. From 1987 to 1996, he was a reporter for the Washington Post, *first as a science writer and then as New York City bureau chief. Since 1996, he has been a staff writer for the* New Yorker. *He is known for writing clearly and engagingly on complex topics, and described his best-selling book,* The Tipping Point (2001), *as "an intellectual adventure story . . . it takes theories and ideas from the social sciences and shows how they can have real relevance to our lives." The following essay is the introduction to* The Tipping Point.

For Hush Puppies—the classic American brushed-suede shoes with the lightweight crepe sole—the Tipping Point came somewhere between late 1994 and early 1995. The brand had been all but dead until that point. Sales were down to 30,000 pairs a year, mostly to backwoods outlets and small-town family stores. Wolverine, the company that makes Hush Puppies, was thinking of phasing out the shoes that made them famous. But then something strange happened. At a fashion shoot, two Hush Puppies executives—Owen Baxter and Geoffrey Lewis—ran into a stylist from New York who told them that the classic Hush Puppies had suddenly become hip in the clubs and bars of downtown Manhattan. "We were being told," Baxter recalls, "that there were resale shops in the Village, in Soho, where the shoes were being sold. People were going to the Ma and Pa stores, the little stores that still carried them, and buying them up." Baxter and Lewis were baffled at first. It made no sense to them that shoes that were so obviously out of fashion could make a comeback. "We were told that Isaac Mizrahi was wearing the shoes himself," Lewis says. "I think it's fair to say that at the time we had no idea who Isaac Mizrahi was."

By the fall of 1995, things began to happen in a rush. First the designer John Bartlett called. He wanted to use Hush Puppies in his spring collection. Then another Manhattan designer, Anna Sui, called, wanting shoes for her show as well. In Los Angeles, the designer Joel Fitzgerald put a twenty-five-foot inflatable basset hound—the symbol of the Hush Puppies brand—on the roof of his Hollywood store and gutted an adjoining art gallery to turn it into a Hush Puppies boutique. While he was still painting and putting up shelves, the actor Pee-wee Herman walked in and asked for a couple of pairs. "It was total word of mouth," Fitzgerald remembers.

In 1995, the company sold 430,000 pairs of the classic Hush Puppies, and the next year it sold four times that, and the year after that still more, until Hush Puppies were once again a staple of the wardrobe of the young American male. In 1996, Hush Puppies won the prize for best accessory at the Council of Fashion Designers awards dinner at Lincoln Center, and the president of the firm stood up on the stage with Calvin Klein and Donna Karan and accepted an award for an achievement that—as he would be the first to admit—his company had almost nothing to do with. Hush Puppies had suddenly exploded, and it all started with a handful of kids in the East Village and Soho.

How did that happen? Those first few kids, whoever they were, weren't deliberately trying to promote Hush Puppies. They were wearing them precisely because no one else would wear them. Then the fad spread to two fashion designers who used the shoes to peddle something else— haute couture. The shoes were an incidental touch. No one was trying to make Hush Puppies a trend. Yet, somehow, that's exactly what happened. The shoes passed a certain point in popularity and they tipped. How does a thirty-dollar pair of shoes go from a handful of downtown Manhattan hipsters and designers to every mall in America in the space of two years?

I

There was a time, not very long ago, in the desperately poor New York City neighborhoods of Brownsville and East New York, when the streets would turn into ghost towns at dusk. Ordinary working people wouldn't walk on the sidewalks. Children wouldn't ride their bicycles on the streets. Old folks wouldn't sit on stoops and park benches. The drug trade ran so rampant and gang warfare was so ubiquitous in that part of Brooklyn that most people would take to the safety of their apartment at nightfall. Police officers who served in Brownsville in the 1980s and early 1990s say that, in those years, as soon as the sun went down their radios exploded with chatter between beat officers and their dispatchers over every conceivable kind of violent and dangerous crime. In 1992, there were 2,154 murders in New York City and 626,182 serious crimes, with the weight of those crimes falling hardest in places like Brownsville and

East New York. But then something strange happened. At some mysterious and critical point, the crime rate began to turn. It tipped. Within five years, murders had dropped 64.3 percent to 770 and total crimes had fallen by almost half to 355,893. In Brownsville and East New York, the sidewalks filled up again, the bicycles came back, and old folks reappeared on the stoops. "There was a time when it wasn't uncommon to hear rapid fire, like you would hear somewhere in the jungle in Vietnam," says Inspector Edward Messadri, who commands the police precinct in Brownsville. "I don't hear the gunfire anymore."[1]

The New York City police will tell you that what happened in New York was that the city's policing strategies dramatically improved. Criminologists point to the decline of the crack trade and the aging of the population. Economists, meanwhile, say that the gradual improvement in the city's economy over the course of the 1990s had the effect of employing those who might otherwise have become criminals. These are the conventional explanations for the rise and fall of social problems, but in the end none is any more satisfying than the statement that kids in the East Village caused the Hush Puppies revival. The changes in the drug trade, the population, and the economy are all long-term trends, happening all over the country. They don't explain why crime plunged in New York City so much more than in other cities around the country, and they don't explain why it all happened in such an extraordinarily short time. As for the improvements made by the police, they are important too. But there is a puzzling gap between the scale of the changes in policing and the size of the effect on places like Brownsville and East New York. After all, crime didn't just slowly ebb in New York as conditions gradually improved. It plummeted. How can a change in a handful of economic and social indices cause murder rates to fall by two-thirds in five years?

II

The idea of the Tipping Point is very simple. It is that the best way to understand the emergence of fashion trends, the ebb and flow of crime waves, or, for that matter, the transformation of unknown books into bestsellers, or the rise of teenage smoking, or the phenomena of word of mouth, or any number of the other mysterious changes that mark everyday life is to think of them as epidemics. Ideas and products and messages and behaviors spread just like viruses do.

[1]For a good summary of New York City crime statistics, see: Michael Massing, "The Blue Revolution," in the *New York Review of Books,* November 19, 1998, pp. 32–34. There is another good discussion of the anomalous nature of the New York crime drop in William Bratton and William Andrews, "What We've Learned About Policing," in *City Journal,* Spring 1999, p. 25.

The rise of Hush Puppies and the fall of New York's crime rate are textbook examples of epidemics in action. Although they may sound as if they don't have very much in common, they share a basic, underlying pattern. First of all, they are clear examples of contagious behavior. No one took out an advertisement and told people that the traditional Hush Puppies were cool and they should start wearing them. Those kids simply wore the shoes when they went to clubs or cafes or walked the streets of downtown New York, and in so doing exposed other people to their fashion sense. They infected them with the Hush Puppies "virus."

The crime decline in New York surely happened the same way. It wasn't that some huge percentage of would-be murderers suddenly sat up in 1993 and decided not to commit any more crimes. Nor was it that the police managed magically to intervene in a huge percentage of situations that would otherwise have turned deadly. What happened is that the small number of people in the small number of situations in which the police or the new social forces had some impact started behaving very differently, and that behavior somehow spread to other would-be criminals in similar situations. Somehow a large number of people in New York got "infected" with an anti-crime virus in a short time.

The second distinguishing characteristic of these two examples is that   10
in both cases little changes had big effects. All of the possible reasons for why New York's crime rate dropped are changes that happened at the margin; they were incremental changes. The crack trade leveled off. The population got a little older. The police force got a little better. Yet the effect was dramatic. So too with Hush Puppies. How many kids are we talking about who began wearing the shoes in downtown Manhattan? Twenty? Fifty? One hundred—at the most? Yet their actions seem to have single-handedly started an international fashion trend.

Finally, both changes happened in a hurry. They didn't build steadily and slowly. It is instructive to look at a chart of the crime rate in New York City from, say, the mid-1960s to the late 1990s. It looks like a giant arch. In 1965, there were 200,000 crimes in the city and from that point on the number begins a sharp rise, doubling in two years and continuing almost unbroken until it hits 650,000 crimes a year in the mid-1970s. It stays steady at that level for the next two decades, before plunging downward in 1992 as sharply as it rose thirty years earlier. Crime did not taper off. It didn't gently decelerate. It hit a certain point and jammed on the brakes.

These three characteristics—one, contagiousness; two, the fact that little causes can have big effects; and three, that change happens not gradually but at one dramatic moment—are the same three principles that define how measles moves through a grade-school classroom or the flu attacks every winter. Of the three, the third trait—the idea that epidemics can rise or fall in one dramatic moment—is the most important, because it is the principle that makes sense of the first two and that permits the greatest insight into why modern change happens the way it does. The name given to that one dramatic moment in an epidemic when everything can change all at once is the Tipping Point.

III

A world that follows the rules of epidemics is a very different place from the world we think we live in now. Think, for a moment, about the concept of contagiousness. If I say that word to you, you think of colds and the flu or perhaps something very dangerous like HIV or Ebola. We have, in our minds, a very specific, biological notion of what contagiousness means. But if there can be epidemics of crime or epidemics of fashion, there must be all kinds of things just as contagious as viruses. Have you ever thought about yawning, for instance? Yawning is a surprisingly powerful act. Just because you read the word "yawning" in the previous two sentences — and the two additional "yawns" in this sentence — a good number of you will probably yawn within the next few minutes. Even as I'm writing this, I've yawned twice. If you're reading this in a public place, and you've just yawned, chances are that a good proportion of everyone who saw you yawn is now yawning too, and a good proportion of the people watching the people who watched you yawn are now yawning as well, and on and on, in an ever-widening, yawning circle.[2]

Yawning is incredibly contagious. I made some of you reading this yawn simply by writing the word "yawn." The people who yawned when they saw you yawn, meanwhile, were infected by the sight of you yawning — which is a second kind of contagion. They might even have yawned it they only heard you yawn, because yawning is also aurally contagious: if you play an audiotape of a yawn to blind people, they'll yawn too. And finally, if you yawned as you read this, did the thought cross your mind — however unconsciously and fleetingly — that you might be tired? I suspect that for some of you it did, which means that yawns can also be emotionally contagious. Simply by writing the word, I can plant a feeling in your mind. Can the flu virus do that? Contagiousness, in other words, is an unexpected property of all kinds of things, and we have to remember that, if we are to recognize and diagnose epidemic change.

The second of the principles of epidemics — that little changes can   15 somehow have big effects — is also a fairly radical notion. We are, as hu-

---

[2]The leader in research on yawning is Robert Provine, a psychologist at the University of Maryland. Among his papers on the subject are:
Robert Provine, "Yawning as a Stereotyped Action Pattern and Releasing Stimulus," *Ethology* (1983), vol. 72, pp. 109–122.
Robert Provine, "Contagious Yawning and Infant Imitation," *Bulletin of the Psychonomic Society* (1989), vol. 27, no. 2, pp. 125–126.

mans, heavily socialized to make a kind of rough approximation between cause and effect. If we want to communicate a strong emotion, if
we want to convince someone that, say, we love them, we realize that we
need to speak passionately and forthrightly. If we want to break bad
news to someone, we lower our voices and choose our words carefully.
We are trained to think that what goes into any transaction or relationship or system must be directly related, in intensity and dimension, to
what comes out. Consider, for example, the following puzzle. I give you
a large piece of paper, and I ask you to fold it over once, and then take
that folded paper and fold it over again, and then again, and again, until
you have refolded the original paper 50 times. How tall do you think the
final stack is going to be? In answer to that question, most people will
fold the sheet in their mind's eye, and guess that the pile would be as
thick as a phone book or, if they're really courageous, they'll say that it
would be as tall as a refrigerator. But the real answer is that the height of
the stack would approximate the distance to the sun. And if you folded
it over one more time, the stack would be as high as the distance to the
sun and back. This is an example of what in mathematics is called a geometric progression. Epidemics are another example of geometric progression: when a virus spreads through a population, it doubles and
doubles again, until it has (figuratively) grown from a single sheet of
paper all the way to the sun in fifty steps. As human beings we have a
hard time with this kind of progression, because the end result—the effect—seems far out of proportion to the cause. To appreciate the power
of epidemics, we have to abandon this expectation about proportional-
ity. We need to prepare ourselves for the possibility that sometimes big
changes follow from small events, and that sometimes these changes can
happen very quickly.

This possibility of sudden change is at the center of the idea of the Tipping Point and might well be the hardest of all to accept. The expression
first came into popular use in the 1970s to describe the flight to the suburbs of whites living in the older cities of the American Northeast. When
the number of incoming African Americans in a particular neighborhood
reached a certain point—20 percent, say—sociologists observed that the
community would "tip": most of the remaining whites would leave almost
immediately. The Tipping Point is the moment of critical mass, the threshold, the boiling point. There was a Tipping Point for violent crime in New
York in the early 1990s, and a Tipping Point for the reemergence of Hush
Puppies, just as there is a Tipping Point for the introduction of any new
technology. Sharp introduced the first low-priced fax machine in 1984,
and sold about 80,000 of those machines in the United States in that first
year. For the next three years, businesses slowly and steadily bought more
and more faxes, until, in 1987, enough people had faxes that it made sense
for everyone to get a fax. Nineteen eighty-seven was the fax machine Tipping Point. A million machines were sold that year, and by 1989 two million new machines had gone into operation. Cellular phones have followed
the same trajectory. Through the 1990s, they got smaller and cheaper, and

service got better until 1998, when the technology hit a Tipping Point and suddenly everyone had a cell phone[3]. . . .

All epidemics have Tipping Points. Jonathan Crane, a sociologist at the University of Illinois, has looked at the effect the number of role models in a community—the professionals, managers, teachers whom the Census Bureau has defined as "high status"—has on the lives of teenagers in the same neighborhood. He found little difference in pregnancy rates or school drop-out rates in neighborhoods of between 40 and 5 percent of high-status workers. But when the number of professionals

[3]The best way to understand the Tipping Point is to imagine a hypothetical outbreak of the flu. Suppose, for example, that one summer 1,000 tourists come to Manhattan from Canada carrying an untreatable strain of twenty-four-hour virus. This strain of flu has a 2 percent infection rate, which is to say that one out of every 50 people who come into close contact with someone carrying it catches the bug himself. Let's say that 50 is also exactly the number of people the average Manhattanite—in the course of riding the subways and mingling with colleagues at work—comes into contact with every day. What we have, then, is a disease in equilibrium. Those 1,000 Canadian tourists pass on the virus to 1,000 new people on the day they arrive. And the next day those 1,000 newly infected people pass on the virus to another 1,000 people, just as the original 1,000 tourists who started the epidemic are returning to health. With those getting sick and those getting well so perfectly in balance, the flu chugs along at a steady but unspectacular clip through the rest of the summer and the fall.

But then comes the Christmas season. The subways and buses get more crowded with tourists and shoppers, and instead of running into an even 50 people a day, the average Manhattanite now has close contact with, say, 55 people a day. All of a sudden, the equilibrium is disrupted. The 1,000 flu carriers now run into 55,000 people a day, and at a 2 percent infection rate, that translates into 1,100 cases the following day. Those 1,100, in turn, are now passing on their virus to 55,000 people as well, so that by day three there are 1,210 Manhattanites with the flu and by day four 1,331 and by the end of the week there are nearly 2,000, and so on up, in an exponential spiral, until Manhattan has a full blown flu epidemic on its hands by Christmas Day. That moment when the average flu carrier went from running into 50 people a day to running into 55 people was the Tipping Point. It was the point at which an ordinary and stable phenomenon—a low-level flu outbreak—turned into a public health crisis. If you were to draw a graph of the progress of the Canadian flu epidemic, the Tipping Point would be the point on the graph where the line suddenly turned upward.

Tipping Points are moments of great sensitivity. Changes made right at the Tipping Point can have enormous consequences. Our Canadian flu became an epidemic when the number of New Yorkers running into a flu carrier jumped from 50 to 55 a day. But had that same small change happened in the opposite direction, if the number had dropped from 50 to 45, that change would have pushed the number of flu victims down to 478 within a week, and within a few weeks more at that rate, the Canadian flu would have vanished from Manhattan entirely. Cutting the number exposed from 70 to 65, or 65 to 60 or 60 to 55 would not have been sufficient to end the epidemic. But a change right at the Tipping Point, from 50 to 45, would.

The Tipping Point model has been described in several classic works of sociology. I suggest:

Mark Granovetter, "Threshold Models of Collective Behavior," *American Journal of Sociology* (1978), vol. 83, pp. 1420–1443.

Mark Granovetter and R. Soong, "Threshold Models of Diffusion and Collective Behavior," *Journal of Mathematical Sociology* (1983), vol. 9, pp. 165–179.

Thomas Schelling, "Dynamic Models of Segregation," *Journal of Mathematical Sociology* (1971), vol. I, pp. 143–186.

Thomas Schelling, *Micromotives and Macrobehavior* (New York: W. W. Norton, 1978).

Jonathan Crane, "The Epidemic Theory of Ghettos and Neighborhood Effects on Dropping Out and Teenage Childbearing," *American Journal of Sociology* (1989), vol. 95, no. 5, pp. 1226–1259.

dropped below 5 percent, the problems exploded. For black schoolchildren, for example, as the percentage of high-status workers falls just 2.2 percentage points—from 5.6 percent to 3.4 percent—drop-out rates more than double. At the same Tipping Point, the rates of childbearing for teenaged girls—which barely move at all up to that point—nearly double. We assume, intuitively, that neighborhoods and social problems decline in some kind of steady progression. But sometimes they may not decline steadily at all; at the Tipping Point, schools can lose control of their students, and family life can disintegrate all at once.

I remember once as a child seeing our family's puppy encounter snow for the first time. He was shocked and delighted and overwhelmed, wagging his tail nervously, sniffing about in this strange, fluffy substance, whimpering with the mystery of it all. It wasn't much colder on the morning of his first snowfall than it had been the evening before. It might have been 34 degrees the previous evening, and now it was 31 degrees. Almost nothing had changed, in other words, yet—and this was the amazing thing—everything had changed. Rain had become something entirely different. Snow! We are all, at heart, gradualists, our expectations set by the steady passage of time. But the world of the Tipping Point is a place where the unexpected becomes expected, where radical change is more than possibility. It is—contrary to all our expectations—a certainty. . . .

The Reader's Presence

1. Gladwell's essay demonstrates in a nutshell nearly every method of explaining a phenomenon: classification, exemplification, causation, comparison and contrast, definition, and analogy. Go through the essay and identify an instance of the author's use of each method. Which method do you think plays the most important role in this essay?

2. Gladwell uses the idea of a "tipping point" to explain a variety of social trends and behavior. Can you think of other examples he might have used to illustrate the way the theory works? Can you think of counterexamples—trends or behavior that can't be explained by the idea of a tipping point?

3. Can you apply the notion of a tipping point to other phenomena described in Part IV of this book? For example, can it help explain the behavior described in Amy Cunningham's essay "Why Women Smile" (page 335)—is smiling, like yawning, "contagious"? How might the theory illuminate the bizarre behavior chronicled in Kai Erikson's "The Witches of Salem Village" (page 369)? Was what happened in Salem an "epidemic" that can be explained by the tipping point idea? Consider the notion of a tipping point in relation to John Hollander's essay "Mess" (page 419): How does a neat room turn into a mess—is it a gradual process or is there a tipping point?

54

Mary Gordon

The Ghosts of Ellis Island

Mary Gordon (b. 1949) is a professor of English at Barnard College and frequently contributes articles and short stories to Harper's, Ladies' Home Journal, Virginia Quarterly Review, *and the* Atlantic Monthly. *Since her first novel,* Final Payments *(1978), earned her critical success, Gordon has published numerous books, including* The Company of Women *(1981),* The Other Side *(1989),* The Shadow Man *(1996),* Spending: A Utopian Divertimento *(1998), and* Reflections on Geography and Identity *(2000). "The Ghosts of Ellis Island" originally appeared in the* New York Times *in 1985.*

I once sat in a hotel in Bloomsbury trying to have breakfast alone. A Russian with a habit of compulsively licking his lips asked if he could join me. I was afraid to say no; I thought it might be bad for détente. He explained to me that he was a linguist, and that he always liked to talk to Americans to see if he could make any connection between their speech and their ethnic background. When I told him about my mixed ancestry—my mother is Irish and Italian, my father a Lithuanian Jew—he began jumping up and down in his seat, rubbing his hands together, and licking his lips even more frantically:

"Ah," he said, "so you are really somebody who comes from what is called the boiling pot of America." Yes, I told him, yes I was, but I quickly rose to leave. I thought it would be too hard to explain to him the relation of the boiling potters to the main course, and I wanted to get to the British Museum. I told him that the only thing I could think of that united people whose backgrounds, histories, and points of view were utterly diverse was that their people had landed at a place called Ellis Island.

I didn't tell him that Ellis Island was the only American landmark I'd ever visited. How could I describe to him the estrangement I'd always felt from the kind of traveler who visits shrines to America's past greatness, those rebuilt forts with muskets behind glass and sabers mounted on the walls and gift shops selling maple sugar candy in the shape of Indian headdresses, those reconstructed villages with tables set for fifty and the

Paul Revere silver gleaming? All that Americana—Plymouth Rock, Gettysburg, Mount Vernon, Valley Forge—it all inhabits for me a zone of blurred abstraction with far less hold on my imagination than the Bastille or Hampton Court. I suppose I've always known that my uninterest in it contains a large component of the willed: I am American, and those places purport to be my history. But they are not mine.

Ellis Island is, though; it's the one place I can be sure my people are connected to. And so I made a journey there to find my history, like any Rotarian traveling in his Winnebago to Antietam to find his. I had become part of that humbling democracy of people looking in some site for a past that has grown unreal. The monument I traveled to was not, however, a tribute to some old glory. The minute I set foot upon the island I could feel all that it stood for: insecurity, obedience, anxiety, dehumanization, the terrified and careful deference of the displaced. I hadn't traveled to the Battery and boarded a ferry across from the Statue of Liberty to raise flags or breathe a richer, more triumphant air. I wanted to do homage to the ghosts.

I felt them everywhere, from the moment I disembarked and saw the   5
building with its high-minded brick, its hopeful little lawn, its ornamental cornices. The place was derelict when I arrived; it had not functioned for more than thirty years—almost as long as the time it had operated at full capacity as a major immigration center. I was surprised to learn what a small part of history Ellis Island had occupied. The main building was constructed in 1892, then rebuilt between 1898 and 1900 after a fire. Most of the immigrants who arrived during the latter half of the nineteenth century, mainly northern and western Europeans, landed not at Ellis Island but on the western tip of the Battery at Castle Garden, which had opened as a receiving center for immigrants in 1855.

By the 1880s the facilities at Castle Garden had grown scandalously inadequate. Officials looked for an island on which to build a new immigration center because they thought that on an island immigrants could be more easily protected from swindlers and quickly transported to railroad terminals in New Jersey. Bedloe's Island was considered, but New Yorkers were aghast at the idea of a "Babel" ruining their beautiful new treasure, "Liberty Enlightening the World." The statue's sculptor, Frédéric Auguste Bartholdi, reacted to the prospect of immigrants landing near his masterpiece in horror; he called it a "monstrous plan." So much for Emma Lazarus.

Ellis Island was finally chosen because the citizens of New Jersey petitioned the federal government to remove from the island an old naval powder magazine that they thought dangerously close to the Jersey shore. The explosives were removed; no one wanted the island for anything. It was the perfect place to build an immigration center.

I thought about the island's history as I walked into the building and made my way to the room that was the center in my imagination of the Ellis Island experience: the Great Hall. It had been made real for me in the stark, accusing photographs of Louis Hine and others who took those pictures to make a point. It was in the Great Hall that everyone had waited—waiting, always, the great vocation of the dispossessed. The room was empty, except for me and a handful of other visitors and the park ranger who showed us around. I felt myself grow insignificant in that room, with its huge semicircular windows, its air, even in dereliction, of solid and official probity.

I walked in the deathlike expansiveness of the room's disuse and tried to think of what it might have been like, filled and swarming. More than sixteen million immigrants came through that room; approximately 250,000 were rejected. Not really a large proportion, but the implications for the rejected were dreadful. For some, there was nothing to go back to, or there was certain death; for others, who left as adventurers, to return would be to adopt in local memory the fool's role, and the failure's. No wonder that the island's history includes reports of three thousand suicides.

Sometimes immigrants could pass through Ellis Island in mere hours, though for some the process took days. The particulars of the experience in the Great Hall were often influenced by the political events and attitudes on the mainland. In the 1890s and the first years of the new century, when cheap labor was needed, the newly built receiving center took in its immigrants with comparatively little question. But as the century progressed, the economy worsened, eugenics became both scientifically respectable and popular, and World War I made American xenophobia seem rooted in fact. 10

Immigration acts were passed; newcomers had to prove, besides moral correctness and financial solvency, their ability to read. Quota laws came into effect, limiting the number of immigrants from southern and eastern Europe to less than 14 percent of the total quota. Intelligence tests were biased against all non-English-speaking persons and medical examinations became increasingly strict, until the machinery of immigration nearly collapsed under its own weight. The Second Quota Law of 1924 provided that all immigrants be inspected and issued visas at American consular offices in Europe, rendering the center almost obsolete.

On the day of my visit, my mind fastened upon the medical inspections, which had always seemed to me most emblematic of the ignominy and terror the immigrants endured. The medical inspectors, sometimes dressed in uniforms like soldiers, were particularly obsessed with a disease of the eyes called trachoma, which they checked for by flipping back the immigrants' top eyelids with a hook used for buttoning gloves—a method that sometimes resulted in the transmission of the disease to healthy people. Mothers feared that if their children cried too much, their red eyes would be mistaken for a symptom of the disease and the whole family would be sent home. Those immigrants suspected of some physical disability had initials chalked on their coats. I remembered the photographs I'd seen of people standing, dumbstruck and innocent as cattle, with their manifest numbers hung around their necks and initials marked in chalk upon their coats: "E" for eye trouble, "K" for hernia, "L" for lameness, "X" for mental defects, "H" for heart disease.

I thought of my grandparents as I stood in the room; my seventeen-year-old grandmother, coming alone from Ireland in 1896, vouched for by a stranger who had found her a place as a domestic servant to some Irish who had done well. I tried to imagine the assault it all must have been for her; I've been to her hometown, a collection of farms with a main street — smaller than the athletic field of my local public school. She must have watched the New York skyline as the first- and second-class passengers were whisked off the gangplank with the most cursory of inspections while she was made to board a ferry to the new immigration center.

What could she have made of it — this buff-painted wooden structure with its towers and its blue slate roof, a place *Harper's Weekly* described as "a latter-day watering place hotel"? It would have been the first time she'd have heard people speaking something other than English. She would have mingled with people carrying baskets on their heads and eating foods unlike any she had ever seen — dark-eyed people, like the Sicilian she would marry ten years later, who came over with his family, responsible even then for his mother and sister. I don't know what they thought, my grandparents, for they were not expansive people, nor romantic; they didn't like to think of what they called "the hard times," and their trip across the ocean was the single adventurous act of lives devoted after landing to security, respectability, and fitting in.

What is the potency of Ellis Island for someone like me — an American, obviously, but one who has always felt that the country really belonged to the early settlers, that, as J. F. Powers wrote in "Morte D'Urban," it had been "handed down to them by the Pilgrims, George Washington and others, and that they were taking a risk in letting you live in it." I have never been the victim of overt discrimination; nothing I have wanted has been denied me because of the accidents of blood. But I suppose it is part of being an American to be engaged in a somewhat tiresome but always self-absorbing process of national definition. And in this process, I have found in traveling to Ellis Island an important piece of evidence that could remind me I was right to feel my differentness. Something had happened to my people on that island, a result of the eternal wrongheadedness of American protectionism and the predictabilities of simple greed. I came to the island, too, so I could tell the ghosts that I was one of them, and that I honored them — their stoicism, and their innocence, the fear that turned them inward, and their pride. I wanted to tell them that I liked them better than the Americans who made them pass through the Great Hall and stole their names and chalked their weaknesses in public on their clothing. And to tell the ghosts what I have always thought: that American history was a very classy party that was not much fun until they arrived, brought the good food, turned up the music, and taught everyone to dance.

The Reader's Presence

1. Gordon contrasts immigrant and mainstream American experiences, although nearly all present-day Americans have immigrant ancestry. How does she define *immigrant?* What imagery does she attach to the immigrant experience? How is this imagery made vivid for the reader? How do you think Gordon would wish a reader like herself to experience the essay? How do you think she would wish a mainstream American to experience the essay?

2. Gordon reveals little-known facts about the Statue of Liberty and Ellis Island. What symbolic meaning do these facts convey in terms of America's reception of immigrants? Ellis Island has since been refashioned into an impressive museum celebrating the history of immigrants in America. Does this development undercut or reinforce Gordon's opposition of official and hidden history?

3. Gordon's description of immigrants' contributions to American culture recalls Ralph Ellison's essay "What America Would Be Like without Blacks" (page 363). What sorts of contributions does Gordon credit immigrants with? In what ways are the two writers' visions of America as a "melting pot" similar? How do they differ?

55 ⸻ ⸻

Stephen Jay Gould

Sex, Drugs, Disasters, and the Extinction of Dinosaurs

Stephen Jay Gould (1941–2002) was professor of geology and zoology at Harvard and curator of invertebrate paleontology at Harvard's Museum of Comparative Zoology. He published widely on evolution and other topics and earned a reputation for making technical subjects readily comprehensible to lay readers without trivializing the material. His The Panda's Thumb *(1980) won the American Book Award, and* The Mismeasure of Man *(1981) won the National Book Critics Circle Award. Gould published over one hundred articles in scientific journals, and contributed to national magazines as well. "Sex, Drugs, Disasters, and the Extinction of Dinosaurs" appeared in* Discover *magazine in 1984. More recently, Gould wrote* Questioning the Millennium: A Rationalist's

Guide to a Precisely Arbitrary Countdown *(1997)*, Leonardo's Mountain of Clams and the Diet of Worms: Essays on Natural History *(1998)*, Rocks of Ages: Science & Religion in the Fullness of Life *(1999)*, The Lying Stones of Marrakesh *(2001)*, and The Structure of Evolutionary Theory *(2001)*. *Among many other honors and awards, he was a fellow of the National Science Foundation and the MacArthur Foundation. In 1999 Gould became president of the American Association for the Advancement of Science. John Updike comments that "Gould, in his scrupulous explication of [other scientists'] carefully wrought half-truths, abolishes the unnecessary distinction between the humanities and science, and honors the latter as a branch of humanistic thought, fallible and poetic."*

When asked if he found it difficult to write about complex scientific concepts in language that is accessible to general readers, Gould replied, "I don't see why it should be that difficult. . . . Every field has its jargon. I think scientists hide behind theirs perhaps more than people in other professions do — it's part of our mythology — but I don't think the concepts of science are intrinsically more difficult than the professional notions in any other field."

Science, in its most fundamental definition, is a fruitful mode of inquiry, not a list of enticing conclusions. The conclusions are the consequence, not the essence.

My greatest unhappiness with most popular presentations of science concerns their failure to separate fascinating claims from the methods that scientists use to establish the facts of nature. Journalists, and the public, thrive on controversial and stunning statements. But science is, basically, a way of knowing — in P. B. Medawar's apt words, "the art of the soluble." If the growing corps of popular science writers would focus on *how* scientists develop and defend those fascinating claims, they would make their greatest possible contribution to public understanding.

Consider three ideas, proposed in perfect seriousness to explain that greatest of all titillating puzzles — the extinction of dinosaurs. Since these three notions invoke the primally fascinating themes of our culture — sex, drugs, and violence — they surely reside in the category of fascinating claims. I want to show why two of them rank as silly speculation, while the other represents science at its grandest and most useful.

Science works with the testable proposals. If, after much compilation and scrutiny of data, new information continues to affirm a hypothesis, we may accept it provisionally and gain confidence as further evidence mounts. We can never be completely sure that a hypothesis is right, though we may be able to show with confidence that it is wrong. The best scientific hypotheses are also generous and expansive: They suggest extensions and implications that enlighten related, and even far distant, subjects. Simply consider how the idea of evolution has influenced virtually every intellectual field.

Useless speculation, on the other hand, is restrictive. It generates no   5
testable hypothesis, and offers no way to obtain potentially refuting evidence. Please note that I am not speaking of truth or falsity. The speculation may well be true; still, if it provides, in principle, no material for

affirmation or rejection, we can make nothing of it. It must simply stand forever as an intriguing idea. Useless speculation turns in on itself and leads nowhere; good science, containing both seeds for its potential refutation and implications for more and different testable knowledge, reaches out. But, enough preaching. Let's move on to dinosaurs, and the three proposals for their extinction.

1. *Sex:* Testes function only in a narrow range of temperature (those of mammals hang externally in a scrotal sac because internal body temperatures are too high for their proper function). A worldwide rise in temperature at the close of the Cretaceous period caused the testes of dinosaurs to stop functioning and led to their extinction by sterilization of males.
2. *Drugs:* Angiosperms (flowering plants) first evolved toward the end of the dinosaurs' reign. Many of these plants contain psychoactive agents, avoided by mammals today as a result of their bitter taste. Dinosaurs had neither means to taste the bitterness nor livers effective enough to detoxify the substances. They died of massive overdoses.
3. *Disasters:* A large comet or asteroid struck the earth some 65 million years ago, lofting a cloud of dust into the sky and blocking sunlight, thereby suppressing photosynthesis and so drastically lowering world temperatures that dinosaurs and hosts of other creatures became extinct.

Before analyzing these three tantalizing statements, we must establish a basic ground rule often violated in proposals for the dinosaurs' demise. *There is no separate problem of the extinction of dinosaurs.* Too often we divorce specific events from their wider contexts and systems of cause and effect. The fundamental fact of dinosaur extinction is its synchrony with the demise of so many other groups across a wide range of habitats, from terrestrial to marine.

The history of life has been punctuated by brief episodes of mass extinction. A recent analysis by University of Chicago paleontologists Jack Sepkoski and Dave Raup, based on the best and most exhaustive tabulation of data ever assembled, shows clearly that five episodes of mass dying stand well above the "background" extinctions of normal times (when we consider all mass extinctions, large and small, they seem to fall in a regular 26-million-year cycle). The Cretaceous debacle, occurring 65 million years ago and separating the Mesozoic and Cenozoic eras of our geological time scale, ranks prominently among the five. Nearly all the marine plankton (single-celled floating creatures) died with geological suddenness; among marine invertebrates, nearly 15 percent of all families perished, including many previously dominant groups, especially the ammonites (relatives of squids in coiled shells). On land, the dinosaurs disappeared after more than 100 million years of unchallenged domination.

In this context, speculations limited to dinosaurs alone ignore the larger phenomenon. We need a coordinated explanation for a system of events that includes the extinction of dinosaurs as one component. Thus it makes little sense, though it may fuel our desire to view mammals as inevitable inheritors of the earth, to guess that dinosaurs died because small mammals ate their eggs (a perennial favorite among untestable speculations). It seems most unlikely that some disaster peculiar to dinosaurs befell these massive beasts—and that the debacle happened to strike just when one of history's five great dyings had enveloped the earth for completely different reasons.

The testicular theory, an old favorite from the 1940s, had its root in an interesting and thoroughly respectable study of temperature tolerances in the American alligator, published in the staid *Bulletin of the American Museum of Natural History* in 1946 by three experts on living and fossil reptiles—E. H. Colbert, my own first teacher in paleontology; R. B. Cowles; and C. M. Bogert.

The first sentence of their summary reveals a purpose beyond alligators: "This report describes an attempt to infer the reactions of extinct reptiles, especially the dinosaurs, to high temperatures as based upon reactions observed in the modern alligator." They studied, by rectal thermometry, the body temperatures of alligators under changing conditions of heating and cooling. (Well, let's face it, you wouldn't want to try sticking a thermometer under a 'gator's tongue.) The predictions under test go way back to an old theory first stated by Galileo in the 1630s—the unequal scaling of surfaces and volumes. As an animal, or an object, grows (provided its shape doesn't change), surface areas must increase more slowly than volumes—since surfaces get larger as length squared, while volumes increase much more rapidly, as length cubed. Therefore, small animals have high ratios of surface to volume, while large animals cover themselves with relatively little surface.

Among cold-blooded animals lacking any physiological mechanism for keeping their temperatures constant, small creatures have a hell of a time keeping warm—because they lose so much heat through their relatively large surfaces. On the other hand, large animals, with their relatively small surfaces, may lose heat so slowly that, once warm, they may maintain effectively constant temperatures against ordinary fluctuations of climate. (In fact, the resolution of the "hot-blooded dinosaur" controversy that burned so brightly a few years back may simply be that, while large dinosaurs possessed no physiological mechanism for constant temperature, and were not therefore warm-blooded in the technical sense, their large size and relatively small surface area kept them warm.)

Colbert, Cowles, and Bogert compared the warming rates of small and large alligators. As predicted, the small fellows heated up (and cooled down) more quickly. When exposed to a warm sun, a tiny 50-gram (1.76-ounce) alligator heated up one degree Celsius every minute and a half,

10

while a large alligator, 260 times bigger at 13,000 grams (28.7 pounds), took seven and a half minutes to gain a degree. Extrapolating up to an adult 10-ton dinosaur, they concluded that a one-degree rise in body temperature would take eighty-six hours. If large animals absorb heat so slowly (through their relatively small surfaces), they will also be unable to shed any excess heat gained when temperatures rise above a favorable level.

The authors then guessed that large dinosaurs lived at or near their optimum temperatures; Cowles suggested that a rise in global temperatures just before the Cretaceous extinction caused the dinosaurs to heat up beyond their optimal tolerance—and, being so large, they couldn't shed the unwanted heat. (In a most unusual statement within a scientific paper, Colbert and Bogert then explicitly disavowed this speculative extension of their empirical work on alligators.) Cowles conceded that this excess heat probably wasn't enough to kill or even to enervate the great beasts, but since testes often function only within a narrow range of temperature, he proposed that this global rise might have sterilized all the males, causing extinction by natural contraception.

The overdose theory has recently been supported by UCLA psychiatrist Ronald K. Siegel. Siegel has gathered, he claims, more than 2,000 records of animals who, when given access, administer various drugs to themselves—from a mere swig of alcohol to massive doses of the big H. Elephants will swill the equivalent of twenty beers at a time, but do not like alcohol in concentrations greater than 7 percent. In a silly bit of anthropocentric speculation, Siegel states that "elephants drink, perhaps, to forget . . . the anxiety produced by shrinking rangeland and the competition for food."

Since fertile imaginations can apply almost any hot idea to the extinction of dinosaurs, Siegel found a way. Flowering plants did not evolve until late in the dinosaurs' reign. These plants also produced an array of aromatic, amino-acid-based alkaloids—the major group of psychoactive agents. Most mammals are "smart" enough to avoid these potential poisons. The alkaloids simply don't taste good (they are bitter); in any case, we mammals have livers happily supplied with the capacity to detoxify them. But, Siegel speculates, perhaps dinosaurs could neither taste the bitterness nor detoxify the substances once ingested. He recently told members of the American Psychological Association: "I'm not suggesting that all dinosaurs OD'd on plant drugs, but it certainly was a factor." He also argued that death by overdose may help explain why so many dinosaur fossils are found in contorted positions. (Do not go gentle into that good night.)

Extraterrestrial catastrophes have long pedigrees in the popular literature of extinction, but the subject exploded again in 1979, after a long lull, when the father-son, physicist-geologist team of Luis and Walter Alvarez proposed that an asteroid, some 10 km in diameter, struck the earth 65 million years ago (comets, rather than asteroids, have since gained favor. Good science is self-corrective).

The force of such a collision would be immense, greater by far than the megatonnage of all the world's nuclear weapons. In trying to reconstruct a scenario that would explain the simultaneous dying of dinosaurs on land and so many creatures in the sea, the Alvarezes proposed that a gigantic dust cloud, generated by particles blown aloft in the impact, would so darken the earth that photosynthesis would cease and temperatures drop precipitously. (Rage, rage against the dying of the light.) The single-celled photosynthetic oceanic plankton, with life cycles measured in weeks, would perish outright, but land plants might survive through the dormancy of their seeds (land plants were not much affected by the Cretaceous extinction, and any adequate theory must account for the curious pattern of differential survival). Dinosaurs would die by starvation and freezing; small, warm-blooded mammals, with more modest requirements for food and better regulation of body temperature, would squeak through. "Let the bastards freeze in the dark," as bumper stickers of our chauvinistic neighbors in sunbelt states proclaimed several years ago during the Northeast's winter oil crisis.

All three theories, testicular malfunction, psychoactive overdosing, and asteroidal zapping, grab our attention mightily. As pure phenomenology, they rank about equally high on any hit parade of primal fascination. Yet one represents expansive science, the others restrictive and untestable speculation. The proper criterion lies in evidence and methodology; we must probe behind the superficial fascination of particular claims.

How could we possibly decide whether the hypothesis of testicular frying is right or wrong? We would have to know things that the fossil record cannot provide. What temperatures were optimal for dinosaurs? Could they avoid the absorption of excess heat by staying in the shade, or in caves? At what temperatures did their testicles cease to function? Were late Cretaceous climates ever warm enough to drive the internal temperatures of dinosaurs close to this ceiling? Testicles simply don't fossilize, and how could we infer their temperature tolerances even if they did? In short, Cowles's hypothesis is only an intriguing speculation leading nowhere. The most damning statement against it appeared right in the conclusion of Colbert, Cowles, and Bogert's paper, when they admitted: "It is difficult to advance any definite arguments against the hypothesis." My statement may seem paradoxical—isn't a hypothesis really good if you can't devise any arguments against it? Quite the contrary. It is simply untestable and unusable.

Siegel's overdosing has even less going for it. At least Cowles extrapolated his conclusion from some good data on alligators. And he didn't completely violate the primary guideline of siting dinosaur extinction in the context of a general mass dying—for rise in temperature could be the root cause of a general catastrophe, zapping dinosaurs by testicular malfunction and different groups for other reasons. But Siegel's speculation cannot touch the extinction of ammonites or oceanic plankton (diatoms

20

make their own food with good sweet sunlight; they don't OD on the chemicals of terrestrial plants). It is simply a gratuitous, attention-grabbing guess. It cannot be tested, for how can we know what dinosaurs tasted and what their livers could do? Livers don't fossilize any better than testicles.

The hypothesis doesn't even make any sense in its own context. An-giosperms were in full flower ten million years before dinosaurs went the way of all flesh. Why did it take so long? As for the pains of a chemical death recorded in contortions of fossils, I regret to say (or rather I'm pleased to note for the dinosaurs' sake) that Siegel's knowledge of geology must be a bit deficient: muscles contract after death and geological strata rise and fall with motions of the earth's crust after burial—more than enough reason to distort a fossil's pristine appearance.

The impact story, on the other hand, has a sound basis in evidence. It can be tested, extended, refined, and, if wrong, disproved. The Alvarezes did not just construct an arresting guess for public consumption. They proposed their hypothesis after laborious geochemical studies with Frank Asaro and Helen Michael had revealed a massive increase of iridium in rocks deposited right at the time of extinction. Iridium, a rare metal of the platinum group, is virtually absent from indigenous rocks of the earth's crust; most of our iridium arrives on extraterrestrial objects that strike the earth.

The Alverez hypothesis bore immediate fruit. Based originally on evidence from two European localities, it led geochemists throughout the world to examine other sediments of the same age. They found abnormally high amounts of iridium everywhere—from continental rocks of the western United States to deep sea cores from the South Atlantic.

Cowles proposed his testicular hypothesis in the mid-1940s. Where has it gone since then? Absolutely nowhere, because scientists can do nothing with it. The hypothesis must stand as a curious appendage to a solid study of alligators. Siegel's overdose scenario will also win a few press notices and fade into oblivion. The Alvarezes' asteroid falls into a different category altogether, and much of the popular commentary has missed this essential distinction by focusing on the impact and its attendant results, and forgetting what really matters to a scientist—the iridium. If you talk just about asteroids, dust, and darkness, you tell stories no better and no more entertaining than fried testicles or terminal trips. It is the iridium—the source of testable evidence—that counts and forges the crucial distinction between speculation and science.

The proof, to twist a phrase, lies in the doing. Cowles's hypothesis has generated nothing in thirty-five years. Since its proposal in 1979, the Alvarez hypothesis has spawned hundreds of studies, a major conference, and attendant publications. Geologists are fired up. They are looking for iridium at all other extinction boundaries. Every week exposes a new wrinkle in the scientific press. Further evidence that the Cretaceous iridium represents extraterrestrial impact and not indigenous volcanism continues to accumulate. As I revise this essay in November 1984 (this paragraph will be out of date when the book is published),[1] new data include chemical "signatures" of other isotopes indicating unearthly provenance, glass spherules of a size and sort produced by impact and not by volcanic eruptions, and high-pressure varieties of silica formed (so far as we know) only under the tremendous shock of impact.

My point is simply this: Whatever the eventual outcome (I suspect it will be positive), the Alvarez hypothesis is exciting, fruitful science because it generates tests, provides us with things to do, and expands outward. We are having fun, battling back and forth, moving toward a resolution, and extending the hypothesis beyond its original scope.

As just one example of the unexpected, distant cross-fertilization that good science engenders, the Alvarez hypothesis made a major contribution to a theme that has riveted public attention in the past few months — so-called nuclear winter. In a speech delivered in April 1982, Luis Alvarez calculated the energy that a ten-kilometer asteroid would release on impact. He compared such an explosion with a full nuclear exchange and implied that all-out atomic war might unleash similar consequences.

This theme of impact leading to massive dust clouds and falling temperatures formed an important input to the decision of Carl Sagan and a group of colleagues to model the climatic consequences of nuclear holocaust. Full nuclear exchange would probably generate the same kind of dust cloud and darkening that may have wiped out the dinosaurs. Temperatures would drop precipitously and agriculture might become impossible. Avoidance of nuclear war is fundamentally an ethical and political imperative, but we must know the factual consequences to make firm judgments. I am heartened by a final link across disciplines and deep concerns — another criterion, by the way, of science at its best.[2] A recognition of the very phenomenon that made our evolution possible by exterminating the previously dominant dinosaurs and clearing a way for the evolution of large mammals, including us, might actually help to save us from joining those magnificent beasts in contorted poses among the strata of the earth.

The Reader's Presence

1. Although the title of Gould's essay focuses on the extinction of dinosaurs, his overriding interest is in demonstrating the way science works, and his purpose is to make that process fully accessible and understandable to the general public. Where does

---

[1]**The Flamingo's Smile** (1985), in which Gould collected this essay. — EDS.
[2]This quirky connection so tickles my fancy that I break my own strict rule about eliminating redundancies from [this essay]. . . .

he lay out this central claim, and how does he demonstrate, clarify, and complicate it as his essay proceeds?

2. Reread Gould's essay, with special attention to his use of tone, diction, syntax, and metaphor. How does he use these compositional strategies to make information accessible to his readers? Point to passages where Gould uses the diction and syntax of a serious scientist. When—and with what effects—does his prose sound more colloquial? Does his tone remain consistent throughout the essay? If not, when and how does it change? With what effects?

3. What distinctions does Gould draw among "testable proposals," "intriguing ideas," and "useless speculation?" What features of each does he identify? How does Gould encourage critical thinking in his reader? Compare his tactics to those of K. C. Cole who, in "Calculated Risks" (page 327), is similarly interested in teaching science to the general reader. Where does each writer use humor to "translate" for the reader facts that might otherwise seem arcane?

56

Jack Hitt

The Hidden Life of SUVs

Jack Hitt, born in 1957, is a contributing writer for the New York Times, Harper's *magazine,* GQ, *and* National Public Radio. *He has written widely on contemporary American life, and is the author of* Off the Road: A Modern-Day Walk Down the Pilgrim's Route into Spain *(1995). Hitt has won many awards and garnered a wide readership for his sharp, observant, and often irreverent style. "The Hidden Life of SUVs" was originally published in* Mother Jones *in July/August 1999.*

What's in a name? What do you make of a passenger vehicle called a Bronco?

Or one dubbed a Cherokee? How about a Wrangler? Are they just chrome-plated expressions of sublimated testosterone flooding the highways? Check out the herd that grazes the average car lot these days: Blazer, Tracker, Yukon, Navigator, Tahoe, Range Rover, Explorer, Mountaineer,

Denali, Expedition, Discovery, Bravada. Besides signaling that we're not Civic or Galant, they indicate there's something else going on here.

These are, of course, all names of sport utility vehicles, the miracle that has resurrected Motown. Think back to the dark days of the previous decade when the Japanese auto industry had nearly buried Detroit. In 1981, only a relative handful of four-wheel-drives traveled the road, and the phrase "sport utility vehicle" hadn't entered the language. Today, they number more than 14 million, and that figure is growing fast. If you include pickups and vans, then quasi trucks now constitute about half of all the vehicles sold in America. Half. They're rapidly displacing cars on the highways of our new unbraking economy.

Go to any car lot and jawbone with a salesman, and you'll find that big is once again better. Any savvy dealer (clutching his copy of Zig Ziglar's *Ziglar on Selling*) will try to talk you up to one of the latest behemoths, which have bloated to such Brobdingnagian[1] dimensions as to have entered the realm of the absurd.

Ford, in fact, unveiled a new monster, the Excursion [in 1999]. With a corporate straight face, its literature touted as selling points that the Excursion is "less than 7 feet tall . . . and less than 20 feet long" and is "more fuel efficient . . . than two average full-size sedans."   5

The Big Berthas have even spawned new vocabulary words. The biggest of the big, for instance, can no longer fit comfortably in a standard-size garage or the average parking space. So salesmen will often sell you on one of the "smaller" SUVs by praising its "garage-ability."

What, then, explains the inexorable advance of these giant SUVs into our lives? Why do we want cars that are, in fact, high-clearance trucks with four-wheel drive, an optional winch, and what amounts to a cow-catcher?

The answer, in part, lies in the vehicles themselves. Cars are not fickle fashions. They are the most expensive and visible purchases in an economy drenched in matters of status and tricked out with hidden meanings.

Some people will tell you that the shift from car to truck can be explained simply: We Americans are getting, um, bigger in the beam. We aren't comfortable in those Camrys, so we trade up to a vehicle we can sit in without feeling scrunched. Here's a new buzzword for Ziglar disciples: fatassability.

But I think the key is found not so much in their size or expense (although both keep ballooning) but in those ersatz Western names. The   10 other day, I saw an acquaintance of mine in a boxy steed called a Durango. Say it out loud for me: "Durango." Can you get the syllables off your tongue without irony? In the post-*Seinfeld* era, can anyone say Durango without giving it an Elaine Benes enunciation at every syllable? Doo-RANG-Go.

---

[1]**Brobdingnagian:** Gigantic; the term derives from *Brobdingnag,* the land of giants in Jonathan Swift's *Gulliver's Travels* (1726). — EDS.

The true irony comes from the fact that this thoroughly market-researched word no longer has any core meaning. No one comprehends its denotation (Colorado town) but only its vague connotations (rugged individualism, mastery over the wilderness, cowboy endurance). The word does not pin down meaning so much as conjure up images.

These names are only the end product of the intense buyer-profiling that the car companies and the marketing firms continuously carry out. By the time they make it to the lot, these cars are streamlined Frankensteinian concoctions of our private anxieties and desires. We consumers don't so much shop for one of these SUVs as they shop for us.

A typical focus-group study might be one like the "cluster analysis" conducted by college students for Washington, D.C.–area car dealers in 1994 and reported in *Marketing Tools*. The analysts coordinated numerous databases, mail surveys, and census information to profile the typical "Bill and Barb Blazers," whose consumer apprehensions can shift from block to block, but can be pinpointed down to the four-digit appendix on the old zip code.

Each Bill and Barb then got tagged as "Young Suburbia" or "Blue-Collar Nursery" or "Urban Gentry." Translation, respectively: "college-educated, upwardly mobile white" or "middle-class, small-town" or "educated black" people. The students next identified what images spoke to the underlying appeal of an SUV for each group (prestige, child space, weekend leisure). Then they developed targeted ads to run in the media most favored by each group: the *Wall Street Journal, National Geographic,* Black Entertainment Television.

Many of the ads they developed were directed at women. For example, the one meant for upscale homeowners depicted a "woman architect standing next to her four-door [Blazer] at a Washington-area construction site" and "conveyed her professional leadership in a city with one of the highest rates of labor force participation for women."

Sport utility vehicles are quickly becoming women's cars. In fact, current statistics show that 40 percent of all SUV sales are to women, and the proportion is growing. (More men, on the other hand, are buying bigger, tougher pickup trucks.) But one wonders what's going on in the mind of that female architect or that soccer mom, high above the world in her soundproof, tinted-glass SUV, chatting on her cellular phone as she steers her mobile fortress down the street.

When GMC decided to launch the Denali (an SUV named for the Alaskan mountain), the auto-trade papers discussed the subtleties of that outdoorsy name: Even though most buyers "will never venture into territory any less trampled than the local country club parking lot," wrote Ward's *Auto World*, "the important goal of the Denali marketing hype is to plant the image in customers' minds that they can conquer rugged terrain. The metaphor of Alaska is particularly apt because SUVs, especially the larger of the species, depend on the myth that we have new frontiers yet to pave. Perhaps we're trying to tame a different

15

kind of wilderness. Indeed, in an age of gated communities the SUV is the perfect transportation shelter to protect us from fears both real and imagined."

In one focus group, female drivers confessed they hesitated even to exit the interstate "because they are afraid of what they are going to find on some surface streets."

G. Clotaire Rapaille, a French medical anthropologist and student of the consumer mind, practices a more advanced marketing technique called "archetype research." In one session he has consumers lie on the floor and lulls them into a relaxed alpha state with soothing music. Then he asks them to free-associate from images of different vehicle designs and write stories about what they hoped the design would become. Overwhelmingly, Rapaille told the *Wall Street Journal,* his participants had the same reaction: "It's a jungle out there. It's Mad Max. People want to kill me, rape me. Give me a big thing like a tank."

More and more, SUVs give us that tanklike security, and part of the   20 feeling derives from their literal altitude. Down there is the old working class, the new peasants who haven't figured out how to snatch a six-figure income out of our roaring economy—the little people who don't own a single Fidelity fund. There's a brutal Darwinian selection at work: They huddle down in their wretched Escorts and their Metros—not merely because they are poor but because they deserve to be.

These are the new savages: people who drive cars. They scrape and fetch about in their tiny compacts, scuttling along on surface streets. But above it all, in their gleaming, skyscraping vehicles, is the new high society—the ambitious, the exurban pioneers, the downtown frontiersmen.

It's been said that the most distinctive feature of the American character is that we continually define ourselves as pilgrims facing a new frontier. In their darkest hearts, the members of the new-money bourgeoisie have convinced themselves that we live in an unforgiving wilderness of marauders and brutes. The hidden meaning of our new conveyances can be found right on the surface. Once upon a time, Trailblazers, Explorers, and Trackers tamed the Wild West. Now, through the sorcery of focus groups, the bull-market gentry have brought the Pathfinders and Mountaineers back into their lives in the belief that they need to conquer the savage land one more time.

The Reader's Presence

1. In his discussion of the marketing behind the name Durango, Hitt remarks: "No one comprehends its *denotation* (Colorado town) but only its vague *connotations*" (paragraph 11, emphasis added). How do connotation and denotation differ? Select five of the

other SUVs Hitt mentions and list the denotations and connotations of each. Which is more important to advertising: denotation or connotation? Why?

2. What does Hitt believe accounts for the success of SUVs? Is it merely their names? How are their names connected to American cultural values and myths? What are some of the myths that help sell SUVs to the American public?

3. Although the exchange occurred nearly half a century before Jack Hitt made his observation about SUVs, how does the correspondence between the poet Marianne Moore and the Ford Motor Company that follows reinforce Hitt's remarks? What issues remain the same? What do you find has changed?

THE WRITER AT WORK

Marianne Moore Assists the Ford Motor Company*

Catchy car names used for marketing purposes didn't begin with the production of SUVs. Almost from the beginning of the automobile industry, manufacturers tried to give their cars names that would appeal to the buying impulses of the American public. These suggestive names would become part of the total marketing package, and many were highly successful: the Ford Mustang and Thunderbird, the Pontiac Le Mans and GTO, the Dodge Dart. In 1955, desperately trying to come up with a compelling name "for a rather important new series of cars," the Ford Motor Company approached the famous American poet, Marianne Moore (1887–1972) asking if she could—given her enormous verbal talent—help the company out. Moore, known for her eccentricities and her love of baseball, had achieved national celebrity as a leading poet of the mid-twentieth century, and Ford contacted her with the idea that someone so gifted with words would be the ideal person to come up with the appropriate name for a new automobile.

The "poetic process" was begun when the head of Ford's Special Products Division wrote Moore in 1955, stating: ". . . we find ourselves with a problem which, strangely enough, is more in the field of words and the fragile meaning of words than in car-making. And we just wonder whether you might be intrigued with it sufficiently to lend us a hand." Over a period of more than one year, Marianne Moore wrote back such suggestions as *The Ford Silver Sword; Hurricane Hirundo; Hurricane Accipiter; The Impeccable; The Resilient Bullet; The Intelligent Whale; Mongoose Civique; Thunder Crester; Pastelogram; Varsity Stroke; Astranaut;* and *Andante con Moto.* Finally, the inspiration ended with *Utopian Turtletop.*

---

*This synopsis of correspondence between the poet Marianne Moore and the Ford Motor Company was written by the editors of this book. Readers can find the original letters reprinted in their entirety in *The Marianne Moore Reader* (Viking Press, 1961).—EDS.

In November of 1956, the head of the Special Products Division wrote Moore to say that the company had finally selected from over 6,000 candidates a name for the new automobile: "It fails somewhat of the resonance, gaiety, and zest we were seeking. But it has a personal dignity and meaning to many of us here. Our name, dear Miss Moore, is—*Edsel*. I hope you will understand."

Introduced in 1958, the *Edsel*—named after the only child of Ford Motor Company founder Henry Ford, later appointed company president in 1919—would soon become one of the automobile industry's most famous flops. Today, however, a vintage 1958 *Edsel Convertible* in good running condition could fetch as much as $65,000.

57

Linda Hogan

Dwellings

The writer and educator Linda Hogan was born in Colorado in 1947. A member of the Chickasaw nation, she is active in Native American communities and in environmental politics. Hogan has published essays, plays, short stories, and many volumes of poetry, including most recently The Book of Medicines *(1993). Her novels* Mean Spirit *(1990) and* Solar Storms *(1995) have been celebrated for their complex and compelling representation of Native Americans. Hogan's interest in narrative and the natural environment are represented in the essay included here, which appears in her book* Dwellings: Reflections on the Natural World *(1995). Her most recent publications include a novel,* Power *(1998),* Intimate Nature: The Bond between Women and Animals *(1997), which she coedited, and a memoir,* The Woman Who Watches over the World *(2001). She has taught at the University of Minnesota and is currently professor of English at the University of Colorado at Boulder.*

Hogan has said, "My writing comes from and goes back to the community, both the human and the global community. I am interested in the deepest questions, those of spirit, of shelter, of growth and movement toward peace and liberation, inner and outer."

Not far from where I live is a hill that was cut into by the moving water of a creek. Eroded this way, all that's left of it is a broken wall of earth that contains old roots and pebbles woven together and exposed. Seen from a distance, it is only a rise of raw earth. But up close it is something wonderful, a small cliff dwelling that looks almost as intricate and well made as those the Anasazi left behind when they vanished mysteriously centuries ago. This hill is a place that could be the starry skies at night turned inward into the thousand round holes where solitary bees have lived and died. It is a hill of tunneling rooms. At the mouths of some of the excavations, half-circles of clay beetle out like awnings shading a doorway. It is earth that was turned to clay in the mouths of the bees and spit out as they mined deeper into their dwelling places.

This place is where the bees reside at an angle safe from rain. It faces the southern sun. It is a warm and intelligent architecture of memory, learned by whatever memory lives in the blood. Many of the holes still contain gold husks of dead bees, their faces dry and gone, their flat eyes gazing out from death's land toward the other uninhabited half of the hill that is across the creek from the catacombs.

The first time I found the residence of the bees, it was dusty summer. The sun was hot, and land was the dry color of rust. Now and then a car rumbled along the dirt road and dust rose up behind it before settling back down on older dust. In the silence, the bees made a soft droning hum. They were alive then, and working the hill, going out and returning with pollen, in and out through the holes, back and forth between daylight and the cooler, darker regions of the inner earth. They were flying an invisible map through air, a map charted by landmarks, the slant of light, and a circling story they told one another about the direction of food held inside the center of yellow flowers.

Sitting in the hot sun, watching the small bees fly in and out around the hill, hearing the summer birds, the light breeze, I felt right in the world. I belonged there. I thought of my own dwelling places, those real and those imagined. Once I lived in a town called Manitou, which means "Great Spirit," and where hot mineral springwater gurgled beneath the streets and rose into open wells. I felt safe there. With the underground movement of water and heat a constant reminder of other life, of what lives beneath us, it seemed to be the center of the world.

A few years after that, I wanted silence. My daydreams were full of places I longed to be, shelters and solitudes. I wanted a room apart from others, a hidden cabin to rest in. I wanted to be in a redwood forest with trees so tall the owls called out in the daytime. I daydreamed of living in a vapor cave a few hours away from here. Underground, warm, and moist, I thought it would be the perfect world for staying out of cold winter, for escaping the noise of living.

And how often I've wanted to escape to a wilderness where a human hand has not been in everything. But those were only dreams of peace, of comfort, of a nest inside stone or woods, a sanctuary where a dream or life wouldn't be invaded.

Years ago, in the next canyon west of here, there was a man who followed one of those dreams and moved into a cave that could only be reached by climbing down a rope. For years he lived there in comfort, like a troglodite. The inner weather was stable, never too hot, too cold, too wet, or too dry. But then he felt lonely. His utopia needed a woman. He went to town until he found a wife. For a while after the marriage, his wife climbed down the rope along with him, but before long she didn't want the mice scurrying about in the cave, or the untidy bats that wanted to hang from the stones of the ceiling. So they built a door. Because of the closed entryway, the temperature changed. They had to put in heat. Then the inner moisture of earth warped the door, so they had to have air-conditioning, and after that the earth wanted to go about life in its own way and it didn't give in to the people.

In other days and places, people paid more attention to the strong-headed will of earth. Once homes were built of wood that had been felled from a single region in a forest. That way, it was thought, the house would hold together more harmoniously, and the family of walls would not fall or lend themselves to the unhappiness or arguments of the inhabitants.

An Italian immigrant to Chicago, Aldo Piacenzi, built birdhouses that were dwellings of harmony and peace. They were the incredible spired shapes of cathedrals in Italy. They housed not only the birds, but also his memories, his own past. He painted them the watery blue of his Mediterranean, the wild rose of flowers in a summer field. Inside them was straw and the droppings of lives that layed eggs, fledglings who grew there. What places to inhabit, the bright and sunny birdhouses in dreary alleyways of the city.

One beautiful afternoon, cool and moist, with the kind of yellow   10
light that falls on earth in these arid regions, I waited for barn swallows to return from their daily work of food gathering. Inside the tunnel where they live, hundreds of swallows had mixed their saliva with mud and clay, much like the solitary bees, and formed nests that were perfect as a potter's bowl. At five in the evening, they returned all at once, a dark, fly-ing shadow. Despite their enormous numbers and the crowding together of nests, they didn't pause for even a moment before entering the nests, nor did they crowd one another. Instantly they vanished into the nests. The tunnel went silent. It held no outward signs of life.

But I knew they were there, filled with the fire of living. And what a marriage of elements was in those nests. Not only mud's earth and water, the fire of sun and dry air, but even the elements contained one another. The bodies of prophets and crazy men were broken down in that soil.

I've noticed often how when a house is abandoned, it begins to sag. Without a tenant, it has no need to go on. If it were a person, we'd say it is depressed or lonely. The roof settles in, the paint cracks, the walls and floorboards warp and slope downward in their own natural ways, telling us that life must stay in everything as the world whirls and tilts and moves through boundless space.

One summer day, cleaning up after long-eared owls where I work at a rehabilitation facility for birds of prey, I was raking the gravel floor of a flight cage. Down on the ground, something looked like it was moving. I bent over to look into the pile of bones and pellets I'd just raked together. There, close to the ground, were two fetal mice. They were new to the planet, pink and hairless. They were so tenderly young. Their faces had swollen blue-veined eyes. They were nestled in a mound of feathers, soft as velvet, each one curled up smaller than an infant's ear, listening to the first sounds of earth. But the ants were biting them. They turned in agony, unable to pull away, not yet having the arms or legs to move, but feeling, twisting away from, the pain of the bites. I was horrified to see them bitten out of life that way. I dipped them in water, as if to take away the sting, and let the ants fall in the bucket. Then I held the tiny mice in the palm of my hand. Some of the ants were drowning in the water. I was trading one life for another, exchanging the lives of the ants for those of mice, but I hated their suffering, and hated even more that they had not yet grown to a life, and already they inhabited the miserable world of pain. Death and life feed each other. I know that.

Inside these rooms where birds are healed, there are other lives besides those of mice. There are fine gray globes the wasps have woven together, the white cocoons of spiders in a corner, the downward tunneling anthills. All these dwellings are inside one small walled space, but I think most about the mice. Sometimes the downy nests fall out of the walls where their mothers have placed them out of the way of their enemies. When one of the nests falls, they are so well made and soft, woven mostly from the chest feathers of birds. Sometimes the leg of a small quail holds the nest together like a slender cornerstone with dry, bent claws. The mice have adapted to life in the presence of their enemies, adapted to living in the thin wall between beak and beak, claw and claw. They move their nests often, as if a new rafter or wall will protect them from the inevitable fate of all our returns home to the deeper, wider nests of earth that houses us all.

One August at Zia Pueblo during the corn dance I noticed tourists   15
picking up shards of all the old pottery that had been made and broken there. The residents of Zia know not to take the bowls and pots left behind by the older ones. They know that the fragments of those earlier lives need to be smoothed back to earth, but younger nations, travelers from continents across the world who have come to inhabit this land, have little of their own to grow on. The pieces of earth that were formed into bowls, even on their way home to dust, provide the new people a lifeline to an unknown land, help them remember that they live in the old nest of earth.

It was in early February, during the mating season of the great horned owl. It was dusk, and I hiked up the back of a mountain to where I'd heard the owls a year before. I wanted to hear them again, the voices so tender, so deep, like a memory of comfort. I was halfway up the trail when I found a soft, round nest. It had fallen from one of the bare-branched trees. It was a delicate nest, woven together of feathers, sage, and strands of wild grass. Holding it in my hand in the rosy twilight, I noticed that a blue thread was entwined with the other gatherings there. I pulled at the thread a little, and then I recognized it. It was a thread from one of my skirts. It was blue cotton. It was the unmistakable color and shape of a pattern I knew. I liked it, that a thread of my life was in an abandoned nest, one that had held eggs and new life. I took the nest home. At home, I held it to the light and looked more closely. There, to my surprise, nestled into the gray-green sage, was a gnarl of black hair. It was also unmistakable. It was my daughter's hair, cleaned from a brush and picked up out in the sun beneath the maple tree, or the pit cherry where the birds eat from the overladen, fertile branches until only the seeds remain on the trees.

I didn't know what kind of nest it was, or who had lived there. It didn't matter. I thought of the remnants of our lives carried up the hill that way and turned into shelter. That night, resting inside the walls of our home, the world outside weighed so heavily against the thin wood of the house. The sloped roof was the only thing between us and the universe. Everything outside of our wooden boundaries seemed so large. Filled with the night's citizens, it all came alive. The world opened in the thickets of the dark. The wild grapes would soon ripen on the vines. The burrowing ones were emerging. Horned owls sat in treetops. Mice scurried here and there. Skunks, fox, the slow and holy porcupine, all were passing by this way. The young of the solitary bees were feeding on the pollen in the dark. The whole world was a nest on its humble tilt, in the maze of the universe, holding us.

The Reader's Presence

1. In each of the vignettes that make up this essay, Hogan contemplates the meaning of various dwellings. What are the specific characteristics of a dwelling place for Hogan? Who lives there? How does each dwelling suit and serve its inhabitants? Why does Hogan describe dwellings for animals as well as dwellings for humans? With what effect(s)? To what extent and in what ways do the two overlap? What are the advantages—and the disadvantages—of Hogan's having chosen to contemplate death as well as life in this essay about where we live? How would you characterize the vision of life, death, and the universe that emerges from this essay?

2. Reread carefully the story about the cave dweller and his wife told in paragraph 7. To what extent does Hogan encourage her readers to take the story literally? At what point does it begin to take on the qualities of myth or fable? Compare and contrast this story with the biblical story of Adam and Eve, and their fall from the Garden of Eden. To whom, or to what impulse(s), can each fall be attributed? How are women characterized in the respective stories? How are the endings similar, and where do they diverge? Based on your comparative analysis of these stories, what inferences might you draw about the Native American and Judeo-Christian worldviews?

3. Identify and discuss the various analogies Hogan draws throughout the essay. Where does she compare dwellings made by animals to human-made artifacts? human-made dwellings to natural phenomena? the animate to the inanimate? What are the effects of this interweaving of processes, objects, and species? In the following essay, John Hollander writes that "such representations of disorder" as lists, paintings, photos, etc., all compromise the purity of true messiness by the verbal or visual order they impose on the confusion" ("Mess," see following selection). What form of order does Hogan's essay "impose" on the natural places in phenomena she discovers? Is "impose" the right word? If not, what verb would you substitute to describe Hogan's writing?

58 _____

John Hollander

Mess

John Hollander (b. 1929) is one of the leading poets in the United States today. His poems and prose appear regularly in the New Yorker, *the* Partisan Review, Esquire, *and other popular and scholarly magazines. The essay "Mess" appeared in the* Yale Review *in 1995. Hollander is the Sterling Professor of English at Yale University, and he has written and edited numerous scholarly works and anthologies. Hollander's most recent collection of literary criticism is* The Work of Poetry *(1997), which won the Robert Penn Warren–Cleanth Brooks award. He has published over twenty volumes of poetry, including* Selected Poetry *(1993),* Animal Poems *(1994), and* Figurehead and Other Poems *(1999).*

Commenting on the experience of writing both poetry and prose, Hollander notes, "Ordinarily, the prose I write is critical or scholarly, where there is some occasion (a lecture to be given, a longish review to be done, etc.) to elicit the piece of writing. My most important writing is my poetry, which is not occasional in these ways. . . . This brief essay was generated more from within, like a poem, than most other prose of mine—nobody asked me to write it, but I felt impelled to observe something about one aspect of life that tends to get swept under the rug, as it were."

Mess is a state of mind. Or rather, messiness is a particular relation between the state of arrangement of a collection of things and a state of mind that contemplates it in its containing space. For example, X's mess may be Y's delight—sheer profusion, uncompromised by any apparent structure even in the representation of it. Or there may be some inner order or logic to A's mess that B cannot possibly perceive. Consider: someone—Alpha—rearranges all the books on Beta's library shelf, which have been piled or stacked, sometimes properly, sometimes not, but all in relevant sequence (by author and, within that, by date of publication), and rearranges them neatly, by size and color. Beta surveys the result, and can only feel, if not blurt out, "WHAT A MESS!" This situation often occurs with respect to messes of the workplace generally.

For there are many kinds of mess, both within walls and outside them: neglected gardens and the aftermath of tropical storms, and the indoor kinds of disorder peculiar to specific areas of our life with, and in and among, *things.* There are messes of one's own making, messes not even of one's own person, places, or things. There are personal states of mind about common areas of messiness—those of the kitchen, the bedroom, the bathroom, the salon (of whatever sort, from half a bed-sitter[1] to some grand public parlor), or those of personal appearance (clothes, hair, etc.). Then, for all those who are in any way self-employed or whose avocations are practiced in some private space—a workshop, a darkroom, a study or a studio—there is a mess of the workplace. It's not the most common kind of mess, but it's exemplary: the eye surveying it is sickened by the rollercoaster of scanning the scene. And, alas, it's the one I'm most afflicted with.

I know that things are really in a mess when—as about ninety seconds ago—I reach for the mouse on my Macintosh and find instead a thick layer of old envelopes, manuscript notes consulted three weeks ago, favorite pens and inoperative ones, folders used hastily and not replaced, and so forth. In order to start working, I brush these accumulated impedimenta aside, thus creating a new mess. But this is, worse yet, absorbed by the general condition of my study: piles of thin books and thick books, green volumes of the Loeb Classical Library and slimy paperbacks of ephemeral spy-thrillers, mostly used notebooks, bills paid and unpaid, immortal letters from beloved friends, unopened and untrashed folders stuffed with things that should be in various other folders, book-mailing

---

[1]*bed-sitter:* A combined bedroom and sitting room.—EDS.

envelopes, unanswered mail whose cries for help and attention are muffled by three months' worth of bank statements enshrouding them in the gloom of continued neglect. Even this fairly orderly inventory seems to simplify the confusion: in actuality, searching for a letter or a page of manuscript in this state of things involves crouching down with my head on one side and searching vertically along the outside of a teetering pile for what may be a thin, hidden layer of it.

Displacement, and lack of design, are obscured in the origins of our very word *mess*. The famous biblical "mess of red pottage" (lentil mush or dal) for which Esau sold his birthright wasn't "messy" in our sense (unless, of course, in the not very interesting case of Esau having dribbled it on his clothing). The word meant a serving of food, or a course in a meal: something *placed* in front of you (from the Latin *missis*, put or placed), hence "messmates" (dining companions) and ultimately "officers' mess" and the like. It also came to mean a dish of prepared mixed food—like an *olla podrida* or a minestrone—then by extension (but only from the early nineteenth century on) any hodge-podge: inedible, and outside the neat confines of a bowl or pot, and thus unpleasant, confusing, and agitating or depressing to contemplate. But for us, the association with food perhaps remains only in how much the state of mind of being messy is like that of being fat: for example, X says, "God, I'm getting gross! I'll have to diet!" Y, *really* fat, cringes on hearing this, and feels that for the slender X to talk that way is an obscenity. Similarly, X: "God, this place is a pigsty!" Y: (ditto). For a person prone to messiness, Cyril Connolly's celebrated observation about fat people is projected onto the world itself: inside every neat arrangement is a mess struggling to break out, like some kind of statue of chaos lying implicit in the marble of apparent organization.

In Paradise, there was no such thing as messiness. This was partly because unfallen, ideal life needed no supplemental *things*—objects of use and artifice, elements of any sort of technology. Thus there was nothing to leave lying around, messily or even neatly, by Adam and Eve—according to Milton—"at their savory dinner set / Of herbs and other country messes." But it was also because order, hence orderliness, was itself so natural that whatever bit of nature Adam and Eve might have been occupied with, or even using in a momentary tool-like way, flew or leapt or crept into place in some sort of reasonable arrangement, even as in our unparadised state things *fall* under the joyless tug of gravity. But messiness may seem to be an inevitable state of the condition of having so many *things*, precious or disposable, in one's life.

As I observed before, even to describe a mess is to impose order on it. The ancient Greek vision of primal chaos, even, was not *messy* in that it was pre-messy: there weren't any categories by which to define order, so that there could be no disorder—no nextness or betweenness, no above, below, here, there, and so forth. "*Let there be light*" meant "Let there be perception of something," and it was then that order became possible, and mess possibly implied. Now, a list or inventory is in itself an orderly

5

literary form, and even incoherent assemblages of items fall too easily into some other kind of order: in *Through the Looking-Glass*, the Walrus's "Of shoes and ships, and sealing wax, / Of cabbages, and kings," is given a harmonious structure by the pairs of alliterating words, and even by the half-punning association of "ships, [sailing] sealing wax." The wonderful catalogue in *Tom Sawyer* of the elements of what must have been, pocketed or piled on the ground, a mess of splendid proportions, is a poem of its own. The objects of barter for a stint of fence whitewashing (Tom, it will be remembered, turns *having* to do a chore into *getting* to do it by sheer con-man's insouciance) comprise

> twelve marbles, part of a jewsharp, a piece of blue bottle-glass to look through, a spool cannon, a key that wouldn't unlock anything, a fragment of chalk, a glass stopper of a decanter, a tin soldier, a couple of tadpoles, six fire-crackers, a kitten with only one eye, a brass door-knob, a dog collar — but no dog — the handle of a knife, four pieces of orange peel, and a dilapidated old window sash.

Thus such representations of disorder as lists, paintings, photos, etc., all compromise the purity of true messiness by the verbal or visual order they impose on the confusion. To get at the mess in my study, for example, a movie might serve best, alternately mixing mid-shot and zoom on a particular portion of the disaster, which would, in an almost fractal way, seem to be a mini-disaster of its own. There are even neatly conventionalized emblems of messiness that are, after all, all too neat: thus, whenever a movie wants to show an apartment or office that has been ransacked by Baddies (cop Baddies or baddy Baddies or whatever) in search of the Thing They Want, the designer is always careful to show at least one picture on the wall hanging carefully askew. All this could possibly tell us about a degree of messiness is that the searchers were so messy (at another level of application of the term) in their technique that they violated their search agenda to run over to the wall and tilt the picture (very messy procedure indeed), or that, hastily leaving the scene to avoid detection, they nonetheless took a final revenge against the Occupant for not having the Thing on his or her premises, and tilted the picture in a fit of pique. And yet a tilted picture gives good cueing mileage: it can present a good bit of disorder at the expense of a minimum of misalignment, after all.

A meditation on mess could be endless. As I struggle to conclude this one, one of my cats regards me from her nest in and among one of the disaster areas that all surfaces in my study soon become. Cats disdain messes in several ways. First, they are proverbially neat about their shit and the condition of their fur. Second, they pick their way so elegantly among my piles of books, papers, and ancillary objects (dishes of paper clips, scissors, functional and dried-out pens, crumpled envelopes, outmoded postage stamps, boxes of slides and disks, staplers, glue bottles, tape dispensers — *you* know) that they cannot even be said to acknowledge the mess's existence. The gray familiar creature currently making her own order out of a region of mess on my desk — carefully disposing herself around and over and among piles and bunches and stacks and crazily oblique layers and thereby reinterpreting it as natural landscape — makes me further despair until I realize that what she does with her body, I must do with my perception of this inevitable disorder — shaping its forms to the disorder and thereby shaping the disorder to its forms. She has taught me resignation.

The Reader's Presence

1. In the second sentence of his essay, Hollander defines "mess" as "a particular relation between the state of arrangement of a collection of things and a state of mind that contemplates it in its containing space." How would you paraphrase Hollander's definition? To what extent does his definition echo proverbs and traditional sayings such as "beauty is in the eye of the beholder"? What does Hollander's definition add to this kind of general insight about the observer? What role do "things" play in messiness, and what role is played by the person who contemplates them? Examine carefully the many observers mentioned in this essay, from the hypothetical X and Y in the first paragraph to the real cat in the final paragraph. What are their various reactions to the seeming disorder around them?

2. Hollander traces the origins of the word *mess* in paragraph 4. What is the connection between its original meaning and the meaning it took on "by extension" in the nineteenth century? According to Hollander, how does the state of mind of being messy correspond to the state of mind of being fat? He follows this association with yet another: the sculpture lying latent within the marble. Examine carefully — and then comment on — the way each analogy leads by association into the next and the effect of this series of associations.

3. Hollander's project is complicated by the fact that he has chosen to define a word that is enmeshed in his own writing process and product. How does the act of describing the "mess" on his desk (paragraph 3) alter the nature of the scene he describes? Is it, according to the author, even possible to do justice to a mess in written terms?

4. Consider the fluctuation between control and lack of control manifested not only in the subject of the essay but in the essay itself. Based on your analysis, how would you compare and contrast the degree of order in Hollander's study and in his writing? Is Hollander's essay a mess? Where are its messy passages? Why does Hollander find himself struggling to end the essay (paragraph 8)? Reread Jamaica Kincaid's brief essay, "Biography of a Dress" (page 154), in the light of Hollander's remarks. How does Kincaid contain or fail to contain the messiness of her memories? Are you bothered by or attracted to writing that is "tilted" or "misaligned"? Why?

59

Helen Keller

Living Words

Helen Keller (1880–1968) was an author, lecturer, and social advocate for the deaf and blind. Born in Tuscumbia, Alabama, Keller suffered the loss of her sight and hearing because of an acute illness when she was nineteen months old. Mute and unable to adequately communicate with others, Keller became a frustrated, willful, and angry child. When she was six years old, her parents sought help from Dr. Alexander Graham Bell, who recommended hiring a teacher from the Perkins Institute for the Blind. Her parents followed his advice and hired Anne Sullivan, Keller's lifelong teacher and friend. With Sullivan's help, Keller learned to read and write in Braille, understood hand symbols, and gained a college degree from Radcliffe. She devoted her life to educating the public about the need for social reform for people with disabilities and received numerous awards for her humanitarian efforts. Keller wrote a number of books, including The Story of My Life *(1902), in which "Living Words" appears as a chapter, and* Helen Keller's Journal *(1938).*

The most important day I remember in all my life is the one on which my teacher, Anne Mansfield Sullivan, came to me. I am filled with wonder when I consider the immeasurable contrasts between the two lives which it connects. It was the third of March, 1887, three months before I was seven years old.

On the afternoon of that eventful day, I stood on the porch, dumb, expectant. I guessed vaguely from my mother's signs and from the hurrying to and fro in the house that something unusual was about to happen, so I went to the door and waited on the steps. The afternoon sun penetrated the mass of honeysuckle that covered the porch, and fell on my upturned face. My fingers lingered almost unconsciously on the familiar leaves and blossoms which had just come forth to greet the sweet southern spring. I did not know what the future held of marvel or surprise for me. Anger and bitterness had preyed upon me continually for weeks and a deep languor had succeeded this passionate struggle.

Have you ever been at sea in a dense fog, when it seemed as if a tangible white darkness shut you in, and the great ship, tense and anxious, groped her way toward the shore with plummet and sounding-line, and you waited with beating heart for something to happen? I was like that ship before my education began, only I was without compass or sounding-line, and had no way of knowing how near the harbour was. "Light! give me light!" was the wordless cry of my soul, and the light of love shone on me in that very hour.

I felt approaching footsteps. I stretched out my hand as I supposed to my mother. Someone took it, and I was caught up and held close in the arms of her who had come to reveal all things to me, and, more than all things else, to love me.

The morning after my teacher came she led me into her room and gave me a doll. The little blind children at the Perkins Institution had sent it and Laura Bridgman[1] had dressed it; but I did not know this until afterward. When I had played with it a little while, Miss Sullivan slowly spelled into my hand the word "d-o-l-l." I was at once interested in this finger play and tried to imitate it. When I finally succeeded in making the letters correctly I was flushed with childish pleasure and pride. Running downstairs to my mother I held up my hand and made the letters for doll. I did not know that I was spelling a word or even that words existed; I was simply making my fingers go in monkey-like imitation. In the days that followed I learned to spell in this uncomprehending way a great many words, among them *pin, hat, cup* and a few verbs like *sit, stand* and *walk*. But my teacher had been with me several weeks before I understood that everything has a name.

One day, while I was playing with my new doll, Miss Sullivan put my big rag doll into my lap also, spelled, "d-o-l-l" and tried to make me understand that "d-o-l-l" applied to both. Earlier in the day we had had a tussle over the words "m-u-g" and "w-a-t-e-r." Miss Sullivan had tried to impress upon me that "m u g" is *mug* and that "w-a-t-e-r" is *water,* but I persisted in confounding the two. In despair she had dropped the subject for the time, only to renew it at the first opportunity. I became impatient at her repeated attempts and, seizing the new doll, I dashed it upon the floor. I was keenly delighted when I felt the fragments of the broken doll at my feet. Neither sorrow nor regret followed my passionate outburst. I had not loved the doll. In the still, dark world in which I lived there was no strong sentiment or tenderness. I felt my teacher sweep the fragments to one side of the hearth and I had a sense of satisfaction that the cause of my discomfort was removed. She brought me my hat, and I knew I was going out into the warm sunshine. This thought, if a wordless sensation may be called a thought, made me hop and skip with pleasure.

---

[1]*Bridgman:* Laura Dewey Bridgman (1829–1889) was the first deaf-blind child to be successfully educated at the now famous Perkins School for the Blind in Boston. Charles Dickens visited her in 1842 and wrote a moving description of her progress. She became internationally celebrated. — EDS.

We walked down the path to the well-house, attracted by the fragrance of the honeysuckle with which it was covered. Someone was drawing water and my teacher placed my hand under the spout. As the cool stream gushed over one hand she spelled into the other the word *water*, first slowly, then rapidly. I stood still, my whole attention fixed upon the motions of her fingers. Suddenly I felt a misty consciousness as of something forgotten—a thrill of returning thought; and somehow the mystery of language was revealed to me. I knew then that "w-a-t-e-r" meant the wonderful cool something that was flowing over my hand. That living word awakened my soul, gave it light, hope, joy, set it free! There were barriers still, it is true, but barriers that could in time be swept away.

I left the well-house eager to learn. Everything had a name, and each name gave birth to a new thought. As we returned to the house every object which I touched seemed to quiver with life. That was because I saw everything with the strange, new sight that had come to me. On entering the door I remembered the doll I had broken. I felt my way to the hearth and picked up the pieces. I tried vainly to put them together. Then my eyes filled with tears; for I realized what I had done, and for the first time I felt repentance and sorrow.

I learned a great many new words that day. I do not remember what they all were; but I do know that *mother, father, sister, teacher* were among them—words that were to make the world blossom for me, "like Aaron's rod, with flowers." It would have been difficult to find a happier child than I was as I lay in my crib at the close of that eventful day and lived over the joys it had brought me, and for the first time longed for a new day to come.

The Reader's Presence

1. The writer treats what for most of us are everyday perceptions and sensations as bizarre and wonderful. How does her narrative style make us aware of experiences we might otherwise take for granted?

2. Keller's experiences are foreign to most of us, yet her account is highly moving. How does the narrative evoke shifts of emotion? How does Keller gain the reader's empathy?

3. Keller's account of her discovery of language—of "the strange, new sight" that had come to her—has the intensity of a religious conversion. In which passages does Keller give the sense of her having been *transported* by the experience? Compare these passages to those in which Frederick Douglass describes his experience in "Learning to Read and Write" (page 112). To what extent can one draw parallels between the two accounts?

60

Stephen King

Everything You Need to Know about Writing Successfully—in Ten Minutes

Stephen King was born in 1947 in Portland, Maine. He began writing stories early in his life, but it was his discovery of a box of horror and science fiction novels in the attic of his aunt's house that made him decide to pursue a career as a writer. He published his first short stories in pulp horror magazines while in high school. After graduating from the University of Maine at Orono in 1970, King, while working at a low-paying job in a laundry, began writing his first novel, Carrie *(1974).* Carrie *was followed by thirty-six more best-sellers, including half a dozen works written under the pen name Richard Bachman, as well as five short story collections and nine screenplays. His critically acclaimed work of nonfiction,* On Writing *(2000), the source of the following essay, was completed while he was recovering painfully from a much-publicized accident.*

Stephen King has commented that, as a creative writer, he always hopes for "that element of inspiration which lifts you past the point where the characters are just you, where you do achieve something transcendental and the people are really people in the story."

I. THE FIRST INTRODUCTION

That's right. I know it sounds like an ad for some sleazy writers' school, but I really am going to tell you everything you need to pursue a successful and financially rewarding career writing fiction, and I really am going to do it in ten minutes, which is exactly how long it took me to learn. It will actually take you twenty minutes or so to read this article, however, because I have to tell you a story, and then I have to write a second introduction. But these, I argue, should not count in the ten minutes.

II. THE STORY, OR, HOW STEPHEN KING LEARNED TO WRITE

When I was a sophomore in high school, I did a sophomoric thing which got me in a pot of fairly hot water, as sophomoric didoes often do. I wrote and published a small satiric newspaper called *The Village Vomit*. In this little paper I lampooned a number of teachers at Lisbon (Maine) High School, where I was under instruction. These were not very gentle lampoons; they ranged from the scatological to the downright cruel.

Eventually, a copy of this paper found its way into the hands of a faculty member, and since I had been unwise enough to put my name on it (a fault, some critics would argue, of which I have still not been entirely cured), I was brought into the office. The sophisticated satirist had by that time reverted to what he really was: a fourteen-year-old kid who was shaking in his boots and wondering if he was going to get a suspension . . . what we called a "three-day vacation" in those dim days of 1964.

I wasn't suspended. I was forced to make a number of apologies — they were warranted, but they tasted like dog-dirt in my mouth — and spent a week in detention hall. And the guidance counselor arranged what he no doubt thought of as a more constructive channel for my talents. This was a job — contingent upon the editor's approval — writing sports for the Lisbon Enterprise, a twelve-page weekly of the sort with which any small-town resident will be familiar. This editor was the man who taught me everything I know about writing in ten minutes. His name was John Gould — not the famed New England humorist or the novelist who wrote *The Greenleaf Fires*, but a relative of both, I believe.

He told me he needed a sports writer, and we could "try each other   5
out," if I wanted.

I told him I knew more about advanced algebra than I did sports.

Gould nodded and said, "You'll learn."

I said I would at least try to learn. Gould gave me a huge roll of yellow paper and promised me a wage of 1/2 [cts.] per word. The first two pieces I wrote had to do with a high school basketball game in which a member of my school team broke the Lisbon High scoring record. One of these pieces was a straight piece of reportage. The second was a feature article.

I brought them to Gould the day after the game, so he'd have them for the paper, which came out Fridays. He read the straight piece, made two minor corrections, and spiked it. Then he started in on the feature piece with a large black pen and taught me all I ever needed to know about my craft. I wish I still had the piece, — it deserves to be framed, editorial corrections and all — but I can remember pretty well how it went and how it looked when he had finished with it. Here's an example:

Last night, in the ~~well-loved~~ gymnasium of Lisbon   10
High School, partisans and Jay Hills fans alike were

stunned by an athletic performance unequalled in
school history: Bob Ransom, ~~known as "Bullet" Bob
for both his size and accuracy,~~ scored thirty-seven
points. Yes, you heard me right. ~~Plus~~ he did it with
grace, and speed...and with an odd courtesy as
well, committing only two personal fouls in his
~~knight-like~~ quest for a record which has eluded Lisbon ~~thinclads~~ since ~~the years of Korea~~...

     players   1953

When Gould finished marking up my copy in the manner I have indicated above, he looked up and must have seen something on my face.
I think he must have thought it was horror, but it was not: It was
revelation.

"I only took out the bad parts, you know," he said. "Most of it's
pretty good."

"I know," I said, meaning both things; yes, most of it was good, and
yes, he had only taken out the bad parts. "I won't do it again."

"If that's true," he said, "you'll never have to work again. You can
do this for a living."

Then he threw back his head and laughed.

And he was right: I am doing this for a living, and as long as I can   15
keep on, I don't expect ever to have to work again.

III. THE SECOND INTRODUCTION

All of what follows has been said before. If you are interested enough
in writing to be a purchaser of this magazine [*Writer*], you will have either heard or read all (or almost all) of it before. Thousands of writing
courses are taught across the United States each year; seminars are con-
vened; guest lecturers talk, then answer questions, and it all boils down to
what follows.

I am going to tell you these things again because often people
will only listen — really listen — to someone who makes a lot of money
doing the thing he's talking about. This is sad but true. And I told you
the story above not to make myself sound like a character out of a
Horatio Alger novel but to make a point: I saw, I listened, and I
learned. Until that day in John Gould's little office, I had been writing
first drafts of stories that might run 2,500 words. The second drafts
were apt to run 3,300 words. Following that day, my 2,500-word first
drafts became 2,200-word second drafts. And two years after that, I
sold the first one.

So here it is, with all the bark stripped off. It'll take ten minutes to
read, and you can apply it right away . . . if you listen.

IV. EVERYTHING YOU NEED TO KNOW
ABOUT WRITING SUCCESSFULLY

1. Be talented

This, of course, is the killer. What is talent? I can hear someone shouting, and here we are, ready to get into a discussion right up there with "What is the meaning of life?" for weighty pronouncements and total uselessness. For the purposes of the beginning writer, talent may as well be defined as eventual success — publication and money. If you wrote something for which someone sent you a check, if you cashed the check and it didn't bounce, and if you then paid the light bill with the money, I consider you talented.

Now some of you are really hollering. Some of you are calling me one crass money-fixated creep. Nonsense. Worse than nonsense, off the subject. We're not talking about good or bad here. I'm interested in telling you how to get your stuff published, not in critical judgments of who's good or bad. As a rule, the critical judgments come after the check's been spent, anyway. I have my own opinions, but most times I keep them to myself. People who are published steadily and are paid for what they are writing may be either saints or trollops, but they are clearly reaching a great many someones who want what they have. Ergo, they are communicating. Ergo, they are talented. The biggest part of writing successfully is being talented, and in the context of marketing, the only bad writer is one who doesn't get paid. If you're not talented, you won't succeed. And if you're not succeeding, you should know when to quit.

When is that? I don't know. It's different for each writer. Not after six rejection slips, certainly, nor after sixty. But after six hundred? Maybe. After six thousand? My friend, after six thousand pinks, it's time you tried painting or computer programming.

Further, almost every aspiring writer knows when he is getting warmer — you start getting little jotted notes on your rejection slips, or personal letters . . . maybe a commiserating phone call. It's lonely out there in the cold, but there are encouraging voices . . . unless there is nothing in your words that warrants encouragement. I think you owe it to yourself to skip as much of the self-illusion as possible. If your eyes are open, you'll know which way to go . . . or when to turn back.

2. Be neat

Type. Double-space. Use a nice heavy white paper. If you've marked your manuscript a lot, do another draft.

3. Be self-critical

If you haven't marked up your manuscript a lot, you did a lazy job. Only God gets things right the first time. Don't be a slob.

4. Remove every extraneous word

You want to get up on a soapbox and preach? Fine. Get one, and try   25
your local park. You want to write for money? Get to the point. And if you remove the excess garbage and discover you can't find the point, tear up what you wrote and start all over again . . . or try something new.

5. Never look at a reference book while doing a first draft

You want to write a story? Fine. Put away your dictionary, your encyclopedias, your *World Almanac,* and your thesaurus. Better yet, throw your thesaurus into the wastebasket. The only things creepier than a thesaurus are those little paperbacks college students too lazy to read the assigned novels buy around exam time. Any word you have to hunt for in a thesaurus is the wrong word. There are no exceptions to this rule. You think you might have misspelled a word? O.K., so here is your choice: Either look it up in the dictionary, thereby making sure you have it right — and breaking your train of thought and the writer's trance in the bargain — or just spell it phonetically and correct it later. Why not? Did you think it was going to go somewhere? And if you need to know the largest city in Brazil and you find you don't have it in your head, why not write in Miami, or Cleveland? You can check it . . . but later. When you sit down to write, write. Don't do anything else except go to the bathroom, and only do that if it absolutely cannot be put off.

6. Know the markets

Only a dimwit would send a story about giant vampire bats surrounding a high school to *McCall's.* Only a dimwit would send a tender story about a mother and daughter making up their differences on Christmas Eve to *Playboy* . . . but people do it all the time. I'm not exaggerating; I have seen such stories in the slush piles of the actual magazines. If you write a good story, why send it out in an ignorant fashion? Would you send your kid out in a snowstorm dressed in Bermuda shorts and a tank top? If you like science fiction, read science fiction novels and magazines. If you want to write mysteries, read the magazines. And so on. It isn't just a matter of knowing what's right for the present story; you can begin to catch on, after a while, to overall rhythms, editorial likes and dislikes, a magazine's slant. Sometimes your reading can influence the next story, and create a sale.

7. Write to entertain

Does this mean you can't write "serious fiction"? It does not. Somewhere along the line pernicious critics have invested the American reading and writing public with the idea that entertaining fiction and serious ideas do not overlap. This would have surprised Charles Dickens, not to mention Jane Austen, John Steinbeck, William Faulkner, Bernard Malarnud, and hundreds of others. But your serious ideas must always serve your story, not the other way around. I repeat: If you want to preach, get a soapbox.

8. Ask yourself frequently, "Am I having fun?"

The answer needn't always be yes. But if it's always no, it's time for a new project or a new career.

9. How to evaluate criticism

Show your piece to a number of people—ten, let us say. Listen carefully to what they tell you. Smile and nod a lot. Then review what was said very carefully. If your critics are all telling you the same thing about some facet of your story—a plot twist that doesn't work, a character who rings false, stilted narrative, or half a dozen other possibles—change it. It doesn't matter if you really like that twist or that character; if a lot of people are telling you something is wrong with your piece, it is. If seven or eight of them are hitting on that same thing, I'd still suggest changing it. But if everyone—or even most everyone—is criticizing something different, you can safely disregard what all of them say.

10. Observe all rules for proper submission

Return postage, self-addressed envelope, etc.

11. An agent? Forget it. For now.

Agents get 10 percent to 15 percent of monies earned by their clients. Fifteen percent of nothing is nothing. Agents also have to pay the rent. Beginning writers do not contribute to that or any other necessity of life. Flog your stories around yourself. If you've done a novel, send around query letters to publishers, one by one, and follow up with sample chapters and/or the complete manuscript. And remember Stephen King's First Rule

30

of Writers and Agent, learned by bitter personal experience: You don't need one until you're making enough for someone to steal . . . and if you're making that much, you'll be able to take your pick of good agents.

12. If it's bad, kill it

When it comes to people, mercy killing is against the law. When it comes to fiction, it is the law.

That's everything you need to know. And if you listened, you can write everything and anything you want. Now I believe I will wish you a pleasant day and sign off.

My ten minutes are up.   35

The Reader's Presence

1. Why does King include sections 1–3, even though they are not part of the "ten minutes"? What does the first introduction actually introduce? the second? How effectively does section 2 work with section 4? For example, how many rules did King learn when John Gould edited his story? Which rules does he break in his own essay? Why do you think he breaks them?

2. King is best known for writing horror novels, stories that scare people. What fears does he play on throughout this essay? How does he go about setting up suspenseful situations? What does he do to frighten people in this essay? If the rules are monsters, which ones do you think are the most frightening? Why?

3. By King's definition, a talented author is one who has been paid for his or her writing. Pick an author in this collection whom you consider talented and evaluate him or her according to King's rules. How successful should this writer be according to King? What other rules of success does the writer's essay suggest should be added to King's list?

4. King's essay represents an approach to an ongoing debate between money and art. Signalled by terms like *practicality* and *popularity,* the money side holds that you should write to make money. Signalled by phrases like *art for art's sake* or *selling out* the art side holds that you should write to please yourself. George Orwell represents another approach to this debate in "Why I Write" (page 492). In the selection, Orwell lists "four great motives for writing" besides earning a living (page 492). Read Orwell's essay and determine how well each of the motives would lead to the kind of successful writing that King imagines. For example, how well—or how poorly—does Orwell's desire to "share an experience which one feels is valuable" (page 493) lead to King's "eventual success—publication and money" (page 430)?

61

Maxine Hong Kingston

No Name Woman

Maxine Hong Kingston (b. 1940) won the National Book Critics Circle Award for nonfiction with her first book, The Woman Warrior: Memoirs of a Girlhood among Ghosts *(1976). "No Name Woman" is the opening chapter of this book, which* Time *magazine named one of the top ten nonfiction works of the 1970s. She has also written* China Men *(1980), which won the American Book Award, and* Trip Master Monkey: His Fake Book *(1988), a picaresque novel. Kingston's writing often blurs the distinction between fiction and nonfiction. Her narratives blend autobiography, history, myth, and legend, drawing on the stories she remembers from her childhood in the Chinese American community of Stockton, California. Kingston's essays, stories, and poems also appear in numerous magazines, and she received the 1997 National Medal for the Humanities. She is currently a senior lecturer at the University of California, Berkeley.*

Kingston has said that before writing The Woman Warrior, *"My life as a writer had been a long struggle with pronouns. For 30 years I wrote in the first person singular. At a certain point I was thinking that I was self-centered and egotistical, solipsistic, and not very developed as a human being, nor as an artist, because I could only see from this one point of view." She began to write in the third person because "I thought I had to overcome this self-centeredness." As she wrote her third novel, Kingston experienced the disappearance of her authorial voice. "I feel that this is an artistic as well as psychological improvement on my part. Because I am now a much less selfish person."*

"You must not tell anyone," my mother said, "what I am about to tell you. In China your father had a sister who killed herself. She jumped into the family well. We say that your father has all brothers because it is as if she had never been born.

"In 1924 just a few days after our village celebrated seventeen hurry-up weddings — to make sure that every young man who went 'out on the road' would responsibly come home — your father and his brothers and your grandfather and his brothers and your aunt's new husband sailed for America, the Gold Mountain. It was your grandfather's last trip. Those lucky enough to get contracts waved good-bye from the decks. They fed and guarded the stowaways and helped them off in Cuba, New York, Bali, Hawaii. 'We'll meet in California next year,' they said. All of them sent money home.

"I remember looking at your aunt one day when she and I were dressing; I had not noticed before that she had such a protruding melon of a stomach. But I did not think, 'She's pregnant,' until she began to look like other pregnant women, her shirt pulling and the white tops of her black pants showing. She could not have been pregnant, you see, because her husband had been gone for years. No one said anything. We did not discuss it. In early summer she was ready to have the child, long after the time when it could have been possible.

"The village had also been counting. On the night the baby was to be born the villagers raided our house. Some were crying. Like a great saw, teeth strung with lights, files of people walked zigzag across our land, tearing the rice. Their lanterns doubled in the disturbed black water, which drained away through the broken bunds. As the villagers closed in, we could see that some of them, probably men and women we knew well, wore white masks. The people with long hair hung it over their faces. Women with short hair made it stand up on end. Some had tied white bands around their foreheads, arms, and legs.

"At first they threw mud and rocks at the house. Then they threw eggs and began slaughtering our stock. We could hear the animals scream their deaths—the roosters, the pigs, a last great roar from the ox. Familiar wild heads flared in our night windows; the villagers encircled us. Some of the faces stopped to peer at us, their eyes rushing like searchlights. The hands flattened against the panes, framed heads, and left red prints.

"The villagers broke in the front and the back doors at the same time, even though we had not locked the doors against them. Their knives dripped with the blood of our animals. They smeared blood on the doors and walls. One woman swung a chicken, whose throat she had slit, splattering blood in red arcs about her. We stood together in the middle of our house, in the family hall with the pictures and tables of the ancestors around us, and looked straight ahead.

"At that time the house had only two wings. When the men came back we would build two more to enclose our courtyard and a third one to begin a second courtyard. The villagers pushed through both wings, even your grandparents' rooms, to find your aunt's, which was also mine until the men returned. From this room a new wing for one of the younger families would grow. They ripped up her clothes and shoes and broke her combs, grinding them underfoot. They tore her work from the loom. They scattered the cooking fire and rolled the new weaving in it. We could hear them in the kitchen breaking our bowls and banging the pots. They overturned the great waist-high earthenware jugs; duck eggs, pickled fruits, vegetables burst out and mixed in acrid torrents. The old woman from the next field swept a broom through the air and loosed the

5

spirits-of-the-broom over our heads. 'Pig.' 'Ghost.' 'Pig,' they sobbed and scolded while they ruined our house.

"When they left, they took sugar and oranges to bless themselves. They cut pieces from the dead animals. Some of them took bowls that were not broken and clothes that were not torn. Afterward we swept up the rice and sewed it back up into sacks. But the smells from the spilled preserves lasted. Your aunt gave birth in the pigsty that night. The next morning when I went up for the water, I found her and the baby plugging up the family well.

"Don't let your father know that I told you. He denies her. Now that you have started to menstruate, what happened to her could happen to you. Don't humiliate us. You wouldn't like to be forgotten as if you had never been born. The villagers are watchful."

Whenever she had to warn us about life, my mother told stories that ran like this one, a story to grow up on. She tested our strength to establish realities. Those in the emigrant generations who could not reassert brute survival died young and far from home. Those of us in the first American generations have had to figure out how the invisible world the emigrants built around our childhoods fit in solid America.

The emigrants confused the gods by diverting their curses, misleading them with crooked streets and false names. They must try to confuse their offspring as well, who, I suppose, threaten them in similar ways — always trying to get things straight, always trying to name the unspeakable. The Chinese I know hide their names; sojourners take new names when their lives change and guard their real names with silence.

Chinese-Americans, when you try to understand what things in you are Chinese, how do you separate what is peculiar to childhood, to poverty, insanities, one family, your mother who marked your growing with stories, from what is Chinese? What is Chinese tradition and what is the movies?

If I want to learn what clothes my aunt wore, whether flashy or ordinary, I would have to begin, "Remember Father's drowned-in-the-well sister?" I cannot ask that. My mother has told me once and for all the useful parts. She will add nothing unless powered by Necessity, a riverbank that guides her life. She plants vegetable gardens rather than lawns; she carries the odd-shaped tomatoes home from the fields and eats food left for the gods.

Whenever we did frivolous things, we used up energy; we flew high kites. We children came up off the ground over the melting cones our parents brought home from work and the American movie on New Year's Day — *Oh, You Beautiful Doll* with Betty Grable one year, and *She Wore a Yellow Ribbon* with John Wayne another year. After the one carnival ride each, we paid in guilt; our tired father counted his change on the dark walk home.

Adultery is extravagance. Could people who hatch their own chicks and eat the embryos and the heads for delicacies and boil the feet in vine-

10

15

gar for party food, leaving only the gravel, eating even the gizzard lin-
ing—could such people engender a prodigal aunt? To be a woman, to
have a daughter in starvation time was a waste enough. My aunt could
not have been the lone romantic who gave up everything for sex. Women
in the old China did not choose. Some man had commanded her to lie
with him and be his secret evil. I wonder whether he masked himself
when he joined the raid on her family.

Perhaps she encountered him in the fields or on the mountain where
the daughters-in-law collected fuel. Or perhaps he first noticed her in the
marketplace. He was not a stranger because the village housed no
strangers. She had to have dealings with him other than sex. Perhaps he
worked an adjoining field, or he sold her the cloth for the dress she sewed
and wore. His demand must have surprised, then terrified her. She obeyed
him; she always did as she was told.

When the family found a young man in the next village to be her husband, she stood tractably beside the best rooster, his proxy, and promised
before they met that she would be his forever. She was lucky that he was
her age and she would be the first wife, an advantage secure now. The
night she first saw him, he had sex with her. Then he left for America. She
had almost forgotten what he looked like. When she tried to envision
him, she only saw the black and white face in the group photograph the
men had had taken before leaving.

The other man was not, after all, much different from her husband.
They both gave orders: she followed. "If you tell your family, I'll beat
you. I'll kill you. Be here again next week." No one talked sex, ever. And
she might have separated the rapes from the rest of living if only she did
not have to buy her oil from him or gather wood in the same forest. I
want her fear to have lasted just as long as rape lasted so that the fear
could have been contained. No drawn-out fear. But women at sex haz-
arded birth and hence lifetimes. The fear did not stop but permeated
everywhere. She told the man, "I think I'm pregnant." He organized the
raid against her.

On nights when my mother and father talked about their life back
home, sometimes they mentioned an "outcast table" whose business they
still seemed to be settling, their voices tight. In a commensal tradition,
where food is precious, the powerful older people made wrongdoers eat
alone. Instead of letting them start separate new lives like the Japanese,
who could become samurais and geishas, the Chinese family, faces
averted but eyes glowering sideways, hung on to the offenders and fed
them leftovers. My aunt must have lived in the same house as my parents
and eaten at an outcast table. My mother spoke about the raid as if she
had seen it, when she and my aunt, a daughter-in-law to a different
household, should not have been living together at all. Daughters-in-law
lived with their husbands' parents, not their own; a synonym for marriage
in Chinese is "taking a daughter-in-law." Her husband's parents could
have sold her, mortgaged her, stoned her. But they had sent her back to

her own mother and father, a mysterious act hinting at disgraces not told me. Perhaps they had thrown her out to deflect the avengers.

She was the only daughter; her four brothers went with her father, husband, and uncles "out on the road" and for some years became western men. When the goods were divided among the family, three of the brothers took land, and the youngest, my father, chose an education. After my grandparents gave their daughter away to her husband's family, they had dispensed all the adventure and all the property. They expected her alone to keep the traditional ways, which her brothers, now among the barbarians, could fumble without detection. The heavy, deep-rooted women were to maintain the past against the flood, safe for returning. But the rare urge west had fixed upon our family, and so my aunt crossed boundaries not delineated in space.

The work of preservation demands that the feelings playing about in one's guts not be turned into action. Just watch their passing like cherry blossoms. But perhaps my aunt, my forerunner, caught in a slow life, let dreams grow and fade and after some months or years went toward what persisted. Fear at the enormities of the forbidden kept her desires delicate, wire and bone. She looked at a man because she liked the way the hair was tucked behind his ears, or she liked the question-mark line of a long torso curving at the shoulder and straight at the hip. For warm eyes or a soft voice or a slow walk—that's all—a few hairs, a line, a brightness, a sound, a pace, she gave up family. She offered us up for a charm that vanished with tiredness, a pigtail that didn't toss when the wind died. Why, the wrong lighting could erase the dearest thing about him.

It could very well have been, however, that my aunt did not take subtle enjoyment of her friend, but, a wild woman, kept rollicking company. Imagining her free with sex doesn't fit, though. I don't know any women like that, or men either. Unless I see her life branching into mine, she gives me no ancestral help.

To sustain her being in love, she often worked at herself in the mirror, guessing at the colors and shapes that would interest him, changing them frequently in order to hit on the right combination. She wanted to look back.

On a farm near the sea, a woman who tended her appearance reaped a reputation for eccentricity. All the married women blunt-cut their hair in flaps about their ears or pulled it back in tight buns. No nonsense. Neither style blew easily into heart-catching tangles. And at their weddings they displayed themselves in their long hair for the last time. "It brushed the back of my knees," my mother tells me. "It was braided, and even so, it brushed the backs of my knees."

At the mirror my aunt combed individuality into her bob. A bun could have been contrived to escape into black streamers blowing in the wind or in quiet wisps about her face, but only the older women in our picture album wear buns. She brushed her hair back from her forehead, tucking the flaps behind her ears. She looped a piece of thread, knotted into a circle between her index fingers and thumbs, and ran the double strand across her forehead. When she closed her fingers as if she were making a pair of shadow geese bite, the string twisted together catching the little hairs. Then she pulled the thread away from her skin, ripping the hairs out neatly, her eyes watering from the needles of pain. Opening her fingers, she cleaned the thread, then rolled it along her hairline and the tops of the eyebrows. My mother did the same to me and my sisters and herself. I used to believe that the expression "caught by the short hairs" meant a captive held with a depilatory string. It especially hurt at the temples, but my mother said we were lucky we didn't have to have our feet bound when we were seven. Sisters used to sit on their beds and cry together, she said, as their mothers or their slave removed the bandages for a few minutes each night and let the blood gush back into their veins. I hope that the man my aunt loved appreciated a smooth brow, that he wasn't just a tits-and-ass man.

Once my aunt found a freckle on her chin, at a spot that the almanac said predestined her for unhappiness. She dug it out with a hot needle and washed the wound with peroxide.

More attention to her looks than these pullings of hairs and pickings at spots would have caused gossip among the villagers. They owned work clothes and good clothes, and they wore good clothes for feasting the new seasons. But since a woman combing her hair hexes beginnings, my aunt rarely found an occasion to look her best. Women looked like great sea snails—the corded wood, babies, and laundry they carried were the whorls on their backs. The Chinese did not admire a bent back; goddesses and warriors stood straight. Still there must have been a marvelous freeing of beauty when a worker laid down her burden and stretched and arched.

Such commonplace loveliness, however, was not enough for my aunt. She dreamed of a lover for the fifteen days of New Year's, the time for families to exchange visits, money, and food. She plied her secret comb. And sure enough she cursed the year, the family, the village, and herself.

Even as her hair lured her imminent lover, many other men looked at her. Uncles, cousins, nephews, brothers would have looked, too, had they been home between journeys. Perhaps they had already been restraining their curiosity, and they left, fearful that their glances, like a field of nesting birds, might be startled and caught. Poverty hurt, and that was their first reason for leaving. But another, final reason for leaving the crowded house was the never-said.

She may have been unusually beloved, the precious only daughter, 30 spoiled and mirror-gazing because of the affection the family lavished on her. When her husband left, they welcomed the chance to take her back from the in-laws; she could live like the little daughter for just a while longer. There are stories that my grandfather was different from other people, "crazy ever since the little Jap bayoneted him in the head." He used to put his naked penis on the dinner table, laughing. And one day he brought home a baby girl, wrapped up inside his brown western-style greatcoat. He had traded one of his sons, probably my father, the youngest, for her. My grandmother made him trade back. When he finally got a daughter of his own, he doted on her. They must have all loved her, except perhaps my father, the only brother who never went back to China, having once been traded for a girl.

Brothers and sisters, newly men and women, had to efface their sexual color and present plain miens. Disturbing hair and eyes, a smile like no other, threatened the ideal of five generations living under one roof. To focus blurs, people shouted face to face and yelled from room to room. The immigrants I know have loud voices, unmodulated to American tones even after years away from the village where they called their friendships out across the fields. I have not been able to stop my mother's screams in public libraries or over telephones. Walking erect (knees straight, toes pointed forward, not pigeon-toed, which is Chinese-feminine) and speaking in an inaudible voice, I have tried to turn myself American-feminine. Chinese communication was loud, public. Only sick people had to whisper. But at the dinner table, where the family members came nearest one another, no one could talk, not the outcasts nor any eaters. Every word that falls from the mouth is a coin lost. Silently they gave and accepted food with both hands. A preoccupied child who took his bowl with one hand got a sideways glare. A complete moment of total attention is due everyone alike. Children and lovers have no singularity here, but my aunt used a secret voice, a separate attentiveness.

She kept the man's name to herself throughout her labor and dying; she did not accuse him that he be punished with her. To save her inseminator's name she gave silent birth.

He may have been somebody in her own household, but intercourse with a man outside the family would have been no less abhorrent. All the village were kinsmen, and the titles shouted in loud country voices never let kinship be forgotten. Any man within visiting distance would have been neutralized as a lover—"brother," "younger brother," "older brother"—115 relationship titles. Parents researched birth charts probably not so much to assure good fortune as to circumvent incest in a population that has but one hundred surnames. Everybody has eight million relatives. How useless then sexual mannerisms, how dangerous.

As if it came from an atavism deeper than fear, I used to add "brother" silently to boys' names. It hexed the boys, who would or would not ask me to dance, and made them less scary and as familiar and deserving of benevolence as girls.

But, of course, I hexed myself also—no dates. I should have stood up, both arms waving, and shouted out across libraries, "Hey, you! Love me back." I had no idea, though, how to make attraction selective, how to control its direction and magnitude. If I made myself American-pretty so that the five or six Chinese boys in the class fell in love with me, everyone else—the Caucasian, Negro, and Japanese boys—would too. Sisterliness, dignified and honorable, made much more sense.

Attraction eludes control so stubbornly that whole societies designed to organize relationships among people cannot keep order, not even when they bind people to one another from childhood and raise them together. Among the very poor and the wealthy, brothers married their adopted sisters, like doves. Our family allowed some romance, paying adult brides' prices and providing dowries so that their sons and daughters could marry strangers. Marriage promises to turn strangers into friendly relatives — a nation of siblings.

In the village structure, spirits shimmered among the live creatures, balanced and held in equilibrium by time and land. But one human being flaring up into violence could open up a black hole, a maelstrom that pulled in the sky. The frightened villagers, who depended on one another to maintain the real, went to my aunt to show her a personal, physical representation of the break she made in the "roundness." Misallying couples snapped off the future, which was to be embodied in true offspring. The villagers punished her for acting as if she could have a private life, secret and apart from them.

If my aunt had betrayed the family at a time of large grain yields and peace, when many boys were born, and wings were being built on many houses, perhaps she might have escaped such severe punishment. But the men — hungry, greedy, tired of planting in dry soil, cuckolded — had been forced to leave the village in order to send food-money home. There were ghost plagues, bandit plagues, wars with the Japanese, floods. My Chinese brother and sister had died of an unknown sickness. Adultery, perhaps only a mistake during good times, became a crime when the village needed food.

The round moon cakes and round doorways, the round tables of graduated size that fit one roundness inside another, round windows and rice bowls — these talismans had lost their power to warn this family of the law: A family must be whole, faithfully keeping the descent line by having sons to feed the old and the dead who in turn look after the family. The villagers came to show my aunt and lover-in-hiding a broken house. The villagers were speeding up the circling of events because she was too shortsighted to see that her infidelity had already harmed the village, that waves of consequences would return unpredictably, sometimes in disguise, as now, to hurt her. This roundness had to be made coin-sized so that she would see its circumference: Punish her at the birth of her baby. Awaken her to the inexorable. People who refused fatalism because they could invent small resources insisted on culpability. Deny accidents and wrest fault from the stars.

After the villagers left, their lanterns now scattering in various directions toward home, the family broke their silence and cursed her. "Aiaa, we're going to die. Death is coming. Death is coming. Look what you've done. You've killed us. Ghost! Dead Ghost! Ghost! You've never been born." She ran out into the fields, far enough from the house so that she could no longer hear their voices, and pressed herself against the earth, her own land no more. When she felt the birth coming, she thought that she had been hurt. Her body seized together. "They've hurt me too

40

much," she thought. "This is gall, and it will kill me." With forehead and knees against the earth, her body convulsed and then relaxed. She turned on her back, lay on the ground. The black well of sky and stars went out and out forever; her body and her complexity seemed to disappear. She was one of the stars, a bright dot in blackness, without home, without a companion, in eternal cold and silence. An agoraphobia rose in her, speeding higher and higher, bigger and bigger; she would not be able to contain it; there would be no end to fear.

Flayed, unprotected against space, she felt pain return, focusing her body. This pain chilled her—a cold, steady kind of surface pain. Inside, spasmodically, the other pain, the pain of the child, heated her. For hours she lay on the ground, alternately body and space. Sometimes a vision of normal comfort obliterated reality: She saw the family in the evening gambling at the dinner table, the young people massaging their elders' backs. She saw them congratulating one another, high joy on the mornings the rice shoots came up. When these pictures burst, the stars drew yet further apart. Black space opened.

She got to her feet to fight better and remembered that old-fashioned women gave birth in their pigsties to fool the jealous, pain-dealing gods, who do not snatch piglets. Before the next spasms could stop her, she ran to the pigsty, each step a rushing out into emptiness. She climbed over the fence and knelt in the dirt. It was good to have a fence enclosing her, a tribal person alone.

Laboring, this woman who had carried her child as a foreign growth that sickened her every day, expelled it at last. She reached down to touch the hot, wet, moving mass, surely smaller than anything human, and could feel that it was human after all—fingers, toes, nails, nose. She pulled it up on to her belly, and it lay curled there, butt in the air, feet precisely tucked one under the other. She opened her loose shirt and buttoned the child inside. After resting, it squirmed and thrashed and she pushed it up to her breast. It turned its head this way and that until it found her nipple. There, it made little snuffling noises. She clenched her teeth at its preciousness, lovely as a young calf, a piglet, a little dog.

She may have gone to the pigsty as a last act of responsibility: She would protect this child as she had protected its father. It would look after her soul, leaving supplies on her grave. But how would this tiny child without family find her grave when there would be no marker for her anywhere, neither in the earth nor the family hall? No one would give her a family hall name. She had taken the child with her into the wastes. At its birth the two of them had felt the same raw pain of separation, a wound that only the family pressing tight could close. A child with no descent line would not soften her life but only trail after her, ghostlike, begging her to give it purpose. At dawn the villagers on their way to the fields would stand around the fence and look.

Full of milk, the little ghost slept. When it awoke, she hardened her breasts against the milk that crying loosens. Toward morning she picked up the baby and walked to the well.   45

Carrying the baby to the well shows loving. Otherwise abandon it. Turn its face into the mud. Mothers who love their children take them along. It was probably a girl; there is some hope of forgiveness for boys.

"Don't tell anyone you had an aunt. Your father does not want to hear her name. She has never been born." I have believed that sex was unspeakable and words so strong and fathers so frail that "aunt" would do my father mysterious harm. I have thought that my family, having settled among immigrants who had also been their neighbors in the ancestral land, needed to clean their name, and a wrong word would incite the kinspeople even here. But there is more to this silence: They want me to participate in her punishment. And I have.

In the twenty years since I heard this story I have not asked for details nor said my aunt's name; I do not know it. People who comfort the dead can also chase after them to hurt them further—a reverse ancestor worship. The real punishment was not the raid swiftly inflicted by the villagers, but the family's deliberately forgetting her. Her betrayal so maddened them, they saw to it that she would suffer forever, even after death. Always hungry, always needing, she would have to beg food from other ghosts, snatch and steal it from those whose living descendants give them gifts. She would have to fight the ghosts massed at crossroads for the buns a few thoughtful citizens leave to decoy her away from village and home so that the ancestral spirits could feast unharassed. At peace, they could act like gods, not ghosts, their descent lines providing them with paper suits and dresses, spirit money, paper houses, paper automobiles, chicken, meat, and rice into eternity—essences delivered up in smoke and flames, steam and incense rising from each rice bowl. In an attempt to make the Chinese care for people outside the family, Chairman Mao encourages us now to give our paper replicas to the spirits of outstanding soldiers and workers, no matter whose ancestors they may be. My aunt remains forever hungry. Goods are not distributed evenly among the dead.

My aunt haunts me—her ghost drawn to me because now, after fifty years of neglect, I alone devote pages of paper to her, though not origamied into houses and clothes. I do not think she always means me well. I am telling on her, and she was a spite suicide, drowning herself in the drinking water. The Chinese are always very frightened of the drowned one, whose weeping ghost, wet hair hanging and skin bloated, waits silently by the water to pull down a substitute.

The Reader's Presence

1. Kingston's account of her aunt's life and death is a remarkable blend of fact and speculation. Consider the overall structure of "No Name Woman." How many versions of the aunt's story do we hear? Where, for example, does the mother's story end? Where does the narrator's begin? Which version do you find more compelling? Why? What does the narrator mean when she says that

her mother's stories "tested our strength to establish realities" (paragraph 10)?

2. The narrator's version of her aunt's story is replete with such words and phrases as *perhaps* and *It could very well have been.* The narrator seems far more speculative about her aunt's life than her mother is. At what point does the narrator raise doubts about the veracity of her mother's version of the aunt's story? What purpose does the mother espouse in telling the aunt's story? Is it meant primarily to express family lore? to issue a warning? Point to specific passages to verify your response. What is the proposed moral of the story? Is that moral the same for the mother as for the narrator? Explain.

3. What line does Kingston draw between the two cultures represented in the story: between the mother, a superstitious, cautious Chinese woman, and the narrator, an American-born child trying to "straighten out" her mother's confusing story? How does the narrator resolve the issue by thinking of herself as neither Chinese nor American, but as Chinese American? How does she imagine her relationship to her distant aunt? Compare Kingston's depiction of relationships across generations and cultures to those in N. Scott Momaday's "The Way to Rainy Mountain" (page 446) and to those in Richard Rodriguez's "Aria: A Memoir of a Bilingual Childhood" (page 221). How does language feature in each writer's family? How do problems of comprehension become occasions for creative play in each essay?

THE WRITER AT WORK

Maxine Hong Kingston on Writing for Oneself

In the fire that raged through the Oakland, California, hills in 1991, Maxine Hong Kingston lost, along with her entire house, all her copies of a work in progress. In the following interview conducted by Diane Simmons at Kingston's new home in 1997, the writer discusses how the fire and the loss of her work have transformed her attitude toward her own writing. Confronted with a similar loss (whether the work was on paper or hard drive), most authors would try to recapture as best they could what they had originally written. Why do you think Kingston wants to avoid that sort of recovery? The following exchange is from the opening of that long interview, which appeared in a literary periodical, The Crab Orchard Review *(Spring/Summer 1998). Diane Simmons is the author of* Maxine Hong Kingston *(New York: Twayne Publishers, 1999).*

I began by asking Ms. Kingston to talk about the book that was lost, and where she was going with her recent work.

Kingston: In the book that I lost in the fire, I was working on an idea of finding the book of peace again. There was a myth that there were three lost books of peace and so I was going to find the book of peace for our time. I imagine that it has to do with how to wage peace on earth and that there would be tactics on how to wage peace and how to stop war. I see that the books of war are popular; they are taught in the military academies; they're translated into all different languages. They [are used to] help corporate executives succeed in business. And people don't even think about the books of peace; people don't even know about them. I'm the only one that knows about it.

And so I was writing this and that was what was burned in the fire. What I'm working on now I'm calling *The Fifth Book of Peace*. I'm not recalling and remembering what I had written. To me it's the pleasure of writing to be constantly discovering, going into the new. To recall word by word what I had written before sounds like torture and agony for me. I know I can do it, I'm sure I can do it if I want to. One of my former students volunteered to hypnotize me so I could recall, but that seemed so wrong to me.

Simmons: How much was lost?

Kingston: About 200 written, rewritten pages, so it was very good.   5
But I had wanted to rewrite it again and I think to recall word by word would freeze me into a version and I didn't want to do that.

Simmons: Is the book you are working on now the same project, the same version?

Kingston: Yes, but it is not the same words. It's not the same story. It's the same idea that I want to work on peace. At one point I called it the global novel. But since then I've been thinking of it as a book of peace. And the one big difference is the Book of Peace was a work of fiction. I was imagining fictional characters. But after the fire I wanted to use writing for my personal self. I wanted to write directly what I was thinking and feeling, not imagining fictional other people. I wanted to write myself. I wanted to write in the way I wrote when I was a child which is to say my deepest feelings and thoughts as they could come out in a personal way and not for public consumption. It's not even for other people to read but for myself, to express myself, and it doesn't matter whether this would be published. I don't even want to think about publication or readers, but this is for my own expression of my own suffering or agony.

Simmons: You've said that that's how you wrote in the beginning.

Kingston: I always begin like that. I always have to begin like that. Getting back to the roots of language in myself. It's almost like diary writing which is not for others.

Simmons: You don't mean that you don't want other people to read   10
it necessarily.

Kingston: That's not a consideration. I don't want to think about any of that. I think of this as going back to a primitive state of what writing is for me, which is that I am finding my own voice again.

Simmons: Was it lost?

Kingston: Well, I started not to think about it anymore. After a while I had such an effective public voice, from childhood to now, I had found it and I had created it.

Simmons: Where do we see that public voice?

Kingston: The public voice is the voice that's in all my books.   15

Simmons: Even *Woman Warrior*?

Kingston: Yes. All my works. That is a public voice. What I mean by the private, personal voice is what I write when I'm trying to figure out things, what I write that's just for me. I get to be the reader and nobody else gets to read this. For years now I have not written in that way. I usually don't write diaries as an adult and so after the fire I needed to get to that again. I had forgotten about it.

Simmons: You are going back to before *Woman Warrior*, to before being a writer.

Kingston: Yes. Before being a writer who publishes.

Simmons: Why do you think the fire caused you to turn away from   20 fiction?

Kingston: At the same time my father died; he died a few weeks before the fire. At that time I felt I'd lost a lot. So I wanted to say what I felt about all that, about all my losses. And I don't see that as writing for publication. I see that as writing for myself, to put into words my losses. And so I started there, and wrote and wrote and wrote. But as I was writing, it became some of the things I was thinking in the book that burned; those would come into the writing, and then of course I go back to that very *id* basic place. I'm old enough and civilized enough now so that the sentences and the words that come out are very elegant, very good, very crafted. I don't return to a place that's not crafted anymore. So all this stuff that I wrote down is going to be part of *The Fifth Book of Peace*.

62

N. Scott Momaday

The Way to Rainy Mountain

N. Scott Momaday (b. 1934) was born on a Kiowa Indian reservation in Oklahoma and grew up surrounded by the cultural traditions of his people. He has taught at the University of California, Berkeley, Stanford University, Columbia University, and Princeton University, and now teaches at the University of Arizona where he has been since 1982. His first novel, House Made of Dawn *(1968), won a Pulitzer Prize. The author of poetry and autobiography, Momaday has edited a collection of Kiowa oral literature. His most recent publications include* In the Bear's House *(1999),* The Man Made of Words: Essays, Stories, Passages *(1997),* Ancestral Voice: Conversations with N. Scott Momaday *(1989),* The Ancient

Child *(1989),* In the Presence of the Sun: Stories and Poems *(1991), and* Circle of Wonder: A Native American Christmas Story *(1994).* "The Way to Rainy Mountain" *appears as the introduction to the book of that name, published in 1969.*

Momaday thinks of himself as a storyteller. When asked to compare his written voice with his speaking voice, he replied, "My physical voice is something that bears on my writing in an important way. I listen to what I write. I work with it until it is what I want it to be in my hearing. I think that the voice of my writing is very much like the voice of my speaking. And I think in both cases it's distinctive. At least, I mean for it to be. I think that most good writers have individual voices, and that the best writers are those whose voices are most distinctive — most recognizably individual."

A single knoll rises out of the plain in Oklahoma, north and west of the Wichita Range. For my people, the Kiowas, it is an old landmark, and they gave it the name Rainy Mountain. The hardest winter in the world is there. Winter brings blizzards, hot tornadic winds arise in the spring, and in summer the prairie is an anvil's edge. The grass turns brittle and brown, and it cracks beneath your feet. There are green belts along the rivers and creeks, linear groves of hickory and pecan, willow and witch hazel. At a distance in July or August, the steaming foliage seems almost to writhe in fire. Great green and yellow grasshoppers are everywhere in the tall grass, popping up like corn to sting the flesh, and tortoises crawl about on the red earth, going nowhere in the plenty of time. Loneliness is an aspect of the land. All things in the plain are isolate; there is no confusion of objects in the eye, but *one* hill or *one* tree or *one* man. To look upon that landscape in the early morning, with the sun at your back, is to lose the sense of proportion. Your imagination comes to life, and this, you think, is where Creation was begun.

I returned to Rainy Mountain in July. My grandmother had died in the spring, and I wanted to be at her grave. She had lived to be very old and at last infirm. Her only living daughter was with her when she died, and I was told that in death her face was that of a child.

I like to think of her as a child. When she was born, the Kiowas were living the last great moment of their history. For more than a hundred years they had controlled the open range from the Smoky Hill River to the Red, from the headwaters of the Canadian to the fork of the Arkansas and Cimarron. In alliance with the Comanches, they had ruled the whole of the southern Plains. War was their sacred business, and they were among the finest horsemen the world has ever known. But warfare for the Kiowas was pre-eminently a matter of disposition rather than of survival, and they never understood the grim, unrelenting advance of the U.S. Cavalry. When at last, divided and ill-provisioned, they were driven onto the Staked Plains in the cold rains of autumn, they fell into panic. In Palo Duro Canyon they abandoned their crucial stores to pillage and had nothing then but their lives. In order to save themselves, they surrendered to the soldiers of Fort Sill and were imprisoned in the old stone corral that now stands as a military museum. My grandmother was spared the humiliation of those high gray walls by eight or ten years, but she must have known from birth the affliction of defeat, the dark brooding of old warriors.

Her name was Aho, and she belonged to the last culture to evolve in North America. Her forebears came down from the high country in western Montana nearly three centuries ago. They were a mountain people, a mysterious tribe of hunters whose language has never been positively classified in any major group. In the late seventeenth century they began a long migration to the south and east. It was a journey toward the dawn, and it led to a golden age. Along the way the Kiowas were befriended by the Crows, who gave them the culture and religion of the Plains. They acquired horses, and their ancient nomadic spirit was suddenly free of the ground. They acquired Tai-me, the sacred Sun Dance doll, from that moment the object and symbol of their worship, and so shared in the divinity of the sun. Not least, they acquired the sense of destiny, therefore courage and pride. When they entered upon the southern Plains they had been transformed. No longer were they slaves to the simple necessity of survival; they were a lordly and dangerous society of fighters and thieves, hunters and priests of the sun. According to their origin myth, they entered the world through a hollow log. From one point of view, their migration was the fruit of an old prophecy, for indeed they emerged from a sunless world.

Although my grandmother lived out her long life in the shadow of Rainy Mountain, the immense landscape of the continental interior lay like memory in her blood. She could tell of the Crows, whom she had never seen, and of the Black Hills, where she had never been. I wanted to see in reality what she had seen more perfectly in the mind's eye, and traveled fifteen hundred miles to begin my pilgrimage.

Yellowstone, it seemed to me, was the top of the world, a region of deep lakes and dark timber, canyons and waterfalls. But, beautiful as it is, one might have the sense of confinement there. The skyline in all directions is close at hand, the high wall of the woods and deep cleavages of shade. There is a perfect freedom in the mountains, but it belongs to the eagle and the elk, the badger and the bear. The Kiowas reckoned their stature by the distance they could see, and they were bent and blind in the wilderness.

Descending eastward, the highland meadows are a stairway to the plain. In July the inland slope of the Rockies is luxuriant with flax and buckwheat, stonecrop and larkspur. The earth unfolds and the limit of the land recedes. Clusters of trees, and animals grazing far in the distance, cause the vision to reach away and wonder to build upon the mind. The sun follows a longer course in the day, and the sky is immense beyond all comparison. The great billowing clouds that sail upon it are shadows that move upon the grain like water, dividing light. Farther down, in the land of the Crows and Blackfeet, the plain is yellow. Sweet clover takes hold of the hills and bends upon itself to cover and seal the soil. There the

Kiowas paused on their way; they had come to the place where they must change their lives. The sun is at home on the plains. Precisely there does it have the certain character of a god. When the Kiowas came to the land of the Crows, they could see the dark lees of the hills at dawn across the Bighorn River, the profusion of light on the grain shelves, the oldest deity ranging after the solstices. Not yet would they veer southward to the caldron of the land that lay below; they must wean their blood from the northern winter and hold the mountains a while longer in their view. They bore Tai-me in procession to the east.

A dark mist lay over the Black Hills, and the land was like iron. At the top of the ridge I caught sight of Devil's Tower upthrust against the gray sky as if in the birth of time the core of the earth had broken through its crust and the motion of the world was begun. There are things in nature that engender an awful quiet in the heart of man; Devil's Tower is one of them. Two centuries ago, because they could not do otherwise, the Kiowas made a legend at the base of the rock. My grandmother said:

> Eight children were there at play, seven sisters and their brother. Suddenly the boy was struck dumb; he trembled and began to run upon his hands and feet. His fingers became claws, and his body was covered with fur. Directly there was a bear where the boy had been. The sisters were terrified; they ran, and the bear ran after them. They came to the stump of a great tree, and the tree spoke to them. It bade them climb upon it, and as they did so it began to rise into the air. The bear came to kill them, but they were just beyond its reach. It reared against the tree and scored the bark all around with its claws. The seven sisters were borne into the sky, and they became the stars of the Big Dipper.

From that moment, and so long as the legend lives, the Kiowas have kinsmen in the night sky. Whatever they were in the mountains, they could be no more. However tenuous their well-being, however much they had suffered and would suffer again, they had found a way out of the wilderness.

My grandmother had a reverence for the sun, a holy regard that now is all but gone out of mankind. There was a wariness in her, and an ancient awe. She was a Christian in her later years, but she had come a long way about, and she never forgot her birthright. As a child she had been to the Sun Dances; she had taken part in those annual rites, and by them she had learned the restoration of her people in the presence of Tai-me. She was about seven when the last Kiowa Sun Dance was held in 1887 in the Washita River above Rainy Mountain Creek. The buffalo were gone. In order to consummate the ancient sacrifice—to impale the head of a buffalo bull upon the medicine tree—a delegation of old men journeyed into Texas, there to beg and barter for an animal from the Goodnight herd. She was ten when the Kiowas came together for the last time as a living Sun Dance culture. They could find no buffalo; they had to hang an old hide from the sacred tree. Before the dance could begin, a company of soldiers rode out from Fort Sill under orders to disperse the tribe. Forbidden without cause the essential act of their faith, having seen the wild herds slaughtered and left to rot upon the ground, the Kiowas backed away forever from the medicine tree. That was July 20, 1890, at the great bend of the Washita. My grandmother was there. Without bitterness, and for as long as she lived, she bore a vision of deicide.

Now that I can have her only in memory, I see my grandmother in   10
the several postures that were peculiar to her: standing at the wood stove on a winter morning and turning meat in a great iron skillet; sitting at the south window, bent above her beadwork, and afterwards, when her vision failed, looking down for a long time into the fold of her hands; going out upon a cane, very slowly as she did when the weight of age came upon her; praying. I remember her most often at prayer. She made long, rambling prayers out of suffering and hope, having seen many things. I was never sure that I had the right to hear, so exclusive were they of all mere custom and company. The last time I saw her she prayed standing by the side of her bed at night, naked to the waist, the light of a kerosene lamp moving upon her dark skin. Her long, black hair, always drawn and braided in the day, lay upon her shoulders and against her breasts like a shawl. I do not speak Kiowa, and I never understood her prayers, but there was something inherently sad in the sound, some merest hesitation upon the syllables of sorrow. She began in a high and descending pitch, exhausting her breath to silence; then again and again—and always the same intensity of effort, of something that is, and is not, like urgency in the human voice. Transported so in the dancing light among the shadows of her room, she seemed beyond the reach of time. But that was illusion; I think I knew then that I should not see her again.

Houses are like sentinels in the plain, old keepers of the weather watch. There, in a very little while, wood takes on the appearance of great age. All colors wear soon away in the wind and rain, and then the wood is burned gray and the grain appears and the nails turn red with rust. The windowpanes are black and opaque; you imagine there is nothing within, and indeed there are many ghosts, bones given up to the land. They stand here and there against the sky, and you approach them for a longer time than you expect. They belong in the distance; it is their domain.

Once there was a lot of sound in my grandmother's house, a lot of coming and going, feasting and talk. The summers there were full of excitement and reunion. The Kiowas are a summer people; they abide the cold and keep to themselves, but when the season turns and the land becomes warm and vital they cannot hold still; an old love of going returns upon them. The aged visitors who came to my grandmother's house when I was a child were made of lean and leather, and they bore themselves upright. They wore great black hats and bright ample shirts that shook in the wind. They rubbed fat upon their hair and wound their braids with strips of colored cloth. Some of them painted their faces and carried the scars of old and cherished enmities. They were an old council of war-lords, come to remind and be reminded of who they were. Their wives and daughters served them well. The women might indulge themselves; gossip was at once the mark and compensation of their servitude. They made loud and elaborate talk among themselves, full of jest and gesture, fright and false alarm. They went abroad in fringed and flowered shawls, bright beadwork and German silver. They were at home in the kitchen, and they prepared meals that were banquets.

There were frequent prayer meetings, and great nocturnal feasts. When I was a child I played with my cousins outside, where the lamplight fell upon the ground and the singing of the old people rose up around us and carried away into the darkness. There were a lot of good things to eat, a lot of laughter and surprise. And afterwards, when the quiet re-turned, I lay down with my grandmother and could hear the frogs away by the river and feel the motion of the air.

Now there is a funeral silence in the rooms, the endless wake of some final word. The walls have closed in upon my grandmother's house. When I returned to it in mourning, I saw for the first time in my life how small it was. It was late at night, and there was a white moon, nearly full. I sat for a long time on the stone steps by the kitchen door. From there I could see out across the land; I could see the long row of trees by the creek, the low light upon the rolling plains, and the stars of the big dip-per. Once I looked at the moon and caught sight of a strange thing. A cricket had perched upon the handrail, only a few inches away from me. My line of vision was such that the creature filled the moon like a fossil. It had gone there, I thought, to live and die, for there, of all places, was its small definition made whole and eternal. A warm wind rose up and purled like the longing within me.

The next morning I awoke at dawn and went out on the dirt road to Rainy Mountain. It was already hot, and the grasshoppers began to fill the air. Still, it was early in the morning, and the birds sang out of the shadows. The long yellow grass on the mountain shone in the bright light, and a scissortail hied above the land. There, where it ought to be, at the end of a long and legendary way, was my grandmother's grave. Here and there on the dark stones were ancestral names. Looking back once, I saw the mountain and came away.

The Reader's Presence

1. Momaday tells several stories in this selection, including the his-tory of the Kiowa people, the story of his grandmother's life and death, the story of his homecoming, and the legend of Devil's Tower. How does each story overlap and intertwine with the oth-ers? What forces compel the telling or creation of each story?

What needs do the stories satisfy? Look, for example, at the legend related in paragraph 8. The Kiowas made this legend "because they could not do otherwise." Why could they have not done otherwise? What does the legend explain for them? How does this embedded legend enhance and complicate the other stories Momaday tells here?

2. From the beginning of this essay, Momaday sets his remarks very firmly in space and then in time. Discuss the importance of physical space in this essay. Why does Momaday take the journey to Rainy Mountain, and the fifteen-hundred-mile "pilgrimage" (paragraph 5)? Why does he say that his grandmother's vision of this landscape is more perfect than his, even though she has never actually seen the landscape he travels? Consider the many remarks about perspective, and change of perspective, that he includes, as well as remarks on proportion. What significance does he attach to these remarks? Where, literally and figuratively, does his grandmother's grave lie? More generally, consider the temporal journeys that run parallel to the spatial journeys: the Kiowas' "journey toward the dawn [that] led to a golden age" (paragraph 4) and Momaday's own journeys that he relates in the essay. How would you characterize the sense of space and time and the relation between the two that are conveyed in this essay?

3. In the interview quoted in the introductory note to this selection, Momaday talks about capturing his speaking voice in his writing. What are some of the phrases and passages that make you hear his distinctive voice as you read? Point to—and analyze—specific words and phrases to discuss how he creates the effect he is aiming for. Compare Momaday's voice to Zora Neale Hurston's in "How It Feels to Be Colored Me" (page 150), and to Calvin Trillin's in "A Traditional Family" (page 561). Despite their differences in tone, what common techniques do these writers use to make their prose appealing to the reader's ear?

63

Bharati Mukherjee

Two Ways to Belong in America

Bharati Mukherjee was born in Calcutta, India, in 1940 and came to the United States at the age of twenty-one to attend the Iowa Writers' Workshop. After she received her Ph.D. at the University of Iowa in 1969, Mukherjee moved to Canada with her husband, Clark Blaise, for several years. Tired of the racist attitudes Mukherjee encountered, she and Blaise eventually returned to the United States, where she has taught at various universities and colleges. She is the author of many novels, including Jasmine *(1989),* The Holder of the World *(1993),* Leave It to Me *(1997), and* Desirable Daughters *(2002). Her two collections of short stories are* Darkness *(1985) and* The Middleman and Other Stories *(1988), which won the National Book Critics' Circle Award. She currently teaches creative writing at the University of California at Berkeley. "Two Ways to Belong in America" originally appeared in the* New York Times *in 1996.*

This is a tale of two sisters from Calcutta, Mira and Bharati, who have lived in the United States for some thirty-five years, but who find themselves on different sides in the current debate over the status of immigrants. I am an American citizen and she is not. I am moved that thousands of long-term residents are finally taking the oath of citizenship. She is not.

Mira arrived in Detroit in 1960 to study child psychology and preschool education. I followed her a year later to study creative writing at the University of Iowa. When we left India, we were almost identical in appearance and attitude. We dressed alike, in saris; we expressed identical views on politics, social issues, love and marriage in the same Calcutta convent-school accent. We would endure our two years in America, secure our degrees, then return to India to marry the grooms of our father's choosing.

Instead, Mira married an Indian student in 1962 who was getting his business administration degree at Wayne State University. They soon acquired the labor certifications necessary for the green card of hassle-free residence and employment.

Mira still lives in Detroit, works in the Southfield, Mich., school system, and has become nationally recognized for her contributions in the fields of pre-school education and parent-teacher relationships. After 36 years as a legal immigrant in this country, she clings passionately to her Indian citizenship and hopes to go home to India when she retires.

In Iowa City in 1963, I married a fellow student, an American of Cana- 5 dian parentage. Because of the accident of his North Dakota birth, I bypassed labor-certification requirements and the race-related "quota" system that favored the applicant's country of origin over his or her merit. I was prepared for (and even welcomed) the emotional strain that came with marrying outside my ethnic community. In thirty-three years of marriage, we have lived in every part of North America. By choosing a husband who was not my father's selection, I was opting for fluidity, self-invention, blue jeans and T-shirts, and renouncing three thousand years (at least) of caste-observant, "pure culture" marriage in the Mukherjee family. My books have often been read as unapologetic (and in some quarters overenthusiastic) texts for cultural and psychological "mongrelization." It's a word I celebrate.

Mira and I have stayed sisterly close by phone. In our regular Sunday morning conversations, we are unguardedly affectionate. I am her only blood relative on this continent. We expect to see each other through the looming crises of aging and ill health without being asked. Long before Vice President Gore's "Citizenship U.S.A." drive, we'd had our polite arguments over the ethics of retaining an overseas citizenship while expecting the permanent protection and economic benefits that come with living and working in America.

Like well-raised sisters, we never said what was really on our minds, but we probably pitied one another. She, for the lack of structure in my life, the erasure of Indianness, the absence of an unvarying daily core. I, for the narrowness of her perspective, her uninvolvement with the mythic depths or the superficial pop culture of this society. But, now, with the scapegoating of "aliens" (documented or illegal) on the increase, and the targeting of long-term legal immigrants like Mira for new scrutiny and new self-consciousness, she and I find ourselves unable to maintain the same polite discretion. We were always unacknowledged adversaries, and we are now, more than ever, sisters.

"I feel used," Mira raged on the phone the other night. "I feel manipulated and discarded. This is such an unfair way to treat a person who was invited to stay and work here because of her talent. My employer went to the I.N.S. and petitioned for the labor certification. For over thirty years, I've invested my creativity and professional skills into the improvement of *this* country's pre-school system. I've obeyed all the rules, I've paid my taxes, I love my work, I love my students, I love the friends I've made. How dare America now change its rules in midstream? If America wants to make new rules curtailing benefits of legal immigrants, they should apply only to immigrants who arrive after those rules are already in place."

To my ears, it sounded like the description of a long-enduring, comfortable yet loveless marriage, without risk or recklessness. Have we the right to demand, and to expect, that we be loved? (That, to me is the subtext of the arguments by immigration advocates.) My sister is an expatriate, professionally generous and creative, socially courteous and gracious, and that's as far as her Americanization can go. She is here to maintain an identity, not to transform it.

I asked her if she would follow the example of others who have decided to become citizens because of the anti-immigration bills in Congress. And here, she surprised me. "If America wants to play the manipulative game, I'll play it too," she snapped. "I'll become a U.S. citizen for now, then change back to Indian when I'm ready to go home. I feel some kind of irrational attachment to India that I don't to America. Until all this hysteria against legal immigrants, I was totally happy. Having my green card meant I could visit any place in the world I wanted to and then come back to a job that's satisfying and that I do very well."

In one family, from two sisters alike as peas in a pod, there could not be a wider divergence of immigrant experience. America spoke to me—I married it—I embraced the demotion from expatriate aristocrat to immigrant nobody, surrendering those thousands of years of "pure culture," the saris, the delightfully accented English. She retained them all. Which of us is the freak?

Mira's voice, I realize, is the voice not just of the immigrant South Asian community but of an immigrant community of the millions who have stayed rooted in one job, one city, one house, one ancestral culture, one cuisine, for the entirety of their productive years. She speaks for greater numbers than I possibly can. Only the fluency of her English and the anger, rather than fear, born of confidence from her education, differentiate her from the seamstresses, the domestics, the technicians, the shop owners, the millions of hard-working but effectively silenced documented immigrants as well as their less fortunate "illegal" brothers and sisters.

Nearly twenty years ago, when I was living in my husband's ancestral homeland of Canada, I was always well-employed but never allowed to feel part of the local Quebec or larger Canadian society. Then, through a Green Paper that invited a national referendum on the unwanted side effects of "nontraditional" immigration, the Government officially turned against its immigrant communities, particularly those from South Asia.

I felt then the same sense of betrayal that Mira feels now. I will never forget the pain of that sudden turning, and the casual racist outbursts the Green Paper elicited. That sense of betrayal had its desired effect and drove me, and thousands like me, from the country.

Mira and I differ, however, in the ways in which we hope to interact with the country that we have chosen to live in. She is happier to live in America as expatriate Indian than as an immigrant American. I need to feel like a part of the community I have adopted (as I tried to feel in Canada as well). I need to put roots down, to vote and make the difference that I can. The price that the immigrant willingly pays, and that the exile avoids, is the trauma of self-transformation.

The Reader's Presence

1. Mukherjee holds a strong opinion, yet strives to represent the opposing side. How is her sister's perspective portrayed? What images does the writer use to describe her sister's lifestyle? Might her sister describe her perspective differently? Does Mukherjee really offer the reader "two ways" of considering the conflict?

2. The essay primarily concerns immigrants and their choices. How are America itself and the citizenship drive portrayed? How does Mukherjee's piece challenge stereotypic views of immigrants as passive and fearful of asserting their rights? To whom does her argument seem directed? Why?

3. Mukherjee's last sentence is provocative, suggesting as it does that the two positions — that of immigrant and that of exile — are necessarily and inherently opposed. Richard Rodriquez, similarly, feels intensely the loss experienced by the second generation of immigrant families in "Aria: A Memoir of a Bilingual Childhood" (page 221). Compare Mukherjee's and Rodriguez's absolute dichotomies to Alberto Ríos's "Green Cards" (page 217). Is Ríos's "discovery of the middle" present in either of the other two essays? If not, can you find places where such ambiguity seems to have been excluded from the essays?

64

Gloria Naylor

A Question of Language

Gloria Naylor (b. 1950) won an American Book Award for her first novel, The Women of Brewster Place *(1982); her most recent novel is a sequel,* The Men of Brewster Place *(1998). Her other works of fiction include* Linden Hills *(1985),* Mama Day *(1988), and* Bailey's Café *(1992), and her nonfiction has been published in* Centennial *(1986). In addition to these books, Naylor contributes essays and articles to many periodicals, including* Southern Review, Essence, Ms., Life, Callaloo, *and the* Ontario Review. *Also, she recently founded One Way Productions, an independent film company that she established to bring the novel* Mama Day *to the screen. Naylor has worked as the "Hers" columnist for the* New York Times *and as a visiting professor and writer at Princeton University, New York University, the University of Pennsylvania, Boston University, and Brandeis Uni-*

versity. In addition, Naylor was a cultural exchange lecturer in India in 1985 and a senior fellow at the Society for the Humanities, Cornell University , in 1988. The article "A Question of Language" first appeared in the New York Times *in 1986.*

Naylor credits her mother's inspiration for her love of books and writing: "Realizing that I was a painfully shy child, she gave me my first diary and told me to write my feelings down in there. Over the years that diary was followed by reams and reams of paper that eventually culminated in The Women of Brewster Place. *And I wrote that book as a tribute to her and other black women who, in spite of very limited personal circumstances, somehow manage to hold fierce belief in the limitless possibilities of the human spirit."*

Language is the subject. It is the written form with which I've managed to keep the wolf away from the door and, in diaries, to keep my sanity. In spite of this, I consider the written word inferior to the spoken, and much of the frustration experienced by novelists is the awareness that whatever we manage to capture in even the most transcendent passages falls far short of the richness of life. Dialogue achieves its power in the dynamics of a fleeting moment of sight, sound, smell, and touch.

I'm not going to enter the debate here about whether it is language that shapes reality or vice versa. That battle is doomed to be waged whenever we seek intermittent reprieve from the chicken and egg dispute. I will simply take the position that the spoken word, like the written word, amounts to a nonsensical arrangement of sounds or letters without a consensus that assigns "meaning." And building from the meanings of what we hear, we order reality. Words themselves are innocuous; it is the consensus that gives them true power.

I remember the first time I heard the word *nigger*. In my third-grade class, our math tests were being passed down the rows, and as I handed the papers to a little boy in back of me, I remarked that once again he had received a much lower mark than I did. He snatched his test from me and spit out that word. Had he called me a nymphomaniac or a necrophiliac, I couldn't have been more puzzled. I didn't know what a nigger was, but I knew that whatever it meant, it was something he shouldn't have called me. This was verified when I raised my hand, and in a loud voice repeated what he had said and watched the teacher scold him for using a "bad" word. I was later to go home and ask the inevitable question that every black parent must face — "Mommy, what does 'nigger' mean?"

And what exactly did it mean? Thinking back, I realize that this could not have been the first time the word was used in my presence. I was part of a large extended family that had migrated from the rural South after World War II and formed a close-knit network that gravitated around my maternal grandparents. Their ground-floor apartment in one of the buildings they owned in Harlem was a weekend mecca for my immediate family, along with countless aunts, uncles, and cousins who brought along assorted friends. It was a bustling and open house with assorted neighbors and tenants popping in and out to exchange bits of gossip, pick up an old quarrel, or referee the ongoing checkers game in which my grandmother cheated shamelessly. They were all there to let down their hair and put up their feet after a week of labor in the factories, laundries, and shipyards of New York.

Amid the clamor, which could reach deafening proportions—two or three conversations going on simultaneously, punctuated by the sound of a baby's crying somewhere in the back rooms or out on the street—there was still a rigid set of rules about what was said and how. Older children were sent out of the living room when it was time to get into the juicy details about "you-know-who" up on the third floor who had gone and gotten herself "p-r-e-g-n-a-n-t!" But my parents, knowing that I could spell well beyond my years, always demanded that I follow the others out to play. Beyond sexual misconduct and death, everything else was considered harmless for our young ears. And so among the anecdotes of the triumphs and disappointments in the various workings of their lives, the word *nigger* was used in my presence, but it was set within contexts and inflections that caused it to register in my mind as something else.

In the singular, the word was always applied to a man who had distinguished himself in some situation that brought their approval for his strength, intelligence, or drive:

"Did Johnny really do that?"

"I'm telling you, that nigger pulled in $6,000 of overtime last year. Said he got enough for a down payment on a house."

When used with a possessive adjective by a woman—"my nigger"—it became a term of endearment for husband or boyfriend. But it could be more than just a term applied to a man. In their mouths it became the pure essence of manhood—a disembodied force that channeled their past history of struggle and present survival against the odds into a victorious statement of being: "Yeah, that old foreman found out quick enough—you don't mess with a nigger."

In the plural, it became a description of some group within the community that had overstepped the bounds of decency as my family defined it: Parents who neglected their children, a drunken couple who fought in public, people who simply refused to look for work, those with excessively dirty mouths or unkempt households were all "trifling niggers." This particular circle could forgive hard times, unemployment, the occasional bout of depression—they had gone through all of that themselves—but the unforgivable sin was lack of self-respect.

A woman could never be a *nigger* in the singular, with its connotation of confirming worth. The noun *girl* was its closest equivalent in that sense, but only when used in direct address and regardless of the gender doing the addressing. *Girl* was a token of respect for a woman. The one-syllable word was drawn out to sound like three in recognition of the extra ounce of wit, nerve, or daring that the woman had shown in the situation under discussion.

"G-i-r-l, stop. You mean you said that to his face?"

5

10

But if the word was used in a third-person reference or shortened so that it almost snapped out of the mouth, it always involved some element of communal disapproval. And age became an important factor in these exchanges. It was only between individuals of the same generation, or from an older person to a younger (but never the other way around), that "girl" would be considered a compliment.

I don't agree with the argument that use of the word *nigger* at this social stratum of the black community was an internalization of racism. The dynamics were the exact opposite: the people in my grandmother's living room took a word that whites used to signify worthlessness or degradation and rendered it impotent. Gathering there together, they transformed *nigger* to signify the varied and complex human beings they knew themselves to be. If the word was to disappear totally from the mouths of even the most liberal of white society, no one in that room was naïve enough to believe it would disappear from white minds. Meeting the word head-on, they proved it had absolutely nothing to do with the way they were determined to live their lives.

So there must have been dozens of times that the word *nigger* was   15
spoken in front of me before I reached the third grade. But I didn't "hear" it until it was said by a small pair of lips that had already learned it could be a way to humiliate me. That was the word I went home and asked my mother about. And since she knew that I had to grow up in America, she took me in her lap and explained.

The Reader's Presence

1. Naylor analyzes the various meanings of the word *nigger*, meanings that are agreed to by consensus and that vary according to the speaker, the audience, and the context within which the word is spoken. Outline the different meanings of *nigger*, and evaluate the effectiveness of the example she provides to illustrate each definition. Do the same for her definitions of *girl*. Can you think of any other examples to reinforce the points she makes in each definition, or any examples that challenge her definitions?

2. Where—and how—does Naylor make her own point of view clear in this essay? How does she reveal her personal stake in the issues addressed in the essay? Consider her use of personal narrative. Comment, for example, on the effectiveness of paragraphs 4 and 5. What do they contribute to the overall point of her essay? What does this description of the circumstances of her extended family in Harlem add to the essay?

3. Naylor creates a two-part structure for her short essay: two generalized, abstract opening paragraphs, followed by a series of extended illustrations of her definitions of the two key words. In the first paragraph she discusses the nature of language and its inade-

quacy in conveying the fullness and complexity of an experience. In the second she asserts that a shared sense of the meanings of words helps to define a social group. Review the usages of *nigger* and *girl* that Naylor provides. What inferences can you draw about the values of the communities she describes? What do these definitions and usages tell us about what kinds of behavior are to be censured or avoided? Compare Naylor's essay to Jamaica Kincaid's short story "Girl" (page 840). How does the story compare with the essay in respect to subject, prose style, and force of argument?

65

Kathleen Norris

The Holy Use of Gossip

Kathleen Norris (b. 1947) is a poet, editor, and author who also manages her family's ranch in Lemmon, South Dakota. Norris has published several collections of poetry, including Falling Off *(1971),* The Middle of the World *(1981), and* Little Girls in Church *(1995). She has recently written* Amazing Grace *(2000), "a poet's journey through language to faith," which recounts the author's religious conversion. Although a poet throughout her writing career, she is most noted for her two spiritual memoirs. In* Dakota: A Spiritual Geography *(1993), which contains "The Holy Use of Gossip," Norris discusses how life in the Great Plains provides her with a source of inspiration and spiritual renewal. The* Cloister Walk *(1996), a follow-up, is a collection of personal meditations on organized religion, her experiences with monasticism, and the value of celibacy.*

> It is the responsibility of writers to listen to gossip and pass it on. It is the way all storytellers learn about life.
>
> —Grace Paley

> If there's anything worth calling theology, it is listening to people's stories, listening to them and cherishing them.
>
> —Mary Pellauer

I once scandalized a group of North Dakota teenagers who had been determined to scandalize me. Working as an artist-in-residence in their school for three weeks, I happened to hit prom weekend. Never much for proms in high school, I helped decorate, cutting swans out of posterboard and sprinkling them with purple glitter as the school gym was festooned with lavender and silver crepe paper streamers.

On Monday morning a group of the school outlaws was gossiping in the library, just loud enough for me to hear, about the drunken exploits that had taken place at a prairie party in the wee hours after the dance: kids meeting in some remote spot, drinking beer and listening to car stereos turned up loud, then, near dawn, going to one girl's house for breakfast. I finally spoke up and said, "See, it's like I told you: the party's not over until you've told the stories. That's where all writing starts." They looked up at me, pretending that it bothered them that I'd heard.

"And," I couldn't resist adding, "everyone knows you don't get piss-drunk and then eat scrambled eggs. If you didn't know it before, you know it now." "You're not going to write about *that,* are you?" one girl said, her eyes wide. "I don't know," I replied, "I might. It's all grist for the mill."

When my husband and I first moved to Dakota, people were quick to tell us about an eccentric young man who came from back East and gradually lost his grip on reality. He shared a house with his sheep until relatives came and took him away. "He was a college graduate," someone would always add, looking warily at us as if to say, we know what can happen to Easterners who are too well educated. This was one of the first tales to go into my West River treasure-house of stories. It was soon joined by the story of the man who shot himself to see what it felt like. He hit his lower leg and later said that while he didn't feel anything for a few seconds, after that it hurt like hell.

There was Rattlesnake Bill, a cowboy who used to carry rattlers in a paper sack in his pickup truck. If you didn't believe him, he'd put his hand in without looking and take one out to show you. One night Bill limped into a downtown bar on crutches. A horse he was breaking had dragged him for about a mile, and he was probably lucky to be alive. He'd been knocked out, he didn't know for how long, and when he regained consciousness he had crawled to his house and changed clothes to come to town. Now Bill thought he'd drink a little whiskey for the pain. "Have you been to a doctor?" friends asked. "Nah, whiskey'll do." 5

Later that night at the steak house I managed to get Bill to eat something—most of my steak, as it turned out, but he needed it more than I. The steak was rare, and that didn't sit well with Bill. A real man eats his steak well done. But when I said, "What's the matter, are you too chicken to eat rare meat?" he gobbled it down. He slept in his pickup that night, and someone managed to get him to a doctor the next day. He had a broken pelvis.

There was another cowboy who had been mauled by a bobcat in a remote horse barn by the Grand River. The animal had leapt from a hayloft as he tied up a horse, and he had managed to grab a rifle and shoot her. He felt terrible afterwards, saying, "I should have realized the only reason she'd have attacked like that was because she was protecting young." He found her two young cubs, still blind, in the loft. In a desperate attempt to save them he called several veterinarians in the hope that they might know of a lactating cat who had aborted. Such a cat was found, but the cubs lived just a few more days.

There was a woman who nursed her husband through a long illness. A dutiful farm daughter and ranch wife, she had never experienced life on her own. When she was widowed, all the town spoke softly about "poor Ida." But when "poor Ida" kicked up her heels and, entering a delayed adolescence in her fifties, dyed her hair, dressed provocatively, and went dancing more than once a week at the steak house, the sympathetic cooing of the gossips turned to outrage. The woman at the center of the storm hadn't changed; she was still an innocent, bewildered by the calumny now directed at her. She lived it down and got herself a steady boyfriend, but she still dyes her hair and dresses flashy. I'm grateful for the color she adds to the town.

Sometimes it seems as if the whole world is fueled by gossip. Much of what passes for hard news today is the Hollywood fluff that was relegated to pulp movie magazines when I was a girl. From the Central Intelligence Agency to *Entertainment Tonight,* gossip is big business. But in small towns, gossip is still small-time. And as bad as it can be — venal, petty, mean — in the small town it also stays closer to the roots of the word. If you look up gossip in the *Oxford English Dictionary* you find that it is derived from the words for God and sibling, and originally meant "akin to God." It was used to describe one who has contracted spiritual kinship by acting as a sponsor at baptism; one who helps "give a name to." Eric Partridge's *Origins,* a dictionary of etymology, tells you simply to "see God," and there you find that the word's antecedents include gospel, godspell, *sippe* (or consanguinity) and "*sabha,* a village community — notoriously inter-related."

We are interrelated in a small town, whether or not we're related by   10
blood. We know without thinking about it who owns what car; inhabitants of a town as small as a monastery learn to recognize each other's footsteps in the hall. Story is a safety valve for people who live as intimately as that; and I would argue that gossip done well can be a holy thing. It can strengthen communal bonds.

Gossip provides comic relief for people under tension. Candidates at one monastery are told of a novice in the past who had such a hot temper that the others loved to bait him. Once when they were studying he closed a window and the other monks opened it; once, twice. When he got up to close the window for the third time, he yelled at them, "Why are you making me sin with this window?"

Gossip can help us give a name to ourselves. The most revealing section of the weekly *Lemmon Leader* is the personal column in the classified ads, where people express thanks to those who helped with the bloodmobile, a 4-H booth at the county fair, a Future Homemakers of America fashion show, a benefit for a family beset by huge medical bills.

If you've been in the hospital or have suffered a death in the family, you take out an ad thanking the doctor, ambulance crew, and wellwishers who visited, sent cards, offered prayers, or brought gifts of food.

Often these ads are quite moving, written from the heart. The parents of a small boy recently thanked those who had remembered their son with

> prayers, cards, balloons, and gifts, and gave moral support to the rest of the family when Ty underwent surgery. . . . It's great to be home again in this caring community, and our biggest task now is to get Ty to eat more often and larger amounts. Where else but Lemmon would we find people who would stop by and have a bedtime snack and milk with Ty or provide good snacks just to help increase his caloric intake, or a school system with staff that take the time to make sure he eats his extra snacks. May God Bless all of you for caring about our "special little" boy — who is going to gain weight!

No doubt it is the vast land surrounding us, brooding on the edge of our consciousness, that makes it necessary for us to call such attention to human activity. Publicly asserting, as do many of these ads, that we live in a caring community helps us keep our hopes up in a hard climate or hard times, and gives us a sense of identity.

Privacy takes on another meaning in such an environment, where you   15
are asked to share your life, humbling yourself before the common wisdom, such as it is. Like everyone else, you become public property and come to accept things that city people would consider rude. A young woman using the pay phone in a West River café is scrutinized by several older women who finally ask her, " Who are you, anyway?" On discovering that she is from a ranch some sixty miles south, they question her until, learning her mother's maiden name, they are satisfied. They know her grandparents by reputation; good ranchers, good people.

The *Leader* has correspondents in rural areas within some fifty miles of Lemmon — Bison, Chance, Duck Creek, Howe, Morristown, Rosebud (on the Grand River), Shadehill, Spring Butte, Thunder Hawk, White Butte — as well as at the local nursing home and in the town of Lemmon itself, who report on "doings." If you volunteer at the nursing home's weekly popcorn party and sing-along, your name appears. If you host a card party at your home, this is printed, along with the names of your guests. If you have guests from out of town, their names appear. Many notices would baffle an outsider, as they require an intimate knowledge of family relationships to decipher. One recent column from White Butte, headed "Neighbors Take Advantage of Mild Winter Weather to Visit Each Other," read in part: "Helen Johanssen spent several afternoons with Gaylene Francke; Mavis Merdahl was a Wednesday overnight guest at the Alvera Ellis home."

Allowing yourself to be a subject of gossip is one of the sacrifices you make, living in a small town. And the pain caused by the loose talk of ignorant people is undeniable. One couple I know, having lost their only child to a virulent pneumonia (a robust thirty-five year old, he was dead in a matter of days) had to endure rumors that he had died of suicide, AIDS, and even anthrax. But it's also true that the gossips don't know all that they think they know, and often misread things in a comical way. My husband was once told that he was having an affair with a woman he hadn't met, and I still treasure the day I was encountered by three people who said, "Have you sold your house yet?" "When's the baby due?" and, "I'm sorry to hear your mother died."

I could trace the sources of the first two rumors: we'd helped a friend move into a rented house, and I'd bought baby clothes downtown when I learned that I would soon become an aunt. The third rumor was easy enough to check; I called my mother on the phone. The flip side, the saving grace, is that despite the most diligent attentions of the die-hard gossips, it is possible to have secrets.

Of course the most important things can't be hidden: birth, sickness, death, divorce. But gossip is essentially democratic. It may be the plumber and his wife who had a screaming argument in a bar, or it could be the bank president's wife who moved out and rented a room in the motel; everyone is fair game. And although there are always those who take delight in the misfortunes of others, and relish a juicy story at the expense of truth and others' feelings, this may be the exception rather than the rule. Surprisingly often, gossip is the way small-town people express solidarity.

I recall a marriage that was on the rocks. The couple had split up,   20
and gossip ran wild. Much sympathy was expressed for the children, and one friend of the couple said to me, "The worst thing she could do is to take him back too soon. This will take time." Those were healing words, a kind of prayer. And when the family did reunite, the town breathed a collective sigh of relief.

My own parents' marriage was of great interest in Lemmon back in the 1930s. My mother, the town doctor's only child, eloped with another Northwestern University student; a musician, of all things. A poor preacher's kid. "This will bear watching," one matriarch said. My parents fooled her. As time went on, the watching grew dull. Now going on fifty-five years, their marriage has outlasted all the gossip.

Like the desert tales that monks have used for centuries as a basis for a theology and way of life, the tales of small-town gossip are often morally instructive, illustrating the ways ordinary people survive the worst that happens to them; or, conversely, the ways in which self-pity, anger, and despair can overwhelm and destroy them. Gossip is theology translated into experience. In it we hear great stories of conversion, like the drunk who turns his or her life around, as well as stories of failure. We can see that pride really does go before a fall, and that hope is essential. We watch closely those who retire, or who lose a spouse, lest they lose interest in living. When we gossip we are also praying, not only for them but for ourselves.

At its deepest level, small-town gossip is about how we face matters of life and death. We see the gossip of earlier times, the story immortalized in ballads such as "Barbara Allen," lived out before our eyes as a young man obsessively in love with a vain young woman nearly self-destructs. We also see how people heal themselves. One of the bravest people I know is a young mother who sewed and embroidered exquisite baptismal clothes for her church with the memorial money she received when her first baby died. When she gave birth to a healthy girl a few years later, the whole town rejoiced.

My favorite gossip takes note of the worst and the best that is in us. Two women I know were diagnosed with terminal cancer. One said, "If I ever get out of this hospital, I'm going to look out for Number One." And that's exactly what she did. Against overwhelming odds, she survived, and it made her mean. The other woman spoke about the blessings of a life that had taken some hard blows: her mother had killed herself when she was a girl, her husband had died young. I happened to visit her just after she'd been told that she had less than a year to live. She was dry-eyed, and had been reading the Psalms. She was entirely realistic about her illness and said to me, "The one thing that scares me is the pain. I hope I die before I turn into an old bitch." I told her family that story after the funeral, and they loved it; they could hear in it their mother's voice, the way she really was.

The Reader's Presence

1. How is gossip generally characterized? How does Norris characterize it? What positive possibilities does it offer? Why is the etymology of the word important to her point?

2. How does Norris describe the small town she lives in? What does she reveal about it through the anecdotes she tells? What is her attitude toward the town? What is her idea of a suitable community? What sort of audience does her description seem to be aimed at? Is she, for example, writing mainly for her own community?

3. This piece is drawn from a book called *Dakota: A Spiritual Biography*. Norris uses many religious terms in the piece and calls gossip "holy." How might her concepts of the sacred differ from conventional ones? How does Norris evoke her sense of the sacred for her readers, and why? Read Bertrand Russell's essay "Why I Am Not a Christian" (page 729), focusing especially on the penultimate paragraph in which he argues that fear is the basis of religious belief. Does Norris understand "the holy use of gossip" as based, in part, on fear? How might Russell's arguments *against* religion help you to understand Norris's arguments *on behalf* of spiritual faith?

THE WRITER AT WORK

Kathleen Norris on the Vocabulary of Religion

Although Kathleen Norris was born and remains a Protestant, she has written extensively of Catholic monasticism and has even become a lay member of the Benedictine Order. In the following passages from an interview with Notre Dame professor and poet Sonia Gernes which appeared in Notre Dame *magazine (Autumn 1998), Norris discusses how important ancestral and religious roots can be to one's writing. Norris acknowledges that many people today are uncomfortable with a religious vocabulary, but she believes that facing those discomforts directly can be a source of creative strength. You might consider some of the religious words you personally think carry (as Norris says) "negative charges." Are you embarrassed to use a religious vocabulary? How does Norris herself use such terms in the interview as well as in the preceding essay, "The Holy Use of Gossip?"*

Gernes: In the mid-1970s, you were a young poet in New York City with connections to the literary world—on the fringe of the Andy Warhol scene, I think you said in one of the books—and you decided to move to a very small town in the Dakotas. I know that your family inherited some property from your grandmother, but aside from that, why did you make that decision?

Norris: It really was largely a family decision. I was the only one of my brother and two sisters who had a job that I could give up. I was the one who could go out there and help manage the ranch and live in the house in town and do all of that. I also had this sneaking suspicion that it would be good for me as a writer to back away from the literary hot house. All my friends were other writers, which was very common in that world, so this was an opportunity for a dramatic change and I thought: Well, we'll see what sorts out here. I also thought [about] getting back to my ancestral roots in a sense, because I had three generations going back in that little town in South Dakota. Partly it was almost a writing experiment—I had a feeling that it would jog some things in my writing. Obviously I was right about that, but I had no idea how right I would be of course.

Gernes: Did you have any inkling that you were not only going back to your roots as a writer but also back to your religious roots?

Norris: Not terribly. What happened—and it was not conscious on my part—was [that] the little Presbyterian church was the church where I had gone to Sunday school every summer when I was a child, so I was familiar with the congregation and I had always known the ministers because of my grandmother. So there was a natural progression toward having the ministers as social friends. I got involved with the church very early on, back in '74, but then it was really a sort of exercise in nostalgia; it didn't really take hold until about ten years later.

Gernes: In *Dakota,* you talk about a "monster God" that was part of   5
your grandmother Norris' Protestant heritage. I grew up—and still am—
Catholic and was a very scrupulous child. I spent a fair amount of my
childhood fearing that I was in mortal sin and would go straight to hell. It
was interesting to me to see you talking about that in terms of Protes-
tantism also. Could you say any more about that?

Norris: I think the concept of the "monster God" was really very
important because in both Catholic and Protestant religions you can
certainly find this. Sometimes when I am on talk shows with people
calling in—and of course when you go on talk shows talking about religion, you are really putting your life into your own hands and going
where angels would fear to tread—but sometimes we will get these calls
from people who are so angry that someone is saying anything good at
all about the Christian religion. They will talk about their own bad experiences, and of course they make that the measure of everything. Their
bottom line is sometimes: How could God let these things happen? And
they might mention the Holocaust or the death of one child. I began to
realize that they really think that God *is* a monster—that God is causing these horrible things to happen to punish us or just because God is
capricious. It's incredible to listen to these calls and try to respond because you really can't get into the depths of it, but that is what I am
often hearing from people who want to talk about God. I think too
many people get raised in religions with that kind of attitude, and
maybe as adults you need to shed some of that and try to figure out
what is really going on there.

Gernes: You've said that for about twenty years you did not attend
church and put "nothing" down in the blanks where it asked for religion.
Do you think you would be where you are today in terms of spirituality if
there hadn't been this fallow period that let you start over?

Norris: I think for me it was necessary; even that is hard to know
for sure. It was also the typical baby boomer thing—drifting away from
religion. I didn't really even think about it that much, I just drifted
away in my late teens when I went to college. I went to Bennington,
which is an extremely secular environment, so there really wasn't anything [religious] on that campus. Arts and psychiatry had replaced religion. But I think in terms of developmental stages with religion,
adolescents do need to shed some of their childish faith and childish religion in order to mature into an adult religion, adult faith. I think that
is really the progression in my three books, and I think in a sense that is
really what I have been writing about. For myself, ironically, that
twenty-year hiatus seems to have been a necessary part of the process. It
was during that twenty years, of course, that I became a writer, and
now I feel that I have sort of come full circle. I am joining all the parts
together of this puzzle because it was becoming a writer that allowed
me to tell this story.

Gernes: In *Dakota,* you make a statement about doctrinal language slamming doors in your face and "words obscuring the *Word."* Was that a motive force behind this "vocabulary of faith" book?

Norris: Oh, yes. I think I really began writing this book the minute I   10 crossed over and decided to go to church on my own. The Presbyterian worship service was like this bombardment with words that I had a very dim memory of, maybe having studied them when I was twelve years old, but never really getting an existential grasp, a deeper meaning of what this word could mean. It took me a long time to work out [an] adult accommodation of a lot of the vocabulary. I think poetry and religion are both taught rather badly in our culture. When I was twelve years old I memorized a lot of words, but they didn't have any real depth or any real meaning or significance in my life. Of course now they do, and of course I am still running into people my own age who just assume that the doctrinal language doesn't mean anything. I think it's a real problem, because to educate young people in the Christian tradition you have to use those words—you can't jettison them. When you do that you end up with something very murky. But how to teach it is really very difficult.

Gernes: I want to ask about the interplay between poetry and spirituality in your life. Does one help feed the other?

Norris: Oh sure. One of the most amazing things that has happened to me as a writer was that after I had finished *Dakota* and survived my book tour, I went back to [the Ecumenical Institute at] Saint John's in Minnesota. I hadn't really been writing any poetry; because of *Dakota* I had really been focusing on prose. I showed up there in fall of '93 and literally, as soon as I began going to the daily liturgy with the monks— morning prayer, noon prayer, evening prayer and usually the Mass— these poems just started coming. I ended up that fall writing almost a whole new book of poems. It was really inspiring and many of my poems that came out during that time really were like a dialogue with the liturgy, with the liturgical readings, with the Psalms, with the homilies sometimes; I mean everything sort of one fabric. It was just an amazing period for me. I have never had a period like that as a writer. I don't know that I ever will again.

Gernes: You mention in the new book that feminist theology became important, that you read a lot of it for a period of time. How did that influence the development of your thought?

Norris: It was very exciting. I read hundreds and hundreds of books on feminist scholarship and then I started reading anti-feminist things, because I wanted to read a whole spectrum of this incredible ferment. This would have been in the early '80s, so I had a lot of catching up to do, and I just immersed myself in reading theology and biblical scholarship for a couple of years. I don't think that anybody gets very good biblical studies, biblical scholarship in Sunday school; I certainly didn't. We learned how to do origami and sing a lot. The singing was very important, but the substantive

look at biblical criticism wasn't allowed, you see, and the kind of questions
that I might have been interested in weren't allowed to be raised.

All of a sudden I am in my early thirties and finding that I am able to   15
read all of this wonderful biblical interpretation, all this exciting stuff, but
ultimately it became a problem for me. I think there is a certain stage of
feminist anger that everyone goes through when you look at the history.
You get so depressed and angry about what is going on in the tradition
but also I think for myself it was a very dangerous overintellectualizing of
religion. The reason that I wrote the book was to just tell my experience
in this little town where most people really don't care much about theology. They care about the church and they care about religion and their
faith is really important to them, but they don't think about theology.
The only people that I really had to talk it over with were the ministers.
Sometimes, some of the feminist critique became an obstacle to simply enjoying the community of this little church and the worship there. I really
had to try to figure out what matters more.

I felt a little scared about [writing the feminist chapter] because I am
really writing about my experience only and not trying to make judgments on anybody — the conservative side, the liberal side, or feminist or
anti-feminist. I will be interested to see what kind of reaction I get. I have
already had women come up to me and say, "You are describing exactly
what happened to me," which is always good to hear.

Gernes: In redefining the childhood terms of religion, you started
fresh because of your twenty years away from church. What about people
for whom some of those old words still carry negative charges but who
have never really left the tradition? Any advice for those of us?

Norris: If words carry negative charges that usually means that there's
some significant relationship there, and I think one of the worst things we do
in American culture with anything negative is try to deny it or shove it aside.
I think one of the more profound spiritual insights that I've gathered from
the Benedictine tradition [is] that if you are angry with someone or you feel
sharp pain over something, that's a significant relationship that you need to
look into. It isn't something that you just have to say "isn't that too bad" or
"isn't that terrible" or you find someone to blame. In fact, this was one of
the things that led me back to church: examining why, the few times that I
did go to church, I had such uncomfortable emotional responses. I could
have simply stayed away and said, "Well, that makes me uncomfortable and
I don't want to go." I learned to say, "No, it makes me *so* uncomfortable I
better find out why." I think with a lot of negative things that's really a much
more fruitful approach than simply walking away or denying or stewing in
anger. The Christian vocabulary still has a lot of pretty scary words in it and
words that are used in scary ways in the culture. I am not trying to write it
off. I think it is one of the things with active faith — you have to keep redefining these words for yourself and adding to your knowledge of them. I
really had to immerse myself in the tradition.

When I hear people just dismiss an ancient word like dogma, without really having any idea of what it means, I go, "Wait a minute! This word has some really interesting history and a derivation and there are reasons why you have dogmas." One of the things that I found out working with the words [was] this volatile mixture of strong emotional reaction with an alarming amount of ignorance on my part. The minute I would look at the way that the word had been interpreted in Christian history, not necessarily in the 1950s Sunday school I went to, but in the Christian tradition, there was so much there that was livable and usable and a whole richer understanding. This whole book in a sense was my way of educating myself, or reeducating myself.

Gernes: One last thing: In *Amazing Grace,* you quote an Anglican monk as saying, "Ambivalence is a sacred emotion." I found that statement consoling because of the scene in the Bible where Jesus talks about people being lukewarm and says, "Because you are neither hot nor cold I will vomit you out of my mouth." Can you say anything more about what you learned from this monk in terms of ambivalence?

Norris: Well, I just loved it when he said ambivalence is a sacred   20
emotion; it was such a strong statement in his monastery newsletter that I really latched onto it. One of my favorite passages, really, in theology, is Emily Dickinson saying, "I believe and disbelieve one hundred times in an hour which keeps believing nimble." That contending with doubt and ambivalence is one of the things that evidently kept her faith alive. In that sort of nice Protestant upbringing, doubts were negative, like having dirty hands. So you didn't want to admit to having doubts, and you wanted everything to be clean and nice, and nice and nice, you see. It doesn't work that way with religious faith.

66

Susan Orlean

The American Man at Age Ten

The journalist and essayist Susan Orlean (b. 1955) began her career writing for the Willamette Week *in Portland, Oregon, before moving to the* Boston Phoenix *and then to the* Boston Globe. *Her first book,* Red Sox, Bluefish, and Other Things That Make New England New England *(1987), collects the columns she published at the* Globe. *From 1987 to 1991, Orlean was a contributing editor at* Rolling Stone *magazine, and since 1987 she has been a staff writer at the* New Yorker. *"The American Man at Age Ten" appeared in* Esquire *in 1992. Her other books include* Saturday Night *(1990), which describes the various ac-*

tivities and entertainments pursued by all kinds of Americans on their Saturday nights; The Orchid Thief *(1998), which examines the obsession with orchid growing, and* The Bullfighter Checks Her Makeup *(2001), which collects her essays published in magazines.*

"For me the biggest step in the writing process," says Orlean, "is to peel away all of the expectations I brought to the story—all of the preconceptions about the subject or the person I'm writing about—and to really find in my heart what I felt like in the moment of reporting. You need to dig into yourself to find your true emotions and thoughts and responses to what you have seen and felt and experienced. . . . Writing is a process of unlearning expectations and paying attention to the genuineness of the moment. How you do that is to reconsider, rethink, recollect, and talk about what you are trying to say. Eventually the writing will emerge out of that—the real thread of truth."

If Colin Duffy and I were to get married, we would have matching superhero notebooks. We would wear shorts, big sneakers, and long, baggy T-shirts depicting famous athletes every single day, even in the winter. We would sleep in our clothes. We would both be good at Nintendo Street Fighter II, but Colin would be better than me. We would have some homework, but it would not be too hard and we would always have just finished it. We would eat pizza and candy for all of our meals. We wouldn't have sex, but we would have crushes on each other and, magically, babies would appear in our home. We would win the lottery and then buy land in Wyoming, where we would have one of every kind of cute animal. All the while, Colin would be working in law enforcement— probably the FBI. Our favorite movie star, Morgan Freeman, would visit us occasionally. We would listen to the same Eurythmics song ("Here Comes the Rain Again") over and over again and watch two hours of television every Friday night. We would both be good at football, have best friends, and know how to drive; we would cure AIDS and the garbage problem and everything that hurts animals. We would hang out a lot with Colin's dad. For fun, we would load a slingshot with dog food and shoot it at my butt. We would have a very good life.

Here are the particulars about Colin Duffy: He is ten years old, on the nose. He is four feet eight inches high, weighs seventy-five pounds, and appears to be mostly leg and shoulder blade. He is a handsome kid. He has a broad forehead, dark eyes with dense lashes, and a sharp, dimply smile. I have rarely seen him without a baseball cap. He owns several, but favors a University of Michigan Wolverines model, on account of its pleasing colors. The hat styles his hair into wild disarray. If you ever managed to get the hat off his head, you would see a boy with a nimbus of golden-brown hair, dented in the back, where the hat hits him.

Colin lives with his mother, Elaine; his father, Jim; his older sister, Megan; and his little brother, Chris, in a pretty pale-blue Victorian house on a bosky street in Glen Ridge, New Jersey. Glen Ridge is a serene and civilized old town twenty miles west of New York City. It does not have much of a commercial district, but it is a town of amazing lawns. Most of the houses were built around the turn of the century and are set back a gracious, green distance from the street. The rest of the town seems to consist of parks and playing fields and sidewalks and backyards—in other words, it is a far cry from South-Central Los Angeles and from Bedford-Stuyvesant and other, grimmer parts of the country where a very different ten-year-old American man is growing up today.

There is a fine school system in Glen Ridge, but Elaine and Jim, who are both schoolteachers, choose to send their children to a parents' cooperative elementary school in Montclair, a neighboring suburb. Currently, Colin is in fifth grade. He is a good student. He plans to go to college, to a place he says is called Oklahoma City State College University. OCSCU satisfies his desire to live out west, to attend a small college, and to study law enforcement, which OCSCU apparently offers as a major. After four years at Oklahoma City State College University, he plans to work for the FBI. He says that getting to be a police officer involves tons of hard work, but working for the FBI will be a cinch, because all you have to do is fill out one form, which he has already gotten from the head FBI office. Colin is quiet in class but loud on the playground. He has a great throwing arm, significant foot speed, and a lot of physical confidence. He is also brave. Huge wild cats with rabies and gross stuff dripping from their teeth, which he says run rampant throughout his neighborhood, do not scare him. Otherwise, he is slightly bashful. This combination of athletic grace and valor and personal reserve accounts for considerable popularity. He has a fluid relationship to many social groups, including the superbright nerds, the ultrajocks, the flashy kids who will someday become extremely popular and socially successful juvenile delinquents, and the kids who will be elected president of the student body. In his opinion, the most popular boy in his class is Christian, who happens to be black, and Colin's favorite television character is Steve Urkel on *Family Matters,* who is black, too, but otherwise he seems uninterested in or oblivious to race. Until this year, he was a Boy Scout. Now he is planning to begin karate lessons. His favorite schoolyard game is football, followed closely by prison dodge ball, blob tag, and bombardo. He's crazy about athletes, although sometimes it isn't clear if he is absolutely sure of the difference between human athletes and Marvel Comics action figures. His current athletic hero is Dave Meggett. His current best friend is named Japeth. He used to have another best friend named Ozzie. According to Colin, Ozzie was found on a doorstep, then changed his name to Michael and moved to Massachusetts, and then Colin never saw him or heard from him again.

He has had other losses in his life. He is old enough to know people who have died and to know things about the world that are worrisome. When he dreams, he dreams about moving to Wyoming, which he has visited with his family. His plan is to buy land there and have some sort of ranch that would definitely include horses. Sometimes when he talks about this, it sounds as ordinary and hard-boiled as a real estate appraisal; other times it can sound fantastical and wifty and achingly naive,

5

informed by the last inklings of childhood—the musings of a balmy real estate appraiser assaying a wonderful and magical landscape that erodes from memory a little bit every day. The collision in his mind of what he understands, what he hears, what he figures out, what popular culture pours into him, what he knows, what he pretends to know, and what he imagines, makes an interesting mess. The mess often has the form of what he will probably think like when he is a grown man, but the content of what he is like as a little boy.

He is old enough to begin imagining that he will someday get married, but at ten he is still convinced that the best thing about being married will be that he will be allowed to sleep in his clothes. His father once observed that living with Colin was like living with a Martian who had done some reading on American culture. As it happens, Colin is not especially sad or worried about the prospect of growing up, although he sometimes frets over whether he should be called a kid or a grown-up; he has settled on the word *kid-up*. Once I asked him what the biggest advantage to adulthood will be, and he said, "The best thing is that grown-ups can go wherever they want." I asked him what he meant, exactly, and he said, "Well, if you're grown-up, you'd have a car, and whenever you felt like it, you could get into your car and drive somewhere and get candy."

Colin loves recycling. He loves it even more than, say, playing with little birds. That ten-year-olds feel the weight of the world and consider it their mission to shoulder it came as a surprise to me. I had gone with Colin one Monday to his classroom at Montclair Cooperative School. The Coop is in a steep, old, sharp-angled brick building that had served for many years as a public school until a group of parents in the area took it over and made it into a private, progressive elementary school. The fifth-grade classroom is on the top floor, under the dormers, which gives the room the eccentric shape and closeness of an attic. It is a rather informal environment. There are computers lined up in an adjoining room and instructions spelled out on the chalkboard—BRING IN: 1) A CUBBY WITH YOUR NAME ON IT, 2) A TRAPPER WITH A 5-POCKET ENVELOPE LABELED SCIENCE, SOCIAL STUDIES, READING/LANGUAGE ARTS, MATH, MATH LAB/COMPUTER; WHITE LINED PAPER; A PLASTIC PENCIL BAG; A SMALL HOMEWORK PAD, 3) LARGE BROWN GROCERY BAGS—but there is also a couch in the center of the classroom, which the kids take turns occupying, a rocking chair, and three canaries in cages near the door.

It happened to be Colin's first day in fifth grade. Before class began, there was a lot of horsing around, but there were also a lot of conversations about whether Magic Johnson had AIDS or just HIV and whether someone falling in a pool of blood from a cut of his would get the disease. These jolts of sobriety in the midst of rank goofiness are a ten-year-old's specialty. Each one comes as a fresh, hard surprise, like finding a razor blade in a candy apple. One day, Colin and I had been discussing horses or dogs or something, and out of the blue he said, "What do you think is better, to dump garbage in the ocean, to dump it on land, or to burn it?" Another time, he asked me if I planned to have children. I had just spent an evening with him and his friend Japeth, during which they put every small, movable object in the house into Japeth's slingshot and fired it at me, so I told him I wanted children but that I hoped they would all be girls, and he said, "Will you have an abortion if you find out you have a boy?"

At school, after discussing summer vacation, the kids began choosing the jobs they would do to help out around the classroom. Most of the jobs are humdrum—putting the chairs up on the tables, washing the chalkboard, turning the computers off or on. Five of the most humdrum tasks are recycling chores—for example, taking bottles or stacks of paper down to the basement, where they would be sorted and prepared for pickup. Two children would be assigned to feed the birds and cover their cages at the end of the day.

I expected the bird jobs to be the first to go. Everyone loved the birds;   10
they'd spent an hour that morning voting on names for them (Tweetie, Montgomery, and Rose narrowly beating out Axl Rose, Bugs, Ol' Yeller, Fido, Slim, Lucy, and Chirpie). Instead, they all wanted to recycle. The recycling jobs were claimed by the first five kids called by Suzanne Nakamura, the fifth-grade teacher; each kid called after that responded by groaning, "Suzanne, aren't there any more recycling jobs?" Colin ended up with the job of taking down the chairs each morning. He accepted the task with a sort of resignation—this was just going to be a job rather than a mission.

On the way home that day, I was quizzing Colin about his world views.
"Who's the coolest person in the world?"
"Morgan Freeman."
"What's the best sport?"
"Football."   15
"Who's the coolest woman?"
"None. I don't know."
"What's the most important thing in the world?"
"Game Boy." Pause. "No, the world. The world is the most important thing in the world."

Danny's Pizzeria is a dark little shop next door to the Montclair Co-   20
operative School. It is not much to look at. Outside, the brick facing is painted muddy brown. Inside, there are some saggy counters, a splintered bench, and enough room for either six teenagers or about a dozen ten-year-olds who happen to be getting along well. The light is low. The air is oily. At Danny's, you will find pizza, candy, Nintendo, and very few girls. To a ten-year-old boy, it is the most beautiful place in the world.

One afternoon, after class was dismissed, we went to Danny's with Colin's friend Japeth to play Nintendo. Danny's has only one game, Street Fighter II Champion Edition. Some teenage boys from a nearby middle school had gotten there first and were standing in a tall, impenetrable thicket around the machine.

"Next game," Colin said. The teenagers ignored him.

"Hey, we get next game," Japeth said. He is smaller than Colin, scrappy, and, as he explained to me once, famous for wearing his hat backward all the time and having a huge wristwatch and a huge bedroom. He stamped his foot and announced again, "Hey, we get next game."

One of the teenagers turned around and said, "Fuck you, *next game*," and then turned back to the machine.

"Whoa," Japeth said.   25

He and Colin went outside, where they felt bigger.

"Which street fighter are you going to be?" Colin asked Japeth.

"Blanka," Japeth said. "I know how to do his head-butt."

"I hate that! I hate the head-butt," Colin said. He dropped his voice a little and growled, "I'm going to be Ken, and I will kill you with my dragon punch."

"Yeah, right, and monkeys will fly out of my butt," Japeth said.   30

Street Fighter II is a video game in which two characters have an explosive brawl in a scenic international setting. It is currently the most popular video-arcade game in America. This is not an insignificant amount of popularity. Most arcade versions of video games, which end up in pizza parlors, malls, and arcades, sell about two thousand units. So far, some fifty thousand Street Fighter II and Street Fighter II Championship Edition arcade games have been sold. Not since Pac-Man, which was released the year before Colin was born, has there been a video game as popular as Street Fighter. The home version of Street Fighter is the most popular home video game in the country, and that, too, is not an insignificant thing. Thirty-two million Nintendo home systems have been sold since 1986, when it was introduced in this country. There is a Nintendo system in seven of every ten homes in America in which a child between the ages of eight and twelve resides. By the time a boy in America turns ten, he will almost certainly have been exposed to Nintendo home games, Nintendo arcade games, and Game Boy, the hand-held version. He will probably own a system and dozens of games. By ten, according to Nintendo studies, teachers, and psychologists, game prowess becomes a fundamental, essential male social marker and a schoolyard boast.

The Street Fighter characters are Dhalsim, Ken, Guile, Blanka, E. Honda, Ryu, Zangief, and Chun Li. Each represents a different country, and they each have their own special weapon. Chun Li, for instance, is from China and possesses a devastating whirlwind kick that is triggered if you push the control pad down for two seconds and then up for two seconds, and then you hit the kick button. Chun Li's kick is money in the bank, because most of the other fighters do not have a good defense against it. By the way, Chun Li happens to be a girl—the only female Street Fighter character.

I asked Colin if he was interested in being Chun Li. There was a long pause. "I'd rather be Ken," he said.

The girls in Colin's class at school are named Cortnerd, Terror, Spacey, Lizard, Maggot, and Diarrhea. "They do have other names, but that's what we call them," Colin told me. "The girls aren't very popular."

"They are about as popular as a piece of dirt," Japeth said. "Or, you know that couch in the classroom? That couch is more popular than any girl. A thousand times more." They talked for a minute about one of the girls in their class, a tall blonde with cheerleader genetic material, who they allowed was not quite as gross as some of the other girls. Japeth said that a chubby, awkward boy in their class was boasting that this girl liked him.

"No way," Colin said. "She would never like him. I mean, not that he's so . . . I don't know. I don't hate him because he's fat, anyway. I hate him because he's nasty."

"Well, she doesn't like him," Japeth said. "She's been really mean to me lately, so I'm pretty sure she likes me."

"Girls are different," Colin said. He hopped up and down on the balls of his feet, wrinkling his nose. "Girls are stupid and weird."

"I have a lot of girlfriends, about six or so," Japeth said, turning contemplative. "I don't exactly remember their names, though."

The teenagers came crashing out of Danny's and jostled past us, so we went inside. The man who runs Danny's, whose name is Tom, was leaning across the counter on his elbows, looking exhausted. Two little boys, holding Slush Puppies, shuffled toward the Nintendo, but Colin and Japeth elbowed them aside and slammed their quarters down on the machine. The little boys shuffled back toward the counter and stood gawking at them, sucking on their drinks.

"You want to know how to tell if a girl likes you?" Japeth said. "She'll act really mean to you. That's a sure sign. I don't know why they do it, but it's always a sure sign. It gets your attention. You know how I show a girl I like her? I steal something from her and then run away. I do it to get their attention, and it works."

They played four quarters' worth of games. During the last one, a teenager with a quilted leather jacket and a fade haircut came in, pushed his arm between them, and put a quarter down on the deck of the machine.

Japeth said, "Hey, what's that?"

The teenager said, "I get next game. I've marked it now. Everyone knows this secret sign for next game. It's a universal thing."

"So now we know," Japeth said. "Colin, let's get out of here and go bother Maggie. I mean Maggot. Okay?" They picked up their backpacks and headed out the door.

Psychologists identify ten as roughly the age at which many boys experience the gender-linked normative developmental trauma that leaves them, as adult men, at risk for specific psychological sequelae often manifest as deficits in the arenas of intimacy, empathy, and struggles with commitment in relationships. In other words, this is around the age when guys get screwed up about girls. Elaine and Jim Duffy, and probably most of the parents who send their kids to Montclair Cooperative School, have done a lot of stuff to try to avoid this. They gave Colin dolls as well as guns. (He preferred guns.) Japeth's father has three motorcycles and two dirt bikes but does most of the cooking and cleaning in their home. Suzanne, Colin's teacher, is careful to avoid sexist references in her presentations. After school, the yard at Montclair Cooperative is filled with as many fathers as mothers—fathers who hug their kids when they come prancing out of the building and are dismayed when their sons clamor for Supersoaker water guns and war toys or take pleasure in beating up girls.

In a study of adolescents conducted by the Gesell Institute of Human Development, nearly half the ten-year-old boys questioned said they thought they had inadequate information about sex. Nevertheless, most ten-year-old boys across the country are subjected to a few months of sex education in school. Colin and his class will get their dose next spring. It is yet another installment in a plan to make them into new, improved men with reconstructed notions of sex and male-female relationships. One afternoon I asked Philip, a schoolmate of Colin's, whether he was looking forward to sex education, and he said, "No, because I think it'll probably make me really, really hyper. I have a feeling it's going to be just like what it was like when some television reporters came to school last year and filmed us in class and I got really hyper. They stood around with all these cameras and asked us questions. I think that's what sex education is probably like."

At a class meeting earlier in the day:

Suzanne: "Today was our first swimming class, and I have one observation to make. The girls went to their locker room, got dressed without a lot of fuss, and came into the pool area. The boys, on the other hand, the *boys* had some sort of problem doing that rather simple task. Can someone tell me exactly what went on in the locker room?"

Keith: "There was a lot of shouting." 50

Suzanne: "Okay, I hear you saying that people were being noisy and shouting. Anything else?"

Christian: "Some people were screaming so much that my ears were killing me. It gave me, like, a huge headache. Also, some of the boys were taking their towels, I mean, after they had taken their clothes off, they had their towels around their waists and then they would drop them really fast and then pull them back up, really fast."

Suzanne: "Okay, you're saying some people were being silly about their bodies."

Christian: "Well, yeah, but it was more like they were being silly about their pants."

Colin's bedroom is decorated simply. He has a cage with his pet para- 55 keet, Dude, on his dresser, a lot of recently worn clothing piled haphazardly on the floor, and a husky brown teddy bear sitting upright in a chair near the foot of his bed. The walls are mostly bare, except for a

Spiderman poster and a few ads torn out of magazines he has thumb-tacked up. One of the ads is for a cologne, illustrated with several small photographs of cowboy hats; another, a feverish portrait of a woman on a horse, is an ad for blue jeans. These inspire him sometimes when he lies in bed and makes plans for the move to Wyoming. Also, he happens to like ads. He also likes television commercials. Generally speaking, he likes consumer products and popular culture. He partakes avidly but not indiscriminately. In fact, during the time we spent together, he provided a running commentary on merchandise, media, and entertainment:

"The only shoes anyone will wear are Reebok Pumps. Big T-shirts are cool, not the kind that are sticky and close to you, but big and baggy and long, not the kind that stop at your stomach."

"The best food is Chicken McNuggets and Life cereal and Frosted Flakes."

"Don't go to Blimpie's. They have the worst service."

"I'm not into Teenage Mutant Ninja Turtles anymore. I grew out of that. I like Donatello, but I'm not a fan. I don't buy the figures anymore."

"The best television shows are on Friday night on ABC. It's called   60
TGIF, and it's *Family Matters, Step by Step, Dinosaurs,* and *Perfect Strangers,* where the guy has a funny accent."

"The best candy is Skittles and Symphony bars and Crybabies and Warheads. Crybabies are great because if you eat a lot of them at once you feel so sour."

"Hyundais are Korean cars. It's the only Korean car. They're not that good because Koreans don't have a lot of experience building cars."

"The best movie is *City Slickers,* and the best part was when he saved his little cow in the river."

"The Giants really need to get rid of Ray Handley. They have to get somebody who has real coaching experience. He's just no good."

"My dog, Sally, costs seventy-two dollars. That sounds like a lot of   65
money but it's a really good price because you get a flea bath with your dog."

"The best magazines are *Nintendo Power,* because they tell you how to do the secret moves in the video games, and also *Mad* magazine and *Money Guide*—I really like that one."

"The best artist in the world is Jim Davis."

"The most beautiful woman in the world is not Madonna! Only Wayne and Garth think that! She looks like maybe a . . . a . . . slut or something. Cindy Crawford looks like she would look good, but if you see her on an awards program on TV she doesn't look that good. I think the most beautiful woman in the world probably is my mom."

Colin thinks a lot about money. This started when he was about nine and a half, which is when a lot of other things started—a new way of walking that has a little macho hitch and swagger, a decision about the Teenage Mutant Ninja Turtles (con) and Eurythmics (pro), and a persistent curiosity about a certain girl whose name he will not reveal. He knows the price of everything he encounters. He knows how much college costs and what someone might earn performing different jobs. Once, he asked me what my husband did; when I answered that he was a lawyer, he snapped, "You must be a rich family. Lawyers make $400,000 a year." His preoccupation with money baffles his family. They are not struggling, so this is not the anxiety of deprivation; they are not rich, so he is not responding to an elegant, advantaged world. His allowance is five dollars a week. It seems sufficient for his needs, which consist chiefly of quarters for Nintendo and candy money. The remainder is put into his Wyoming fund. His fascination is not just specific to needing money or having plans for money: It is as if money itself, and the way it makes the world work, and the realization that almost everything in the world can be assigned a price, has possessed him. "I just pay attention to things like that," Colin says. "It's really very interesting."

He is looking for a windfall. He tells me his mother has been notified   70
that she is in the fourth and final round of the Publisher's Clearinghouse Sweepstakes. This is not an ironic observation. He plays the New Jersey lottery every Thursday night. He knows the weekly jackpot; he knows the number to call to find out if he has won. I do not think this presages a future for Colin as a high-stakes gambler; I think it says more about the powerful grasp that money has on imagination and what a large percentage of a ten-year-old's mind is made up of imaginings. One Friday, we were at school together, and one of his friends was asking him about the lottery, and he said, "This week it was $4 million. That would be I forget how much every year for the rest of your life. It's a lot, I think. You should play. All it takes is a dollar and a dream."

Until the lottery comes through and he starts putting together the Wyoming land deal, Colin can be found most of the time in the backyard. Often, he will have friends come over. Regularly, children from the neighborhood will gravitate to the backyard, too. As a technical matter of real-property law, title to the house and yard belongs to Jim and Elaine Duffy, but Colin adversely possesses the backyard, at least from 4:00 each afternoon until it gets dark. As yet, the fixtures of teenage life—malls, video arcades, friends' basements, automobiles—either hold little interest for him or are not his to have.

He is, at the moment, very content with his backyard. For most intents and purposes, it is as big as Wyoming. One day, certainly, he will grow and it will shrink, and it will become simply a suburban backyard and it won't be big enough for him anymore. This will happen so fast that one night he will be in the backyard, believing it a perfect place, and by the next night he will have changed and the yard as he imagined it will be gone, and this era of his life will be behind him forever.

Most days, he spends hours in the backyard building an Evil Spider-Web Trap. This entails running a spool of Jim's fishing line from every surface in the yard until it forms a huge web. Once a garbageman picking up the Duffy's trash got caught in the trap. Otherwise, the Evil Spider-Web Trap mostly has a deterrent effect, because the kids in the neighborhood who might roam over know that Colin builds it back there. "I do it all the time," he says. "First I plan who I'd like to catch in it, and then we get started. Trespassers have to beware."

One afternoon when I came over for a few rounds of Street Fighter at Danny's, Colin started building a trap. He selected a victim for inspiration—a boy in his class who had been pestering him—and began wrapping. He was entirely absorbed. He moved from tree to tree, wrapping; he laced fishing line through the railing of the deck and then back to the shed; he circled an old jungle gym, something he'd outgrown and abandoned a few years ago, and then crossed over to a bush at the back of the yard. Briefly, he contemplated making his dog, Sally, part of the web. Dusk fell. He kept wrapping, paying out fishing line an inch at a time. We could hear mothers up and down the block hooting for their kids; two tiny children from next door stood transfixed at the edge of the yard, uncertain whether they would end up inside or outside the web. After a while, the spool spun around in Colin's hands one more time and then stopped; he was out of line.

It was almost too dark to see much of anything, although now and   75
again the light from the deck would glance off a length of line, and it would glint and sparkle. "That's the point," he said. "You could do it with thread, but the fishing line is invisible. Now I have this perfect thing and the only one who knows about it is me." With that, he dropped the spool, skipped up the stairs of the deck, threw open the screen door, and then bounded into the house, leaving me and Sally the dog trapped in his web.

The Reader's Presence

1. Orlean begins the essay with a description of what life would be like if she and Colin Duffy got married. From whose perspective is she writing? How does this introduction set the tone for the rest of the essay?

2. Consider the role of gender in the essay. Do you think it makes any difference that the author is a woman? How might her tone and approach be different if Orlean had once been a ten-year-old boy? Why do you think she chose to title the essay "The American *Man* at Age Ten" rather than "The American *Boy* at Age Ten"? What is Orlean trying to say about the way that men learn cultural attitudes and beliefs?

3. By most standards, Colin Duffy's life is relatively privileged. How does Orlean acknowledge this fact? Is she presenting Colin as a representative American ten-year-old boy? Compare Orlean's por-

trait of Colin to Scott Russell Sanders's portrait of the men he knew as a child in "The Men We Carry in Our Minds" (page 742). How does social class figure in both essays? How does Orlean's final image—of herself and the dog "trapped in [Colin's] web"—compare to Sanders's realization that the women he met as an adult saw him "as an enemy to their desires" (paragraph 21)? How does each writer express the relations between men and women?

67

George Orwell

Politics and the English Language

During his lifetime, George Orwell was well known for the political positions he laid out in his essays. The events that inspired Orwell to write his essays have long since passed, but his writing continues to be read and enjoyed. Orwell demonstrates that political writing need not be narrowly topical—it can speak to enduring issues and concerns. He suggested as much in 1946 when he wrote, "What I have most wanted to do throughout the past ten years is to make political writing into an art. My starting point is always a feeling of partisanship, a feeling of injustice. . . . But I could not do the work of writing a book, or even a long magazine article, if it were not also an aesthetic experience." "Politics and the English Language" appears in Shooting an Elephant and Other Essays *(1950).*

For more information about Orwell, see page 198.

Most people who bother with the matter at all would admit that the English language is in a bad way, but it is generally assumed that we cannot by conscious action do anything about it. Our civilization is decadent and our language—so that argument runs—must inevitably share in the general collapse. It follows that any struggle against the abuse of language is a sentimental archaism, like preferring candles to electric light or hansom cabs to airplanes. Underneath this lies the half-conscious belief that language is a natural growth and not an instrument which we shape for our own purposes.

Now, it is clear that the decline of a language must ultimately have political and economic causes: It is not due simply to the bad influence of this or that individual writer. But an effect can become a cause, reinforcing the original cause and producing the same effect in an intensified form, and so on indefinitely. A man may take to drink because he feels himself to be a failure, and then fail all the more completely because he drinks. It is rather the same thing that is happening to the English language. It becomes ugly and inaccurate because our thoughts are foolish, but the slovenliness of our language makes it easier for us to have foolish thoughts. The point is that the process is reversible. Modern English, especially written English, is full of bad habits which spread by imitation and which can be avoided if one is willing to take the necessary trouble. If one gets rid of these habits one can think more clearly, and to think clearly is a necessary first step towards political regencration: so that the fight against bad English is not frivolous and is not the exclusive concern of professional writers. I will come back to this presently, and I hope that by that time the meaning of what I have said here will have become clearer. Meanwhile, here are five specimens of the English language as it is now habitually written.

These five passages have not been picked out because they are especially bad—I could have quoted far worse if I had chosen—but because they illustrate various of the mental vices from which we now suffer. They are a little below the average, but are fairly representative samples. I number them so that I can refer back to them when necessary:

(1) I am not, indeed, sure whether it is true to say that the Milton who once seemed not unlike a seventeenth-century Shelley had not become, out of an experience ever more bitter in each year, more alien [*sic*] to the founder of that Jesuit sect which nothing could induce him to tolerate.
                    Professor Harold Laski (Essay in *Freedom of Expression*).

(2) Above all, we cannot play ducks and drakes with a native battery of idioms which prescribes such egregious collections of vocals as the Basic *put up with* for *tolerate* or *put at a loss* for *bewilder*.
                    Professor Lancelot Hogben (*Interglossa*).

(3) On the one side we have the free personality: By definition it is not neurotic, for it has neither conflict nor dream. Its desires, such as they are, are transparent, for they are just what institutional approval keeps in the forefront of consciousness; another institutional pattern would alter their number and intensity; there is little in them that is natural, irreducible, or culturally dangerous. But *on the other side,* the social bond itself is nothing but the mutual reflection of these self-secure integrities. Recall the definition of love. Is not this the very picture of a small academic? Where is there a place in this hall of mirrors for either personality or fraternity?
                    Essay on psychology in *Politics* (New York).

(4) All the "best people" from the gentlemen's clubs, and all the frantic fascist captains, united in common hatred of Socialism and bestial horror of the rising tide of the mass revolutionary movement, have turned to acts of provocation, to foul incendiarism, to medieval legends of poisoned wells, to legalize their own destruction of proletarian organizations, and rouse the agitated petty-bourgeoisie to chauvinistic fervor on behalf of the fight against the revolutionary way out of the crisis.
                    Communist pamphlet.

(5) If a new spirit *is* to be infused into this old country, there is one thorny and contentious reform which must be tackled, and that is the humanization and galvanization of the B.B.C. Timidity here will bespeak cancer and atrophy of the soul. The heart of Britain may be sound and of strong beat, for instance, but the British lion's roar at present is like that of Bottom in Shakespeare's *Midsummer Night's Dream*—as gentle as any sucking dove. A virile new Britain cannot continue indefinitely to be traduced in the eyes or rather ears, of the world by the effete languors of Langham Place, brazenly masquerading as "standard English." When the Voice of Britain is heard at nine o'clock, better far and infinitely less ludicrous to hear aitches honestly dropped than the present priggish, inflated, inhibited, school-ma'amish arch braying of blameless bashful mewing maidens!

Letter in Tribune.

Each of these passages has faults of its own, but, quite apart from avoidable ugliness, two qualities are common to all of them. The first is staleness of imagery: The other is lack of precision. The writer either has a meaning and cannot express it, or he inadvertently says something else, or he is almost indifferent as to whether his words mean anything or not. This mixture of vagueness and sheer incompetence is the most marked characteristic of modern English prose, and especially of any kind of political writing. As soon as certain topics are raised, the concrete melts into the abstract and no one seems able to think of turns of speech that are not hackneyed: Prose consists less and less of *words* chosen for the sake of their meaning, and more and more of *phrases* tacked together like the sections of a prefabricated hen-house. I list below, with notes and examples, various of the tricks by means of which the work of prose-construction is habitually dodged:

Dying Metaphors. A newly invented metaphor assists thought by evoking a visual image, while on the other hand a metaphor which is technically "dead" (e.g., *iron resolution*) has in effect reverted to being an ordinary word and can generally be used without loss of vividness. But in between these two classes there is a huge dump of worn-out metaphors which have lost all evocative power and are merely used because they save people the trouble of inventing phrases for themselves. Examples are: *Ring the changes on, take up the cudgels for, toe the line, ride roughshod over, stand shoulder to shoulder with, play into the hands of, no axe to grind, grist to the mill, fishing in troubled waters, rift within the lute, on the order of the day, Achilles' heel, swan song, hotbed.* Many of these are used without knowledge of their meaning (what is a "rift," for instance?), and incompatible metaphors are frequently mixed, a sure sign that the writer is not interested in what he is saying. Some metaphors now current have been twisted out of their original meaning without those who use them even being aware of the fact. For example, *toe the line* is sometimes written *tow the line.* Another example is *the hammer and the anvil*, now always used with the implication that the anvil gets the worst of it. In real life it is always the anvil that breaks the hammer, never the other way about: A writer who stopped to think what he was saying would be aware of this, and would avoid perverting the original phrase.

Operators or Verbal False Limbs. These save the trouble of picking out appropriate verbs and nouns, and at the same time pad each sentence with extra syllables which give it an appearance of symmetry. Characteristic phrases are *render inoperative, militate against, make contact with, be subjected to, give rise to, give grounds for, have the effect of, play a leading part (role) in, make itself felt, take effect, exhibit a tendency to, serve the purpose of, etc., etc.* The keynote is the elimination of simple verbs. Instead of being a single word, such as *break, stop, spoil, mend, kill,* a verb becomes a *phrase,* made up of a noun or adjective tacked on to some general-purpose verb such as *prove, serve, form, play, render.* In addition, the passive voice is wherever possible used in preference to the active, and noun constructions are used instead of gerunds (*by examination of* instead of *by examining*). The range of verbs is further cut down by means of the *-ize* and *de-* formation, and the banal statements are given an appearance of profundity by means of the *not un-* formation. Simple conjunctions and prepositions are replaced by such phrases as *with respect to, having regard to, the fact that, by dint of, in view of, in the interests of, on the hypothesis that;* and the ends of sentences are saved from anticlimax by such resounding commonplaces as *greatly to be desired, cannot be left out of account, a development to be expected in the near future, deserving of serious consideration, brought to a satisfactory conclusion,* and so on and so forth.

Pretentious Diction. Words like *phenomenon, element, individual* (as noun), *objective, categorical, effective, virtual, basic, primary, promote, constitute, exhibit, exploit, utilize, eliminate, liquidate,* are used to dress up simple statements and give an air of scientific impartiality to biased judgments. Adjectives like *epoch-making, epic, historic, unforgettable, triumphant, age-old, inevitable, inexorable, veritable,* are used to dignify the sordid processes of international politics, while writing that aims at glorifying war usually takes on an archaic color, its characteristic words being: *realm, throne, chariot, mailed fist, trident, sword, shield, buckler, banner, jackboot, clarion.* Foreign words and expressions such as *cul de sac, ancien régime, deus ex machina, mutatis mutandis, status quo, gleichschaltung, weltanschauung,* are used to give an air of culture and elegance. Except for the useful abbreviations *i.e., e.g.,* and *etc.,* there is no real need for any of the hundreds of foreign phrases now current in English. Bad writers, and especially scientific, political, and sociological writers, are nearly always haunted by the notion that Latin or Greek words are grander than Saxon ones, and unnecessary words like *expedite, ameliorate, predict, extraneous, deracinated, clandestine, subaqueous,* and hundreds of others constantly gain ground from their Anglo-Saxon opposite numbers.[1] The jargon peculiar to Marxist writing (*hyena, hangman, cannibal, petty bourgeois, these gentry, lackey, flunkey, mad dog, White Guard, etc.*) consists largely of words and phrases translated from Russian, German, or French; but the normal way of coining a new word is to use a Latin or Greek root with the appropriate affix and, where necessary, the *-ize* formation. It is often easier to make up words of this kind (*deregionalize, impermissible, extramarital, nonfragmentary,* and so forth) than to think up the English words that will cover one's meaning. The result, in general, is an increase in slovenliness and vagueness.

Meaningless Words. In certain kinds of writing, particularly in art criticism and literary criticism, it is normal to come across long passages which are almost completely lacking in meaning.[2] Words like *romantic, plastic, values, human, dead, sentimental, natural, vitality,* as used in art criticism, are strictly meaningless, in the sense that they not only do not point to any discoverable object, but are hardly ever expected to do so by the reader. When one critic writes, "The outstanding feature of Mr. X's work is its living quality," while another writes, "The immediately striking thing about Mr. X's work is its peculiar deadness," the reader accepts this as a simple difference of opinion. If words like *black* and *white* were involved, instead of the jargon words *dead* and *living,* he would see at once that language was being used in an improper way. Many political words are similarly abused. The word *Fascism* has now no meaning except in so far as it signifies "something not desirable." The words *democracy, socialism, freedom, patriotic, realistic, justice,* have each of them several different meanings which cannot be reconciled with one another. In the case of a word like *democracy,* not only is there no agreed definition, but the attempt to make one is resisted from all sides. It is almost universally felt that when we call a country democratic we are praising it: Consequently the defenders of every kind of regime claim that it is a democracy, and fear that they might have to stop using the word if it were tied down to any one meaning. Words of this kind are often used in a consciously dishonest way. That is, the person who uses them has his own private definition, but allows his hearer to think he means something

---

[1]An interesting illustration of this is the way in which the English flower names which were in use till very recently are being ousted by Greek ones, *snapdragon* becoming *antirrhinum, forget-me-not* becoming *myosotis,* etc. It is hard to see any practical reason for this change of fashion: It is probably due to an instinctive turning away from the more homely word and a vague feeling that the Greek word is scientific.

[2]Example: "Comfort's catholicity of perception and image, strangely Whitmanesque in range, almost the exact opposite in aesthetic compulsion, continues to evoke that trembling atmospheric accumulative hinting at a cruel, an inexorably serene timelessness. . . . Wrey Gardiner scores by aiming at simple bull's-eyes with precision. Only they are not so simple, and through this contented sadness runs more than the surface bitter-sweet of resignation." (*Poetry Quarterly.*)

quite different. Statements like *Marshal Pétain[3] was a true patriot, The Soviet Press is the freest in the world, The Catholic Church is opposed to persecution,* are almost always made with intent to deceive. Other words used in variable meanings, in most cases more or less dishonestly, are: *class, totalitarian, science, progressive, reactionary, bourgeois, equality.*

Now that I have made this catalogue of swindles and perversions, let me give another example of the kind of writing that they lead to. This time it must of its nature be an imaginary one. I am going to translate a passage of good English into modern English of the worst sort. Here is a well-known verse from *Ecclesiastes:*

> I returned and saw under the sun, that the race is not to the swift, nor the battle to the strong, neither yet bread to the wise, nor yet riches to men of understanding, nor yet favor to men of skill; but time and chance happeneth to them all.

Here it is in modern English:

> Objective consideration of contemporary phenomena compels the conclusion that success or failure in competitive activities exhibits no tendency to be commensurate with innate capacity, but that a considerable element of the unpredictable must invariably be taken into account.

This is a parody, but not a very gross one. Exhibit (3), above, for instance, contains several patches of the same kind of English. It will be seen that I have not made a full translation. The beginning and ending of the sentence follow the original meaning fairly closely, but in the middle the concrete illustrations—race, battle, bread—dissolve into the vague phrase "success or failure in competitive activities." This had to be so, because no modern writer of the kind I am discussing—no one capable of using phrases like "objective consideration of contemporary phenomena"—would ever tabulate his thoughts in that precise and detailed way. The whole tendency of modern prose is away from concreteness. Now analyze these two sentences a little more closely. The first contains forty-nine words but only sixty syllables, and all its words are those of everyday life. The second contains thirty-eight words of ninety syllables: Eighteen of its words are from Latin roots, and one from Greek. The first sentence contains six vivid images, and only one phrase ("time and chance") that could be called vague. The second contains not a single fresh, arresting phrase, and in spite of its ninety syllables it gives only a shortened version of the meaning contained in the first. Yet without a doubt it is the second kind of sentence that is gaining ground in modern

10

---

[3]***Pétain:*** Henri Philippe Pétain was a World War I French military hero who served as chief of state in France from 1940 to 1945, after France surrendered to Germany. A controversial figure, Pétain was regarded by some to be a patriot who had sacrificed himself for his country, while others considered him to be a traitor. He was sentenced to life imprisonment in 1945, the year before Orwell wrote his essay.—EDS.

English. I do not want to exaggerate. This kind of writing is not yet universal, and outcrops of simplicity will occur here and there in the worst-written page. Still, if you or I were told to write a few lines on the uncertainty of human fortunes, we should probably come much nearer to my imaginary sentences than to the one from *Ecclesiastes*.

As I have tried to show, modern writing at its worst does not consist in picking out words for the sake of their meaning and inventing images in order to make the meaning clearer. It consists in gumming together long strips of words which have already been set in order by someone else, and making the results presentable by sheer humbug. The attraction of this way of writing is that it is easy. It is easier—even quicker once you have the habit—to say *In my opinion it is a not unjustifiable assumption that* than to say *I think*. If you use ready-made phrases, you not only don't have to hunt about for words; you also don't have to bother with the rhythms of your sentences, since these phrases are generally so arranged as to be more or less euphonious. When you are composing in a hurry—when you are dictating to a stenographer, for instance, or making a public speech—it is natural to fall into a pretentious, Latinized style. Tags like *a consideration which we should do well to bear in mind* or *a conclusion to which all of us would readily assent* will save many a sentence from coming down with a bump. By using stale metaphors, similes, and idioms, you save much mental effort, at the cost of leaving your meaning vague, not only for your reader but for yourself. This is the significance of mixed metaphors. The sole aim of a metaphor is to call up a visual image. When these images clash—as in *The Fascist octopus has sung its swan song, the jackboot is thrown into the melting pot*—it can be taken as certain that the writer is not seeing a mental image of the objects he is naming; in other words he is not really thinking. Look again at the examples I gave at the beginning of this essay. Professor Laski (1) uses five negatives in fifty-three words. One of these is superfluous, making nonsense of the whole passage, and in addition there is the slip—*alien* for akin—making further nonsense, and several avoidable pieces of clumsiness which increase the general vagueness. Professor Hogben (2) plays ducks and drakes with a battery which is able to write prescriptions, and, while disapproving of the everyday phrase *put up with*, is unwilling to look *egregious* up in the dictionary and see what it means; (3), if one takes an uncharitable attitude towards it, is simply meaningless: Probably one could work out its intended meaning by reading the whole of the article in which it occurs. In (4), the writer knows more or less what he wants to say, but an accumulation of stale phrases chokes him like tea leaves blocking a sink. In (5), words and meaning have almost parted company. People who write in this manner usually have a general emotional meaning—they dislike one thing and want to express solidarity with another—but they are not interested in the detail of what they are saying. A scrupulous writer, in every sentence that he writes, will ask himself at least four questions, thus: What am I trying to say? What words will express it? What image or idiom will make it clearer? Is this image fresh enough to have an effect? And he will probably ask himself two more: Could I put it more shortly? Have I said anything that is avoidably ugly? But you are not obliged to go to all this trouble. You can shirk it by simply throwing your mind open and letting the ready-made phrases come crowding in. They will construct your sentences for you—even think your thoughts for you, to a certain extent—and at need they will perform the important service of partially concealing your meaning even from yourself. It is at this point that the special connection between politics and the debasement of language becomes clear.

In our time it is broadly true that political writing is bad writing. Where it is not true, it will generally be found that the writer is some kind of rebel, expressing his private opinions and not a "party line." Orthodoxy, of whatever color, seems to demand a lifeless, imitative style. The political dialects to be found in pamphlets, leading articles, manifestos, White Papers, and the speeches of under-secretaries do, of course, vary from party to party, but they are all alike in that one almost never finds in them a fresh, vivid, home-made turn of speech. When one watches some tired hack on the platform mechanically repeating the familiar phrases— *bestial atrocities, iron heel, bloodstained tyranny, free peoples of the world, stand shoulder to shoulder*—one often has a curious feeling that one is not watching a live human being but some kind of dummy: a feeling which suddenly becomes stronger at moments when the light catches the speaker's spectacles and turns them into blank discs which seem to have no eyes behind them. And this is not altogether fanciful. A speaker who uses that kind of phraseology has gone some distance towards turning himself into a machine. The appropriate noises are coming out of his larynx, but his brain is not involved as it would be if he were choosing his words for himself. If the speech he is making is one that he is accustomed to make over and over again, he may be almost unconscious of what he is saying, as one is when one utters the responses in church. And this reduced state of consciousness, if not indispensable, is at any rate favorable to political conformity.

In our time, political speech and writing are largely the defense of the indefensible. Things like the continuance of British rule in India, the Russian purges and deportations, the dropping of the atom bombs on Japan, can indeed be defended, but only by arguments which are too brutal for most people to face, and which do not square with the professed aims of political parties. Thus political language has to consist largely of euphemism, question-begging, and sheer cloudy vagueness. Defenseless villages are bombarded from the air, the inhabitants driven out into the countryside, the cattle machine-gunned, the huts set on fire with incendiary bullets: This is called *pacification*. Millions of peasants are robbed of their farms and sent trudging along the roads with no more than they can carry: This is called *transfer of population* or *rectification of frontiers*. People are imprisoned for years without trial, or shot in the back of the neck or sent to die of scurvy in Arctic lumber camps:[4] This is called *elimination of unreliable elements*. Such phraseology is needed if one wants to name things without calling up mental pictures of them. Consider for instance some comfortable English professor defending Russian totalitarianism. He cannot say outright, "I believe in killing off your opponents when you get good results by doing so." Probably, therefore, he will say something like this:

"While freely conceding that the Soviet régime exhibits certain features which the humanitarian may be inclined to deplore, we must, I think, agree that a certain curtailment of the right to political opposition is an unavoidable concomitant of transitional periods, and that the rigors which the Russian people have been called upon to undergo have been amply justified in the sphere of concrete achievement."

The inflated style is itself a kind of euphemism. A mass of Latin words falls upon the facts like soft snow, blurring the outlines and covering up all the details. The great enemy of clear language is insincerity. When there is a gap between one's real and one's declared aims, one turns as it were instinctively to long words and exhausted idioms, like a cuttlefish squirting out ink. In our age there is no such thing as "keeping out of politics." All issues are political issues, and politics itself is a mass of lies, evasions, folly, hatred, and schizophrenia. When the general atmosphere is bad, language must suffer. I should expect to find—this is a guess which I have not sufficient knowledge to verify—that the German, Russian, and Italian languages have all deteriorated in the last ten or fifteen years, as a result of dictatorship.

But if thought corrupts language, language can also corrupt thought. A bad usage can spread by tradition and imitation, even among people who should and do know better. The debased language that I have been discussing is in some ways very convenient. Phrases like *a not unjustifiable assumption, leaves much to be desired, would serve no good purpose, a consideration which we should do well to bear in mind*, are a continuous temptation, a packet of aspirins always at one's elbow. Look back through this essay, and for certain you will find that I have again and again committed the very faults I am protesting against. By this morning's post I have received a pamphlet dealing with conditions in Germany. The author tells me that he "felt impelled" to write it. I open it at random, and here is almost the first sentence that I see: "(The Allies) have an opportunity not only of achieving a radical transformation of Germany's social and political structure in such a way as to avoid a nationalistic reaction in Germany itself, but at the same time of laying the foundations of a co-operative and unified Europe." You see, he "feels impelled" to write—feels, presumably, that he has something new to say—and yet his words, like cavalry horses answering the bugle, group themselves auto-

15

[4]*People . . . camps:* Though Orwell is decrying all totalitarian abuse of language, his examples are mainly pointed at the Soviet purges under Stalin.—EDS.

matically into the familiar dreary pattern. The invasion of one's mind by ready-made phrases (*lay the foundations, achieve a radical transformation*) can only be prevented if one is constantly on guard against them, and every such phrase anaesthetizes a portion of one's brain.

I said earlier that the decadence of our language is probably curable. Those who deny this would argue, if they produced an argument at all, that language merely reflects existing social conditions, and that we cannot influence its development by any direct tinkering with words and constructions. So far as the general tone or spirit of a language goes, this may be true, but it is not true in detail. Silly words and expressions have often disappeared, not through any evolutionary process but owing to the conscious action of a minority. Two recent examples were *explore every avenue* and *leave no stone unturned,* which were killed by the jeers of a few journalists. There is a long list of flyblown metaphors which could similarly be got rid of if enough people would interest themselves in the jobs; and it should also be possible to laugh the *not un-* formation out of existence,[5] to reduce the amount of Latin and Greek in the average sentence, to drive out foreign phrases and strayed scientific words, and, in general, to make pretentiousness unfashionable. But all these are minor points. The defense of the English language implies more than this, and perhaps it is best to start by saying what it does *not* imply.

To begin with it has nothing to do with archaism, with the salvaging of obsolete words and turns of speech, or with the setting up of a "standard English" which must never be departed from. On the contrary, it is especially concerned with the scrapping of every word or idiom which has outworn its usefulness. It has nothing to do with correct grammar and syntax, which are of no importance so long as one makes one's meaning clear, or with the avoidance of Americanisms, or with having what is called a "good prose style." On the other hand it is not concerned with fake simplicity and the attempt to make written English colloquial. Nor does it even imply in every case preferring the Saxon word to the Latin one, though it does imply using the fewest and shortest words that will cover one's meaning. What is above all needed is to let the meaning choose the word, and not the other way about. In prose, the worst thing one can do with words is to surrender to them. When you think of a concrete object, you think wordlessly, and then, if you want to describe the thing you have been visualizing you probably hunt about till you find the exact words that seem to fit. When you think of something abstract you are more inclined to use words from the start, and unless you make a conscious effort to prevent it, the existing dialect will come rushing in and do the job for you, at the expense of blurring or even changing your meaning. Probably it is better to put off using words as long as possible and get one's meaning as clear as one can through pictures or sensations.

---

[5]One can cure oneself of the *not un-* formation by memorizing this sentence: *A not unblack dog was chasing a not unsmall rabbit across a not ungreen field.*

Afterwards one can choose—not simply *accept*—the phrases that will best cover the meaning, and then switch round and decide what impression one's words are likely to make on another person. This last effort of the mind cuts out all stale or mixed images, all prefabricated phrases, needless repetitions, and humbug and vagueness generally. But one can often be in doubt about the effect of a word or a phrase, and one needs rules that one can rely on when instinct fails. I think the following rules will cover most cases:

(i)   Never use a metaphor, simile, or other figure of speech which you are used to seeing in print.

(ii) Never use a long word where a short one will do.

(iii) If it is possible to cut a word out, always cut it out.

(iv) Never use the passive where you can use the active.

(v)   Never use a foreign phrase, a scientific word, or a jargon word if you can think of an everyday English equivalent.

(vi) Break any of these rules sooner than say anything outright barbarous.

These rules sound elementary, and so they are, but they demand a deep change in attitude in anyone who has grown used to writing in the style now fashionable. One could keep all of them and still write bad English, but one could not write the kind of stuff that I quoted in those five specimens at the beginning of this article.

I have not here been considering the literary use of language, but merely language as an instrument for expressing and not for concealing or preventing thought. Stuart Chase and others have come near to claiming that all abstract words are meaningless, and have used this as a pretext for advocating a kind of political quietism. Since you don't know what Fascism is, how can you struggle against Fascism? One need not swallow such absurdities as these, but one ought to recognize that the present political chaos is connected with the decay of language, and the one can probably bring about some improvement by starting at the verbal end. If you simplify your English, you are freed from the worst follies of orthodoxy. You cannot speak any of the necessary dialects, and when you make a stupid remark its stupidity will be obvious, even to yourself. Political language—and with variations this is true of all political parties, from Conservatives to Anarchists—is designed to make lies sound truthful and murder respectable, and to give an appearance of solidity to pure wind. One cannot change this all in a moment, but one can at least change one's own habits, and from time to time one can even, if one jeers loudly enough, send some worn-out and useless phrase—some *jackboot, Achilles' heel, hotbed, melting pot, acid test, veritable inferno,* or other lump of verbal refuse—into the dustbin where it belongs.

The Reader's Presence

1. What characteristics of Orwell's own writing demonstrate his six rules for writing good prose? Can you identify five examples in which Orwell practices what he preaches? Can you identify any moments when he seems to slip?

2. Note that Orwell does not provide *positive* examples of political expression. Why do you think this is so? Is Orwell implying that all political language—regardless of party or position—is corrupt? From this essay can you infer his political philosophy? Explain your answer.

3. Look carefully at Orwell's five examples of bad prose. Would you have identified this writing as "bad" if you had come across it in your college reading? Compare Orwell's list of rules for writing, and the ideas expressed in paragraph 16, to Langston Hughes's "How to Be a Bad Writer (in Ten Easy Lessons)" (page 149). How does each writer use humor to persuade the reader of the serious effects of writing badly? What does each writer seem to think is at stake in how one writes?

THE WRITER AT WORK

George Orwell on the Four Reasons for Writing

As the preceding essay shows, George Orwell spent much time considering the art of writing. He believed it was of the utmost political importance to write clearly and accurately. In the following passage from another essay, "Why I Write," Orwell considers a more fundamental aspect of writing: the reasons behind why people write at all. You may observe that he doesn't list the reason most college students write—to respond to an assignment. Why do you think he omitted assigned writing? Can you think of other motives he doesn't take into account?

Putting aside the need to earn a living, I think there are four great motives for writing, at any rate for writing prose. They exist in different degrees in every writer, and in any one writer the proportions will vary from time to time, according to the atmosphere in which he is living. They are:

1. Sheer egoism. Desire to seem clever, to be talked about, to be remembered after death, to get your own back on grown-ups who snubbed you in childhood, etc., etc. It is humbug to pretend that this is not a motive, and a strong one. Writers share this characteristic with scientists, artists, politicians, lawyers, soldiers, successful businessmen—in short, with the whole top crust of humanity. The great mass of human beings are not acutely selfish. After the age of thirty they abandon individual ambition—in many cases, indeed, they almost abandon the sense of

being individuals at all—and live chiefly for others, or are simply smothered under drudgery. But there is also the minority of gifted, willful people who are determined to live their own lives to the end, and writers belong in this class. Serious writers, I should say, are on the whole more vain and self-centered than journalists, though less interested in money.

2. Aesthetic enthusiasm. Perception of beauty in the external world, or, on the other hand, in words and their right arrangement. Pleasure in the impact of one sound on another, in the firmness of good prose or the rhythm of a good story. Desire to share an experience which one feels is valuable and ought not to be missed. The aesthetic motive is very feeble in a lot of writers, but even a pamphleteer or a writer of textbooks will have pet words and phrases which appeal to him for non-utilitarian reasons; or he may feel strongly about typography, width of margins, etc. Above the level of a railway guide, no book is quite free from aesthetic considerations.

3. Historical impulse. Desire to see things as they are, to find out true facts and store them up for the use of posterity.

4. Political purpose—using the word "political" in the widest possible sense. Desire to push the world in a certain direction, to alter other people's idea of the kind of society that they should strive after. Once again, no book is genuinely free from political bias. The opinion that art should have nothing to do with politics is itself a political attitude.

5

68

Katha Pollitt

Why Boys Don't Play with Dolls

Katha Pollitt was born in 1949 in New York City and is considered one of the leading poets of her generation. Her 1982 collection of poetry, Antarctic Traveller, *won a National Book Critics Circle Award. Her poetry has received many other honors and has appeared in the* Atlantic *and the* New Yorker. *Pollitt also writes essays, and she has gained a reputation for incisive analysis and persuasive argument. She contributes reviews and essays to many national magazines and is an associate editor and columnist for the* Nation. *Her column, "Subject to Debate," appears every other week. "Why Boys Don't Play with Dolls" appeared in the* New York Times *Magazine in 1995. Her essays can also be found in* Reasonable Creatures: Feminism and Society in American Culture at the End of the Twentieth Century *(1994) and* Subject to Debate: Sense and Dissents on Women, Politics, and Culture *(2001).*

Pollitt thinks of writing poems and political essays as two distinct endeavors.
"What I want in a poem—one that I read or one that I write—is not an argu-
ment, it's not a statement, it has to do with language. . . . There isn't that much
political poetry that I find I even want to read once, and almost none that I would
want to read again."

It's twenty-eight years since the founding of NOW, and boys still like
trucks and girls still like dolls. Increasingly, we are told that the source of
these robust preferences must lie outside society—in prenatal hormonal
influences, brain chemistry, genes—and that feminism has reached its
natural limits. What else could possibly explain the love of preschool girls
for party dresses or the desire of toddler boys to own more guns than
Mark from Michigan.[1]

True, recent studies claim to show small cognitive differences between
the sexes: he gets around by orienting himself in space, she does it by remembering landmarks. Time will tell if any deserve the hoopla with which
each is invariably greeted, over the protests of the researchers themselves.
But even if the results hold up (and the history of such research is not encouraging), we don't need studies of sex-differentiated brain activity in
reading, say, to understand why boys and girls still seem so unalike.

The feminist movement has done much for some women, and something for every woman, but it has hardly turned America into a playground free of sex roles. It hasn't even got women to stop dieting or men
to stop interrupting them.

Instead of looking at kids to "prove" that differences in behavior by
sex are innate, we can look at the ways we raise kids as an index to how
unfinished the feminist revolution really is, and how tentatively it is embraced even by adults who fully expect their daughters to enter previously
male-dominated professions and their sons to change diapers.

I'm at a children's birthday party. "I'm sorry," one mom silently   5
mouths to the mother of the birthday girl, who has just torn open her
present—Tropical Splash Barbie. Now, you can love Barbie or you can
hate Barbie, and there are feminists in both camps. But *apologize* for Barbie? Inflict Barbie, against your own convictions, on the child of a friend
you know will be none too pleased?

Every mother in that room had spent years becoming a person who
had to be taken seriously, not least by herself. Even the most attractive,
I'm willing to bet, had suffered over her body's failure to fit the impossible American ideal. Given all that, it seems crazy to transmit Barbie to
the next generation. Yet to reject her is to say that what Barbie represents—being sexy, thin, stylish—is unimportant, which is obviously not
true, and children know it's not true.

Women's looks matter terribly in this society, and so Barbie, however

[1]*Mark from Michigan:* Mark Koernke, a former right-wing talk-show host who supports the militia movement's resistance to federal government. —EDS.

ambivalently, must be passed along. After all, there are worse toys. The Cut and Style Barbie styling head, for example, a grotesque object intended to encourage "hair play." The grown-ups who give that probably apologize, too.

How happy would most parents be to have a child who flouted sex conventions? I know a lot of women, feminists, who complain in a comical, eyeball-rolling way about their sons' passion for sports: the ruined weekends, obnoxious coaches, macho values. But they would not think of discouraging their sons from participating in this activity they find so foolish. Or do they? Their husbands are sports fans, too, and they like their husbands a lot.

Could it be that even sports-resistant moms see athletics as part of manliness? That if their sons wanted to spend the weekend writing up their diaries, or reading, or baking, they'd find it disturbing? Too antisocial? Too lonely? Too gay?

Theories of innate differences in behavior are appealing. They let parents off the hook—no small recommendation in a culture that holds moms, and sometimes even dads, responsible for their children's every misstep on the road to bliss and success.   10

They allow grown-ups to take the path of least resistance to the dominant culture, which always requires less psychic effort, even if it means more actual work: just ask the working mother who comes home exhausted and nonetheless finds it easier to pick up her son's socks than make him do it himself. They let families buy for their children, without *too* much guilt, the unbelievably sexist junk that the kids, who have been watching commercials since birth, understandably crave.

But the thing that theories do most of all is tell adults that the *adult* world—in which moms and dads still play by many of the old rules even as they question and fidget and chafe against them—is the way it's supposed to be. A girl with a doll and a boy with a truck "explain" why men are from Mars and women are from Venus, why wives do housework and husbands just don't understand.

The paradox is that the world of rigid and hierarchical sex roles evoked by determinist theories is already passing away. Three-year-olds may indeed insist that doctors are male and nurses female, even if their own mother is a physician. Six-year-olds know better. These days, something like half of all medical students are female, and male applications to nursing school are inching upward. When tomorrow's three-year-olds play doctor, who's to say how they'll assign the roles?

With sex roles, as in every area of life, people aspire to what is possible, and conform to what is necessary. But these are not fixed, especially today. Biological determinism may reassure some adults about their present, but it is feminism, the ideology of flexible and converging sex roles, that fits our children's future. And the kids, somehow, know this.

That's why, if you look carefully, you'll find that for every kid who   15
fits a stereotype, there's another who's breaking one down. Sometimes it's

the same kid—the boy who skateboards *and* takes cooking in his after-school program; the girl who collects stuffed animals *and* A-pluses in science.

Feminists are often accused of imposing their "agenda" on children. Isn't that what adults always do, consciously and unconsciously? Kids aren't born religious, or polite, or kind, or able to remember where they put their sneakers. Inculcating these behaviors, and the values behind them, is a tremendous amount of work, involving many adults. We don't have a choice, really, about *whether* we should give our children messages about what it means to be male and female—they're bombarded with them from morning till night.

The question, as always, is what do we want those messages to be?

The Reader's Presence

1. Pollitt notes in her opening paragraph that "it's twenty-eight years since the founding of NOW, and boys still like trucks and girls still like dolls." What does Pollitt identify as the competing theories to explain these differences between boys and girls? Which theory does Pollitt prefer, and how does she express her support of it?

2. As you reread the essay, consider carefully the role of the media in upholding the status quo with regard to differentiated roles for girls and boys. As you develop a response to this question, examine carefully both the media directed principally to children and the media targeted at adults. In the latter category, for instance, Pollitt refers to the media version of scientific research studies into gender differences (paragraph 2) and alludes to popular books that discuss the differences between men and women, such as *Men Are from Mars, Women Are from Venus,* and *You Just Don't Understand* (paragraph 12). Drawing on Pollitt's essay and on your own experience, identify—and discuss—the specific social responsibilities you would like to see America's mass media take more seriously.

3. How would you characterize Pollitt's stance toward today's parents? What are some of the reasons she gives to explain parents' choices and actions? Consider Pollitt's argument in the light of Bernard Cooper's essay "A Clack of Tiny Sparks: Remembrances of a Gay Boyhood" (page 104). How does Cooper's account of his parents' attitudes compare with Pollitt's portrait of parents? Do a similar comparative reading of Pollitt's polemic and Adrienne Rich's portrait of her parents in "Split at the Root: An Essay on Jewish Identity" (page 205). What general points about childrearing can you draw from the contrasts and commonalities between the essays? How does parenting figure in the transmission of beliefs and practices in America, according to these authors?

69

Elayne Rapping

Daytime Inquiries

Elayne Rapping (b. 1938) is a professor of women's and cultural studies at the State University of New York, Buffalo. A media critic and analyst, Rapping has been writing about television, popular culture, and women's issues since the early 1970s, and she contributes regularly to the Nation, *the* Progressive, *the* Village Voice, *and the* Women's Review of Books. *Her publications include* The Looking Glass World of Nonfiction TV *(1987),* The Movie of the Week: Private Stories/Public Events *(1992),* Media-tions: Forays into the Culture and Gender Wars *(1994), and* The Culture of Recovery: Making Sense of the Self-Help Movement in Women's Lives *(1996). "Daytime Inquiries" appeared in 1991 in the* Progressive. *Although some of the talk shows she examines are no longer on the air, the cultural and social issues she raises are still highly relevant, perhaps more so than when the essay first appeared.*

"On *Oprah* today: women who sleep with their sisters' husbands!"

"Donahue talks to women married to bisexuals!"

"Today—Sally Jessy Raphael talks with black women who have bleached their hair blond!"

These are only three of my personal favorites of the past television season. Everyone's seen these promos and laughed at them. "What next?" we wonder to each other with raised eyebrows. And yet, these daytime talk shows are enormously popular and—more often than we like to admit—hard to stop watching once you start.

As with so much else about today's media, the knee-jerk response to this state of affairs is to hold one's nose, distance oneself from those who actually watch this stuff, and moan about the degradation and sleaze with which we're bombarded. But this doesn't tell us much about what's really going on in America—and television's role in it. Worse, it blinds us to what's actually interesting about these shows, what they tell us about the way television maneuvers discussions of controversial and contested topics.

It's no secret that television has *become* the public sphere for Americans, the one central source of information and public debate on matters

of national import. Ninety-eight percent of us live in homes in which the
TV set is on, and therefore in one way or another being experienced and
absorbed, an average of seven-and-a-half hours a day; 67 percent of us
get *all* our information from TV. This is not a matter of laziness, stupidity, or even the seductive power of the tube. It is a tragic fact that illiteracy—actual and functional—is rampant. It is difficult if not impossible
for more and more of us to read, even when we try. Television, in such
cases, is a necessity, even a godsend.

In the early 1950s, when TV emerged as the dominant cultural form,
it presented to us a middle-aged, middle-class, white-male image of authority. Network prime time *was* TV, and what it gave us, from dusk to
bedtime, was a series of white middle-class fathers—Walter Cronkites
and Ward Cleavers—assuring us night after night that they knew best,
that all was in good hands, that we needn't worry about the many scary,
confusing changes wrought by postwar capitalism.

Network prime time still plays that role, or tries to. The fathers sometimes are black now, the authority occasionally shared with mothers, a
voice from the ideological fringes invited from time to time to be a
"guest" (and behave appropriately or not get asked back). But prime time
is still the home of Official, Authoritative Truth as presented by experts
and institutional power brokers. Whatever oppositional voices are heard
are always controlled by the Great White Fathers in charge, who get paid
six- and seven-figure salaries for their trouble.

The money value of these guys to the media—the Koppels, the Jen-
ningses—is so high because their jobs are increasingly difficult. TV, in a
sense, was developed to put a reassuring, controlling facade over the
structural fault lines of American life.

Ever since the 1960s, however, this has been harder and harder to   10
manage. The breakdown of the family, the crises in education, religion,
and the credibility of the state, the growing visibility and vocality of minority groups and ideas—all these took the country and media by storm.
The most recent dramatic proof of the impact of social crises and the progressive movements they spawned is the amazing media hullabaloo over
"multiculturalism" and "political correctness" on campuses. The Left,
people of color, women, gays, and lesbians are apparently making the old
white men extremely nervous.

At night, all of this tumult is being handled more or less as it has always been handled. Things seem to be under control. *MacNeil/Lehrer*
and *Nightline* have their panels of experts, which now often include
women, blacks, and—on rare occasions—"leftists" who really are leftists. But the structure of these shows makes it impossible seriously to
challenge the host and, therefore, seriously to challenge TV hegemony.

A much juicier and, in many ways, more encouraging kind of ideological battle rages before 5 P.M., however. Daytime, women's time, has
always been delegated to "domestic matters." If Father Knew Best in the

evening, on the soaps the women always ruled the roost and what mattered were family and relationship issues — sex, adultery, childbirth, marriage, and the negotiating of the social and domestic end of life in a class-
and race-divided society.

This is still true on daytime. In fact, the soaps are more likely to treat
such social issues as rape, incest, aging, and interracial relationships with
depth and seriousness than any prime-time series. In the sexual division of
labor, these matters of emotional and relational caretaking and socialization have always been seen as "women's domain." And so it goes in TV
Land. Daytime equals women equals "soft" issues. Prime time equals men
and the "hard" stuff.

Except that what used to be soft isn't so soft anymore. The social
movements of the 1960s — especially feminism, with its insistence that
"the personal is political" — changed all that. Everyone who isn't brain-
dead knows — and feels with great intensity — that all the old rules for
living one's life are up for grabs. Relations between the sexes, the generations, the races, among co-workers, neighbors, family members — all of
these are matters of confusion and anxiety.

What is the line, in the workplace, between being friendly and sexual   15
harassment? How do we deal with our children, who are increasingly
media-savvy and street-savvy and whose social environments are radically
different from ours? What about sex education? Drugs? Condoms? Interracial dating? How do we handle social interactions with gay men and
lesbians, now that more and more people are out and proud?

These are just the obvious issues. But they grow out of changes in the
larger political and economic environments and they resonate into every
crevice of our lives in far stranger, more confusing ways. In the breakdown of accepted views about things, and of the ties that kept us on the
straight and narrow in spite of ourselves, unconventional behavior is both
more common and more visible.

Women do, in fact, sleep with their sisters' husbands or find themselves married to bisexuals. Or perhaps they always did these things but
never dreamed of discussing it, never saw it as a social topic, a matter for
debate and disagreement about right and wrong. The same is true of
something as seemingly trivial as one's choice of hair color. For black
women, such tensions are rife, reflecting divisions brought on by political
and cultural issues raised by black liberation movements.

The personal is ever more political, and inquiring minds not only
want to know, they need to know. Or at least they need to talk and listen
about these things. And so the coming of daytime talk shows, a financial
gold mine for the media and a sensationalized, trivialized "political"
event for confused and frightened people everywhere.

The political roots of this form are apparent. In structure, in process,
and in subject matter, they take their cues from an important political institution of the 1960s: the women's consciousness-raising movement. In
those small groups, through which hundreds of thousands of women

passed during a brief, highly charged four- or five-year period starting in about 1968, we invented a democratic, emotionally safe way of bringing out in the open things we never before spoke of. We found we were not alone in our experiences and analyzed their meanings.

Of course, the purpose of these consciousness-raising groups was   20
empowerment, political empowerment. The idea that the personal was political led to a strategy for social change. We hoped that when previously isolated and privatized women recognized common sources of our unhappiness in the larger political world, we could organize to change things.

The words "political" and "organize" do not, of course, occur on daytime TV. The primary goal of talk shows as a television form is to lure curious audiences and sell them products, not revolution. Thus the circus-like atmosphere and the need for bizarre and giggle-inducing topics and participants.

Still, the influence of feminism (and other social and cultural movements) is there, and the result is more interesting and contradictory because of it. Donahue, Oprah, and pals have reproduced, in a plasticized format, the experience of being in a group and sharing deeply personal and significant matters with others in the same boat. Consciousness-raising, unfortunately, is long gone. But from 9 to 11 A.M. and from 3 to 5 P.M. on weekdays, there is a remarkable facsimile thereof.

One reason these shows appeal is because, in line with the democratic thrust of 1960s feminism, their structure approaches the nonhierarchical. The host is still the star, of course. But in terms of authority, she or he is far from central. The physical set enforces this fact. Audiences and participants sit in a circular form and—this is the only TV format in which this happens—speak out, sometimes without being called on. They yell at each other and at the host, disagree with experts, and come to no authoritative conclusions. There is something exhilarating about watching people who are usually invisible—because of class, race, gender, status— having their say and, often, being wholly disrespectful to their "betters."

The discussion of black women with blond hair, for example, ignited a shouting match between those for whom such behavior meant a disavowal of one's "blackness," a desire to "be white," and those who insisted it was simply a matter of choosing how one wished to look, no different from the behavior of white women who dye their hair or tan their bodies. The audience, selected from the black community, took issue with everything that was said. Both participants and audience members attacked the "expert," a black writer committed to the natural—to BLACK IS BEAUTIFUL.

This is as close as television gets to open discourse on serious issues.   25
But it is only possible because the issues discussed are not taken seriously by those in power. And that is why the sensationalism of these shows is double-edged. If they were more respectable in their style and choice of issues, they'd be reined in more. By allowing themselves to seem frivolous

and trashy, they manage to carry on often-serious discussions without being cut off the air or cleaned up.

This may seem contradictory, but it's not. The truth is that the fringy, emotional matters brought up on Oprah, Donahue, Sally, and the others are almost always related in some way to deep cultural and structural problems in our society. Most of us, obviously, wouldn't go on these shows and spill our guts or open ourselves to others' judgments. But the people on these shows are an emotional vanguard, blowing the lid off the idea that America is anything like the place Ronald Reagan pretended to live in.

A typical recent program, for instance, featured a predictably weird ratings lure as topic: FAMILIES WHO DATE PRISONERS. It featured a family of sisters, and some other women, who sought out relationships with convicts. The chance for humor at guests' expense was not spared; Procter & Gamble doesn't care if people watch just to feel superior, as long as they watch. But in the course of the program, important political points came out.

Two issues were of particular interest. The "expert," a psychologist, pushed the protofeminist line that these women had low self-esteem— "women who love too much." Some admitted to it. Others, however, refused to accept that analysis, at least in their own cases. They stressed the prejudice against prisoners in society and went on to discuss the injustices of the criminal-justice system and to insist that their men were good people who had either made a mistake or were treated unfairly by the courts.

Our discomfort on watching what seems to be gross exhibitionism is understandable. We are taught, as children, that we don't air our dirty laundry in public. We learn to be hypocritical and evasive, to keep secret our own tragedies and sorrows, to feign shock when a public official is exposed for his or hers. It is not easy, even today, for most of us to reveal difficulties to neighbors. We are rightly self-protective. But the result of this sense of decorum is to isolate us, to keep us frightened and alone, unwilling to seek out help or share problems.

And so we sit at home, from Omaha to Orlando, and watch Oprah in order to get some sense of what it all means and how we might begin to handle it, whatever it is. These talk shows are safe. They let it all hang out. They don't judge anyone. They don't get shocked by anything. They admit they don't know what's right or wrong for anyone else. They are, for many people, a great relief.

Let me give one final example of how these shows operate as forums for opposing views. A recent segment of *Donahue* concerned women and eating disorders. This show was a gem. It seems Phil had not yet gotten the word, or understood it, that eating disorders are serious matters from which women suffer and die. Nor had he grasped that this is a feminist issue, the result of highly sexist stereotypes imposed upon women who want to succeed at work or love.

Donahue's approach was to make light of the topic. His guests were actresses from Henry Jaglom's film *Eating*, which concerns women, food,

30

and body image, and he teased them about their own bouts with food compulsions. After all, they were all beautiful and thin; how bad could it be?

First the call-in audience, then the studio audience, and finally the actresses themselves, rebelled. Women called in to describe tearfully how they had been suicidal because of their weight. Others rebuked the host's frivolous attitude. Still others offered information about feminist counseling services and support groups. And finally, one by one, those downstage and then those on stage—the celebrities—rose to tell their stories of bulimia, anorexia, self-loathing, many with tears streaming down their faces.

Donahue was chastened and, I think, a bit scared. Ted Koppel would never have allowed such a thing to happen. He would have several doctors, sociologists, or whatever, almost all of them white and male, answer *his* questions about what medical and academic professionals know about eating disorders. There would be no audience participation and very little dialogue among guests. Certainly none would yell or cry or show any other "excessive" emotional involvement in the matter. If they did, Koppel, the smoothest of network journalists, would easily take control and redirect the show. For that matter, only when such a subject as eating disorders is deemed nationally important by the media gatekeepers will it ever get on *Nightline* anyway. Daytime is less cautious.

I have been stressing the positive side of these shows primarily because of their differences from their highbrow, prime-time counterparts, which are far more reactionary in form and content. It is, in the grand scheme of things as they are, a good thing to have these arenas of ideological interaction and open-endedness.   35

But, finally, these shows are a dead end, and they're meant to be. They lead nowhere but to the drug store for more Excedrin. In fact, what's most infuriating about them is not that they are sleazy or in bad taste. It is that they work to co-opt and contain real political change. What talk shows have done is take the best insights and traditions of a more politicized time and declaw them. They are all talk and no action. Unless someone yells something from the floor (as a feminist did during the eating discussion), there will be no hint that there is a world of political action, or of politics at all.

This makes perfect sense. It is the nature of the mass media in a contradictory social environment to take progressive ideas, once they gain strength, and contain them in the large, immobilizing structure of the political status quo.

We are allowed to voice our woes. We are allowed to argue, cry, shout, whatever. We are even allowed to hear about approved services and institutions that might help with this or that specific bruise or wound. But we are not allowed to rock the political or economic boat of television by suggesting that things could be different. That would rightly upset the sponsors and network heads. Who would buy their Excedrin if the headaches of American life went away?

The Reader's Presence

1. What is the conventional attitude toward daytime television, as Rapping characterizes it? How does Rapping challenge this characterization? What rhetorical techniques does she use in her attempt to demonstrate the value of the shows?

2. The writer draws many oppositions between male and female areas of power and speech. How are the different realms evoked? What images and issues pertain to each? She positions "politics" as occurring in the cultural rather than in the governmental arena. What are the characteristics of this politics? What does she believe can be accomplished in it? Is her argument convincing to you? Why or why not?

3. In paragraph 37 Rapping refers to "the large, immobilizing structure of the political status quo"; in the following paragraph she suggests that television's "sponsors and network heads" are somehow to blame for this immobilization. How exactly does Rapping explain the link between media and politics? Compare her understanding of television's ideological power (that is, its capacity to shape or even to determine viewers' opinions and beliefs) to Katha Pollitt's argument about the media in "Why Boys Don't Play with Dolls" (page 493). Do these writers think there are ways to escape the media's control? If so, what are they? If not, why not? To what extent might each essayist think of her own writing as a form of political intervention?

70 ———————————————————

Salman Rushdie

The Ground Beneath My Feet

Salman Rushdie was born in Bombay, India, in 1947. He was educated in Bombay and England, and received a degree in history at King's College, Cambridge. He worked for about a year as a stage actor in London and then became a freelance advertising copywriter. His first novel, Midnight's Children *(1981), won the Booker Prize and was immediately acclaimed as a classic. In 1983 he was selected as one of Granta's Best Young Novelists. He has since published seven more novels, a collection of short stories, a book of nonfiction reportage, and a work of film criticism, and has also received an enormous array of literary and*

...tural awards. When Iranian fundamentalists issued a fatwa, or religious *...ct,* *...gainst* Rushdie condemning him to death for his satirical literary treatment *...f the* prophet Mohammed in The Satanic Verses (1989), he was forced to go *in* hiding and instantly became a cause célèbre in Europe and America. Rush*...,* who lives in New York City, has most recently published the novel Fury (20*...)*. "The Ground Beneath My Feet" was originally published in the Nation in Ju*...* 2001.

In the summer of 1986 I was traveling in Nicaragua, working on the book of reportage that was published six months later as *The Jaguar Smile*. It was the seventh anniversary of the Sandinista revolution, and the war against the U.S.-backed *contra* forces was intensifying almost daily. I was accompanied by my interpreter, Margarita, an improbably glamorous and high-spirited blonde with more than a passing resemblance to Jayne Mansfield. Our days were filled with evidence of hardship and struggle: the scarcity of produce in the markets of Managua, the bomb crater on a country road where a school bus had been blown up by a *contra* mine. One morning, however, Margarita seemed unusually excited.

"Bono's coming!" she cried, bright-eyed as any fan, and then added, without any change in vocal inflection or dulling of ocular glitter, "Tell me: Who is Bono?"

In a way, the question was as vivid a demonstration of her country's beleaguered isolation as anything I heard or saw in the frontline villages, the destitute Atlantic Coast bayous or the quake-ravaged city streets. In July 1986, the release of U2's monster album *The Joshua Tree* was still eight months away, but they were already, after all, the masters of War. Who was Bono? He was the fellow who sang, "I can't believe the news today, I can't close my eyes and make it go away." And Nicaragua was one of the places where the news had become unbelievable, and you couldn't shut your eyes to it, and so of course he was there.

I didn't meet Bono in Nicaragua, but he did read *The Jaguar Smile*. Five years later, when I was involved in some difficulties of my own, my friend the composer Michael Berkeley asked if I wanted to go to a U2 *Achtung Baby* gig, with its hanging psychedelic Trabants. In those days it was hard for me to go most places, but I said yes and was touched by the enthusiasm with which the request was greeted by U2's people. And so there I was at Earl's Court, standing in the shadows, listening.

Backstage, after the show, I was shown into a mobile home full of sandwiches and children. There were no groupies at U2 gigs; just crèches. Bono came in and was instantly festooned with daughters. My memory of that first chat is that I wanted to talk about music and he was keen to talk politics—Nicaragua, an upcoming protest against unsafe nuclear waste disposal at Sellafield in northern England, his support for me and my work. We didn't spend long together, but we both enjoyed it. Bono was less taken with Michael Berkeley, however. Years afterward he told me he'd felt condescended to by the classical composer. My own view is that there was a misunderstanding—Michael isn't a condescending man, but a high culture/low culture rift had opened, and that was that.

5

Two years later, when the giant *Zooropa* tour arrived at Wembley Stadium, Bono called to ask if I'd like to come out on stage. U2 wanted to make a gesture of solidarity, and this was the biggest one they could think of. When I told my then–14-year-old son about the plan, he said, "Just don't sing, Dad. If you sing, I'll have to kill myself." There was no question of my being allowed to sing—U2 aren't stupid people—but I did go out there and feel, for a moment, what it's like to have 80,000 fans cheering you on. The audience at the average book reading is a little smaller. Girls tend not to climb onto their boyfriends' shoulders during them, and stage-diving is discouraged. Even at the very best book readings, there are only one or two supermodels dancing by the mixing desk. Anton Corbijn took a photograph that day for which he persuaded Bono and me to exchange glasses. There I am looking godlike in Bono's wraparound Fly shades, while he peers benignly over my uncool literary specs. There could be no more graphic expression of the difference between our two worlds.

It was inevitable that both U2 and I would be criticized in Britain in bringing these two worlds together. They have been accused of trying to acquire some borrowed intellectual "cred," and I of course am supposedly star-struck. None of this matters very much. I've been crossing frontiers all my life—physical, social, intellectual, artistic borderlines—and I spotted, in Bono and Edge, whom I've come to know better than the others so far, an equal hunger for the new, for whatever nourishes. I think, too, that the band's involvement in religion—as inescapable a subject in Ireland as it is in India—gave us, when we first met, a subject and an enemy (fanaticism) in common.

An association with U2 is good for one's anecdote stock. Some of these anecdotes are risibly apocryphal: A couple of years ago, for example, a front-page Irish press report confidently announced that I had been living in "the folly"—the guest house with a spectacular view of Killiney Bay that stands in the garden of Bono's Dublin home—for four whole years! Apparently I arrived and departed at dead of night in a helicopter that landed on the beach below the house. Other stories that sound apocryphal are unfortunately true. It is true, for example, that I once danced—or, to be precise, pogoed—with Van Morrison in Bono's living room. It is also true that in the small hours of the following morning I was treated to the rough end of the great man's tongue. (Van Morrison has been known to get a little grumpy toward the end of a long evening. It's possible that my pogoing wasn't up to his exacting standards.)

Over the years U2 and I discussed collaborating on various projects. Bono mentioned an idea he had for a stage musical, but my imagination failed to spark. There was another long Dublin night (a bottle of Jameson's was involved) during which the film director Neil Jordan, Bono, and I conspired to make a film of my novel *Haroun and the Sea of Stories*. To my great regret this never came to anything either.

Then, in 1999, I published my novel *The Ground Beneath Her Feet*, 10 in which the Orpheus myth winds through a story set in the world of rock music. Orpheus is the defining myth for singers and writers—for the Greeks, he was the greatest singer as well as the greatest poet—and it was my Orphic tale that finally made possible the collaboration we'd been kicking around.

It happened, like many good things, without being planned. I sent Bono and U2's manager, Paul McGuinness, prepublication copies of the novel in typescript, hoping they would tell me if the thing worked or not. Bono said afterward that he had been very worried on my behalf, believing that I had taken on an impossible task, and that he began reading the book in the spirit of a "policeman"—that is, to save me from my mistakes. Fortunately, the novel passed the test. Deep inside it is the lyric of what Bono called the novel's "title track," a sad elegy written by the novel's main male character about the woman he loved, who has been swallowed up in an earthquake: a contemporary Orpheus' lament for his lost Eurydice.

Bono called me. "I've written this melody for your words, and I think it might be one of the best things I've done." I was astonished. One of the novel's principal images is that of the permeable frontier between the world of the imagination and the one we inhabit, and here was an imaginary song crossing that frontier. I went to McGuinness's place near Dublin to hear it. Bono took me away from everyone else and played the demo CD to me in his car. Only when he was sure that I liked it—and I liked it right away—did we go back indoors to play it for the assembled company.

There wasn't much after that that one would properly call "collaboration." There was a long afternoon when Daniel Lanois, who was producing the song, brought his guitar and sat down with me to work out the lyrical structure. And there was the Day of the Lost Words, when I was called urgently by a woman from Principle Management, which looks after U2. "They're in the studio and they can't find the lyrics. Could you fax them over?" Otherwise, silence, until the song was ready.

I wasn't expecting it to happen, but I'm proud of it. It's called "The Ground Beneath Her Feet." For U2, too, it was a departure. They haven't often used anyone's lyrics but their own, and they don't usually start with the lyrics; typically, the words come at the very end. But somehow it all worked out. I suggested facetiously that they might consider renaming the band U2+1, or, even better, Me2, but I think they'd heard all those gags before.

There was a long al fresco lunch in Killiney at which the film director Wim Wenders startlingly announced that artists must no longer use irony. Plain speaking, he argued, was necessary now: Communication should be direct, and anything that might create confusion should be eschewed. Irony, in the rock world, has acquired a special meaning. The multimedia self-consciousness of U2's *Achtung Baby-Zooropa* phase,

15

which simultaneously embraced and debunked the mythology and gob-bledygook of rock stardom, capitalism, and power, and of which Bono's white-faced, gold-lamé-suited, red-velvet-horned MacPhisto incarnation was the emblem, is what Wenders was criticizing. Characteristically, U2 responded by taking this approach even further, pushing it further than it would bear, in the less-well-received POP-Mart tour. After that, it seems, they took Wender's advice. The new album, and the Elevation tour, is the spare, impressive result.

There was a lot riding on this album, this tour. If things hadn't gone well it might have been the end of U2. They certainly discussed that possi-bility, and the album was much delayed as they agonized over it. Ex-tracurricular activities, mainly Bono's, also slowed them down, but since these included getting David Trimble and John Hume to shake hands on a public stage and reducing Jesse Helms—Jesse Helms!—to tears, winning his support for the campaign against Third World debt, it's hard to argue that these were self-indulgent irrelevances. At any event, *All That You Can't Leave Behind* turned out to be a strong album, a renewal of cre-ative force and, as Bono put it, there's a lot of good will flowing toward the band right now.

I've seen them three times this year: in the "secret" pre-tour gig in London's little Astoria Theatre and then twice in America, in San Diego and Anaheim. They've come down out of the giant stadiums to play arena-sized venues that seem tiny after the gigantism of their recent past. The act has been stripped bare; essentially, it's just the four of them out there, playing their instruments and singing their songs. For a person of my age, who remembers when rock music was always like this, the show feels simultaneously nostalgic and innovative. In the age of choreo-graphed, instrumentless little-boy and little-girl bands (yes, I know the Supremes didn't play guitars, but they were the Supremes!) it's exhilarat-ing to watch a great, grown-up quartet do the fine, simple things so well. Direct communication, as Wim Wenders said. It works.

And they're playing my song.

The Reader's Presence

1. In paragraph 15 Rushdie uses the word *emblem*. What is an em-blem? How is the word used in that sentence? Earlier, in para-graph 6, Rushdie describes a photograph of himself and Bono in which the two had exchanged eyeglasses. "There could be no more graphic expression of the difference between our two worlds," he writes. What are the two worlds to which Rushdie refers? In what ways is this photograph an emblem of the dis-tance between them?

2. Rushdie alludes in paragraph 4 to "some difficulties of [his] own." To what is he referring? Why might he keep the particulars out of this essay? How does the knowledge of Rushdie's history affect your understanding of paragraph 6 in which he stands before 80,000 U2 fans? How does it affect your appreciation of Rushdie's developing friendship with Bono?

3. Why might Wim Wenders have said that "artists must no longer use irony" (paragraph 15)? Does Rushdie use irony in this piece? Does Bono? Where, and to what effect? Rushdie describes one of U2's albums as "simultaneously embrac[ing] and debunk [ing] the mythology and gobbledygook of rock stardom, capitalism, and power" (paragraph 15). Does Rushdie do something similar in this essay, or is U2's brand of celebrity (with which Rushdie is now associated) seen to be beyond common critiques of capitalism?

71

Luc Sante

What Secrets Tell

As a child, Luc Sante (b. 1954) moved back and forth between Belgium and the United States several times until his family settled in New Jersey. While in his early twenties, Sante got a job at a bookstore and began reading obscure stories about New York City's seedy history from the late 1800s to the early 1900s. These accounts of prostitutes, corrupt police officers, thieves, gamblers, and drug dealers provided rich material for his first two books, Low Life: Lures and Snares of Old New York *(1991) and* Evidence *(1992). His most recent work is a memoir titled* The Factory of Facts *(1998).*

Sante has written extensively on photography and popular culture; his next book will be about the famous American photographer Walker Evans.

"Secrets," writes Sante, "are a permanent feature of the human condition." In "What Secrets Tell," he provides a summary of the many types of human secrets and examines the role they play in a world increasingly dominated by computer technology and mass media. With so much private information readily available and with so many people eager to bare their souls for daily public entertainment, what can we possibly have secrets about?

Sante is a frequent contributor to the New York Times Magazine, *where "What Secrets Tell" was originally published (December 3, 2000).*

Once, it was believed that a wholesale revelation of secrets would not occur until the Day of Judgment, when graves would be opened and the tongues of the dead at last loosened. Nowadays you might almost get the impression that the time had arrived, so profuse has been the unsealing of lips, the unlocking of vaults, the uncovering of caches. Secrets, some of them moss-covered with age, have one after another been stripped naked in public. There are two major catalysts for this phenomenon. The dissolution of the Soviet empire, first of all, opened a tremendous number of lead-lined rooms. We now know where various bodies are buried, who spied and for whom, and what they transmitted. Because to Westerners the U.S.S.R. was for more than 70 years the No. 1 sphinx, the serial release of KGB documents over the past decade has solved whole shelves' worth of longstanding mysteries and promoted an atmosphere of real or imaginary worldwide openness.

And then there is the Internet, which has proved a nemesis to secrecy official and unofficial at home. Nothing of major importance, it would seem, can remain hidden for long before someone in on the deal feels the urge to post the details online. The Web is the universal souk, where fans, zealots, voyeurs, lonely crusaders, congenital meddlers, dirt brokers, disgruntled ex-employees, and the idly curious can trade facts, as well as rumors and fantasies posing as facts, in relative safety and anonymity. A secret posted on the Web can reach an astonishing number of eyes in no time at all; deniability doesn't count for much when you've got a few million eager witnesses. The secret, once an important, gold-backed currency, appears in danger of rapid devaluation as the screens of the world are flooded with industrial quantities of the skinny.

A third factor, meanwhile, has been coursing through American culture since before either of the other two became relevant. The urge to confess one's hidden transgressions before an audience of strangers, a peculiar phenomenon that came to our attention in the 1980s, has wildly miscellaneous roots: revival-tent epiphanies, Alcoholics Anonymous, psychotherapy and its many cousins, televised trials and certain odd game shows of the past, the poetry of Robert Lowell and Sylvia Plath, the memoirs of Mafiosi and Hollywood lechers and Watergate spear-carriers. Baring all in public attracts attention and at least used to assure forgiveness. Today it's all about entertainment value, with maybe some cathartic relief thrown in, and the secrets revealed have become more inconsequential even as they have become more sordid. The taboo-busting memoir, which was the intellectuals' outlet, seems to have dried up recently, but the TV confession shows are still strong after more than a decade—television thrives on repetition. Anyway, the phenomenon builds momentum, and the measure of normality is subject to continual revision; the more rubber fetishists reveal all before a live studio audience, the more additional rubber fetishists will feel impelled to do the same. At this rate, the last living American with a hidden vice will surrender to Jerry Springer in about eight years.

So are we in the midst of a new era of candor? Not likely. We need secrets far too much to jettison them. Just as it is possible that today secrets are being manufactured for the express purpose of revealing them amid trumpet flourishes, so it has happened and will happen again that secrets are constructed simply to answer a pressing need for secrets. Secrets are a permanent feature of the human condition. We need secrets the way we need black holes, for their mystery; the way we need land-speed records, for their enlargement of scale; the way we need sexy models in advertisements, for their seductively false promises; the way we need lotteries, for their vague possibility. We also need them the way we need bank vaults and sock drawers and glove compartments. Anybody who doesn't carry around one or two secrets probably has all the depth of a place mat.

But then the word "secret" conceals under its mantle a teeming and motley population of types. Secrets cater to the entire range of human susceptibilities, from the laughably trivial to the terrifying fundamental. Principal landmarks along the way include:

Personal Secrets. In other words, those secrets that are chiefly of interest to the persons who carry them around. You know the sort: you pick your nose when no one's looking; your real first name is Eustace; you wear a truss for nonmedical reasons. If such things were revealed, your ego might take a beating and your intimates could gain a weapon for use in squabbles or extortions, but the foundations of your house would not be shaken.

Romantic Secrets. They run the gamut. That interval of passion you once shared with your dentist when the two of you were stuck in an elevator with a bottle of Cherry Kijafa may remain swathed in gauze for all eternity, although your partner might eventually demand to know the identity of this "Shirley" whose name you utter in your sleep. That you enjoy above all the erotic sensation of being pinched with tweezers until you bleed might not matter a whole lot to anyone, unless you decide to run for office, and then you will find yourself sending discreet sums of money to people you haven't thought of in years. Couples often tacitly erect a whole edifice of secrets, based on real or imagined causes for jealousy. This can be relatively harmless, or it can be a symptom of the relationship's becoming a regime.

Secrets in Gossip. That is, the wheat left over when gossip's chaff is sifted out. Secrets that surface as gossip are usually of the mildest sort, personal eccentricities and romantic peccadilloes not of much interest outside a closed circle. (It is understood that there is a direct correlation between the degree of triviality of the secret transmitted as gossip and the rank of the gossip's subject within that circle.) Gossip, though, demonstrates how secrets can become currency, as the teller invests the hearer with power in exchange for esteem. The possession of a secret concerning another is, like all forms of power, something of a burden, a weight pressing one's lips together, which can be relieved only by telling someone else. This, added to a hunger for knowledge on the part of all within the gossip circle, keeps the wheel of the secret-fueled gossip economy turning.

Trade Secrets. The monetary economy, meanwhile, revolves around a wide and diverse range of secrets. A business strategy is a secret until it becomes a *fait accompli.* The details of the financial health of a company are kept as secret as the law allows. Anyone with a degree of power in the market is continually keeping secrets — from competitors, from the press, from anyone who is an outsider, including friends and family, but sometimes from colleagues and office mates. The reasons are obvious: everyone is naked in a cutthroat world, and secrets are clothing. It goes without saying that secrets protect innovations and that they also hide various extralegal undertakings — the ostensibly respectable bank that takes in laundry on the side, for example. Business also employs secrets strategically, as secrets qua secrets, usually painting the word "secret" in letters 10-stories tall. Naturally the new car model will differ little from the previous year's, but a bit of cloak-and-dagger about it will increase public interest. The "secret recipe" is on a par with "new and improved" as a carny barker's hook. The cake mix or soft drink or laundry soap may, of course, actually include a secret ingredient, known only to staff chemists and highly placed executives, but very often a "secret ingredient" is rumored or bruited about primarily as a lure to the gulls of the public.

Secret Formulas. The public hunger for secrets is primordial. It is   10
first and foremost a matter of curiosity, but it also springs from a painful awareness of rank and a belief that things are different upstairs, with a more or less fanciful idea of the specifics. These days, with fortune-building running at a pitch not seen since the 1920s, there is widespread demand for financial folklore. You can make a lot of money catering to the suspicion that there exist shortcuts known only to a few. That some people are richer, thinner, more charismatic or whiter of teeth may be a result of a variety of imponderable factors, but for everyone who in moments of desperation has imagined that there must be some simple trick, some formula or high sign or investment routine or hidden spa, there is an author with a book aimed at the exact combination of vulnerability and prurient imagination. Such publications run along the entire span of implied legitimacy based upon demographics, from the crudities aimed at the supermarket-tabloid constituency (diets centered on junk food named in the Bible, for instance) to the overpriced hardcover pamphlets catering to the anxieties of the managerial class by dressing up received ideas with slogans and numbered lists. For centuries, the secret has been a sure-fire sales gimmick. All you have to do is combine the banal and the esoteric.

Secret Societies. There are probably a lot fewer than there once were, but somewhere in America, no doubt, insurance adjusters and trophy engravers still gather once a month in acrylic gowns and button-flap underwear to exchange phrases in pseudobiblical Double Dutch and then get down to the business of drinking beer. It helps them feel special to be the only ones in town who know the three-finger handshake. The setup descends from the heresies of the Middle Ages by way of the pecking order of the playground. We can laugh at them, now that they are so enfeebled, but there was a time not long ago when they dominated the social life of male middle-class America, and in many ways their pretensions are not so far removed from those of the Mafia or the CIA.

Mystical Secrets. The secret is bait. The secret leads votaries by the nose through a maze of connected chambers, in each of which they must ante up. Only when they have finally tumbled to there being no secret (and they have run through the better part of their inheritances) can they truly be counted as initiates. But few have the stamina to get that far, and most instead spend their spare afternoons consuming one tome after another promoting the secrets of, variously, the pyramids, the Templars, the ascended masters, the elders of Mu, the Essene scrolls, and so on through greater and lesser degrees of perceived legitimacy, all of which flutter around the edges of the secret, none of which make so bold as to suggest what it might consist of.

State Secrets. "Our laws are not generally known; they are kept secret by the small group of nobles who rule us," wrote Kafka in one of his miniature stories. "We are convinced that these ancient laws are scrupulously administered; nevertheless it is an extremely painful thing to be ruled by laws that one does not know." This is the essence of state secrets. A government does not have to be totalitarian, particularly, to possess a stratum of laws whose existence cannot be generally known because they describe the limits of the knowable. It is forbidden for unauthorized persons to possess certain kinds of information. What kinds of information? Well, that's the trouble; if you knew that, you would already know too much. State secrets range all the way from banal prohibitions on photographing customs booths and power plants to the highest levels of technical esoterica.

Atomic Secrets. "Stop me if you've heard this atomic secret," cracked William Burroughs in "Naked Lunch." Atomic secrets may be the world's most famous class of secret, an oxymoron, surely, but for the fact that few enough people would recognize or understand an atomic secret if it landed in their mailboxes. The workaday state secret may be a matter of mere protocol or protection of resources, not unlike industries safeguarding the peculiarities of their production methods. The atomic secret, however, ascends to the level of the sacred because it manifests in concrete form the terror that mystics can only suggest: the end of the world. The secret of life may be an empty proposition, but the secret of death is actually legible to those who possess the language and the tools.

The existence of the Internet, too, has increased the fluidity of secrets.   15
Suddenly no one knows the difference between fact and folklore. Maybe secrets are posted all the time on fixed or fleeting sites, or maybe those are just clever counterfeits of secrets. Maybe the real deal is available on some site no one has thought to access yet. The Web, after all, offers the

possibility that every iota of information in the world will sooner or later appear, but it may be that, like Jorge Luis Borges's library of Babel, the Web will eventually serve up every possible combination of words, so that finally no one at all will be able to tell a secret from its chance approximation.

Confessional culture further devalues the secret. It may be a big deal to the one making a clean breast of things, but to the audience it's *Grand Guignol,* rated on its novelty quotient or on how much carnage it inspires on the set. Secrets are loose change—celebrities keep bagfuls in the storm cellar for when they need to score some publicity by leaking a few to the tabs. The daytime-TV guests each have one, but each greatly resembles others previously broadcast by other guests, and there is a limitless supply of new guests eating doughnuts in the greenroom. Anyway, whole classes of lifestyle deviations that used to be secret are now strictly ho-hum, will inspire yawns, have support groups devoted to them right down the street. That truly private shame of yours, meanwhile, probably requires too much context to be particularly negotiable, and the only three people who will care enough are not very likely to derive much entertainment from it. And what good is a secret then? That kind of secret will remain impervious to trends.

There is a deep human need for secrets that transcends all rational explanations. The revelation of a secret can be liberating, even intoxicating, at least at first, but to those on the receiving end, it is finally disappointing. This is in part because few secrets can live up to their packaging. Secrets need to mature some to be truly effective—a point too often missed in today's climate—but secrets known of long before they are divulged are especially susceptible to anticlimax. Witness the recent publication by the Catholic Church of the final prophecy of Fatima. It fell with a thud, especially because its revelation was way ex post facto—the papal assassination attempt, nearly 20 years stone cold! Holy secrets have an obligation to lie beyond human understanding and, if unveiled, to produce a physically overwhelming effect.

People need secrets because they need the assurance that there is something left to discover, that they have not exhausted the limits of their environment, that a prize might lie in wait like money in the pocket of an old jacket, that the existence of things beyond their ken might propose as a corollary that their own minds contain unsuspected corridors. People need uncertainty and destabilization the way they need comfort and security. It's not that secrets make them feel small but that they make the world seem bigger—a major necessity these days, when sensations need to be extreme to register at all. Secrets reawaken that feeling from childhood that the ways of the world were infinitely mysterious, unpredictable and densely packed, and that someday you might come to know and master them. Secrets purvey affordable glamour, suggest danger without presenting an actual threat. If there were no more secrets, an important motor of life would be stopped, and the days would merge into a continuous blur. Secrets hold out the promise, false but necessary, that death will be deferred until their unveiling.

The Reader's Presence

1. Sante's essay relies heavily on a method of classification: He breaks secrets down into a number of different types. How do you think he developed his system of classification? Do you think he borrowed it from a sociological study or an encyclopedia? How thorough do you find it? Are there types of secrets you can think of that he doesn't include?

2. Why does Sante believe that people need secrets? What do secrets offer that a world of total candor and openness does not? Do you agree with his assessment?

3. Try applying Sante's analysis of secrets to other examples of secrets found in this collection. For example, what sort of secret does Eric Schlosser refer to in "Why McDonald's Fries Taste So Good" (see following selection), or does Elayne Rapping write about in "Daytime Inquiries" (page 497)? How would you describe Bernard Cooper's secrets in "A Clack of Tiny Sparks" (page 104) or Langston Hughes's in "Salvation" (page 146)? How well do these secrets fit into Sante's classification?

72

Eric Schlosser

Why McDonald's Fries Taste So Good

Eric Schlosser is a correspondent for the Atlantic Monthly. *His articles and essays about contemporary America have won numerous journalistic honors and awards, including a National Magazine Award for an article he wrote on marijuana.* Fast Food Nation: The Dark Side of the All-American Meal, *Schlosser's controversial and widely reviewed first book, has prompted a reexamination of current practices of the meat-processing industry.*

Of writing Fast Food Nation, *Schlosser said, "I care about the literary aspects of the book. I tried to make it as clear as possible, and make it an interesting thing to read, but I sacrificed some of that, ultimately, in order to get this out to people and let them know what's going on."*

The french fry was "almost sacrosanct for me," Ray Kroc, one of the founders of McDonald's, wrote in his autobiography, "its preparation a ritual to be followed religiously." During the chain's early years french fries were made from scratch every day. Russet Burbank potatoes were peeled, cut into shoestrings, and fried in McDonald's kitchens. As the chain expanded nationwide, in the mid-1960s, it sought to cut labor costs, reduce the number of suppliers, and ensure that its fries tasted the same at every restaurant. McDonald's began switching to frozen french fries in 1966 — and few customers noticed the difference. Nevertheless, the change had a profound effect on the nation's agriculture and diet. A familiar food had been transformed into a highly processed industrial commodity. McDonald's fries now come from huge manufacturing plants that can peel, slice, cook, and freeze two million pounds of potatoes a day. The rapid expansion of McDonald's and the popularity of its low-cost, mass-produced fries changed the way Americans eat. In 1960 Americans consumed an average of about eighty-one pounds of fresh potatoes and four pounds of frozen french fries. In 2000 they consumed an average of about fifty pounds of fresh potatoes and thirty pounds of frozen fries. Today McDonald's is the largest buyer of potatoes in the United States.

The taste of McDonald's french fries played a crucial role in the chain's success — fries are much more profitable than hamburgers — and was long praised by customers, competitors, and even food critics. James Beard loved McDonald's fries. Their distinctive taste does not stem from the kind of potatoes that McDonald's buys, the technology that processes them, or the restaurant equipment that fries them: other chains use Russet Burbanks, buy their french fries from the same large processing companies, and have similar fryers in their restaurant kitchens. The taste of a french fry is largely determined by the cooking oil. For decades McDonald's cooked its french fries in a mixture of about seven percent cottonseed oil and 93 percent beef tallow. The mixture gave the fries their unique flavor — and more saturated beef fat per ounce than a McDonald's hamburger.

In 1990, amid a barrage of criticism over the amount of cholesterol in its fries, McDonald's switched to pure vegetable oil. This presented the company with a challenge: how to make fries that subtly taste like beef without cooking them in beef tallow. A look at the ingredients in McDonald's french fries suggests how the problem was solved. Toward the end of the list is a seemingly innocuous yet oddly mysterious phrase: "natural flavor." That ingredient helps to explain not only why the fries taste so good but also why most fast food — indeed, most of the food Americans eat today — tastes the way it does.

Open your refrigerator, your freezer, your kitchen cupboards, and look at the labels on your food. You'll find "natural flavor" or "artificial flavor" in just about every list of ingredients. The similarities between these two broad categories are far more significant than the differences. Both are man-made additives that give most processed food most of its taste. People usually buy a food item the first time because of its packaging or appearance. Taste usually determines whether they buy it again. About 90 percent of the money that Americans now spend on food goes to buy processed food. The canning, freezing, and dehydrating techniques used in processing destroy most of food's flavor — and so a vast industry has arisen in the United States to make processed food palatable. Without this flavor industry today's fast food would not exist. The names of the leading American fast-food chains and their best-selling menu items have become embedded in our popular culture and famous worldwide. But few people can name the companies that manufacture fast food's taste.

The flavor industry is highly secretive. Its leading companies will not   5 divulge the precise formulas of flavor compounds or the identities of clients. The secrecy is deemed essential for protecting the reputations of beloved brands. The fast-food chains, understandably, would like the public to believe that the flavors of the food they sell somehow originate in their restaurant kitchens, not in distant factories run by other firms. A McDonald's french fry is one of countless foods whose flavor is just a component in a complex manufacturing process. The look and the taste of what we eat now are frequently deceiving — by design.

THE FLAVOR CORRIDOR

The New Jersey Turnpike runs through the heart of the flavor industry, an industrial corridor dotted with refineries and chemical plants. International Flavors & Fragrances (IFF), the world's largest flavor company, has a manufacturing facility off Exit 8A in Dayton, New Jersey; Givaudan, the world's second-largest flavor company, has a plant in East Hanover. Haarmann & Reimer, the largest German flavor company, has a plant in Teterboro, as does Takasago, the largest Japanese flavor company. Flavor Dynamics has a plant in South Plainfield; Frutarom is in North Bergen; Elan Chemical is in Newark. Dozens of companies manufacture flavors in the corridor between Teaneck and South Brunswick. Altogether the area produces about two thirds of the flavor additives sold in the United States.

The IFF plant in Dayton is a huge pale-blue building with a modern office complex attached to the front. It sits in an industrial park, not far from a BASF plastics factory, a Jolly French Toast factory, and a plant that manufactures Liz Claiborne cosmetics. Dozens of tractor-trailers were parked at the IFF loading dock the afternoon I visited, and a thin cloud of steam floated from a roof vent. Before entering the plant, I signed a nondisclosure form, promising not to reveal the brand names of foods that contain IFF flavors. The place reminded me of Willy Wonka's chocolate factory. Wonderful smells drifted through the hallways, men and women in neat white lab coats cheerfully went about their work, and hundreds of little glass bottles sat on laboratory tables and shelves. The bottles contained powerful but fragile flavor chemicals, shielded from light by brown glass and round white caps shut tight. The long chemical names on the little white labels were as mystifying to me as medieval Latin. These odd-sounding things would be mixed and poured and turned into new substances, like magic potions.

I was not invited into the manufacturing areas of the IFF plant, where, it was thought, I might discover trade secrets. Instead I toured various laboratories and pilot kitchens, where the flavors of well-established brands are tested or adjusted, and where whole new flavors are created. IFF's snack-and-savory lab is responsible for the flavors of potato chips, corn chips, breads, crackers, breakfast cereals, and pet food. The confectionary lab devises flavors for ice cream, cookies, candies, toothpastes, mouthwashes, and antacids. Everywhere I looked, I saw famous, widely advertised products sitting on laboratory desks and tables. The beverage lab was full of brightly colored liquids in clear bottles. It comes up with flavors for popular soft drinks, sports drinks, bottled teas, and wine coolers, for all-natural juice drinks, organic soy drinks, beers, and malt liquors. In one pilot kitchen I saw a dapper food technologist, a middle-aged man with an elegant tie beneath his crisp lab coat, carefully preparing a batch of cookies with white frosting and pink-and-white sprinkles. In another pilot kitchen I saw a pizza oven, a grill, a milk-shake machine, and a french fryer identical to those I'd seen at innumerable fast-food restaurants.

In addition to being the world's largest flavor company, IFF manufactures the smells of six of the ten best-selling fine perfumes in the United States, including Estée Lauder's Beautiful, Clinique's Happy, Lancôme's Trésor, and Calvin Klein's Eternity. It also makes the smells of household products such as deodorant, dishwashing detergent, bath soap, shampoo, furniture polish, and floor wax. All these aromas are made through essentially the same process: the manipulation of volatile chemicals. The basic science behind the scent of your shaving cream is the same as that governing the flavor of your TV dinner.

"NATURAL" AND "ARTIFICIAL"

Scientists now believe that human beings acquired the sense of taste as a way to avoid being poisoned. Edible plants generally taste sweet, harmful ones bitter. The taste buds on our tongues can detect the presence of half a dozen or so basic tastes, including sweet, sour, bitter, salty, astringent, and umami, a taste discovered by Japanese researchers—a rich and full sense of deliciousness triggered by amino acids in foods such

10

as meat, shellfish, mushrooms, potatoes, and seaweed. Taste buds offer a limited means of detection, however, compared with the human olfactory system, which can perceive thousands of different chemical aromas. Indeed, "flavor" is primarily the smell of gases being released by the chemicals you've just put in your mouth. The aroma of a food can be responsible for as much as 90 percent of its taste.

The act of drinking, sucking, or chewing a substance releases its volatile gases. They flow out of your mouth and up your nostrils, or up the passageway in the back of your mouth, to a thin layer of nerve cells called the olfactory epithelium, located at the base of your nose, right between your eyes. Your brain combines the complex smell signals from your olfactory epithelium with the simple taste signals from your tongue, assigns a flavor to what's in your mouth, and decides if it's something you want to eat.

A person's food preferences, like his or her personality, are formed during the first few years of life, through a process of socialization. Babies innately prefer sweet tastes and reject bitter ones; toddlers can learn to enjoy hot and spicy food, bland health food, or fast food, depending on what the people around them eat. The human sense of smell is still not fully understood. It is greatly affected by psychological factors and expectations. The mind focuses intently on some of the aromas that surround us and filters out the overwhelming majority. People can grow accustomed to bad smells or good smells; they stop noticing what once seemed overpowering. Aroma and memory are somehow inextricably linked. A smell can suddenly evoke a long-forgotten moment. The flavors of childhood foods seem to leave an indelible mark, and adults often return to them, without always knowing why. These "comfort foods" become a source of pleasure and reassurance—a fact that fast-food chains use to their advantage. Childhood memories of Happy Meals, which come with french fries, can translate into frequent adult visits to McDonald's. On average, Americans now eat about four servings of french fries every week.

The human craving for flavor has been a largely unacknowledged and unexamined force in history. For millennia royal empires have been built, unexplored lands traversed, and great religions and philosophies forever changed by the spice trade. In 1492 Christopher Columbus set sail to find seasoning. Today the influence of flavor in the world marketplace is no less decisive. The rise and fall of corporate empires—of soft-drink companies, snack-food companies, and fast-food chains—is often determined by how their products taste.

The flavor industry emerged in the mid-nineteenth century, as processed foods began to be manufactured on a large scale. Recognizing the need for flavor additives, early food processors turned to perfume companies that had long experience working with essential oils and volatile aromas. The great perfume houses of England, France, and the Netherlands produced many of the first flavor compounds. In the early part of the twentieth century Germany took the technological lead in flavor production, owing to its powerful chemical industry. Legend has it that a German scientist discovered methyl anthranilate, one of the first artificial flavors, by accident while mixing chemicals in his laboratory. Suddenly the lab was filled with the sweet smell of grapes. Methyl anthranilate later became the chief flavor compound in grape Kool-Aid. After World War II much of the perfume industry shifted from Europe to the United States, settling in New York City near the garment district and the fashion houses. The flavor industry came with it, later moving to New Jersey for greater plant capacity. Man-made flavor additives were used mostly in baked goods, candies, and sodas until the 1950s, when sales of processed food began to soar. The invention of gas chromatographs and mass spectrometers—machines capable of detecting volatile gases at low levels—vastly increased the number of flavors that could be synthesized. By the mid-1960s flavor companies were churning out compounds to supply the taste of Pop Tarts, Bac-Os, Tab, Tang, Filet-O-Fish sandwiches, and literally thousands of other new foods.

The American flavor industry now has annual revenues of about $1.4 billion. Approximately 10,000 new processed-food products are introduced every year in the United States. Almost all of them require flavor additives. And about nine out of ten of these products fail. The latest flavor innovations and corporate realignments are heralded in publications such as *Chemical Market Reporter, Food Chemical News, Food Engineering,* and *Food Product Design.* The progress of IFF has mirrored that of the flavor industry as a whole. IFF was formed in 1958, through the merger of two small companies. Its annual revenues have grown almost fifteenfold since the early 1970s, and it currently has manufacturing facilities in twenty countries.   15

Today's sophisticated spectrometers, gas chromatographs, and headspace-vapor analyzers provide a detailed map of a food's flavor components, detecting chemical aromas present in amounts as low as one part per billion. The human nose, however, is even more sensitive. A nose can detect aromas present in quantities of a few parts per trillion—an amount equivalent to about 0.000000000003 percent. Complex aromas, such as those of coffee and roasted meat, are composed of volatile gases from nearly a thousand different chemicals. The smell of a strawberry arises from the interaction of about 350 chemicals that are present in minute amounts. The quality that people seek most of all in a food—flavor—is usually present in a quantity too infinitesimal to be measured in traditional culinary terms such as ounces or teaspoons. The chemical that provides the dominant flavor of bell pepper can be tasted in amounts as low as 0.02 parts per billion; one drop is sufficient to add flavor to five average-size swimming pools. The flavor additive usually comes next to last in a processed food's list of ingredients and often costs less than its packaging. Soft drinks contain a larger proportion of flavor additives than most products. The flavor in a twelve-ounce can of Coke costs about half a cent.

The color additives in processed foods are usually present in even smaller amounts than the flavor compounds. Many of New Jersey's flavor companies also manufacture these color additives, which are used to make processed foods look fresh and appealing. Food coloring serves many of the same decorative purposes as lipstick, eye shadow, mascara — and is often made from the same pigments. Titanium dioxide, for example, has proved to be an especially versatile mineral. It gives many processed candies, frostings, and icings their bright white color; it is a common ingredient in women's cosmetics; and it is the pigment used in many white oil paints and house paints. At Burger King, Wendy's, and McDonald's coloring agents have been added to many of the soft drinks, salad dressings, cookies, condiments, chicken dishes, and sandwich buns.

Studies have found that the color of a food can greatly affect how its taste is perceived. Brightly colored foods frequently seem to taste better than bland-looking foods, even when the flavor compounds are identical. Foods that somehow look off-color often seem to have off tastes. For thousands of years human beings have relied on visual cues to help determine what is edible. The color of fruit suggests whether it is ripe, the color of meat whether it is rancid. Flavor researchers sometimes use colored lights to modify the influence of visual cues during taste tests. During one experiment in the early 1970s people were served an oddly tinted meal of steak and french fries that appeared normal beneath colored lights. Everyone thought the meal tasted fine until the lighting was changed. Once it became apparent that the steak was actually blue and the fries were green, some people became ill.

The federal Food and Drug Administration does not require companies to disclose the ingredients of their color or flavor additives so long as all the chemicals in them are considered by the agency to be GRAS ("generally recognized as safe"). This enables companies to maintain the secrecy of their formulas. It also hides the fact that flavor compounds often contain more ingredients than the foods to which they give taste. The phrase "artificial strawberry flavor" gives little hint of the chemical wizardry and manufacturing skill that can make a highly processed food taste like strawberries.

A typical artificial strawberry flavor, like the kind found in a Burger King strawberry milk shake, contains the following ingredients: amyl acetate, amyl butyrate, amyl valerate, anethol, anisyl formate, benzyl acetate, benzyl isobutyrate, butyric acid, cinnamyl isobutyrate, cinnamyl valerate, cognac essential oil, diacetyl, dipropyl ketone, ethyl acetate, ethyl amyl ketone, ethyl butyrate, ethyl cinnamate, ethyl heptanoate, ethyl heptylate, ethyl lactate, ethyl methylphenylglycidate, ethyl nitrate, ethyl propionate, ethyl valerate, heliotropin, hydroxyphenyl-2-butanone (10 percent solution in alcohol), α-ionone, isobutyl anthranilate, isobutyl butyrate, lemon essential oil, maltol, 4-methylacetophenone, methyl anthranilate, methyl benzoate, methyl cinnamate, methyl heptine carbonate, methyl naphthyl ketone, methyl salicylate, mint essential oil, neroli essential oil, nerolin, neryl isobutyrate, orris butter, phenethyl alcohol, rose, rum ether, γ-undecalactone, vanillin, and solvent.

Although flavors usually arise from a mixture of many different volatile chemicals, often a single compound supplies the dominant aroma. Smelled alone, that chemical provides an unmistakable sense of the food. Ethyl-2-methyl butyrate, for example, smells just like an apple. Many of today's highly processed foods offer a blank palette: whatever chemicals are added to them will give them specific tastes. Adding methyl-2-pyridyl ketone makes something taste like popcorn. Adding ethyl-3-hydroxy butanoate makes it taste like marshmallow. The possibilities are now almost limitless. Without affecting appearance or nutritional value, processed foods could be made with aroma chemicals such as hexanal (the smell of freshly cut grass) or 3-methyl butanoic acid (the smell of body odor).

The 1960s were the heyday of artificial flavors in the United States. The synthetic versions of flavor compounds were not subtle, but they did not have to be, given the nature of most processed food. For the past twenty years food processors have tried hard to use only "natural flavors" in their products. According to the FDA, these must be derived entirely from natural sources—from herbs, spices, fruits, vegetables, beef, chicken, yeast, bark, roots, and so forth. Consumers prefer to see natural flavors on a label, out of a belief that they are more healthful. Distinctions between artificial and natural flavors can be arbitrary and somewhat absurd, based more on how the flavor has been made than on what it actually contains.

"A natural flavor," says Terry Acree, a professor of food science at Cornell University, "is a flavor that's been derived with an out-of-date technology." Natural flavors and artificial flavors sometimes contain exactly the same chemicals, produced through different methods. Amyl acetate, for example, provides the dominant note of banana flavor. When it is distilled from bananas with a solvent, amyl acetate is a natural flavor. When it is produced by mixing vinegar with amyl alcohol and adding sulfuric acid as a catalyst, amyl acetate is an artificial flavor. Either way it smells and tastes the same. "Natural flavor" is now listed among the ingredients of everything from Health Valley Blueberry Granola Bars to Taco Bell Hot Taco Sauce.

A natural flavor is not necessarily more healthful or purer than an artificial one. When almond flavor—benzaldehyde—is derived from natural sources, such as peach and apricot pits, it contains traces of hydrogen cyanide, a deadly poison. Benzaldehyde derived by mixing oil of clove and amyl acetate does not contain any cyanide. Nevertheless, it is legally considered an artificial flavor and sells at a much lower price. Natural and artificial flavors are now manufactured at the same chemical plants, places that few people would associate with Mother Nature.

A TRAINED NOSE AND A POETIC SENSIBILITY

The small and elite group of scientists who create most of the flavor   25
in most of the food now consumed in the United States are called "flavorists." They draw on a number of disciplines in their work: biology,
psychology, physiology, and organic chemistry. A flavorist is a chemist
with a trained nose and a poetic sensibility. Flavors are created by blending scores of different chemicals in tiny amounts — a process governed by
scientific principles but demanding a fair amount of art. In an age when
delicate aromas and microwave ovens do not easily co-exist, the job of
the flavorist is to conjure illusions about processed food and, in the words
of one flavor company's literature, to ensure "consumer likeability." The
flavorists with whom I spoke were discreet, in keeping with the dictates
of their trade. They were also charming, cosmopolitan, and ironic. They
not only enjoyed fine wine but could identify the chemicals that give each
grape its unique aroma. One flavorist compared his work to composing
music. A well-made flavor compound will have a "top note" that is often
followed by a "dry-down" and a "leveling-off," with different chemicals
responsible for each stage. The taste of a food can be radically altered by
minute changes in the flavoring combination. "A little odor goes a long
way," one flavorist told me.

In order to give a processed food a taste that consumers will find appealing, a flavorist must always consider the food's "mouthfeel" — the
unique combination of textures and chemical interactions that affect how
the flavor is perceived. Mouthfeel can be adjusted through the use of various fats, gums, starches, emulsifiers, and stabilizers. The aroma chemicals
in a food can be precisely analyzed, but the elements that make up
mouthfeel are much harder to measure. How does one quantify a pret-
zel's hardness, a french fry's crispness? Food technologists are now conducting basic research in rheology, the branch of physics that examines
the flow and deformation of materials. A number of companies sell sophisticated devices that attempt to measure mouthfeel. The TA.XT2i
Texture Analyzer, produced by the Texture Technologies Corporation, of
Scarsdale, New York, performs calculations based on data derived from
as many as 250 separate probes. It is essentially a mechanical mouth. It
gauges the most-important rheological properties of a food — bounce,
creep, breaking point, density, crunchiness, chewiness, gumminess, lumpi-
ness, rubberiness, springiness, slipperiness, smoothness, softness, wetness,
juiciness, spreadability, springback, and tackiness.

Some of the most important advances in flavor manufacturing are
now occurring in the field of biotechnology. Complex flavors are being
made using enzyme reactions, fermentation, and fungal and tissue cultures. All the flavors created by these methods — including the ones being
synthesized by fungi — are considered natural flavors by the FDA. The
new enzyme-based processes are responsible for extremely true-to-life
dairy flavors. One company now offers not just butter flavor but also

fresh creamy butter, cheesy butter, milky butter, savory melted butter, and super-concentrated butter flavor, in liquid or powder form. The development of new fermentation techniques, along with new techniques for heating mixtures of sugar and amino acids, have led to the creation of much more realistic meat flavors.

The McDonald's Corporation most likely drew on these advances when it eliminated beef tallow from its french fries. The company will not reveal the exact origin of the natural flavor added to its fries. In response to inquiries from *Vegetarian Journal,* however, McDonald's did acknowledge that its fries derive some of their characteristic flavor from "an animal source." Beef is the probable source, although other meats cannot be ruled out. In France, for example, fries are sometimes cooked in duck fat or horse tallow.

Other popular fast foods derive their flavor from unexpected ingredients. McDonald's Chicken McNuggets contain beef extracts, as does Wendy's Grilled Chicken Sandwich. Burger King's BK Broiler Chicken Breast Patty contains "natural smoke flavor." A firm called Red Arrow Products specializes in smoke flavor, which is added to barbecue sauces, snack foods, and processed meats. Red Arrow manufactures natural smoke flavor by charring sawdust and capturing the aroma chemicals released into the air. The smoke is captured in water and then bottled, so that other companies can sell food that seems to have been cooked over a fire.

The Vegetarian Legal Action Network recently petitioned the FDA to   30
issue new labeling requirements for foods that contain natural flavors. The group wants food processors to list the basic origins of their flavors on their labels. At the moment vegetarians often have no way of knowing whether a flavor additive contains beef, pork, poultry, or shellfish. One of the most widely used color additives—whose presence is often hidden by the phrase "color added"—violates a number of religious dietary restrictions, may cause allergic reactions in susceptible people, and comes from an unusual source. Cochineal extract (also known as carmine or carminic acid) is made from the desiccated bodies of female *Dactylopius coccus Costa,* a small insect harvested mainly in Peru and the Canary Islands. The bug feeds on red cactus berries, and color from the berries accumulates in the females and their unhatched larvae. The insects are collected, dried, and ground into a pigment. It takes about 70,000 of them to produce a pound of carmine, which is used to make processed foods look pink, red, or purple. Dannon strawberry yogurt gets its color from carmine, and so do many frozen fruit bars, candies, and fruit fillings, and Ocean Spray pink-grapefruit juice drink.

In a meeting room at IFF, Brian Grainger let me sample some of the company's flavors. It was an unusual taste test—there was no food to taste. Grainger is a senior flavorist at IFF, a soft-spoken chemist with graying hair, an English accent, and a fondness for understatement. He could easily be mistaken for a British diplomat or the owner of a West End brasserie with two Michelin stars. Like many in the flavor industry, he has an Old World, old-fashioned sensibility. When I suggested that IFF's policy of secrecy and discretion was out of step with our mass-marketing, brand-conscious, self-promoting age, and that the company should put its own logo on the countless products that bear its flavors, instead of allowing other companies to enjoy the consumer loyalty and affection inspired by those flavors, Grainger politely disagreed, assuring me that such a thing would never be done. In the absence of public credit or acclaim, the small and secretive fraternity of flavor chemists praise one another's work. By analyzing the flavor formula of a product, Grainger can often tell which of his counterparts at a rival firm devised it. Whenever he walks down a supermarket aisle, he takes a quiet pleasure in seeing the well-known foods that contain his flavors.

Grainger had brought a dozen small glass bottles from the lab. After he opened each bottle, I dipped a fragrance-testing filter into it — a long white strip of paper designed to absorb aroma chemicals without producing off notes. Before placing each strip of paper in front of my nose, I closed my eyes. Then I inhaled deeply, and one food after another was conjured from the glass bottles. I smelled fresh cherries, black olives, sautéed onions, and shrimp. Grainger's most remarkable creation took me by surprise. After closing my eyes, I suddenly smelled a grilled hamburger. The aroma was uncanny, almost miraculous — as if someone in the room were flipping burgers on a hot grill. But when I opened my eyes, I saw just a narrow strip of white paper and a flavorist with a grin.

The Reader's Presence

1. What do McDonald's french fries have to do with Eric Schlosser's primary aim in this selection? Why does he feature them in the title and use them in the opening to the essay? Why, in your opinion, didn't he use a different example?

2. Describe Schlosser's attitude toward "natural" and "artificial" flavoring. Does he think one is superior to the other? How critical does he appear toward food additives in general? Do you read his essay as a condemnation of fast food? How does his account of his laboratory visit color your response? Overall, were his laboratory experiences positive or negative? Explain what in his account makes you feel one way or the other.

3. Compare and contrast Schlosser's investigative techniques with those of James Fallows (page 378), Amy Cunningham (page 335), Susan Orlean (page 470), or Andrew Sullivan (page 533). How does each writer establish a question to investigate, provoke your interest in the issue, gather information, and conduct the investigation? How important are sources and interviews? What information about sources and interviews is omitted from the essays?

73

Benjamin Spock

Should Children Play with Guns?

The pediatrician and Vietnam antiwar activist Dr. Benjamin Spock (1903–1998) became America's most respected expert on child care with the publication of The Common Sense Book of Baby and Child Care *in 1946. His book offered a new approach to the subject and challenged previous views such as those expressed in Dr. John B. Watson's* Psychological Care of Infant and Child *(1928), which advised parents to "never, never kiss your child. Never hold it on your lap. Never rock its carriage." Spock was both widely applauded and criticized for his relatively relaxed attitude toward childrearing, and he has even been blamed for fueling the countercultural youth movement of the 1960s. His publications include* Decent and Indecent: Our Personal and Political Behavior *(1970),* Raising Children in a Difficult Time *(1974),* Spock on Spock: A Memoir of Growing Up with the Century *(1989), and* A Better World for Our Children: Rebuilding American Family Values *(1994). "Should Children Play with Guns?" is taken from the 1976 edition of* Baby and Child Care.

Is gun play good or bad for children? For many years I emphasized its harmlessness. When thoughtful parents expressed doubt about letting their children have pistols and other warlike toys, because they didn't want to encourage them in the slightest degree to become delinquents or militarists, I would explain how little connection there was. In the course of growing up, children have a natural tendency to bring their aggressiveness more and more under control provided their parents encourage this. One- to two-year-olds, when they're angry with another child, may bite the child's arm without hesitation. But by three or four they have already learned that crude aggression is not right. However, they like to pretend to shoot a pretend bad guy. They may pretend to shoot their mother or father, but grinning to assure them that the gun and the hostility aren't to be taken seriously.

In the six- to twelve-year-old period, children will play an earnest game of war, but it has lots of rules. There may be arguments and rough-housing, but real fights are relatively infrequent. At this age children don't shoot at their mother or father, even in fun. It's not that the parents have turned stricter; the children's own conscience has. They say, "Step on a crack; break your mother's back," which means that even the thought of wishing harm to their parents now makes them uncomfortable. In adolescence, aggressive feelings become much stronger, but well-brought-up children sublimate them into athletics and other competition or into kidding their pals.

In other words, I'd explain that playing at war is a natural step in the disciplining of the aggression of young children; that most clergymen and pacifists probably did the same thing; that an idealistic parent doesn't really need to worry about producing a scoundrel; that the aggressive delinquent was not distorted in personality by being allowed to play bandit at five or ten, he was neglected and abused in his first couple of years, when his character was beginning to take shape; that he was doomed before he had any toys worthy of the name.

But nowadays I'd give parents much more encouragement in their inclination to guide their child away from violence. A number of occurrences have convinced me of the importance of this.

One of the first things that made me change my mind, several years   5
ago, was an observation that an experienced nursery school teacher told me about. Her children were crudely bopping each other much more than previously, without provocation. When she remonstrated with them, they would protest, "But that's what the Three Stooges do." (This was a children's TV program full of violence and buffoonery which had recently been introduced and which immediately became very popular.) This attitude of the children showed me that watching violence can lower a child's standards of behavior. Recent psychological experiments have shown that being shown brutality on film stimulates cruelty in adults, too.

What further shocked me into reconsidering my point of view was the assassination of President Kennedy, and the fact that some school-children cheered about this. (I didn't so much blame the children as I blamed the kind of parents who will say about a President they dislike, "I'd shoot him if I got the chance!")

These incidents made me think of other evidences that Americans have often been tolerant of harshness, lawlessness, and violence. We were ruthless in dealing with the Indians. In some frontier areas we slipped into the tradition of vigilante justice. We were hard on the later waves of immigrants. At times we've denied justice to groups with different religions or political views. We have crime rates way above those of other, comparable nations. A great proportion of our adult as well as our child population has been endlessly fascinated with dramas of Western violence and with brutal crime stories, in movies and on television. We have had a shameful history of racist lynchings and murders, as well as regular abuse and humiliation. In recent years it has been realized that infants and small children are being brought to hospitals with severe injuries caused by gross parental brutality.

Of course, some of these phenomena are characteristic of only a small percentage of the population. Even the others that apply to a majority of people don't necessarily mean that we Americans on the average have more aggressiveness inside us than the people of other nations. I think rather that the aggressiveness we have is less controlled, from childhood on.

To me it seems very clear that in order to have a more stable and civilized national life we should bring up the next generation of Americans with a greater respect for law and for other people's rights and sensibilities than in the past. There are many ways in which we could and should teach these attitudes. One simple opportunity we could utilize in the first half of childhood is to show our disapproval of lawlessness and violence in television programs and in children's gun play.

I also believe that the survival of the world now depends on a much   10
greater awareness of the need to avoid war and to actively seek peaceful agreements. There are enough nuclear arms to utterly destroy all civilization. One international incident in which belligerence or brinkmanship was carried a small step too far could escalate into annihilation within a few hours. This terrifying situation demands a much greater stability and self-restraint on the part of national leaders and citizens than they have ever shown in the past. We owe it to our children to prepare them very deliberately for this awesome responsibility. I see little evidence that this is being done now.

When we let people grow up feeling that cruelty is all right provided they know it is make-believe, or provided they sufficiently disapprove of certain individuals or groups, or provided the cruelty is in the service of their country (whether the country is right or wrong), we make it easier for them to go berserk when the provocation comes.

But can we imagine actually depriving American children of their guns or of watching their favorite Western or crime programs? I think we should consider it—to at least a partial degree.

I believe that parents should firmly stop children's war play or any other kind of play that degenerates into deliberate cruelty or meanness. (By this I don't mean they should interfere in every little quarrel or tussle.)

If I had a three- or four-year-old son who asked me to buy him a gun, I'd tell him—with a friendly smile, not a scowl—that I don't want to give him a gun for even pretend shooting because there is too much meanness and killing in the world, that we must all learn how to get along in a friendly way together. I'd ask him if he didn't want some other present instead.

If I saw him, soon afterward, using a stick for a pistol in order to join   15
a gang that was merrily going "bang-bang" at each other, I wouldn't rush out to remind him of my views. I'd let him have the fun of participating as long as there was no cruelty. If his uncle gave him a pistol or a soldier's helmet for his birthday, I myself wouldn't have the nerve to take it away from him. If when he was seven or eight he decided he wanted to spend his own money for battle equipment, I wouldn't forbid him. I'd remind him that I myself don't want to buy war toys or give them as presents; but

from now on he will be playing more and more away from home and making more of his own decisions; he can make this decision for himself. I wouldn't give this talk in such a disapproving manner that he wouldn't dare decide against my policy. I would feel I'd made my point and that he had been inwardly influenced by my viewpoint as much as I could influence him. Even if he should buy weapons then, he would be likely to end up—in adolescence and adulthood—as thoughtful about the problems of peace as if I'd prohibited his buying them, perhaps more so.

One reason I keep backing away from a flat prohibition is that it would have its heaviest effect on the individuals who need it least. If all the parents of America became convinced and agreed on a toy-weapons ban on the first of next month, this would be ideal from my point of view. But this isn't going to happen for a long time, unless one nuclear missile goes off by accident and shocks the world into a banning of all weapons, real and pretend. A small percentage of parents—those most thoughtful and conscientious—will be the first ones who will want to dissuade their children from war toys; but their children will be most apt to be the sensitive, responsible children anyway. So I think it's carrying the issue unnecessarily far for those of us who are particularly concerned about peace and kindliness to insist that our young children demonstrate a total commitment to our cause while all their friends are gun toters. (It might be practical in a neighborhood where a majority of parents had the same conviction.) The main ideal is that children should grow up with a fond attitude toward all humanity. That will come about basically from the general atmosphere of our families. It will be strengthened by the attitude that we teach specifically toward other nations and groups. The elimination of war play would have some additional influence, but not as much as the two previous factors.

I feel less inclined to compromise on brutality on television and in movies. The sight of a real human face being apparently smashed by a fist has a lot more impact on children than what they imagine when they are making up their own stories. I believe that parents should flatly forbid programs that go in for violence. I don't think they are good for adults either. Young children can only partly distinguish between dramas and reality. Parents can explain, "It isn't right for people to hurt each other or kill each other and I don't want you to watch them do it."

Even if children cheat and watch such a program in secret, they'll know very well that their parents disapprove, and this will protect them to a degree from the coarsening effect of the scenes.

The Reader's Presence

1. Spock's advice on guns appears in his well-known book on baby and child care. Does building a more peaceable society count as a

form of child care? Why or why not? Do you consider the doctor's political views valid in this context? Why or why not?

2. The essay includes personal reflections and detailed hypothetical scenarios. Suppose Spock offered only advice? How might the reader's approach to that advice differ?

3. The writer discusses his earlier opinions in depth before explicating his current views. What is the effect for the reader of learning his reasoning? Is the argument weakened or strengthened through the presentation of conflicting positions? Because of recent shootings in America's schools, the issue of children and guns is far more serious today than it was when Spock offered his opinion in 1976. Do you find Spock's position relevant today? Why or why not?

4. Compare Spock's tactic of self-examination to that of George Orwell in "Shooting an Elephant" (page 198). By the end of Orwell's essay, what does he think of British imperialism? What do you, the reader, think of British imperialism by the end of the essay? Did your ideas change in the process of reading the essay? By the end of Spock's essay, what does he think are the consequences of children playing with guns? Having read Spock's essay, what do you think are the consequences of children playing with guns? How do Spock and Orwell get themselves—and their readers—through ethical problems?

74

Robert Stone

In the Mind's Eye of the Bomber

Robert Stone, born in Brooklyn in 1937, dropped out of high school to enlist in the U.S. Navy and travel the world. In 1962 Stone won a Stegner fellowship to the creative writing program at Stanford University. Shortly after moving to California, he joined Ken Kesey's Merry Pranksters and traveled by bus across the country. Stone's first novel, Hall of Mirrors, *appeared in 1967, winning the Faulkner Award for a "notable first novel." In 1971, Stone spent two months as a correspondent in Vietnam. His experiences there led to the writing of* Dog Soldiers *(1974), a novel that won the National Book Award about the way Vietnam affected American life. Stone's other novels include* Children of Light *(1986),* Outerbridge Reach *(1992), and* Damascus Gate *(1998)—the last dealing presciently with religion and terrorism in the Middle East. He has also authored a short story collection,* The Bear and His Daughter *(1997). Stone has received numerous awards, including Guggenheim fellowships and a National Endowment for the Humanities fellowship. He teaches creative writing at Yale University.*

Put yourself in the mind's eye of the conspirator. Whoever he is, it's likely he first saw the city from the air, looked out and saw the Twin Towers mirroring each other's dizzying rise. Maybe he stood at the window of some safe house in Queens or Jersey and looked at them. Thrusting so immodestly more than a thousand feet in the air, they mocked his passionate intensity, he no doubt thought.

The World Trade Center towers don't have much poetry in them. It might be harder psychologically to bomb one of the old cathedrals of commerce, like the Empire State or the Chrysler Building. These seem to contain some transcendent urge to aspire beyond Mammon belonging essentially to a bygone era; they no longer challenge the world. The *Michelin Guide to New York* describes them for the bargain-hunting foreign tourists of the Nineties in virtually archeological terms.

The World Trade Center towers were built for an age that for a number of reasons will probably never come to pass. They represent an ultimate reduction of the American Dream: America as home of unadorned Economic Man—practical, rational, powerful, even brutal. They can be seen as the external expression of an aspect of America our true-believing enemies have learned to hate and fear.

Now, as our influence contracts, the world returns to its old romances. In Europe, blood and soil are back. In what used to be called the Third World, religion flourishes. In our radical interpretation of democracy, our rejection of elites, our well-nigh demagogic respect for the opinions of the unlearned, we are essentially alone.

Nobody loves you when you're down and out. Our country has been   5
so long identified with its wealth and power that a sense seems to grow abroad that the United States will eventually somehow disappear, as though we were no more than our own compulsive communicating, a media phenomenon, a pop artifact going out of style.

Although every president since Roosevelt has denied it, we did set out, years ago, to be the world's policeman. The image was of Uncle Sam, rolling up his sleeves and wading in to do the right things. The unheralded corollary was that we might do well by doing it. After all, the original Uncle Sam was a defense contractor.

On the international scene these days, our trumpets have sounded slightly sour and uncertain. Our pro bono military operations have been conducted with noticeable diffidence. And it *has* been noticed, in friendly and unfriendly quarters. Cops make enemies. The best cops are good diplomats, which we have not always been. The impression of weakness, even relative weakness, always invites predation.

Malcolm X, exercising his customary cruel wit, called the assassination of President John Kennedy a case of the "chickens coming home to roost." His allusion was to the murder of President Diem of South Vietnam, in which some felt the United States had colluded. The world is so much smaller now than even during Malcolm's lifetime. The poor are poorer and more restless. Entire populations are on the move. The migration of the world's poor in the late twentieth century has been compared to the "barbarian" migrations of the fifth century A.D. Borders are porous; in jet planes and on rafts, desperate people cross oceans.

Literally and figuratively, our cities have no walls. We have lived for a long time like ancient Rome, relying on our far-flung power for defense. To a degree, we have claimed exemption from the forces of history. Now, history has come for us, presenting old half-forgotten due bills. In striking at symbols, terrorists destroy the real lives of American working people, traumatize actual American children.

In the face of this, we will learn to cope as other nations have; we are good at coping. Eventually few Americans will remember the country as it was before the X-ray machines appeared at airports and at the vestibules of public buildings, before the minimum-wage security guards were deployed at every other corporate door.   10

When I imagined the conspirators' "passionate intensity," I was thinking of "The Second Coming," by Yeats, the chilling, prophetic dream of "mere anarchy" loosed on the world. "The best lack all conviction," Yeats wrote, "while the worst are filled with passionate intensity." A dozen or so individuals, as human as we, fly planes full of doomed, terrified people into the Pentagon and into the Trade Center, a teeming city in the air. Are they moral monsters? Are they really the worst, driven by sheer evil?

Though we are being judged, despite our grief and loss, we cannot really judge. We are steeped in relativism, as confined by our narratives as the murderers are confined by theirs. History is a story we have accepted, our lives are the stories we tell ourselves about the experience of life.

In the Middle East, where gods were born, where narratives were sacred and the books in which they were inscribed considered sacramental, the ancient narratives are glorified again. After the 1967 war, for example, Jewish settlers awaiting the Messiah founded settlements among their ancestral stones, risking their lives and the lives of their families, ready to kill and to die in the name of a sacred narrative soon to be vindicated.

So in the Muslim world, the sacred historical destiny of Islam is reasserted. The will of God is to be done on earth. One narrative contained in the Koran speaks of the people of Ad. "Their sin is arrogance," the book says. The people of Ad rely on their power and their material wealth to prevail in the world. "They," says the Holy Koran, "will be brought low."

The dreadful sights of September 11th took on a surreal edge.   15
All the horrors—planes hitting towers out of a cloudless sky, all the
rest—seemed somehow unreal. I don't think it was their utter unfamil-
iarity that caused our vertiginous denial, made us refuse to believe what
we were seeing. I think it was déjà vu and a weird recognition that these
images had been half-seen before. Rendered by movies, imagined,
described in novels. The unreality we experienced was of something
fictive. We saw in the shocking elemental collision that our conscious
minds denied the violent assault of one narrative system upon another.
People deeply enclosed in their sanctified worldview were carrying
out what they experienced as a sacred command to annihilate the
Other.

The expressions from Washington are nothing surprising—
assurances of "resolve" and retribution. But in various ways our internal
narrative, our social and political foundations, circumscribe our capacity
for revenge as they limited our capacity for a surer defense. The internal
narrative of our enemies, their absolute ruthless devotion to an invisible
world, makes them strong. Our system too is a state of mind. We need to
find in it the elements that will serve our actual survival.

The power of narrative is shattering, overwhelming. We are the
stories we believe, we are who we believe we are. All the reasoning of
the world cannot set us free of our mythic systems. We live and die by
them.

During the Cold War, we lived in fear of nuclear holocaust. Now we
know that if a nuclear device ever goes off in an American city, it will not
likely come launched from some Siberian silo. More probably it will have
been assembled by a few people, perhaps in the guise of immigrants, in
that safe house with a view of lower Manhattan. These days people are
dying again for their national or religious identity. The new breed of terrorists may be those whose cause we have offended perhaps by simply
being what we are.

The Reader's Presence

1. What does Stone see through "the mind's eye of the conspirator"
   (paragraph 1)? Why does he choose to observe what he does from
   this perspective? What else might he have looked at? Think back
   to what you thought as you watched the towers at the World
   Trade Center collapse. In what ways does Stone's description of
   the American worldview in the final three paragraphs reflect your
   thoughts? In what ways does it not?

2. Look carefully at Stone's use of visual images. How many of them
   are metaphoric? How does he connect the metaphoric images, for

example "world*view*" (emphasis added) with the literal images—
for example, "the dreadful sights of September 11" (paragraph
15)? Which do you think are more important to this article, the
metaphors or the literal sights?

3. Stone ends his essay by noting that people "whose cause we have
   offended" are "dying again for their national or religious identity"
   (paragraph 17). Look at another essay in this collection in which
   someone has been deeply offended (for example, Sojourner
   Truth's "And Ain't I a Woman?" page 787). How did the offended person respond? What strategies did he or she use? persuasion? laughter? compassion? Looking through Stone's suggested
   "mind's eye," would such responses work for the conspirators?
   Explain why or why not.

75

Andrew Sullivan

The "He" Hormone

*Andrew Sullivan was born in 1963 in southern England, and grew up near
his birthplace. He attended Oxford, where he studied modern history and modern
languages. In 1984, he won a Harkness Fellowship to the John F. Kennedy School
of Government at Harvard, and graduated with a master's degree in Public
Administration in 1986. Upon graduation, he began Ph.D. work at Harvard in
political science, and from 1991 to 1996 he was acting editor of the* New Republic. *Sullivan became known for his open embrace of a gay lifestyle and his* New
Republic *essay, "The Politics of Homosexuality," which remains one of the most
influential articles of the decade on the subject of gay rights and his 1999 essay,
"Why Men Are Different," provoked a furor of controversy. Sullivan, a contributing writer for the* New York Times Magazine *and a senior editor at the* New
Republic, *is the author of several books on sexuality and is currently at work on a
book on science and human differences, provisionally titled* Nature, *forthcoming
in 2003.*

It has a slightly golden hue, suspended in an oily substance and injected in a needle about half as thick as a telephone wire. I have never
been able to jab it suddenly in my hip muscle, as the doctor told me to.
Instead, after swabbing a small patch of my rump down with rubbing

alcohol, I push the needle in slowly until all three inches of it are submerged. Then I squeeze the liquid in carefully, as the muscle often spasms to absorb it. My skin sticks a little to the syringe as I pull it out, and then an odd mix of oil and blackish blood usually trickles down my hip.

I am so used to it now that the novelty has worn off. But every now and again the weirdness returns. The chemical I am putting in myself is synthetic testosterone: a substance that has become such a metaphor for manhood that it is almost possible to forget that it has a physical reality. Twenty years ago, as it surged through my pubescent body, it deepened my voice, grew hair on my face and chest, strengthened my limbs, made me a man. So what, I wonder, is it doing to me now?

There are few things more challenging to the question of what the difference between men and women really is than to see the difference injected into your hip. Men and women differ biologically mainly because men produce 10 to 20 times as much testosterone as most women do, and this chemical, no one seriously disputes, profoundly affects physique, behavior, mood, and self-understanding. To be sure, because human beings are also deeply socialized, the impact of this difference is refracted through the prism of our own history and culture. But biology, it is all too easy to forget, is at the root of this process. As more people use testosterone medically, as more use testosterone-based steroids in sports and recreation and as more research explores the behavioral effects of this chemical, the clearer the power of that biology is. It affects every aspect of our society, from high divorce rates and adolescent male violence to the exploding cults of bodybuilding and professional wrestling. It helps explain, perhaps better than any other single factor, why inequalities between men and women remain so frustratingly resilient in public and private life. This summer, when an easy-to-apply testosterone gel hits the market, and when more people experience the power of this chemical in their own bodies, its social importance, once merely implicit, may get even harder to ignore.

My own encounter with testosterone came about for a simple medical reason. I am HIV-positive, and two years ago, after a period of extreme fatigue and weight loss, I had my testosterone levels checked. It turned out that my body was producing far less testosterone than it should have been at my age. No one quite knows why, but this is common among men with long-term HIV. The usual treatment is regular injection of artificial testosterone, which is when I experienced my first manhood supplement.

At that point I weighed around 165 pounds. I now weigh 185   5
pounds. My collar size went from a 15 to a 17½ in a few months; my chest went from 40 to 44. My appetite in every sense of that word expanded beyond measure. Going from napping two hours a day, I now rarely sleep in the daytime and have enough energy for daily workouts and a hefty work schedule. I can squat more than 400 pounds. Depres-

sion, once a regular feature of my life, is now a distant memory. I feel better able to recover from life's curveballs, more persistent, more alive. These are the long-term effects. They are almost as striking as the short-term ones.

Because the testosterone is injected every two weeks, and it quickly leaves the bloodstream, I can actually feel its power on almost a daily basis. Within hours, and at most a day, I feel a deep surge of energy. It is less edgy than a double espresso, but just as powerful. My attention span shortens. In the two or three days after my shot, I find it harder to concentrate on writing and feel the need to exercise more. My wit is quicker, my mind faster, but my judgment is more impulsive. It is not unlike the kind of rush I get before talking in front of a large audience, or going on a first date, or getting on an airplane, but it suffuses me in a less abrupt and more consistent way. In a word, I feel braced. For what? It scarcely seems to matter.

And then after a few days, as the testosterone peaks and starts to decline, the feeling alters a little. I find myself less reserved than usual, and more garrulous. The same energy is there, but it seems less directed toward action than toward interaction, less toward pride than toward lust. The odd thing is that, however much experience I have with it, this lust peak still takes me unawares. It is not like feeling hungry, a feeling you recognize and satiate. It creeps up on you. It is only a few days later that I look back and realize that I spent hours of the recent past socializing in a bar or checking out every potential date who came vaguely over my horizon. You realize more acutely than before that lust is a chemical. It comes; it goes. It waxes; it wanes. You are not helpless in front of it, but you are certainly not fully in control.

Then there's anger. I have always tended to bury or redirect my rage. I once thought this an inescapable part of my personality. It turns out I was wrong. Late last year, mere hours after a T shot, my dog ran off the leash to forage for a chicken bone left in my local park. The more I chased her, the more she ran. By the time I retrieved her, the bone had been consumed, and I gave her a sharp tap on her rear end. "Don't smack your dog!" yelled a burly guy a few yards away. What I found myself yelling back at him is not printable in this magazine, but I have never used that language in public before, let alone bellow it at the top of my voice. He shouted back, and within seconds I was actually closer to hitting him. He backed down and slunk off. I strutted home, chest puffed up, contrite beagle dragged sheepishly behind me. It wasn't until half an hour later that I realized I had been a complete jerk and had nearly gotten into the first public brawl of my life. I vowed to inject my testosterone at night in the future.

That was an extreme example, but other, milder ones come to mind: losing my temper in a petty argument; innumerable traffic confrontations; even the occasional slightly too prickly column or e-mail flameout. No doubt my previous awareness of the mythology of testosterone had subtly primed me for these feelings of irritation and impatience. But when I place them in the larger context of my new testosterone-associated energy, and of what we know about what testosterone tends to do to people, then it seems plausible enough to ascribe some of this increased edginess and self-confidence to that biweekly encounter with a syringe full of manhood.

Testosterone, oddly enough, is a chemical closely related to choles-   10
terol. It was first isolated by a Dutch scientist in 1935 from mice testicles and successfully synthesized by the German biologist Adolf Butenandt. Although testosterone is often thought of as the definition of maleness, both men and women produce it. Men produce it in their testicles; women produce it in their ovaries and adrenal glands. The male body converts some testosterone to estradiol, a female hormone, and the female body has receptors for testosterone, just as the male body does. That's why women who want to change their sex are injected with testosterone and develop male characteristics, like deeper voices, facial hair, and even baldness. The central biological difference between adult men and women, then, is not that men have testosterone and women don't. It's that men produce much, much more of it than women do. An average woman has 40 to 60 nanograms of testosterone in a deciliter of blood plasma. An average man has 300 to 1,000 nanograms per deciliter.

Testosterone's effects start early — really early. At conception, every embryo is female and unless hormonally altered will remain so. You need testosterone to turn a fetus with a Y chromosome into a real boy, to masculinize his brain and body. Men experience a flood of testosterone twice in their lives: in the womb about six weeks after conception and at puberty. The first fetal burst primes the brain and the body, endowing male fetuses with the instinctual knowledge of how to respond to later testosterone surges. The second, more familiar adolescent rush — squeaky voices, facial hair and all — completes the process. Without testosterone, humans would always revert to the default sex, which is female. The Book of Genesis is therefore exactly wrong. It isn't women who are made out of men. It is men who are made out of women. Testosterone, to stretch the metaphor, is Eve's rib.

The effect of testosterone is systemic. It engenders both the brain and the body. Apart from the obvious genital distinction, other differences between men's and women's bodies reflect this: body hair, the ratio of muscle to fat, upper-body strength and so on. But testosterone leads to behavioral differences as well. Since it is unethical to experiment with human embryos by altering hormonal balances, much of the evidence for this idea is based on research conducted on animals. A Stanford research group, for example, as reported in Deborah Blum's book "Sex on the Brain," injected newborn female rats with testosterone. Not only did the female rats develop penises from their clitorises, but they also appeared fully aware of how to use them, trying to have sex with other females with merry abandon. Male rats who had their testosterone blocked after birth, on the other hand, saw their penises wither or disappear entirely and presented themselves to the female rats in a passive, receptive way. Other scientists, theorizing that it was testosterone that enabled male zebra finches to sing, injected mute female finches with testosterone. Sure enough, the females sang. Species in which the female is typically more aggressive, like hyenas in female-run clans, show higher levels of testosterone among the females than among the males. Female sea snipes, which impregnate the males, and leave them to stay home and rear the young, have higher testosterone levels than their mates. Typical "male" behavior, in other words, corresponds to testosterone levels, whether exhibited by chromosomal males or females.

Does this apply to humans? The evidence certainly suggests that it does, though much of the "proof" is inferred from accidents. Pregnant women who were injected with progesterone (chemically similar to testosterone) in the 1950s to avoid miscarriage had daughters who later reported markedly tomboyish childhoods. Ditto girls born with a disorder that causes their adrenal glands to produce a hormone like testosterone rather than the more common cortisol. The moving story, chronicled in John Colapinto's book "As Nature Made Him," of David Reimer, who as an infant was surgically altered after a botched circumcision to become a girl, suggests how long-lasting the effect of fetal testosterone can be. Despite a ruthless attempt to socialize David as a girl, and to give him the correct hormonal treatment to develop as one, his behavioral and psychological makeup was still ineradicably male. Eventually, with the help of more testosterone, he became a full man again. Female-to male transsexuals report a similar transformation when injected with testosterone. One, Susan/Drew Seidman, described her experience in the *Village Voice* last November. "My sex-drive went through the roof," Seidman recalled. "I felt like I had to have sex once a day or I would die. . . . I was into porn as a girl, but now I'm *really* into porn." For Seidman, becoming a man was not merely physical. Thanks to testosterone, it was also psychological. "I'm not sure I can tell you what makes a man a man," Seidman averred. "But I know it's not a penis."

The behavioral traits associated with testosterone are largely the cliché-ridden ones you might expect. The Big T correlates with energy, self-confidence, competitiveness, tenacity, strength and sexual drive.

When you talk to men in testosterone therapy, several themes recur. "People talk about extremes," one man in his late 30s told me. "But that's not what testosterone does for me. It makes me think more clearly. It makes me think more positively. It's my Saint John's Wort." A man in his 20s said: "Usually, I cycle up the hill to my apartment in 12th gear. In the days after my shot, I ride it easily in 16th." A 40-year-old executive who took testosterone for bodybuilding purposes told me: "I walk into a business meeting now and I just exude self-confidence. I know there are lots of other reasons for this, but my company has just exploded since my treatment. I'm on a roll. I feel capable of almost anything."

When you hear comments like these, it's no big surprise that strutting   15
peacocks with their extravagant tails and bright colors are supercharged
with testosterone and that mousy little male sparrows aren't. "It turned
my life around," another man said. "I felt stronger—and not just in a
physical sense. It was a deep sense of being strong, almost spiritually
strong." Testosterone's antidepressive power is only marginally understood. It doesn't act in the precise way other antidepressants do, and it
probably helps alleviate gloominess primarily by propelling people into
greater activity and restlessness, giving them less time to think and reflect.
(This may be one reason women tend to suffer more from depression
than men.) Like other drugs, T can also lose potency if overused. Men
who inject excessive amounts may see their own production collapse and
experience shrinkage of their testicles and liver damage.

Individual effects obviously vary, and a person's internal makeup is
affected by countless other factors—physical, psychological, and external. But in this complex human engine, testosterone is gasoline. It revs
you up. A 1997 study took testosterone samples from 125 men and 128
women and selected the 12 with the lowest levels of testosterone and the
15 with the highest. They gave them beepers, asked them to keep diaries
and paged them 20 times over a four-day period to check on their actions, feelings, thoughts, and whereabouts. The differences were striking.
High-testosterone people "experienced more arousal and tension than
those low in testosterone," according to the study. "They spent more time
thinking, especially about concrete problems in the immediate present.
They wanted to get things done and felt frustrated when they could not.
They mentioned friends more than family or lovers."

Unlike Popeye's spinach, however, testosterone is also, in humans at
least, a relatively subtle agent. It is not some kind of on-off switch by
which men are constantly turned on and women off. For one thing, we all
start out with different base-line levels. Some women may have remarkably high genetic T levels, some men remarkably low, although the male-
female differential is so great that no single woman's T level can exceed
any single man's, unless she, or he, has some kind of significant hormonal
imbalance. For another, and this is where the social and political ramifi-
cations get complicated, testosterone is highly susceptible to environment.
T levels can rise and fall depending on external circumstances—short
term and long term. Testosterone is usually elevated in response to con-
frontational situations—a street fight, a marital spat, a presidential debate—or in highly charged sexual environments, like a strip bar or a
pornographic Web site. It can also be raised permanently in continuously
combative environments, like war, although it can also be suddenly lowered by stress.

Because testosterone levels can be measured in saliva as well as in
blood, researchers like Alan Booth, Allan Mazur, Richard Udry and particularly James M. Dabbs, whose book "Heroes, Rogues and Lovers" will
be out this fall [2000], have compiled quite a database on these varia-

tions. A certain amount of caution is advisable in interpreting the results of these studies. There is some doubt about the validity of onetime samples to gauge underlying testosterone levels. And most of the studies of the psychological effects of testosterone take place in culturally saturated environments, so that the difference between cause and effect is often extremely hard to disentangle. Nevertheless, the sheer number and scale of the studies, especially in the last decade or so, and the strong behavioral correlations with high testosterone, suggest some conclusions about the social importance of testosterone that are increasingly hard to gainsay.

Testosterone is clearly correlated in both men and women with psychological dominance, confident physicality and high self-esteem. In most combative, competitive environments, especially physical ones, the person with the most T wins. Put any two men in a room together and the one with more testosterone will tend to dominate the interaction. Working women have higher levels of testosterone than women who stay at home, and the daughters of working women have higher levels of testosterone than the daughters of housewives. A 1996 study found that in lesbian couples in which one partner assumes the male, or "butch," role and another assumes the female, or "femme," role, the "butch" woman has higher levels of testosterone than the "femme" woman. In naval medical tests, midshipmen have been shown to have higher average levels of testosterone than plebes. Actors tend to have more testosterone than ministers, according to a 1990 study. Among 700 male prison inmates in a 1995 study, those with the highest T levels tended to be those most likely to be in trouble with the prison authorities and to engage in unprovoked violence. This is true among women as well as among men, according to a 1997 study of 87 female inmates in a maximum security prison. Although high testosterone levels often correlate with dominance in interpersonal relationships, it does not guarantee more social power. Testosterone levels are higher among blue-collar workers, for example, than among white-collar workers, according to a study of more than 4,000 former military personnel conducted in 1992. A 1998 study found that trial lawyers—with their habituation to combat, conflict, and swagger—have higher levels of T than other lawyers.

The salient question, of course, is, How much of this difference in aggression and dominance is related to environment? Are trial lawyers naturally more testosteroned, and does that lead them into their profession? Or does the experience of the courtroom raise their levels? Do working women have naturally higher T levels, or does the prestige of work and power elevate their testosterone? Because of the limits of researching such a question, it is hard to tell beyond a reasonable doubt. But the social context clearly matters. It is even possible to tell who has won a tennis match not by watching the game, but by monitoring testosterone-filled saliva samples throughout. Testosterone levels rise for both players before the match. The winner of any single game sees his T production rise; the

20

loser sees it fall. The ultimate winner experiences a postgame testosterone surge, while the loser sees a collapse. This is true even for people watching sports matches. A 1998 study found that fans backing the winning side in a college basketball game and a World Cup soccer match saw their testosterone levels rise; fans rooting for the losing teams in both games saw their own T levels fall. There is, it seems, such a thing as vicarious testosterone.

One theory to explain this sensitivity to environment is that testosterone was originally favored in human evolution to enable successful hunting and combat. It kicks in, like adrenaline, in anticipation of combat, mental or physical, and helps you prevail. But a testosterone crash can be a killer too. Toward the end of my two-week cycle, I can almost feel my spirits dragging. In the event of a just-lost battle, as Matt Ridley points out in his book "The Red Queen," there's a good reason for this to occur. If you lose a contest with prey or a rival, it makes sense not to pick another fight immediately. So your body wisely prompts you to withdraw, filling your brain with depression and self-doubt. But if you have made a successful kill or defeated a treacherous enemy, your hormones goad you into further conquest. And people wonder why professional football players get into postgame sexual escapades and violence. Or why successful businessmen and politicians often push their sexual luck.

Similarly, testosterone levels may respond to more long-term stimuli. Studies have shown that inner-city youths, often exposed to danger in high-crime neighborhoods, may generate higher testosterone levels than unthreatened, secluded suburbanites. And so high T levels may not merely be responses to a violent environment; they may subsequently add to it in what becomes an increasingly violent, sexualized cycle. (It may be no accident that testosterone-soaked ghettos foster both high levels of crime and high levels of illegitimacy.) In the same way, declines in violence and crime may allow T levels to drop among young inner-city males, generating a virtuous trend of further reductions in crime and birth rates. This may help to explain why crime can decline precipitously, rather than drift down slowly, over time. Studies have also shown that men in long-term marriages see their testosterone levels progressively fall and their sex drives subsequently decline. It is as if their wives successfully tame them, reducing their sexual energy to a level where it is more unlikely to seek extramarital outlets. A 1993 study showed that single men tended to have higher levels of testosterone than married men and that men with high levels of testosterone turned out to be more likely to have had a failed marriage. Of course, if you start out with higher T levels, you may be more likely to fail at marriage, stay in the sexual marketplace, see your testosterone increase in response to this and so on.

None of this means, as the scientists always caution, that testosterone is directly linked to romantic failure or violence. No study has found a simple correlation, for example, between testosterone levels and crime. But there may be a complex correlation. The male-prisoner study, for example, found no general above-normal testosterone levels among inmates. But murderers and armed robbers had higher testosterone levels than mere car thieves and burglars. Why is this not surprising? One of the most remarkable, but least commented on, social statistics available is the sex differential in crime. For decades, arrest rates have shown that an overwhelmingly disproportionate number of arrestees are male. Although the sex differential has narrowed since the chivalrous 1930s, when the male-female arrest ratio was 12 to 1, it remains almost 4 to 1, a close echo of the testosterone differential between men and women. In violent crime, men make up an even bigger proportion. In 1998, 89 percent of murders in the United States, for example, were committed by men. Of course, there's a nature-nurture issue here as well, and the fact that the sex differential in crime has decreased over this century suggests that environment has played a part. Yet despite the enormous social changes of the last century, the differential is still 4 to 1, which suggests that underlying attributes may also have a great deal to do with it.

This, then, is what it comes down to: testosterone is a facilitator of risk—physical, criminal, personal. Without the influence of testosterone, the cost of these risks might seem to far outweigh the benefits. But with testosterone charging through the brain, caution is thrown to the wind. The influence of testosterone may not always lead to raw physical confrontation. In men with many options it may influence the decision to invest money in a dubious enterprise, jump into an ill-advised sexual affair or tell an egregiously big whopper. At the time, all these decisions may make some sort of testosteroned sense. The White House, anyone?

The effects of testosterone are not secret; neither is the fact that men   25
have far more of it than women. But why? As we have seen, testosterone is not synonymous with gender; in some species, it is the female who has most of it. The relatively new science of evolutionary psychology offers perhaps the best explanation for why that's not the case in humans. For neo Darwinians, the aggressive and sexual aspects of testosterone are related to the division of labor among hunter-gatherers in our ancient but formative evolutionary past. This division—men in general hunted, women in general gathered—favored differing levels of testosterone. Women need some testosterone—for self-defense, occasional risk-taking, strength—but not as much as men. Men use it to increase their potential to defeat rivals, respond to physical threats in strange environments, maximize their physical attractiveness, prompt them to spread their genes as widely as possible, and defend their home if necessary.

But the picture, as most good evolutionary psychologists point out, is more complex than this. Men who are excessively testosteroned are not that attractive to most women. Although they have the genes that turn women on—strong jaws and pronounced cheekbones, for example, are correlated with high testosterone—they can also be precisely the unstable, highly sexed creatures that childbearing, stability-seeking women want to avoid. There are two ways, evolutionary psychologists hazard, that women have successfully squared this particular circle. One is to marry the sweet class nerd and have an affair with the college quarterback: that way you get the good genes, the good sex, and the stable home. The other is to find a man with variable T levels, who can be both stable and nurturing when you want him to be and yet become a muscle-bound, bristly gladiator when the need arises. The latter strategy, as Emma Bovary realized, is sadly more easily said than done.

So over millennia, men with high but variable levels of testosterone were the ones most favored by women and therefore most likely to produce offspring, and eventually us. Most men today are highly testosteroned, but not rigidly so. We don't have to live at all times with the T levels required to face down a woolly mammoth or bed half the village's young women. We can adjust so that our testosterone levels make us more suitable for co-parenting or for simply sticking around our mates when the sexual spark has dimmed. Indeed, one researcher, John Wingfield, has found a suggestive correlation in bird species between adjustable testosterone levels and males that have an active role to play in rearing their young. Male birds with consistently high testosterone levels tend to be worse fathers; males with variable levels are better dads. So there's hope for the new man yet.

From the point of view of men, after all, constantly high testosterone is a real problem, as any 15-year-old boy trying to concentrate on his homework will tell you. I missed one deadline on this article because it came three days after a testosterone shot and I couldn't bring myself to sit still long enough. And from a purely genetic point of view, men don't merely have an interest in impregnating as many women as possible; they also have an interest in seeing that their offspring are brought up successfully and their genes perpetuated. So for the male, the conflict between sex and love is resolved, as it is for the female, by a compromise between the short-term thrill of promiscuity and the long-term rewards of nurturing children. Just as the female does, he optimizes his genetic outcome by a stable marriage and occasional extramarital affairs. He is just more likely to have these affairs than a woman. Testosterone is both cause and effect of this difference.

And the difference is a real one. This is so obvious a point that we sometimes miss it. But without that difference, it would be hard to justify separate sports leagues for men and women, just as it would be hard not to suspect judicial bias behind the fact that of the 98 people executed last year in the United States, 100 percent came from a group that composes a little less than 50 percent of the population; that is, men. When the discrepancy is racial, we wring our hands. That it is sexual raises no red flags. Similarly, it is not surprising that 55 percent of everyone arrested in 1998 was under the age of 25—the years when male testosterone levels are at their natural peak.

It is also controversial yet undeniable that elevating testosterone lev-   30 els can be extremely beneficial for physical and mental performance. It depends, of course, on what you're performing in. If your job is to whack home runs, capture criminals, or play the market, then testosterone is a huge advantage. If you're a professional conciliator, office manager, or teacher, it is probably a handicap. Major League Baseball was embarrassed that Mark McGwire's 1998 season home-run record might have been influenced by his use of androstenedione, a legal supplement that helps increase the body's own production of testosterone. But its own study into andro's effects concluded that regular use of it clearly raises T levels and so improves muscle mass and physical strength, without serious side effects. Testosterone also accelerates the rate of recovery from physical injury. Does this help make sense of McGwire's achievement? More testosterone obviously didn't give him the skill to hit 70 home runs, but it almost certainly contributed to the physical and mental endurance that helped him do so.

Since most men have at least 10 times as much T as most women, it therefore makes sense not to have coed baseball leagues. Equally, it makes sense that women will be underrepresented in a high-testosterone environment like military combat or construction. When the skills required are more cerebral or more endurance-related, the male-female gap may shrink, or even reverse itself. But otherwise, gender inequality in these fields is primarily not a function of sexism, merely of common sense. This is a highly controversial position, but it really shouldn't be. Even more unsettling is the racial gap in testosterone. Several solid studies, published in publications like *Journal of the National Cancer Institute,* show that black men have on average 3 to 19 percent more testosterone than white men. This is something to consider when we're told that black men dominate certain sports because of white racism or economic class rather than black skill. This reality may, of course, feed stereotypes about blacks being physical but not intellectual. But there's no evidence of any trade-off between the two. To say that someone is physically gifted is to say nothing about his mental abilities, as even NFL die-hards have come to realize. Indeed, as Jon Entine points out in his new book, *Taboo,* even the position of quarterback, which requires a deft mix of mental and physical strength and was once predominantly white, has slowly become less white as talent has been rewarded. The percentage of blacks among NFL quarterbacks is now twice the percentage of blacks in the population as a whole.

But fears of natural difference still haunt the debate about gender equality. Many feminists have made tenacious arguments about the lack of any substantive physical or mental differences between men and women as if the political equality of the sexes depended on it. But to rest the equality of women on the physical and psychological equivalence of the sexes is to rest it on sand. In the end, testosterone bites. This year, for example, Toys "R" Us announced it was planning to redesign its toy stores to group products most likely to be bought by the same types of consumers: in marketing jargon, "logical adjacencies." The results? Almost total gender separation. "Girl's World" would feature Easy-Bake Ovens and Barbies; "Boy's World," trucks and action figures. Though Toys "R" Us denied that there was any agenda behind this—its market research showed that gender differences start as young as 2 years old— such a public outcry ensued that the store canceled its plans. Meanwhile, Fox Family Channels is about to introduce two new, separate cable channels for boys and girls, boyzChannel and girlzChannel, to attract advertisers and consumers more efficiently. Fox executives told the *Wall Street Journal* that their move is simply a reflection of what Nielsen-related research tells them about the viewing habits of boys and girls: that, "in general terms, girls are more interested in entertainment that is relationship-oriented," while boys are "more action-oriented." T anyone? After more than two decades of relentless legal, cultural, and ideological attempts to negate sexual difference between boys and girls, the market has turned around and shown that very little, after all, has changed.

Advocates of a purely environmental origin for this difference between the sexes counter that gender socialization begins very early and is picked up by subtle inferences from parental interaction and peer pressure, before being reinforced by the collective culture at large. Most parents observing toddlers choosing their own toys and play patterns can best judge for themselves how true this is. But as Matt Ridley has pointed out, there is also physiological evidence of very early mental differences between the sexes, most of it to the advantage of girls. Ninety-five percent of all hyperactive kids are boys; four times as many boys are dyslexic and learning-disabled as girls. There is a greater distinction between the right and left brain among boys than girls, and worse linguistic skills. In general, boys are better at spatial and abstract tasks, girls at communication. These are generalizations, of course. There are many, many boys who are great linguists and model students, and vice versa. Some boys even prefer, when left to their own devices, to play with dolls as well as trucks. But we are talking of generalities here, and the influence of womb-given testosterone on those generalities is undeniable.

Some of that influence is a handicap. We are so used to associating testosterone with strength, masculinity, and patriarchal violence that it is easy to ignore that it also makes men weaker in some respects than women. It doesn't correlate with economic power: in fact, as we have seen, blue-collar workers have more of it than white-collar workers. It gets men into trouble. For reasons no one seems to understand, testosterone may also be an immune suppressant. High levels of it can correspond, as recent studies have shown, not only with baldness but also with heart disease and a greater susceptibility to infectious diseases. Higher levels of prostate cancer among blacks, some researchers believe, may well be related to blacks' higher testosterone levels. The aggression it can foster and the risks it encourages lead men into situations that often wound or kill them. And higher levels of testosterone-driven promiscuity make men more prone to sexually transmitted diseases. This is one reason that men live shorter lives on average than women. There is something, in other words, tragic about testosterone. It can lead to a certain kind of male glory; it may lead to valor or boldness or impulsive romanticism. But it also presages a uniquely male kind of doom. The cockerel with the brightest comb is often the most attractive and the most testosteroned, but it is also the most vulnerable to parasites. It is as if it has sacrificed quantity of life for intensity of experience, and this trade-off is a deeply male one.

So it is perhaps unsurprising that those professions in which this 35 trade-off is most pronounced—the military, contact sports, hazardous exploration, venture capitalism, politics, gambling—tend to be disproportionately male. Politics is undoubtedly the most controversial because it is such a critical arena for the dispersal of power. But consider for a moment how politics is conducted in our society. It is saturated with combat, ego, conflict, and risk. An entire career can be lost in a single gaffe or an unexpected shift in the national mood. This ego-driven roulette is almost as highly biased toward the testosteroned as wrestling. So it makes some sense that after almost a century of electorates made up by as many women as men, the number of female politicians remains pathetically small in most Western democracies. This may not be endemic to politics; it may have more to do with the way our culture constructs politics. And it is not to say that women are not good at government. Those qualities associated with low testosterone—patience, risk aversion, empathy—can all lead to excellent governance. They are just lousy qualities in the crapshoot of electoral politics.

If you care about sexual equality, this is obviously a challenge, but it need not be as depressing as it sounds. The sports world offers one way out. Men and women do not compete directly against one another; they have separate tournaments and leagues. Their different styles of physical excellence can be appreciated in different ways. At some basic level, of course, men will always be better than women in many of these contests. Men run faster and throw harder. Women could compensate for this by injecting testosterone, but if they took enough to be truly competitive, they would become men, which would somewhat defeat the purpose.

The harder cases are in those areas in which physical strength is important but not always crucial, like military combat or manual labor. And here the compromise is more likely to be access but inequality in numbers. Finance? Business? Here, where the testosterone-driven differences may well be more subtly psychological, and where men may dominate by discrimination rather than merit, is the trickiest arena. Testosterone-induced impatience may lead to poor decision-making, but low-testosterone risk aversion may lead to an inability to seize business opportunities. Perhaps it is safest to say that unequal numbers of men and women in these spheres is not prima facie evidence of sexism. We should do everything we can to ensure equal access, but it is foolish to insist that numerical inequality is always a function of bias rather than biology. This doesn't mean we shouldn't worry about individual cases of injustice; just that we shouldn't be shocked if gender inequality endures. And we should recognize that affirmative action for women (and men) in all arenas is an inherently utopian project.

Then there is the medical option. A modest solution might be to give more women access to testosterone to improve their sex drives, aggression, and risk affinity and to help redress their disadvantages in those areas as compared with men. This is already done for severely depressed women, or women with hormonal imbalances, or those lacking an adequate sex drive, especially after menopause. Why not for women who simply want to rev up their will to power? Its use needs to be carefully monitored because it can also lead to side effects, like greater susceptibility to cancer, but that's what doctors are there for. And since older men also suffer a slow drop-off in T levels, there's no reason they should be cold-shouldered either. If the natural disadvantages of gender should be countered, why not the natural disadvantages of age? In some ways, this is already happening. Among the most common drugs now available through Internet doctors and pharmacies, along with Viagra and Prozac, is testosterone. This summer [2000], with the arrival of AndroGel, the testosterone gel created as a medical treatment for those four to five million men who suffer from low levels of testosterone, recreational demand may soar.

Or try this thought experiment: what if parents committed to gender equity opted to counteract the effect of testosterone on boys in the womb by complementing it with injections of artificial female hormones? That way, structural gender difference could be eradicated from the beginning. Such a policy would lead to "men and women with normal bodies but identical feminine brains," Matt Ridley posits. "War, rape, boxing, car racing, pornography, and hamburgers and beer would soon be distant memories. A feminist paradise would have arrived." Today's conservative cultural critics might also be enraptured. Promiscuity would doubtless decline, fatherhood improve, crime drop, virtue spread. Even gay men might start behaving like lesbians, fleeing the gym and marrying for life. This is a fantasy, of course, but our increasing control and understanding of the scientific origins of our behavior, even of our culture, is fast making those fantasies things we will have to actively choose to forgo.

But fantasies also tell us something. After a feminist century, we may   40
be in need of a new understanding of masculinity. The concepts of manliness, of gentlemanly behavior, of chivalry have been debunked. The New Age bonding of the men's movement has been outlived. What our increasing knowledge of testosterone suggests is a core understanding of what it is to be a man, for better and worse. It is about the ability to risk for good and bad; to act, to strut, to dare, to seize. It is about a kind of energy we

often rue but would surely miss. It is about the foolishness that can lead to courage or destruction, the beauty that can be strength or vanity. To imagine a world without it is to see more clearly how our world is inseparable from it and how our current political pieties are too easily threatened by its reality.

And as our economy becomes less physical and more cerebral, as women slowly supplant men in many industries, as income inequalities grow and more highly testosteroned blue-collar men find themselves shunted to one side, we will have to find new ways of channeling what nature has bequeathed us. I don't think it's an accident that in the last decade there has been a growing focus on a muscular male physique in our popular culture, a boom in crass men's magazines, an explosion in violent computer games or a professional wrestler who has become governor. These are indications of a cultural displacement, of a world in which the power of testosterone is ignored or attacked, with the result that it reemerges in cruder and less social forms. Our main task in the gender wars of the new century may not be how to bring women fully into our society, but how to keep men from seceding from it, how to reroute testosterone for constructive ends, rather than ignore it for political point-making.

For my part, I'll keep injecting the Big T. Apart from how great it makes me feel, I consider it no insult to anyone else's gender to celebrate the uniqueness of one's own. Diversity need not mean the equalization of difference. In fact, true diversity requires the acceptance of difference. A world without the unruly, vulnerable, pioneering force of testosterone would be a fairer and calmer, but far grayer and duller, place. It is certainly somewhere I would never want to live. Perhaps the fact that I write this two days after the injection of another 200 milligrams of testosterone into my bloodstream makes me more likely to settle for this colorful trade-off than others. But it seems to me no disrespect to womanhood to say that I am perfectly happy to be a man, to feel things no woman will ever feel to the degree that I feel them, to experience the world in a way no woman ever has. And to do so without apology or shame.

The Reader's Presence

1. Sullivan begins and ends his essay with references to his own injections of testosterone. Reread the first and last paragraphs: How does personal detail function in both passages? How does Sullivan merge his experience of the hormone with his larger argument? What is his argument? What is the tone of his conclusion? What might be its sources?

2. In paragraph 10 Sullivan begins an historical account of the study of testosterone, and then moves into a biological account of how

testosterone variously affects males and females. In the midst of this objective writing, however, he interjects jokey sentences ("Testosterone's effects start early—really early," paragraph 11) and slightly off-color phrases (female rats "trying to have sex with other females with merry abandon," paragraph 12). How does this variation of tone and diction affect your reaction to Sullivan's essay? Does it make you more or less likely to be persuaded by his argument?

3. In paragraph 32 Sullivan writes that "fears of natural difference still haunt the debate about gender equality." How does this "fear" haunt Sullivan's essay? Where in the essay does Sullivan attempt to refute the argument that gender difference is a matter of social environment, of nurture rather than nature? What are the social implications of Sullivan's argument? Reread Judy Ruiz's essay about her brother who undergoes a sex-change operation ("Oranges and Sweet Sister Boy," page 241). How might Ruiz respond to Sullivan's essay, and vice versa?

76

Deborah Tannen

Listening to Men, Then and Now

Deborah Tannen (b. 1945) is University Professor of Linguistics at Georgetown University. She writes both for general and academic readers, and her many books and articles have been popular with both audiences. Her specialty is sociolinguistics, and in her research Tannen focuses on the different ways men and women communicate—and on the difficulties of communicating across gender. Her 1990 book You Just Don't Understand *was a best-seller and has been translated into twenty-four languages. In spite of the title, the book was written with the faith that men and women can understand each other better if they take the time to consider how gender influences communication styles. More recently she published* Gender and Conversational Interaction *(1993),* Gender and Discourse *(1994),* Talking from 9 to 5 *(1995),* The Argument Culture *(1998), and* I Only Say This Because I Love You *(2001). "Listening to Men, Then and Now" first appeared in the* New York Times Magazine *for May 16, 1999.*

Reflecting on the experience of writing, Tannen says, "Writing is hard to begin—it's much easier to return a phone call or check E-mail for messages—but once underway, if it's going well, it's joy, exhilaration, intense pleasure."

A woman and a man meet at the end of the day. He asks how her day was, and she replies with a long report of what she did, whom she met, what they said, and what that made her think and feel. Then she eagerly turns to him:

She: How was your day?

He: Same old rat race.

She: Didn't anything happen?

He: Nah, nothing much.   5

Her disappointment is deepened when that evening they go out to dinner with friends and suddenly he regales the group with an amusing account of something that happened at work. She is cut to the quick, crestfallen at hearing this story as part of an audience of strangers. "How could he have said nothing happened?" she wonders. "Why didn't he tell me this before? What am I? Chopped liver?"

The key to this frustration is that women and men typically have different ideas about what makes people friends. For many women, as for girls, talk is the glue of close relationships; your best friend is the one you tell your secrets to, the one you discuss your troubles with. For many men, as for boys, activities are central; your best friend is the one you do everything with (and the one who will stick up for you if there is a fight).

As the millennium approaches and commentators examine how our lives have changed in the last thousand years, I find myself wondering about the change in relations between the sexes. Clearly there has been a transformation. In the past, the woman was deferential, subordinate. Now we are not trying to be partners in a societal arrangement with a clearly defined separation of labor, but rather hoping to be each other's best friends. Yet at least two aspects of women's and men's relations have endured—our differing expectations about the importance of talk in intimacy, and the tendency of women to take the role of listener in conversation with men.

In the absence of tape recordings from earlier times, we can look to conversations in literature. For a glimpse of how a sixteenth-century couple might have talked to each other, I turned to Shakespeare—and my earliest memory of his plays. When I was at Ditmas Junior High in Brooklyn, my classmates were all atitter: our teacher had us reading "Julius Caesar" aloud, and, having read ahead, we knew that the next day some poor girl would have to stand and read a passage in which Brutus's wife uses the word "harlot." Susan Ehrlich had the bad luck to be chosen, and I can still see her, tall and brown-haired, reading, "Portia is Brutus's harlot, not his wife."

Revisiting those lines today, what strikes me is how similar the senti-   10
ment is to what I hear from contemporary women. Portia wants to be Brutus's best friend—and her idea of what this means is very similar to ours. Waking up to discover that her husband has left their bed, she finds him pacing, and implores him to say what is worrying him. Like the modern woman who feels that best friends tell each other secrets, Portia pleads:

Within the bond of marriage, tell me, Brutus,
Is it excepted I should know no secrets
That appertain to you?
*   Am I yourself*
But, as it were, in sort or limitation,
To keep with you at meals, comfort your bed,
And talk to you sometimes? Dwell I but in the suburbs
Of your good pleasure? If it be no more,
Portia is Brutus's harlot, not his wife.

A similar sentiment emerges in an even more distant conversation—in the Arabian romance of the Bedouin hero Antar, believed to have been written between 1080 and 1400. In one episode, a character named al-Minhal, escaping a king he has wronged, comes upon a ruined castle inhabited by a female demon named Dahiya. She gives him shelter, feeds him, falls in love with him and wins his love by her attentions, which include her conversation. Sounding rather like Portia, Dahiya says: "I want you to be my companion and to be my lord, and I will be your wife. Disclose to me what is in your heart. Do not believe that I will ever let you go. Open your mind to me for I have need to know your thoughts." They are married on the spot, and, we are told, "Long was their companionship, and they loved each other dearly."

I am not suggesting that relationships between women and men were the same then as now. But it's intriguing to think that what women regard as intimacy, talking about what's on your mind, has been a common thread right through the millennium. There's another, related pattern that seems to have endured. It, too, is evident in the case of the husband who can't think of anything to tell his wife but comes up with an amusing story to entertain a dinner gathering. To her, it's a failure of intimacy: if we're truly close, I should hear everything first. To him, I think, the situation of being home with someone he feels close to does not call for a story performance. This creates a paradox. Many women were drawn to the men they fell in love with because the men told captivating stories. After marriage, the women expect that the closer they get, the more the men will open up and tell. Instead, to their deep disappointment, after marriage the men clam up.

Once again, looking at how boys and girls are socialized provides a key. Boys' groups are hierarchical; low-status boys are pushed around. One way boys earn and keep status is to hold center stage by verbal performance—boasting, telling jokes, or recounting mesmerizing stories. And this seems to work well in winning maidens as well.

This aspect of storytelling can be seen as far back as "Beowulf," that Anglo-Saxon saga, usually dated to the eighth century. The hero, a member of a Swedish tribe known as the Geats, wins the attention of Wealhtheow, queen of Hrothgar, who is serving beer to a gathering of men:

Beowulf spoke, the son of Ecgtheow: "I resolved, when I set out on
the sea, sat down in the sea-boat with my band of men, that I should al-

together fulfill the will of your people or else fall in slaughter, fast in the
foe's grasp. I shall achieve a deed of manly courage or else have lived to
see in the mead-hall my ending day." These words were well-pleasing to
the woman, the boast of the Geat. Gold-adorned, the noble folk-queen
went to sit by her lord.

Boasting, my colleague Catherine Ball tells me, was a customary male   15
activity in the Anglo-Saxon mead-hall, so it is not surprising that Wealhtheow was well pleased, even though the exploits Beowulf boasts of have
not yet taken place. (In fact, he sounds a little like Cassius Clay predicting
what he will do to Sonny Liston.)

This scenario—a woman wooed by a man's boasts of exploits in
battle—brings us back to Shakespearean icons: Desdemona and Othello.
As Othello tells "how I did thrive in this fair lady's love," he explains that
she became entranced when she heard him telling "the story of my life":

Wherein I spoke of most disastrous chances:
Of moving accidents by flood and field,
Of hair-breadth scapes i'th'imminent deadly breach;
Of being taken by the insolent foe. . . .

And so on, until:

My story being done,
She gave me for my pains a world of kisses. . . .
And bad me, if I had a friend that lov'd her,
I should but teach him how to tell my story,
And that would woo her.

As we know, he wooed her himself with his own story.

In our era, the tactic of wooing by verbal performance takes a funny
turn. Etiquette books of the 50s instructed young women to be good
listeners if they wanted to win their men, and you need only look around
a restaurant to see many women attentively listening to talking men. In
place of battle yarns, what I hear, over and over, is that a woman fell in
love because "he makes me laugh." That's why Michelle Pfeiffer said in
1992 she picked a particular boyfriend, and why Joanne Woodward fell
for Paul Newman. I don't hear the same explanation from men as to why
they fall in love. What I hear is the corresponding one, as for example
when Woody Allen said of his relationship with Soon-Yi Previn: "She's a
marvel. And she laughs at all my jokes."

We seem to have a situation of *plus ça change.*[1] Even as relationships   20
between men and women have changed, our contrasting expectations
about the meaning of closeness still cause confusion and disappointment.
And though the performance has shifted from heroic tales to amusing en-

---

[1]*Plus ça change:* Tannen refers to the well-known French saying, *le plus ça change, le plus*
c'est la même chose, meaning: "the more things change, the more they remain the same." —
EDS.

tertainment, more often than not the apportionment of roles has stayed the same: Women are the audience and men are the show.

The Reader's Presence

1. How does Tannen characterize most women's talk and need for talk? How does she characterize most men's talk and preference for silence with their partners? Does this reflect your own experience? Why or why not?

2. Tannen uses statistical evidence to back up her claims about current-day talk, but she must rely on works of literature to assemble a sense of talk in history. Does the latter methodology seem valid? reliable? Why or why not? What differences can you think of between the way Shakespeare's female characters speak and real-life women would have spoken at the time? In your opinion, how do these differences affect your evaluation of Tannen's historical argument?

3. Do you think Tannen values male and female speech behavior equally, or does she favor one over the other? How can you tell? Given the essay's logic, does an understanding of the natural or societal basis of male or female behaviors lead one to accept either position? Or does the essay suggest that we need to work to change male or female speech behavior? Consider Tannen's perspective alongside Andrew Sullivan's in "The 'He' Hormone" (see page 533). Compare the ways that they treat gender in their essays.

77

Sallie Tisdale

Mean Cuisine

Sallie Tisdale was born in 1957 in California and has lived in Oregon for many years. A nurse by profession, her medical training has shaped her career as a writer. Her first books, The Sorcerer's Apprentice: Tales of the Modern Hospital *(1986) and* Harvest Moon: Portrait of a Nursing Home *(1987), discuss the ethical issues that complicate the relationship between caregivers and patients. Tisdale takes up the subject of health from quite a different angle in her book*

Lot's Wife: Salt and the Human Condition *(1988). This book uses the issue of salt consumption to reflect on the interconnections between people and the natural environment they inhabit. Tisdale's thoughts on these matters are further developed in* Stepping Westward: The Long Search for Home in the Pacific Northwest *(1991). She has also published* Talk Dirty to Me: An Intimate Philosophy of Sex *(1994), and* The Best Thing I Ever Tasted: The Secret of Food *(2000). Tisdale has taught writing at the University of Portland and the University of California at Davis; she currently lives in Portland, Oregon.*

According to surveys, about half of American households have at least one person on a diet at any given time. Dieting is normal—more normal than eating what you want to eat. How many of us now live on various versions of Lean Cuisine during the work week and pay premium for a plate of swordfish and greens on Saturday night? (We have the sauce and dressing on the side—of course.) Stouffer's Lean Cuisine (now a Nestlé product)—is little more than smaller portions for a higher price; the consumer pays for the corporate mother to dole out the proper foods in their proper amounts. A man told me he's never had to worry about his weight, he can eat whatever he wants. "People resent me," he said. "They don't want to go out to eat with me." He paused. "It's *lonely.*"

If an alien landed here, it would see a strange world—a world with much food and many starving people. Most of the starvation is forced on whole populations by power brokers and distant agendas. But what could visitors from afar think of the hundreds of thousands, the millions of healthy, wealthy people who starve voluntarily? Who go at least a little hungry all the time? They take on the mantle of hunger with pride and self satisfaction, complaining of the deprivation, seeking sympathy.

The marriage of desires—between sensual pleasure and the pleasure of denial—is a tense marriage. We buy asceticism at a decadent price, spend thousands of dollars a week to be supervised eating fewer than a thousand calories a day, hands slapped if we stray. Starvation, paid for with hard work. But both indulgence and sacrifice are limited to the privileged few who can afford to throw away what others literally die to have. If I take any comfort in the painful dead end in which we find ourselves, it is the rather petty one that very thin people with reduced body fat are people who have been in a self-induced famine for a long time. And they didn't have to do this—there is no reason to do this. The next time a real famine comes along, dieters are going to lose. They have nothing left to give.

My own life has been marked by a perilous and disturbing terror of my own body—a pendulum swinging, inexorably, forward and back. I ate too much, I ate too little, I dieted for dieting's sake—simply to resist, to conquer food. I dieted because I did not deserve not to be hungry, to hunger, to yearn. I made food both fetish and taboo; I felt secret appetites and attended to them in private, with shame, while the words of television commercials and magazine headlines echoed in the shadows.

To the extent that my mother disliked cooking, she was fond of eating sweets. She was perpetually dieting in a casual random way, though
she wasn't heavy. She made no sense of it and didn't seem to mind even
that, relishing her Mounds bar after the Saturday grocery shopping was
done and eating a bowl of ice cream every night. "It's really ice *milk*," she
would say. "Not so fattening." She bought box upon box of AYDS diet
candy (I'd eat half a dozen at a time when she wasn't looking) and diet
breakfast milk shakes and Hershey's chocolate syrup to pour on top of
her ice *milk* while she watched television.

I didn't diet like that. In my twenties I starved, I took pills, I picked at
tiny portions of dreadful, frozen, reconstituted diet food. I fasted. In my
thirties I mostly worried at food, skipping meals and snacking when no one
saw. Dieting is credit and debt. For many years I caught myself wondering
if I could "afford" to eat something, if I'd "earned" it through activity or
earlier deprivation, if I "owed" more denial. When I was dieting I would
haunt the kitchen hour by hour, gazing, grazing, tracking, noting—keeping
the books. Now that I no longer diet, I sometimes forget to eat, look up
from work or play surprised by the clock. When I eat, I try to eat with relish and attention. But I can't always do that; eating became more than sustenance and less than nourishment the longer I worried about eating this
way. It became something else, not quite metaphor. More symptom. I still
tend to eat certain "bad" foods with half-averted eyes, flinching, haunted.

I write today as a woman who dieted "successfully." I lost quite a lot
of weight, and kept it off for several years. I was thinner at twenty-eight
than I was at puberty. I look at photographs of myself from that time—I
see the cheekbones, collarbones, the apricot-sized breasts, the tight jeans.
The tight smile. The dead eyes. What I remember (besides the counting,
besides the scales and measuring cups and careful, constant planning and
the hunger) is sadness. I had come to believe that I was unhappy because I
was too big, and when I was smaller and still unhappy, I could not for a
long time figure out what was wrong. When I finally started to relax, and
the weight gradually, inevitably, returned to my body, another kind of
weight slowly rose off me and disappeared.

Dieting utterly disrupts one's relationship to food, to all food at all
times. Eating takes on a sinister power and food an animate spirit—
mostly malevolent. The way one thinks on a diet is the way people in
famine think about food—obsessively, with great care—but turned upside down. Instead of being desired and out of reach, food is desired and
within reach, but just as potently remains fantasy.

Dieting is about being good and bad; the eater is either obedient or
naughty, compliant or resistant. (Dieting was once considered a sin simply because it is rooted in vanity.) Food is good or bad for you—but
more important, in eating any given food, *you* are good or bad. When I
dieted a lot I liked being hungry because it meant I was being good. A
childish dichotomy, but one that can take up the whole world for a time.

Dieting is control. The word *anorexia* is rooted in the Greek *orex*,   10
meaning appetite, desire, to reach after. Anorexia means literally not to do

so—not to long for, to stretch out in need for, not to reach, not to want. And when we finally can't control our desires, we can control what our body does with food—we can vomit, take laxatives, have surgery, swallow pills, exercise into oblivion. We can always find another way to say *No*.

Processed diet food is successful because it allows us to relinquish control for a moment, to be, in a tiny way, uncontrolled. It doesn't matter that a frozen diet dinner doesn't taste good, doesn't satisfy hunger, and lacks any nutrients to speak of—we eat them because they allow us to eat without thinking, without planning, without keeping the books. Michelle Stacey, in *Consumed*, her book on modern American food, says they let us be children. "To talk about simple moderation—good, satisfying food in normal amounts—is to talk like an adult, a parent . . ."

In the thin joke of chronic dieting, people conspire to pretend that what they are eating is actually delicious. (Spas advertise their hedonism without a wink. The Golden Door recipes are "sybaritic" and "sumptuous," the Rancho La Puerta meals are "flavor-packed.") If you diet all the time, like many women do, dieting is often vaguely masked as a sensible approach to health. The customer nods and smiles and says, oh, it's *good*, isn't it good? Of course, it's dreadful; no one can make 800 calories taste like 2,000, and even if the miracle of modern chemistry breaks through with the final equation, no one can make 800 calories and 15 grams of fat *feel* like 2,000 calories and 40 grams of fat. The body isn't fooled.

Robert Farrar Capon, an Episcopal priest, remembers his big uncles as "sacred groves, as *places* in my history." The "diet-mongers" who force such uncles to slim "dwell only upon what they would like a man to conform to; they never come within a hundred miles of knowing what a man *is* . . . dieting is wrong because it is not priestly. It is a way of using food without using it, bringing it into your history without letting it get involved with your history."

In such a way does dieting become a profound reduction of selfhood. When we shrink the body from shame at its size, we are literally *reduced*—encaged by our failure. Anger, demands, selfish insistence on personal freedom, escape, resistance—lost, put aside, inside. Our bigness disappears not only in fact but from sight, disappears inside, and we become inside-out people. All our weight and shape and meaning are withheld—all that anger, that insistence, those demands. When I was thin the emptiness in me felt bottomless. I don't mean the hunger. I stopped being hungry, or stopped minding. The emptiness I felt, the hollowness, was psychic, spiritual—it was the opposite of feeling big, strong, safe. I had gotten hungry for the sake of others, for their opinion of me, and so the hunger I felt was a bottomless hunger, one that could never be satisfied.

Recently, a new fashion in soap has appeared: great chunks of translucent perfumed soap made to look like food. Peach bars filled with candied "fruit," and chocolate bars and coconut cream bars, aromatic of the grocer's. They are sold individually by weight, like good cheese. Instead of real food we buy false food, products to soothe and pamper the "self"—that is, the body, in its long days of hunger.

15

Dieting is hatred—of self and others. Women, fat and thin both, hate fat women. We hate one another, say cruel things to and about one another, judge, cut apart. We sympathize with one another but the battle is about survival. In such a world, as Sally Cline says, eating disorders are an "extreme but *orderly* response."

I catch myself thinking, *I should lose a little weight.* I catch myself spiraling downward; I catch myself turning toward an ill-tasting frozen dinner because it promises "under 300 calories"; I catch myself denigrating my own *experience* of happiness. I remember that I actually am happy and that I do not need to turn helplessly through this spiral; I remember that there could hardly be anything less important in the world than whether or not I lose a few pounds, and I feel like I've caught my breath after being held under water, pleading for air.

It is a chronic disease, though: To this day, there are certain foods I do not allow myself. Such divisions down the middle of the world are the core truth of dieting. There are foods I like and almost never touch— good, fun food like doughnuts and milk shakes and onion rings. Most of the food I don't allow myself to eat is the sort of thing one might say has *no redeeming value.* But there's nothing consistent about it. I cheerfully make and eat brownies, pies, pizza, rich and creamy sauces. I find myself contemplating doughnuts, looking at one single doughnut on a plate, and I hear shrill voices chorus together in my head, voices crying out, *calories, fat, nasty, bad. Bad girl; mustn't touch.*

Other voices tell me what to do at restaurants, at parties, at the grocery store. Go ahead, laugh—if you don't recognize this, I go to the grocery store. I buy all kinds of things—vegetables, juice, toilet paper, bread. But what I want are potato chips. Will I buy them? Won't I? Yes. No. Yes. I grab them on the fly as I approach the register, refusing to think clearly, not looking, and then, back home, I don't eat them. I just keep the unopened bag in the cupboard. This is grotesque behavior. But even this behavior isn't what I think of as the real sickness—it's not the eating or not-eating, the buying or not-buying, not the wanting or not-wanting that matters. Not even the shame about eating or the shame about being ashamed. The sickness I want to be shod of for good is the continual *thinking-about-food* in all these joyless ways. I want back the room dieting has made food take up in my life without regard for pleasure—the terrible space this grotesqueness fills.

Several years ago, I consciously stopped dieting—and sometimes not   20
dieting was as hard as the dieting had been, harder. The entire question of whether a person is "too big" (or too small) is rarely asked in objective terms—objective measures for such things simply don't exist. Some very big (and very small) people defy the apparently objective medical criteria behind which judgment often resides. Even these criteria change frequently. To ask such a question—Am I the "right" size?—of oneself or another is to ask only whether one is too big or too small, too tall, thin, dark, or light, to meet another person's standard. I weigh myself only once or twice a year, and my weight has been the same for many years,

about eight pounds more than I weighed in high school. This is, in the general scheme of female physiology, normal, healthy, nothing to worry about. My weight stays the same through illness and holidays, vacations and surgery, in happiness and sadness. And still—*still*—I think, *If I just cut back a little I could probably lose a little weight.*

The act of dieting is the act of creating a mental world of struggle, a struggle most people expect to lose even as they begin. In the last few years, an anti-dieting movement has slowly gained strength, empowered by a great deal of careful research showing that almost everything we think about dieting and food attitudes and weight is wrong. The journalist Laura Fraser, in *Losing It,* a tour through the dieting industry, describes a world clearly outside logic and outside ordinary human experience. By the time the reader passes through the strange environments inhabited by Weight Watchers, Susan Powter, and a host of self-styled thinness gurus, the world of dieting has ceased to make sense. She ends with a discussion of what it means *not* to diet—new gurus giving power back. Viewed in the whole context of obsession with ounces and inches, anti-dieting becomes the truest pro-life philosophy I know.

Some of the most important research has been done by Janet Polivy and Peter Herman, who have carefully studied the mental world of the dieter for more than twenty years. The dieter, Polivy and Herman write, is occupied continually with food and meals and lives in an "entrenchment of dichotomous thinking." In their article "Dieting and Bingeing: A Causal Analysis," they propose that "dieting causes bingeing by promoting the adoption of a cognitively regulated eating style." In other words, dieting makes you so obsessed with food that you eat too much. Polivy and Herman have found that "non-dieters eat less when they are anxious than when they are calm . . . Dieters, however, eat small, diet-maintaining amounts when calm, but eat somewhat *more* when distressed . . ." Nondieters lose weight when depressed; dieters gain. Nondieters eat less when drinking alcohol; dieters eat more. Depression and alcohol are "disinhibitors" for dieters—these and other factors interrupt the fragile mental control dieters must constantly exert upon themselves.

Polivy and Herman did an experiment wherein several men starved themselves down to 74 percent of their starting weight on a very-low-calorie diet. "When food was later made available in unlimited quantities and the men had returned to their initial weights, they exhibited a persistent tendency to binge, gorging at meals to the limit of their physical capacity. Such behavior was never observed in these men prior to their 'diet' experience. Not only that, the men weren't overweight to begin with, didn't "need" to lose weight. They were part of an experiment and under no social pressure of any kind. This is what Polivy and Herman call "counter-regulation." Dieters diet until the diet is interrupted and then they give up completely and overeat.

In another experiment, the researchers gave people "preload" milk shakes. Some shakes were low in calories and fat grams, some were rich. The subjects were sometimes told the truth about what they were drinking and sometimes not. Only their bodies knew for sure if the milk shake they'd had was a "diet" drink or real dessert.

When a self-declared dieter thought she'd had a diet shake, she ate lit-   25
tle of the rich treats offered later. When she thought—correctly or not—
that she'd drunk a rich milk shake, she gorged on the treats. This happened again and again. The sense of having "blown" the diet for the day
was followed by "lusty eating," say the researchers. Dieters responded to
the food psychologically. On the other hand, people who said they didn't
diet responded *physiologically*—their bodies balanced the fat in their
diets by regulating their appetite for it.

Much research supports the fact that many, perhaps most, people
can't wholly regulate their eating. The body insistently regulates itself. Secretly fed low-fat diets, people unconsciously seek out fatty foods later, in
one study after another. There may be a purely biological response to dieting involving a disrupted sympathomimetic and endocrinological system. Polivy points out that "restrained eaters salivate more than do
unrestrained eaters in the presence of attractive food cues . . ."

This research reveals a world already quite familiar to me, one I am
nevertheless glad to see validated this way. It is so hard to explain, and its
distorted logic is so often displayed as the prevailing point of view. Physiological reactions aside, Polivy and Herman believe most of the behavior
is cognitive. Dieters respond to their perceptions; nondieters to the facts.
Moreover, the crash of cognitive control is socially specific. Dieters
binged more when they thought they were unobserved. If they had an official observer, dieters acted much like nondieters did all the time, neither
restricting nor indulging. "Unfortunately, such socially induced 'sensible'
eating lasted only as long as the observer was present," note the researchers. When the observer pretended to be another experimental subject, the dieters followed her carefully, eating more only if she did first.
Dieters ate least of all if their companion claimed to be on a diet, too.

A few years after this experiment, Polivy and Herman published a survey article called "Diagnosis and Treatment of Normal Eating." Their deliberately paradoxical title was the point: Chronic, often obsessive dieting is
now the normal way for many people to eat; in certain segments of the population, far more people are actively dieting to lose weight than are not. "It
is now 'normal' for individuals in our society to express concern about their
weight and to engage in fitful attempts to change it," and so "the meaning of
a phrase such as *normal eating* is no longer obvious." This is only a rumor,
but I'm told by a good source that there's a sign in the women's bathroom
of a leading fashion magazine that reads, PLEASE DON'T VOMIT HERE.

Polivy and Herman propose the possibility of a continuum of disor-
dered thinking. Based on their own and others' research, Polivy and Herman believe that dieters lose the ability to understand both hunger and
satisfaction. Normal boundaries between cognitive, social, and bodily desires exist only in the *"undisturbed* organism"—not in the overeater,
who is unusually sensitive to external cues, and especially not in the di-

eter, who has created an artificial boundary closer to hunger than satiety. That boundary is a painful one, almost constantly present, and it is frail, requiring continual vigilance. "In fact, the sorts of disinhibited eating that the dieter fears actually arise from dieting itself."

When one exercises a continual (as opposed to occasional) restriction on any natural desire, one loses the ability to make rational decisions about that desire. This is one of the paradoxes of living in a human body, this need to give up control at some point and trust in an invisible and immeasurable wisdom—part biology, part something rather more ethereal, perhaps. Constant conscious control makes us the puppet of physiological systems we barely understand. The only way out of the downward spiral is to stop basing one's hungers entirely on nutrient dosages, calorie counts, and what the person next to you will think. I needed to learn, and continue to learn, to listen to my own appetite for food, and I am always surprised. There is newness here, curiosity, the unexpected. I am still learning what satisfaction is. I am still learning that trusting in the often irrational pleasures of the body is not only normal but wise.

A few years ago in New York City, I ate dinner with three women I know there. It was a lot like a Polivy and Herman experiment. We met in the restaurant of a trendy midtown hotel. All three of my friends came from work and they all were wearing black—short black skirts, black tops, sheer black stockings, and black shoes. Their hair was neat and carefully combed and pulled back. They all were thin. I was the contrast, the out-of-towner, out of touch—my unruly plumpness, my loose long hair, my pink blazer and blue jeans. We talked throughout the meal about their pressured lives, the impossibility of it all, their stressful jobs, the crazy city full of noise and tension. "Oh, if I don't get out of town on the weekends, I go out of my mind!" said one.

Anyone who looks at so-called women's magazines now knows how to order in restaurants so as to protect one's special dietary needs: no oil, no sauces, dressing on the side, steamed vegetables, grilled everything. We used to go out to a good restaurant in order to enjoy a chef's unique creations; now we go out and try to avoid them. That night, we ate up-to-date eclectic cuisine of some kind or other, all shellfish and portobellos and bits of pasta—I ate, they dabbled. Everyone oohed and aahed at the dessert tray, and each of us ordered something off it. But when the desserts came, I was the only one who ate. The other women poked and sipped and stared, and stole a few bites of my crème caramel. Their reward was the virtue of resistance, the tight spring's long-held tension still holding. Denial is what some women have come to desire most, and that's nothing new. Certain emotions are dangerous to people who live by denial, by need and hunger. The relaxed happiness of a good table is one. Another is gratitude, in any form.

I find it difficult to explain the twin position I seem to occupy in this scene. I am inside and outside at once. I am watching four women around a table, three of one world and a visitor from another—so clearly for-

30

eign, so unable to fit in. I am watching the strangeness of a rich, noisy, seductively vibrant city I love, which demands so much of people, and the smaller worlds within it where codes of dress and conduct and appearance are strictly, harshly enforced. And I am inside, nervous, aware of my differences, my inability to meet the standard these other women meet every day. And we all are living in times so detached that "lighten up" is used when people are more thoughtful than their fellows want them to be. There is no way to point out these self-contained contradictions and not be guilty of something or other.

I ate my dessert, all of it, and I ate in a glaring spotlight, a complex concoction of feelings. I ate my dessert because I had wanted it, but it went down hard. I didn't feel guilty about their hunger; I resented it. But what I felt besides resentment was shame. Shame at my bigness, the big space I took up in my chair, the lack of restraint in my hair and my clothes and my desire. I felt shame not that I ate dessert but that I failed at not eating. I failed not to *want* too much.

The Reader's Presence

1. Note the many metaphors Tisdale uses to talk about food and dieting throughout her essay. Which of these do you use to talk about food in everyday life? For example, Tisdale writes that dieting is "credit and debt" (paragraph 6). Do you *count* calories, *save* food, or *earn* a treat after working out? How do these metaphoric ways of thinking about food affect how Tisdale interacts with food? Which metaphors do you identify with? What metaphors about food and dieting can you identify that are not mentioned in the essay? Would they add to, or detract from, the points Tisdale makes here? Explain your thinking.

2. Tisdale uses several types of irony to communicate her points about dieting and food. Look up the word *irony* in a dictionary and match the different definitions you find to different types of irony in the essay. Explain why Tisdale uses the type of irony that she does at particular points in her essay. What makes one type more effective for her than another? Why do you think that irony is a particularly effective tool to use when writing about dieting?

3. In some ways, Tisdale's descriptions of food are very limited; smell, texture, preparation, and the like play small or nonexistent parts in her essay. Which essay in *The Writer's Presence* has the richest writing about food? How does the author's attitude differ from Tisdale's? How does this difference manifest itself in the writing? Where are the thematic and stylistic differences most clear between the two writers' treatment of food?

Calvin Trillin

A Traditional Family

The journalist, critic, novelist, and humorist Calvin Trillin was born in Kansas City in 1935, but has lived in New York City for many years. He works as a staff writer at the New Yorker *and contributes to many other magazines, including the* Atlantic Monthly, Harper's, Life, *and the* Nation. *Trillin is especially well known for his nonfiction. His magazine columns are collected in* Uncivil Liberties *(1982),* With All Disrespect: More Uncivil Liberties *(1985),* If You Can't Say Something Nice *(1987), and* Enough's Enough *(1990); Trillin has also published a series of very popular books dealing with food and eating. In* American Fried *(1974) he paints a revealing portrait of American life through his discussion of regional and national eating habits. His love of traveling and eating in the company of his wife Alice also led him to write* Alice, Let's Eat *(1978),* Third Helpings *(1983), and* Travels with Alice *(1989). More recently Trillin has forsworn the temptation to eat for a living and has taken his keen sense of humor to the stage in one-man shows. "A Traditional Family" is excerpted from his book* Too Soon to Tell *(1995); his other recent publications include* Deadline Poet: My Life as a Doggerelist *(1994),* Messages from My Father *(1996),* Family Man *(1998), and* Tepper Isn't Going Out *(2001).*

When asked to describe the process he goes through when writing factual as opposed to imaginative columns, Trillin replied, "In a nonfiction piece . . . you really have to carry around a lot of baggage. You have what happened, your understanding of what happened, what you want to get across about what happened, all kinds of burdens of being fair to whatever sides there are. The facts are terribly restricting." Trillin typically writes at least four drafts of nonfiction articles, but finds that imaginative writing is less predictable. When writing his humor columns, for example, "it's a much less rigid system than that of writing nonfiction. Sometimes it only takes two drafts; sometimes it takes five."

I just found out that our family is no longer what the Census Bureau calls a traditional American family, and I want everyone to know that this is not our fault.

We now find ourselves included in the statistics that are used constantly to show the lamentable decline of the typical American household from something like Ozzie and Harriet and the kids to something like a bunch of kooks and hippies.

I want everyone to know right at the start that we are not kooks. Oh sure, we have our peculiarities, but we are not kooks. Also, we are not hippies. We have no children named Goodness. I am the first one to admit that reasonable people may differ on how to characterize a couple of my veteran sportcoats, and there may have been a remark or two passed in the neighborhood from time to time about the state of our front lawn. But no one has ever seriously suggested that we are hippies.

In fact, most people find us rather traditional. My wife and I have a marriage certificate, although I can't say I know exactly where to put my hands on it right at the moment. We have two children. We have a big meal on Christmas. We put on costumes at Halloween. (What about the fact that I always wear an ax murderer's mask on Halloween? That happens to be one of the peculiarities.) We make family decisions in the traditional American family way, which is to say the father is manipulated by the wife and the children. We lose a lot of socks in the wash. At our house, the dishes are done and the garbage is taken out regularly — after the glass and cans and other recyclable materials have been separated out. We're not talking about a commune here.

So why has the Census Bureau begun listing us with households that   5
consist of, say, the ex-stepchild of someone's former marriage living with someone who is under the mistaken impression that she is the aunt of somebody or other? Because the official definition of a traditional American family is two parents and one or more children under age eighteen. Our younger daughter just turned nineteen. Is that our fault?

As it happens, I did everything in my power to keep her from turning nineteen. When our daughters were about two and five, I decided that they were the perfect age, and I looked around for some sort of freezing process that might keep them there. I discovered that there was no such freezing process on the market. Assuming, in the traditional American way, that the technology would come along by and by, I renewed my investigation several times during their childhoods — they always seemed to be at the perfect age — but the freezing process never surfaced. Meanwhile, they kept getting older at what seemed to me a constantly accelerating rate. Before you could say "Zip up your jacket," the baby turned nineteen. What's a parent to do?

Ask for an easement. That's what a parent's to do. When I learned about the Census Bureau's definition of a traditional family — it was mentioned in an Associated Press story about how the latest census shows the traditional family declining at a more moderate pace than "the rapid and destabilizing rate" at which it declined between 1970 and 1980 — it occurred to me that we could simply explain the situation to the Census Bureau and ask that an exception be made in our case.

I realize that the Census Bureau would probably want to send out an inspector. I would acknowledge to him that our daughters are more or

less away from home, but remind him that we have been assured by more experienced parents that we can absolutely count on their return. I would take the position, in other words, that we are just as traditional as any American family, just slightly undermanned at the moment—like a hockey team that has a couple of guys in the penalty box but is still a presence on the ice. We could show the official our Christmas tree decorations and our Halloween costumes and a lot of single socks. We might, in the traditional American way, offer him a cup of coffee and a small bribe.

I haven't decided for sure to approach the Census Bureau. For one thing, someone might whisper in the inspector's ear that I have been heard to refer to my older daughter's room—the room where we now keep the exercise bike—as "the gym," and that might take some explaining. Also, I haven't discussed the matter with my wife. I would, of course, abide by her wishes. It's traditional.

The Reader's Presence

1. According to Trillin, how does the Census Bureau define "a traditional American family"? How does Trillin discover that his family would no longer be included in the Census Bureau's statistical compilations about "traditional" American families? Why does his family no longer satisfy the Census Bureau's criteria? What does Trillin try to do about this "problem"?

2. What characteristics of his family's behavior does Trillin identify as "traditional"? Examine the effect(s) of Trillin's verb choices. What patterns do you notice? What other patterns do you notice that he has woven into his word choices? When—and how—does Trillin poke fun at himself and the members of his family? To what extent does his humor depend on irony? on wit? Point to specific words and phrases to support your response.

3. When—and how—does Trillin use gender and familial stereotypes to reinforce the points he makes? Compare his light piece to the far more serious essay by David Mamet about his "new, cobbled-together family" who live in a new suburban development ("The Rake," page 192). How do both writers play with the reader's sense of the normative or the ideal? Can you imagine a comic version of Mamet's essay, and a serious version of Trillin's? If so, what might they look like?

79

Barbara Tuchman

"This Is the End of the World": The Black Death

Barbara Tuchman (1912–1989) was an acclaimed historian who was noted for writing historical accounts in a literary style. Believing that most historians alienate their readers by including minute details and by ignoring the elements of well-written prose, Tuchman hoped to engage a broad audience with a well-told narrative. As she explained during a speech at the National Portrait Gallery in 1978, "I want the reader to turn the page and keep on turning to the end. . . . This is accomplished only when the narrative moves steadily ahead, not when it comes to a weary standstill, overloaded with every item uncovered in the research." Tuchman, a 1933 Radcliffe College graduate, never received formal training as a historian but developed an ability to document history early in her career while working as a research assistant for the Institute of Pacific Relations, a writer for the Nation, *a foreign correspondent during the Spanish Civil War, and an editor for the Office of War Information during World War II. Tuchman earned critical attention when her third book,* The Zimmermann Telegram, *became a best-seller in 1958. She received a Pulitzer Prize for* The Guns of August *(1962), a description of the early days of World War I, and for* Stilwell and the American Experience in China, 1911–1945, *a biographical account of Joseph Warren Stilwell, an American military officer during China's shift from feudalism to communism. Other books include* The Proud Tower: A Portrait of the World before the War, 1890–1914 *(1966);* A Distant Mirror: The Calamitous Fourteenth Century *(1978), from which "'This Is the End of the World': The Black Death" is taken; and* The March of Folly: From Troy to Vietnam *(1984).*

In October 1347, two months after the fall of Calais,* Genoese trading ships put into the harbor of Messina in Sicily with dead and dying men at the oars. The ships had come from the Black Sea port of Caffa (now Feodosiya) in the Crimea, where the Genoese maintained a trading post.

---

*After a year-long siege, Calais surrendered to Edward III, king of England and self-declared king of France. — EDS.

564

The diseased sailors showed strange black swellings about the size of an egg or an apple in the armpits and groin. The swellings oozed blood and pus and were followed by spreading boils and black blotches on the skin from internal bleeding. The sick suffered severe pain and died quickly within five days of the first symptoms. As the disease spread, other symptoms of continuous fever and spitting of blood appeared instead of the swellings or buboes. These victims coughed and sweated heavily and died even more quickly, within three days or less, sometimes in 24 hours. In both types everything that issued from the body — breath, sweat, blood from the buboes and lungs, bloody urine, and blood-blackened excrement — smelled foul. Depression and despair accompanied the physical symptoms, and before the end "death is seen seated on the face."[1]

The disease was bubonic plague, present in two forms: one that infected the bloodstream, causing the buboes and internal bleeding, and was spread by contact; and a second, more virulent pneumonic type that infected the lungs and was spread by respiratory infection. The presence of both at once cause the high mortality and speed of contagion. So lethal was the disease that cases were known of persons going to bed well and dying before they woke, of doctors catching the illness at a bedside and dying before the patient. So rapidly did it spread from one to another that to a French physician, Simon de Covino, it seemed as if one sick person "could infect the whole world."[2] The malignity of the pestilence appeared more terrible because its victims knew no prevention and no remedy.

The physical suffering of the disease and its aspect of evil mystery were expressed in a strange Welsh lament[3] which saw "death coming into our midst like black smoke, a plague which cuts off the young, a rootless phantom which has no mercy for fair countenance. Woe is me of the shilling in the armpit! It is seething, terrible . . . a head that gives pain and causes a loud cry . . . a painful angry knob . . . Great is its seething like a burning cinder . . . a grievous thing of ashy color." Its eruption is ugly like the "seeds of black peas, broken fragments of brittle sea-coal . . . the early ornaments of black death, cinders of the peelings of the cockle weed, a mixed multitude, a black plague like halfpence, like berries . . . ."

Rumors of a terrible plague supposedly arising in China and spreading through Tartary (Central Asia) to India and Persia, Mesopotamia, Syria, Egypt, and all of Asia Minor had reached Europe in 1346. They told of a death toll so devastating that all of India was said to be depopulated, whole territories covered by dead bodies, other areas with no one left alive. As added up by Pope Clement VI at Avignon, the total of reported dead reached 23,840,000. In the absence of a concept of contagion, no serious alarm was felt in Europe until the trading ships brought their black burden of pestilence into Messina while other infected ships from the Levant carried it to Genoa and Venice.

By January 1348 it penetrated France via Marseille, and North Africa via Tunis. Shipborne along coasts and navigable rivers, it spread westward from Marseille through the ports of Languedoc to Spain and northward

5

up the Rhône to Avignon, where it arrived in March. It reached Narbonne, Montpellier, Carcassonne, and Toulouse between February and May, and at the same time in Italy spread to Rome and Florence and their hinterlands. Between June and August it reached Bordeaux, Lyon, and Paris, spread to Burgundy and Normandy, and crossed the Channel from Normandy into southern England. From Italy during the same summer it crossed the Alps into Switzerland and reached eastward to Hungary.

In a given area the plague accomplished its kill within four to six months and then faded, except in the larger cities, where, rooting into the close-quartered population, it abated during the winter, only to reappear in the spring and rage for another six months.

In 1349 it resumed in Paris, spread to Picardy, Flanders, and the Low Countries, and from England to Scotland and Ireland as well as to Norway, where a ghost ship with a cargo of wool and a dead crew drifted offshore until it ran aground near Bergen. From there the plague passed into Sweden, Denmark, Prussia, Iceland, and as far as Greenland. Leaving a strange pocket of immunity in Bohemia, and Russia unattacked until 1351, it had passed from most of Europe by mid-1350. Although the mortality rate was erratic, ranging from one fifth in some places to nine tenths or almost total elimination in others, the overall estimate of modern demographers has settled—for the area extending from India to Iceland—around the same figure expressed in Froissart's casual words: "a third of the world died." His estimate, the common one at the time, was not an inspired guess but a borrowing of St. John's figure for mortality from plague in Revelation, the favorite guide to human affairs of the Middle Ages.

A third of Europe would have meant about 20 million deaths. No one knows in truth how many died. Contemporary reports were an awed impression, not an accurate count. In crowded Avignon, it was said, 400 died daily; 7,000 houses emptied by death were shut up; a single graveyard received 11,000 corpses in six weeks; half the city's inhabitants reportedly died, including 9 cardinals or one third of the total, and 70 lesser prelates. Watching the endlessly passing death carts, chroniclers let normal exaggeration take wings and put the Avignon death toll at 62,000 and even at 120,000 although the city's total population was probably less than 50,000.

When graveyards filled up, bodies at Avignon were thrown into the Rhône until mass burial pits were dug for dumping the corpses. In London in such pits corpses piled up in layers until they overflowed. Everywhere reports speak of the sick dying too fast for the living to bury. Corpses were dragged out of homes and left in front of doorways. Morning light revealed new piles of bodies. In Florence the dead were gathered up by the Compagnia della Misericordia—founded in 1244 to care for the sick—whose members wore red robes and hoods masking the face except for the eyes. When their efforts failed, the dead lay putrid in the streets for days at a time. When no coffins were to be had, the bodies were laid on boards, two or three at once, to be carried to graveyards or common pits. Families dumped their own relatives into the pits, or buried them so hastily and thinly "that dogs dragged them forth and devoured their bodies."[4]

Amid accumulating death and fear of contagion, people died without last rites and were buried without prayers, a prospect that terrified the last hours of the stricken. A bishop in England gave permission to laymen to make confession to each other as was done by the Apostles, "or if no man is present then even to a woman,"[5] and if no priest could be found to administer extreme unction, "then faith must suffice." Clement VI found it necessary to grant remissions of sin to all who died of the plague because so many were unattended by priests. "And no bells tolled,"[6] wrote a chronicler of Siena, "and nobody wept no matter what his loss because almost everyone expected death.... And people said and believed, 'This is the end of the world.'"

In Paris, where the plague lasted through 1349, the reported death rate was 800 a day, in Pisa 500, in Vienna 500 to 600. The total dead in Paris numbered 50,000 or half the population. Florence, weakened by the famine of 1347, lost three to four fifths of its citizens, Venice two thirds, Hamburg and Bremen, though smaller in size, about the same proportion. Cities, as centers of transportation, were more likely to be affected than villages, although once a village was infected, its death rate was equally high. At Givry, a prosperous village in Burgundy of 1,200 to 1,500 people, the parish register records 615 deaths in the space of fourteen weeks, compared to an average of thirty deaths a year in the previous decade.[7] In three villages of Cambridgeshire, manorial records show a death rate of 47 percent, 57 percent, and in one case 70 percent.[8] When the last survivors, too few to carry on, moved away, a deserted village sank back into the wilderness and disappeared from the map altogether, leaving only a grass-covered ghostly outline to show where mortals once had lived.

In enclosed places such as monasteries and prisons, the infection of one person usually meant that of all, as happened in the Franciscan convents of Carcassonne and Marseille, where every inmate without exception died. Of the 140 Dominicans at Montpellier only seven survived. Petrarch's brother Gherardo, member of a Carthusian monastery, buried the prior and 34 fellow monks one by one, sometimes three a day, until he was left alone with his dog and fled to look for a place that would take him in.[9] Watching every comrade die, men in such places could not but wonder whether the strange peril that filled the air had not been sent to exterminate the human race. In Kilkenny, Ireland, Brother John Clyn of the Friars Minor, another monk left alone among dead men, kept a record of what had happened lest "things which should be remembered perish with time and vanish from the memory of those who come after us."[10] Sensing "the whole world, as it were, placed within the grasp of the Evil One," and waiting for death to visit him too, he wrote, "I leave

10

parchment to continue this work, if perchance any man survive and any of the race of Adam escape this pestilence and carry on the work which I have begun." Brother John, as noted by another hand, died of the pestilence, but he foiled oblivion.

The largest cities of Europe, with populations of about 100,000, were Paris and Florence, Venice and Genoa. At the next level, with more than 50,000, were Ghent and Bruges in Flanders, Milan, Bologna, Rome, Naples, and Palermo, and Cologne. London hovered below 50,000 the only city in England except York with more than 10,000. At the level of 20,000 to 50,000 were Bordeaux, Toulouse, Montpellier, Marseille, and Lyon in France, Barcelona, Seville, and Toledo in Spain, Siena, Pisa, and other secondary cities in Italy, and the Hanseatic trading cities of the Empire. The plague raged through them all, killing anywhere from one third to two thirds of their inhabitants. Italy, with a total population of 10 to 11 million, probably suffered the heaviest toll. Following the Florentine bankruptcies, the crop failures and workers' riots of 1346–47, the revolt of Cola di Rienzi that plunged Rome into anarchy, the plague came as the peak of successive calamities. As if the world were indeed in the grasp of the Evil One, its first appearance on the European mainland in January 1348 coincided with a fearsome earthquake that carved a path of wreckage from Naples up to Venice. Houses collapsed, church towers toppled, villages were crushed, and the destruction reached as far as Germany and Greece. Emotional response, dulled by horrors, underwent a kind of atrophy epitomized by the chronicler who wrote, "And in these days was burying without sorrowe and wedding without friendschippe."[11]

In Siena, where more than half the inhabitants died of the plague, work was abandoned on the great cathedral, planned to be the largest in the world, and never resumed, owing to loss of workers and master masons and "the melancholy and grief" of the survivors. The cathedral's truncated transept still stands in permanent witness to the sweep of death's scythe. Agnolo di Tura, a chronicler of Siena, recorded the fear of contagion that froze every other instinct. "Father abandoned child, wife husband, one brother another," he wrote, "for this plague seemed to strike through the breath and sight.[12] And so they died. And no one could be found to bury the dead for money or friendship. . . . And I, Angolo di Tura, called the Fat, buried my five children with my own hands, and so did many others likewise."

There were many to echo his account of inhumanity and few to balance it, for the plague was not the kind of calamity that inspired mutual help. Its loathsomeness and deadliness did not herd people together in mutual distress, but only prompted their desire to escape each other. "Magistrates and notaries refused to come and make the wills of the dying," reported a Franciscan friar of Piazza in Sicily;[13] what was worse, "even the priests did not come to hear their confessions."[14] A clerk of the Archbishop of Canterbury reported the same of English priests who "turned away from the care of their benefices from fear of death." Cases

15

of parents deserting children and children their parents were reported across Europe from Scotland to Russia.[15] The calamity chilled the hearts of men, wrote Boccaccio° in his famous account of the plague in Florence that serves as introduction to the *Decameron*. "One man shunned another ... kinsfolk held aloof, brother was forsaken by brother, oftentimes husband by wife; nay, what is more, and scarcely to be believed, fathers and mothers were found to abandon their own children to their fate, untended, unvisited as if they had been strangers." Exaggeration and literary pessimism were common in the fourteenth century, but the Pope's physician, Guy de Chauliac, was a sober, careful observer who reported the same phenomenon: "A father did not visit his son, nor the son his father. Charity was dead."[16]

Yet not entirely. In Paris, according to the chronicler Jean de Venette, the nuns of the Hôtel Dieu or municipal hospital, "having no fear of death, tended the sick with all sweetness and humility."[17] New nuns repeatedly took the places of those who died, until the majority "many times renewed by death now rest in peace with Christ as we may piously believe."

When the plague entered northern France in July 1348, it settled first in Normandy and, checked by winter, gave Picardy a deceptive interim until the next summer. Either in mourning or warning, black flags were flown from church towers of the worst-stricken villages of Normandy. "And in that time," wrote a monk of the abbey of Fourcarment, "the mortality was so great among the people of Normandy that those of Picardy mocked them."[18] The same unneighborly reaction was reported of the Scots, separated by a winter's immunity from the English. Delighted to hear of the disease that was scourging the "southrons," they gathered forces for an invasion, "laughing at their enemies." Before they could move, the savage mortality fell upon them too, scattering some in death and the rest in panic to spread the infection as they fled.

In Picardy in the summer of 1349 the pestilence penetrated the castle of Coucy to kill Enguerrand's* mother, Catherine, and her new husband.[19] Whether her nine-year-old son escaped by chance or was perhaps living elsewhere with one of his guardians is unrecorded. In nearby Amiens, tannery workers, responding quickly to losses in the labor force, combined to bargain for higher wages.[20] In another place villagers were seen dancing to drums and trumpets, and on being asked the reason, answered that, seeing their neighbors die day by day while their village remained immune, they believed they could keep the plague from entering "by the jollity that is in us. That is why we dance."[21] Further north in Tournai on the border of Flanders, Gilles li Muisis, Abbot of St. Martin's,

---

°*Giovanni Boccaccio* (1313–1375): Italian writer best known for his collection of stories about the Black Death, *The Decameron*. —EDS.

*Enguerrand de Coucy is the historical figure on which Tuchman focuses in her account of the fourteenth century. —EDS.

kept one of the epidemic's most vivid accounts. The passing bells rang all day and all night, he recorded, because sextons were anxious to obtain their fees while they could. Filled with the sound of mourning, the city became oppressed by fear, so that the authorities forbade the tolling of bells and the wearing of black and restricted funeral services to two mourners. The silencing of funeral bells and of criers' announcements of deaths was ordained by most cities. Siena imposed a fine on the wearing of mourning clothes by all except widows.

Flight was the chief recourse of those who could afford it or arrange it. The rich fled to their country places like Boccaccio's young patricians of Florence, who settled in a pastoral palace "removed on every side from the roads" with "wells of cool water and vaults of rare wines." The urban poor died in their burrows, "and only the stench of their bodies informed neighbors of their death." That the poor were more heavily afflicted than the rich was clearly remarked at the time, in the north as in the south. A Scottish chronicler, John of Fordun, stated flatly that the pest "attacked especially the meaner sort and common people—seldom the magnates."[22] Simon de Covino of Montpellier made the same observation.[23] He ascribed it to the misery and want and hard lives that made the poor more susceptible, which was half the truth. Close contact and lack of sanitation was the unrecognized other half. It was noticed too that the young died in greater proportion than the old; Simon de Covino compared the disappearance of youth to the withering of flowers in the fields.[24]

In the countryside peasants dropped dead on the roads, in the fields,   20
in their houses. Survivors in growing helplessness fell into apathy, leaving ripe wheat uncut and livestock untended. Oxen and asses, sheep and goats, pigs and chickens ran wild and they too, according to local reports, succumbed to the pest. English sheep, bearers of the precious wool, died throughout the country. The chronicler Henry Knighton, canon of Leicester Abbey, reported 5,000 dead in one field alone, "their bodies so corrupted by the plague that neither beast nor bird would touch them," and spreading an appalling stench.[25] In the Austrian Alps wolves came down to prey upon sheep and then, "as if alarmed by some invisible warning, turned and fled back into the wilderness."[26] In remote Dalmatia bolder wolves descended upon a plague-stricken city and attacked human survivors. For want of herdsmen, cattle strayed from place to place and died in hedgerows and ditches. Dogs and cats fell like the rest.[27]

The dearth of labor held a fearful prospect because the fourteenth century lived close to the annual harvest both for food and for next year's seed. "So few servants and laborers were left," wrote Knighton, "that no one knew where to turn for help." The sense of a vanishing future created a kind of dementia of despair. A Bavarian chronicler of Neuberg on the Danube recorded that "Men and women . . . wandered around as if mad" and let their cattle stray "because no one had any inclination to concern themselves about the future."[28] Fields went uncultivated, spring seed unsown. Second growth with nature's awful energy crept back over cleared land, dikes crumbled, salt water reinvaded and soured the low-lands. With so few hands remaining to restore the work of centuries, people felt, in Walsingham's words, that "the world could never again regain its former prosperity."[29]

Though the death rate was higher among the anonymous poor, the known and the great died too. King Alfonso XI of Castile was the only reigning monarch killed by the pest, but his neighbor King Pedro of Aragon lost his wife, Queen Leonora, his daughter Marie, and a niece in the space of six months. John Cantacuzene, Emperor of Byzantium, lost his son. In France the lame Queen Jeanne and her daughter-in-law Bonne de Luxemburg, wife of the Dauphin, both died in 1349 in the same phase that took the life of Enguerrand's mother. Jeanne, Queen of Navarre, daughter of Louis X, was another victim. Edward III's second daughter, Joanna, who was on her way to marry Pedro, the heir of Castile, died in Bordeaux. Women appear to have been more vulnerable than men, perhaps because, being more housebound, they were more exposed to fleas. Boccaccio's mistress Fiammetta, illegitimate daughter of the King of Naples, died, as did Laura, the beloved—whether real or fictional—of Petrarch. Reaching out to us in the future, Petrarch cried, "Oh happy posterity who will not experience such abysmal woe and will look upon our testimony as a fable."[30]

In Florence Giovanni Villani, the great historian of his time, died at 68 in the midst of an unfinished sentence: "... *e dure questo pistolenza fino a* ... (in the midst of this pestilence there came to an end ...)."[31] Siena's master painters, the brothers Ambrogio and Pietro Lorenzetti, whose names never appear after 1348, presumably perished in the plague, as did Andrea Pisano, architect and sculptor of Florence. William of Ockham and the English mystic Richard Rolle of Hampole both disappear from mention after 1349. Francisco Datini, merchant of Prato, lost both his parents and two siblings. Curious sweeps of mortality afflicted certain bodies of merchants in London. All eight wardens of the Company of Cutters, all six wardens of the Hatters, and four wardens of the Goldsmiths died before July 1350. Sir John Pulteney, master draper and four times Mayor of London, was a victim, likewise Sir John Montgomery, Governor of Calais.

Among the clergy and doctors the mortality was naturally high because of the nature of their professions. Out of 24 physicians in Venice, 20 were said to have lost their lives in the plague, although, according to another account, some were believed to have fled or to have shut themselves up in their houses.[32] At Montpellier, site of the leading medieval medical school, the physician Simon de Covino reported that, despite the great number of doctors, "hardly one of them escaped."[33] In Avignon, Guy de Chauliac confessed that he performed his medical visits only because he dared not stay away for fear of infamy, but "I was in continual fear."[34] He claimed to have contracted the disease but to have cured himself by his own treatment; if so, he was one of the few who recovered.

Clerical mortality varied with rank. Although the one-third toll of car-

25

dinals reflects the same proportion as the whole, this was probably due to their concentration in Avignon. In England, in strange and almost sinister procession, the Archbishop of Canterbury, John Stratford, died in August 1348, his appointed successor died in May 1349, and the next appointee three months later, all three within a year. Despite such weird vagaries, prelates in general managed to sustain a higher survival rate than the lesser clergy. Among bishops the deaths have been estimated at about one in twenty. The loss of priests, even if many avoided their fearful duty of attending the dying, was about the same as among the population as a whole.

Government officials, whose loss contributed to the general chaos, found, on the whole, no special shelter. In Siena four of the nine members of the governing oligarchy died, in France one third of the royal notaries, in Bristol 15 out of the 52 members of the Town Council or almost one third. Tax-collecting obviously suffered, with the result that Philip VI was unable to collect more than a fraction of the subsidy granted him by the Estates in the winter of 1347–48.

Lawlessness and debauchery accompanied the plague as they had during the great plague of Athens of 430 B.C., when according to Thucydides, men grew bold in the indulgence of pleasure: "For seeing how the rich died in a moment and those who had nothing immediately inherited their property, they reflected that life and riches were alike transitory and they resolved to enjoy themselves while they could."[35] Human behavior is timeless. When St. John had his vision of plague in Revelation, he knew from some experience or race memory that those who survived "repented not of the work of their hands. . . . Neither repented they of their murders, nor of their sorceries, nor of their fornication, nor of their thefts."

Ignorance of the cause augmented the sense of horror. Of the real carriers, rats and fleas, the fourteenth century had no suspicion, perhaps because they were so familiar. Fleas, though a common household nuisance, are not once mentioned in contemporary plague writings, and rats only incidentally, although folklore commonly associated them with pestilence. The legend of the Pied Piper arose from an outbreak of 1284. The actual plague bacillus, *Pasturella pestis,* remained undiscovered for another 500 years. Living alternately in the stomach of the flea and the bloodstream of the rat who was the flea's host, the bacillus in its bubonic form was transferred to humans and animals by the bite of either rat or flea. It traveled by virtue of *Rattus rattus,* the small medieval black rat that lived on ships, as well as by the heavier brown or sewer rat. What precipitated the turn of the bacillus from innocuous to virulent form is unknown, but the occurrence is now believed to have taken place not in China but somewhere in central Asia and to have spread along the caravan routes. Chinese origin was a mistaken notion of the fourteenth century based on real but belated reports of huge death tolls in China from drought, famine, and pestilence which have since been traced to the 1330s, too soon to be responsible for the plague that appeared in India in 1346.[36]

The phantom enemy had no name. Called the Black Death only in later recurrences, it was known during the first epidemic simply as the Pestilence or Great Mortality. Reports from the East, swollen by fearful imaginings, told of strange tempests and "sheets of fire" mingled with huge hailstones that "slew almost all," or a "vast rain of fire" that burned up men, beasts, stones, trees, villages, and cities.[37] In another version, "foul blasts of wind" from the fires carried the infection to Europe "and now as some suspect it cometh round the seacoast." Accurate observation in this case could not make the mental jump to ships and rats because no idea of animal- or insect-borne contagion existed.

The earthquake was blamed for releasing sulfurous and foul fumes   30 from the earth's interior, or as evidence of a titanic struggle of planets and oceans causing waters to rise and vaporize until fish died in masses and corrupted the air. All these explanations had in common a factor of poisoned air, of miasmas and thick, stinking mists traced to every kind of natural or imagined agency from stagnant lakes to malign conjunction of the planets, from the hand of the Evil One to the wrath of God. Medical thinking, trapped in the theory of astral influences, stressed air as the communicator of disease, ignoring sanitation or visible carriers. The existence of two carriers confused the trail, the more so because the flea could live and travel independently of the rat for as long as a month and, if infected by the particularly virulent septicemic form of the bacillus, could infect humans without reinfecting itself from the rat. The simultaneous presence of the pneumonic form of the disease, which was indeed communicated through the air, blurred the problem further.

The mystery of the contagion was "the most terrible of all the terrors," as an anonymous Flemish cleric in Avignon wrote to a correspondent in Bruges. Plagues had been known before, from the plague of Athens (believed to have been typhus) to the prolonged epidemic of the sixth century A.D., to the recurrence of sporadic outbreaks in the twelfth and thirteenth centuries, but they had left no accumulated store of understanding.[38] That the infection came from contact with the sick or with their houses, clothes, or corpses was quickly observed but not comprehended. Gentile da Foligno, renowned physician of Perugia and doctor of medicine at the universities of Bologna and Padua, came close to respiratory infection when he surmised that poisonous material was "communicated by means of air breathed out and in."[39] Having no idea of microscopic carriers, he had to assume that the air was corrupted by planetary influences. Planets, however, could not explain the ongoing contagion. The agonized search for an answer gave rise to such theories as transference by sight. People fell ill, wrote Guy de Chauliac, not only by remaining with the sick but "even by looking at them." Three hundred years later Joshua Barnes, the seventeenth century biographer of Edward III, could write that the power of infection had entered into beams of light and "darted death from the eyes."

Doctors struggling with the evidence could not break away from the terms of astrology, to which they believed all human physiology was subject. Medicine was the one aspect of medieval life, perhaps because of its links with the Arabs, not shaped by Christian doctrine. Clerics detested astrology, but could not dislodge its influence. Guy de Chauliac, physician to three popes in succession, practiced in obedience to the zodiac. While his *Cirurgia* was the major treatise on surgery of its time, while he understood the use of anesthesia made from the juice of opium, mandrake, or hemlock, he nevertheless prescribed bleeding and purgatives by the planets and divided chronic from acute diseases on the basis of one being under the rule of the sun and the other of the moon.

In October 1348 Philip VI asked the medical faculty of the University of Paris for a report on the affliction that seemed to threaten human survival.[40] With careful thesis, antithesis, and proofs, the doctors ascribed it to a triple conjunction of Saturn, Jupiter, and Mars in the fortieth degree of Aquarius said to have occurred on March 20, 1345. They acknowledged, however, effects "whose cause is hidden from even the most highly trained intellects." The verdict of the masters of Paris became the official version. Borrowed, copied by scribes, carried abroad, translated from Latin into various vernaculars, it was everywhere accepted, even by the Arab physicians of Cordova and Granada, as the scientific if not the popular answer. Because of the terrible interest of the subject, the translations of the plague tracts stimulated use of national languages. In that one respect, life came from death.

To the people at large there could be but one explanation—the wrath of God. Planets might satisfy the learned doctors, but God was closer to the average man. A scourge so sweeping and unsparing without any visible cause could only be seen as Divine punishment upon mankind for its sins. It might even be God's terminal disappointment in his creature. Matteo Villani compared the plague to the Flood in ultimate purpose and believed he was recording "the extermination of mankind."[41] Efforts to appease Divine wrath took many forms, as when the city of Rouen ordered that everything that could anger God, such as gambling, cursing, and drinking, must be stopped.[42] More general were the penitent processions authorized at first by the Pope, some lasting as long as three days, some attended by as many as 2,000, which everywhere accompanied the plague and helped to spread it.

Barefoot in sackcloth, sprinkled with ashes, weeping, praying, tearing   35
their hair, carrying candles and relics, sometimes with ropes around their necks or beating themselves with whips, the penitents wound through the streets, imploring the mercy of the Virgin and saints at their shrines. In a vivid illustration for the *Très Riches Heures* of the Duc de Berry, the Pope is shown in a penitent procession attended by four cardinals in scarlet from hat to hem. He raises both arms in supplication to the angel on top of the Castel Sant'Angelo, while white-robed priests bearing banners and relics in golden cases turn to look as one of their number, stricken by the

plague, falls to the ground, his face contorted with anxiety. In the rear, a gray-clad monk falls beside another victim already on the ground as the townspeople gaze in horror. (Nominally the illustration represents a sixth century plague in the time of Pope Gregory the Great, but as medieval artists made no distinction between past and present, the scene is shown as the artist would have seen it in the fourteenth century.) When it became evident that these processions were sources of infection, Clement VI had to prohibit them.

In Messina, where the plague first appeared, the people begged the Archbishop of neighboring Catania to lend them the relics of St. Agatha.[43] When the Catanians refused to let the relics go, the Archbishop dipped them in holy water and took the water himself to Messina, where he carried it in a procession with prayers and litanies through the streets. The demonic, which shared the medieval cosmos with God, appeared as "demons in the shape of dogs" to terrify the people. "A black dog with a drawn sword in his paws appeared among them, gnashing his teeth and rushing upon them and breaking all the silver vessels and lamps and candlesticks on the altars and casting them hither and thither. . . . So the people of Messina, terrified by this prodigious vision, were all strangely overcome by fear."

The apparent absence of earthly cause gave the plague a supernatural and sinister quality. Scandinavians believed that a Pest Maiden emerged from the mouth of the dead in the form of a blue flame and flew through the air to infect the next house.[44] In Lithuania the Maiden was said to wave a red scarf through the door or window to let in the pest. One brave man, according to legend, deliberately waited at his open window with drawn sword and, at the fluttering of the scarf, chopped off the hand. He died of his deed, but his village was spared and the scarf long preserved as a relic in the local church.

Beyond demons and superstition the final hand was God's. The Pope acknowledged it in a Bull° of September 1348, speaking of the "pestilence with which God is afflicting the Christian people." To the Emperor John Cantacuzene it was manifest that a malady of such horrors, stenches, and agonies, and especially one bringing the dismal despair that settled upon its victims before they died, was not a plague "natural" to mankind but "a chastisement from Heaven."[45] To Piers Plowman "these pestilences were for pure sin."[46]

The general acceptance of this view created an expanded sense of guilt, for if the plague were punishment there had to be terrible sin to have occasioned it. What sins were on the fourteenth century conscience? Primarily greed, the sin of avarice, followed by usury, worldliness, adultery, blasphemy, falsehood, luxury, irreligion. Giovanni Villani, attempting to account for the cascade of calamity that had fallen upon Florence, concluded that it was retribution for the sins of avarice and usury that op-

---

°A bull is a formal papal document. —EDS.

pressed the poor. Pity and anger about the condition of the poor, especially victimization of the peasantry in war, was often expressed by writers of the time and was certainly on the conscience of the century. Beneath it all was the daily condition of medieval life, in which hardly an act or thought, sexual, mercantile, or military, did not contravene the dictates of the Church. Mere failure to fast or attend mass was sin. The result was an underground lake of guilt in the soul that the plague now tapped.

That the mortality was accepted as God's punishment may explain in part the vacuum of comment that followed the Black Death. An investigator has noticed that in the archives of Périgord references to the war are innumerable, to the plague few. Froissart mentions the great death but once, Chaucer gives it barely a glance. Divine anger so great that it contemplated the extermination of man did not bear close examination.   40

NOTES

1. "Death Is Seen Seated": Simon de Covino, q. Campbell, 80.
2. "Could Infect the World": q. Gasquet, 41.
3. Welsh Lament: q. Ziegler, 190.
4. "Dogs Dragged Them Forth": Agnolo di Tura, q. Ziegler, 58.
5. "Or if No Man Is Present": Bishop of Bath and Wells, q. Ziegler, 125.
6. "No Bells Tolled": Agnolo di Tura, q. Schevill, *Siena,* 211. The same observation was made by Gabriel de Muisis, notary of Piacenza, q. Crawford, 113.
7. Givry Parish Register: Renouard, 111.
8. Three Villages of Cambridgeshire: Saltmarsh.
9. Petrarch's Brother: Bishop, 273.
10. Brother John Clyn: q. Ziegler, 195.
11. Apathy; "And in These Days": q. Deaux, 143, citing only "an old northern chronicle."
12. Agnolo di Tura, "Father Abandoned Child": q. Ziegler, 58.
13. "Magistrates and Notaries": q. Deaux, 49.
14. English Priests Turned Away: Ziegler, 261.
15. Parents Deserting Children: Hecker, 30.
16. Guy de Chauliac, "A Father": q. Gasquet, 50–51.
17. Nuns of the Hotel Dieu: *Chron. Jean de Venette,* 49.
18. Picards and Scots Mock Mortality of Neighbors: Gasquet, 53, and Ziegler, 198.
19. Catherine de Coucy: *L'Art de verifier,* 237.
20. Amiens Tanners: Gasquet, 57.
21. "By the Jollity That Is in Us": *Grandes Chrons.,* VI, 486–87.
22. John of Fordun: q. Ziegler, 199.
23. Simon de Covino on the Poor: Gasquet, 42.
24. On Youth: Cazelles, *Peste.*
25. Knighton on Sheep: q. Ziegler, 175.
26. Wolves of Austria and Dalmatia: ibid., 84, 111.
27. Dogs and Cats: Muisis, q. Gasquet, 44, 61.
28. Bavarian Chronicler of Neuberg: q. Ziegler, 84.
29. Walsingham, "The World Could Never": Denifle, 273.
30. "Oh Happy Posterity": q. Ziegler, 45.
31. Giovanni Villani, *"e dure questo"*: q. Snell, 334.
32. Physicians of Venice: Campbell, 98.
33. Simon de Covino: ibid., 31.
34. Guy de Chauliac, "I Was in Fear": q. Thompson, *Ec. and Soc.,* 379.
35. Thucydides: q. Crawfurd, 30–31.
36. Chinese Origin: Although the idea of Chinese origin is still being repeated (e.g., by William H. McNeill, *Plagues and People,* New York, 1976, 161–63), it is disputed by L.

Carrington Goodrich of the Association for Asian Studies, Columbia Univ., in letters to the author of 18 and 26 October 1973. Citing contemporary Chinese and other sources, he also quotes Dr. George A. Perera of the College of Physicians and Surgeons, an authority on communicable diseases, who "agrees with me that the spaces between epidemics in China (1334), Semirechyé (1338–9) and the Mediterranean basin (1347–9) seem too long for the first to be responsible for the last."

37. Reports from the East: Barnes, 432; Coulton, *Black Death*, 9–11.
38. Anonymous Flemish Cleric, "Most Terrible": His correspondence was edited in the form of a chronicle by De Smet, in *Recueil des chroniques de Flandres*, III, q. Ziegler, 22.
39. Gentile da Foligno, "Communicated by air": Campbell, 38.
40. Report of the University of Paris: Hecker, 51–53; Campbell, 15.
41. M. Villani, "Extermination of Mankind": q. Meiss, *Painting . . . After the Black Death*, 66.
42. Rouen Prohibits Gambling: Nohl, 74.
43. At Messina, Demons Like Dogs: Coulton, *Black Death*, 22–27.
44. Pest Maiden: Ziegler, 85.
45. Cantacuzene: Barnes, 435.
46. Piers Plowman, "Pure Sin": B text, V, 13.

BIBLIOGRAPHY

L'Art de verifier les dates des faits historiques, par un Religieux de la Congregation de St. Maur, vol. XII. Paris, 1818.
Barnes, Joshua, *The History of Edward III.* Cambridge, 1688.
Campbell, Anna M., *The Black Death and Men of Learning.* Columbia University Press, 1931.
Chronicle of Jean de Venette. Trans. Jean Birdsall. Ed. Richard A. Newhall. Columbia University Press, 1853.
Crawfurd, Raymond, *Plague and Pestilence in Literature and Art.* Oxford, 1914.
Coulton, G. G., *The Black Death.* London, 1929.
Deaux, George, *The Black Death, 1347.* London, 1969.
Denifle, Henri, *La Désolation des églises, monastères et hôpitaux en France pendant la guerre de cent ans,* vol. I. Paris, 1899.
Gasquet, Francis Aidan, Abbot, *The Black Death of 1348 and 1349,* 2nd ed. London, 1908.
Grandes Chroniques de France, vol. VI (to 1380). Ed. Paulin Paris. Paris, 1838.
Hecker, J. F. C., *The Epidemics of the Middle Ages.* London, 1844.
Meiss, Millard, *Painting in Florence and Siena After the Black Death.* Princeton, 1951.
Nohl, Johannes, *The Black Death: A Chronicle of the Plague Compiled from Contemporary Sources.* Trans. C. H. Clarke. London, 1971.
Saltmarsh, John, "Plague and Economic Decline in England in the Latter Middle Ages," *Cambridge Historical Journal,* vol. VII, no. 1, 1941.
Schevill, Ferdinand, *History of Florence.* New York, 1961.
Snell, Frederick, *The Fourteenth Century.* Edinburgh, 1899.
Thompson, James Westfall, *Economic and Social History of Europe in the Later Middle Ages.* New York, 1931.
Ziegler, Philip, *The Black Death.* New York, 1969. (The best modern study.)

The Reader's Presence

1. History is a form of story. Which elements of Tuchman's account seem to pertain to pure fact, and which to storytelling? Events are related in an objective tone. Is the writer's approval or disapproval ever evident? If so, where and in what ways?

2. This piece is drawn from a book titled *A Distant Mirror: The Calamitous Fourteenth Century.* In what ways does Tuchman's

account suggest that fourteenth-century behaviors reflect our behaviors today?

3. At times Tuchman recounts history in the aggregate; at times she
   traces history through a specific figure. Find a few instances of
   this latter technique. Why might she have chosen to augment the
   general with the particular and vice-versa? What is the effect of
   this technique on the reader?

4. "Ignorance of the cause augmented the sense of horror," Tuchman
   writes of the fourteenth century plague (paragraph 28), but her
   statement can be taken as universally true. Use Tuchman's insight
   to sharpen your perception of the emotions expressed in Michihiko
   Hachiya's journal ("From *Hiroshima Diary*," page 29) and in Don
   DeLillo's essay ("In the Ruins of the Future," page 341). How does
   each of these writers respond to problems of unspeakable horror?
   How do their approaches to narrating disaster compare?

80

John Updike

Car Talk

*Over the course of his career as a novelist, short story writer, poet, essayist,
and dramatist, John Updike (b. 1932) has been awarded every major American
literary award; in 1998 he was awarded the National Book Foundation Medal for
Distinguished Contribution to American Letters. For one novel alone,* Rabbit Is
Rich *(1981), he won the Pulitzer Prize, the American Book Award, and the National Book Critics Circle Award. Among over a dozen published novels, his recurring themes include religion, sexuality, and middle-class experience. In his
essays, Updike's concerns range widely over literary and cultural issues. One volume of his collected essays,* Hugging the Shore: Essays and Criticism *(1983), was
awarded a National Book Critics Circle Award. His most recent publications include* More Matter: Essays and Criticism *(1999),* Licks of Love: Short Stories and
a Sequel *(2000), and* Gertrude and Claudius *(2000). "Car Talk" first appeared in
the* New Yorker *in 1997.*

*Updike has said, "I began my writing career with a fairly distinct set of prin-
ciples which, one by one, have eroded into something approaching shapeless-
ness." He does maintain one principle, however: "You should attempt to write
things that you would like to read." Writing, he continues, is a process of rendering "your vision of reality into the written symbol. Out of this, living art will
come."*

A human being has vocal cords, a tongue, teeth, and, for expressive reinforcement, eyes and hands; a car has nothing but its horn and lights. Yet
cars do talk; they can say "Howdy!" (a brief, deft toot) and "I hate you!"
(a firmer, sustained blast) and "Do it!" (a flicker of the headlights). As their
drivers are sealed ever more inaccessibly into a casing of audiotapes, cell
phones, and deafening air-conditioning, automobiles for the sake of their
own survival are evolving increasingly complex speech patterns. There is a
distinct difference, to the attuned ear, between the highly respectful honk
used in a service station during an annual car inspection in response to the
command "Sound your horn" and the just perceptibly more urgent, less
deferential beep that announces to the inhabitants of a domicile that a summoned taxi or car-pool van somewhat impatiently awaits.

Meaning is often, as with other languages, a matter of context. The
polite, minimal sounding of the horn—the automotive equivalent of a
throat-clearing—that declares simple presence ("Howdy!") in nonthreatening circumstances, becomes, while one is passing on a four-lane
highway an automobile that has an aura of wanting to change lanes with
an abrupt swerve, more admonitory—something like "Watch it, buddy!
You've got two tons of moving metal right here in your blind spot!"

If no response is indicated, the same utterance, more insistently intoned,
takes on a suggestion of rebuke and heightened anxiety: "Hey, you're riding
me into the median strip!" And if the swerve does take place, within inches
of one's front fender, a strengthened intonation moderates the meaning to,
roughly, "You crazy blind idiot, go back to driving school!" Then, if no
penitent reverse-swerve communicates regret, the next level of volume declares, "You bastard—you cut me off! Drivers like you should be in jail,
and I'd ram you right in your saucy little vanity plate if I didn't hate fussing
with the insurance agent and weren't already late for the dentist!"

As with birdsong and insect stridulation, impressive amounts of information are packed into virtually indistinguishable sounds. In city traffic, one moderate toot, not quite deferential, informs the car ahead at an
intersection that the light has changed from red to green. "Let's go, day-
dreamer!" might be a translation. The same toot, amplified by a few decibels, point out to a truck being slowly unloaded that double parking is
illegal and obstructive, or to a taxi that passengers should not be dumped
in the middle of Fifth Avenue. Another few decibels suggest to an errant
pedestrian, "I'd be within my rights to run you over," or to a messenger
on a bicycle, "Having thin wheels, Lycra shorts, and a Walkman on your
head doesn't make you immune to the laws of physics. Someday you're
going to get squashed, and don't look for me among the mourners!"

The highest, most prolonged volume of the horn transcends commu-   5
nication. It expresses—at, say, the mouth of the Lincoln Tunnel—
frustration to the point of insanity. The noise can be read as existential
protest, a frantic desire on the part of automobiles to opt out of their very
condition of car-ness, as cattle at the chute of the slaughterhouse bellow
to be released from their condition of steer-ness.

Car lights, too, say more than they used to. Having the controls on a stalk behind the steering wheel has considerably enhanced their eloquence. Flashed lights, for instance, once only hinted that a police car was lurking around the corner, but now, flicked demurely, say "Do it" and "Thank you," much as the Italian word *prego* says both "Here you are" and "You're welcome."

Headlights lit in broad daylight used to mean, "We're all in a funeral procession. Don't muscle in." But now such headlights, enlarging in the rearview mirror, cry out, "Here I come, hell for leather, and possibly crazed on drugs! Get out of my way!" Red tail-lights, braked into luminescence, can mean not only "I'm braking" but "Stop tailgating, I do beg you!" The latter can be reacted to before it is consciously understood. As in other highly evolved languages, signifiers can signify opposites: at night, high-beam lights in your eyes either mean that the offending driver has forgotten to switch to the low beam or he is telling you that *you* have. Even turned-off lights can say something: in a locked car parked in your favorite curbside spot near home, their message reads, "Tough luck, kid. I got here first."

Thus a situational and gestural linguistics of considerable complexity has grown up in a mere hundred years of automobile traffic. In the next century, we may expect vocabulary to increase and grammar to ramify to the point that human drivers can spare themselves the vocal outbursts and exchanges which occasionally still mar the subtle conversational pattern of the streets.

The Reader's Presence

1. Updike's essay is a humor piece, distinguished by its light tone. In the middle of the first paragraph, however, he seems to be making a serious statement about the increasing presence of technology in our lives. How seriously should we take this point? Is this a case of a writer using humor to level a social critique? How can the reader determine Updike's aims?

2. At the beginning of paragraph 2, Updike writes, "Meaning is, as with other languages, a matter of context." Give some thought to what this statement means. How does Updike build upon this general truth? What does this sentence do for the essay as a whole? Would the essay work as well without this sentence?

3. It is notoriously difficult to describe how a joke works, but Updike's humor here relies on a relatively simple technique. How would you describe the humor of this piece to someone who hasn't read it? Find the funniest sentence and determine what exactly makes it funny. Compare Updike's style to that of Ian Frazier in "Tracks" (page 384) and David Sedaris in "Me Talk Pretty One Day" (page 249).

81

Marie Winn

TV Addiction

Born in 1936 in Prague, Czechoslovakia, Marie Winn came to the United States with her family in 1939. After receiving her education at Radcliffe College and Columbia University, Winn became a freelance writer specializing in children's literature. In addition to having written over a dozen books for children or for parents and teachers of children, she has contributed to the New York Times, the New York Times Book Review, and the Wall Street Journal. Her publications include Children without Childhood *(1983),* Unplugging the Plug-In Drug *(1987), and* Redtails in Love: A Wildlife Drama in Central Park *(1998). "TV Addiction" is from* The Plug-In Drug: Television, Children and the Family *(originally published in 1977 and revised in 2000).*

The word "addiction" is often used loosely and wryly in conversation. People will refer to themselves as "mystery-book addicts" or "cookie addicts." E. B. White wrote of his annual surge of interest in gardening: "We are hooked and are making an attempt to kick the habit." Yet nobody really believes that reading mysteries or ordering seeds by catalogue is serious enough to be compared with addictions to heroin or alcohol. In these cases the word "addiction" is used jokingly to denote a tendency to overindulge in some pleasurable activity.

People often refer to being "hooked on TV." Does this, too, fall into the lighthearted category of cookie eating and other pleasures that people pursue with unusual intensity? Or is there a kind of television viewing that falls into the more serious category of destructive addiction?

Not unlike drugs or alcohol, the television experience allows the participant to blot out the real world and enter into a pleasurable and passive mental state. To be sure, other experiences, notably reading, also provide a temporary respite from reality. But it's much easier to stop reading and return to reality than to stop watching television. The entry into another world offered by reading includes an easily accessible return ticket. The entry via television does not. In this way television viewing, for those vulnerable to addiction, is more like drinking or taking drugs—once you start it's hard to stop.

Just as alcoholics are only vaguely aware of their addiction, feeling that they control their drinking more than they really do ("I can cut it out any time I want—I just like to have three or four drinks before dinner"), many people overestimate their control over television watching. Even as they put off other activities to spend hour after hour watching television, they feel they could easily resume living in a different, less passive style. But somehow or other while the television set is present in their homes, it just stays on. With television's easy gratifications available, those other activities seem to take too much effort.

A heavy viewer (a college English instructor) observes:

> I find television almost irresistible. When the set is on, I cannot ignore it. I can't turn it off. I feel sapped, will-less, enervated. As I reach out to turn off the set, the strength goes out of my arms. So I sit there for hours and hours.

Self-confessed television addicts often feel they "ought" to do other things—but the fact that they don't read and don't plant their garden or sew or crochet or play games or have conversations means that those activities are no longer as desirable as television viewing. In a way, the lives of heavy viewers are as unbalanced by their television "habit" as drug addicts' or alcoholics' lives. They are living in a holding pattern, as it were, passing up the activities that lead to growth or development or a sense of accomplishment. This is one reason people talk about their television viewing so ruefully, so apologetically. They are aware that it is an unproductive experience, that by any human measure almost any other endeavor is more worthwhile.

It is the adverse effect of television viewing on the lives of so many people that makes it feel like a serious addiction. The television habit distorts the sense of time. It renders other experiences vague and curiously unreal while taking on a greater reality for itself. It weakens relationships by reducing and sometimes eliminating normal opportunities for talking, for communicating.

And yet television does not satisfy, else why would the viewer continue to watch hour after hour, day after day? "The measure of health," wrote the psychiatrist Lawrence Kubie, "is flexibility . . . and especially the freedom to cease when sated." But heavy television viewers can never be sated with their television experiences. These do not provide the true nourishment that satiation requires, and thus they find that they cannot stop watching.

The Reader's Presence

1. How does Winn characterize addiction? How does she apply that characterization to television watching? Do you think watching television is a genuine addiction, similar to addiction to drugs, alcohol, or tobacco? Why or why not?

2. Does Winn rely more heavily on evidence or opinion for her argument? Is her methodology convincing? What evidence do you find most persuasive?

3. What other forms of addiction, legitimate and humorous, does Winn mention? How would mystery-book reading or frequent telephone calling or use of the Internet differ from TV watching? What arguments, if any, might be offered to class TV addiction with these lesser ills rather than with drug abuse and alcoholism? Reread Benjamin Spock's essay "Should Children Play with Guns?" (page 525). How does he use television in his argument? How might Winn respond to his essay? How might Spock, a physician, respond to Winn's medicalization of television viewing? Is Winn's understanding of this "addiction," finally, an analogy?

82 _____

Virginia Woolf

The Death of the Moth

One of the most important writers of the twentieth century, Virginia Woolf (1882–1941) explored innovations in indirect narration and the impressionistic use of language that are now considered hallmarks of the modern novel and continue to influence novelists on both sides of the Atlantic. Together with her husband, Leonard Woolf, she founded the Hogarth Press, which published many experimental works that have now become classics, including her own. A central figure in the Bloomsbury group of writers, Woolf established her reputation with the novels Mrs. Dalloway *(1925),* To the Lighthouse *(1927), and* The Waves *(1931). The feminist movement has helped to focus attention on her work, and Woolf's nonfiction has provided the basis for several important lines of argument in contemporary feminist theory.* A Room of One's Own *(1929),* Three Guineas *(1938), and* The Common Reader *(1938) are the major works of nonfiction published in Woolf's lifetime; posthumously, her essays have been gathered together in* The Death of the Moth *(where the essay reprinted here appears) and in the four-volume* Collected Essays.

Reflecting on her own writing life, Woolf wrote, "The novelist — it is his distinction and his danger — is terribly exposed to life. . . . He can no more cease to receive impressions than a fish in mid-ocean can cease to let the water rush through his gills." To turn those impressions into writing, Woolf maintained, requires solitude and the time for thoughtful selection. Given tranquility, a writer can, with effort, discover art in experience. "There emerges from the mist something stark, formidable and enduring, the bone and substance upon which our rush of indiscriminating emotion was founded."

For more on Virginia Woolf, see page 55.

Moths that fly by day are not properly to be called moths; they do not excite that pleasant sense of dark autumn nights and ivy-blossom which the commonest yellow-underwing asleep in the shadow of the curtain never fails to rouse in us. They are hybrid creatures, neither gay like butterflies nor somber like their own species. Nevertheless the present specimen, with his narrow hay-colored wings, fringed with a tassel of the same color, seemed to be content with life. It was a pleasant morning, mid-September, mild, benignant, yet with a keener breath than that of the summer months. The plough was already scoring the field opposite the window, and where the share had been, the earth was pressed flat and gleamed with moisture. Such vigor came rolling in from the fields and the down beyond that it was difficult to keep the eyes strictly turned upon the book. The rooks too were keeping one of their annual festivities; soaring round the tree tops until it looked as if a vast net with thousands of black knots in it had been cast up into the air; which, after a few moments sank slowly down upon the trees until every twig seemed to have a knot at the end of it. Then, suddenly, the net would be thrown into the air again in a wider circle this time, with the utmost clamor and vociferation, as though to be thrown into the air and settle slowly down upon the tree tops were a tremendously exciting experience.

The same energy which inspired the rooks, the ploughmen, the horses, and even, it seemed, the lean bare-backed downs, sent the moth fluttering from side to side of his square of the windowpane. One could not help watching him. One, was, indeed, conscious of a queer feeling of pity for him. The possibilities of pleasure seemed that morning so enormous and so various that to have only a moth's part in life, and a day moth's at that, appeared a hard fate, and his zest in enjoying his meager opportunities to the full, pathetic. He flew vigorously to one corner of his compartment, and after waiting there a second, flew across to the other. What remained for him but to fly to a third corner and then to a fourth? That was all he could do, in spite of the size of the downs, the width of the sky, the far-off smoke of houses, and the romantic voice, now and then, of a steamer out at sea. What he could do he did. Watching him, it seemed as if a fiber, very thin but pure, of the enormous energy of the world had been thrust into his frail and diminutive body. As often as he crossed the pane, I could fancy that a thread of vital light became visible. He was little or nothing but life.

Yet, because he was so small, and so simple a form of the energy that was rolling in at the open window and driving its way through so many narrow and intricate corridors in my own brain and in those of other human beings, there was something marvelous as well as pathetic about him. It was as if someone had taken a tiny bead of pure life and decking it as lightly as possible with down and feathers, had set it dancing and zigzagging to show us the true nature of life. Thus displayed one could not get over the strangeness of it. One is apt to forget all about life, seeing it humped and bossed and garnished and cumbered so that it has to move with the greatest circumspection and dignity. Again, the thought of all that life might have been had he been born in any other shape caused one to view his simple activities with a kind of pity.

After a time, tired by his dancing apparently, he settled on the window ledge in the sun, and, the queer spectacle being at an end, I forgot about him. Then, looking up, my eye was caught by him. He was trying to resume his dancing, but seemed either so stiff or so awkward that he could only flutter to the bottom of the windowpane; and when he tried to fly across it he failed. Being intent on other matters I watched these futile attempts for a time without thinking, unconsciously waiting for him to resume his flight, as one waits for a machine, that has stopped momentarily, to start again without considering the reason of its failure. After perhaps a seventh attempt he slipped from the wooden ledge and fell, fluttering his wings, on to his back on the windowsill. The helplessness of his attitude roused me. It flashed upon me that he was in difficulties; he could no longer raise himself; his legs struggled vainly. But, as I stretched out a pencil, meaning to help him to right himself, it came over me that the failure and awkwardness were the approach of death. I laid the pencil down again.

The legs agitated themselves once more. I looked as if for the enemy   5 against which he struggled. I looked out of doors. What had happened there? Presumably it was midday, and work in the fields had stopped. Stillness and quiet had replaced the previous animation. The birds had taken themselves off to feed in the brooks. The horses stood still. Yet the power was there all the same, massed outside, indifferent, impersonal, not attending to anything in particular. Somehow it was opposed to the little hay-colored moth. It was useless to try to do anything. One could only watch the extraordinary efforts made by those tiny legs against an oncoming doom which could, had it chosen, have submerged an entire city, not merely a city, but masses of human beings; nothing, I knew had any chance against death. Nevertheless after a pause of exhaustion the legs fluttered again. It was superb this last protest, and so frantic that he succeeded at last in righting himself. One's sympathies, of course, were all on the side of life. Also, when there was nobody to care or to know, this gigantic effort on the part of an insignificant little moth, against a power of such magnitude, to retain what no one else valued or desired to keep, moved one strangely. Again, somehow, one saw life, a pure bead. I lifted the pencil again, useless though I knew it to be. But even as I did so, the unmistakable tokens of death showed themselves. The body relaxed, and instantly grew stiff. The struggle was over. The insignificant little creature now knew death. As I looked at the dead moth, this minute wayside triumph of so great a force over so mean an antagonist filled me with wonder. Just as life had been strange a few minutes before, so death was now as strange. The moth having righted himself now lay most decently and uncomplainingly composed. O yes, he seemed to say, death is stronger than I am.

The Reader's Presence

1. Woolf calls her essay "The Death of *the* Moth" rather than "The Death of *a* Moth." Describe what difference this makes. What quality does the definite article add to the essay?

2. Reread the essay, paying special attention not to the moth but to the writer. What presence does Woolf establish for herself in the essay? How does the act of writing itself get introduced? Of what significance is the pencil? Can you discover any connection between the essay's subject and its composition? Can you find any connection between this essay and the author's ideas about the writing process in *A Writer's Diary* (see page 55)?

3. Reread Woolf's concluding paragraph and paragraph 11 of George Orwell's "Shooting an Elephant." How do the passages compare on the level of physical detail? How vivid is the death of each creature? Reread the paragraphs again, paying special attention to point of view. How do the writers implicate themselves in the deaths they witness? How do they appeal to the reader? Is the reader made into an "innocent bystander" or is he or she more intimately involved? If so, how does this intimacy come about?

Part IV

Argumentative Writing: Contending with Issues

83

Dorothy Allison

This Is Our World

Dorothy Allison (b. 1949) was born in Greenville, South Carolina, and received an M.A. in anthropology from the New School for Social Research in New York City. A versatile writer, Allison has published poems, short stories, essays, and novels. Her first collection of short stories, Trash *(1988), won the Lambda Book Award for the best work of lesbian fiction. She gained mainstream attention with her first novel,* Bastard Out of Carolina *(1992), which was a finalist for the National Book Award. Her most recent work,* Cavedweller *(1998), is an epic novel about the lives of four women in a small town in Georgia. Allison also contributes to many periodicals, including* Harper's, *the* New York Times, Village Voice, *and* Southern Exposure. *"This Is Our World" first appeared in the summer 1998 issue of* DoubleTake, *a magazine featuring creative writing and photography.*

The first painting I ever saw up close was at a Baptist church when I was seven years old. It was a few weeks before my mama was to be baptized. From it, I took the notion that art should surprise and astonish, and hopefully make you think something you had not thought until you saw it. The painting was a mural of Jesus at the Jordan River done on the wall behind the baptismal font. The font itself was a remarkable creation—a swimming pool with one glass side set into the wall above and behind the pulpit so that ordinarily you could not tell the font was there, seeing only the painting of Jesus. When the tank was flooded with water, little lights along the bottom came on, and anyone who stepped down the steps seemed to be walking past Jesus himself and descending into the Jordan River. Watching baptisms in that tank was like watching movies at the drive-in, my cousins had told me. From the moment the deacon walked us around the church, I knew what my cousin had meant. I could not take my eyes off the painting or the glass-fronted tank. It looked every moment as if Jesus were about to come alive, as if he were about to step out onto the water of the river. I think the way I stared at the painting made the deacon nervous.

The deacon boasted to my mama that there was nothing like that baptismal font in the whole state of South Carolina. It had been designed, he told her, by a nephew of the minister—a boy who had gone on to build a shopping center out in New Mexico. My mama was not sure that someone who built shopping centers was the kind of person who should have been designing baptismal fonts, and she was even more uncertain about the steep steps by Jesus' left hip. She asked the man to let her practice going up and down, but he warned her it would be different once the water poured in.

"It's quite safe though," he told her. "The water will hold you up. You won't fall."

I kept my attention on the painting of Jesus. He was much larger than I was, a little bit more than life-size, but the thick layer of shellac applied to protect the image acted like a magnifying glass, making him seem larger still. It was Jesus himself that fascinated me, though. He was all rouged and pale and pouty as Elvis Presley. This was not my idea of the son of God, but I liked it. I liked it a lot.

"Jesus looks like a girl," I told my mama.   5

She looked up at the painted face. A little blush appeared on her cheekbones, and she looked as if she would have smiled if the deacon were not frowning so determinedly. "It's just the eyelashes," she said. The deacon nodded. They climbed back up the stairs. I stepped over close to Jesus and put my hand on the painted robe. The painting was sweaty and cool, slightly oily under my fingers.

"I liked that Jesus," I told my mama as we walked out of the church. "I wish we had something like that." To her credit, Mama did not laugh.

"If you want a picture of Jesus," she said, "we'll get you one. They have them in nice frames at Sears." I sighed. That was not what I had in mind. What I wanted was a life-size, sweaty painting, one in which Jesus looked as hopeful as a young girl—something other-worldly and peculiar, but kind of wonderful at the same time. After that, every time we went to church I asked to go up to see the painting, but the baptismal font was locked tight when not in use.

The Sunday Mama was to be baptized, I watched the minister step down into that pool past the Son of God. The preacher's gown was tailored with little weights carefully sewn into the hem to keep it from rising up in the water. The water pushed up at the fabric while the weights tugged it down. Once the minister was all the way down into the tank, the robe floated up a bit so that it seemed to have a shirred ruffle all along the bottom. That was almost enough to pull my eyes away from the face of Jesus, but not quite. With the lights on in the bottom of the tank, the eyes of the painting seemed to move and shine. I tried to point it out to my sisters, but they were uninterested. All they wanted to see was Mama.

Mama was to be baptized last, after three little boys, and their gowns   10
had not had any weights attached. The white robes floated up around their necks so that their skinny boy bodies and white cotton underwear were perfectly visible to the congregation. The water that came up above

the hips of the minister lapped their shoulders, and the shortest of the boys seemed panicky at the prospect of gulping water, no matter how holy. He paddled furiously to keep above the water's surface. The water started to rock violently at his struggles, sweeping the other boys off their feet. All of them pumped their knees to stay upright and the minister, realizing how the scene must appear to the congregation below, speeded up the baptismal process, praying over and dunking the boys at high speed.

Around me the congregation shifted in their seats. My little sister slid forward off the pew, and I quickly grabbed her around the waist and barely stopped myself from laughing out loud. A titter from the back of the church indicated that other people were having the same difficulty keeping from laughing. Other people shifted irritably and glared at the noisemakers. It was clear that no matter the provocation, we were to pretend nothing funny was happening. The minister frowned more fiercely and prayed louder. My mama's friend Louise, sitting at our left, whispered a soft "Look at that" and we all looked up in awe. One of the hastily blessed boys had dog-paddled over to the glass and was staring out at us, eyes wide and his hands pressed flat to the glass. He looked as if he hoped someone would rescue him. It was too much for me. I began to giggle helplessly, and not a few of the people around me joined in. Impatiently the minister hooked the boy's robe, pulled him back, and pushed him toward the stairs.

My mama, just visible on the staircase, hesitated briefly as the sodden boy climbed up past her. Then she set her lips tightly together, and reached down and pressed her robe to her thighs. She came down the steps slowly, holding down the skirt as she did so, giving one stern glance to the two boys climbing past her up the steps, and then turning her face deliberately up to the painting of Jesus. Every move she made communicated resolution and faith, and the congregation stilled in respect. She was baptized looking up stubbornly, both hands holding down that cotton robe while below, I fought so hard not to giggle, tears spilled down my face.

Over the pool, the face of Jesus watched solemnly with his pink, painted cheeks and thick, dark lashes. For all the absurdity of the event, his face seemed to me startlingly compassionate and wise. That face understood fidgety boys and stubborn women. It made me want the painting even more, and to this day I remember it with longing. It had the weight of art, that face. It had what I am sure art is supposed to have — the power to provoke, the authority of a heartfelt vision.

I imagine the artist who painted the baptismal font in that Baptist church so long ago was a man who did not think himself much of an artist. I have seen paintings like his many times since, so perhaps he worked from a model. Maybe he traced that face off another he had seen in some other church. For a while, I tried to imagine him a character out of a Flannery O'Connor[1] short story, a man who traveled around the South in the fifties painting Jesus wherever he was needed, giving the Son of God the long lashes and pink cheeks of a young girl. He would be the kind of man who would see nothing blasphemous in painting eyes that followed the congregation as they moved up to the pulpit to receive a blessing and back to the pews to sit chastened and still for the benediction. Perhaps he had no sense of humor, or perhaps he had one too refined for intimidation. In my version of the story, he would have a case of whiskey in his van, right behind the gallon containers of shellac and buried notebooks of his own sketches. Sometimes, he would read thick journals of art criticism while sitting up late in cheap hotel rooms and then get roaring drunk and curse his fate.

"What I do is wallpaper," he would complain. "Just wallpaper." But   15
the work he so despised would grow more and more famous as time passed. After his death, one of those journals would publish a careful consideration of his murals, calling him a gifted primitive. Dealers would offer little churches large sums to take down his walls and sell them as installations to collectors. Maybe some of the churches would refuse to sell, but grow uncomfortable with the secular popularity of the paintings. Still, somewhere there would be a little girl like the girl I had been, a girl who would dream of putting her hand on the cool, sweaty painting while the Son of God blinked down at her in genuine sympathy. Is it a sin, she would wonder, to put together the sacred and the absurd? I would not answer her question, of course. I would leave it, like the art, to make everyone a little nervous and unsure.

I love black-and-white photographs, and I always have. I have cut photographs out of magazines to paste in books of my own, bought albums at yard sales, and kept collections that had one or two images I wanted near me always. Those pictures tell me stories — my own and others, scary stories sometimes, but more often simply everyday stories, what happened in that place at that time to those people. The pictures I collect leave me to puzzle out what I think about it later. Sometimes, I imagine my own life as a series of snapshots taken by some omniscient artist who is just keeping track — not interfering or saying anything, just capturing the moment for me to look back at it again later. The eye of God, as expressed in a Dorothea Lange or Wright Morris.[2] This is the way it is, the photograph says, and I nod my head in appreciation. The power of art is in that nod of appreciation, though sometimes I puzzle nothing out, and the nod is more a shrug. No, I do not understand this one, but I see it. I take it in. I will think about it. If I sit with this image long enough, this

---

[1]*Flannery O'Connor:* For an example of her fiction, see page 854. — EDS.
[2]*Dorothea Lange* (1895–1965) was an American photographer known for her depictions of rural poverty. *Wright Morris* (1910–1998) was a prominent midwestern novelist also known for his photography; he often published books that combined text and photographs. — EDS.

story, I have the hope of understanding something I did not understand before. And that, too, is art, the best art.

My friend Jackie used to call my photographs sentimental. I had pinned them up all over the walls of my apartment, and Jackie liked a few of them but thought on the whole they were better suited to being tucked away in a book. On her walls, she had half a dozen bright prints in bottle-cap metal frames, most of them bought from Puerto Rican artists at street sales when she was working as a taxi driver and always had cash in her pockets. I thought her prints garish and told her so when she made fun of my photographs.

"They remind me of my mama," she told me. I had only seen one photograph of Jackie's mother, a wide-faced Italian matron from Queens with thick, black eyebrows and a perpetual squint.

"She liked bright colors?" I asked.

Jackie nodded. "And stuff you could buy on the street. She was al-   20
ways buying stuff off tables on the street, saying that was the best stuff. Best prices. Cheap skirts that lost their dye after a couple of washes, shoes with cardboard insoles, those funky little icons, weeping saints and long-faced Madonnas. She liked stuff to be really colorful. She painted all the ceilings in our apartment red and white. Red-red and white-white. Like blood on bone."

I looked up at my ceiling. The high tin ceiling was uniformly bloody when I moved in, with paint put on so thick, I could chip it off in lumps. I had climbed on stacks of boxes to paint it all cream white and pale blue.

"The Virgin's colors," Jackie told me. "You should put gold roses on the door posts."

"I'm no artist," I told her.

"I am," Jackie laughed. She took out a pencil and sketched a leafy vine above two of my framed photographs. She was good. It looked as if the frames were pinned to the vine. "I'll do it all," she said, looking at me to see if I was upset.

"Do it," I told her.   25

Jackie drew lilies and potato vines up the hall while I made tea and admired the details. Around the front door she put the Virgin's roses and curious little circles with crosses entwined in the middle. "It's beautiful," I told her.

"A blessing," she told me. "Like a bit of magic. My mama magic." Her face was so serious, I brought back a dish of salt and water, and we blessed the entrance. "Now the devil will pass you by," she promised me.

I laughed, but almost believed.

For a few months last spring I kept seeing an ad in all the magazines that showed a small child high in the air dropping toward the upraised arms of a waiting figure below. The image was grainy and distant. I could not tell if the child was laughing or crying. The copy at the bottom of the page read: "Your father always caught you."

"Look at this," I insisted the first time I saw the ad. "Will you look at   30
this?"

A friend of mine took the magazine, looked at the ad, and then up into my shocked and horrified face.

"They don't mean it that way," she said.

I looked at the ad again. They didn't mean it that way? They meant it innocently? I shuddered. It was supposed to make you feel safe, maybe make you buy insurance or something. It did not make me feel safe. I dreamed about the picture, and it was not a good dream.

I wonder how many other people see that ad the way I do. I wonder how many other people look at the constant images of happy families and make wry faces at most of them. It's as if all the illustrators have television sitcom imaginations. I do not believe in those families. I believe in the exhausted mothers, frightened children, numb and stubborn men. I believe in hard-pressed families, the child huddled in fear with his face hidden, the father and mother confronting each other with their emotions hidden, dispassionate passionate faces, and the unsettling sense of risk in the baby held close to that man's chest. These images make sense to me. They are about the world I know, the stories I tell. When they are accompanied by wry titles or copy that is slightly absurd or unexpected, I grin and know that I will puzzle it out later, sometimes a lot later.

I think that using art to provoke uncertainty is what great writing   35
and inspired images do most brilliantly. Art should provoke more questions than answers and, most of all, should make us think about what we rarely want to think about at all. Sitting down to write a novel, I refuse to consider if my work is seen as difficult or inappropriate or provocative. I choose my subjects to force the congregation to look at what they try so stubbornly to pretend is not happening at all, deliberately combining the horribly serious with the absurd or funny, because I know that if I am to reach my audience I must first seduce their attention and draw them into the world of my imagination. I know that I have to lay out my stories, my difficult people, each story layering on top of the one before it with care and craft, until my audience sees something they had not expected. Frailty—stubborn, human frailty—that is what I work to showcase. The wonder and astonishment of the despised and ignored, that is what I hope to find in art and in the books I write—my secret self, my vulnerable and embattled heart, the child I was and the woman I have become, not Jesus at the Jordan but a woman with only her stubborn memories and passionate convictions to redeem her.

"You write such mean stories," a friend once told me. "Raped girls, brutal fathers, faithless mothers, and untrustworthy lovers—meaner than the world really is, don't you think?"

I just looked at her. Meaner than the world really is? No. I thought about showing her the box under my desk where I keep my clippings. Newspaper stories and black-and-white images—the woman who drowned her children, the man who shot first the babies in her arms and then his wife, the teenage boys who led the three-year-old away along the train track, the homeless family recovering from frostbite with their eyes glazed and indifferent while the doctor scowled over their shoulders. The world is meaner than we admit, larger and more astonishing. Strength appears in the most desperate figures, tragedy when we have no reason to expect it. Yes, some of my stories are fearful, but not as cruel as what I see in the world. I believe in redemption, just as I believe in the nobility of the despised, the dignity of the outcast, the intrinsic honor among misfits, pariahs, and queers. Artists—those of us who stand outside the city gates and look back at a society that tries to ignore us—we have an angle of vision denied to whole sectors of the sheltered and indifferent population within. It is our curse and our prize, and for everyone who will tell us our work is mean or fearful or unreal, there is another who will embrace us and say with tears in their eyes how wonderful it is to finally feel as if someone else has seen their truth and shown it in some part as it should be known.

"My story," they say. "You told my story. That is me, mine, us." And it is.

We are not the same. We are a nation of nations. Regions, social classes, economic circumstances, ethical systems, and political convictions—all separate us even as we pretend they do not. Art makes that plain. Those of us who have read the same books, eaten the same kinds of food as children, watched the same television shows, and listened to the same music, we believe ourselves part of the same nation—and we are continually startled to discover that our versions of reality do not match. If we were more the same, would we not see the same thing when we look at a painting? But what is it we see when we look at a work of art? What is it we fear will be revealed? The artist waits for us to say. It does not matter that each of us sees something slightly different. Most of us, confronted with the artist's creation, hesitate, stammer, or politely deflect the question of what it means to us. Even those of us from the same background, same region, same general economic and social class, come to "art" uncertain, suspicious, not wanting to embarrass ourselves by revealing what the work provokes in us. In fact, sometimes we are not sure. If we were to reveal what we see in each painting, sculpture, installation, or little book, we would run the risk of exposing our secret selves, what we know and what we fear we do not know, and of course incidentally what it is we truly fear. Art is the Rorschach test for all of us, the projective hologram of our secret lives. Our emotional and intellectual lives are laid bare. Do you like hologram roses? Big, bold, brightly painted canvases? Representational art? Little boxes with tiny figures posed precisely? Do you dare say what it is you like?

For those of us born into poor and working-class families, these are   40
not simple questions. For those of us who grew up hiding what our home
life was like, the fear is omnipresent — particularly when that home life
was scarred by physical and emotional violence. We know if we say anything about what we see in a work of art we will reveal more about ourselves than the artist. What do you see in this painting, in that one? I see a
little girl, terrified, holding together the torn remnants of her clothing. I
see a child, looking back at the mother for help and finding none. I see a
mother, bruised and exhausted, unable to look up for help, unable to believe anyone in the world will help her. I see a man with his fists raised,
hating himself but making those fists tighter all the time. I see a little girl,
uncertain and angry, looking down at her own body with hatred and contempt. I see that all the time, even when no one else sees what I see. I
know I am not supposed to mention what it is I see. Perhaps no one else
is seeing what I see. If they are, I am pretty sure there is some cryptic
covenant that requires that we will not say what we see. Even when looking at an image of a terrified child, we know that to mention why that
child might be so frightened would be a breach of social etiquette. The
world requires that such children not be mentioned, even when so many
of us are looking directly at her.

There seems to be a tacit agreement about what it is not polite to
mention, what it is not appropriate to portray. For some of us, that polite
behavior is set so deeply we truly do not see what seems outside that tacit
agreement. We have lost the imagination for what our real lives have
been or continue to be, what happens when we go home and close the
door on the outside world. Since so many would like us to never mention
anything unsettling anyway, the impulse to be quiet, the impulse to deny
and pretend, becomes very strong. But the artist knows all about that impulse. The artist knows that it must be resisted. Art is not meant to be polite, secret, coded, or timid. Art is the sphere in which that impulse to hide
and lie is the most dangerous. In art, transgression is holy, revelation a
sacrament, and pursuing one's personal truth the only sure validation.

Does it matter if our art is canonized, if we become rich and successful, lauded and admired? Does it make any difference if our pictures become popular, our books made into movies, our creations win awards?
What if we are the ones who wind up going from town to town with our
notebooks, our dusty boxes of prints or Xeroxed sheets of music, never
acknowledged, never paid for our work? As artists, we know how easily
we could become a Flannery O'Connor character, reading those journals
of criticism and burying our faces in our hands, staggering under the
weight of what we see that the world does not. As artists, we also know
that neither worldly praise not critical disdain will ultimately prove the
worth of our work.

Some nights I think of that sweating, girlish Jesus above my mother's
determined features, those hands outspread to cast benediction on those
giggling uncertain boys, me in the congregation struck full of wonder and
love and helpless laughter. If no one else ever wept at that image, I did. I

wished the artist who painted that image knew how powerfully it touched me, that after all these years his art still lives inside me. If I can wish for anything for my art, that is what I want—to live in some child forever—and if I can demand anything of other artists, it is that they attempt as much.

The Reader's Presence

1. You may have heard the old writing advice to "say what you're going to say, say it, and then say what you've said." How does the structure of Allison's argument diverge from this rule? How does the essay begin? Where is her argument first explicitly stated? How is it developed?

2. What is the relation between the painting of Jesus and Allison's argument? Does the scene of her mother's baptism serve merely as an interesting anecdote, or can it be tied in some way to the questions she raises regarding the function and value of art? In your opinion, do Allison's personal stories contribute to or detract from her central argument? In what ways?

3. Pay close attention to Allison's ideas about the role of the artist (see especially paragraphs 35, 37, and 41). "Artists—those of us who stand outside the city gates and look back at a society that tries to ignore us—we have an angle of vision denied to whole sectors of the sheltered and indifferent population within" (paragraph 37). Does Allison see the artist's position in society as privileged? Why or why not? Compare her sense of artistic mission ("trangression," "revelation," "personal truth," paragraph 41) to that of Gloria Anzaldúa in "How to Tame a Wild Tongue" (page 299). What is the place of beauty in each writer's understanding of art?

84

James Baldwin
Equal in Paris

James Baldwin (1924–1987) grew up in New York City but moved to France in 1948 because he felt personally and artistically stifled as a gay African American man in the United States. His first novels, Go Tell It on the Mountain *(1956) and* Giovanni's Room *(1956), and his first collection of essays,* Notes of a Native

Son (1955), were published during Baldwin's first stay abroad, where he was able to write critically about race, sexual identity, and social injustice in America. In 1949, an impoverished, twenty-five-year-old Baldwin, who was trying to launch his career as a writer, experienced a part of France that most tourists never see: its prison system. In "Equal in Paris," a chance encounter with another American sets off a sequence of events that, in Baldwin's terms, has all the elements of a "comic-opera." The essay originally appeared in Commentary *in 1955 and was collected in Baldwin's* Notes of a Native Son.

After nearly a decade in France, he returned to New York and became a national figure in the civil rights movement. Henry Louis Gates Jr. eulogized Baldwin as the conscience of the nation, for he "educated an entire generation of Americans about the civil-rights struggle and the sensibility of Afro-Americans as we faced and conquered the final barriers in our long quest for civil rights." Baldwin continues to educate through his essays, collected in The Price of the Ticket: Collected Nonfiction *(1985).*

When asked if he approached the writing of fiction and nonfiction in different ways, Baldwin responded, "Every form is different, no one is easier than another. . . . An essay is not simpler, though it may seem so. An essay is clearly an argument. The writer's point of view in an essay is always absolutely clear. The writer is trying to make the readers see something, trying to convince them of something. In a novel or a play you're trying to show them something. The risks, in any case, are exactly the same."

On the nineteenth of December, in 1949, when I had been living in Paris for a little over a year, I was arrested as a receiver of stolen goods and spent eight days in prison. My arrest came about through an American tourist whom I had met twice in New York, who had been given my name and address and told to look me up. I was then living on the top floor of a ludicrously grim hotel on the rue du Bac, one of those enormous dark, cold, and hideous establishments in which Paris abounds that seem to breathe forth, in their airless, humid, stone-cold halls, the weak light, scurrying chambermaids, and creaking stairs, an odor of gentility long long dead. The place was run by an ancient Frenchman dressed in an elegant black suit which was green with age, who cannot properly be described as bewildered or even as being in a state of shock, since he had really stopped breathing around 1910. There he sat at his desk in the weirdly lit, fantastically furnished lobby, day in and day out, greeting each one of his extremely impoverished and *louche*[1] lodgers with a stately inclination of the head that he had no doubt been taught in some impossibly remote time was the proper way for a *propriétaire*[2] to greet his guests. If it had not been for his daughter, an extremely hardheaded *tricoteuse*[3]—the inclination of *her* head was chilling and abrupt, like the downbeat of an ax—the hotel would certainly have gone bankrupt long before. It was said that this old man had not gone farther than the door of his hotel for

---

[1]*louche:* Shady; suspicious (French). — EDS.
[2]*propriétaire:* Hotel proprietor (French). — EDS.
[3]*tricoteuse:* A knitter; the sense here is of a knitting machine (French). — EDS.

thirty years, which was not at all difficult to believe. He looked as though the daylight would have killed him.

I did not, of course, spend much of my time in this palace. The moment I began living in French hotels I understood the necessity of French cafés. This made it rather difficult to look me up, for as soon as I was out of bed I hopefully took notebook and fountain pen off to the upstairs room of the Flore, where I consumed rather a lot of coffee and, as evening approached, rather a lot of alcohol, but did not get much writing done. But one night, in one of the cafés of Saint Germain des Prés, I was discovered by this New Yorker and only because we found ourselves in Paris we immediately established the illusion that we had been fast friends back in the good old U.S.A. This illusion proved itself too thin to support an evening's drinking, but by that time it was too late. I had committed myself to getting him a room in my hotel the next day, for he was living in one of the nest of hotels near the Gare Saint Lazare, where, he said, the *propriétaire* was a thief, his wife a repressed nymphomaniac, the chambermaids "pigs," and the rent a crime. Americans are always talking this way about the French and so it did not occur to me that he meant what he said or that he would take into his own hands the means of avenging himself on the French Republic. It did not occur to me, either, that the means which he *did* take could possibly have brought about such dire results, results which were not less dire for being also comic-opera.

It came as the last of a series of disasters which had perhaps been made inevitably by the fact that I had come to Paris originally with a little over forty dollars in my pockets, nothing in the bank, and no grasp whatever of the French language. It developed, shortly, that I had no grasp of the French character either. I considered the French an ancient, intelligent, and cultured race, which indeed they are. I did not know, however, that ancient glories imply, at least in the middle of the present century, present fatigue and, quite probably, paranoia; that there is a limit to the role of the intelligence in human affairs; and that no people come into possession of a culture without having paid a heavy price for it. This price they cannot, of course, assess, but it is revealed in their personalities and in their institutions. The very word "institutions," from my side of the ocean, where, it seemed to me, we suffered so cruelly from the lack of them, had a pleasant ring, as of safety and order and common sense; one had to come into contact with these institutions in order to understand that they were also outmoded, exasperating, completely impersonal, and very often cruel. Similarly, the personality which had seemed from a distance to be so large and free had to be dealt with before one could see that, if it was large, it was also inflexible and, for the foreigner, full of strange, high, dusty rooms which could not be inhabited. One had, in short, to come into contact with an alien culture in order to understand that a culture was not a community basket-weaving project, nor yet an act of God; was something neither desirable nor undesirable in itself, being inevitable, being nothing more or less than the recorded and visible effects on a body of people of the vicissitudes with which they had been forced to deal. And their great men are revealed as simply another of these vicissitudes, even if, quite against their will, the brief battle of their great men with them has left them richer.

When my American friend left his hotel to move to mine, he took with him, out of pique, a bedsheet belonging to the hotel and put it in his suitcase. When he arrived at my hotel I borrowed the sheet, since my own were filthy and the chambermaid showed no sign of bringing me any clean ones, and put it on my bed. The sheets belonging to *my* hotel I put out in the hall, congratulating myself on having thus forced on the attention of the Grand Hôtel du Bac the unpleasant state of its linen. Thereafter, since, as it turned out, we kept very different hours—I got up at noon, when, as I gathered by meeting him on the stairs one day, he was only just getting in—my new-found friend and I saw very little of each other.

On the evening of the nineteenth I was sitting thinking melancholy   5
thoughts about Christmas and staring at the walls of my room. I imagine that I sold something or that someone had sent me a Christmas present, for I remember that I had a little money. In those days in Paris, though I floated, so to speak, on a sea of acquaintances, I knew almost no one. Many people were eliminated from my orbit by virtue of the fact that they had more money than I did, which placed me, in my own eyes, in the humiliating role of a free-loader; and other people were eliminated by virtue of the fact that they enjoyed their poverty, shrilly insisting that this wretched round of hotel rooms, bad food, humiliating concierges, and unpaid bills was the Great Adventure. It couldn't, however, for me, end soon enough, this Great Adventure; there was a real question in my mind as to which would end soonest, the Great Adventure or me. This meant, however, that there were many evenings when I sat in my room, knowing that I couldn't work there, and not knowing what to do, or whom to see. On this particular evening I went down and knocked on the American's door.

There were two Frenchmen standing in the room, who immediately introduced themselves to me as policemen; which did not worry me. I had got used to policemen in Paris bobbing up at the most improbable times and places, asking to see one's *carte d'identité*.[4] These policemen, however, showed very little interest in my papers. They were looking for something else. I could not imagine what this would be and, since I knew I certainly didn't have it, I scarcely followed the conversation they were having with my friend. I gathered that they were looking for some kind of gangster and since I wasn't a gangster and knew that gangsterism was not, insofar as he had one, my friend's style, I was sure that the two policemen would presently bow and say *Merci, messieurs,* and leave. For by this time, I remember very clearly, I was dying to have a drink and go to dinner.

I did not have a drink or go to dinner for many days after this, and when I did my outraged stomach promptly heaved everything up again.

---

[4]*carte d'identité:* Identity papers or I.D. (French). — EDS.

For now one of the policemen began to exhibit the most vivid interest in me and asked, very politely, if he might see my room. To which we mounted, making, I remember, the most civilized small talk on the way and even continuing it for some moments after we were in the room in which there was certainly nothing to be seen but the familiar poverty and disorder of that precarious group of people of whatever age, race, country, calling, or intention which Paris recognizes as *les étudiants*[5] and sometimes, more ironically and precisely, as *les nonconformistes*. Then he moved to my bed, and in a terrible flash, not quite an instant before he lifted the bedspread, I understood what he was looking for. We looked at the sheet, on which I read, for the first time, lettered in the most brilliant scarlet I have ever seen, the name of the hotel from which it had been stolen. It was the first time the word *stolen* entered my mind. I had certainly seen the hotel monogram the day I put the sheet on the bed. It had simply meant nothing to me. In New York I had seen hotel monograms on everything from silver to soap and towels. Taking things from New York hotels was practically a custom, though, I suddenly realized, I had never known anyone to take a *sheet*. Sadly, and without a word to me, the inspector took the sheet from the bed, folded it under his arm, and we started back downstairs. I understood that I was under arrest.

And so we passed through the lobby, four of us, two of us very clearly criminal, under the eyes of the old man and his daughter, neither of whom said a word, into the streets where a light rain was falling. And I asked, in French, "But is this very serious?"

For I was thinking, it is, after all, only a sheet, not even new.

"No," said one of them. "It's not serious."   10

"It's nothing at all," said the other.

I took this to mean that we would receive a reprimand at the police station and be allowed to go to dinner. Later on I concluded that they were not being hypocritical or even trying to comfort us. They meant exactly what they said. It was only that they spoke another language.

In Paris everything is very slow. Also, when dealing with the bureaucracy, the man you are talking to is never the man you have to see. The man you have to see has just gone off to Belgium, or is busy with his family, or has just discovered that he is a cuckold; he will be in next Tuesday at three o'clock, or sometime in the course of the afternoon, or possibly tomorrow, or, possibly, in the next five minutes. But if he is coming in the next five minutes he will be far too busy to be able to see you today. So that I suppose I was not really astonished to learn at the commissariat that nothing could possibly be done about us before The Man arrived in the morning. But no, we could not go off and have dinner and come back in the morning. Of course he knew that we *would* come back — that was not the question. Indeed, there was no question: we would simply have to stay there for the night. We were placed in a cell which rather resembled a

[5]*les étudiants:* College students (French). — EDS.

chicken coop. It was now about seven in the evening and I relinquished the thought of dinner and began to think of lunch.

I discouraged the chatter of my New York friend and this left me alone with my thoughts. I was beginning to be frightened and I bent all my energies, therefore, to keeping my panic under control. I began to realize that I was in a country I knew nothing about, in the hands of a people I did not understand at all. In a similar situation in New York I would have had some idea of what to do because I would have had some idea of what to expect. I am not speaking now of legality which, like most of the poor, I had never for an instant trusted, but of the temperament of the people with whom I had to deal. I had become very accomplished in New York at guessing and, therefore, to a limited extent manipulating to my advantage the reactions of the white world. But this was not New York. None of my old weapons could serve me here. I did not know what they saw when they looked at me. I knew very well what Americans saw when they looked at me and this allowed me to play endless and sinister variations on the role which they had assigned me; since I knew that it was, for them, of the utmost importance that they never be confronted with what, in their own personalities, made this role so necessary and gratifying to them, I knew that they could never call my hand or, indeed, afford to know what I was doing; so that I moved into every crucial situation with the deadly and rather desperate advantages of bitterly accumulated perception, of pride and contempt. This is an awful sword and shield to carry through the world, and the discovery that, in the game I was playing, I did myself a violence of which the world, at its most ferocious, would scarcely have been capable, was what had driven me out of New York. It was a strange feeling, in this situation, after a year in Paris, to discover that my weapons would never again serve me as they had.

It was quite clear to me that the Frenchmen in whose hands I found   15
myself were no better or worse than their American counterparts. Certainly their uniforms frightened me quite as much, and their impersonality, and the threat, always very keenly felt by the poor, of violence, was as present in that commissariat as it had ever been for me in any police station. And I had seen, for example, what Paris policemen could do to Arab peanut vendors. The only difference here was that I did not understand these people, did not know what techniques their cruelty took, did not know enough about their personalities to see danger coming, to ward it off, did not know on what ground to meet it. That evening in the commissariat I was not a despised black man. They would simply have laughed at me if I had behaved like one. For them, I was an American. And here it was they who had the advantage, for that word, *Américain*, gave them some idea, far from inaccurate, of what to expect from me. In order to corroborate none of their ironical expectations I said nothing and did nothing—which was not the way any Frenchman, white or black, would have reacted. The question thrusting up from the bottom of my mind was not *what* I was, but *who*. And this question, since a *what*

can get by with skill but a *who* demands resources, was my first real intimation of what humility must mean.

In the morning it was still raining. Between nine and ten o'clock a black Citroën took us off to the Ile de la Cité, to the great, gray Préfecture. I realize now that the questions I put to the various policemen who escorted us were always answered in such a way as to corroborate what I wished to hear. This was not out of politeness, but simply out of indifference—or, possibly, an ironical pity—since each of the policemen knew very well that nothing would speed or halt the machine in which I had become entangled. They knew I did not know this and there was certainly no point in their telling me. In one way or another I would certainly come out at the other side—for they also knew that being found with a stolen bedsheet in one's possession was not a crime punishable by the guillotine. (They had the advantage over me there, too, for there were certainly moments later on when I was not so sure.) If I did *not* come out at the other side—well, that was just too bad. So, to my question, put while we were in the Citroën—"Will it be over today?"—I received a *"Oui, bien sûr."*[6] He was not lying. As it turned out, the *procès-verbal*[7] was over that day. Trying to be realistic, I dismissed, in the Citroën, all thoughts of lunch and pushed my mind ahead to dinner.

At the Préfecture we were first placed in a tiny cell, in which it was almost impossible either to sit or to lie down. After a couple of hours of this we were taken down to an office, where, for the first time, I encountered the owner of the bedsheet and where the *procès-verbal* took place. This was simply an interrogation, quite chillingly clipped and efficient (so that there was, shortly, no doubt in one's own mind that one *should* be treated as a criminal), which was recorded by a secretary. When it was over, this report was given to us to sign. One had, of course, no choice but to sign it, even though my mastery of written French was very far from certain. We were being held, according to the law in France, incommunicado, and all my angry demands to be allowed to speak to my embassy or to see a lawyer met with a stony *"Oui, oui. Plus tard."*[8] The *procès-verbal* over, we were taken back to the cell, before which, shortly, passed the owner of the bedsheet. He said he hoped we had slept well, gave a vindictive wink, and disappeared.

By this time there was only one thing clear: that we had no way of controlling the sequence of events and could not possibly guess what this sequence would be. It seemed to me, since what I regarded as the high point—the *procès-verbal*—had been passed and since the hotel-keeper was once again in possession of his sheet, that we might reasonably expect to be released from police custody in a matter of hours. We had been detained now for what would soon be twenty-four hours, during which

---

[6]*Oui, bien sûr:* "Yes, of course." (French). — EDS.
[7]*procès-verbal:* Statement (French). — EDS.
[8]*Oui, oui. Plus tard:* "Yes, yes. Later." (French). — EDS.

time I had learned only that the official charge against me was *receleur*.[9]
My mental shifting, between lunch and dinner, to say nothing of the
physical lack of either of these delights, was beginning to make me dizzy.
The steady chatter of my friend from New York, who was determined to
keep my spirits up, made me feel murderous; I was praying that some
power would release us from this freezing pile of stone before the impulse
became the act. And I was beginning to wonder what was happening in
that beautiful city, Paris, which lived outside these walls. I wondered how
long it would take before anyone casually asked, "But where's Jimmy?
He hasn't been around"—and realized, knowing the people I knew, that
it would take several days.

Quite late in the afternoon we were taken from our cells; handcuffed,
each to a separate officer; led through a maze of steps and corridors to the
top of the building; fingerprinted; photographed. As in movies I had seen,
I was placed against a wall, facing an old-fashioned camera, behind which
stood one of the most completely cruel and indifferent faces I had ever
seen, while someone next to me and, therefore, just outside my line of vision, read off in a voice from which all human feeling, even feeling of the
most base description, had long since fled, what must be called my public
characteristics—which, at that time and in that place, seemed anything
but that. He might have been roaring to the hostile world secrets which I
could barely, in the privacy of midnight, utter to myself. But he was only
reading off my height, my features, my approximate weight, my color—
that color which, in the United States, had often, odd as it may sound,
been my salvation—the color of my hair, my age, my nationality. A light
then flashed, the photographer and I staring at each other as though there
was murder in our hearts, and then it was over. Handcuffed again, I was
led downstairs to the bottom of the building, into a great enclosed shed in
which had been gathered the very scrapings off the Paris streets. Old, old
men, so ruined and old that life in them seemed really to prove the miracle of the quickening power of the Holy Ghost—for clearly their life was
no longer their affair, it was no longer even their burden, they were simply the clay which had once been touched. And men not so old, with faces
the color of lead and the consistency of oatmeal, eyes that made me think
of stale *café-au-lait* spiked with arsenic, bodies which could take in food
and water—any food and water—and pass it out, but which could not
do anything more, except possibly, at midnight, along the riverbank
where rats scurried, rape. And young men, harder and crueler than the
Paris stones, older by far than I, their chronological senior by some five to
seven years. And North Africans, old and young, who seemed the only
living people in this place because they yet retained the grace to be bewildered. But they were not bewildered by being in this shed: they were simply bewildered because they were no longer in North Africa. There was a
great hole in the center of this shed which was the common toilet. Near it,

---

[9]*receleur:* Receiver of stolen goods (French). — EDS.

though it was impossible to get very far from it, stood an old man with white hair, eating a piece of camembert. It was at this point, probably, that thought, for me, stopped, that physiology, if one may say so, took over. I found myself incapable of saying a word, not because I was afraid I would cry but because I was afraid I would vomit. And I did not think any longer of the city of Paris but my mind flew back to that home from which I had fled. I was sure that I would never see it any more. And it must have seemed to me that my flight from home was the cruelest trick I had ever played on myself, since it had led me here, down to a lower point than any I could ever in my life have imagined—lower, far, than anything I had seen in that Harlem which I had so hated and so loved, the escape from which had soon become the greatest direction of my life. After we had been here an hour or so a functionary came and opened the door and called out our names. And I was sure that *this* was my release. But I was handcuffed again and led out of the Préfecture into the streets—it was dark now, it was still raining—and before the steps of the Préfecture stood the great police wagon, doors facing me, wide open. The handcuffs were taken off, I entered the wagon, which was peculiarly constructed. It was divided by a narrow aisle, and on each side of the aisle was a series of narrow doors. These doors opened on a narrow cubicle, beyond which was a door which opened onto another narrow cubicle: three or four cubicles, each private, with a locking door. I was placed in one of them; I remember there was a small vent just above my head which let in a little light. The door of my cubicle was locked from the outside. I had no idea where this wagon was taking me and, as it began to move, I began to cry. I suppose I cried all the way to prison, the prison called Fresnes, which is twelve kilometers outside of Paris.

For reasons I have no way at all of understanding, prisoners whose last initial is A, B, or C are always sent to Fresnes; everybody else is sent to a prison called, rather cynically it seems to me, La Santé. I will, obviously, never be allowed to enter La Santé, but I was told by people who certainly seemed to know that it was infinitely more unbearable than Fresnes. This arouses in me, until today, a positive storm of curiosity concerning what I promptly began to think of as The Other Prison. My colleague in crime, occurring lower in the alphabet, had been sent there and I confess that the minute he was gone I missed him. I missed him because he was not French and because he was the only person in the world who knew that the story I told was true.

For, once locked in, divested of shoelaces, belt, watch, money, papers, nailfile, in a freezing cell in which both the window and the toilet were broken, with six other adventurers, the story I told of *l'affaire du drap de lit*[10] elicited only the wildest amusement or the most suspicious disbelief. Among the people who shared my cell the first three days no one, it is true, had been arrested for anything much more serious—or, at

20

[10]*l'affaire du . . . lit:* The affair of the bedsheet (French). — EDS.

least, not serious in my eyes. I remember that there was a boy who had stolen a knitted sweater from a *monoprix*,[11] who would probably, it was agreed, receive a six-month sentence. There was an older man there who had been arrested for some kind of petty larceny. There were two North Africans, vivid, brutish, and beautiful, who alternated between gaiety and fury, not at the fact of their arrest but at the state of the cell. None poured as much emotional energy into the fact of their arrest as I did; they took it, as I would have liked to take it, as simply another unlucky happening in a very dirty world. For, though I had grown accustomed to thinking of myself as looking upon the world with a hard, penetrating eye, the truth was that they were far more realistic about the world than I, and more nearly right about it. The gap between us, which only a gesture I made could have bridged, grew steadily, during thirty-six hours, wider. I could not make any gesture simply because they frightened me. I was unable to accept my imprisonment as a fact, even as a temporary fact. I could not, even for a moment, accept my present companions as *my* companions. And they, of course, felt this and put it down, with perfect justice, to the fact that I was an American.

There was nothing to do all day long. It appeared that we would one day come to trial but no one knew when. We were awakened at seven-thirty by a rapping on what I believe is called the Judas, that small opening in the door of the cell which allows the guards to survey the prisoners. At this rapping we rose from the floor—we slept on straw pallets and each of us was covered with one thin blanket—and moved to the door of the cell. We peered through the opening into the center of the prison, which was, as I remember, three tiers high, all gray stone and gunmetal steel, precisely that prison I had seen in movies, except that, in the movies, I had not known that it was cold in prison. I had not known that when one's shoelaces and belt have been removed one is, in the strangest way, demoralized. The necessity of shuffling and the necessity of holding up one's trousers with one hand turn one into a rag doll. And the movies fail, of course, to give one any idea of what prison food is like. Along the corridor, at seven-thirty, came three men, each pushing before him a great garbage can, mounted on wheels. In the garbage can of the first was the bread—this was passed to one through the small opening in the door. In the can of the second was the coffee. In the can of the third was what was always called *la soupe,* a pallid paste of potatoes which had certainly been bubbling on the back of the prison stove long before that first, so momentous revolution. Naturally, it was cold by this time and, starving as I was, I could not eat it. I drank the coffee—which was not coffee—because it was hot, and spent the rest of the day, huddled in my blanket, munching on the bread. It was not the French bread one bought in bakeries. In the evening the same procession returned. At ten-thirty the lights went out. I had a recurring dream, each night, a nightmare which always

---

[11]*monoprix:* Inexpensive department store (French). — EDS.

involved my mother's fried chicken. At the moment I was about to eat it came the rapping at the door. Silence is really all I remember of those first three days, silence and the color gray.

I am not sure now whether it was on the third or the fourth day that I was taken to trial for the first time. The days had nothing, obviously, to distinguish them from one another. I remember that I was very much aware that Christmas Day was approaching and I wondered if I was really going to spend Christmas Day in prison. And I remember that the first trial came the day before Christmas Eve.

On the morning of the first trial I was awakened by hearing my name called. I was told, hanging in a kind of void between my mother's fried chicken and the cold prison floor, "*Vous préparez. Vous êtes extrait*"[12]— which simply terrified me, since I did not know what interpretation to put on the word "*extrait*," and since my cellmates had been amusing themselves with me by telling terrible stories about the inefficiency of French prisons, an inefficiency so extreme that it had often happened that someone who was supposed to be taken out and tried found himself on the wrong line and was guillotined instead. The best way of putting my reaction to this is to say that, though I knew they were teasing me, it was simply not possible for me to totally *disbelieve* them. As far as I was concerned, once in the hands of the law in France, anything could happen. I shuffled along with the others who were *extrait* to the center of the prison, trying, rather, to linger in the office, which seemed the only warm spot in the whole world, and found myself again in that dreadful wagon, and was carried again to the Ile de la Cité, this time to the Palais de Justice. The entire day, except for ten minutes, was spent in one of the cells, first waiting to be tried, then waiting to be taken back to prison.

For I was *not* tried that day. By and by I was handcuffed and led through the halls, upstairs to the courtroom where I found my New York friend. We were placed together, both stage-whisperingly certain that this was the end of our ordeal. Nevertheless, while I waited for our case to be called, my eyes searched the courtroom, looking for a face I knew, hoping, anyway, that there was someone there who knew *me*, who would carry to someone outside the news that I was in trouble. But there was no one I knew there and I had had time to realize that there was probably only one man in Paris who could help me, an American patent attorney for whom I had worked as an office boy. He could have helped me because he had a quite solid position and some prestige and would have testified that, while working for him, I had handled large sums of money regularly, which made it rather unlikely that I would stoop to trafficking in bedsheets. However, he was somewhere in Paris, probably at this very moment enjoying a snack and a glass of wine and as far as the possibility of reaching him was concerned, he might as well have been on Mars. I tried to watch the proceedings and to make my mind a blank. But the

25

---

[12]*Vous préparez . . . extrait:* "Get ready. You are taken out." (French). — EDS.

proceedings were not reassuring. The boy, for example, who had stolen the sweater *did* receive a six-month sentence. It seemed to me that all the sentences meted out that day were excessive; though, again, it seemed that all the people who were sentenced that day had made, or clearly were going to make, crime their career. This seemed to be the opinion of the judge, who scarcely looked at the prisoners or listened to them; it seemed to be the opinion of the prisoners, who scarcely bothered to speak in their own behalf; it seemed to be the opinion of the lawyers, state lawyers for the most part, who were defending them. The great impulse of the courtroom seemed to be to put these people where they could not be seen—and not because they were offended at the crimes, unless, indeed, they were offended that the crimes were so petty, but because they did not wish to know that their society could be counted on to produce, probably in greater and greater numbers, a whole body of people for whom crime was the only possible career. Any society inevitably produces its criminals, but a society at once rigid and unstable can do nothing whatever to alleviate the poverty of its lowest members, cannot present to the hypothetical young man at the crucial moment that so-well-advertised right path. And the fact, perhaps, that the French are the earth's least sentimental people and must also be numbered among the most proud aggravates the plight of their lowest, youngest, and unluckiest members, for it means that the idea of rehabilitation is scarcely real to them. I confess that this attitude on their part raises in me sentiments of exasperation, admiration, and despair, revealing as it does, in both the best and the worst sense, their renowned and spectacular hard-headedness.

Finally our case was called and we rose. We gave our names. At the point that it developed that we were American the proceedings ceased, a hurried consultation took place between the judge and what I took to be several lawyers. Someone called out for an interpreter. The arresting officer had forgotten to mention our nationalities and there was, therefore, no interpreter in the court. Even if our French had been better than it was we would not have been allowed to stand trial without an interpreter. Before I clearly understood what was happening, I was handcuffed again and led out of the courtroom. The trial had been set back for the twenty-seventh of December.

I have sometimes wondered if I would *ever* have got out of prison if it had not been for the older man who had been arrested for the mysterious petty larceny. He was acquitted that day and when he returned to the cell—for he could not be released until morning—he found me sitting numbly on the floor, having just been prevented, by the sight of a man, all blood, being carried back to *his* cell on a stretcher, from seizing the bars and screaming until they let me out. The sight of the man on the stretcher proved, however, that screaming would not do much for me. The petty-larceny man went around asking if he could do anything in the world outside for those he was leaving behind. When he came to me I, at first, responded, "No, nothing"—for I suppose I had by now retreated into the attitude, the earliest I remember, that of my father, which was simply (since I had lost his God) that nothing could help me. And I suppose I will remember with gratitude until I die the fact that the man now insisted: *"Mais, êtes-vous sûr?"*[13] Then it swept over me that he was going *outside* and he instantly became my first contact since the Lord alone knew how long with the outside world. At the same time, I remember, I did not really believe that he would help me. There was no reason why he should. But I gave him the phone number of my attorney friend and my own name.

So, in the middle of the next day, Christmas Eve, I shuffled downstairs again, to meet my visitor. He looked extremely well fed and sane and clean. He told me I had nothing to worry about any more. Only not even he could do anything to make the mill of justice grind any faster. He would, however, send me a lawyer of his acquaintance who would defend me on the 27th, and he would himself, along with several other people, appear as a character witness. He gave me a package of Lucky Strikes (which the turnkey took from me on the way upstairs) and said that, though it was doubtful that there would be any celebration in the prison, he would see to it that I got a fine Christmas dinner when I got out. And this, somehow, seemed very funny. I remember being astonished at the discovery that I was actually laughing. I was, too, I imagine, also rather disappointed that my hair had not turned white, that my face was clearly not going to bear any marks of tragedy, disappointed at bottom, no doubt, to realize, facing him in that room, that far worse things had happened to most people and that, indeed, to paraphrase my mother, if this was the worst thing that ever happened to me I could consider myself among the luckiest people ever to be born. He injected—my visitor—into my solitary nightmare common sense, the world, and the hint of blacker things to come.

The next day, Christmas, unable to endure my cell, and feeling that, after all, the day demanded a gesture, I asked to be allowed to go to Mass, hoping to hear some music. But I found myself, for a freezing hour and a half, locked in exactly the same kind of cubicle as in the wagon which had first brought me to prison, peering through a slot placed at the level of the eye at an old Frenchman, hatted, overcoated, muffled, and gloved, preaching in this language which I did not understand, to this row of wooden boxes, the story of Jesus Christ's love for men.

The next day, the twenty-sixth, I spent learning a peculiar kind of game, played with matchsticks, with my cellmates. For, since I no longer felt that I would stay in this cell forever, I was beginning to be able to make peace with it for a time. On the twenty-seventh I went again to trial and, as had been predicted, the case against us was dismissed. The story of the *drap de lit,*[14] finally told, caused great merriment in the courtroom, whereupon my friend decided that the French were "great." I was chilled

30

---

[13]*Mais . . . sûr?:* "But, are you certain?" (French). — EDS.
[14]*drap de lit:* Bedsheet (French). — EDS.

by their merriment, even though it was meant to warm me. It could only remind me of the laughter I had often heard at home, laughter which I had sometimes deliberately elicited. This laughter is the laughter of those who consider themselves to be at a safe remove from all the wretched, for whom the pain of the living is not real. I had heard it so often in my native land that I had resolved to find a place where I would never hear it any more. In some deep, black, stony, and liberating way, my life, in my own eyes, began during that first year in Paris, when it was borne in on me that this laughter is universal and never can be stilled.

The Reader's Presence

1. What does Baldwin learn from his experiences in Paris? What does he learn about equality? What does he discover about the French? Explain what you think equality means to Baldwin, and why it serves as the basis of his title.

2. Consider Baldwin's final paragraph. What is the laughter he refers to? Who is laughing at whom? What comic elements has Baldwin introduced throughout the essay?

3. Compare Baldwin's essay to another essay about a writer living in a foreign culture, such as Richard Wright's "I Choose Exile" (page 288) or George Orwell's "Shooting an Elephant" (page 198). What similarities in style and subject do you find? How does each writer encounter cultural differences that he must try to understand? What similarities and differences do you see between the ways the writers handle the cultural dissonance they find in a strange place? Compare what these writers ultimately learn from their encounters with another culture.

THE WRITER AT WORK

James Baldwin on Black English

In the following piece, Baldwin takes up a subject that is periodically scrutinized by the American mass media: Is Black English a language and, if so, what kind of language is it? The debate over the legitimacy of Ebonics flared in the 1990s when, for example, some Oakland, California, schools recognized as a second language a codified version of Black English. Ebonics has since been abandoned by most of even its most zealous supporters. Whatever its current status in the eyes of the dominant society, Black English is an indisputable fact of everyday life for many Americans. When Baldwin writes that blacks have "endured and transcended" American racism by means of language, he echoes William Faulkner's belief that our compulsion to talk is what will save the human race.

*Since Baldwin wrote this piece over twenty years ago, the language he so ar-
dently defends as necessary to African American strength in the face of "brutal
necessity" (that is, in defense against racism) has entered the mainstream through
the spread of hip-hop culture. What might Baldwin say about white speakers of
Black English? Are they simply another example of the appropriation of subcul-
tural forms by the dominant culture, a means of containing or defusing resistance? The "rules of the language are dictated by what the language must convey," Baldwin writes. Who is using Black English today? And for what purposes?*

St. Paul de Vence, France—The argument concerning the use, or the
status, or the reality, of black English is rooted in American history and
has absolutely nothing to do with the question the argument supposes itself to be posing. The argument has nothing to do with language itself but
with the *role* of language. Language, incontestably, reveals the speaker.
Language, also, far more dubiously, is meant to define the other—and, in
this case, the other is refusing to be defined by a language that has never
been able to recognize him.

People evolve a language in order to describe and thus control their
circumstances, or in order not to be submerged by a reality that they cannot articulate. (And, if they cannot articulate it, they *are* submerged.) A
Frenchman living in Paris speaks a subtly and crucially different language
from that of the man living in Marseilles; neither sounds very much like a
man living in Quebec; and they would all have great difficulty in appre-
hending what the man from Guadeloupe, or Martinique, is saying, to say
nothing of the man from Senegal—although the "common" language of
all these areas is French. But each has paid, and is paying, a different
price for this "common" language, in which, as it turns out, they are not
saying, and cannot be saying, the same things: They each have very different realities to articulate, or control.

What joins all languages, and all men, is the necessity to confront life,
in order, not inconceivably, to outwit death: The price for this is the acceptance, and achievement, of one's temporal identity. So that, for example, though it is not taught in the schools (and this has the potential of becoming a political issue) the south of France still clings to its ancient and
musical Provençal, which resists being described as a "dialect." And
much of the tension in the Basque countries, and in Wales, is due to the
Basque and Welsh determination not to allow their languages to be destroyed. This determination also feeds the flames in Ireland for among the
many indignities the Irish have been forced to undergo at English hands is
the English contempt for their language.

It goes without saying, then, that language is also a political instrument, means, and proof of power. It is the most vivid and crucial key to
identity: It reveals the private identity, and connects one with, or divorces
one from, the larger, public, or communal identity. There have been, and
are, times, and places, when to speak a certain language could be dangerous, even fatal. Or, one may speak the same language, but in such a way
that one's antecedents are revealed, or (one hopes) hidden. This is true in

France, and is absolutely true in England: The range (and reign) of accents on that damp little island make England coherent for the English and totally incomprehensible for everyone else. To open your mouth in England is (if I may use black English) to "put your business in the street": You have confessed your parents, your youth, your school, your salary, your self-esteem, and, alas, your future.

Now, I do not know what white Americans would sound like if there had never been any black people in the United States, but they would not sound the way they sound. *Jazz,* for example, is a very specific sexual term, as in *jazz me, baby,* but white people purified it into the Jazz Age. *Sock it to me,* which means, roughly, the same thing, has been adopted by Nathaniel Hawthorne's descendants with no qualms or hesitations at all, along with *let it all hang out* and *right on! Beat to his socks* which was once the black's most total and despairing image of poverty, was transformed into a thing called the Beat Generation, which phenomenon was, largely, composed of *uptight,* middle-class white people, imitating poverty, trying to *get down,* to get *with it,* doing their *thing,* doing their despairing best to be *funky,* which we, the blacks, never dreamed of doing—we *were* funky, baby, like *funky* was going out of style.

Now, no one can eat his cake, and have it, too, and it is late in the day to attempt to penalize black people for having created a language that permits the nation its only glimpse of reality, a language without which the nation would be even more *whipped* than it is.

I say that the present skirmish is rooted in American history, and it is. Black English is the creation of the black diaspora. Blacks came to the United States chained to each other, but from different tribes: Neither could speak the other's language. If two black people, at that bitter hour of the world's history, had been able to speak to each other, the institution of chattel slavery could never have lasted as long as it did. Subsequently, the slave was given, under the eye, and the gun, of his master, Congo Square, and the Bible—or in other words, and under these conditions, the slave began the formation of the black church, and it is within this unprecedented tabernacle that black English began to be formed. This was not, merely, as in the European example, the adoption of a foreign tongue, but an alchemy that transformed ancient elements into a new language: *A language comes into existence by means of brutal necessity, and the rules of the language are dictated by what the language must convey.*

There was a moment, in time, and in this place, when my brother, or my mother, or my father, or my sister, had to convey to me, for example, the danger in which I was standing from the white man standing just behind me, and to convey this with a speed, and in a language, that the white man could not possibly understand, and that, indeed, he cannot understand, until today. He cannot afford to understand it. This understanding would reveal to him too much about himself, and smash that mirror before which he has been frozen for so long.

Now, if this passion, this skill, this (to quote Toni Morrison) "sheer intelligence," this incredible music, the mighty achievement of having brought a people utterly unknown to, or despised by "history" — to have brought this people to their present, troubled, troubling, and unassailable and unanswerable place — if this absolutely unprecedented journey does not indicate that black English is a language, I am curious to know what definition of language is to be trusted.

A people at the center of the Western world, and in the midst of so   10 hostile a population, has not endured and transcended by means of what is patronizingly called a "dialect." We, the blacks, are in trouble, certainly, but we are not doomed, and we are not inarticulate because we are not compelled to defend a morality that we know to be a lie.

The brutal truth is that the bulk of white people in America never had any interest in educating black people, except as this could serve white purposes. It is not the black child's language that is in question, it is not his language that is despised: It is his experience. A child cannot be taught by anyone who despises him, and a child cannot afford to be fooled. A child cannot be taught by anyone whose demand, essentially, is that the child repudiate his experience, and all that gives him sustenance, and enter a limbo in which he will no longer be black, and in which he knows that he can never become white. Black people have lost too many black children that way.

And, after all, finally, in a country with standards so untrustworthy, a country that makes heroes of so many criminal mediocrities, a country unable to face why so many of the nonwhite are in prison, or on the needle, or standing, futureless, in the streets — it may very well be that both the child, and his elder, have concluded that they have nothing whatever to learn from the people of a country that has managed to learn so little.

85

Harold Bloom

In Praise of the Greats

Harold Bloom, born in 1930, grew up in New York City and was educated at Cornell and Yale. He has taught at Yale since 1955, and also — since 1988 — at New York University. A prolific writer, Bloom has published over twenty works of literary and religious criticism as well as hundreds of essays, articles, and prefaces. He first gained attention with a series of groundbreaking studies of English Romantic poets, including Shelley's Mythmaking *(1959),* The Visionary Company

(1961), and Blake's Apocalypse *(1963). He then wrote the influential* Yeats *(1970) and* The Ringers in the Tower *(1971), tracing the continuity between Romantic and modernist poets. He followed these volumes with two books establishing a unique reading of poetic tradition:* The Anxiety of Influence *(1973) and* A Map of Misreading *(1975). Bloom is often classed as a literary theorist, but he maintains that literary writing manifests a heroism that cannot be reduced to dogmatic conceptions. His* Western Canon *(1994) attacks Marxist, feminist, and multiculturalist critics for reducing literature to politics. More recently, Bloom authored* Shakespeare and the Invention of the Human *(1999) and* How to Read and Why *(2000), which includes the following essay, "In Praise of the Greats."* Genius: A Mosaic of One Hundred Exemplary Creative Minds *appeared in 2002.*

Bloom has said, "What vanishes in most ideological ways of reading and most politicizing of literature is irony, individual irony . . . By irony I mean that aspect of literature that, rhetorically speaking, is a matter of saying one thing while meaning something quite different . . . If you lose the ability to handle irony, you lose the ability to read."

There is no single way to read well, though there is a prime reason why we should read. Information is endlessly available to us; where shall wisdom be found? If you are fortunate, you encounter a particular teacher who can help, yet finally you are alone, going on without further mediation. Reading well is one of the great pleasures that solitude can afford you, because it is, at least in my experience, the most healing of pleasures. It returns you to otherness, whether in yourself or in friends, or in those who may become friends. Imaginative literature is otherness, and as such alleviates loneliness. We read not only because we cannot know enough people, but because friendship is so vulnerable, so likely to diminish or disappear, overcome by space, time, imperfect sympathies, and all the sorrows of familial and passional life.

I try to teach how to read and why, proceeding by a multitude of examples and instances: poems short and long; stories and novels and plays. I do not consider my selections an exclusive list of what to read, but rather a sampling of works that best illustrate why to read. Reading well is best pursued as an implicit discipline; finally there is no method but yourself, when your self has been fully molded. Literary criticism, as I have learned to understand it, ought to be experiential and pragmatic, rather than theoretical.

The critics who are my masters—Dr. Samuel Johnson and William Hazlitt in particular—practice their art in order to make what is implicit in a book finely explicit. In what follows, whether I deal with a lyric by A. E. Housman or a play by Oscar Wilde, with a story by Jorge Luis Borges or a novel by Marcel Proust, my principal concern will be with ways of noticing and realizing what can and should be made explicit. Because, for me, the question of how to read always leads on to the motives and uses of reading, I shall never separate the "how" and they "why" of this book's subject. Virginia Woolf, in "How Should One Read a Book?"—the final brief essay in *The Common Reader, Second Series*—

charmingly warns: "The only advice, indeed, that one person can give another about reading is to take no advice. . . ." But she then adds many codicils to the reader's enjoyment of freedom, culminating in the grand question "Where are we to begin?" To get the deepest and widest pleasures of reading, "[w]e must not squander our powers, helplessly and ignorantly. . . ." So it seems that, until we become wholly ourselves, some advice about reading may be helpful, even perhaps essential.

Woolf herself had found that advice in Walter Pater (whose sister had tutored her), and also in Dr. Johnson and in the Romantic critics Thomas De Quincey and William Hazlitt, of whom she wonderfully remarked: "He is one of those rare critics who have thought so much that they can dispense with reading." Woolf thought incessantly, and never would stop reading. She herself had a good deal of advice to give to other readers, and I have happily taken it throughout this book. Her best advice is to remind us that "there is always a demon in us who whispers, 'I hate, I love,' and we cannot silence him." I cannot silence my demon, but in this work anyway I will listen to him only when he whispers, "I love," as I intend no polemic here, but only to teach reading.

It matters, if individuals are to retain any capacity to form their own judgments and opinions, that they continue to read for themselves. How they read, well or badly, and what they read, cannot depend wholly upon themselves, but why they read must be for and in their own interest. You can read merely to pass the time, or you can read with an overt urgency, but eventually you will read against the clock. Bible readers, those who search the Bible for themselves, perhaps exemplify the urgency more plainly than readers of Shakespeare, yet the quest is the same. One of the uses of reading is to prepare ourselves for change, and the final change alas is universal.

I turn to reading as a solitary praxis, rather than as an educational   5
enterprise. The way we read now, when we are alone with ourselves, retains considerable continuity with the past, however it is performed in the academies. My ideal reader (and lifelong hero), Dr. Samuel Johnson, knew and expressed both the power and the limitation of incessant reading. Like every other activity of the mind, it must satisfy Johnson's prime concern, which is with "what comes near to ourselves, what we can turn to use." Sir Francis Bacon, who provided some of the ideas that Johnson put to use, famously gave the advice: "Read not to contradict and confute, nor to believe and take for granted, nor to find talk and discourse, but to weigh and consider." I add to Bacon and Johnson a third sage of reading, Emerson, fierce enemy of history and of all historicisms, who remarked that the best books "impress us with the conviction, that one nature wrote and the same reads." Let me fuse Bacon, Johnson, and Emerson into a formula of how to read: Find what comes near to you that can be put to the use of weighing and considering, and that addresses you as though you share the one nature, free of time's tyranny. Pragmatically

that means, first find Shakespeare, and let him find you. If *King Lear* is fully to find you, then weigh and consider the nature it shares with you; its closeness to yourself. I do not intend this as an idealism, but as a pragmatism. Putting the tragedy to use as a complaint against patriarchy is to forsake your own prime interests, particularly as a young woman, which sounds rather more ironical than it is. Shakespeare, more than Sophocles, is the inescapable authority upon intergenerational conflict, and more than anyone else, upon the differences between women and men. Be open to a full reading of *King Lear*, and you will understand better the origins of what you judge to be patriarchy.

Ultimately we read—as Bacon, Johnson, and Emerson agree—in order to strengthen the self, and to learn its authentic interests. We experience such augmentations as pleasure, which may be why aesthetic values have always been deprecated by social moralists, from Plato through our current campus Puritans. The pleasures of reading indeed are selfish rather than social. You cannot directly improve anyone else's life by reading better or more deeply. I remain skeptical of the traditional social hope that care for others may be stimulated by the growth of individual imagination, and I am wary of any arguments whatsoever that connect the pleasures of solitary reading to the public good.

The sorrow of professional reading is that you recapture only rarely the pleasure of reading you knew in youth, when books were a Hazlittian gusto. The way we read now partly depends upon our distance, inner or outer, from the universities, where reading is scarcely taught as a pleasure, in any of the deeper senses of the aesthetics of pleasure. Opening yourself to a direct confrontation with Shakespeare at his strongest, as in *King Lear*, is never an easy pleasure, whether in youth or in age, and yet not to read *King Lear* fully (which means without ideological expectations) is to be cognitively as well as aesthetically defrauded. A childhood largely spent watching television yields to an adolescence with a computer, and the university receives a student unlikely to welcome the suggestion that we must endure our going hence even as our going hither: Ripeness is all. Reading falls apart, and much of the self scatters with it. All this is past lamenting, and will not be remedied by any vows or programs. What is to be done can only be performed by some version of elitism, and that is now unacceptable, for reasons both good and bad. There are still solitary readers, young and old, everywhere, even in the universities. If there is a function of criticism at the present time, it must be to address itself to the solitary reader, who reads for herself, and not for the interests that supposedly transcend the self.

Value, in literature as in life, has much to do with the idiosyncratic, with the excess by which meaning gets started. It is not accidental that historicists—critics who believe all of us to be overdetermined by societal history—should also regard literary characters as marks upon a page, and nothing more. *Hamlet* is not even a case history if our thoughts are not at all our own. I come then to the first principle if we are to restore the way we read now, a principle I appropriate from Dr. Johnson: Clear your mind of cant. Your dictionary will tell you that cant in this sense is speech overflowing with pious platitudes, the peculiar vocabulary of a sect or coven. Since the universities have empowered such covens as "gender and sexuality" and "multiculturalism," Johnson's admonition thus becomes "Clear your mind of academic cant." A university culture where the appreciation of Victorian women's underwear replaces the appreciation of Charles Dickens and Robert Browning sounds like the outrageousness of a new Nathanael West, but is merely the norm. A side product of such "cultural poetics" is that there can be no new Nathanael West, for how could such an academic culture sustain parody? The poems of our climate have been replaced by the body stockings of our culture. Our new Materialists tell us that they have recovered the body for historicism, and assert that they work in the name of the Reality Principle. The life of the mind must yield to the death of the body, yet that hardly requires the cheerleading of an academic sect.

Clear your mind of cant leads on to the second principle of restoring reading: Do not attempt to improve your neighbor or your neighborhood by what or how you read. Self-improvement is a large enough project for your mind and spirit: There are no ethics of reading. The mind should be kept at home until its primal ignorance has been purged; premature excursions into activism have their charm, but are time-consuming, and for reading there will never be enough time. Historicizing, whether of past or present, is a kind of idolatry, an obsessive worship of things in time. Read therefore by the inner light that John Milton celebrated and that Emerson took as a principle of reading, which can be our third: A scholar is a candle which the love and desire of all men will light. Wallace Stevens, perhaps forgetting his source, wrote marvelous variations upon that metaphor, but the original Emersonian phrasing makes for a clearer statement of the third principle of reading. You need not fear that the freedom of your development as a reader is selfish, because if you become an authentic reader, then the response to your labors will confirm you as an illumination to others. I ponder the letters that I receive from strangers these last seven or eight years, and generally I am too moved to reply. Their pathos, for me, is that all too often they testify to a yearning for canonical literary study that universities disdain to fulfill. Emerson said that society cannot do without cultivated men and women, and prophetically he added: "The people, and not the college, is the writer's home." He meant strong writers, representative men and women, who represented themselves, and not constituencies, since his politics were those of the spirit.

The largely forgotten function of a university education is caught forever in Emerson's address "The American Scholar," when he says of the scholar's duties: "They may all be comprised in self-trust." I take from Emerson also my fourth principle of reading: One must be an inventor to

10

read well. "Creative reading" in Emerson's sense I once named as "misreading," a word that persuaded opponents that I suffered from a voluntary dyslexia. The ruin or blank that they see when they look at a poem is in their own eye. Self-trust is not an endowment, but is the Second Birth of the mind, which cannot come without years of deep reading. There are no absolute standards for the aesthetic. If you wish to maintain that Shakespeare's ascendancy was a product of colonialism, then who will bother to confute you? Shakespeare after four centuries is more pervasive than ever he was before; they will perform him in outer space, and on other worlds, if those worlds are reached. He is not a conspiracy of Western culture; he contains every principle of reading. . . . Borges attributed this universalism to Shakespeare's apparent selflessness, but that quality is a large metaphor for Shakespeare's difference, which finally is cognitive power as such. We read, frequently if unknowingly, in quest of a mind more original than our own.

Since ideology, particularly in its shallower versions, is peculiarly destructive of the capacity to apprehend and appreciate irony, I suggest that the recovery of the ironic might be our fifth principle for the restoration of reading. Think of the endless irony of Hamlet, who when he says one thing almost invariably means another, frequently indeed the opposite of what he says. But with this principle, I am close to despair, since you can no more teach someone to be ironic than you can instruct them to become solitary. And yet the loss of irony is the death of reading, and of what had been civilized in our natures.

> I stepped from Plank to Plank
> A slow and cautious way
> The Stars about my Head I felt
> About my Feet the Sea.
>
> I knew not but the next
> Would be my final inch —
> This gave me that precarious Gait
> Some call Experience.

Women and men can walk differently, but unless we are regimented we all tend to walk somewhat individually. Dickinson, master of the precarious Sublime, can hardly be apprehended if we are dead to her ironies. She is walking the only path available, "from Plank to Plank," but her slow caution ironically juxtaposes with a titanism in which she feels "The Stars about my Head," though her feet very nearly are in the sea. Not knowing whether the next step will be her "final inch" gives her "that precarious Gait" she will not name, except to tell us that "some" call it Experience. She had read Emerson's essay "Experience," a culmination much in the way "Of Experience" was for his master Montaigne, and her irony is an amiable response to Emerson's opening: "Where do we find ourselves?

In a series of which we do not know the extremes, and believe that it has none." The extreme, for Dickinson, is the not knowing whether the next step is the final inch. "If any of us knew what we were doing, or where we are going, then when we think we best know!" Emerson's further reverie differs from Dickinson's in temperament, or as she words it, in gait. "All things swim and glitter," in Emerson's realm of experience, and his genial irony is very different from her irony of precariousness. Yet neither is an ideologue, and they live still in the rival power of their ironies.

At the end of the path of lost irony is a final inch, beyond which literary value will be irrecoverable. Irony is only a metaphor, and the irony of one literary age can rarely be the irony of another, yet without the renaissance of an ironic sense more than what we once called imaginative literature will be lost. Thomas Mann, most ironic of this century's great writers, seems to be lost already. New biographies of him appear, and are reviewed almost always on the basis of his homoeroticism, as though he can be saved for our interest only if he can be certified as gay, and so gain a place in our curriculum. That is akin to studying Shakespeare mostly for his apparent bisexuality, but the vagaries of our current counter-Puritanism seem limitless. Shakespeare's ironies, as we would expect, are the most comprehensive and dialectical in all of Western literature, and yet they do not always mediate his characters' passions for us, so vast and intense is their emotional range. Shakespeare therefore will survive our era; we will lose his ironies, and hold on to the rest of him. But in Thomas Mann every emotion, narrative or dramatic, is mediated by an ironic aestheticism; to teach *Death in Venice* or *Disorder and Early Sorrow* to most current undergraduates, even the gifted, is nearly impossible. When authors are destroyed by history, we rightly call their work period pieces, but when they are made unavailable through historicized ideology, I think that we encounter a different phenomenon.

Irony demands a certain attention span, and the ability to sustain antithetical ideas, even when they collide with one another. Strip irony away from reading and it loses at once all discipline and all surprise. Find now what comes near to you, that can be used for weighing and considering, and it very likely will be irony, even if many of your teachers will not know what it is, or where it is to be found. Irony will clear your mind of the cant of the ideologues, and help you to blaze forth as the scholar of one candle.

Going on 70, one doesn't want to read badly any more than live badly, since time will not relent. I don't know that we owe God or nature a death, but nature will collect anyway, and we certainly owe mediocrity nothing, whatever collectively it purports to advance or at least represent.   15

Because my ideal reader, for half a century, had been Dr. Samuel Johnson, I turn next to my favorite passage in his *Preface to Shakespeare:*

> This therefore is the praise of Shakespeare, that his drama is the
> mirror of life; that he who has mazed his imagination, in following the

phantoms which other writers raise up before him, may here be cured of his delirious ecstasies, by reading human sentiments in human language; by scenes from which a hermit may estimate the transactions of the world, and a confessor predict the progress of the passions.

To read human sentiments in human language you must be able to read humanly, with all of you. You are more than an ideology, whatever your convictions, and Shakespeare speaks to as much of you as you can bring to him. That is to say: Shakespeare reads you more fully than you can read him, even after you have cleared your mind of cant. No writer before or since Shakespeare has had anything like his control of perspectivism, which outleaps any contextualizations we impose upon the plays. Johnson, admirably perceiving this, urges us to allow Shakespeare to cure us of our "delirious ecstasies." Let me extend Johnson by also urging us to recognize the phantoms that the deep reading of Shakespeare will exorcise. One such phantom is the Death of the Author; another is the assertion that the self is a fiction; yet another is the opinion that literary and dramatic characters are so many marks upon a page. A fourth phantom, and the most pernicious, is that language does the thinking for us.

Still, my love for Johnson, and for reading, turns me at last away from polemic, and towards a celebration of the many solitary readers I keep encountering, whether in the classroom or in messages I receive. We read Shakespeare, Dante, Chaucer, Cervantes, Dickens, Proust, and all their peers because they more than enlarge life. Pragmatically, they have become the Blessing, in its true Yahwistic sense of "more life into a time without boundaries." We read deeply for varied reasons, most of them familiar: that we cannot know enough people profoundly enough; that we need to know ourselves better; that we require knowledge, not just of self and others, but of the way things are. Yet the strongest, most authentic motive for deep reading of the now much-abused traditional canon is the search for a difficult pleasure. I am not exactly an erotics-of-reading purveyor, and a pleasurable difficulty seems to me a plausible definition of the Sublime, but a higher pleasure remains the reader's quest. There is a reader's Sublime, and it seems the only secular transcendence we can ever attain, except for the even more precarious transcendence we call "falling in love." I urge you to find what truly comes near to you, that can be used for weighing and for considering. Read deeply, not to believe, not to accept, not to contradict, but to learn to share in that one nature that writes and reads.

The Reader's Presence

1. According to Bloom, what are the characteristics that a reader has or should have? He mentions Dr. Samuel Johnson as his ideal reader. What makes Dr. Johnson an ideal reader? What would Bloom's worst reader be like? What characteristics would he or

she have? How would he or she read in ways that Bloom wouldn't like? Think about how you read. How might Bloom characterize you as a reader?

2. Bloom suggests that the job of a critical reader is "to make what is implicit in a book finely explicit" (paragraph 3). What does he mean by this? What, more specifically, does it mean to make something "finely" explicit? How many implicit points can you identify in Bloom's essay? How would you go about making them explicit (finely or not)? What do you make, for example, of such aphoristic pronouncements as "Ultimately we read . . . in order to strengthen the self" (paragraph 7) or "[w]e read . . . in quest of a mind more original than our own" (paragraph 11)?

3. Of all the essays that you have read in this collection, which was most filled with irony? You might consider Sallie Tisdale's "Mean Cuisine" (page 552). Reread whichever essay you select and pay attention to how you read ironic passages. What in your reading experience leads you to agree or disagree with Bloom's claim: "Irony will clear your mind of the cant of the ideologues, and help you to blaze forth as the scholar of one candle" (paragraph 15)? Choose one of these ironic passages and rewrite it, eliminating the irony (that is, make explicit what was implicit). Then compare and contrast your reading experience of the two passages. How accurate is Bloom's claim that a passage stripped of irony "loses at once all discipline and all surprise" (paragraph 15)? What would you add about how the loss of irony affects writing?

86

Edwidge Danticat

We Are Ugly, but We Are Here

Edwidge Danticat was born in Port-au-Prince, Haiti, in 1969 and was raised to the age of twelve by her aunt, finally joining her family in Brooklyn, New York, in 1981. She earned a B.A. from Barnard College and an M.F.A. from Brown University in 1993, and one year later published her reworked M.F.A. thesis, the critically acclaimed Breath, Eyes, Memory *(1994). She followed this novel with a collection of short stories about the Haitian experience,* Krik? Krak! *(1995) and another novel,* The Farming of Bones *(1998), which is set on the Caribbean island of Hispaniola in 1937, when hostilities between Haiti and the Dominican Republic exploded into a bloody massacre.*

Danticat, who is regarded as one of the best young authors in the United States, has won a Pushcart Short Story Prize and, in 1995, was a finalist for the National Book Award. She confesses to drawing her subject material from her native country's "rich landscape of memory." Her writing is often praised for its lushness and its appeal to the senses, but also deals honestly with poverty, violence, and the political history of Haiti. Recently, Danticat edited The Butterfly's Way: Voices from the Haitian Dyaspora *(2001). "We Are Ugly, but We Are Here" was originally published in the* Caribbean Writer *in 1996.*

One of the first people murdered on our land was a queen. Her name was Anacaona and she was an Arawak Indian. She was a poet, dancer, and even a painter. She ruled over the western part of an island so lush and green that the Arawaks called it Ayiti—land on high. When the Spaniards came from across the seas to look for gold, Anacaona was one of their first victims. She was raped and killed and her village pillaged. Anacaona's land is now the poorest country in the Western hemisphere, a place of continuous political unrest. Thus, for some, it is easy to forget that this land was the first Black Republic, home to the first people of African descent to uproot slavery and create an independent nation in 1804.

I was born under Haiti's dictatorial Duvalier regime. When I was four, my parents left Haiti to seek a better life in the United States. I must admit that their motives were more economic than political. But as anyone who knows Haiti will tell you, economics and politics are very intrinsically related in Haiti. Who is in power determines to a great extent whether or not people will eat.

I am twenty-six years old now and have spent more than half of my life in the United States. My most vivid memories of Haiti involve incidents that once represented the general situation there. In Haiti, there are a lot of "blackouts," sudden power failures. At those times, you can't read or study or watch TV, so you sit around a candle and listen to stories from the elders in the house. My grandmother was an old country woman who always felt displaced in the city of Port-au-Prince—where we lived—and had nothing but her patched-up quilts and her stories to console her. She was the one who told me about Anacaona. I used to share a room with her. I was in the room when she died. She was over a hundred years old. She died with her eyes wide open and I was the one who closed her eyes. I still miss the countless mystical stories that she told us. However, I accepted her death very easily because during my childhood death was always around us.

As a little girl, I attended more than my share of funerals. My uncle and legal guardian was a Baptist minister and his family was expected to attend every funeral he presided over. I went to all the funerals he presided over. I went to all the funerals in the same white lace dress. Perhaps it was because I attended so many funerals that I have such a strong feeling that death is not the end, that the people we bury are going off to live somewhere else. But at the same time, they will always be hovering around to watch over us and guide us through our journeys.

When I was eight, my uncle's brother-in-law went on a long journey to 5
cut cane in the Dominican Republic. He came back, deathly ill. I remember
his wife twirling feathers inside his nostrils and rubbing black pepper on
his upper lip to make him sneeze. She strongly believed that if he sneezed,
he would live. At night, it was my job to watch the sky above the house for
signs of falling stars. In Haitian folklore, when a star falls out of the sky, it
means someone will die. A star did fall out of the sky and he did die.

I have memories of Jean Claude "Baby Doc" Duvalier and his wife,
racing by in their Mercedes Benz and throwing money out of the window
to the very poor children in our neighborhood. The children nearly killed
each other trying to catch a coin or a glimpse of Baby Doc. One Christmas, they announced on the radio that the first lady, Baby Doc's wife,
was giving away free toys at the palace. My cousins and I went and were
nearly killed in the mob of children who flooded the palace lawns.

All of this now brings many questions buzzing to my head. Where
was really my place in all of this? What was my grandmother's place?
What is the legacy of the daughters of Anacaona? What do we all have
left to remember, the daughters of Haiti?

Watching the news reports, it is often hard to tell whether there are
real living and breathing women in conflict-stricken places like Haiti. The
evening news broadcasts only allow us a brief glimpse of presidential
coups, rejected boat people, and sabotaged elections. The women's stories
never manage to make the front page. However they do exist.

Today, I know women who, when the soldiers came to their homes in
Haiti, would tell their daughters to lie still and play dead. I once met a
woman whose sister was shot in her pregnant stomach because she was
wearing a t-shirt with an "anti-military image." I know a mother who
was arrested and beaten for working with a pro-democracy group. Her
body remains laced with scars where the soldiers put out their cigarettes
on her flesh. At night, this woman still smells the ashes of the cigarette
butts that were stuffed lit inside her nostrils. In the same jail cell, she
watched as paramilitary "attachés" raped her fourteen-year-old daughter
at gun point. When mother and daughter took a tiny boat to the United
States, the mother had no idea that her daughter was pregnant. Nor did
she know that the child had gotten the HIV virus from one of the paramilitary men who had raped her. The grandchild—the offspring of the
rape—was named Anacaona, after the queen, because that family of
women is from the same region where Anacaona was murdered. The infant Anacaona has a face which no longer shows any trace of indigenous
blood; however, her story echoes back to the first flow of blood on a land
that has seen much more than its share.

There is a Haitian saying which might upset the aesthetic images of 10
most women. *Nou led, Nou la,* it says. We are ugly, but we are here. This
saying makes a deeper claim for poor Haitian women than maintaining
beauty, be it skin deep or otherwise. For most of us, what is worth celebrating is the fact that we are here, that we—against all the odds—exist. To the
women who might greet each other with this saying when they meet along

the countryside, the very essence of life lies in survival. It is always worth reminding our sisters that we have lived yet another day to answer the roll call of an often painful and very difficult life. It is in this spirit that to this day a woman remembers to name her child Anacaona, a name which resonates both the splendor and agony of a past that haunts so many women.

When they were enslaved, our foremothers believed that when they died their spirits would return to Africa, most specifically to a peaceful land we call *Guinen,* where gods and goddesses live. The women who came before me were women who spoke half of one language and half another. They spoke the French and Spanish of their captors mixed in with their own African language. These women seemed to be speaking in tongues when they prayed to their old gods, the ancient African spirits. Even though they were afraid that their old deities would no longer understand them, they invented a new language—our Kreyòl—with which to describe their new surroundings, a language from which colorful phrases blossomed to fit the desperate circumstances. When these women greeted each other, they found themselves speaking in codes.

— How are we today, Sister?

— I am ugly, but I am here.

These days, many of my sisters are greeting each other away from the homelands where they first learned to speak in tongues. Many have made it to other shores, after traveling endless miles on the high seas, on rickety boats that almost took their lives. Two years ago, a mother jumped into the sea when she discovered that her baby daughter had died in her arms on a journey which they had hoped would take them to a brighter future. Mother and child, they sank to the bottom of an ocean which already holds millions of souls from the middle passage—the holocaust of the slave trade—that is our legacy. That woman's sacrifice moved then-deposed Haitian President Jean Bertrand Aristide to the brink of tears. However, like the rest of us, he took comfort in the past sacrifices that were made for all of us, so that we could be here.

The past is full of examples when our foremothers and forefathers   15 showed such deep trust in the sea that they would jump off slave ships and let the waves embrace them. They too believed that the sea was the beginning and the end of all things, the road to freedom and their entrance to *Guinen.* These women have been part of the very construction of my being ever since I was a little girl. Women like my grandmother who had taught me the story of Anacaona, the queen.

My grandmother believed that if a life is lost, then another one springs up replanted somewhere else, the next life even stronger than the last. She believed that no one really dies as long as someone remembers, someone who will acknowledge that this person had—in spite of everything—been here. We are part of an endless circle, the daughters of Anacaona. We have stumbled, but have not fallen. We are ill-favored, but we still endure. Every once in a while, we must scream this as far as the wind can carry our voices: We are ugly, but we are here! And here to stay.

The Reader's Presence

1. Danticat begins the essay with the story of Anacaona. How is Anacaona characterized? Where does this legend reappear in the essay? What relation does it bear to the essay's message of hope and strength? What sort of hope and strength does the figure of Anacaona represent?

2. Danticat describes daily existence in Haiti: funerals, folk medicine, money thrown from a car. What tones does the writer use in evoking these scenes of her homeland? What moods do those tones convey? How might the essay's title tie into these everyday scenarios?

3. The saying that Danticat puts at the center of her essay epitomizes for her a profound truth about Haitian women. What is the truth? How is writing itself linked for Danticat to survival, "the very essense of life" (paragraph 10)? How is writing linked to endurance? Whose endurance? How does Danticat's sense of art as cultural memory compare with that of Julia Alvarez in "My English" (see page 65)? How do these writers link their words to the needs of women more generally? What do they think is the relation between literature and social change?

THE WRITER AT WORK

Edwidge Danticat on Becoming a Writer

As the previous selection shows, Edwidge Danticat is a writer concerned deeply with Haitian legend and legacy. These concerns, especially when combined with her political ideals, have been the chief stimulus for her writing. In the following brief interview that appeared in Essence *magazine (May 1996), Danticat discusses how she became a writer and the motives that have inspired and guided her career. In an earlier "Writer at Work" selection, George Orwell (see page 492) outlines what he believes are the chief motives for why people write. How closely do you think Danticat's motives conform to Orwell's list? Does she offer any reasons for writing that you think should be added to Orwell's outline?*

While I was growing up, most of the writers I knew were either in hiding, missing, or dead. We were living under the brutal Duvalier dictatorship in Haiti, and silence was the law of the land. I learned that code of silence early on. It was as real as the earth beneath our feet, which was full of blood of martyrs, among them many novelists, poets, journalists, and playwrights who had criticized our government.

Writing was a dangerous activity. Perhaps it was that danger that attracted me, the feeling of doing a high-wire act between stretching the limits of silence and telling the whole truth.

Even though I now live in a country where people are not persecuted for their words, I still feel as though I am always balancing between the personal dangers of writing and the comfort and healing it offers me.

I write to communicate with my ancestors, to explore the truth of their lives and to link it to my own. When I write, I think of my fore-mothers, who as Zora Neale Hurston [see page 150] observed, were considered "the mules of the earth." I think of wives who were separated from their husbands by poverty and political violence, children who lived off other people's trash, mothers and daughters, fathers and sons, all linked by centuries of pillage and slaughter. These men and women sacrificed their own enjoyment and pleasures so that the next generation—my generation—would have a voice and a future.

I wrote my first short story when I was nine years old, on a few white   5
pages folded to form a tiny notebook. The story was about a little girl who was visited every night by a clan of women just like the overburdened and underappreciated creatures who were part of my own lineage.

When I moved to the United States at age twelve, I was temporarily floating between languages—Creole and English—so I stopped writing for a while. At fourteen I was asked by a New York City–based newspaper, *New Youth Connections,* to write about my experiences as a new immigrant. I wrote a short essay about adapting to my new life in Brooklyn, and my public writing career began.

People often ask me, "How can I become a writer?" In response I tell them the story of a Haitian painter I know. He is a very poor man who often gives up food to buy materials to paint with. He lives in a worn-out house in a slum. He never shows his paintings, and you have to fight him to buy one from him.

One day while in his studio, pleading with him to sell me a piece, I asked him, "Why create anything if you won't put it out there for the world to see and enjoy?"

To that he replied, "I don't do this for the world. I do it because I have no choice. I do it to save my life."

Now when I write, I realize that I'm writing to save my life. I write to   10
unearth all those things that scare me, to reach those places in my soul that may seem remote and dark to others. I write to preserve my sanity and to honor the sacrifices made by all those who came before me. The way I figure, it's a privilege just to be given a voice to speak and to be heard. God and the universe will take care of the rest.

87

Annie Dillard

Living Like Weasels

Annie Dillard (b. 1945) was awarded the Pulitzer Prize for general nonfiction in 1974 for Pilgrim at Tinker Creek, *which she describes (borrowing from Henry David Thoreau) as "a meteorological journal of the mind." She has also published poetry in* Tickets for a Prayer Wheel *(1975) and* Mornings Like This: Found Poems *(1995), literary theory in* Living by Fiction *(1982), essays in* Teaching a Stone to Talk *(1982) and* For the Time Being *(1999), and autobiography in* An American Childhood *(1987). Dillard published her first novel,* The Living, *in 1992, and* The Annie Dillard Reader *appeared in 1994. From 1973 to 1982 she served as contributing editor to* Harper's *magazine, and since 1979 she has taught creative writing at Wesleyan University. "Living Like Weasels" appears in her book* Teaching a Stone to Talk.

In her book The Writing Life *(1989), Dillard writes, "One of the few things I know about writing is this: spend it all, shoot it, play it, lose it, all, right away, every time. . . . Something more will arise for later, something better. These things fill from behind, like well water. Similarly, the impulse to keep to yourself what you have learned is not only shameful, it is destructive. Anything you do not give freely and abundantly becomes lost to you."*

A weasel is wild. Who knows what he thinks? He sleeps in his underground den, his tail draped over his nose. Sometimes he lives in his den for two days without leaving. Outside, he stalks rabbits, mice, muskrats, and birds, killing more bodies than he can eat warm, and often dragging the carcasses home. Obedient to instinct, he bites his prey at the neck, either splitting the jugular vein at the throat or crunching the brain at the base of the skull, and he does not let go. One naturalist refused to kill a weasel who was socketed into his hand deeply as a rattlesnake. The man could in no way pry the tiny weasel off, and he had to walk half a mile to water, the weasel dangling from his palm, and soak him off like a stubborn label.

And once, says Ernest Thompson Seton[1] — once, a man shot an eagle

---

[1]*Ernest Thompson Seton* (1860–1946): American author and naturalist who founded the wildlife organization upon which the Boy Scout movement was later patterned. — EDS.

out of the sky. He examined the eagle and found the dry skull of a weasel fixed by the jaws to his throat. The supposition is that the eagle had pounced on the weasel and the weasel swiveled and bit as instinct taught him, tooth to neck, and nearly won. I would like to have seen that eagle from the air a few weeks or months before he was shot. Was the whole weasel still attached to his feathered throat, a fur pendant? Or did the eagle eat what he could reach, gutting the living weasel with his talons before his breast, bending his beak, cleaning the beautiful airborne bones?

I have been reading about weasels because I saw one last week. I startled a weasel who startled me, and we exchanged a long glance.

Near my house in Virginia is a pond—Hollins Pond. It covers two acres of bottomland near Tinker Creek with six inches of water and six thousand lily pads. There is a fifty-five mph highway at one end of the pond, and a nesting pair of wood ducks at the other. Under every bush is a muskrat hole or a beer can. The far end is an alternating series of fields and woods, fields and woods, threaded everywhere with motorcycle tracks—in whose bare clay wild turtles lay eggs.

One evening last week at sunset, I walked to the pond and sat on a   5 downed log near the shore. I was watching the lily pads at my feet tremble and part over the thrusting path of a carp. A yellow warbler appeared to my right and flew behind me. It caught my eye; I swiveled around—and the next instant, inexplicably, I was looking down at a weasel, who was looking up at me.

Weasel! I'd never seen one wild before. He was ten inches long, thin as a curve, a muscled ribbon, brown as fruitwood, soft-furred, alert. His face was fierce, small and pointed as a lizard's; he would have made a good arrowhead. There was just a dot of chin, maybe two brown hairs' worth, and then the pure white fur began that spread down his underside. He had two black eyes I didn't see, any more than you see a window.

The weasel was stunned into stillness as he was emerging from beneath an enormous shaggy wild rose bush four feet away. I was stunned into stillness twisted backward on the tree trunk. Our eyes locked, and someone threw away the key.

Our look was as if two lovers, or deadly enemies, met unexpectedly on an overgrown path when each had been thinking of something else: a clearing blow to the gut. It was also a bright blow to the brain, or a sudden beating of brains, with all the charge and intimate grate of rubbed balloons. It emptied our lungs. It felled the forest, moved the fields, and drained the pond; the world dismantled and tumbled into that black hole of eyes. If you and I looked at each other that way, our skulls would split and drop to our shoulders. But we don't. We keep our skulls.

He disappeared. This was only last week, and already I don't remember what shattered the enchantment. I think I blinked, I think I retrieved

my brain from the weasel's brain, and tried to memorize what I was seeing, and the weasel felt the yank of separation, the careening splashdown
into real life and the urgent current of instinct. He vanished under the
wild rose. I waited motionless, my mind suddenly full of data and my
spirit with pleadings, but he didn't return.

Please do not tell me about "approach-avoidance conflicts." I tell you   10
I've been in that weasel's brain for sixty seconds, and he was in mine.
Brains are private places, muttering through unique and secret tapes —
but the weasel and I both plugged into another tape simultaneously, for a
sweet and shocking time. Can I help it if it was a blank?

What goes on in his brain the rest of the time? What does a weasel
think about? He won't say. His journal is tracks in clay, a spray of feathers, mouse blood and bone: uncollected, unconnected, loose-leaf, and
blown.

I would like to learn, or remember, how to live. I come to Hollins
Pond not so much to learn how to live as, frankly, to forget about it. That
is, I don't think I can learn from a wild animal how to live in particular —
shall I suck warm blood, hold my tail high, walk with my footprints precisely over the prints of my hands? — but I might learn something of
mindlessness, something of purity of living in the physical senses and the
dignity of living without bias or motive. The weasel lives in necessity and
we live in choice, hating necessity and dying at the last ignobly in its
talons. I would like to live as I should, as the weasel lives as he should.
And I suspect that for me the way is like the weasel's: open to time and
death painlessly, noticing everything, remembering nothing, choosing the
given with a fierce and pointed will.

I missed my chance. I should have gone for the throat. I should have
lunged for that streak of white under the weasel's chin and held on, held on
through mud and into the wild rose, held on for a dearer life. We could live
under the wild rose wild as weasels, mute and uncomprehending. I could
very calmly go wild. I could live two days in the den, curled, leaning on
mouse fur, sniffing bird bones, blinking, licking, breathing musk, my hair
tangled in the roots of grasses. Down is a good place to go, where the mind
is single. Down is out, out of your ever-loving mind and back to your careless senses. I remember muteness as a prolonged and giddy fast, where
every moment is a feast of utterance received. Time and events are merely
poured, unremarked, and ingested directly, like blood pulsed into my gut
through a jugular vein. Could two live that way? Could two live under the
wild rose, and explore by the pond, so that the smooth mind of each is as
everywhere present to the other, and as received and as unchallenged, as
falling snow?

We could, you know. We can live any way we want. People take
vows of poverty, chastity, and obedience — even of silence — by choice.

The thing is to stalk your calling in a certain skilled and supple way, to locate the most tender and live spot and plug into that pulse. This is yielding, not fighting. A weasel doesn't "attack" anything; a weasel lives as
he's meant to, yielding at every moment to the perfect freedom of single
necessity.

I think it would be well, and proper, and obedient, and pure, to   15
grasp your one necessity and not let it go, to dangle from it limp wherever it takes you. Then even death, where you're going no matter how
you live, cannot you part. Seize it and let it seize you up aloft even, till
your eyes burn out and drop; let your musky flesh fall off in shreds,
and let your very bones unhinge and scatter, loosened over fields, over
fields and woods, lightly, thoughtless, from any height at all, from as
high as eagles.

The Reader's Presence

1. Dillard begins her essay with two documented accounts of
   weasels, presumably drawn from her reading. What do these accounts have in common? How do they establish the dominant
   characteristic of weasels and the theme of the essay?
2. "Our eyes locked," Dillard says in describing her encounter with
   the weasel. Why is this an appropriate image? How does the idea
   of "locking" run through the essay? She also uses the word *wild*.
   How does she characterize the wild? Could the wild be thought of
   differently, and in what ways?
3. Dillard's understanding of wild animals suggests a high degree of
   empathy on her part. Does she give the impression that her wish
   to live like a weasel is sincere? If not, what is the significance of
   this hypothetical argument? How does Dillard's sense of what she
   can learn from animals (in paragraph 14 especially) compare to
   Linda Hogan's in "Dwellings" (page 414). Might Hogan agree
   with Dillard's distinction between animals (who live "in necessity") and humans (who live "in choice")? What might each
   writer think her writing can do for the reader?

THE WRITER AT WORK

Annie Dillard on the Writing Life

*One of the nation's outstanding nonfiction writers—who prefers to think of
herself as an "all-purpose writer" rather than an essayist—Annie Dillard is also a
prominent creative writing teacher at Wesleyan University. Dillard said recently*

that a commitment to writing is "like living any dedicated life." How is this idea reflected in the following excerpt from her book The Writing Life *(1989)? What is it that Dillard believes drives the creative artist and writer? Does her tough-minded advice apply only to artistic expression? In what other areas of human activity or expression might it also apply?*

Push it. Examine all things intensely and relentlessly. Probe and search each object in a piece of art. Do not leave it, do not course over it, as if it were understood, but instead follow it down until you see it in the mystery of its own specificity and strength. Giacometti's drawings and paintings show his bewilderment and persistence. If he had not acknowledged his bewilderment, he would not have persisted. A twentieth-century master of drawing, Rico Lebrun, taught that "the draftsman must aggress; only by persistent assault will the live image capitulate and give up its secret to an unrelenting line." Who but an artist fierce to know — not fierce to seem to know — would suppose that a live image possessed a secret? The artist is willing to give all his or her strength and life to probing with blunt instruments those same secrets no one can describe in any way but with those instruments' faint tracks.

Admire the world for never ending on you — as you would admire an opponent, without taking your eyes from him, or walking away.

One of the few things I know about writing is this: spend it all, shoot it, play it, lose it, all, right away, every time. Do not hoard what seems good for a later place in the book, or for another book; give it, give it all, give it now. The impulse to save something good for a better place later is the signal to spend it now. Something more will arise for later, something better. These things fill from behind, from beneath, like well water. Similarly, the impulse to keep to yourself what you have learned is not only shameful, it is destructive. Anything you do not give freely and abundantly becomes lost to you. You open your safe and find ashes.

After Michelangelo died, someone found in his studio a piece of paper on which he had written a note to his apprentice, in the handwriting of his old age: "Draw, Antonio, draw, Antonio, draw and do not waste time."

88

Gregg Easterbrook
The Myth of Fingerprints

Gregg Easterbrook was educated at Colorado College and Northwestern University, earning an M.A. in journalism in 1977 and quickly gaining a national reputation for his investigative reporting. Many of his articles and essays have been published by the Atlantic Monthly *where he is a contributing editor, but he has also published work in the* New York Times, *the* Washington Post, *the* Los Angeles Times, *the* New Yorker, *and the* New Republic. *His novel* This Magic Moment *appeared in 1987; and his nonfiction books include* A Moment on the Earth *(1995),* Beside Still Waters *(1996), and* Tuesday Morning Quarterback *(2001).*

False convictions have been an important story this year [2000]. The reason? Genetic testing. So far, DNA tests have shown that at least sixty-eight people imprisoned by state and federal courts—including some sent to death row (though none executed)—were innocent. As a result, criminal defense lawyers Barry Scheck and Peter Neufeld are spearheading a national drive to make the tests available to thousands of inmates. They have dubbed their campaign the Innocence Project—creating the impression that DNA tests will serve mainly to exonerate.

In fact, genetic evidence will serve mainly to lock people up. In England, where DNA fingerprinting was invented and has been in widespread use for a decade, law enforcement agencies have already used genetic evidence to solve some 70,000 cases. In the fairly near future, a standard item in the trunks of American police cruisers—perhaps even on each officer's belt—may be a DNA analyzer. As a suspect is arrested, police will quickly swipe the inside of his cheek with a cotton swab and pop the results into the scanner. Within minutes the machine will produce a stream of data describing the suspect's unique genetic structure. The data will be uploaded to state or national DNA databases to determine whether the suspect's DNA matches that of blood, sweat, semen, or similar bodily fluids found at the scene of unsolved crimes around the nation. Such a procedure will be good for public safety and make our legal system more just, but in the long run it will be exactly the opposite of an "innocence project"—it will result in a steady stream of inmates about whose guilt we can be almost entirely certain.

The most striking effect of genetic fingerprinting may be on capital punishment, with some opponents suggesting that DNA exonerations could shift the debate in their favor. They're probably mistaken. Of the four people on Texas's death row who have been granted extra DNA testing, three have been executed anyway when genetic evidence either failed to clear them or confirmed their guilt. The fourth, Ricky McGinn, last month received a stay of execution from Governor George W. Bush so he too could be extended the tests—and they reportedly help support his conviction as well. The two big laboratories that process DNA tests, Cellmark Diagnostics and Forensic Science Associates, have exonerated an estimated 40 percent of the inmates whose "post-conviction" genetic evidence they have reviewed, but the other 60 percent have had their guilt confirmed—and what's being reviewed here is the genetic evidence from those with the strongest claims of mistaken conviction.

During the next few years, post-conviction DNA testing will analyze the evidence of death-row inmates convicted before genetic fingerprinting became practical, and some innocent people will surely be freed. But over time—as the system works through the backlog of those tried before genetic analysis was common—the test's main effect will be to increase society's confidence that the man or woman being strapped to the death gurney really did commit the crime. There are two basic arguments against capital punishment: that it is inherently wrong and that it might be used against the wrong person. Death-penalty opponents have been placing more and more emphasis in recent months on the second—precisely the one genetic fingerprinting will undermine.

DNA testing is not the first anti-crime device touted as infallible. Similar claims were made for fingerprinting, also developed in England, when it was introduced at the end of the nineteenth century. But criminals learned to wear gloves or to wipe the crime scene clean. What's more, because fingerprints don't readily convert into the kind of digital data that can be rapidly accessed and shared by police—searching files for a print match is laborious and expensive—regular fingerprints may solve one particular crime but are not usually much help in matching a suspect to others.

Genetic fingerprinting, however, may really allow close-to-infallible identification. In the early '80s, English geneticist Alec Jeffreys realized that the "markers" on human chromosomes—short, structural areas of the genome—are unique from person to person, except for identical twins. Jeffreys developed a test that converts gene markers into a readout similar to a bar code, which can be easily loaded into computers. Not only has the Jeffreys test proved extremely reliable in identifying individuals, but, because it generates a digital result, computers can cross-reference one genetic fingerprint with thousands or millions of others, quickly and cheaply linking suspects to past crimes.

In recent years, DNA-fingerprinting technology has advanced to the point that, rather than requiring a good sample of blood or semen—which often meant securing warrants to jab suspects with needles—a speck of sweat or a swab from the inside of the mouth will do the trick. A test of mitochondrial DNA—which, while not unique to each individual, tells whether the DNA comes from a particular family's maternal line—can even be conducted on a strand of hair or "degraded" blood and bodily fluid samples that have been kept in storage. The cost of DNA fingerprinting has also dropped dramatically, from about $5,000 when the tests were first developed to about $100 for the newest versions, and is still falling.

Though very reliable, DNA fingerprinting won't solve every crime. It is useful mainly for what might be called intimate violent crimes, in which the perpetrator struggles with the victim and leaves behind blood, semen, or something else testable. (In the recent controversy over Bush's execution of Gary Graham, for instance, genetic evidence was moot—the victim was shot from a distance, leaving nothing of the killer's to test.) At other times, DNA in itself may neither exculpate nor damn. A hair from the murderer of Ricky McGinn's twelve-year-old stepdaughter was found on her corpse, for instance, and a DNA test is believed to show that this hair came from either McGinn or a close maternal relative of his. So, although a prosecutor could not convict McGinn on the DNA evidence alone, it could be a critical component of a larger case.

While there is currently no way to beat a DNA test, that could change, especially if criminals grow more careful with bodily fluids—say, abandoning knives for guns shot from afar. And people won't be researching biotech just to cure diseases—perhaps some enterprising chemist will invent a pill that scrambles the genetic markers in sweat and semen. But for now, at least, genetic fingerprinting is just shy of foolproof.

For that reason, it is vital that DNA testing be used to exonerate the   10
innocent. There are two main questions about genetic evidence: whether people convicted before such tests were available can reopen their cases for post-conviction DNA reviews and whether genetic fingerprinting should become a standard element of new arrests, as it already is in England.

Today only a few states, among them New York and Illinois, unambiguously grant those already imprisoned access to additional DNA testing. Courts have traditionally put strict deadlines on how long after conviction someone can introduce new evidence, in part because experience teaches that the longer ago something happened, the easier it is to find someone willing to commit perjury about it. Prosecutors traditionally fight requests for post-conviction testing, too—which is shortsighted, since a false conviction not only imprisons an innocent person but lets the real perpetrator go free. The Justice Department recommends that post-conviction testing be allowed when it could prove "actual" innocence but not permitted in cases built on claims of technicalities or reversible error.

This would be a substantial improvement, and a bill offered by Senator Patrick Leahy of Vermont would basically make it law.

Many states have compiled DNA databases and are scanning them to see if evidence from tested suspects matches evidence from unsolved cases. Virginia, which has enacted a law requiring convicted felons to submit to DNA analysis, now has about 120,000 DNA samples on record. It has already found 177 matches between suspects and genetic material at the scenes of past crimes. This June, Virginia detectives took the gene markers of a man convicted of robbing a local gas station and ran them through the state database; they matched the DNA fingerprint to blood found and stored after a horribly gruesome—and until then unsolved—1992 murder. The gas-station robber was promptly arrested for the murder as well.

Yet, for routine police work, many states actually forbid DNA fingerprinting or, nonsensically, allow it only after crimes of extreme violence— as though violent criminals should be caught but not mere thieves or carjackers. Leahy's bill, or something like it, would make genetic evidence more standard and also establish a national databank: had the accused murderer in the 1992 Virginia case robbed a gas station in another state and given his DNA sample there instead, Virginia detectives might never have found him. Fighting efforts to more effectively use genetic evidence is the American Civil Liberties Union, which is lobbying against testing laws on the grounds that chromosome material deserves privacy protection because it might reveal such things as sexual orientation.

Why a murderer has a right to sexual privacy (or any kind of privacy) isn't clear, but in any case the ACLU claim evinces confusion about what Jeffreys-style DNA tests can show. The "markers" analyzed in police tests constitute only a small, structural part of the genome. Just as a traditional fingerprint doesn't tell you anything about the suspect's personality—it just tells you about the shape of his or her finger ridges—genetic markers don't reveal anything about IQ or disease disposition or sexual orientation. Analyzing such complex traits, assuming it can be done at all, would require far more sophisticated tests, along the lines of the years-long human genome initiative. Perhaps someday there will be a quick, cheap test that gives police personal information derived from genes; that may be a reason to enact legal safeguards. . . . For now, the main reason the ACLU seems to fear DNA fingerprinting is that it works.

And that should give death-penalty opponents pause as well. Expanded use of DNA evidence will free a few death-row innocents, which would be a blessing. But the new technology will also make society much more confident that those receiving their last meals really are guilty of a mortal sin. Suspicions that the innocent are being executed will not grow stronger as DNA testing spreads—they will grow weaker. And so opponents of capital punishment will lose the offensive they have claimed in recent months. They will be forced back to their real argument, the one that technology can't undermine: the inherent wickedness of execution itself.

15

The Reader's Presence

1. Who does Easterbrook think should be subject to mandatory DNA testing? According to him, why should these people be tested? Do you agree or disagree that mandatory genetic testing can "exonerate the innocent" (paragraph 10)? Why?

2. What is Easterbrook's position on the death penalty? In what ways does his position on this issue influence his position on mandatory DNA testing? How does he relate the two issues? Who do you think would be more likely to support Easterbrook's ideas about DNA testing: an innocent person falsely accused of a crime or a guilty person who was rightly accused of a crime? Explain why.

3. Like Easterbrook, the essayist Lewis Thomas ("On Cloning a Human Being," page 784) takes on an issue of science and tries to convince the reader to share his point of view. Compare the arguments made by these two essayists. What strategies do the authors use to convince you? What evidence do they introduce and how do they present it? How do they deal with possible objections? What would you say were "fair" argumentative strategies in the respective essays? Unfair? What, in particular, do you think makes one author more effective than the other?

89

Barbara Ehrenreich

Family Values

The writer, feminist, and Socialist Party leader Barbara Ehrenreich (b. 1941) wrote some of her first articles and books on the inefficiency and inhumanity of the American health care system. In Complaints and Disorders: The Sexual Politics of Sickness *(coauthored with Deirdre English, 1973) she critiques the unjust and unequal treatment women receive in the medical system. She has written over a dozen books, among them* The Hearts of Men: American Dreams and the Flight from Commitment *(1983),* The Worst Years of Our Lives: Irreverent Notes from a Decade of Greed *(1990), from which "Family Values" is taken, and* Kipper's Game *(1993). Ehrenreich is a contributing editor at the* Progressive *and the* Nation, *and her essays also appear regularly in magazines as varied as* Radical America, Time,*

Vogue, *and the* New York Times Magazine. *Her most recent books are* The Snarling Citizen: Essays *(1995),* Blood Rites: Origins and History of the Passions of War *(1997), and* Nickel and Dimed: On (Not) Getting By in America *(2001).*

Asked whether she writes in a different voice for the alternative and the mainstream press, Ehrenreich replied, "I don't think it's really a different voice. . . . Obviously I assume more political sympathy for my views if I'm writing for Z or the Guardian *in England or the* Nation *than* Time, *but it might be the exact basic argument." She added, "An essay is like a little story, a short story, and I will obsess about what is the real point, what are the real connections, a long time before I ever put finger to keyboard."*

Sometime in the eighties, Americans had a new set of "traditional values" installed. It was part of what may someday be known as the "Reagan renovation," that finely balanced mix of cosmetic refinement and moral coarseness which brought $200,000 china to the White House dinner table and mayhem to the beleaguered peasantry of Central America. All of the new traditions had venerable sources. In economics, we borrowed from the Bourbons; in foreign policy, we drew on themes fashioned by the nomad warriors of the Eurasian steppes. In spiritual matters, we emulated the braying intolerance of our archenemies and esteemed customers, the Shi'ite fundamentalists.

A case could be made, of course, for the genuine American provenance of all these new "traditions." We've had our own robber barons, military adventures, and certainly more than our share of enterprising evangelists promoting ignorance and parochialism as a state of grace. From the vantage point of the continent's original residents, or, for example, the captive African laborers who made America a great agricultural power, our "traditional values" have always been bigotry, greed, and belligerence, buttressed by wanton appeals to a God of love.

The kindest—though from some angles most perverse—of the era's new values was "family." I could have lived with "flag" and "faith" as neotraditional values—not happily, but I could have managed—until "family" was press-ganged into joining them. Throughout the eighties, the winning political faction has been aggressively "profamily." They have invoked "the family" when they trample on the rights of those who hold actual families together, that is, women. They have used it to justify racial segregation and the formation of white-only, "Christian" schools. And they have brought it out, along with flag and faith, to silence any voices they found obscene, offensive, disturbing, or merely different.

Now, I come from a family—was raised in one, in fact—and one salubrious effect of right-wing righteousness has been to make me hew ever more firmly to the traditional values of my own progenitors. These were not people who could be accused of questionable politics or ethnicity. Nor were they members of the "liberal elite" so hated by our current conservative elite. They were blue-eyed, Scotch-Irish Democrats. They were small farmers, railroad workers, miners, shopkeepers, and migrant farm workers. In short, they fit the stereotype of "real" Americans; and their values, no matter how unpopular among today's opinion-shapers, are part of America's tradition, too. To my mind, of course, the finest part.

But let me introduce some of my family, beginning with my father, who was, along with my mother, the ultimate source of much of my radicalism, feminism, and, by the standards of the eighties, all-around bad attitude.

One of the first questions in a test of mental competency is "Who is the president of the United States?" Even deep into the indignities of Alzheimer's disease, my father always did well on that one. His blue eyes would widen incredulously, surprised at the neurologist's ignorance, then he would snort in majestic indignation, "Reagan, that dumb son of a bitch." It seemed to me a good deal—two people tested for the price of one.

Like so many of the Alzheimer's patients he came to know, my father enjoyed watching the president on television. Most programming left him impassive, but when the old codger came on, his little eyes twinkling piggishly above the disciplined sincerity of his lower face, my father would lean forward and commence a wickedly delighted cackle. I think he was prepared, more than the rest of us, to get the joke.

But the funniest thing was Ollie North. For an ailing man, my father did a fine parody. He would slap his hand over his heart, stare rigidly at attention, and pronounce, in his deepest bass rumble, "God Bless Am-ar-ica!" I'm sure he couldn't follow North's testimony—who can honestly say that they did?—but the main themes were clear enough in pantomime: the watery-eyed patriotism, the extravagant self-pity, the touching servility toward higher-ranking males. When I told my father that many people considered North a hero, a representative of the finest American traditions, he scowled and swatted at the air. Ollie North was the kind of man my father had warned me about, many years ago, when my father was the smartest man on earth.

My father had started out as a copper miner in Butte, Montana, a tiny mountain city famed for its bars, its brawls, and its distinctly unservile work force. In his view, which remained eagle-sharp even after a stint of higher education, there were only a few major categories of human beings. There were "phonies" and "decent" people, the latter group having hardly any well-known representative outside of Franklin Delano Roosevelt and John L. Lewis, the militant and brilliantly eloquent leader of the miners' union. "Phonies," however, were rampant, and, for reasons I would not understand until later in life, could be found clustered especially thick in the vicinity of money or power.

Well before he taught me other useful things, like how to distinguish fool's gold, or iron pyrite, from the real thing, he gave me some tips on the detection of phonies. For one thing, they broadened the *e* in "America" to a reverent *ahh*. They were the first to leap from their seats at the playing of "The Star Spangled Banner," the most visibly moved participants in any prayer. They espoused clean living and admired war. They preached hard work and paid for it with nickels and dimes. They loved their country above all, but despised the low-paid and usually invisible men and women who built it, fed it, and kept it running.

Two other important categories figured in my father's scheme of things. There were dumb people and smart ones: a distinction which had nothing to do with class or formal education, the dumb being simply all those who were taken in by the phonies. In his view, dumbness was rampant, and seemed to increase in proportion to the distance from Butte, where at least a certain hard-bodied irreverence leavened the atmosphere. The best prophylactic was to study and learn all you could, however you could, and, as he adjured me over and over: always ask *why*.

Finally, there were the rich and the poor. While poverty was not seen as an automatic virtue—my parents struggled mightily to escape it—wealth always carried a presumption of malfeasance. I was instructed that, in the presence of the rich, it was wise to keep one's hand on one's wallet. "Well," my father fairly growled, "how do you think they got their money in the first place?"

It was my mother who translated these lessons into practical politics. A miner's daughter herself, she offered two overarching rules for comportment: never vote Republican and never cross a union picket line. The pinnacle of her activist career came in 1964, when she attended the Democratic Convention as an alternate delegate and joined the sit-in staged by civil rights leaders and the Mississippi Freedom Democratic Party. This was not the action of a "guilt-ridden" white liberal. She classified racial prejudice along with superstition and other manifestations of backward thinking, like organized religion and overcooked vegetables. The worst thing she could find to say about a certain in-law was that he was a Republican and a churchgoer, though when I investigated these charges later in life, I was relieved to find them baseless.

My mother and father, it should be explained, were hardly rebels. The values they imparted to me had been "traditional" for at least a generation before my parents came along. According to my father, the first great steps out of mental passivity had been taken by his maternal grandparents, John Howes and Mamie O'Laughlin Howes, sometime late in the last century. You might think their rebellions small stuff, but they provided our family with its "myth of origins" and a certain standard to uphold.

I knew little about Mamie O'Laughlin except that she was raised as a   15
Catholic and ended up in western Montana sometime in the 1880s. Her father, very likely, was one of those itinerant breadwinners who went west to prospect and settled for mining. At any rate, the story begins when her father lay dying, and Mamie dutifully sent to the next town for a priest. The message came back that the priest would come only if twenty-five dollars was sent in advance. This being the West at its wildest, he may have been justified in avoiding house calls. But not in the price, which was probably more cash than my great-grandmother had

ever had at one time. It was on account of its greed that the church lost the souls of Mamie O'Laughlin and all of her descendents, right down to the present time. Futhermore, whether out of filial deference or natural intelligence, most of us have continued to avoid organized religion, secret societies, astrology, and New Age adventures in spiritualism.

As the story continues, Mamie O'Laughlin herself lay dying a few years later. She was only thirty-one, the mother of three small children, one of them an infant whose birth, apparently, led to a mortal attack of pneumonia. This time, a priest appeared unsummoned. Because she was too weak to hold the crucifix, he placed it on her chest and proceeded to administer the last rites. But Mamie was not dead yet. She pulled herself together at the last moment, flung the crucifix across the room, fell back, and died.

This was my great-grandmother. Her husband, John Howes, is a figure of folkloric proportions in my memory, well known in Butte many decades ago as a powerful miner and a lethal fighter. There are many stories about John Howes, all of which point to a profound inability to accept authority in any of its manifestations, earthly or divine. As a young miner, for example, he caught the eye of the mine owner for his skill at handling horses. The boss promoted him to an aboveground driving job, which was a great career leap for the time. Then the boss committed a foolish and arrogant error. He asked John to break in a team of horses for his wife's carriage. Most people would probably be flattered by such a request, but not in Butte, and certainly not John Howes. He declared that he was no man's servant, and quit on the spot.

Like his own wife, John Howes was an atheist or, as they more likely put it at the time, a freethinker. He, too, had been raised as a Catholic—on a farm in Ontario—and he, too, had had a dramatic, though somehow less glorious, falling out with the local clergy. According to legend, he once abused his position as an altar boy by urinating, covertly of course, in the holy water. This so enhanced his enjoyment of the Easter communion service that he could not resist letting a few friends in on the secret. Soon the priest found out and young John was defrocked as an altar boy and condemned to eternal damnation.

The full weight of this transgression hit a few years later, when he became engaged to a local woman. The priest refused to marry them and forbade the young woman to marry John anywhere, on pain of excommunication. There was nothing to do but head west for the Rockies, but not before settling his score with the church. According to legend, John's last act in Ontario was to drag the priest down from his pulpit and slug him, with his brother, presumably, holding the scandalized congregation at bay.

I have often wondered whether my great-grandfather was caught up   20
in the radicalism of Butte in its heyday: whether he was an admirer of Joe Hill, Big Bill Haywood, or Mary "Mother" Jones, all of whom passed

through Butte to agitate, and generally left with the Pinkertons on their tails. But the record is silent on this point. All I know is one last story about him, which was told often enough to have the ring of another "traditional value."

According to my father, John Howes worked on and off in the mines after his children were grown, eventually saving enough to buy a small plot of land and retire to farming. This was his dream, anyway, and a powerful one it must have been for a man who had spent so much of his life underground in the dark. So he loaded up a horse-drawn cart with all his money and belongings and headed downhill, toward Montana's eastern plains. But along the way he came to an Indian woman walking with a baby in her arms. He offered her a lift and ascertained, pretty easily, that she was destitute. So he gave her his money, all of it, turned the horse around, and went back to the mines.

Far be it from me to interpret this gesture for my great-grandfather, whom I knew only as a whiskery, sweat-smelling, but straight-backed old man in his eighties. Perhaps he was enacting his own uncompromising version of Christian virtue, even atoning a little for his youthful offenses to the faithful. But at another level I like to think that this was one more gesture of defiance of the mine owners who doled out their own dollars so grudgingly—a way of saying, perhaps, that whatever they had to offer, he didn't really need all that much.

So these were the values, sanctified by tradition and family loyalty, that I brought with me to adulthood. Through much of my growing-up, I thought of them as some mutant strain of Americanism, an idiosyncracy which seemed to grow rarer as we clambered into the middle class. Only in the sixties did I begin to learn that my family's militant skepticism and oddball rebelliousness were part of a much larger stream of American dissent. I discovered feminism, the antiwar movement, the civil rights movement. I learned that millions of Americans, before me and around me, were "smart" enough, in my father's terms, to have asked "Why?"—and, beyond that, the far more radical question, "Why not?"

These are also the values I brought into the Reagan-Bush era, when all the dangers I had been alerted to as a child were suddenly realized. The "phonies" came to power on the strength, aptly enough, of a professional actor's finest performance. The "dumb" were being led and abetted by low-life preachers and intellectuals with expensively squandered educations. And the rich, as my father predicted, used the occasion to dip deep into the wallets of the desperate and the distracted.

It's been hard times for a traditionalist of my persuasion. Long-standing moral values—usually claimed as "Judeo-Christian" but actually of much broader lineage—were summarily tossed, along with most familiar forms of logic. We were told, at one time or another, by the president or his henchpersons, that trees cause pollution, that welfare causes poverty,

25

and that a bomber designed for mass destruction may be aptly named the *Peacemaker*. "Terrorism" replaced missing children to become our national bugaboo and—simultaneously—one of our most potent instruments of foreign policy. At home, the poor and the middle class were shaken down, and their loose change funneled blithely upwards to the already overfed.

Greed, the ancient lubricant of commerce, was declared a wholesome stimulant. Nancy Reagan observed the deep recession of '82 and '83 by redecorating the White House, and continued with this Marie Antoinette theme while advising the underprivileged, the alienated, and the addicted to "say no." Young people, mindful of their elders' Wall Street capers, abandoned the study of useful things for finance banking and other occupations derived, ultimately, from three-card monte. While the poor donned plastic outerware and cardboard coverings, the affluent ran nearly naked through the streets, working off power meals of goat cheese, walnut oil, and crème fraîche.

Religion, which even I had hoped would provide a calming influence and reminder of mortal folly, decided to join the fun. In an upsurge of piety, millions of Americans threw their souls and their savings into evangelical empires designed on the principle of pyramid scams. Even the sleazy downfall of our telemessiahs—caught masturbating in the company of ten-dollar prostitutes or fornicating in their Christian theme parks—did not discourage the faithful. The unhappily pregnant were mobbed as "baby-killers"; sexual nonconformists—gay and lesbian— were denounced as "child molesters"; atheists found themselves lumped with "Satanists," Communists, and consumers of human flesh.

Yet somehow, despite it all, a trickle of dissent continued. There were homeless people who refused to be shelved in mental hospitals for the crime of poverty, strikers who refused to join the celebration of unions in faraway countries and scabs at home, women who insisted that their lives be valued above those of accidental embryos, parents who packed up their babies and marched for peace, students who protested the ongoing inversion of normal, nursery-school-level values in the name of a more habitable world.

I am proud to add my voice to all these. For dissent is also a "traditional value," and in a republic founded by revolution, a more deeply native one than smug-faced conservatism can ever be. Feminism was practically invented here, and ought to be regarded as one of our proudest exports to the world. Likewise, it tickles my sense of patriotism that Third World insurgents have often borrowed the ideas of our own African-American movement. And in what ought to be a source of shame to some and pride to others, our history of labor struggle is one of the hardest-fought and bloodiest in the world.

No matter that patriotism is too often the refuge of scoundrels. 30 Dissent, rebellion, and all-around hell-raising remain the true duty of patriots.

The Reader's Presence

1. Do you believe, with Ehrenreich, that different periods in American history have carried different social values? Why or why not? What is your impression of the 1980s, and what sources have you derived it from? How does Ehrenreich characterize the 1980s? What elements of 1980s culture does she recall in supporting her claims?

2. One catch phrase frequently heard during Ehrenreich's radical college years was "the personal is political." In what ways were Ehrenreich's father's personal principles political, in her view? How does Ehrenreich's use of her father as a model make the personal political and the political personal? Does this intermingling of the personal and the political undermine or enhance her larger argument? Why?

3. Ehrenreich uses her own impressions and experience as evidence in her argument. How might the essay read if it were argued in more objective terms (historical facts, statistics, etc.)? What sorts of examples does she use to make her point? Can you think of examples contrary to hers (counterexamples)? Contrast the type of evidence used by Ehrenreich with that used by Calvin Trillin ("A Traditional Family," page 561).

90

Stanley Fish

When Principles Get in the Way

Stanley Fish was born in Providence, Rhode Island, in 1938, grew up in Philadelphia, and received his B.A. at the University of Pennsylvania in 1959 and his Ph.D at Yale in 1962. Much of Fish's writing focuses on such topics as popular culture, critical theory, political theory, race, law, and religion, and many of his more provocative essays have been collected in The Stanley Fish Reader *(1999). His critical essays on First Amendment issues are collected in such works as* Self-Consuming Artifacts *(1972),* There's No Such Thing as Free Speech and It's a Good Thing, Too *(1994), and* Professional Correctness: Literary Studies and Political Change *(1995).*

Fish is most widely known for his claim that the response of readers, organized into "interpretive communities," ultimately determines the meaning of texts. During his long and often controversial career, Fish has held teaching posi-

tions at the University of California at Berkeley, Johns Hopkins University, Duke University, and most recently at the University of Illinois at Chicago, where he still teaches. His most recent work is The Trouble with Principle *(1999).*

Suppose you were arguing for something but were told that you would have to make your case without the facts that supported it. This is the situation proponents of affirmative action face when they find themselves defending their position in terms of principle rather than policy.

A policy is a response to actual historical circumstances; it is directed at achieving a measurable result—like an increase in the representation of minorities in business and education. A principle scorns actual historical circumstances and moves quickly to a level of generalization and abstraction so high that the facts of history can no longer be seen.

Affirmative action is an attempt to deal with a real-world problem. If that problem is recharacterized in the language of principle—if you stop asking, "What's wrong and how can we fix it?" and ask instead, "Is it fair?"—the real world fades away and is replaced by the arid world of philosophical puzzles.

The recipe for making real-world problems disappear behind a smokescreen of philosophizing was given to us years ago by the legal scholar Herbert Wechsler in his enormously influential 1959 Harvard Law Review article "Toward Neutral Principles." Wechsler was trying to justify the Supreme Court's decision in Brown v. Board of Education, which declared segregated schools unconstitutional. What troubled Wechsler about Brown was that the Justices, in reaching their decision, seemed moved by a practical desire to secure a result they favored (integrated schools) rather than by some general principle whose application would yield that result independently.

Unable to find any such principle spelled out in the Court's arguments, Wechsler was driven to provide one himself: the "right of freedom of association." But in attempting to make this case, he soon realized that the principle of freedom of association turned out not to justify Brown but to make it even more of a puzzle. "If the freedom of association is denied by segregation, integration forces an association upon those for whom it is . . . repugnant," he wrote. And "given a choice between denying the association to those . . . who wish it and imposing it on those who would avoid it," he was unable to find a principle that would justify either the one or the other.

Here in as naked a form as one might like (or not like) is the logic of neutral principle. When Wechsler characterizes the choice as being between the rights of those who wish to associate and the rights of those who wish not to, these two wishes have lost all contact with the issue that made their opposition meaningful—whether the schoolhouse door should be open or shut. Once the historical specificity of that issue is lost, there no longer seems to be any moral difference between the two sides,

5

although the difference was perfectly clear before Wechsler began his tortured analysis.

In other words, the puzzle of Brown is only a puzzle if you forget everything that made the case urgent in the first place—the long history of racism and its effects. You have substituted philosophical urgencies for social urgencies. This is what the demand for principle does, and what opponents of affirmative action intend it to do. After all, isn't it convenient to be able to deny a remedy for longstanding injustices by invoking the higher name of principle?

It is a very bad game, but it is alive and well in the phrase "reverse racism," which does in an instant what Wechsler needed an entire essay to do. The phrase makes the actions of college admissions officers who give preference to minority candidates equivalent to the hate crimes of the Ku Klux Klan. It does so by claiming that each is motivated by race con- sciousness, an argument that makes sense only if the very thought of race, no matter the content or context, is considered the sin. Like the freedom of association in Wechsler's argument, race-consciousness invoked as an abstraction rides roughshod over history while laying claim to the noblest of motives.

That is in effect what Justice Clarence Thomas did in his concurring opinion in Adarand v. Pena, in which the Court struck down the policy of giving incentives to Federal contractors who hired minority subcontractors. "It is irrelevant," he wrote, "whether a government's racial classifications are drawn by those who wish to oppress a race or by those who have a sincere desire to help those thought to be disadvantaged. In each instance, it is racial discrimination, plain and simple."

But both the plainness and the simplicity are apparent only if the 10
complex facts of history have been suppressed or declared out of bounds. In his dissent, Justice John Paul Stevens returned to history to make the *truly* plain and simple point: "There is no moral or Constitutional equivalence between a policy that is designed to perpetuate a caste system and one that seeks to eradicate racial subordination."

The important word in Justice Stevens's statement is "moral," for it shows that the choice here is not between the principled and the non-principled. It is between neutral principles, which refuse to acknowledge the dilemmas we face as a society, and moral principles, which begin with an awareness of those dilemmas and demand that we address them.

Those who favor affirmative action are moved by moral principles—principles that recognize the reality and persistence of historical inequities. And yet those who favor affirmative action are often maneuvered into using a vocabulary designed to remove from sight the very realities on which their case depends.

Of course, you could also try to work within that vocabulary and fight over its terms, arguing that "fairness," "equality" and "colorblindness" really belong on your side. But even if you got good at the game, you would be playing on your opponent's field and thus buying into his position, and why would you want to do that?

It would be far wiser to refuse the lure of "fairness," "merit" and "equality," now code words for ignoring the effects of the long history of racial oppression. Let's be done with code words and concentrate on the problems we face and on possible ways of solving them. Those who support affirmative action should give up searching for theoretical consistency—a goal at once impossible and unworthy—and instead seek strategies with the hope of relieving the pain of people who live in the world and not in the never-never land of theory.

Let's stop asking, "Is it fair or is it reverse racism?" and start asking,   15
"Does it work and are there better ways of doing what needs to be done?" Merely asking these questions does not guarantee that affirmative action will be embraced, but it does guarantee that the shell game of the search for neutral principle will no longer stand between us and doing the right thing.

The Reader's Presence

1. Fish's essay appeared on the "Op-Ed" page of the *New York Times*. What does this tell you about the kind of essay you are reading? How does he communicate his position on affirmative action in the first three paragraphs? Identify the particular words he uses in these paragraphs to convey his position. Where in the essay does he come closest to stating his opinion? Does he ever use the first person pronoun? If not, how does the reader know when Fish is expressing his own views?

2. One of Fish's rhetorical strategies is to reduce "the arid world of philosophical puzzles" (paragraph 3) to simple questions. Find the places in the article where he does this. Are you convinced by these phrases? How does Fish use Justice Thomas's phrase *plain and simple* against Thomas's decision in *Adarand v. Pena* (paragraph 9)? How does he redirect that phrase in the following paragraph in support of Justice Steven's dissent? Is Fish's argument itself a plain and simple argument? What is the difference between *simple* and *simplistic*?

3. Fish draws a distinction between moral principles and what he calls "neutral principles." Reread his definitions of both (paragraphs 11–12) and come to your own understanding of their meanings. Review Martin Luther King Jr.'s "Letter from Birmingham Jail" (page 692) in which he discusses the moral responsibility of civil disobedience (paragraphs 13–14). Both Fish and King allude to the landmark decision of *Brown v. Board of Education*. How does that 1954 decision enter into each writer's argument? How is affirmative action related to the racial integration of schools?

91

Paul Fussell

A Well-Regulated Militia

A well-established English professor who taught at Rutgers before accepting a distinguished professorship at the University of Pennsylvania in 1983, Paul Fussell (b. 1924) did not successfully break with academic prose until he tired of writing what he was "supposed to write." After twenty years of writing critical works such as Poetic Meter and Poetic Form *(1965) and* The Rhetorical World of Augustan Humanism *(1965), Fussell published his first work of nonfiction for a general audience.* The Great War and Modern Memory *(1975) won the National Book Award and the National Book Critics Circle Award and received wide critical acclaim for its examination of how World War I changed what Frank Kermode called "the texture of our culture." Fussell continued to touch upon the subject of war in his subsequent books,* Abroad: British Literary Traveling between the Wars *(1980) and* The Boy Scout Handbook and Other Observations *(1982). Fussell then wrote* Class: A Guide through the American Status System *(1983) and edited* The Norton Book of Travel *(1987). Fussell returned to his favorite subject in his collection of essays* Thank God for the Atom Bomb and Other Essays *(1988), from which this selection is taken. His most recent publications are* Bad, or The Dumbing of America *(1991),* The Anti-Egoist, Kingsley Amis, Man of Letters *(1994), and* Doing Battle: The Making of a Skeptic *(1996).*

In the spring Washington swarms with high school graduating classes. They come to the great pulsating heart of the Republic—which no one has yet told them is Wall Street—to be impressed by the White House and the Capitol and the monuments and the Smithsonian and the space capsules. Given the state of public secondary education, I doubt if many of these young people are at all interested in language and rhetoric, and I imagine few are fascinated by such attendants of power and pressure as verbal misrepresentation and disingenuous quotation. But any who are can profit from a stroll past the headquarters of the National Rifle Association of America, its slick marble façade conspicuous at 1600 Rhode Island Avenue, NW.

There they would see an entrance flanked by two marble panels offering language, and language more dignified and traditional than that customarily associated with the Association's gun-freak constituency, with its T-shirts reading GUNS, GUTS, AND GLORY ARE WHAT MADE AMERICA GREAT and its belt buckles proclaiming I'LL GIVE UP MY GUN WHEN THEY PRY MY COLD DEAD FINGERS FROM AROUND IT. The marble panel on the right reads, "The right of the people to keep and bear arms shall not be infringed," which sounds familiar. So familiar that the student naturally expects the left-hand panel to honor the principle of symmetry by presenting the first half of the quotation, namely: "A well-regulated Militia, being necessary to the security of a free state, . . ." But looking to the left, the inquirer discovers not that clause at all but rather this lame list of NRA functions and specializations: "Firearms Safety Education. Marksmanship Training. Shooting for Recreation." It's as if in presenting its well-washed, shiny public face the NRA doesn't want to remind anyone of the crucial dependent clause of the Second Amendment, whose latter half alone it is so fond of invoking to urge its prerogatives. (Some legible belt buckles of members retreat further into a seductive vagueness, reading only, "Our American Heritage: the Second Amendment.") We infer that for the Association, the less emphasis on the clause about the militia, the better. Hence its pretence on the front of its premises that the quoted main clause is not crucially dependent on the now unadvertised subordinate clause — indeed, it's meaningless without it.

Because flying .38- and .45-caliber bullets rank close to cancer, heart disease, and AIDS as menaces to public health in this country, the firearm lobby, led by the NRA, comes under liberal attack regularly, and with special vigor immediately after an assault on some conspicuous person like Ronald Reagan or John Lennon. Thus the *New Republic,* in April 1981, deplored the state of things but offered as a solution only the suggestion that the whole Second Amendment be perceived as obsolete and amended out of the Constitution. This would leave the NRA with not a leg to stand on.

But here as elsewhere a better solution would be not to fiddle with the Constitution but to take it seriously, the way we've done with the First Amendment, say, or with the Thirteenth, the one forbidding open and avowed slavery. And by taking the Second Amendment seriously I mean taking it literally. We should "close read" it and thus focus lots of attention on the grammatical reasoning of its two clauses. This might shame the NRA into pulling the dependent clause out of the closet, displaying it on its façade, and accepting its not entirely pleasant implications. These could be particularized in an Act of Congress providing:

(1) that the Militia shall now, after these many years, be "well-regulated," as the Constitution requires.

(2) that any person who has chosen to possess at home a gun of any kind, and who is not a member of the police or the military or an appropriate government agency, shall be deemed to have enrolled automatically in the Militia of the United States. Members of the Militia, who will be issued identifying badges, will be organized in units of battalion, company, or platoon size representing coun-

ties, towns, or boroughs. If they bear arms while not proceeding to or from scheduled exercises of the Militia, they will be punished "as a court martial may direct."

(3) that any gun owner who declines to join the regulated Militia may opt out by selling his firearms to the federal government for $1,000 each. He will sign an undertaking that if he ever again owns firearms he will be considered to have enlisted in the Militia.

(4) that because the Constitution specifically requires that the Militia shall be "well regulated," a regular training program, of the sort familiar to all who have belonged to military units charged with the orderly management of small arms, shall be instituted. This will require at least eight hours of drill each Saturday at some convenient field or park, rain or shine or snow or ice. There will be weekly supervised target practice (separation from the service, publicly announced, for those who can't hit a barn door). And there will be ample practice in digging simple defense works, like foxholes and trenches, as well as necessary sanitary installations like field latrines and straddle trenches. Each summer there will be a six-week bivouac (without spouses), and this, like all the other exercises, will be under the close supervision of long service non commissioned officers of the United States Army and the Marine Corps. On bivouac, liquor will be forbidden under extreme penalty, but there will be an issue every Friday night of two cans of 3.2 beer, and feeding will follow traditional military lines, the cuisine consisting largely of shit-on-a-shingle, sandwiches made of bull dick (baloney) and choke-ass (cheese), beans, and fatty pork. On Sundays and holidays, powdered eggs for breakfast. Chlorinated water will often be available, in Lister Bags. Further obligatory exercises designed to toughen up the Militia will include twenty-five-mile hikes and the negotiation of obstacle courses. In addition, there will be instruction of the sort appropriate to other lightly armed, well-regulated military units: in map-reading, the erection of double-apron barbed-wire fences, and the rudiments of military courtesy and the traditions of the Militia, beginning with the Minute Men. Per diem payments will be made to those participating in these exercises.

(5) that since the purpose of the Militia is, as the Constitution says, to safeguard "the security of a free state," at times when invasion threatens (perhaps now the threat will come from Nicaragua, national security no longer being menaced by North Vietnam) all units of the Militia will be trucked to the borders for the duration of the emergency, there to remain in field conditions (here's where the practice in latrine-digging pays off) until Congress declares that the emergency has passed. Congress may also order the Militia to perform other duties consistent with its constitutional identity as a regulated volunteer force: for example, flood

and emergency and disaster service (digging, sandbag filling, rescuing old people); patrolling angry or incinerated cities; or controlling crowds at large public events like patriotic parades, motor races, and professional football games.

(6) that failure to appear for these scheduled drills, practices, bivouacs, and mobilizations shall result in the Militiaperson's dismissal from the service and forfeiture of badge, pay, and firearm.

Why did the Framers of the Constitution add the word *bear* to the phrase "keep and bear arms?" Because they conceived that keeping arms at home implied the public obligation to bear them in a regulated way for "the security of" not a private household but "a free state." If interstate bus fares can be regulated, it is hard to see why the Militia can't be, especially since the Constitution says it must be. The *New Republic* has recognized that "the Second Amendment to the Constitution clearly connects the right to bear arms to the eighteenth-century national need to raise a militia." But it goes on: "That need is now obsolete, and so is the amendment." And it concludes: "If the only way this country can get control of firearms is to amend the Constitution, then it's time for Congress to get the process under way."

I think not. Rather, it's time not to amend Article II of the Bill of Rights (and Obligations) but to read it, publicize it, embrace it, and enforce it. That the Second Amendment stems from concerns that can be stigmatized as "eighteenth-century" cuts little ice. The First Amendment stems precisely from such concerns, and no one but Yahoos wants to amend it. Also "eighteenth-century" is that lovely bit in Section 9 of Article I forbidding any "Title of Nobility" to be granted by the United States. That's why we've been spared Lord Annenberg and Sir Leonard Bernstein, Knight. Thank God for the eighteenth century, I say. It understood not just what a firearm is and what a Militia is. It also understood what "well regulated" means. It knew how to compose a constitutional article and it knew how to read it. And it assumed that everyone, gun lobbyists and touring students alike, would understand and correctly quote it. Both halves of it.

The Reader's Presence

1. Here is the Second Amendment of the Bill of Rights: "A well-regulated Militia being necessary to the security of a free state, the right of the people to keep and bear arms shall not be infringed." Why does Fussell point out that the first part of the amendment does not appear on the marble facade of the National Rifle Association headquarters in Washington, D.C.? Why does he believe that the first half of the amendment is crucial to a correct understanding of the second half? Do you agree? Can you think of an alternative interpretation?

2. Though he is a proponent of gun control, why doesn't Fussell believe the Second Amendment should be repealed or revised? In what ways does his interpretation preserve the Second Amendment? Do you think the National Rifle Association would endorse Fussell's proposal? Do you think it would support any aspects of it? Explain.

3. Fussell's argument turns on rereading a familiar (and in his eyes, misunderstood) text, rather than modifying it. What does Fussell mean when he says that we should "close read" the Second Amendment? How does a basic analysis of grammar and syntax support his point? What does he mean when he writes that "verbal misrepresentation and disingenuous quotation" are "attendants of power and pressure" (paragraph 1)? What might George Orwell say about Fussell's essay in light of his comments in "Politics and the English Language" (page 481)? Do Fussell and Orwell share certain assumptions? If so, what are they?

92

William Gibson

The Net Is a Waste of Time

William Gibson was born in 1948 in Conway, South Carolina, and now lives with his wife and children in Vancouver, British Columbia. Since Gibson coined the term cyberspace *and used it in his 1984* Neuromancer—*a debut novel that won all three major science fiction awards (the Hugo, Nebula, and Philip K. Dick awards)—he has been the foremost practitioner of the "cyberpunk" genre. Gibson's other novels include* Count Zero *(1986),* Mona Lisa Overdrive *(1988),* Virtual Light *(1993),* Idoru *(1999), and his latest work,* All Tomorrow's Parties *(1999). He has also written a screenplay,* Johnny Mnemonic *(1995), and an episode of the television show* The X-Files. *Gibson is known for writing slowly, and for being somewhat reclusive. Although he believes "most social change is technology-driven," until recently he did not have an e-mail address.*

I coined the word "cyberspace" in 1981 in one of my first science fiction stories and subsequently used it to describe something that people insist on seeing as a sort of literary forerunner of the Internet. This being so, some think it remarkable that I do not use E-mail. In all truth, I have avoided it because I am lazy and enjoy staring blankly into space (which is also the space where novels come from) and because unanswered mail, e- or otherwise, is a source of discomfort.

But I have recently become an avid browser of the World Wide Web. Some people find this odd. My wife finds it positively perverse. I, however, scent big changes afoot, possibilities that were never quite as manifest in earlier incarnations of the Net.

I was born in 1948. I can't recall a world before television, but I know I must have experienced one. I do, dimly, recall the arrival of a piece of brown wooden furniture with sturdy Bakelite knobs and a screen no larger than the screen on this Powerbook.

Initially there was nothing on it but "snow," and then the nightly advent of a targetlike device called "the test pattern," which people actually gathered to watch.

Today I think about the test pattern as I surf the Web. I imagine that   5
the World Wide Web and its modest wonders are no more than the test pattern for whatever the twenty-first century will regard as its equivalent medium. Not that I can even remotely imagine what that medium might actually be.

In the age of wooden television in the South where I grew up, leisure involved sitting on screened porches, smoking cigarettes, drinking iced tea, engaging in conversation and staring into space. It might also involve fishing.

Sometimes the Web does remind me of fishing. It never reminds me of conversation, although it can feel a lot like staring into space. "Surfing the Web" (as dubious a metaphor as "the information highway") is, as a friend of mind has it, "like reading magazines with the pages stuck together." My wife shakes her head in dismay as I patiently await the downloading of some Japanese Beatles fan's personal catalogue of bootlegs. "But it's from Japan!" She isn't moved. She goes out to enjoy the flowers in her garden.

I stay in. Hooked. Is this leisure—this browsing, randomly linking my way through these small patches of virtual real-estate—or do I somehow imagine that I am performing some more dynamic function? The content of the Web aspires to absolute variety. One might find anything there. It is like rummaging in the forefront of the collective global mind. Somewhere, surely, there is a site that contains . . . everything we have lost?

The finest and most secret pleasure afforded new users of the Web rests in submitting to the search engine of Alta Vista the names of people we may not have spoken aloud in years. Will she be here? Has he survived unto this age? (She isn't there. Someone with his name has recently posted to a news group concerned with gossip about soap stars.) What is this casting of the nets of identity? Do we engage here in something of a tragic seriousness?

In the age of wooden television, media were there to entertain, to sell   10
an advertiser's product, perhaps to inform. Watching television, then, could indeed be considered a leisure activity. In our hypermediated age, we have come to suspect that watching television constitutes a species of

work. Post-industrial creatures of an information economy, we increasingly sense that accessing media is what we do. We have become terminally self-conscious. There is no such thing as simple entertainment. We
watch ourselves watching. We watch ourselves watching Beavis and Butt-
head, who are watching rock videos. Simply to watch, without the buffer
of irony in place, might reveal a fatal naïveté.

But that is our response to aging media like film and television, survivors from the age of wood. The Web is new, and our response to it has
not yet hardened. That is a large part of its appeal. It is something half-
formed, growing. Larval. It is not what it was six months ago; in another
six months it will be something else again. It was not planned; it simply
happened, is happening. It is happening the way cities happened. It *is* a city.

Toward the end of the age of wooden televisions the futurists of the
Sunday supplements announced the advent of the "leisure society." Technology would leave us less and less to do in the Marxian sense of yanking
the levers of production. The challenge, then, would be to fill our days
with meaningful, healthful, satisfying activity. As with most products of an
earlier era's futurism, we find it difficult today to imagine the exact coordi-
nates from which this vision came. In any case, our world does not offer us
a surplus of leisure. The word itself has grown somehow suspect, as quaint
and vaguely melancholy as the battered leather valise in a Ralph Lauren
window display. Only the very old or the economically disadvantaged
(provided they are not chained to the schedules of their environment's
more demanding addictions) have a great deal of time on their hands. To
be successful, apparently, is to be chronically busy. As new technologies
search out and lace over every interstice in the net of global communication, we find ourselves with increasingly less excuse for . . . slack.

And that, I would argue, is what the World Wide Web, the test pattern for whatever will become the dominant global medium, offers us.
Today, in its clumsy, larval, curiously innocent way, it offers us the opportunity to waste time, to wander aimlessly, to daydream about the
countless other lives, the other people, on the far sides of however many
monitors in that postgeographical meta-country we increasingly call
home. It will probably evolve into something considerably less random,
and less fun—we seem to have a knack for that—but in the meantime,
in its gloriously unsorted Global Ham Television Postcard Universes
phase, surfing the Web is a procrastinator's dream. And people who see
you doing it might even imagine you're working.

The Reader's Presence

1. Of what importance is the age of television to Gibson's point about
   the World Wide Web? Why is television an "aging" medium? In
   what ways does he believe the Web differs from television?

2. How does Gibson reach his conclusion that the best thing about the Web is that it "offers us the opportunity to waste time" (paragraph 13)? Why is that an advantage of this new "global medium"? Go back through the essay and explain how Gibson establishes the grounds for his conclusion.

3. Read Gibson's essay in conjunction with Marie Winn's "TV Addiction" (see page 581). Do you find any similarities between the way these two writers describe television? Winn was writing before the Internet had become a household reality. Does her description of television support Gibson's argument? Would you say that people are no longer addicted to television but are addicted now to the Internet?

93

Jane Eaton Hamilton

Twenty-One Questions

Jane Eaton Hamilton was born and grew up in Ontario and moved about frequently before settling in Vancouver with her partner, Etusko Joy Masuhara, and their two daughters. Her fiction, poetry, and essays have appeared in many magazines and journals, including the New York Times, Maclean's, *and* Seventeen. *She has won literary awards from a number of publications, including* Yellow Silk, Paragraph, Event, *and* Belles-Letters. *Hamilton's books include* July Nights and Other Stories *(1992),* Steam-Cleaning Love *(1993), and* Going Santa Fe *(1997). She has commented, "I'll be learning how to write until the day I put down my pen."*

One: The question that engenders all the rest.

Two homosexual women shiver in February at Long Beach, on the west coast of Vancouver Island, beachcombing during low tide, wearing anoraks, fleeces, heavy boots. They are not whispery, vaporous, gauzy. The waves crash behind them, wild and combustible. There is an unholy wind, which has driven heterosexuals indoors to moon at each other over oysters Rockefeller. In the case of our women, the wind does not whip hair, because our women have short hair. Very short, in fact, with razor trims above their ears. Gelled tufts atop. Already we are in the realm of queer. Shyly, one woman asks the other woman if she thinks they should maybe get married. Maybe. It sounds like a castoff comment, like nothing special. Except that it is Valentine's Day.

"Married?" says the second woman, her voice sucked away by the wind. She does not understand this as a proposal; her lover is hardly on bended knee.

"I want to be with you all my life," says the first woman.

The second woman just frowns. "I want to be with you, too," she says. "But, jiminy crickets, do you have to call it marriage?"

"But marriage is what I want," says the first woman. "I think." She 5 sighs. She is the first to admit it. For lesbians, the words are clumsy, the institution clumsier. "I think it's what I want. I want to marry you."

The women are drawn to each other like moths to light bulbs, like fingers to sea anemones. They are gooily in love.

"Oh, heck." The second woman laughs, joy surging through her. Though they are on uneasy footing there among the rocks, she lifts the first woman, swings her and shouts, "Yes, yes, yes!"

Two: Marriage? But what is marriage between women?

What are the women intending to say to each other by marrying? What are they saying to their community? Neither of them really knows. They just have an inchoate longing toward a deep, secure future. They sit over dinner discussing it, falling silent, mooning.

"But marriage! Isn't marriage—" The second woman thinks to herself that it's goofy. Just downright goofy. To mimic heterosexuals? Isn't it just embracing rituals that haven't even brought heterosexuals much joy? Isn't it selling out lezzie culture? Anyhow, don't marriages fall apart at a heady clip? What's the failure rate—50 percent? That's something to ape?

The women talk about marriage versus commitment ceremonies, but 10 here they agree: They are already as committed as they would be following such a ceremony. Marriage must hold more meaning, or hets wouldn't bother. Why do they, though? What's the draw? "Divorce?" asks the second woman. "Maybe people head into marriage more seriously because it's hard to get back out."

"Or maybe they just love each other more," says the first woman, "and they have to find a way to express it."

The second woman says, "I love you more."

"Honeybunch," says the first woman, taking her lover's hand. "I love you more, too."

Marriage, then. The women settle, hesitantly, on marriage.

But now what? Where do they go from here? Back to Vancouver, for 15 starters, because they both have work in the morning. And, also, they want to look at rings, those walkabout symbols that tell everyone else what has transpired. But what kind of rings? Should there be one, or two? If they try to toe the heterosexual line, they will have to choose a diamond (a girl's best friend) for at least one of them. But neither of our women is femme. Neither of them is butch. They cling to the amorphous muddle at the middle where diamonds and dresses—well, ugh. All right, then. Two simple silver bands as engagement rings, and each of them can choose her own accompanying wedding band.

"My fiancée," breathes the first bride that night in bed as she strokes her lover's face.

"My fiancée," whispers the second bride back and giggles.

They cannot get used to the ludicrous sound of the word on their tongues. "Are we really engaged?" asks the first bride.

Are they? That's a question about queer marriage: Is there even any such thing? If you think there's an easy answer, you're mistaken. In heterosexual marriage, traditions are a given, and they add a significance that's understood by a wider community. Nothing is that simple with queer marriage. Arguments start up.

Three: For instance, what is the best month for a wedding?

"June," says the first bride without hesitation.   20

"I hate June," says the second bride. "It always rains in Vancouver in June."

"August, then," says the first bride.

"Uh, no," says the second bride after an obvious hesitation.

"Why not?"

"I just can't, okay?"   25

"Tell me. I want to know why not."

"It doesn't matter, really," says the second bride.

"It does matter. To me it matters."

"Carol and I held our commitment ceremony in August."

Silence.   30

"Honey?" says the second bride. "Does that bother you? What's wrong? That shouldn't bother you. It wasn't a wedding, at least."

"Nothing," says the first bride, turning away her face.

"Nothing?"

"Nothing, all right? I said nothing. Didn't you hear me? I'm glad you had your ceremony in August, therefore wrecking the month for me for all time."

"Snookums?"   35

"Leave me alone."

"Honeybunch? Let's just do it in July."

Four: What should the brides wear?

"White wedding gowns?" jokes the second bride.

The first bride hoots and says, "That'd work for you, because technically, you're a virgin. But me! I've had sex so often I'd have to wear—well, all right, let's say it: black."

The second bride is absurdly hurt. "Are you ridiculing me? You are.   40
You are ridiculing me. I shouldn't be put down just because I don't like

penetration. Just because I haven't had the sleazy kind of past you have. Just because I've never slept with a man."

The same question again: What should the women wear?

They could both wear gowns. They could both wear tuxedos. One could wear a gown and one could wear a tuxedo. They could flip for it. But neither of them has worn a dress in ten years. They could just wear everyday clothes, but would that signal to their guests how much all this means? How would that say wedding?

And also, what should the maids of honor wear? Should they even be called maids of honor? Would coupled lesbians be matrons of honor, or only if they'd been through a commitment ceremony?

"Why can't we just call them 'best women?'" asks the second bride.

"Fine by me," says the first bride, grinning devilishly. "As long as we get to dress them in ruffled pink gowns."   45

Five: What is a queer wedding for?

It's not licensed. There's no marriage certificate, after all. The government doesn't suddenly open up with spousal pension benefits. There are still no joint tax returns. There's no financial incentive—no community property laws. It is merely a cleaving. Unto each other. Of two brides. Do the brides care about sickness and health?

"What if I had an accident and became a paraplegic?" says the first bride. "Would you stay with me then?"

"Of course I would, snookums," says fiancée two.

"The law wouldn't make you."

"The law wouldn't make me if we were straight, either."   50

"They'd make you pay alimony," says the first bride. "So what if I were a quadriplegic? Then?"

"Well, yeah, I think so."

"You think so?" The first bride gives the second bride a little kick.

"I know so. Okay? I know so."

"No, you don't. You'd leave me. I can tell you'd leave me. The stress   55
would get to be too great and you'd run off with what's-her-name. Your ex. The French one. Fifi."

"Well, what would you do if I were the one who had the accident?"

"I'd run off with Fifi."

Six: Do our brides care about richer or poorer?

"Share money?" says the first bride. "But I earn three times as much as you do! You expect me just to fork it over?"

"Fork it over?" says the second bride.

"I'm sorry. But still, how is that fair?"   60

"That's what heterosexuals do. It deepens the commitment, don't you think? One for all and all for one."

"Can't we be a little progressive here? We're not heterosexual, or hadn't you noticed? My money is mine. Your money is yours."

"Fine," says the second bride through gritted teeth.

"You're mad. Are you mad? You're always mad, lately."

"I'm not mad. Why would I be mad? Just because my wife will have   65
to take her tropical vacations without me because I can't afford to go?
Honestly, I'm not mad. Good golly, no. Don't be absurd."

"I'm just against you getting too dependent on me," says the first bride.

"Screw you," says the second bride." "And screw the bank account
you rode in on."

Seven: What about the vow "until death us do part"?

"Death, whoa," says the second bride. "'Til death us do part. That's
a really long time."

There. It is finally out. This is what they are talking about when they
talk about marriage. Forsaking—all others. Forsaking the ones with
giddy laughs. The ones who snake around the dance floor at the club.
The ones with snapping eyes. The ones who are short and just slightly
overweight. The exes, with whom it is possible to tumble accidentally
into bed. The tall chunky ones. The lithe ones. The ones who wear
dresses and high heels. The ones who wear black jackets. The one who
pitches in the all-girl softball league, with whom the second bride has
been flirting recently.

"What?" says the first bride." Did you just say what I think   70
you just said? How could you be so cruel? I thought you loved me, but let
me tell you, lately I'm questioning the depth of your commitment.
I didn't twist your arm here. You said yes. You said you wanted to
do this."

There is a long pause, then: "Occasionally, once in a while," admits
the second bride, "maybe I have a doubt or two. Don't you?"

"I don't. No way. I don't."

"You're always mad lately. You're mad every time I come home from
softball."

"So? So? I mean, geez Louise. You're gone a lot. Are you going to be
gone this much after we're married? I mean, yeah. I wish you'd hang out
with me instead of going to play ball. Why does it have to be all day every
Sunday?"

"I thought you liked that I play ball. I thought maintaining our inde-   75
pendence was so important to you."

"I'm a softball widow, that's all."

"How could you possibly be a widow? We aren't even married yet.
And besides, why should I stay home, when all you do all day long on
Sunday is clean?"

"Someone has to wash the floors. We don't have time all week. But
oh no: You think I should do all the grunt work, don't you? You do,
don't you?"

"The grunt work? I take out the garbage. I fix the washing machine.
That's the real grunt work."

Eight: Where should the ceremony be performed?

And what kind of ceremony? How many guests should the brides   80
invite?

"Listen," says the second bride, "I know we talked about a church wedding. But I have to tell you, I've been having real qualms. It feels wrong when I'm an atheist. It goes against everything I believe in. I know it would seem more formal, but—"

"You're not an atheist," says the first bride. "You're agnostic. You're keeping an open mind. At least, that's what you told me. There's a big difference between atheism and agnosticism."

"Well, you believe in reincarnation. You've been dabbling in Wicca."

"Outdoors, then. We can get married at Jericho Beach with just our nearest and dearest present. No fuss. Less expense. We can limit the guest list to—"

"Ten," says the second bride.   85

"Ten? I have six married brothers and thirteen nieces and nephews. Fifty, maybe, though a hundred would be more realistic."

"My mother won't come."

"She'd let you get married and not attend?" says the first bride.

"You know she thinks it's not a real marriage. You know she just thinks I need to meet the right young fellow."

"Aren't I your nice young fellow?"   90

"Oh, you are, little snooglebums. My honeybunch bruiser. I love you so, so much."

"I love you too, popsicle. Pumpkin. Puddingdrop."

Nine: Here's a basic question. Are there really two brides?

Or are there a bride and groom? Or two grooms? Let's face it, neither of these women is particularly feminine. They divide the labor around the house according to preference. The first bride cooks because the second bride stinks at it. The second bride takes the garbage out when the first bride doesn't get to it. The second bride does all the mending. The first bride does the laundry and changes the spark plugs in the car. Neither wears dresses, ever. Who knows why? They're dykes. They don't like them.

"I don't mind being called a bride," says the first bride.

"Ugh," says the second. "It sounds like you're a Barbie doll."   95

The first bride says, "Well, you be the groom. Do you want to be the groom?"

"I don't think of myself as a man. I'm a woman. But I'm not a dippy woman."

"You're saying brides are dippy?"

"It's a dippy word. It comes from when women were considered their husband's property. What about 'marrying partner'?'

"Oh, that's just great. Very simple, easy on the tongue: 'Aunt Sylvia,   100
I'd like you to meet my "marrying partner,"' yup. Very nice ring to it.

Very nice indeed." The first bride thinks a minute. "Nope, I think I'd rather be your property."

Ten: Will they register a china pattern?

"I don't like those plates. Too many roses. Look at these. Brown. Plain. I like these ones more," says the second bride.

"Do you think anybody's going to buy us china anyhow?"

"Of course they'll buy us china. Heterosexuals aren't totally stupid. They'll know we have to eat."

"We don't eat," says the first bride. "Lesbians just have sex. Everybody knows that. All day every day."

"Yum," says the second bride and squeezes her fiancée's hand.   105

The first bride says, "I still like that pattern best."

"I don't even see why we have to register."

"People want to know what to get us. Anyhow, isn't that half the point of marriage? The presents? Don't you have a dowry?"

The second bride laughs. "One left-handed baseball glove, one pair of slightly worn cleats, a huge Visa bill, an '82 Honda. Lucky you."

The first bride squeezes her hand. "I *am* lucky. I'm really lucky."   110

The second bride smiles. "Do you think people will get us good presents? I mean, we're queer. It isn't actually legal. Won't they just expect us to break up eventually? They might not want to spend much. They might just hedge their bets."

Eleven: Who will officiate? And what will the brides say to each other?

There is also the question, and it is a big one, of whether the second bride's Uncle Thomas should be invited. Last Thanksgiving, Uncle Thomas was heard hooting when the brides (at that point girlfriends, now life as opposed to marrying partners) kissed.

"What are you doing there?" asks the second bride.

"I'm addressing the invitations. Someone has to get to it."

"But you're using a Bic."   115

"So?" says the first bride.

"I just thought we decided on calligraphy. I know we talked about this, and we said calligraphy would be more elegant."

"Did we? I'm so tired." The first bride swipes a hand over her face. "Honey, you smell like sweat. Did you win? Sometimes I wish we'd just—"

"What?"

"Elope."

The second bride holds her shoulders. "There's a lesbian minister at   120
the United Church who could officiate."

"Is there? How do you know that?"

The second bride shrugs. "She married Mary and Sue."

"Mary and Sue got married? When?"

"Before your time. Back when you lived in Montreal."   125

"That's—fifteen years ago. Sixteen. They're still together."

"Of course they're still together, silly. They're married."

Twelve: What about flowers?

"I'm not carrying flowers," says the second bride adamantly. "No way I'm going down the aisle carrying a bouquet like some simpering straight girl."

"You're walking down the aisle?"

"Well, I don't know. I never really thought about it. Aren't you?"   130

"I never thought about it either. Maybe I'll wait at the altar."

"There isn't an altar. It's outside. There isn't an aisle, either."

"Well, at the seagull poop then. Whatever, we still need bouquets," says the first bride. "We can't get married and not have any flowers."

"Why can't we?"

"I love flowers. They're very hopeful. I always saw myself carrying   135 stephanotis."

"You did? You're not kidding? You know what? You're a closet femme. I'll bet you played with Barbie dolls."

"I had two Barbie dolls. They were queer. They got married and had babies together. They harvested one Barbie's eggs, fertilized them in a petri dish and implanted them in the other Barbie. They had three daughters. Barbie, Barbie and Barbie. They lived happily ever after."

Thirteen: Who will pay for the wedding?

The brides themselves, proportionate to their earnings—or split expenses down the middle?

"I talked to my father today," says the first bride. "He's going to pay for everything."

"Your father is going to pay for you to marry a woman?"   140

"Yes, he is," insists the first bride. "Even the honeymoon."

"We're going on a honeymoon?"

"Now we are."

"I've always dreamed of going mountain climbing," says the second bride.

The first bride replies, "You know where I've always dreamed of   145 honeymooning?"

"You've dreamed of honeymooning?"

"Niagara Falls."

Fourteen: There is still the question of who will stand up with them.

"Who do you want to be your maid of honor?" asks the first bride.

"I thought we were calling them best women."

"Best women, then. Are you still thinking about asking Dorothy? Be-   150 cause she was really snotty to me at the party on Sunday."

"But Dorothy's my best friend," says the second bride.

"I'm just saying."

"What are you saying?"

"I'm saying: If we're a team now, shouldn't we be making joint decisions?"

"About who I want to stand up for me?!"   155

"If we're a team. Are we a team?"

"We're a team, but I still want Dorothy," says the second bride. "You're asking Claire."

"What's wrong with Claire? Suddenly there's something wrong with Claire? Claire happens to be one of the best people I know."

"Well, so is Dorothy, if you'd give her half a chance. And she's the most important person in the world to me."

"I thought I was."   160

Fifteen: Is queer marriage even safe?

The second bride's mother is convinced it might not be. She tries to convince the women to reconsider having an outdoor ceremony. They have to apply for a permit—what if word gets out? Bystanders could take exception. The press could show up. Wackos could bring guns.

"Because of two people pledging their undying love?" says the second bride.

"Don't pretend you don't know what I mean," says her mother. "You know very well what I mean."

"We have the right to do this in front of everyone. We won't hide."

"People might not like it, is all I'm saying."   165

"That's their problem, then."

"Unless they pump bullets into you. Then it's yours."

"I plan to say I love this woman. I plan to say it right out loud. This is our marriage, Mom." The second bride reaches for the first bride's hand.

"I don't like it," says her mother. "It's not what I wanted for you."

Sixteen: There is always, always, the question about shaving.

"Are you planning to shave your armpits?" asks the second bride.   170

"Are you out of your mind? Why would I do that? I thought I might shave my mustache, is all. Or maybe wax it."

"I thought I'd shave my armpits. Along with my legs. I mean, if you're going to slide a garter down my leg—"

"I could go for that."

"Mmm," says the second bride . "Me too. Now that I think about it. Me too. But wouldn't we have to take our pants off first?"

Seventeen: And the question about names.

"Are you going to take my last name?" asks the first bride.   175

"Are you going to take mine?" asks the second.

"We could hyphenate."

"Let's just keep our own names," says the second bride.

"You don't want my name? But you could become Mrs. Squat."
"Well, you could become Mrs. Idono."   180
"Mrs. and Mrs. Idono Squat!"

Eighteen: Should the brides hire a professional photographer?
Or just someone they know?
Oops. It seems the first bride neglected to tell the second that once, in
a life far away (Kelowna—a day's drive to the interior) and long ago
(two years earlier), she and the photographer happened to be lovers.
"It was not a serious affair," says the first bride. "Merely a fling."
But the second bride is not mollified. She feels defiled. "When were   185
you going to tell me? When I was grinning into the lens? Everyone at the
wedding would have known but me!"
"So?"
"So! How many women have there been? Honestly, now. Is it more
than ten? More than twenty? More than fifty?"

Nineteen: There are too many questions and too few answers.
To reach the simplest of answers proves exhausting.
The second bride throws herself across the bed and says she wants to
call the whole thing off. "I can't do this," she wails. "It's not even legal."
"It's legal in my heart," says the first bride.   190
"I don't want to get married unless I can really get married. Other-
wise, what's the point?"
"I thought *I* was the point."
"I can cleave without a wedding," says the second bride, sniffling.
"Don't cry," says the first bride. "If it means that much to you, we
don't have to go through with it."
"You don't want to go through with it? Is that what you're saying?   195
You don't want to be my wife?"
"I want to be your husband."
"Very funny."
"I'm sorry. I do want to marry you. That's not what I was saying."
"You do want to? I want to, too. I do. I really do."
"C'mere. Give me a hug."   200

Twenty: Finally, it's time—July 14.
If there are questions now, other than on the lips of the guests milling
about near the duck ponds at Jericho Beach, it's too late to ask. It's
sunny; the ocean is as flat as a mirror. Gulls wheel across the sky calling
raucously. The mountains in the distance look like blue reclining nudes.
Tables of food are set up.
But look—the second bride's mother wasn't wrong. There are protesters, fortunately held back by police.
The second bride wears a tux, and the first bride wears a very off-
white gown. This is because the second bride is pretending to be butch

(she is packing), and the other, femme (she is also packing, but only for the honeymoon trip to Niagara Falls). The first bride's mother sits on a white folding chair in the front row dabbing her eyes with a tissue. The first bride's father nods his head sagely.

The second bride's mother is there, but out of sight behind some bushes, peeking in, also weeping.

The brides promise a justice of the peace that they will love, honor,   205
and cherish each other forever. A small emerald is placed on the ring finger of the first bride. A labyris is slid onto the ring finger of the second bride.

Protesters hold up placecards saying, "God hates fags." Saying, "Die, Sodomites." They try to drown out the ceremony with their shouts.

When the women kiss, the guests clap and cheer.

So do the protesters, only their cheers are jeers.

At the reception, the brides sign a registry (which isn't really anything more than a form printed out on the second bride's computer) on the dotted line, but not quite on the dotted line. Being queer, they sign a little outside the line, and it is requested that they use crayons. The usual color is of course lavender, a vibrant, solidaritous lavender, but they are free to choose whichever color most pleases them. There are no thought police here! Except suddenly there's horrid Uncle Thomas—where did he come from?—holding apples against his chest, dancing around the floor air-kissing men.

Twenty-one:
They have ordered up the honeymoon suite at a Niagara Falls hotel,   210
but when they register the clerk says, "I have Mr. and Mrs. Idono Squat registered. There must be some mistake, ladies. That suite is reserved for honeymooners."

Us!" say the brides, exultant.

The clerk's lips thin. "Oh, I don't think so. Perhaps—we have a room on the first floor that surely would be perfect."

"We paid for the honeymoon suite," insists the first bride. "We reserved it."

"I'll have to talk to my manager."

Finally, after tears and threats of legal action, the matter is sorted   215
out. The brides are shown, holding hands, into the honeymoon suite, where a vase of red roses waits beside a bottle of chilled champagne and two champagne flutes. The bed is red and heart shaped. There is a red whirlpool bath.

"Holy toots," says the first bride and throws down her backpack.

"Jesus Christ," says the second bride and flops down on the bed on her back.

"Could you believe that jerk? I couldn't believe that jerk. Like lesbians aren't allowed to fall in love. Like there's something unsavory about us."

"Never mind him." The second bride rolls on her side. "Are you unsavory? I'm feeling a little unsavory. In fact, never mind unsavory. I'm feeling a little perverted. A little — married."

"Are we really married?" says the first bride, grinning, clambering   220 onto the bed.

And that, of course, is the last question: Are they?

The Reader's Presence

1. Why do you think Hamilton constructed her essay on lesbian marriage as a series of twenty-one questions with dialogue? How else might she have handled this topic? In what other ways have you seen it covered in print? How effective do you think Hamilton's method is? What advantages does it give her in writing about this topic?

2. In what ways do the two women differ? Go through the essay and make a list of their differences. How would you characterize the personality of each woman? How does their way of talking express their different personalities? Do you think this is a personal essay, in which one of the women is the author? Or has the author invented two women for the sake of the argument? Or is the author describing a relationship between two women other than herself? Explain your response.

3. Read Hamilton's essay in relation to June Jordan's "A New Politics of Sexuality" (page 678). Do you think Jordan's ideas are relevant to the sexual politics expressed in Hamilton's essay? Would one or both of the women planning their marriage agree or disagree with Jordan?

94

Vicki Hearne

What's Wrong with Animal Rights

Vicki Hearne (1946–2001) had a unique career as a poet, author, and animal trainer, and taught creative writing at Yale University and at the University of California. She published three volumes of poetry, Nervous Horses *(1980),* In the Absence of Horses *(1983), and* The Parts of Light *(1994). Hearne was known for her ability to train aggressive dogs (particularly pit bull terriers), and she wrote an account of her experiences in* Bandit: Dossier of a Dangerous Dog *(1991). Her other books include* Adam's Task: Calling Animals by Name *(1987),* The White German Shepherd *(1988), and* Animal Happiness *(1994). "What's Wrong with Animal Rights" was originally published in* Harper's *in 1991 and was selected for* The Best American Essays 1992.

Not all happy animals are alike. A Doberman going over a hurdle after a small wooden dumbbell is sleek, all arcs of harmonious power. A basset hound cheerfully performing the same exercise exhibits harmonies of a more lugubrious nature. There are chimpanzees who love precision the way musicians or fanatical housekeepers or accomplished hypochondriacs do; others for whom happiness is a matter of invention and variation — chimp vaudevillians. There is a rhinoceros whose happiness, as near as I can make out, is in needing to be trained every morning, all over again, or else he "forgets" his circus routine, and in this you find a clue to the slow, deep, quiet chuckle of his happiness and to the glory of the beast. Happiness for Secretariat is in his ebullient bound, that joyful length of stride. For the draft horse or the weight-pull dog, happiness is of a different shape, more awesome and less obviously intelligent. When the pulling horse is at its most intense, the animal goes into himself, allocating all of the educated power that organizes his desire to dwell in fierce and delicate intimacy with that power, leans into the harness, and MAKES THAT SUCKER MOVE.

If we are speaking of human beings and use the phrase "animal happiness," we tend to mean something like "creature comforts." The emblems of this are the golden retriever rolling in the grass, the horse with his nose deep in the oats, the kitty by the fire. Creature comforts are important to animals — "Grub first, then ethics" is a motto that would describe many a wise Labrador retriever, and I have a pit bull named Annie whose continual quest for the perfect pillow inspires her to awesome feats. But there is something more to animals, a capacity for satisfactions that come from work in the fullest sense — what is known in philosophy and in this country's Declaration of Independence as "happiness." This is a sense of personal achievement, like the satisfaction felt by a good woodcarver or a dancer or a poet or an accomplished dressage horse. It is a happiness that, like the artist's must come from something within the animal, something trainers call "talent." Hence, it cannot be imposed on the animal. But it is also something that does not come *ex nihilo*. If it had not been a fairly ordinary thing, in one part of the world, to teach young children to play the pianoforte, it is doubtful that Mozart's music would exist.

Happiness is often misunderstood as a synonym for pleasure or as an antonym for suffering. But Aristotle associated happiness with ethics — codes of behavior that urge us toward the sensation of getting it right, a kind of work that yields the "click" of satisfaction upon solving a problem or surmounting an obstacle. In his *Ethics,* Aristotle wrote, "If happiness is activity in accordance with excellence, it is reasonable that it should be in accordance with the highest excellence." Thomas Jefferson identified the capacity for happiness as one of the three fundamental rights on which all others are based: "life, liberty, and the pursuit of happiness."

I bring up this idea of happiness as a form of work because I am an animal trainer, and work is the foundation of the happiness a trainer and an animal discover together. I bring up these words also because they cannot be found in the lexicon of the animal-rights movement. This absence accounts for the uneasiness toward the movement of most people, who sense that rights advocates have a point but take it too far when they liberate snails or charge that goldfish at the county fair are suffering. But the problem with the animal-rights advocates is not that they take it too far; it's that they've got it all wrong.

Animal rights are built upon a misconceived premise that rights were   5
created to prevent us from unnecessary suffering. You can't find an animal-rights book, video, pamphlet, or rock concert in which someone doesn't mention the Great Sentence, written by Jeremy Bentham in 1789. Arguing in favor of such rights, Bentham wrote: "The question is not, Can they *reason?* nor, can they *talk?* but, can they suffer?"

The logic of the animal-rights movement places suffering at the iconographic center of a skewed value system. The thinking of its proponents—given eerie expression in a virtually sado-pornographic sculpture of a tortured monkey that won a prize for its compassionate vision—has collapsed into a perverse conundrum. Today the loudest voices calling for—demanding—the destruction of animals are the humane organizations. This is an inevitable consequence of the apotheosis of the drive to relieve suffering: death is the ultimate release. To compensate for their contradictions, the humane movement has demonized, in this century and the last, those who made animal happiness their business: veterinarians, trainers, and the like. We think of Louis Pasteur as the man whose work saved you and me and your dog and cat from rabies, but antivivisectionists of the time claimed that rabies increased in areas where there were Pasteur Institutes.

An anti-rabies public relations campaign mounted in England in the 1880s by the Royal Society for the Prevention of Cruelty to Animals and other organizations led to orders being issued to club any dog found not wearing a muzzle. England still has her cruel and unnecessary law that requires an animal to spend six months in quarantine before being allowed loose in the country. Most of the recent propaganda about pit bulls—the crazy claim that they "take hold with their front teeth while they chew away with their rear teeth" (which would imply, incorrectly, that they have double jaws)—can be traced to literature published by the Humane Society of the United States during the fall of 1987 and earlier. If your neighbors want your dog or horse impounded and destroyed because he is a nuisance—say the dog barks, or the horse attracts flies—it will be the local Humane Society to whom your neighbors turn for action.

In a way, everyone has the opportunity to know that the history of the humane movement is largely a history of miseries, arrests, prosecutions, and death. The Humane Society is the pound, the place with the decompression chamber or the lethal injections. You occasionally find worried letters about this in Ann Landers's column.

Animal-rights publications are illustrated largely with photographs of two kinds of animals—"Helpless Fluff" and "Agonized Fluff," the two conditions in which some people seem to prefer their animals, because any other version of an animal is too complicated for propaganda. In the introduction to his book *Animal Liberation*, Peter Singer says somewhat smugly that he and his wife have no animals and, in fact, don't much care for them. This is offered as evidence of his objectivity and ethical probity. But it strikes me as an odd, perhaps, obscene underpinning for an ethical project that encourages university and high school students to cherish their ignorance of, say, great bird dogs as proof of their devotion to animals.

I would like to leave these philosophers behind, for they are inept   10
connoisseurs of suffering who might revere my Airedale for his capacity to scream when subjected to a blowtorch but not for his wit and courage, not for his natural good manners that are a gentle rebuke to ours. I want to celebrate the moment not long ago when, at his first dog show, my Airedale, Drummer, learned that there can be a public place where his work is respected. I want to celebrate his meticulousness, his happiness upon realizing at the dog show that no one would swoop down upon him and swamp him with the goo-goo excesses known as the "teddy-bear complex" but that people actually got out of his way, gave him room to work. I want to say, "There can be a six-and-a-half-month-old puppy who can care about accuracy, who can be fastidious, and whose fastidiousness will be a foundation for courage later." I want to say, "Leave my puppy alone!"

I want to leave the philosophers behind, but I cannot, in part because the philosophical problems that plague academicians of the animal-rights movement are illuminating. They wonder, do animals have rights or do they have interests? Or, if these rightists lead particularly unexamined lives, they dismiss that question as obvious (yes, of course animals have rights, prima facie) and proceed to enumerate them, James Madison style. This leads to the issuance of bills of rights—the right to an environment, the right not to be used in medical experiments—and other forms of trivialization.

The calculus of suffering can be turned against the philosophers of festering flesh, even in the case of food animals, or exotic animals who perform in movies and circuses. It is true that it hurts to be slaughtered by man, but it doesn't hurt nearly as much as some of the cunningly cruel arrangements, meted out by "Mother Nature." In Africa, 75 percent of the lions cubbed do not survive to the age of two. For those who make it to two, the average age at death is ten years. Asali, the movie and TV lioness, was still working at age twenty-one. There are fates worse than death, but twenty-one years of a close working relationship with Hubert Wells, Asali's trainer, is not one of them. Dorset sheep and polled Herefords would not exist at all were they not in a symbiotic relationship with human beings.

A human being living in the "wild"—somewhere, say, without the benefits of medicine and advanced social organization—would probably have a life expectancy of from thirty to thirty-five years. A human being living in "captivity"—in, say, a middle-class neighborhood of what the Centers for Disease Control call a Metropolitan Statistical Area—has a life expectancy of seventy or more years. For orangutans in the wild in Borneo and Malaysia, the life expectancy is thirty-five years; in captivity, fifty years. The wild is not a suffering-free zone or all that frolicsome a location.

The questions asked by animal-rights activists are flawed, because they are built on the concept that the origin of rights is in the avoidance of suffering rather than in the pursuit of happiness. The question that needs to be asked—and that will put us in closer proximity to the truth—is not, do they have rights? or, what are those rights? but rather, what is a right?

Rights originate in committed relationships and can be found, both   15
intact and violated, wherever one finds such relationships—in social compacts, within families, between animals, and between people and nonhuman animals. This is as true when the nonhuman animals in question are lions or parakeets as when they are dogs. It is my Airedale whose excellencies have my attention at the moment, so it is with reference to him that I will consider the question, what is a right?

When I imagine situations in which it naturally arises that A defends or honors or respects B's rights, I imagine situations in which the relationship between A and B can be indicated with a possessive pronoun. I might say, "Leave her alone, she's my daughter" or "That's what she wants, and she is my daughter. I think I am bound to honor her wants." Similarly, "Leave her alone, she's my mother." I am more tender of the happiness of my mother, my father, my child, than I am of other people's family members; more tender of my friends' happinesses than your friends' happinesses, unless you and I have a mutual friend.

Possession of a being by another has come into more and more disrepute, so that the common understanding of one person possessing another is slavery. But the important detail about the kind of possessive pronoun that I have in mind is reciprocity: if I have a friend, she has a friend. If I have a daughter, she has a mother. The possessive does not bind one of us while freeing the other; it cannot do that. Moreover, should the mother reject the daughter, the word that applies is "disown." The form of disowning that most often appears in the news is domestic violence. Parents abuse children; husbands batter wives.

Some cases of reciprocal possessives have built-in limitations, such as "my patient / my doctor" or "my student / my teacher" or "my agent / my client." Other possessive relations are extremely limited but still remarkably binding: "my neighbor" and "my country" and "my president."

The responsibilities and the ties signaled by reciprocal possession typically are hard to dissolve. It can be as difficult to give up an enemy as to give up a friend, and often the one becomes the other, as though the logic of the possessive pronoun outlasts the forms it chanced to take at a given moment, as though we were stuck with one another. In these bindings, nearly inextricable, are found the origin of our rights. They imply a possessiveness but also recognize an acknowledgment by each side of the other's existence.

The idea of democracy is dependent on the citizens' having knowledge of the government; that is, realizing that the government exists and knowing how to claim rights against it. I know this much because I get mail from the government and see its "representatives" running about in uniforms. Whether I actually have any rights in relationship to the government is less clear, but the idea that I do is symbolized by the right to vote. I obey the government, and, in theory, it obeys me, by counting my ballot, reading the *Miranda* warning to me, agreeing to be bound by the Constitution. My friend obeys me as I obey her; the government "obeys" me to some extent, and, to a different extent, I obey it.   20

What kind of thing can my Airedale, Drummer, have knowledge of? He can know that I exist and through that knowledge can claim his happinesses, with varying degrees of success, both with me and against me. Drummer can also know about larger human or dog communities than the one that consists only of him and me. There is my household—the other dogs, the cats, my husband. I have had enough dogs on campuses to know that he can learn that Yale exists as a neighborhood or village. My older dog, Annie, not only knows that Yale exists but can tell Yalies from townies, as I learned while teaching there during labor troubles.

Dogs can have elaborate conceptions of human social structures, and even of something like their rights and responsibilities within them, but these conceptions are never elaborate enough to construct a rights relationship between a dog and the state, or a dog and the Humane Society. Both of these are concepts that depend on writing and memoranda, officers in uniform, plaques and seals of authority. All of these are literary constructs, and all of them are beyond a dog's ken, which is why the mail carrier who doesn't also happen to be a dog's friend is forever an intruder—this is why dogs bark at mailmen.

It is clear enough that natural rights relations can arise between people and animals. Drummer, for example, can insist, "Hey, let's go outside and do something!" if I have been at my computer several days on end. He can both refuse to accept various of my suggestions and tell me when he fears for his life—such as the time when the huge, white flapping flag appeared out of nowhere, as it seemed to him, on the town green one evening when we were working. I can (and do) say to him either, "Oh, you don't have to worry about that" or, "Uh oh, you're right, Drum, that guy looks dangerous." Just as the government and I—two different species of organism—have developed improvised ways of communicating, such as the vote, so Drummer and I have worked out a number of ways to make our expressions known. Largely through obedience, I have taught him a fair amount about how to get responses from me. Obedience is reciprocal; you cannot get responses from a dog to whom you do not respond accurately. I have enfranchised him in a relationship to me by educating him, creating the conditions by which he can achieve a certain happiness specific to a dog, maybe even specific to an Airedale, inasmuch as this same relationship has allowed me to plumb the happiness of being a trainer and writing this article.

Instructions in this happiness are given terms that are alien to a culture in which liver treats, fluffy windup toys, and miniature sweaters are confused with respect and work. Jack Knox, a sheepdog trainer originally from Scotland, will shake his crook at a novice handler who makes a promiscuous move to praise a dog, and will call out in his Scottish accent, "Eh! Eh! Get back, get BACK! Ye'll no be abusin' the dogs like that in my clinic." America is a nation of abused animals. Knox says, because we are always swooping at them with praise, "no gi'ing them their freedom." I am reminded of Rainer Maria Rilke's account in which the Prodigal Son leaves—has to leave—because everyone loves him, even the dogs love him, and he has no path to the delicate and fierce truth of himself. Unconditional praise and love, in Rilke's story, disenfranchise us, distract us from what truly excites our interest.

In the minds of some trainers and handlers, praise is dishonesty. 25 Paradoxically, it is a kind of contempt for animals that masquerades as a reverence for helplessness and suffering. The idea of freedom means that you do not, at least not while Jack Knox is nearby, helpfully guide your dog through the motions of, say, herding over and over—what one trainer calls "explainy-wainy." This is rote learning. It works tolerably well on some handlers, because people have vast unconscious minds and can store complex preprogrammed behaviors. Dogs, on the other hand, have almost no unconscious minds, so they can learn only by thinking. Many children are like this until educated out of it.

If I tell my Airedale to sit and stay on the town green, and someone comes up and burbles, "What a pretty thing you are," he may break his stay to go for a caress. I pull him back and correct him for breaking. Now he holds his stay because I have blocked his way to movement but not because I have punished him. (A correction blocks one path as it opens another for desire to work; punishment blocks desire and opens nothing.) He holds his stay now, and—because the stay opens this possibility of work, new to a heedless young dog—he watches. If the person goes on talking, and isn't going to gush with praise, I may heel Drummer out of his stay and give him an "Okay" to make friends. Sometimes something about the person makes Drummer feel that reserve is in order. He responds to an insincere approach by sitting still, going down into himself, and thinking, "This person has no business pawing me. I'll sit very still, and he will go away." If the person doesn't take the hint from Drummer, I'll give the pup a little backup by saying. "Please don't pet him, he's working," even though he was not under any command.

The pup reads this, and there is a flicker of a working trust now stirring in the dog. Is the pup grateful? When the stranger leaves, does he lick my hand, full of submissive blandishments? This one doesn't. This one says nothing at all, and I say nothing much to him. This is a working trust we are developing, not a mutual congratulation society. My backup is praise enough for him; the use he makes of my support is praise enough for me.

Listening to a dog is often praise enough. Suppose it is just after dark and we are outside. Suddenly there is a shout from the house. The pup and I both look toward the shout and then toward each other: "What do you think?" I don't so much as cock my head, because Drummer is growing up, and I want to know what he thinks. He takes a few steps toward the house, and I follow. He listens again and comprehends that it's just Holly, who at fourteen is much given to alarming cries and shouts. He shrugs at me and goes about his business. I say nothing. To praise him for this performance would make about as much sense as praising a human being for the same thing. Thus:

A. What's that?

B. I don't know. [Listens] Oh, it's just Holly.

A. What a goooooood human being!

B. Huh?

This is one small moment in a series of like moments that will culminate in an Airedale who on a Friday will have the discrimination and confidence required to take down a man who is attacking me with a knife and on Saturday clown and play with the children at the annual Orange Empire Dog Club Christmas party.

People who claim to speak for animal rights are increasingly devoted   30
to the idea that the very keeping of a dog or a horse or a gerbil or a lion is in and of itself an offense. The more loudly they speak, the less likely they are to be in a rights relation to any given animal, because they are spending so much time in airplanes or transmitting fax announcements of the latest Sylvester Stallone anti-fur rally. In a 1988 *Harper's* forum, for example, Ingrid Newkirk, the national director of People for the Ethical Treatment of Animals, urged that domestic pets be spayed and neutered and ultimately phased out. She prefers, it appears, wolves—and wolves someplace else—to Airedales and, by a logic whose interior structure is

both emotionally and intellectually forever closed to Drummer, claims thereby to be speaking for "animal rights."

She is wrong. I am the only one who can own up to my Airedale's inalienable rights. Whether or not I do it perfectly at any given moment is no more refutation of this point than whether I am perfectly my husband's mate at any given moment refutes the fact of marriage. Only people who know Drummer, and whom he can know, are capable of this relationship. PETA and the Humane Society and the ASPCA and the Congress and NOW—as institutions—do have the power to affect my ability to grant rights to Drummer but are otherwise incapable of creating conditions or laws or rights that would increase his happiness. Only Drummer's owner has the power to obey him—to obey who he is and what he is capable of—deeply enough to grant him his rights and open up the possibility of happiness.

The Reader's Presence

1. Hearne writes from an "expert" perspective as an animal trainer. Suppose she were not an expert. How would that change your reading of her argument?

2. Hearne takes issue both with the common definition of "animal," protesting that not all animals are alike, and with the common notion of "happiness" as comfort (paragraphs 1 and 2). How do questions of these definitions form the basis of her argument? Is it possible to disagree with Hearne's definitions and still support her overall argument, or vice-versa? Why or why not?

3. Throughout her essay, Hearne attends to the political dimensions of her argument. In paragraph 20, for example, she introduces "the idea of democracy" and in the final paragraph she refers to her "Airedale's inalienable rights." Find other such examples. How does Hearne incorporate American political history into her essay? Do you find her allusion to slavery (paragraph 17) persuasive? necessary? Compare Hearne's ideas about dogs to Annie Dillard's understanding of wild animals in "Living Like Weasels" (page 627). Is Dillard's essay as philosophical as Hearne's? as political? as poetical? How does each essay address the reader? What are their respective goals?

95

Thomas Jefferson
The Declaration of Independence

Thomas Jefferson (1743–1826) was born and raised in Virginia and attended William and Mary College. After being admitted to the bar, he entered politics and served in the Virginia House of Burgesses and the Continental Congress of 1775. During the Revolutionary War he was elected governor of Virginia, and after independence was appointed special minister to France and later secretary of state. As the nation's third president he negotiated the Louisiana Purchase. Of all his accomplishments as an inventor, architect, diplomat, scientist, and politician, Jefferson counted his work in designing the University of Virginia among the most important, along with his efforts to establish separation of church and state and the composition of the Declaration of Independence.

In May and June 1776, the Continental Congress had been vigorously debating the dangerous idea of independence and felt the need to issue a document that clearly pointed out the colonial grievances against Great Britain. A committee was appointed to "prepare a declaration" that would summarize the specific reasons for colonial discontent. The committee of five included Thomas Jefferson, Benjamin Franklin, and John Adams. Jefferson, who was noted for his skills in composition and, as Adams put it, "peculiar felicity of expression," was chosen to write the first draft. The assignment took Jefferson about two weeks, and he submitted the draft first to the committee, which made a few verbal alterations, and then on June 28 to Congress, where, after further alterations mainly relating to slavery, it was finally approved on July 4, 1776.

Jefferson claims to have composed the document without research, working mainly from ideas he felt were commonly held at the time. As Jefferson recalled many years later, he drafted the document as "an appeal to the tribunal of the world" and hoped "to place before mankind the common sense of the subject, in terms so plain and firm as to command their assent." He claims that "neither aiming at originality of principle or sentiment . . . it was intended to be an expression of the American mind, and to give to that expression the proper tone and spirit called for by the occasion."

When in the Course of human events, it becomes necessary for one people to dissolve the political bands which have connected them with another, and to assume among the Powers of the earth, the separate and equal station to which the Laws of Nature and of Nature's God entitle them, a decent respect to the opinions of mankind requires that they should declare the causes which impel them to the separation.

We hold these truths to be self-evident, that all men are created equal, that they are endowed by their Creator with certain inalienable Rights, that among these are Life, Liberty and the pursuit of Happiness. That to secure these rights, Governments are instituted among Men, deriving their just powers from the consent of the governed. That whenever any Form of Government becomes destructive of these ends, it is the Right of the People to alter or to abolish it, and to institute new Government, laying its foundation on such principles and organizing its powers in such form, as to them shall seem most likely to effect their Safety and Happiness. Prudence, indeed, will dictate that Governments long established should not be changed for light and transient causes; and accordingly all experience hath shown, that mankind are more disposed to suffer, while evils are sufferable, than to right themselves by abolishing the forms to which they are accustomed. But when a long train of abuses and usurpations, pursuing invariably the same Object evinces a design to reduce them under absolute Despotism, it is their right, it is their duty, to throw off such Government, and to provide new Guards for their future security. — Such has been the patient sufferance of these Colonies; and such is now the necessity which constrains them to alter their former Systems of Government. The history of the present King of Great Britain is a history of repeated injuries and usurpations, all having in direct object the establishment of an absolute Tyranny over these States. To prove this, let Facts be submitted to a candid world.

He has refused his Assent to Laws, the most wholesome and necessary for the public good.

He has forbidden his Governors to pass Laws of immediate and pressing importance, unless suspended in their operation till his Assent should be obtained; and when so suspended, he has utterly neglected to attend to them.

He has refused to pass other laws for the accommodation of large   5
districts of people, unless those people would relinquish the right of Representation in the Legislature, a right inestimable to them and formidable to tyrants only.

He has called together legislative bodies at places unusual, uncomfortable, and distant from the depository of their Public Records, for the sole purpose of fatiguing them into compliance with his measures.

He has dissolved Representative Houses repeatedly, for opposing with manly firmness his invasions on the rights of the people.

He has refused for a long time, after such dissolutions, to cause others to be elected; whereby the Legislative Powers, incapable of Annihilation, have returned to the People at large for their exercise; the State remaining in the mean time exposed to all the dangers of invasion from without, and convulsions within.

He has endeavoured to prevent the population of these States;[1] for that purpose obstructing the Laws for Naturalization of Foreigners; refusing to pass others to encourage their migration hither, and raising the conditions of new Appropriations of Lands.

He has obstructed the Administration of Justice, by refusing his Assent to Laws for establishing Judiciary Powers.   10

He has made Judges dependent on his Will alone, for the tenure of their offices, and the amount and payment of their salaries.

He has erected a multitude of New Offices, and sent hither swarms of Officers to harass our People, and eat out their substance.

He has kept among us, in times of peace, Standing Armies without the Consent of our legislature.

He has affected to render the Military independent of and superior to the Civil Power.

He has combined with others to subject us to a jurisdiction foreign to   15
our constitution, and unacknowledged by our laws; giving his Assent to their acts of pretended Legislation:

For quartering large bodies of armed troops among us:

For protecting them, by a mock Trial, from Punishment for any Murders which they should commit on the Inhabitants of these States:

For cutting off our Trade with all parts of the world:

For imposing taxes on us without our Consent:

For depriving us in many cases, of the benefits of Trial by Jury: 20

For transporting us beyond Seas to be tried for pretended offenses:

For abolishing the free System of English Laws in a neighbouring Province, establishing therein an Arbitrary government, and enlarging its Boundaries so as to render it at once an example and fit instrument for introducing the same absolute rule into these Colonies:

For taking away our Charters, abolishing our most valuable Laws, and altering fundamentally the Forms of our Governments:

For suspending our own Legislatures, and declaring themselves invested with Power to legislate for us in all cases whatsoever.

He has abdicated Government here, by declaring us out of his Protec-   25
tion and waging War against us.

He has plundered our seas, ravaged our Coasts, burnt our towns, and destroyed the lives of our people.

He is at this time transporting large armies of foreign mercenaries to compleat the works of death, desolation and tyranny, already begun with circumstances of Cruelty & perfidy scarcely paralleled in the most barbarous ages, and totally unworthy of the Head of a civilized nation.

---

[1]*prevent the population of these States:* This meant limiting emigration to the Colonies, thus controlling their growth. —EDS.

He has constrained our fellow Citizens taken Captive on the high Seas to bear Arms against their Country, to become the executioners of their friends and Brethren, or to fall themselves by their Hands.

He has excited domestic insurrections amongst us, and has endeavoured to bring on the inhabitants of our frontiers, the merciless Indian Savages, whose known rule of warfare, is an undistinguished destruction of all ages, sexes and conditions.

In every stage of these Oppressions We have Petitioned for Readdress 30 in the most humble terms: Our repeated Petitions have been answered only by repeated injury. A Prince, whose character is thus marked by every act which may define a Tyrant, is unfit to be the ruler of a free People.

Nor have We been wanting in attention to our British brethren. We have warned them from time to time of attempts by their legislature to extend an unwarrantable jurisdiction over us. We have reminded them of the circumstances of our emigration and settlement here. We have appealed to their native justice and magnanimity, and we have conjured them by the ties of our common kindred to disavow these usurpations, which, would inevitably interrupt our connections and correspondence. They too have been deaf to the voice of justice and of consanguinity. We must, therefore, acquiesce in the necessity, which denounces our Separation, and hold them, as we hold the rest of mankind, Enemies in War, in Peace Friends.

We, therefore, the Representatives of the United States of America, in General Congress, Assembled, appealing to the Supreme Judge of the world for the rectitude of our intentions, do in the Name, and by Authority of the good People of these Colonies, solemnly publish and declare, That these United Colonies are, and of Right ought to be Free and Independent States, that they are Absolved from all Allegiance to the British Crown, and that all political connection between them and the State of Great Britain, is and ought to be totally dissolved; and that as Free and Independent States, they have full Power to levy War, conclude Peace, contract Alliances, establish Commerce, and to do all other Acts and Things which Independent States may of right do. And for the support of this Declaration, with a firm reliance on the Protection of Divine Providence, we mutually pledge to each other our Lives, our Fortunes and our sacred Honor.

The Reader's Presence

1. How does Jefferson seem to define *independence?* Whom does the definition include? Whom does it exclude? How does Jefferson's definition of independence differ from your own? It has been pointed out that Jefferson disregards "interdependence." Can you formulate an argument contrary to Jefferson's?

2. Examine the Declaration's first sentence. Who is the speaker here? What is the effect of the omniscient tone of the opening? Why does the first paragraph have no personal pronouns or references to specific events? What might Jefferson's argument stand to gain in generalizing the American situation?

3. As in classical epics and the Bible, Jefferson frequently relies on the rhetorical devices of repetition and lists. What is the effect of such devices? Can you find another essay in this anthology that relies on similar strategies? What do these essays have in common? What sets them apart? Paul Fussell refers to "the Framers of the Constitution" in his essay on the right to bear arms ("A Well-Regulated Militia," page 647). "Thank God for the eighteenth century," Fussell writes (paragraph 6), following an appreciation of the phraseology and the spirit of the Second Amendment to the Bill of Rights. What about the Declaration strikes you as representative of eighteenth-century ideas and language? Do you share Fussell's opinion about the continuing applicability of such texts?

96 ⸻⸻⸻⸻⸻⸻⸻⸻⸻⸻⸻⸻

June Jordan

A New Politics of Sexuality

June Jordan (1936–2002) was professor of African American studies at the University of California, Berkeley. She was the award-winning author of novels, short stories, poetry, children's fiction, and biography and is considered one of the most prominent contemporary women writers. Her essays can be found in collections such as On Call *(1986),* Moving Toward Home: Political Essays *(1989),* Technical Difficulties: African American Notes on the State of the Union *(1992), and* Affirmative Acts: Political Essays *(1998). Jordan also wrote a musical,* I Was Looking at the Ceiling and Then I Saw the Sky: Earthquake-Romance *(1995), for which John Adams wrote the music. She also published stories and poems in numerous national magazines; her latest collection of poems is* Kissing God Goodbye: Poems, 1991–97 *(1997). Her most recent work includes her memoir,* Soldier: A Poet's Childhood *(2000) and* Some of Us Did Not Die: Selected Essays of June Jordan *(2002). The essay "A New Politics of Sexuality" is from* Technical Difficulties.

Jordan considered writing, and especially poetry, to be a way toward empowerment. "Why should power and language coalesce in poetry? Because poetry is the medium for telling the truth, and because a poem is antithetical to lies/eva-sions and superficiality, anyone who becomes a practicing poet has an excellent chance of becoming somebody real, somebody known, self-defined and attuned to and listening and hungering for kindred real voices utterly/articulately different from his or her own voice."

As a young worried mother, I remember turning to Dr. Benjamin Spock's *Common Sense Book of Baby and Child Care* just about as often as I'd pick up the telephone. He was God. I was ignorant but striving to be good: a good Mother. And so it was there, in that best-seller pocket-book of do's and dont's, that I came upon this doozie of a guideline. Do not wear miniskirts or other provocative clothing because that will upset your child, especially if your child happens to be a boy. If you give your offspring "cause" to think of you as a sexual being, he will, at the least, become disturbed; you will derail the equilibrium of his notions about your possible identity and meaning in the world.

It had never occurred to me that anyone, especially my son, might look upon me as an asexual being. I had never supposed that "asexual" was some kind of positive designation I should, so to speak, lust after. I was pretty surprised by Dr. Spock. However, I was also, by habit, a crea-ture of obedience. For a couple of weeks I actually experimented with lus-terless colors and dowdy tops and bottoms, self-consciously hoping thereby to prove myself as a lusterless and dowdy and, therefore, excel-lent female parent.

Years would have to pass before I could recognize the familiar, by then, absurdity of a man setting himself up as the expert on a subject that presupposed women as the primary objects for his patriarchal dis-course — on motherhood, no less! Years passed before I came to perceive the perversity of dominant power assumed by men, and the perversity of self-determinating power ceded to men by women.

A lot of years went by before I understood the dynamics of what any-one could summarize as the Politics of Sexuality.

I believe the Politics of Sexuality is the most ancient and probably the most profound arena for human conflict. Increasingly, it seems clear to me that deeper and more pervasive than any other oppression, than any other bitterly contested human domain, is the oppression of sexuality, the exploitation of the human domain of sexuality for power.

When I say sexuality, I mean gender: I mean male subjugation of human beings because they are female. When I say sexuality I mean het-erosexual institutionalization of rights and privileges denied to homosex-ual men and women. When I say sexuality I mean gay or lesbian con-tempt for bisexual modes of human relationship.

The Politics of Sexuality therefore subsumes all of the different ways in which some of us seek to dictate to others of us what we should do, what we should desire, what we should dream about, and how we should behave ourselves, generally, on the planet. From China to Iran, from

5

Nigeria to Czechoslovakia, from Chile to California, the politics of sexuality—enforced by traditions of state-sanctioned violence plus religion and the law—reduces to male domination of women, heterosexist tyranny, and, among those of us who are in any case deemed despicable or deviant by the powerful, we find intolerance for those who choose a different, a more complicated—for example, an interracial or bisexual—mode of rebellion and freedom.

We must move out from the shadows of our collective subjugation—as people of color/as women/as gay/as lesbian/as bisexual human beings.

I can voice my ideas without hesitation or fear because I am speaking, finally, about myself. I am black and I am female and I am a mother and I am bisexual and I am a nationalist and I am an antinationalist. And I mean to be fully and freely all that I am!

Conversely, I do not accept that any white or black or Chinese men—   10
I do not accept that, for instance, Dr. Spock—should presume to tell me, or any other woman, how to mother a child. He has no right. He is not a mother. My child is not his child. And, likewise, I do not accept that anyone—any woman or any man who is not inextricably part of the subject he or she dares to address—should attempt to tell any of us, the objects of her or his presumptuous discourse, what we should do or what we should not do.

Recently, I have come upon gratuitous and appalling pseudoliberal pronouncements on sexuality. Too often, these utterances fall out of the mouths of men and women who first disclaim any sentiment remotely related to homophobia, but who then proceed to issue outrageous opinions like the following:

- That it is blasphemous to compare the oppression of gay, lesbian, or bisexual people to the oppression, say, of black people, or of the Palestinians.

- That the bottom line about gay or lesbian or bisexual identity is that you can conceal it whenever necessary and, so, therefore, why don't you do just that? Why don't you keep your deviant sexuality in the closet and let the rest of us—we who suffer oppression for reasons of our ineradicable and always visible components of our personhood such as race or gender—get on with our more necessary, our more beleaguered struggle to survive?

Well, number one: I believe I have worked as hard as I could, and then harder than that, on behalf of equality and justice—for African Americans, for the Palestinian people, and for people of color everywhere.

And, no, I do not believe it is blasphemous to compare oppressions of sexuality to oppressions of race and ethnicity: Freedom is indivisible or it is nothing at all besides sloganeering and temporary, short-sighted, and short-lived advancement for a few. Freedom is indivisible, and either we are working for freedom or you are working for the sake of your self-interests and I am working for mine.

If you can finally go to the bathroom, wherever you find one, if you can finally order a cup of coffee and drink it wherever coffee is available, but you cannot follow your heart—you cannot respect the response of your own honest body in the world—then how much of what kind of freedom does any one of us possess?

Or, conversely, if your heart and your honest body can be controlled by the state, or controlled by community taboo, are you not then, and in that case, no more than a slave ruled by outside force?

What tyranny could exceed a tyranny that dictates to the human heart, and that attempts to dictate the public career of an honest human body?

Freedom is indivisible; the Politics of Sexuality is not some optional "special-interest" concern for serious, progressive folk.

And, on another level, let me assure you: If every single gay or lesbian or bisexual man or woman active on the Left of American politics decided to stay home, there would be *no* Left left.

One of the things I want to propose is that we act on that reality: that we insistently demand reciprocal respect and concern from those who cheerfully depend upon our brains and our energies for their, and our, effective impact on the political landscape.

Last spring, at Berkeley, some students asked me to speak at a rally against racism. And I did. There were 400 or 500 people massed on Sproul Plaza, standing together against that evil. And, on the next day, on that same Plaza, there was a rally for bisexual and gay and lesbian rights, and students asked me to speak at that rally. And I did. There were fewer than seventy-five people stranded, pitiful, on that public space. And I said then what I say today: That was disgraceful! There should have been just one rally. One rally: Freedom is indivisible.

As for the second, nefarious pronouncement on sexuality that now enjoys mass-media currency: the idiot notion of keeping yourself in the closet—that is very much the same thing as the suggestion that black folks and Asian Americans and Mexican Americans should assimilate and become as "white" as possible—in our walk/talk/music/food/values—or else. Or else? Or else we should, deservedly, perish.

Sure enough, we have plenty of exposure to white everything so why would we opt to remain our African/Asian/ Mexican selves? The answer is that suicide is absolute, and if you think you will survive by hiding who you really are, you are sadly misled: There is no such thing as partial or intermittent suicide. You can only survive if you—who you really are—do survive.

Likewise, we who are not men and we who are not heterosexist—we, sure enough, have plenty of exposure to male-dominated/heterosexist this and that.

But a struggle to survive cannot lead to suicide: Suicide is the opposite of survival. And so we must not conceal/assimilate/integrate into the

15

20

would-be dominant culture and political system that despises us. Our survival requires that we alter our environment so that we can live and so that we can hold each other's hands and so that we can kiss each other on the streets, and in the daylight of our existence, without terror and without violence and sometimes fatal reactions from the busybodies of America.

Finally, I need to speak on bisexuality. I do believe that the analogy is   25
interracial or multiracial identity. I do believe that the analogy for bisexuality is a multicultural, multi-ethnic, multiracial world view. Bisexuality follows from such a perspective and leads to it, as well.

Just as there are many men and women in the United States whose parents have given them more than one racial, more than one ethnic identity and cultural heritage to honor; and just as these men and women must deny no given part of themselves except at the risk of self-deception and the insanities that must issue from that; and just as these men and women embody the principle of equality among races and ethnic communities; and just as these men, and women falter and anguish and choose and then falter again and then anguish and then choose yet again how they will honor the irreducible complexity of their God-given human being—even so, there are many men and women, especially young men and women, who seek to embrace the complexity of their total, always-changing social and political circumstance.

They seek to embrace our increasing global complexity on the basis of the heart and on the basis of an honest human body. Not according to ideology. Not according to group pressure. Not according to anybody's concept of "correct."

This is a New Politics of Sexuality. And even as I despair of identity politics—because identity is given and principles of justice/equality/freedom cut across given gender and given racial definitions of being, and because I will call you my brother, I will call you my sister, on the basis of what you *do* for justice, what you *do* for equality, what you *do* for freedom and *not* on the basis of who you are, even so I look with admiration and respect upon the new, bisexual politics of sexuality.

This emerging movement politicizes the so-called middle ground: Bisexuality invalidates either/or formulation, either/or analysis. Bisexuality means I am free and I am as likely to want and to love a woman as I am likely to want and to love a man, and what about that? Isn't that what freedom implies?

If you are free, you are not predictable and you are not controllable.   30
To my mind, that is the keenly positive, politicizing significance of bisexual affirmation: To insist upon complexity, to insist upon the validity of all of the components of social/sexual complexity, to insist upon the equal validity of all of the components of social/sexual complexity.

This seems to me a unifying, 1990s mandate for revolutionary Americans planning to make it into the twenty-first century on the basis of the heart, on the basis of an honest human body, consecrated to every struggle for justice, every struggle for equality, every struggle for freedom.

The Reader's Presence

1. What does Jordan mean by a "new" politics of sexuality? What is the "old" politics and how does it differ? Who was included and excluded in the old politics, and who stands most to benefit from a new politics of sexuality?

2. In paragraph 10, Jordan writes that she does "not accept that anyone—any woman or any man who is not inextricably part of the subject he or she dares to address—should attempt to tell any of us, the objects of her or his presumptuous discourse, what we should do or what we should not do." What are the logical implications of this statement? Who would be prohibited from speaking to whom about what—and who would do the prohibiting? Do you think Jordan herself, by her own reasoning, is "presumptuous" two paragraphs later in speaking on behalf of the Palestinians, since she is not one of them? Explain why or why not.

3. Why is Jordan critical of Dr. Spock's *Common Sense Book of Baby and Child Care?* Read the selection from that book, "Should Children Play with Guns?" reprinted on page 525. How do you evaluate Spock's position in light of Jordan's comments about him? Do you agree that he is unqualified to address the issue of children and violence? Explain why or why not.

97

Michiko Kakutani

The Word Police

Michiko Kakutani (b. 1955) was born in New Haven, Connecticut, and received a B.A. from Yale University in 1976. After graduation Kakutani worked as a reporter at the Washington Post *and later as a staff writer for* Time. *In 1979 she joined the cultural news department of the* New York Times *and has been the paper's senior book critic since 1983. She received the 1998 Pulitzer Prize for criticism for her "passionate, intelligent writing on books and contemporary literature." Kakutani has also published a collection of interviews,* The Poet at the Piano: Portraits of Writers, Filmmakers, Playwrights, and Other Artists *(1988). "The Word Police" appeared in the* New York Times *in January 1993.*

This month's inaugural festivities, with their celebration, in Maya Angelou's words, of "humankind" — "the Asian, the Hispanic, the Jew/ The African, the Native American, the Sioux, / The Catholic, the Muslim, the French, the Greek / The Irish, the Rabbi, the Priest, the Sheik, / The Gay, the Straight, the Preacher, / The privileged, the homeless, the Teacher" — constituted a kind of official embrace of multiculturalism and a new politics of inclusion.

The mood of political correctness, however, has already made firm inroads into popular culture. Washington boasts a store called Politically Correct that sells pro-whale, anti-meat, ban-the-bomb T-shirts, bumper stickers, and buttons, as well as a local cable television show called "Politically Correct Cooking" that features interviews in the kitchen with representatives from groups like People for the Ethical Treatment of Animals.

The Coppertone suntan lotion people are planning to give their long-time cover girl, Little Miss (Ms.?) Coppertone, a male equivalent, Little Mr. Coppertone. And even Superman (Superperson?) is rumored to be returning this spring, reincarnated as four ethnically diverse clones: an African-American, an Asian, a Caucasian and a Latino.

Nowhere is this P.C. mood more striking than in the increasingly noisy debate over language that has moved from university campuses to the country at large — a development that both underscores Americans' puritanical zeal for reform and their unwavering faith in the talismanic power of words.

Certainly no decent person can quarrel with the underlying impulse 5 behind political correctness: a vision of a more just, inclusive society in which racism, sexism, and prejudice of all sorts have been erased. But the methods and fervor of the self-appointed language police can lead to a rigid orthodoxy — and unintentional self-parody — opening the movement to the scorn of conservative opponents and the mockery of cartoonists and late-night television hosts.

It's hard to imagine women earning points for political correctness by saying "ovarimony" instead of "testimony" — as one participant at the recent Modern Language Association convention was overheard to suggest. It's equally hard to imagine people wanting to flaunt their lack of prejudice by giving up such words and phrases as "bull market," "kaiser roll," "Lazy Susan," and "charley horse."

Several books on bias-free language have already appeared, and the 1991 edition of the *Random House Webster's College Dictionary* boasts an appendix titled "Avoiding Sexist Language." The dictionary also includes such linguistic mutations as "womyn" (women, "used as an alternative spelling to avoid the suggestion of sexism perceived in the sequence m-e-n") and "waitron" (a gender-blind term for waiter or waitress).

Many of these dictionaries and guides not only warn the reader against offensive racial and sexual slurs, but also try to establish and enforce a whole new set of usage rules. Take, for instance, *The Bias-Free*

Word Finder, a Dictionary of Nondiscriminatory Language by Rosalie Maggio (Beacon Press) — a volume often indistinguishable, in its meticulous solemnity, from the tongue-in-cheek *Official Politically Correct Dictionary and Handbook* put out last year by Henry Beard and Christopher Cerf (Villard Books). Ms. Maggio's book supplies the reader intent on using kinder, gentler language with writing guidelines as well as a detailed listing of more than 5,000 "biased words and phrases."

Whom are these guidelines for? Somehow one has a tough time picturing them replacing *Fowler's Modern English Usage* in the classroom, or being adopted by the average man (sorry, individual) in the street.

The "pseudogeneric 'he,'" we learn from Ms. Maggio, is to be   10
avoided like the plague, as is the use of the word "man" to refer to humanity. "Fellow," "king," "lord" and "master" are bad because they're "male-oriented words," and "king," "lord" and "master" are especially bad because they're also "hierarchical, dominator society terms." The politically correct lion becomes the "monarch of the jungle," new-age children play "someone on the top of the heap," and the "Mona Lisa" goes down in history as Leonardo's "acme of perfection."

As for the word "black," Ms. Maggio says it should be excised from terms with a negative spin: she recommends substituting words like "mouse" for "black eye," "ostracize" for "blackball," "payola" for "blackmail" and "outcast" for "black sheep." Clearly, some of these substitutions work better than others: somehow the "sinister humor" of Kurt Vonnegut or *Saturday Night Live* doesn't quite make it; nor does the "denouncing" of the Hollywood 10.

For the dedicated user of politically correct language, all these rules can make for some messy moral dilemmas. Whereas "battered wife" is a gender-biased term, the gender-free term "battered spouse," Ms. Maggio notes, incorrectly implies "that men and women are equally battered."

On one hand, say Francine Wattman Frank and Paula A. Treichler in their book *Language, Gender, and Professional Writing* (Modern Language Association), "he or she" is an appropriate construction for talking about an individual (like a jockey, say) who belongs to a profession that's predominantly male — it's a way of emphasizing "that such occupations are not barred to women or that women's concerns need to be kept in mind." On the other hand, they add, using masculine pronouns rhetorically can underscore ongoing male dominance in those fields, implying the need for change.

And what about the speech codes adopted by some universities in recent years? Although they were designed to prohibit students from uttering sexist and racist slurs, they would extend, by logic, to blacks who want to use the word "nigger" to strip the term of its racist connotations, or homosexuals who want to use the word "queer" to reclaim it from bigots.

In her book, Ms. Maggio recommends applying bias-free usage   15
retroactively: she suggests paraphrasing politically incorrect quotations,

or replacing "the sexist words or phrases with ellipsis dots and/or brack-
eted substitutes," or using "*sic*" "to show that the sexist words come
from the original quotation and to call attention to the fact that they are
incorrect."

Which leads the skeptical reader of *The Bias-Free Word Finder* to
wonder whether "All the King's Men" should be retitled "All the Ruler's
People"; "Pet Semetary," "Animal Companion Graves"; "Birdman of Alcatraz," "Birdperson of Alcatraz"; and "The Iceman Cometh," "The Ice
Route Driver Cometh"?

Will making such changes remove the prejudice in people's minds?
Should we really spend time trying to come up with non-male-based alter-
natives to "Midas touch," "Achilles' heel," and "Montezuma's revenge"?
Will tossing out Santa Claus—whom Ms. Maggio accuses of reinforcing
"the cultural male-as-norm system"—in favor of Belfana, his Italian female alter ego, truly help banish sexism? Can the avoidance of "violent
expressions and metaphors" like "kill two birds with one stone," "sock it
to 'em" or "kick an idea around" actually promote a more harmonious
world?

The point isn't that the excesses of the word police are comical. The
point is that their intolerance (in the name of tolerance) has disturbing
implications. In the first place, getting upset by phrases like "bullish on
America" or "the City of Brotherly Love" tends to distract attention from
the real problems of prejudice and injustice that exist in society at large,
turning them into mere questions of semantics. Indeed, the emphasis currently put on politically correct usage has uncanny parallels with the academic movement of deconstruction—a method of textual analysis that
focuses on language and linguistic pyrotechnis—which has become
firmly established on university campuses.

In both cases, attention is focused on surfaces, on words and
metaphors; in both cases, signs and symbols are accorded more importance than content. Hence, the attempt by some radical advocates to remove *The Adventures of Huckleberry Finn* from curriculums on the
grounds that Twain's use of the word "nigger" makes the book a racist
text—never mind the fact that this American classic (written in 1884) depicts the spiritual kinship achieved between a white boy and a runaway
slave, never mind the fact that the "nigger" Jim emerges as the novel's
most honorable, decent character.

Ironically enough, the P.C. movement's obsession with language is   20
accompanied by a strange Orwellian willingness to warp the meaning of
words by placing them under a high-powered ideological lens. For instance, the *Dictionary of Cautionary Words and Phrases*—a pamphlet issued by the University of Missouri's Multicultural Management Program
to help turn "today's journalists into tomorrow's multicultural newsroom
managers"—warns that using the word "articulate" to describe members
of a minority group can suggest the opposite, "that 'those people' are not
considered well educated, articulate and the like."

The pamphlet patronizes minority groups, by cautioning the reader against using the words "lazy" and "burly" to describe any member of such groups; and it issues a similar warning against using words like "gorgeous" and "petite" to describe women.

As euphemism proliferates with the rise of political correctness, there is a spread of the sort of sloppy, abstract language that Orwell said is "designed to make lies sound truthful and murder respectable, and to give an appearance of solidity to pure wind." "Fat" becomes "big boned" as "differently sized"; "stupid" becomes "exceptional"; "stoned" becomes "chemically inconvenienced."

Wait a minute here! Aren't such phrases eerily reminiscent of the euphemisms coined by the government during Vietnam and Watergate? Remember how the military used to speak of "pacification," or how President Richard M. Nixon's press secretary, Ronald L. Ziegler, tried to get away with calling a lie an "inoperative statement"?

Calling the homeless "the underhoused" doesn't give them a place to live; calling the poor "the economically marginalized" doesn't help them pay the bills. Rather, by playing down their plight, such language might even make it easier to shrug off the seriousness of their situation.

Instead of allowing free discussion and debate to occur, many gung-ho 25 advocates of politically correct language seem to think that simple suppression of a word or concept will magically make the problem disappear. In the *Bias-Free Word Finder,* Ms. Maggio entreats the reader not to perpetuate the negative stereotype of Eve. "Be extremely cautious in referring to the biblical Eve," she writes; "this story has profoundly contributed to negative attitudes toward women throughout history, largely because of misogynistic and patriarchal interpretations that labeled her evil, inferior, and seductive."

The story of Bluebeard, the rake (whoops!—the libertine) who killed his seven wives, she says, is also to be avoided, as is the biblical story of Jezebel. Of Jesus Christ, Ms. Maggio writes: "There have been few individuals in history as completely androgynous as Christ, and it does his message a disservice to overinsist on his maleness." She doesn't give the reader any hints on how this might be accomplished; presumably, one is supposed to avoid describing him as the Son of God.

Of course the P.C. police aren't the only ones who want to proscribe what people should say or give them guidelines for how they may use an idea; Jesse Helms and his supporters are up to exactly the same thing when they propose to patrol the boundaries of the permissible in art. In each case, the would-be censor aspires to suppress what he or she finds distasteful—all, of course, in the name of the public good.

In the case of the politically correct, the prohibition of certain words, phrases and ideas is advanced in the cause of building a brave new world free of racism and hate, but this vision of harmony clashes with the very ideals of diversity and inclusion that the multicultural movement holds dear, and it's purchased at the cost of freedom of expression and freedom of speech.

In fact, the utopian world envisioned by the language police would be bought at the expense of the ideas of individualism and democracy articulated in the "The [*sic*] Gettysburg Address": "Fourscore and seven years ago our fathers brought forth on this continent a new nation, conceived in liberty and dedicated to the proposition that all men are created equal."

Of course, the P.C. police have already found Lincoln's words hopelessly "phallocentric." No doubt they would rewrite the passage: "Fourscore and seven years ago our foremothers and forefathers brought forth on this continent a new nation, formulated with liberty, and dedicated to the proposition that all humankind is created equal."   30

The Reader's Presence

1. Kakutani begins by dissecting what she sees as a current state of affairs. What kinds of words does she use to describe this state of affairs in paragraphs 1–3? Is she merely stating the facts or beginning her argument? Why do you say so? Kakutani uses the word *police* (paragraph 5) to describe those who would alter the English language. What does this word imply? Is it justified?

2. The author humorously cites rather awkward word substitutions from *The Bias-Free Word Finder*. Is this example sufficient and fair as evidence? Why or why not? Does mockery strengthen or weaken Kakutani's case? Why? What response might a proponent of language change propose to counter her argument?

3. In paragraph 20 Kakutani refers to "a strange Orwellian willingness to warp the meaning of words by placing them under a high-powered ideological lens." What do you think she is saying here? In what sense is such linguistic scrutiny "Orwellian"? Where else does Kakutani allude to Orwell's writing? Read George Orwell's "Politics and the English Language" (page 481). If Kakutani hadn't suggested the connection, would you associate Orwell with the "P.C. movement" or the "word police"?

98

Wendy Kaminer

Let's Talk about Gender, Baby

Wendy Kaminer (b. 1949), lawyer, author, and social critic, is the president of the National Coalition against Censorship, a public policy fellow at Radcliffe College, and a frequent commentator for National Public Radio's "Morning Edition." Kaminer's books include I'm Dysfunctional, You're Dysfunctional *(1992),* It's All the Rage: Crime and Culture *(1995),* True Love Waits: Essays and Criticism *(1996), and* Sleeping with Extra-Terrestrials: The Rise of Irrationalism and Perils of Piety *(1999). Her most recent book is* Free for All: Defending Liberty in America *(2002). She received a Guggenheim fellowship (1983) and has written numerous essays and reviews for such publications as the* New York Times, *the* New Republic, *and the* Nation, *and is a contributing editor at the* Atlantic Monthly.

Feminists have long been ridiculed for their efforts to purge sexism from language by using words like *chairperson* and avoiding the use of male pronouns as universal signifiers of both sexes. The results have not always been pretty: "He knows what's good for him" is a far more felicitous phrase than "He/she knows what's good for him/her." And we can probably achieve equality without ever using the word *herstory*. Still, I'm grateful that common usage no longer completely ignores the existence of women with words like *mankind*.

Besides, I grew up in a predigital age, when concern about grammar and usage was not dismissed as pedantry. So in my view, while feminist language police are sometimes hypervigilant, sometimes they're not vigilant enough. Why do they tolerate, and even promote, use of the word *woman* (or the plural *women*) as an adjective? It's a noun. We have "women doctors" and "women senators" but no "men doctors" or "men senators." We do, however, have "manservants." It's not hard to figure out why. Servants are presumptively female, just as senators are presumptively male. When we incorrectly describe a female politician as a "woman politician," we confirm that, like a "man-child," she's an oddity, an oxymoron.

Equally irritating is our conflation of *sex* and *gender*. In a society that vacillates between Puritanism and permissiveness, there are obvious reasons to avoid using the word *sex*. People fear that it arouses prurient interest by recalling what teenagers do in the backseats of cars or what hookers do in the front. But in addition to various acts, *sex* refers to the biological categories male and female; *gender* refers (or used to refer) to cultural norms of masculinity and femininity. To say that you're a member of the female sex is simply to say that you're a woman. To say that you're a member of the female gender is to say that you behave the way a woman is supposed to behave. Sexual differences can only be accommodated; gender differences can and do change. Men can't get pregnant, but they can learn to type, as the computer age has shown.

So I don't think my complaint is mere pedantry. When we use these terms interchangeably, we lose important distinctions between biology and culture and risk confusing our standards of law. We shouldn't use the term *gender discrimination* to describe discrimination against a person because she's a female. Instead, it means (or should mean) discrimination against a woman who dresses like a man, for example, or has adopted a masculine style. A sign that says "No men need apply" constitutes sex discrimination. Gender discrimination is a sign that says "No men in skirts need apply."

Fortunately, the U.S. Supreme Court has managed, barely, to outlaw   5
discrimination based on gender, without ever recognizing how it differs from discrimination based on sex. In the 1989 case *Price Waterhouse v. Hopkins,* a plurality of the Court ruled in favor of a woman who had been passed over for partnership at the accounting firm of Price Waterhouse because she was deemed insufficiently ladylike. One partner advised her to "walk more femininely, talk more femininely, dress more femininely, wear make-up, have her hair styled, and wear jewelry."

Or consider the 1998 case of Joseph Oncale, a former oil rig worker who claimed to have been subjected to highly sexualized, physical assaults and threatened with rape by his male colleagues. In *Oncale v. Sundowner Offshore Services,* the Supreme Court allowed Oncale to pursue his "same-sex" harassment case under federal equal-employment law. The Court stressed that federal law prohibits sex discrimination, even when practiced by members of the same sex against one another. The trouble is that Oncale suffered gender discrimination, not sex discrimination. He was reportedly singled out for abuse not because he is a man but because he is a relatively slight man whose masculinity was questioned. There was no general hostility toward men in Oncale's all-male workplace; there was, it seems, hostility toward men deemed to possess insufficient machismo.

Misuse of *sex* and *gender* is steadily worsening: As if "single-sex" schools" weren't bad enough, we now have "single-gender schools," which I imagine as places in which men learn to walk like women and women learn to whistle. Instead of "transsexuals," we have "transgendered people"—a term that might apply to any woman who exercises authority in what is labeled a masculine style or to any man who carries a purse. We even have surveys asking us to specify our "sex or gender." "Male gender," I replied once, when I was wearing a mannish suit; "female sex."

How did we get so confused? Supreme Court Justice Ruth Bader Ginsburg is sometimes blamed or credited for introducing the term *gender discrimination* in the early 1970s, when she was arguing landmark sexual-equality cases before the Supreme Court. According to my favorite rumor, she did not want to use the word *sex* before the Court and so offered up the word *gender*. I've always been quite grateful to Justice Ginsburg for the rights she helped secure, and I understand that every revolution has its casualties. But why must language always be among them?

The Reader's Presence

1. How would you describe Kaminer's attitude toward feminist language? Does she ridicule efforts to purge the English language of sexism? Where does she appear to draw the line between excessive and legitimate usage? Why, for example, does she object to use of the word *woman* as an adjective?

2. What distinction does Kaminer draw between *sex* and *gender?* Why does she complain that these two terms are being used interchangeably? What harm does it do? Consult a dictionary or encyclopedia and look up the word *gender*. What is the primary definition? Does your quick research support or contradict Kaminer's argument? Do you think that *gender* is generally used today as a euphemism for *sex* by people who would rather not say that word directly, or do you think it has a distinct meaning in itself?

3. Compare Kaminer's essay with one on a similar topic, Michiko Kakutani's "The Word Police" (see page 683). Are these writers complaining about similar problems? Do you think Kaminer's objections are mainly against politically correct language, or do you think she has different concerns? Explain the differences you see between Kaminer and Kakutani. You may also want to read Kaminer's essay in the context of George Orwell's classic "Politics and the English Language" (page 481). How might Orwell regard the use of the word *gender* today? How does his argument anticipate the issue Kaminer raises?

99

Martin Luther King Jr.

Letter from Birmingham Jail

Martin Luther King Jr. (1929–1968) was born in Atlanta, Georgia, and after training for the ministry became pastor of the Dexter Avenue Baptist Church in Montgomery, Alabama. He became active in the civil rights movement in 1956 when he was elected president of the Montgomery Improvement Association, the group which organized a transportation boycott in response to the arrest of Rosa Parks. King later became president of the Southern Christian Leadership Conference, and under his philosophy of nonviolent direct action he led marches and protests throughout the South, to Chicago, and to Washington, D.C. In 1963 King delivered his most famous speech, "I Have a Dream," before 200,000 people in front of the Lincoln Memorial in Washington, D.C., and in 1964 he was awarded the Nobel Peace Prize. King was assassinated on April 3, 1968, in Memphis, Tennessee.

King was a masterful orator and a powerful writer. Along with his many speeches, King wrote several books, including Why We Can't Wait *(1963),* Where Do We Go from Here: Chaos or Community? *(1967),* The Measure of a Man *(1968), and* Trumpet of Conscience *(1968). "Letter from Birmingham Jail" appeared in* Why We Can't Wait.

King's best-known writings and speeches, including the letter reprinted here, are designed to educate his audiences and inspire them to act. "Through education we seek to break down the spiritual barriers to integration," he once said, and "through legislation and court orders we seek to break down the physical barriers to integration. One method is not a substitute for the other, but a meaningful and necessary supplement."

MARTIN LUTHER KING JR.
Birmingham City Jail
April 16, 1963

Bishop C. C. J. CARPENTER
Bishop JOSEPH A. DURICK
Rabbi MILTON L. GRAFMAN
Bishop PAUL HARDIN

Bishop NOLAN B. HARMON
The Rev. GEORGE M. MURRAY
The Rev. EDWARD V. RAMAGE
The Rev. EARL STALLINGS

My dear Fellow Clergymen,

While confined here in the Birmingham City Jail, I came across your recent statement calling our present activities "unwise and untimely." Seldom, if ever, do I pause to answer criticism of my work and ideas. If I sought to answer all of the criticisms that cross my desk, my secretaries would be engaged in little else in the course of the day and I would have no time for constructive work. But since I feel that you are men of genuine good will and your criticisms are sincerely set forth, I would like to answer your statement in what I hope will be patient and reasonable terms.

I think I should give the reason for my being in Birmingham, since you have been influenced by the argument of "outsiders coming in." I have the honor of serving as president of the Southern Christian Leadership Conference, an organization operating in every Southern state with headquarters in Atlanta, Georgia. We have some eighty-five affiliate organizations all across the South—one being the Alabama Christian Movement for Human Rights. Whenever necessary and possible we share staff, educational, and financial resources with our affiliates. Several months ago our local affiliate here in Birmingham invited us to be on call to engage in a nonviolent direct action program if such were deemed necessary. We readily consented and when the hour came we lived up to our promises. So I am here, along with several members of my staff, because we were invited here. I am here because I have basic organizational ties here. Beyond this, I am in Birmingham because injustice is here. Just as the eighth century prophets left their little villages and carried their "thus saith the Lord" far beyond the boundaries of their home town, and just as the Apostle Paul left his little village of Tarsus and carried the gospel of Jesus Christ to practically every hamlet and city of the Graeco-Roman world, I too am compelled to carry the gospel of freedom beyond my particular home town. Like Paul, I must constantly respond to the Macedonian call for aid.

Moreover, I am cognizant of the interrelatedness of all communities and states. I cannot sit idly by in Atlanta and not be concerned about what happens in Birmingham. Injustice anywhere is a threat to justice everywhere. We are caught in an inescapable network of mutuality tied in a single garment of destiny. Whatever affects one directly affects all indirectly. Never again can we afford to live with the narrow, provincial "outside agitator" idea. Anyone who lives inside the United States can never be considered an outsider anywhere in this country.

You deplore the demonstrations that are presently taking place in Birmingham. But I am sorry that your statement did not express a similar concern for the conditions that brought the demonstrations into being. I am sure that each of you would want to go beyond the superficial social analyst who looks merely at effects, and does not grapple with underlying causes. I would not hesitate to say that it is unfortunate that so-called demonstrations are taking place in Birmingham at this time, but I would say in more emphatic terms it is even more unfortunate that the white power structure of this city left the Negro community with no other alternative.

In any nonviolent campaign there are four basic steps: (1) collection   5
of the facts to determine whether injustices are alive; (2) negotiation; (3) self-purification; and (4) direct action. We have gone through all of these steps in Birmingham. There can be no gainsaying of the fact that racial injustice engulfs this community. Birmingham is probably the most thoroughly segregated city in the United States. Its ugly record of police brutality is known in every section of this country. Its unjust treatment of Negroes in the courts is a notorious reality. There have been more unsolved bombings of Negro homes and churches in Birmingham than any city in this nation. These are the hard, brutal, and unbelievable facts. On the basis of these conditions Negro leaders sought to negotiate with the city fathers. But the political leaders consistently refused to engage in good faith negotiation.

Then came the opportunity last September to talk with some of the leaders of the economic community. In these negotiating sessions certain promises were made by the merchants — such as the promise to remove the humiliating racial signs from the stores. On the basis of these promises Rev. Shuttlesworth and the leaders of the Alabama Christian Movement for Human Rights agreed to call a moratorium on any type of demonstrations. As the weeks and months unfolded we realized that we were the victims of a broken promise. The signs remained. As in so many experiences of the past we were confronted with blasted hopes, and the dark shadow of a deep disappointment settled upon us. So we had no alternative except that of preparing for direct action, whereby we would present our very bodies as a means of laying our case before the conscience of the local and national community. We were not unmindful of the difficulties involved. So we decided to go through a process of self-purification. We started having workshops on nonviolence and repeatedly asked ourselves the questions, "Are you able to accept blows without retaliating?" "Are you able to endure the ordeals of jail?"

We decided to set our direct action program around the Easter season, realizing that with the exception of Christmas, this was the largest shopping period of the year. Knowing that a strong economic withdrawal program would be the by-product of direct action, we felt that this was the best time to bring pressure on the merchants for the needed changes. Then it occurred to us that the March election was ahead, and so we speedily decided to postpone action until after election day. When we discovered that Mr. Connor[1] was in the run-off, we decided again to postpone so that the demonstrations could not be used to cloud the issues. At this time we agreed to begin our nonviolent witness the day after the run-off.

This reveals that we did not move irresponsibly into direct action. We too wanted to see Mr. Connor defeated; so we went through postponement after postponement to aid in this community need. After this we felt that direct action could be delayed no longer.

You may well ask, "Why direct action? Why sit-ins, marches, etc.? Isn't negotiation a better path?" You are exactly right in your call for negotiation. Indeed, this is the purpose of direct action. Nonviolent direct action seeks to create such a crisis and establish such creative tension that a community that has constantly refused to negotiate is forced to confront the issue. It seeks so to dramatize the issue that it can no longer be ignored. I just referred to the creation of tension as a part of the work of the nonviolent resister. This may sound rather shocking. But I must confess that I am not afraid of the word tension. I have earnestly worked and preached against violent tension, but there is a type of constructive nonviolent tension that is necessary for growth. Just as Socrates felt that it was necessary to create a tension in the mind so that individuals could rise from the bondage of myths and half-truths to the unfettered realm of creative analysis and objective appraisal, we must see the need of having nonviolent gadflies to create the kind of tension in society that will help men rise from the dark depths of prejudice and racism to the majestic heights of understanding and brotherhood. So the purpose of the direct action is to create a situation so crisis-packed that it will inevitably open the door to negotiation. We, therefore, concur with you in your call for negotiation. Too long has our beloved Southland been bogged down in the tragic attempt to live in monologue rather than dialogue.

One of the basic points in your statement is that our acts are un-   10
timely. Some have asked, "Why didn't you give the new administration time to act?" The only answer that I can give to this inquiry is that the new administration must be prodded about as much as the outgoing one before it acts. We will be sadly mistaken if we feel that the election of Mr. Boutwell will bring the millennium to Birmingham. While Mr. Boutwell is much more articulate and gentle than Mr. Connor, they are both segregationists dedicated to the task of maintaining the status quo. The hope I see in Mr. Boutwell is that he will be reasonable enough to see the futility of massive resistance to desegregation. But he will not see this without

---

[1]*Mr. Connor:* Eugene "Bull" Connor and Albert Boutwell ran for mayor of Birmingham, Alabama, in 1963. Although Boutwell, the more moderate candidate, was declared the winner, Connor, the city commissioner of public safety, refused to leave office, claiming that he had been elected to serve until 1965. While the issue was debated in the courts, Connor was on the street ordering the police to use force to suppress demonstrations against segregation. — EDS.

pressure from the devotees of civil rights. My friends, I must say to you that we have not made a single gain in civil rights without determined legal and nonviolent pressure. History is the long and tragic story of the fact that privileged groups seldom give up their privileges voluntarily. Individuals may see the moral light and voluntarily give up their unjust posture; but as Reinhold Niebuhr has reminded us, groups are more immoral than individuals.

We know through painful experience that freedom is never voluntarily given by the oppressor; it must be demanded by the oppressed. Frankly I have never yet engaged in a direct action movement that was "well timed," according to the timetable of those who have not suffered unduly from the disease of segregation. For years now I have heard the word "Wait!" It rings in the ear of every Negro with a piercing familiarity. This "wait" has almost always meant "never." It has been a tranquilizing thaliodomide, relieving the emotional stress for a moment, only to give birth to an ill-formed infant of frustration. We must come to see with the distinguished jurist of yesterday that "justice too long delayed is justice denied." We have waited for more than three hundred and forty years for our constitutional and God-given rights. The nations of Asia and Africa are moving with jet-like speed toward the goal of political independence, and we still creep at horse and buggy pace toward the gaining of a cup of coffee at a lunch counter.

I guess it is easy for those who have never felt the stinging darts of segregation to say wait. But when you have seen vicious mobs lynch your mothers and fathers at will and drown your sisters and brothers at whim; when you have seen hate-filled policemen curse, kick, brutalize, and even kill your black brothers and sisters with impunity; when you see the vast majority of your twenty million Negro brothers smothering in an air-tight cage of poverty in the midst of an affluent society; when you suddenly find your tongue twisted and your speech stammering as you seek to explain to your six-year-old daughter why she can't go to the public amusement park that has just been advertised on television, and see tears welling up in her little eyes when she is told that Funtown is closed to colored children, and see the depressing clouds of inferiority begin to form in her little mental sky, and see her begin to distort her little personality by unconsciously developing a bitterness toward white people; when you have to concoct an answer for a five-year-old son asking in agonizing pathos: "Daddy, why do white people treat colored people so mean?"; when you take a cross country drive and find it necessary to sleep night after night in the uncomfortable corners of your automobile because no motel will accept you; when you are humiliated day in and day out by nagging signs reading "white" men and "colored"; when your first name becomes "nigger" and your middle name becomes "boy" (however old you are) and your last name becomes "John," and when your wife and mother are never given the respected title "Mrs."; when you are harried by day and haunted by night by the fact that you are a Negro, living constantly at tip-toe stance never quite knowing what to expect next, and plagued with inner fears and outer resentments; when you are forever fighting a degenerating sense of "nobodiness";—then you will understand why we find it difficult to wait. There comes a time when the cup of endurance runs over, and men are no longer willing to be plunged into an abyss of injustice where they experience the bleakness of corroding despair. I hope, sirs, you can understand our legitimate and unavoidable impatience.

You express a great deal of anxiety over our willingness to break laws. This is certainly a legitimate concern. Since we so diligently urge people to obey the Supreme Court's decision of 1954 outlawing segregation in the public schools, it is rather strange and paradoxical to find us consciously breaking laws. One may well ask, "How can you advocate breaking some laws and obeying others?" The answer is found in the fact that there are two types of laws. There are *just* laws and there are *unjust* laws. I would be the first to advocate obeying just laws. One has not only a legal but moral responsibility to obey just laws. Conversely, one has a moral responsibility to disobey unjust laws. I would agree with Saint Augustine that "An unjust law is no law at all."

Now what is the difference between the two? How does one determine when a law is just or unjust? A just law is a man-made code that squares with the moral law or the law of God. An unjust law is a code that is out of harmony with the moral law. To put it in the terms of Saint Thomas Aquinas, an unjust law is a human law that is not rooted in eternal and natural law. Any law that uplifts human personality is just. Any law that degrades human personality is unjust. All segregation statutes are unjust because segregation distorts the soul and damages the personality. It gives the segregator a false sense of superiority and the segregated a false sense of inferiority. To use the words of Martin Buber, the great Jewish philosopher, segregation substitutes an "I-it" relationship for the "I-thou" relationship, and ends up relegating persons to the status of things. So segregation is not only politically, economically, and sociologically unsound, but it is morally wrong and sinful. Paul Tillich[2] has said that sin is separation. Isn't segregation an existential expression of man's tragic separation, an expression of his awful estrangement, his terrible sinfulness? So I can urge men to obey the 1954 decision of the Supreme Court[3] because it is morally right, and I can urge them to disobey segregation ordinances because they are morally wrong.

Let us turn to a more concrete example of just and unjust laws. An   15
unjust law is a code that a majority inflicts on a minority that is not binding on itself. This is *difference* made legal. On the other hand a just law is

---

[2]*Paul Tillich* (1886–1965): Theologian and philosopher.—EDS.

[3]*1954 decision of the Supreme Court: Brown v. Board of Education,* the case in which the Supreme Court ruled racial segregation in the nation's public schools unconstitutional.—EDS.

a code that a majority compels a minority to follow that it is willing to follow itself. This is *sameness* made legal.

Let me give another explanation. An unjust law is a code inflicted upon a minority which that minority had no part in enacting or creating because they did not have the unhampered right to vote. Who can say the legislature of Alabama which set up the segregation laws was democratically elected? Throughout the state of Alabama all types of conniving methods are used to prevent Negroes from becoming registered voters and there are some counties without a single Negro registered to vote despite the fact that the Negro constitutes a majority of the population. Can any law set up in such a state be considered democratically structured?

These are just a few examples of unjust and just laws. There are some instances when a law is just on its face but unjust in its application. For instance, I was arrested Friday on a charge of parading without a permit. Now there is nothing wrong with an ordinance which requires a permit for a parade, but when the ordinance is used to preserve segregation and to deny citizens the First Amendment privilege of peaceful assembly and peaceful protest, then it becomes unjust.

I hope you can see the distinction I am trying to point out. In no sense do I advocate evading or defying the law as the rabid segregationist would do. This would lead to anarchy. One who breaks an unjust law must do it *openly, lovingly* (not hatefully as the white mothers did in New Orleans when they were seen on television screaming "nigger, nigger, nigger") and with a willingness to accept the penalty. I submit that an individual who breaks a law that conscience tells him is unjust, and willingly accepts the penalty by staying in jail to arouse the conscience of the community over its injustice, is in reality expressing the very highest respect for law.

Of course there is nothing new about this kind of civil disobedience. It was seen sublimely in the refusal of Shadrach, Meshach, and Abednego to obey the laws of Nebuchadnezzar because a higher moral law was involved. It was practiced superbly by the early Christians who were willing to face hungry lions and the excruciating pain of chopping blocks, before submitting to certain unjust laws of the Roman Empire. To a degree academic freedom is a reality today because Socrates practiced civil disobedience.

We can never forget that everything Hitler did in Germany was 20
"legal" and everything the Hungarian freedom fighters[4] did in Hungary was "illegal." It was "illegal" to aid and comfort a Jew in Hitler's Germany. But I am sure that, if I had lived in Germany during that time, I would have aided and comforted my Jewish brothers even though it was illegal. If I lived in a communist country today where certain principles dear to the Christian faith are suppressed, I believe I would openly advocate disobeying those antireligious laws.

---

[4]*Hungarian freedom fighters:* Those who fought in the unsuccessful 1956 revolt against Soviet oppression. — EDS.

I must make two honest confessions to you, my Christian and Jewish brothers. First I must confess that over the last few years I have been gravely disappointed with the white moderate. I have almost reached the regrettable conclusion that the Negroes' great stumbling block in the stride toward freedom is not the White Citizens' "Counciler" or the Ku Klux Klanner, but the white moderate who is more devoted to "order" than to justice; who prefers a negative peace which is the absence of tension to a positive peace which is the presence of justice; who constantly says "I agree with you in the goal you seek, but I can't agree with your methods of direct action"; who paternalistically feels that he can set the timetable for another man's freedom; who lives by the myth of time and who constantly advises the Negro to wait until a "more convenient season." Shallow understanding from people of good will is more frustrating than absolute misunderstanding from people of ill will. Lukewarm acceptance is much more bewildering than outright rejection.

I had hoped that the white moderate would understand that law and order exist for the purpose of establishing justice, and that when they fail to do this they become the dangerously structured dams that block the flow of social progress. I had hoped that the white moderate would understand that the present tension in the South is merely a necessary phase of the transition from an obnoxious negative peace, where the Negro passively accepted his unjust plight, to a substance-filled positive peace, where all men will respect the dignity and worth of human personality. Actually, we who engage in nonviolent direct action are not the creators of tension. We merely bring to the surface the hidden tension that is already alive. We bring it out in the open where it can be seen and dealt with. Like a boil that can never be cured as long as it is covered up but must be opened with all its pus-flowing ugliness to the natural medicines of air and light, injustice must likewise be exposed, with all of the tension its exposing creates, to the light of human conscience and the air of national opinion before it can be cured.

In your statement you asserted that our actions, even though peaceful, must be condemned because they precipitate violence. But can this assertion be logically made? Isn't this like condemning the robbed man because his possession of money precipitated the evil act of robbery? Isn't this like condemning Socrates because his unswerving commitment to truth and his philosophical delvings precipitated the misguided popular mind to make him drink the hemlock? Isn't this like condemning Jesus because His unique God consciousness and never-ceasing devotion to His will precipitated the evil act of crucifixion? We must come to see, as federal courts have consistently affirmed, that it is immoral to urge an individual to withdraw his efforts to gain his basic constitutional rights because the quest precipitates violence. Society must protect the robbed and punish the robber.

I had also hoped that the white moderate would reject the myth of time. I received a letter this morning from a white brother in Texas which

said: "All Christians know that the colored people will receive equal
rights eventually, but is it possible that you are in too great of a religious
hurry? It has taken Christianity almost 2000 years to accomplish what it
has. The teachings of Christ take time to come to earth." All that is said
here grows out of a tragic misconception of time. It is the strangely irrational notion that there is something in the very flow of time that will inevitably cure all ills. Actually time is neutral. It can be used either destruc-
tively or constructively. I am coming to feel that the people of ill will have
used time much more effectively than the people of good will. We will
have to repent in this generation not merely for the vitriolic words and
actions of the bad people, but for the appalling silence of the good
people. We must come to see that human progress never rolls in on
wheels of inevitability. It comes through the tireless efforts and persistent
work of men willing to be co-workers with God, and without this hard
work time itself becomes an ally of the forces of social stagnation.

We must use time creatively, and forever realize that the time is al-   25
ways ripe to do right. Now is the time to make real the promise of
democracy, and transform our pending national elegy into a creative
psalm of brotherhood. Now is the time to lift our national policy from
the quicksand of racial injustice to the solid rock of human dignity.

You spoke of our activity in Birmingham as extreme. At first I was
rather disappointed that fellow clergymen would see my nonviolent efforts as those of the extremist. I started thinking about the fact that I
stand in the middle of two opposing forces in the Negro community. One
is a force of complacency made up of Negroes who, as a result of long
years of oppression, have been so completely drained of self-respect and a
sense of "somebodiness" that they have adjusted to segregation, and of a
few Negroes in the middle class who, because of a degree of academic
and economic security, and because at points they profit by segregation,
have unconsciously become insensitive to the problems of the masses. The
other force is one of bitterness and hatred and comes perilously close to
advocating violence. It is expressed in the various black nationalist
groups that are springing up over the nation, the largest and best known
being Elijah Muhammad's Muslim movement.[5] This movement is nourished by the contemporary frustration over the continued existence of
racial discrimination. It is made up of people who have lost faith in
America, who have absolutely repudiated Christianity, and who have
concluded that the white man is an incurable "devil." I have tried to
stand between these two forces saying that we need not follow the "do-
nothing-ism" of the complacent or the hatred and despair of the black nationalist. There is the more excellent way of love and nonviolent protest.
I'm grateful to God that, through the Negro church, the dimension of

---

[5]*Elijah Muhammad's Muslim Movement:* Led by Elijah Muhammad, the Black Muslims opposed integration and promoted the creation of a black nation within the United
States. — EDS.

nonviolence entered our struggle. If this philosophy had not emerged I am convinced that by now many streets of the South would be flowing with floods of blood. And I am further convinced that if our white brothers dismiss us as "rabble rousers" and "outside agitators"—those of us who are working through the channels of nonviolent direct action—and refuse to support our nonviolent efforts, millions of Negroes, out of frustration and despair, will seek solace and security in black nationalist ideologies, a development that will lead inevitably to a frightening racial nightmare.

Oppressed people cannot remain oppressed forever. The urge for freedom will eventually come. This is what has happened to the American Negro. Something within has reminded him of his birthright of freedom; something without has reminded him that he can gain it. Consciously and unconsciously, he has been swept in by what the Germans call the *Zeitgeist*,[6] and with his black brothers of Africa, and his brown and yellow brothers of Asia, South America, and the Caribbean, he is moving with a sense of cosmic urgency toward the promised land of racial justice. Recognizing this vital urge that has engulfed the Negro community, one should readily understand public demonstrations. The Negro has many pent-up resentments and latent frustrations. He has to get them out. So let him march sometime; let him have his prayer pilgrimages to the city hall; understand why he must have sit-ins and freedom rides. If his repressed emotions do not come out in these nonviolent ways, they will come out in ominous expressions of violence. This is not a threat; it is a fact of history. So I have not said to my people, "Get rid of your discontent." But I have tried to say that this normal and healthy discontent can be channeled through the creative outlet of nonviolent direct action. Now this approach is being dismissed as extremist. I must admit that I was initially disappointed in being so categorized.

But as I continued to think about the matter I gradually gained a bit of satisfaction from being considered an extremist. Was not Jesus an extremist in love? "Love your enemies, bless them that curse you, pray for them that despitefully use you." Was not Amos an extremist for justice—"Let justice roll down like waters and righteousness like a mighty stream." Was not Paul an extremist for the gospel of Jesus Christ—"I bear in my body the marks of the Lord Jesus." Was not Martin Luther an extremist—"Here I stand; I can do none other so help me God." Was not John Bunyan an extremist—"I will stay in jail to the end of my days before I make a butchery of my conscience." Was not Abraham Lincoln an extremist—"This nation cannot survive half slave and half free." Was not Thomas Jefferson an extremist—"We hold these truths to be self-evident, that all men are created equal." So the question is not whether we will be extremist but what kind of extremist will we be. Will we be extremists for hate or will we be extremists for love? Will we be extremists for the preservation of injustice—

---

[6]*Zeitgeist:* A German word meaning "spirit of the time."—EDS.

or will we be extremists for the cause of justice? In that dramatic scene on Calvary's hill three men were crucified. We must never forget that all three were crucified for the same crime—the crime of extremism. Two were extremists for immorality, and thus fell below their environment. The other, Jesus Christ, was an extremist for love, truth, and goodness, and thereby rose above His environment. So, after all, maybe the South, the nation, and the world are in dire need of creative extremists.

I had hoped that the white moderate would see this. Maybe I was too optimistic. Maybe I expected too much. I guess I should have realized that few members of a race that has oppressed another race can understand or appreciate the deep groans and passionate yearnings of those that have been oppressed, and still fewer have the vision to see that injustice must be rooted out by strong, persistent, and determined action. I am thankful, however, that some of our white brothers have grasped the meaning of this social revolution and committed themselves to it. They are still all too small in quantity, but they are big in quality. Some like Ralph McGill, Lillian Smith, Harry Golden, and James Dabbs have written about our struggle in eloquent, prophetic, and understanding terms. Others have marched with us down nameless streets of the South. They have languished in filthy, roach-infested jails, suffering the abuse and brutality of angry policemen who see them as "dirty nigger lovers." They, unlike so many of their moderate brothers and sisters, have recognized the urgency of the moment and sensed the need for powerful "action" antidotes to combat the disease of segregation.

Let me rush on to mention my other disappointment. I have been so 30 greatly disappointed with the white Church and its leadership. Of course there are some notable exceptions. I am not unmindful of the fact that each of you has taken some significant stands on this issue. I commend you, Rev. Stallings, for your Christian stand on this past Sunday, in welcoming Negroes to your worship service on a nonsegregated basis. I commend the Catholic leaders of this state for integrating Springhill College several years ago.

But despite these notable exceptions I must honestly reiterate that I have been disappointed with the Church. I do not say that as one of those negative critics who can always find something wrong with the Church. I say it as a minister of the gospel, who loves the Church; who was nurtured in its bosom; who has been sustained by its spiritual blessings and who will remain true to it as long as the cord of life shall lengthen.

I had the strange feeling when I was suddenly catapulted into the leadership of the bus protest in Montgomery[7] several years ago that we would have the support of the white Church. I felt that the white minis-

---

[7]*bus protest in Montgomery:* After Rosa Parks was arrested on December 1, 1955, in Montgomery, Alabama, for refusing to give her seat on a bus to a white male passenger, a bus boycott began, which lasted nearly one year and was supported by nearly all of the city's black residents.—EDS.

ters, priests, and rabbis of the South would be some of our strongest allies. Instead, some have been outright opponents, refusing to understand the freedom movement and misrepresenting its leaders; all too many others have been more cautious than courageous and have remained silent behind the anesthetizing security of stained glass windows.

In spite of my shattered dreams of the past, I came to Birmingham with the hope that the white religious leadership of the community would see the justice of our cause and, with deep moral concern, serve as the channel through which our just grievances could get to the power structure. I had hoped that each of you would understand. But again I have been disappointed.

I have heard numerous religious leaders of the South call upon their worshippers to comply with a desegregation decision because it is the law, but I have longed to hear white ministers say follow this decree because integration is morally right and the Negro is your brother. In the midst of blatant injustices inflicted upon the Negro, I have watched white churches stand on the sideline and merely mouth pious irrelevancies and sanctimonious trivialities. In the midst of a mighty struggle to rid our nation of racial and economic injustice, I have heard so many ministers say, "Those are social issues with which the Gospel has no real concern," and I have watched so many churches commit themselves to a completely otherworldly religion which made a strange distinction between body and soul, the sacred and the secular.

So here we are moving toward the exit of the twentieth century with a religious community largely adjusted to the status quo, standing as a tail-light behind other community agencies rather than a headlight leading men to higher levels of justice.   35

I have travelled the length and breadth of Alabama, Mississippi, and all the other Southern states. On sweltering summer days and crisp autumn mornings I have looked at her beautiful churches with their spires pointing heavenward. I have beheld the impressive outlay of her massive religious education buildings. Over and over again I have found myself asking: "Who worships here? Who is their God? Where were their voices when the lips of Governor Barnett[8] dripped with words of interposition and nullification? Where were they when Governor Wallace[9] gave the clarion call for defiance and hatred? Where were their voices of support when tired, bruised, and weary Negro men and women decided to rise from the dark dungeons of complacency to the bright hills of creative protest?"

Yes, these questions are still in my mind. In deep disappointment, I have wept over the laxity of the Church. But be assured that my tears have been tears of love. There can be no deep disappointment where there

[8]*Governor Barnett:* Ross R. Barnett, governor of Mississippi from 1960 to 1964.—EDS.

[9]*Governor Wallace:* George C. Wallace served as governor of Alabama from 1963 to 1966, 1971 to 1979, and 1983 to 1987.—EDS.

is not deep love. Yes, I love the Church; I love her sacred walls. How could I do otherwise? I am in the rather unique position of being the son, the grandson, and the great grandson of preachers. Yes, I see the Church as the body of Christ. But, oh! How we have blemished and scarred that body through social neglect and fear of being nonconformists.

There was a time when the Church was very powerful. It was during that period when the early Christians rejoiced when they were deemed worthy to suffer for what they believed. In those days the Church was not merely a thermometer that recorded the ideas and principles of popular opinion; it was a thermostat that transformed the mores of society. Wherever the early Christians entered a town the power structure got disturbed and immediately sought to convict them for being "disturbers of the peace" and "outside agitators." But they went on with the conviction that they were a "colony of heaven" and had to obey God rather than man. They were small in number but big in commitment. They were too God-intoxicated to be "astronomically intimidated." They brought an end to such ancient evils as infanticide and gladiatorial contest.

Things are different now. The contemporary Church is so often a weak, ineffectual voice with an uncertain sound. It is so often the arch-supporter of the status quo. Far from being disturbed by the presence of the Church, the power structure of the average community is consoled by the Church's silent and often vocal sanction of things as they are.

But the judgment of God is upon the Church as never before. If the Church of today does not recapture the sacrificial spirit of the early Church, it will lose its authentic ring, forfeit the loyalty of millions, and be dismissed as an irrelevant social club with no meaning for the twentieth century. I am meeting young people every day whose disappointment with the Church has risen to outright disgust.   40

Maybe again I have been too optimistic. Is organized religion too inextricably bound to the status quo to save our nation and the world? Maybe I must turn my faith to the inner spiritual Church, the church within the Church, as the true *ecclesia*[10] and the hope of the world. But again I am thankful to God that some noble souls from the ranks of organized religion have broken loose from the paralyzing chains of conformity and joined us as active partners in the struggle for freedom. They have left their secure congregations and walked the streets of Albany, Georgia, with us. They have gone through the highways of the South on torturous rides for freedom. Yes, they have gone to jail with us. Some have been kicked out of their churches and lost the support of their bishops and fellow ministers. But they have gone with the faith that right defeated is stronger than evil triumphant. These men have been the leaven in the lump of the race. Their witness has been the spiritual salt that has preserved the true meaning of the Gospel in these troubled times. They have carved a tunnel of hope through the dark mountain of disappointment.

[10]*ecclesia:* The Latin word for church. — EDS.

I hope the Church as a whole will meet the challenge of this decisive hour. But even if the Church does not come to the aid of justice, I have no despair about the future. I have no fear about the outcome of our struggle in Birmingham, even if our motives are presently misunderstood. We will reach the goal of freedom in Birmingham and all over the nation, because the goal of America is freedom. Abused and scorned though we may be, our destiny is tied up with the destiny of America. Before the pilgrims landed at Plymouth, we were here. Before the pen of Jefferson etched across the pages of history the majestic words of the Declaration of Independence, we were here. For more than two centuries our foreparents labored in this country without wages; they made cotton "king"; and they built the homes of their masters in the midst of brutal injustice and shameful humiliation—and yet out of a bottomless vitality they continued to thrive and develop. If the inexpressible cruelties of slavery could not stop us, the opposition we now face will surely fail. We will win our freedom because the sacred heritage of our nation and the eternal will of God are embodied in our echoing demands.

I must close now. But before closing I am impelled to mention one other point in your statement that troubled me profoundly. You warmly commended the Birmingham police force for keeping "order" and "preventing violence." I don't believe you would have so warmly commended the police force if you had seen its angry violent dogs literally biting six unarmed, nonviolent Negroes. I don't believe you would so quickly commend the policemen if you would observe their ugly and inhuman treatment of Negroes here in the city jail; if you would watch them push and curse old Negro women and young Negro girls; if you would see them slap and kick old Negro men and young Negro boys; if you will observe them, as they did on two occasions, refuse to give us food because we wanted to sing our grace together. I'm sorry that I can't join you in your praise for the police department.

It is true that they have been rather disciplined in their public handling of the demonstrators. In this sense they have been rather publicly "nonviolent." But for what purpose? To preserve the evil system of segregation. Over the last few years I have consistently preached that nonviolence demands that the means we use must be as pure as the ends we seek. So I have tried to make it clear that it is wrong to use immoral means to attain moral ends. But now I must affirm that it is just as wrong, or even more so, to use moral means to preserve immoral ends. Maybe Mr. Connor and his policemen have been rather publicly nonviolent, as Chief Pritchett[11] was in Albany, Georgia, but they have used the moral means of nonviolence to maintain the immoral end of flagrant racial injustice.

---

[11]*Chief Pritchett:* Pritchett served as police chief in Albany, Georgia, during nonviolent demonstrations in 1961 and 1962. Chief Pritchett responded to the nonviolent demonstrations with nonviolence, refusing to allow his officers to physically or verbally abuse the demonstrators.—EDS.

T. S. Eliot has said that there is no greater treason than to do the right deed for the wrong reason.

I wish you had commended the Negro sit-inners and demonstrators   45
of Birmingham for their sublime courage, their willingness to suffer, and their amazing discipline in the midst of the most inhuman provocation. One day the South will recognize its real heroes. They will be the James Merediths,[12] courageously and with a majestic sense of purpose, facing jeering and hostile mobs and the agonizing loneliness that characterizes the life of the pioneer. They will be old, oppressed, battered Negro women, symbolized in a seventy-two year old woman of Montgomery, Alabama, who rose up with a sense of dignity and with her people decided not to ride the segregated buses, and responded to one who inquired about her tiredness with ungrammatical profundity: "My feets is tired, but my soul is rested." They will be young high school and college students, young ministers of the gospel and a host of the elders, courageously and nonviolently sitting in at lunch counters and willingly going to jail for conscience sake. One day the South will know that when these disinherited children of God sat down at lunch counters they were in reality standing up for the best in the American dream and the most sacred values in our Judeo-Christian heritage, and thus carrying our whole nation back to great wells of democracy which were dug deep by the founding fathers in the formulation of the Constitution and the Declaration of Independence.

Never before have I written a letter this long (or should I say a book?). I'm afraid that it is much too long to take your precious time. I can assure you that it would have been much shorter if I had been writing from a comfortable desk, but what else is there to do when you are alone for days in the dull monotony of a narrow jail cell other than write long letters, think strange thoughts, and pray long prayers?

If I have said anything in this letter that is an overstatement of the truth and is indicative of an unreasonable impatience, I beg you to forgive me. If I have said anything in this letter that is an understatement of the truth and is indicative of my having a patience that makes me patient with anything less than brotherhood, I beg God to forgive me.

I hope this letter finds you strong in the faith. I also hope that circumstances will soon make it possible for me to meet each of you, not as an integrationist or a civil rights leader, but as a fellow clergyman and a Christian brother. Let us all hope that the dark clouds of racial prejudice will soon pass away and the deep fog of misunderstanding will be lifted from our fear-drenched communities and in some not too distant tomor-

---

[12]*James Merediths:* Under the protection of federal marshals and the National Guard in 1962, James Meredith was the first black man to enroll at the University of Mississippi. — EDS.

row the radiant stars of love and brotherhood will shine over our great
nation with all of their scintillating beauty.

> *Yours for the cause of*
> *Peace and Brotherhood*
> MARTIN LUTHER KING JR.

The Reader's Presence

1. King wrote this letter in response to the eight clergymen identified
   at the beginning of the letter, who had declared that the civil
   rights activities of King and his associates were "unwise and untimely." What does King gain by characterizing his "Fellow Clergymen" as "men of genuine good will," whose criticisms are "sincerely set forth"? What evidence can you point to in King's letter
   to verify the claim that his audience extends far beyond the eight
   clergymen he explicitly addresses? Comment on the overall structure of King's letter. What principle of composition underpins the
   structure of his response?

2. King establishes the tone of his response to the criticisms of the
   clergymen at the end of the opening paragraph: "I would like to
   answer your statement in what I hope will be patient and reasonable terms." As you reread his letter, identify specific words and
   phrases—as well as argumentative strategies—that satisfy these
   self-imposed criteria. In what specific sense does King use the
   word *hope* here? As you reread his letter, point to each subsequent reference to hope. How does King emphasize the different
   meanings and connotations of the word as he unfolds his argument?

3. This letter has the ring of the oratory for which King was widely
   known and justly praised. Read passages aloud and note the ways
   that King appeals to his reader's ear (for example, with the balanced clauses of many of his sentences). In paragraph 42, King repeats the refrain "we were here," speaking of the essential place of
   African Americans in the making of American freedom. How does
   King enlarge the scope of his political vision in this paragraph?
   How does he relate the 1963 crisis of African American oppression to the founding of the American republic? How do the ca-
   dences of King's prose help to make his point? Compare King's
   letter to Edwidge Danticat's essay about Haitan immigrants, "We
   Are Ugly, but We Are Here" (page 621). How do these writers in-
   still hope into their writing?

THE WRITER AT WORK

Martin Luther King Jr. on Self-Importance

*In the following piece, the famous African American political leader ex-
presses his profound mistrust of the individual voice that rises above those for
whom that voice speaks. In this, as in so many respects, King joins a long tradition of wrestling with the question of how to reconcile one's own creativity with
the larger—and vastly more important—word and mission of God. King's spiritual mission was, of course, a social vision as well: that of racial equality in America. In speaking for those who believed with him in the possibility of making this
dream a reality, King drew upon his consummate skills as a preacher, orator, and
organizer. Throughout his short public life (spanning only twelve years, ending
with his assassination on April 4, 1968, in Memphis, Tennessee), King struggled
with the competing claims of personal celebrity and of the community he so forcefully represented. How do King's ideas about representation (standing for and
speaking on behalf of others) resonate with the ideas of other notable Americans
included in this anthology, for example, Thomas Jefferson (page 674) and Malcolm X (page 178)?*

Would you allow me to share a personal experience with you this
morning? And I say it only because I think it has bearing on this message.
One of the problems that I have to face and even fight every day is this problem of self-centeredness, this tendency that can so easily come to my life now
that I'm something special, that I'm something important. Living over the
past year, I can hardly go into any city or any town in this nation where I'm
not lavished with hospitality by peoples of all races and of all creeds. I can
hardly go anywhere to speak in this nation where hundreds and thousands
of people are not turned away because of lack of space. And then after
speaking, I often have to be rushed out to get away from the crowd rushing
for autographs. I can hardly walk the street in any city of this nation where
I'm not confronted with people running up on the street, "Isn't this Reverend King of Alabama?" Living under this it's easy, it's a dangerous tendency that I will come to feel that I'm something special, that I stand somewhere in this universe because of my ingenuity and that I'm important, that
I can walk around life with a type of arrogance because of an importance
that I have. And one of the prayers that I pray to God every day is: "O God,
help me to see my self in my true perspective. Help me, O God, to see that
I'm just a symbol of a movement. Help me to see that I'm the victim of what
the Germans call a *Zeitgeist* and that something was getting ready to happen in history; history was ready for it. And that a boycott would have
taken place in Montgomery, Alabama, if I had never come to Alabama.
Help me to realize that I'm where I am because of the forces of history and
because of the fifty thousand Negroes of Alabama who will never get their
names in the papers and in the headline. O God, help me to see that where I
stand today, I stand because others helped me to stand there and because the
forces of history projected me there. And this movement would have come

in history even if M. L. King had never been born." And when we come to see that, we stand with humility. This is the prayer I pray to God every day, "Lord help me to see M. L. King as M. L. King in his true perspective." Because if I don't see that, I will become the biggest fool in America.

100

Barbara Kingsolver

Stone Soup

Barbara Kingsolver (b. 1955) writes about middle-American lives, and in both her fiction and her essays she searches for the common threads that bind people together. She has published stories in Homeland *(1989), poetry in* Another America *(1994), and five novels,* The Bean Trees *(1988),* Animal Dreams *(1990),* Pigs in Heaven *(1993),* The Poisonwood Bible *(1998), which was nominated for the 1999 PEN/Faulkner Award for Fiction, and* The Prodigal Summer *(2000). She also contributes to numerous periodicals, including the* Progressive, Smithsonian, *the* New York Times Book Review, *and the* Los Angeles Times Book Review. *Her nonfiction works include* Holding the Line: Women in the Great Arizona Mine Strike of 1983 *(1989; revised 1999) and* High Tide in Tucson: Essays for Now or Never *(1995), in which "Stone Soup" appears.*

Regarding her work, Kingsolver remarks, "To me, writing is writing. . . . I believe there are some truths that are better told as fiction, and other truths that are most jarring and moving when you know they really did happen—like the Holding the Line *strike. There are moments of light that are best revealed in a poem, or a short story. . . . But the techniques, for me, remain the same."*

In the catalog of family values, where do we rank an occasion like this? A curly-haired boy who wanted to run before he walked, age seven now, a soccer player scoring a winning goal. He turns to the bleachers with his fists in the air and a smile wide as a gap-toothed galaxy. His own cheering section of grown-ups and kids all leap to their feet and hug each other, delirious with love for this boy. He's Andy, my best friend's son. The cheering section includes his mother and her friends, his brother, his father and stepmother, a stepbrother and stepsister, and a grandparent. Lucky is the child with this many relatives on hand to hail a proud accomplishment. I'm there too, witnessing a family fortune. But in spite of myself, defensive words take shape in my head. I am thinking: I dare *anybody* to call this a broken home.

Families change, and remain the same. Why are our names for home so slow to catch up to the truth of where we live?

When I was a child, I had two parents who loved me without cease. One of them attended every excuse for attention I ever contrived, and the other made it to the ones with higher production values, like piano recitals and appendicitis. So I was a lucky child too, I played with a set of paper dolls called "The Family of Dolls," four in number, who came with the factory-assigned names of Dad, Mom, Sis, and Junior. I think you know what they looked like, at least before I loved them to death and their heads fell off.

Now I've replaced the dolls with a life. I knit my days around my daughter's survival and happiness, and am proud to say her head is still on. But we aren't the Family of Dolls. Maybe you're not, either. And if not, even though you are statistically no oddity, it's probably been suggested to you in a hundred ways that yours isn't exactly a real family, but an impostor family, a harbinger of cultural ruin, a slapdash substitute — something like counterfeit money. Here at the tail end of our century, most of us are up to our ears in the noisy business of trying to support and love a thing called family. But there's a current in the air with ferocious moral force that finds its way even into political campaigns, claiming there is only one right way to do it, the Way It Has Always Been.

In the face of a thriving, particolored world, this narrow view is so   5
pickled and absurd I'm astonished that it gets airplay. And I'm astonished that it still stings.

Every parent has endured the arrogance of a child-unfriendly grump sitting in judgment, explaining what those kids of ours really need (for example, "a good licking"). If we're polite, we move our crew to another bench in the park. If we're forthright (as I am in my mind, only, for the rest of the day), we fix them with a sweet imperious stare and say, "Come back and let's talk about it after you've changed a thousand diapers."

But it's harder somehow to shrug off the Family-of-Dolls Family Values crew when they judge (from their safe distance) that divorced people, blended families, gay families, and single parents are failures. That our children are at risk, and the whole arrangement is messy and embarrassing. A marriage that ends is not called "finished," it's called *failed*. The children of this family may have been born to a happy union, but now they are called *the children of divorce*.

I had no idea how thoroughly these assumptions overlaid my culture until I went through divorce myself. I wrote to a friend: "This might be worse than being widowed. Overnight I've suffered the same losses — companionship, financial and practical support, my identity as a wife and partner, the future I'd taken for granted. I am lonely, grieving, and hard-pressed to take care of my household alone. But instead of bringing casseroles, people are acting like I had a fit and broke up the family china."

Once upon a time I held these beliefs about divorce: that everyone who does it could have chosen not to do it. That it's a lazy way out of marital problems. That it selfishly puts personal happiness ahead of family integrity. Now I tremble for my ignorance. It's easy, in fortunate times, to forget about the ambush that could leave your head reeling: serious mental or physical illness, death in the family, abandonment, financial calamity, humiliation, violence, despair.

I started out like any child, intent on being the Family of Dolls. I set   10
upon young womanhood believing in most of the doctrines of my generation: I wore my skirts four inches above the knee. I had that Barbie with her zebra-striped swimsuit and a figure unlike anything found in nature. And I understood the Prince Charming Theory of Marriage, a quest for Mr. Right that ends smack dab where you find him. I did not completely understand that another whole story *begins* there, and no fairy tale prepared me for the combination of bad luck and persistent hope that would interrupt my dream and lead me to other arrangements. Like a cancer diagnosis, a dying marriage is a thing to fight, to deny, and finally, when there's no choice left, to dig in and survive. Casseroles would help. Likewise, I imagine it must be a painful reckoning in adolescence (or later on) to realize one's own true love will never look like the soft-focus fragrance ads because Prince Charming (surprise!) is a princess. Or vice versa. Or has skin the color your parents didn't want you messing with, except in the Crayola box.

It's awfully easy to hold in contempt the straw broken home, and that mythical category of persons who toss away nuclear family for the sheer fun of it. Even the legal terms we use have a suggestion of caprice. I resent the phrase "irreconcilable differences," which suggest a stubborn refusal to accept a spouse's little quirks. This is specious. Every happily married couple I know has loads of irreconcilable differences. Negotiating where to set the thermostat is not the point. A nonfunctioning marriage is a slow asphyxiation. It is waking up despised each morning, listening to the pulse of your own loneliness before the radio begins to blare its raucous gospel that you're nothing if you aren't loved. It is sharing your airless house with the threat of suicide or other kinds of violence, while the ghost that whispers, "Leave here and destroy your children," has passed over every door and nailed it shut. Disassembling a marriage in these circumstances is as much *fun* as amputating your own gangrenous leg. You do it, if you can, to save a life — or two, or more.

I know of no one who really went looking to hoe the harder row, especially the daunting one of single parenthood. Yet it seems to be the most American of customs to blame the burdened for their destiny. We'd like so desperately to believe in freedom and justice for all, we can hardly name that rogue bad luck, even when he's a close enough snake to bite us. In the wake of my divorce, some friends (even a few close ones) chose to vanish, rather than linger within striking distance of misfortune.

But most stuck around, bless their hearts, and if I'm any the wiser for my trials, it's from having learned the worth of steadfast friendship. And also, what not to say. The least helpful question is: "Did you want the divorce, or didn't you?" Did I want to keep that gangrenous leg, or not? How to explain, in a culture that venerates choice: two terrifying options are much worse than none at all. Give me any day the quick hand of cruel fate that will leave me scarred but blameless. As it was, I kept thinking of that wicked third-grade joke in which some boy comes up behind you and grabs your ear, starts in with a prolonged tug, and asks, "Do you want this ear any longer?"

Still, the friend who holds your hand and says the wrong thing is made of dearer stuff than the one who stays away. And generally, through all of it, you live. My favorite fictional character, Kate Vaiden (in the novel by Reynolds Price), advises: "Strength just comes in one brand—you stand up at sunrise and meet what they send you and keep your hair combed."

Once you've weathered the straits, you get to cross the tricky juncture from casualty to survivor. If you're on your feet at the end of a year or two, and have begun putting together a happy new existence, those friends who were kind enough to feel sorry for you when you needed it must now accept you back to the ranks of the living. If you're truly blessed, they will dance at your second wedding. Everybody else, for heaven's sake, should stop throwing stones.   15

Arguing about whether nontraditional families deserve pity or tolerance is a little like the medieval debate about left-handedness as a mark of the devil. Divorce, remarriage, single parenthood, gay parents, and blended families simply are. They're facts of our time. Some of the reasons listed by sociologists for these family reconstructions are: the idea of marriage as a romantic partnership rather than a pragmatic one; a shift in women's expectations, from servility to self-respect and independence; and longevity (prior to antibiotics no marriage was expected to last many decades—in Colonial days the average couple lived to be married less than twelve years). Add to all this, our growing sense of entitlement to happiness and safety from abuse. Most would agree these are all good things. Yet their result—a culture in which serial monogamy and the consequent reshaping of families are the norm—gets diagnosed as "failing."

For many of us, once we have put ourselves Humpty-Dumpty-wise back together again, the main problem with our reorganized family is that other people think we have a problem. My daughter tells me the only time she's uncomfortable about being the child of divorced parents is when her friends say they feel sorry for her. It's a bizarre sympathy, given that half the kids in her school and nation are in the same boat, pursuing childish happiness with the same energy as their married-parent peers. When anyone asks how *she* feels about it, she spontaneously lists the benefits: our house is in the country and we have a dog, but she can go to her dad's neighborhood for the urban thrills of a pool and sidewalks for roller-skating. What's more, she has three sets of grandparents!

Why is it surprising that a child would revel in a widened family and the right to feel at home in more than one house? Isn't it the opposite that should worry us—a child with no home at all, or too few resources to feel safe? The child at risk is the one whose parents are too immature themselves to guide wisely; too diminished by poverty to nurture; too far from opportunity to offer hope. The number of children in the U.S. living in poverty at this moment is almost unfathomably large: twenty percent. There are families among us that need help all right, and by no means are they new on the landscape. The rate at which teenage girls had babies in 1957 (ninety-six per thousand) was twice what it is now. That remarkable statistic is ignored by the religious right—probably because the teen birth rate was cut in half mainly by legalized abortion. In fact, the policy gatekeepers who coined the phrase "family values" have steadfastly ignored the desperation of too-small families, and since 1979 have steadily reduced the amount of financial support available to a single parent. But, this camp's most outspoken attacks seem aimed at the notion of families getting too complex, with add-ons and extras such as a gay parent's partner, or a remarried mother's new husband and his children.

To judge a family's value by its tidy symmetry is to purchase a book for its cover. There's no moral authority there. The famous family comprised of Dad, Mom, Sis, and Junior living as an isolated economic unit is not built on historical bedrock. In *The Way We Never Were*, Stephanie Coontz writes, "Whenever people propose that we go back to the traditional family, I always suggest that they pick a ballpark date for the family they have in mind." Colonial families were tidily disciplined, but their members (meaning everyone but infants) labored incessantly and died young. Then the Victorian family adopted a new division of labor, in which women's role was domestic and children were allowed time for study and play, but this was an upper-class construct supported by myriad slaves. Coontz writes, "For every nineteenth-century middle-class family that protected its wife and child within the family circle, there was an Irish or German girl scrubbing floors . . . a Welsh boy mining coal to keep the home-baked goodies warm, a black girl doing the family laundry, a black mother and child picking cotton to be made into clothes for the family, and a Jewish or an Italian daughter in a sweatshop making 'ladies' dresses or artificial flowers for the family to purchase."

The abolition of slavery brought slightly more democratic arrangements, in which extended families were harnessed together in cottage industries; at the turn of the century came a steep rise in child labor in mines and sweatshops. Twenty percent of American children lived in orphanages at the time; their parents were not necessarily dead, but couldn't afford to keep them.

During the Depression and up to the end of World War II, many mil-

20

lions of U.S. households were more multigenerational than nuclear. Women my grandmother's age were likely to live with a fluid assortment of elderly relatives, in-laws, siblings, and children. In many cases they spent virtually every waking hour working in the company of other women—a companionable scenario in which it would be easier, I imagine, to tolerate an estranged or difficult spouse. I'm reluctant to idealize a life of so much hard work and so little spousal intimacy, but its advantage may have been resilience. A family so large and varied would not easily be brought down by a single blow: it could absorb a death, long illness, an abandonment here or there, and any number of irreconcilable differences.

The Family of Dolls came along midcentury as a great American experiment. A booming economy required a mobile labor force and demanded that women surrender jobs to returning soldiers. Families came to be defined by a single breadwinner. They struck out for single-family homes at an earlier age than ever before, and in unprecedented numbers they raised children in suburban isolation. The nuclear family was launched to sink or swim.

More than a few sank. Social historians corroborate that the suburban family of the postwar economic boom, which we have recently selected as our definition of "traditional," was no panacea. Twenty-five percent of Americans were poor in the mid-1950s, and as yet there were no food stamps. Sixty percent of the elderly lived on less than $1,000 a year, and most had no medical insurance. In the sequestered suburbs, alcoholism and sexual abuse of children were far more widespread than anyone imagined.

Expectations soared, and the economy sagged. It's hard to depend on one other adult for everything, come what may. In the last three decades, that amorphous, adaptable structure we call "family" has been reshaped once more by economic tides. Compared with fifties families, mothers are far more likely now to be employed. We are statistically more likely to divorce, and to live in blended families or other extra-nuclear arrangements. We are also more likely to plan and space our children, and to rate our marriages as "happy." We are less likely to suffer abuse without recourse, or to stare out at our lives through a glaze of prescription tranquilizers. Our aged parents are less likely to become destitute, and we're half as likely to have a teenage daughter turn up a mother herself. All in all, I would say that if "intact" in modern family-values jargon means living quietly desperate in the bell jar, then hip-hip-hooray for "broken." A neat family model constructed to service the Baby Boom economy seems to be returning gradually to a grand, lumpy shape that human families apparently have tended toward since they first took root in the Olduvai Gorge. We're social animals, deeply fond of companionship, and children love best to run in packs. If there is a *normal* for humans, at all, I expect it looks like two or three Families of Dolls, connected variously by kinship and passion, shuffled like cards and strewn over several shoeboxes.

The sooner we can let go the fairy tale of families functioning perfectly   25 in isolation, the better we might embrace the relief of community. Even the admirable parents who've stayed married through thick and thin are very likely, at present, to incorporate other adults into their families—household help and baby-sitters if they can afford them, or neighbors and grandparents if they can't. For single parents, this support is the rock-bottom definition of family. And most parents who have split apart, however painfully, still manage to maintain family continuity for their children, creating in many cases a boisterous phenomenon that Constance Ahrons in her book *The Good Divorce* calls the "binuclear family." Call it what you will—when ex-spouses beat swords into plowshares and jump up and down at a soccer game together, it makes for happy kids.

Cinderella, look, who needs her? All those evil stepsisters? That story always seemed like too much cotton-picking fuss over clothes. A childhood tale that fascinated me more was the one called "Stone Soup," and the gist of it is this: Once upon a time, a pair of beleagured soldiers straggled home to a village empty-handed, in a land ruined by war. They were famished, but the villagers had so little they shouted evil words and slammed their doors. So the soldiers dragged out a big kettle, filled it with water, and put it on a fire to boil. They rolled a clean round stone into the pot, while the villagers peered through their curtains in amazement.

"What kind of soup is that?" they hooted.

"Stone soup," the soldiers replied. "Everybody can have some when it's done."

"Well, thanks," one matron grumbled, coming out with a shriveled carrot. "But it'd be better if you threw this in."

And so on, of course, a vegetable at a time, until the whole suspicious 30
village managed to feed itself grandly.

Any family is a big empty pot, save for what gets thrown in. Each stew turns out different. Generosity, a resolve to turn bad luck into good, and respect for variety—these things will nourish a nation of children. Name-calling and suspicion will not. My soup contains a rock or two of hard times, and maybe yours does too. I expect it's a heck of a bouillabaisse.

The Reader's Presence

1. In paragraph 2, Kingsolver asks, "Why are our names for home so slow to catch up to the truth of where we live?" What are some of the old, outworn labels or buzzwords that Kingsolver identifies directly or indirectly in this essay? What are some of the phrases she offers to replace them? What difference(s) might these new terms make?

2. Kingsolver draws on Stephanie Koontz's book *The Way We Never Were* to support her idea that the good old days for which many feel nostalgic were not really all that "good." What are some of the advantages, according to Kingsolver, of living in the

contemporary world as opposed to in the past? In what particular ways have women's and children's lives changed for the better? What are some of the remaining social problems that Kingsolver believes the "policy gatekeepers" (paragraph 18) would do better to address?

3. One of the more powerful aspects of Kingsolver's essay is her self-indictment; she realizes, after the fact, that she, too, had misjudged families that fell short of her ideal of the "Family of Dolls." "Once upon a time," she begins paragraph 9, describing her former ignorance. How else does Kingsolver use fairy-tale language and imagery in her essay? Why does she borrow from this story form? Compare Kingsolver's meditation upon "stone soup" families to Barbara Ehrenreich's essay "Family Values" (page 636) or to Calvin Trillin's "A Traditional Family" (page 561). How does each writer approach the problem of measuring oneself against the "normative"? Kingsolver writes that she now imagines how painful it must be to realize that one's "Prince Charming (surprise!) is a princess" (paragraph 10). How does Bernard Cooper's essay about his homosexuality ("A Clack of Tiny Sparks," page 104) confirm Kingsolver's intuition?

101

Paul Monette

Can Gays and Straights Be Friends?

A passionate advocate for a humane, swift, and urgent response to the AIDS crisis, Paul Monette (1945–1995) first became a national literary figure with his book Borrowed Time: An AIDS Memoir *(1988). In this book and in a collection of poems,* Love Alone: Eighteen Elegies for Rog *(1988), he mourned the loss of his partner Roger Horwitz and chronicled the early years of the epidemic. He continued to explore his rage against the AIDS crisis in two novels —* Afterlife *(1990) and* Halfway Home *(1991) — in which he also affirmed the experience of living with AIDS and fighting back against ignorance, prejudice, and fear. In 1992 Monette received a National Book Award for his autobiography,* Becoming a Man: Half a Life Story, *and shortly before his death from the disease he completed a collection of essays,* Last Watch of the Night: Essays Too Personal and Otherwise *(1994). "Can Gays and Straights Be Friends?" appeared in* Playboy *in 1993.*

Monette published a number of novels and volumes of poetry during the

1970s and 1980s, but endured many rejection notices in the process. In Last Watch of the Night *he wrote, "I spent twenty years being turned down because my work was considered 'too gay.' Which I came to regard as a compliment, and proof I was on the right track." Even after receiving his National Book Award, some of his essays were turned down by publishers because they were considered "too personal," which, Monette wrote, "I couldn't help but feel was even better than a compliment. For I grew up in a culture in which the personal was* verboten, *especially in polite company—a company I've long since sold my stock in."*

Radio call-ins are the worst, especially during drive time. Commuters sit gridlocked in traffic, their only way out by cellular phone to the local radio show. Some callers practically foam at the mouth, saying I deserve to die and my kind makes them want to puke. Usually, I've been talking about the skyrocketing rates of teen suicide, a third of which involves gays and lesbians. Or I'm describing the tyranny of the closet, the stunting of the heart by cruel stereotypes. "Excuse me," I said to the caller in Houston, "do I make you want to puke because I'm gay or because I have AIDS?"

It's not a meaningful distinction to your weed-variety homophobe. Over my desk hangs a picture of a young woman whose wet T-shirt reads: THANK GOD FOR AIDS. Such hatred pours across the airwaves daily from preachers wringing their hands over the sins of Sodom. Their diatribes rarely mention lesbians. To them it is a fight unto death between two breeds of men—the "real" ones and the "sick" ones.

Where do they come by this virulence? Is it an inherent code of pumped-up self-regard passed from dugout and locker room to cover a straight man's fear of being misperceived as queer? Is it a primal fear of being penetrated? A Seattle boy called in once, so cocksure at the age of 11, and asked with disdain, "Why would anyone want to be gay?" All he thought he needed was to score with a girl and his sexual issues would be eternally resolved. "In ten or fifteen years," I promised him, "you will grapple as hard as anyone, gay or straight, with problems of intimacy"— the lifelong struggle to somehow integrate *fuck* and *love*.

As for wanting to be gay, every young man who knows that he's "different" has already internalized society's ugly message. Gay kids become locked in a self-hatred that renders them meek, apologetic, and invisible—their only safety the prison walls of their secret.

It's crucial to understand the difference between homophobia and   5
what I call homo-ignorance. There's much more of the latter, especially as gay and lesbian issues have surfaced more prominently in the news. Instinctively, people of goodwill rejected the paranoid philippic delivered in Houston by Pat Buchanan—a walking hate crime all by himself.

A straight friend of mine considers himself completely unhomophobic, he's that secure in his own manhood. Yet, when pinned down, he'll admit that the tactics of Queer Nation and Act Up make him, well, uncomfortable.

Uncomfortable is how the activists want him to feel. Even gays and lesbians juggle conflicting feelings about the guerrilla warriors in our midst. Sometimes I'm engulfed in the minutiae of political correctedness, labeled an enemy of my own people because I'm white, prosperous, and published. But I also feel juiced to have been part of the FDA takeover action in 1988 demanding the release of AIDS drugs. Our movement is only a generation old, and we've done it almost entirely without role models. Harvey Milk[1] was our Martin Luther King, but history texts have erased him. I studied Whitman at Yale for two years without hearing a mention of his homosexuality. Let alone Eleanor Roosevelt's. Or J. Edgar Hoover's.

It's easy to stay ignorant if gay never speaks its name. We need our straight allies to understand the nature of our struggle. It used to be said that a faggot was a homosexual gentleman who had just left the room. That can cease if enough heteros speak up and say "That's not funny" to fag jokes. Our families raise us the best they can, but it's a rare man who reaches adulthood without some legacy of racism, sexism, and homophobia. We must confront these demons in ourselves, tolerance being the minimum goal of self-examination.

There's this thing that many straight men have about being on the team, one of the guys. This is the argument of the military brass who want to keep us out. What they really want is for us to continue hiding and lying. While the Joint Chiefs of Staff deliberate the earth-shattering problem of queers taking showers with straight men, the Armed Forces drown in sexual-harassment cover-ups. And the only thing they can offer by way of sensitivity training is "Don't bend over to pick up the soap."

I don't want to do it with a straight man any more that I want to "indoctrinate" his sons. I have no problem with straight men's sexuality, unless it harms or belittles women. I experience none of the homophobe's obsession with what others do in bed. That's sexual compulsion all its own, as if gay or lesbian had only carnal meaning. I think what disorients straight men today is how happy and fulfilled many gay lives are. We're supposed to be miserable, after all.

We all have closets to come out of. Gay isn't the enemy of straight. Heterosexual men have told me for years that, since college, they have no male friends to talk with. The emotional isolation caused by fear of intimacy is indifferent to sexual orientation. We're not boys anymore, trapped in the insecurities of the schoolyard. Our common enemy is ignorance, a sex-phobic bitterness and name-calling purveyed by those who are jealous of the joy of others because they have none of their own.

10

---

[1]*Harvey Milk* (1930–1978): An openly gay politician, Milk was elected to the San Francisco Board of Supervisors in 1977. He and Mayor George Moscone were assassinated in 1978 by former city supervisor and police officer Don White. — EDS.

Nothing is more important to me than the freedom of being "out." I won't live to see 50, yet not even that can take away the happiness of having lived my life for real. Of course, you must realize you are in a closet before you can open the door. As gay and straight men, we can help one another over the great divide. We make terrific friends, we queers, perhaps because we have traveled so far to reach the free country of the heart. All men deserve to live there.

The Reader's Presence

1. The title of this essay poses a question: "Can Gays and Straights Be Friends?" How and where does Monette answer this question? What are some of the common grounds between gays and straights that Monette mentions or implies in his essay? What actions might heterosexual people take to ease gay-straight relations? What might homosexuals do? In what ways does Monette's essay itself further the cause of gay-straight friendships?

2. What are the causes of homophobia? In developing your response, draw on both the essay and your own personal experience. This essay was first published in *Playboy* magazine, which caters to heterosexual men. What signs do you find in the essay to suggest that Monette anticipates a measure of potential homophobia in his readers? Point to specific words and phrases to support your response. How effectively do you think he deals with the possible homophobia of his readers? Compare and contrast, for example, the discomfort felt by the radio call-ins in paragraph 1 and the discomfort intentionally caused by gay activists discussed in paragraph 7.

3. Monette describes the self-hatred that many gays experience, having "already internalized society's ugly message" (paragraph 4). What are the relations Monette sees between society's views of gay men and gay men's view of themselves? At one point Monette calls Pat Buchanan "a walking hate crime all by himself" (paragraph 5). What does this mean? What is a "paranoid philippic"? In "Just Walk on By: A Black Man Ponders His Power to Alter Public Space" (page 254), Brent Staples writes about the experience of scaring fellow pedestrians simply because he is a black man. What do racism and homophobia have in common? (note, too, June Jordan's essay on page 678.) How are they distinct? Compare how Staples and Monette identify the social problems at hand and their possible solutions. What is the role of the individual who is the object of hatred?

102

Martha Nussbaum

Can Patriotism Be Compassionate?

Martha Nussbaum (b. 1947) received her B.A. from New York University and her Ph.D. from Harvard, and has taught at Harvard, Brown, and Oxford universities. She has published many books, including The Fragility of Goodness: Luck and Ethics in Greek Tragedy and Philosophy *(1986/2001),* Love's Knowledge: Essays on Philosophy and Literature *(1990), and her latest work,* Upheavals of Thought: The Intelligence of Emotions *(2001). The Ernst Freund Distinguished Professor at the University of Chicago, Nussbaum teaches in the law school, the philosophy department, the divinity school, and the classics department. She has said that, in order to act ethically on the global stage, it is necessary to cultivate "the ability to imagine what it might be like to be in the shoes of someone who's different from yourself."*

In the aftermath of September 11, we have all experienced strong emotions for our country: fear, outrage, grief, astonishment. Our media portray the disaster as a tragedy that has happened to our nation, and that is how we very naturally see it. So too the ensuing war: It is called "America's New War," and most news reports focus on the meaning of events for us and our nation. We think these events are important because they concern us—not just human lives, but American lives. In one way, the crisis has expanded our imaginations. We find ourselves feeling sympathy for many people who did not even cross our minds before: New York firefighters, that gay rugby player who helped bring down the fourth plane, bereaved families of so many national and ethnic origins. We even sometimes notice with a new attention the lives of Arab-Americans among us, or feel sympathy for a Sikh taxi driver who complains about customers who tell him to go home to "his country," even though he came to the United States as a political refugee from Punjab. Sometimes our compassion even crosses that biggest line of all, the national boundary. Events have led many Americans to sympathize with the women and girls of Afghanistan, for example, in a way that many feminists had been trying to get people to do for a long time, without success.

All too often, however, our imaginations remain oriented to the local; indeed, this orientation is implicit in the unusual level of our alarm. The world has come to a stop in a way that it never has for Americans when disaster has befallen human beings in other places. Floods, earthquakes, cyclones—and the daily deaths of thousands from preventable malnutrition and disease—none of these typically make the American world come to a standstill, none elicit a tremendous outpouring of grief and compassion. The plight of innocent civilians in the current war evokes a similarly uneven and flickering response.

And worse: Our sense that the "us" is all that matters can easily flip over into a demonizing of an imagined "them," a group of outsiders who are imagined as enemies of the invulnerability and the pride of the all-important "us." Just as parents' compassion for their own children can all too easily slide into an attitude that promotes the defeat of other people's children, so too with patriotism: Compassion for our fellow Americans can all too easily slide over into an attitude that wants America to come out on top, defeating or subordinating other peoples or nations. Anger at the terrorists themselves is perfectly appropriate; so is the attempt to bring them to justice. But "us versus them" thinking doesn't always stay focused on the original issue; it too easily becomes a general call for American supremacy, the humiliation of "the other."

One vivid example of this slide took place at a baseball game I went to at Chicago's Comiskey Park, the first game played there after September 11—and a game against the Yankees, so there was a heightened awareness of the situation of New York and its people. Things began well, with a moving ceremony commemorating the firefighters who had lost their lives and honoring local firefighters who had gone to New York afterward to help out. There was even a lot of cheering when the Yankees took the field, a highly unusual transcendence of local attachments. But as the game went on and the beer flowed, one heard, increasingly, "U-S-A, U-S-A," echoing the chant from the 1980 Olympic hockey match in which the United States defeated Russia. This chant seemed to express a wish for America to defeat, abase, humiliate its enemies. Indeed, it soon became a general way of expressing the desire to crush one's enemies, whoever they were. When the umpire made a bad call that went against the Sox, the same group in the stands turned to him, chanting "U-S-A." In other words, anyone who crosses us is evil, and should be crushed. It's not surprising that Stoic philosopher and Roman emperor Marcus Aurelius, trying to educate himself to have an equal respect for all human beings, reported that his first lesson was "not to be a fan of the Greens or Blues at the races, or the light-armed or heavy-armed gladiators at the Circus."

Compassion is an emotion rooted, probably, in our biological heritage. (Although biologists once portrayed animal behavior as egoistic, primatologists by now recognize the existence of altruistic emotion in apes, and it may exist in other species as well.) But this history does not mean that compassion is devoid of thought. In fact, as Aristotle argued long ago, human compassion standardly requires three thoughts: that a serious bad thing has happened to someone else; that this bad event was not (or not entirely) the person's own fault; and that we ourselves are vulnerable in similar ways. Thus compassion forms a psychological link between our own self-interest and the reality of another person's good or ill. For that reason it is a morally valuable emotion—when it gets things right. Often, however, the thoughts involved in the emotion, and therefore the emotion itself, go astray, failing to link people at a distance to ones' own current possibilities and vulnerabilities. (Rousseau said that kings don't feel compassion for their subjects because they count on never being human, subject to the vicissitudes of life.) Sometimes, too, compassion goes wrong by getting the seriousness of the bad event wrong: Sometimes, for example, we just don't take very seriously the hunger and illness of people who are distant from us. These errors are likely to be built into the nature of compassion as it develops in childhood and then adulthood: We form intense attachments to the local first, and only gradually learn to have compassion for people who are outside our own immediate circle. For many Americans, that expansion of moral concern stops at the national boundary.

Most of us are brought up to believe that all human beings have equal worth. At least the world's major religions and most secular philosophies tell us so. But our emotions don't believe it. We mourn for those we know, not for those we don't know. And most of us feel deep emotions about America, emotions we don't feel about India or Russia or Rwanda. In and of itself, this narrowness of our emotional lives is probably acceptable and maybe even good. We need to build outward from meanings we understand, or else our moral life would be empty of urgency. Aristotle long ago said, plausibly, that the citizens in Plato's ideal city, asked to care for all citizens equally, would actually care for none, since care is learned in small groups with their more intense attachments. Reading Marcus Aurelius bears this out: The project of weaning his imagination from its intense erotic attachments to the familial and the local gradually turns into the rather alarming project of weaning his heart from deep investment in the world. He finds that the only way to be utterly evenhanded is to cultivate a kind of death within life, seeing all people as distant and shadowlike, "vain images in a procession." If we want our life with others to contain strong passions—for justice in a world of injustice, for aid in a world where many go without what they need—we would do well to begin, at least, with our familiar strong emotions toward family, city and country. But concern should not stop with these local attachments.

Americans, unfortunately, are prone to such emotional narrowness. So are all people, but because of the power and geographical size of America, isolationism has particularly strong roots here. When at least some others were finding ways to rescue the Jews during the Holocaust, America's inactivity and general lack of concern were culpable, especially in proportion to American power. It took Pearl Harbor to get us even to come to the aid of our allies. When genocide was afoot in Rwanda, our own sense of self-sufficiency and invulnerability stopped us from imagining the Rwandans as people who might be us; we were therefore culpably inactive toward them. So too in the present situation. Sometimes we see a very laudable recognition of the interconnectedness of all peoples, and of the fact that we must join forces with people in all nations to defeat terrorists and bring them to justice. At other times, however, we see simplifying slogans ("America Fights Back") that portray the situation in terms of a good "us" crusading against an evil "them"—failing to acknowledge, for instance, that people in all nations have strong reasons to oppose terrorism, and that the fight has many active allies.

Such simplistic thinking is morally wrong, because it encourages us to ignore the impact of our actions on innocent civilians and to focus too little on the all-important project of humanitarian relief. It is also counterproductive. We now understand, or ought to, that if we had thought more about support for the educational and humanitarian infrastructure of Pakistan, for example, funding good local nongovernmental organizations there the way several European nations have done in India, young people in Pakistan might possibly have been educated in a climate of respect for religious pluralism, the equality of women and other values that we rightly prize instead of having fundamentalist *madrassahs** as their only educational option. Our policy in South Asia has exhibited for many years a gross failure of imagination and sympathy; we basically thought in terms of cold war values, ignoring the real lives of people to whose prospects our actions could make a great difference. Such crude thinking is morally obtuse; it is also badly calculated to advance any good cause we wish to embrace, in a world where all human lives are increasingly interdependent.

Compassion begins with the local. But if our moral natures and our emotional natures are to live in any sort of harmony, we must find devices through which to extend our strong emotions—and our ability to imagine the situation of others—to the world of human life as a whole. Since compassion contains thought, it can be educated. We can take this disaster as occasion for narrowing our focus, distrusting the rest of the world, and feeling solidarity with Americans alone. Or we can take it as an occasion for expansion of our ethical horizons. Seeing how vulnerable our great country is, we can learn something about the vulnerability that all human beings share, about what it is like for distant others to lose those they love to a disaster not of their own making, whether it is hunger or flood or war.

madrassahs: A group of buildings used for teaching Islamic theology and religious law, typically including a mosque.—EDS.

Because human beings find the meaning of life in attachments that   10
are local, we should not ask of people that they renounce patriotism, any
more than we now ask them to renounce the love of their parents and
children. But we typically do ask parents not to try to humiliate or thwart
other people's children, and we work (at least sometimes) for schools that
develop the abilities of all children, that try to make it possible for everyone to support themselves and find rewarding work. So too with the
world: We may love our own nation most, but we should also strive for a
world in which the capacities of human beings will not be blighted by
hunger or misogyny or lack of education—or by being in the vicinity
of a war one has not caused. We should therefore demand an education
that does what it can to encourage the understanding of human predicaments—and also to teach children to recognize the many obstacles to
that pursuit, the many pitfalls of the self-centered imagination as it tries
to be just. There are hopeful signs in the present situation, particularly in
attempts to educate the American public about Islam, about the histories
of Afghanistan and Pakistan, and about the situation and attitudes of
Arab-Americans in this country. But we need to make sure these educational efforts are consistent and systematic, not just fear-motivated responses to an immediate crisis.

Our media and our systems of education have long given us far too
little information about lives outside our borders, stunting our moral
imaginations. The situation of America's women and its racial, ethnic,
and sexual minorities has to some extent worked its way into curricula
at various levels, and into our popular media. We have done less well
with parts of the world that are unfamiliar. This is not surprising, because such teaching requires a lot of investment in new curricular initia-
tives, and such television programming requires a certain temporary
inattention to the competition for ratings. But we now know that we
live in a complex, interconnected world, and we know our own ignorance. As Socrates said, this is at least the beginning of progress. At this
time of national crisis we can renew our commitment to the equal
worth of humanity, demanding media, and schools, that nourish and
expand our imaginations by presenting non-American lives as deep,
rich, and compassion-worthy. "Thus from our weakness," said Rousseau
of such an education, "our fragile happiness is born." Or, at least, it
might be born.

The Reader's Presence

1. Evaluate the validity of Nussbaum's claim that becoming compassionate requires an "expansion of our ethical horizons" (paragraph 9) by looking at the instances where she sees a lack of compassion. For each instance, how would you expand people's

horizons? According to Nussbaum, what conditions are necessary to make people feel compassionate? Which do you think would work? Which wouldn't? Why and why not?

2. Beginning with a twenty-first century United States' perspective, Nussbaum expands and contracts her temporal focus several times. For example, she talks about recent events (a baseball game) and then immediately switches to a discussion of Aristotle's argument about compassion. By writing this way, she broadens the "emotional narrowness" which she feels constricts America. In what other ways does she try to broaden our horizons? In how many other ways does she contract and expand her focus? Which ways create compassion most effectively? Why?

3. Nussbaum writes that "we must find devices through which to extend our strong emotions—and our ability to imagine the situation of others" (paragraph 9). Read Robert Stone's "In the Mind's Eye of the Bomber" (page 529). Examine the devices Stone uses to extend his readers' ability to see from a perspective that is different from the American mind's eye. How does he make us extend our emotions? Compare the techniques he uses with those Nussbaum uses. Which author made you feel more strongly? How did he or she manage to affect you so deeply? How did this help, or hinder, you from accepting other points of view?

103

Orlando Patterson

Race Over

Orlando Patterson was educated at London University and the London School of Economics, and has taught at Harvard University since 1971. His dissertation on Jamaican slave society was published in 1967 as The Sociology of Slavery: Jamaica, 1655–1838. *He served as special advisor for social policy and development to Jamaican prime minister Michael Manley from 1972–1980 and published his book on the effects of slavery on economic and social development,* Slavery and Social Death, *in 1982. He is the author of four other scholarly books. Before fully committing himself to sociology, Patterson pursued a parallel career as a novelist and critic, publishing three novels and a number of anthologized short stories, along with many reviews and critical essays. He was awarded the National Book Award in nonfiction for volume 1 of his two-volume* Freedom: Freedom in the Making of Western Culture *(1991).*

> *Patterson has remarked, in describing his views of historical development,*
> *"Progress always is accompanied by friction. I am suspicious of any historical*
> *change not accompanied by conflict."*

One can quibble with W. E. B. Du Bois's famous prediction for the twentieth century. This has been not simply the century of the color line but a century of Jim Crow and myriad other persecutions — many within color boundaries. But, if Du Bois's epigraph was only half right, his modern-day disciples, who insist the color line will define the next one hundred years as well, are altogether wrong. The racial divide that has plagued America since its founding is fading fast — made obsolete by migratory, sociological, and biotechnological developments that are already under way. By the middle of the twenty-first century, America will have problems aplenty. But no racial problem whatsoever.

For this we can thank four social patterns, each indigenous to a particular region of the country but which together will reshape the nation as a whole. The strongest and clearest might be called the California system. Cultural and somatic mixture will be its hallmark. A hybrid population, mainly Eurasian — but with a growing Latin element — will come to dominate the middle and upper classes and will grow exponentially, especially after the 2020s. Lower-class Caucasians, middle-class racial purists, and most African Americans, under pressure from an endless stream of unskilled Mexican workers, will move away. Those African Americans who remain will be rapidly absorbed into the emerging mixed population. The California system will come to dominate the American and Canadian Pacific Rim.

The second major pattern might be called the Caribbean-American system. Increasingly, the countries of the Caribbean basin will be socially and economically integrated with the United States. As their fragile and already declining economies collapse (most dramatically in post-Castro Cuba), they will swarm the mainland by legal and illegal means. Florida will be the metropolitan center of this system, although Caribbean colonies will sprout all over the Northeast. Caribbean peoples will bring their distinctive concept of race and color to America, one in which people marry lighter and "white" as they move up the social ladder. This system will differ from the California one in that the dominant element will be Afro-Latin rather than Eurasian. Since the Caribbean is much closer than Asia, this system will also create a distinctive social type: genuinely transnational and post-national communities in which people feel equally at home in their native and American locations. Increasingly, people will spend their childhoods and retirements in the Caribbean and their productive years in America. The Caribbean-American system will compete with the African American community not only in the lower reaches of the labor force but as the nation's major source of popular culture, especially in music and sports. But, despite these differences, the Caribbean-American system, like the California one, will render the "one drop" rule obsolete.

The third and most problematic system will be the one now emerging in the Northeast and urban Midwest. Here, the economic situation for all classes of African Americans and native-born Latinos is likely to deteriorate—with the ending of affirmative action, a shrinking public sector, and competition from skilled and unskilled (mainly Caribbean basin) immigrant labor. The rise of workfare without compensating provision for child care, combined with the growing pattern of paternal abandonment of children, will further undermine traditional family norms among African American, Latino, and, increasingly, the European American lower classes. Reversing the pattern that emerged after World War II, African Americans, Latinos, and the poorest Caucasians will move into the inner and secondary rings of what are now mainly European American middle-class suburbs. The middle classes will move to either gated exurbs or gentrified central cities—leaving a European American underclass that resembles other ethnic underclasses more and more.

But, although these developments will at first exacerbate racial conflict, they will ultimately transform racial frustrations into class ones. Indeed, for the first time in the nation's history, young, poor, and alienated Caucasians, African Americans, and Latinos will find common ground—based on social resentment and a common lumpen-proletarian, hip-hop culture. Even as these young people periodically engage in murderous racial gang fights, intermarriage and miscegenation will escalate as the young poor of all races break away from present gender and racial taboos. In contrast to the California and Florida systems, the growing hybrid population in the Northeast and industrial Midwest will be lower-class, alienated, and out of control. But it will be hybrid nonetheless.

The exception will be in the Southeast, in what may be called the Atlanta pattern. African Americans and European Americans will cling to notions of racial purity and will remain highly (and voluntarily) segregated from each other. Affirmative action will be the bulwark of this system, the price the European American elite willingly pays for "racial" stability and the reassuring presence of a culturally familiar but socially distant African American group and a pliant working class. The old Confederacy will remain a place where everyone knows who is white and who is black and need reckon with no in-between. But, as opposed to the nineteenth and twentieth centuries, when the South defined the terms of racial engagement on which the entire nation interacted (more or less brutally), in the twenty-first century the Southern model will become an increasingly odd and decreasingly relevant anachronism.

For the decline of race as a factor in American life will result not only from immigration, which can perhaps be halted, but also from biotechnology. More and more in the coming decades, Americans will gain the means to genetically manipulate human appearance. The foundations of genetic engineering are already in place. Given the interest of the affluent population in male-pattern baldness, the restoration of hair loss after cancer treatment, and cancer-free tanning, science is likely to create dramatic new methods of changing hair texture and skin color. Indeed, last No-

5

vember, scientists at Columbia University transplanted scalp cells from one person to another. I don't expect many African Americans to chose straight-haired whiteness for themselves or their progeny, but many will opt for varying degrees of hybridity. In a world dominated by mass culture, many will embrace changes that enhance their individuality. Once dramatically manipulable by human action, "race" will lose its social significance, and the myth of racial purity will be laid to rest.

By the middle of the next century, the social virus of race will have gone the way of smallpox. The twenty-first century, relieved of the obscuring blinkers of race, will be a century of class and class consciousness, forcing the nation to finally take seriously its creed that all are created equal. It should be interesting.

The Reader's Presence

1. Patterson's essay addresses how racial distinctions have been conceived and defined throughout the history of this country. Review some of the phrases and passages in which Patterson alludes to precise historical events or legal decisions. What was the "one drop" rule (paragraph 3)? What was "the pattern that emerged after World War II" (paragraph 4)? How did "the South [define] the terms of racial engagement on which the entire nation interacted (more or less brutally)" in the nineteenth and twentieth centuries (paragraph 6)? More generally, why is the past necessary to Patterson's argument?

2. A commonplace idea about Americans is that they are always on the move, that mobility is more important than being rooted in a particular place. Although Patterson includes many patterns of movement in his analysis—especially migration from and back to the Caribbean, his four systems are regionally defined. In each of the four systems—the California, the Caribbean-American, the Northeast/urban Midwest, and the Atlanta—how do the phenomena of racial mixing and resettlement emerge from the particular location? For example, what is it about California's geographical location and sociopolitical history that makes "cultural and somatic mixture . . . its hallmark" (paragraph 2)?

3. Patterson's first real metaphor is that of epidemic: "The racial divide that has plagued America since its founding is fading fast" (paragraph 1). What does this metaphor suggest? How is it carried through the essay, repeated, or revised or replaced? What does Patterson mean by "the social virus of race" (paragraph 8)? How does Patterson's discussion of race compare with that of Cornel West (page 799) or of Arthur Schlesinger (page 749)? Do either of these authors use the metaphor of virus or contagion? If so, why? If not, why not?

104

Bertrand Russell
Why I Am Not a Christian

Mathematician, philosopher, logician, and social critic, Bertrand Russell (1872–1970) was born in England and is regarded as one of the greatest thinkers of modern times. Russell was an extremely prolific and influential writer, and his books, many of them highly readable, include Principia Mathematica, *a three-volume set published in 1910, 1912, and 1913;* Marriage and Morals *(1929);* A History of Western Philosophy *(1945);* Why I Am Not a Christian *(1957); and* The Autobiography of Bertrand Russell *(3 vols.: 1967–69). Russell is also known for his outspoken views on pacifism, advocacy of free love, and criticism of American foreign policy. "Why I Am Not a Christian," one of his most famous essays, was delivered as a lecture in 1927 to the National Secular Society.*

As your Chairman has told you, the subject about which I am going to speak to you tonight is "Why I Am Not a Christian." Perhaps it would be as well, first of all, to try to make out what one means by the word *Christian*. It is used these days in a very loose sense by a great many people. Some people mean no more by it than a person who attempts to live a good life. In that sense I suppose there would be Christians in all sects and creeds; but I do not think that that is the proper sense of the word, if only because it would imply that all the people who are not Christians—all the Buddhists, Confucians, Mohammedans, and so on—are not trying to live a good life. I do not mean by a Christian any person who tries to live decently according to his lights. I think that you must have a certain amount of definite belief before you have a right to call yourself a Christian. The word does not have quite such a full-blooded meaning now as it had in the times of St. Augustine and St. Thomas Aquinas. In those days, if a man said that he was a Christian it was known what he meant. You accepted a whole collection of creeds which were set out with great precision, and every single syllable of those creeds you believed with the whole strength of your convictions.

WHAT IS A CHRISTIAN?

Nowadays it is not quite that. We have to be a little more vague in our meaning of Christianity. I think, however, that there are two different items which are quite essential to anybody calling himself a Christian. The first is one of a dogmatic nature — namely, that you must believe in God and immortality. If you do not believe in those two things, I do not think that you can properly call yourself a Christian. Then, further than that, as the name implies, you must have some kind of belief about Christ. The Mohammedans, for instance, also believe in God and in immortality, and yet they would not call themselves Christians. I think you must have at the very lowest the belief that Christ was, if not divine, at least the best and wisest of men. If you are not going to believe that much about Christ, I do not think you have any right to call yourself a Christian. Of course, there is another sense, which you find in *Whitaker's Almanack* and in geography books, where the population of the world is said to be divided into Christians, Mohammedans, Buddhists, fetish worshipers, and so on; and in that sense we are all Christians. The geography books count us all in, but that is a purely geographical sense, which I suppose we can ignore. Therefore I take it that when I tell you why I am not a Christian I have to tell you two different things: first, why I do not believe in God and in immortality; and, secondly, why I do not think that Christ was the best and wisest of men, although I grant him a very high degree of moral goodness.

But for the successful efforts of unbelievers in the past, I could not take so elastic a definition of Christianity as that. As I said before, in olden days it had a much more full-blooded sense. For instance, it included the belief in hell. Belief in eternal hell-fire was an essential item of Christian belief until pretty recent times. In this country, as you know, it ceased to be an essential item because of a decision of the Privy Council, and from that decision the Archbishop of Canterbury and the Archbishop of York dissented; but in this country our religion is settled by Act of Parliament, and therefore the Privy Council was able to override their Graces and hell was no longer necessary to a Christian. Consequently I shall not insist that a Christian must believe in hell.

THE EXISTENCE OF GOD

To come to this question of the existence of God: It is a large and serious question, and if I were to attempt to deal with it in any adequate manner I should have to keep you here until Kingdom Come, so that you will have to excuse me if I deal with it in a somewhat summary fashion. You know, of course, that the Catholic Church has laid it down as a dogma that the existence of God can be proved by the unaided reason. That is a somewhat curious dogma, but it is one of their dogmas. They had to introduce it because at one time the freethinkers adopted the habit of saying that there were such and such arguments which mere reason might urge against the existence of God, but of course they knew as a matter of faith that God did exist. The arguments and the reasons were set out at great length, and the Catholic Church felt that they must stop it. Therefore they laid it down that the existence of God can be proved by the unaided reason and they had to set up what they considered were arguments to prove it. There are, of course, a number of them, but I shall take only a few.

THE FIRST CAUSE ARGUMENT

Perhaps the simplest and easiest to understand is the argument of the   5
First Cause. (It is maintained that everything we see in this world has a cause, and as you go back in the chain of causes further and further you must come to a First Cause, and to that First Cause you give the name of God.) That argument, I suppose, does not carry very much weight nowadays, because, in the first place, cause is not quite what it used to be. The philosophers and the men of science have got going on cause, and it has not anything like the vitality it used to have; but, apart from that, you can see that the argument that there must be a First Cause is one that cannot have any validity. I may say that when I was a young man and was debating these questions very seriously in my mind, I for a long time accepted the argument of the First Cause, until one day, at the age of eighteen, I read John Stuart Mill's *Autobiography,* and I there found this sentence: "My father taught me that the question 'Who made me?' cannot be answered, since it immediately suggests the further question 'Who made God?'" That very simple sentence showed me, as I still think, the fallacy in the argument of the First Cause. If everything must have a cause, then God must have a cause. If there can be everything without a cause, it may just as well be the world as God, so that there cannot be any validity in that argument. It is exactly of the same nature as the Hindu's view that the world rested upon an elephant and the elephant rested upon a tortoise; and when they said, "How about the tortoise?" the Indian said, "Suppose we change the subject." The argument is really no better than that. There is no reason why the world could not have come into being without a cause; nor, on the other hand, is there any reason why it should not have always existed. There is no reason to suppose that the world had a beginning at all. The idea that things must have a beginning is really due to the poverty of our imagination. Therefore, perhaps, I need not waste any more time upon the argument about the First Cause.

THE NATURAL LAW ARGUMENT

Then there is a very common argument from natural law. That was a favorite argument all through the eighteenth century, especially under the influence of Sir Isaac Newton and his cosmogony. People observed the planets going around the sun according to the law of gravitation, and they thought that God had given a behest to these planets to move in that particular fashion, and that was why they did so. That was, of course, a convenient and simple explanation that saved them the trouble of looking any further for explanations of the law of gravitation. Nowadays we explain the law of gravitation in a somewhat complicated fashion that Einstein has introduced. I do not propose to give you a lecture on the law of gravitation, as interpreted by Einstein, because that again would take some time; at any rate, you no longer have the sort of natural law that you had in the Newtonian system, where, for some reason that nobody could understand, nature behaved in a uniform fashion. We now find that a great many things we thought were natural laws are really human conventions. You know that even in the remotest depths of stellar space there are still three feet to a yard. That is, no doubt, a very remarkable fact, but you would hardly call it a law of nature. And a great many things that have been regarded as laws of nature are of that kind. On the other hand, where you can get down to any knowledge of what atoms actually do, you will find they are much less subject to law than people thought, and that the laws at which you arrive are statistical averages of just the sort that would emerge from chance. There is, as we all know, a law that if you throw dice you will get double sixes only about once in thirty-six times, we do not regard that as evidence that the fall of the dice is regulated by design; on the contrary, if the double sixes came every time we should think that there was design. The laws of nature are of that sort as regards a great many of them. They are statistical averages such as would emerge from the laws of chance; and that makes this whole business of natural law much less impressive than it formerly was. Quite apart from that, which represents the momentary state of science that may change tomorrow, the whole idea that natural laws imply a lawgiver is due to a confusion between natural and human laws. Human laws are behests commanding you to behave a certain way, in which way you may choose to behave, or you may choose not to behave; but natural laws are a description of how things do in fact behave, and being a mere description of what they in fact do, you cannot argue that there must be somebody who told them to do that, because even supposing that there were, you are then faced with the question "Why did God issue just those natural laws and no others?" If you say that he did it simply from his own good pleasure, and without any reason, you then find that there is something which is not subject to law, and so your train of natural law is interrupted. If you say, as more orthodox theologians do, that in all the laws which God issues he had a reason for giving those laws rather than others—the reason, of course, being to create the best universe, although you would never think it to look at it—if there were a reason for the laws which God gave, then God himself was subject to law, and therefore you do not get any advantage by introducing God as an intermediary. You have really a law outside and anterior to the divine edicts, and God does not serve your purpose, because he is not the ultimate lawgiver. In short, this whole argument about natural law no longer has anything like the strength that it used to have. I am traveling on in time in my review of the arguments. The arguments that are used for the existence of God change their character as time goes on. They were at first hard intellectual arguments embodying certain quite definite fallacies. As we come to modern times they become less respectable intellectually and more and more affected by a kind of moralizing vagueness.

THE ARGUMENT FROM DESIGN

The next step in this process brings us to the argument from design. You all know the argument from design: Everything in the world is made just so that we can manage to live in the world, and if the world was ever so little different, we could not manage to live in it. That is the argument from design. It sometimes takes a rather curious form; for instance, it is argued that rabbits have white tails in order to be easy to shoot. I do not know how rabbits would view that application. It is an easy argument to parody. You all know Voltaire's remark, that obviously the nose was designed to be such as to fit spectacles. That sort of parody has turned out to be not nearly so wide of the mark as it might have seemed in the eighteenth century, because since the time of Darwin we understand much better why living creatures are adapted to their environment. It is not that their environment was made to be suitable to them but that they grew to be suitable to it, and that is the basis of adaptation. There is no evidence of design about it.

When you come to look into this argument from design, it is a most astonishing thing that people can believe that this world, with all the things that are in it, with all its defects, should be the best that omnipotence and omniscience have been able to produce in millions of years. I really cannot believe it. Do you think that, if you were granted omnipotence and omniscience and millions of years in which to perfect your world, you could produce nothing better than the Ku Klux Klan or the Fascists? Moreover, if you accept the ordinary laws of science, you have to suppose that human life and life in general on this planet will die out in due course: It is a stage in the decay of the solar system; at a certain stage of decay you get the sort of conditions of temperature and so forth which are suitable to protoplasm, and there is life for a short time in the life of the whole solar system. You see in the moon the sort of thing to which the earth is tending—something dead, cold, and lifeless.

I am told that that sort of view is depressing, and people will sometimes tell you that if they believed that, they would not be able to go on living. Do not believe it; it is all nonsense. Nobody really worries much about what is going to happen millions of years hence. Even if they think they are worrying much about that, they are really deceiving themselves. They are worried about something much more mundane, or it may merely be a bad digestion; but nobody is really seriously rendered unhappy by the thought of something that is going to happen to this world millions and millions of years hence. Therefore, although it is of course a gloomy view to suppose that life will die out — at least I suppose we may say so, although sometimes when I contemplate the things that people do with their lives I think it is almost a consolation — it is not such as to render life miserable. It merely makes you turn your attention to other things.

THE MORAL ARGUMENTS FOR DEITY

Now we reach one stage further in what I shall call the intellectual descent that the Theists have made in their argumentations, and we come to what are called the moral arguments for the existence of God. You all know, of course, that there used to be in the old days three intellectual arguments for the existence of God, all of which were disposed of by Immanuel Kant in the *Critique of Pure Reason;* but no sooner had he disposed of those arguments than he invented a new one, a moral argument, and that quite convinced him. He was like many people: In intellectual matters he was skeptical, but in moral matters he believed implicitly in the maxims that he had imbibed at his mother's knee. That illustrates what the psychoanalysts so much emphasize — the immensely stronger hold upon us that our very early associations have than those of later times.

Kant, as I say, invented a new moral argument for the existence of God, and that in varying forms was extremely popular during the nineteenth century. It has all sorts of forms. One form is to say that there would be no right or wrong unless God existed. I am not for the moment concerned with whether there is a difference between right and wrong, or whether there is not: That is another question. The point I am concerned with is that, if you are quite sure there is a difference between right and wrong, you are then in this situation: Is that difference due to God's fiat or is it not? If it is due to God's fiat, then for God himself there is no difference between right and wrong, and it is no longer a significant statement to say that God is good. If you are going to say, as theologians do, that God is good, you must then say that right and wrong have some meaning which is independent of God's fiat, because God's fiats are good and not bad independently of the mere fact that he made them. If you are going to say that, you will then have to say that it is not only through God that right and wrong came into being, but that they are in their essence logically anterior to God. You could, of course, if you liked, say that there was a superior deity who gave orders to the God who made this world, or could take up the line that some of the gnostics took up — a line which I often thought was a very plausible one — that as a matter of fact this world that we know was made by the devil at a moment when

10

God was not looking. There is a good deal to be said for that, and I am not concerned to refute it.

THE ARGUMENT FOR THE REMEDYING OF INJUSTICE

Then there is another very curious form of moral argument, which is this: They say that the existence of God is required in order to bring justice into the world. In the part of this universe that we know there is great injustice, and often the good suffer, and often the wicked prosper, and one hardly knows which of those is the more annoying; but if you are going to have justice in the universe as a whole you have to suppose a future life to redress the balance of life here on earth. So they say that there must be a God, and there must be heaven and hell in order that in the long run there may be justice. That is a very curious argument. If you looked at the matter from a scientific point of view, you would say, "After all, I know only this world. I do not know about the rest of the universe, but so far as one can argue at all on probabilities one would say that probably this world is a fair sample, and if there is injustice here the odds are that there is injustice elsewhere also." Supposing you got a crate of oranges that you opened, and you found all the top layer of oranges bad, you would not argue, "The underneath ones must be good, so as to redress the balance." You would say, "Probably the whole lot is a bad consignment"; and that is really what a scientific person would argue about the universe. He would say, "Here we find in this world a great deal of injustice, and so far as that goes that is a reason for supposing that justice does not rule in the world; and therefore so far as it goes it affords a moral argument against deity and not in favor of one." Of course I know that the sort of intellectual arguments that I have been talking to you about are not what really moves people. What really moves people to believe in God is not any intellectual argument at all. Most people believe in God because they have been taught from early infancy to do it, and that is the main reason.

Then I think that the next most powerful reason is the wish for safety, a sort of feeling that there is a big brother who will look after you. That plays a very profound part in influencing people's desire for a belief in God.

THE CHARACTER OF CHRIST

I now want to say a few words upon a topic which I often think is not quite sufficiently dealt with by Rationalists, and that is the question whether Christ was the best and the wisest of men. It is generally taken for granted that we should all agree that that was so. I do not myself. I think that there are a good many points upon which I agree with Christ a great deal more than the professing Christians do. I do not know that I could go with Him all the way, but I could go with Him much further than most professing Christians can. You will remember that He said, "Resist not evil: But whosoever shall smite thee on thy right cheek, turn to him the other also." That is not a new precept or a new principle. It was used by Lao-tse and Buddha some 500 or 600 years before Christ, but it is not a principle which as a matter of fact Christians accept. I have no doubt that the present Prime Minister,[1] for instance, is a most sincere Christian, but I should not advise any of you to go and smite him on one cheek. I think you might find that he thought this text was intended in a figurative sense.

Then there is another point which I consider excellent. You will re- 15 member that Christ said, "Judge not lest ye be judged." That principle I do not think you would find was popular in the law courts of Christian countries. I have known in my time quite a number of judges who were very earnest Christians, and none of them felt that they were acting contrary to Christian principles in what they did. Then Christ says, "Give to him that asketh of thee, and from him that would borrow of thee turn not thou away." That is a very good principle. Your Chairman has reminded you that we are not here to talk politics, but I cannot help observing that the last general election was fought on the question of how desirable it was to turn away from him that would borrow of thee, so that one must assume that the Liberals and Conservatives of this country are composed of people who do not agree with the teaching of Christ, because they certainly did very emphatically turn away on that occasion.

Then there is one other maxim of Christ which I think has a great deal in it, but I do not find that it is very popular among some of our Christian friends. He says, "If thou wilt be perfect, go and sell that which thou hast, and give to the poor." That is a very excellent maxim, but, as I say, it is not much practiced. All these, I think, are good maxims, although they are a little difficult to live up to. I do not profess to live up to them myself; but then, after all, it is not quite the same thing as for a Christian.

DEFECTS IN CHRIST'S TEACHING

Having granted the excellence of these maxims, I come to certain points in which I do not believe that one can grant either the superlative wisdom or the superlative goodness of Christ as depicted in the Gospels; and here I may say that one is not concerned with the historical question. Historically it is quite doubtful whether Christ ever existed at all, and if He did we do not know anything about Him, so that I am not concerned with the historical question, which is a very difficult one. I am concerned

[1]Stanley Baldwin (1867–1947). — EDS.

with Christ as He appears in the Gospels, taking the Gospel narrative as it stands, and there one does find some things that do not seem to be very wise. For one thing, He certainly thought that His second coming would occur in clouds of glory before the death of all the people who were living at that time. There are a great many texts that prove that. He says, for instance, "Ye shall not have gone over the cities of Israel till the Son of Man be come." Then He says, "There are some standing here which shall not taste death till the Son of Man comes into His kingdom"; and there are a lot of places where it is quite clear that He believed that His second coming would happen during the lifetime of many then living. That was the belief of His earlier followers, and it was the basis of a good deal of His moral teaching. When He said, "Take no thought for the morrow," and things of that sort, it was very largely because He thought that the second coming was going to be very soon, and that all ordinary mundane affairs did not count. I have, as a matter of fact, known some Christians who did believe that the second coming was imminent. I knew a parson who frightened his congregation terribly by telling them that the second coming was very imminent indeed, but they were much consoled when they found that he was planting trees in his garden. The early Christians did really believe it, and they did abstain from such things as planting trees in their gardens, because they did accept from Christ the belief that the second coming was imminent. In that respect, clearly He was not so wise as some other people have been, and He was certainly not superlatively wise.

THE MORAL PROBLEM

Then you come to moral questions. There is one very serious defect to my mind in Christ's moral character, and that is that He believed in hell. I do not myself feel that any person who is really profoundly human can believe in everlasting punishment. Christ certainly as depicted in the Gospels did believe in everlasting punishment, and one does find repeatedly a vindictive fury against those people who would not listen to His preaching—an attitude which is not uncommon with preachers, but which does somewhat detract from superlative excellence. You do not, for instance, find that attitude in Socrates. You find him quite bland and urbane toward the people who would not listen to him; and it is, to my mind, far more worthy of a sage to take that line than to take the line of indignation. You probably all remember the sort of things that Socrates was saying when he was dying, and the sort of things that he generally did say to people who did not agree with him.

You will find that in the Gospels Christ said, "Ye serpents, ye generation of vipers, how can ye escape the damnation of hell." That was said to people who did not like His preaching. It is not really to my mind quite the best tone, and there are a great many of these things about hell. There is, of course, the familiar text about the sin against the Holy Ghost: "Whosoever speaketh against the Holy Ghost it shall not be forgiven him neither in this World nor in the world to come." That text has caused an unspeakable amount of misery in the world, for all sorts of people have imagined that they have committed the sin against the Holy Ghost, and thought that it would not be forgiven them either in this world or in the world to come. I really do not think that a person with a proper degree of kindliness in his nature would have put fears and terrors of that sort into the world.

Then Christ says, "The Son of Man shall send forth His angels, and they shall gather out of His kingdom all things that offend, and them which do iniquity, and shall cast them into a furnace of fire; there shall be wailing and gnashing of teeth"; and He goes on about the wailing and gnashing of teeth. It comes in one verse after another, and it is quite manifest to the reader that there is a certain pleasure in contemplating wailing and gnashing of teeth, or else it would not occur so often. Then you all, of course, remember about the sheep and the goats; how at the second coming He is going to divide the sheep from the goats, and He is going to say to the goats, "Depart from me, ye cursed, into everlasting fire." He continues, "And these shall go away into everlasting fire." Then He says again, "If thy hand offend thee, cut it off; it is better for thee to enter into life maimed, than having two hands to go into hell, into the fire that never shall be quenched; where the worm dieth not and the fire is not quenched." He repeats that again and again also. I must say that I think all this doctrine, that hell-fire is a punishment for sin, is a doctrine of cruelty. It is a doctrine that put cruelty into the world and gave the world generations of cruel torture; and the Christ of the Gospels, if you could take Him as His chroniclers represent Him, would certainly have to be considered partly responsible for that.

There are other things of less importance. There is the instance of the Gadarene swine, where it certainly was not very kind to the pigs to put the devils into them and make them rush down the hill to the sea. You must remember that He was omnipotent, and He could have made the devils simply go away; but He chose to send them into the pigs. Then there is the curious story of the fig tree, which always rather puzzled me. You remember what happened about the fig tree. "He was hungry; and seeing a fig tree afar off having leaves, He came if haply He might find anything thereon; and when He came to it He found nothing but leaves, for the time of figs was not yet. And Jesus answered and said unto it: 'No man eat fruit of thee hereafter for ever' . . . and Peter . . . saith unto Him: 'Master, behold the fig tree which thou cursedst is withered away.'" This is a very curious story, because it was not the right time of year for figs, and you really could not blame the tree. I cannot myself feel that either in the matter of wisdom or in the matter of virtue Christ stands quite as high as some other people known to history. I think I should put Buddha and Socrates above Him in those respects.

20

THE EMOTIONAL FACTOR

As I said before, I do not think that the real reason why people accept religion has anything to do with argumentation. They accept religion on emotional grounds. One is often told that it is a very wrong thing to attack religion, because religion makes men virtuous. So I am told; I have not noticed it. You know, of course, the parody of that argument in Samuel Butler's book, *Erewhon Revisited*. You will remember that in *Erewhon* there is a certain Higgs who arrives in a remote country, and after spending some time there he escapes from that country in a balloon. Twenty years later he comes back to that country and finds a new religion in which he is worshipped under the name of the "Sun Child," and it is said that he ascended into heaven. He finds that the Feast of the Ascension is about to be celebrated, and he hears Professors Hanky and Panky say to each other that they never set eyes on the man Higgs, and they hope they never will; but they are the high priests of the religion of the Sun Child. He is very indignant, and he comes up to them, and he says, "I am going to expose all this humbug and tell the people of Erewhon that it was only I, the man Higgs, and I went up in a balloon." He was told, "You must not do that, because all the morals of this country are bound round this myth, and if they once know that you did not ascend into heaven they will all become wicked"; and so he is persuaded of that and he goes quietly away.

That is the idea—that we should all be wicked if we did not hold to the Christian religion. It seems to me that the people who have held to it have been for the most part extremely wicked. You find this curious fact, that the more intense has been the religion of any period and the more profound has been the dogmatic belief, the greater has been the cruelty and the worse has been the state of affairs. In the so-called ages of faith, when men really did believe the Christian religion in all its completeness, there was the Inquisition, with its tortures; there were millions of unfortunate women burned as witches; and there was every kind of cruelty practiced upon all sorts of people in the name of religion.

You find as you look around the world that every single bit of progress in humane feeling, every improvement in the criminal law, every step toward the diminution of war, every step toward better treatment of the colored races, or every mitigation of slavery, every moral progress that there has been in the world, has been consistently opposed by the organized churches of the world. I say quite deliberately that the Christian religion, as organized in its churches, has been and still is the principal enemy of moral progress in the world.

HOW THE CHURCHES HAVE
RETARDED PROGRESS

You may think that I am going too far when I say that that is still so. I do not think that I am. Take one fact. You will bear with me if I mention it. It is not a pleasant fact, but the churches compel one to mention

25

facts that are not pleasant. Supposing that in this world that we live in today an inexperienced girl is married to a syphilitic man; in that case the Catholic Church says, "This is an indissoluble sacrament. You must endure celibacy or stay together. And if you stay together, you must not use birth control to prevent the birth of syphilitic children." Nobody whose natural sympathies have not been warped by dogma, or whose moral nature was not absolutely dead to all sense of suffering, could maintain that it is right and proper that that state of things should continue.

That is only an example. There are a great many ways in which, at the present moment, the church, by its insistence upon what it chooses to call morality, inflicts upon all sorts of people undeserved and unnecessary suffering. And of course, as we know, it is in its major part an opponent still of progress and of improvement in all the ways that diminish suffering in the world, because it has chosen to label as morality a certain narrow set of rules of conduct which have nothing to do with human happiness; and when you say that this or that ought to be done because it would make for human happiness, they think that has nothing to do with the matter at all. "What has human happiness to do with morals? The object of morals is not to make people happy."

FEAR, THE FOUNDATION OF RELIGION

Religion is based, I think, primarily and mainly upon fear. It is partly the terror of the unknown and partly, as I have said, the wish to feel that you have a kind of elder brother who will stand by you in all your troubles and disputes. Fear is the basis of the whole thing—fear of the mysterious, fear of defeat, fear of death. Fear is the parent of cruelty, and therefore it is no wonder if cruelty and religion have gone hand in hand. It is because fear is at the basis of those two things. In this world we can now begin a little to understand things, and a little to master them by help of science, which has forced its way step by step against the Christian religion, against the churches, and against the opposition of all the old precepts. Science can help us to get over this craven fear in which mankind has lived for so many generations. Science can teach us, and I think our own hearts can teach us, no longer to look around for imaginary supports, no longer to invent allies in the sky, but rather to look to our own efforts here below to make this world a fit place to live in, instead of the sort of place that the churches in all these centuries have made it.

WHAT WE MUST DO

We want to stand upon our own feet and look fair and square at the world—its good facts, its bad facts, its beauties, and its ugliness; see the world as it is and be not afraid of it. Conquer the world by intelligence and not merely by being slavishly subdued by the terror that comes from it. The whole conception of God is a conception derived from the ancient Oriental despotisms. It is a conception quite unworthy of free men. When you hear people in church debasing themselves and saying that they are miserable sinners, and all the rest of it, it seems contemptible and not worthy of self-respecting human beings. We ought to stand up and look the world frankly in the face. We ought to make the best we can of the world, and if it is not so good as we wish, after all it will still be better than what these others have made of it in all these ages. A good world needs knowledge, kindliness, and courage; it does not need a regretful hankering after the past or a fettering of the free intelligence by the words uttered long ago by ignorant men. It needs a fearless outlook and a free intelligence. It needs hope for the future, not looking back all the time toward a past that is dead, which we trust will be far surpassed by the future that our intelligence can create.

The Reader's Presence

1. Summarize Russell's first and second paragraphs, each in a sentence. In a third sentence, describe and evaluate his strategy in opening with these paragraphs. What might be Russell's intention? What tone does Russell use in pursuing his points? Is this an expected tone for the subject matter? Does Russell's tone enhance or undermine the seriousness of his argument?

2. How does Russell characterize the "First Cause" argument? Is this how its originators are likely to have characterized it? Can you understand the original argument from Russell's version of it? What sense of Russell's perspective do you gain from his "reading" of the original argument? What sort of audience do you think Russell was addressing? Why?

3. Russell's essay is, among other things, a review of arguments on behalf of Christianity, each of which he carefully dismantles. Russell also devotes several pages to the figure of Christ—his character, his maxims, his moral stature, and his wisdom. The climax of his essay, however may be his critique of the church: "I say quite deliberately that the Christian religion, *as organized in its churches,* has been and still is the principal enemy of moral progress in the world" (paragraph 24, emphasis added). Both Russell and Martin Luther King Jr. were pacifists. Compare Russell's use of Christ and the church to the way King uses both in his "Letter from Birmingham Jail" (page 692). King's letter is not, strictly speaking, a defense of Christianity, but how might you read it as a response to Russell's polemic?

Scott Russell Sanders

The Men We Carry in Our Minds

Scott Russell Sanders (b. 1945) writes in a variety of genres: science fiction, realistic fiction, folktales, children's stories, essays, and historical novels. In all his work, however, he is concerned with the ways in which people live in communities. Some of his books include The Paradise of Bombs *(1987), from which "The Men We Carry in Our Minds" is taken;* Staying Put: Making a Home in a Restless World *(1993);* Here Comes the Mystery Man *(1993);* Writing from the Center *(1995);* Hunting for Hope: A Father's Journey *(1998); and* The Country of Language *(1999). Sanders contributes to both literary and popular magazines. He is a professor of English at Indiana University.*

Sanders has said, "I believe that a writer should be a servant of language, community, and nature. Language is the creation and sustenance of community.... My writing is driven by a deep regard for particular places and voices, persons and tools, plants and animals, for human skills and stories.... If my writing does not help my neighbors to live more alertly, pleasurably, or wisely, then it is worth little."

"This must be a hard time for women," I say to my friend Anneke. "They have so many paths to choose from, and so many voices calling them."

"I think it's a lot harder for men," she replies.

"How do you figure that?"

"The women I know feel excited, innocent, like crusaders in a just cause. The men I know are eaten up with guilt."

We are sitting at the kitchen table drinking sassafras tea, our hands   5
wrapped around the mugs because this April morning is cool and drizzly. "Like a Dutch morning," Anneke told me earlier. She is Dutch herself, a writer and midwife and peacemaker, with the round face and sad eyes of a woman in a Vermeer painting who might be waiting for the rain to stop, for a door to open. She leans over to sniff a sprig of lilac, pale lavender, that rises from a vase of cobalt blue.

"Women feel such pressure to be everything, do everything," I say.

"Career, kids, art, politics. Have their babies and get back to the office a week later. It's as if they're trying to overcome a million years' worth of evolution in one lifetime."

"But we help one another. We don't try to lumber on alone, like so many wounded grizzly bears, the way men do." Anneke sips her tea. I gave her the mug with the owls on it, for wisdom. "And we have this deep-down sense that we're in the *right*—we've been held back, passed over, used—while men feel they're in the wrong. Men are the ones who've been discredited, who have to search their souls."

I search my soul. I discover guilty feelings aplenty—toward the poor, the Vietnamese, Native Americans, the whales, an endless list of debts—a guilt in each case that is as bright and unambiguous as a neon sign. But toward women I feel something more confused, a snarl of shame, envy, wary tenderness, and amazement. This muddle troubles me. To hide my unease I say, "You're right, it's tough being a man these days."

"Don't laugh." Anneke frowns at me, mournful-eyed, through the sassafras steam. "I wouldn't be a man for anything. It's much easier being the victim. All the victim has to do is break free. The persecutor has to live with his past."

How deep is that past? I find myself wondering after Anneke has left.   10
How much of an inheritance do I have to throw off? Is it just the beliefs I breathed in as a child? Do I have to scour memory back through father and grandfather? Through St. Paul? Beyond Stonehenge and into the twilit caves? I'm convinced the past we must contend with is deeper even than speech. When I think back on my childhood, on how I learned to see men and women, I have a sense of ancient, dizzying depths. The back roads of Tennessee and Ohio where I grew up were probably closer, in their sexual patterns, to the campsites of Stone Age hunters than to the genderless cities of the future into which we are rushing.

The first men, besides my father, I remember seeing were black convicts and white guards, in the cottonfield across the road from our farm on the outskirts of Memphis. I must have been three or four. The prisoners wore dingy gray-and-black zebra suits, heavy as canvas, sodden with sweat. Hatless, stooped, they chopped weeds in the fierce heat, row after row, breathing the acrid dust of boll-weevil poison. The overseers wore dazzling white shirts and broad shadowy hats. The oiled barrels of their shotguns flashed in the sunlight. Their faces in memory are utterly blank. Of course those men, white and black, have become for me an emblem of racial hatred. But they have also come to stand for the twin poles of my early vision of manhood—the brute toiling animal and the boss.

When I was a boy, the men I knew labored with their bodies. They were marginal farmers, just scraping by, or welders, steelworkers, carpenters; they swept floors, dug ditches, mined coal, or drove trucks, their forearms ropy with muscle; they trained horses, stoked furnaces, built tires, stood on assembly lines wrestling parts onto cars and refrigerators. They got up before light, worked all day long whatever the weather, and when they came home at night they looked as though somebody had been whipping them. In the evenings and on weekends they worked on their own places, tilling gardens that were lumpy with clay, fixing broken-down cars, hammering on houses that were always too drafty, too leaky, too small.

The bodies of the men I knew were twisted and maimed in ways visible and invisible. The nails of their hands were black and split, the hands tattooed with scars. Some had lost fingers. Heavy lifting had given many of them finicky backs and guts weak from hernias. Racing against conveyor belts had given them ulcers. Their ankles and knees ached from years of standing on concrete. Anyone who had worked for long around machines was hard of hearing. They squinted, and the skin of their faces was creased like the leather of old work gloves. There were times, studying them, when I dreaded growing up. Most of them coughed, from dust or cigarettes, and most of them drank cheap wine or whiskey, so their eyes looked bloodshot and bruised. The fathers of my friends always seemed older than the mothers. Men wore out sooner. Only women lived into old age.

As a boy I also knew another sort of men, who did not sweat and break down like mules. They were soldiers, and so far as I could tell they scarcely worked at all. During my early school years we lived on a military base, an arsenal in Ohio, and every day I saw GIs in the guardshacks, on the stoops of barracks, at the wheels of olive drab Chevrolets. The chief fact of their lives was boredom. Long after I left the Arsenal I came to recognize the sour smell the soldiers gave off as that of souls in limbo. They were all waiting—for wars, for transfers, for leaves, for promotions, for the end of their hitch—like so many braves waiting for the hunt to begin. Unlike the warriors of older tribes, however, they would have no say about when the battle would start or how it would be waged. Their waiting was broken only when they practiced for war. They fired guns at targets, drove tanks across the churned-up fields of the military reservation, set off bombs in the wrecks of old fighter planes. I knew this was all play. But I also felt certain that when the hour for killing arrived, they would kill. When the real shooting started, many of them would die. This was what soldiers were *for*, just as a hammer was for driving nails.

Warriors and toilers: those seemed, in my boyhood vision, to be the chief destinies for men. They weren't the only destinies, as I learned from having a few male teachers, from reading books, and from watching television. But the men on television—the politicians, the astronauts, the generals, the savvy lawyers, the philosophical doctors, the bosses who gave orders to both soldiers and laborers—seemed as remote and unreal to me as the figures in tapestries. I could no more imagine growing up to become one of these cool, potent creatures than I could imagine becoming a prince.

A nearer and more hopeful example was that of my father, who had escaped from a red-dirt farm to a tire factory, and from the assembly line

15

to the front office. Eventually he dressed in a white shirt and tie. He carried himself as if he had been born to work with his mind. But his body, remembering the earlier years of slogging work, began to give out on him in his fifties, and it quit on him entirely before he turned sixty-five. Even such a partial escape from man's fate as he had accomplished did not seem possible for most of the boys I knew. They joined the army, stood in line for jobs in the smoky plants, helped build highways. They were bound to work as their fathers had worked, killing themselves or preparing to kill others.

A scholarship enabled me not only to attend college, a rare enough feat in my circle, but even to study in a university meant for the children of the rich. Here I met for the first time young men who had assumed from birth that they would lead lives of comfort and power. And for the first time I met women who told me that men were guilty of having kept all the joys and privileges of the earth for themselves. I was baffled. What privileges? What joys? I thought about the maimed, dismal lives of most of the men back home. What had they stolen from their wives and daughters? The right to go five days a week, twelve months a year, for thirty or forty years to a steel mill or a coal mine? The right to drop bombs and die in war? The right to feel every leak in the roof, every gap in the fence, every cough in the engine, as a wound they must mend? The right to feel, when the lay-off comes or the plant shuts down, not only afraid but ashamed?

I was slow to understand the deep grievances of women. This was because, as a boy, I had envied them. Before college, the only people I had ever known who were interested in art or music or literature, the only ones who read books, the only ones who ever seemed to enjoy a sense of ease and grace were the mothers and daughters. Like the menfolk, they fretted about money, they scrimped and made-do. But, when the pay stopped coming in, they were not the ones who had failed. Nor did they have to go to war, and that seemed to me a blessed fact. By comparison with the narrow, ironclad days of fathers, there was an expansiveness, I thought, in the days of mothers. They went to see neighbors, to shop in town, to run errands at school, at the library, at church. No doubt, had I looked harder at their lives, I would have envied them less. It was not my fate to become a woman, so it was easier for me to see the graces. Few of them held jobs outside the home, and those who did filled thankless roles as clerks and waitresses. I didn't see, then, what a prison a house could be, since houses seemed to me brighter, handsomer places than any factory. I did not realize—because such things were never spoken of—how often women suffered from men's bullying. I did learn about the wretchedness of abandoned wives, single mothers, widows; but I also learned about the wretchedness of lone men. Even then I could see how exhausting it was for a mother to cater all day to the needs of young children. But if I had been asked, as a boy, to choose between tending a baby and tending a machine, I think I would have chosen the baby. (Having now tended both, I know I would choose the baby.)

So I was baffled when the women at college accused me and my sex of having cornered the world's pleasures. I think something like my bafflement has been felt by other boys (and by girls as well) who grew up in dirt-poor farm country, in mining country, in black ghettos, in Hispanic barrios, in the shadows of factories, in Third World nations — any place where the fate of men is as grim and bleak as the fate of women. Toilers and warriors. I realize now how ancient these identities are, how deep the tug they exert on men, the undertow of a thousand generations. The miseries I saw, as a boy, in the lives of nearly all men I continue to see in the lives of many — the body-breaking toil, the tedium, the call to be tough, the humiliating powerlessness, the battle for a living and for territory.

When the women I met at college thought about the joys and privileges of men, they did not carry in their minds the sort of men I had known in my childhood. They thought of their fathers, who were bankers, physicians, architects, stockbrokers, the big wheels of the big cities. These fathers rode the train to work or drove cars that cost more than any of my childhood houses. They were attended from morning to night by female helpers, wives, and nurses and secretaries. They were never laid off, never short of cash at month's end, never lined up for welfare. These fathers made decisions that mattered. They ran the world.   20

The daughters of such men wanted to share in this power, this glory. So did I. They yearned for a say over their future, for jobs worthy of their abilities, for the right to live at peace, unmolested, whole. Yes, I thought, yes yes. The difference between me and these daughters was that they saw me, because of my sex, as destined from birth to become like their fathers, and therefore as an enemy to their desires. But I knew better. I wasn't an enemy, in fact or in feeling. I was an ally. If I had known, then, how to tell them so, would they have believed me? Would they now?

The Reader's Presence

1. Sanders begins the essay by jumping directly into a conversation (paragraphs 1–9). What initial effect does this conversation have on the reader? What does Sanders want you to think of him as you read the dialogue? How does he move from the conversation to the body of the essay (paragraphs 10 and following)? How might you describe the transition? Does Sanders's voice change at paragraph 10? Does Sanders return to Anneke's distinction between the victim and the persecutor (end of paragraph 9)? If so, how? Finally, how do you understand the opening dialogue by the end of the essay, having encountered the full passion of Sanders's beliefs about his legacy of masculinity?

2. Consider the title of the essay. Why does Sanders use the word *carry*? What image does the word convey? How is that image reinforced throughout the essay?

3. Sanders's essay is as much about class as it is about gender. Discuss the roles of privation and privilege, of physical labor and higher education in the essay. Sanders is in many respects a compatriot of Dorothy Allison; the two writers share a strong sense of the ethical responsibility of the artist. Reread Allison's essay, "This Is Our World" (page 589) and Sanders's thoughts about writing that follow, and compare the two writers' understanding of their roles as writers in American society. How do class issues enter into each essay?

THE WRITER AT WORK

Scott Russell Sanders on Writing Essays

The well-known American essayist Scott Russell Sanders is also a professor of English at the University of Indiana and the author of several novels, short story collections, and books of criticism. In the following passage from "The Singular First Person," which was originally delivered as a keynote talk at an academic conference on the essay at Seton Hall University in 1988, Sanders argues for the relevance of essay writing in a society that increasingly relies on abstract and formulaic language. If you compare this passage with the style of argument Sanders makes in the preceding essay, you will see that he is a writer who practices what he preaches. He also raises an interesting question about the difference between essays and fiction that you might consider when reading the stories in Part V: Do essayists put more of themselves at risk than novelists and short story writers?

The essay is a haven for the private, idiosyncratic voice in an era of anonymous babble. Like the blandburgers served in their millions along our highways, most language served up in public these days is textureless, tasteless mush. On television, over the phone, in the newspaper, wherever humans bandy words about, we encounter more and more abstractions, more empty formulas. Think of the pablum ladled out by politicians. Think of the fluffy white bread of advertising. Think, Lord help us, of committee reports. In contrast, the essay remains stubbornly concrete and particular: it confronts you with an oil-smeared toilet at the Sunoco station, a red vinyl purse shaped like a valentine heart, a bow-legged dentist hunting deer with an elephant gun. As Orwell forcefully argued,[1] and as

---

[1]See "Politics and the English Language," page 481. —EDS.

dictators seem to agree, such a bypassing of abstractions, such an insistence on the concrete, is a politically subversive act. Clinging to this door, that child, this grief, following the zigzag motions of an inquisitive mind, the essay renews language and clears trash from the springs of thought. A century and a half ago, Emerson called on a new generation of writers to cast off the hand-me-down rhetoric of the day, to "pierce this rotten diction and fasten words again to visible things." The essayist aspires to do just that.

As if all these virtues were not enough to account for a renaissance of this protean genre, the essay has also taken over some of the territory abdicated by contemporary fiction. Pared down to the brittle bones of plot, camouflaged with irony, muttering in brief sentences and grade-school vocabulary, today's fashionable fiction avoids disclosing where the author stands on anything. Most of the trends in the novel and short story over the past twenty years have led away from candor—toward satire, artsy jokes, close-lipped coyness, metafictional hocus-pocus, anything but a direct statement of what the author thinks and feels. If you hide behind enough screens, no one will ever hold you to an opinion or demand from you a coherent vision or take you for a charlatan.

The essay is not fenced round by these literary inhibitions. You may speak without disguise of what moves and worries and excites you. In fact, you had better speak from a region pretty close to the heart, or the reader will detect the wind of phoniness whistling through your hollow phrases. In the essay you may be caught with your pants down, your ignorance and sentimentality showing, while you trot recklessly about on one of your hobbyhorses. You cannot stand back from the action, as Joyce instructed us to do, and pare your fingernails. You cannot palm off your cockamamie notions on some hapless character. If the words you put down are foolish, everyone knows precisely who the fool is.

To our list of the essay's contemporary attractions we should add the perennial ones of verbal play, mental adventure, and sheer anarchic high spirits. The writing of an essay is like finding one's way through a forest without being quite sure what game you are chasing, what landmark you are seeking. You sniff down one path until some heady smell tugs you in a new direction, and then off you go, dodging and circling, lured on by the songs of unfamiliar birds, puzzled by the tracks of strange beasts, leaping from stone to stone across rivers, barking up one tree after another. Much of the pleasure in writing an essay—and, when the writing is any good, the pleasure in reading it—comes from this dodging and leaping, this movement of the mind. It must not be idle movement, however, if the essay is to hold up; it must be driven by deep concerns. The surface of a river is alive with lights and reflections, the breaking of foam over rocks, but beneath that dazzle it is going somewhere. We should expect as much from an essay: the shimmer and play of mind on the surface and in the depths a strong current.

Arthur M. Schlesinger Jr.

The Cult of Ethnicity, Good and Bad

One of the most widely known historians, Arthur M. Schlesinger Jr. (b. 1917) has been a professor at Harvard University and at the Graduate Center of the City University of New York. Politically liberal, Schlesinger served as a special adviser to President Kennedy from 1961 to 1963. He has received numerous awards, including over two dozen honorary degrees, both a National Book Award and a Pulitzer Prize for A Thousand Days: John F. Kennedy in the White House *(1965), and a Pulitzer for* The Age of Jackson *(1945). His major historical work on the life of Franklin D. Roosevelt,* The Age of Roosevelt, *was published in three volumes:* The Crisis of the Old Order, 1919–1933 *(1957),* The Coming of the New Deal *(1958), and* The Politics of Upheaval *(1960). Most recently, Schlesinger has published* The Disuniting of America *(1991),* Running for President: The Candidates and Their Images *(1994), and* A Life in the Twentieth Century: Innocent Beginnings, *1917–1950 (2000). "The Cult of Ethnicity, Good and Bad" appeared in* Time *in 1991.*

The history of the world has been in great part the history of the mixing of peoples. Modern communication and transport accelerate mass migrations from one continent to another. Ethnic and racial diversity is more than ever a salient fact of the age.

But what happens when people of different origins, speaking different languages and professing different religions, inhabit the same locality and live under the same political sovereignty? Ethnic and racial conflict — far more than ideological conflict — is the explosive problem of our times.

On every side today ethnicity is breaking up nations. The Soviet Union, India, Yugoslavia, Ethiopia, are all in crisis. Ethnic tensions disturb and divide Sri Lanka, Burma, Indonesia, Iraq, Cyprus, Nigeria, Angola, Lebanon, Guyana, Trinidad — you name it. Even nations as stable and civilized as Britain and France, Belgium and Spain, face growing ethnic troubles. Is there any large multiethnic state that can be made to work?

The answer to that question has been, until recently, the United States. "No other nation," Margaret Thatcher[1] has said, "has so successfully combined people of different races and nations within a single culture." How have Americans succeeded in pulling off this almost unprecedented trick?

We have always been a multiethnic country. Hector St. John de   5
Crèvecoeur, who came from France in the eighteenth century, marveled at the astonishing diversity of the settlers—"a mixture of English, Scotch, Irish, French, Dutch, Germans, and Swedes . . . this promiscuous breed." He propounded a famous question: "What then is the American, this new man?" And he gave a famous answer: "Here individuals of all nations are melted into a new race of men." *E pluribus unum.*[2]

The United States escaped the divisiveness of a multiethnic society by a brilliant solution: the creation of a brand-new national identity. The point of America was not to preserve old cultures but to forge a new *American* culture. "By an intermixture with our people," President George Washington told Vice President John Adams, immigrants will "get assimilated to our customs, measures and laws: in a word, soon become one people." This was the ideal that a century later Israel Zangwill crystallized in the title of his popular 1908 play *The Melting Pot.* And no institution was more potent in molding Crèvecoeur's "promiscuous breed" into Washington's "one people" than the American public school.

The new American nationality was inescapably English in language, ideas, and institutions. The pot did not melt everybody, not even all the white immigrants; deeply bred racism put black Americans, yellow Americans, red Americans, and brown Americans well outside the pale. Still, the infusion of other stocks, even of nonwhite stocks, and the experience of the New World reconfigured the British legacy and made the United States, as we all know, a very different country from Britain.

In the twentieth century, new immigration laws altered the composition of the American people, and a cult of ethnicity erupted both among non-Anglo whites and among nonwhite minorities. This had many healthy consequences. The American culture at last began to give shamefully overdue recognition to the achievements of groups subordinated and spurned during the high noon of Anglo dominance, and it began to acknowledge the great swirling world beyond Europe. Americans acquired a more complex and invigorating sense of their world—and of themselves.

But, pressed too far, the cult of ethnicity has unhealthy consequences. It gives rise, for example, to the conception of the United States as a nation composed not of individuals making their own choices but of inviolable ethnic and racial groups. It rejects the historic American goals of assimilation and integration. And, in an excess of zeal, well-intentioned people seek to transform our system of education from a means of

---

[1]*Margaret Thatcher:* Former prime minister of Great Britain.—EDS.
[2]*E pluribus unum:* Latin phrase and U.S. motto meaning "out of many, one."—EDS.

creating "one people" into a means of promoting, celebrating, and per-petuating separate ethnic origins and identities. The balance is shifting from *unum* to *pluribus*.

That is the issue that lies behind the hullabaloo over "multicultural-   10
ism" and "political correctness," the attack on the "Eurocentric" curricu-lum and the rise of the notion that history and literature should be taught not as disciplines but as therapies whose function is to raise minority self-esteem. Group separatism crystallizes the differences, magnifies tensions, intensifies hostilities. Europe—the unique source of the liberating ideas of democracy, civil liberties, and human rights—is portrayed as the root of all evil, and non-European cultures, their own many crimes deleted, are presented as the means of redemption.

I don't want to sound apocalyptic about these developments. Education is always in ferment, and a good thing, too. The situation in our universities, I am confident, will soon right itself. But the impact of separatist pressures on our public schools is more troubling. If a Kleagle[3] of the Ku Klux Klan wanted to use the schools to disable and handicap black Americans, he could hardly come up with anything more effective than the "Afrocentric" curriculum. And if separatist tendencies go unchecked, the result can only be the fragmentation, resegregation, and tribalization of American life.

I remain optimistic. My impression is that the historic forces driving toward "one people" have not lost their power. The eruption of ethnicity is, I believe, a rather superficial enthusiasm stirred by romantic ideologues on the one hand and by unscrupulous con men on the other: self-appointed spokesmen whose claim to represent their minority groups is carelessly accepted by the media. Most American-born members of mi-nority groups, white or nonwhite, see themselves primarily as Americans rather than primarily as members of one or another ethnic group. A notable indicator today is the rate of intermarriage across ethnic lines, across religious lines, even (increasingly) across racial lines. "We Ameri-cans," said Theodore Roosevelt, "are children of the crucible."

The growing diversity of the American population makes the quest for unifying ideals and a common culture all the more urgent. In a world sav-agely rent by ethnic and racial antagonisms, the United States must continue as an example of how a highly differentiated society holds itself together.

The Reader's Presence

1. Why does the author use a Latin phrase in paragraph 5? Evaluate the use of this phrase. Is it a common phrase? Do you think most readers know what it means in English? Why does he use it twice in varying forms?

---

[3]*Kleagle:* An organizer or recruiter for the Ku Klux Klan.—EDS.

2. Schlesinger agrees that, historically, America has faced difficulties with ethnicity and assimilation, yet feels that in the current situation events have gone too far. Does he propose a different solution? Is this "commonsense" approach valid? Would a more fact-based approach be more, or less, convincing? Why? Can you think of an opposing argument? It might be counterargued that Schlesinger, hailing from a past generation of immigrants, is insensitive to the needs of current-day groups. How might Schlesinger answer that response? Can you think of an answer?

3. Why does Schlesinger discuss both the positive and negative aspects of what he calls "the cult of ethnicity"? Why does he present the positive points first? What does he conclude about this trend? What is the relation between ethnicity and race in Schlesinger's essay? Trace that distinction through the essay—what is the ideal role of language of our "highly differentiated society"? Compare Schlesinger's view of integration and assimilation as "historic American goals" to that of Richard Rodriguez in "Aria" (page 221) and Gloria Anzaldúa in "How to Tame a Wild Tongue" (page 299). How might each of these three writers respond to the others' viewpoints?

107

Leslie Marmon Silko

In the Combat Zone

Poet, novelist, screenwriter, and storyteller Leslie Marmon Silko (b. 1948) is of mixed heritage, part Pueblo Indian, part Mexican, and part white. She was raised on the Laguna Pueblo and educated at the University of New Mexico, where she now teaches English. Her publications include a montage of stories, legends, poems, and photographs called Storyteller *(1981), several works of fiction, the screenplay for Marlon Brando's film* Black Elks, *an illustrated autobiographical narrative called* Sacred Water Narratives and Pictures *(1993), and* Yellow Woman and a Beauty of the Spirit: Essays on Native American Life Today *(1996). Her work has been extensively anthologized and published in magazines and journals. "In the Combat Zone" appeared in* Hungry Mind Review *in 1995. In 1981, Silko was awarded a MacArthur grant for her writing.*

When asked by an interviewer why she writes, she replied, "I don't know what I know until it comes out in narrative." Speaking specifically of the process of composing her novel Almanac of the Dead *(1991), she said, "It's like*

*a do-it-yourself psychoanalysis. It's sort of dangerous to be a novelist . . .
you're working with language and all kinds of things can escape with the words
of a narrative."*

Women seldom discuss our wariness or the precautions we take after
dark each time we leave the apartment, car, or office to go on the most
brief errand. We take for granted that we are targeted as easy prey by
muggers, rapists, and serial killers. This is our lot as women in the United
States. We try to avoid going anywhere alone after dark, although economic necessity sends women out night after night. We do what must be
done, but always we are alert, on guard, and ready. We have to be aware
of persons walking on the sidewalk behind us; we have to pay attention
to others who board an elevator we're on. We try to avoid all staircases
and deserted parking garages when we are alone. Constant vigilance requires considerable energy and concentration seldom required of men.

I used to assume that most men were aware of this fact of women's
lives, but I was wrong. They may notice our reluctance to drive at night
to the convenience store alone, but they don't know or don't want to
know the experience of a woman out alone at night. Men who have been
in combat know the feeling of being a predator's target, but it is difficult
for men to admit that we women live our entire lives in a combat zone.
Men have the power to end violence against women in the home, but they
feel helpless to protect women from violent strangers. Because men feel
guilt and anger at their inability to shoulder responsibility for the safety
of their wives, sisters, and daughters, we don't often discuss random acts
of violence against women.

When we were children, my sisters and I used to go to Albuquerque
with my father. Sometimes strangers would tell my father it was too bad
that he had three girls and no sons. My father, who has always preferred
the company of women, used to reply that he was glad to have girls and
not boys, because he might not get along as well with boys. Furthermore,
he'd say, "My girls can do anything your boys can do, and my girls can
do it better." He had in mind, of course, shooting and hunting.

When I was six years old, my father took me along as he hunted deer;
he showed me how to walk quietly, to move along, and then to stop and
listen carefully before taking another step. A year later, he traded a pistol
for a little single shot .22 rifle just my size.

He took me and my younger sisters down to the dump by the river   5
and taught us how to shoot. We rummaged through the trash for bottles
and glass jars; it was great fun to take aim at a pickle jar and watch it
shatter. If the Rio San Jose had water running in it, we threw bottles for
moving targets in the muddy current. My father told us that a .22 bullet
can travel a mile, so we had to be careful where we aimed. The river was
a good place because it was below the villages and away from the houses;
the high clay riverbanks wouldn't let any bullets stray. Gun safety was
drilled into us. We were cautioned about other children whose parents

might not teach them properly; if we ever saw another child with a gun, we knew to get away. Guns were not toys. My father did not approve of BB guns because they were classified as toys. I had a .22 rifle when I was seven years old. If I felt like shooting, all I had to do was tell my parents where I was going, take my rifle and a box of .22 shells and go. I was never tempted to shoot at birds or animals because whatever was killed had to be eaten. Now, I realize how odd this must seem; a seven year old with a little .22 rifle and a box of ammunition, target shooting alone at the river. But that was how people lived at Laguna when I was growing up; children were given responsibilities from an early age.

Laguna Pueblo people hunted deer for winter meat. When I was thirteen, I carried George Pearl's saddle carbine, a .30–30, and hunted deer for the first time. When I was fourteen, I killed my first mule deer buck with one shot through the heart.

Guns were for target shooting and guns were for hunting, but also I knew that Grandma Lily carried a little purse gun with her whenever she drove alone to Albuquerque or Los Lunas. One night my mother and my grandmother were driving the fifty miles from Albuquerque to Laguna down Route 66 when three men in a car tried to force my grandmother's car off the highway. Route 66 was not so heavily traveled as Interstate 40 is now, and there were many long stretches of highway where no other car passed for minutes on end. Payrolls at the Jackpile Uranium Mine were large in the 1950s, and my mother or my grandmother had to bring home thousands from the bank in Albuquerque to cash the miners' checks on paydays.

After that night, my father bought my mother a pink nickel-plated snub-nose .22 revolver with a white bone grip. Grandma Lily carried a tiny Beretta as black as her prayer book. As my sisters and I got older, my father taught us to handle and shoot handguns, revolvers mostly, because back then, semiautomatic pistols were not as reliable—they frequently jammed. I will never forget the day my father told us three girls that we never had to let a man hit us or terrorize us because no matter how big and strong the man was, a gun in our hand equalized all differences of size and strength.

Much has been written about violence in the home and spousal abuse. I wish to focus instead on violence from strangers toward women because this form of violence terrifies women more, despite the fact that most women are murdered by a spouse, relative, fellow employee, or next-door neighbor, not a stranger. Domestic violence kills many more women and children than strangers kill, but domestic violence also follows more predictable patterns and is more familiar: He comes home drunk and she knows what comes next. A good deal of the terror of a stranger's attack comes from its suddenness and unexpectedness. Attacks by strangers occur with enough frequency that battered women and children often cite their fears of such attacks as reasons for remaining in abusive domestic situations. They fear the violence they imagine strangers will inflict on them more than they fear the abusive home. More than one feminist has pointed out that rapists and serial killers help keep the patriarchy securely in place.

An individual woman may be terrorized by her spouse, but women   10
are not sufficiently terrorized that we avoid marriage. Yet many women I know, including myself, try to avoid going outside of their homes alone after dark. Big deal, you say; well, yes, it is a big deal since most lectures, performances, and films are presented at night; so are dinners and other social events. Women out alone at night who are assaulted by strangers are put on trial by public opinion: Any woman out alone after dark is asking for trouble. Presently, for millions of women of all socioeconomic backgrounds, sundown is lockdown. We are prisoners of violent strangers.

Daylight doesn't necessarily make the streets safe for women. In the early 1980s, a rapist operated in Tucson in the afternoon near the University of Arizona campus. He often accosted two women at once, forced them into residential alleys, then raped each one with a knife to her throat and forced the other to watch. Afterward the women said that part of the horror of their attack was that all around them, everything appeared normal. They could see people inside their houses and cars going down the street—all around them life was going on as usual while their lives were being changed forever.

The afternoon rapist was not the only rapist in Tucson at that time; there was the prime-time rapist, the potbellied rapist, and the apologetic rapist all operating in Tucson in the 1980s. The prime-time rapist was actually two men who invaded comfortable foothills homes during television prime time when residents were preoccupied with television and eating dinner. The prime-time rapists terrorized entire families; they raped the women and sometimes they raped the men. Family members were forced to go to automatic bank machines to bring back cash to end the ordeal. Potbelly rapist and apologetic rapist need little comment, except to note that the apologetic rapist was good looking, well educated, and smart enough to break out of jail for one last rape followed by profuse apologies and his capture in the University of Arizona library. Local papers recounted details about Tucson's last notorious rapist, the red bandanna rapist. In the late 1970s, this rapist attacked more than twenty women over a three-year period, and Tucson police were powerless to stop him. Then one night, the rapist broke into a midtown home where the lone resident, a woman, shot him four times in the chest with a .38 caliber revolver.

In midtown Tucson, on a weekday afternoon, I was driving down Campbell Avenue to the pet store. Suddenly the vehicle behind me began to weave into my lane, so I beeped the horn politely. The vehicle swerved back to its lane, but then in my rearview mirror I saw the small late-model truck change lanes and begin to follow my car very closely. I drove a few blocks without looking in the rearview mirror, but in my sideview mirror I saw the compact truck was right behind me. OK. Some motorists stay upset for two or three blocks, some require ten blocks or more to recover their senses. Stoplight after stoplight, when I glanced into the rearview mirror I saw the man — in his early thirties, tall, white, brown hair, and dark glasses. This guy must not have a job if he has the time to follow me for miles — oh, ohhh! No beast more dangerous in the U.S.A. than an unemployed white man.

At this point I had to make a decision: Do I forget about the trip to the pet store and head for the police station downtown, four miles away? Why should I have to let this stranger dictate my schedule for the afternoon? The man might dare to follow me to the police station, but by the time I reach the front door of the station, he'd be gone. No crime was committed; no Arizona law forbids tailgating someone for miles or for turning into a parking lot behind them. What could the police do? I had no license plate number to report because Arizona requires only one license plate, on the rear bumper of the vehicle. Anyway, I was within a block of the pet store where I knew I could get help from the pet store owners. I would feel better about this incident if it was not allowed to ruin my trip to the pet store.

The guy was right on my rear bumper; if I'd had to stop suddenly for   15 any reason, there'd have been a collision. I decide I will not stop even if he does ram into the rear of my car. I study this guy's face in my rearview mirror; six feet two inches tall, 175 pounds, medium complexion, short hair, trimmed moustache. He thinks he can intimidate me because I am a woman, five feet five inches tall, 140 pounds. But I am not afraid, I am furious. I refuse to be intimidated. I won't play his game. I can tell by the face I see in the mirror this guy has done this before, he enjoys using his truck to menace lone women.

I keep thinking he will quit, or he will figure that he's scared me enough, but he seems to sense that I am not afraid. It's true. I am not afraid because years ago my father taught my sisters and me that we did not have to be afraid. He'll give up when I turn into the parking lot outside the pet store, I think. But I watch in my rearview mirror; he's right on my rear bumper. As his truck turns into the parking lot behind my car, I reach over and open the glove compartment. I take out the holster with my .38 special and lay it on the car seat beside me.

I turned my car into a parking spot so quickly that I was facing my stalker who had momentarily stopped his truck and was watching me. I slid the .38 out of its holster onto my lap. I watched the stranger's face, trying to determine whether he would jump out of his truck with a baseball bat or gun and come after me. I felt calm. No pounding heart or rapid breathing. My early experience deer hunting had prepared me well. I did not panic because I felt I could stop him if he tried to harm me. I was in no hurry. I sat in the car and waited to see what choice my stalker would make. I looked directly at him without fear because I had my .38 and I was ready to use it. The expression on my face must have been unfamiliar to him; he was used to seeing terror in the eyes of the women he followed. The expression on my face communicated a warning: If he approached the car window, I'd kill him.

He took a last look at me then sped away. I stayed in my car until his truck disappeared in the traffic of Campbell Avenue.

I walked into the pet store shaken. I had felt able to protect myself throughout the incident, but it left me emotionally drained and exhausted. The stranger had only pursued me—how much worse to be battered or raped.

Years before, I was unarmed the afternoon that two drunken deer   20 hunters threatened to shoot me off my horse with razor-edged hunting arrows from fiberglass crossbows. I was riding a colt on a national park trail near my home in the Tucson Mountains. These young white men in their late twenties were complete strangers who might have shot me if the colt had not galloped away erratically bucking and leaping—a moving target too difficult for the drunken bow hunters to aim at. The colt brought me to my ranch house where I called the county sheriff's office and the park ranger. I live in a sparsely populated area where my nearest neighbor is a quarter-mile away. I was afraid the men might have followed me back to my house so I took the .44 magnum out from under my pillow and strapped it around my waist until the sheriff or park ranger arrived. Forty five minutes later, the park ranger arrived; the deputy sheriff arrived fifteen minutes after him. The drunken bow hunters were apprehended on the national park and arrested for illegally hunting; their bows and arrows were seized as evidence for the duration of bow hunting season. In southern Arizona that is enough punishment; I didn't want to take a chance of stirring up additional animosity with these men because I lived alone then; I chose not to make a complaint about their threatening words and gestures. I did not feel that I backed away by not pressing charges; I feared that if I pressed assault charges against these men, they would feel that I was challenging them to all-out war. I did not want to have to kill either of them if they came after me, as I thought they might. With my marksmanship and my .243 caliber hunting rifle from the old days, I am confident that I could stop idiots like these. But to have to take the life of another person is a terrible experience I will always try to avoid.

It isn't height or weight or strength that make women easy targets; from infancy women are taught to be self-sacrificing, passive victims. I was taught differently. Women have the right to protect themselves from death or bodily harm. By becoming strong and potentially lethal individuals, women destroy the fantasy that we are sitting ducks for predatory strangers.

In a great many cultures, women are taught to depend on others, not themselves, for protection from bodily harm. Women are not taught to defend themselves from strangers because fathers and husbands fear the consequences themselves. In the United States, women depend on the courts and the police, but as many women have learned the hard way, the police cannot be outside your house twenty-four hours a day. I don't want more police. More police on the streets will not protect women. A few policemen are rapists and killers of women themselves; their uniforms and squad cars give them an advantage. No, I will be responsible for my own safety, thank you.

Women need to decide who has the primary responsibility for the health and safety of their bodies. We don't trust the State to manage our reproductive organs, yet most of us blindly trust that the State will protect us (and our reproductive organs) from predatory strangers. One look at the rape and murder statistics for women (excluding domestic incidents) and it is clear that the government FAILS to protect women from the violence of strangers. Some may cry out for a "stronger" State, more police, mandatory sentences, and swifter executions. Over the years we have seen the U.S. prison population become the largest in the world, executions take place every week now, inner-city communities are occupied by the National Guard, and people of color are harassed by police, but guess what? A woman out alone, night or day, is confronted with more danger of random violence from strangers than ever before. As the U.S. economy continues "to downsize," and the good jobs disappear forever, our urban and rural landscapes will include more desperate, angry men with nothing to lose.

Only women can put a stop to the "open season" on women by strangers. Women are TAUGHT to be easy targets by their mothers, aunts, and grandmothers, who themselves were taught that "a woman doesn't kill" or "a woman doesn't learn how to use a weapon." Women must learn how to take aggressive action individually, apart from the police and the courts.

Presently, twenty-one states issue permits to carry concealed   25 weapons; most states require lengthy gun safety courses and a police security check before issuing a permit. Inexpensive but excellent gun safety and self-defense courses designed for women are also available from every quality gun dealer who hopes to sell you a handgun at the end of the course. Those who object to firearms need trained companion dogs or collectives of six or more women to escort one another day and night. We must destroy the myth that women are born to be easy targets.

The Reader's Presence

1. What does Silko mean by a "combat zone"? What is the origin of the term? How does she apply it to women's experiences? Do you think the term is applicable? What behavior does the term legit-

imize? Why do you think she concentrates on violence from strangers instead of domestic violence?

2. Why do you think Silko introduces stories about hunting experiences? In what ways do those experiences shape her background? Do you think they have shaped her present attitude? How do the experiences help reinforce her point about gun ownership? In what ways do they make her more qualified to speak on the issue?

3. How do you think Silko would respond to Dr. Spock's essay "Should Children Play with Guns?" (see page 525) and Paul Fussell's essay "A Well-Regulated Militia" (see page 647)? What do you think her position is on gun control?

108

Peter Singer

The Singer Solution to World Poverty

Peter Singer, born in Melbourne, Australia, in 1946, has had a long career as the dean of the animal rights movement, and is one of today's most controversial contemporary philosophers. He has taught at the University of Colorado at Boulder, the University of California at Irvine, and is now the DeCamp Professor of Bioethics at Princeton University's Center for Human Values. His book Animal Liberation, *first published in 1975 and reprinted many times since, has become a basic sourcebook for animal rights activists. His* Practical Ethics (1979) *is one of the most widely recognized works of applied ethics. He has also written* Rethinking Life and Death, *which received an award from the National Book Council in 1995. In 2000 Singer published* Writings on an Ethical Life *and* A Darwinian Left: Politics, Evolution, and Cooperation, *which argues that the left should replace Marx with Darwin.*

A reviewer of Writings on an Ethical Life *commented: "Singer argues that value judgments should be matters of rational scrutiny and not matters of taste about which argument is futile. . . . For Singer, living ethically is living a meaningful life. It is a life that makes a difference in the world. It is a life that reduces the sum total of suffering."*

In the Brazilian film *Central Station*, Dora is a retired schoolteacher who makes ends meet by sitting at the station writing letters for illiterate people. Suddenly she has an opportunity to pocket $1,000. All she has to do is persuade a homeless nine-year-old boy to follow her to an address she has been given. (She is told he will be adopted by wealthy foreigners.) She delivers the boy, gets the money, spends some of it on a television set, and settles down to enjoy her new acquisition. Her neighbor spoils the fun, however, by telling her that the boy was too old to be adopted — he will be killed and his organs sold for transplantation. Perhaps Dora knew this all along, but after her neighbor's plain speaking, she spends a troubled night. In the morning Dora resolves to take the boy back.

Suppose Dora had told her neighbor that it is a tough world, other people have nice new TVs too, and if selling the kid is the only way she can get one, well, he was only a street kid. She would then have become, in the eyes of the audience, a monster. She redeems herself only by being prepared to bear considerable risks to save the boy.

At the end of the movie, in cinemas in the affluent nations of the world, people who would have been quick to condemn Dora if she had not rescued the boy go home to places far more comfortable than her apartment. In fact, the average family in the United States spends almost one-third of its income on things that are no more necessary to them than Dora's new TV was to her. Going out to nice restaurants, buying new clothes because the old ones are no longer stylish, vacationing at beach resorts — so much of our income is spent on things not essential to the preservation of our lives and health. Donated to one of a number of charitable agencies, that money could mean the difference between life and death for children in need.

All of which raises a question: In the end, what is the ethical distinction between a Brazilian who sells a homeless child to organ peddlers and an American who already has a TV and upgrades to a better one — knowing that the money could be donated to an organization that would use it to save the lives of kids in need?

Of course, there are several differences between the two situations   5 that could support different moral judgments about them. For one thing, to be able to consign a child to death when he is standing right in front of you takes a chilling kind of heartlessness; it is much easier to ignore an appeal for money to help children you will never meet. Yet for a utilitarian philosopher like myself — that is, one who judges whether acts are right or wrong by their consequences — if the upshot of the American's failure to donate the money is that one more kid dies on the streets of a Brazilian city, then it is, in some sense, just as bad as selling the kid to the organ peddlers. But one doesn't need to embrace my utilitarian ethic to see that, at the very least, there is a troubling incongruity in being so quick to condemn Dora for taking the child to the organ peddlers while, at the same time, not regarding the American consumer's behavior as raising a serious moral issue.

In his 1996 book, *Living High and Letting Die,* the New York University philosopher Peter Unger presented an ingenious series of imaginary examples designed to probe our intuitions about whether it is wrong to live well without giving substantial amounts of money to help people who are hungry, malnourished, or dying from easily treatable illnesses like diarrhea. Here's my paraphrase of one of these examples:

Bob is close to retirement. He has invested most of his savings in a very rare and valuable old car, a Bugatti, which he has not been able to insure. The Bugatti is his pride and joy. In addition to the pleasure he gets from driving and caring for his car, Bob knows that its rising market value means that he will always be able to sell it and live comfortably after retirement. One day when Bob is out for a drive, he parks the Bugatti near the end of a railway siding and goes for a walk up the track. As he does so, he sees that a runaway train, with no one aboard, is running down the railway track. Looking farther down the track, he sees the small figure of a child very likely to be killed by the runaway train. He can't stop the train and the child is too far away to warn of the danger, but he can throw a switch that will divert the train down the siding where his Bugatti is parked. Then nobody will be killed—but the train will destroy his Bugatti. Thinking of his joy in owning the car and the financial security it represents, Bob decides not to throw the switch. The child is killed. For many years to come, Bob enjoys owning his Bugatti and the financial security it represents.

Bob's conduct, most of us will immediately respond, was gravely wrong. Unger agrees. But then he reminds us that we, too, have opportunities to save the lives of children. We can give to organizations like Unicef or Oxfam America. How much would we have to give one of these organizations to have a high probability of saving the life of a child threatened by easily preventable diseases? (I do not believe that children are more worth saving than adults, but since no one can argue that children have brought their poverty on themselves, focusing on them simplifies the issues.) Unger called up some experts and used the information they provided to offer some plausible estimates that include the cost of raising money, administrative expenses, and the cost of delivering aid where it is most needed. By his calculation, $200 in donations would help a sickly two-year-old transform into a healthy six-year-old—offering safe passage through childhood's most dangerous years. To show how practical philosophical argument can be, Unger even tells his readers that they can easily donate funds by using their credit card and calling one of these toll-free numbers: (800) 367-5437 for Unicef; (800) 693-2687 for Oxfam America.

Now you, too, have the information you need to save a child's life. How should you judge yourself if you don't do it? Think again about Bob and his Bugatti. Unlike Dora, Bob did not have to look into the eyes of the child he was sacrificing for his own material comfort. The child was a complete stranger to him and too far away to relate to in an intimate, personal way. Unlike Dora, too, he did not mislead the child or initiate the chain of events imperiling him. In all these respects, Bob's situation resembles that of people able but unwilling to donate to overseas aid and differs from Dora's situation.

If you still think that it was very wrong of Bob not to throw the   10
switch that would have diverted the train and saved the child's life, then it
is hard to see how you could deny that it is also very wrong not to send
money to one of the organizations listed above. Unless, that is, there is
some morally important difference between the two situations that I have
overlooked.

Is it the practical uncertainties about whether aid will really reach the
people who need it? Nobody who knows the world of overseas aid can
doubt that such uncertainties exist. But Unger's figure of $200 to save a
child's life was reached after he had made conservative assumptions about
the proportion of the money donated that will actually reach its target.

One genuine difference between Bob and those who can afford to
donate to overseas aid organizations but don't is that only Bob can save
the child on the tracks, whereas there are hundreds of millions of people
who can give $200 to overseas aid organizations. The problem is that
most of them aren't doing it. Does this mean that it is all right for you
not to do it?

Suppose that there were more owners of priceless vintage cars—
Carol, Dave, Emma, Fred, and so on, down to Ziggy—all in exactly the
same situation as Bob, with their own siding and their own switch, all sacrificing the child in order to preserve their own cherished car. Would that
make it all right for Bob to do the same? To answer this question affirma-
tively is to endorse follow-the-crowd ethics—the kind of ethics that led
many Germans to look away when the Nazi atrocities were being committed. We do not excuse them because others were behaving no better.

We seem to lack a sound basis for drawing a clear moral line between
Bob's situation and that of any reader of this article with $200 to spare
who does not donate it to an overseas aid agency. These readers seem to
be acting at least as badly as Bob was acting when he chose to let the runaway train hurtle toward the unsuspecting child. In the light of this conclusion, I trust that many readers will reach for the phone and donate
that $200. Perhaps you should do it before reading further.

Now that you have distinguished yourself morally from people who   15
put their vintage cars ahead of a child's life, how about treating yourself
and your partner to dinner at your favorite restaurant? But wait. The
money you will spend at the restaurant could also help save the lives of
children overseas! True, you weren't planning to blow $200 tonight, but
if you were to give up dining out just for one month, you would easily
save that amount. And what is one month's dining out, compared to a
child's life? There's the rub. Since there are a lot of desperately needy children in the world, there will always be another child whose life you could
save for another $200. Are you therefore obliged to keep giving until you
have nothing left? At what point can you stop?

Hypothetical examples can easily become farcical. Consider Bob.
How far past losing the Bugatti should he go? Imagine that Bob had got
his foot stuck in the track of the siding, and if he diverted the train, then

before it rammed the car it would also amputate his big toe. Should he still throw the switch? What if it would amputate his foot? His entire leg?

As absurd as the Bugatti scenario gets when pushed to extremes, the point it raises is a serious one: Only when the sacrifices become very significant indeed would most people be prepared to say that Bob does nothing wrong when he decides not to throw the switch. Of course, most people could be wrong; we can't decide moral issues by taking opinion polls. But consider for yourself the level of sacrifice that you would demand of Bob, and then think about how much money you would have to give away in order to make a sacrifice that is roughly equal to that. It's almost certainly much, much more than $200. For most middle-class Americans, it could easily be more like $200,000.

Isn't it counterproductive to ask people to do so much? Don't we run the risk that many will shrug their shoulders and say that morality, so conceived, is fine for saints but not for them? I accept that we are unlikely to see, in the near or even medium-term future, a world in which it is normal for wealthy Americans to give the bulk of their wealth to strangers. When it comes to praising or blaming people for what they do, we tend to use a standard that is relative to some conception of normal behavior. Comfortably off Americans who give, say, 10 percent of their income to overseas aid organizations are so far ahead of most of their equally comfortable fellow citizens that I wouldn't go out of my way to chastise them for not doing more. Nevertheless, they should be doing much more, and they are in no position to criticize Bob for failing to make the much greater sacrifice of his Bugatti.

At this point various objections may crop up. Someone may say: "If every citizen living in the affluent nations contributed his or her share I wouldn't have to make such a drastic sacrifice, because long before such levels were reached, the resources would have been there to save the lives of all those children dying from lack of food or medical care. So why should I give more than my fair share?" Another, related objection is that the government ought to increase its overseas aid allocations, since that would spread the burden more equitably across all taxpayers.

Yet the question of how much we ought to give is a matter to be decided in the real world—and that, sadly, is a world in which we know that most people do not, and in the immediate future will not, give substantial amounts to overseas aid agencies. We know, too, that at least in the next year, the United States government is not going to meet even the very modest United Nations–recommended target of 0.7 percent of gross national product; at the moment it lags far below that, at 0.09 percent, not even half of Japan's 0.22 percent or a tenth of Denmark's 0.97 percent. Thus, we know that the money we can give beyond that theoretical "fair share" is still going to save lives that would otherwise be lost. While the idea that no one need do more than his or her fair share is a powerful one, should it prevail if we know that others are not doing their fair share

20

and that children will die preventable deaths unless we do more than our fair share? That would be taking fairness too far.

Thus, this ground for limiting how much we ought to give also fails. In the world as it is now, I can see no escape from the conclusion that each one of us with wealth surplus to his or her essential needs should be giving most of it to help people suffering from poverty so dire as to be life-threatening. That's right: I'm saying that you shouldn't buy that new car, take that cruise, redecorate the house, or get that pricey new suit. After all, a $1,000 suit could save five children's lives.

So how does my philosophy break down in dollars and cents? An American household with an income of $50,000 spends around $30,000 annually on necessities, according to the Conference Board, a nonprofit economic research organization. Therefore, for a household bringing in $50,000 a year, donations to help the world's poor should be as close as possible to $20,000. The $30,000 required for necessities holds for higher incomes as well. So a household making $100,000 could cut a yearly check for $70,000. Again, the formula is simple: Whatever money you're spending on luxuries, not necessities, should be given away.

Now, evolutionary psychologists tell us that human nature just isn't sufficiently altruistic to make it plausible that many people will sacrifice so much for strangers. On the facts of human nature, they might be right, but they would be wrong to draw a moral conclusion from those facts. If it is the case that we ought to do things that, predictably, most of us won't do, then let's face that fact head-on. Then, if we value the life of a child more than going to fancy restaurants, the next time we dine out we will know that we could have done something better with our money. If that makes living a morally decent life extremely arduous, well, then that is the way things are. If we don't do it, then we should at least know that we are failing to live a morally decent life—not because it is good to wallow in guilt but because knowing where we should be going is the first step toward heading in that direction.

When Bob first grasped the dilemma that faced him as he stood by that railway switch, he must have thought how extraordinarily unlucky he was to be placed in a situation in which he must choose between the life of an innocent child and the sacrifice of most of his savings. But he was not unlucky at all. We are all in that situation.

The Reader's Presence

1. How convincing do you find Singer's hypothetical examples, such as Bob and his (apparently uninsured) Bugatti? Do you think the examples support his basic argument or weaken it? Explain your response.

2. In paragraph 5, Singer defines a utilitarian philosopher as one who "judges whether acts are right or wrong by their consequences." Can you think of utilitarian solutions other than Singer's to the problems of world poverty? For example, would population control methods that drastically reduced the number of impoverished children born into the world also be a utilitarian solution? Would donations to organizations that fund population control be more effective than charitable donations that directly assist children? If Singer's solution were adopted and more and more children were assisted, would that eventually encourage higher birth rates and thus worsen the very problem Singer wants to solve?

3. Consider Singer's essay in conjunction with Jonathan Swift's classic satirical essay on poverty, "A Modest Proposal" (see page 776). In what ways does Swift's essay also take a utilitarian position? How do you think Swift would react to Singer's solution to world poverty?

109

Wole Soyinka

Every Dictator's Nightmare

Wole Soyinka was born in western Nigeria in 1934, and educated both in Nigeria and the United Kingdom. He received a degree in English literature from the University of Leeds in 1957. After graduation, he served as a play reader for the Royal Court Theatre while writing his own plays attacking colonial oppression and racism. In 1960 he returned to Nigeria to begin his own acting company and, in 1964, cofounded the Drama Association of Nigeria. His plays have since been performed in every major city in the world. From 1967–69 Soyinka was imprisoned in Nigeria for his political views, spending much of his time in solitary confinement—a harrowing experience that he recounts in his autobiographical work, The Man Died *(1972). In 1986 Soyinka received the Nobel Prize in Literature. In his most famous work,* The Open Sore of a Continent *(1996), Soyinka traces Nigeria's political decline and exposes the brutality of its series of military governments. As punishment for his political outspokenness, the government of Nigeria condemned him to death in 1997. He lives in the United States and is a professor of the arts at Emory University.*

Soyinka is a vocal advocate of traditional African religious cultures that he feels exemplify the humane values of justice and tolerance. As he proclaimed in his Nobel Prize acceptance speech: "There is a deep lesson for the world in the black race's capacity to forgive."

With the blood-soaked banner of religious fanaticism billowing across the skies as one prominent legacy of this millennium, Martin Luther's famous theses against religious absolutism struck me early as a strong candidate for the best idea of the last thousand years. By progressive association, so did the microprocessor and its implications—the liberalization of access to knowledge, and a quantum boost for the transmission of ideas. There is, however, a nobler idea that has spread by its own power in this millennium and that has now begun to flourish: the idea that certain fundamental rights are inherent to all humanity.

Humankind has always struggled to assert certain values in their own right, values that the individual intuitively felt belonged to each person as part of natural existence. It is difficult to imagine a period when such values were not pursued in spasmodic acts of dissent from norms that appeared to govern society even in its most rudimentary form. Even after years of conformity to hallowed precedents, a few dissidents always arise, and they obtain their primary impulse in crucial instances from the individual's seizure of his or her subjective worth.

In the devolution of authority to one individual as the head of a collective, a system of checks on arbitrary authority is prevalent. Take, for instance, monarchical rule among the Yoruba, the people now concentrated in western Nigeria. At the apex is a quasi-deified personage, endowed with supreme authority over his subjects. To preserve the mystic aura of such a ruler, he is never seen to eat or drink. In earlier times, he was not permitted to speak directly to his people but had to employ an intermediary voice, a spokesman. For the highest-ranked kings in the Yoruban world, the *ekeji orisa* (companions to the deities), it was forbidden even to see their faces. Despite the social and psychological distance between the leader and his subjects, the monarch was pledged to rule within a strict contract of authority. Transgression of a taboo, say, or failure to fulfill ceremonial duties on time, resulted in fines, rituals of appeasement, or a period of ostracism. The major crime, however, was abuse of power, excessive authoritarianism, and a trampling on the rights of the citizenry. For this category of crimes, there was only one response: the king, on being found guilty, was given a covered calabash and invited to retreat to his inner chambers. He understood the sentence: he must never again be seen among the living.

Sometimes, of course, an individual manages to convert collective authority into a personal monopoly. In these instances, society is characterized by tensions, palpable or hidden, between the suppressed rights of the people and the power rapacity of one individual. But where does society ground its claims, its resistant will, in such circumstances? We know that rebellion may be triggered by recollections of more equitable relationships, by material expropriation or by a cultural transgression that affects the spiritual well-being of the community or individual. Such rebellion finds its authority in the belief, in one citizen after another, that the ruler has violated a fundamental condition of human existence.

The *droit du seigneur,* the "right" that confers on the lord the plea-   5
sure of deflowering, on her marriage night, the bride of any of his vassals—on what does the ritually cuckolded groom finally ground his rebellion other than a subjective sense of self-worth? What of the Yoruban
monarch who, even today in certain parts of the world, tries to exercise
his "right" to *gbese le*—that is, to place his royal slipper, symbolically,
on any woman who catches his fancy, and thus assign her to his harem?
The manor lord's entitlement to compulsory labor from his peasants, the
ownership of another being as a slave, the new age of enslavement of
womanhood in countries like Afghanistan—the challenges to these and
other so-called rights surely commence with the interrogation of self-
worth, expanding progressively toward an examination of the common
worth of the human entity as a unit of irreducible properties and rights.

It took centuries for societies to influence one another to the critical
extent needed to incite the philosophic mind to address the concept of the
human race in general, and not simply as members of a specific race or
occupants of a geographical space. In its rudimentary beginnings, each
society remained limited by a process that codified its own now-recogniz-
able collective interests against all others, like the Magna Carta and the
Bill of Rights. Such oaths of fealty by petty chieftains imposed duties on
the suzerain but also entrenched their own equally arbitrary mechanisms
of authority and coercion over the next level of society. This sometimes
resulted in the bizarre alliance of the monarch with his lowest vassals
against his overreaching barons and chieftains.

Like race and citizenship, religion was not far behind in the exclu-
sionist philosophy of rights, formulating codes to protect the rights of the
faithful but denying the same to others—the Cross against the Crescent,
Buddhist versus Hindu, the believer against the infidel. Or simply religion
versus secularism. Ground into powder beneath the hooves of the contending behemoths of religion, ideology and race, each social unit ponders, at least periodically, how he or she differs from cattle or sheep, from
the horses that pull the carriages of majesty, even when such choices are
the mere expressions of the collective will. If order alone, ornamentation,
social organization, technology, bonding and even productive structures
were all that defined the human species, then what significant properties
marked out Homo sapiens as distinct from the rest of the living species?

Polarizations within various micro-worlds—us versus the inferior
them—have long been armed with industrious rationalizations. Christian
and Islamic theologians throughout history have quarried their scriptures
for passages that stress the incontestable primacy of an unseen and unknowable Supreme Deity who has conferred authority on them. And to
what end? Largely to divide the world into us and the rest. The great
philosophical minds of Europe, like Hume, Hegel, and Kant, bent their

prodigious talents to separating the species into those with rights and those with none, founded on the convenient theory that some people were human and others less so. The Encyclopedists of France, products of the so-called Age of Reason, remain the most prolific codifiers of the human (and other) species on an ambitiously comprehensive scale, and their scholarly industry conferred a scientific benediction on a purely commercial project that saw millions of souls dragged across the ocean to serve as beasts of burden. Religion and commerce — far older professions than the one that is sometimes granted that distinction, but of an often-identical temperament — were reinforced by the authority of new scientific theories to divide humanity into higher and lower manifestations of the species. The dichotomy of the world was complete.

It took the near triumph of fascism to bring the world to its senses. The horror of the Holocaust finally took the rulers of the world back to the original question: what is the true value of humanity? It is to be doubted if the victorious three meeting in Yalta actually went into any profound philosophical niceties in the discussions that resulted in the United Nations, that partial attempt to reverse the dichotomizing course of humanity. That course, taken to its ultimate conclusion, had just resulted in an attempted purification of the species, the systemic elimination of millions in gas chambers and a war that mired the potential of Europe in the blood of its youth. After all, the concept of the master race was not new, but it was never before so obsessively articulated and systematically pursued. It was time to rethink the entire fate of humanity. The conversations at Yalta, conversations that led to the birth of the United Nations, were a partial answer to that question.

The first stage was to render the new thinking in concrete terms, to enshrine in a charter of rights the product of the bruising lessons of the immediate past: the United Nations and the Universal Declaration of Human Rights. The informing recognition is that long-suppressed extract of the intuition that humanity had guarded through evolution, one that had been proposed, compromised, amended, vitiated, subverted but never abandoned: that, for all human beings, there do exist certain fundamental rights. 10

The idea already exists in the Bible, in the Koran, in the Bhagavad-Gita, in the Upanishads, but always in curtailed form, relativist, patriarchal, always subject to the invisible divine realms whose interpreters are mortals with distinct, secular agendas, usually allied to the very arbitrary controls that are a contradiction to such ideas. Quiet, restrained, ignored by but also blissfully indifferent to the so-called world religions, Ifa, the corpus of Yoruban spiritual precepts and secular philosophy, its origins lost in antiquity but preserved and applied till today, annunciates identical ideas through Orunmila, the god of divination:

> *Dandan enia l'ayan ko mu ire lo s'aye . . . Ipo rere naa ni aye-amotan ohungbogbo, ayo nnigbagbogbo, igbesi laisi ominu tabi iberu ota.*

> *Certainly, it is the human being that was elected to bring values to the world . . . and his place of good is the knowledge of all things, joy at all times, freedom from anxiety, and freedom from fear of the enemy.* [Irosu Wori]

Humanity has been straining to seize the fullness of this doctrine, the right to knowledge, the freedom from anxiety, the right to security of existence as inherent to the species. It is only the process of promulgating its pertinence to all mankind that has been long and costly. The kernel of the idea, therefore, is both timeless and new. Its resurrection—the concrete seizure of the idea within this millennium, answering the exigencies of politics, religion and power and securing it within the bedrock of universality—was a destiny that would first be embraced by France.

There, alas, the events that gave new life to this idea did not encourage its adoption on a universal scale, indeed not even durably within France itself. The restoration of slavery by Napoleon was surely the most blatant contradiction of the idea, but this did not much trouble the Emperor.

Still, the idea had taken hold, the idea of the rights of man as a universal principle. It certainly motored the passion of the genuine idealists in the abolition of the slave trade, who must always be distinguished from those to whom abolition was simply a shrewd commercial calculation. The idea of the American Declaration of Independence—an idea that still lacks full realization—that "all men are created equal, that they are endowed by their Creator with certain unalienable Rights" is an adumbration of that original idea from which the French Revolution obtained its inspiration, one that has continued to convulse the unjust order of the world wherever it has been grasped: the fundamental rights of man.

It is an idea whose suppression is the main occupation of dictatorships—be these military or civilian, of the right or the left, secular or theocratic. It is, however, their nightmare, their single province of terror, one that they cannot exorcise, not even through the most unconscionable pogroms, scorched-earth campaigns and crimes against humanity. It is an idea that has transformed the lives of billions and remains poised to liberate billions more, since it is an idea that will not settle for tokenism or for relativism—it implicitly links the liberation of one to the liberation of all. Its gospel of universalism is anchored in the most affective impulse that cynics attribute to the choices made by humanity, self-love, but one that now translates humanity as one's own self.   15

The Reader's Presence

1. Soyinka gives a sweeping account of the impediments to and the progress of human rights throughout world history. What does he hold up as the high points of this history? How does slavery figure into this historical narrative? What was the role of France? of

America, Afghanistan, and Yoruba? of the talks at Yalta? of the United Nations? How does Soyinka see the doctrine of human rights working at present in the world? Why does he write this essay now?

2. A natural problem, Soyinka suggests, is that a society or sect defines its rights in opposition to those of other societies or sects. How does polarization follow? To what, exactly, does Soyinka refer when he writes, "The dichotomy of the world was complete" (paragraph 8)? When? Where? In his view, is this statement still true?

3. Soyinka states that the doctrine of universal human rights "implicitly links the liberation of one to the liberation of all" (paragraph 15). Several of the essayists in this anthology write from the same assumption. How might you link the ideas of Thomas Jefferson (page 674) and Martin Luther King Jr. (page 692) to those Soyinka puts forward in this essay? Does Soyinka seem to share with King a sense of universal freedom as inevitable destiny? Was the Declaration of Independence an expression of "every dictator's nightmare"? In what ways did the nation fail to live up to its ideals, according to King? How might Soyinka describe the relation between American democracy and slavery at the time of the republic's founding?

110

Cass Sunstein

Media and Democracy: A "Daily Me" or a "Daily We"?

Cass Sunstein (b. 1954) was educated at Harvard University. After graduating from Harvard Law School in 1978, he clerked for Justice Thurgood Marshall of the Supreme Court and worked as an attorney-advisor for the Department of Justice. He now teaches at the University of Chicago, in both the law school and the department of political science. Sunstein has been involved in constitution-making and law reform activities in many foreign nations, and has testified before congressional committees on various subjects. He is the author of many articles and books on constitutional law and free speech. This essay is adapted from his most recent book, Republic.com *(2001).*

It is some time in the future. Technology has greatly increased people's ability to "filter" what they want to read, see, and hear. General-interest newspapers and magazines are largely a thing of the past. The same is true of broadcasters. The idea of choosing "Channel 4" instead of "Channel 7" seems positively quaint. With the aid of the Internet and a television or computer screen, you are able to design your own newspapers and magazines. Having dispensed with broadcasters, you can choose your own video programming, with movies, game shows, sports, shopping, and news of your choice. You mix and match. You need not come across topics and views that you have not sought out. Without any difficulty, you are able to see exactly what you want to see, no more and no less.

Maybe you want to focus on sports all the time, and to avoid anything dealing with business or government. It is easy for you to do exactly that. Perhaps you choose replays of famous football games in the early evening, live baseball from New York at night, and college basketball on the weekends. If you hate sports, and want to learn about the Middle East in the evening and watch old situation comedies late at night, that is easy, too. If you care only about the United States, and want to avoid international issues entirely, you can restrict yourself to material involving the United States. So, too, if you care only about New York City, or Chicago, or California, or Long Island.

Perhaps you have no interest at all in "news." Maybe you find news impossibly boring. If so, you need not see it at all. Maybe you select programs and stories involving only music and weather. Or perhaps you are more specialized still, emphasizing opera, or Beethoven, or the Rolling Stones, or modern dance, or some subset of one or more of the above.

If you are interested in politics, you may want to restrict yourself to certain points of view, by hearing only from people you like. In designing your preferred newspaper, you choose among conservatives, moderates, liberals, vegetarians, the religious right, and socialists. You have your favorite columnists; perhaps you want to hear from them and from no one else. If so, that is entirely feasible with a simple "point and click." Or perhaps you are interested in only a few topics. If you believe that the most serious problem is gun control, or global warming, or lung cancer, you might spend most of your time reading about that problem—if you wish, from the point of view that you like best.

Of course, everyone else has the same freedom that you do. Many   5
people choose to avoid news altogether. Many people restrict themselves to their own preferred points of view—liberals watch and read mostly, or only, liberals; moderates, moderates; conservatives, conservatives; neo-Nazis, neo-Nazis. People in different states, and in different countries, make predictably different choices.

The resulting divisions run along many lines—of race, religion, ethnicity, nationality, wealth, age, political conviction, and more. Most white people avoid news and entertainment options designed for African-Americans. Many African-Americans focus largely on options specifically designed for them. So, too, with Hispanics. With the reduced importance of the general-interest magazine and newspaper, and the flowering of individual programming, different groups make fundamentally different choices.

The market for news, entertainment, and information has finally been perfected. Consumers are able to see exactly what they want. When the power to filter is unlimited, people can decide, in advance and with perfect accuracy, what they will and will not encounter. They can design something very much like a communications universe of their own choosing.

Our communications market is rapidly moving in the direction of this apparently utopian picture. As of this writing, many newspapers, including the *Wall Street Journal,* allow subscribers to create "personalized" electronic editions, containing exactly what each reader wants, and excluding what each does not want. If you are interested in getting help with the design of an entirely personalized paper, you can consult an ever growing number of Web sites, including http://www.individual.com (helpfully named!) and http://www.crayon.net (a less helpful name, but evocative in its own way).

In reality, we are not so very far from complete personalization of the entire system of communications.

If you put the words "personalized news" in any search engine, you will find vivid evidence of what is happening. And that is only the tip of the iceberg. Thus Nicholas Negroponte, director of the Media Laboratory at the Massachusetts Institute of Technology, prophesies the emergence of the "Daily Me"—a communications package that is personally designed, with each component chosen in advance. Many of us applaud those developments, which obviously increase individual convenience and entertainment.

But in the midst of the applause, we should insist on asking some questions. How will the increasing power of private control affect democracy? How will the Internet, the new forms of television, and the explosion of communications options alter the capacity of citizens to govern themselves? What are the social preconditions for a well-functioning system of democratic deliberation, or for individual freedom itself? We need to ensure that new communications technologies serve democracy, rather than the other way around.

Perhaps above all, the growing power of consumers to filter what they see demands a better understanding of the meaning of freedom of speech in a democratic society. To obtain that understanding, we must explore what makes for a well-functioning system of free expression. Such a system requires far more than restraints on government censorship and respect for individual choices. For the last few decades, those topics have been the preoccupation of American law and politics, and the law and politics of many other nations as well, including England, Germany, France, and Israel. Censorship is indeed a threat to democracy and freedom. But an exclusive focus on government censorship produces serious blind spots. In particular, a well-functioning system of free expression must meet two distinctive requirements.

First, people should be exposed to materials that they would not have chosen in advance. Unplanned, unanticipated encounters are central to democracy itself. Such encounters often involve topics and points of view that people have not sought out and, perhaps, find quite irritating; they are important because they ensure against fragmentation and extremism, which are predictable outcomes of any situation in which like-minded people speak only with each other. I do not suggest that government should force people to see things that they wish to avoid. But I do contend that, in a democracy deserving the name, people often come across views and topics that they have not specifically selected.

Second, many—or most—citizens should have a range of common experiences. Without shared experiences, a heterogeneous society will have a much more difficult time in addressing social problems. People may even find it hard to understand one another. Common experiences, emphatically including the common experiences made possible by the media, provide a form of social glue. A system of communications that radically diminishes the number of such experiences will create numerous problems, not least an increase in social fragmentation.

As preconditions for a well-functioning democracy, these require- 15 ments hold in any large nation. They are especially important in a heterogeneous nation, which is bound to face an occasional risk of fragmentation. They have all the more importance as each nation becomes increasingly global, and each citizen becomes, to a greater or lesser degree, a "citizen of the world."

An insistence on these two requirements should not be rooted in nostalgia for some supposedly idyllic past. With respect to communications, the past was hardly idyllic. Compared with any other period in human history, we are in the midst of many extraordinary gains, particularly from the standpoint of democracy itself. For us, nostalgia is not only unproductive but also senseless.

Nor should anything here be taken as a reason for "optimism" or "pessimism," two great obstacles to clear thinking about new technological developments. If we must choose between them, by all means let us choose optimism. But, in view of the many potential gains and losses inevitably associated with massive technological change, any attitude of optimism or pessimism is far too general to make sense. What we need to have is not a basis for pessimism, but a lens through which we might understand, a bit better than before, what makes a system of freedom of expression successful in the first place. That improved understanding will equip us to appreciate a free nation's own aspirations, and thus help in evaluating continuing changes in the system of communications. It will also point the way toward a clearer understanding of the nature of citizenship, and toward social reforms if emerging developments disserve our aspirations, as they threaten to do.

To make progress on this issue, we must take a stand on some large questions in democratic theory. Some political theorists are pure populists. They focus on improving people's ability to influence government directly. Pure populists tend to welcome the Internet as a wonderful boon, and for one simple reason: For the first time in the history of the world, millions of people can make their views known, immediately, to elected representatives. Indeed, considerable academic thinking about democracy celebrates the technological capacity of the Internet to provide stronger citizen control over government.

But many other theorists are nervous about populism. Following Edmund Burke, they believe that representatives should be largely insulated from the ebb and flow of public opinion, to ensure that elected officials can deliberate wisely on the issues of the day. For faithful Burkeans, the Internet is, in many ways, a threat to wise rule.

In American constitutional thought, and to a significant extent in modern political theory, a distinctive conception of democracy has risen to prominence in the past decade. According to this conception, it is best to have a deliberative democracy—one that combines elements of accountability and inclusiveness with a commitment to reflection and providing reasons. Deliberative democrats reject populism on the ground that it is likely to give too little space for deliberation, but they reject Burkeanism, too, on the ground that, in most forms, it devalues the importance of ensuring public checks on official behavior—and even on official thought. The influential German philosopher Jürgen Habermas, for one, has developed the argument for deliberative democracy in particular detail.

From the standpoint of deliberative democracy, the Internet is both a promise and a threat. It is a promise insofar as it allows so many diverse people to learn and to reflect and to exchange reasons with each other. But it is a threat insofar as it allows instantaneous reactions to have a large influence on policy—and even more insofar as it promotes the "Daily Me," allowing so many people to create communications universes of their own choosing.

As Habermas has stressed, one of the preconditions of a deliberative democracy is a large set of "public forums" (including streets and parks) in which diverse people encounter each other, often by chance. If public forums become increasingly specialized, many people might substitute technological echo chambers for the streets and parks in which diverse people meet. In fact, that is already happening.

It follows that, in the long run, the most serious "digital divides" that we will face might not involve the exclusion of poor people from communications technologies, but the creation of numerous free-speech enclaves, in practice walled off from each other. A great advantage of general-interest newspapers and magazines is that they ensure that people will see topics and ideas that they might not have specifically chosen in advance. If the role of such media diminishes, democracy may be impoverished, if only because people will understand their fellow citizens less well—and possibly not at all.

If this is right, there is all the reason in the world to reject the view

20

that free markets, as embodied in the notion of "consumer sovereignty," are the appropriate foundation for communications policy. Free markets have many virtues, but, in the area of communications, they will serve democracy imperfectly. They might even compromise the preconditions for citizenship.

Above all, it is important to see that, in well-functioning democracies,   25
public forums of various stripes—from streets and parks to daily news-
papers—expose people to a variety of (sometimes unexpected) ideas and topics. Unanticipated, chance encounters—with people and ideas—are fundamental to democracy. This is not the place to set out a specific agenda, but we might consider the possibility of building on the precedents we already have and providing creative links among Web sites; or, perhaps, of setting up, under public or private auspices, deliberative fo-
rums on the Internet for people who would not otherwise "meet."

The crucial step will be to recognize the problem. The imagined world of the "Daily Me" is the farthest thing from a utopian dream, and it would create serious problems from the democratic point of view.

The Reader's Presence

1. Sunstein suggests that citizens require "a better understanding of the meaning of freedom of speech in a democratic society" (paragraph 12). What would such an understanding be? To what ex-
   tent does he think our current understanding of free speech is lim-
   ited? What doesn't it take into account? How has it encouraged "consumer sovereignty" and why, according to Sunstein, is that a problem in today's society?

2. What is a "deliberative democracy" (paragraph 20)? What extremes does it avoid? Where is it found? In what way does the theory of a deliberative democracy serve as the intellectual frame-
   work of Sunstein's argument? In your opinion, is a deliberative democracy possible or is it an unrealizable ideal? Consider, too, whether a deliberative democracy as Sunstein describes it would be less democratic or more democratic than what we have in the United States today.

3. "In reality," Sunstein maintains, "we are not so very far from complete personalization of the entire system of communications (paragraph 9). Consider this statement and Sunstein's evidence that this is happening in connection with Malcolm Gladwell's "The Tipping Point" (see page 389). What might be the tipping point in this case? Using Gladwell's theory and Sunstein's evidence, construct a tipping point scenario that would result in the triumph of the "Daily Me."

111

Jonathan Swift

A Modest Proposal

For Preventing the Children of Poor People in Ireland from Being a Burden to Their Parents or Country, and for Making Them Beneficial to the Public

Jonathan Swift (1667–1745) was born and raised in Ireland, the son of English parents. He was ordained an Anglican priest, and although as a young man he lived a literary life in London, he was appointed against his wishes to be dean of St. Patrick's Cathedral in Dublin. Swift wrote excellent poetry, but is remembered principally for his essays and political pamphlets, most of which were published under pseudonyms. Swift received payment for only one work in his entire life, Gulliver's Travels *(1726), for which he earned £200. Swift's political pamphlets were very influential in his day; among other issues, he spoke out against English exploitation of the Irish. Some of Swift's more important publications include* A Tale of a Tub *(1704),* The Importance of the Guardian Considered *(1713),* The Public Spirit of the Whigs *(1714), and* A Modest Proposal *(1729).*

Writing to his friend Alexander Pope, Swift commented that "the chief end I propose to my self in all my labors is to vex the world rather than divert it, and if I could compass that design without hurting my own person or Fortune I would be the most Indefatigable writer you have ever seen."

It is a melancholy object to those who walk through this great town[1] or travel in the country, when they see the streets, the roads, and cabin doors, crowded with beggars of the female sex, followed by three, four, or six children, all in rags and importuning every passenger for an alms. These mothers instead of being able to work for their honest livelihood, are forced to employ all their time in strolling to beg sustenance for their helpless infants: who as they grow up either turn thieves for want of

---

[1]*this great town:* Dublin. —EDS.

work, or leave their dear native country to fight for the pretender in Spain,[2] or sell themselves to the Barbadoes.[3]

I think it is agreed by all parties that this prodigious number of children in the arms, or on the backs, or at the heels of their mothers, and frequently of their fathers, is in the present deplorable state of the kingdom a very great additional grievance; and, therefore, whoever could find out a fair, cheap, and easy method of making these children sound, useful members of the commonwealth, would deserve so well of the public as to have his statute set up for a preserver of the nation.

But my intention is very far from being confined to provide only for the children of professed beggars; it is of a much greater extent, and shall take in the whole number of infants at a certain age who are born of parents in effect as little able to support them as those who demand our charity in the streets.

As to my own part, having turned my thoughts for many years upon this important subject, and maturely weighed the several schemes of our projectors,[4] I have always found them grossly mistaken in their computation. It is true, a child just dropped from its dam may be supported by her milk for a solar year, with little other nourishment; at most not above the value of 2s.,[5] which the mother may certainly get, or the value in scraps, by her lawful occupation of begging; and it is exactly at one year old that I propose to provide for them in such a manner as instead of being a charge upon their parents or the parish, or wanting food and raiment for the rest of their lives, they shall on the contrary contribute to the feeding, and partly to the clothing, of many thousands.

There is likewise another great advantage in my scheme, that it will   5
prevent those voluntary abortions, and that horrid practice of women murdering their bastard children, alas! too frequent among us! sacrificing the poor innocent babes I doubt more to avoid the expense than the shame, which would move tears and pity in the most savage and inhuman breast.

The number of souls in this kingdom being usually reckoned one million and a half, of these I calculate there may be about 200,000 couple whose wives are breeders; from which number I subtract 30,000 couple who are able to maintain their own children (although I apprehend there cannot be so many, under the present distress of the kingdom); but this being granted, there will remain 170,000 breeders. I again subtract 50,000 for those women who miscarry, or whose children die by accident or dis-

---

[2]*pretender in Spain:* James Stuart (1688–1766); exiled in Spain, he laid claim to the English crown and had the support of many Irishmen who had joined an army hoping to restore him to the throne. — EDS.

[3]*the Barbadoes:* Inhabitants of the British colony in the Caribbean where Irishmen emigrated to work as indentured servants in exchange for their passage. — EDS.

[4]*projectors:* Planners. — EDS.

[5]*2s.:* Two shillings; in Swift's time one shilling was worth less than twenty-five cents. Other monetary references in the essay are to pounds sterling ("£"), pence ("d."), a crown, and a groat. A pound consisted of twenty shillings; a shilling of twelve pence; a crown was five shillings; a groat was worth a few cents. — EDS.

ease within the year. There only remain 120,000 children of poor parents annually born. The question therefore is, how this number shall be reared and provided for? which, as I have already said, under the present situation of affairs, is utterly impossible by all the methods hitherto proposed. For we can neither employ them in handicraft or agriculture; we neither build houses (I mean in the country) nor cultivate land; they can very seldom pick up a livelihood by stealing, till they arrive at six years old, except where they are of towardly parts,[6] although I confess they learn the rudiments much earlier; during which time they can, however, be properly looked upon only as probationers; as I have been informed by a principal gentleman in the county of Cavan, who protested to me that he never knew above one or two instances under the age of six, even in a part of the kingdom so renowned for the quickest proficiency in that art.

I am assured by our merchants, that a boy or a girl before twelve years old is no salable commodity; and even when they come to this age they will not yield above 3£. or 3£. 2s. 6d. at most on the exchange; which cannot turn to account either to the parents or kingdom, the charge of nutriment and rags having been at least four times that value.

I shall now therefore humbly propose my own thoughts, which I hope will not be liable to the least objection.

I have been assured by a very knowing American of my acquaintance in London, that a young healthy child well nursed is at a year old a most delicious, nourishing, and wholesome food, whether stewed, roasted, baked, or broiled; and I make no doubt that it will equally serve in a fricassee or a ragout.[7]

I do therefore humbly offer it to public consideration that of the 120,000 children already computed, 20,000 may be reserved for breed, whereof only one-fourth part to be males; which is more than we allow to sheep, black cattle, or swine; and my reason is, that these children are seldom the fruits of marriage, a circumstance not much regarded by our savages; therefore one male will be sufficient to serve four females. That the remaining 100,000 may, at a year old, be offered in sale to the persons of quality and fortune through the kingdom; always advising the mother to let them suck plentifully in the last month, so as to render them plump and fat for a good table. A child will make two dishes at an entertainment for friends; and when the family dines alone, the fore and hind quarter will make a reasonable dish, and seasoned with a little pepper or salt will be very good boiled on the fourth day, especially in winter. 10

I have reckoned upon a medium that a child just born will weigh 12 pounds, and in a solar year, if tolerably nursed, will increase to 28 pounds.

I grant this food will be somewhat dear, and therefore very proper for landlords, who, as they have already devoured most of the parents, seem to have the best title to the children.

---

[6]*towardly parts:* Natural abilities. —EDS.
[7]*ragout:* A stew. —EDS.

Infants' flesh will be in season throughout the year, but more plentiful in March, and a little before and after: for we are told by a grave author, an eminent French physician,[8] that fish being a prolific diet, there are more children born in Roman Catholic countries about nine months after Lent than at any other season; therefore, reckoning a year after Lent, the markets will be more glutted than usual, because the number of popish infants is at least three to one in this kingdom: and therefore it will have one other collateral advantage, by lessening the number of papists among us.

I have already computed the charge of nursing a beggar's child (in which list I reckon all cottagers, laborers, and four-fifths of the farmers) to be about 2s. per annum, rags included; and I believe no gentleman would repine to give 10s. for the carcass of a good fat child, which, as I have said, will make four dishes of excellent nutritive meat, when he has only some particular friend or his own family to dine with him. Thus the squire will learn to be a good landlord, and grow popular among the tenants; the mother will have 8s. net profit, and be fit for work till she produces another child.

Those who are more thrifty (as I must confess the times require) may   15
flay the carcass; the skin of which artificially[9] dressed will make admirable gloves for ladies, and summer boots for fine gentlemen.

As to our city of Dublin, shambles[10] may be appointed for this purpose in the most convenient parts of it, and butchers we may be assured will not be wanting: although I rather recommend buying the children alive, and dressing them hot from the knife as we do roasting pigs.

A very worthy person, a true lover of his country, and whose virtues I highly esteem, was lately pleased in discoursing on this matter to offer a refinement upon my scheme. He said that many gentlemen of this kingdom, having of late destroyed their deer, he conceived that the want of venison might be well supplied by the bodies of young lads and maidens, not exceeding fourteen years of age nor under twelve; so great a number of both sexes in every country being now ready to starve for want of work and service; and these to be disposed of by their parents, if alive, or otherwise by their nearest relations. But with due deference to so excellent a friend and so deserving a patriot, I cannot be altogether in his sentiments; for as to the males, my American acquaintance assured me from frequent experience that their flesh was generally tough and lean, like that of our schoolboys by continual exercise, and their taste disagreeable; and to fatten them would not answer the charge. Then as to the females, it would, I think, with humble submission be a loss to the public, because

---

[8]*French physician:* François Rabelais (c. 1494–1553), the great Renaissance humanist and author of the comic masterpiece *Gargantua and Pantagruel.* Swift is being ironic in calling Rabelais "grave." —EDS.
   [9]*artificially:* Artfully. —EDS.
   [10]*shambles:* Slaughterhouses. —EDS.

they soon would become breeders themselves: and besides, it is not improbable that some scrupulous people might be apt to censure such a practice (although indeed very unjustly), as a little bordering upon cruelty; which, I confess, has always been with me the strongest objection against any project, how well soever intended.

But in order to justify my friend, he confessed that this expedient was put into his head by the famous Psalmanazar[11] a native of the island Formosa, who came from thence to London about twenty years ago: and in conversation told my friend, that in his country when any young person happened to be put to death, the executioner sold the carcass to persons of quality as a prime dainty; and that in his time the body of a plump girl of fifteen, who was crucified for an attempt to poison the emperor, was sold to his imperial majesty's prime minister of state, and other great mandarins of the court, in joints from the gibbet, at 400 crowns. Neither indeed can I deny, that if the same use were made of several plump young girls in this town, who without one single groat to their fortunes cannot stir abroad without a chair,[12] and appear at the playhouse and assemblies in foreign fineries which they never will pay for, the kingdom would not be the worse.

Some persons of a desponding spirit are in great concern about the vast number of poor people, who are aged, diseased, or maimed, and I have been desired to employ my thoughts what course may be taken to ease the nation of so grievous an encumbrance. But I am not in the least pain upon that matter, because it is very well known that they are every day dying and rotting by cold and famine, and filth and vermin, as fast as can be reasonably expected. And as to the young laborers, they are now in as hopeful condition: They cannot get work, and consequently pine away for want of nourishment, to a degree that if at any time they are accidentally hired to common labor, they have not strength to perform it; and thus the country and themselves are happily delivered from the evils to come.

I have too long digressed, and therefore shall return to my subject. I   20
think the advantages by the proposal which I have made are obvious and many, as well as of the highest importance.

For first, as I have already observed, it would greatly lessen the number of papists, with whom we are yearly overrun, being the principal breeders of the nation as well as our most dangerous enemies; and who stay at home on purpose to deliver the kingdom to the Pretender, hoping to take their advantage by the absence of so many good Protestants, who have chosen rather to leave their country than stay at home and pay tithes against their conscience to an Episcopal curate.

---

[11]*Psalmanazar:* George Psalmanazar (c. 1679–1763) was a Frenchman who tricked London society into believing he was a native of Formosa (now Taiwan). — EDS.
[12]*a chair:* A sedan chair in which one is carried about. — EDS.

Secondly, The poor tenants will have something valuable of their own, which by law may be made liable to distress[13] and help to pay their landlord's rent, their corn and cattle being already seized, and money a thing unknown.

Thirdly, Whereas the maintenance of 100,000 children from two years old and upward, cannot be computed at less that 10s. a-piece per annum, the nation's stock will be thereby increased £50,000 per annum, beside the profit of a new dish introduced to the tables of all gentlemen of fortune in the kingdom who have any refinement in taste. And the money will circulate among ourselves, the goods being entirely of our own growth and manufacture.

Fourthly, The constant breeders beside the gain of 8s. sterling per annum by the sale of their children, will be rid of the charge of maintaining them after the first year.

Fifthly, This food would likewise bring great custom to taverns, where the vintners will certainly be so prudent as to procure the best receipts[14] for dressing it to perfection, and consequently have their houses frequented by all the fine gentlemen, who justly value themselves upon their knowledge in good eating; and a skilful cook who understands how to oblige his guests, will contrive to make it as expensive as they please.

Sixthly, This would be a great inducement to marriage, which all wise nations have either encouraged by rewards or enforced by laws and penalties. It would increase the care and tenderness of mothers toward their children, when they were sure of a settlement for life to the poor babes, provided in some sort by the public, to their annual profit instead of expense. We should see an honest emulation among the married women, which of them would bring the fattest child to the market. Men would become as fond of their wives during the time of their pregnancy as they are now of their mares in foal, their cows in calf, their sows when they are ready to farrow, nor offer to beat or kick them (as is too frequent a practice) for fear of a miscarriage.

Many other advantages might be enumerated. For instance, the addition of some thousand carcasses in our exportation of barreled beef, the propagation of swine's flesh, and improvement in the art of making good bacon, so much wanted among us by the great destruction of pigs, too frequent at our table; which are no way comparable in taste or magnificence to a well-grown, fat, yearling child, which roasted whole will make a considerable figure at a lord mayor's feast or any other public entertainment. But this and many others I omit, being studious of brevity.

Supposing that 1,000 families in this city would be constant customers for infants' flesh, besides others who might have it at merry-meetings, particularly at weddings and christenings, I compute that Dublin would take off annually about 20,000 carcasses; and the rest of

25

---

[13]*distress:* Seizure for payment of debt. —EDS.
[14]*receipts:* Recipes. —EDS.

the kingdom (where probably they will be sold somewhat cheaper) the remaining 80,000.

I can think of no one objection that will possibly be raised against this proposal unless it should be urged that the number of people will be thereby much lessened in the kingdom. This I freely own, and it was indeed one principal design in offering it to the world. I desire the reader will observe, that I calculate my remedy for this one individual kingdom of Ireland and for no other that ever was, is, or I think ever can be upon earth. Therefore let no man talk to me of other expedients: of taxing our absentees at 5s. a pound: of using neither clothes nor household furniture except what is of our own growth and manufacture: of utterly rejecting the materials and instruments that promote foreign luxury: of curing the expensiveness of pride, vanity, idleness, and gaming in our women: of introducing a vein of parsimony, prudence, and temperance: of learning to love our country, in the want of which we differ even from Laplanders and the inhabitants of Topinamboo:[15] of quitting our animosities and factions, nor acting any longer like the Jews, who were murdering one another at the very moment their city was taken:[16] of being a little cautious not to sell our country and conscience for nothing: of teaching landlords to have at least one degree of mercy toward their tenants: lastly, of putting a spirit of honesty, industry, and skill into our shopkeepers; who, if a resolution could now be taken to buy only our native goods, would immediately unite to cheat and exact upon us in the price the measure, and the goodness, nor could ever yet be brought to make one fair proposal of just dealing, though often and earnestly invited to it.

Therefore I repeat, let no man talk to me of these and the like expedients, till he has at least some glimpse of hope that there will be ever some hearty and sincere attempt to put them in practice.   30

But as to myself, having been wearied out for many years with offering vain, idle, visionary thoughts, and at length utterly despairing of success, I fortunately fell upon this proposal; which, as it is wholly new, so it has something solid and real, of no expense and little trouble, full in our own power, and whereby we can incur no danger in disobliging England. For this kind of commodity will not bear exportation, the flesh being of too tender a consistence to admit a long continuance in salt, although perhaps I could name a country which would be glad to eat up our whole nation without it.

After all, I am not so violently bent upon my own opinion as to reject any offer proposed by wise men, which shall be found equally innocent, cheap, easy, and effectual. But before something of that kind shall be advanced in contradiction to my scheme, and offering a better, I desire the author or authors will be pleased maturely to consider two points. First,

---

[15]*Laplanders and the inhabitants of Topinamboo:* Lapland is the area of Scandinavia above the Arctic Circle; Topinamboo, in Brazil, was known in Swift's time for the savagery of its tribes. — EDS.

[16]*was taken:* A reference to the Roman seizure of Jerusalem (A.D. 70). — EDS.

as things now stand, how they will be able to find food and raiment for 100,000 useless mouths and backs. And secondly, there being a round million of creatures in human figure throughout this kingdom, whose subsistence put into a common stock would leave them in debt 2,000,000£. sterling, adding those who are beggars by profession to the bulk of farmers, cottagers, and laborers, with the wives and children who are beggars in effect; I desire those politicians who dislike my overture, and may perhaps be so bold as to attempt an answer, that they will first ask the parents of these mortals, whether they would not at this day think it a great happiness to have been sold for food at a year old in the manner I prescribe, and thereby have avoided such a perpetual scene of misfortunes as they have since gone through by the oppression of landlords, the impossibility of paying rent without money or trade, the want of common sustenance, with neither house nor clothes to cover them from the inclemencies of the weather, and the most inevitable prospect of entailing the like or greater miseries upon their breed for ever.

I profess, in the sincerity of my heart, that I have not the least personal interest in endeavoring to promote this necessary work, having no other motive than the public good of my country, by advancing our trade, providing for infants, relieving the poor, and giving some pleasure to the rich. I have no children by which I can propose to get a single penny; the youngest being nine years old, and my wife past childbearing.

The Reader's Presence

1. Consider Swift's title. In what sense is the proposal "modest"? What is modest about it? What synonyms would you use for *modest* that appear in the essay? In what sense is the essay a "proposal"? Does it follow any format that resembles a proposal? What aspects of its language seem to resemble proposal writing?

2. For this essay Swift invents a speaker, an unnamed, fictional individual who "humbly" proposes a plan to relieve poverty in Ireland. What attitudes and beliefs in the essay do you attribute to the speaker? Which do you attribute to Swift, the author? Having considered two authors (the speaker of the proposal and Swift), now consider two readers—the reader the speaker imagines and the reader Swift imagines. How do these two readers differ? Reread the final paragraph of the essay from the perspective of each of these readers. How do you think each reader is expected to respond?

3. In the introductory comment Swift is quoted as wanting "to vex the world rather than divert it" with his writing. Where in the essay do you find Swift most vexing? How does he attempt to provoke the reader's outrage? Is paragraph 9 the first, most

visceral indication of the speaker's plan? Does he heighten the essay's effect after this point? If so, where and how? How does Swift mount a serious political argument in the midst of such hyperbole? What other essayists in this collection use hyperbole or satire in the presentation of their arguments?

112

Lewis Thomas

On Cloning a Human Being

Lewis Thomas (1913–1993) was trained as a physician and scientist, but his intellectual curiosity and his publications took him far beyond the practice of medicine. In 1971 he became a regular contributor to the New England Journal of Medicine, *writing a column called "Notes of a Biology Watcher." Several of these essays are collected in* The Lives of the Cell *(1974), which explores the many ways in which organisms relate to one another for their mutual benefit. Joyce Carol Oates praised this book, saying that it "anticipates the kind of writing that will appear more and more frequently, as scientists take on the language of poetry in order to communicate human truths too mysterious for old-fashioned common sense."*

Thomas also published The Medusa and the Snail: More Notes of a Biology Watcher *(1979), from which "On Cloning a Human Being" is taken. His later books expanded the range of his investigations into natural and social processes and include* Late Night Thoughts on Listening to Mahler's Ninth Symphony *(1984) and a collection of essays on language,* Et Cetera, Et Cetera: Notes of a Word Watcher *(1990).*

It is important to remember that Thomas wrote this essay in the late 1970s, long before cloning living creatures became a scientific actuality.

It is now theoretically possible to recreate an identical creature from any animal or plant, from the DNA contained in the nucleus of any somatic cell. A single plant root-tip cell can be teased and seduced into conceiving a perfect copy of the whole plant; a frog's intestinal epithelial cell possesses the complete instructions needed for a new, same frog. If the technology were further advanced, you could do this with a human being, and there are now startled predictions all over the place that this will in fact be done, someday, in order to provide a version of immortality for carefully selected, especially valuable people.

The cloning of humans is on most of the lists of things to worry about from Science, along with behavior control, genetic engineering, transplanted heads, computer poetry, and the unrestrained growth of plastic flowers.

Cloning is the most dismaying of prospects, mandating as it does the elimination of sex with only a metaphoric elimination of death as compensation. It is almost no comfort to know that one's cloned, identical surrogate lives on, especially when the living will very likely involve edging one's real, now aging self off to the side, sooner or later. It is hard to imagine anything like filial affection or respect for a single, unmated nucleus; harder still to think of one's new, self-generated self as anything but an absolute, desolate orphan. Not to mention the complex interpersonal relationship involved in raising one's self from infancy, teaching the language, enforcing discipline, instilling good manners and the like. How would you feel if you became an incorrigible juvenile delinquent by proxy, at the age of fifty-five?

The public questions are obvious. Who is to be selected, and on what qualifications? How to handle the risks of misused technology, such as self-determined cloning by the rich and powerful but socially objectionable, or the cloning by governments of dumb, docile masses for the world's work? What will be the effect on all the uncloned rest of us of human sameness? After all, we've accustomed ourselves through hundreds of millennia to the continual exhilaration of uniqueness; each of us is totally different, in a fundamental sense, from all the other four billion. Selfness is an essential fact of life. The thought of human nonselfness, precise sameness, is terrifying, when you think about it.

Well, don't think about it, because it isn't a probable possibility, not   5 even as a long shot for the distant future, in my opinion. I agree that you might clone some people who would look amazingly like their parental cell donors, but the odds are that they'd be almost as different as you or me, and certainly more different than any of today's identical twins.

The time required for the experiment is only one of the problems, but a formidable one. Suppose you wanted to clone a prominent, spectacularly successful diplomat, to look after the Middle East problems of the distant future. You'd have to catch him and persuade him, probably not very hard to do, and extirpate a cell. But then you'd have to wait for him to grow up through embryonic life and then for at least forty years more, and you'd have to be sure all observers remained patient and unmeddlesome through his unpromising, ambiguous childhood and adolescence.

Moreover, you'd have to be sure of recreating his environment, perhaps down to the last detail. "Environment" is a word which really means people, so you'd have to do a lot more cloning than just the diplomat himself.

This is a very important part of the cloning problem, largely overlooked in our excitement about the cloned individual himself. You don't have to agree all the way with B. F. Skinner to acknowledge that the environment does make a difference, and when you examine what we really mean by the word "environment" it comes down to other human beings. We use euphemisms and jargon for this, like "social forces," "cultural influences," even Skinner's "verbal community," but what is meant is the dense crowd of nearby people who talk to, listen to, smile or frown at, give to, withhold from, nudge, push, caress, or flail out at the individual. No matter what the genome says, these people have a lot to do with shaping a character. Indeed, if all you had was the genome, and no people around, you'd grow a sort of vertebrate plant, nothing more.

So, to start with, you will undoubtedly need to clone the parents. No question about this. This means the diplomat is out, even in theory, since you couldn't have gotten cells from both his parents at the time when he was himself just recognizable as an early social treasure. You'd have to limit the list of clones to people already certified as sufficiently valuable for the effort, with both parents still alive. The parents would need cloning and, for consistency, their parents as well. I suppose you'd also need the usual informed-consent forms, filled out and signed, not easy to get if I know parents, even harder for grandparents.

But this is only the beginning. It is the whole family that really influ-   10
ences the way a person turns out, not just the parents, according to current psychiatric thinking. Clone the family.

Then what? The way each member of the family develops has already been determined by the environment set around him, and this environment is more people, people outside the family, schoolmates, acquaintances, lovers, enemies, car-pool partners, even, in special circumstances, peculiar strangers across the aisle on the subway. Find them, and clone them.

But there is no end to the protocol. Each of the outer contacts has his own surrounding family, and his and their outer contacts. Clone them all.

To do the thing properly, with any hope of ending up with a genuine duplicate of a single person, you really have no choice. You must clone the world, no less.

We are not ready for an experiment of this size, nor, I should think, are we willing. For one thing, it would mean replacing today's world by an entirely identical world to follow immediately, and this means no new, natural, spontaneous, random, chancy children. No children at all, except for the manufactured doubles of those now on the scene. Plus all those identical adults, including all of today's politicians, all seen double. It is too much to contemplate.

Moreover, when the whole experiment is finally finished, fifty years   15
or so from now, how could you get a responsible scientific reading on the outcome? Somewhere in there would be the original clonee, probably lost and overlooked, now well into middle age, but everyone around him would be precise duplicates of today's everyone. It would be today's same world, filled to overflowing with duplicates of today's people and their same, duplicated problems, probably all resentful at having had to go

through our whole thing all over, sore enough at the clonee to make endless trouble for him, if they found him.

And obviously, if the whole thing were done precisely right, they would still be casting about for ways to solve the problem of universal dissatisfaction, and sooner or later they'd surely begin to look around at each other, wondering who should be cloned for his special value to society, to get us out of all this. And so it would go, in regular cycles, perhaps forever.

I once lived through a period when I wondered what Hell could be like, and I stretched my imagination to try to think of a perpetual sort of damnation. I have to confess, I never thought of anything like this.

I have an alternative suggestion, if you're looking for a way out. Set cloning aside, and don't try it. Instead, go in the other direction. Look for ways to get mutations more quickly, new variety, different songs. Fiddle around, if you must fiddle, but never with ways to keep things the same, no matter who, not even yourself. Heaven, somewhere ahead, has got to be a change.

The Reader's Presence

1. As a biologist, Thomas writes as an "expert." How would you read this essay differently if it were written by a nonscientist, reasoning through common sense rather than inside knowledge of the subject? What sort of audience does Thomas appear to be writing for? What sorts of fears does he address? What is his general argument?

2. Thomas concludes with advice pertinent both to genetic engineering and life in general. How does Thomas link cellular and greater human concerns? Is this leap from biology to everyday life convincing? Why or why not? Does it undermine or enhance Thomas's authority?

3. In paragraphs 6–12 Thomas outlines a hypothetical scenario that quickly becomes ridiculous. What is the effect of such exaggeration? Why might Thomas have pursued this technique? How does it compare, in tone and effect, to what precedes this section? Can you compare Thomas's essay to Jonathan Swift's "A Modest Proposal" (page 776)? Is Thomas's essay more usefully compared with Stephen Jay Gould's "Sex, Drugs, Disasters, and the Extinction of Dinosaurs" (page 401)? How does each of these three essayists use scientific evidence (or the simulation thereof) to support his argument? To what extent is each writer describing a situation and/or staking a claim?

113

Sojourner Truth

And Ain't I a Woman?

Sojourner Truth was born Isabella Baumfree in New York, circa 1797. After being liberated from slavery by the New York State Emancipation Act of 1827, she lived briefly in New York, working as a domestic servant. She took the name Sojourner Truth as a sign of her religious vocation and soon became famous as a wandering preacher, spellbinding crowds wherever she spoke. Eventually she joined the abolitionist movement and lectured on her experiences as a slave before white audiences throughout the North. She became friendly with the major abolitionist of the era, including Harriet Beecher Stowe, who called her "the Libyan sibyl." She lived for many years in Florence, Massachusetts, and in the 1850s relocated to Battle Creek, Michigan, where she spent the rest of her life. During the Civil War she helped to raise relief funds for escaped slaves and to gather supplies for black volunteer regiments. In 1864, she was received warmly at the White House by President Abraham Lincoln. Sojourner Truth's autobiography, The Narrative of Sojourner Truth *(narrated to Olive Gilbert) was published in 1850. She died in 1883. "And Ain't I a Woman" is a speech she gave at the Women's Rights Convention in 1851.*

The leaders of the movement trembled on seeing a tall, gaunt black woman in a gray dress and white turban, surmounted with an uncouth sun-bonnet, march deliberately into the church, walk with the air of a queen up the aisle, and take her seat upon the pulpit steps. A buzz of disapprobation was heard all over the house, and there fell on the listening ear, "An abolition affair!" "Woman's rights and niggers!" "I told you so!" . . .

I chanced on that occasion to wear my first laurels in public life as president of the meeting. At my request order was restored, and the business of the Convention went on. Morning, afternoon, and evening exercises came and went. Through all these sessions old Sojourner, quiet and reticent as the "Lybian Statue," sat crouched against the wall on the corner of the pulpit stairs, her sun-bonnet shading her eyes, her elbows on her knees, her chin resting upon her broad, hard palms. At intermission she was busy selling the "Life of Sojourner Truth," a narrative of her own strange and adventurous life. Again and again, timorous and trembling ones came to me and said, with earnestness, "Don't let her speak, Mrs. Gage, it will ruin us. Every newspaper in the land will have our cause mixed up with abolition and niggers, and we shall be utterly denounced." My only answer was, "We shall see when the time comes."

The second day the work waxed warm. Methodist, Baptist, Episcopal, Presbyterian, and Universalist ministers came in to hear and discuss the resolutions presented. One claimed superior rights and privileges for man, on the ground of "superior intellect"; another, because of the "manhood of Christ; if God had desired the equality of woman, He would have given some token of His will through the birth, life, and death of the Saviour." Another gave us a theological view of the "sin of our first mother."

There were very few women in those days who dared to "speak in meeting"; and the august teachers of the people were seemingly getting the better of us, while the boys in the galleries, and the sneerers among the pews, were hugely enjoying the discomfiture, as they supposed, of the "strong-minded." Some of the tender-skinned friends were on the point of losing dignity, and the atmosphere betokened a storm. When, slowly from her seat in the corner rose Sojourner Truth, who, till now, had scarcely lifted her head. "Don't let her speak!" gasped half a dozen in my ear. She moved slowly and solemnly to the front, laid her old bonnet at her feet, and turned her great speaking eyes to me. There was a hissing sound of disapprobation above and below. I rose and announced "Sojourner Truth," and begged the audience to keep silence for a few moments.

The tumult subsided at once, and every eye was fixed on this almost   5 Amazon form, which stood nearly six feet high, head erect, and eyes piercing the upper air like one in a dream. At her first word there was a profound hush. She spoke in deep tones, which, though not loud, reached every ear in the house, and away through the throng at the doors and windows.

"Wall, chilern, whar dar is so much racket dar must be somethin' out o' kilter. I tink dat 'twixt de niggers of de Souf and de womin at de Norf, all talkin' 'bout rights, de white men will be in a fix pretty soon. But what's all dis here talkin' 'bout?

"Dat man ober dar say dat womin needs to be helped into carriages, and lifted ober ditches, and to hab de best place everywhar. Nobody eber helps me into carriages, or ober mud-puddles, or gibs me any best place!" And raising herself to her full height, and her voice to a pitch like rolling thunder, she asked, "And a'n't I a woman? Look at me! Look at my arm! (and she bared her right arm to the shoulder, showing her tremendous muscular power). I have ploughed, and planted, and gathered into barns, and no man could head me! And a'n't I a woman? I could work as much and eat as much as a man—when I could get it—and bear de lash as well! And a'n't I a woman? I have borne thirteen chilern, and seen 'em mos' all sold off to slavery, and when I cried out with my mother's grief, none but Jesus heard me! And a'n't I a woman?

"Den dey talks 'bout dis ting in de head; what dis dey call it?" ("Intellect," whispered some one near.) "Dat's it, honey. What's dat got to do wid womin's rights or nigger's rights? If my cup won't hold but a pint, and yourn holds a quart, wouldn't ye be mean not to let me have my little half-measure full?" And she pointed her significant finger, and sent a keen glance at the minister who had made the argument. The cheering was long and loud.

"Den dat little man in black dar, he say women can't have as much rights as men, 'cause Christ wan't a woman! Whar did your Christ come from?" Rolling thunder couldn't have stilled that crowd, as did those deep, wonderful tones, as she stood there with outstretched arms and eyes of fire. Raising her voice still louder, she repeated, "Whar did your Christ come from? From God and a woman! Man had nothin' to do wid Him." Oh, what a rebuke that was to that little man.

Turning again to another objector, she took up the defense of Mother   10
Eve. I can not follow her through it all. It was pointed, and witty, and solemn; eliciting at almost every sentence deafening applause; and she ended by asserting: "If de fust woman God ever made was strong enough to turn de world upside down all alone, dese women togedder (and she glanced her eye over the platform) ought to be able to turn it back, and get it right side up again! And now dey is asking to do it, de men better let 'em." Long-continued cheering greeted this. " 'Bleeged to ye for hearin' on me, and now ole Sojourner han't got nothin' more to say."

Amid roars of applause, she returned to her corner, leaving more than one of us with streaming eyes, and hearts beating with gratitude. She had taken us up in her strong arms and carried us safely over the slough of difficulty turning the whole tide in our favor. I have never in my life seen anything like the magical influence that subdued the mobbish spirit of the day, and turned the sneers and jeers of an excited crowd into notes of respect and admiration. Hundreds rushed up to shake hands with her, and congratulate the glorious old mother, and bid her God-speed on her mission of "testifyin' agin concerning the wickedness of this 'ere people."

The Reader's Presence

1. Imagine yourself as the two men whom Sojourner Truth directly addresses: "[that] man over there" and "[that] little man in black" (paragraphs 7 and 9). Continue the conversation. What might each one have said in reply to her points? How would she have responded? In developing your dialogue, focus on maintaining Sojourner's style and rhythm as much as possible. How convincing was your Sojourner? What was the most difficult challenge you

faced in making her voice sound "right"? What was the easiest aspect of recreating her voice?

2. Sojourner Truth was illiterate when she spoke at the Women's Rights Convention in 1851. Recollecting the speech in 1863 — twelve years later — the convention's president, Frances Gage, wrote what has become the official version of Truth's words. Reread the speech carefully. What indications do you find that the speech has been changed from spoken language to written word? How do these changes affect the overall meaning of the speech? In answering this question, think about what has been left out of the written version (for example, facial expressions, gestures, tone). What has been added (for example, punctuation, asides)? Do you think the changes make the speech more powerful and successful, or less powerful? How?

3. Why has Sojourner Truth's speech continued to be popular for over 150 years? Examine another selection that is dated from at least 20 years ago, such as Martin Luther King Jr.'s "Letter from Birmingham Jail" (page 692) or Thomas Jefferson's "Declaration of Independence" (page 674). What characteristics do the selections share? How do the pieces continue to be relevant to a world very different from the world in which they were written? What indications do you find that the essays are past their time? How long do you think the essays will continue to be important? Why?

114

Mark Twain

Corn-pone Opinions

Mark Twain, the pseudonym of Samuel Clemens (1835–1910), was a master satirist, journalist, novelist, orator, and steamboat pilot. He grew up in Hannibal, Missouri, a frontier setting which appears in different forms in several of his novels, most notably in his masterpiece Adventures of Huckleberry Finn *(1869). His satirical eye spared very few American political or social institutions including slavery, and for this reason, as well as because it violated conventional standards of taste,* Huckleberry Finn *created a minor scandal when it was published. Nonetheless, with such books as* The Innocents Abroad *(1869),* Roughing It *(1872),* Old Times on the Mississippi *(1875),* The Adventures of Tom Sawyer *(1876), and* The Prince and the Pauper *(1882), Twain secured himself a position as one of the most popular authors in American history. Twain built his career upon his experiences in the western states and his travels in Europe and the Middle East, but he eventually settled in Hartford, Connecticut. His last years were spent as one of the most celebrated public speakers and social figures in the United States.*

Reflecting upon the experience of writing, Twain once wrote in his notebook, "The time to begin writing an article is when you have finished it to your satisfaction. By that time you begin to clearly and logically perceive what it is that you really want to say."

Fifty years ago, when I was a boy of fifteen and helping to inhabit a Missourian village on the banks of the Mississippi, I had a friend whose society was very dear to me because I was forbidden by my mother to partake of it. He was a gay and impudent and satirical and delightful young black man—a slave—who daily preached sermons from the top of his master's woodpile, with me for sole audience. He imitated the pulpit style of the several clergymen of the village, and did it well, and with fine passion and energy. To me he was a wonder. I believed he was the greatest orator in the United States and would some day be heard from. But it did not happen; in the distribution of rewards he was overlooked. It is the way, in this world.

He interrupted his preaching, now and then, to saw a stick of wood; but the sawing was a pretense—he did it with his mouth; exactly imitating the sound the bucksaw makes in shrieking its way through the wood. But it served its purpose; it kept his master from coming out to see how the work was getting along. I listened to the sermons from the open window of a lumber room at the back of the house. One of his texts was this:

"You tell me whar a man gits his corn pone[1], en I'll tell you what his 'pinions is."

I can never forget it. It was deeply impressed upon me. By my mother. Not upon my memory, but elsewhere. She had slipped in upon me while I was absorbed and not watching. The black philosopher's idea was that a man is not independent, and cannot afford views which might interfere with his bread and butter. If he would prosper, he must train with the majority; in matters of large moment, like politics and religion, he must think and feel with the bulk of his neighbors, or suffer damage in his social standing and in his business prosperities. He must restrict himself to corn-pone opinions—at least on the surface. He must get his opinions from other people; he must reason out none for himself; he must have no first-hand views.

I think Jerry was right, in the main, but I think he did not go far   5
enough.

---

[1]*Corn pone:* Southern expression that dates from the mid-nineteenth century for a simple corn bread or muffin; *pone* comes from a Native American word for something baked. —EDS.

1. It was his idea that a man conforms to the majority view of his locality by calculation and intention.

This happens, but I think it is not the rule.

2. It was his idea that there is such a thing as a first-hand opinion; an original opinion; an opinion which is coldly reasoned out in a man's head, by a searching analysis of the facts involved, with the heart unconsulted, and the jury room closed against outside influences. It may be that such an opinion has been born somewhere, at some time or other, but I suppose it got away before they could catch it and stuff it and put it in the museum.

I am persuaded that a coldly-thought-out and independent verdict upon a fashion in clothes, or manners, or literature, or politics, or religion, or any other matter that is projected into the field of our notice and interest, is a most rare thing—if it has indeed ever existed.

A new thing in costume appears—the flaring hoopskirt, for example—and the passers-by are shocked, and the irreverent laugh. Six months later everybody is reconciled; the fashion has established itself; it is admired, now, and no one laughs. Public opinion resented it before, public opinion accepts it now, and is happy in it. Why? Was the resentment reasoned out? Was the acceptance reasoned out? No. The instinct that moves to conformity did the work. It is our nature to conform; it is a force which not many can successfully resist. What is its seat? The inborn requirement of self-approval. We all have to bow to that; there are no exceptions. Even the woman who refuses from first to last to wear the hoopskirt comes under that law and is its slave; she could not wear the skirt and have her own approval; and that she *must* have, she cannot help herself. But as a rule our self-approval has its source in but one place and not elsewhere—the approval of other people. A person of vast consequences can introduce any kind of novelty in dress and the general world will presently adopt it—moved to do it, in the first place, by the natural instinct to passively yield to that vague something recognized as authority, and in the second place by the human instinct to train with the multitude and have its approval. An empress introduced the hoopskirt, and we know the result. A nobody introduced the bloomer, and we know the result. If Eve should come again, in her ripe renown, and reintroduce her quaint styles—well, we know what would happen. And we should be cruelly embarrassed, along at first.

The hoopskirt runs its course and disappears. Nobody reasons about it. One woman abandons the fashion; her neighbor notices this and follows her lead; this influences the next woman; and so on and so on, and presently the skirt has vanished out of the world, no one knows how nor why, nor cares, for that matter. It will come again, by and by and in due course will go again.

Twenty-five years ago, in England, six or eight wine glasses stood grouped by each person's plate at a dinner party, and they were used, not left idle and empty; to-day there are but three or four in the group, and

10

the average guest sparingly uses about two of them. We have not adopted this new fashion yet, but we shall do it presently. We shall not think it out; we shall merely conform, and let it go at that. We get our notions and habits and opinions from outside influences; we do not have to study them out.

Our table manners, and company manners, and street manners change from time to time, but the changes are not reasoned out; we merely notice and conform. We are creatures of outside influences; as a rule we do not think, we only imitate. We cannot invent standards that will stick; what we mistake for standards are only fashions, and perishable. We may continue to admire them, but we drop the use of them. We notice this in literature. Shakespeare is a standard, and fifty years ago we used to write tragedies which we couldn't tell from—from somebody else's; but we don't do it any more, now. Our prose standard, three quarters of a century ago, was ornate and diffuse; some authority or other changed it in the direction of compactness and simplicity, and conformity followed, without argument. The historical novel starts up suddenly, and sweeps the land. Everybody writes one, and the nation is glad. We had historical novels before; but nobody read them, and the rest of us conformed—without reasoning it out. We are conforming in the other way, now, because it is another case of everybody.

The outside influences are always pouring in upon us, and we are always obeying their orders and accepting their verdicts. The Smiths like the new play; the Joneses go to see it, and they copy the Smith verdict. Morals, religions, politics, get their following from surrounding influences and atmospheres, almost entirely; not from study, not from thinking. A man must and will have his own approval first of all, in each and every moment and circumstance of his life—even if he must repent of a self-approved act the moment after its commission, in order to get his self-approval *again:* but, speaking in general terms, a man's self-approval in the large concerns of life has its source in the approval of the peoples about him, and not in a searching personal examination of the matter. Mohammedans are Mohammedans because they are born and reared among that sect, not because they have thought it out and can furnish sound reasons for being Mohammedans; we know why Catholics are Catholics; why Presbyterians are Presbyterians; why Baptists are Baptists; why Mormons are Mormons; why thieves are thieves; why monarchists are monarchists; why Republicans are Republicans and Democrats, Democrats. We know it is a matter of association and sympathy, not reasoning and examination; that hardly a man in the world has an opinion upon morals, politics, or religion which he got otherwise than through his associations and sympathies. Broadly speaking, there are none but corn-pone opinions. And broadly speaking, corn-pone stands for self-approval. Self-approval is acquired mainly from the approval of other people. The result is conformity. Sometimes conformity has a sordid business interest—the bread-and-butter interest—but not in most cases, I think. I think that in the majority of cases it is unconscious and not calculated; that it is born of the human being's natural yearning to stand well with his fellows and have their inspiring approval and praise—a yearning which is commonly so strong and so insistent that it cannot be effectually resisted, and must have its way.

A political emergency brings out the corn-pone opinion in fine force 15 in its two chief varieties—the pocketbook variety, which has its origin in self-interest, and the bigger variety, the sentimental variety—the one which can't bear to be outside the pale; can't bear to be in disfavor; can't endure the averted face and the cold shoulder; wants to stand well with his friends, wants to be smiled upon, wants to be welcome, wants to hear the precious words, "*He's* on the right track!" Uttered, perhaps by an ass, but still an ass of high degree, an ass whose approval is gold and diamonds to a smaller ass, and confers glory and honor and happiness, and membership in the herd. For these gauds many a man will dump his lifelong principles into the street, and his conscience along with them. We have seen it happen. In some millions of instances.

Men think they think upon great political questions, and they do; but they think with their party, not independently; they read its literature, but not that of the other side; they arrive at convictions, but they are drawn from a partial view of the matter in hand and are of no particular value. They swarm with their party, they feel with their party, they are happy in their party's approval; and where the party leads they will follow, whether for right and honor, or through blood and dirt and a mush of mutilated morals.

In our late canvass half of the nation passionately believed that in silver lay salvation, the other half as passionately believed that that way lay destruction. Do you believe that a tenth part of the people, on either side, had any rational excuse for having an opinion about the matter at all? I studied that mighty question to the bottom—came out empty. Half of our people passionately believe in high tariff, the other half believe otherwise. Does this mean study and examination, or only feeling? The latter, I think. I have deeply studied that question, too—and didn't arrive. We all do no end of feeling, and we mistake it for thinking. And out of it we get an aggregation which we consider a boon. Its name is Public Opinion. It is held in reverence. It settles everything. Some think it the Voice of God.

The Reader's Presence

1. "Corn pone" was a dish eaten, in Twain's time, by poor Southerners. How might this image of a lowly, common foodstuff be tied to the opinions of Twain's commonsense slave "philosopher"? What is Twain's position on Jerry's everyday wisdom? What sort of audience does Twain appear to be writing for? How does Twain "translate" Jerry's statement?

2. Twain agrees with Jerry's statement, but feels he "did not go far enough." How do Twain's opinions differ from Jerry's? How does Twain use Jerry's opinions, starting in paragraph 9, to launch his own? Twain does not return to Jerry in the essay. How does the dramatic technique of ending the essay with topics far from those with which it was begun affect your reading of it?

3. About ten years after Samuel Clemens was born in Missouri, the New England philosopher, Ralph Waldo Emerson, wrote an essay called "Self-Reliance" in which he sharply criticized *his* fellow Americans' tendency toward conformism. "If I know your sect," he wrote, "I anticipate your argument." How does Twain invoke the ideal of self-reliance? Twain calls Jerry's mode of oratory a kind of "pulpit style"; Emerson, too, was a preacher whose essays loosely resemble sermons. What does Twain's essay have in common with the structure of a traditional sermon? Compare the essay to that of another preacher, Martin Luther King Jr.'s "Letter from Birmingham Jail" (page 692). Why might Twain, a deeply irreverent writer, participate in the American sermon tradition? What is the effect of this "sermon" on you as reader? Is Twain's essay as sharp a piece of oratory as King's? How does it appeal to the reader's ear?

115

Gore Vidal

Drugs

Gore Vidal (b. 1925), author, playwright, screenwriter, essayist, and reviewer, is known for his satirical observations, acerbic wit, and eloquence. He is a prolific author of more than twenty books, including The City and the Pillar *(1948),* Myra Breckinridge *(1968),* Myron *(1974),* Palimpsest: A Memoir *(1995), and* The Smithsonian Institution *(1998). Among Gore's irreverent historical novels are* Julian *(1964),* Burr *(1973),* 1876 *(1976),* Lincoln *(1984), and* The Golden Age *(2000). His best-known dramatic work is* Visit to a Small Planet *(1957), which was made into a movie. Vidal has published collections of his writings in* The Essential Gore Vidal *(1999) and* Gore Vidal, Sexually Speaking *(1999). The essay "Drugs" originally appeared in 1970 as an editorial in the* New York Times *and was later included in his book* Homage to Daniel Shays: Collected Essays 1952–1972 *(1972).*

It is possible to stop most drug addiction in the United States within a very short time. Simply make all drugs available and sell them at cost. Label each drug with a precise description of what effect—good and bad—the drug will have on the taker. This will require heroic honesty. Don't say that marijuana is addictive or dangerous when it is neither, as millions of people know—unlike "speed," which kills most unpleasantly, or heroin, which is addictive and difficult to kick.

For the record, I have tried—once—almost every drug and liked none, disproving the popular Fu Manchu theory that a single whiff of opium will enslave the mind. Nevertheless many drugs are bad for certain people to take and they should be told why in a sensible way.

Along with exhortation and warning, it might be good for our citizens to recall (or learn for the first time) that the United States was the creation of men who believed that each man has the right to do what he wants with his own life as long as he does not interfere with his neighbor's pursuit of happiness. (That his neighbor's idea of happiness is persecuting others does confuse matters a bit.)

This is a startling notion to the current generation of Americans. They reflect a system of public education which has made the Bill of Rights, literally, unacceptable to a majority of high school graduates (see the annual Purdue reports) who now form the "silent majority"—a phrase which that underestimated wit Richard Nixon took from Homer, who used it to describe the dead.

Now one can hear the warning rumble begin: If everyone is allowed   5
to take drugs everyone will and the GNP will decrease, the Commies will stop us from making everyone free, and we shall end up a race of zombies, passively murmuring "groovy" to one another. Alarming thought. Yet it seems most unlikely that any reasonably sane person will become a drug addict if he knows in advance what addiction is going to be like.

Is everyone reasonably sane? No. Some people will always become drug addicts just as some people will always become alcoholics, and it is just too bad. Every man, however, has the power (and should have the legal right) to kill himself if he chooses. But since most men don't, they won't be mainliners either. Nevertheless, forbidding young people things they like or think they might enjoy only makes them want those things all the more. This psychological insight is, for some mysterious reason, perennially denied our governors.

It is a lucky thing for the American moralist that our country has always existed in a kind of time-vacuum: We have no public memory of anything that happened before last Tuesday. No one in Washington today recalls what happened during the years alcohol was forbidden to the people by a Congress that thought it had a divine mission to stamp out Demon Rum—launching, in the process, the greatest crime wave in the country's history, causing thousands of deaths from bad alcohol, and creating a general (and persisting) contempt among the citizenry for the laws of the United States.

The same thing is happening today. But the government has learned nothing from past attempts at prohibition, not to mention repression.

Last year when the supply of Mexican marijuana was slightly curtailed by the Feds, the pushers got the kids hooked on heroin and deaths increased dramatically, particularly in New York. Whose fault? Evil men like the Mafiosi? Permissive Dr. Spock? Wild-eyed Dr. Leary? No.

The government of the United States was responsible for those   10
deaths. The bureaucratic machine has a vested interest in playing cops and robbers. Both the Bureau of Narcotics and the Mafia want strong laws against the sale and use of drugs because if drugs are sold at cost there would be no money in it for anyone.

If there was no money in it for the Mafia, there would be no friendly playground pushers, and addicts would not commit crimes to pay for the next fix. Finally, if there was no money in it, the Bureau of Narcotics would wither away, something they are not about to do without a struggle.

Will anything sensible be done? Of course not. The American people are as devoted to the idea of sin and its punishment as they are to making money—and fighting drugs is nearly as big a business as pushing them. Since the combination of sin and money is irresistible (particularly to the professional politician), the situation will only grow worse.

The Reader's Presence

1. Writing in 1970, Vidal admits to having tried "almost every drug." What might the impact of such an admission by a public figure have been at that time? Would the impact be the same today? What sort of audience might Vidal's piece be directed to? Does his admission seem casual or calculated? Does it strengthen or weaken his argument? Why?

2. In paragraph 5, Vidal constructs a hypothetical scenario of what would happen if drugs were not illegal. Does he endorse or mock this scenario? Whose opinion does he seem to be representing? What sorts of words does he use to describe a drug-addicted world? Does his use of humor enhance or undermine his argument?

3. Vidal asserts that the U.S. government profits from drug sales and prosecution, and links the government to organized crime. He argues, finally, that drugs will continue to be a problem in this society as long as Americans are "devoted" to making money: For all their dangers, drugs are big business. How does Vidal support these claims? What is his view of the American people? How does it compare to Martha Nussbaum's portrait of American compassion in "Can Patriotism Be Compassionate?" (see page 720)? Cite specific examples from each text.

116 _____

Cornel West

Race Matters

Philosopher, author, and social critic, Cornel West (b. 1953) taught for many years in the Afro-American Studies Department at Harvard University and at Harvard Divinity School. He is now on the faculty of Princeton University. Regarded as an inspiring and popular speaker, West has delivered speeches at churches, political rallies, and lecture halls, and has appeared on such television programs as The MacNeil/Lehrer Newshour *and William F. Buckley's* Firing Line. *As a scholar and author, he has fought persistently for the continuing relevance of Christianity and Marxism as means for battling white racism and oppression. He has also fought against what he calls "the closing of ranks" among African Americans who place racial allegiances before moral principles. He has published more than a dozen books, including* The Ethical Dimensions of Marxist Thought *(1991);* Race Matters *(1993), in which the following essay originally appeared;* Keeping Faith: Philosophy and Race in America *(1993);* The Future of American Progressivism: An Initiative for Political and Economic Reform *(1998), and* The Cornel West Reader *(2000).*

Since the beginning of the nation, white Americans have suffered from a deep inner uncertainty as to who they really are. One of the ways that has been used to simplify the answer has been to seize upon the presence of black Americans and use them as a marker, a symbol of limits, a metaphor for the "outsider." Many whites could look at the social position of blacks and feel that color formed an easy and reliable gauge for determining to what extent one was or was not American.

Perhaps that is why one of the first epithets that many European immigrants learned when they got off the boat was the term "nigger" — it made them feel instantly American. But this is tricky magic. Despite his racial difference and social status, something indisputably American about Negroes not only raised doubts about the white man's value system but aroused the troubling suspicion that whatever else the true American is, he is also somehow black.

(Ralph Ellison,
"What America Would Be Like without Blacks" [1970])[1]

_____

[1]For the full essay, see page 363. — EDS.

What happened in Los Angeles in April of 1992 was neither a race riot nor a class rebellion. Rather, this monumental upheaval was a multiracial, trans-class, and largely male display of justified social rage. For all its ugly, xenophobic resentment, its air of adolescent carnival, and its downright barbaric behavior, it signified the sense of powerlessness in American society. Glib attempts to reduce its meaning to the pathologies of the black underclass, the criminal actions of hoodlums, or the political revolt of the oppressed urban masses miss the mark. Of those arrested, only 36 percent were black, more than a third had full-time jobs, and most claimed to shun political affiliation. What we witnessed in Los Angeles was the consequence of a lethal linkage of economic decline, cultural decay, and political lethargy in American life. Race was the visible catalyst, not the underlying cause.

The meaning of the earthshaking events in Los Angeles is difficult to grasp because most of us remain trapped in the narrow framework of the dominant liberal and conservative views of race in America, which with its worn-out vocabulary leaves us intellectually debilitated, morally disempowered, and personally depressed. The astonishing disappearance of the event from public dialogue is testimony to just how painful and distressing a serious engagement with race is. Our truncated public discussions of race suppress the best of who and what we are as a people because they fail to confront the complexity of the issue in a candid and critical manner. The predictable pitting of liberals against conservatives, Great Society Democrats against self-help Republicans, reinforces intellectual parochialism and political paralysis.

The liberal notion that more government programs can solve racial problems is simplistic — precisely because it focuses *solely* on the economic dimension. And the conservative idea that what is needed is a change in the moral behavior of poor black urban dwellers (especially poor black men, who, they say, should stay married, support their children, and stop committing so much crime) highlights immoral actions while ignoring public responsibility for the immoral circumstances that haunt our fellow citizens.

The common denominator of these views of race is that each still sees black people as a "problem people," in the words of Dorothy I. Height, president of the National Council of Negro Women, rather than as fellow American citizens with problems. Her words echo the poignant "unasked question" of W. E. B. Du Bois, who, in *The Souls of Black Folk* (1903), wrote:

> They approach me in a half-hesitant sort of way, eye me curiously or compassionately, and then instead of saying directly, How does it feel to be a problem? they say, I know an excellent colored man in my town.... Do not these Southern outrages make your blood boil? At these I smile, or am interested, or reduce the boiling to a simmer, as the occasion may require. To the real question, How does it feel to be a problem? I answer seldom a word.

Nearly a century later, we confine discussions about race in America to the "problems" black people pose for whites, rather than consider what this way of viewing black people reveals about us as a nation.

This paralyzing framework encourages liberals to relieve their guilty   5
consciences by supporting public funds directed at "the problems"; but at the same time, reluctant to exercise principled criticism of black people, liberals deny them the freedom to err. Similarly, conservatives blame the "problems" on black people themselves—and thereby render black social misery invisible or unworthy of public attention.

Hence, for liberals, black people are to be "included" and "integrated" into "our" society and culture, while for conservatives they are to be "well behaved" and "worthy of acceptance" by "our" way of life. Both fail to see that the presence and predicaments of black people are neither additions to nor defections from American life, but rather *constitutive elements of that life.*

To engage in a serious discussion of race in America, we must begin not with the problems of black people but with the flaws of American society—flaws rooted in historic inequalities and longstanding cultural stereotypes. How we set up the terms for discussing racial issues shapes our perception and response to these issues. As long as black people are viewed as a "them," the burden falls on blacks to do all the "cultural" and "moral" work necessary for healthy race relations. The implication is that only certain Americans can define what it means to be American—and the rest must simply "fit in."

The emergence of strong black-nationalist sentiments among blacks, especially among young people, is a revolt against this sense of having to "fit in." The variety of black-nationalist ideologies, from the moderate views of Supreme Court Justice Clarence Thomas in his youth to those of Louis Farrakhan today, rest upon a fundamental truth: white America has been historically weak-willed in ensuring racial justice and has continued to resist fully accepting the humanity of blacks. As long as double standards and differential treatment abound—as long as the rap performer Ice-T is harshly condemned while former Los Angeles Police Chief Daryl F. Gates's antiblack comments are received in polite silence, as long as Dr. Leonard Jeffries's anti-Semitic statements are met with vitriolic outrage while presidential candidate Patrick J. Buchanan's anti-Semitism receives a genteel response—black nationalisms will thrive.

Afrocentrism, a contemporary species of black nationalism, is a gallant yet misguided attempt to define an African identity in a white society perceived to be hostile. It is gallant because it puts black doings and sufferings, not white anxieties and fears, at the center of discussion. It is misguided because—out of fear of cultural hybridization and through silence on the issue of class, retrograde views on black women, gay men, and lesbians, and a reluctance to link race to the common good—it reinforces the narrow discussions about race.

To establish a new framework, we need to begin with a frank ac- 10
knowledgment of the basic humanness and Americanness of each of us.
And we must acknowledge that as a people — *E Pluribus Unum* — we are
on a slippery slope toward economic strife, social turmoil, and cultural
chaos. If we go down, we go down together. The Los Angeles upheaval
forced us to see not only that we are not connected in ways we would like
to be but also, in a more profound sense, that this failure to connect binds
us even more tightly together. The paradox of race in America is that our
common destiny is more pronounced and imperiled precisely when our
divisions are deeper. The Civil War and its legacy speak loudly here. And
our divisions are growing deeper. Today, 86 percent of white suburban
Americans live in neighborhoods that are less than 1 percent black, meaning that the prospects for the country depend largely on how its cities fare
in the hands of a suburban electorate. There is no escape from our interracial interdependence, yet enforced racial hierarchy dooms us as a nation
to collective paranoia and hysteria — the unmaking of any democratic
order.

The verdict in the Rodney King case, which sparked the incidents in
Los Angeles, was perceived to be wrong by the vast majority of Americans. But whites have often failed to acknowledge the widespread mistreatment of black people, especially black men, by law enforcement
agencies, which helped ignite the spark. The verdict was merely the occasion for deep-seated rage to come to the surface. This rage is fed by the
"silent" depression ravaging the country — in which real weekly wages of
all American workers since 1973 have declined nearly 20 percent, while
at the same time wealth has been upwardly distributed.

The exodus of stable industrial jobs from urban centers to cheaper
labor markets here and abroad, housing policies that have created
"chocolate cities and vanilla suburbs" (to use the popular musical artist
George Clinton's memorable phrase), white fear of black crime, and the
urban influx of poor Spanish-speaking and Asian immigrants — all have
helped erode the tax base of American cities just as the federal government has cut its support and programs. The result is unemployment,
hunger, homelessness, and sickness for millions.

And a pervasive spiritual impoverishment grows. The collapse of
meaning in life — the eclipse of hope and absence of love of self and others, the breakdown of family and neighborhood bonds — leads to the social deracination and cultural denudement of urban dwellers, especially
children. We have created rootless, dangling people with little link to the
supportive networks — family, friends, school — that sustain some sense
of purpose in life. We have witnessed the collapse of the spiritual communities that in the past helped Americans face despair, disease, and death
and that transmit through the generations dignity and decency, excellence
and elegance.

The result is lives of what we might call "random nows," of fortuitous and fleeting moments preoccupied with "getting over" — with ac-

quiring pleasure, property, and power by any means necessary. (This is not what Malcolm X meant by this famous phrase.) Post-modern culture is more and more a market culture dominated by gangster mentalities and self-destructive wantonness. This culture engulfs all of us—yet its impact on the disadvantaged is devastating, resulting in extreme violence in everyday life. Sexual violence against women and homicidal assaults by young black men on one another are only the most obvious signs of this empty quest for pleasure, property, and power.

Last, this rage is fueled by a political atmosphere in which images,   15
not ideas, dominate, where politicians spend more time raising money than debating issues. The functions of parties have been displaced by public polls, and politicians behave less as thermostats that determine the climate of opinion than as thermometers registering the public mood. American politics has been rocked by an unleashing of greed among opportunistic public officials—who have followed the lead of their counterparts in the private sphere, where, as of 1989, 1 percent of the population owned 37 percent of the wealth and 10 percent of the population owned 86 percent of the wealth—leading to a profound cynicism and pessimism among the citizenry.

And given the way in which the Republican Party since 1968 has appealed to popular xenophobic images—playing the black, female, and homophobic cards to realign the electorate along race, sex, and sexual-orientation lines—it is no surprise that the notion that we are all part of one garment of destiny is discredited. Appeals to special interests rather than to public interests reinforce this polarization. The Los Angeles upheaval was an expression of utter fragmentation by a powerless citizenry that includes not just the poor but all of us.

What is to be done? How do we capture a new spirit and vision to meet the challenges of the post-industrial city, post-modern culture, and post-party politics?

First, we must admit that the most valuable sources for help, hope, and power consist of ourselves and our common history. As in the ages of Lincoln, Roosevelt, and King, we must look to new frameworks and languages to understand our multilayered crisis and overcome our deep malaise.

Second, we must focus our attention on the public square—the common good that undergirds our national and global destinies. The vitality of any public square ultimately depends on how much we *care* about the quality of our lives together. The neglect of our public infrastructure, for example—our water and sewage systems, bridges, tunnels, highways, subways, and streets—reflects not only our myopic economic policies, which impede productivity, but also the low priority we place on our common life.

The tragic plight of our children clearly reveals our deep disregard for   20
public well-being. About one out of every five children in this country

lives in poverty, including one out of every two black children and two out of every five Hispanic children. Most of our children—neglected by overburdened parents and bombarded by the market values of profit-hungry corporations—are ill-equipped to live lives of spiritual and cultural quality. Faced with these facts, how do we expect ever to constitute a vibrant society?

One essential step is some form of large-scale public intervention to ensure access to basic social goods—housing, food, health care, education, child care, and jobs. We must invigorate the common good with a mixture of government, business, and labor that does not follow any existing blueprint. After a period in which the private sphere has been sacrilized and the public square gutted, the temptation is to make a fetish of the public square. We need to resist such dogmatic swings.

Last, the major challenge is to meet the need to generate new leadership. The paucity of courageous leaders—so apparent in the response to the events in Los Angeles—requires that we look beyond the same elites and voices that recycle the older frameworks. We need leaders—neither saints nor sparkling television personalities—who can situate themselves within a larger historical narrative of this country and our world, who can grasp the complex dynamics of our peoplehood and imagine a future grounded in the best of our past, yet who are attuned to the frightening obstacles that now perplex us. Our ideals of freedom, democracy, and equality must be invoked to invigorate all of us, especially the landless, propertyless, and luckless. Only a visionary leadership that can motivate "the better angels of our nature," as Lincoln said, and activate possibilities for a freer, more efficient, and stable America—only that leadership deserves cultivation and support.

This new leadership must be grounded in grass-roots organizing that highlights democratic accountability. Whoever *our* leaders will be as we approach the twenty-first century, their challenge will be to help Americans determine whether a genuine multiracial democracy can be created and sustained in an era of global economy and a moment of xenophobic frenzy.

Let us hope and pray that the vast intelligence, imagination, humor, and courage of Americans will not fail us. Either we learn a new language of empathy and compassion, or the fire this time will consume us all.

The Reader's Presence

1. West is a Princeton professor and a well-respected figure in the African American religious community. Would you read the essay differently if it were written by an unknown author, or a white author? Why? Does West present evidence for his case? Does ex-

perience or expertise serve as a form of evidence in the piece? Is it convincing? Why or why not?

2. West's argument begins in a fairly accessible manner but subtly becomes complicated. Summarize each paragraph in a sentence, stopping at concepts you do not understand to note your questions. Through what steps does West's argument proceed? What is his final conclusion? Examine your first and last summary statements. How does tracing West's logical process enhance your understanding of his reasoning?

3. What is the relation of the quotation from Ralph Ellison at the beginning of the essay to the rest of West's piece? Compare West's essay with Ellison's "What America Would Be Like without Blacks" (page 363). How might West's piece be seen to respond directly to Ellison's? In his final sentence West alludes to the title of an essay by James Baldwin, "The Fire Next Time." Reread Baldwin's essay in this anthology, "Equal in Paris" (page 597). How might West be responding to Baldwin? Also in the final sentence, West calls for "a new language of empathy and compassion." How does West's sense of compassion compare with that of Martha Nussbaum in her essay on patriotism after September 11, 2001 ("Can Patriotism Be Compassionate?" page 720)? What do West's and Nussbaum's views of America have in common? How do they differ?

117

John Edgar Wideman

The Night I Was Nobody

John Edgar Wideman was born in 1941 in Washington, D.C., and grew up in Homewood, a Pittsburgh ghetto. Much of his fiction is set in Homewood or neighborhoods like it, and it explores issues facing the black urban poor in America. He has published over a dozen books, including Brothers and Keepers *(1984), a memoir that focuses on his brother Robby; the novel* Philadelphia Fire *(1990); The Stories of John Edgar Wideman *(1992);* Fatheralong: A Meditation on Fathers and Sons, Race and Society *(1994); and* Hoop Roots *(2001), a memoir about his obsession with basketball. Other recent novels include* The Cattle Killing *(1996) and* Two Cities *(1998). Wideman was a Rhodes scholar at Oxford University (1963) and a Kent fellow at the University of Iowa Writing Workshop*

(1966). He is also an athlete and a member of the Philadelphia Big Five Basketball Hall of Fame. "The Night I Was Nobody" appeared in Speak My Name: Black Men on Masculinity and the American Dream *(1995).*

When Wideman lived in Cheyenne and taught at the University of Wyoming (1975–1986), an interviewer inquired whether he felt a distance between his life and his fiction. "My particular imagination has always worked well in a kind of exile," he responded. "It fits the insider-outsider view I've always had. It helps to write away from the center of action." Currently he is affiliated with the University of Massachusetts at Amherst and lectures at colleges all over the United States.

On July 4th, the fireworks day, the day for picnics and patriotic speeches, I was in Clovis, New Mexico, to watch my daughter, Jamila, and her team, the Central Massachusetts Cougars, compete in the Junior Olympics Basketball national tourney. During our ten-day visit to Clovis the weather had been bizarre. Hailstones as large as golf balls. Torrents of rain flooding streets hubcap deep. Running through the pelting rain from their van to a gym, Jamila and several teammates cramming through a doorway had looked back just in time to see a funnel cloud touch down a few blocks away. Continuous sheet lightning had shattered the horizon, crackling for hours night and day. Spectacular, off-the-charts weather flexing its muscles, reminding people what little control they had over their lives.

Hail rat-tat-tatting against our windshield our first day in town wasn't exactly a warm welcome, but things got better fast. Clovis people were glad to see us and the mini-spike we triggered in the local economy. Hospitable, generous, our hosts lavished upon us the same hands-on affection and attention to detail that had transformed an unpromising place in the middle of nowhere into a very livable community.

On top of all that, the Cougars were kicking butt, so the night of July 3rd I wanted to celebrate with a frozen margarita. I couldn't pry anybody else away from "Bubba's," the movable feast of beer, chips, and chatter the adults traveling with the Cougars improvised nightly in the King's Inn Motel parking lot, so I drove off alone to find one perfect margarita.

Inside the door of Kelley's Bar and Lounge I was flagged by a guy collecting a cover charge and told I couldn't enter wearing my Malcolm X hat. I asked why; the guy hesitated, conferred for a moment with his partner, then declared that Malcolm X hats were against the dress code. For a split second I thought it might be that *no* caps were allowed in Kelley's. But the door crew and two or three others hanging around the entranceway all wore the billed caps ubiquitous in New Mexico, duplicates of mine, except theirs sported the logos of feed stores and truck stops instead of a silver X.

What careened through my mind in the next couple of minutes is essentially unsayable but included scenes from my own half-century of life as a black man, clips from five hundred years of black/white meetings on   5 slave ships, auction blocks, plantations, basketball courts, in the Supreme Court's marble halls, in beds, back alleys and back rooms, kisses and lynch ropes and contracts for millions of dollars so a black face will grace a cereal box. To tease away my anger I tried joking with folks in other places. Hey, Spike Lee. That hat you gave me on the set of the Malcolm movie in Cairo ain't legal in Clovis.

But nothing about these white guys barring my way was really funny. Part of me wanted to get down and dirty. Curse the suckers. Were they prepared to do battle to keep me and my cap out? Another voice said, Be cool. Don't sully your hands. Walk away and call the cops or a lawyer. Forget these chumps. Sue the owner. Or should I win hearts and minds? Look, fellas, I understand why the X on my cap might offend or scare you. You probably don't know much about Malcolm. The incredible metamorphoses of his thinking, his soul. By the time he was assassinated he wasn't a racist, didn't advocate violence. He was trying to make sense of America's impossible history, free himself, free us from the crippling legacy of race hate and oppression.

While all the above occupied my mind, my body, on its own, had assumed a gunfighter's vigilance, hands ready at sides, head cocked, weight poised, eyes tight and hard on the doorkeeper yet alert to anything stirring on the periphery. Many other eyes, all in white faces, were checking out the entranceway, recognizing the ingredients of a racial incident. Hadn't they witnessed Los Angeles going berserk on their TV screens just a couple months ago? That truck driver beaten nearly to death in the street, those packs of black hoodlums burning and looting? Invisible lines were being drawn in the air, in the sand, invisible chips bristled on shoulders.

The weather again. Our American racial weather, turbulent, unchanging in its changeability, its power to rock us and stun us and smack us from our routines and tear us apart as if none of our cities, our pieties, our promises, our dreams, ever stood a chance of holding on. The racial weather. Outside us, then suddenly, unforgettably, unforgivingly inside, reminding us of what we've only pretended to have forgotten. Our limits, our flaws. The lies and compromises we practice to avoid dealing honestly with the contradictions of race. How dependent we are on luck to survive—*when* we survive—the racial weather.

One minute you're a person, the next moment somebody starts treating you as if you're not. Often it happens just that way, just that suddenly. Particularly if you are a black man in America. Race and racism are a force larger than individuals, more powerful than law or education or government or the church, a force able to wipe these institutions away in the charged moments, minuscule or mountainous, when black and white come face to face. In Watts in 1965, or a few less-than-glorious minutes in Clovis, New Mexico, on the eve of the day that commemorates our country's freedom, our inalienable right as a nation, as citizens, to life, liberty, equality, the pursuit of happiness, those precepts and principles that still look good on paper but are often as worthless as a sheet of newspaper to protect you in a storm if you're a black man at the wrong time in the wrong place.

None of this is news, is it? Not July 3rd in Clovis, when a tiny misfire   10
occurred, or yesterday in your town or tomorrow in mine? But haven't we made progress? Aren't things much better than they used to be? Hasn't enough been done?

We ask the wrong questions when we look around and see a handful of fabulously wealthy black people, a few others entering the middle classes. Far more striking than the positive changes are the abiding patterns and assumptions that have not changed. Not all black people are mired in social pathology, but the bottom rung of the ladder of opportunity (and the space *beneath* the bottom rung) is still defined by the color of the people trapped there—and many *are* still trapped there, no doubt about it, because their status was inherited, determined generation after generation by blood, by color. Once, all black people were legally excluded from full participation in the mainstream. Then fewer. Now only some. But the mechanisms of disenfranchisement that originally separated African Americans from other Americans persist, if not legally, then in the apartheid mind-set, convictions and practices of the majority. The seeds sleep but don't die. Ten who suffer from exclusion today can become ten thousand tomorrow. Racial weather can change that quickly.

How would the bouncer have responded if I'd calmly declared, "This is a free country, I can wear any hat I choose"? Would he thank me for standing up for our shared birthright? Or would he have to admit, if pushed, that American rights belong only to *some* Americans, white Americans?

We didn't get that far in our conversation. We usually don't. The girls' faces pulled me from the edge—girls of all colors, sizes, shapes, gritty kids bonding through hard clean competition. Weren't these guys who didn't like my X cap kids too? Who did they think I was? What did they think they were protecting? I backed out, backed down, climbed in my car and drove away from Kelley's. After all, I didn't want Kelley's. I wanted a frozen margarita and a mellow celebration. So I bought plenty of ice and the ingredients for a margarita and rejoined the festivities at Bubba's. Everybody volunteered to go back with me to Kelley's, but I didn't want to spoil the victory party, taint our daughters' accomplishments, erase the high marks Clovis had earned hosting us.

But I haven't forgotten what happened in Kelley's. I write about it now because this is my country, the country where my sons and daughter are growing up, and your daughters and sons, and the crisis, the affliction, the same ole, same ole waste of life continues across the land, the nightmarish weather of racism, starbursts of misery in the dark.

The statistics of inequality don't demonstrate a "black crisis"—that   15
perspective confuses cause and victim, solutions and responsibility. When the rain falls, it falls on us all. The bad news about black men—that they

die sooner and more violently than white men, are more ravaged by unemployment and lack of opportunity, are more exposed to drugs, disease, broken families, and police brutality, more likely to go to jail than college, more cheated by the inertia and callousness of a government that represents and protects the most needy the least—this is not a "black problem," but a *national* shame affecting us all. Wrenching ourselves free from the long nightmare of racism will require collective determination, countless individual acts of will, gutsy, informed, unselfish. To imagine the terrible cost of not healing ourselves, we must first imagine how good it would feel to be healed.

The Reader's Presence

1. The incident Wideman recounts in this essay takes place on the eve of July Fourth, "the fireworks day, the day for picnics and patriotic speeches" (paragraph 1). Look closely at the modifiers he chooses to describe the Fourth of July. Given the events that took place in Clovis that night, comment on the significance of each phrase. How else might he have described this holiday, and why might he have intentionally discarded those descriptions? Identify—and comment on the effectiveness of—other moments in the essay when Wideman refers to the Fourth of July in related themes.

2. An extended metaphor of weather runs through this essay. Trace the analogy through the comparisons and contrasts Wideman makes or implies. In what specific ways, for instance, are the townsfolk described in paragraph 2 like or unlike the weather? How does this change as the essay progresses? How does racism resemble and differ from the weather? Given this guiding metaphor, does Wideman leave his reader with much hope for an end to racism?

3. Wideman's Malcolm X hat is the object that sparks the inciting incident of the essay. The hat, Wideman tells his reader, was a gift from Spike Lee during the making of the film *Malcolm X* in 1992. Wideman's allusion to the famous African American leader, Malcolm X, is not trivial. What does Malcolm X's "presence" in the essay do for Wideman's argument? Compare Wideman's essay to the excerpt from Malcolm X's autobiography included in this anthology ("Homeboy," page 178). How do these authors express their emotions about racism? How does each writer employ vernacular language (everyday speech), and to what effects? How does each of them justify the recording of their experiences for others to read? Compare how the two discuss ideas of rage, violence, shame, and hope.

118 _____

Patricia J. Williams
Hate Radio

Patricia J. Williams (b. 1951) is a law professor at Columbia University. She was an undergraduate at Wellesley College, received her J.D. from Harvard University, and was a fellow in the prestigious School of Criticism and Theory at Dartmouth College. She is a contributing editor to the Nation, *where she writes a column, "Diary of a Mad Law Professor." She has published* The Alchemy of Race and Rights *(1990),* The Rooster's Egg: On the Persistence of Prejudice *(1995), and* Seeing a Color-Blind Future: The Paradox of Race *(1997). "Hate Radio" appeared in* Ms. *magazine in March/April 1994.*

Three years ago [1991] I stood at my sink, washing the dishes and listening to the radio. I was tuned to rock and roll so I could avoid thinking about the big news from the day before—George Bush had just nominated Clarence Thomas to replace Thurgood Marshall on the Supreme Court. I was squeezing a dot of lemon Joy into each of the wine glasses when I realized that two smoothly radiocultured voices, a man's and a woman's, had replaced the music.

"I think it's a stroke of genius on the president's part," said the female voice.

"Yeah," said the male voice. "Then those blacks, those African Americans, those Negroes—hey 'Negro' is good enough for Thurgood Marshall—whatever, they can't make up their minds [what] they want to be called. I'm gonna call them Blafricans. Black Africans. Yeah, I like it. Blafricans. Then they can get all upset because now the president appointed a Blafrican."

"Yeah, well, that's the way those liberals think. It's just crazy."

"And then after they turn down his nomination the president can say   5
he tried to please 'em, and then he can appoint someone with some intelligence."

Back then, this conversation seemed so horrendously unusual, so singularly hateful, that I picked up a pencil and wrote it down. I was certain

810

that a firestorm of protest was going to engulf the station and purge those foul radio mouths with the good clean soap of social outrage.

I am so naive. When I finally turned on the radio and rolled my dial to where everyone else had been tuned while I was busy watching Cosby reruns, it took me a while to understand that there's a firestorm all right, but not of protest. In the two and a half years since Thomas has assumed his post on the Supreme Court, the underlying assumptions of the conversation I heard as uniquely outrageous have become commonplace, popularly expressed, and louder in volume. I hear the style of that snide polemicism everywhere, among acquaintances, on the street, on television in toned-down versions. It is a crude demagoguery that makes me heartsick. I feel more and more surrounded by that point of view, the assumptions of being without intelligence, the coded epithets, the "Blafrican"-like stand-ins for "nigger," the mocking angry glee, the endless tirades filled with nonspecific, nonempirically based slurs against "these people" or "those minorities" or "feminazis" or "liberals" or "scumbags" or "pansies" or "jerks" or "sleazeballs" or "loonies" or "animals" or "foreigners."

At the same time I am not so naive as to suppose that this is something new. In clearheaded moments I realize I am not listening to the radio anymore, I am listening to a large segment of white America think aloud in ever louder resurgent thoughts that have generations of historical precedent. It's as though the radio has split open like an egg, Morton Downey, Jr.'s[1] clones and Joe McCarthy's[2] ghost spilling out, broken yolks, a great collective of sometimes clever, sometimes small, but uniformly threatened brains—they have all come gushing out. Just as they were about to pass into oblivion, Jack Benny and his humble black side-kick Rochester get resurrected in the ungainly bodies of Howard Stern and his faithful black henchwoman, Robin Quivers. The culture of Amos and Andy has been revived and reassembled in Bob Grant's radio minstrelry and radio newcomer Darryl Gates's[3] sanctimonious imprecations on behalf of decent white people. And in striking imitation of Jesse Helm's nearly forgotten days as a radio host, the far Right has found its undisputed king in the personage of Rush Limbaugh—a polished demagogue with a weekly radio audience of at least twenty million, a television show that vies for ratings with the likes of Jay Leno, a newsletter with a circulation of 380,000, and two best-selling books whose combined sales are closing in on six million copies.

From Churchill to Hitler to the old Soviet Union, it's clear that radio and television have the power to change the course of history, to prosely-

---

[1]*Morton Downey Jr.* was a talk-show host of the 1980s who often ridiculed his guests and took up controversial topics. — EDS.

[2]*U.S. Senator Joseph R. McCarthy* (1909–1957), chair of the House Un-American Activities Committee, hunted and prosecuted suspected Communists and Communist sympathizers in the 1950s. — EDS.

[3]*Darryl Gates* was Los Angeles police commissioner during the Rodney King beating affair of the early 1990s. — EDS.

tize, and to coalesce not merely the good and the noble but the very worst in human nature as well. Likewise, when Orson Welles made his famous radio broadcast "witnessing" the landing of a spaceship full of hostile Martians, the United States ought to have learned a lesson about the power of radio to appeal to mass instincts and incite mass hysteria. Radio remains a peculiarly powerful medium even today, its visual emptiness in a world of six trillion flashing images allowing one of the few remaining playgrounds for the aural subconscious. Perhaps its power is attributable to our need for an oral tradition after all, some conveying of stories, feelings, myths of ancestors, epics of alienation, and the need to rejoin ancestral roots, even ignorant bigoted roots. Perhaps the visual quiescence of radio is related to the popularity of E-mail or electronic networking. Only the voice is made manifest, unmasking worlds that cannot — or dare not? — be seen. Just yet. Nostalgia crystallizing into a dangerous future. The preconscious voice erupting into the expressed, the prime time.

What comes out of the modern radio mouth could be the *Iliad,* the   10
Rubaiyat, the griot's song of our times. If indeed radio is a vessel for the American "Song of Songs," then what does it mean that a manic, adolescent Howard Stern is so popular among radio listeners, that Rush Limbaugh's wittily smooth sadism has gone the way of prime-time television, and that both vie for the number one slot on all the best-selling book lists? What to make of the stories being told by our modern radio evangelists and their tragic unloved chorus of callers? Is it really just a collapsing economy that spawns this drama of grown people sitting around scaring themselves to death with fantasies of black feminist Mexican able-bodied gay soldiers earning $100,000 a year on welfare who are so criminally depraved that Hillary Clinton or the Antichrist-of-the-moment had no choice but to invite them onto the government payroll so they can run the country? The panicky exaggeration reminds me of a child's fear. . . . *And then, and then, a huge lion jumped out of the shadows and was about to gobble me up, and I can't ever sleep again for a whole week.*

As I spin the dial on my radio, I can't help thinking that this stuff must be related to that most poignant of fiber-optic phenomena, phone sex. Aural Sex. Radio Racism with a touch of S & M. High-priest hosts with the power and run-amok ego to discipline listeners, to smack with the verbal back of the hand, to smash the button that shuts you up once and for all. "Idiot!" shouts New York City radio demagogue Bob Grant and then the sound of droning telephone emptiness, the voice of dissent dumped out some trapdoor in aural space.

As I listened to a range of such programs what struck me as the most unifying theme was not merely the specific intolerance on such hot topics as race and gender but a much more general contempt for the world, a verbal stoning of anything different. It is like some unusually violent game of "Simon Says," this mockery and shouting down of callers, this roar of incantations, the insistence on agreement.

But, ah, if you *will* but only agree, what sweet and safe reward, what soft enfolding by a stern and angry radio god. And as an added bonus, the invisible shield of an AM community of fans who are Exactly Like You, to whom you can express, in anonymity, all the filthy stuff you imagine "them" doing to you. The comfort and relief of being able to ejaculate, to those who understand, about the dark imagined excess over-taking, robbing, needing to be held down and taught a good lesson, need-ing to put it in its place before the ravenous demon enervates all that is true and good and pure in this life.

The audience for this genre of radio flagellation is mostly young, white, and male. Two thirds of Rush Limbaugh's audience is male. Ac-cording to *Time* magazine, 75 percent of Howard Stern's listeners are white men. Most of the callers have spent their lives walling themselves off from any real experience with blacks, feminists, lesbians, or gays. In this regard, it is probably true, as former Secretary of Education William Bennett says, that Rush Limbaugh "tells his audience that what you be-lieve inside, you can talk about in the marketplace." Unfortunately, what's "inside" is then mistaken for what's outside, treated as empirical and political reality. The *National Review* extols Limbaugh's conserva-tive leadership as no less than that of Ronald Reagan, and the Republican party provides Limbaugh with books to discuss, stories, angles, and pub-lic support. "People were afraid of censure by gay activists, feminists, en-vironmentalists—now they are not because Rush takes them on," says Bennett.

U.S. history has been marked by cycles in which brands of this or   15
that hatred come into fashion and go out, are unleashed, and then re-strained. If racism, homophobia, jingoism, and woman-hating have been features of national life in pretty much all of modern history, it rather begs the question to spend a lot of time wondering if right-wing radio is a symptom or a cause. For at least four-hundred years, prevail-ing attitudes in the West have considered African Americans less intelli-gent. Recent statistics show that 53 percent of people in the United States agree that blacks and Latinos are less intelligent than whites, and a majority believe that blacks are lazy, violent, welfare-dependent, and unpatriotic.

I think that what has made life more or less tolerable for "out" groups have been those moments in history when those "inside" feel-ings were relatively restrained. In fact, if I could believe that right-wing radio were only about idiosyncratic, singular, rough-hewn individuals thinking those inside thoughts, I'd be much more inclined to agree with Columbia University media expert Everette Dennis, who says that Stern's and Limbaugh's popularity represents the "triumph of the indi-vidual," or with *Time* magazine's bottom line that "the fact that either is seriously considered a threat . . . is more worrisome than Stern or Limbaugh will ever be." If what I was hearing had even a tad more to do with real oppressions, with real white *and* black levels of joblessness and homelessness, or with the real problems of real white men, then I wouldn't have bothered to slog my way through hours of Howard Stern's miserable obsessions.

Yet at the heart of my anxiety is the worry that Stern, Limbaugh, Grant, et al. represent the very antithesis of individualism's triumph. As the *National Review* said of Limbaugh's ascent, "It was a feat not only of the loudest voice but also of a keen political brain to round up, as Rush did, the media herd and drive them into the conservative corral." When asked about his political aspirations, Bob Grant gloated to the *Washington Post,* "I think I would make rather a good dictator."

The polemics of right-wing radio are putting nothing less than hate onto the airwaves, into the marketplace, electing it to office, teaching it in schools, and exalting it as freedom. What worries me is the increasing-to-constant commerce of retribution, control, and lashing out, fed not by fact but fantasy. What worries me is the re-emergence, more powerfully than at any time since the institution of Jim Crow, of a sociocentered self that excludes, "the likes of," well, me for example, from the civic circle and that would rob me of my worth and claim and identity as a citizen. As the *Economist* rightly observes, "Mr. Limbaugh takes a mass market—white, mainly male, middle-class, ordinary America—and talks to it as an endangered minority."

I worry about this identity whose external reference is a set of beliefs, ethics, and practices that excludes, restricts, and acts in the world on me, or mine, as the perceived if not real enemy. I am acutely aware of losing *my* mythic individualism to the surface shapes of my mythic group fearsomeness as black, as female, as left wing. "I" merge not fluidly but irretrievably into a category of "them." I become a suspect self, a moving target of loathsome properties, not merely different but dangerous. And that worries me a lot.

What happens in my life with all this translated license, this permission to be uncivil? What happens to the social space that was supposed at the sweet mountaintop of the civil rights movement's trail? Can I get a seat on the bus without having to be reminded that I *should* be standing? Did the civil rights movement guarantee us nothing more than to use public accommodations while surrounded by raving lunatic bigots? "They didn't beat this idiot [Rodney King] enough," says Howard Stern.   20

Not long ago I had the misfortune to hail a taxicab in which the driver was listening to Howard Stern undress some woman. After some blocks, I had to get out. I was, frankly, afraid to ask the driver to turn it off—not because I was afraid of "censoring" him, which seems to be the only thing people will talk about anymore, but because the driver was stripping me too, as he leered through the rearview mirror. "Something the matter?" he demanded, as I asked him to pull over and let me out well short of my destination. (I'll spare you the full story of what happened from there—trying to get another cab, as the cabbies stopped for all the white businessmen who so much as scratched their heads near the curb; a nice young white man, seeing my plight, giving me his cab, having to thank him, he hero, me saved-but-humiliated, cabdriver pissed and surly. I fight my way to my destination, finally arriving in bad mood, militant black woman, cranky feminazi.)

When Yeltsin blared rock music at his opponents holed up in the parliament building in Moscow, in imitation of the U.S. Marines trying to torture Manuel Noriega in Panama, all I could think of was that it must be like being trapped in a crowded subway car when all the portable stereos are tuned to Bob Grant or Howard Stern. With Howard Stern's voice a tinny, screeching backdrop, with all the faces growing dreamily mean as though some soporifically evil hallucinogen were gushing into their bloodstreams, I'd start begging to surrender.

Surrender to what? Surrender to the laissez-faire resegregation that is the metaphoric significance of the hundreds of "Rush rooms" that have cropped up in restaurants around the country; rooms broadcasting Limbaugh's words, rooms for your listening pleasure, rooms where bigots can capture the purity of a Rush-only lunch counter, rooms where all those unpleasant others just "choose" not to eat? Surrender to the naughty luxury of a room in which a Ku Klux Klan meeting could take place in orderly, First Amendment fashion? Everyone's "free" to come in (and a few of you outsiders do), but mostly the undesirable nonconformists are gently repulsed away. It's a high-tech world of enhanced choice. Whites choose mostly to sit in the Rush room. Feminists, blacks, lesbians, and gays "choose" to sit elsewhere. No need to buy black votes, you just pay them not to vote; no need to insist on white-only schools, you just sell the desirability of black-only schools. Just sit back and watch it work, like those invisible shock shields that keep dogs cowering in their own backyards.

How real is the driving perception behind all the Sturm und Drang of this genre of radio-harangue — the perception that white men are an oppressed minority, with no power and no opportunity in the land that they made great? While it is true that power and opportunity are shrinking for all but the very wealthy in this country (and would that Limbaugh would take that issue on), the fact remains that white men are still this country's most privileged citizens and market actors. To give just a small example, according to the *Wall Street Journal,* blacks were the only racial group to suffer a net job loss during the 1990–91 economic downturn at the companies reporting to the Equal Employment Opportunity Commission. Whites, Latinos, and Asians, meanwhile, gained thousands of jobs. While whites gained 71,144 jobs at these companies, Latinos gained 60,040, Asians gained 55,104, and blacks lost 59,479. If every black were hired in the United States tomorrow, the numbers would not be sufficient to account for white men's expanding balloon of fear that they have been specifically dispossessed by African Americans.

Given deep patterns of social segregation and general ignorance of   25
history, particularly racial history, media remain the principal source of

most Americans' knowledge of each other. Media can provoke violence or induce passivity. In San Francisco, for example, a radio show on KMEL called *Street Soldiers* has taken this power as a responsibility with great consequence: "Unquestionably," writes Ken Auletta in the *New Yorker,* "the show has helped avert violence. When a Samoan teenager was slain, apparently by Filipino gang members, in a drive-by shooting, the phones lit up with calls from Samoans wanting to tell [the hosts] they would not rest until they had exacted revenge. Threats filled the air for a couple of weeks. Then the dead Samoan's father called in, and, in a poignant exchange, the father said he couldn't tolerate the thought of more young men senselessly slaughtered. There would be no retaliation, he vowed. And there was none." In contrast, we must wonder at the phenomenon of the very powerful leadership of the Republican party, from Ronald Reagan to Robert Dole to William Bennett, giving advice, counsel, and friendship to Rush Limbaugh's passionate divisiveness.

The outright denial of the material crisis at every level of U.S. society, most urgently in black inner-city neighborhoods but facing us all, is a kind of political circus, dissembling as it feeds the frustrations of the moment. We as a nation can no longer afford to deal with such crises by *imagining* an excess of bodies, of babies, of job-stealers, of welfare mothers, of overreaching immigrants, of too-powerful (Jewish, in whispers) liberal Hollywood, of lesbians and gays, of gang members ("gangsters" remain white, and no matter what the atrocity, less vilified than "gang members," who are black), of Arab terrorists, and uppity women. The reality of our social poverty far exceeds these scapegoats. This right-wing backlash resembles, in form if not substance, phenomena like anti-Semitism in Poland: There aren't but a handful of Jews left in that whole country, but the giant balloon of heated anti-Semitism flourishes apace, Jews blamed for the world's evils.

The overwhelming response to right-wing excesses in the United States has been to seek an odd sort of comfort in the fact that the First Amendment is working so well that you can't suppress this sort of thing. Look what's happened in Eastern Europe. Granted. So let's not talk about censorship or the First Amendment for the next ten minutes. But in Western Europe, where fascism is rising at an appalling rate, suppression is hardly the problem. In Eastern and Western Europe as well as the United States, we must begin to think just a little bit about the fiercely coalescing power of media to spark mistrust, to fan it into forest fires of fear, and revenge. We must begin to think about the levels of national and social complacence in the face of such resolute ignorance. We must ask ourselves what the expected result is, not of censorship or suppression but of so much encouragement, so much support, so much investment in the fashionability of hate. What future is it that we are designing with the devotion of such tremendous resources to the disgraceful propaganda of bigotry?

The Reader's Presence

1. Reread Williams's opening paragraph. Why do you think she begins her essay this way? What does the paragraph tell you about her? How does it prepare you for the rest of the essay? Suppose Williams began with an anecdote from her experience in law or teaching. Would the effect differ? How and why?

2. Williams writes: "It's clear that radio and television have the power to change the course of history, to proselytize, and to coalesce not merely the good and the noble, but the very worst in human nature as well" (paragraph 9). What is the significance of this statement relative to Williams's general argument? Williams cites the Orson Welles example. What correlation is implied between this and the "hate mongers" of radio?

3. Compare Williams's argument about "the fiercely coalescing power of media" (paragraph 27) to that of Marie Winn in "TV Addiction" (page 581). How do the two essays compare in substance (that is, in the points they make) and in structure and style (that is, in the way they build their cases)? Whose argument do you find most persuasive, and why? How might you write an essay on a similar theme? What governs your decisions?

119

Terry Tempest Williams

The Clan of One-Breasted Women

The environmentalist and writer Terry Tempest Williams (b. 1953) lives in Utah, where she is active in the movement to expand federally protected wilderness areas. She has been a professor of English at the University of Utah and naturalist-in-residence at the Utah Museum of Natural History. In Refuge: An Unnatural History of Family and Place *(1991), she documents the epidemic of cancer caused by nuclear weapons tested in Utah during the 1950s and meditates upon the meaning of this tragedy for her family. "The Clan of One-Breasted Women" appears in* Refuge. *Her first book,* Pieces of a White Shell: A Journey to Navajoland *(1984), received a Southwest Book Award. Other books include,* Coyote's Canyon *(1989),* An Unspoken Hunger: Stories from the Field *(1994),* Desert Quartet *(1995),* Leap *(2000), and* Red: Passion and Patience in the Desert *(2001). She also coedited* Testimony: Writers of the West Speak on Behalf of Utah

Wilderness *(1996) and* New Genesis: Mormons Writing on the Environment
(1999).
    *Reflecting upon her motivation for writing about her personal experience
with cancer, Williams notes, "Perhaps I am telling this story in an attempt to heal
myself, to confront what I do not know, to create a path for myself with the idea
that 'memory is the only way home.'"*

    I belong to a Clan of One-Breasted Women. My mother, my grand-
mothers, and six aunts have all had mastectomies. Seven are dead. The
two who survive have just completed rounds of chemotherapy and radiation.
    I've had my own problems: two biopsies for breast cancer and a small
tumor between my ribs diagnosed as a "borderline malignancy."
    This is my family history.
    Most statistics tell us that breast cancer is genetic, hereditary, with
rising percentages attached to fatty diets, childlessness, or becoming pregnant after thirty. What they don't say is that living in Utah may be the
greatest hazard of all.
    We are a Mormon family with roots in Utah since 1847. The "word   5
of wisdom" in my family aligned us with good foods—no coffee, no tea,
tobacco, or alcohol. For the most part, our women were finished having
their babies by the time they were thirty. And only one faced breast cancer prior to 1960. Traditionally, as a group of people, Mormons have a
low rate of cancer.
    Is our family a cultural anomaly? The truth is, we didn't think about
it. Those who did, usually the men, simply said, "bad genes." The
women's attitude was stoic. Cancer was part of life. On February 16,
1971, the eve of my mother's surgery, I accidentally picked up the telephone and overheard her ask my grandmother what she could expect.
    "Diane, it is one of the most spiritual experiences you will ever en-
counter."
    I quietly put down the receiver.
    Two days later, my father took my brothers and me to the hospital to
visit her. She met us in the lobby in a wheelchair. No bandages were
visible. I'll never forget her radiance, the way she held herself in a purple
velvet robe, and how she gathered us around her.
    "Children, I am fine. I want you to know I felt the arms of God   10
around me."
    We believed her. My father cried. Our mother, his wife, was thirty-
eight years old.
    A little over a year after Mother's death, Dad and I were having din-
ner together. He had just returned from St. George, where the Tempest
Company was completing the gas lines that would service southern Utah.
He spoke of his love for the country, the sandstoned landscape, bare-
boned and beautiful. He had just finished hiking the Kolob trail in Zion

National Park. We got caught up in reminiscing, recalling with fondness our walk up Angel's Landing on his fiftieth birthday and the years our family had vacationed there.

Over dessert, I shared a recurring dream of mine. I told my father that for years, as long as I could remember, I saw this flash of light in the night in the desert—that this image had so permeated my being that I could not venture south without seeing it again, on the horizon, illuminating buttes and mesas.

"You did see it," he said.

"Saw what?"   15

"The bomb. The cloud. We were driving home from Riverside, California. You were sitting on Diane's lap. She was pregnant. In fact, I remember the day, September 7, 1957. We had just gotten out of the Service. We were driving north, past Las Vegas. It was an hour or so before dawn, when this explosion went off. We not only heard it, but felt it. I thought the oil tanker in front of us had blown up. We pulled over and suddenly, rising from the desert floor, we saw it, clearly, this golden-stemmed cloud, the mushroom. The sky seemed to vibrate with an eerie pink glow. Within a few minutes, a light ash was raining on the car."

I stared at my father.

"I thought you knew that," he said. "It was a common occurrence in the fifties."

It was at this moment that I realized the deceit I had been living under. Children growing up in the American Southwest, drinking contaminated milk from contaminated cows, even from the contaminated breasts of their mothers, my mother—members, years later, of the Clan of One-Breasted Women.

It is a well-known story in the Desert West, "The Day We Bombed   20
Utah," or more accurately, the years we bombed Utah: above ground atomic testing in Nevada took place from January 27, 1951 through July 11, 1962. Not only were the winds blowing north covering "low-use segments of the population" with fallout and leaving sheep dead in their tracks but the climate was right. The United States of the 1950s was red, white, and blue. The Korean War was raging. McCarthyism[1] was rampant. Ike[2] was it, and the cold war was hot. If you were against nuclear testing, you were for a communist regime.

Much has been written about this "American nuclear tragedy." Public health was secondary to national security. The Atomic Energy Commissioner, Thomas Murray, said, "Gentlemen, we must not let anything interfere with this series of tests, nothing."

---

[1]*McCarthyism:* The practice of publicizing accusations of political disloyalty or subversion without sufficient regard to evidence. Associated with Senator Joseph McCarthy (1908–1957).—EDS.

[2]*Ike:* President Dwight D. Eisenhower (1890–1969) was known as "Ike."—EDS.

Again and again, the American public was told by its government, in spite of burns, blisters, and nausea, "It has been found that the tests may be conducted with adequate assurance of safety under conditions prevailing at the bombing reservations." Assuaging public fears was simply a matter of public relations. "Your best action," an Atomic Energy Commission booklet read, "is not to be worried about fallout." A news release typical of the times stated, "We find no basis for concluding that harm to any individual has resulted from radioactive fallout."

On August 30, 1979, during Jimmy Carter's presidency, a suit was filed, *Irene Allen v. The United States of America*. Mrs. Allen's case was the first on an alphabetical list of twenty-four test cases, representative of nearly twelve hundred plaintiffs seeking compensation from the United States government for cancers caused by nuclear testing in Nevada.

Irene Allen lived in Hurricane, Utah. She was the mother of five children and had been widowed twice. Her first husband, with their two oldest boys, had watched the tests from the roof of the local high school. He died of leukemia in 1956. Her second husband died of pancreatic cancer in 1978.

In a town meeting conducted by Utah Senator Orrin Hatch, shortly   25
before the suit was filed, Mrs. Allen said, "I am not blaming the government, I want you to know that, Senator Hatch. But I thought if my testimony could help in any way so this wouldn't happen again to any of the generations coming up after us . . . I am happy to be here this day to bear testimony of this."

God-fearing people. This is just one story in an anthology of thousands.

On May 10, 1984, Judge Bruce S. Jenkins handed down his opinion. Ten of the plaintiffs were awarded damages. It was the first time a federal court had determined that nuclear tests had been the cause of cancers. For the remaining fourteen test cases, the proof of causation was not sufficient. In spite of the split decision, it was considered a landmark ruling. It was not to remain so for long.

In April 1987, the Tenth Circuit Court of Appeals overturned Judge Jenkins's ruling on the ground that the United States was protected from suit by the legal doctrine of sovereign immunity, a centuries-old idea from England in the days of absolute monarchs.

In January 1988, the Supreme Court refused to review the Appeals Court decision. To our court system it does not matter whether the United States government was irresponsible, whether it lied to its citizens, or even that citizens died from the fallout of nuclear testing. What matters is that our government is immune: "The King can do no wrong."

In Mormon culture, authority is respected, obedience is revered, and   30
independent thinking is not. I was taught as a young girl not to "make waves" or "rock the boat."

"Just let it go," Mother would say. "You know how you feel, that's what counts."

For many years, I have done just that—listened, observed, and quietly formed my own opinions, in a culture that rarely asks questions because it has all the answers. But one by one, I have watched the women in my family die common, heroic deaths. We sat in waiting rooms hoping for good news, but always receiving the bad. I cared for them, bathed their scarred bodies, and kept their secrets. I watched beautiful women become bald as Cytoxan, cisplatin, and Adriamycin were injected into their veins. I held their foreheads as they vomited green-black bile, and I shot them with morphine when the pain became inhuman. In the end, I witnessed their last peaceful breaths, becoming a midwife to the rebirth of their souls.

The price of obedience has become too high.

The fear and inability to question authority that ultimately killed rural communities in Utah during atmospheric testing of atomic weapons is the same fear I saw in my mother's body. Sheep. Dead sheep. The evidence is buried.

I cannot prove that my mother, Diane Dixon Tempest, or my grand- 35 mothers, Lettie Romney Dixon and Kathryn Blackett Tempest, along with my aunts developed cancer from nuclear fallout in Utah. But I can't prove they didn't.

My father's memory was correct. The September blast we drove through in 1957 was part of Operation Plumbbob, one of the most intensive series of bomb tests to be initiated. The flash of light in the night in the desert, which I had always thought was a dream, developed into a family nightmare. It took fourteen years, from 1957 to 1971, for cancer to manifest in my mother—the same time, Howard L. Andrews, an authority in radioactive fallout at the National Institutes of Health, says radiation cancer requires to become evident. The more I learn about what it means to be a "downwinder," the more questions I drown in.

What I do know, however, is that as a Mormon woman of the fifth generation of Latter-day Saints, I must question everything, even if it means losing my faith, even if it means becoming a member of a border tribe among my own people. Tolerating blind obedience in the name of patriotism or religion ultimately takes our lives.

When the Atomic Energy Commission described the country north of the Nevada Test Site as "virtually uninhabited desert terrain," my family and the birds at Great Salt Lake were some of the "virtual uninhabitants."

One night, I dreamed women from all over the world circled a blazing fire in the desert. They spoke of change, how they hold the moon in their bellies and wax and wane with its phases. They mocked the presumption of even-tempered beings and made promises that they would never fear the witch inside themselves. The women danced wildly as sparks broke away from the flames and entered the night sky as stars.

And they sang a song given to them by Shoshone grandmothers: 40

Ah ne nah, nah	Consider the rabbits
nin nah nah—	How gently they walk on the earth—
ah ne nah, nah	Consider the rabbits
nin nah nah—	How gently they walk on the earth—
Nyaga mutzi	We remember them
oh ne nay—	We can walk gently also—
Nyaga mutzi	We remember them
oh ne nay	We can walk gently also

The women danced and drummed and sang for weeks, preparing themselves for what was to come. They would reclaim the desert for the sake of their children, for the sake of the land.

A few miles downwind from the fire circle, bombs were being tested. Rabbits felt the tremors. Their soft leather pads on paws and feet recognized the shaking sands, while the roots of mesquite and sage were smoldering. Rocks were hot from the inside out and dust devils hummed unnaturally. And each time there was another nuclear test, ravens watched the desert heave. Stretch marks appeared. The land was losing its muscle.

The women couldn't bear it any longer. They were mothers. They had suffered labor pains but always under the promise of birth. The red hot pains beneath the desert promised death only, as each bomb became a stillborn. A contract had been made and broken between human beings and the land. A new contract was being drawn by the women, who understood the fate of the earth as their own.

Under the cover of darkness, ten women slipped under a barbed-wire fence and entered the contaminated country. They were trespassing. They walked toward the town of Mercury, in moonlight, taking their cues from coyote, kit fox, antelope squirrel, and quail. They moved quietly and deliberately through the maze of Joshua trees. When a hint of daylight appeared they rested, drinking tea and sharing their rations of food. The women closed their eyes. The time had come to protest with the heart, that to deny one's genealogy with the earth was to commit treason against one's soul.

At dawn, the women draped themselves in mylar, wrapping long streamers of silver plastic around their arms to blow in the breeze. They wore clear masks, that became the faces of humanity. And when they arrived at the edge of Mercury, they carried all the butterflies of a summer day in their wombs. They paused to allow their courage to settle.

The town that forbids pregnant women and children to enter because   45
of radiation risks was asleep. The women moved through the streets as winged messengers, twirling around each other in slow motion, peeking inside homes and watching the easy sleep of men and women. They were astonished by such stillness and periodically would utter a shrill note or low cry just to verify life.

The residents finally awoke to these strange apparitions. Some simply stared. Others called authorities, and in time, the women were apprehended by wary soldiers dressed in desert fatigues. They were taken to a

white, square building on the edge of Mercury. When asked who they
were and why they were there, the women replied, "We are mothers and
we have come to reclaim the desert for our children."

The soldiers arrested them. As the ten women were blindfolded and
handcuffed, they began singing:

You can't forbid us everything
You can't forbid us to think—
You can't forbid our tears to flow
And you can't stop the songs that we sing.

The women continued to sing louder and louder, until they heard the
voices of their sisters moving across the mesa:

Ah ne nah, nah
nin nah nah—
Ah ne nah, nah
nin nah nah—
Nyaga mutzi
oh ne nay—
Nyaga mutzi
oh ne nay—

"Call for reinforcements," one soldier said.

"We have," interrupted one woman, "we have—and you have no
idea of our numbers."

I crossed the line at the Nevada Test Site and was arrested with nine
other Utahns for trespassing on military lands. They are still conducting
nuclear tests in the desert. Ours was an act of civil disobedience. But as I
walked toward the town of Mercury, it was more than a gesture of peace.
It was a gesture on behalf of the Clan of One-Breasted Women.

As one officer cinched the handcuffs around my wrists, another   50
frisked my body. She found a pen and a pad of paper tucked inside my
left boot.

"And these?" she asked sternly.

"Weapons," I replied.

Our eyes met. I smiled. She pulled the leg of my trousers back over
my boot.

"Step forward, please," she said as she took my arm.

We were booked under an afternoon sun and bused to Tonopah,   55
Nevada. It was a two-hour ride. This was familiar country. The Joshua
trees standing their ground had been named by my ancestors, who believed they looked like prophets pointing west to the Promised Land.
These were the same trees that bloomed each spring, flowers appearing
like white flames in the Mojave. And I recalled a full moon in May, when
Mother and I had walked among them, flushing out mourning doves
and owls.

The bus stopped short of town. We were released.

The officials thought it was a cruel joke to leave us stranded in the desert with no way to get home. What they didn't realize was that we were home, soul-centered and strong, women who recognized the sweet smell of sage as fuel for our spirits.

The Reader's Presence

1. Paragraph 3 reads, "This is my family history." Which parts of Williams's essay are particular to her family, and what do they add to the larger social history of her time and place? How does her family's religion, Mormonism, play into the family history? What does she gain by drawing on the earlier spiritual tradition of the Shoshones, which is rooted in the same geographical area? What other "families," besides her nuclear and extended family, might Williams belong to?

2. Examine carefully—and discuss in detail—the roles of dream and reality in this essay. Characterize the power of each. Consider also the relationship between dream and nightmare. How do you read the "dream" Williams recounts in paragraph 39 and following? Characterize the relationship between that dream and the "civil disobedience" she recounts in the following section (paragraph 49 and following).

3. Discuss the role of language in the essay. You might begin by examining instances of what could be termed Orwellian doublespeak. (In this context you might refer to Orwell's "Politics and the English Language" on page 481.) What are the dangers and ironies inherent in this euphemistic, obfuscating prose? Examine carefully Williams's own language and that of the Shoshones, as well as the written doctrines and documents to which Williams alludes or refers. Finally, reread paragraph 52, where she refers to her pen and paper as "weapons." How effective a weapon is this essay itself in the battle for social justice?

Part V

The Voices of Fiction: Ten Modern Short Stories

120

Sherman Alexie

The Toughest Indian in the World

When asked in an interview about the recurring theme of Native American identity in his work, Sherman Alexie responded: "Literature is all about the search for identity, regardless of ethnicity." The following selection is the title story of Alexie's recent collection of short stories The Toughest Indian in the World *(2000). Of this story, Alexie has commented "In 'The Toughest Indian,' the journalist's primary struggle is not ethnic identity, but his sexuality. I don't think he knows any of his identities. One of the points I was trying to make in that story is that being Indian is just part of who we are."*

For additional information on Sherman Alexie, see pages 61 and 836.

Being a Spokane Indian, I only pick up Indian hitchhikers. I learned this particular ceremony from my father, a Coeur d'Aléne, who always stopped for those twentieth-century aboriginal nomads who refused to believe the salmon were gone. I don't know what they believed in exactly, but they wore hope like a bright shirt. My father never taught me about hope. From an early age, I was told that our salmon would never come back, and though such lessons may seem cruel, I learned to cover my heart in a crowd of white people.

"They'll kill you if they get the chance," my father said. "Love you or hate you, white people will shoot you in the heart. Even after all these years, they'll still smell the salmon on you, the dead salmon, and that will make white people dangerous."

All of us, Indian and white, are haunted by salmon.

When I was a boy, I leaned over the edge of one dam or another — perhaps Long Lake or Little Falls or the great gray dragon known as the Grand Coulee — and watched the ghosts of salmon rise from the water to the sky and become constellations. Believe me, for most Indians stars are nothing more than white tombstones scattered across a dark graveyard.

But the Indian hitchhikers my father picked up refused to admit the   5
existence of sky, let alone the possibility that salmon might be stars. They were common people who believed only in the thumb and the foot. My

827

father envied those simple Indian hitchhikers. He wanted to change their minds about salmon; he wanted to break open their hearts and see the future in their blood, because he loved them.

Driving along one highway or another, my father would point out a hitchhiker standing beside the road a mile or two in the distance.

"Indian," he would say, and he was never wrong, though I could never tell if the distant figure was male or female, let alone Indian or not.

If that distant figure happened to be white, my father would drive by without comment. That was how I learned to be silent in the presence of white people. The silence is not about hate or pain or fear. Indians just like to believe that white people will vanish, perhaps explode into smoke, if they are ignored enough times. Perhaps a thousand white families are still waiting for their sons and daughters to return home, and can't recognize them when they float back as morning fog.

"Indian," my father would say again as we approached one of those dream filled hitchhikers. Hell, those hitchhikers' faces grew red and puffy with the weight of their dreams.

"We better stop," my mother would say from the passenger seat. She   10
was one of those Spokane women who always wore a purple bandanna tied tightly around their heads. These days, her bandanna is usually red. There are reasons, motives, traditions behind the choice of color, but my mother keeps them secret.

"Make room," my father would say to my siblings and me as we sat on the floor in the cavernous passenger area of our blue van. We sat on carpet samples because my father had torn out the seats in a sober rage not long after he bought the van from a crazy white man.

I have three brothers and three sisters now. Back then, I had four of each. I missed one of the funerals and cried myself sick during the other one.

"Make room," my father would say again—he said everything twice and only then would we scramble to make space for the Indian hitchhiker.

Of course, it was easy enough to make room for one hitchhiker, but Indians usually travel in packs. Once or twice, we picked up entire all-Indian basketball teams, along with their coaches, girlfriends, and cousins. Fifteen, twenty Indian strangers squeezed into the back of a blue van with nine wide-eyed Indian kids.

Back in those days, I loved the smell of Indians, and of Indian hitch-   15
hikers in particular. They were usually in some stage of drunkenness, often in need of soap and towel, and always ready to sing.

Oh, the songs! Indian blues bellowed at the highest volumes. We called them "49s," those cross-cultural songs that combined Indian lyrics and rhythms with country-and-Western and blues melodies. It seemed that every Indian knew all the lyrics to every Hank Williams song ever recorded. Hank was our Jesus, Patsy Cline was our Madonna, and Freddy Fender, George Jones, Conway Twitty, Loretta Lynn, Tammy

Wynette, Charlie Pride, Ronnie Milsap, Tanya Tucker, Marty Robbins, Johnny Horton, Donna Fargo, and Charlie Rich were our disciples.

We all know that nostalgia is dangerous, but I remember those days with a clear conscience. We live in different days now, and there aren't as many Indian hitchhikers as there used to be.

Today, I drive my own car, a 1998 Toyota Camry, the best-selling automobile in the United States, and therefore the one most often stolen. *Consumer Reports* has named it the most reliable family sedan for sixteen years running, and I believe them.

With my Camry I pick up three or four Indian hitchhikers a week. Mostly men. They're usually headed home, back to their reservations or somewhere close to their reservations. Indians hardly ever travel in a straight line, so a Crow Indian might hitchhike west when his reservation is back east in Montana. He has some people to see in Seattle, he might explain if I ever asked him. But I never ask Indians their reasons for hitchhiking. They were Indian, walking, raising a thumb, and I was there to pick them up.

At the newspaper where I work, my fellow reporters think I'm crazy   20
to pick up hitchhikers. They're all white and never stop to pick up anybody, let alone an Indian. After all, we're the ones who write the stories and headlines: "HITCHHIKER KILLS HUSBAND AND WIFE," "MISSING GIRL'S BODY FOUND," "RAPIST STRIKES AGAIN." If I really tried, maybe I could explain to them why I pick up any Indian, but who wants to try? Instead, if they ask I just give them a smile and turn back to my computer. My coworkers smile back and laugh loudly. They're always laughing loudly at me, at one another, at themselves, at goofy typos in the newspaper, at the idea of hitchhikers.

I dated one of them for a few months. Cindy. She covered the local courts: speeding tickets and divorces, drunk driving and embezzlement. Cindy firmly believed in the who-what-where-when-why-and-how of journalism. In daily conversation, she talked like she was writing the lead of her latest story. Hell, she talked like that in bed.

"How does that feel?" I would ask, quite possibly becoming the only Indian man who has ever asked that question.

"I love it when you touch me there," she would answer. "But it would help if you rubbed it about thirty per cent lighter and with your thumb instead of your middle finger. And could you maybe turn the radio to a different station? KYZY would be good. I feel like soft jazz will work better for me right now. A minor chord, a C or G flat, or something like that. O.K., honey?"

During lovemaking, I would get so exhausted by the size of her vocabulary that I would fall asleep before my orgasm, continue pumping away as if I were awake, and then regain consciousness with a sudden start when I finally did come, more out of reflex than passion.

Don't get me wrong. Cindy was a good one, cute and smart, funny as   25 hell, a good catch no matter how you define it, but she was also one of those white women who only date brown-skinned guys. Indians like me, black dudes, Mexicans, even a few Iranians. I started to feel like a trophy, or like one of those entries in a personal ad. I asked Cindy why she never dated pale boys.

"White guys bore me," she said. "All they want to talk about is their fathers."

"What do brown guys talk about?" I asked her.

"Their mothers," she said and laughed, then promptly left me for a public defender who was half Japanese and half African—a combination that left Cindy dizzy with the interracial possibilities.

Since Cindy, I haven't dated anyone. I live in my studio apartment with the ghosts of two dogs. Felix and Oscar, and a laptop computer stuffed with bad poems, the aborted halves of three novels, and some three-paragraph personality pieces I wrote for the newspaper.

I'm a features writer, and an Indian at that, so I get all the shit jobs.　30
Not the dangerous shit jobs or the monotonous shit jobs. No, I get to write the articles designed to please the eye, ear, and heart. And there is no journalism more soul-endangering to write than journalism that aims to please.

So it was with reluctance that I hopped into my car last week and headed down Highway 2 to write some damn pleasant story about some damn pleasant people. Then I saw the Indian hitchhiker standing beside the road. He looked the way Indian hitchhikers usually look. Long, straggly black hair. Brown eyes and skin. Missing a couple of teeth. Bad complexion. Crooked nose that had been broken more than once. Big, misshapen ears. A few whiskers masquerading as a mustache. Even before he climbed into my car, I could tell he was tough. He had some serious muscles that threatened to rip through his blue jeans and denim jacket. When he was in the car, I could see his hands up close and they told the whole story. His fingers were twisted into weird shapes, and his knuckles were covered with layers of scar tissue.

"Jeez," I said. "You're a fighter, enit?"

The hitchhiker looked down at his hands, flexed them into fists. I could tell it hurt him to do that.

"Yeah," he said.

I pulled back onto the highway, looking over my shoulder to check　35
my blind spot.

"What tribe are you?" I asked him.

"Lummi," he said. "What about you?"

"Spokane."

"I know some Spokanes. Haven't seen them in a long time."

He clutched his backpack in his lap like he didn't want to let it go for　40
nothing. He reached inside a pocket and pulled out a piece of deer jerky. I recognized it by the smell.

"Want some?" he asked.

"Sure."

It had been a long time since I'd eaten jerky. The salt, the gamy taste. I felt as Indian as Indian gets, driving down the road in a fast car, chewing on jerky, talking to an indigenous fighter.

"Where you headed?" I asked.

"Home. Back to the rez."   45

I nodded my head as I passed a big truck. The driver gave us a smile as we went by. I tooted the horn.

"Big truck," said the fighter.

I haven't lived on my reservation for years. But I live in Spokane, which is only an hour's drive from the rez. Still, I hardly ever go there. I don't know why not. I don't think about it much, I guess, but my mom and dad still live in the same house where I grew up. My brothers and sisters, too. The ghosts of my two dead siblings share an apartment in the converted high school. Believe me. It's just a local call from Spokane to the rez, so I talk to all of them once or twice a week. Smoke signals courtesy of the U.S. West Communications. Sometimes they call me up to talk about the stories they've seen that I write for the newspaper. Pet pigs and support groups and science fairs. Once in a while, I used to fill in for the obituaries writer when she was sick. Then she died, and I had to write her obituary.

"How far you going?" asked the fighter, meaning how much closer was he going to get to his reservation than he was now.

"Up to Wenatchee," I said. "I've got some people to interview there."   50

"Interview? What for?"

"I'm a reporter. I work for the newspaper."

"No," said the fighter, looking at me like I was stupid for thinking he was stupid. "I mean, what's the story about?"

"Oh, not much. There's two sets of twins who work for the fire department. Human interest stuff, you know?"

"Two sets of twins, enit? That's weird."   55

He offered me more deer jerky, but I was too thirsty from the salty meat, so I offered him a Pepsi instead. It's a little known fact that Indians can be broken up into two distinct groups: Pepsi tribes and Coke tribes.

"Don't mind if I do," he said. He was obviously a member of a Pepsi tribe.

"They're in a cooler on the back seat," I said. "Grab me one, too."

He maneuvered his backpack carefully and found room enough to reach into the back seat for the soda pop. He opened my can first and handed it to me. I took a big mouthful and hiccupped loudly.

"That always happens to me when I drink cold things," he said.   60

We sipped slowly after that. I kept my eyes on the road while he stared out his window into the wheat fields. We were quiet for many miles.

"Who do you fight?" I asked as we passed through another anonymous small town.

"Mostly Indians," he said. "Money fights, you know? I go from rez to rez, fighting the best they have. Winner takes all."

"Jeez, I never heard of that."

"Yeah, I guess it's illegal."   65

He rubbed his hands together. I could see fresh wounds.

"Man," I said. "Those fights must be rough."

The fighter stared out the window. I watched him for a little too long and almost drove off the road. Car horns sounded all around us.

"Jeez," the fighter said. "Close one, enit?"

"Close enough," I said.   70

He pulled his backpack closer to him, using it as a barrier between his chest and the dashboard. An Indian hitchhiker's version of a passenger-side air bag.

"Who'd you fight last?" I asked, trying to concentrate on the road.

"Some Flathead kid," he said. "In Arlee. He was supposed to be the toughest Indian in the world."

"Was he?"

"Nah, no way. Wasn't even close. Wasn't even tougher than me."   75

He told me how big the Flathead kid was, way over six feet tall and two hundred and some pounds. Big buck Indian. Had hands as big as this and arms as big as that. Had a chin like a damn buffalo. The fighter told me that he hit the Flathead kid harder than he ever hit anybody before.

"I hit him like he was a white man," the fighter said. "I hit him like he was two or three white men rolled into one."

But the Flathead kid would not go down, even though his face swelled up so bad that he looked like the Elephant Man. There were no referees, no judge, no bells to signal the end of the round. The winner was the Indian still standing. Punch after punch, man, and the kid would not go down.

"I was so tired after a while," said the fighter, "that I just took a step back and watched the kid. He stood there with his arms down, swaying from side to side like some toy, you know? Head bobbing on his neck like there was no bone at all. You couldn't even see his eyes no more. He was all messed up."

"What'd you do?" I asked.   80

"Ah, hell, I couldn't fight him no more. That kid was planning to die before he ever went down. So I just sat on the ground while they counted me out. Dumb Flathead kid didn't even know what was happening. I just sat on the ground while they raised his hand. While all the winners collected their money and all the losers cussed me out. I just sat there, man."

"Jeez," I said. "What happened next?"

"Not much. I sat there until everybody was gone. Then I stood up and headed for home. I'm tired of this shit. I just want to go home for a while. I got enough money to last me a long time. I'm a rich Indian, you hear? I'm a rich Indian."

The fighter finished his Pepsi with one last swallow, rolled down his window, and pitched the can out. I almost protested, but decided against it. I kept my empty can wedged between my legs.

"That's a hell of a story," I said.   85

"Ain't no story," he said. "It's what happened."

"Jeez," I said. "You would've been a warrior in the old days, enit? You would've been a killer. You would've stolen everybody's goddamn horses. That would've been you. You would've been it."

I was excited. I wanted the fighter to know how much I thought of him. He didn't even look at me.

"A killer," he said. "Sure."

We didn't talk much after that. I pulled into Wenatchee just before   90
sundown, and the fighter seemed happy to be leaving me.

"Thanks for the ride, cousin," he said as he climbed out. Indians always call each other cousin, especially if they're strangers.

"Wait," I said.

He looked at me, waiting impatiently.

I wanted to know if he had a place to sleep that night. It was supposed to get cold. There was a mountain range between Wenatchee and his reservation. Big mountains that used to be volcanoes. Big mountains that were still volcanoes. It could all blow up at any time. We wrote about it once in the newspaper. Things can change so quickly. So many emergencies and disasters that we can barely keep track. I wanted to tell him how much I cared about my job, even if I had to write about small town firemen. I wanted to tell the fighter that I always picked up every Indian hitchhiker, young and old, men and women. Believe me, I pick them up and get them all a little closer to home, even if I can't get them all the way. I wanted to tell him that the night sky was a graveyard. I wanted to know if he was the toughest Indian in the world.

"It's late," I finally said. "You can crash with me, if you want."   95

He studied my face and then looked down the long road toward his reservation.

"O.K.," he said. "That sounds good."

We got a room at the Pony Soldier Motel, and both of us laughed at the irony of it all. Inside the room, in a generic watercolor hanging above the bed, the U.S. Cavalry was kicking the crap out of a band of renegade Indians.

"What tribe you think they are?" I asked the fighter.

"All of them," he said.   100

The fighter crashed on the floor while I curled up in the uncomfortable bed. I couldn't sleep for the longest time. I listened to the fighter talk in his sleep. I stared up at the water-stained ceiling. I don't know what time it was when I finally drifted off, and I don't know what time it was when the fighter got into bed with me. He was naked and his penis was hard. I could feel it press against my back as he snuggled up close to me, reached inside my underwear, and took my penis in his hand. Neither of us said a word. He just continued to stroke me as he rubbed himself against my back. That went on for a long time. I had never been that close to another man, but the fighter's callused fingers felt better than I would have imagined if I had ever allowed myself to imagine such things.

"This isn't working," he whispered. "I can't come."

Without thinking, I reached around and took the fighter's penis in my hand. He was surprisingly small.

"No," he said. "I want to be inside you."

"I don't know," I said. "I've never done this before."   105

"It's O.K.," he said. "I'll be careful. I have rubbers."

Without waiting for my answer, he released me and got up from the bed. I turned to look at him. He was beautiful and scarred. So much brown skin marked with bruises, badly healed wounds, and tattoos. His long black hair was unbraided and hung down to his thin waist. My slacks and dress shirt were carefully folded and draped over the chair near the window. My shoes were sitting on the table. Blue light filled the room. The fighter bent down to his pack and searched for his condoms. For reasons I could not explain then and cannot explain now, I kicked off my underwear and rolled over on my stomach. I could not see him, but I could hear him breathing heavily as he found the condoms, tore open a package, and rolled one over his penis. He crawled onto the bed, between my legs, and slid a pillow beneath my belly.

"Are you ready?" he asked.

"I'm not gay," I said.

"Sure," he said as he pushed himself into me. He was small but it   110
hurt more than I expected, and I knew I would be sore for days after-ward. But I wanted him to save me. He didn't say anything. He just pumped into me for a few minutes, came with a loud sigh, and then pulled out. Believe me. I wanted him to save me. I quickly rolled off the bed and went into the bathroom. I locked the door behind me and stood there in the dark. I smelled like salmon.

"Hey," the fighter said through the door. "Are you O.K.?"

"Yes," I said. "I'm fine."

A long silence.

"Hey," he said. "Would you mind if I slept in the bed with you?"

I had no answer to that.   115

"Listen," I said. "That Flathead boy you fought? You know, the one you really beat up? The one who wouldn't fall down?"

In my mind, I could see the fighter pummeling that boy. Punch after punch. The boy too beaten to fight back but too strong to fall down.

"Yeah, what about him?" asked the fighter.

"What was his name?"

"His name?"   120

"Yeah, his name."

"Elmer something or other."

"Did he have an Indian name?"

"I have no idea. How the hell would I know that?"

I stood there in the dark for a long time. I was chilled. I wanted to get   125
into bed and fall asleep.

"Hey," I said. "I think, I think maybe—well, I think you should
leave now."

"Yeah," the fighter said. He was not surprised. I could hear him
softly singing as he dressed and stuffed all of his belongings into his pack.
I couldn't tell what he was singing, but I wanted to know. I opened the
bathroom door just as he was opening the door to leave. He stopped,
looked back at me, and smiled.

"Hey, tough guy," he said. "You were good."

The fighter walked out the door then, leaving it open, and walked
away. I stood in the doorway and watched him continue his walk down
the highway, past the city limits. I watched him rise from earth to sky and
become a new constellation. I closed the door and wondered what was
going to happen next. Feeling uncomfortable and cold, I went back into
the bathroom. I ran the shower with the hottest water possible. I stared at
myself in the mirror. Steam quickly filled the room. I threw a few shadow
punches. Feeling stronger, I got in the shower and searched my body for
changes. A middle-aged man needs to look for tumors. I dried myself
with a towel too small for the job. Then I crawled naked into bed. I wondered if I was a warrior in this life and if I had been a warrior in a previous life. Lonely and laughing, I fell asleep. I didn't dream at all, not one
bit. Or perhaps I did dream, but I can't remember any of it. Instead, I
woke early the next morning, before sunrise, and went out into the
world. I walked past my car. I stepped onto the pavement, still warm
from the previous day's sun. I started walking. In bare feet, I traveled up-
river toward the place where I was born and will someday die. Believe
me. At that moment, if you had broken open my heart you could have
looked inside and seen the thin white skeletons of a thousand salmon.

The Reader's Presence

1. What kind of person do you think the narrator is? How would
   you describe him to someone? Did you feel as if you were reading
   about a real person or a character in a story? What made you feel
   that way? Look closely at three particular passages that made you
   believe that this story was truth or fiction. What was there about
   each of these passages that prompted you to believe that the story
   was truth or fiction?

2. Even though he's reluctant to have sex with the fighter, the narrator explains the encounter by writing: "I wanted him to save me"
   (paragraph 110). What did the narrator want to be saved from and
   how is he saved in the story? What was it about the fighter that

made him a likely savior for the narrator? After the encounter, the narrator writes that he smelled "like salmon" (paragraph 110) and that inside him were "the thin white skeletons of a thousand salmon" (paragraph 129). What symbolic roles do salmon play throughout this story? How do salmon connect with sexuality? with gender? with being Indian?

3. Why does Alexie often describe people as "Indian" rather than as Native American or as being from particular tribes? Choose three specific sentences and substitute the phrase *Native American* for the word *Indian*. What differences do the substitutions make? How does the tone change? the rhythm? the meaning? Keeping these differences in mind, choose an essay or story in this collection that identifies an ethnicity by a single term (for example, Latino/a, white, or Asian American). Substitute another common but not derogatory term (for example, Mexican, Caucasian, or Chinese). How do these sentences change? What similarities and/or differences do you find between the way *Native American* affected Alexie's writing and the way the other term you chose as a substitute affected the other story or essay?

THE WRITER AT WORK

Sherman Alexie on the Responsibilities of Native Writers

One of Sherman Alexie's most recent books, The Toughest Indian in the World *(the title story of which precedes this selection), has received a wide range of responses: enthusiastic praise for his mastery of craft as well as criticism for his use of what have become his trademark effects of surprise or shock, and of characters who sometimes go too far to make a human connection. Throughout his career, Alexie has had to negotiate his relation to his Indian and white audiences. "[Indians] ask me to represent them, until the point where I'm not an artist. I'm a politician, or even a propagandist. . . . That kind of pressure is terrible." White readers ask him why he "hates whites." Alexie refuses to conform to simple expectations; he writes from a sense of responsibility to Indians and non-Indians who are trying to overcome the stereotypes they have been assigned. (See also the introduction to "The Joy of Reading and Writing: Superman and Me," page 61.)*

EK: Would you speak to what you see as our responsibility as Native writers? Do you see that responsibility restricting/constricting certain avenues of creativity?

SA: We do have a cultural responsibility above and beyond what other people do, more than other ethnic groups, simply because we are so misrepresented and misunderstood and appropriated. We have a serious responsibility to tell the truth. And to act as . . . role models. We are more than just writers. We are storytellers. We are spokespeople. We are cultural ambassadors. We are politicians. We are activists. We are all of these simply by nature of what we do, without even wanting to be. So we're not like these other writers who can just pick up and choose their expressions. They've chosen for us, and we have to be aware of that. I also think that we have a responsibility to live up to our words. As Native writers, we certainly talk the talk about the things that everybody should do, but if you're going to write about racism, I don't think you should be a racist.

If you're going to write about sexism and exploitation, then I don't think you should be sleeping around. If you're going to write about violence and colonialism, then I don't think you should be doing it to your own family. So, I think we have a serious responsibility as Native writers to live traditionally in a contemporary world. And I don't think that a lot of us do.

EK: What do you think prevents us from doing that?

SA: A lot of it is our own dysfunctions. While we may have more responsibilities because of what we do, that does not automatically make us healthy. Part of the danger in being an artist of whatever color is that you fall in love with your wrinkles. The danger is that if you fall in love with your wrinkles then you don't want to get rid of them. You start to glorify them and perpetuate them. If you write about pain, you can end up searching for more pain to write about, that kind of thing; that self-destructive route. We need to get away from that. We can write about pain and anger without having it consume us, and we have to learn how to do that in our lives as individuals before we can start doing that as writers.

121

Raymond Carver

Popular Mechanics

Raymond Carver (1938–1988) is best known for his tightly crafted, spare, and often grim short stories. In fact, his mastery of dialogue and his fine eye for detail have made his collections of short stories best-sellers in the United States and abroad. These collections include Will You Please Be Quiet, Please? *(1976);* What We Talk about When We Talk about Love *(1981), in which "Popular Mechanics" can be found;* Cathedral *(1984); and* Where I'm Calling From *(1988). In 1993 Robert Altman made the critically acclaimed film* Short Cuts *based on a number of Carver's short stories.*

Describing the process of writing fiction, Carver says, "I never start with an idea. I always see something. I start with an image, a cigarette being put out in a jar of mustard, for instance, or the remains, the wreckage, of a dinner left on the table. Pop cans in the fireplace, that sort of thing. And a feeling goes with that. And that feeling seems to transport me back to that particular time and place, and the ambience of time. But it is the image, and the emotion that goes with that image—that's what's important."

For more information on Raymond Carver, see page 86.

Early that day the weather turned and the snow was melting into dirty water. Streaks of it ran down from the little shoulder-high window that faced the backyard. Cars slushed by on the street outside, where it was getting dark. But it was getting dark on the inside too.

He was in the bedroom pushing clothes into a suitcase when she came to the door.

I'm glad you're leaving! I'm glad you're leaving! she said. Do you hear?

He kept on putting his things into the suitcase.

Son of a bitch! I'm so glad you're leaving! She began to cry. You   5
can't even look me in the face, can you?

Then she noticed the baby's picture on the bed and picked it up.

He looked at her and she wiped her eyes and stared at him before turning and going back to the living room.

Bring that back, he said.

Just get your things and get out, she said.

He did not answer. He fastened the suitcase, put on his coat, looked   10
around the bedroom before turning off the light. Then he went out to the living room.

She stood in the doorway of the little kitchen, holding the baby.

I want the baby, he said.

Are you crazy?

No, but I want the baby. I'll get someone to come by for his things.

You're not touching this baby, she said.   15

The baby had begun to cry and she uncovered the blanket from around his head.

Oh, oh, she said, looking at the baby.

He moved toward her.

For God's sake! she said. She took a step back into the kitchen.

I want the baby.   20

Get out of here!

She turned and tried to hold the baby over in a corner behind the stove.

But he came up. He reached across the stove and tightened his hands on the baby.

Let go of him, he said.

Get away, get away! she cried.   25

The baby was red-faced and screaming. In the scuffle they knocked down a flowerpot that hung behind the stove.

He crowded her into the wall then, trying to break her grip. He held on to the baby and pushed with all his weight.

Let go of him, he said.

Don't, she said. You're hurting the baby, she said.

I'm not hurting the baby, he said. 30

The kitchen window gave no light. In the near-dark he worked on her fisted fingers with one hand and with the other hand he gripped the screaming baby up under an arm near the shoulder.

She felt her fingers being forced open. She felt the baby going from her.

No! she screamed just as her hands came loose.

She would have it, this baby. She grabbed for the baby's other arm. She caught the baby around the wrist and leaned back.

But he would not let go. He felt the baby slipping out of his hands 35 and he pulled back very hard.

In this manner, the issue was decided.

The Reader's Presence

1. Carver begins his story in the middle of the action, without properly introducing his characters or the story's setting. What clues do you find within the opening ten paragraphs as to the characters' natures and relationship? What questions remain? How does this lack of detail affect your reading of the story? How might a more detailed opening description affect your reading? Why might Carver have chosen this narrative technique? The story also ends on a note of mystery. What do you think has happened at the end?

2. In the first paragraph, Carver writes: "Cars slushed by on the street outside, where it was getting dark. But it was getting dark on the inside too." In paragraph 31 he writes: "The kitchen window gave no light." How does this description of the objective factor of light enhance the story's mood and influence your understanding of the characters' subjective experience?

3. Carver writes his dialogue without quotation marks. Does this make the dialogue seem different from that in most short stories? If so, in what ways? Would the dialogue read differently for you with quotation marks? If so, describe the difference. Jamaica Kincaid's story "Girl" (page 840) adopts the same convention as Carver's story (page 837). Her story is one long sentence comprising bits of speech. Compare the two stories in this respect: Does the lack of quotation marks establish a stronger sense of the author's voice than there would be if quotation marks were used? John Updike's story "A&P" (page 888) is also narrated directly in the first person. Compare these stories by Carver, Updike, and Kincaid to Flannery O'Connor's "A Good Man is Hard to Find" (page 854), which is written from an omniscient and impersonal point of view.

122

Jamaica Kincaid

Girl

Jamaica Kincaid became a professional writer almost by accident. Living in New York City in the 1970s, she befriended one of the staff writers at the New Yorker *and began to accompany him as he conducted research for the "Talk of the Town" section. Before long, she discovered that she could write and that her writing impressed the editors of the magazine. When her first piece of nonfiction was published, Kincaid remembers, "That is when I realized what my writing was. My writing was the thing that I thought. Not something else. Just what I thought." After working as a staff writer at the* New Yorker *for four years, she began to turn to fiction. "Girl" is the first piece of fiction she published; it appeared in the* New Yorker *in 1978.*

For more information on Jamaica Kincaid, see page 154.

Wash the white clothes on Monday and put them on the stone heap; wash the color clothes on Tuesday and put them on the clothesline to dry; don't walk barehead in the hot sun; cook pumpkin fritters in very hot sweet oil; soak your little clothes right after you take them off; when buying cotton to make yourself a nice blouse, be sure that it doesn't have gum on it, because that way it won't hold up well after a wash; soak salt fish overnight before you cook it; is it true that you sing benna[1] in Sunday School?; always eat your food in such a way that it won't turn someone else's stomach; on Sundays try to walk like a lady and not like the slut you are so bent on becoming; don't sing benna in Sunday School; you mustn't speak to wharf-rat boys, not even to give directions; don't eat fruits on the street—flies will follow you; *but I don't sing benna on Sundays at all and never in Sunday School;* this is how to sew on a button; this is how to make a buttonhole for the button you have just sewed on; this is how to hem a dress when you see the hem coming down and so to prevent yourself from looking like the slut I know you are so bent on becoming; this is how you iron your father's khaki shirt so that it doesn't have a crease; this is how you iron your father's khaki pants so that they don't have a crease; this is how you grow

[1]*benna:* Popular calypso-like music.—EDS.

okra—far from the house, because okra tree harbors red ants; when you are growing dasheen,[2] make sure it gets plenty of water or else it makes your throat itch when you are eating it; this is how you sweep a corner; this is how you sweep a whole house; this is how you sweep a yard; this is how you smile to someone you don't like too much; this is how you smile to someone you don't like at all; this is how you smile to someone you like completely; this is how you set a table for tea; this is how you set a table for dinner; this is how you set a table for dinner with an important guest; this is how you set a table for lunch; this is how you set a table for breakfast; this is how to behave in the presence of men who don't know you very well, and this way they won't recognize immediately the slut I have warned you against becoming; be sure to wash every day, even if it is with your own spit; don't squat down to play marbles—you are not a boy, you know; don't pick people's flowers—you might catch something; don't throw stones at blackbirds, because it might not be a blackbird at all; this is how to make a bread pudding; this is how to make doukona;[3] this is how to make pepper pot; this is how to make a good medicine for a cold; this is how to make a good medicine to throw away a child before it even becomes a child; this is how to catch a fish; this is how to throw back a fish you don't like, and that way something bad won't fall on you; this is how to bully a man; this is how a man bullies you; this is how to love a man, and if this doesn't work there are other ways, and if they don't work don't feel too bad about giving up; this is how to spit up in the air if you feel like it, and this is how to move quick so that it doesn't fall on you; this is how to make ends meet; always squeeze bread to make sure it's fresh; *but what if the baker won't let me feel the bread?;* you mean to say that after all you are really going to be the kind of woman who the baker won't let near the bread?

The Reader's Presence

1. Whose voice dominates this story? To whom is the monologue addressed? What effect(s) does the speaker seek to have on the listener? Where does the speaker appear to have acquired her values? Categorize the kinds of advice you find in the story. Identify sentences in which one category of advice merges into another. How are the different kinds of advice alike, and to what extent are they contradictory?

2. "Girl" speaks only two lines, both of which are italicized. In each case, what prompts her to speak? What is the result? Stories generally create the expectation that at least one main character will undergo a change. What differences, if any, do you notice between her first and second lines of dialogue (and the replies she elicits),

[2]*dasheen:* A starchy vegetable. —EDS.
[3]*doukona:* Cornmeal. —EDS.

differences that might suggest that such a change has taken place? If so, in whom? Analyze the girl's character based not only on what she says but on what she hears (if one can assume that this monologue was not delivered all in one sitting, but is rather the distillation of years' worth of advice, as heard by the girl).

3. Consider the role of gender in this story. What gender stereotypes are perpetuated by the main speaker? Look not only at the stereotypes that affect women, but also at those that define the roles of men. What can you infer about the males, who remain behind the scenes? Two other short stories in this anthology directly concern the relationship between mother and daughter, and the powerful effect that relationship has upon the daughter's sense of her gender. Compare "Girl" to Tillie Olsen's "I Stand Here Ironing" (page 870) and to Alice Walker's "Everyday Use" (page 895). In each case, what can you infer about the author's (as opposed to the narrator's) attitude toward these gender issues?

THE WRITER AT WORK

Jamaica Kincaid on "Girl"

To many readers, "Girl" appears to be an odd and confusing short story. It's far shorter than most published stories and consists almost entirely of a monologue spoken by a mother to her daughter. Readers may wonder: "What makes this a story?" In the following passage from an interview with Jamaica Kincaid, Allan Varda asks the author some questions about this intriguing little story and discovers behind its composition a larger agenda than we might not perceive from a single reading. Do Kincaid's answers to Varda's questions help you better understand what's happening in the story? In what ways? After considering the story and interview, you also might want to turn (or return) to Kincaid's essay, "Biography of a Dress" (see page 154) and see how they enhance its autobiographical and social significance.

AV: There is a litany of items in "Girl" from a mother to her daughter about what to do and what *not* to do regarding the elements of being "a nice young lady." Is this the way it was for you and other girls in Antigua?

JK: In a word, yes.

AV: Was that good or bad?

JK: I don't think it's the way I would tell my daughter, but as a mother I would tell her what I think would be best for her to be like. This mother in "Girl" was really just giving the girl an idea about the things she would need to be a self-possessed woman in the world.

AV: But you didn't take your mother's advice?

JK: No, because I had other ideas on how to be a self-possessed woman in the world. I didn't know that at the time. I only remember

5

these things. What the mother in the story sees as aids to living in the world, the girl might see as extraordinary oppression, which is one of the things I came to see.

AV: Almost like she's Mother England.

JK: I was just going to say that. I've come to see that I've worked through the relationship of the mother and the girl to a relationship between Europe and the place that I'm from, which is to say, a relationship between the powerful and the powerless. The girl is powerless and the mother is powerful. The mother shows her how to be in the world, but at the back of her mind she thinks she never will get it. She's deeply skeptical that this child could ever grow up to be a self-possessed woman and in the end she reveals her skepticism; yet even within the skepticism is, of course, dismissal and scorn. So it's not unlike the relationship between the conquered and the conqueror.

123

Stephen King

The Hotel Story: Two Versions

Stephen King is a one-man literary industry, having produced hundreds of novels, short stories, essays, and interviews under his own name and under the pseudonym Richard Bachman. Born in Portland, Maine, in 1947, King lived as a young child in several other states, but returned to Maine with his family when he was eleven and has made Maine his home ever since. Some of King's best-known novels, including Carrie *(1974) and* The Shining *(1977) have been made into popular films starring some of Hollywood's most famous actors. King is one of America's savviest writers about the changing nature of publishing in the age of the Internet. He was one of the first well-known writers to experiment with self-publishing on an industrial scale. His novel,* The Green Mile *(1999), was made available on the Web for readers to download, chapter by chapter. Even in this experiment, however, King showed his understanding of the ethics of the market: Readers would only be able to download subsequent chapters if 80 percent of the readers of chapter one had paid for it. Two of the main themes of King's life have been (1) his interest in controlling the publication of his work, both in terms of profit and in terms of distribution; and (2) his desire to be considered a literary writer and not a prolific horror novelist. His novel* Misery *(1987) is one of the best parables ever written of the sadistic interdependence between a writer and his voracious, demanding reader; few readers escape King's writing feeling comfortably distant from the experience.*

"The Hotel Story: Two Versions" is from one of the final chapters of On Writing: A Memoir of the Craft *(2000), where it originally appeared under the title "And Furthermore, Part I, Door Shut, Door Open."*

THE HOTEL STORY

Earlier in this book,* when writing about my brief career as a sports reporter for the Lisbon Weekly Enterprise (I was, in fact, the entire sports department; a small-town Howard Cosell), I offered an example of how the editing process works. That example was necessarily brief, and dealt with nonfiction. The passage that follows is fiction. It is completely raw, the sort of thing I feel free to do with the door shut—it's the story undressed, standing up in nothing but its socks and undershorts. I suggest that you look at it closely before going on to the edited version.

Mike Enslin was still in the revolving door when he saw Ostermeyer, the manager of the Hotel Dolphin, sitting in one of the overstuffed lobby chairs. Mike's heart sank a little. *Maybe should have brought the damned lawyer along again, after all,* he thought. Well, too late now. And even if Ostermeyer had decided to throw up another roadblock or two between Mike and room 1408, that wasn't all bad; it would simply add to the story when he finally told it.

Ostermeyer saw him, got up, and was crossing the room with one pudgy hand held out as Mike left the revolving door. The Dolphin was on Sixty-first Street, around the corner from Fifth Avenue; small but smart. A man and woman dressed in evening clothes passed Mike as he reached out and took Ostermeyer's hand, switching his small overnight case to his left hand in order to do it. The woman was blonde, dressed in black, of course, and the light, flowery smell of her perfume seemed to summarize New York. On the mezzanine level, someone was playing "Night and Day" in the bar, as if to underline the summary.

"Mr. Enslin. Good evening."

"Mr. Ostermeyer. Is there a problem?"

Ostermeyer looked pained. For a moment he glanced around the small, smart lobby, as if for help. At the concierge's stand, a man was discussing theater tickets with his wife while the concierge himself watched them with a small, patient smile. At the front desk, a man with the rumpled look one only got after long hours in Business Class was discussing his reservation with a woman in a smart black suit that could itself have doubled for evening wear. It was business as usual at the Hotel Dolphin. There was help for everyone except poor Mr. Ostermeyer, who had fallen into the writer's clutches.

"Mr. Ostermeyer?" Mike repeated, feeling a little sorry for the man.

"No," Ostermeyer said at last. "No problem. But, Mr. Enslin . . . could I speak to you for a moment in my office?"

So, Mike thought. *He wants to try one more time.*

Under other circumstances he might have been impatient. Now he

5

---

*This piece is reprinted from *On Writing: A Memoir of the Craft,* by Stephen King (2000).—EDS.

was not. It would help the section on room 1408, offer the proper ominous tone the readers of his books seemed to crave—it was to be One Final Warning—but that wasn't all. Mike Enslin hadn't been sure until now, in spite of all the backing and filling; now he was. Ostermeyer wasn't playing a part. Ostermeyer was really afraid of room 1408, and what might happen to Mike there tonight.

"Of course, Mr. Ostermeyer. Should I leave my bag at the desk, or bring it?"   10

"Oh, we'll bring it along, shall we?" Ostermeyer, the good host, reached for it. Yes, he still held out some hope of persuading Mike not to stay in the room. Otherwise, he would have directed Mike to the desk . . . or taken it there himself. "Allow me."

"I'm fine with it," Mike said. "Nothing but a change of clothes and a toothbrush."

"Are you sure?"

"Yes," Mike said, holding his eyes. "I'm afraid I am."

For a moment Mike thought Ostermeyer was going to give up. He sighed, a little round man in a dark cutaway coat and a neatly knotted tie, and then he squared his shoulders again. "Very good, Mr. Enslin. Follow me."   15

The hotel manager had seemed tentative in the lobby, depressed, almost beaten. In his oak-paneled office, with the pictures of the hotel on the walls (the Dolphin had opened in October of 1910—Mike might publish without the benefit of reviews in the journals or the big-city papers, but he did his research), Ostermeyer seemed to gain assurance again. There was a Persian carpet on the floor. Two standing lamps cast a mild yellow light. A desk-lamp with a green lozenge-shaped shade stood on the desk, next to a humidor. And next to the humidor were Mike Enslin's last three books. Paperback editions, of course; there had been no hardbacks. Yet he did quite well. *Mine host has been doing a little research of his own,* Mike thought.

Mike sat down in one of the chairs in front of the desk. He expected Ostermeyer to sit behind the desk, where he could draw authority from it, but Ostermeyer surprised him. He sat in the other chair on what he probably thought of as the employees' side of the desk, crossed his legs, then leaned forward over his tidy little belly to touch the humidor.

"Cigar, Mr. Enslin? They're not Cuban, but they're quite good."

"No, thank you. I don't smoke."

Ostermeyer's eyes shifted to the cigarette behind Mike's right ear— parked there on a jaunty jut the way an oldtime wisecracking New York reporter might have parked his next smoke just below his fedora with the PRESS tag stuck in the band. The cigarette had become so much a part of him that for a moment Mike honestly didn't know what Ostermeyer was looking at. Then he remembered, laughed, took it down, looked at it himself, then looked back at Ostermeyer.   20

"Haven't had a cigarette in nine years," he said. "I had an older brother who died of lung cancer. I quit shortly after he died. The cigarette behind the ear . . ." He shrugged. "Part affectation, part superstition, I guess. Kind of like the ones you sometimes see on people's desks or walls, mounted in a little box with a sign saying BREAK GLASS IN CASE OF EMERGENCY. I sometimes tell people I'll light up in case of nuclear war. Is 1408 a smoking room, Mr. Ostermeyer? Just in case nuclear war breaks out?"

"As a matter of fact, it is."

"Well," Mike said heartily, "that's one less worry in the watches of the night."

Mr. Ostermeyer sighed again, unamused, but this one didn't have the disconsolate quality of his lobby-sigh. Yes, it was the room, Mike reckoned. *His* room. Even this afternoon, when Mike had come accompanied by Robertson, the lawyer, Ostermeyer had seemed less flustered once they were in here. At the time Mike had thought it was partly because they were no longer drawing stares from the passing public, partly because Ostermeyer had given up. Now he knew better. It was the room. And why not? It was a room with good pictures on the walls, a good rug on the floor, and good cigars—although not Cuban—in the humidor. A lot of managers had no doubt conducted a lot of business in here since October of 1910; in its own way it was as New York as the blonde woman in her black off-the-shoulder dress, her smell of perfume and her unarticulated promise of sleek sex in the small hours of the morning—New York sex. Mike himself was from Omaha, although he hadn't been back there in a lot of years.

"You still don't think I can talk you out of this idea of yours, do   25
you?" Ostermeyer asked.

"I know you can't," Mike said, replacing the cigarette behind his ear.

What follows is revised copy of this same opening passage—it's the story putting on its clothes, combing its hair, maybe adding just a small dash of cologne. Once these changes are incorporated into my document, I'm ready to open the door and face the world.

~~The Hotel Story~~ **1408** ①

By Stephen King

② Mike Enslin was still in the revolving door when he saw ~~Ostermeyer,~~ **Olin** the manager of the Hotel Dolphin, sitting in one of the overstuffed lobby chairs. Mike's heart sank ~~a little~~. *Maybe should have brought the damned lawyer along again, after all,* he thought. Well, too late now. And even if ~~Ostermeyer~~ **Olin** had decided to throw up another roadblock or two between Mike and room 1408, that wasn't all bad; ~~it~~ there were compensations. ~~would simply add to the story when he finally told it~~

Olin ~~Ostermeyer saw him, got up, and~~ was crossing the room with one pudgy hand held out as Mike left the revolving door. The Dolphin was on Sixty-first Street, around the corner from Fifth Avenue, small but smart. A man and woman dressed in evening clothes passed Mike as he reached out and took Olin's ~~Ostermeyer's~~ hand, switching his small overnight case to his left hand in order to do it. The woman was blonde, dressed in black, of course, and the light, flowery smell of her perfume seemed to summarize New York. On the mezzanine level, someone was playing "Night and Day" in the bar, as if to underline the summary.

"Mr. Enslin. Good evening."

"Mr. ~~Ostermeyer.~~ Olin. Is there a problem?"   30

Olin ~~Ostermeyer~~ looked pained. For a moment he glanced around the small, smart lobby, as if for help. At the concierge's stand, a man was discussing theater tickets with his wife while the concierge himself watched ~~them~~ with a small, patient smile. At the front desk, a man with the rumpled look one only got after long hours in Business Class was discussing his reservation with a woman in a smart black suit that could itself have doubled for evening wear. It was business as usual at the Hotel Dolphin. There was help for everyone except poor Mr. [Olin] ~~Ostermeyer~~, who had fallen into the writer's clutches.

③ "Mr. ~~Ostermeyer~~ [Olin]?" Mike repeated~~, feeling a little sorry for the man.~~

"No," Ostermeyer said at last. "No problem. But, [¶] Mr. Enslin . . . could I speak to you for a moment in my office?"

So, Mike thought. ~~He wants to try one more time~~ [¶ Well, and why not?] ~~Under other circumstances he might have been impatient. Now he was not.~~ It would help the section on room 1408, ~~offer~~ [add to] the ~~proper~~ ominous tone the readers of his books seemed to crave~~, it was to be One Final Warning—but that wasn't all~~ [and that wasn't all.] Mike Enslin hadn't been sure until now, in spite of all the backing and filling; now he was. ~~Ostermeyer~~ [Olin] wasn't playing a part. ~~Ostermeyer~~ [Olin] was really afraid of room 1408, and what might happen to Mike there tonight.

"Of course, Mr. ~~Ostermeyer~~ [Olin]."~~Should I leave my bag at the desk, or bring it?~~

④ ["Olin,] "Oh, we'll bring it along, shall we?" ~~Ostermeyer,~~ the good host, reached for ~~it.~~ [Mike's bag.] ~~Yes, he still held out some hope of persuading Mike not to stay in the room. Otherwise, he would have directed Mike to the desk . . . or taken it there himself.~~ "Allow me."

35

"I'm fine with it," Mike said. "Nothing but a change of clothes and a toothbrush."

"Are you sure?"

"Yes," Mike said, holding his eyes. "I'm ~~afraid I am.~~ already wearing my lucky Hawaiian shirt." He smiled. "It's the one with the ghost repellent."

⑤ 40

~~For a moment Mike thought Ostermeyer was going to give up. He~~ A Olin sighed, a little round man in a dark cutaway coat and a neatly knotted tie, ~~and then he squared his shoulders again.~~ "Very good, Mr. Enslin. Follow me."

The hotel manager had seemed tentative in the lobby, ~~depressed,~~ almost beaten. In his oak-paneled office, with the pictures of the hotel on the walls (the Dolphin had opened in October of 1910—Mike might publish without the benefit of reviews in the journals or the big-city papers, but he did his research), ~~Ostermeyer~~ Olin seemed to gain assurance again. There was a Persian carpet on the floor. Two standing lamps cast a mild yellow light. A desk-lamp with a green lozenge-shaped shade stood on the desk, next to a humidor. And next to the humidor were Mike Enslin's last three books. Paperback editions, of course; there had been no hardbacks. ~~Yet he did quite well.~~ *Mine host has been doing a little research of his own,* Mike thought.

Mike sat down ~~in one of the chairs~~ in front of the desk. He expected ~~Ostermeyer~~ Olin to sit behind the desk, ~~where he could draw~~ authority from ~~it~~, but ~~Ostermeyer~~ Olin surprised him. He ~~sat in the other chair~~ took the chair ~~on what he probably thought of as the employees'~~ beside Mike, ~~side of the desk,~~ crossed his legs, then leaned forward over his tidy little belly to touch the humidor.

"Cigar, Mr. Enslin? ~~They're not Cuban, but~~ ~~they're quite good.~~"

"No, thank you. I don't smoke."   45

~~Ostermeyer~~ Olin's's eyes shifted to the cigarette behind Mike's right ear—parked ~~there~~ on a jaunty jut the way an oldtime wisecracking New York reporter might have parked his next smoke just below ~~his~~ of his fedora. ~~fedora with~~ the PRESS tag stuck in the band. The cigarette had become so much a part of him that for a moment Mike honestly didn't know what ~~Oster~~ Olin ~~meyer~~ was looking at. Then he ~~remembered,~~ laughed, took it down, looked at it himself, then looked back at ~~Ostermeyer~~ Olin.

"Haven't had ~~a cigarette~~ one in nine years," he said. "I had an older brother who died of lung cancer. I quit ~~shortly~~ after he died. The cigarette behind the ear . . ." He shrugged. "Part affectation, part superstition, I guess. ~~Kind of like the ones~~ Like the Hawaiian shirt. Or the cigarettes you sometimes see on people's desks or walls, mounted in a little box with a sign saying BREAK GLASS IN CASE OF

EMERGENCY. Is 1408 a smoking room, Mr. Olin? Just in case nuclear war breaks out?"

"As a matter of fact, it is."

"Well," Mike said heartily, "that's one less worry in the watches of the night."

Mr. Olin sighed again, but this sigh didn't have the disconsolate quality of his lobby-sigh. Yes, it was the office, Mike reckoned. *His* office. Even this afternoon, when Mike had come accompanied by Robertson, the lawyer, Olin had seemed less flustered once they were in here. Where else could you feel in charge, if not in your special place? Olin's office was a room with good pictures on the walls, a good rug on the floor, and good cigars—although not Cuban—in the humidor. A lot of managers had no doubt conducted a lot of business in here since 1910; in its own way it was as New York as the blonde woman in her black off-the-shoulder dress, her smell of perfume and her unarticulated promise of sleek New York sex in the small hours of the morning. Mike himself was from Omaha, although he hadn't been back there in years.

"You still don't think I can talk you out of this

                Olin

idea of yours, do you?" ~~Ostermeyer~~ asked.

"I know you can't," Mike said, replacing the cig-

arette behind his ear.

The reasons for the majority of the changes are self-evident; if you flip back and forth between the two versions, I'm confident that you'll understand almost all of them, and I'm hopeful that you'll see how raw the first-draft work of even a so-called "professional writer" is once you really examine it.

Most of the changes are cuts, intended to speed the story. I have cut with Strunk in mind — "Omit needless words" — and also to satisfy the formula stated earlier: 2nd Draft = 1st Draft –10%.

I have keyed a few changes for brief explanation: 55

1. Obviously, "The Hotel Story" is never going to replace "Kill-dozer!" or *Norma Jean, the Termite Queen* as a title. I simply slotted it into the first draft, knowing a better one would occur as I went along. (If a better title doesn't occur, an editor will usually supply his or her idea of a better one, and the results are usually ugly.) I like "1408" because this is a "thirteenth floor" story, and the numbers add up to thirteen.

2. Ostermeyer is a long and galumphing name. By changing it to Olin via global replace, I was able to shorten my story by about fifteen lines at a single stroke. Also, by the time I finished "1408," I had realized it was probably going to be part of an audio collection. I would read the stories myself, and didn't want to sit there in the little recording booth, saying Ostermeyer, Ostermeyer, Ostermeyer all day long. So I changed it.

3. I'm doing a lot of the reader's thinking for him here. Since most readers can think for themselves, I felt free to cut this from five lines to just two.

4. Too much stage direction, too much belaboring of the obvious, and too much clumsy back story. Out it goes.

5. Ah, here is the lucky Hawaiian shirt. It shows up in the first draft, but not until about page thirty. That's too late for an important prop, so I stuck it up front. There's an old rule of theater that goes, "If there's a gun on the mantel in Act I, it must go off in Act III." The reverse is also true; if the main character's lucky Hawaiian shirt plays a part at the end of a story, it must be introduced early. Otherwise it looks like a *deus ex machina* (which of course it is).

6. The first-draft copy reads "Mike sat down in one of the chairs in front of the desk." Well, duh — where else is he going to sit? On the floor? I don't think so, and out it goes. Also out is the business of the Cuban cigars. This is not only trite, it's the sort of thing bad guys are always saying in bad movies. "Have a cigar! They're Cuban!" Fuhgeddaboudit!

7. The first- and second-draft ideas and basic information are the same, but in the second draft, things have been cut to the bone. And look! See that wretched adverb, that "shortly"? Stomped it, didn't I? No mercy!

8. And here's one I didn't cut . . . not just an adverb but a Swiftie: **"Well," Mike said heartily** . . . But I stand behind my choice not to cut in this case, would argue that it's the exception which proves the rule. "Heartily" has been allowed to stand because I want the reader to understand that Mike is making fun of poor Mr. Olin. Just a little, but yes, he's making fun.

9. This passage not only belabors the obvious but repeats it. Out it goes. The concept of a person's feeling comfortable in one's own special place, however, seemed to clarify Olin's character, and so I added it.

I toyed with the idea of including the entire finished text of "1408" in this book, but the idea ran counter to my determination to be brief, for once in my life. If you would like to listen to the entire thing, it's available as part of a three-story audio collection, *Blood and Smoke*. You may access a sample on the Simon and Schuster Web site, http://www.Simon-Says.com. And remember, for our purposes here, you don't need to finish the story. This is about engine maintenance, not joyriding.

The Reader's Presence

1. For over twenty years King has lamented the way many critics have dismissed his work as genre fiction. Judging from the excerpts printed here, what kind of a writer does Mike Enslin seem to be, and how does King describe him? Do we imagine he comes to grief in the story ultimately? And if so, what point might King be making?

2. King's prose style in this story is efficient and straightforward, suggesting that he is good at taking his own suggestions. But would those suggestions work for all, or even most, writers of fiction? Reread a page or two from a work by a literary stylist such as Flannery O'Connor (page 854), E. B. White (page 281), or Don DeLillo (page 341), and mentally edit it according to King's prescriptions. Does the result seem to be an improvement?

3. King's comments about the revision process are resolutely practical (omit needless words; if a character's name is hard to say, change it, etc.) and accord closely with the advice about writing he gives in "Everything You Need to Know about Writing Successfully — in Ten Minutes." But King says close to nothing about such fundamental questions as: How does a story generate curiosity? suspense? fear? Look again at the revised pages of King's story and try to identify the specific tools King uses to generate the reader's anxious interest.

124

Flannery O'Connor

A Good Man Is Hard to Find

Flannery O'Connor (1925–1964) was born in Savannah, Georgia, the only child of devout Catholic parents. At the age of thirteen, O'Connor moved with her parents to her mother's ancestral home in Milledgeville, Georgia, after her father became terminally ill with lupus. In 1945 she received an A.B. degree from Georgia State College for Women, where she contributed regularly to the school's literary magazine. While earning an M.F.A. from the Writers' Workshop at the University of Iowa, O'Connor published her first short story, "The Geranium," in 1946. After graduation O'Connor was a resident at Yaddo, an artists' retreat in New York, and lived in New York City and in Connecticut until 1951, when she was diagnosed with lupus and returned to Georgia for treatment. She and her mother moved a short distance from Milledgeville to their family farm, Andalusia, where O'Connor lived until her death at the age of thirty-nine, raising peafowl, painting, and writing daily. During her short yet distinguished life, O'Connor published two novels, Wise Blood *(1952) and* The Violent Bear It Away *(1960), and a collection of short stories,* A Good Man Is Hard to Find *(1955) the title story of which appears here. A book of essays,* Mystery and Manners *(1969); two other short story collections,* Everything That Rises Must Converge *(1965) and* The Complete Stories of Flannery O'Connor *(1971), winner of a National Book Award; and a collection of letters,* The Habit of Being *(1979), were published posthumously.*

The grandmother didn't want to go to Florida. She wanted to visit some of her connections in east Tennessee and she was seizing at every chance to change Bailey's mind. Bailey was the son she lived with, her only boy. He was sitting on the edge of his chair at the table, bent over the orange sports section of the *Journal.* "Now look here, Bailey," she said, "see here, read this," and she stood with one hand on her thin hip and the other rattling the newspaper at his bald head. "Here this fellow that calls himself The Misfit is aloose from the Federal Pen and headed toward Florida and you read here what it says he did to these people. Just you read it. I wouldn't take my children in any direction with a criminal like that aloose in it. I couldn't answer to my conscience if I did."

Bailey didn't look up from his reading so she wheeled around then and faced the children's mother, a young woman in slacks, whose face was as broad and innocent as a cabbage and was tied around with a green head-kerchief that had two points on the top like a rabbit's ears. She was sitting on the sofa, feeding the baby his apricots out of a jar. "The children have been to Florida before," the old lady said. "You all ought to take them somewhere else for a change so they would see different parts of the world and be broad. They never have been to east Tennessee."

The children's mother didn't seem to hear her but the eight-year-old boy, John Wesley, a stocky child with glasses, said, "If you don't want to go to Florida, why dontcha stay at home?" He and the little girl, June Star, were reading the funny papers on the floor.

"She wouldn't stay at home to be queen for a day," June Star said without raising her yellow head.

"Yes and what would you do if this fellow, The Misfit, caught you?" 5 the grandmother asked.

"I'd smack his face," John Wesley said.

"She wouldn't stay at home for a million bucks," June Star said. "Afraid she'd miss something. She has to go everywhere we go."

"All right, Miss," the grandmother said. "Just remember that the next time you want me to curl your hair."

June Star said her hair was naturally curly.

The next morning the grandmother was the first one in the car, ready 10 to go. She had her big black valise that looked like the head of a hippopotamus in one corner, and underneath it she was hiding a basket with Pitty Sing, the cat, in it. She didn't intend for the cat to be left alone in the house for three days because he would miss her too much and she was afraid he might brush against one of the gas burners and accidentally asphyxiate himself. Her son, Bailey, didn't like to arrive at a motel with a cat.

She sat in the middle of the back seat with John Wesley and June Star on either side of her. Bailey and the children's mother and the baby sat in front and they left Atlanta at eight forty-five with the mileage on the car at 55890. The grandmother wrote this down because she thought it would be interesting to say how many miles they had been when they got back. It took them twenty minutes to reach the outskirts of the city.

The old lady settled herself comfortably, removing her white cotton gloves and putting them up with her purse on the shelf in front of the back window. The children's mother still had on slacks and still had her head tied up in a green kerchief, but the grandmother had on a navy blue straw sailor hat with a bunch of white violets on the brim and a navy blue dress with a small white dot in the print. Her collars and cuffs were white organdy trimmed with lace and at her neckline she had pinned a purple spray of cloth violets containing a sachet. In case of an accident, anyone seeing her dead on the highway would know at once that she was a lady.

She said she thought it was going to be a good day for driving, neither too hot nor too cold, and she cautioned Bailey that the speed limit was fifty-five miles an hour and that the patrolmen hid themselves behind billboards and small clumps of trees and sped out after you before you had a chance to slow down. She pointed out interesting details of the scenery: Stone Mountain; the blue granite that in some places came up to both sides of the highway; the brilliant red clay banks slightly streaked with purple; and the various crops that made rows of green lace-work on the ground. The trees were full of silver-white sunlight and the meanest of them sparkled. The children were reading comic magazines and their mother had gone back to sleep.

"Let's go through Georgia fast so we won't have to look at it much," John Wesley said.

"If I were a little boy," said the grandmother, "I wouldn't talk about   15 my native state that way. Tennessee has the mountains and Georgia has the hills."

"Tennessee is just a hillbilly dumping ground," John Wesley said, "and Georgia is a lousy state too."

"You said it," June Star said.

"In my time," said the grandmother, folding her thin veined fingers, "children were more respectful of their native states and their parents and everything else. People did right then. Oh look at the cute little pickaninny!" she said and pointed to a Negro child standing in the door of a shack. "Wouldn't that make a picture, now?" she asked and they all turned and looked at the little Negro out of the back window. He waved.

"He didn't have any britches on," June Star said.

"He probably didn't have any," the grandmother explained. "Little   20 niggers in the country don't have things like we do. If I could paint, I'd paint that picture," she said.

The children exchanged comic books.

The grandmother offered to hold the baby and the children's mother passed him over the front seat to her. She set him on her knee and bounced him and told him about the things they were passing. She rolled her eyes and screwed up her mouth and stuck her leathery thin face into his smooth bland one. Occasionally he gave her a faraway smile. They passed a large cotton field with five or six graves fenced in the middle of it, like a small island. "Look at the graveyard!" the grandmother said, pointing it out. "That was the old family burying ground. That belonged to the plantation."

"Where's the plantation?" John Wesley asked.

"Gone With the Wind," said the grandmother. "Ha. Ha."

When the children finished all the comic books they had brought, they   25 opened the lunch and ate it. The grandmother ate a peanut butter sandwich and an olive and would not let the children throw the box and the paper napkins out the window. When there was nothing else to do they played a game by choosing a cloud and making the other two guess what shape it suggested. John Wesley took one the shape of a cow and June Star guessed a cow and John Wesley said, no, an automobile, and June Star said he didn't play fair, and they began to slap each other over the grandmother.

The grandmother said she would tell them a story if they would keep quiet. When she told a story, she rolled her eyes and waved her head and was very dramatic. She said once when she was a maiden lady she had been courted by a Mr. Edgar Atkins Teagarden from Jasper, Georgia. She said he was a very good-looking man and a gentleman and that he brought her a watermelon every Saturday afternoon with his initials cut in it, E. A. T. Well, one Saturday, she said, Mr. Teagarden brought the watermelon and there was nobody at home and he left it on the front porch and returned in his buggy to Jasper, but she never got the watermelon, she said, because a nigger boy ate it when he saw the initials, E. A. T.! This story tickled John Wesley's funny bone and he giggled and giggled but June Star didn't think it was any good. She said she wouldn't marry a man that just brought her a watermelon on Saturday. The grandmother said she would have done well to marry Mr. Teagarden because he was a gentleman and had bought Coca-Cola stock when it first came out and that he had died only a few years ago, a very wealthy man.

They stopped at The Tower for barbecued sandwiches. The Tower was a part stucco and part wood filling station and dance hall set in a clearing outside of Timothy. A fat man named Red Sammy Butts ran it and there were signs stuck here and there on the building and for miles up and down the highway saying, TRY RED SAMMY'S FAMOUS BARBE-CUE. NONE LIKE FAMOUS RED SAMMY'S! RED SAM! THE FAT BOY WITH THE HAPPY LAUGH! A VETERAN! RED SAMMY'S YOUR MAN!

Red Sammy was lying on the bare ground outside The Tower with his head under a truck while a gray monkey about a foot high, chained to a small chinaberry tree, chattered nearby. The monkey sprang back into the tree and got on the highest limb as soon as he saw the children jump out of the car and run toward him.

Inside, The Tower was a long dark room with a counter at one end and tables at the other and dancing space in the middle. They all sat down at a board table next to the nickelodeon and Red Sam's wife, a tall burnt-brown woman with hair and eyes lighter than her skin, came and took their order. The children's mother put a dime in the machine and played "The Tennessee Waltz," and the grandmother said that tune always made her want to dance. She asked Bailey if he would like to dance but he only glared at her. He didn't have a naturally sunny disposition like she did and trips made him nervous. The grandmother's brown eyes were very bright. She swayed her head from side to side and pretended she was dancing in her chair. June Star said play something she could tap to so the children's mother put in another dime and played a fast number and June Star stepped out onto the dance floor and did her tap routine.

"Ain't she cute?" Red Sam's wife said, leaning over the counter. 30 "Would you like to come be my little girl?"

"No I certainly wouldn't," June Star said. "I wouldn't live in a broken-down place like this for a million bucks!" and she ran back to the table.

"Ain't she cute?" the woman repeated, stretching her mouth politely.

"Aren't you ashamed?" hissed the grandmother.

Red Sam came in and told his wife to quit lounging on the counter and hurry up with these people's order. His khaki trousers reached just to his hip bones and his stomach hung over them like a sack of meal swaying under his shirt. He came over and sat down at a table nearby and let out a combination sigh and yodel. "You can't win," he said. "You can't win," and he wiped his sweating red face off with a gray handkerchief. "These days you don't know who to trust," he said. "Ain't that the truth?"

"People are certainly not nice like they used to be," said the grand-   35
mother.

"Two fellers come in here last week," Red Sammy said, "driving a Chrysler. It was a old beat-up car, but it was a good one and these boys looked all right to me. Said they worked at the mill and you know I let them fellers charge the gas they bought? Now why did I do that?"

"Because you're a good man!" the grandmother said at once.

"Yes'm, I suppose so," Red Sam said as if he were struck with this answer.

His wife brought the orders, carrying the five plates all at once without a tray, two in each hand and one balanced on her arm. "It isn't a soul in this green world of God's that you can trust," she said. "And I don't count nobody out of that, not nobody," she repeated, looking at Red Sammy.

"Did you read about that criminal, The Misfit, that's escaped?"   40
asked the grandmother.

"I wouldn't be a bit surprised if he didn't attact this place right here," said the woman. "If he hears about it being here, I wouldn't be none surprised to see him. If he hears it's two cent in the cash register, I wouldn't be a tall surprised if he . . ."

"That'll do," Red Sam said. "Go bring these people their Co'-Colas," and the woman went off to get the rest of the order.

"A good man is hard to find," Red Sammy said. "Everything is getting terrible. I remember the day you could go off and leave your screen door unlatched. Not no more."

He and the grandmother discussed better times. The old lady said that in her opinion Europe was entirely to blame for the way things were now. She said the way Europe acted you would think we were made of money and Red Sam said it was no use talking about it, she was exactly right. The children ran outside into the white sunlight and looked at the monkey in the lacy chinaberry tree. He was busy catching fleas on himself and biting each one carefully between his teeth as if it were a delicacy.

They drove off again into the hot afternoon. The grandmother took   45
cat naps and woke up every few minutes with her own snoring. Outside of Toombsboro she woke up and recalled an old plantation that she had visited in this neighborhood once when she was a young lady. She said the house had six white columns across the front and that there was an avenue of oaks leading up to it and two little wooden trellis arbors on

either side in front where you sat down with your suitor after a stroll in the garden. She recalled exactly which road to turn off to get to it. She knew that Bailey would not be willing to lose any time looking at an old house, but the more she talked about it, the more she wanted to see it once again and find out if the little twin arbors were still standing. "There was a secret panel in this house," she said craftily, not telling the truth but wishing that she were, "and the story went that all the family silver was hidden in it when Sherman came through but it was never found . . ."

"Hey!" John Wesley said. "Let's go see it! We'll find it! We'll poke all the woodwork and find it! Who lives there? Where do you turn off at? Hey Pop, can't we turn off there?"

"We never have seen a house with a secret panel!" June Star shrieked. "Let's go to the house with the secret panel! Hey Pop, can't we go see the house with the secret panel!"

"It's not far from here, I know," the grandmother said. "It wouldn't take over twenty minutes."

Bailey was looking straight ahead. His jaw was as rigid as a horseshoe. "No," he said.

The children began to yell and scream that they wanted to see the house with the secret panel. John Wesley kicked the back of the front seat and June Star hung over her mother's shoulder and whined desperately into her ear that they never had any fun even on their vacation, that they could never do what THEY wanted to do. The baby began to scream and John Wesley kicked the back of the seat so hard that his father could feel the blows in his kidney.

"All right!" he shouted and drew the car to a stop at the side of the road. "Will you all shut up? Will you all just shut up for one second? If you don't shut up, we won't go anywhere."

"It would be very educational for them," the grandmother murmured.

"All right," Bailey said, "but get this: this is the only time we're going to stop for anything like this. This is the one and only time."

"The dirt road that you have to turn down is about a mile back," the grandmother directed. "I marked it when we passed."

"A dirt road," Bailey groaned.

After they had turned around and were headed toward the dirt road, the grandmother recalled other points about the house, the beautiful glass over the front doorway and the candle-lamp in the hall. John Wesley said that the secret panel was probably in the fireplace.

"You can't go inside this house," Bailey said. "You don't know who lives there."

"While you all talk to the people in front, I'll run around behind and get in a window," John Wesley suggested.

"We'll all stay in the car," his mother said.

They turned onto the dirt road and the car raced roughly along in a swirl of pink dust. The grandmother recalled the times when there were no paved roads and thirty miles was a day's journey. The dirt road was hilly and there were sudden washes in it and sharp curves on dangerous embankments. All at once they would be on a hill, looking down over the blue tops of trees for miles around, then the next minute, they would be in a red depression with the dust-coated trees looking down on them.

"This place had better turn up in a minute," Bailey said, "or I'm going to turn around."

The road looked as if no one had traveled on it in months.

"It's not much farther," the grandmother said and just as she said it, a horrible thought came to her. The thought was so embarrassing that she turned red in the face and her eyes dilated and her feet jumped up, upsetting her valise in the corner. The instant the valise moved, the newspaper top she had over the basket under it rose with a snarl and Pitty Sing, the cat, sprang onto Bailey's shoulder.

The children were thrown to the floor and their mother, clutching the baby, was thrown out the door onto the ground; the old lady was thrown into the front seat. The car turned over once and landed right-side-up in a gulch off the side of the road. Bailey remained in the driver's seat with the cat—gray-striped with a broad white face and an orange nose—clinging to his neck like a caterpillar.

As soon as the children saw they could move their arms and legs, they scrambled out of the car, shouting, "We've had an ACCIDENT!" The grandmother was curled up under the dashboard, hoping she was injured so that Bailey's wrath would not come down on her all at once. The horrible thought she had had before the accident was that the house she had remembered so vividly was not in Georgia but in Tennessee.

Bailey removed the cat from his neck with both hands and flung it out the window against the side of a pine tree. Then he got out of the car and started looking for the children's mother. She was sitting against the side of the red gutted ditch, holding the screaming baby, but she only had a cut down her face and a broken shoulder. "We've had an ACCIDENT!" the children screamed in a frenzy of delight.

"But nobody's killed," June Star said with disappointment as the grandmother limped out of the car, her hat still pinned to her head but the broken front brim standing up at a jaunty angle and the violet spray hanging off the side. They all sat down in the ditch, except the children, to recover from the shock. They were all shaking.

"Maybe a car will come along," said the children's mother hoarsely.

"I believe I have injured an organ," said the grandmother, pressing her side, but no one answered her. Bailey's teeth were clattering. He had on a yellow sport shirt with bright blue parrots designed in it and his face was as yellow as the shirt. The grandmother decided that she would not mention that the house was in Tennessee.

The road was about ten feet above and they could see only the tops of the trees on the other side of it. Behind the ditch they were sitting in there were more woods, tall and dark and deep. In a few minutes they saw a car some distance away on top of a hill, coming slowly as if the oc-

65

70

cupants were watching them. The grandmother stood up and waved both arms dramatically to attract their attention. The car continued to come on slowly, disappeared around a bend and appeared again, moving even slower, on top of the hill they had gone over. It was a big black battered hearselike automobile. There were three men in it.

It came to a stop just over them and for some minutes, the driver looked down with a steady expressionless gaze to where they were sitting, and didn't speak. Then he turned his head and muttered something to the other two and they got out. One was a fat boy in black trousers and a red sweat shirt with a silver stallion embossed on the front of it. He moved around on the right side of them and stood staring, his mouth partly open in a kind of loose grin. The other had on khaki pants and a blue striped coat and a gray hat pulled down very low, hiding most of his face. He came around slowly on the left side. Neither spoke.

The driver got out of the car and stood by the side of it, looking down at them. He was an older man than the other two. His hair was just beginning to gray and he wore silver-rimmed spectacles that gave him a scholarly look. He had a long creased face and didn't have on any shirt or undershirt. He had on blue jeans that were too tight for him and was holding a black hat and a gun. The two boys also had guns.

"We've had an ACCIDENT!" the children screamed.

The grandmother had the peculiar feeling that the bespectacled man was someone she knew. His face was as familiar to her as if she had known him all her life but she could not recall who he was. He moved away from the car and began to come down the embankment, placing his feet carefully so that he wouldn't slip. He had on tan and white shoes and no socks, and his ankles were red and thin. "Good afternoon," he said. "I see you all had you a little spill."

"We turned over twice!" said the grandmother. 75

"Oncet," he corrected. "We seen it happen. Try their car and see will it run, Hiram," he said quietly to the boy with the gray hat.

"What you got that gun for?" John Wesley asked. "Whatcha gonna do with that gun?"

"Lady," the man said to the children's mother, "would you mind calling them children to sit down by you? Children make me nervous. I want all you all to sit down right together there where you're at."

"What are you telling US what to do for?" June Star asked.

Behind them the line of woods gaped like a dark open mouth. "Come 80 here," said their mother.

"Look here now," Bailey began suddenly, "we're in a predicament! We're in . . ."

The grandmother shrieked. She scrambled to her feet and stood staring. "You're The Misfit!" she said. "I recognized you at once!"

"Yes'm," the man said, smiling slightly as if he were pleased in spite of himself to be known, "but it would have been better for all of you, lady, if you hadn't of reckernized me."

Bailey turned his head sharply and said something to his mother that shocked even the children. The old lady began to cry and The Misfit reddened.

"Lady," he said, "don't you get upset. Sometimes a man says things   85
he don't mean. I don't reckon he meant to talk to you thataway."

"You wouldn't shoot a lady, would you?" the grandmother said and removed a clean handkerchief from her cuff and began to slap at her eyes with it.

The Misfit pointed the toe of his shoe into the ground and made a little hole and then covered it up again. "I would hate to have to," he said.

"Listen," the grandmother almost screamed, "I know you're a good man. You don't look a bit like you have common blood. I know you must come from nice people!"

"Yes mam," he said, "finest people in the world." When he smiled he showed a row of strong white teeth. "God never made a finer woman than my mother and my daddy's heart was pure gold," he said. The boy with the red sweat shirt had come around behind them and was standing with his gun at his hip. The Misfit squatted down on the ground. "Watch them children, Bobby Lee," he said. "You know they make me nervous." He looked at the six of them huddled together in front of him and he seemed to be embarrassed as if he couldn't think of anything to say. "Ain't a cloud in the sky," he remarked, looking up at it. "Don't see no sun but don't see no cloud neither."

"Yes, it's a beautiful day," said the grandmother. "Listen," she said,   90
"you shouldn't call yourself The Misfit because I know you're a good man at heart. I can just look at you and tell."

"Hush!" Bailey yelled. "Hush! Everybody shut up and let me handle this!" He was squatting in the position of a runner about to sprint forward but he didn't move.

"I pre-chate that, lady," The Misfit said and drew a little circle in the ground with the butt of his gun.

"It'll take a half a hour to fix this here car," Hiram called, looking over the raised hood of it.

"Well, first you and Bobby Lee get him and that little boy to step over yonder with you," The Misfit said, pointing to Bailey and John Wesley. "The boys want to ast you something," he said to Bailey. "Would you mind stepping back in them woods there with them?"

"Listen," Bailey began, "we're in a terrible predicament! Nobody re-   95
alizes what this is," and his voice cracked. His eyes were as blue and intense as the parrots in his shirt and he remained perfectly still.

The grandmother reached up to adjust her hat brim as if she were going to the woods with him but it came off in her hand. She stood staring at it and after a second she let it fall on the ground. Hiram pulled Bailey up by the arm as if he were assisting an old man. John Wesley caught hold of his father's hand and Bobby Lee followed. They went off toward the woods and just as they reached the dark edge, Bailey turned and supporting himself against a gray naked pine trunk, he shouted, "I'll be back in a minute, Mamma, wait on me!"

"Come back this instant!" his mother shrilled but they all disappeared into the woods.

"Bailey Boy!" the grandmother called in a tragic voice but she found she was looking at The Misfit squatting on the ground in front of her. "I just know you're a good man," she said desperately. "You're not a bit common!"

"Nome, I ain't a good man," The Misfit said after a second as if he had considered her statement carefully, "but I ain't the worst in the world neither. My daddy said I was a different breed of dog from my brothers and sisters. 'You know,' Daddy said, 'it's some that can live their whole life out without asking about it and it's others has to know why it is, and this boy is one of the latters. He's going to be into everything!'" He put on his black hat and looked up suddenly and then away deep into the woods as if he were embarrassed again. "I'm sorry I don't have on a shirt before you ladies," he said, hunching his shoulders slightly. "We buried our clothes that we had on when we escaped and we're just making do until we can get better. We borrowed these from some folks we met," he explained.

"That's perfectly all right," the grandmother said. "Maybe Bailey has   100
an extra shirt in his suitcase."

"I'll look and see terrectly," The Misfit said.

"Where are they taking him?" the children's mother screamed.

"Daddy was a card himself," The Misfit said. "You couldn't put anything over on him. He never got in trouble with the Authorities though. Just had the knack of handling them."

"You could be honest too if you'd only try," said the grandmother. "Think how wonderful it would be to settle down and live a comfortable life and not have to think about somebody chasing you all the time."

The Misfit kept scratching in the ground with the butt of his gun as if   105
he were thinking about it. "Yes'm, somebody is always after you," he murmured.

The grandmother noticed how thin his shoulder blades were just behind his hat because she was standing up looking down on him. "Do you ever pray?" she asked.

He shook his head. All she saw was the black hat wiggle between his shoulder blades. "Nome," he said.

There was a pistol shot from the woods, followed closely by another. Then silence. The old lady's head jerked around. She could hear the wind move through the tree tops like a long satisfied insuck of breath. "Bailey Boy!" she called.

"I was a gospel singer for a while," The Misfit said. "I been most everything. Been in the arm service, both land and sea, at home and abroad, been twict married, been an undertaker, been with the railroads, plowed Mother Earth, been in a tornado, seen a man burnt alive oncet," and looked up at the children's mother and the little girl who were sitting close together, their faces white and their eyes glassy; "I even seen a woman flogged," he said.

"Pray, pray," the grandmother began, "pray, pray . . ." 110

"I never was a bad boy that I remember of," The Misfit said in an almost dreamy voice, "but somewheres along the line I done something wrong and got sent to the penitentiary. I was buried alive," and he looked up and held her attention to him by a steady stare.

"That's when you should have started to pray," she said. "What did you do to get sent to the penitentiary that first time?"

"Turn to the right, it was a wall," The Misfit said, looking up again at the cloudless sky. "Turn to the left, it was a wall. Look up it was a ceiling, look down it was a floor. I forget what I done, lady. I set there and set there, trying to remember what it was I done and I ain't recalled it to this day. Oncet in a while, I would think it was coming to me, but it never come."

"Maybe they put you in by mistake," the old lady said vaguely.

"Nome," he said. "It wasn't no mistake. They had the papers on 115 me."

"You must have stolen something," she said.

The Misfit sneered slightly. "Nobody had nothing I wanted," he said. "It was a head-doctor at the penitentiary said what I had done was kill my daddy but I known that for a lie. My daddy died in nineteen ought nineteen of the epidemic flu and I never had a thing to do with it. He was buried in the Mount Hopewell Baptist churchyard and you can go there and see for yourself."

"If you would pray," the old lady said, "Jesus would help you."

"That's right," The Misfit said.

"Well then, why don't you pray?" she asked trembling with delight 120 suddenly.

"I don't want no hep," he said. "I'm doing all right by myself."

Bobby Lee and Hiram came ambling back from the woods. Bobby Lee was dragging a yellow shirt with bright blue parrots in it.

"Throw me that shirt, Bobby Lee," The Misfit said. The shirt came flying at him and landed on his shoulder and he put it on. The grandmother couldn't name what the shirt reminded her of. "No, lady," The Misfit said while he was buttoning it up, "I found out the crime don't matter. You can do one thing or you can do another, kill a man or take a tire off his car, because sooner or later you're going to forget what it was you done and just be punished for it."

The children's mother had begun to make heaving noises as if she couldn't get her breath. "Lady," he asked, "would you and that little girl like to step off yonder with Bobby Lee and Hiram and join your husband?"

"Yes, thank you," the mother said faintly. Her left arm dangled help- 125 lessly and she was holding the baby, who had gone to sleep, in the other.

"Hep that lady up, Hiram," The Misfit said as she struggled to climb out of the ditch, "and Bobby Lee, you hold onto that little girl's hand."

"I don't want to hold hands with him," June Starr said. "He reminds me of a pig."

The fat boy blushed and laughed and caught her by the arm and pulled her off into the woods after Hiram and her mother.

Alone with The Misfit, the grandmother found that she had lost her voice. There was not a cloud in the sky nor any sun. There was nothing around her but woods. She wanted to tell him that he must pray. She opened and closed her mouth several times before anything came out. Finally she found herself saying, "Jesus, Jesus," meaning, Jesus will help you, but the way she was saying it, it sounded as if she might be cursing.

"Yes'm," the Misfit said as if he agreed. "Jesus thown everything off balance. It was the same case with Him as with me except He hadn't committed any crime and they could prove I had committed one because they had the papers on me. Of course," he said, "they never shown me my papers. That's why I sign myself now. I said long ago, you get you a signature and sign everything you do and keep a copy of it. Then you'll know what you done and you can hold up the crime to the punishment and see do they match and in the end you'll have something to prove you ain't been treated right. I call myself The Misfit," he said, "because I can't make what all I done wrong fit what all I gone through in punishment."

There was a piercing scream from the woods, followed closely by a   130 pistol report. "Does it seem right to you, lady, that one is punished a heap and another ain't punished at all?"

"Jesus!" the old lady cried. "You've got good blood! I know you wouldn't shoot a lady! I know you come from nice people! Pray! Jesus, you ought not to shoot a lady. I'll give you all the money I've got!"

"Lady," The Misfit said, looking beyond her far into the woods, "there never was a body that give the undertaker a tip."

There were two more pistol reports and the grandmother raised her head like a parched old turkey hen crying for water and called, "Bailey Boy, Bailey Boy!" as if her heart would break.

"Jesus was the only One that ever raised the dead." The Misfit continued, "and He shouldn't have done it. He thown everything off balance. If He did what He said, then it's nothing for you to do but thow away everything and follow Him, and if He didn't, then it's nothing for you to do but enjoy the few minutes you got left the best way you can—by killing somebody or burning down his house or doing some other meanness to him. No pleasure but meanness," he said and his voice had become almost a snarl.

"Maybe He didn't raise the dead," the old lady mumbled, not know-   135 ing what she was saying and feeling so dizzy that she sank down in the ditch with her legs twisted under her.

"I wasn't there so I can't say He didn't," The Misfit said. "I wisht I had of been there," he said, hitting the ground with his fist. "It ain't right I wasn't there because if I had of been there I would of known. Listen lady," he said in a high voice, "if I had of been there I would of known and I wouldn't be like I am now." His voice seemed about to crack and the grandmother's head cleared for an instant. She saw the man's face twisted close to her own as if he was going to cry and she murmured, "Why you're one of my babies. You're one of my own children!" She reached out and touched him on the shoulder. The Misfit sprang back as if a snake had bitten him and shot her three times through the chest. Then he put his gun down on the ground and took off his glasses and began to clean them.

Hiram and Bobby Lee returned from the woods and stood over the ditch, looking down at the grandmother who half sat and half lay in a puddle of blood with her legs crossed under her like a child's and her face smiling up at the cloudless sky.

Without his glasses, The Misfit's eyes were red-rimmed and pale and defenseless-looking. "Take her off and thow her where you thown the others," he said, picking up the cat that was rubbing itself against his leg.

"She was a talker, wasn't she?" Bobby Lee said, sliding down the ditch with a yodel.

"She would of been a good woman," The Misfit said, "if it had been   140 somebody there to shoot her every minute of her life."

"Some fun!" Bobby Lee said.

"Shut up, Bobby Lee," The Misfit said. "It's no real pleasure in life."

The Reader's Presence

1. The grandmother is described only indirectly, through her words, actions, and interactions with others. Reread paragraphs 1–9. How does the grandmother appear to see herself? How do you see her? In what ways does the writer's "voice" influence your impression of the character?

2. What might the Misfit figure symbolize in relation to the grandmother and her family? Does his nickname have any significance? What sort of tone does O'Connor establish in the Misfit encounter? Is it eerie, comedic, or somewhere in between? Imagine the story as presented in a different tone; how would it differ? What does O'Connor's position on the characters and events appear to be? What clues in her approach lead you to your conclusion? (See also O'Connor's commentary on the story.)

3. In "The Writer at Work" that follows, O'Connor discusses the crucial action or gesture that makes a story work. "[I]t is probably some action, some gesture of a character that is unlike any other in the story, one which indicates where the real heart of the story lies. . . . It would be a gesture which somehow made contact with mystery" (paragraph 12). O'Connor locates this key moment in

paragraph 136 of "A Good Man Is Hard to Find" (page 865), when the grandmother's "head cleared for an instant." Locate the crucial gesture or action in Raymond Carver's story "Popular Mechanics" (page 837) and in Amy Tan's story "Jing-Mei Woo: Two Kinds" (page 878). Is O'Connor's description of such a gesture and its key role in "making a story hold up" applicable to stories by writers other than herself? Is "mystery" as important to Carver and to Tan as it is to O'Connor?

THE WRITER AT WORK

Flannery O'Connor on Her Own Work

Flannery O'Connor's "A Good Man Is Hard to Find" ranks as one of American fiction's most durable short stories. It has been reprinted and analyzed in critical periodicals hundreds of times since it first appeared in 1953. Ten years after its first publication and shortly before her untimely death, O'Connor was invited to read the story at Hollins College in Virginia, where she made the following remarks. Her comments on the story were then included in a collection of nonfiction published by her editor in 1969 under the very appropriate title "Mystery and Manners." As you consider the story, you may want to focus on these terms: mystery and manners. How does each word describe an important aspect of the story? How are they interrelated? You should also consider the story from the perspective O'Connor herself provides in the following selection. Do you think her comments on her own story are critically persuasive? Did you come away from the story with a different sense of its significance? Do you think that what an author says about his or her own work must always be the final word?

Last fall I received a letter from a student who said she would be "graciously appreciative" if I would tell her "just what enlightenment" I expected her to get from each of my stories. I suspect she had a paper to write. I wrote her back to forget about the enlightenment and just try to enjoy them. I knew that was the most unsatisfactory answer I could have given because, of course, she didn't want to enjoy them, she just wanted to figure them out.

In most English classes the short story has become a kind of literary specimen to be dissected. Every time a story of mine appears in a Freshman anthology, I have a vision of it, with its little organs laid open, like a frog in a bottle.

I realize that a certain amount of this what-is-the-significance has to go on, but I think something has gone wrong in the process when, for so many students, the story becomes simply a problem to be solved, something which you evaporate to get Instant Enlightenment.

A story really isn't any good unless it successfully resists paraphrase, unless it hangs on and expands in the mind. Properly, you analyze to enjoy, but it's equally true that to analyze with any discrimination, you have to have enjoyed already, and I think that the best reason to hear a story read is that it should stimulate that primary enjoyment.

I don't have any pretensions to being an Aeschylus or Sophocles and providing you in this story with a cathartic experience out of your mythic background, though this story I'm going to read certainly calls up a good deal of the South's mythic background, and it should elicit from you a degree of pity and terror, even though its way of being serious is a comic one. I do think, though, that like the Greeks you should know what is going to happen in this story so that any element of suspense in it will be transferred from its surface to its interior.

I would be most happy if you had already read it, happier still if you knew it well, but since experience has taught me to keep my expectations along these lines modest, I'll tell you that this is the story of a family of six which, on its way driving to Florida, gets wiped out by an escaped convict who calls himself the Misfit. The family is made up of the Grandmother and her son, Bailey, and his children, John Wesley and June Star and the baby, and there is also the cat and the children's mother. The cat is named Pitty Sing, and the Grandmother is taking him with them, hidden in a basket.

Now I think it behooves me to try to establish with you the basis on which reason operates in this story. Much of my fiction takes its character from a reasonable use of the unreasonable, though the reasonableness of my use of it may not always be apparent. The assumptions that underlie this use of it, however, are those of the central Christian mysteries. These are assumptions to which a large part of the modern audience takes exception. About this I can only say that there are perhaps other ways than my own in which this story could be read, but none other by which it could have been written. Belief, in my own case anyway, is the engine that makes perception operate.

The heroine of this story, the Grandmother, is in the most significant position life offers the Christian. She is facing death. And to all appearances she, like the rest of us, is not too well prepared for it. She would like to see the event postponed. Indefinitely.

I've talked to a number of teachers who use this story in class and who tell their students that the Grandmother is evil, that in fact, she's a witch, even down to the cat. One of these teachers told me that his students, and particularly his Southern students, resisted this interpretation with a certain bemused vigor, and he didn't understand why. I had to tell him that they resisted it because they all had grandmothers or great-aunts just like her at home, and they knew, from personal experience, that the old lady lacked comprehension, but that she had a good heart. The Southerner is usually tolerant of those weaknesses that proceed from innocence, and he knows that a taste for self-preservation can be readily combined with the missionary spirit.

This same teacher was telling his students that morally the Misfit was several cuts above the Grandmother. He had a really sentimental attachment to the Misfit. But then a prophet gone wrong is almost always more interesting than your grandmother, and you have to let people take their pleasures where they find them.

It is true that the old lady is a hypocritical old soul; her wits are no match for the Misfit's, nor is her capacity for grace equal to his; yet I think the unprejudiced reader will feel that the Grandmother has a special kind of triumph in this story which instinctively we do not allow to someone altogether bad.

I often ask myself what makes a story work, and what makes it hold up as a story, and I have decided that it is probably some action, some gesture of a character that is unlike any other in the story, one which indicates where the real heart of the story lies. This would have to be an action or a gesture which was both totally right and totally unexpected; it would have to be one that was both in character and beyond character; it would have to suggest both the world and eternity. The action or gesture I'm talking about would have to be on the anagogical level, that is, the level which has to do with the Divine life and our participation in it. It would be a gesture that transcended any neat allegory that might have been intended or any pat moral categories a reader could make. It would be a gesture which somehow made contact with mystery.

There is a point in this story where such a gesture occurs. The Grandmother is at last alone, facing the Misfit. Her head clears for an instant and she realizes, even in her limited way, that she is responsible for the man before her and joined to him by ties of kinship which have their roots deep in the mystery she has been merely prattling about so far. And at this point, she does the right thing, she makes the right gesture.

I find that students are often puzzled by what she says and does here, but I think myself that if I took out this gesture and what she says with it, I would have no story. What was left would not be worth your attention. Our age not only does not have a very sharp eye for the almost imperceptible intrusions of grace, it no longer has much feeling for the nature of the violences which precede and follow them. The devil's greatest wile, Baudelaire has said, is to convince us that he does not exist.

I suppose the reasons for the use of so much violence in modern fiction will differ with each writer who uses it, but in my own stories I have found that violence is strangely capable of returning my characters to reality and preparing them to accept their moment of grace. Their heads are so hard that almost nothing else will do the work. This idea, that reality is something to which we must be returned at considerable cost, is one which is seldom understood by the casual reader, but it is one which is implicit in the Christian view of the world.   15

I don't want to equate the Misfit with the devil. I prefer to think that, however unlikely this may seem, the old lady's gesture, like the mustard-seed, will grow to be a great crow-filled tree in the Misfit's heart, and will be enough of a pain to him there to turn him into the prophet he was meant to become. But that's another story.

This story has been called grotesque, but I prefer to call it literal. A good story is literal in the same sense that a child's drawing is literal. When a child draws, he doesn't intend to distort but to set down exactly what he sees, and as his gaze is direct, he sees the lines that create motion. Now the lines of motion that interest the writer are usually invisible. They are lines of spiritual motion. And in this story you should be on the lookout for such things as the action of grace in the Grandmother's soul, and not for the dead bodies.

We hear many complaints about the prevalence of violence in modern fiction, and it is always assumed that this violence is a bad thing and meant to be an end in itself. With the serious writer, violence is never an end in itself. It is the extreme situation that best reveals what we are essentially, and I believe these are times when writers are more interested in what we are essentially than in the tenor of our daily lives. Violence is a force which can be used for good or evil, and among other things taken by it is the kingdom of heaven. But regardless of what can be taken by it, the man in the violent situation reveals those qualities least dispensable in his personality, those qualities which are all he will have to take into eternity with him; and since the characters in this story are all on the verge of eternity, it is appropriate to think of what they take with them. In any case, I hope that if you consider these points in connection with the story, you will come to see it as something more than an account of a family murdered on the way to Florida.

125

Tillie Olsen

I Stand Here Ironing

Strongly influenced by her politically active Jewish parents and by her experiences as a union laborer, Tillie Olsen (b. 1912 or 1913) writes about the struggles of the working class, the poor, and women. While raising four children and working a variety of jobs to support her family, Olsen was unable to devote herself to writing until 1956, when she received a Stanford University Creative Writing Fellowship after taking a writing course at San Francisco State University. Other recognition for her work includes an O. Henry Award for best short story, a Guggenheim Fellowship, a Rea Award for short fiction, and several honorary degrees. She has taught at various colleges, such as Amherst College, Massachusetts Institute of Technology, Kenyon College, and University of California at Los Angeles. "I Stand Here Ironing" is from Olsen's first book, a collection of four short stories titled Tell Me a Riddle *(1961). Her only novel,* Yonnondio: From the Thirties *(1974), describes the plight of a poor family during the Depression. In her book of essays,* Silences *(1978), Olsen explores the difficulties writers encounter as a result of economic factors, racial prejudice, gender bias, or familial obligations. She is also editor of* Mother to Daughter, Daughter to Mother *(1984) and coeditor of* Mothers and Daughters, That Special Quality *(1995).*

I stand here ironing, and what you asked me moves tormented back and forth with the iron.

"I wish you would manage the time to come in and talk with me about your daughter. I'm sure you can help me understand her. She's a youngster who needs help and whom I'm deeply interested in helping."

"Who needs help." . . . Even if I came, what good would it do? You think because I am her mother I have a key, or that in some way you could use me as a key? She has lived for nineteen years. There is all that life that has happened outside of me, beyond me.

And when is there time to remember, to sift, to weigh, to estimate, to total? I will start and there will be an interruption and I will have to gather it all together again. Or I will become engulfed with all I did or did not do, with what should have been and what cannot be helped.

She was a beautiful baby. The first and only one of our five that was   5 beautiful at birth. You do not guess how new and uneasy her tenancy in her now-loveliness. You did not know her all those years she was thought homely, or see her poring over her baby pictures, making me tell her over and over how beautiful she had been—and would be, I would tell her— and was now, to the seeing eye. But the seeing eyes were few or nonexistent. Including mine.

I nursed her. They feel that's important nowadays, I nursed all the children, but with her, with all the fierce rigidity of first motherhood, I did like the books then said. Though her cries battered me to trembling and my breasts ached with swollenness, I waited till the clock decreed.

Why do I put that first? I do not even know if it matters, or if it explains anything.

She was a beautiful baby. She blew shining bubbles of sound. She loved motion, loved light, loved color and music and textures. She would lie on the floor in her blue overalls patting the surface so hard in ecstasy her hands and feet would blur. She was a miracle to me, but when she was eight months old I had to leave her daytimes with the woman downstairs to whom she was no miracle at all, for I worked or looked for work and for Emily's father, who "could no longer endure" (he wrote in his good-bye note) "sharing want with us."

I was nineteen. It was pre-relief, pre-WPA world of the depression. I would start running as soon as I got off the streetcar, running up the stairs, the place smelling sour, and awake or asleep to startle awake, when she saw me she would break into a clogged weeping that could not be comforted, a weeping I can hear yet.

After a while I found a job hashing at night so I could be with her   10
days, and it was better. But it came to where I had to bring her to his
family and leave her.

It took a long time to raise the money for her fare back. Then she got
chicken pox and I had to wait longer. When she finally came, I hardly
knew her, walking quick and nervous like her father, looking like her father, thin, and dressed in a shoddy red that yellowed her skin and glared
at the pockmarks. All the baby loveliness gone.

She was two. Old enough for nursery school they said, and I did not
know then what I know now—the fatigue of the long day, and the lacer-
ations of group life in the kinds of nurseries that are only parking places
for children.

Except that it would have made no difference if I had known. It was
the only place there was. It was the only way we could be together, the
only way I could hold a job.

And even without knowing, I knew. I knew the teacher that was evil
because all these years it has curdled into my memory, the little boy
hunched in the corner, her rasp, "why aren't you outside, because Alvin
hits you? that's no reason, go out, scaredy." I knew Emily hated it even if
she did not clutch and implore "don't go Mommy" like the other children, mornings.

She always had a reason why we should stay home. Momma, you   15
look sick. Momma, I feel sick. Momma, the teachers aren't there today,
they're sick. Momma, we can't go, there was a fire last night. Momma,
it's a holiday today, no school, they told me.

But never a direct protest, never rebellion. I think of our others in
their three-, four-year-oldness—the explosions, the tempers, the denunci-
ations, the demands—and I feel suddenly ill. I put the iron down. What
in me demanded that goodness in her? And what was the cost, the cost to
her of such goodness?

The old man living in the back once said in his gentle way: "You
should smile at Emily more when you look at her." What *was* in my face
when I looked at her? I loved her. There were all the acts of love.

It was only with the others I remembered what he said, and it was the
face of joy, and not of care or tightness or worry I turned to them—too
late for Emily. She does not smile easily, let alone almost always as her
brothers and sisters do. Her face is closed and sombre, but when she
wants, how fluid. You must have seen it in her pantomimes, you spoke of
her rare gift for comedy on the stage that rouses laughter out of the audience so dear they applaud and applaud and do not want to let her go.

Where does it come from, that comedy? There was none of it in her
when she came back to me that second time, after I had to send her away
again. She had a new daddy now to learn to love, and I think perhaps it
was a better time.

Except when we left her alone nights, telling ourselves she was old   20
enough.

"Can't you go some other time, Mommy, like tomorrow?" she would ask. "Will it be just a little while you'll be gone? Do you promise?"

The time we came back, the front door open, the clock on the floor in the hall. She rigid awake. "It wasn't just a little while. I didn't cry. Three times I called you, just three times, and then I ran downstairs to open the door so you could come faster. The clock talked loud. I threw it away, it scared me what it talked."

She said the clock talked loud again that night I went to the hospital to have Susan. She was delirious with the fever that comes before red measles, but she was fully conscious all the week I was gone and the week after we were home when she could not come near the new baby or me.

She did not get well. She stayed skeleton thin, not wanting to eat, and night after night she had nightmares. She would call for me, and I would rouse from exhaustion to sleepily call back: "You're all right, darling, go to sleep, it's just a dream," and if she still called, in a sterner voice, "now go to sleep, Emily, there's nothing to hurt you." Twice, only twice, when I had to get up for Susan anyhow, I went in to sit with her.

Now when it is too late (as if she would let me hold her and comfort her like I do the others) I get up and go to her at once at her moan or restless stirring. "Are you awake, Emily? Can I get you something?" And the answer is always the same: "No, I'm all right, go back to sleep, Mother."   25

They persuaded me at the clinic to send her away to a convalescent home in the country where "she can have the kind of food and care you can't manage for her, and you'll be free to concentrate on the new baby." They still send children to that place. I see pictures on the society page of sleek young women planning affairs to raise money for it, or dancing at the affairs, or decorating Easter eggs or filling Christmas stockings for the children.

They never have a picture of the children so I do not know if the girls still wear those gigantic red bows and the ravaged looks on the every other Sunday when parents can come to visit "unless otherwise notified" — as we were notified the first six weeks.

Oh it is a handsome place, green lawns and tall trees and fluted flower beds. High up on the balconies of each cottage the children stand, the girls in their red bows and white dresses, the boys in white suits and giant red ties. The parents stand below shrieking up to be heard and the children shriek down to be heard, and between them the invisible wall "Not To Be Contaminated by Parental Germs or Physical Affection."

There was a tiny girl who always stood hand in hand with Emily. Her parents never came. One visit she was gone. "They moved her to Rose Cottage," Emily shouted in explanation. "They don't like you to love anybody here."

She wrote once a week, the labored writing of a seven-year-old. "I am   30 fine. How is the baby. If I write my leter nicly I will have a star. Love."

There never was a star. We wrote every other day, letters she could never hold or keep but only hear read—once. "We simply do not have room for children to keep any personal possessions," they patiently explained when we pieced one Sunday's shrieking together to plead how much it would mean to Emily, who loved so to keep things, to be allowed to keep her letters and cards.

Each visit she looked frailer. "She isn't eating," they told us.

(They had runny eggs for breakfast or mush with lumps, Emily said later, I'd hold it in my mouth and not swallow. Nothing ever tasted good, just when they had chicken.)

It took us eight months to get her released home, and only the fact that she gained back so little of her seven lost pounds convinced the social worker.

I used to try to hold and love her after she came back, but her body would stay stiff, and after a while she'd push away. She ate little. Food sickened her, and I think much of life too. Oh she had physical lightness and brightness, twinkling by on skates, bouncing like a ball up and down up and down over the jump rope, skimming over the hill; but these were momentary.

She fretted about her appearance, thin and dark and foreign-looking   35 at a time when every little girl was supposed to look or thought she should look a chubby blonde replica of Shirley Temple. The doorbell sometimes rang for her, but no one seemed to come and play in the house or to be a best friend. Maybe because we moved so much.

There was a boy she loved painfully through two school semesters. Months later she told me how she had taken pennies from my purse to buy him candy. "Licorice was his favorite and I brought him some every day, but he still liked Jennifer better'n me. Why, Mommy?" The kind of question for which there is no answer.

School was a worry for her. She was not glib or quick in a world where glibness and quickness were easily confused with ability to learn. To her overworked and exasperated teachers she was an overconscientious "slow learner" who kept trying to catch up and was absent entirely too often.

I let her be absent, though sometimes the illness was imaginary. How different from my now-strictness about attendance with the others. I wasn't working. We had a new baby. I was home anyhow. Sometimes, after Susan grew old enough, I would keep her home from school, too, to have them all together.

Mostly Emily had asthma, and her breathing, harsh and labored, would fill the house with a curiously tranquil sound. I would bring the two old dresser mirrors and her boxes of collections to her bed. She would select beads and single earrings, bottle tops and shells, dried flowers and pebbles, old postcards and scraps, all sorts of oddments; then she and Susan would play Kingdom, setting up landscapes and furniture, peopling them with action.

Those were the only times of peaceful companionship between her   40
and Susan. I have edged away from it, that poisonous feeling between
them, that terrible balancing of hurts and needs I had to do between the
two, and did so badly, those earlier years.

Oh there were conflicts between the others too, each one human,
needing, demanding, hurting, taking—but only between Emily and
Susan, no, Emily toward Susan that corroding resentment. It seems so obvious on the surface, yet it is not obvious; Susan, the second child, Susan,
golden- and curly-haired and chubby, quick and articulate and assured,
everything in appearance and manner Emily was not; Susan, not able to
resist Emily's precious things, losing or sometimes clumsily breaking
them; Susan telling jokes and riddles to company for applause while
Emily sat silent (to say to me later: that was *my* riddle, Mother, I told it
to Susan); Susan, who for all the five years' difference in age was just a
year behind Emily in developing physically.

I am glad for that slow physical development that widened the difference between her and her contemporaries, though she suffered over it.
She was too vulnerable for that terrible world of youthful competition, of
preening and parading, of constant measuring of yourself against every
other, of envy, "If I had that copper hair," "If I had that skin. . . ." She
tormented herself enough about not looking like the others, there was
enough of unsureness, the having to be conscious of words before you
speak, the constant caring—what are they thinking of me? without having it all magnified by the merciless physical drives.

Ronnie is calling. He is wet and I change him. It is rare there is such a
cry now. That time of motherhood is almost behind me when the ear is
not one's own but must always be racked and listening for the child cry,
the child call. We sit for a while and I hold him, looking out over the city
spread in charcoal with its soft aisles of light. "*Shoogily,*" he breathes and
curls closer. I carry him back to bed, asleep. *Shoogily.* A funny word, a
family word, inherited from Emily, invented by her to say: *comfort.*

In this and other ways she leaves her seal, I say aloud. And startle at
my saying it. What do I mean? What did I start to gather together, to try
and make coherent? I was at the terrible, growing years. War years. I do
not remember them well. I was working, there were four smaller ones
now, there was not time for her. She had to help be a mother, and housekeeper, and shopper. She had to get her seal. Mornings of crisis and near
hysteria trying to get lunches packed, hair combed, coats and shoes
found, everyone to school or Child Care on time, the baby ready for
transportation. And always the paper scribbled on by a smaller one, the
book looked at by Susan then mislaid, the homework not done. Running
out to that huge school where she was one, she was lost, she was a drop;
suffering over the unpreparedness, stammering and unsure in her
classes.

There was so little time left at night after the kids were bedded down.   45
She would struggle over books, always eating (it was in those years she

developed her enormous appetite that is legendary in our family) and I would be ironing, or preparing food for the next day, or writing V-mail to Bill, or tending the baby. Sometimes, to make me laugh, or out of her despair, she would imitate happenings or types at school.

I think I said once: "Why don't you do something like this in the school amateur show?" One morning she phoned me at work, hardly understandable through the weeping: "Mother, I did it. I won, I won; they gave me first prize; they clapped and clapped and wouldn't let me go."

Now suddenly she was Somebody, and as imprisoned in her difference as she had been in anonymity.

She began to be asked to perform at other high schools, even in colleges, then at city and statewide affairs. The first one we went to, I only recognized her that first moment when thin, shy, she almost drowned herself into the curtains. Then: Was this Emily? The control, the command, the convulsing and deadly clowning, the spell, then the roaring, stamping audience, unwilling to let this rare and precious laughter out of their lives.

Afterwards: You ought to do something about her with a gift like that—but without money or knowing how, what does one do? We have left it all to her, and the gift has so often eddied inside, clogged and clotted, has been used and growing.

She is coming. She runs up the stairs two at a time with her light   50
graceful step, and I know she is happy tonight. Whatever it was that occasioned your call did not happen today.

"Aren't you ever going to finish the ironing, Mother? Whistler painted his mother in a rocker. I'd have to paint mine standing over an ironing board." This is one of her communicative nights and she tells me everything and nothing as she fixes herself a plate of food out of the icebox.

She is so lovely. Why did you want me to come in at all? Why were you concerned? She will find her way.

She starts up the stairs to bed. "Don't get me up with the rest in the morning." "But I thought you were having midterms." "Oh, those," she comes back in, kisses me, and says quite lightly, "in a couple of years when we'll all be atom-dead they won't matter a bit."

She has said it before. She *believes* it. But because I have been dredging the past, and all that compounds a human being is so heavy and meaningful in me, I cannot endure it tonight.

I will never total it all. I will never come in to say: She was a child sel-   55
dom smiled at. Her father left me before she was a year old. I had to work her first six years when there was work, or I sent her home and to his relatives. There were years she had care she hated. She was dark and thin and foreign-looking in a world where the prestige went to blondeness and curly hair and dimples, she was slow where glibness was prized. She was a child of anxious, not proud, love. We were poor and could not afford for her the soil of easy growth. I was a young mother, I was a dis-

tracted mother. There were other children pushing up, demanding. Her younger sister seemed all that she was not. There were years she did not want me to touch her. She kept too much in herself, her life was such she had to keep too much in herself. My wisdom came too late. She has much to her and probably little will come of it. She is a child of her age, of depression, of war, of fear.

Let her be. So all that is in her will not bloom but in how many does it? There is still enough left to live by. Only help her to know—help make it so there is cause for her to know—that she is more than this dress on the ironing board, helpless before the iron.

The Reader's Presence

1. Olsen introduces the narrator solely through her own words. Reread paragraphs 1–7. What sort of person is she? To whom is she speaking? Can you understand more about her and her situation than she does? Through what means? What clues in the narrative lead you to distinguish the writer's "voice" from the narrator's?

2. The reader's view of the narrator's past is filtered both through her perspective and through time. In a few lines, recount Emily's growing-up as the narrator describes it. How might the narrator have viewed it at the time? What does hindsight seem to have added to or taken from it? Is the narrator a reliable source of information? Why or why not? Should the narrator's later version of the past be taken as more, or less, accurate? Does Olsen suggest a different interpretation than the one the narrator offers? If so, where do you see this division of "voice"?

3. The narrator compares her daughter to "this dress on the ironing board, helpless before the iron." What might the iron signify? Is the daughter the only helpless one? What does the writer refrain from saying? Do these omissions seem significant? If so, in what ways? Alice Walker's story "Everyday Use" (page 895) is also about a mother and her daughter, but it ends on a very different note than Olsen's. How would you characterize the difference between the endings? How do the different endings continue the deep contrasts between the two stories?

126

Amy Tan

Jing-Mei Woo: Two Kinds

"Two Kinds" is one of sixteen stories that compose Amy Tan's best-selling novel, The Joy Luck Club *(1989). Tan's success as a writer seemed to come about overnight, but she reminds us that writing is a process that can consume large amounts of time, energy, patience, and paper. When writing her second novel, Tan recalls, she started by writing—and throwing away—at least one thousand pages of manuscript that could have become several books. "But those books were not meant to become anything more than a lesson to me on what it takes to write fiction: persistence imposed by a limited focus. . . . The focus required of a priest, a nun, a convict serving a life's sentence."*

For more information on Amy Tan, see page 260.

My mother believed you could be anything you wanted to be in America. You could open a restaurant. You could work for the government and get good retirement. You could buy a house with almost no money down. You could become rich. You could become instantly famous.

"Of course you can be prodigy, too," my mother told me when I was nine. "You can be best anything. What does Auntie Lindo know? Her daughter, she is only best tricky."

America was where all my mother's hopes lay. She had come here in 1949 after losing everything in China: her mother and father, her family home, her first husband, and two daughters, twin baby girls. But she never looked back with regret. There were so many ways for things to get better.

We didn't immediately pick the right kind of prodigy. At first my mother thought I could be a Chinese Shirley Temple. We'd watch Shirley's old movies on TV as though they were training films. My mother would poke my arm and say, *"Ni kan"*—You watch. And I would see Shirley tapping her feet, or singing a sailor song, or pursing her lips in a very round O while saying, "Oh my goodness."

"*Ni kan,*" said my mother as Shirley's eyes flooded with tears. "You   5
already know how. Don't need talent for crying!"

Soon after my mother got this idea about Shirley Temple, she took
me to a beauty training school in the Mission district and put me in the
hands of a student who could barely hold the scissors without shaking.
Instead of getting big fat curls, I emerged with an uneven mass of crinkly
black fuzz. My mother dragged me off to the bathroom and tried to wet
down my hair.

"You look like Negro Chinese," she lamented, as if I had done this
on purpose.

The instructor of the beauty training school had to lop off these
soggy clumps to make my hair even again. "Peter Pan is very popular
these days," the instructor assured my mother. I now had hair the length
of a boy's, with straight-across bangs that hung at a slant two inches
above my eyebrows. I liked the haircut and it made me actually look forward to my future fame.

In fact, in the beginning, I was just as excited as my mother, maybe
even more so. I pictured this prodigy part of me as many different images,
trying each one on for size. I was a dainty ballerina girl standing by the
curtains, waiting to hear the right music that would send me floating on
my tiptoes. I was like the Christ child lifted out of the straw manger, crying with holy indignity. I was Cinderella stepping from her pumpkin carriage with sparkly cartoon music filling the air.

In all of my imaginings, I was filled with a sense that I would soon   10
become *perfect.* My mother and father would adore me. I would be beyond reproach. I would never feel the need to sulk for anything.

But sometimes the prodigy in me became impatient. "If you don't
hurry up and get me out of here, I'm disappearing for good," it warned.
"And then you'll always be nothing."

Every night after dinner, my mother and I would sit at the Formica
kitchen table. She would present new tests, taking her examples from stories of amazing children she had read in *Ripley's Believe It or Not,* or
Good Housekeeping, Reader's Digest, and a dozen other magazines she
kept in a pile in our bathroom. My mother got these magazines from
people whose houses she cleaned. And since she cleaned many houses
each week, we had a great assortment. She would look through them all,
searching for stories about remarkable children.

The first night she brought out a story about a three-year-old boy
who knew the capitals of all the states and even most of the European
countries. A teacher was quoted as saying the little boy could also pronounce the names of the foreign cities correctly.

"What's the capital of Finland?" my mother asked me, looking at the
magazine story.

All I knew was the capital of California, because Sacramento was the   15
name of the street we lived on in Chinatown. "Nairobi!" I guessed, saying

the most foreign word I could think of. She checked to see if that was possibly one way to pronounce "Helsinki" before showing me the answer.

The tests got harder—multiplying numbers in my head, finding the queen of hearts in a deck of cards, trying to stand on my head without using my hands, predicting the daily temperatures in Los Angeles, New York, and London.

One night I had to look at a page from the Bible for three minutes and then report everything I could remember. "Now Jehoshaphat had riches and honor in abundance and . . . that's all I remember, Ma," I said.

And after seeing my mother's disappointed face once again, something inside of me began to die. I hated the tests, the raised hopes and failed expectations. Before going to bed that night, I looked in the mirror above the bathroom sink and when I saw only my face staring back— and that it would always be this ordinary face—I began to cry. Such a sad, ugly girl! I made high-pitched noises like a crazed animal, trying to scratch out the face in the mirror.

And then I saw what seemed to be the prodigy side of me—because I had never seen that face before. I looked at my reflection, blinking so I could see more clearly. The girl staring back at me was angry, powerful. This girl and I were the same. I had new thoughts, willful thoughts, or rather thoughts filled with lots of won'ts. I won't let her change me, I promised myself. I won't be what I'm not.

So now on nights when my mother presented her tests, I performed   20
listlessly, my head propped on one arm. I pretended to be bored. And I was. I got so bored I started counting the bellows of the foghorns out on the bay while my mother drilled me in other areas. The sound was comforting and reminded me of the cow jumping over the moon. And the next day, I played a game with myself, seeing if my mother would give up on me before eight bellows. After a while I usually counted only one, maybe two bellows at most. At last she was beginning to give up hope.

Two or three months had gone by without any mention of my being a prodigy again. And then one day my mother was watching *The Ed Sullivan Show* on TV. The TV was old and the sound kept shorting out. Every time my mother got halfway up from the sofa to adjust the set, the sound would go back on and Ed would be there talking. As soon as she sat down, Ed would go silent again. She got up, the TV broke into loud piano music. She sat down. Silence. Up and down, back and forth, quiet and loud. It was like a stiff embraceless dance between her and the TV set. Finally she stood by the set with her hand on the sound dial.

She seemed to be entranced by the music, a little frenzied piano piece with this mesmerizing quality, sort of quick passages and then teasing lilting ones before it returned to the quick playful parts.

"*Ni kan*," my mother said, calling me over with hurried hand gestures, "Look here."

I could see why my mother was fascinated by the music. It was being pounded out by a little Chinese girl, about nine years old, with a Peter Pan haircut. The girl had the sauciness of a Shirley Temple. She was proudly modest like a proper Chinese child. And she also did this fancy sweep of a curtsy, so that the fluffy skirt of her white dress cascaded slowly to the floor like the petals of a large carnation.

In spite of these warning signs, I wasn't worried. Our family had no 25 piano and we couldn't afford to buy one, let alone reams of sheet music and piano lessons. So I could be generous in my comments when my mother bad-mouthed the little girl on TV.

"Play note right, but doesn't sound good! No singing sound," complained my mother.

"What are you picking on her for?" I said carelessly. "She's pretty good. Maybe she's not the best, but she's trying hard." I knew almost immediately I would be sorry I said that.

"Just like you," she said. "Not the best. Because you not trying." She gave a little huff as she let go of the sound dial and sat down on the sofa.

The little Chinese girl sat down also to play an encore of "Anitra's Dance" by Grieg. I remember the song, because later on I had to learn how to play it.

Three days after watching *The Ed Sullivan Show,* my mother told me 30 what my schedule would be for piano lessons and piano practice. She had talked to Mr. Chong, who lived on the first floor of our apartment building. Mr. Chong was a retired piano teacher and my mother traded house-cleaning services for weekly lessons and a piano for me to practice on every day, two hours a day, from four until six.

When my mother told me this, I felt as though I had been sent to hell. I whined and then kicked my foot a little when I couldn't stand it anymore.

"Why don't you like me the way I am? I'm *not* a genius! I can't play the piano. And even if I could, I wouldn't go on TV if you paid me a million dollars!" I cried.

My mother slapped me. "Who ask you to be genius?" she shouted. "Only ask you to be your best. For your sake. You think I want you to be genius? Hunh! What for! Who ask you!"

"So ungrateful," I heard her mutter in Chinese. "If she had as much talent as she has temper, she would be famous now."

Mr. Chong, whom I secretly nicknamed Old Chong, was very 35 strange, always tapping his fingers to the silent music of an invisible orchestra. He looked ancient in my eyes. He had lost most of the hair on top of his head and he wore thick glasses and had eyes that always looked tired and sleepy. But he must have been younger than I thought, since he lived with his mother and was not yet married.

I met old lady Chong once and that was enough. She had this peculiar smell like a baby that had done something in its pants. And her fingers felt like a dead person's, like an old peach I once found in the back of the refrigerator, the skin just slid off the meat when I picked it up.

I soon found out why Old Chong had retired from teaching piano. He was deaf. "Like Beethoven!" he shouted to me. "We're both listening only in our head!" And he would start to conduct his frantic silent sonatas.

Our lessons went like this. He would open the book and point to different things, explaining their purpose: "Key! Treble! Bass! No sharps or flats! So this is C major! Listen now and play after me!"

And then he would play the C scale a few times, a simple chord, and then, as if inspired by an old, unreachable itch, he gradually added more notes and running trills and a pounding bass until the music was really something quite grand.

I would play after him, the simple scale, the simple chord, and then I just played some nonsense that sounded like a cat running up and down on top of garbage cans. Old Chong smiled and applauded and then said, "Very good! But now you must learn to keep time!"   40

So that's how I discovered that Old Chong's eyes were too slow to keep up with the wrong notes I was playing. He went through the motions in half-time. To help me keep rhythm, he stood behind me, pushing down on my right shoulder for every beat. He balanced pennies on top of my wrists so I would keep them still as I slowly played scales and arpeggios. He had me curve my hand around an apple and keep that shape when playing chords. He marched stiffly to show me how to make each finger dance up and down, staccato like an obedient little soldier.

He taught me all these things, and that was how I also learned I could be lazy and get away with mistakes, lots of mistakes. If I hit the wrong notes because I hadn't practiced enough, I never corrected myself. I just kept playing in rhythm. And Old Chong kept conducting his own private reverie.

So maybe I never really gave myself a fair chance. I did pick up the basics pretty quickly, and I might have become a good pianist at that young age. But I was so determined not to try, not to be anybody different that I learned to play only the most ear-splitting preludes, the most discordant hymns.

Over the next year, I practiced like this, dutifully in my own way. And then one day I heard my mother and her friend Lindo Jong both talking in a loud bragging tone of voice so others could hear. It was after church, and I was leaning against the brick wall wearing a dress with stiff white petticoats. Auntie Lindo's daughter, Waverly, who was about my age, was standing farther down the wall about five feet away. We had grown up together and shared all the closeness of two sisters squabbling over crayons and dolls. In other words, for the most part, we hated each other. I thought she was snotty. Waverly Jong had gained a certain amount of fame as "Chinatown's Littlest Chinese Chess Champion."

"She bring home too many trophy," lamented Auntie Lindo that Sunday. "All day she play chess. All day I have no time do nothing but dust off her winnings." She threw a scolding look at Waverly, who pretended not to see her.   45

"You lucky you don't have this problem," said Auntie Lindo with a sigh to my mother.

And my mother squared her shoulders and bragged: "Our problem worser than yours. If we ask Jing-mei wash dish, she hear nothing but music. It's like you can't stop this natural talent."

And right then, I was determined to put a stop to her foolish pride.

A few weeks later, Old Chong and my mother conspired to have me play in a talent show which would be held in the church hall. By then, my parents had saved up enough to buy me a secondhand piano, a black Wurlitzer spinet with a scarred bench. It was the showpiece of our living room.

For the talent show, I was to play a piece called "Pleading Child" from   50 Schumann's *Scenes from Childhood*. It was a simple, moody piece that sounded more difficult than it was. I was supposed to memorize the whole thing, playing the repeat parts twice to make the piece sound longer. But I dawdled over it, playing a few bars and then cheating, looking up to see what notes followed. I never really listened to what I was playing. I daydreamed about being somewhere else, about being someone else.

The part I liked to practice best was the fancy curtsy: right foot out, touch the rose on the carpet with a pointed foot, sweep to the side, left leg bends, look up and smile.

My parents invited all the couples from the Joy Luck Club to witness my debut. Auntie Lindo and Uncle Tin were there. Waverly and her two older brothers had also come. The first two rows were filled with children both younger and older than I was. The littlest ones got to go first. They recited simple nursery rhymes, squawked out tunes on miniature violins, twirled Hula Hoops, pranced in pink ballet tutus, and when they bowed or curtsied, the audience would sigh in unison, "Awww," and then clap enthusiastically.

When my turn came, I was very confident. I remember my childish excitement. It was as if I knew, without a doubt, that the prodigy side of me really did exist. I had no fear whatsoever, no nervousness. I remember thinking to myself, This is it! This is it! I looked out over the audience, at my mother's blank face, my father's yawn, Auntie Lindo's stiff-lipped smile, Waverly's sulky expression. I had on a white dress layered with sheets of lace, and a pink bow in my Peter Pan haircut. As I sat down I envisioned people jumping to their feet and Ed Sullivan rushing up to introduce me to everyone on TV.

And I started to play. It was so beautiful. I was so caught up in how lovely I looked that at first I didn't worry how I would sound. So it was a surprise to me when I hit the first wrong note and I realized something didn't sound quite right. And then I hit another and another followed that. A chill started at the top of my head and began to trickle down. Yet I couldn't stop playing, as though my hands were bewitched. I kept thinking my fingers would adjust themselves back, like a train switching to the right track. I played this strange jumble through two repeats, the sour notes staying with me all the way to the end.

When I stood up, I discovered my legs were shaking. Maybe I had 55 just been nervous and the audience, like Old Chong, had seen me go through the right motions and had not heard anything wrong at all. I swept my right foot out, went down on my knee, looked up and smiled. The room was quiet, except for Old Chong, who was beaming and shouting "Bravo! Bravo! Well done!" But then I saw my mother's face, her stricken face. The audience clapped weakly, and as I walked back to my chair, with my whole face quivering as I tried not to cry, I heard a little boy whisper loudly to his mother, "That was awful," and the mother whispered back, "Well, she certainly tried."

And now I realized how many people were in the audience, the whole world it seemed. I was aware of eyes burning into my back. I felt the shame of my mother and father as they sat stiffly throughout the rest of the show.

We could have escaped during the intermission. Pride and some strange sense of honor must have anchored my parents to their chairs. And so we watched it all: the eighteen-year-old boy with a fake mustache who did a magic show and juggled flaming hoops while riding a unicycle. The breasted girl with white makeup who sang from *Madame Butterfly* and got honorable mention. And the eleven-year-old boy who won first prize playing a tricky violin song that sounded like a busy bee.

After the show, the Hsus, the Jongs, and the St. Clairs from the Joy Luck Club came up to my mother and father.

"Lots of talented kids," Auntie Lindo said vaguely, smiling broadly.

"That was somethin' else," said my father, and I wondered if he was 60 referring to me in a humorous way, or whether he even remembered what I had done.

Waverly looked at me and shrugged her shoulders. "You aren't a genius like me," she said matter-of-factly. And if I hadn't felt so bad, I would have pulled her braids and punched her stomach.

But my mother's expression was what devastated me: a quiet, blank look that said she had lost everything. I felt the same way, and it seemed as if everybody were now coming up, like gawkers at the scene of an accident, to see what parts were actually missing. When we got on the bus to go home, my father was humming the busy-bee tune and my mother was silent. I kept thinking she wanted to wait until we got home before shouting at me. But when my father unlocked the door to our apartment, my mother walked in and then went to the back, into the bedroom. No accusations. No blame. And in a way, I felt disappointed. I had been waiting for her to start shouting, so I could shout back and cry and blame her for all my misery.

I assumed my talent-show fiasco meant I never had to play the piano again. But two days later, after school, my mother came out of the kitchen and saw me watching TV.

"Four clock," she reminded me as if it were any other day. I was stunned, as though she were asking me to go through the talent-show torture again. I wedged myself more tightly in front of the TV.

"Turn off TV," she called from the kitchen five minutes later.   65

I didn't budge. And then I decided. I didn't have to do what my mother said anymore. I wasn't her slave. This wasn't China. I had listened to her before and look what happened. She was the stupid one.

She came out from the kitchen and stood in the arched entryway of the living room. "Four clock," she said once again, louder.

"I'm not going to play anymore," I said nonchalantly. "Why should I? I'm not a genius."

She walked over and stood in front of the TV. I saw her chest was heaving up and down in an angry way.

"No!" I said, and I now felt stronger, as if my true self had finally   70
emerged. So this was what had been inside me all along.

"No! I won't!" I screamed.

She yanked me by the arm, pulled me off the floor, snapped off the TV. She was frighteningly strong, half pulling, half carrying me toward the piano as I kicked the throw rugs under my feet. She lifted me up and onto the hard bench. I was sobbing by now, looking at her bitterly. Her chest was heaving even more and her mouth was open, smiling crazily as if she were pleased I was crying.

"You want me to be someone that I'm not!" I sobbed. "I'll never be the kind of daughter you want me to be!"

"Only two kinds of daughters," she shouted in Chinese. "Those who are obedient and those who follow their own mind! Only one kind of daughter can live in this house! Obedient daughter!"

"Then I wish I wasn't your daughter. I wish you weren't my mother,"   75
I shouted. As I said these things I got scared. It felt like worms and toads and slimy things crawling out of my chest, but it also felt good, as if this awful side of me had surfaced, at last.

"Too late change this," said my mother shrilly.

And I could sense her anger rising to its breaking point. I wanted to see it spill over. And that's when I remembered the babies she had lost in China, the ones we never talked about. "Then I wish I'd never been born!" I shouted. "I wish I were dead! Like them."

It was as if I had said the magic words. Alakazam! — and her face went blank, her mouth closed, her arms went slack, and she backed out of the room, stunned, as if she were blowing away like a small brown leaf, thin, brittle, lifeless.

It was not the only disappointment my mother felt in me. In the years that followed, I failed her so many times, each time asserting my own will, my right to fall short of expectations. I didn't get straight As. I didn't become class president. I didn't get into Stanford. I dropped out of college.

For unlike my mother, I did not believe I could be anything I wanted   80
to be. I could only be me.

And for all those years, we never talked about the disaster at the recital or my terrible accusations afterward at the piano bench. All that remained unchecked, like a betrayal that was now unspeakable. So I never found a way to ask her why she had hoped for something so large that failure was inevitable.

And even worse, I never asked her what frightened me the most: Why had she given up hope?

For after our struggle at the piano, she never mentioned my playing again. The lessons stopped. The lid to the piano was closed, shutting out the dust, my misery, and her dreams.

So she surprised me. A few years ago, she offered to give me the piano, for my thirtieth birthday. I had not played in all those years. I saw the offer as a sign of forgiveness, a tremendous burden removed.

"Are you sure?" I asked shyly. "I mean, won't you and Dad miss it?"   85

"No, this your piano," she said firmly. "Always your piano. You only one can play."

"Well, I probably can't play anymore," I said. "It's been years."

"You pick up fast," said my mother, as if she knew this was certain. "You have natural talent. You could been genius if you want to."

"No I couldn't."

"You just not trying," said my mother. And she was neither angry   90
nor sad. She said it as if to announce a fact that could never be disproved. "Take it," she said.

But I didn't at first. It was enough that she had offered it to me. And after that, every time I saw it in my parents' living room, standing in front of the bay windows, it made me feel proud, as if it were a shiny trophy I had won back.

Last week I sent a tuner over to my parents' apartment and had the piano reconditioned, for purely sentimental reasons. My mother had died a few months before and I had been getting things in order for my father, a little bit at a time. I put the jewelry in special silk pouches. The sweaters she had knitted in yellow, pink, bright orange—all the colors I hated—I put those in moth-proof boxes. I found some old Chinese silk dresses, the kind with the little slits up the sides. I rubbed the old silk against my skin, then wrapped them in tissue and decided to take them home with me.

After I had the piano tuned, I opened the lid and touched the keys. It sounded even richer than I imagined. Really, it was a very good piano. Inside the bench were the same exercise notes with handwritten scales, the same secondhand books with their covers held together with yellow tape.

I opened up the Schumann book to the dark little piece I had played at the recital. It was on the left-hand side of the page, "Pleading Child." It looked more difficult than I remembered. I played a few bars, surprised at how easily the notes came back to me.

And for the first time, or so it seemed, I noticed the piece on the   95
right-hand side. It was called "Perfectly Contented." I tried to play this

one as well. It had a lighter melody but the same flowing rhythm and turned out to be quite easy. "Pleading Child" was shorter but slower; "Perfectly Contented" was longer, but faster. And after I played them both a few times, I realized they were two halves of the same song.

The Reader's Presence

1. The story opens with background information on the mother. What objective facts about her are conveyed in the opening section? What subjective impressions of her do you derive from this section? Whose "voice" is evident in this section—the writer's, the narrator's, the mother's, or a mix? Reread the section sentence by sentence; which voices and perspectives do you hear in each? What is the effect of this writing technique for the reader?

2. Tan writes in the first person. Are the writer and narrator exactly the same? What leads you to your conclusion? Reread the second section, supposing that all the events recounted actually occurred to the young Tan. How are they edited and arranged to form a coherent, meaningful whole? What sorts of details are preserved? What sorts of details are left out?

3. Paragraph 62 is a great example of anti-climax: The narrator (and the reader) expects her mother to lose her temper, as she has often in the story up to this point, but instead she disappears silently into the back of the house. The argument takes place in the next section (paragraphs 63–78). How do you describe the tension between these two moments in the story? What is their relation to one another, and to the eventual end of the story? Can you imagine the ending without one section or the other preceding it? How would removing paragraph 62 or the section following it affect your overall sense of the narrator and her parents? Do a similar experiment with Flannery O'Connor's story: "A Good Man Is Hard to Find" (page 854). Remove paragraph 136, and reimagine the ending. How would you describe the role of such swerves in plot and character in a story's overall success?

THE WRITER AT WORK

Amy Tan on Being an Asian American Writer

Voicing a familiar problem for American writers today, Amy Tan speaks of her "responsibilities" to society as a writer. Unlike Harold Bloom, who argues in "In Praise of the Greats" (page 613) that literature is above all a solitary experience with no predictable or measurable social effects, Tan reaches out through her writing—to her family and her heritage, as well as her readers of the present and future. But Tan, like Sherman Alexie, will not be constrained by the expectations of her readers for her to serve as a "representative" or to "right moral wrongs." When asked about the political dimensions of his poetry, John Ashbery, one of America's most important living poets, said, "Well . . . I'm a democrat." Do Bloom's and Ashbery's opinions about literature's political effects reflect the privileged position of white critics and artists? Are "ethnic" writers like Tan and Alexie unreasonably burdened by a sense of social responsibility? Are there writers who successfully escape or counteract this dichotomy?

I believe that a writer does have to think about the responsibilities [to society], but make them individually and never have them dictated to him or her. I think about the reasons I write and I have to be true to them. I want to write about how I've evolved as a person through the history of my family, or I want to write about the things that I believe and act them out in the way of a narrative. I can have characters who speak thoughts that may or may not be my own, but I always know the distinction between my thoughts and those of the narrator or the characters.

I also am conscious, more so as a result of being published, that people will sometimes interpret my work as being representational and therefore they think my role as a writer is to speak out about this issue of what the role of literature should be and should not be. But I don't think that writers should censor themselves and I don't think that readers should censor writers. Readers also have a responsibility to be intelligent and not to interpret everything in a book as necessarily serving as a model or being representational of a particular culture and that literature is not meant to right the moral wrongs of a past society or the current one.

127

John Updike

A & P

"A&P" is one of nineteen stories from John Updike's 1962 collection titled Pigeon Feathers and Other Stories, *which appeared early in the writer's long and impressive career. In a 2001 interview, Updike commented on his goals as a writer and what he appreciates in other writing: "I've just tried to write in a way that would entertain and please me, if I were the reader. . . the kind of writer I'm attracted to is a writer who gives pleasure—the prose writer who does a little more than what is strictly called for to deliver the image or the facts. I'm not a very fast reader, so I like to open up a book and feel some whiff of poetry or of*

extra effort or of something inventive going on, so that even read backwards, a paragraph of prose will yield something to the sense." Updike has said humorously of his approach to reading: "My purpose in reading has ever secretly been not to come and judge but to come and steal."

For Updike, his presence as a writer is inevitable: "You can't really control your writer's voice. It's a lot like your handwriting—you can't stop it. You can try to alter it, but it always comes out as you. My prose tends to come out as me..."

For more information on John Updike, see page 578.

In walks these three girls in nothing but bathing suits. I'm in the third checkout slot, with my back to the door, so I don't see them until they're over by the bread. The one that caught my eye first was the one in the plaid green two-piece. She was a chunky kid, with a good tan and a sweet broad soft-looking can with those two crescents of white just under it, where the sun never seems to hit, at the top of the backs of her legs. I stood there with my hand on a box of HiHo crackers trying to remember if I rang it up or not. I ring it up again and the customer starts giving me hell. She's one of these cash-register-watchers, a witch about fifty with rouge on her cheekbones and no eyebrows, and I know it made her day to trip me up. She'd been watching cash registers for fifty years and probably never seen a mistake before.

By the time I got her feathers smoothed and her goodies into a bag—she gives me a little snort in passing, if she'd been born at the right time they would have burned her over in Salem—by the time I get her on her way the girls had circled around the bread and were coming back, without a pushcart, back my way along the counters, in the aisle between the checkouts and the Special bins. They didn't even have shoes on. There was this chunky one, with the two-piece—it was bright green and the seams on the bra were still sharp and her belly was still pretty pale so I guessed she just got it (the suit)—there was this one, with one of those chubby berry-faces, the lips all bunched together under her nose, this one, and a tall one, with black hair that hadn't quite frizzed right, and one of these sunburns right across under the eyes, and a chin that was too long—you know, the kind of girl other girls think is very "striking" and "attractive" but never quite makes it, as they very well know, which is why they like her so much—and then the third one, that wasn't quite so tall. She was the queen. She kind of led them, the other two peeking around and making their shoulders round. She didn't look around, not this queen, she just walked straight on slowly, on these long white prima-donna legs. She came down a little hard on her heels, as if she didn't walk in her bare feet that much, putting down her heels and then letting the weight move along to her toes as if she was testing the floor with every step, putting a little deliberate extra action into it. You never know for sure how girls' minds work (do you really think it's a mind in there or just a little buzz like a bee in a glass jar?) but you got the idea she had talked the other two into coming in here with her, and now she was showing them how to do it, walk slow and hold yourself straight.

She had on a kind of dirty-pink—beige maybe, I don't know—bathing suit with a little nubble all over it and, what got me, the straps were down. They were off her shoulders looped loose around the cool tops of her arms, and I guess as a result the suit had slipped a little on her, so all around the top of the cloth there was this shining rim. If it hadn't been there you wouldn't have known there could have been anything whiter than those shoulders. With the straps pushed off, there was nothing between the top of the suit and the top of her head except just *her,* this clean bare plane of the top of her chest down from the shoulder bones like a dented sheet of metal tilted in the light. I mean, it was more than pretty.

She had sort of oaky hair that the sun and salt had bleached, done up in a bun that was unraveling, and a kind of prim face. Walking into the A & P with your straps down, I suppose it's the only kind of face you *can* have. She held her head so high her neck, coming up out of those white shoulders, looked kind of stretched, but I didn't mind. The longer her neck was, the more of her there was.

She must have felt in the corner of her eye me and over my shoulder Stokesie in the second slot watching, but she didn't tip. Not this queen. She kept her eyes moving across the racks, and stopped, and turned so slow it made my stomach rub the inside of my apron, and buzzed to the other two, who kind of huddled against her for relief, and then they all three of them went up the cat-and-dog-food-breakfast-cereal-macaroni-rice-raisins-seasonings-spreads-spaghetti-soft-drinks-crackers-and-cookies aisle. From the third slot I look straight up this aisle to the meat counter, and I watched them all the way. The fat one with the tan sort of fumbled with the cookies, but on second thought she put the package back. The sheep pushing their carts down the aisle—the girls were walking against the usual traffic (not that we have one-way signs or anything)—were pretty hilarious. You could see them, when Queenie's white shoulders dawned on them, kind of jerk, or hop, or hiccup, but their eyes snapped back to their own baskets and on they pushed. I bet you could set off dynamite in an A & P and the people would by and large keep reaching and checking oatmeal off their lists and muttering "Let me see, there was a third thing, began with A, asparagus, no, ah, yes, applesauce!" or whatever it is they do mutter. But there was no doubt, this jiggled them. A few houseslaves in pin curlers even looked around after pushing their carts past to make sure what they had seen was correct.

You know, it's one thing to have a girl in a bathing suit down on the beach, where what with the glare nobody can look at each other much anyway, and another thing in the cool of the A & P, under the fluorescent lights, against all those stacked packages, with her feet paddling along naked over our checkerboard green-and-cream rubber-tile floor.

"Oh Daddy," Stokesie said beside me. "I feel so faint."

"Darling," I said. "Hold me tight." Stokesie's married, with two babies chalked up on his fuselage already, but as far as I can tell that's the only difference. He's twenty-two, and I was nineteen this April.

"Is it done?" he asks, the responsible married man finding his voice. I forgot to say he thinks he's going to be manager some sunny day, maybe in 1990 when it's called the Great Alexandrov and Petrooshki Tea Company or something.

What he meant was, our town is five miles from a beach, with a big   10
summer colony out on the Point, but we're right in the middle of town, and the women generally put on a shirt or shorts or something before they get out of the car into the street. And anyway these are usually women with six children and varicose veins mapping their legs and nobody, including them, could care less. As I say, we're right in the middle of town, and if you stand at our front doors you can see two banks and the Congregational church and the newspaper store and three real-estate offices and about twenty-seven old freeloaders tearing up Central Street because the sewer broke again. It's not as if we're on the Cape, we're north of Boston and there's people in this town haven't seen the ocean for twenty years.

The girls had reached the meat counter and were asking McMahon something. He pointed, they pointed, and they shuffled out of sight behind a pyramid of Diet Delight peaches. All that was left for us to see was old McMahon patting his mouth and looking after them sizing up their joints. Poor kids, I began to feel sorry for them, they couldn't help it.

Now here comes the sad part of the story, at least my family says it's sad, but I don't think it's so sad myself. The store's pretty empty, it being Thursday afternoon, so there was nothing much to do except lean on the register and wait for the girls to show up again. The whole store was like a pinball machine and I didn't know which tunnel they'd come out of. After a while they come around out of the far aisle, around the light bulbs, records at discount of the Caribbean Six or Tony Martin Sings or some such gunk you wonder they waste the wax on, sixpacks of candy bars, and plastic toys done up in cellophane that fall apart when a kid looks at them anyway. Around they come, Queenie still leading the way, and holding a little gray jar in her hands. Slots Three through Seven are unmanned and I could see her wondering between Stokes and me, but Stokesie with his usual luck draws an old party in baggy gray pants who stumbles up with four giant cans of pineapple juice (what do these bums *do* with all that pineapple juice? I've often asked myself). So the girls come to me. Queenie puts down the jar and I take it into my fingers icy cold. Kingfish Fancy Herring Snacks in Pure Sour Cream: 49¢. Now her hands are empty, not a ring or a bracelet, bare as God made them, and I wonder where the money's coming from. Still with that prim look she lifts a folded dollar bill out of the hollow at the center of her nubbled pink top. The jar went heavy in my hand. Really, I thought that was so cute.

Then everybody's luck begins to run out. Lengel comes in from haggling with a truck full of cabbages on the lot and is about to scuttle into that door marked MANAGER behind which he hides all day when the girls touch his eye. Lengel's pretty dreary, teaches Sunday school and the rest, but he doesn't miss that much. He comes over and says, "Girls, this isn't the beach."

Queenie blushes, though maybe it's just a brush of sunburn I was noticing for the first time, now that she was so close. "My mother asked me to pick up a jar of herring snacks." Her voice kind of startled me, the way voices do when you see the people first, coming out so flat and dumb yet kind of tony, too, the way it ticked over "pick up" and "snacks." All of a sudden I slid right down her voice into the living room. Her father and the other men were standing around in ice-cream coats and bow ties and the women were in sandals picking up herring snacks on toothpicks off a big glass plate and they were all holding drinks the color of water with olives and sprigs of mint in them. When my parents have somebody over they get lemonade and if it's a real racy affair Schlitz in tall glasses with "They'll Do It Every Time" cartoons stenciled on.

"That's all right," Lengel said. "But this isn't the beach." His repeat-   15
ing this struck me as funny, as if it had just occurred to him, and he had been thinking all these years the A & P was a great big dune and he was the head lifeguard. He didn't like my smiling—as I say he doesn't miss much—but he concentrates on giving the girls that sad Sunday-school-superintendent stare.

Queenie's blush is no sunburn now, and the plump one in plaid, that I liked better from the back—a really sweet can—pipes up, "We weren't doing any shopping. We just came in for the one thing."

"That makes no difference," Lengel tells her, and I could see from the way his eyes went that he hadn't noticed she was wearing a two-piece be-fore. "We want you decently dressed when you come in here."

"We *are* decent," Queenie says suddenly, her lower lip pushing, get-ting sore now that she remembers her place, a place from which the crowd that runs the A & P must look pretty crummy. Fancy Herring Snacks flashed in her very blue eyes.

"Girls, I don't want to argue with you. After this come in here with your shoulders covered. It's our policy." He turns his back. That's policy for you. Policy is what the kingpins want. What the others want is juve-nile delinquency.

All this while, the customers had been showing up with their carts   20
but, you know, sheep, seeing a scene, they had all bunched up on Stoke-sie, who shook open a paper bag as gently as peeling a peach, not want-ing to miss a word. I could feel in the silence everybody getting nervous, most of all Lengel, who asks me, "Sammy, have you rung up their pur-chase?"

I thought and said "No" but it wasn't about that I was thinking. I go through the punches, 4, 9, GROC. TOT—it's more complicated than you think, and after you do it often enough, it begins to make a little song, that you hear words to, in my case "Hello (*bing*) there, you (*gung*) hap-py *pee*-pul (*splat*)!"—the *splat* being the drawer flying out. I uncrease the bill, tenderly as you may imagine, it just having come from between the two smoothest scoops of vanilla I had ever known were there, and pass a half and a penny into her narrow pink palm, and nestle the herrings in a bag and twist its neck and hand it over, all the time thinking.

The girls, and who'd blame them, are in a hurry to get out, so I say "I quit" to Lengel quick enough for them to hear, hoping they'll stop and watch me, their unsuspected hero. They keep right on going, into the electric eye; the door flies open and they flicker across the lot to their car, Queenie and Plaid and Big Tall Goony-Goony (not that as raw material she was so bad), leaving me with Lengel and a kink in his eyebrow.

"Did you say something, Sammy?"

"I said I quit."

"I thought you did." 25

"You didn't have to embarrass them."

"It was they who were embarrassing us."

I started to say something that came out "Fiddle-de-doo." It's a saying of my grandmother's, and I know she would have been pleased.

"I don't think you know what you're saying," Lengel said.

"I know you don't," I said. "But I do." I pull the bow at the back of 30 my apron and start shrugging it off my shoulders. A couple customers that had been heading for my slot begin to knock against each other, like scared pigs in a chute.

Lengel sighs and begins to look very patient and old and gray. He's been a friend of my parents for years. "Sammy, you don't want to do this to your Mom and Dad," he tells me. It's true, I don't. But it seems to me that once you begin a gesture it's fatal not to go through with it. I fold the apron, "Sammy" stitched in red on the pocket, and put it on the counter, and drop the bow tie on top of it. The bow tie is theirs, if you've ever wondered. "You'll feel this for the rest of your life," Lengel says, and I know that's true, too, but remembering how he made the pretty girl blush makes me so scrunchy inside I punch the No Sale tab and the machine whirs "pee-pul" and the drawer splats out. One advantage to this scene taking place in summer, I can follow this up with a clean exit, there's no fumbling around getting your coat and galoshes, I just saunter into the electric eye in my white shirt that my mother ironed the night before, and the door heaves itself open, and outside the sunshine is skating around on the asphalt.

I look around for my girls, but they're gone, of course. There wasn't anybody but some young married screaming with her children about some candy they didn't get by the door of a powder-blue Falcon station wagon. Looking back in the big windows, over the bags of peat moss and aluminum lawn furniture stacked on the pavement, I could see Lengel in my place in the slot, checking the sheep through. His face was dark gray and his back stiff, as if he'd just had an injection of iron, and my stomach kind of fell as I felt how hard the world was going to be to me hereafter.

The Reader's Presence

1. The story is written in colloquial language. Reread the first two paragraphs. What does the narrator's style of expression convey about him? What effect does the narrator's style of expression have upon your reading of the story? Are you more, or less, inclined to believe his words? Suppose the same story were recounted in more conventional English. Would its meaning differ? If so, in what ways? How do you think Updike wishes the reader to view the narrator? Does Updike seem to agree, partially agree, or disagree with the narrator's point of view? What clues in the narrative lead you to your conclusion?

2. A great deal of the story hinges upon what the narrator doesn't know or say. Is the girls' attire the only issue in the confrontation? What other tensions are evident in the store and in the town? What impression of the situation do you glean "between the lines"? How does the writer convey information beyond the scope of what the narrator is able to articulate?

3. Reread the final paragraph, beginning in the present tense and ending with the narrator's retrospective estimation of "how hard the world was going to be to me hereafter." How do the present and past tenses mingle in the paragraph? How do present and past perceptions intersect in the story? Tillie Olsen does something similar in her story, "I Stand Here Ironing" (page 870). Near the end of the story (paragraph 54), the mother says: "But because I have been dredging the past, and all that compounds a human being is so heavy and meaningful in me, I cannot endure it tonight." Compare the effects of the two endings: What kinds of actions and feelings does each story's end anticipate? What are the trajectories the reader is left to imagine for each character? Imagine how a sequel to each story might begin. Who would narrate it? Why?

128

Alice Walker

Everyday Use

Alice Walker is well known for both her essays and her fiction. Her novel
The Color Purple *(1982) received many prestigious awards, including the Pulitzer
Prize and the American Book Award, and was made into a successful film. One
of her most famous essays, "Beauty: When the Other Dancer Is the Self" appears
in Part II of this book and offers an interesting comparison with the following
short story. "Everyday Use" is from Walker's 1973 short story collection* In Love
and Trouble: Stories of Black Women.

For additional information on Alice Walker, see page 274.

For Your Grandmama

I will wait for her in the yard that Maggie and I made so clean and
wavy yesterday afternoon. A yard like this is more comfortable than most
people know. It is not just a yard. It is like an extended living room.
When the hard clay is swept clean as a floor and the fine sand around the
edges lined with tiny, irregular grooves, anyone can come and sit and
look up into the elm tree and wait for the breezes that never come inside
the house.

Maggie will be nervous until after her sister goes: She will stand
hopelessly in corners, homely and ashamed of the burn scars down her
arms and legs, eying her sister with a mixture of envy and awe. She thinks
her sister has held life always in the palm of one hand, that "no" is a
word the world never learned to say to her.

You've no doubt seen those TV shows where the child who has
"made it" is confronted, as a surprise, by her own mother and father, tot-
tering in weakly from backstage. (A pleasant surprise, of course: What
would they do if parent and child came on the show only to curse out and
insult each other?) On TV mother and child embrace and smile into each
other's faces. Sometimes the mother and father weep, the child wraps

them in her arms and leans across the table to tell how she would not have made it without their help. I have seen these programs.

Sometimes I dream a dream in which Dee and I are suddenly brought together on a TV program of this sort. Out of a dark and soft-seated limousine I am ushered into a bright room filled with many people. There I meet a smiling, gray, sporty man like Johnny Carson who shakes my hand and tells me what a fine girl I have. Then we are on the stage and Dee is embracing me with tears in her eyes. She pins on my dress a large orchid, even though she has told me once that she thinks orchids are tacky flowers.

In real life I am a large, big-boned woman with rough, man-working   5
hands. In the winter I wear flannel nightgowns to bed and overalls during the day. I can kill and clean a hog as mercilessly as a man. My fat keeps me hot in zero weather. I can work outside all day, breaking ice to get water for washing; I can eat pork liver cooked over the open fire minutes after it comes steaming from the hog. One winter I knocked a bull calf straight in the brain between the eyes with a sledge hammer and had the meat hung up to chill before nightfall. But of course all this does not show on television. I am the way my daughter would want me to be: a hundred pounds lighter, my skin like an uncooked barley pancake. My hair glistens in the hot bright lights. Johnny Carson has much to do to keep up with my quick and witty tongue.

But that is a mistake. I know even before I wake up. Who ever knew a Johnson with a quick tongue? Who can even imagine me looking a strange white man in the eye? It seems to me I have talked to them always with one foot raised in flight, with my head turned in whichever way is farthest from them. Dee, though. She would always look anyone in the eye. Hesitation was no part of her nature.

"How do I look, Mama?" Maggie says, showing just enough of her thin body enveloped in pink skirt and red blouse for me to know she's there, almost hidden by the door.

"Come out into the yard," I say.

Have you ever seen a lame animal, perhaps a dog run over by some careless person rich enough to own a car, sidle up to someone who is ignorant enough to be kind to him? That is the way my Maggie walks. She has been like this, chin on chest, eyes on ground, feet in shuffle, ever since the fire that burned the other house to the ground.

Dee is lighter than Maggie, with nicer hair and a fuller figure. She's a   10
woman now, though sometimes I forget. How long ago was it that the other house burned? Ten, twelve years? Sometimes I can still hear the flames and feel Maggie's arms sticking to me, her hair smoking and her dress falling off her in little black papery flakes. Her eyes seemed stretched open, blazed open by the flames reflected in them. And Dee. I see her standing off under the sweet gum tree she used to dig gum out of;

a look of concentration on her face as she watched the last dingy gray board of the house fall in toward the red-hot brick chimney. Why don't you do a dance around the ashes? I'd wanted to ask her. She had hated the house that much.

I used to think she hated Maggie, too. But that was before we raised the money, the church and me, to send her to Augusta to school. She used to read to us without pity; forcing words, lies, other folks' habits, whole lives upon us two, sitting trapped and ignorant underneath her voice. She washed us in a river of make-believe, burned us with a lot of knowledge we didn't necessarily need to know. Pressed us to her with the serious way she read, to shove us away at just the moment, like dimwits, we seemed about to understand.

Dee wanted nice things. A yellow organdy dress to wear to her graduation from high school; black pumps to match a green suit she'd made from an old suit somebody gave me. She was determined to stare down any disaster in her efforts. Her eyelids would not flicker for minutes at a time. Often I fought off the temptation to shake her. At sixteen she had a style of her own: and knew what style was.

I never had an education myself. After second grade the school was closed down. Don't ask me why: In 1927 colored asked fewer questions than they do now. Sometimes Maggie reads to me. She stumbles along good-naturedly but can't see well. She knows she is not bright. Like good looks and money, quickness passed her by. She will marry John Thomas (who has mossy teeth in an earnest face) and then I'll be free to sit here and I guess just sing church songs to myself. Although I never was a good singer. Never could carry a tune. I was always better at a man's job. I used to love to milk till I was hooked in the side in '49. Cows are soothing and slow and don't bother you, unless you try to milk them the wrong way.

I have deliberately turned my back on the house. It is three rooms, just like the one that burned, except the roof is tin; they don't make shingle roofs any more. There are no real windows, just some holes cut in the sides, like the portholes in a ship, but not round and not square, with rawhide holding the shutters up on the outside. This house is in a pasture, too, like the other one. No doubt when Dee sees it she will want to tear it down. She wrote me once that no matter where we "choose" to live, she will manage to come see us. But she will never bring her friends. Maggie and I thought about this and Maggie asked me, "Mama, when did Dee ever *have* any friends?"

She had a few. Furtive boys in pink shirts hanging about on washday 15 after school. Nervous girls who never laughed. Impressed with her they worshiped the well-turned phrase, the cute shape, the scalding humor that erupted like bubbles in lye. She read to them.

When she was courting Jimmy T she didn't have much time to pay to us, but turned all her faultfinding power on him. He *flew* to marry a cheap city girl from a family of ignorant flashy people. She hardly had time to recompose herself.

When she comes I will meet—but there they are!

Maggie attempts to make a dash for the house, in her shuffling way, but I stay her with my hand. "Come back here," I say. And she stops and tries to dig a well in the sand with her toe.

It is hard to see them clearly through the strong sun. But even the first glimpse of leg out of the car tells me it is Dee. Her feet were always neat-looking, as if God himself had shaped them with a certain style. From the other side of the car comes a short, stocky man. Hair is all over his head a foot long and hanging from his chin like a kinky mule tail. I hear Maggie suck in her breath. "Uhnnnh," is what it sounds like. Like when you see the wriggling end of a snake just in front of your foot on the road. "Uhnnnh."

Dee next. A dress down to the ground, in this hot weather. A dress so   20
loud it hurts my eyes. There are yellows and oranges enough to throw back the light of the sun. I feel my whole face warming from the heat waves it throws out. Earrings gold, too, and hanging down to her shoulders. Bracelets dangling and making noises when she moves her arm up to shake the folds of the dress out of her armpits. The dress is loose and flows, and as she walks closer, I like it. I hear Maggie go "Uhnnnh" again. It is her sister's hair. It stands straight up like the wool on a sheep. It is black as night and around the edges are two long pigtails that rope about like small lizards disappearing behind her ears.

"Wa-su-zo-Tean-o!" she says, coming on in that gliding way the dress makes her move. The short stocky fellow with the hair to his navel is all grinning and he follows up with "Asalamalakim, my mother and sister!" He moves to hug Maggie but she falls back, right up against the back of my chair. I feel her trembling there and when I look up I see the perspiration falling off her chin.

"Don't get up," says Dee. Since I am stout it takes something of a push. You can see me trying to move a second or two before I make it. She turns, showing white heels through her sandals, and goes back to the car. Out she peeks next with a Polaroid. She stoops down quickly and lines up picture after picture of me sitting there in front of the house with Maggie cowering behind me. She never takes a shot without making sure the house is included. When a cow comes nibbling around the edge of the yard she snaps it and me and Maggie *and* the house. Then she puts the Polaroid in the back seat of the car, and comes up and kisses me on the forehead.

Meanwhile Asalamalakim is going through motions with Maggie's hand. Maggie's hand is as limp as a fish, and probably as cold, despite the sweat, and she keeps trying to pull it back. It looks like Asalamalakim wants to shake hands but wants to do it fancy. Or maybe he don't know how people shake hands. Anyhow, he soon gives up on Maggie.

"Well," I say. "Dee."

"No, Mama," she says. "Not 'Dee,' Wangero Leewanika Kemanjo!"   25

"What happened to 'Dee'?" I wanted to know.

"She's dead," Wangero said. "I couldn't bear it any longer, being named after the people who oppress me."

"You know as well as me you was named after your aunt Dicie," I said. Dicie is my sister. She named Dee. We called her "Big Dee" after Dee was born.

"But who was *she* named after?" asked Wangero.

"I guess after Grandma Dee," I said.   30

"And who was she named after?" asked Wangero.

"Her mother," I said, and saw Wangero was getting tired. "That's about as far back as I can trace it," I said. Though, in fact, I probably could have carried it back beyond the Civil War through the branches.

"Well," said Asalamalakim, "there you are."

"Uhnnnh," I heard Maggie say.

"There I was not," I said, "before 'Dicie' cropped up in our family,   35
so why should I try to trace it that far back?"

He just stood there grinning, looking down on me like somebody inspecting a Model A car. Every once in a while he and Wangero sent eye signals over my head.

"How do you pronounce this name?" I asked.

"You don't have to call me by it if you don't want to," said Wangero.

"Why shouldn't I?" I asked. "If that's what you want us to call you, we'll call you."

"I know it might sound awkward at first," said Wangero.   40

"I'll get used to it," I said. "Ream it out again."

Well, soon we got the name out of the way. Asalamalakim had a name twice as long and three times as hard. After I tripped over it two or three times he told me to just call him Hakim-a-barber. I wanted to ask him was he a barber, but I didn't really think he was, so I didn't ask.

"You must belong to those beef-cattle peoples down the road," I said. They said "Asalamalakim" when they met you, too, but they didn't shake hands. Always too busy: feeding the cattle, fixing the fences, putting up salt-lick shelters, throwing down hay. When the white folks poisoned some of the herd the men stayed up all night with rifles in their hands. I walked a mile and a half just to see the sight.

Hakim-a-barber said, "I accept some of their doctrines, but farming and raising cattle is not my style." (They didn't tell me, and I didn't ask, whether Wangero (Dee) had really gone and married him.)

We sat down to eat and right away he said he didn't eat collards and   45
pork was unclean. Wangero, though, went on through the chitlins and corn bread, the greens and everything else. She talked a blue streak over the sweet potatoes. Everything delighted her. Even the fact that we still used the benches her daddy made for the table when we couldn't afford to buy chairs.

"Oh, Mama!" she cried. Then turned to Hakim-a-barber. "I never knew how lovely these benches are. You can feel the rump prints," she said, running her hands underneath her and along the bench. Then she gave a sigh and her hand closed over Grandma Dee's butter dish. "That's it!" she said. "I knew there was something I wanted to ask you if I could have." She jumped up from the table and went over in the corner where the churn stood, the milk in it clabber by now. She looked at the churn and looked at it.

"This churn top is what I need," she said. "Didn't Uncle Buddy whittle it out of a tree you all used to have?"

"Yes," I said.

"Uh huh," she said happily. "And I want the dasher, too."

"Uncle Buddy whittle that, too?" asked the barber.   50

Dee (Wangero) looked up at me.

"Aunt Dee's first husband whittled the dash," said Maggie so low you almost couldn't hear her. "His name was Henry, but they called him Stash."

"Maggie's brain is like an elephant's," Wangero said, laughing. "I can use the churn top as a centerpiece for the alcove table," she said, sliding a plate over the churn, "and I'll think of something artistic to do with the dasher."

When she finished wrapping the dasher the handle stuck out. I took it for a moment in my hands. You didn't even have to look close to see where hands pushing the dasher up and down to make butter had left a kind of sink in the wood. In fact, there were a lot of small sinks; you could see where thumbs and fingers had sunk into the wood. It was beautiful light yellow wood, from a tree that grew in the yard where Big Dee and Stash had lived.

After dinner Dee (Wangero) went to the trunk at the foot of my bed   55
and started rifling through it. Maggie hung back in the kitchen over the dishpan. Out came Wangero with two quilts. They had been pieced by Grandma Dee and then Big Dee and me had hung them on the quilt frames on the front porch and quilted them. One was in the Lone Star pattern. The other was Walk Around the Mountain. In both of them were scraps of dresses Grandma Dee had worn fifty and more years ago. Bits and pieces of Grandpa Jarrell's Paisley shirts. And one teeny faded blue piece, about the size of a penny matchbox, that was from Great Grandpa Ezra's uniform that he wore in the Civil War.

"Mama," Wangero said sweet as a bird. "Can I have these old quilts?"

I heard something fall in the kitchen, and a minute later the kitchen door slammed.

"Why don't you take one or two of the others?" I asked. "These old things was just done by me and Big Dee from some tops your grandma pieced before she died."

"No," said Wangero. "I don't want those. They are stitched around the borders by machine."

"That'll make them last better," I said.   60

"That's not the point," said Wangero. "These are all pieces of dresses Grandma used to wear. She did all this stitching by hand. Imagine!" She held the quilts securely in her arms, stroking them.

"Some of the pieces, like those lavender ones, come from old clothes her mother handed down to her," I said, moving up to touch the quilts. Dee (Wangero) moved back just enough so that I couldn't reach the quilts. They already belonged to her.

"Imagine!" she breathed again, clutching them closely to her bosom.

"The truth is," I said, "I promised to give them quilts to Maggie, for when she marries John Thomas."

She gasped like a bee had stung her.   65

"Maggie can't appreciate these quilts!" she said. "She'd probably be backward enough to put them to everyday use."

"I reckon she would," I said. "God knows I been saving 'em for long enough with nobody using 'em. I hope she will!" I didn't want to bring up how I had offered Dee (Wangero) a quilt when she went away to college. Then she had told me they were old-fashioned, out of style.

"But they're *priceless*!" she was saying now, furiously; for she has a temper. "Maggie would put them on the bed and in five years they'd be in rags. Less than that!"

"She can always make some more," I said. "Maggie knows how to quilt."

Dee (Wangero) looked at me with hatred. "You just will not under   70
stand. The point is these quilts, *these* quilts!"

"Well," I said, stumped. "What would *you* do with them?"

"Hang them," she said. As if that was the only thing you *could* do with quilts.

Maggie by now was standing in the door. I could almost hear the sound her feet made as they scraped over each other.

"She can have them, Mama," she said, like somebody used to never winning anything, or having anything reserved for her. "I can 'member Grandma Dee without the quilts."

I looked at her hard. She had filled her bottom lip with checkerberry   75
snuff and it gave her face a kind of dopey, hangdog look. It was Grandma Dee and Big Dee who taught her how to quilt herself. She stood there with her scarred hands hidden in the folds of her skirt. She looked at her sister with something like fear but she wasn't mad at her. This was Maggie's portion. This was the way she knew God to work.

When I looked at her like that something hit me in the top of my head and ran down to the soles of my feet. Just like when I'm in church and the spirit of God touches me and I get happy and shout. I did something I never had done before: hugged Maggie to me, then dragged her on into the room, snatched the quilts out of Miss Wangero's hands and dumped them into Maggie's lap. Maggie just sat there on my bed with her mouth open.

"Take one or two of the others," I said to Dee.

But she turned without a word and went out to Hakim-a-barber.

"You just don't understand," she said, as Maggie and I came out to the car.

"What don't I understand?" I wanted to know.   80

"Your heritage," she said. And then she turned to Maggie, kissed her, and said, "You ought to try to make something of yourself, too, Maggie. It's really a new day for us. But from the way you and Mama still live you'd never know it."

She put on some sunglasses that hid everything above the tip of her nose and her chin.

Maggie smiled; maybe at the sunglasses. But a real smile, not scared. After we watched the car dust settle I asked Maggie to bring me a dip of snuff. And then the two of us sat there just enjoying, until it was time to go in the house and go to bed.

The Reader's Presence

1. The story is told in the first person. Are the writer and narrator the same person? What sort of person is the narrator? Which clues lead you to your conclusions? Reread the first and second sections. Whose "voice" do you hear — the writer's, the narrator's, or a mix? How do you think Walker wishes the reader to view the narrator?

2. How might the fire and its aftermath (section 3) symbolize other elements of the story? How is this external event used to mirror the internal states of the characters? Reread the last section. What might the quilt symbolize? How might the fire and the quilt be related to the theme of "tradition" and "heritage"? Do these elements seem coincidental to the events in the story, or carefully chosen? Where can you see the writer's "craft" at work in this seemingly straightforward narrative?

3. Both Walker and Amy Tan write stories about daughters and their relationships with their mothers. Though both stories turn on painful confrontations and realizations, they end in relative harmony. Tan's narrator plays a piano piece called "Perfectly Contented" to complement the "Pleading Child"; "And then the two of us sat there just enjoying," writes Walker's narrator at the end of her story (paragraph 83). How do these endings work for you? Do they close off the stories too neatly, or do you find their resolutions satisfying? How do you compare the endings of these stories with the unresolved endings of Updike's "A&P" (page 888) and Carver's "Popular Mechanics" (page 837)?

129

John Edgar Wideman
Weight

When asked about his approach to fiction and nonfiction and the relationship between reality and imagination, John Edgar Wideman has responded that the lines between fiction and nonfiction are not "hard and fast." In his stories and novels, Wideman frequently blurs the lines of reality by weaving into his imaginative narratives the names of family members. He has commented: "I think that what we call imaginative reality has just as much place in how we see ourselves and put ourselves together as material reality. . . . Where is someone when they're saying a prayer? Where are you when you are thinking about another time or another place than your body happens to be, or when you are addressing a lover, a family member who's not around? These moments when you're suspended between worlds or shuttling indiscriminately, seamlessly back and forth, in both at once, are as real as any I've encountered, and I insist on those being part of what's designated as reality."

Consider Wideman's ideas on reality and imagination as you read the following story.

For more information about John Edgar Wideman, see pages 805 and 914.

My mother is a weightlifter. You know what I mean. She understands that the best laid plans, the sweetest beginnings have a way of turning to shit. Bad enough when life fattens you up just so it can turn around and gobble you down. Worse for the ones like my mother life keeps skinny, munching on her daily, one cruel, little, needle-toothed bite at a time so the meal lasts and lasts. Mom understands life don't play so spends beaucoup time and energy getting ready for the worst. She lifts weights to stay strong. Not barbells or dumbbells, though most of the folks she deals with, especially her sons, act just that way, like dumbbells. No. The weights she lifts are burdens, her children's, her neighbors, yours. Whatever awful calamities arrive on her doorstep or howl in the news, my mom squeezes her frail body beneath them. Grips, hoists, holds the weight. I swear sometimes I can hear her sinews squeaking and singing under a load of invisible tons.

I ought to know since I'm one of the burdens bowing her shoulders. She loves heavy, hopeless me unconditionally. Before I was born. Mom loved me, forever and ever till death do us part. I'll never be anyone else's darling, darling boy so it's her fault, her doing, isn't it, that neither of us can face the thought of losing the other. How could I resist reciprocating her love. Needing her. Draining her. Feeling her straining underneath me, the pop and cackle of her arthritic joints, her gray hair sizzling with static electricity, the hissing friction, tension and pressure as she lifts more than she can bear. Bears more than she can possibly lift. You have to see it to believe it. Like the flying Wallendas or Houdini's spine-chilling escapes. One of the greatest shows on earth.

My mother believes in a god whose goodness would not permit him to inflict more troubles than a person can handle. A god of mercy and salvation. A sweaty, bleeding god presiding over a fitness class in which his chosen few punish their muscles. She should wear a T-shirt: *God's Gym.*

In spite of a son in prison for life, twin girls born dead, a mind blown son who roams the streets with everything he owns in a shopping cart, a strung out daughter with a crack baby, a good daughter who'd miscarried the only child her dry womb ever produced, in spite of me and the rest of my limp-along, near to normal siblings and their children — my nephews doping and gangbanging, nieces unwed, underage, dropping babies as regularly as the seasons — in spite of breast cancer, sugar diabetes, hypertension, failing kidneys, emphysema, gout, all resident in her body and epidemic in the community, knocking off one by one her girlhood friends, in spite of corrosive poverty and a neighborhood whose streets are no longer safe even for gray, crippled up folks like her, my mom loves her god, thanks him for the blessings he bestows, keeps her faith he would not pile on more troubles than she could bear. Praises his name and prays for strength, prays for more weight so it won't fall on those around her less able to bear up.

You've seen those iron pumping, musclebound brothers fresh out the slam who show up at the playground to hoop and don't get picked on a team cause they can't play a lick, not before they did their bit, and sure not now, back on the set, stiff and stone-handed as Frankenstein, but finally some old head goes on and chooses one on his squad because the brother's so huge and scary looking sitting there with his jaws tight, lip poked out you don't want him freaking out and kicking everybody's ass just because the poor baby's feelings is hurt, you know what I mean, the kind so buff looks like his coiled-up insides about to bust through his skin or his skin's stripped clean off his body so he's a walking anatomy lesson. Well, that's how my mom looks to me sometimes, her skin peeled away, no secrets, every taut nerve string on display.

I can identify the precise moment during a trip with her one afternoon to the supermarket on Walnut Street in Shadyside, a Pittsburgh, Pennsylvania, white community with just a few families of us colored sprinkled at the bottom ends of a couple of streets, when I began to mar-

5

vel at my mother's prodigious strength. I was very young, young enough not to believe I'd grow old, just bigger. A cashier lady who seemed to be acquainted with my mother asked very loudly, Is this your son, and Mom smiled in reply to the cashier's astonishment saying calmly, Yes, he is, and the doughy white lady in her yellow Krogers' smock with her name on the breast tried to match my mother's smile but only managed a fake grin like she'd just discovered shit stinks but didn't want anybody else to know she knew. Then she blurted, He's a tall one, isn't he.

Not a particularly unusual moment as we unloaded our shopping cart and waited for the bad news to ring up on the register. The three of us understood, in spite of the cashier's quick shuffle, what had seized her attention. In public situations the sight of my pale, caucasian featured mother and her variously colored kids disconcerted strangers. They gulped. Stared. Muttered insults. We were visible proof somebody was sneaking around after dark, breaking the apartheid rule, messy mulatto exceptions to the rule, trailing behind a woman who could be white.

Nothing special about the scene in Krogers. Just an ugly moment temporarily reprieved from turning uglier by the cashier's remark that attributed her surprise to a discrepancy in height not color. But the exchange alerted me to a startling fact—I was taller than my mother. The brown boy, me, could look down at the crown of his light-skinned mother's head. Obsessed by size, like most adolescent boys, size in general and the size of each and every particular part of my body and how mine compared to others, I was always busily measuring and keeping score, but somehow I'd lost track of my mother's size, and mine relative to hers. Maybe because she was beyond size. If someone had asked me my mother's height or weight I probably would have replied, *Huh*. Ubiquitous I might say now. A tiny, skin-and-bone woman way too huge for size to pin down.

The moment in Krogers is also when I began to marvel at my mother's strength. Unaccountably, unbeknownst to me, my body had grown larger than hers, yes, and the news was great in a way, but more striking and not so comforting was the fact, never mind my advantage in size, I felt hopelessly weak standing there beside my mom in Krogers. A wimpy shadow next to her solid flesh and bones. I couldn't support for one hot minute a fraction of the weight she bore on her shoulders twenty-four hours a day. The weight of the cashier's big-mouthed disbelief. The weight of hating the pudgy white woman forever because she tried to steal my mother from me. The weight of cooking and cleaning and making do with no money, the weight of fighting and loving us iron-headed, ungrateful brats. Would I always feel puny and inadequate when I looked up at the giant fist hovering over our family, the first of God or the Devil, ready to squash us like bugs if my mother wasn't always on duty, spreading herself thin as an umbrella over our heads, her bones its steel ribs keeping the sky from falling.

Reaching down for the brass handle of this box I must lift to my   10 shoulder, I need the gripping strength of my mother's knobby-knuckled fingers, her superhero power to bear impossible weight.

Since I was reading her this story over the phone (I called it a story but Mom knew better), I stopped at the end of the paragraph above you just completed, if you read that far, stopped because the call was long distance, daytime rates, and also because the rest had yet to be written. I could tell by her silence she was not pleased. Her negative reaction didn't surprise me. Plenty in the piece I didn't like either. Raw, stuttering stuff I intended to improve in subsequent drafts, but before revising and trying to complete it, I needed her blessing.

Mom's always been my best critic. I depend on her honesty. She tells the truth yet never affects the holier-than-thou superiority of some people who believe they occupy the high ground and let you know in no uncertain terms that you nor nobody else like you ain't hardly coming close. Huh-uh. My mother smiles as often as she groans or scolds when she hears gossip about somebody behaving badly. *My, my, my* she'll say and nod and smile and gently broom you, the sinner, and herself into the same crowded heap, no one any better than they should be, could be, absolute equals in a mellow sputter of laughter she sometimes can't suppress, hiding it, muffling it with her fist over her mouth, nodding, remembering, how people's badness can be too good to be true, *my, my, my.*

Well, my story didn't tease out a hint of laugh, and forget the 550 miles separating us, I could tell she wasn't smiling either. Why was she holding back the sunshine that could forgive the worst foolishness. Absolve my sins. Retrieve me from the dead end corners into which I paint myself. Mama, please. Please, please, please, don't you weep. And tell ole Martha not to moan. Don't leave me drowning like Willie Boy in the deep blue sea. Smile, Mom. Laugh. Send that healing warmth through the wire and save poor me.

Was it the weightlifting joke, Mom. Maybe you didn't think it was funny.

Sorry. Tell the truth, I didn't see nothing humorous about any of it.   15
God's t-shirt. You know better. Ought to be ashamed of yourself. Taking the Lord's name in vain.

Where do you get such ideas, boy. I think I know my children. God knows I should by now, shouldn't I. How am I not supposed to know youall after all you've put me through beating my brains out to get through to you. *Yes, yes, yes.* Then one youall goes and does something terrible I never would have guessed was in you. Won't say you break my heart. Heart's been broke too many times. In too many little itty-bitty pieces can't break down no more, but youall sure ain't finished with me, are you. Still got some new trick in you to lay on your weary mother before she leaves here.

Guess I ought to be grateful to God an old fool like me's still around to be tricked, Weightlifter. Well, it's different. Nobody ain't called me nothing like weightlifter before. It's different, sure enough.

Now here's where she should have laughed. She'd picked up the stone I'd bull's-eyed right into the middle of her wrinkled brow, between her tender, brown, all-seeing eyes, lifted it and turned it over in her hands like a jeweler with a tiny telescope strapped around his skull inspecting a jewel, testing its heft and brilliance, the marks of god's hands, god's will, the hidden truths sparkling in its depths, multiplied, splintered through mirroring facets. After such a brow scrunching examination, isn't it time to smile. Kiss and make up. Wasn't that Mom's way. Wasn't that how she handled the things that hurt us and hurt her. Didn't she ease the pain of our worst injuries with the balm of her everything's-going-to-be-alright-in-the-morning smile. The smile that takes the weight, every hurt-ful ounce and forgives, the smile licking our wounds so they scab over, and she can pick them off our skin, stuff their lead weight into the bulging sack of all sorrows slung across her back.

The possibility my wannabe story had actually hurt her dawned on me. Or should I say bopped me upside my head like the Br'er Bear club my middle brother loads in his cart to discourage bandits. I wished I was sitting at the kitchen table across from her so I could check for damage, her first, then check myself in the mirror of those soft, brown, incredibly loving mother's eyes. If I'd hurt her even a teeny-bit, I'd be broken forever unless those eyes repaired me. Yet even as I regretted reading her the clumsy passage and prepared myself to surrender wholly, happily to the hounds of hell if I'd harmed one hair on her tender, gray head, I couldn't deny a sneaky, smarting tingle of satisfaction at the thought that maybe, maybe words I'd written had touched another human being, mama mia or not.

Smile, Mom. It's just a story. Just a start. I know it needs more work.   20
You were supposed to smile at the weightlifting part.

God not something to joke about.

C'mon, mom. How many times have I heard Reverend Fitch cracking you up with his corny God jokes.

Time and a place.

Maybe stories are my time and place, Mom. You know. My time and place to say things I need to say.

No matter how bad it comes out sounding, right. No matter you   25
make a joke of your poor mother . . .

Poor mother's suffering. You were going to say, *Poor mother's suffering,* weren't you.

You heard what I said.

And heard what you didn't say. I hear those words, too. The unsaid ones, Mom. Louder sometimes. Drowning out what gets said, Mom.

Whoa. We gon let it all hang out this morning, ain't we. Son. First that story. Now you accusing me of *your* favorite trick, that muttering under your breath. Testing me this morning, aren't you. What makes you think a sane person would ever pray for more weight. Ain't those the words you put in my mouth. More weight.

And the building shook. The earth rumbled. More weight descended   30 like god's fist on his Hebrew children. Like in Lamentations. The Book in the Bible. The movie based on the Book based on what else, the legend of my mother's long suffering back.

Because she had a point.

People with no children can be cruel. Had I heard it first from Oprah, the diva of suffering my mother could have become if she'd pursued showbiz instead of weightlifting. Or was the damning phrase a line from one of Gwen Brooks's abortion blues. Whatever their source, the words fit and I was ashamed. I do know better. A bachelor and nobody's daddy, but still my words have weight. Like sticks and stones, words can break bones. Metaphors can pull you apart and put you back together all wrong. I know what you mean, Mom. My entire life I've had to listen to people trying to tell me I'm just a white man in a dark skin.

Give me a metaphor long enough and I'll move the earth. Somebody famous said it. Or said something like that. And everybody, famous or not knows words sting. Words change things. Step on a crack, break your mother's back.

On the other hand, Mom, metaphor's just my way of trying to say two things, be in two places at once. Saying goodbye and hello and good-bye. Many things, many places at once. You know, like James Cleveland singing our favorite gospel tune, *Stood on the Bank of Jordan.* Metaphors are very short songs. Mini-mini stories. Rivers between like the Jordan where ships sail on, sail on and you stand and wave goodbye-hello, hello-goodbye.

Weightlifter just a word, just play. I was only teasing, Mom. I didn't   35 mean to upset you. I certainly intended no harm. I'd swallow every stick of dynamite it takes to pay for a Nobel prize before I'd accept one if it cost just one of your soft, curly hairs.

Smile. Let's begin again.

It's snowing in Massachusetts / The ground's white in O-Hi-O. Yes, it's snowing in Massachusetts / And ground's white in O-Hi-O. Shut my eyes, Mr. Weatherman / Can't stand to see my baby go.

When I called you last Thursday evening and didn't get an answer I started worrying. I didn't know why. We'd talked Tuesday and you sounded fine. Better than fine. A lift and lilt in your voice. After I hung up the phone Tuesday said to myself, Mom's in good shape. Frail but her spirit's strong. Said those very words to myself more than once Tuesday. *Frail but her spirit's strong.* The perkiness I sensed in you helped make my Wednesday super. Early rise. Straight to my desk. Two pages before noon and you know me, Mom. Two pages can take a week, a month. I've had two pages years. I've had decades dreaming the one perfect page I never got around to writing. Thursday morning reams of routine and no pages but not to worry I told myself. After Wednesday's productivity, wasn't I entitled to some down time. Just sat at my desk, pleased as punch with myself till I got bored feeling so good and started a nice novel, *Call It Sleep*. Dinner at KFC buffet. Must have balled up fifty napkins trying to keep my chin decent. Then home to call you before I snuggled up again with the little jewish boy, his mama and their troubles in old N.Y.C.

Let your phone ring and ring. Too late for you to be out unless you had a special occasion. And you always let me know well ahead of time when something special coming up. I tried calling a half hour later and again twenty minutes after that. By then nearly nine, close to your bed-time. I was getting really worried now. Couldn't figure where you might be. Nine-fifteen and still no answer, no clue what was going on.

Called Sis. Called Aunt Chloe. Nobody knew where you were. Chloe   40
said she'd talked with you earlier just like every other morning. Sis said you called her at work after she got back from lunch. Both of them said you sounded fine. Chloe said you'd probably fallen asleep in your recliner and left the phone in the bedroom or bathroom and your hearing's to the point you can be wide-awake but if the TV's on and the phone's not be-side you or the ringer's not turned to high she said sometimes she has to ring and hang up, ring and hang up two, three times before she catches you.

Chloe promised to keep calling every few minutes till she reached you. Said they have a prayer meeting Thursdays in your mother's building and she's been saying she wants to go and I bet she's there, honey. She's alright, honey. Don't worry yourself, O.K. We're old and fuddleheaded now, but we're tough old birds. Your mother's fine. I'll tell her to call you soon's I get through to her. Your mom's okay, baby. God keeps an eye on us.

You know Aunt Chloe. She's your sister. Five hundred miles away and I could hear her squeezing her large self through the telephone line, see her pillow arms reaching for the weight before it comes down on me.

Why would you want to hear any of this. You know what happened. Where you were. You know how it all turned out.

You don't need to listen to my conversation with Sis. Dialing her back after we'd been disconnected. The first time in life I think my sister ever phoned me later than ten o'clock at night. First time a lightning bolt ever disconnected us. Ever disconnected me from anybody ever.

Did you see Eva Wallace first, Mom, coming through your door, or   45
was it the busybody super you've never liked since you moved in. Some-thing about the way she speaks to her granddaughter you said. Little girl's around the building all day because her mother's either in the street or the slam and the father takes the child so rarely he might as well live in Timbuctoo so you know the super doesn't have it easy and on a couple of occasions you've offered to keep the granddaughter when the super needs both hands and her mind free for an hour. You don't hold the way she busies up in everybody's business or the fact the child has to look out for herself too many hours in the day against the super, and you're sure she loves her granddaughter you said but the short way she talks sometimes to a child that young just not right.

Who'd you see first pushing open your door. Eva said you didn't show up after you said you'd stop by for her. She waited awhile she said then phoned you and got no answer and then a friend called her and they got to running their mouths and Eva said she didn't think again about you not showing up when you were supposed to until she hung up the phone. And not right away then. Said as soon as she missed you, soon as she remembered youall had planned on attending the Thursday prayer meeting together she got scared. She knows how dependable you are. Even though it was late, close to your bedtime, she called you anyway and let the phone ring and ring. Way after nine by then. Pulled her coat on over her housedress, scooted down the hall and knocked on your door cause where else you going to be. No answer so she hustled back to her place and phoned downstairs for the super and they both pounded on your door till the super said we better have a look just in case and unlocked your apartment. Stood there staring after she turned the key, trying to see through the door, then slid it open a little and both of them Eva said tiptoeing in like a couple of fools after all that pounding and hollering in the hall. Said she never thought about it at the time but later, after everything over and she drops down on her couch to have that cigarette she knew she shouldn't have with her lungs rotten as they are and hadn't smoked one for more than a year but sneaks the Camel she'd been saving out its hiding place in a Baggie in the freezer and sinks back in the cushions and lights up, real tired, real shook up and teary she said but couldn't help smiling at herself when she remembered all that hollering and pounding and then tipping in like a thief.

It might have happened that way. Being right or wrong about what happened is less important sometimes than finding a good way to tell it. What's anybody want to hear anyway. Not the truth people want. No-no-no. People want the best told story, the lie that entertains and turns them on. No question about it, is there. What people want. What gets people's attention. What sells soap. Why else do the biggest, most barefaced liars rule the world.

Hard to be a mother, isn't it Mom. I can't pretend to be yours, not even a couple minutes' worth before I go to pieces. I try to imagine a cradle with you lying inside, cute, miniature bedding tucked around the tiny doll of you. I can almost picture you asleep in it, snuggled up, your eyes shut, maybe your thumb in your mouth but then you cry out in the night, you need me to stop whatever I'm doing and rush in and scoop you up and press you to my bosom, lullabye you back to sleep. I couldn't manage it. Not the easy duty I'm imagining, let alone you bucking and wheezing and snot, piss, vomit, shit, blood, you hot and throbbing with fever, steaming in my hands like the heart ripped fresh from some poor soul's chest.

Too much weight. Too much discrepancy in size. As big a boy as I've grown to be, I can't lift you.

Will you forgive me if I cheat, Mom. Dark suited, strong men in   50 somber ties and white shirts will lug you out of the church, down the stone steps, launch your gleaming barge into the black river of the Cadillac's bay. My brothers won't miss me not handling my share of the weight. How much weight could there be. Tiny, scooped out you. The tinny, fake wood shell. The entire affair's symbolic. Heavy with meaning not weight. You know. Like metaphors. Like words interchanged as if they have no weight or too much weight, as if words are never required to bear more than they can stand. As if words, when we're finished mucking with them, go back to just being words.

The word *trouble*. The word *sorrow*. The word *bye-and-bye*.

I was wrong and you were right, as usual, Mom. So smile. Certain situations, yours for instance, being a mother, suffering what mothers suffer, why would anyone want to laugh at that. Who could stand in your shoes a heartbeat—*shoes, shoes, everybody got to have shoes*—bear your burdens one instant and think it's funny. Who ever said it's O.K. to lie and kill as long as it makes a good story.

Smile. Admit you knew from the start it would come to this. Me trembling, needing your strength. It has, Mom, so please, please, a little, bitty grin of satisfaction. They say curiosity kills the cat and satisfaction brings it back. Smiling. Smile Mom. Come back. You know I've always hated spinach but please spoonfeed me a canful so those Popeye muscles pop in my arms. I meant shapeshifter not weightlifter. I meant the point of this round, spinningtop earth must rest somewhere, on something or someone. I meant you are my sunshine. My only sunshine.

The problem never was the word *weightlifter*, was it. If you'd been insulted by my choice of metaphor you would have let me know, not by silence, but nailing me with a quick, funny signifying dig, and then you would have smiled or laughed and we'd have gone on to the next thing. What must have bothered you, stunned you was what I said into the phone before I began reading. Said this is about a man scared he won't survive his mother's passing.

That's what upset you, wasn't it. Saying goodbye to you. Practicing for your death in a story. Trying on for size a world without you. Ignoring like I did when I was a boy, your size. Saying aloud terrible words with no power over us as long as we don't speak them.

So when you heard me let the cat out the bag, you were shocked, weren't you. Speechless. Smileless. What could you say. The damage had been done. I heard it in your first words after you got back your voice. And me knowing your lifelong, deathly fear of cats. Like the big, furry orange Tom you told me about, how it curled up on the porch just outside your door, trapping you a whole August afternoon inside the hotbox shanty in Washington, D.C., when I lived in your belly.

Why would I write a story that risks your life. Puts our business in the street. I'm the oldest child, supposed to be the man of the family now. No wonder you cried, Oh father. Oh son. Oh holy ghost. Why hath thou forsaken me. I know you didn't cry that. You aren't Miss Oprah. But I

55

sure did mess up, didn't I. Didn't I, Mom. Up to my old tricks. Crawling up inside you. My weight twisting you all out of shape.

I asked you once about the red sailor cap hanging on the wall inside your front door. Knew it was my brother's cap on the nail, but why that particular hat I asked and not another of his countless, fly sombreros on display. Rob, Rob, man of many lids. For twenty years in the old house, now in your apartment, the hat a shrine no one allowed to touch. You never said it but everybody understood the red hat your good luck charm, your mojo for making sure Rob would get out the slam one day and come bopping through the door, pluck the hat from the wall and pull it down over his bean head. Do you remember me asking why the sailor cap. You probably guessed I was fishing. Really didn't matter which cap, did it. Point was you chose the red one and *why* must always be your secret. You could have made up a nice story to explain why the red sailor cap wound up on the nail and I would have listened as I always listened all ears but you knew part of me would be trying to peek through the words at your secret. Always a chance you might slip up and reveal too much. So the hat story and plenty others never told. The old folks had taught you that telling another person your secret wish strips it of its power, a wish's small, small chance, as long as it isn't spoken, to influence what might happen next in the world. You'd never tell anyone the words sheltered in the shadow of your heart. Still, I asked about the red sailor cap because I needed to understand your faith, your weightlifting power, how you can believe a hat, any fucking kind of hat, could bring my baby brother home safe and sound from prison. I needed to spy and pry. Wiretap the telephone in your bosom. Hear the words you would never say to another soul, not even on pain of death.

How would such unsaid words sound, what would they look like on a page. And if you had uttered them, surrendered your stake in them, forfeited their meager, silent claim to work miracles, would it have been worth the risk, even worth the loss, to finally hear the world around you cracking, collapsing, changing as you spoke your little secret tale.

Would you have risen an inch or two from this cold ground. Would   60
you have breathed easier after releasing the heaviness of silent words hoarded so unbearably, unspeakably long. Let go, Mom. Shed the weight just once.

Not possible for you, I know. It would be cheating, I know. The man of unbending faith did not say to the hooded inquisitors piling a crushing load of stones on his chest, *More light. More light.* No, I'm getting my quotes mixed up again. Just at the point the monks thought they'd broken his will, just as spiraling fractures started splintering his bones, he cried, *More bricks. More bricks.*

I was scared, Mom. Scared every cotton picking day of my life I'd lose you. The fear a sing-song taunt like tinnitus ringing in my ear. No wonder I'm a little crazy. But don't get me wrong. Not your fault. I don't blame you for my morbid fears, my unhappiness. It's just that I should have confessed sooner, long, long ago, the size of my fear of losing you. I wish you'd heard me say the words. How fear made me keep my distance, hide how much I depended on your smile. The sunshine of your smiling laughter that could also send me silently screaming out the room in stories I never told you because you'd taught me as you'd been taught, not to say anything aloud I didn't want to come true. Not say out loud the things I wished to come true. Doesn't leave a hell of a lot to say, does it. No wonder I'm tongue-tied, scared shitless.

But would it be worth the risk, worth failing, if I could find words to tell our story and also keep us covered inside it, work us invisibly into the fret, the warp and woof of the story's design, safe there, connected there as words in perfect poems, the silver apples of the moon, golden apples of the sun, blue guitars. The two of us like those rhyming pairs *never* and *forever, heart* and *part,* in the doo-wop songs I harmonized with the fellas in the alley around the corner from Henderson's barber shop up on Frankstown Avenue, first me then lost brother Sonny and his crew then baby brother Rob and his cut buddy hoodlums rapping and now somebody else black and young and wild and pretty so the song lasts forever and never ever ends even though the voices change back there in the alley where you can hear bones rattling in the men's fists, *fever in the funkhouse looking for a five* and hear wine bottles exploding and hear the rusty shopping cart squeak over the cobblestones of some boy ferrying an old lady's penny-ante groceries home for a nickel once, then a dime, a quarter, four quarters now.

Would it be worth the risk, worth failing.

Shouldn't I try even if I know the strength's not in me. No, you say.   65
Yes. Hold on, let go. Do I hear you saying, Everything's gonna be alright. Saying, Do what you got to do, baby, smiling as I twist my fingers into the brass handle. As I lift.

The Reader's Presence

1. What does Wideman mean when he writes "metaphor's just my way of trying to say two things, be in two places at once" (paragraph 34)? Identify four of his "weight" metaphors. What two things does he say with each metaphor? In which two places does each metaphor help him to be? What do these double meanings allow him to accomplish in the essay that he couldn't accomplish with simpler statements?

2. Wideman breaks numerous conventions of writing. For example, in paragraphs 16–17 and 45–46 he doesn't end his questions with question marks. In paragraph 6 he quotes the cashier without putting quotation marks around what she says. He also addresses the reader directly, changes tense in strange places, and punctuates

irregularly. How did these rule violations affect your reading experience? Find passages or phrases where Wideman breaks major traditional rules of writing. Rewrite these passages or phrases, adding the proper punctuation. How does the experience of reading the rewritten passage compare with reading the passage that breaks the rules? What does Wideman gain — or lose — by breaking the rules where he does?

3. This story uses a technique known as "the false start": Wideman begins writing about one topic only to change to another halfway through the story. Find other stories or essays in this collection that also use the false start. Why do the authors introduce a subject, and then quickly shift to another subject? How would the essays be different if the authors either continued writing on the same subject or simply started with the subject they ended up writing about? What different kinds of false starts are there? How do the techniques for beginning again vary with different authors? Cite an example from another essay to support your argument.

THE WRITER AT WORK

John Edgar Wideman on the Value of Storytelling

John Edgar Wideman's fiction is full of characters who encounter in unexpected and often extremely intimate ways the limits of human connection in communities riven by hatred and fear. And yet his writing carries considerable hope, often conveyed by humor and irony. Wideman's ideas about writing are equally intense. When he describes mediocre writing as that in which there is "[n]o necessity to change ourselves," he underscores what his fiction shows: Like those rare moments of genuine, human connection, real writing is necessary, and it is necessarily mysterious and risky. Like Rainer Maria Rilke — whose famous poem "Archaic Torso of Apollo" ends with the line, "You must change your life" — Wideman's sense of art is visceral, personal, and moral. Compare what Wideman has to say about mystery with Flannery O'Connor's remarks on the same subject (page 867). For more on Wideman, see page 805).

Good writing teases us with the possibility/impossibility of sharing the intimacy and power of someone else's invisible vision. Mediocre writing works similar turf but compromises the invisibility, the mystery, the distance, the integrity of the "other" with the promise and pretense of delivering a final revelation: the last veil discarded. Exotic locales, an extraordinary chain of coincidence, drastic reversals of fortune, intricately convoluted plots, the impossible task, the unresolvable conflict, tragic accidents, virtue unrewarded, evil triumphant, turn out not to be what they seemed. We find ourselves at the conclusion of a docudrama or in a melodramatic story's epiphany exactly where we knew we were going all along. A familiar place. No surprises. No necessity to change ourselves.

Difference resolved, dissolved. What had been hidden beneath the veil becomes commonplace, unthreatening, valueless the moment it's revealed.

Most of what passes for art, particularly narrative art, advertises mainstream values and culture. An ad for itself. Product endorsing product, creating a seamless web of resemblance and reinforcement. This art tells us that other peoples' lives aren't actually invisible, not intrinsically unknowable. We learn that anybody's story can be reduced to familiar terms, *our* terms, the terms our way of living prioritizes. Black people are just white people in darker skins, aren't they? In such art, disguise, illusion, technique, trickery, are deployed as delaying tactics, mystification that deadens our awareness of mystery.

Stories that don't acknowledge the mystery at the center of things, don't challenge the version of reality most consenting adults rely upon day by day, are stories that disappear swiftly into the ever-present buzz of entertainment. Stories that do mount a challenge to our everyday conventions and assumptions stir my blood. Not only because they are exciting formally and philosophically, but because they retain for fiction its special subversive, radically democratic role. The Ibo of West Africa put it this way: "All stories are true." Their proverb declares the value of storytelling, the value of every storyteller's unique access to the world.

Working hard, taking chances, having fun, failing, suffering, the storyteller through the tale makes us aware of a larger, unfinished story, the collective, collaborative utterance never completed because there's always another voice worth hearing.

Alternate Tables of Contents

Selections Arranged by Common Rhetorical Modes and Patterns of Development

CONSTRUCTING NARRATIVES

SUPPLYING INSTANCES AND EXAMPLES

CLASSIFYING IDEAS

ANALYZING AND DESCRIBING PROCESSES

ESTABLISHING CAUSES AND EFFECTS

FORMING ANALOGIES

FASHIONING ARGUMENTS: EIGHT METHODS

Arguing from Personal Experience

Arguing from Factual Evidence

Correcting Popular Misconceptions

Countering Other Arguments

Arguing from Personal Authority and Expertise

Arguing with Humor, Irony, and Satire

Urging Changes in Public Policy

Finding Common Ground

Selections Arranged by Contemporary Issues

IMMIGRATION

GENDER DIFFERENCES

SOCIAL JUSTICE

THE CHANGING AMERICAN FAMILY

THE POWER OF THE MEDIA

Selections Arranged by Research Techniques and Use of Information

EMPLOYING SUMMARY AND PARAPHRASE

OBTAINING INFORMATION THROUGH INTERVIEWS
AND ORAL HISTORY

Acknowledgments (continued from page iv)

Julia Alvarez, "My English." Copyright © 1982, 1998 by Julia Alvarez. Published in *Something to Declare*, Algonquin Books of Chapel Hill, 1998. Originally published in *Brújula/Compass*, Fall 1992. "Dona Aida, with Your Permission." Copyright © 1998 by Julia Alvarez. Published in *Something to Declare*, Algonquin Books of Chapel Hill, 1998. Originally published in *Brújula/Compass*, Winter 1998. Both selections reprinted by permission of Susan Bergholz Literary Services, New York. All rights reserved.

Maya Angelou, "What's Your Name, Girl?" from *I Know Why the Caged Bird Sings* by Maya Angelou. Copyright © 1969, renewed 1997 by Maya Angelou. Used by permission of Random House, Inc.

Gloria Anzaldúa, "How to Tame a Wild Tongue" from *Borderlands/La Frontera: The New Mestiza* by Gloria Anzaldúa. Copyright © 1987, 1999 by Gloria Anzaldúa. Reprinted by permission of Aunt Lute Books.

Russell Baker, "Gumption" from *Growing Up* by Russell Baker. Copyright © 1982 by Russell Baker. Reprinted by permission of Don Congdon Associates, Inc.

James Baldwin, "Equal in Paris" from *Notes of a Native Son* by James Baldwin. Copyright © 1955, renewed 1983 by James Baldwin. Reprinted by permission of Beacon Press, Boston. "James Baldwin on Black English." Originally published as "If Black English Isn't a Language, Then Tell Me, What Is?" in *The New York Times*, March 29, 1998. Copyright © 1998 by The New York Times Co. Reprinted by permission of The New York Times.

Harold Bloom, "In Praise of the Greats" extracted from "Preface and Prologue" of *How to Read and Why* by Harold Bloom. Copyright © 2000 by Harold Bloom. Reprinted with the permission of Scribner, an imprint of Simon & Schuster Adult Publishing Group.

Veronica Boix-Mansilla and Howard Gardner, "Cognition and Understanding." Originally published as "Of Kinds of Disciplines and Kinds of Understanding" in *Phi Delta Kappan*, January 1997. Copyright © 1997 by Veronica Boix-Mansilla and Howard Gardner. Reprinted by permission of the authors.

Stephen L. Carter, "The Insufficiency of Honesty" from *Integrity* by Stephen L. Carter. Copyright © 1996 by Stephen L. Carter. Reprinted by permission of Basic Books, a member of Perseus Books, L.L.C.

Raymond Carver, "My Father's Life." Copyright © 1984 by Tess Gallagher. First appeared in *Esquire*. Reprinted by permission of International Creative Management, Inc. "Popular Mechanics" from *What We Talk About When We Talk About Love* by Raymond Carver. Copyright © 1981 by Raymond Carver. Used by permission of Alfred A. Knopf, a division of Random House, Inc.

Judith Ortiz Cofer, "Silent Dancing" and "Preface" are reprinted with permission from the publisher of *Silent Dancing: A Partial Remembrance of a Puerto-Rican Childhood* (Houston: Arte Público Press—University of Houston, 1990).

K. C. Cole, "Calculated Risks" from *The Universe and the Teacup: The Mathematics of Truth and Beauty* by K. C. Cole. Copyright © 1998 by K. C. Cole. Reprinted by permission of Harcourt, Inc.

Bernard Cooper, "A Clack of Tiny Sparks: Remembrances of a Gay Boyhood." Copyright © 1990 by *Harper's Magazine*. All rights reserved. Reproduced from the January 1991 issue by special permission.

Amy Cunningham, "Why Women Smile." Copyright © 1993 by Amy Cunningham. First published in *Lear's* and edited by Nelson Aldrich. Reprinted by permission of the author.

Edwidge Danticat, "We Are Ugly, But We Are Here" from *The Caribbean Writer*, Summer 1996. Copyright © 1996 by Edwidge Danticat. "Edwidge Danticat on Becoming a Writer" excerpted from an interview in *Essence*, May 1996. Copyright © 1996 by Edwidge Danticat. Both selections reprinted by permission of the author.

Don DeLillo, "In the Ruins of the Future: Reflections on Terror, Loss, and Time in the Shadow of September." Copyright © 2001 by Don DeLillo. First published in *Harper's Magazine*. Used by permission of the Wallace Literary Agency, Inc.

Toi Derricotte, "October" and "July" from *The Black Notebooks: An Interior Journey* by Toi Derricotte. Copyright © 1997 by Toi Derricotte. Used by permission of W. W. Norton & Company, Inc.

Joan Didion, "On Keeping a Notebook" from *Slouching Towards Bethlehem* by Joan Didion. Copyright © 1966, 1968 and renewed 1996 by Joan Didion. Reprinted by permission of Farrar, Straus & Giroux, LLC.

Annie Dillard, "Living Like Weasels" from the HarperPerennial 1992 edition of *Teaching a Stone to Talk: Expeditions and Encounters* by Annie Dillard. Copyright © 1982 by Annie Dillard. Excerpt from *The Writing Life* by Annie Dillard. Copyright © 1989 by Annie Dillard. Both selections reprinted by permission of HarperCollins Publishers, Inc.

Gregg Easterbrook, "The Myth of Fingerprints" from *The New Republic*, July 31, 2000. Copyright © 2000 by The New Republic, LLC. Reprinted by permission of The New Republic, LLC.

Barbara Ehrenreich, "Family Values" from *The Worst Years of Our Lives* by Barbara Ehrenreich. Copyright © 1990 by Barbara Ehrenreich. Reprinted by permission of International Creative Management, Inc.

Lars Eighner, "On Dumpster Diving" from *Travels With Lizbeth* by Lars Eighner. Copyright © 1993 by Lars Eighner. Reprinted by permission of St. Martin's Press, LLC.

Ralph Ellison, "What America Would Be Like Without Blacks" from *Going to the Territory* by Ralph Ellison. Copyright © 1986 by Ralph Ellison. Used by permission of Random House, Inc.

Nora Ephron, "A Few Words About Breasts" from *Crazy Salad* by Nora Ephron. Copyright © 1972 by Nora Ephron. Reprinted by permission of International Creative Management, Inc.

Kai Erikson, "The Witches of Salem Village" from *Wayward Puritans: A Study on the Sociology of Deviance* by Kai Erikson. Published by Allyn and Bacon, Boston, MA. Copyright © 1966 by Pearson Education. Reprinted by permission of the author.

James Fallows, "Throwing Like a Girl" from *The Atlantic Monthly*, August 1996. Copyright © 1996 by James Fallows. Reprinted by permission of the author.

Stanley Fish, "When Principles Get in the Way." Copyright © 1996 by Stanley Fish. Originally published in *The New York Times*. Reprinted by permission of the author.

Anne Frank, "Things That Lie Buried Deep in My Heart," "Back to My Diary" and "A Sweet Secret" from *Diary of a Young Girl* by Anne Frank, translated by B. M. Mooyaart-Doubleday. Copyright © 1952 by Otto H. Frank. Used by permission of Doubleday, a division of Random House, Inc.

Ian Frazier, "Tracks" from *Audubon Magazine*, November/December 1996. Copyright © 1996 by Ian Frazier. Reprinted with the permission of the Wylie Agency.

Paul Fussell, "A Well-Regulated Militia" from *Class* by Paul Fussell. Copyright © 1983 by Paul Fussell. Reprinted with the permission of Simon & Schuster.

Henry Louis Gates Jr., "In the Kitchen" and excerpt from "Introduction" from *Colored People* by Henry Louis Gates Jr. Copyright © 1994 by Henry Louis Gates Jr. Used by permission of Alfred A. Knopf, a division of Random House, Inc.

William Gibson, "The Net Is A Waste of Time (And That's Probably What's Right About It)" from *The New York Times Magazine*, July 14, 1996. Copyright © 1996 by The New York Times Co. Reprinted by permission of The New York Times.

Malcolm Gladwell, "Introduction" from *The Tipping Point* by Malcolm Gladwell. Copyright © 2000, 2002 by Malcolm Gladwell. By permission of Little, Brown and Company, Inc.

Mary Gordon, "The Ghosts of Ellis Island." Originally published as "More Than Just a Shrine: Paying Homage to the Ghosts of Ellis Island" in *The New York Times Magazine*, Part 2, November 3, 1985. Copyright © 1985 by Mary Gordon. Reprinted by permission of Sterling Lord Literistic, Inc.

Stephen Jay Gould, "Sex, Drugs, Disaster, and the Extinction of Dinosaurs" from *The Flamingo's Smile: Reflections in Natural History* by Stephen Jay Gould. Copyright © 1984 by Stephen Jay Gould. Used by permission of W. W. Norton & Company, Inc.

Michihiko Hachiya, "What Had Happened?" and "Pikadon" from *Hiroshima Diary: The Journal of a Japanese Physician, August 6–September 30, 1945* by Michihiko Hachiya, translated by Warner Wells, M.D. Copyright © 1955 by The University of North Carolina Press, renewed 1995. Used by permission of the publisher.

Jane Eaton Hamilton, "Twenty-One Questions." Copyright © 2001 by Jane Eaton Hamilton. First appeared in *Young Wives' Tales*, Seal Press, 2001. Reprinted by permission of the author.

Vicki Hearne, "What's Wrong With Animal Rights" from *Harper's Magazine*. Copyright © 1991 by Harper's Magazine. All rights reserved. Reprinted from the September 1991 issue by special permission.

Jack Hitt, "The Hidden Life of SUVs" from *Mother Jones*, July–August 1999. Copyright © 1999 by The Foundation for National Progress. Reprinted with permission of The Foundation for National Progress.

Edward Hoagland, "On Stuttering." Originally published as "The Football Game In My Head" from *US News & World Report*, April 2, 2001. Copyright © 2001 by US News & World Report, L.P. Reprinted with permission. "To the Point: Truths Only Essays Can Tell." Copyright © 1993 by Harper's Magazine. All rights reserved. Reprinted from the March 1993 issue by special permission.

Linda Hogan, "Dwellings" from *Dwellings: A Spiritual History of the Living World* by Linda Hogan. Copyright © 1995 by Linda Hogan. Used by permission of W. W. Norton & Company, Inc.

John Hollander, "Mess" from *The Yale Review* 83:2, April 1995. Copyright © 1995 by John Hollander. Reprinted by permission of the author and Blackwell Publishing.

bell hooks, "Learning in the Shadow of Race and Class" from *The Chronicle of Higher Education*, November 17, 2000. Adapted from *Where We Stand: Class Matters* by bell hooks. Copyright © 2000. Reproduced by permission of Routledge, Inc., part of the Taylor & Francis Group.

Langston Hughes, "Salvation" from *The Big Sea* by Langston Hughes. Copyright © renewed 1968 by Arna Bontemps & George Huston Bass. Reprinted by permission of Hill and Wang, a division of Farrar, Straus and Giroux, LLC. "How to Be a Bad Writer (In Ten Easy Lessons)" from *The Langston Hughes Reader*. Copyright © 1950 by Langston Hughes. Reprinted by permission of Harold Ober Associates Incorporated.

June Jordan, "A New Politics of Sexuality" from *Technical Difficulties* by June Jordan. Copyright © 1992 by June Jordan. Reprinted by permission of the Literary Estate of June M. Jordan.

Michiko Kakutani, "The Word Police" from *The New York Times*, February 1, 1993. Copyright © 1993 by The New York Times Co. Reprinted by permission of The New York Times.

Wendy Kaminer, "Let's Talk About Gender, Baby" from *The American Prospect*, August 13, 2001. Copyright © 2001 by Wendy Kaminer. Reprinted by permission of the author.

Jamaica Kincaid, "Biography of a Dress" from *Grand Street* 43, vol. 11, #3, 1992. Copyright © 1992 by Jamaica Kincaid. Reprinted by permission of the Wylie Agency. "Girl" from *At the Bottom of the River* by Jamaica Kincaid. Copyright © 1993 by Jamaica Kincaid. Reprinted by permission of Farrar, Straus & Giroux, LLC.

Martin Luther King Jr., "Letter from Birmingham Jail." Copyright © 1963 by Dr. Martin Luther King Jr., renewed 1991 by Coretta Scott King. "King on Self-Importance" excerpted from "Conquering Self-Centeredness." Copyright © 1957 by Dr. Martin Luther King, Jr., copyright renewed 1985 by Coretta Scott King. Both selections reprinted by arrangement with the Estate of Martin Luther King Jr., c/o Writers House, Inc., as agent for the proprietor New York, NY.

Stephen King, "The Hotel Story: Two Versions." Originally published as "And Furthermore, Part I: Door Shut, Door Open" from *On Writing: A Memoir of the Craft* by Stephen King. Copyright © 2000 by Stephen King. Reprinted with the permission of Scribner, an imprint of Simon & Schuster Adult Publishing Group. "Everything You Need to Know About Writing Successfully—in Ten Minutes" from *The Writer*, March 2000. Copyright © 2000 by Stephen King. All rights reserved. Reprinted with permission of Arthur B. Greene & Co. and the author.

Barbara Kingsolver, "Stone Soup" from *High Tide in Tucson: Essays from Now or Never* by Barbara Kingsolver. Copyright © 1995 by Barbara Kingsolver. Reprinted by permission of HarperCollins Publishers Inc.

Maxine Hong Kingston, "No Name Woman" from *The Woman Warrior* by Maxine Hong Kingston. Copyright © 1975, 1976 by Maxine Hong Kingston. Used by permission of Alfred A. Knopf, a division of Random House, Inc. "Maxine Hong Kingston on Writing for Oneself," excerpted from "'Pig in a Poke': An Interview with Maxine Hong Kingston" by Diane Simmons, *Crab Orchard Review* 3:2, Spring/Summer 1998. Copyright © 1998 by Diane Simmons. Reprinted with permission of Diane Simmons.

Eric Liu, "Creating an Asian American Identity" excerpted from "The Accidental Asian: Variations on a Theme" from *The Accidental Asian: Notes of a Native Speaker* by Eric Liu. Copyright © 1998 by Eric Liu. Used by permission of Random House, Inc.

Nancy Mairs, "On Being a Cripple" from *Plain Text* by Nancy Mairs. Copyright © 1986 by The Arizona Board of Regents. Reprinted by permission of the University of Arizona Press. "On Finding a Voice" from *Voice Lessons* by Nancy Mairs. Copyright © 1994 by Nancy Mairs. Reprinted by permission of Beacon Press, Boston.

Malcolm X, "Homeboy" from *The Autobiography of Malcolm X* by Malcolm X and Alex Haley. Copyright © 1964 by Alex Haley and Malcolm X, copyright © 1965 by Alex Haley and Betty Shabazz. Used by permission of Random House, Inc.

David Mamet, "The Rake: A Few Scenes From My Childhood" from *The Cabin* by David Mamet. Copyright © 1992 by David Mamet. Used by permission of Vintage Books, a division of Random House, Inc.

Adam Mayblum, "The Price We Pay" from *DoubleTake,* Special Edition 2001. Copyright © 2001 by Adam Mayblum. Reprinted by permission of the author.

N. Scott Momaday, "The Way to Rainy Mountain." Copyright © 1969, 1997 by the University of New Mexico Press. First published in *The Reporter,* January 26, 1967. Reprinted by permission of the University of New Mexico Press.

Paul Monette, "Can Gays and Straights Be Friends?" Copyright © 1993 by Paul Monette. First published in *Playboy Magazine,* May 1993. Reprinted by permission of the Wendy Weil Agency, Inc.

Bharati Mukherjee, "Two Ways to Belong in America." Copyright © 1996 by The New York Times Co. Originally published in *The New York Times,* September 2, 1996. Reprinted by permission of The New York Times.

Gloria Naylor, "A Question of Language." Copyright © 1986 by Gloria Naylor. Reprinted by permission of Sterling Lord Literistic, Inc.

Kathleen Norris, "The Holy Use of Gossip" from *Dakota* by Kathleen Norris. Copyright © 1993 by Kathleen Norris. Reprinted by permission of Houghton Mifflin Company. All rights reserved. "Kathleen Norris and the Vocabulary of Religion," excerpted from an interview with Kathleen Norris by Sonia Gernes, *Notre Dame Magazine,* Autumn 1998. Reprinted by permission of Sonia Gernes.

Martha Nussbaum, "Can Patriotism Be Compassionate?" Copyright © 2001 by The Nation. Reprinted with permission from the December 17, 2001 issue of *The Nation.*

Flannery O'Connor, "A Good Man Is Hard to Find" from *A Good Man Is Hard to Find and Other Stories* by Flannery O'Connor. Copyright © 1953 by Flannery O'Connor and renewed 1981 by Regina O'Connor. Reprinted by permission of Harcourt, Inc. "On Her Own Work" from "A Reasonable Use of the Unreasonable" from *Mystery and Manners* by Flannery O'Connor. Copyright © 1969 by The Estate of Mary Flannery O'Connor. Reprinted by permission of Farrar, Straus & Giroux, LLC.

Tillie Olsen, "I Stand Here Ironing" from *Tell Me a Riddle* by Tillie Olsen, introduction by John Leonard. Copyright © 1956, 1957, 1960, 1961 by Tillie Olsen. Used by permission of Dell Publishing, a division of Random House, Inc.

Susan Orlean, "The American Man at Age Ten" from *Esquire,* December 1992. Copyright © 1992 by Susan Orlean. Permission granted by Arthur Pine Associates, Inc., New York, NY.

George Orwell, "Shooting an Elephant" from *Shooting an Elephant and Other Essays* by George Orwell. Copyright © 1950 by Sonia Brownell Orwell and renewed 1978 by Sonia Pitt-Rivers. "Politics and the English Language" from *Shooting an Elephant and Other Essays* by George Orwell. Copyright © 1946 by Sonia Brownell Orwell and renewed 1974 by Sonia Orwell. Excerpt from "Why I Write" from *Such, Such Were the Joys* by George Orwell. Copyright © 1953 by Sonia Brownell Orwell and renewed 1981 by Mrs. George K. Perutz, Mrs. Miriam Gross, and Dr. Michael Dickson, Executors of the Estate of Sonia Brownell Orwell. All selections reprinted by permission of Harcourt, Inc., Bill Hamilton as Literary Executor of the Estate of the Late Sonia Brownell Orwell, and Secker & Warburg Ltd.

Orlando Patterson, "Race Over" from *The New Republic,* January 10, 2000. Copyright © 1999 by Orlando Patterson. Reprinted by permission of the author.

Sylvia Plath, "Bitter Strawberries" from *Collected Poems* by Sylvia Plath. Copyright © 1960, 1965, 1971, 1981 by the Estate of Sylvia Plath. Reprinted by permission of HarperCollins Publishers Inc. and Faber and Faber Ltd. Excerpt from *The Unabridged Journals of Sylvia Plath* by Sylvia Plath, edited by Karen V. Kukil. Copyright © 2000 by The Estate of Sylvia Plath. Preface, notes, and index copyright © 2000 by Karen V. Kukil. Used by permission of Random House, Inc.

Katha Pollitt, "Why Boys Don't Play With Dolls," from *The New York Times Magazine,* October 8, 1995. Copyright © 1995 by The New York Times Co. Reprinted by permission of The New York Times.

Elayne Rapping, "Daytime Inquiries" from *The Progressive,* October 1991. Copyright

© 1991 by The Progressive. Reprinted by permission from The Progressive, 409 E. Main St., Madison, WI, 53703.

Adrienne Rich, "Split at the Root: An Essay on Jewish Identity (abridged)" from *Blood, Bread, and Poetry: Selected Prose 1979–1985* by Adrienne Rich. Copyright © 1986 by Adrienne Rich. Used by permission of the author and W. W. Norton & Company, Inc.

Alberto Alvaro Ríos, "Green Cards" from *Indiana Review*, October 1, 1995. Copyright © 1995 by Alberto Alvaro Ríos. Reprinted by permission of the author.

Richard Rodriguez, "Aria: A Memoir of a Bilingual Childhood." Copyright © 1980 by Richard Rodriguez. Originally appeared in *The American Scholar*. Reprinted by permission of Georges Borchardt, Inc., Literary Agency, for the author. "On a Writer's Identity" excerpted from "Crossing Borders: An Interview with Richard Rodriguez" by Scott London, *The Sun* 260 (August 1997). Copyright © 1997 by Scott London. Reprinted by permission of Scott London.

Judy Ruiz, "Oranges and Sweet Sister Boy" from *Iowa Woman*, Summer 1988. Copyright © 1988 by Judy Ruiz. Reprinted by permission of the author.

Salman Rushdie, "The Ground Beneath My Feet" from *The Nation*, July 9, 2001. Copyright © 2001 by Salman Rushdie. Reprinted with the permission of the Wylie Agency.

Bertrand Russell, "Why I Am Not a Christian" from *Why I Am Not a Christian* by Bertrand Russell. Copyright © 1957 by George Allen & Unwin Ltd. Reprinted with the permission of Simon & Schuster Adult Publishing Group and the Bertrand Russell Peace Foundation, Ltd.

Scott Russell Sanders, "The Men We Carry in Our Minds" from *The Paradise of Bombs* by Scott Russell Sanders. Copyright © 1984 by Scott Russell Sanders. First appeared in *Milkweed Chronicle*. Reprinted by permission of the author and the author's agent, the Virginia Kidd Agency, Inc. "Scott Russell Sanders on Writing Essays," excerpt from "The Singular First Person." Copyright © 1988 by Scott Russell Sanders. First appeared in *Sewanee Review*. Reprinted by permission of the author.

Luc Sante, "What Secrets Tell" from *The New York Times Magazine*, December 3, 2000. Copyright © 2000 by The New York Times Co. Reprinted by permission of the author.

Arthur Schlesinger Jr., "The Cult of Ethnicity, Good and Bad" from *Time*, July 8, 1991. Copyright © 1991 by Arthur Schlesinger Jr. Reprinted by permission of the author.

Eric Schlosser, "Why McDonald's Fries Taste So Good" from *Fast Food Nation: The Dark Side of the All American Meal* by Eric Schlosser. First published in the Atlantic Monthly, January 2001. Excerpted and reprinted by permission of Houghton Mifflin Company. All rights reserved.

David Sedaris, "Me Talk Pretty One Day" from *Me Talk Pretty One Day* by David Sedaris. Copyright © 2000 by David Sedaris. By permission of Little, Brown and Company, Inc.

Leslie Marmon Silko, "In the Combat Zone" from *Hungry Mind Review*, Fall 1995. Copyright © 1995 by Leslie Marmon Silko. Reprinted by permission of the Wylie Agency.

Peter Singer, "The Singer Solution to World Poverty" from *The New York Times Magazine*, September 5, 1999. Copyright © 1999 by The New York Times Co. Reprinted by permission of The New York Times.

Wole Soyinka, "Every Dictator's Nightmare." Copyright © 1999 by Wole Soyinka. First appeared in *The New York Times Magazine*. Reprinted by permission of the Melanie Jackson Agency, L.L.C.

Benjamin Spock, "Should Children Play With Guns?" from *Baby and Child Care* by Benjamin Spock. Copyright © 1945, 1946, 1957, 1968, 1976, 1985, 1992 and renewed 1973, 1974, 1985, 1996 by Benjamin Spock, M.D. Reprinted with the permission of *Pocket Books*, an imprint of Simon & Schuster Adult Publishing Group.

Brent Staples, excerpt from *Parallel Time* by Brent Staples. Copyright © 1994 by Brent Staples. Used by permission of Pantheon Books, a division of Random House, Inc. "Just Walk On By: A Black Man Ponders His Power to Alter Public Space." Copyright © 1986 by Brent Staples. Reprinted by permission of the author.

Robert Stone, "In the Mind's Eye of the Bomber" from *Rolling Stone*, October 25, 2001. Copyright © 2001 by Mario Puzo. Reprinted by permission of Donadio & Olson, Inc.

Andrew Sullivan, "The 'He' Hormone" from *The New York Times Magazine*, April 2, 2000. Copyright © 2000 by Andrew Sullivan. Reprinted by permission of the Wylie Agency.

Cass Sunstein, "Media and Democracy: A 'Daily Me' or a 'Daily We'?" from *Republic.com* by Cass Sunstein. Copyright © 2001 by Princeton University Press. Originally

Tempest Williams. Used by permission of Pantheon Books, a division of Random House, Inc.

Marie Winn, "TV Addiction." Originally titled "Cookies or Heroin?" from *The Plug-In Drug, Revised and Updated 25ᵗʰ Anniversary Edition* by Marie Winn. Copyright 1977, 1985, 2002 by Marie Winn Miller. Used by permission of Viking Penguin, a division of Penguin Putnam, Inc.

Virginia Woolf, "This Loose, Drifting Material of Life," "Chained to My Rock," and "They Get Closer Every Time" from *A Writer's Diary* by Virginia Woolf. Copyright © 1954 by Leonard Woolf, renewed 1982 by Quentin Bell and Angela Garnett. Reprinted by permission of Harcourt, Inc. "The Death of the Moth" from *The Death of the Moth and Other Essays* by Virginia Woolf. Copyright © 1942 by Harcourt, Inc. and renewed 1970 by Marjorie T. Parsons, Executrix. Reprinted by permission of the publisher.

Richard Wright, "I Choose Exile." Copyright © 1951. Reprinted by permission of John Hawkins and Associates, Inc.

Index of Authors and Titles ———

Online Research and Reference Aids for Students

The English Research Room
bedfordstmartins.com/english_research
Mike Palmquist, *Colorado State University*

A good starting place for all researchers, this site offers advice on how to search and evaluate online sources. Interactive tutorials take you step-by-step through searches of databases, online catalogs, and the Web.

Research and Documentation Online
bedfordstmartins.com/resdoc
Diana Hacker, *Prince George's Community College*

This online version of Hacker's popular booklet provides clear guidelines on how to integrate outside material into a paper, how to cite sources correctly, and how to format sources according to MLA, APA, Chicago, or CBE documentation styles.

After September 11: An Online Reader for Writers
bedfordstmartins.com/september11
Eric Crump, *Interversity.com*

This free online reader by Eric Crump, a nationally recognized online teacher and scholar, offers instructors and students up-to-date links to some of the best-written and most diverse articles, commentary, and news stories about the events and consequences of September 11, 2001.